SIXTH EDITION

TAYLOR TRADE PUBLISHING
Lanham • New York • Boulder • Toronto • Plymouth, UK

SIXTH EDITION

Why Stop?

A GUIDE TO
Texas Roadside
Historical Markers

BETTY DOOLEY AWBREY AND STUART AWBREY
AND THE TEXAS HISTORICAL COMMISSION

Published by Taylor Trade Publishing
An imprint of The Rowman & Littlefield Publishing Group, Inc.
4501 Forbes Boulevard, Suite 200, Lanham, Maryland 20706
www.rowman.com

10 Thornbury Road, Plymouth PL6 7PP, United Kingdom

Distributed by National Book Network

British Library Cataloguing in Publication Information Available

Library of Congress Cataloging-in-Publication Data
Dooley-Awbrey, Betty.
  Why stop? : a guide to Texas roadside historical markers / Betty Awbrey and Stuart Awbrey. — Sixth Edition.
    pages cm
    Includes index.
    ISBN 978-1-58979-789-5 (pbk. : alk. paper) — ISBN 978-1-58979-790-1 (electronic) 1. Historical markers—Texas—Guidebooks. 2. Texas—History, Local. 3. Legends—Texas. 4. Texas—Guidebooks. I. Awbrey, Stuart, 1937– II. Title.
  F387.D68 2013
  976.4—dc23

                                                              2012050584

♾™ The paper used in this publication meets the minimum requirements of American National Standard for Information Sciences—Permanence of Paper for Printed Library Materials, ANSI/NISO Z39.48-1992.

Contents

In loving memory
of Betty's father,
Claude W. Dooley,
whose enthusiasm
for Texas history
inspired this book.

Dedicated to
The Texas Historical Commission
and all other organizations whose research
and recordings have enriched
our knowledge of the history of Texas.

Acknowledgments

We wish to express our appreciation to the Texas Historical Commission for making its files available and for the courtesy and assistance of its members in compiling this book, especially—

Mark Wolfe, Executive Director, Texas Historical Commission
Bratten Thomason, Director, History Programs Division
Bob Brinkman, Marker Program Coordinator
Sarah McCleskey, Historian
and
the staff of the Texas Historical Commission

The Commission maintains an excellent website at **www.thc.state.tx.us**
and has a database of all historical markers at **http://atlas.thc.state.tx.us**

We also thank the members of the Texas Historical Commission in each of the counties.

About Texas Historical Markers . . .

The markers you will encounter are designated Official Texas Historical Markers by the Texas Historical Commission. Markers are erected to commemorate historical sites, buildings, and events; institutions such as churches, businesses, and organizations; and individuals whose achievements have been recognized.

The most common types of markers are those pictured. Many of the earlier markers are made of stone, usually granite, featuring either engraved lettering or a metal plate with inscription. The familiar aluminum marker with raised lettering on a black background is more commonly used now. Also, there is the round medallion, which identifies a structure as a Recorded Texas Historic Landmark. An interpretive plate offering historical background of the building often accompanies the medallion.

Preface

From the Panhandle to the Gulf Coast, from Texarkana to El Paso, this vast area that once was a sovereign nation holds an enviable history that intrigues all who are fascinated by its legends. Much of this history endures through the inscriptions on historical markers that recount an array of interesting facts about people, places, and events that shaped the history of this state.

The original purpose of this book was to include the text of markers located along highways and country roads so that hurried travelers could "meet" the fascinating individuals, "experience" the dramatic events, and "see" the historical places of Texas without having to stop to read the markers. That purpose continues with the sixth edition.

When the first edition of *Why Stop?* was published in 1978, there were more than 6,000 recorded historical markers in Texas. By the time the second edition was published in 1985, that number had increased to nearly 10,000. The Texas Historical Commission (THC) to date has more than 15,000 markers and boasts markers across other southern states, as well as a few Texas markers in Europe.

Each year the THC adds several hundred markers. To accommodate new markers, it is necessary to delete some markers from the book. With each new edition the decision of selecting markers to delete becomes increasingly difficult. During the third revision of *Why Stop?* the decision was made to feature markers located on more heavily traveled U.S. and state highways without omitting city markers, especially since those markers tell the unique stories of their local history. We also include markers at state parks for their value to the history of Texas—just in case your travel plans do not include a stopping visit "until the next time" you are in the area.

While the purpose of *Why Stop?* is to give readers the pleasure of learning about the colorful history of Texas without having to delay a trip, we believe that these inscriptions about the great, near-great, and not-so-great events and people that made this legendary state what it is will inspire you to learn more and maybe even stop awhile. When there is time to stop and read the markers, you will want to go to the courthouse squares, local museums, and city parks where markers are often located. Also, be advised that the historical commissions of many counties publish brochures and have websites that include the locations of the markers in their counties.

Inscriptions on roadside markers are written by the Texas Historical Commission staff, based upon research done by county historical commissions. To the best of our knowledge the inscriptions are quoted as they appear on the markers. Any errors are unintentional, and corrections reported to us will be considered in future editions of *Why Stop?*

Betty and Stuart Awbrey
Fair Oaks Ranch, Texas

To Our Readers

We would like you to let us know how you use the book, along with any suggestions for future editions. Remember that not all markers can be included.

Betty and Stuart Awbrey

txwhystop@gmail.com

How to Use This Guide

The marker inscriptions selected for this book have been compiled for the convenience and enjoyment of both the traveler and the history enthusiast. They are arranged in the book by the city or town where they are located. Begin by searching for a nearby city or town. Locations of markers are shown in italics. Indicated distances are measured from the nearest town within the county in which the marker is located. Some entries reference two or more highways. Read them as follows:

CITY (County Co.) *SH 33, 10 mi. E of US 60/83, 7 mi. S*
This marker is on SH 33, 10 mi. E of its intersection with US 60/83 (which is) 7 mi. S of City.

The Texas Historical Commission (THC) files contain the locations of the markers. This is our primary source of information. We also consult online sources to check the accuracy of the locations. You may report errors to either:
the authors—**txwhystop@gmail.com**
or the THC History Programs—**www.thc.state.tx.us/contactus/cotdefault.shtml**

Questions we are often asked:

Why do I sometimes see markers that are not in the book?
The Texas Historical Commission now has over 15,000 markers. A book this size accommodates approximately 2,500 inscriptions. The decision was made thirty-five years ago when *Why Stop?* was first published to feature the roadside markers and additionally, to include a selection of markers in cities and towns.

Why are markers arranged by city instead of by highway number?
A collection of markers along the highways near a city or town tells a story about the local area. Readers report that they read not only the inscription of the marker they have just spotted, but also about nearby markers in the area.

How do you decide which markers to include in the book?
We try to include almost every marker on a state or U.S. highway, as well as a few markers on highways within towns and cities, with the intention of giving the reader a brief history of the area. Additionally, we select a few non-highway markers that highlight events and personalities that are closely associated with the identity of the area.

ABBOTT (Hill Co.)   *IH 35 Access Road*
Czech Settlers in Hill County
One of the most influential and numerous national groups to settle in Hill County, Czechs came to this area from Fayette County and the Province of Moravia in Austria-Hungary. Many sought greater freedom due to barriers to attaining national status in the old country, political restraints, introduction of German into the schools, and compulsory military service. Land agents painted a rosy picture of opportunities awaiting those who purchased cheap state university lands in this region. The first immigrants arrived in the 1870s and found the soil so fertile that they induced many others to join them. Building of the Texas Central and "Katy" Railroads boosted immigration. Capital of Czech settlement in the area is Abbott, named for Jo Abbott (1840–1908), judge, legislator, and lawyer. Surrounding towns are Zee Vee (so called for the local ZV cattle brand), Penelope, and Aquilia. Neighbors admired the Czechs for their neat, well-managed farms and their thrift and industry. For many years they retained a strong group spirit, speaking their own language and observing old world customs. In recent decades they have mixed more with other groups and today fill many public and professional offices as well as continuing to farm.   (1970)

ABERNATHY (Hale Co.)   *off IH 27 on Loop 369 at City Hall*
Town of Abernathy
Founded when Santa Fe Railroad was extended from Plainview to Lubbock, 1909. Named for Monroe G. Abernathy (1868–1962), treasurer of South Plains Investment Company, firm which promoted townsite. Community prospered, becoming a major railhead for shipping of cattle. Several buildings from the defunct town of Bartonsite were moved here and new ones built. Center of civic activities was the "Old Tabernacle" (1918–1947), located on city square. In early days, before roads were built, broad plowed furrows marked way to house of town doctor. Economy is agriculture-based.   (1973)

ABILENE (Taylor Co.)   *US 277, 35 mi. SW at Shep Community*
Valley Creek Station
(site located 2 mi. northwest)
Near this site, an important link in the frontier transportation system was an area landmark. The Butterfield Overland Mail maintained a stage stop at the falls and crossing of Valley Creek beginning in 1858. The twice-weekly mail and passenger line stretched from San Francisco to St. Louis, crossing the southwest corner of Taylor County and passing six miles west of present Abilene. The path through Texas, known as the oxbow route, added about 600 miles to the 2,800 mile trip. The line moved out of Texas in March 1861, leaving this area sparsely settled. Ranchers later settled near Spring, Cottonwood and Valley creeks, and established the nearby community of Shep in the 1880s.   (2007)

ABILENE (Taylor Co.)   *US 277, at FM 89, 15 mi. SW*
In Vicinity of Coronado's Camp
In 1541, the Spanish explorer Coronado is thought to have passed this way en route from New Mexico to the fabled Indian village of "Quivira," though his path across vast Texas plains is now difficult to determine. Upon finding that his Indian guide, "The Turk," had taken him too far south, Coronado halted at a small canyon or barranca. Here he conferred with his captains and decided to follow the compass directly north. When they reached "Quivira" (possibly in Kansas), no gold was found—only the poor, grass huts of a Wichita village.   (1968)

ABILENE (Taylor Co.)   *US 277, at site, about 8 mi. SW*
Camp Barkeley
(February 15, 1941–March 21, 1945)
Site of main entrance to Camp Barkeley, one of the nation's largest military camps of World War II. At peak, 60,000 men were in training here. Named for Pvt. David B. Barkeley of the 89th Division, who died on a secret scouting expedition behind German lines during the Meuse-Argonne Battle of World War I. Among famous units trained here were the 45th and 90th Infantry Divisions and the 11th and 12th Armored. A medical replacement training center, the largest in the country, was also established here, with 15 battalions. In May, 1942, the Medical Administrative Corps Officer Candidate School was activated and graduated about 12,500 candidates. Camp Barkeley eventually grew to be a complete city unit twice the size of Abilene in the 1940s. It had a 2,300-bed

hospital, 2 cold storage plants, a bakery, 4 theaters, 2 service clubs for enlisted men, 15 chapels, and 35 post exchange buildings. The military personnel were housed in hutments, except for some 4,000 in barracks. Part of the post was also a German prisoner-of-war camp. Once some of the prisoners escaped, to the alarm of Abilene citizens, and others attempted to tunnel under the fences. Camp Barkeley was declared surplus in 1945. (1969)

ABILENE (Taylor Co.) *US 83 at SH 36, 2.3 mi. E of intersection*
Lindbergh in West Texas
(September 26, 1927)
Four months after his record-setting trans-Atlantic solo flight, Charles Augustus Lindbergh (1902–1974) landed here for one hour and thirty-six minutes during a nationwide publicity tour. Touching down at Kinsolving Field (now the site of Abilene Zoo) after an almost nine-hour flight from Santa Fe, "Lucky Lindy" was given a hero's welcome by thousands of West Texans. His famous Ryan monoplane, "Spirit of St. Louis," was taxied into a fenced area and surrounded by National Guard troops for protection. An escort plane landed later. Heading a parade into Abilene were seventy-one mayors and countless officials. Lindbergh was escorted by Mrs. Mildred Moody (1897–1983), wife of Gov. Dan Moody and an Abilene native; Mayor Thomas Edward Hayden (1891–1949); and Chamber of Commerce President Charles William Bacon (1871–1947). The young pilot reportedly balked at a "throne" rigged for him in an open Nash automobile, and rode with Mrs. Moody through the town to Federal Lawn. Lindbergh delivered a brief speech over loud speakers praising the ideal terrain and weather in Texas for developing civil and military aviation. He was escorted back to his plane and flew two hours and forty-two minutes to his next stop in Fort Worth. (Texas Sesquicentennial 1836–1986)

ABILENE (Taylor Co.) *N. 1st St. at Pine St., 1 blk. N of IH 20*
Texas & Pacific Railway; First Railroad Across West Texas
Chartered March 3, 1871, by Act of U.S. Congress, to build a railroad to the Pacific Coast, the Texas & Pacific Railway Company, under leadership of Colonel Thomas A. Scott, president, began construction across West Texas in 1880. General Grenville M. Dodge, civil engineer and builder of the Union Pacific, was in charge. The first train reached the Abilene area in early January 1881 and a station opened for business here on February 28, 1881. The office was in a boxcar at the present Pine Street overpass. As a policy during its era of construction, the Texas & Pacific promoted the settlement of West Texas. Encouraged by local ranchers, agents of the railway held on March 15, 1881, the first auction of lots in Abilene townsite. On that day 178 lots were sold for $27,550.00. The wisdom of the purchasers has since been well confirmed for Abilene is now the business, agricultural, transportation, medical, educational and cultural center for Central West Texas. (1968)

ABILENE (Taylor Co.) *S. 1st St. (IH 20 Bus./US80) at S. Leggett St.*
Site of Western Cattle Trail
The main route—1876 to 1887—for several hundred thousand longhorns driven north to stock ranches and Indian reservations and to supply beef market. Was also called Dodge City Trail, for its main terminus; or Fort Griffin Trail, for the site where feeder trails joined. This major branch began in South Texas, passed the western outskirts of Abilene, and from here moved northeast to Fort Griffin. An alternate route ran to the Red River, then to Kansas. Use of the trail ceased after fenced ranges blocked route, and Texas & Pacific Railway arrived. (1968)

ABILENE (Taylor Co.) *IH 20, .25 mi. W of Tye*
Butterfield Mail and Stage Line
One of major horse-drawn transportation projects of history. Was authorized by act of Congress on March 3, 1857. Contract for semi-weekly service overland to San Francisco, Calif., was awarded to company headed by John Butterfield; another stockholder in the $2,000,000 venture was express pioneer Wm. G. Fargo. The line employed some 2,000 people and used hundreds of stagecoaches and thousands of animals. In addition to receipts from freight and passengers it had a $600,000 annual subsidy for carrying U.S. mail. Company operated from Sept. 1858 to Feb. 1861 with a 25-day schedule for the 2,795-mile trip (8 to 9 days were allowed for crossing Texas). Route began in Tipton, Mo., and Memphis, Tenn., uniting at Fort Smith, Ark., entering Texas near Sherman, thence westward through the Comanche-held frontier, leaving the state at El Paso. Stage stations were

4

located about every 20 miles, and the best known in this vicinity were Fort Belknap, Fort Phantom Hill, Mountain Pass and Fort Chadbourne. Between Fort Belknap and Tucson, Arizona mules were used to pull the coaches as they were less appealing to Indians. Each coach accommodated four to ten passengers at an average fare of $200 each; mail and freight charges were ten cents per one-half ounce. (1969)

ABILENE (Taylor Co.)
US 83/84, 12 mi. S in roadside park
Taylor County
Created 1858. Named for Edward, James and George Taylor, 18, 20, and 22, Tennesseans who came to Texas in 1833 and died at the Alamo, March 6, 1836. Organized 1878, with county seat at Buffalo Gap, through which went the Fort Concho to Fort Belknap stagecoach and longhorns on western trail up to Kansas. County seat was moved to Abilene in 1883. Of the 254 Texas counties, 42 bear Indian, French or Spanish names. 10 honor such colonizers as Stephen F. Austin, "Father of Texas". 12 were named for Washington, Clay and other American patriots. 96 were named for men like the Taylors who fought in the Texas War for Independence (15 dying at the Alamo), signed the Declaration of Independence, or served as statesmen in the Republic of Texas. 23 have the names of frontiersmen and pioneers. 11 honor American statesmen who worked for the annexation of Texas; 10, leaders in Texas since statehood, including jurists, ministers, educators, historians, statesmen; and 36, men prominent in the Confederacy during the Civil War. El Paso and 8 others have geographical names, San Jacinto and Val Verde were named for battles; Live Oak and Orange, for trees; and Mason for a fort. (1964)

ADAMSVILLE (Lampasas Co.)
US 281
John Patterson Home
Built 1879–1880 by John Patterson, first man to cultivate (in 1854) land in county, and a minute-man during Civil War. (1965)

ADRIAN (Oldham Co.)
IH 40, 4 mi. W at picnic area
Fort Smith–Santa Fe Trail
What came to be known as the Fort Smith–Santa Fe Trail was first blazed in 1840 by Josiah Gregg, a trader seeking a route to Santa Fe along the south side of the Canadian River. In 1849, Gregg's route was closely followed by a military escort led by Capt. Randolph B. Marcy (1812–1857). Marcy's group traveled from Fort Smith, Arkansas to Santa Fe with about 500 pioneers heading for California. The party entered Oldham County on June 13th, and on June 14th ascended to the Llano Estacado near this site. Reaching the top, Marcy found the plains "as boundless . . . and trackless as the ocean . . . a desolate waste of uninhabited solitude." Eighty-five days after leaving Fort Smith, the party reached Santa Fe. After passing the plains, Marcy remarked, "I have never passed a country where wagons could move along with as much ease and facility, without expenditure of any labor in making a road, as upon this route." Marcy advocated the trail as a prospective route for a transcontinental railroad, which was built after the Civil War. Later, as the country entered the automobile age and the interstate highway system was developed, U.S. Highway 66 (Route 66) and Interstate 40 were laid close to the trail. (1991)

AGUA DULCE (Nueces Co.)
SH 44, E
Battle of Agua Dulce
During the Texas Revolution, Dr. James Grant (1793–1836), a Scottish-born physician, and Francis W. Johnson (1799–1884) recruited an army of volunteers to invade Mexico and capture the town of Matamoros. After Sam Houston expressed disapproval of the poorly-organized venture, many recruits left the expedition before it reached the settlement of San Patricio along the Nueces River in January 1836. Mexican General Santa Anna, who was organizing an army to attack Texan forces at the Alamo in San Antonio, discovered the Matamoros plan and dispatched General Jose Urrea to stop the advancing expedition. Urrea's cavalry, reinforced with 300 infantrymen, crossed the Rio Grande on February 16. Meanwhile, Grant and Johnson divided their troops to hunt for horses. Johnson's men were camped at San Patricio when Urrea attacked on the morning of February 27. Johnson and 4 others escaped, while 18 Texans were killed and 32 captured. On March 2, Urrea's soldiers surprised Grant's company at Agua Dulce Creek (3.25 Mi. NW). Grant was among the 12 Texans killed; 6 were taken prisoner, and 6 escaped. The brief skirmish occurred on the same day the Texas Declaration of Independence was signed at Washington-on-the-Brazos. (1976)

5

ALAMO (Hidalgo Co.)   *1341 W US 83 Bus.*
Camp Ebenezer
From 1902 to 1909, Peter Ebenezer Blalock and George L. Hawkins bought 32,000 acres of land here. By 1908 they had built shipping pens at this site and named the railroad depot Ebenezer. Their ranching plans ended in 1909 when the tract was sold to the Alamo Land and Sugar Company. Under the direction of C. H. Swallow (1868–1957), the company colonized the land after 1914. Excursion trains brought prospective farmers, housed here at "Camp Ebenezer." The depot was moved one mile east in 1919 to serve the new town of Alamo. The camp served until the 1930s as temporary housing for land buyers.   (Texas Sesquicentennial 1836–1986)

ALBANY (Shackelford Co.)   *US 283, 14 mi. N, Fort Griffin State Historic Site*
Family Forts, C.S.A.
Few in numbers and with little protection from the military but refusing to abandon their country, certain families of courageous and determined people on the Texas frontier during the Civil War gathered together in hastily constructed stockades and held out against the threats of hostile Indians and renegade whites known as "forting up." This plan was encouraged by the military for this part of the state. Most of the men 18 to 45 were away in Confederate service, and those 17 and over 45 were subject to periodic militia duty for frontier protection. Family forts gave settlers a way to protect stock, farms and provide some schooling for their children. Best-known family fort in this sector was Fort Davis, located 8 miles east on bank Clear Fork of Brazos in Stephens County, where some 120 people lived during last year of Civil War. Named for Confederate President Jefferson Davis, it was laid off in lots. Log houses with dirt roofs, mud in cracks, dirt floors, were connected by pickets driven into ground. A blockhouse was used by women and children during raids. There were no luxuries, little food; all clothes, soap, soda, candles were made. Nearest supplies were 100 miles away, doctor 65 miles. Yet, there were dances, candy pulls, weddings, "feasts," Sunday school, occasional sermons and blue-backed spellers. Other family forts near were Lynch and Green ranches, Shackelford County; Blair's Fort, Allen's ranch, Eastland County; Buffalo Springs, Clay County; Bragg's, Murray's, Young County; Picketville, Mugginsville, Owls Head, Stephens County.   (1963)

ALBANY (Shackelford Co.)   *US 180 at SH 6, courthouse*
Shackelford County
First inhabited by Nomadic Indian tribes, Shackelford County was created in 1858 and named for Dr. John Shackelford (1790–1857). The first permanent Anglo-American settlers in this area included J. C. Lynch (1828–1912), a native of Ireland who moved here in 1858; W. H. Ledbetter (1833–1884), who arrived in 1859 and later started the Ledbetter Salt Works; T. E. Jackson (b. 1820), a merchant who settled in the northern part of the county before 1860; and G. W. Greer (1812–1893), who operated a stage station on Hubbard Creek after 1861. During the Civil War (1861–1865), settlers took refuge at "family forts" such as Fort Mugginsville and Fort Hubbard. They gained military protection from frontier perils when the U.S. Army established Fort Griffin in 1867. Griffin, the lawless settlement that grew up around the fort, attracted buffalo hide hunters and cattlemen driving herds up the western cattle trail. Shackelford County was organized Sept. 12, 1874, with Fort Griffin as temporary county seat. Albany was chosen permanent county seat in Nov. 1874. The county's population increased sharply after the arrival of the Texas Central Railroad in 1881. Petroleum production generated an economic boom, 1910–1930. Chief industries today (1976) are petroleum and ranching.   (1976)

ALBANY (Shackelford Co.)   *US 180 at US 283, Albany City Park*
The Cook Ranch Oil Field (5 mi. NW on FM 1084)
William Ivy Cook (1857–1923) and his wife Matilda moved to this county in 1895. With a brother-in-law, J. H. Nail, Cook purchased a 27.75 section ranch. The Cooks bought out Nail in 1898, and have owned the ranch ever since. During the 1918 Breckenridge and Ranger booms, Cook sold leases but prophesied he could drink from his hat all of the oil under his land. In 1925 his widow leased all open acreage to Charles Roeser, Tol Pendleton, and Marshall R. Young, of Roeser & Pendleton, Inc. This firm's second well in 1926 struck oil at 1241 feet and flowed at 1,000 barrels a day. This prolific flow of oil at such a shallow depth has been one of Cook ranch field's remarkable features. Commercial low pressure gas injection was started on the ranch in 1927 and helped elevate recovery standards internationally. With the oil wealth, Mrs. Cook founded the W. I.

Cook Memorial Hospital in Fort Worth in 1929. Cook field enriched Albany and its trade area by expanding petroleum-related business activities. Of the 1087 wells drilled on the ranch, 825 yielded oil and four gas. Production has now exceeded thirty million barrels. Marshall R. Young remains owner of the oil firm. (1976)

ALBANY (Shackelford Co.) *US 180, 12.5 mi. W*
Butterfield Overland Mail Trail
The trail of the Butterfield Overland mail passed this point 1858.

ALBANY (Shackelford Co.) *SH 180, 14 mi. W*
Bud Matthews Switch of the Texas Central Railway
In 1900, the Texas Central Railway extended a line northwest from Albany across this portion of Rose Ella (Matthews) Conrad's cattle ranch. Ella and her Brother John A. "Budi" Matthews, for whom this site is named, promptly constructed cattle pens and a loading chute at this location. Surrounding ranchers soon were shipping their cattle from this switch to markets in Fort Worth. As many as 105,000 head of cattle were shipped annually until the railroad ceased operations in 1967. Since that year local ranchers have continued to load cattle onto trucks from this site. (1993)

ALICE (Jim Wells Co.) *US 281, 14.4 mi. N*
Vicinity of Texas Rangers' Battle of May 29, 1850
A gallant fight in an era after the Mexican War, while the Federals and Texans were ridding Nueces to Rio Grande area of marauders. Texas Rangers under Capt. John S. "Rip" Ford surprised a camp of Comanches near this site on May 29, 1850. In numbers, Rangers and Indians were about equal. Seven Comanches were wounded, four slain; one ranger was killed and two were wounded. Comanche Chief Otto Cuero was wounded by Capt. Ford and slain by a bullet from the gun of Ranger David Steele, who sent Chief's regalia to Governor P. H. Bell, an ex-Texas Ranger. (1969)

ALICE (Jim Wells Co.) *US 281 at SH 44*
Jim Wells County
Formed from Nueces County, created March 11, 1911; organized May 6, 1911; named for Judge James B. Wells, an able lawyer, born near Aransas Pass, Texas, July 12, 1854; died at Brownsville December 21, 1923. Alice, the county seat.

ALICE (Jim Wells Co.) *SH 44/359 at FM 1931*
Archelaus Bynum Dodson (December 31, 1807–March 10, 1898)
Texas patriot famed as man who introduced the Lone Star flag during the Texas Revolution. Born in North Carolina, Dodson came to Texas with his parents in 1827. He served as a delegate to the 1832 convention seeking governmental reforms. On May 17, 1835, he married Sarah Rudolph Bradley. Later in the year 1835, Dodson was first lieutenant in Texas defense unit under Capt. Andrew Robinson. To Robinson's company his bride presented her handiwork—a red, white and blue flag with a single star, launching tradition of Lone Star Flag of Texas. This banner flew at Washington-on-the Brazos when Declaration of Independence was signed March 2, 1836. Dodson continued to fight in the Texas Revolution until after victory at San Jacinto. He located his headright of land Grimes County, moving family there in 1844. Mrs. Sarah Bradley Dodson, flag maker and mother of six children, died in 1848. Her grave is in Bethel cemetery, near Bedias, Grimes County. Dodson in 1850 married Louisa McWhorter, a widow. In 1860 he moved his family west to another Texas frontier, on the Nueces River. In this vicinity he lived to a respected old age. At death he was buried in Collins cemetery, a half-mile south of here. (1969)

ALLEN (Collin Co.) *Exchange Parkway, Allen Station Park*
Allen
Fertile land and plentiful water drew settlers to this area from as early as the 1840s. This part of Collin County was well populated by 1876 when the Houston and Texas Central Railroad built a water supply stop on Cottonwood Creek near this site. The railroad stop and newly created town lots established a center of commerce for local farmers and their families and provided better equipment and broader markets for agricultural production. The surrounding open prairie soon was developed into small family farms. The Houston and Texas Central Railroad filed documents to create the town of Allen from the James L. Read survey in 1876. The village was named for Ebenezer Allen, a former Republic and State of Texas attorney general and a founder of the Houston

and Texas Central Railroad. A dry goods store, barber shop, and school soon opened in the rapidly growing town. Sam Bass reportedly led an outlaw gang that robbed the Allen Depot on February 22, 1878. This was probably the first successful train robbery in Texas. By 1884, the town of Allen had three churches, a flour mill, and a population of 350. In 1908, the Texas Traction Company built an electric railway through town, calling it the Interurban, the citizenry numbered 550 by 1915. Allen was incorporated in 1953 with 400 residents. Electric railway service ended in 1948, but railway freight service continued. Strong economic growth in the Dallas–Fort Worth area helped the town's population grow to include more than 19,000 citizens in the 1990s. (1998)

ALPINE (Brewster Co.)
US 90 at US 67, 8 mi. E, at roadside park
Ancient Rocks Boundary
The mountains toward the east are limestone reef beds deposited in the Cretaceous and Permian Seas about 135 million years and 250 million years ago, respectively. The limestone reefs overlie deformed rocks in the Ouachita Fold Belt, which is visible along the highway to the east, near Marathon. To the south are younger limestone beds deposited about 125 to 135 million years ago. They also rest above the Ouachita Fold Belt (so named for the Ouachita Mountains of Arkansas-Oklahoma, where the formation was first studied by geologists). Toward the west, northwest, and southwest are layers of lava and associated volcanic rocks 25 to 35 million years old. These were thrust upward, into, and over most of the older sedimentary rock layers. Many of the molten rock masses cooled and hardened underneath, while vast quantities poured over the surface in the form of lava flows and volcanic debris up to a mile in thickness. Subsequent erosion has sculptured these highlands by removing much of the younger volcanic rock, and cutting deeply into the older sea deposits. Out of the lower, igneous hills grow yucca and other cacti, contrasting with juniper and piñon on the higher elevations. (1970)

ALPINE (Brewster Co.)
US 67/90, 8 mi. E
Brewster County
Formed from Presidio County, created February 2, 1887, organized February 14, 1887. In 1897 the territory of Buchel and Foley Counties was added to Brewster. Named for Henry Percy Brewster, 1816–1884 soldier and statesman, a hero of San Jacinto. Murphyville, county seat, 1887, name changed to Alpine, 1889. Largest county in area in the state.

ALPINE (Brewster Co.)
US 67/90, 2.3 mi. E
Alpine
Original name Osborne. Central gateway to Big Bend National Park. Largest city in largest county in Texas. Center for mining, livestock, travel. Named for its mountainous setting. Site well known for its spring during Indian days. First settled in 1882 as a Southern Pacific railroad stop. Called Murphyville, 1883–1887, for owner of the waterhole. Originally in Presidio County. Was made county seat 1887 when Brewster County was created. Historic sites marked. Western lore displayed at museum, Sul Ross State College. (1965)

ALTO (Cherokee Co.)
SH 294, 9 mi. W
Box's Fort
John M. and Sally Box, along with John's brother Stephen F. and his wife Keziah Box and their families, came to Texas from Alabama in 1834. John and Sally's son, Roland W. Box, and his wife Mary Hallmark Box purchased ⅓ of the Stephen Burnham land grant and built a log fort on a hill near its northern boundary. Within the enclosure they built a log house and a dugout, and Box's Fort became the center of a settlement as the extended Box families made their own homes in and near the fort. John A. Stillwell, Thomas G., and Nelson Box and their cousins Samuel C. and James E. Box fought in the Texas Revolution. The home of John A. and Letty T. Box was a post office called Box's Creek from 1851 to 1866. Over time, several churches and stores operated in the vicinity, but by 1900 Box's Fort no longer appeared on area maps. (2000)

ALTO (Cherokee Co.)
US 69 to CR 2405, 2 mi. N
Chief Bowles' Last Homesite
In 1836, General Sam Houston negotiated a treaty with the Cherokees in Texas allowing possession of the lands they occupied in East Texas. The leading figure among the Cherokees at that time was Duwali (also known as Bowl, Chief Bowles and Bold Hunter). After the Texas Revolution, the

8

Senate of the Republic of Texas declared the treaty invalid. Near this site in 1839, Chief Bowles learned of Texas President Mirabeau B. Lamar's orders to remove the Cherokee from Texas. Bowl mobilized his people to resist the expulsion, but they were defeated and the chief was killed at the Battle of the Neches on July 16, 1839, in what is now Van Zandt County.   (2001)

ALTO (Cherokee Co.)   *US 69, 1 mi. S, then 1 mi. E*
Cherokee Home of Grand Xinesi
In the present county of Cherokee was the home of the Grand Xinesi, chief priest and custodian of the sacred fire of the Hasinai Confederacy of Indians. If fire was allowed to die out, it was his duty to carry more fire with proper ceremony to their homes to be rekindled. It was to the Hasinai, the principal tribe of this Confederacy, that the word "Texas" was generally applied.

ALTO (Cherokee Co.)   *US 69 & FM 1911, 10.5 mi. S*
Homer-Alto Road
As the population increased in Angelina and Cherokee counties in the 1860s, a formal system of roads began to take shape. Until that time, roads were usually forged by farmers and other pioneers carrying goods to market or traveling to new homes, as in other areas of Texas. Construction of a road from Homer (at that time Angelina County seat) to Alto began in 1860. The survey crew followed buffalo and Indian trails to determine the best route for the new road. Once open, it was the official mail route from Homer to Alto, and then on to Rusk, the Cherokee County seat. It led through a community known as Denman Springs until 1882 when Lufkin was created there and the road became Denman Avenue. The main part of the Homer-Alto Road became State Highway 40 in the 1930s and later U. S. Highway 69.   (1999)

ALTO (Cherokee Co.)   *SH 21, 7 mi. E at Angelina River*
Angelina River
Early Texas artery of travel and transportation. Ran through land of civilized Indians whose word "Tejas," for friend, gave name to northern part of New Spain, then to the Republic and State of Texas. Here in 1690, Spanish explorers and missionaries found a young girl eager to learn Christianity. For her sweet disposition, she was called Angelina. Her name soon was used for the river where she lived. Though French and Spaniards were enemies, Angelina befriended all, and for years acted as interpreter. Angelina River by 1779 was route for settlers to come from the coast to East Texas. It was crossed by El Camino Real (King's Highway to Mexico) and by Smugglers' Road, for those dodging tax collectors. In the 1830s, John Durst promoted on the Angelina, just south of here, a port for shipping cotton to New Orleans and receiving merchandise in return. Other Texas Rivers named by Spaniards include the Blanco, Brazos (River of the Arms of God), Colorado, Concho, Comal (a pan), Frio, Guadalupe, Lavaca, Llano, Medina, Navidad, Navasota, Neches, Nueces, Pedernales, Pecos Rio Grande, San Antonio, San Gabriel, Trinity and San Jacinto. Anglo-American names for streams include Canadian, Pease, Red and Devil's River.   (1965)

ALTO (Cherokee Co.)   *SH 21, 7 mi. E*
Site of Linwood
On land inherited by Delilah Dill Durst from Helena Kimble Dill, whose daughter born in 1804 was thought to be first white child native to Texas. Built about 1830 by Delilah's husband, Joseph Durst, who settled in Texas in early 1800's and rose by 1826 to office of alcalde in Nacogdoches. During troubles of 1832, the Battle of Nacogdoches ended here with surrender of Colonel Piedras' army to 17 Texans. Later was home of Geo. Whitfield Terrell (1802–1846), who served Republic of Texas as attorney-general and as minister to England, France, and Spain. Birthplace of Geo. B. Terrell (1862–1947), state representative, commissioner of agriculture, and congressman-at-large.   (1965)

ALTO (Cherokee Co.)   *SH 21 at CR 2610, 2 mi. E*
Ellis P. Bean, June 8, 1783–October 3, 1846
Born in Tennessee, Ellis P. Bean came to Texas with Philip Nolan's mustang hunters in 1800. He was captured by Spanish troops in 1801, and taken to Mexico as a prisoner. In 1810 he was freed in exchange for service to the Royalist Army, but he quickly deserted to the rebels under Morelos. Fifteen years later, Bean returned to the U. S. as a Mexican colonel to seek aid for the rebel cause. He joined Andrew Jackson's army at the Battle of New Orleans, but returned to Mexico within the

year. In 1816 he barely escaped the Royalists by leaving his wife to flee to the U. S. He married a Tennessean in 1818. They moved to Texas in 1823, where Bean served Mexico as an Indian agent. After Texas independence, Bean made his home near this site. He disappeared in 1843 to return to Mexico, dying in the home of his first wife in 1846.   (1999)

ALTO (Cherokee Co.)   *SH 21, 2.5 mi. SW*
Cherokee
In the present county of Cherokee was the home of the exalted Grand Xinesi—Chief Priest and Custodian of the Sacred Fire of the Hasinai Confederacy of Indians. If fire was allowed to die out, it was his duty to carry more fire with proper ceremony to their homes to be rekindled. It was to the Hasinai—the principal tribe of this Confederacy—that the word "Texas" was generally applied.

ALTO (Cherokee Co.)   *SH 21, 2.5 mi. SW*
Site of Delaware Indian Village
Noted as interpreters and messengers of peace, the Delaware were chiefly instrumental in bringing the other tribes to the general treaty at Bird's Fort (in the present county of Tarrant) in 1843.

ALTO (Cherokee Co.)   *SH 21, 2.5 mi. SW*
Site of Lacy's Fort
Built before 1835 as a home and trading post by Martin Lacy, Indian agent for the Mexican government. Used as a place of refuge after the massacre of the Killough family, October 5, 1838.

ALTO (Cherokee Co.)   *Caddoan Mound State Historic Site, SH 21, 6 mi. SW*
Zebulon Pike Campsite
In 1807, under commission from Gen. James Wilkinson, Governor of the Louisiana Territory, Lt. Zebulon Pike led an expedition to explore the headwaters of the Arkansas and Red Rivers and to report on Spanish settlements in the New Mexico area. Heading south from present Colorado, where the party saw the mountain later named Pike's Peak for the expedition's leader, they were arrested by Spanish authorities. Under escort back to the United States, the party camped near this site on June 23, 1807. The Pike Expedition furnished an important account of Spanish Texas and New Mexico.   (1982)

ALTO (Cherokee Co.)   *SH 21, 8 mi. SW*
Site of Neches Indian Village
Here at the opening of the 18th century stood a village of the Neches Indians. Their name was given to the river and later a mission, San Francisco de los Neches, established near by. With the Cherokees, the Neches Indians were expelled from Texas, 1839.

ALTO (Cherokee Co.)   *SH 21, 8 mi. SW*
Mound Prairie
Bulging out of the earth a few yards from this point, three prehistoric Indian mounds interrupt the prevailing flat terrain. Long overgrown with grass, the mounds and adjacent village (covering about 11 acres) constitute one of the major aboriginal sites in North America. From about 500 to 1100 A.D., Caddoan Indians inhabited the village, which lay near the southwest edge of a great mound-building culture. Called "Mississippian," this culture once flourished throughout the present Eastern United States. Excavations during 1939–1941 and 1968–1969 showed two of the mounds to have had ceremonial purposes. One may have been capped with bright yellow clay and both apparently supported temples. The tallest mound (about 20 feet) revealed several major burials. The village surrounding the mounds but settled before they were built, contained many round houses that probably resembled giant beehives. Thousands of pot fragments, some pipes, charred corncobs and nuts, and flint points were found in the area. Centuries after its abandonment by the Indians, this region was again a center of civilization when, in 1690, the first Spanish mission in East Texas was built nearby to minister to the Tejas Indians.   (1970)

ALVARADO (Johnson Co.)   *6921 US 67 at IH-35*
Site of Norman Springs & Norman Grove
William Balch (1804–1870) claimed land around this site as a member of the Peters Colony in 1849. When he returned with his family in 1851, they found a group of Caddo Indians camping on

one side of the springs. The Balch family built their cabin on the other side and lived peaceably with their neighbors. Other Caddo were living in the area that became Alvarado. Like the new settlers, they were attracted by the abundance of fresh water. The springs were located on the road from Birdville and Fort Worth to Hillsboro, Waco, Ft. Graham and other destinations. William Balch founded the town of Alvarado in 1854 and the family moved into town. Joe (1798–1882) and Sarah (1797–1897) Shaw and their family settled here and farmed the land. Joe Shaw was a three-term county sheriff. With settlers coming in increasing numbers, the Caddo Indians moved to the Oklahoma territory or further west, and by 1860 the area was dominated by new settlers. Tennessee native Lafayette Norman (1826–1904), veteran of the U. S. war with Mexico and later the Confederate Army, purchased 245 acres around this site with his third wife Julia in 1872. The Normans supplied thirsty and weary travelers with access to their spring; the site became known as Norman Springs and Norman Grove. A seven-year drought in the 1930s and a five-year drought in the 1950s significantly reduced the water table in this region. Norman Springs slowly became little more than a muddy patch. By the dawn of the 21st century, the once free-flowing spring that provided priceless fresh water to the early Indians and pioneer settlers of the Johnson County frontier was marked only by a willow tree. (2000)

ALVIN (Brazoria Co.) *SH 35, 6 mi. S in roadside park*
Vicinity of Oyster Creek and Chocolate Bayou
Most early Texas homes and towns were built along streams that provided water for people and livestock, and travel for boats said to be capable of "floating on a heavy dew." Oyster Creek served, 1822–1861, as such a homesite-highway. Its boat landings were piled high with sugar, cotton, cane and other products of some of America's richest plantations. Chocolate Bayou was an area of early-day cattle raising. These were 2 of 50 streams and 10 bays that made this coast a network of useful waterways. (1968)

ALVORD (Wise Co.) *US 287 near N city limit*
NE at 606 Washington Street Is Birthplace of General Ernest O. Thompson (1892–1966)
Acknowledged world leader in petroleum conservation. A third generation Texan, born here in Alvord. Left college to enter service in World War I, earning a battlefield commission as lieutenant colonel—at the time the youngest in American Army. In 1930, he gained national acclaim as crusading mayor of Amarillo. Appointed (1932) to Texas Railroad Commission; served by election until 1966. From prior career of lawyer-hotel owner, he stepped into public duty which sent him at once into East Texas during the world's greatest oil boom, to enforce proration. At peril of his life, he shut off non-complying wells and made the petroleum industry respect Texas laws. He became a pioneer in conservation practices. With promptings from President Franklin Roosevelt, he led in 1934 in founding of the Interstate Oil Compact Commission. In Paris in 1937, he represented the United States at the World Petroleum Congress. By presidential order he was returned to Texas by the army in World War II, to ensure oil supplies for allied military forces. He was awarded American Petroleum Institute Gold Medal for distinguished achievement, in 1951. As an international authority on oil—a key to world trade—he had great influence on the course of history. (1972)

ALVORD (Wise Co.) *US 287 in Alvord*
City of Alvord
By 1882, when the Fort Worth & Denver Railroad built a line to this area, a small agricultural community had developed here on an old Indian trail. First known as Nina, the town was renamed Alvord in 1883, probably in honor of J. B. Alvord, president of the railroad. Early businesses here included mercantile stores, a drugstore, a variety store, a bank, hotels, and a saloon with a second floor opera house. The first school was established at Briar Branch in 1890. Alvord has continued to develop as a center of farming, ranching, and oil production. (1982)

AMARILLO (Potter Co.) *Located on highways leading into Amarillo*
Amarillo
County seat, Potter County; founded in 1887. Incorporated 1892. Named for Arroyo Amarillo, Spanish name of nearby creek. Transportation, financial, cultural and medical center. Gateway to Alibates Flint Quarry National Monument, Lake Meredith, Palo Duro State Park, Panhandle-Plains Historical Museum, Boys Ranch. (1965)

11

AMARILLO (Potter Co.)   *Hollywood Rd. (FM 2186) just W of Loop 335*
Amarillo Helium Plant
This plant, operated by the United States Bureau of Mines, was the first to produce helium from the extensive helium resources in the Texas Panhandle. From 1929 until 1943, it furnished almost all of the world's supply of helium. Operating around the clock, the plant extracts helium by liquifying the natural gas and separating helium from it at temperatures 300 degrees below zero.

The natural reserves in these fields and in extensions into adjacent states contain more than 95 percent of the world's known supply of helium. This is also the site of the world renowned research center which provides fundamental data on the production and uses of helium. Helium is used for a variety of purposes: lighter-than-air craft, low-temperature research, shielded-arc welding; and in national defense, nuclear energy programs and space exploration.   (1965)

AMARILLO (Potter Co.)   *SH 136, about 40 mi. NE*
                                                   (Overlooking Lake Meredith)
Pioneer in Texas Geology and Paleontology
Dr. Charles Newton Gould (1868–1949)
One of early scientists to use geology in search for oil and gas. This region's rapid economic growth in 1920s and '30s was result of Gould's selection of drill site for Hapgood No. 1-Masterson, discovery well of the vast Panhandle-Hugoton gas field, the world's largest known source for helium. Gould was born in Ohio; grew up in Kansas, where he began teaching; gained scientific background in summer schools and in covered wagon and horseback field trips; by 25 was a widely-known paleontologist; became a professor at the University of Oklahoma. In 1903–1905 he made studies of Texas Panhandle water resources, for the United States geological survey. A geological structure he observed (1904) and named Alibates Dolomite in 1907 led him to suggest to Amarillo merchants and ranchmen the drilling site in 1918 for Hapgood No. 1-Masterson Well. In 1919 he set the location for Gulf No. 2, first oil well in the Texas Panhandle and high plains region.

Gould was the scientist who first identified these quarries (now Alibates National Monument) as source for flint artifacts made by ice age Folsom man—a major North American anthropological discovery.   (1967)

AMARILLO (Potter Co.)   *SH 136, 20 mi. NE*
The Fort Smith–Santa Fe Trail, Marcy Route, 1849
Clearly visible to the northeast and southwest are ruts of the old Fort Smith–Santa Fe Trail, the overland route connecting river ports of Fort Smith and Van Buren, Arkansas, with Santa Fe, New Mexico. Route gained national fame when Col. R. B. Marcy, U.S. Army, escorted party of 500 Arkansans—professional and business men and families—over this road in June 1849, on the way to California's gold fields. Scores of goldseekers in smaller groups also used the route that year. Old trail became proposed route in 1853 for first Transcontinental Railroad as surveyed by Lt. A. W. Whipple. Prior to the Civil War, this route had won congressional support, but the war shifted sentiment so that Union Pacific, to the northward, actually was built first. During the war, a mail line left the old Butterfield stage route in eastern Oklahoma and went by way of this point over to Las Vegas and Santa Fe. In 1878 began usage of this link of road for a mail-stage line from the Federal fort at Mobeetie, in the Texas Panhandle, to Las Vegas, New Mexico. The trail has not been used since 1888.   (1965)

AMARILLO (Potter Co.)   *SH 136, 12 mi. NE*
Fort Smith–Santa Fe Trail, Gregg Route, 1840
This marks the site of the nationally known Overland Trail that connected the river ports of Fort Smith and Van Buren, Arkansas, with Santa Fe, center of travel and trade since 1609. This road was pioneered by Josiah Gregg, a Santa Fe trader who first passed this point on March 15, 1840. Many goldseekers later used his route, beginning in the summer of 1849, after gold was found in California. Before barbed wire fences, regular travelers here were military parties and traders.   (1964)

AMARILLO (Potter Co.)   *SH 136, 7.5 mi. NE*
Canadian River Project
The Canadian River Municipal Water Authority was authorized by a Texas constitutional amendment on May 27, 1953. It was approved, by vote of citizens of eleven West Texas cities, for purpose of supplying municipal and industrial water to Amarillo, Borger, Brownfield, Lamesa, Leveland,

Lubbock, O'Donnell, Pampa, Plainview, Slaton and Tahoka. Construction was supervised by the United States Bureau of Reclamation. Sanford Dam (located 34 mi. NE of here) is the impounding structure for Lake Meredith. The aqueduct system consists of 322 miles of concrete pressure pipe—the longest pipeline supervised by the Reclamation Bureau to this date. Construction costs ($83,799,000) covered the following items: municipal and industrial water, $76,975,000; flood control, $2,833,000; fish and wildlife, $2,891,000; recreation $1,100,000. Water cost will be repaid to Federal government, with interest, over a 50-year period. This is largest repayment contract ever made between a water authority and the U.S. government. This section of pipe is identical to that utilized in segment of the aqueduct two miles west of this marker. This pipe section is 78 inches in diameter, 22 feet in length and weighs 36,000 pounds. (1968)

AMARILLO (Potter Co.)   US 287, 30 mi. N
First Gas Well in the Panhandle of Texas
The discovery well in the vast Panhandle-Hugoton Gas Field, largest known gas field in the world, is located one mile east of this point on the east slope of John Ray Butte. The geological structure was discovered by Dr. Charles N. Gould in 1905 while in the employ of the United States Geological Survey, and the well was located by him in 1917. This well, the Hapgood-Masterson No. 1, was started December 1, 1917, and completed at a cost of $70,000 as a gas well December 7, 1918, at a depth of 2,605 feet. It produced about 5,000,000 cubic feet of gas per day. This discovery initiated the development of this great gas field and of the Panhandle oil fields. The gas field now extends 275 miles from the Texas Panhandle north into Kansas, with a width in places of more than 90 miles. Pipelines from this field transmit gas to Denver, Kansas City, St. Louis, Chicago, Detroit, and to most of the cities and towns of the Mid-West. Lines also carry gas to Los Angeles and to other cities and towns on the West Coast. (1965)

AMARILLO (Potter Co.)   US 87/287, 22 mi. N
The LX, First Ranch in Potter County
Established by W. H. Bates and D. T. Beals, Colorado merchants and ranchers on the Arkansas River since 1870. "Crowded conditions" there resulted in moving herd and brand to the Panhandle of Texas in 1877—three years after Indians were expelled from this region. LX cattle were being driven to Dodge City for shipment to market or to ranges in Montana and Wyoming as the Buffalo were being exterminated in the area. The ranch extended from present cities of Dumas (30 mi. N) to Amarillo (20 mi. S), and was 20 miles wide—1,000 square miles of open range. The ranch was sold in 1884 to the American Pastoral Company, LTD., London. Ownership included 210,597 acres of land, 45,000 cattle, and 1,000 horses. Famous LX cowboys included Allie Bates and John Ray, whose names are on geological maps, and Charles Siringo, author of *Western Americana* and *Cattle Rustler Detective*. Potter County was organized on Aug. 30, 1887, by 53 qualified electors. By unanimous vote of the 38 LX Cowboys Amarillo was elected the county seat. In 1906 the Pastoral Company began liquidating. Heirs of large purchasers now own the properties. (1971)

AMARILLO (Potter Co.)   US 87/287 right of way, 19 mi. N
The United States Topographical Engineers in the High Plains of Texas
This region and much of Western America was mapped under adversity, as territory held by hostile Indians. With the dual aims of compiling scientific data and opening the way for settlers, U.S. Army topographers covered ground earlier traversed by conquistadors and mountain men. Earlier travelers mentioned their experiences. The topographers mapped the terrain. The United States Army Topographical Corps from 1838 to 1863 consisted of 36 officers. Barometer, compass, sextant, and pencil were their instruments for handling data on climate, geographical features, soil, feasible routes for wagons or railroads, and sites for towns and industrial developments. Three topographical parties investigated the land that is now Potter County: Lt. James W. Abert invaded this Indian region in 1845 to survey environs of the Canadian and other rivers; Lt. James H. Simpson in 1849 reconnoitered a proposed railroad route from Fort Smith to Santa Fe; Lt. Amiel W. Whipple in 1853 mapped another railroad route from the Mississippi to the Pacific. The United States owes great honor to these and other topographers. (1973)

AMARILLO (Potter Co.)   US 87, 16 mi. N at Canadian River Bridge
Great Spanish Road
Near course of the Canadian River, early as days of the American Revolution, men from Santa Fe went past this spot on trips to meet traders from San Augustine, Nacogdoches and other Spanish

towns of East Texas. In 1786, Pedro Vial was commissioned by the Spanish governor at Santa Fe to establish this route, and secure direct connection from Santa Fe to San Antonio, Texas with access to East Texas towns. The great Spanish road served well colonial Texas and foreshadowed 20th century usage of the route for a segment of a great international highway.

First Ranch in Potter County
Established 1877 at point 1½ miles east of this site, by Bates and Beals, northern investors. Ran the LX brand, and once had a cowboy named Will Rogers, later internationally famous as a humorist.

First Store in Potter County
Opened 1878 a few hundred feet west of this marker, by William Pitcher, whose name was given to nearby creek, and who figured in a desperate robbery from which LX cowhands "rescued him."   (1964)

AMARILLO (Potter Co.)   *2705 SW. 6th Ave. (SH 279)*
Amarillo Natatorium ("The Nat")
The Natatorium, an open air building surrounding a swimming pool that measured 36' by 101', opened in July 1922. "The Nat" was enclosed in 1923 for year round use. In 1926 the building was converted into a dance hall with 10,000 square feet of maple flooring covering the pool area. "The Nat" also provided dining and at its peak employed 40 staff members. Well known bands traveling along Route 66 often stopped here to entertain. Though closed as a public dance hall in the 1960's, "The Nat" served the Amarillo area as a significant social center for decades.   (1996)

AMARILLO (Potter Co.)   *SW. 6th Ave. (SH 279) at S. Georgia St.*
Route 66 in Amarillo
Commonly called the "Main Street of America" and also the "Mother Road," Route 66 became the first paved transcontinental highway in the U.S. spanning from Chicago to Los Angeles; the route in Texas crossed 7 panhandle counties over 177 miles. Route 66 was popular with automobile tourists. The road was important in the development of Sixth Street and the San Jacinto area in Amarillo, which was the only large urban city on the Texas route. In 1994 the area was listed in the National Register of historic places, and has become the focus of local preservation efforts.(1996)

ANAHUAC (Chambers Co.)   *IH 10, 8 mi. NW at Trinity River Bridge*
Taylor White Ranch
On this ranch, a part of the grant of James Taylor White who came to Texas in 1828, the Texas force camped before Anahuac and the colonists drew up the Turtle Bayou Resolutions, June 13, 1832.

ANAHUAC (Chambers Co.)   *IH 10, .25 mi. E of the Trinity River Bridge*
Mission Nuestra Señora de la Luz Del Orcoquisac
and Presidio San Agustín de Ahumada
Two of the most misfortune-ridden outposts of Spain in Texas, "Our Lady of the Light" Mission and its auxiliary fort, were founded near here in 1756 to guard against French encroachment from the east. The two friars who were to minister to members of the Orcoquisac tribe arrived shortly after the 30 soldiers who were to man the fort. Soon, however, the elder friar died. The younger, asking to be relieved of his duties, complained vividly of biting insects, extremes of heat and cold, and the thick and stinking water in the lake near the lonely mission. The 50 families who were to establish a town at the site never arrived, and although valiant efforts were made at improvement, conditions instead became worse. A woeful lack of training among the soldiers sparked unrest among the Indians. Meager supplies of food, clothing, and ammunition were the rule, and some commanders treated their men with great cruelty. In 1767, an official inspector reported that due to the terrain, discord among the staff, and failure to convert the Indians, the presidio and mission should be closed. In 1771, fearing an invasion of Apaches, the authorities withdrew the personnel, and these two remote outposts of Spain were totally abandoned.   (1970)

ANAHUAC (Chambers Co.)   *SH 61 and FM 1724 exits, 9 mi. NE*
James Taylor White
A veteran of the War of 1812, James Taylor White (b. 1789) migrated to this area from Louisiana in 1828. As a rancher, he developed one of the largest herds of longhorn cattle in Southeast Texas.

On White's ranch in June 1832, area colonists signed the Turtle Bayou Resolutions. Written to protest the actions of Captain Juan Davis Bradburn, commander of Mexican troops at Anahuac (9 mi. SW), the resolutions were an early sign of the growing dissatisfaction with Mexican governmental policies which limited the rights of colonists. Four years later, during the Texas Revolution, White provided aid and shelter for settlers fleeing the advancing Mexican forces under General Santa Anna. He also helped the Republic of Texas by supplying cattle for the Texas army. Following the revolution, White began driving his cattle overland to markets in New Orleans. His early cattle drives, utilizing sections of the Opelousas Trail, preceded development of post–Civil War routes, including the Dodge City and Chisholm Trails. White died in 1852 and was buried near his home (200 yds. S). His cattle brand, the "Crossed W," inherited from his father in 1806, is still used by members of the White family. (1980)

ANAHUAC (Chambers Co.) *SH 61 at IH 10, 5 mi. NE*
Site—Mission Nuestra Señora de la Luz
Established in 1757 by Franciscan missionaries with the purpose of civilizing and Christianizing the Orcoquiza and Bidai Indians. Abandoned in 1772.

ANAHUAC (Chambers Co.) *SH 61, 5 mi. N*
Near Site of the Signing of Turtle Bayou Resolutions
Drafted and signed at Turtle Bayou on June 13, 1832; this first formal protest of Texas colonists against Mexican tyranny formed an early step in events that led eventually to the Texas Revolution of 1836. The settlers were protesting recent restrictive laws of Mexico designed to limit immigration and trade between the United States and Texas, passed because Mexico feared losing Texas to the U.S. In particular, citizens of Anahuac were enraged by unreasonable acts of Col. Juan Davis Bradburn, a local agent of the Mexican government. Alarm spread after Bradburn unjustly imprisoned several Texans, one of whom was the later Alamo hero, William B. Travis. Fighting broke out on June 9 and 12, 1832, between citizens and Bradburn's militia. Following this, the Texans met at Turtle Bayou to plan future action. Here they drew up resolutions censuring violations of Mexico's constitution of President Bustamante, encouraging resistance to his regime, and inviting all Texans to uphold the cause of civil liberty. Signers of the document, most of whom later served with valor in the 1835 revolution and in the Texas Republic, were John Austin, W. H. Jack, Hugh B. Johnson, Luke Lesassier, Wylie Martin, and R. M. Williamson.

ANAHUAC (Chambers Co.) *Main St., Fort Anahuac Park*
Fort Anahuac
Known as Perry's Point until 1825, Anahuac was a port of entry for early Texas colonists. In 1830 the Mexican government established a military post here to collect customs duties and to enforce the law of April 6, 1830, which curtailed further Anglo-American colonization. Situated on a high bluff at the mouth of the Trinity River, Fort Anahuac controlled access to East Texas settlements. Two 18-pound guns topped the 7-foot-thick brick walls of the bastion. 4-foot-thick walls protected the adjacent barracks, and an underground tunnel led to a nearby powder magazine. Col. Juan Davis Bradburn, commander of the Anahuac garrison, angered Texas colonists by conscripting labor and supplies to construct the fort and by failing to control his disorderly troops. In 1832 he unjustly imprisoned William B. Travis, Patrick C. Jack, and other settlers here. When he refused to release the men, armed conflict erupted between Texas and Mexican forces. The confrontation here, which also sparked fighting at Velasco and adoption of the Turtle Bayou Resolutions, resulted in Bradburn's dismissal and the removal of Mexican troops from the post. Today the ruins of Fort Anahuac are a physical reminder of events that kindled the drive for Texas Independence. (1976)

ANAHUAC (Chambers Co.) *Miller St. (SH 61) at Magnolia St.*
Events at Anahuac Leading to the Texas Revolution
In the spring of 1832, Wm. B. Travis, Patrick C. Jack and other American settlers in Texas were unjustly imprisoned by Col. Juan Bradburn, commander of the Mexican garrison at Anahuac. Bradburn's refusal to deliver his prisoners for civil trial caused alarm throughout the American settlements, resulting in the organization of an armed force of citizens for intervention to save their friends from trial by a military court in Mexico. Rallying at Liberty, the Texans on June 10 went to Anahuac to parley with Bradburn, who agreed to free the colonists in exchange for Mexican soldiers held by the Texans. When Bradburn refused to keep his word, the Texans resolved to fight,

and sent to Brazoria for reinforcements of men and cannon, thus precipitating the Battle of Velasco on June 26, 1832. These events were climaxed by the arrival of the Mexican military commander from Nacogdoches, who resolved the conflict by releasing the colonists and placing Bradburn under arrest. Mexican resentment aroused over the events at Anahuac and Velasco was a contributing factor in the development of the Texas Revolution. (1965)

ANDERSON (Grimes Co.) — *2 blks. S of Main St. at SH 90 Intersection*
Steinhagen Log Cabin
Built before 1860. Log walls are unspliced. Slaves hand-hewed the timbers, stones; made doors, window shutters. (1965)

ANDERSON (Grimes Co.) — *Off SH 90 at 101 S. Main St.*
Grimes County Courthouse
Unique Victorian Texas public building. Third courthouse here. Site, in an 1824 land grant from Mexico, was donated 1850 by Henry Fanthorp, first permanent settler in county. Built 1891 of hand-molded brick with native stone trim. Vault is same one used in previous buildings; has twice withstood fires. Tried here in 1930s, a Clyde Barrow gang member vowed he'd see court in infernal regions. (1965)

ANDREWS (Andrews Co.) — *SH 176, 12 mi. W in roadside park*
Andrews County Created August 21, 1876
Organized May 11, 1910. Named for Richard Andrews. Killed at the Battle of Concepcion, October 28, 1835. The first man to fall in the Texas Revolution. County Seat, Andrews.

ANDREWS (Andrews Co.) — *US 385, courthouse*
Billionth Barrel
On May 25, 1965 from one of 7,400 producing oil wells in the county's 196 fields, came the billionth barrel of Andrews County crude oil. In the 35 years and 5 months since oil flowed from the county's discovery well, C. E. Ogden No. 1 in Dec. 1929, Andrews has attained a new place in history. In 1929, the county had about 400 people. Its wealth mostly in land and livestock, amounted to $8,109,399. Five persons in the county filed income tax returns. There were fewer than 100 children in school. Highway bonds in the amount of $200,000 were about to be issued, as a measure of county improvement. By 1956, Andrews County produced more than 60,000,000 barrels of oil annually—gaining recognition as number one in Texas and the United States. Of great significance is the fact that presently proven reserves underlying the county total more than one billion barrels, without any consideration for additional recoveries by secondary methods. Andrews is more than a product of the billion barrels of crude oil it has produced, more than the gasoline plants working through the night, more than modern highways, paved streets, homes, schools, dreams. Its destiny is great in human resources and oil. (1965)

ANDREWS (Andrews Co.) — *700 W. Broadway St. (SH 115/176)*
Original Townsite of Andrews
Founded when Andrews County was organized in 1910, on land owned by Robert Madison Means (b. 1878). With his father, J. S. Means, "Bob" Means began homesteading here in 1899 and organized an abstract company in 1909. When Andrews battled Shafter City to acquire county seat, Means donated lots to local cowboys so they could vote; helped win election. Married Atwood Wilder, 1910; was county clerk, 1918–1922; civic leader throughout life. Town has grown through many gifts of real estate and funds from Means, who retired after finding oil on his land in 1934. (1970)

ANDREWS (Andrews Co.) — *700 W. Broadway (SH 115/176)*
Early Settlers of Andrews County
One of last frontiers of Texas. Anglo settlement here lagged 60 years behind rest of state due to Indians and scarcity of water. In 1886 O. B. Holt became first man to file for county land. First settlers included the Cowden brothers and Peter Von Holebeke. In 1900 county had 87 people; it was finally organized in 1910. With windmill pumps and drift fences, ranching became feasible, although soil was so dry that a grazing cow crashed through a dugout roof into a bed one day. In 1930 the discovery of oil brought wealth and rewarded the tenacity of first pioneers. (1970)

ANDREWS (Andrews Co.)   *Main St. (US 385) at SW 1st St.*
Shafter's Trail
In 1875, Col. Wm. R. Shafter and a company of soldiers traveled from Fort Concho (where San Angelo is today) to Monument Springs, New Mexico, charting the arid plains, mapping all the vital watering places. This marker is in the only town of today through which Shafter's Trail passes. Here Col. Shafter, defending his party, chased Indians who ran 12 miles to the northwest. Thus he found the salt lake known ever after by his name. His expedition's maps of this formerly unknown land opened the Permian Basin to settlement.   (1965)

ANDREWS (Andrews Co.)   *SH 176, 6 mi. W*
Andrews County Discovery Well (½ mi. S & ½ mi. W)
C. E. Ogden No. 1, producing 200 barrels a day from San Andrew lime formation was brought in Dec. 1929 by Deep Rock Oil Co.—the Andrews County Discovery Well and first of 730 wells in Fuhrman–Masco Oil Field. Bought Feb. 1932, by Tripplehorn Brothers, of Fort Worth. Has now pumped for more than 35 years. Since 1956, Andrews has been top producing county in Texas and U.S. Fuhrman-Masco Field has produced 55 million barrels of oil—its contribution to total of more than a billion barrels for Andrews County in May, 1965.   (1965)

ANDREWS (Andrews Co.)   *SH 176 at FM 181, 16 mi. W*
Frankel City
In 1941, the Fullerton Oil Company of California struck oil near this site, and by 1945 more than 100 drilling rigs were in operation. The discovery brought great numbers of workers into the area, resulting in the establishment of the town of Fullerton. Located approximately one mile north, Fullerton provided newcomers with two churches, two cafes, two filling stations, a grocery store, delicatessen, beauty shop, and Andrews Telephone Exchange. Buses transported children to and from school in Andrews (16 mi. SE). By the end of World War II, the boom town also boasted supply stores, oil field service companies, welding shops, and an electric plant. Fullerton's name was changed to Frankel City when the U.S. Post Office was established in 1948. At one time the post office served as many as 500 area families. By 1976, however, most of the oil had been taken from the ground, and workers in the field were laid off or transferred to other jobs. The town was abandoned as the post office and other businesses closed. The old Prairie Schooner Cafe, moved to this site from its original location, is all that is left of Frankel City. The ghost town, however, remains an important part of West Texas history.   (1984)

ANGLETON (Brazoria Co.)   *S. Front St. (SH 274/288) at W. Cedar St.*
Old Brazoria County Courthouse
Angleton's first permanent courthouse was built in 1897, a year after the city was chosen Brazoria County seat. Constructed from plans originally drawn for the Matagorda County courthouse, the structure was enlarged and extensively remodeled in 1927. After the building suffered some structural damage in a 1932 storm, the county erected a new courthouse but maintained offices here until the 1970s.   (1983)

ANNA (Collin Co.)   *SH 5, 2 mi. N*
Site of Collin McKinney Homestead
Collin McKinney, a delegate to the General Convention at Washington-on-the-Brazos who helped draft the Texas Declaration of Independence from Mexico and later the Constitution of the Republic of Texas, settled in this area about 1846. On July 10, 1848, McKinney bought the Rob Whitaker survey around this site from Anna Whitaker, paying $500 for 640 acres. The McKinney family was active in the region: They were instrumental in building the Mantua Road and the organization of the town of Mantua and the Van Alstyne Christian Church. Collin McKinney divided his land among his heirs in 1857. He died in 1861. The McKinney family gave his house to the city of McKinney in 1936. The structure burned in 1980. Collin McKinney's legacy continues to influence the history of North Texas.   (2000)

ANNONA (Red River Co.)   *US 82, 2.5 mi. E*
Warthan Cemetery
George Washington Warthan came to Texas from Tuscaloosa, Alabama with brothers Thomas I. and Robert J. in 1852. G. W. wed Amanda Johnson, and the couple settled in the Red River Valley

in 1855. In 1861, he mustered into Company E of the 32nd Texas Cavalry and during his service saw action in more than 30 Civil War battles. Captured in 1864 and held as a prisoner of war until 1865, he returned to Texas at the age of 29, and through grants and land purchases he expanded his Red River County landholdings. Warthan's acquisitions included land in this area, north of the farming community of Garland. It included a cemetery used by area residents, with graves believed to predate the Republic of Texas. In 1881, he set aside what he dubbed Warthan Cemetery and encouraged his family to preserve the site. By the late 1960s, early grave indicators, including bois d'arc markers and loose stones, had disappeared. The cemetery land was formally deeded in 1951 and later enlarged. The earliest marked grave dates to 1881, and today the cemetery remains as a tie to generations of Warthans and other area residents.   (2005)

ANSON (Jones Co.)   US 83, N of Taylor-Jones Co. Line
Butterfield Trail Marker
Butterfield Trail, US Mail Route, St. Louis to San Francisco. Crossed here 1858–1861.

ANSON (Jones Co.)   11th St. at Commercial (US 277/83)
Jones County Courthouse
The Seventh Texas Legislature created Jones County in 1858 and named it for Anson Jones, the last president of the Republic of Texas. The Civil War, Reconstruction, and the area's untamed wilderness combined to postpone the county's formal organization until 1881. Voters selected Jones City, later renamed Anson, as permanent county seat. The first permanent courthouse was a small frame building, which served until the county purchased a hotel in 1884 for use as a courthouse. An 1886 brick courthouse served the county for the next 24 years. In late 1909, the Jones County Commissioners Court, led by County Judge J. R. Stinson, determined that the growth of the county called for a larger courthouse. They selected Elmer G. Withers of Stamford (15 mi. N) and the Texas Building Company of Fort Worth as architect and contractor, respectively. Completed in 1910, the Jones County courthouse is an excellent example of Beaux Arts styling, with influences from the Arts and Crafts movement found in the decorative painting uncovered during 1990s rehabilitation on the ceiling of the district courtroom. Other notable features include the statue of Lady Justice atop the domed clock tower and the pedimented porticoes with flanking pairs of Ionic columns on each façade. Constructed of brick and Pecos red sandstone, the Jones County courthouse continues to stand as an important part of Anson's architectural heritage and a center of politics and government for the citizens of the county.   (2000)

ANSON (Jones Co.)   US 277 at US 180, courthouse
Fort Phantom Hill, CSA
Located 10 miles east, 9 miles south on Old Butterfield Stageline. Upon secession, company of First Regiment Texas Mounted Rifles used it as an outpost to give protection against Indians. Stopover on way west for some Union sympathizers and people wanting to avoid conflict of war. In 1862 the frontier defense line was pulled back more than 30 miles east. However, scouting parties and patrols of Confederate and state troops intermittently visited the post in aggressive warfare to keep Indians near their camps and away from settlements and to check on invasion by Union forces. Usually supplying their own mounts, guns and sustenance, these men guarded the frontier until war's end. Texas Civil War Frontier Defense—Texas had 2000 miles of coastline and frontier to defend from Union attack, Indian raids, marauders. Defense lines were set to give maximum protection with the few men left in the state. One line stretched from El Paso to Brownsville. Another had posts set a day's horseback ride apart from Red River to the Rio Grande. Phantom Hill and other U. S. forts used by scouting parties lay in a line between. Behind these lines and to the east organized militia, citizens' posses from nearby settlements backed the Confederate and state troops to curb Indian raids. A memorial to Texans who served the Confederacy.   (1963)

ANSON (Jones Co.)   US 277 at US 180, courthouse
Jones County
Site of emigrant trail, the frontier military road, and Fort Phantom Hill, founded in 1851 to guard the military road. County created 1858 from Bexar and Bosque counties. Named for Anson Jones (1798–1858), a veteran of San Jacinto, minister to the U.S., Secretary of State and last President of the Texas Republic. Phantom Hill, in 1858–1861, a Butterfield Overland Mail Station, was in

1861–1865 a Civil War patrol point, trying to curb frontier raids by Indians. The county was recreated in 1876, organized 1881. Anson (at first called Jones City) is county seat.   (1965)

ANSON (Jones Co.)   *US 180E at FM 126*
Boyd Chapel Community
Settlements began to develop in Jones County by the mid-1800s, first around the abandoned Fort Phantom Hill site and then around ranches founded in the 1880s and farms established shortly thereafter. At this site in 1895, Reese Davis, Joe Swent and Alex Boyd built the Boyd School. The community that developed nearby came to be known as Boyd Chapel. Over the next decades, Boyd Chapel was shaped by early area landowners. These included Guy Arthur Hillier, a New York native who herded sheep from south Texas to this area, where he met and married Minnie Estes. Alexander Brown Young and his wife came to this area in 1897 from East Texas. They settled in the Boyd Chapel community with five sons, including their oldest, Thomas O. Young, who had a wife and family of his own. The Young family deeded land for Methodist and Baptist churches, and a tabernacle, school and teacherage. Judge L. Crow and his wife Dora built a unique house on a rise, using concrete, as well as stone gathered from around the U.S.; they cultivated an orchard and berry fields. In 1916, Raymond Young built a general store and gas station, the only one in Boyd Chapel. As the farming community grew, cotton became its primary crop. As in much of rural Texas, World War II greatly impacted the community's population, with young adults serving in the Armed Forces or finding work in urban centers in support of the war. In 1947, the school consolidated into the Anson school district. Today, only burials in the nearby Neinda Cemetery link the present agricultural fields to the community known as Boyd Chapel.   (2006)

ANTELOPE (Jack Co.)   *SH 187 in business district*
Town of Antelope
Named for Springs where herds of antelope watered and Kiowa Indians had a campsite. In 1875, Walter S. Jones platted townsite on Henrietta-Graham mail route. By 1887, place had 400 people, a general store, post office, a school, doctors, hotel, and spa built around its mineral wells. Town was overnight stop and supply point for cattle trails leading north. The G. R. Christian camp No. 703, United Confederate Veterans, active 1895–1941, served as city's park association. Economy is based on ranch and oil income; area is known for its churches and hospitality.   (1970)

ARANSAS PASS (Aransas Co.)   *SH 35 Bus., 0.9 mi. N*
Cementerio San Antonio de Padua
According to local lore, George Lewis (1859–1895) donated one-half acre of land at this site to the Hispanic citizens of the area for use as a cemetery, provided that he be buried in the center of the land. Handmade stones indicate burials dating from the 19th century; the first recorded deed was signed in 1933. Years of wind and rain have rendered many stones illegible. A number of children who died in an influenza epidemic in 1940 and many veterans of U. S. and international conflicts are interred here. A statue of San Antonio holding a child, crafted in Mexico, was brought across the border by the local priest for placement in an open chapel on the cemetery grounds. It is revered by the families of those interred here.   (1998)

ARANSAS PASS (San Patricio Co.)   *SH 361 (Goodnight Ave.)*
Terminal Railroad
Built in 1892, the Aransas Harbor Terminal Railroad ("Old Terminal Railroad") provided a means for transporting rock from mainland quarries to jetties under construction in the pass. In 1909, the Aransas Pass Channel and Dock Company was chartered to build a channel from the first South Texas deep water port at Harbor Island to Aransas Pass. As the channel was dredged, the displaced sediment was piled along one side and became the basis for a railroad bed. Opened in 1912, the new terminal railroad extended along the roadbed and a series of eight trestles. It connected with the San Antonio and Aransas Pass Railroad in Aransas Pass, and was an important cotton shipping tool. Passenger service was inaugurated with the "Toonerville Trolley," passenger coaches pulled by a converted Model T Ford truck which transported workers from the mainland to a new shipyard on Harbor Island during World War I. After Corpus Christi was designated a deep water port in 1922, business declined for Harbor Island and the railroad. In 1931, the rail line was converted to a road for automobiles, which was in turn replaced by a new highway in 1960. Hurricanes in 1961 and 1970 left few visible remnants of the terminal railroad.   (1989)

ARCHER CITY (Archer Co.)   *SH 79, 15 mi. NE*
Old Buffalo Road
Named for traffic in buffalo hides and bones, road from plains hunting grounds crossed this site. Hunters hauled thousands of hides to market in 1870s. The first settlers in late 1870s–1880s sold bones for fertilizer and bought supplies to sustain life during hard times.   (1973)

ARCHER CITY (Archer Co.)   *SH 79, 6 mi. S*
Archer County
A part of Peter's grant 1841, created January 22, 1858. Organized July 27, 1880. Named in honor of Dr. Branch Tanner Archer 1790–1856. Texas Commissioner to the United States, 1835, member of Congress, Secretary of War of the Republic of Texas. First permanent settlement, 1874, first railroad 1890. Archer City, the county seat.

ARCHER CITY (Archer Co.)   *SH 79, 7 mi. S at roadside park*
Cimmaron (Persimmon) Springs
(Four miles east off Cowan Road) The natural springs that flow near this site first appeared on early maps of the area as Cimmaron Springs. European immigrants who settled here in the early 1890s were unfamiliar with the word cimmaron and called it Persimmon Springs. The water source served early Native Americans, settlers and military parties and was a factor in settlement patterns and immigration routes. A garden spot in the midst of a dry, windy area, Cimmaron (Persimmon) Springs has been a well-known landmark since the earliest days of occupation in Archer County.   (1986)

ARCHER CITY (Archer Co.)   *SH 79, 8 mi. S*
Extinct Town of Anarene
Landowner Charles E. Graham (1872–1937) in 1908 granted the Wichita Falls and Southern Railroad a route across his property and platted a town at this site. Anarene was named for his wife Annie Lawrene Graham, daughter of pioneer cattleman J. Marion Keen. Graham built a hotel and obtained a post office, cattle pens, dipping vat and other facilities. The town schoolhouse was used for religious services. In 1921 oil was discovered nearby. A refinery was built in 1938. When oil production ceased and the trains stopped running in 1954, Anarene quickly declined.   (1976)

ARCHER CITY (Archer Co.)   *SH 25, 4.5 mi. NW*
Archer County Copper Mines (¼ mi. NE and 5 mi. SSE)
The civilized world first heard of copper in this area from Texas Rangers after an 1860 campaign against Comanches on the Pease River, about 100 miles to the northwest. The Ranger captain, Lawrence S. ("Sul") Ross, later to serve Texas as Governor, had nuggets picked off the surface of the ground and hauled to Austin. In 1861, assistant state geologist, S. B. Buckley, charted the mineral site. The Rangers' ore haul was processed and used in gun caps for Confederate forces during the Civil War. To get more of the needed metal, the Texas Copper Mining & Manufacturing Company was founded on May 28, 1864, but wartime shortage of men apparently prevented recovery of copper at the time. The T.C.M. & M. Co., based in Dallas, sent W. F. Cummings to Archer County in 1880 to open mining sites. Although the Texas Commissioner of Agriculture and Statistics reported in 1882 that no mining had commenced, ore eventually was hauled out and shipped to smelters in the East. No central vein or deposit could be found. The Boston & Texas Copper Company of Tucson, Ariz., leased the mine site here in 1899. It produced some copper ore which was processed in El Paso, but again the project failed to meet expectations.   (1971)

ARCHER CITY (Archer Co.)   *SH 25 at FM 210, 2 mi. W at roadside park*
Battle of the Little Wichita
In reaction to an Indian attack on a mail stage, Capt. Curwen B. McLellan set out on July 6, 1870, from Fort Richardson with 56 men of the 6th Cavalry. On July 12, McLellan's command encountered a war party of 250 Kiowas led by "Kicking Bird" near the north fork of the Little Wichita (6 miles NW). After a brief skirmish, McLellan ordered his troops into retreat, fighting a defensive battle across the middle and south forks of the Little Wichita. The Indians gave up the chase on the 13th. Corporal John Given and Private George Blume were killed. 13 medals of honor were awarded for heroism.   (1974)

ARCHER CITY (Archer Co.)   *SH 25 at FM 210, 2 mi. W at roadside park*
In Vicinity of French Trading Area (4.5 mi. W)
In the mid-1700s, Indians of this region met at a trading ground near this site with Frenchmen who brought them manufactured goods, sometimes including guns and ammunition—products denied them by the Spanish who held sovereignty, but could not prevent intrusions from Louisiana. The Spanish explorer Jose Mares on a road-mapping expedition here in 1787 saw evidences of the French. Among noted early-day visitors were Captain R. B. Marcy of the U.S. Army and Indian agent R. S. Neighbors, who camped nearby in 1854 while seeking a good site for an Indian reservation.   (1974)

ARGYLE (Denton Co.)   *506 N. Fort Worth Dr. (US 377)*
Argyle
This area was first settled in the 1850s by members of the Peters Colony. In 1881 the town of Argyle was started by Galveston developer James Morrill, when a rail line was built through the area. Early residents came from neighboring settlements. Schools consolidated with Argyle included Beulah, Pilot Knob, Stoney Ridge, Lane, and parts of the Prairie Mound and Litsey Districts. An 1895 fire destroyed the business area, but it was soon rebuilt. The growth of nearby urban areas, which led to a decline before World War II, has resulted in recent population increases.   (1981)

ARLINGTON (Tarrant Co.)   *3001 W. Division (SH 180)*
Top O' Hill Terrace
Beulah Adams Marshall bought land here along the Bankhead highway in the early 1920s and opened a tea room, hosting teas and serving dinners to Dallas and Fort Worth patrons. In 1926, Fred and Mary Browning purchased the property and shortly began converting the facilities into a casino, adding an escape tunnel and secret room for hiding the gambling paraphernalia during raids. Known as Top O' Hill Terrace, the popular spot attracted gamblers as well as visitors who were often unaware of the gaming activities. The restaurant, along with the tea garden that exists today, was a legitimate business, operating alongside a brothel as well as the casino, which benefited from the nearby Arlington Downs Racetrack. Top O' Hill Terrace facilities included a horse barn and a private stable for Browning's prized stud, Royal Ford, purchased from oilman and Arlington Downs owner W.T. Waggoner. Contemporary to the Top O' Hill heyday was the outspoken Dr. J. Frank Norris (d. 1952), longtime pastor of first Baptist Church of Fort Worth. The conservative Norris, co-founder of fundamental Baptist Bible Institute, later known as Bible Baptist Seminary and later as the Arlington Baptist College, was an ardent proponent of prohibition and gambling reform. One of his targets was Top O' Hill Terrace, which he reportedly vowed one day to own. In 1947, Texas Ranger Captain M.T. "Lone Wolf" Gonzaullas led a raid on Top O' Hill, catching the gambling operation in full swing. In late 1956, under the leadership of Earl K. Oldham, the Bible Baptist Seminary bought the property and relocated here, fulfilling Norris' promise, although neither he nor Browning (d. 1953) had lived to see it. Today, the Arlington Baptist College continues to use the site, which retains many of its original structures and features a statue of Norris by noted sculptor Pompeo Coppini.   (2003)

ARLINGTON (Tarrant Co.)   *400 W. Sanford St., 3 blks. N of SH 180*
The Hill
A roughly five-block area of Arlington known as "The Hill" was the only addition specifically set aside for the city's African American residents. In the 1890s, the community began developing on land that once belonged to Martin V. and Rebecca A. Thomas. Also during this time, several churches organized in the emerging community. The Church of God in Christ, Mt. Olive Baptist Church and the African Methodist Episcopal (AME) Church, now known as Armstrong Chapel AME, became leading institutions in the neighborhood. Mt. Olive, in particular, became a center for spiritual life while also hosting many community and social events. In 1907, Arlington resident Edward F. Wilkerson subdivided land known as the Wilkerson Addition that became the core of The Hill. Growth occurred in the following years as a vibrant community emerged including grocery stores, clubs and restaurants opening by the 1920s. Other important institutions included a school, which the county first established for Arlington's African American children in the 1890s. The last segregated school in The Hill, named for Booker T. Washington, was built in 1953 and closed as integration took place in the 1960s. Another vital part of the neighborhood was this park, which the city opened in the mid-1950s and named for George Stevens, principal of Booker T. Washington

School. Although The Hill was originally a rural community, it became more densely populated and urban as the city grew out to meet it by the 1930s. From the mid-1940s through the 1960s, The Hill began to decline as job opportunities and social changes led residents to other areas. Today, The Hill has become an ethnically diverse community. (2006)

ART (Mason Co.) *SH 29 at Lower Willow Creek Rd.*
Kothmann Homesite and Cemetery
Heinrich Conrad Kothmann (1798–1881) and his wife Ilse Katherine Pahlmann (1810–1905) and their family sailed from Germany to Indianola, Texas in 1845. Among the first families to settle in Fredericksburg, the Kothmanns were issued a 640-acre land grant in Mason County in 1848. In 1856 they moved to Art and were among the first immigrant families in this area. A trained cabinetmaker and musician, Kothmann began ranching and acquired another 640-acre tract of land. Located on their former homestead, the Kothmann Cemetery is all that remains of the original ranch site. Containing only five graves, all of Kothmann family members, the graveyard began with the burial of Heinrich Conrad Kothmann in 1881. His wife Ilse is buried beside him. Their son Karl, the first of their family born in Texas, is buried here along with his wife Katherine (Hoerster) Kothmann. A fifth unmarked grave is thought to be that of a grandchild. Though most of the land was sold after Ilse's death in 1905, the family retained one acre including the cemetery property. The concrete wall and slab were constructed after 1937 to provide protection and ease in maintenance for the five graves. The family maintains the cemetery. (1996)

ASPERMONT (Stonewall Co.) *US 380, 7.5 mi. E*
Site of the Courthouse at Rayner
First county seat of Stonewall County. Erected in 1888. County seat removed to Aspermont in 1898.

ASPERMONT (Stonewall Co.) *US 83 at US 380*
Stonewall County
Explored 1541 on behalf of Spain by Francisco de Coronado. Visited by Texans early as the 1840s. Mapped by U.S. Army expedition of Capt. Randolph Marcy 1849. Yielded salt for use of early settlers and hunters. Was site of buffalo hunters' capital, Rath City, 1876–1879. County created in 1876; organized 1888. Named in honor of Confederate General Thomas Jonathan "Stonewall" Jackson (1824–1863), whose courage and fighting skill inspired Texas soldiers in the Civil War. First county seat, Rayner, replaced 1898 by Aspermont, named for high location. (1965)

ASPERMONT (Stonewall Co.) *US 83 at US 380*
County Named for Confederate Hero General "Stonewall" Jackson 1824–1863
Gen. Barnard E. Bee, a Texan, gave him the famous sobriquet in first battle of Manassas. Jackson was rallying his men for a charge as other units retreated. Bee, seeing him, cried to his men, "There is Jackson standing like a stone wall. Let us determine to die here, and we will conquer." In battles of Gaines Mill and Malvern Hill, Hood's famous Texas Brigade fought under his command. After Gaines Mill when Jackson saw the strong Union fortified position which the Texans had overrun, he—not known to give praise—said, "The men that took this position were soldiers indeed."

Texas in the Civil War
Texas made an all-out effort for the Confederacy after a 3 to 1 popular vote for secession. 90,000 troops, famed for mobility and daring, fought on every battlefront. A 2,000-mile frontier and coast were successfully defended from Union troop invasion and savage Indians. Texas was the storehouse of western Confederacy. Wagon trains laden with cotton—life blood of the South—crossed the state to Mexico to trade for medical supplies. State and private industry produced guns, ammunition, wagons, pots, kettles, leather goods, salt, hospital supplies. Wives, sons, daughters, slaves provided corn, cotton, cloth, cattle, hogs, cured meats to the army, giving much, keeping little for themselves. (1963)

ASPERMONT (Stonewall Co.) *US 83, 10 mi. S in roadside park*
Rath City (4 mi. SW)
In 1876, during an international demand for buffalo hides, Charles Rath (1836–1902) founded this town. He opened the Rath, Lee & Reynolds Mercantile Store. He sold supplies and bought the hides from the buffalo hunters. On one occasion in 1877, there were 1,100,000 hides at his trading

post. The town, also known as "Reynolds City," boasted a corral, hide yard, saloon, and restaurant. Skins stretched across poles sheltered the hunters. A tower beside the corral was used as a lookout to ward off Indian attacks. By 1879, the buffalo disappeared and the town vanished.   (1979)

ATHENS (Henderson Co.) — *US 175, 6 mi. NW*
William Richardson (Dec. 6, 1805–May 30, 1864)
Born in South Carolina, William Richardson moved to Pickens County, Alabama in 1830. There he married Mary "Polly" Kilpatrick (1813–1889) on Feb. 13, 1834. Children born to them were John K., James J., Sara F., Margaret C., Martha E., William A., Peter M., Andrew J., Franklin P., Ann, Allen, Texana, Mary M., and Judeth. Richardson moved his family, slaves, and the families of his brothers, Steven Madison and Matthias, to Texas by wagon train, arriving at this location on Dec. 12, 1855. Richardson built a home (1 mi. NE) and became a successful planter. His "Three Circles" cattle brand was recorded in 1855. He was appointed to lay out one of the first roads between Athens and Kaufman. Highway 175 follows much of his original route. He and his brothers helped found the First Baptist Church in Athens. The slaves he brought to Texas were Dinah, Charles, Gin, Rachel, Washington, Henry, Tom, Harrison, Kate, Easter, Til, Carolina, Jane, Sam, Congo, Marion, Mimm, and Jube. All took the Richardson name, and most stayed on with the family after being freed. Later they and their descendants established the Sand Flat community (1 mi. NNE). William Richardson is buried in the family cemetery (1 mi. NE) along with his wife, two sons, and two grandchildren. Some of the slaves are buried there also.   (1984)

ATHENS (Henderson Co.) — *204 W. Corsicana St. (US 175)*
Site of Hawn Lumber Company
As the geographic center of the newly redrawn Henderson County lines, Athens became the county seat in 1850. Charles H. and Lillian (Barksdale) Hawn arrived with a load of lumber on the first train to stop in Athens in 1881. Charles Hawn quickly established a role for himself and his family in the village. Called "adept as an architect and master builder" by the Athens Register, Hawn built a new county courthouse in 1885. He also is credited with the design and construction of many early houses in and around Athens, including the residence of Senator J. J. Faulk and his wife in 1882. In December 1886 Charles and Lillian Hawn purchased two acres on this site in order to establish the Hawn Lumber Company. Hawn continued to provide lumber and labor for many of the buildings around the town square as well as settlers' homes. He is credited with constructing the Faulk-Gaunt building and the Gaunt Brothers buildings in downtown Athens, as well as the home of Joseph Thomas La Rue. Charles and Lillian Hawn's second son, William A. Hawn, became president of the company. He inherited family holdings including Charles' several sawmills upon his father's death in 1922. W. A. Hawn served as city commissioner and mayor, postmaster and school board member for the city of Athens. Under his direction, the Hawn Lumber Company remained a strong fixture in the city's building trade. William A. Hawn died in 1960; the company remained in the family until it closed in 1997. From the early development of Athens to the end of the 20th century, the Hawn Lumber Company was instrumental in the city's growth.   (1999)

ATHENS (Henderson Co.) — *3700 US 175E*
Site of Gum Creek School
Following the close of the Civil War in 1865, Armstead Barker brought his family to this area. Other African American families followed, and their settlement became known as Gum Creek. By the mid-1880s, African American children in the area attended Gum Creek School, which offered classes through the eighth grade. Students met in a one-room frame building. Early teachers included P. H. Eddings, S. H. Wilhite and J. M. Donnell. J. T. Dunnington, Sam Frank, W. H. Barker and C. S. Sharp served as trustees. As in many rural schools, students attended classes from October through March so they could work in the fields for planting and harvesting seasons. The school was part of County District Two. When area white schools combined to form the Baxter School, the Gum Creek facility was sometimes also called Baxter Colored School. In 1902, J. I. Richardson bought land in this vicinity that included the school location. Wade's Chapel A.M.E. Church also used the school building, and in 1920, when Richardson's widow, Nannie, sold the property to school district trustees, the deed stipulated that it continue to be used for both school and church purposes. Following the 1938–39 school term, Gum Creek School closed. Students transferred to Blackshear Public School and Fisher High School in Athens, and the school district sold the property to Wade's Chapel Methodist Church. Dunnington heirs later bought the property,

and the building burned in 1942. Today, the history of Gum Creek School represents early efforts to educate the area's African American youth. In the many decades between emancipation and integration, parents and educators strived to provide education as a means to true freedom. (2005)

ATHENS (Henderson Co.) *SH 19 at Bryson Ave.*
Henderson County
Formed from Houston and Nacogdoches Counties. Created April 27, 1846. Organized August 4, 1846. Named in honor of James Pinckney Henderson (1808–1858). First Governor of the State of Texas. Buffalo, Centerville and Athens since 1850 have served as county seats.

ATHENS (Henderson Co.) *SH 19 at Bryson Ave.*
Athens
Founded 1850. Named for Athens, Greece. Supply and military training headquarters during Civil War. Sent army about 1,000 men. Center for manufacturing and agriculture. Home of annual Old Fiddlers' Contest and of Henderson County Junior College. Black-eyed peas capital of the world.

ATHENS (Henderson Co.) *SH 19 at Bryson Ave.*
Henderson County Pottery Industry
Prehistoric Caddoan Indians utilized the abundant deposits of rich clays in this region to make their fine pottery vessels. The modern pottery industry in Henderson County began in 1857, when Levi S. Cogburn (1812–1866), one of a family of potters from Georgia, started making cups, saucers, and plates in Athens. Cogburn's plant operated until shortly after his death in 1866. Industry was reactivated in 1885 by M. K. Miller, who with his sons, started the Athens Pottery Company, first of many tile, brick, and pottery plants in the area. (1973)

ATHENS (Henderson Co.) *SH 19 at Bryson Ave.*
Machinery from First Factory in Athens
Established 1882 (at site 1.5 mi. NE) by local planter H. M. Morrison, to make building brick. Total original machinery consisted of this press and plunger. Press was hand-operated. A mule-drawn swivel ran the plunger, mixing clay dug at the plant site. C. H. Coleman bought into firm in 1891; after Morrison's death in 1899 he became sole owner. Harbison-Walker Refractories Company bought business in 1940; continued making Coleman brick and enriching economy until closing in 1968. These machines are a permanent loan to city of Athens from Harbison-Walker. (1968)

ATHENS (Henderson Co.) *SH 19 at FM 59*
Henderson County, C.S.A.
Voted 400–49 for secession. Sent about 1,000 into Confederate Army with one detachment of 150 having only 13 live to return. Caldwell's farm three miles northeast and Fincastle 19 miles southeast of Athens, had camps of instruction. Confederate supply depot, Fincastle had stores of grain, meat in charge of Captain Thomas F. Murchison, who also was county enrolling officer. Wartime manufactures included earthenware, jugs and dishes. Other products for C.S.A. were cotton, corn beef, pork, timber. Cynthia Ann Parker, delivered from Indian captivity 1860 by Sul Ross Ranger Unit lived during war at Athens. Postmaster General of Confederacy was John H. Reagan, who had been surveyor and first probate judge in Henderson.

ATLANTA (Cass Co.) *101 N. East St., off Main St. (SH 249)*
Bessie Coleman (1892–1926)
The tenth of 13 children born to tenant farmers Susan and George Coleman, famed aviatrix Bessie Coleman was a native of Atlanta, Texas. The family moved to Waxahachie when Bessie was two years old. She followed her brothers to Chicago in 1915 and developed an interest in flying. Because she could find no one in the United States who would teach an African-American woman, Coleman learned to fly in France and obtained her international pilot's license in 1921. Upon her return to the United States, she was hailed as the first black woman to pilot an airplane. Bessie Coleman died in an air accident in Jacksonville, Florida, in 1926 and is buried near Chicago. (2002)

AUSTIN (Travis Co.) *Loop 1, Under MoPac Bridge*
Travis County
Created January 25, 1840. Organized April 8, 1843. Named in honor of William Barrett Travis. Born Edgefield district South Carolina, August 1, 1809. Came to Texas in 1831. Commander at

the Alamo where he was killed March 6, 1836. Austin, the county seat, selected as the capital of the Republic of Texas in 1839 and by a vote of the people in 1850 made the permanent capital of the State of Texas.

AUSTIN (Travis Co.)   *1st St. W, W bank of Waller Creek at*
                                                 Town Lake in Austin City Park area
The Grinninger Fence
First known use of barbed wire in Texas (1857), by John Grinninger, immigrant from Europe, worker in an early Austin iron foundry. Grinninger, who lived on Waller Creek (NE of here) grew fruit, vegetables and flowers. To protect garden, he ran homemade barbed wire along top of his fence. Noted peace officer and sometime outlaw Ben Thompson is said to have recalled years later that in youth he tore jeans on that fence. Grinninger was murdered in 1862. In 1867 first U.S. patent on barbed wire was issued. Expansion of the cattle industry in 1870s led to business for wire-makers, for Midwest and Western America lacked timber for fences. John Warne "Bet-A-Million" Gates created a sensation in the 70s in San Antonio by penning wild cattle with barbed wire. Joseph F. Glidden and Isaac L. Ellwood, of Illinois, were most successful barbed wire manufacturers in the United States. Their Texas manager, H. B. Sanborn, erected "model" fences in 1870s–1880s in Grayson and Potter Counties, showing ranchers the practicality of enclosing vast acreages. Barbed wire is said to have saved ranching from extinction; it gave each landowner control of cattle breeding and property. Wire's many styles are now prized by collectors.   (1969)

AUSTIN (Travis Co.)   *Capitol grounds*
The Texas Capitol
Austin became the capital of Texas Jan. 19, 1840, and this hill was platted as Capitol Square. A modest statehouse built here in the 1850s soon developed structural flaws. The Constitutional Convention of 1876 set aside about 3,000,000 acres of public land to finance another building. This was authorized after the 1850s capitol burned on Nov. 9, 1881. Architect E. E. Myers of Detroit won a national competition with his plans for this capitol. The contractor was Mattheas Schnell of Rock Island, Ill. Basement excavation began early in 1882. Railroads built especially for this project hauled limestone from the Oatmanville quarries in Travis County as well as stone donated by the owners of the Granite Mountain in Burnet County. The 900 workmen on the project included 86 granite cutters brought from Scotland. Charles B. and John V. Farwell, Chicago bankers, funded the construction and were repaid in land in ten Panhandle counties, on which they founded the famous XIT ranch. At dedication ceremonies on May 18, 1888, the capitol was accepted on behalf of the people by State Senator Temple Houston, son of Texas hero Sam Houston. He called it "A structure that shall stand as a sentinel of eternity."   (1976)

AUSTIN (Travis Co.)   *Capitol grounds*
Moses Austin (October 4, 1761–June 10, 1821)
The initiator of Anglo-American settlement in Texas, Moses Austin was a native of Durham, Connecticut. After his marriage to Mary Brown in 1785, Austin became a leading figure in the development of the American lead industry. His business took him to Virginia and then west to the Mississippi Valley. A colonizer and pioneer as well, Austin helped establish several frontier communities. Moses Austin's decision to venture into a colonization enterprise in the Spanish territory of Texas led him to San Antonio de Bexar in 1820. With the help of Felipe Neri, Baron de Bastrop, Austin requested permission from the Spanish governor, Antonio Martinez, to settle a colony of 300 Anglo-American families in his province. Austin returned to Missouri, where he learned in March 1821 that his petition had been granted. Although ill from the effects of his journey, he began making plans to raise a colony. Three months later, Moses Austin died in the Hazel Run settlement, where he was buried. He was later reinterred in Potosi, Missouri. In response to his father's dying wish, Stephen F. Austin continued the colonization project and led the first of the "Old 300" colonists into Texas in late 1821.   (Texas Sesquicentennial 1836–1986)

AUSTIN (Travis Co.)   *1201 Brazos, at front of State Archives and Library*
The Archive War
In 1839, Austin became the capital of the Republic of Texas. The national archives—state papers and land titles—were housed on Congress Avenue. In 1842, after Mexican armies seized San Antonio and seemed likely to capture Austin, many residents fled in what was called "the breakup."

From his home in Galveston, President Sam Houston ordered removal of the government papers. A local "Archive Committee" responded by burying them. The President then tried unsuccessfully to have Congress create a new capital near the coast. Later his men came secretly to haul the papers to the interim capital, Washington-on-the-Brazos, loading them before dawn on Dec. 30, 1842. Mrs. Angelina Eberly, a noted innkeeper and one of the few women in Austin during the breakup, found the men loading the archives in darkness. Running to the city cannon on Congress Avenue at Pecan (6th) Street, she fired at the wagons. The 26 men departed with the records. About 68 citizens rode after them, hauling along the city cannon. Some 20 miles from Austin they retrieved the archives without bloodshed. Because the archives remained here, the President and the Congress returned in 1845, preserving Austin as the capital of the Republic and (later) the state.   (1978)

AUSTIN (Travis Co.)   *1201 Brazos*
Texas and the Civil War Secession Convention
The election of Abraham Lincoln in 1860 caused unrest and drastic action all over the South and in many Texas counties. Despite petitions, editorials and political pressure, Gov. Sam Houston refused to call a special legislative session to consider the position Texas should take. On Dec. 3, 1860, a group of secession leaders took matters into their own hands and called on the people to elect delegates to a convention to meet in Austin on Jan. 28, 1861. Counties sent 177 delegates, and the convention met in the capitol from Jan. 28 to Feb. 4 and March 2 to March 25. A committee on public safety, with broad powers, acted for the convention between sessions. By vote of 166 to 7, the convention adopted the ordinance of secession and called for a statewide election—the first state in the Confederacy to let voters have a direct voice. 108 of the 122 counties favored secession by a vote of 46,129 to 14, 697. The convention voted to join the Confederacy, send delegates to its congress, gear for war and raise troops to protect the frontier. When Gov. Sam Houston refused to take the oath supporting the Confederacy, the convention replaced him with the Lieutenant Governor Edward Clark.   (1965)

AUSTIN (Travis Co.)   *1010 Colorado St.*
The Governor's Mansion
Official residence of the Governor of Texas. By law, each chief executive must live here during his term of office. Before the erection of this structure in 1855–1856, the only official executive home had been the rough, two-story frame "President's House" at present Seventh and San Jacinto Streets. Within these walls, many decisions of statewide import have taken place. Here in 1861 Gov. Sam Houston decided not to support the Confederacy. Also, like numerous 19th-century houses, the mansion acquired a ghost story after the nephew of Gov. Pendleton Murrah (1863–1865) committed suicide here. Built some thirty years before the pink granite capitol, this structure was first occupied by Gov. Elisha M. Pease, who selected the site and design. Pioneer architect-contractor Abner Cook supervised the construction of the stately residence in Greek Revival style. Austin-made bricks were used, and huge pine logs were hauled from Bastrop, then adzed to form the six massive pillars with Ionic capitals. Distinguished visitors have included U.S. Presidents and heads of state from other countries. More than perhaps any other residence in Texas, the Governor's mansion is a repository of Texas history.   (1969)

AUSTIN (Travis Co.)   *N. Congress at W 1st*
Austin, C.S.A.
An active place during the Civil War, Austin was the site of the Secession Convention, March 2, 1861, and legislative sessions which lasted until June 1865. City visitors during the early 1860s included lobbyists, cotton speculators, military leaders, and businessmen seeking to aid the war effort. Five stage lines and a pony express to the railhead at Brenham provided communications. Also located here was the Texas Military Board, an agency created to obtain arms and munitions for 33 militia districts. A city arsenal was set up on Waller Creek in southeast Austin. A gun cap factory in the old land office on 11th Street made 14,000 shells a day, and a foundry produced guns and cannon. Factories for shoes and gunpowder, and a sewing room in the basement of the capitol, furnished goods for the Confederate Army. The city also maintained a military fort. During the war citizens endured Indian raids, epidemics of fever and diphtheria, rumors of slave uprisings, and a scarcity of food. Hotels refused room and board, even to state legislators, unless payment was made in gold, silver, or goods such as nails and tobacco. As a result, some lawmakers lived in their wagons and cooked over open fires.   (1965)

26

AUSTIN (Travis Co.)   *601 N. Congress*
Littlefield Building
George Washington Littlefield (1842–1920) came to Texas from Mississippi in 1850. After serving in Terry's Texas Rangers in the Civil War, he made his fortune ranching and driving cattle. He moved to Austin in 1883 and, in 1890, established the American National Bank, which included a ladies' banking department. He hired architect C. H. Page, Jr., to design this Beaux Arts Classical building, which opened in 1912 with a rooftop garden. His bank was on the ground floor. For the corner entrance, he commissioned Tiffany's of New York to cast bronze, Bas Relief doors by sculptor Daniel Webster. These were later donated to the University of Texas, of which Littlefield was a major benefactor.   (2002)

AUSTIN (Travis Co.)   *Barton Springs Rd. at entrance to pool house*
Barton Springs
Clear and icy, these springs over the years have drawn Indians, pioneers, and tourists to this spot. The waters are brought from limestone strata to the surface by the Balcones Fault, which bisects Central Texas. Average flow is 27,000,000 gallons daily. During 1730–1731, Spanish friars located three missions here (see marker, SE side of pool). Colorful settler William "Uncle Billy" Barton patented the land about 1837, naming two of the springs for his daughters Parthenia and Eliza. His two tame baby buffaloes soon began to attract sight-seers to his place, in spite of constant danger from Indian attacks. As the place gained in popularity, one astute Austin merchant installed a merry-go-round here and rented bathing suits to swimmers. In 1871, he and several others built ice-making machines at the springs. In addition, flour mills, sawmills, and a quarry appeared along the creek banks. About 1875, the riverboat "Sunbeam" ran excursions to Barton's at 50 cents a round trip. At one period a ferry was located here on a main road to Austin. Between 1901 and 1913 A. J. Zilker, leading merchant, bought this land and in 1918 and 1931 deeded it to the people of Austin for use as a park.   (1970)

AUSTIN (Travis Co.)   *2100 Barton Springs Rd.*
Andrew Jackson Zilker
Voted Austin's most worthy citizen twice, Indiana native Andrew Jackson Zilker (1858–1934) grew up with a strong respect for the laborers along the Ohio River. He came to Austin penniless in 1876 but quickly became a businessman and bank director. He contributed to his community at the neighborhood, city and county levels. Believing in the importance of "practical" education, he indirectly funded school industrial programs when he sold 366 acres of parkland, including Barton Springs, to the city. The payments on the land were required to go to the school district. A gift of 32 additional acres in 1934 added to the city's most cherished recreation area, Zilker Park. (2003)

AUSTIN (Travis Co.)   *909 Navasota St., off IH 35 at 7th St.*
State Cemetery of Texas
Burial ground for the honored dead of Texas, this cemetery contains the remains of Stephen F. Austin, the "Father of Texas"; nine governors of Texas (as of 1968); and representatives of every period of state history and every department of state government. Statuary at the graves includes a marble figure of Albert Sidney Johnston by Elisabet Ney and bronzes of Austin and Joanna Troutman by Pompeo Coppini. The cemetery was founded in 1851 when Gen. Edward Burleson, hero of the Texas Revolution, was interred on this tract. In 1854, the state purchased the land, which had once belonged to Andrew Jackson Hamilton, provisional Governor of Texas from 1865 to 1866. The cemetery was seldom used, however, until the 1860s, when some officers of the Confederate Army of Texas were buried here. Today small, white marble headstones mark the graves of about 1,583 soldiers and 515 graves of members of their families. Through the untiring efforts of Louis W. Kemp, a state official (1881–1956), the remains of over 100 prominent persons were reinterred here after 1930. Since 1951, those eligible for burial here include designated state officials, Confederate veterans, and certain others. In 1968 there were 2,389 graves.   (1968)

AUSTIN (Travis Co.)   *100 N. IH 35 at E. 1st St.*
Palm School
When Edwin Waller platted Austin in 1839, he set aside this site for construction of an armory that would offer protection for the new capital of the Republic of Texas. In 1845, Texas joined the United States and the armory became a federal installation. By 1888, it was no longer in use and

the United States government donated the land to the city of Austin as the site for a new public school. The Tenth Ward school building was completed here in 1892. One of the first Austin schools built after legislative authorization of city-operated school systems, Tenth Ward opened under the leadership of Principal Florence Ralston Brooke (1858–1944), a native of England. The name of the school was changed in 1902 to honor Swante Palm (1815–1899), Sweden's former Consul to the State of Texas and a prominent Austin resident and University of Texas benefactor. Miss Brooke remained as principal until 1912 when she was transferred to Austin High School. In 1976, after 84 years of operation, Palm School was closed. Former students here include many of Austin's business, civic, and professional leaders, and reflect the school's dramatic impact on the city's development. (1982)

AUSTIN (Travis Co.) *IH 35 E frontage road, between 15th & 16th Sts.*
Swedish Hill
Residential development of this area began in the 1870s when a number of Swedish immigrants erected homes near their downtown businesses. Initially bounded by Red River, 14th, 18th, and Navasota Streets, the neighborhood became known as Svenska Kullen (Swedish Hill). A Swedish Methodist and other Swedish churches were built in the area, which was later divided by the inter-state highway. A number of historic houses remain in the section of Swedish Hill that is east of the interstate. The neighborhood was listed in the National Register of Historic Places in 1986. (1990)

AUSTIN (Travis Co.) *Loop 360 just W of Spicewood Springs Rd.*
Balcones Fault Aids Colonization of Texas
Curving through the center of Texas from Hill County south and west to Uvalde County is the rugged escarpment-fault called Balcones. The abundance of natural resources associated with this geologic formation affected the pattern of colonization in Texas. The numerous springs and wooded hills of the escarpment and adjacent fertile prairies attracted Indian tribes and Spanish colonists before the area was permanently settled by Anglo-American pioneers. Spanish explorer Bernardo de Miranda in 1756 named the formation "Los Balcones," meaning "balconies." Part of El Camino Real, the "King's Highway," it skirted the fault line. Spanish missions and presidios were located at springs near San Antonio, Austin, and elsewhere, but many Spanish settlements disappeared before 1800. Anglo-Americans led by Stephen F. Austin began to settle near the Balcones Escarpment before 1830. Through their courage and determination, early pioneer settlements grew into the towns and cities that today dot the fault line. The town of Austin, with its combination of beauty and natural resources, was chosen capital of the independent Republic of Texas, which became the 28th state of the United States. (1976)

AUSTIN (Travis Co.) *903 S Capital of Texas Hwy. (Loop 360)*
Eanes-Marshall Ranch
Alexander Eanes (1806–1888) moved to Texas from Mississippi in 1845 and acquired this ranch by 1857. In 1873, he sold the property to his brother, Robert Eanes (1805–1895), who had moved to the area following the Civil War. A log cabin built on the Eanes Ranch was the first Eanes school, and the community also assumed the Eanes name. Robert Eanes sold the ranch to his son-in-law, Hudson Boatner Marshall (1862–1951) in 1883. Marshall dismantled the ranch house and moved it to a site adjacent to the nearby creek. (Texas Sesquicentennial 1836–1986)

AUSTIN (Travis Co.) *US 183, 11693 Research Blvd.*
Aynesworth-Wright House
Isaiah Hezekiah Aynesworth (b. 1797), a Baptist preacher and cabinetmaker, constructed this Greek Revival residence about 1852. Originally located at 4507 East Avenue, it was a two-room house with an enclosed dog-run hallway. Additional rooms were later attached to the back porch. Dr. Joseph Wright (1798–1898) purchased the property from Aynesworth in 1855. A physician and surveyor, Wright practiced medicine in a log building near his home. The house was moved to this location and restored in 1978 by the Franklin Savings Association. (1980)

AUSTIN (Travis Co.) *US 183 at FM 1625, 5 mi. S*
Pilot Knob
Pilot Knob, the only example of an exposed submarine volcano in Texas, appears today as a prominent hill one mile northwest. It was formed some 80 million years ago on the bottom of a

warm, shallow sea which covered much of the continent during the Cretaceous Period. The molten rock which it spewed forth rose to the surface from deep within the earth's crust, following a channel opened by a belt of fractures known as the Balcones Fault Zone. Reef organisms were attracted to the irregularity on the sea floor. Seeking food and protection on its slopes they multiplied rapidly, not unlike coral reefs form now in the South Pacific Ocean. As corals, starfish, oysters, and other marine life died, their shells and skeletons were fossilized around the volcano. Outcroppings of the small reefs which they formed can be seen today along the banks of Onion Creek, immediately north of Pilot Knob. As the Cretaceous sea receded, the volcano was exposed in its entirety. The long weathering to which it was subjected eroded much of the mass, leaving only the central portion or vent. Today, it rises 710 feet above sea level, 180 feet above the surrounding valley. Diameter of its rim is 1.5 miles. The Pilot Knob area, 29 square miles around the volcano, is probably the best known igneous (volcanic) rock locality in the entire Balcones zone. Principal component of both the central knob and the several smaller knolls on its south and east is basalt, a dark gray to black volcanic rock. Weathered volcanic ash, similar in composition to basalt, underlies the valley around Pilot Knob and makes the land rich for farming.

AUSTIN (Travis Co.)
US 290, at roadside park in Oak Hill
Oak Hill
First settlers arrived in area in 1840s. The community founded here in 1856 was called Live Oak Springs; in 1865 it was renamed Shiloh. Later schools known as Live Oak and Oatmanville gave names temporarily to the settlement. It has been known as Oak Hill since 1900. Limestone quarries were opened, 1882, to supply stone for capitol building in Austin. By 1886, ten carloads of stone were shipped daily over railroad which joined quarries with capitol grounds. It is estimated that one-third of capitol's walls are lined with limestone from Oak Hill quarries.   (1969)

AUSTIN (Travis Co.)
FM 1431, 1.3 mi. N at Nameless Church and Cemetery
Site of Community of Nameless
First surveyed in the 1850s, this area attracted numerous settlers by 1868. A community grew up, and in 1880 townspeople applied for a post office. After postal authorities rejected six names, the citizens replied in disgust, "Let the post office be Nameless and be d—d." The implied "name" was accepted. Besides the post office (1880–1890), town had store, meat market, and school, which also served as a church. The present school was erected in 1909; classes were discontinued in 1945. Today only school, cemetery, and ruins mark site of once active community.   (1970)

AUSTONIO (Houston Co.)
SH 21, .3 mi. W
The Homesite of Samuel Cartmill Hiroms
One of this community's pioneer settlers, Samuel Cartmill Hiroms (1836–1920) was born in Polk County. His parents were among Stephen F. Austin's "Old three hundred" colonists. Hiroms taught school and served as Polk County surveyor. He served in the Confederate Army during the Civil War (1861–1865). After his first wife died, he married Emily Ann Johnston (1853–1948) in 1869 and moved his family to Houston County. In 1878, Hiroms settled here in the Creek community, which later became Austonio. He received land for his teaching services and was an early leader in the Methodist Church.   (1978)

AUSTWELL (Refugio Co.)
SH 239 at Proctor St.
Preston Rose Austin (November 11, 1872–September 29, 1929)
A far-sighted businessman who contributed much to the development of South Texas, Preston Rose Austin was born in Harrison County and grew up in Victoria County. After achieving prominence as a stock raiser, Austin became a partner in the Refugio Land and Irrigation Company, which acquired large landholdings in this area in 1902. Austin conducted a series of agricultural experiments and determined that the land was best suited to raising cotton. The company divided the property into small cotton farms for sale to German and Bohemian farmers. Austin then founded two market towns to serve the settlers. The townsite of Tivoli was platted in 1907 by J. W. Ward. Austwell, named for Austin and one of his partners, Jesse McDowell of Pennsylvania, was platted in 1912 by L. A. Gueringer. The company provided each community with a church, school, store, hotel, and cotton gin and mill, as well as modern conveniences such as electricity and a telephone system. Austin and his associates also financed a branch line of the Missouri Pacific Railroad,

which connected Tivoli and Austwell with Victoria when it was completed in 1912. Austin's energetic ventures resulted in extensive settlement of northern Refugio County. (1976)

AZLE (Tarrant Co.)
FM 730, .6 mi. N of SH 199
Kiowa Raid on Walnut Creek
In April 1867, a band of about sixty Kiowa Indians, led by Chiefs Satank and Satanta, raided the home of William Hamleton on Walnut Creek. Hamleton was away when the Kiowas killed his wife, Sally, and captured two children, Lavina and Mary. Lavina was released from captivity after six months, but Mary was given to an Indian family and grew to adulthood among the Kiowas. Called To-goam-gat-ty, she became an accepted tribal member and married another captive, Calisay. The site of the 1867 Kiowa raid is now under the waters of Eagle Mountain Reservoir. (1983)

BAILEY'S PRAIRIE (Brazoria Co.)
SH 35, 3 mi. E at roadside park
"Brit" Bailey Plantation
Established in 1818 as an individual claim by James Briton Bailey, a member later of Austin's colony. Born 1779, Bailey was tall, fearless, of Irish stock. At his request, he was buried (1833) standing up, facing west, gun at side. His restless ghost is said to walk this prairie. (1968)

BAIRD (Callahan Co.)
US 80, in city limits
The Dr. John Collier Residence
This home was constructed in the early 1880's soon after Baird was selected as the county seat of Callahan Co. It was first the home of Elias Norton, an early merchant of Callahan Co. It later became the home of Dr. John Collier, prominent educator in the early days of the county and founder of the Baird College and its president for a number of years.

BAIRD (Callahan Co.)
100 W. 4th St. (IH 20T Bus.)
Callahan County
Formed from Bexar Territory, created February 1, 1858; recreated August 21, 1876; organized July 3, 1877. Named in Honor of James H. Callahan, 1812–1856 soldier in the Texas Revolution, captain of the Texas Rangers. County Seat, Callahan City, 1877; Belle Plain, 1877–1883; Baird, since two early military roads, the Chisholm Trail, and the first government telegraph line traversed this region. (1936)

BAIRD (Callahan Co.)
Loop 425 at courthouse
Callahan County Courthouse
The county seat moved from Belle Plain to Baird in 1883, and a courthouse, designed by noted architect F. E. Ruffini, was built at this site. The county hired another noted architect, J. Riely Gordon, in 1900 for a larger courthouse; J. E. Flanders was the supervising architect. In 1928, the growing county hired Voelcker & Dixon Architects & Engineers of Wichita Falls, who designed this Classical Revival courthouse, completed the next year. Suggs and Dunlap contractors constructed the building, which features intricate detailing, including acanthus leaves, rosettes, medallions and cartouches. (2003)

BAIRD (Callahan Co.)
Loop 425 at courthouse
Camp Pecan, C.S.A.
This Civil War camp of the Texas frontier regiment was located 21 miles southeast. Established in 1862 as one of a line of posts a day's horseback ride apart. The number of men guarding the frontier were few. Trouble came from all directions with Indian threats and raids from the west and plundering renegades and deserters from the east. Food, supplies, clothing and horses were constantly scarce. But in spite of all obstacles, these Confederates managed to effectively hold the frontier line of settlement. A Memorial to Texans who served the Confederacy, erected by the State of Texas 1963. (1963)

BALLINGER (Runnels Co.)
US 83, 7 mi. S
San Clemente Mission (Site 10 mi. SE)
The first mission known to have been established in Texas east of the Pecos River, San Clemente was a hastily built, two-room structure located on a hill about 17 mi. S of present Ballinger. (Some historians place the site farther south, near Junction.) Although earlier than the great Spanish mis-

sion movement, this was one of the first (1684) in Texas and was founded by Juan Dominguez de Mendoza and Fray Nicolas Lopez. Named for the San Clemente River (actually the Colorado), the mission was founded at the request of the Jumano Indians, who desired Christianity and the friendship of the Spanish. The building was probably constructed of logs, its lower story serving as a chapel and its upper story as a lookout post. Though they stayed only from March 15 to May 1, awaiting envoys from 48 tribes (bands), the Spaniards baptized many of their several thousand Indian allies. Finally, being attacked by hostile Apaches, Mendoza returned with his men to El Paso six months after he had left. Although Mendoza did not know it, French explorer La Salle had landed on the Gulf Coast, 1684. This fact, plus Mendoza's report of seeing a French flag among the Indians, quickly led to other Spanish expeditions being sent to chart the Texas wilderness. (1968)

BALLINGER (Runnels Co.)   *0.8 mi. E of intersection of US 83 at US 67*
Site of Picketteville
First civilian settlement in Runnels County. Founded 1862 by frontiersmen whose picket houses and corrals gave place its name. Original settlers included Mr. and Mrs. John W. Guest and three sons; Henry and R. K. Wylie, their cowboys and Negro servant; Mrs. Felicia Gordon and five sons. In 1862 "Rich" Coffey's family also moved here. Indian hostilities of Civil War years (1861–1865) caused these ranchers to band together for protection. In 1866 they left with cattle for open range. Their picket corral later penned the trail herds of John Hittson, John and Joseph Henderson, and others. (1973)

BALLINGER (Runnels Co.)   *S. 7th St. (US 83) at Hutchings Ave. (US 67)*
Charles H. Noyes (1896–1917)
Charles H. Noyes, 21, died when his horse fell while rounding up cattle on the Noyes' ranch. His father and mother, Gus and Lula Noyes, erected monument in 1919 as a tribute to their son and all Texas cowboys. Pompeo Coppini of Chicago studied horses two years before sculpturing the statue. (1966)

BALLINGER (Runnels Co.)   *S. 7th St. (US 83) at Hutchings Ave. (US 67)*
Ballinger
Originally called Hutchins City. Promoted by Santa Fe Rwy. Named for Judge William Pitt Ballinger (1825–1888), railroad attorney and townsite official. Distinguished Texas statesman, veteran of the Mexican War. In the Civil War helped establish defenses of Galveston, served as Confederate receiver of enemy aliens property, was sent to negotiate peace for Texas. Ballinger is county seat, and farm-ranch center. Industries include dairying, meat products, leather goods manufacturing. Has annual rodeo, livestock and quarterhorse shows. (1964)

BALLINGER (Runnels Co.)   *SH 158, 13.5 mi. W*
Maverick
Founded in the 1870s. Named for Samuel A. Maverick (1803–1870), who came to Texas 1835. Fought in the Texas War for Independence. In Secession Convention, 1861, he was made one of the commissioners to negotiate surrender of United States troops in San Antonio. In 1853 he had land in this important ranching area. (1964)

BALMORHEA (Reeves Co.)   *SH 17, 4 mi. S in state park*
San Salomon Springs
Called "Mescalero Spring" in 1849, when watering corn and peaches of the Mescalero Apaches. To Ft. Davis soldiers, 1856, was "Head Spring". Present name given by first permanent settlers, Mexican farmers. Miller, Lyles and Murphy in 1871 began large-scale commercial irrigation. Murphy built first canals. (1964)

BANDERA (Bandera Co.)   *SH 173/FM 689, 10 mi. N*
Bandera Pass
Celebrated Indian pass known from the earliest days of Spanish settlement. Identified with many a frontier fight and many a hostile inroad. Old Ranger trail from the Medina to the Guadalupe River and the United States Army route between frontier posts followed this route through the mountains.

BANDERA (Bandera Co.)   *SH 16, .8 mi. W; also, SH 16, 1 mi. E*
Bandera County
A strategic Indian point in early days. Rangers and Comanches struggled here in 1843. In 1854 Elder Lyman Wight settled Mormon Colony. In 1855 Poles settled here. From early days a part of Bexar County, created and organized in 1856. Bandera, the county seat founded by John James, Charles de Montel and John Herndon in 1853.

BANDERA (Bandera Co.)   *SH 173 between RR 3240 and Cottonwood*
Bandera Cemetery
The Bandera Cemetery has served the town of Bandera since the 1850s. The site's oldest burial dates to 1851, before the town's establishment several years later. Many former community leaders of the area are buried in the cemetery. In addition, there are a number of veterans interred here, some involved in military conflicts dating to the Mexican American War (1846–1848) and earlier. Members of fraternal organizations are also among those represented here. Ownership of the land can be traced back to Hendrick Arnold, a free African American who was a guide and spy during the Texas Revolution. He joined the revolt with his father-in-law, Erastus (Deaf) Smith, who led the celebrated spy company of which Arnold was part. After several transactions over the years, the section of Arnold's land which became the burial ground was deeded to the Bandera Cemetery Association, which seven women organized in 1907. Today, the burial ground continues to serve the community as an active cemetery and remains an important part of Bandera's history.   (2006)

BANDERA (Bandera Co.)   *SH 16, on public square across the*
                                                              street from courthouse
Old Texas Ranger Trail
This winding, 100-mile trail from San Antonio to Kerrville was, during the 19th century, a strategic patrol road traveled by Texas Rangers to protect the surrounding area from hostile Indian attacks. During uneasy pioneer days roads such as this, regularly scouted by Rangers, helped promote early white settlement by strengthening frontier defense. Because Bandera was located midway on the trail and because Bandera Pass, 10 miles north, frequently harbored Indian ambushers, the town became a focal point for Ranger activities along the road. Perhaps the best-known battle to occur on the old route happened in Bandera Pass in the spring of 1841. At that time a company of 40 Texas Rangers under intrepid Indian fighter Capt. "Jack" Hays was on a scouting mission in the Guadalupe Mountains. Halfway through the pass, they were suddenly attacked by several hundred wild Comanches who lay hidden in the brush and behind boulders in the narrow gorge. A bloody fight ensued, much of it hand-to-hand combat with Bowie knives; but after their chief was slain, the Indians withdrew and finally escaped. Thus the Rangers and this trail helped remove the Indian menace and open the frontier across Texas.   (1968)

BANQUETE (Nueces Co.)   *FM 666, 9 mi. N at bridge over Nueces River*
Santa Margarita Crossing
Ranchers occupying the 1804 Spanish Land Grant of Jose Herrera established this crossing of the Nueces and named the scattered settlement Santa Margarita. In 1828, John McMullen and James McGloin received a land grant from the Mexican government for an Irish colony north of the river and founded the town of San Patricio. This site soon became a major crossing on the Matamoros Road into Texas. To protect the crossing, the Mexican Army, in 1831, established nearby Fort Lipentitlan, which was captured Nov. 4, 1835, by insurgent Texians. On Feb. 27, 1836, Gen. Jose Urrea's army defeated the Texian forces of James Grant and F. W. Johnson here before marching to Goliad. After Texas won independence, Gen. Vicente Filisola led the defeated Mexican troops back to Mexico along this road. After crossing the river here in summer of 1845, Gen. Zachary Taylor held his army in this region until March 1846, when he moved to the Rio Grande, the action which precipitated the U.S. War with Mexico (1846–1848). During the Civil War the Old Matamoros Road, then called the "Cotton Road," served as a trade outlet for the Confederacy. Texas products were transported via the Santa Margarita Crossing to Mexico, circumventing the Federal blockade of Confederate ports.   (1973)

BANQUETE (Nueces Co.)   *SH 44 at FM 666*
Banquete, C.S.A.
In the critical Civil War years, Banquete meant water, supplies, repairs and defenses to thousands on arid trips along the Cotton Road to Mexico. The Cotton Road was well known, for it followed

a segment of the historic "King's Highway" of early explorers. Yet its vital role for 4 years in supplying the Confederacy earned it undying fame. It was the way to Mexico's border towns of Bagdad and Matamoros, where 20,000 speculators clamored for cotton, using valuable European goods to make attractive bargains. To get guns, ammunition, shoes, clothing, medicines—necessities scarce at home—the Confederacy sent to neutral Mexico long trains of 5 to 15 wagons or ox carts that lumbered for many weeks over the desert. Sometimes to lighten a load for an exhausted team, cotton bales might be hidden in roadside brush. The traffic left signs in the wilds. Often the landscape would whiten with the lint thrown off passing loads. Banquete's water made possible the long hauls to Mexico and back to the goods-hungry Confederate population. Thus the town named for an 1832 fiesta honoring Texas colonists served a strategic role in the history of the Civil War, 1861–1865.

BARKER (Harris Co.)   *211 Baker Rd. (IH 10)*
Barker Post Office
The settlement that became Barker developed on the Missouri-Kansas-Texas railroad in the late 1890s. G. T. Miller applied for a post office in 1898. It occupied a corner of his store, which also was used as a saloon. The structure was damaged in the 1900 storm, and postmaster Miller moved it to the east side of the Barker-Clodine Road and rebuilt it. He remained postmaster until 1911. Moved to a new location on the Katy Freeway (Interstate Highway 10) in 1967, it was designated a third-class post office in 1969 and a second-class office in 1977. In 1978 the postal service considered closing it, but residents rallied and saved it. Designated first class in 1981, the post office moved to Baker Road in 1984.   (2001)

BARKSDALE (Edwards Co.)   *SH 55 in Barksdale*
The Pioneer Coalsons (Cedar Creek Ranch and Graves about 9 mi.)
Indians attacked goat camp of Nick Coalson on June 1, 1877; son Arthur, 10, was killed; Johnny, 14, wounded. Coalson escaped after 3 hours of hard fighting. One year later he lost his wife Alice, a daughter, Etta Elizabeth (twin of Arthur), and infant stepson in another Indian raid. Captains Pat Dolan and Dan Roberts with Texas Ranger units, S. D. Coalson (Nick's son), U.S. Army scout Jim Hill, Jim and John Welch, and Henry and Sam Wells pursued but failed to find the Indians. The victims' graves are near old homesite, on Half-Moon Prairie. Coalson descendants are prominent in Texas history.   (1972)

BARKSDALE (Edwards Co.)   *SH 55 in Barksdale*
Dixie Settlement (Forerunner of Barksdale)
Named for Camp Dixie, a Texas Ranger post near military road to Fort Inge (42 mi. SE). First civilian settler was Jerusha Sanchez, midwife for Nueces Canyon area widowed by Indians in the 1870s. Next came Elizabeth Hill, whose eldest son Jim was a military scout. Lewis Barksdale, a veteran of Republic of Texas wars, opened a ranch on his 1876 land grant. The J. R. (Bob) Sweeten family established a store that became the focus for the expanding community. When a post office was created in 1882 and named for Lewis Barksdale, the name Dixie disappeared from use.   (1974)

BARKSDALE (Edwards Co.)   *SH 55 in Barksdale*
Site of Nix Mill (1885–1926)
Built by John L. Nix (1842–1915) to cut rawhide lumber, grind corn and wheat, and gin cotton. Upper floor housed gin; lower, grist mill. On east side was sawmill with wood furnace and boiler to furnish steam power. Furnace was fed cedar and oak wood. Spanish oaks, white oaks, and elms from Nueces River watercourse were sawed into the rawhide lumber from which were built town's wagon yard feed stalls, a dance hall, and other structures. After Nix, successive owners were J. L. Jackson, W. D. Hutcherson, Edward Miller, Matthew Taylor, and O. C. Henderson.   (1972)

BARNHART (Irion Co.)   *US 67*
Barnhart
Named for William F. Barnhart, an agent of the Kansas City, Mexico & Orient Railroad, this community was founded in 1910. During the 1920s and 1930s it was a major freighting center and considered by many the largest inland livestock shipping point. The Ozona-Barnhart Trap Co. set up cattle holding pens (traps) along the trails into town to protect area ranches. Barnhart declined with decreased rail traffic. It was once the site of a school, post office, newspaper, drugstore, theater, bank, four cafes, two hotels, three groceries, and a variety of other businesses.   (1981)

BARTLETT (Bell Co.)   *SH 95, 1 mi. N*
St. John Lutheran Church
The first Lutheran worship services in this area were held at the home of early German settler J. E. Pietzsch, who had moved from Austin County. In 1880, a small school and church building was erected on land donated by John Bartlett, for whom the nearby town of Bartlett was named. St. John Lutheran Church was formally organized on December 16, 1883. A year later the Rev. Immanuel Glatzle arrived to become the first resident pastor. By 1896 the congregation had acquired more land and erected a small white frame sanctuary. All written records were destroyed in a 1922 fire which burned the parsonage and two outbuildings. Larger facilities were needed by 1931, so a new church structure was built that year. Dedication services were held January 10, 1932. On August 12, 1951, the congregation dedicated its new pipe organ, which at the time was the largest in any Texas Lutheran church. From its beginning St. John Lutheran Church has served the spiritual and educational needs of the surrounding communities. Although the last German service was conducted in 1942, the church continues to reflect the ideals and traditions of its founders.   (1983)

BARTLETT (Bell Co.)   *SH 95, 1 mi. N*
Site of German-English School (50 yds. W)
Established by German immigrants in 1880, the German-English School was an early school in the Bartlett area. First called Indian Creek School, the name was changed due to popular usage and the nature of instruction, which was in English during the winter and German during the summer. Closely associated with St. John's Lutheran Church, the school shared facilities with the church until 1896, when a church sanctuary was built. The school was closed in 1948, but the building remained in use for community functions until the early 1960s.   (1988)

BARTLETT (Bell Co.)   *Old US 281 (Old Austin-Belton Rd.), 2 mi. S*
Lampasas River Bridge
Erected to replace an 1875 toll bridge at this site, this was one of several bridges authorized by the Bell County Commissioners Court in 1889. Built by the Penn Bridge Company of Beaver Falls, Pennsylvania, it is a rare surviving example of a double-intersection Pratt Truss Bridge (also known as Whipple Truss Bridge, after the engineer who patented the design in the 19th century). Measuring over 196 feet in length, the bridge consists of eleven pin-connected panels. Large pieces of native rock were used to form the abutments, and the floor is made of heavy timber planking.   (Recorded Texas Historic Landmark—1990)

BASTROP (Bastrop Co.)   *SH 304, 1 mi. S of SH 71, 2 mi. W*
Aldridge-Fitzwilliam Home
Built 1852 on part of league granted in 1831 by the Mexican government to Mozea Rousseau, a member of Austin's second colony. First portion was erected by John Aldridge, farmer, whose family lived here until about 1865. The 2-story part was built about 1872 by J. W. Fitzwilliam, captain in Confederate Army and plantation owner. House is called "Wexford" after town in Ireland where he was born. Home is still owned by the Fitzwilliam family.   (1968)

BASTROP (Bastrop Co.)   *SH 71 W, 2 mi. E in roadside park*
Mrs. R. T. P. Allen
Resident of Bastrop County, 1857–1863. Wife of Col. Robert Thomas Pritchard Allen (1812–1888), graduate of West Point, civil engineer, mathematics professor, Methodist preacher, U.S. mail agent and co-publisher "Pacific News," San Francisco, 1849–1850; founder and commandant of Kentucky Military Institute and of Bastrop Military Institute. Their family visitors from time to time in Bastrop included Governor Sam Houston, whose son, Sam Junior, was a B. M. I. cadet. Mrs. Allen, during the Civil War, was an angel of mercy to prisoners at Camp Ford, Tyler, where her husband, at that time colonel of the 17th Texas Infantry, was commandant, 1863–1864. She nursed the ill, consoled the homesick, cheered the despondent, attended church services with the prisoners. She was so much esteemed and loved that one of the Federals wrote a poem in her honor. After the war, returned with her husband to state of Kentucky. There Col. Allen resumed operation of Kentucky Military Institute. His brother-in-law, Jay Cooke, of Philadelphia, who had won international fame as the United States' financier for the Civil War, backed Allen and K.M.I. until his 1873 business failure known as the Jay Cooke money panic.   (1965)

BASTROP (Bastrop Co.)   *SH 71 at Loop 150*
Early History of the City of Bastrop
Long before white men arrived, this region was inhabited by Tonkawa and Comanche Indians. In 1691 the first Spanish explorers crossed this territory en route to East Texas. From their route, parts of "El Camino Real" (The King's Highway) were blazed, thus placing Bastrop on a major early travel artery. Because El Camino Real crossed the Colorado River here, this was a strategic spot. In 1805 the fort "Puesta de Colorado" and accompanying community were founded here to protect commerce on the road. In 1825 this area became "Mina," one of the first settlements in the Colony of Stephen F. Austin. It was named for revolutionary leader Xavier Mina. In the years that followed, many members of its first 100 families served in the Texas Revolution (1836), the Mexican War (1846–1848), and were active in political life in the Republic and State of Texas. In 1837 when the town incorporated, the name was changed to "Bastrop" to honor the Baron de Bastrop, influential early land agent and statesman. The city was also designated county seat in 1837. From 1851–1870, this was seat of Bastrop Military Academy, an important Texas school. First courthouse was built in 1853; present one in 1883 on same spot.   (1968)

BASTROP (Bastrop Co.)   *SH 71 at CR 154, 7 mi. W*
Alum Creek Cemetery
In the 1820s, several families answered Stephen F. Austin's call to settle this part of Texas, then a part of Mexico. The Cottle, Highsmith, Grimes, Craft, Ridgeway, White and Parks families were among those who arrived in this area from Missouri in 1828. Three years later, Sarah (Turner) Cottle, whose husband had died during the journey to Texas, received title to her land, situated along Alum Creek. After her death in 1843, the property was divided among her heirs. In 1857, Newton and Mary (Cottle) Alsup deeded land to the Alum Creek community for a cemetery and a Methodist Episcopal Church, South. Other denominations held services in the building, which was also used for a community school. The first marked graves in the cemetery date to 1875, and a number of burials are marked by fieldstones. In 1950, community members formed an association. It continues to maintain the cemetery, which remains a link to the settlers who arrived in the years before Texas independence and to the generations that have since been a part of the Alum Creek community.   (2004)

BASTROP (Bastrop Co.)   *SH 71, at entrance to state park*
Bastrop County
A part of Austin's grant in 1821 created the Municipality of Mina 1834, became the County of Mina in the Republic of Texas 1836. Name changed to "Bastrop" December 18, 1837, in honor of Felipe Enrique Neri Baron de Bastrop, 1770–1829 land commissioner of Austin's colony, member of the Congress of Coahuila and Texas. Bastrop, the county seat.

BASTROP (Bastrop Co.)   *Loop 150, 2 mi. E on Park Rd. 1A*
Felipe Enrique Nerí de Bastrop (1770–1829)
Erected in recognition of the distinguished service to Texas. Pioneer Red River empresario. Land commissioner of Austin's colony. Member of the Congress of Coahuila and Texas. In his honor this county and county seat have been named.   (1936)

BASTROP (Bastrop Co.)   *SH 21, 1 mi. NE (Bastrop State Park)*
The Gotier Trace
Originated in 1820s. Crossed the present counties of Austin, Washington, Fayette, Lee, Bastrop; joined San Felipe, capital of Stephen F. Austin's colony, with Bastrop. Marked by James Gotier, a settler who (with several in his family) died in Indian massacre near this site in 1837. Like most early Texas roads, this was only a marked route which travelers could follow—dusty in droughts, boggy in rains. From such traces, wagon roads and cattle trails, Texas has developed over 67,000 miles of fine paved highways—a system recognized as nation's finest.   (1967)

BASTROP (Bastrop Co.)   *SH 21, 1 mi. NE (Bastrop State Park)*
Erected in Recognition of the Distinguished Service to Texas of
Felipe Enrique Nerí, Baron de Bastrop 1770–1829
Pioneer Red River empresario. Land commissioner of Austin's colony. Member of the Congress of Coahuila and Texas. In his honor this county and county seat have been named.

BASTROP (Bastrop Co.)   *SH 21, 1 mi. NE at entrance to Bastrop State Park*
Lost Pines of Texas
    Located 80 miles west of the main pine belt of Texas, these trees probably were once part of vast prehistoric pine forests. As land areas gradually rose, possibly due to glacier activity, most of the forests moved east. Ideal local conditions have kept the "lost pines" intact. One of the first records of the trees was made in 1807 by Zebulon Pike, explorer for whom Pike's Peak was named. In the 19th century, these loblolly pines supported the county's main industry. Local lumber was shipped by riverboat and ox-wagon to points all over Texas.   (1969)

BASTROP (Bastrop Co.)   *SH 21 at Loop 150, 2 mi. E,*
                                             at Bastrop State Park Refectory
The CCC at Bastrop State Park
    President Franklin D. Roosevelt and the U.S. Congress, as part of the "New Deal" efforts to offer unemployed workers jobs on public projects, created the Civilian Conservation Corps (CCC) in March 1933. Due to decades of lumbering activities, Bastrop County's "Lost Pines" forest was a prime candidate for the CCC's reforestation program and a logical site for the establishment of a park, and two hundred recruits of the CCC's company #1805 arrived in Bastrop in November 1933. With the help of Austin architect Arthur Fehr and a group of "local experienced men" or L.E.M.s, the men worked to create a state recreational park in the forest. Built of native materials in the "NPS rustic" style promoted by the National Park Service, the park structures, particularly the central refectory, reflect the expert craftsmanship of the CCC. A second CCC company, #1811, arrived in November 1934 to assist with reforestation work and development of nearby Buescher State Park. Additional activities included making native wood furniture for this and other Texas state parks, and building roads, trails, bridges, and small lakes. CCC work at Bastrop ended with the park substantially complete in 1939.   (1991)

BASTROP (Bastrop Co.)   *SH 21, 12 mi. NE*
King's Highway, Camino Real
    Old San Antonio Road marked by the Daughters of the American Revolution and the State of Texas; A.D. 1918.

BATESVILLE (Zavala Co.)   *Main St., 1 blk. off US 57*
Site of First Zavala County Courthouse
    Zavala County was created in 1858 from Maverick and Uvalde Counties. Named for Lorenzo de Zavala, a veteran of the Battle of San Jacinto, the county was not organized for judicial purposes until 1884. In that year citizens elected county officials and selected Batesville as the county seat. Batesville originally was known as the Bates Ditch Community or Bates City. Elijah A. and Ellen J. Bates are credited with its founding. They came to the area in the late 1860s and became a prominent ranching family. Bates, who is credited with the first irrigation project in the area, began selling two-acre plots of the irrigated farmland, and a settlement grew up near his home. After the selection of Batesville as the Zavala County seat, Bates conveyed a portion of his land for use as a courthouse square. The first county courthouse and jail were constructed at this site in 1885. Built of burnt bricks made from Leona River soil, the two-story courthouse featured offices downstairs and a courtroom upstairs. The structure was used as the county courthouse until 1928, when the seat of government was moved to Crystal City. The old courthouse then was used for a variety of purposes until it was torn down in 1947.   (1984)

BAY CITY (Matagorda Co.)   *SH 35, courthouse*
Matagorda County
    Organized March 6, 1834, into the Mexican municipality of Matagorda. Created a county of the same name in 1836. Organized in 1837. Named for the bay on which it fronts. County seat, Matagorda 1837–1894. Bay City, since.

BAY CITY (Matagorda Co.)   *SH 35, east side of Colorado River Bridge*
Elliott's Ferry
    During the early days of Anglo-American colonization in Texas, the Matagorda Bay prairie area was an important route for people traveling between settlements. A convenient river crossing was a necessity, and a ferry was established on the Thomas Cayce league of land near this site. Known

as Cayce's Ferry, the site was garrisoned by a small army post. In January 1839, George Elliott (1806–1862) purchased land on the west bank of the Colorado River from Thomas Cayce, and from that time the ferry crossing was known as Elliott's Ferry. George Elliott was assisted in his endeavors by two nephews, William Elliott and John Elliott, who continued the ferry business after George Elliott's death. By 1863, a small settlement had grown up around Elliott's Ferry. A small mercantile business and a post office known as Elliott's Ferry, Texas, were in operation in 1872. In 1893, the post office name was changed to Elliott, Texas, and a year later was moved to Bay City. In 1902, a bridge was built over the Colorado River two miles northwest of Bay City. Known as the "Old River Bridge," its completion resulted in the demise of Elliott's Ferry.

(Texas Sesquicentennial 1836–1986)

BAYTOWN (Harris Co.)   *SH 146, E of Hartman Bridge*
Bayland Orphanage (Site ½ mi. SE)

Established in 1866 by Texas Confederate veterans for children of deceased soldiers. Had capacity for 250. Rev. Henry F. Gillette was first superintendent. C.S.A. Col. Ashbel Smith, diplomat, soldier, and statesman, was staff doctor. Trustees included leading citizens. Donations from Harris and Galveston Counties started the home, but later gifts came from as far away as New Orleans. After the Confederate children grew up, home and school were opened to others. Bayland was forerunner of the De Pelchin Faith Home of Houston.   (1964)

BAYTOWN (Harris Co.)   *SH 146, 1.8 mi. E of Hartman Bridge*
Ashbel Smith, M.D. (1805–1886)

Born in Hartford, Connecticut, this prominent physician, statesman, soldier, and educator received his degree from Yale Medical College in 1828. After a period of study in France, Smith returned to the United States to practice medicine in the state of North Carolina. He determined to go to Texas upon hearing news of the events of the mid-1830s and arrived in 1837, too late to participate in the Revolution. He soon, however, was appointed Surgeon-General of the Texas Army and established a home, known as Evergreen Plantation, one mile east of this site. Smith later served the Republic of Texas as Secretary of State and as Minister to Great Britain, France, Belgium, and Spain. After Texas attained statehood, Smith served several terms in the state legislature. A Civil War veteran, he was elected Captain of the Bayland Guards and Colonel of the 2nd Texas Infantry of the Confederate Army. Also noted for his work in higher education, Ashbel Smith served as president of the first Board of Regents of the University of Texas and led support for establishment of its medical branch in Galveston. A significant leader during Texas' formative years, Ashbel Smith died at his home on Evergreen Plantation and is buried in the State Cemetery in Austin.   (1984)

BAYTOWN (Harris Co.)   *2641 S SH 146*
Bayland Guards

On April 27, 1861, Dr. Ashbel Smith organized a group of volunteers from Bayland (now Baytown) and Cedar Bayou in Harris County, and Barbers Hill in Chambers County. The group, known as the Bayland Guards, drilled on Smith's Evergreen Plantation and worked in local defense of Galveston Bay. On August 13, 1861, they mustered into the Confederate forces as Company C of the Galveston Infantry Regiment. The regiment was redesignated in October as the Second Texas Infantry Regiment and that December, it moved to Camp Bee in Houston. Among the Bayland Guards were three sons of Republic of Texas presidents Sam Houston and Anson Jones: Samuel Houston, Jr., Charles Elliot Jones and Samuel Edward Jones. The Bayland Guards fought with the rest of the regiment at the Battles of Shiloh, Corinth and Hatchie Bridge in 1862. At the Battle of Shiloh, half of Company C was wounded or killed. During the Vicksburg campaign in 1863, the Second Texas distinguished itself by defending a crescent-shaped fortification in the center of the line of Confederate defense while withstanding Union assaults and 46 days and nights of shelling and bombardment. The Second Texas infantry and the other defenders were surrendered at Vicksburg on July 4, 1863 and were promptly paroled to make their way back to Texas. The decimated regiment reorganized at Houston in the fall of 1863 and served out the war on the Texas coast from Matagorda to Galveston, helping to deter General Banks' attempt to invade Texas early in 1864. The regiment was surrendered on May 26, 1865. After the war, many members of the Bayland Guards became leaders and respected individuals in their communities.   (2009)

37

BAYTOWN (Harris Co.)   *2641 S SH 146*
Confederate Naval Works at Goose Creek
In 1854, brothers Thomas and John Chubb bought land in the William Scott League on the east bank of Goose Creek at the mouth of Tabbs Bay. On this site, they established the Chubb Shipyard prior to the Civil War. At the time, Texas shipbuilding was a developing industry. During the war, however, in an effort to compensate for the Union's industrial advantage, the Confederate government encouraged Texans to engage in manufacturing ventures that would aid its military effort. The Chubb brothers responded to this call with the Confederate Naval Works at Goose Creek, which built and repaired vessels during the war. Thomas Chubb also served in the Texas Marine Department, an element of the Confederate States Army operating independently of the Confederate Navy. He obtained the rank of Captain and later became superintendent of the Confederate Naval Works. The design and structure of ships built at the Goose Creek shipyard were integral to the Department's effectiveness in running the Union blockade. The shallow draft of the centerboard schooners made them suitable for blockade running in shallow areas of the Gulf of Mexico, where deep draft vessels could not pass. These successful ships included the Royal Yacht, Bagdad, Phoebe, Henrietta, Marguereta and Altha Brooks. An important contributor to the Texas naval and industrial effort during the Civil War, the Goose Creek shipyard later built ships for the federal government and private mariners until Thomas Chubb left the business in 1869. The following year, the Thomas B. Gaillard family purchased the former shipyard and established Gaillard's Landing. Later, the site became part of the Goose Creek oil fields.   (2007)

BEAUMONT (Jefferson Co.)   *University St. between Florida St.*
and US 287/96/69
The Lucas Gusher
Discovery well of the Spindletop Oil Field and the first important well on the Gulf Coast. It blew in on Jan. 10, 1901, flowing 100,000 barrels of oil a day from a depth of 1020 feet. The oil production which resulted made Beaumont a city and the Sabine District a major oil refining and exporting center of the world. The Lucas Gusher was drilled by the Hamill Brothers, contractors, under the direct supervision of Captain Anthony F. Lucas for Guffey and Galey of Pittsburgh, on the McFaddin, Weiss and Kyle lease.   (1936)

BEDIAS (Grimes Co.)   *SH 90, 4 mi. N at roadside park*
Sarah Bradley Dodson
Born in Kentucky in 1812, eleven-year-old Sarah Bradley and her parents arrived in Texas in 1823 with Stephen F. Austin's Old Three Hundred colonists, settling near Brazoria. Sarah married Archelaus Bynum Dodson of nearby Harrisburg on May 17, 1835. As tensions mounted between Mexico and the Texian colonists, a call for military volunteers was circulated in September 1835, and Archelaus Dodson became First Lt. in Captain Andrew Robinson's Harrisburg Volunteers. Sarah offered to design and make a flag for her husband's company. Using blue, white, and red calico, she fashioned a flag of three equal squares, with a five pointed white star in the center of the blue square. Reportedly the first Lone Star flag, the banner was displayed in the town of Gonzales in October 1835, and in December flew during the siege of Bexar. When the Declaration of Independence was signed, two flags were seen flying over Convention Hall. One was described as a Lone Star flag and is believed to have been the one made by Sarah Dodson. Following the Texan victory at San Jacinto, the Dodsons lived in Fort Bend County, then moved in 1844 to Grimes County. They donated the land for Bethel Cemetery (5 mi. N) where Sarah was buried in 1848.
(Texas Sesquicentennial 1836–1986)

BEDIAS (Grimes Co.)   *3652 Main St., off SH 90*
Town of Bedias
Named for North and South Bedias Creeks, which in turn were named for the Bidai Indians, an agricultural people reputed to have been the oldest inhabitants of the area. "Bidai" means "brushwood," which may refer to the building material used in their dwellings. The first white settlement in this vicinity was founded 1835 by Thomas P. Plaster, and for a while it was called Plasterville. In 1903, the community of "Old" Bedias surrendered most of its population to "New" Bedias after a branch of the International & Great Northern Railroad was built to the northeast. Townspeople from Pankey and Cotton also moved here. The name "Bedias" was retained, but only after a heated struggle in which determined citizens refused to have the town named for a railroad official. A fa-

mous, early resident of the Bedias area was Sarah Dodson, who in 1835 made the first "Lone Star" flag in Texas. She lived here from 1844 to 1848 and is buried in old Bethel Cemetery, seven miles west. One of the most unique features of this region is the large number of Tektites (also called Bediasites) found here. These are beautiful, glassy, meteor-like stones which fell to earth 34 million years ago. Amazingly, Indians called them "jewels of the moon."   (1968)

BEEVILLE (Bee Co.)   *US 181, 5 mi. N at roadside park*
Captain A. C. Jones
One of builders of Southwest. Born in Nacogdoches County, son of very early settlers. Became a cattleman; served as sheriff of Goliad County in 1858–1860. In Civil War cavalry of Col. John S. "Rip" Ford for 4 years. Fought at Palmito Hill, war's last battle, 34 days after the surrender of Gen. Robt. E. Lee. In 1886, raised $75,000 to build SA and AP railroad from San Antonio to Beeville. Aided in getting GH and SA to extend line from Victoria to here in 1890. Was county treasurer, banker and the president and general manager of Beeville Oil Mill.   (1965)

BEEVILLE (Bee Co.)   *US 181, 3.6 mi. N in roadside park*
Early Trails in Bee County
From pack trails and wagon roads that marked this area at least 300 years have developed such modern roads as US Highway 181. The old trails of Indians, wild cattle, and mustang horses formed highways for 17th-, 18th-, and 19th-century expeditions coming from Mexico to claim sovereignty for Spain over land of Texas. When pioneers established land grants in this section, they also found Indian trails useful, placing towns along them. Beeville, the county seat, was situated at the natural intersection of San Patricio–Helena Road with Goliad-Laredo Road. About 20 miles south, the Matamoros-Goliad Road ("Camino Real" to old-timers) was probably the most historic road in this area. In the years 1861–1865, the "Cotton Road"—called "Lifeline of the Southern Confederacy"—crossed Bee County. A later route of great value was a cattle trail that channeled thousands of Longhorns north from the Rio Grande to the Red River and up the Dodge City Trail or the Chisholm Trail to northern markets. In this area were also La Para (or Grapevine) Road; the Indianola-Papalote Road; and a road to now-vanished St. Mary's, a port on Copano Bay, off the Gulf of Mexico.   (1968)

BEEVILLE (Bee Co.)   *105 W. Corpus St. (US 59)*
Bee County Courthouse
Bee County was created in 1857 from parts of five neighboring counties. The first county seat was located seven miles east of this site, and the first commissioners court was held on the banks of Medio Creek in February 1858. The city's earliest courthouse consisted of a box frame structure. In 1912, local architect W. C. Stephenson designed this, the county's fourth courthouse. A native of Buffalo, New York, Stephenson aided in the design of the death mask of President William McKinley. He was the architect of several Beeville buildings, including the Rialto Theater, two churches and several houses, and later designed the Classical Revival McMullen County courthouse. W. C. Whitney, builder of three other Texas courthouses, contracted to build the Bee County courthouse for $72,050. Whitney died during construction and W. C. Stephenson's partner, Fritz Heldenfels, completed the project. Stephenson drew upon the strong contemporary influence of the French Beaux Arts School with a level of grandeur previously nonexistent in Bee County. Some original Beaux Arts features such as the cast stone balustrade originally outlining the roof were later removed, and the 1943 addition partially obscured the symmetrical plan and façade of the edifice. The Bee County courthouse is a fine example of the Classical Revival style. Of particular significance are the grand portico and projecting pediment entry with Corinthian columns and dentils along the roofline. The Chicago-style windows, comprised of one glass pane flanked by two narrower ones, with transoms above, are noteworthy. Also unusual is Stephenson's Lady of Justice; unlike most such symbols, she is not depicted as blind.   (2002)

BELLAIRE (Harris Co.)   *Bellaire Blvd. at 2nd St.*
Texan Capture of Mexican Dispatches
The San Jacinto Campaign in Southwest Harris County
After the fall of the Alamo on March 6, 1836, Gen. Sam Houston led the Texan Army in retreat from Gonzales. The Mexican Army under Gen. Santa Anna followed eastward from San Antonio. On April 14, while Houston's army was north of him, Santa Anna led a division of his army from the Brazos River near present Richmond to Harrisburg. He crossed present southwest Harris

County, then an uninhabited prairie, and reached Harrisburg (12 mi. E of this site) on April 15. The Mexicans burned Harrisburg on April 17 and continued marching east. Houston's army, arriving at Buffalo Bayou opposite Harrisburg on April 18, found the town in ruins, but did not know the whereabouts of the Mexican Army. That day, Texan scouts led by Erastus "Deaf" Smith captured three Mexicans, including Capt. Miguel Bachiller, a courier, and a guide in this vicinity. The prisoners and their dispatches revealed the location, size, and plans of the Mexican Army. With this vital intelligence, Houston intercepted Santa Anna's march on April 20 and defeated his division with a surprise attack on April 21 at the San Jacinto River. The Battle of San Jacinto ended the Texas Revolution and secured the Independent Republic of Texas. (1989)

BELLS (Grayson Co.) US 69 at US 82
First Baptist Church of Bells
Originally known as Bell Plain Baptist Church, this congregation was organized in 1879 at the home of J. A. Lindsay. The first services were conducted in the Bailey Junction Schoolhouse by the Rev. Isaac Reed. In 1884, soon after the school building burned, the members constructed a sanctuary on property donated by A. T. Wilson. They worshiped there as the Baptist Church of Christ until about 1896, when high winds destroyed the structure. Later that year the congregation built a chapel at this location. The present sanctuary was completed in 1954. (1980)

BELLVILLE (Austin Co.) SH 36 at SH 159
Austin County
A part of the grant to Stephen F. Austin in 1821. Created a municipality under the Mexican government in 1828. Became a county of the Republic of Texas, March 17, 1836. Named in honor of Stephen Fuller Austin, 1793–1836, pioneer empresario founder of Anglo-American Texas. San Felipe De Austin, Capital of Austin's colony, 1824–1836. Seat of provisional government of Texas, 1835–1836. County seat, 1837–1848, Beeville, since.

BELLVILLE (Austin Co.) 30 S. Holland St., off SH 36
Bellville
Brothers Thomas and James Bell came to this area from Florida in 1822 with Stephen F. Austin's colony and acquired about 2,000 acres of land in 1837. Thomas Bell offered a portion of his land at this site for a new townsite to replace San Felipe as the county seat; his offer was accepted by voters in 1846. Pioneers from such faraway places as England, Germany, Connecticut, Maryland and Georgia were drawn to the new town, which was platted in 1848 and soon called Bellville by popular vote. A courthouse and jail were erected in 1848 and Bellville's first hotel opened in 1849. Within ten years, the booming town boasted about fifteen businesses. The Civil War left the town nearly deserted, and as in many similar Texas towns it was difficult to rebuild during the Reconstruction era. Positive growth began about 1877 as new business ventures took root. In 1880 the Gulf, Colorado and Santa Fe Railway arrived in Bellville, and the population doubled rapidly. The Episcopal and German Methodist churches organized about 1881, and the Bellville Standard newspaper was established in 1882. A telephone company began operations and a library was established by 1886. Cotton production rose in the late 1890s and more than 10,000 bales were shipped each growing season. By the turn of the century Bellville was thriving both culturally and economically. Oil replaced cotton as the area's major industry in 1915 when black gold was discovered around Bellville. Development of local oil fields further spurred the town's growth and continued to help support Bellville throughout the 20th century. (1999)

BELTON (Bell Co.) IH 35, 2 mi. N
Little River Fort
Site of a picket fort on Little River commonly called Fort Griffin. Also known as Fort Smith and Little River Fort. Erected by Geo. B. Erath and 20 Texas Rangers in November, 1836 as a protection against Indians. Abandoned as a military post before the Santa Fe Expedition camped here, June 24–29, 1841, but used by settlers many years as a place of defense against the Indians.

BELTON (Bell Co.) 6870 S. IH-35
Gulf, Colorado and Santa Fe Railway Planing Mill
Built in 1912 at the Santa Fe rail yards in Temple, this planing mill was part of a complex of buildings that housed repair facilities for the railroad. Workers at the mill manufactured replacement parts

for wooden elements of the Santa Fe's boxcars and early wooden passenger cars. Heavy timbers used in the building's construction were assembled in such a manner to handle the pounding of heavy machinery inside. In use until the late 1940s, the mill was moved to this location in 1989 to save it from demolition. Although no longer sited along the railroad route, it still serves as a reminder of the significant role the Santa Fe played in the industrial development of Bell County.   (2001)

BELTON (Bell Co.)   *IH 35, 2 mi. S in roadside park*
Bell County
Settlement began on Lampasas River, 1847. Created Jan. 22, organized Aug. 1, 1850. Named for Peter Hansbrough Bell (1812–1898), native of Virginia; veteran of Battle of San Jacinto; served in Somervell expedition to stop Mexico's raids into Texas; officer in Mexican War; Governor of Texas 1849–1853; U.S. Congressman, 1853–1857. First county seat Nolanville, moved Dec. 16, 1851, to Belton. By 1860 population was 4,799. Sent 12 troop companies into Civil War. Furnished goods from flour mills, hat factory, tanyard, leather works, blacksmith shops, cabinet shop, beef slaughter pens.   (1965)

BELTON (Bell Co.)   *506 N. Main (SH 317)*
First Baptist Church of Belton
The First Baptist Church of Belton was organized in the summer of 1853 under the leadership of the Rev. Solomon G. O'Bryan and the Rev. David Fisher. There were eight charter members, and the congregation met in a small frame building on Pearl Street on the north side of Nolan Creek. Early visiting preachers included John Clabaugh and Judge R. E. B. Baylor. Clabaugh was called as permanent pastor of the church in 1856 and held services once a month until the beginning of the Civil War. Visiting ministers served the congregation during the war. A revival held in 1864 at the courthouse by the Rev. W. W. Harris resulted in many new members for the church. The Rev. M. V. Smith began an eighteen-year pastorate in Belton in January 1875. The congregation, which had been meeting in other churches, built a stone structure on the east side of Main Street, south of the present church buildings. After the stone church was destroyed by fire in 1947, construction began on the present structure at 506 N. Main. The facilities have been enlarged over the years to serve the growing congregation. With service to its congregation and the community, the church has contributed to Belton's history.   (Texas Sesquicentennial 1836–1986)

BEN FRANKLIN (Delta Co.)   *FM 128, 3 mi. SW*
Giles Academy
Early settlers, who came to this area from Giles County, Tenn., founded an academy at this site in 1859, hired fellow-Tennessean Thomas Hart Benton Hockaday (1835–1918) as the first teacher, and named the new school in memory or their Southern Tennessee homeland. Hockaday taught at Giles until his enlistment in the Confederate Army in 1862, and after the Civil War for several years before moving to Franklin County in 1870s. He presented a curriculum emphasizing arithmetic, reading the classics, and use of the English language. His daughter, Ela Hockaday (1876–1956), founded the well known Hockaday school for girls in Dallas in 1913. School expenses, including teachers' salaries, were paid by parents of the students. A small community center, with a black-smith shop, general merchandise store, and church, grew up around the large log schoolhouse. After the organization of common school districts in Texas in 1883, the academy became Giles School, District No. 4. The old log house was replaced with a frame structure in 1886. A more modern building, erected on this site in 1924, was badly damaged by a tornado in 1936. The Giles School never reopened, and its students were distributed between the Ben Franklin and Pecan Gap Schools.   (1973)

BEN WHEELER (Van Zandt Co.)   *SH 64, 2 mi. W*
Prairie Springs Cemetery
Associated for many years with the Prairie Springs Methodist Episcopal Church, South, this cemetery dates to 1866, when the infant grandson of R. W. Berry was buried here. Berry formally deeded land for the graveyard in 1880, although several other burials took place here before that time. The Prairie Springs Church moved to the town of Ben Wheeler (2 mi. SE) in 1893, but title to the cemetery was not formally transferred to the Prairie Springs Cemetery Association until 1949. The large graveyard is the burial ground for many of the area's pioneers and their descendants.   (1985)

BENCHLEY (Robertson Co.)   *SH 6 at Old San Antonio Rd.*
El Camino Real
(Also Known as Old San Antonio Road and Old Spanish Trail)
A trail of adventure, hardships, opportunity and freedom, over which history stalked into Texas. To the Spanish, El Camino Real was a road traveled for the King—to colonize, Christianize, seek adventure or look for riches. This road became the most famous. Its many parts were made, discovered or known hundreds of years before 1691, when Domingo Teran de los Rios, first Governor of Texas, joined and marked the different trails for the king. It was the route from Monclova (crossing the Rio Grande near Eagle Pass) to the Missions of East Texas. Probably its trailblazers were buffalo and Indians, or Aztecs on trading expeditions. It was also possibly traveled, described and changed in part by French explorer La Salle; by Alonso de Leon and Father Damian Massanet planting missions in East Texas; and by the French nobleman St. Denis seeking trade along the Rio Grande. As the years wore on, it was traveled in 1820 by Moses Austin, as well as by thousands of settlers who followed him. San Augustine, Nacogdoches and San Antonio were its principal cities; inns sprang up along the way. Soldiers and supply trains used it during the Texas Revolution, Mexican War and Civil War. It is still followed in part by this highway.

BENCHLEY (Robertson Co.)   *SH 6, 1 mi. E*
Staggers Point
Earliest large community in Robertson's colony. Settled by Irishmen who came to America in 1821; lived in South Carolina and then in Alabama; and in 1829 sent west an emissary, Robert Henry, to find a permanent location. In 1833, their ox-wagon train arrived, and log cabins were built. By 1836, kinsmen had joined early arrivals, to strengthen settlement. Community name, meaning "Strivers' Point" in dialect, was probably given for rugged zeal of settlers in face of hardships. James Dunn built a fort, to give neighborhood a refuge during Indian raids. In War for Independence, 1835–1836, Staggers Point men fought in major actions, including the April 21, 1836, Battle of San Jacinto, which freed Texas from Mexico. In 1830s and '40s, the Irish were compelled to keep up their defenses against the Indians. Women as well as men earned respect for skill with "long guns." In time their village had a church, stores, cotton gin, race track, and taverns, and was invaded by gamblers and ruffians drawn to the races. Until the settlers subdued the lawless, duels and gunplay were common. This remained a progressive community until 1868, when Houston & Texas Central Railway bypassed it, and business waned. Descendants still honor the settlers.   (1973)

BEND (San Saba Co.)   *FM 580*
Dr. Edward D. Doss
Edward D. Doss (1849–1928) beloved pioneer doctor in this area for 40 years; served as pharmacist, general practitioner, obstetrician, dentist & on occasion surgeon & nurse. Traveled horse back, two wheel cart, horse & buggy ('Old Ross' in picture). Crossed river by ferry boat. Wore out 3 Ford cars. Came to Bend with wife Arebell Tomblinson, 1882. Owned & operated general merchandise store with son, Lawrence. "No night too dark or road too long to serve his fellow man." Erected by those who loved him—July 1965.
*Picture of doctor at hitched buggy is posted on granite marker.

BENJAMIN (Knox Co.)   *US 82, 6 mi. E in roadside park*
The Narrows
This crest separates the drainage basins of the Wichita River, whose waters flow into the Mississippi, and the Brazos River, which winds through Texas to the Gulf of Mexico. Known as good hunting grounds because of buffalo grass, fresh springs and herds of mustangs from which to get mounts, the narrows were crossed by the Comanche, Wichita, Kiowa, Apache, Seminole and Tonkawa Indians. Evidences of battles and camps are still being found. Later, settlers used the well-worn paths. Today its canyons and ravines are used for ranching.   (1965)

BENJAMIN (Knox Co.)   *US 82, 3.5 mi. E*
Texas Business Pioneer Pleasant C. Sams (1845–1921)
In 1850s came to Texas from Arkansas. At 16, on outbreak of Civil War, was left in charge of family mills, instructed by his father to give entire flour output to widows of Confederates. In 1862, captured in Missouri, as he went through enemy lines to get his bride; escaped from Federal who also admired bride. Wedding trip was horseback ride to Texas. He served 1864–65 in Confederate

Frontier Regiment. Pioneer cattleman; business and financial leader. Founder and president, Benjamin Commercial Company, president and director, First National Bank, Benjamin.   (1965)

BENJAMIN (Knox Co.)   *US 82/SH114 at Stewart St., courthouse*
Knox County
Formed from Young and Bexar Territories. Created February 1, 1858. Recreated August 21, 1876. Organized March 20, 1886. Named in honor of General Henry Knox, 1750–1806. Major General of the Continental Army, 1781, Secretary of War, 1785–1794. Benjamin, the county seat.   (1936)

BENJAMIN (Knox Co.)   *US 82/SH114 at Stewart St., courthouse*
First Settlement in Knox County
In the immediate area of the L Bar Ranch were 12 families, most of them stockholders in the Wichita & Brazos Cattle Company. To assure them church and school privileges, in 1885 H. G. Bedford started the town of Benjamin, located 6 miles west of The Narrows, naming it for his eldest son. In 1886 he was instrumental in getting Knox County organized with Benjamin as county seat. FOUNDERS of BENJAMIN H. G. Bedford, Rufus Browder, G. B. Stewart, L. W. Ricketts, R. P. Dimmett, W. W. Wetherly, T. G. Stewart, Ed W. Bedford, J. W. Hinton, A. E. Brannin, R. D. Goree, H. C. Thompson. Other side:

L - Ranch, Hilory Green Bedford
In 1884, Hilory G. Bedford formed Wichita & Brazos Stock Company to own and operate the L Bar Ranch. Retaining 51% stock, he became president with R. P. Dimmitt, secretary. This company had a herd of some 8,000 cattle, grazing on the open range, centered north to south at The Narrows, between Wichita & Brazos rivers, branding S on neck and L - on left side. Headquarters of ranch was 4 miles northeast of The Narrows on north bank S. Wichita River, about center of present John Ed Jones ranch. 1886–1887 loss of many cattle by severe drought and blizzards and sharp drop in prices caused dissolution of W & B Stock Company and disposal of ranch in 1887. Erected by some descendants of first settlers in tribute to settlers and their leader, H. G. Bedford.   (1967)

BERGHEIM (Kendall Co.)   *SH 46 on Bergheim General Store*
The Engel Store
A native of Austria, Andreas Engel (b. 1864) migrated to Texas in 1885. In 1900 he purchased land here and built a cotton gin, around which an agricultural community developed. When the area post office was moved here in 1901 and Engel became postmaster, he named the town Bergheim, German for "home in the hills". He and his wife Eva opened a store at this site in 1903. Their son Alfred added later services, including a cedar yard, to meet community needs and aid local development. A symbol of Bergheim's pioneers, the store has remained in the Engel family.   (1983)

BERTRAM (Burnet Co.)   *SH 29 West, Vaughan Highway Park*
Bertram
The town of Bertram was founded in 1882 when the Austin and Northwestern Railroad established a route through the area. The community was named for Rudolph Bertram, an Austin merchant who was instrumental in the development of the rail line. Many early residents were from the settlement of South Gabriel (2 mi. SE). Homes and commercial buildings of the pioneer settlers were moved here by brothers L. R. and J. W. Gray. The first store, also relocated from South Gabriel, was run by James D. Riley and Capt. Tom D. Vaughan. Bertram developed as a marketing center for the area's diversified agricultural production. Continued growth came during World War I when the demand for farm and ranch products increased. By the 1920s, it was the site of auto dealerships, four banks, a newspaper, a hotel and a variety of other businesses. The economic depression of the 1930s, World War II and improved methods of transportation combined to limit Bertram's growth. Incorporated in the 1970s, the town remains an agricultural center. It serves as a reminder of the pioneers who settled here over a century ago. Many of their descendants still live in the area and serve as leaders of the community.   (1982)

BIG LAKE (Reagan Co.)   *SH 137 right-of-way, 18 mi. NW*
Stiles Cemetery (1 mi. W)
Established about 1903. Site is on land then owned by early settlers G. W. and Lizzie Stiles. Plot summarizes much frontier history, as it holds graves of cowboys who died in accidents of cattle range; one Spanish-American War veteran; victims of shootings, rattlesnake bites, epidemic

dysentery. Most were pioneers of steady habits and quiet lives. Already in use for many years, the 3-acre plot was deeded to county in 1920 by J. D. Wagner, an adventuring man, who lived for years alternately in Texas and in South America.   (1970)

BIG LAKE (Reagan Co.)   *US 67 at SH 137*
City of Big Lake
The land on which the original townsite of Big Lake was located was owned in 1903 by T. H. Taylor, who sold 320 acres to the Orient Land Company, which agreed to build a railroad station and lay out a town to be called Big Lake. The city took its name from a lake created by rain which gathers in a natural land depression about one and one half miles from here. Once filled by spring-fed water, it is now the largest dry lake in Texas. In pioneer days it was the only known fresh water between the Concho River and springs at Fort Stockton and was a campsite for Indians, Mexican traders and cattle drivers. Oldest house in Reagan County, the John Gardner house, is located near its banks. The town was established in 1911. Its first economic activity was a stockpen built by the Kansas City, Mexico & Orient Railroad, a hotel, and a grocery store. It grew up around the line of the railroad and by 1915 had about fifty families. Big Lake was incorporated on May 28, 1923, and in 1925 became the seat of Reagan County. Land additions were made in 1914 and 1925. Today the city is a center for the oil and gas industry.   (1967)

BIG LAKE (Reagan Co.)   *E. 2nd St. (US 67) at Main*
This County Named in 1903 for John H. Reagan
(First Chairman of Railroad Commission of Texas)
As Congressman, 1876–1887, sponsored bill creating Interstate Commerce Commission; re-signed 1891 from United States Senate to head newly-formed Railroad Commission, modeled after I.C.C., and created to regulate shipping rates and practices. In his term, 1891–1903, railway transportation of petroleum became important in Texas. The Commission was given jurisdiction in 1917 over pipelines. This led to formation of the oil and gas division. The legislature made the Commission responsible in 1919 for oil and gas conservation. Proration began in 1920s. Complete regulation came in the 1930s with 1,700,000-barrel-a-day production in East Texas. Commission policies were acclaimed when in World War II Texas was able to supply the Allies with great stores of oil necessary for victory. The Commission's goal is to prevent waste and protect oil and gas re-serves by orderly regulation of exploration, production and transportation. Such men as Chairman Reagan have set high ethical standards that have continued in the Commission, causing it to merit the confidence of the people and of the petroleum industry.   (1966)

BIG LAKE (Reagan Co.)   *US 67 at Main Ave.*
Martin-Castillo Expedition
Explored the Concho River, 32 miles north of here, gathering information on Jumano Indians and searching for pearls, 1650. Setting out from Santa Fe, Capts. Hernan Martin and Diego Del Castillo traveled about 600 miles to the Jumano territory, where they stayed for 6 months. Further travels took them to the edge of the Texas nation, where they obtained the first information definitely about the tribe that gave Texas its name. The "discoveries" of their journey—pearls and the Texas nation—sparked later important Spanish expeditions to East Texas.   (1970)

BIG LAKE (Reagan Co.)   *US 67, 3 mi. W in roadside park*
Reagan County
Formed from Tom Green County. Created March 7, 1903, organized April 20, 1903. Named in honor of John H. Reagan (1818–1905). Indian fighter and surveyor, member of Texas Legislature and United States Congress. Postmaster General of the Southern Confederacy. County seat, Stiles, 1903–1925. Big Lake since.   (1925)

BIG LAKE (Reagan Co.)   *US 67, 13 mi. W*
Santa Rita No. 1
Discovery well for Big Lake Oil Field. First gusher in Permian Basin; first University of Texas producer. On land once thought almost worthless. Fruit of the faith of Big Lake lawyer Rupert Ricker. Though in 1919 no oil had been found within 100 miles, Ricker got leases on 431,360 acres of University of Texas land in Crockett, Irion, Reagan and Upton Counties. Soon working with him were P. G. Stokes, Big Spring; Frank Pickrell and Hyman Krupp, El Paso; and others. Their

wildcat well, ½ mile south of this site, on Ollie Parker's ranch, was drilled by Carl Cromwell. Dee Locklin was tooldresser. Slow and hard drilling made crew name well for Santa Rita, patronness of the impossible. 4 years, 2 months and a day after permit was filed, and at 3,055 feet, well pressure tossed the rig's bucket high into the air. Santa Rita was a producer! The date was May 28, 1923. This day the Permian Basin, since acclaimed one of the greatest oil regions in the world, had its first big find. Other spectacular fields were to follow. Multi-millions in royalty dollars have since made the University of Texas one of the world's most heavily endowed schools. Original rig that brought in Santa Rita now is on the university campus.   (1965)

BIG SANDY (Upshur Co.)   *SH 155, 1 mi. SW*
Walters' Bluff Ferry (Site Located 1.3 mi. SE)
Located at a noted early-day crossing on Sabine River, this pioneer ferry carried settlers traveling north or south into Upshur or Smith Counties. It was begun before 1849 by Robt. Walters, a Texas Revolutionary veteran, and used until a bridge was built, 1903. Town of Florence was once situated near ferry on south bank of the Sabine. Ferriage rates in 1860 were 50¢ for a wagon drawn by two horses or oxen; 75¢ for a wagon and more than two animals. A pleasure carriage was charged 40¢; a man and horse, 10¢; loose livestock, 5¢ per head.   (1968)

BIG SPRING (Howard Co.)   *US 87 at FM 821, 8 mi. S*
First Commercial Oil Well in Howard County
On Nov. 9, 1925, this wildcat well No. 1 H. R. Clay, drilled by Fred Hyer, began pumping oil in a venture that hinted at vast oil resources in West Texas. The well on Clay's land hit pay dirt at 1,508 feet. Soon oil land speculators developed a great interest in this formerly "worthless" territory and other wildcatters flocked to the area. As a result of efforts here, the Permian Basin—one of the richest oil repositories in the state—was developed. Since 1925 Howard County has produced more than 300 million barrels.   (1968)

BIG SPRING (Howard Co.)   *US 87, 5 mi. S in roadside park*
Howard County
Formed from Young and Bexar Territories. Created August 21, 1876, organized June 15, 1882. Named in honor of Volney Erskine Howard (1809–1889). Came to Texas in 1844, delegate to the First State Constitutional Convention. Member of the Texas legislature. Member of the United States Congress. Big Spring, the county seat.

BIG SPRING (Howard Co.)   *Big Spring State Park, S of IH 20 Bus.*
Big Spring State Park on Route of Old Comanche War Trail
For Comanche war parties, about 1750 to 1875, the Big Spring was an oasis. Here paths from northeast, north and northwest twined into the war trail that led to San Antonio and other Texas points, and down into Mexico. At the Big Spring, parties from far away as the Arkansas Valley could rest their horses. At this point on return trips northward, their weary captives might find water, rest, and possibly food. The Comanches harassed settlements, robbing and burning stores, mills, farms, ranches; killing men and capturing women and children to be held for ransom, slavery, or adoption into the tribe. The war trail was well marked, for warriors took on their long expeditions numerous pack and riding horses, hordes of dogs, and their women and children to wait upon the men and assist in the looting. Indians in the Civil War years, 1861–1865, had much freedom to invade Texas. By 1866 they were selling to New Mexico traders thousands of cattle stolen from Texas ranchmen. Most of the Comanches were put on reservations in 1875. Afterward their old trails were used by white settlers and by hunting parties on special leave. In 1881 a hunting party attacked builders of the T. & P. Railroad working near here.   (1966)

BIG SPRING (Howard Co.)   *200 N. Gregg St. (US 87)*
Potton House
Joseph Potton (1847–1920), a native of England and master mechanic for Texas & Pacific Railroad, built this Victorian residence in 1901. Designed by the Fort Worth firm of S. B. Haggart and Son, the house was constructed of Pecos sandstone with iron pillars and zinc gable decorations. Potton, a school board trustee, and his wife occupied the home after he retired in 1912 and often entertained here. Later their daughter, Mrs. Henry R. Hayden, and her family resided here.   (1976)

BLANCO (Blanco Co.)
US 281, Main and 3rd St.
Old Blanco County Courthouse
Designed in Victorian style by architect F. D. Ruffini. Erected in 1886 as first permanent county courthouse. Building served only four years—until 1890. County seat then moved to Johnson City. Purchased by Chas. E. Crist, the structure entered varied career as school, Blanco National Bank, office of "Blanco County News," opera house, Farmers Union Hall, and hospital (1936–1970). Now houses Blanco Museum of Early West.   (Recorded Texas Historic Landmark—1972)

BLANCO (Blanco Co.)
FM 165, 8 mi. NE in roadside park
Peyton Colony Lime Kiln
Peyton Colony was a freedmen's community established in the 1860s under the leadership of former slave Peyton Roberts. In addition to homes, the community included a local school and Mt. Horeb Baptist Church. This lime kiln was built by Peyton Roberts and his neighbors to provide high-quality materials with which to make mortar for buildings in Blanco County, some of which remain today. The kiln was restored in the 1960s in conjunction with the construction of a roadside park at the site. It stands as a reminder of the efforts of ex-slaves to begin new lives.   (1988)

BLEAKWOOD (Newton Co.)
SH 87, 1 mi. N
Bleakwood Cemetery
Pioneers who settled the Bleakwood community after the Civil War established thriving mill and cotton gin businesses. Mill-owner Reuben Bennington donated an acre of land for this cemetery to serve area residents. The oldest marked grave, that of Doulie Lee, is dated Jan. 24, 1871. In 1940 J. K. Wilson gave an additional acre of land to the cemetery in memory of his wife Minnie Lee. Veterans of wars from the Civil War to the Korean War are buried here. The graves are given full care by the Bleakwood Cemetery Association, incorporated in 1975.   (1981)

BLEAKWOOD (Newton Co.)
SH 87, 1 mi. S
Watson Chapel Cemetery
Prominent early settler George Adams and his wife, Orinda Hester Scott, donated land for this cemetery in 1883. Although the gravestone of Tilman Scott Ingram, who was reinterred here from another cemetery, bears an earlier death dated (1880), the first recorded burials were those of John Edwards in 1883 and Orinda Adams' parents, Hester Ann Scott in 1885 and James M. Scott in 1887. Many people who worked in the area's lumber industry are interred here. Watson Chapel Cemetery is maintained by an association of descendants of persons buried here.   (1993)

BLEAKWOOD (Newton Co.)
SH 87, 1.5 mi. S
Watson Chapel Methodist Church
On 5-acre site given by George Adams (1842–1906). This church has been in continuous use since its construction in 1883 by men of community. According to tradition, a man named Watson financed the project. Square nails were used. Heart pine lumber for structure was shipped by steam-boat on the Sabine River from Orange to town of Salem, then hauled by ox-teams to this site. Belfry and Sunday school rooms were added later.   (1972)

BLEAKWOOD (Newton Co.)
SH 87, 9 mi. S
Swift Cemetery (2.7 Mi. E)
The trading village of Salem was founded in 1835 by Seth Swift. A quaker and whaling merchant, Swift had moved to this area from Massachusetts with his wife, Lydia, and six children. When Lydia died about 1852, Swift set aside an acre of land for a cemetery. Upon his death in 1869, Swift was buried beside his wife in a pink marble casket he had brought from Massachusetts. Several other members of the community are believed to be interred in the cemetery, as well. Lost to forest overgrowth for many years, the graveyard has been restored.   (1988)

BLEDSOE (Cochran Co.)
SH 125 at FM 595
Town of Bledsoe
Promoted and founded in July 1925 by South Plains & Santa Fe Railroads. Named for rail-road president S. T. Bledsoe. In later 1920s became important cattle shipping point. It was also county's largest town. Population hit 750. Began decline after rail freight traffic decreased in 1930s.   (1970)

BLESSING (Matagorda Co.)   *SH 35 NE, 1 mi. E of intersection with SH 71*
Old Hawley Cemetery
Known 1838–1899 as Demin's Bridge Cemetery. Second post office in Matagorda County was located nearby in 1858. Two acres donated by Emelius Savage and his son Norman for the cemetery and Tres Palacios Baptist Church, founded 1852. More land given by Jonathan E. Pierce, who in 1900 named area Hawley, honoring United States Senator Robert Bradley Hawley. Buried here are the brothers Jonathan E. and Abel H. ("Shang") Pierce and many other famous early cattlemen; also, more than 50 veterans of Civil War and all U.S. wars since 1865.   (1967)

BLUM (Hill Co.)   *SH 174, 3 mi. N*
Erected in Memory of Phillip Nolan
Born in Ireland. First came to Texas and established residence at Nacogdoches in 1791. When killed was a resident of Natchez, Miss. Was killed near this site March 21, 1801 by the Spaniards. Was buried there by Negro slaves Caesar and Robert. Nolan's death aroused a wave of indignation that led to the independence of Texas.

BLUM (Hill Co.)   *SH 174, .5 mi. E of Brazos River Bridge*
Site of Early Cattle Trail
Often called Chisholm Trail, since it connected with that famous route lying to the north. At Kimball Crossing (1.3 mi. SW) this trail entered Hill County. Drovers rested and reshod horses at Towash and Fort Graham, and then forded the Nolan River into Johnson County.   (1967)

BOERNE (Kendall Co.)   *US 87 N at county line*
Confederate Army Chaplain Andrew Jackson Potter (1830–1895)
Born in Missouri. Orphaned at age 10, was a jockey, gambler, ruffian. Fought in Mexican War, 1846–1847. Was a Texas Ranger later. Converted in a camp meeting, he learned to write and became a Methodist minister. Served 4 years in the Confederate Army. Like any chaplain, had pay and rations of a private. In camp he conducted regular religious services, counseled, taught men to read and write, handled mail, visited the sick. Once whipped an editor for libeling the army. In battle line, until firing order came, he had Bible in hand, preaching to his men "on the brink of eternity." Fought to end of battle, then took down from lips of dying men words of family or friends; prayed for the passing soul; aided the wounded. After war, with Bible in left hand, pistol in right, preached 30 years on Texas frontiers. Gave many a wild town its first sermon, sometimes preaching in a settlement's only public building—a saloon. Founded several churches. From enforcing respect for his work with fists and guns, was called "the fighting parson." At home he owned on this site, 1868–1883, several of his 15 children were born. He died in his pulpit, and was buried in Caldwell County.   (1965)

BOERNE (Kendall Co.)   *E. San Antonio Ave., 1 blk. E US 87 Bus. at old courthouse*
Kendall County
Created January 10, 1862. Organized February 18, 1862. Named in honor of George Wilkins Kendall, 1809–1867, poet, journalist, author and farmer. One of the founders of the "New Orleans Picayune." Member of the Santa Fe Expedition. Most successful sheep raiser in the Southwest. Boerne, the county seat.   (1936)

BOERNE (Kendall Co.)   *Main St. (US 87 Bus.) at city square bandstand*
German Music in Boerne
German music professor Karl Dienger, who immigrated to Boerne in 1855, organized a singing club (gesang verein) and band in Boerne in 1860. Dienger's music group consisted of musicians from throughout the area and was commonly known as the Boerne Village Band. The band reflected traditional German music, heritage, and culture and performed at various area festivals, functions, and events. Since the 1860s a number of musical groups similar to the village band have flourished in Boerne and other area communities. Boerne's German-style bands have gained statewide recognition.   (1995)

BOERNE (Kendall Co.)   *106 W. Blanco at US 87 Bus.*
Joseph Dienger Building
This limestone commercial structure was built for Joseph Dienger (1859–1950) shortly after he purchased the site in 1884. The ground floor housed his grocery and the second floor provided

living quarters for his family. A later addition was used for the dry goods store of Dienger's sisters Lina and Louise. Owned by family members until 1967, the double galleried building features Victorian styling with German influences.   (Recorded Texas Historic Landmark—1980)

BOERNE (Kendall Co.)   *128 W. Blanco Rd., just W of Main St. (US 87 Bus.)*
Ye Kendall Inn
The center section of Kendall Inn is the old Reed house, built by Erastus Reed and his wife, Sarah Conning Reed, who purchased the land April 23, 1859, and later leased to Henry Chipman. After 1869 its fame grew as the "King Place" under ownership of Colonel & Senator Henry C. King. By 1878 the Boerne climate had attracted large numbers of health seekers to find relief from asthma, sinus, etc. To accommodate them, C. J. Roundtree & N. L. Wadsworth extended the old building to its present size and adopted the new name the Boerne Hotel. This was the stagecoach stop during the early 1880s. In 1909 Dr. H. D. Barnitz changed the name to "Ye Kendall Inn."

BOERNE (Kendall Co.)   *402 E. Blanco Rd. (RR 474) at city hall*
Early Boerne Schoolhouses
The origins of public schools in Boerne date to 1873, when the Boerne Gesangenverein donated land on which to erect a schoolhouse. A two-room stone building was completed in 1874 and served children in all grades. A small frame building was added to the property around the turn of the century, and the upper and lower grades were separated. In 1910 a new two-story stone school was built. It served students of all ages until a high school was built on Johns Road in 1929. The 1910 building was sold to the City of Boerne Utilities in 1951.
(Texas Sesquicentennial 1836–1986)

BOERNE (Kendall Co.)   *334 S. Main St. (US 87 Bus.)*
Staffel Family and the Staffel Store
German immigrant August Staffel arrived in Texas in 1852 and in due course made his way to Boerne, where he purchased property at this site in 1854. When Boerne was granted a postal station in 1856, Staffel served as first postmaster and housed the post office on his property. Staffel's other businesses included the Staffel store, stagecoach office, saloon, livery stable and wagon yard. After August's death in 1870, his wife, Bertha, operated the post office out of the Staffel store until 1881 and sold the property in 1905. Reminders of early economic development in Boerne, the Staffel store and the Staffel family played a significant role in that heritage.   (2001)

BOERNE (Kendall Co.)   *N of IH 10 at Cascade Cavern Rd.,*
entrance to cavern, 3.3 mi. S
Cascade Cavern
Probably formed during the Pleistocene epoch by the underground passage of the Cibolo River, Cascade Cavern presents an interesting mix of geological, archeological, and historical features. It exhibits a combination of the joint and the dip and strike types of caverns, and is the home of a number of unusual animals, including cliff and leopard frogs, Mexican brown bats, and Cascade Cavern salamanders. Archeological evidence uncovered near the cave indicates the presence of two Indian sites. It is probable that the Indians used the cave for shelter, and soot found on the side of a natural chimney suggests that they had fires. Commercial development of the cave, known earlier as Hester's Cave, began in the 1930s. The current name, taken from the seven waterfalls at the entrance to the cathedral room, officially was adopted in a 1932 ceremony led by State Attorney General, and later Governor of Texas, James V. Allred. Over the years, Cascade Cavern has provided visitors and Boerne area residents with many opportunities for recreation and exploration, and it remains one of the state's important geological sites.   (1984)

BOMARTON (Baylor Co.)   *SH 277, access road*
St. John Catholic Church (of Bomarton)
Established in 1908, when services and masses were held in Mary's Creek schoolhouse or in home of Matt Marak. First church edifice was built 1909, with John Cocek, Marak, Leopold Skrehot, and Alois Sykora, trustees. Father Paul Mosler was installed as first pastor in 1910. Brick church was built in 1936.   (1970)

BON WIER (Newton Co.)   *US 190*
Bon Wier
W. H. Stark settled here in 1836 and established a ferry and warehouse business on the Sabine River known as Stark's Landing. It served as a wharf for steamboats and a point from which large quantities of timber were rafted to sawmills downriver. Development in this area began after T. J. Trotti established a company logging town nearby in 1898. The Trotti Sawmill gained access to the railroad when the Jasper and Eastern Railroad extended track through here in 1905. The Santa Fe Townsite Company platted a town here in 1906 named Bon Wier for Kirby Lumber Company officials B. F. Bonner and R. W. Wier. T. A. Campbell's General Store, established in 1905, served as an unofficial town center for decades. Bon Wier was granted a post office in 1907. About 1912 T. M. Hughes built a sizeable sawmill which began a Hughes family lumber business which continues today. Bon Wier's Sabine River Bridge was completed in 1931. A number of mills, established along the Sabine River in or near Bon Wier, helped to sustain the town's economy. Bon Wier boasted several stores and its own school system until 1956. Although lumber activity continues in the area, Bon Wier is supported by a thriving farm, market, and commercial river economy.   (1993)

BONHAM (Fannin Co.)   *US 82, 4 mi. E in rest area*
Fannin County
This area was first settled by Anglo-Americans who traveled up the Red River by steamboat in 1836. Fannin County was created in 1837, organized 1838, and named for James W. Fannin (1805–1836), who was massacred with his soldiers at Goliad (March 27, 1836) after surrendering to the Mexican Army. County officials first met at Jacob Black's cabin on the Red River. The county seat was moved in 1840 to Warren and in 1843 to Bois D'Arc, which was renamed in 1844 in honor of James Butler Bonham (1807–1836), a hero of the siege of the Alamo.   (1975)

BONHAM (Fannin Co.)   *US 82, 1.5 mi. W*
Congressman Sam Rayburn
Born in Tennessee on Jan. 6, 1882, Samuel Taliaferro Rayburn came to North Texas with his parents in 1887. His political career began in 1906 with his election to the Texas House of Representatives, where he was Speaker of the 1911–1913 session. Rayburn was elected to the U.S. Congress from the 4th District in 1912, the first of his 25 consecutive terms there. Rising quickly to a leadership position, he was chairman of the Democratic party caucus in 1921. As head of the House Interstate and Foreign Commerce Committee (1931–1937) and then Majority Leader (1937–1940), Rayburn sponsored much of President Franklin D. Roosevelt's New Deal legislation. On Sept. 16, 1940 Rayburn was elected Speaker of the House of Representatives. Except for the 80th (1947–1949) and 83rd (1953–1955) Congresses, when he was Minority Leader, Rayburn held the speakership until 1961, longer than anyone in the nation's history. A party leader as well, he was chairman of the Democratic National Conventions of 1948, 1952, and 1956. Rayburn died on Nov. 16, 1961, and Presidents Harry S. Truman, Dwight Eisenhower, and John F. Kennedy, along with Lyndon B. Johnson, were among national figures at his funeral. He is buried in Willow Wild Cemetery.   (1975)

BONHAM (Fannin Co.)   *US 82, 1.5 mi. W*
Sam Rayburn House
In 1916, three years after he began his career in the U.S. Congress, Sam Rayburn built this home for his parents, who had left their farm at Windom. The 2-story house had a front porch on each floor. In 1934 architect W. B. Yarborough enlarged "the home place," turning the porches into 2-story portico. When not in Washington, Rayburn lived here with other members of the family. Deeded to the Texas Historical Commission in 1972, the house is now (1974) a museum.
(Recorded Texas Historic Landmark—1965)

BONHAM (Fannin Co.)   *SH 78 at FM 274, 10.5 mi. N*
Joseph Sowell
In September 1836, Joseph Sowell (1804–1841) came to Texas shortly after the Republic was established. Settling on his 1280-acre land grant just south of the Red River, Sowell made his home about 1.5 miles northwest of this site. In the short time he lived in Texas, Sowell was closely involved with the creation and development of Fannin County and with the protection of the frontier

settlers. Upon the creation of Fannin County in 1837 and its organization the following year, Sowell was appointed to the county board of land commissioners and served as county treasurer. He and fellow pioneer J.S. Scott built a tavern at Warren, the first county seat, where Sowell had served as postmaster. As leader of his militia company to defend the frontier and its settlers, Sowell led several attacks against the region's Native Americans. Additionally, he served as quartermaster for the Army of the Republic of Texas. On October 31, 1841, a band of Indians raided the horse stable at the tavern in Warren. In the ensuing struggle, which involved the guests and proprietors of the tavern as well, Joseph Sowell was killed, leaving behind a widow and four children. He was buried near his homesite. As an early settler in northeast Texas whose interest and concern for his duty as a citizen was realized in the positions he held and his active involvement in local affairs, Joseph Sowell played a significant role in Fannin County's early development.   (2003)

BONHAM (Fannin Co.)   SH 56 at Chinner St.
Bailey Inglish (ca. 1797–1867)
In 1837, Bailey Inglish moved his family to this area from western Arkansas, where he had been an influential leader of pioneer settlers. Here he was active in the formation of Fannin County, serving on the land board and later as Chief Justice. To guard against repeated Indian raids, he built a fort on his land for area residents. The settlement that developed, first known as Bois d'Arc, became Bonham. Inglish was instrumental in its early growth through active public service and donations of land for town lots, a cemetery, and a female seminary.   (Texas Sesquicentennial 1836–1986)

BONHAM (Fannin Co.)   SH 56 at Star St.
Old Home of Pioneer Banker A. B. Scarborough
Built 1897. The massive architecture combines Gothic, Grecian and 17th century features in arches, balconies, cupola, turrets, gables. An example of Victorian Romanesque, bought 1937 and preserved by Joe C. Denton.   (1966)

BONHAM (Fannin Co.)   Katy Blvd., 1 blk. N of SH 56
Site of Booker T. Washington School
According to local tradition, the Bonham Colored School began in a one-room structure in northwest Bonham in the early 1890s. Enrollment in the 4-teacher school grew from 40 pupils in 1904 to 216 in 1911. By 1920, the school offered 11 grades and was called Booker T. Washington. A new school complex, funded in part by the Rosenwald Foundation, was built on 10 acres here in 1928; Ray Seay served as principal. School expanded to 12 grades in 1940. Until 1966, when it closed due to school integration, the school served as a focal point for Bonham's entire African American community.   (Sesquicentennial of Texas Statehood 1845–1995)

BONHAM (Fannin Co.)   SH 78, 4.5 mi. S
Arledge Ridge Cemetery
Among the early settlers of this area were Joseph and William Arledge, brothers who arrived from Alabama in the 1850s. Both established successful farms in the area, and the growing settlement became known as Arledge Ridge. Joseph Arledge operated one of the earliest freight lines in Fannin County, with regular routes to the port city of Jefferson. William Arledge established a cotton gin in the central part of the county and later sold an acre of land to be used for a community school and church. A tract of land, deeded by William Arledge in 1876, was designated as a community burial ground. According to local tradition, burials may have taken place in the cemetery as early as the 1840s, but the oldest documented grave is that of Joseph Arledge, who died in 1855. Interred in the Arledge Ridge Cemetery are many early settlers, as well as a number of Civil War veterans. Additional land acquisitions in 1893, 1948, and 1965 enlarged the cemetery tract. The Arledge Ridge Cemetery Association, organized in 1948, maintains the historic graveyard and sponsors an annual homecoming event.   (1988)

BOOKER (Lipscomb Co.)   SH 23, 1.5 mi. S
Heart Cemetery
Heart Cemetery has served the community of Booker since 1929. The town was platted in 1917 and named for B. F. Booker, a civil engineer for the Panhandle and Santa Fe Railway, which extended their line through this area. The community consisted of residents from La Kemp, Oklahoma, who relocated here to the new railroad town. A local cemetery became necessary as the community

grew. In 1925, Harry Herbert and Mary Agnes (Mullinex) Mitchell donated land to the town for use as a graveyard. In 1929, the City of Booker dedicated the land as Heart Cemetery; the name comes from its heart-shaped design. Historically, the burial ground has also been known as Booker Cemetery. The earliest marked grave is that of Y. E. Winn (d. 1911), reinterred here from his original burial site in Missouri. Notable gravesites include those of the town's first physician, Dr. I. T. Smith; businessman William Vernon Shouse, who was involved in oil, real estate and manufacturing; and the property donors, the Mitchells. Community doctors, teachers, ministers, farmers, ranchers and other residents are also buried here. Other graves include veterans of military conflicts dating from World War I. In 1966, a park and cemetery board formed to oversee the property. The board dissolved in 1975, leaving the operation under the direction of the City of Booker, which still cares for the burial ground. Heart Cemetery continues to serve the community of Booker and the surrounding area, chronicling the lives of residents dating to the pioneer days of settlement.   (2007)

BOOKER (Lipscomb Co.)   *SH 15 at SH 23*
Booker
Platted 1917 by Thomas C. Spearman, Santa Fe Railway official. Named for railroad locating engineer, B. F. Booker, town of La Kemp, Okla., (6 mi. North) moved here 1919. First train arrived July 4, 1919, official birthdate of Booker. Economy based on farming, cattle and (since 1956) oil and gas production.   (1969)

BOOKER (Lipscomb Co.)   *SH 15 at SH 23*
Route of Jones and Plummer Trail
Established about 1874, when used by the freighting firm of Ed Jones and Joe Plummer to haul tons of buffalo hides from their general store in Lipscomb County to Dodge City, Kansas. Also in its early days, this trail carried crucial supplies to Generals Nelson Miles and Philip Sheridan during their famous 1874 Indian campaign. Materials for building Fort Elliott, at Mobeetie, also came over trail. The fort then became southern terminus for the route, Dodge City, Northern. In its later years (until 1885), it became a cattle trail.   (1968)

BORGER (Hutchinson Co.)   *SH 136, 6 mi. N*
Battle of Adobe Walls
Fifteen miles to the site of the Battle of Adobe Walls. Fought on November 25, 1864 between Kiowa and Comanche Indians and United States troops commanded by Colonel Christopher Carson, 1809–1868. This was "Kit" Carson's last fight.   (1936)

BORGER (Hutchinson Co.)   *SH 136, 6 mi. N in roadside park*
Bents Creek (About 15 mi. E)
Named for Charles (1799–1847) and William Bent (1809–1869), famed for frontier trading with mountain men and "wild" Indians. As early as 1835 they came from their headquarters near present La Junta, Colo., to trade with the Kiowas and Comanches along the Canadian River, in this vicinity. They built at least three posts along the river and tributary creeks; most permanent post was Fort Adobe, built 1843–1844. In the ruins of this fort (NE of here) Kit Carson fought his last big Indian battle (1864), and buffalo hunters and Indians fought the battle of Adobe Walls in 1874.   (1971)

BORGER (Hutchinson Co.)   *SH 136, .5 mi. W of intersection with SH 207*
The Marcy Trail
Captain R. B. Marcy was commissioned in 1849 by the Federal government to establish a less hazardous route with good water supply, on an even terrain, to be more direct from Fort Smith thru Santa Fe to the gold fields of California. This historical marker was dedicated on the path by the Rotary Club of Borger, Texas, 19 June, 1956.

BORGER (Hutchinson Co.)   *SH 136, 4.5 mi. W*
Antelope Creek Ruins
Plains Village Native Americans occupied a series of interconnected rock dwellings near here from about 1200–1500. Called "Texas' first apartment house," the ruins have been the focus of numerous excavations through the years. Made of native dolomite, the rock and slab dwellings averaged about 12 feet by 15 feet in size with a single opening, a long crawlway, on the east side. Other rooms contained a central hearth under four roof-support posts, while smaller rooms were thought

to be for storage. Adobe platforms may have been an altar for ceremonial purposes. The ruins are located near a branch of the Canadian River, providing a perennial source of water. The creek bottom soil of sandy loam allowed residents to harvest crops including corn, beans, squash and pumpkin. The semi-sedentary natives also hunted bison, antelope, deer, and small animals as evidenced by the bones and tools found at the site. Artifacts recovered include small arrow points, beveled and oval knives, bone implements, grinding stones, and cord marked ceramics. Considerable information on the artifact assemblage and village structure was gained from the Works Progress Administration excavations from 1938–41, and subsequent interpretive works in 1946.   (1997)

BOVINA (Parmer Co.)   *US 60, 5.5 mi. NE*
Site of Parmerton (Elevation 4,202 Feet)
Founded as Parmer Switch on Pecos & Northern Texas Railroad in 1898. In 1906, became site of a model farm, using Campbell dry farming method, run by Capitol Freehold Land & Investment Co. In 1907 Parmerton Townsite Co. bought 200 acres of the farm and laid out a town, which was designated first county seat that same year. A post office was soon established. When, in late 1907, Farwell was elected new county seat, Parmerton's citizens departed, taking homes and other buildings with them. Only the railroad switch marks the site today.   (1971)

BOVINA (Parmer Co.)   *US 60 in Bovina*
Bovina (Elevation: 4070 ft.)
Early in the 20th century, this was one of largest cattle shipping points in the United States. Originated as the Hay Hook line camp of the XIT—famed ranch that received over 3,000,000 acres of land in payment for building Texas State Capitol, 1882–1888. One of the earliest structures in Parmer County division number eight headquarters of XIT, stood 400 yards northeast of site of this marker. The shipping pasture, 640 acres in area, was 1 mile east. The Pecos & Northern Texas Railroad built to this point in 1898, and cattle for eastern markets were loaded here. Train crews called the place "Bull Town," but the community chose the name "Bovina" when establishing the post office in 1899. This was the first post office in Parmer County, created 1876, named for Martin Parmer (1778–1850), patriot and signer of Texas Declaration of Independence. Although known to explorers early as 18th century, county had few inhabitants before 1907, when it was organized, with Bovina one of its leading towns. By 1915, Bovina had 200 people, 2 churches, a bank, a school, and a hotel for prospective settlers. It is now market and supply center for rich area of irrigated farms, and still produces fine cattle.   (1968)

BOWIE (Montague Co.)   *US 81, .5 mi. NW in city park*
Montague County
Created December 24, 1857. Organized August 2, 1858. Named in honor of Daniel Montague, 1798–1876. Pioneer Texas surveyor and Indian fighter, commander of a company in the Mexican War.

BOWIE (Montague Co.)   *US 81, .5 mi. NW in city park*
Home County of Governor James V. Allred
(March 29, 1899–Sept. 24, 1959)
Vigorous, forthright and humane chief executive of Texas in years 1935–1939. Born in Bowie, one of nine children of Renne and Mary Henson Allred. Worked in youth as a soda pop bottler, shoeshine boy, newsboy. Attended local schools, Rice University, Cumberland Law School; was in U.S. Navy during World War I. Admitted to the bar in 1921, his early law practice was with firm of Bernard Martin and Ben G. ONeal, Wichita Falls. After experience as assistant district attorney, was named in 1923 by Governor Pat Neff to office of district attorney, 30th district, where he earned a strong reputation in fight against Ku Klux Klan. Married Joe Betsy Miller, of Wichita Falls, and had three sons: James V. Jr., William David, and Sam Houston Allred. As Texas Attorney General 1931–1935, won many victories over monopolies; put "teeth" into gasoline tax law, to halt evasions; corrected a number of unfair trade practices; defended oil proration laws, winning the very first test case; successfully fought attempts of Federal officials to tax the income of Texas schools; established school fund's title to West Texas oil royalties worth over twenty million dollars. In 1934 race for Governor, James V. Allred was victorious over five opponents. In 1935 he was named "outstanding young man in America" by the National Junior Chamber of Commerce. Won second term by landslide, in 1936. As governor, 1935–1939, he implemented strong executive, legislative and

judicial programs to correct social and economic ills; led fight that outlawed pari-mutuel gambling in Texas. During his administration, Social Security amendments were added to Texas Constitution, and on Nov. 19, 1935, he signed the state's first old-age assistance bill; soon instituted aid to dependent children, aid to needy blind, and a teachers' retirement fund. Secured for schools the greatest per capita apportionment that they had known; obtained for the instructors fairer salaries; advanced building programs for colleges and other state institutions. Set up a board of pardons and paroles to correct old system whereby it was alleged a governor might "sell" pardons; initiated prison reforms; revised Industrial Labor Commission; instituted unemployment insurance system. Combined Texas Rangers and highway patrol to form State Department of Public Safety. In 1937 gave encouragement to an aspiring statesman, Lyndon B. Johnson, then running for Congress and later to be 36th President of the United States. Befriended many others seeking high public office, including later U.S. Senator Ralph Yarborough, Secretary of Treasury Robert B. Anderson, and Chief Justice of Texas Supreme Court Robert Calvert. Named to Texas Judiciary its first woman member—Judge Sarah T. Hughes, of Dallas. After his two terms as Governor, Allred was twice appointed United States District Judge, and was on bench at time of his death. He is buried in Riverside Cemetery, Wichita Falls.   (Outstanding Texas Statesmen Series, 1968)

BOYS RANCH (Oldham Co.)   *US 385 at Boys Ranch*
Tascosa Courthouse, 1884
Served 12 counties in Panhandle. Site of trials for killings that had filled Boothill cemetery. Until 1915 Oldham County seat. Many years headquarters, Julian Bivins ranch. Birthplace of Cal Farley's Boys Ranch, 1939.   (1965)

BRACKETTVILLE (Kinney Co.)   *US 90, 5 mi. E, Fritter Park*
Kinney County
Formed from Bexar County; created January 28, 1850; recreated February 2, 1856; organized December 3, 1869. Named in honor of Henry L. Kinney (1813–1861), founder of Corpus Christi. Member of the first state constitutional convention. Brackettville, county seat a leading wool and mohair producing county.

BRACKETTVILLE (Kinney Co.)   *US 90 at entrance to Ft. Clark*
Fort Clark
A strategic installation in the U.S. Army's line of forts along the military road stretching from San Antonio to El Paso, Fort Clark was established in June 1852. Located near natural springs and Las Moras Creek, its site was considered a point of primary importance to the defense of frontier settlements and control of the U.S. Mexico border. Many infantry regiments and almost all cavalry regiments were at one time based at Fort Clark, as well as companies of Texas Rangers and Confederate troops during the Civil War. The Army's Seminole-Negro Indian Scouts also were assigned to Fort Clark, and with black troops of the 10th Cavalry and 24th and 25th infantry played a decisive role in the Indian campaigns of the 1870s. Prominent military leaders who served here include Col. Ranald S. MacKenzie, Gen. Wesley Merritt, Gen. William R. Shafter, Gen. John L. Bullis, Gen. Zenas R. Bliss, Gen. Jonathan M. Wainwright, and Gen. George S. Patton, Jr. Fort Clark remained a horse-cavalry post for the U.S. Army through World War II and finally was inactivated in 1946. The fort property, including many native stone buildings constructed by civilian craftsmen in the 1870s, was listed in the National Register of Historic Places in 1979.   (1994)

BRACKETTVILLE (Kinney Co.)   *US 90, at entrance to Fort Clark*
Military Roads in Texas
The routes that moved troops in early Texas often followed old Indian trails and were usually little more than deep wagon ruts. This one, the Chihuahua Road, joining Fort Clark with other Southwest posts, was widely used, 1850–1880. The Comanche War Trail, part of the Chihuahua Road, carried women, children, and horses stolen by Indians, from Mexico to the north. The Spanish era opened El Camino Real (the Old San Antonio Road) in 1691 to join Louisiana to Mexico. After 1836, Republic of Mexico settlers demanded forts for safety from Indians; a main 1840 supply road followed present Austin-Dallas highway. Central National Road, 1844, linked Trinity and Red Rivers. (Its rules required all trees to be cut 12 inches or less from the ground). From 1848–1860, surveys by U.S. led to a network of military roads in West Texas. In 1849, Captain Randolph B. Marcy blazed a West Texas trail used by California gold hunters. Famed U.S. 2nd

Cavalry made Fort Belknap–San Antonio Road a military artery in 1850s. During Civil War supplies moved from Mexico to Texas over the Cotton Road. The Indian campaigns of Captain R. S. Mackenzie in 1870's opened trails across the Staked Plains; but by 1881, the railroad had begun to replace Texas's once famous military routes.

BRACKETTVILLE (Kinney Co.)   *S. Ann St. (RM 674) at courthouse*
Fort Clark, C.S.A.
Located southwest edge of town. Upon secession and surrender of U.S. posts, Texas troops occupied the fort to give protection against Indians. They seized the four 24-pounders and two 8-inch Howitzers located there and sent the cannon for use in defense of the Texas coast. On supply line for Arizona, New Mexico campaign to make the South an ocean to ocean nation. Although the frontier defense line was pulled east more than 50 miles in 1862 and posts set a day's horseback ride apart from the Red River to Rio Grande, Fort Clark remained occupied by Confederate and State troops to keep Indian uprisings in check, to protect against bandits from Mexico, and to constantly watch for U.S. invasion along the Rio Grande.

BRACKETTVILLE (Kinney Co.)   *S. Ann St. (RM 674) at courthouse*
Fort Clark, U.S.A.
1852–1946. Founded June, 1852. Guarded California road, rebuffed Indians, outlaws. Named for Maj. J. B. Clark, killed in Mexican War. Companies of infantry, artillery, cavalry stationed here. Clothing issued proved too warm for summer. Buildings were too cold for winter until chimneys were built in 1856. Troops routed Indians to Pecos River mouth, helped expel bandit Cortinas from Brownsville, 1859 Union gave up Clark, 1861, after Texas seceded—reoccupied it 1866. Used Seminole Scout Company. Indian reservation established near post. Duty here, decade after Civil War, was said to be equivalent to honorable mention. Practically all U.S. Cavalry regiments served here. 5th Cavalry served 1920–41. In World War II, 2nd and 11th Cavalry trained here. Post inactivated Feb. 9, 1946.   (1963)

BRACKETTVILLE (Kinney Co.)   *2 mi. S. of US 90 in Fort Clark Springs*
Seminole Scout Camp on Fort Clark
Under Spanish rule, Florida was a haven for freed or escaped slaves in the 1700s. Once there, many integrated into the Seminole tribe, intermarrying and adapting to the culture. Florida became a U.S. territory in 1821, and after approximately 30 years of warfare, the majority of the Seminoles were forced to relocate to the Indian Territory (Oklahoma). Tribal leaders Coacoochee (Wild Cat) and John Horse gathered a group of Seminoles in 1850 and left the Indian Territory for Mexico. There, under an agreement with the Mexican government, they settled and fought against raiding tribes along the Rio Grande. In 1870, the U.S. Army offered the group pay and rations to move to Fort Clark, established in 1852 to protect settlers along the border. The Black Seminoles became scouts for the Army, serving under Lt. John L. Bullis and other noted officers during Texas' Indian wars. The Seminole-Negro Indian scouts, as they were known, lived on the fort in a settlement referred to as "The Camp." They built homes in the Mexican jacal style, using wattle and daub construction and thatched roofs. The scouts and their families also built dams and irrigation systems along Las Moras Creek for farming. The Seminoles lived on the fort until 1914, when the scouts were disbanded. Some returned to Mexico, many stayed in the Brackettville area and some moved to Oklahoma, where the Seminole nation was granted sovereignty. Still others remained, buried in the scouts' cemetery (1.5 mi. SW), which was established in 1872. Among those buried there are four scouts who earned Congressional Medals of Honor: Adam Payne (Paine), Isaac Payne, John Ward and Pompey Factor.   (2002)

BRACKETTVILLE (Kinney Co.)   *RR 3348, 3 mi. SW*
Seminole Indian Scouts Cemetery
(Founded on Fort Clark Reservation, Sept. 1, 1872)
Burial site of heroic U.S. Army men, families, and heirs. These Seminoles came mainly from Florida about 1850; lived in northern Mexico or Texas; joined Lt. (later a General) John L. Bullis and Col. Ranald S. Mackenzie in ridding Texas of hostile Indians, 1870s.   (1971)

Incise on plate on back of marker:
The following are among the many scouts buried here:

John Bowlegs	George Kibbit
Elijah Daniels	Issac Payne
Pompey Factor	Pompey Perryman
Renty Grayson	Joseph Phillips
John Jefferson	Billie Wilson
Billy July	Issac Wilson
Sampson July	Kelina Wilson

BRACKETTVILLE (Kinney Co.)
US 90W, about 8 mi. W
Dolores Townsite (About 8 mi. S)
Only settlement founded in John Charles Beales' ill-fated Rio Grande colony of 1834–1836. Beales (1804–1878)—empresario of 70,000,000 acres in present southern and western Texas and New Mexico—was Texas' largest known land king. In 1833 he and a partner brought 59 settlers here to colonize a town to be named for Beales' Mexican wife. Indian raids and drouth soon took their toll, but the death blow came in 1836. As the group fled the Mexican Army during the Texas Revolution, Comanches killed all but 7 of one party. This ended the town's existence. (1970)

BRADY (McCulloch Co.)
US 283, 10 mi. N near Cow Gap
Western Trail
Through this gap in hills called "Brady Mountains" passed the Western Cattle Trail, also known as "Dodge City Trail," "Fort Griffin Trail," or "The Beef Trail." Said to have originated in 1876, this was the last of the old-time Texas cattle trails, those east of here having been closed by farmers. Large numbers of cattle were driven up this trail 1876 to 1886—over 200,000 head in 1881 alone. This trail started near Brownsville and came up to San Antonio, then northwest through or near Uvalde and Kerrville. Skirting the Nueces River, it came over the divide, crossing headwaters of the South Llano River, fording San Saba River at Pegleg Crossing, going downriver about six miles, then turning north. Near Brady, feeder trails came from Fort McKavett and points west, and from San Saba, to the east. After leaving Cow Gap (likely so named from Cow Creek, about 500 yds. W. of this marker), it went northwest and over the Colorado at "Beef Crossing" in Waldrip's Bend, then to Coleman, Baird, Fort Griffin and Vernon, spanning Red River at Doan's Crossing. Northward through Indian country it went to Dodge City, Kans., and later into Wyoming and Montana. This trail was of great worth to the territories it traversed. (1970)

BRADY (McCulloch Co.)
US 377, 20.8 mi. N
Geographic Center of Texas
Five miles northwest is the geographic center of Texas, an imaginary point whose coordinates divide the state into four equal areas. In straight-line distance it is 437 miles from the state's most westerly point on the Rio Grande River above El Paso, 412 miles from the most northerly point in the northwest corner of the Panhandle near Texline, 401 miles from the most southerly point on the Rio Grande near Brownsville and 341 miles from the most easterly point on the Sabine River near Burkeville. Maximum border-to-border distance is 801 miles from north to south and 773 miles from east to west. Enclosed within the 4,137-mile perimeter of the state are 267,339 square miles or 7.4 per cent of the nation's total area. Fifteen of the 50 states could be readily accommodated within Texas' borders—with more than 1,000 square miles left over. Brewster, in southwest Texas, is the largest of the state's 254 counties with 6,208 square miles, an area larger than the state of Connecticut. Smallest county is Rockwall in northeast Texas with 147 square miles. Texas elevations rise from sea level along the 624-mile coast of the Gulf of Mexico to 8,751 feet atop Guadalupe Peak in the Guadalupe Mountains. Altitude at this point is 1,545 feet. Terrain varies from the subtropic Rio Grande Valley to the trackless Great Plains, from the lush forests of East Texas to the rugged Trans-Pecos region where mountain ranges thrust 90 peaks a mile or more into the sky. But perhaps nowhere are Texas contrasts more pronounced than in average annual rainfall: from more than 56 inches along the Sabine River, nearly as much as Miami's, to less than 8 inches in the extreme west, as little as Phoenix's.

BRADY (McCulloch Co.)
US 377, 2 mi. N at municipal airport
Curtis Airfield
Named for Harry Lamar Curtis, mayor of Brady who instigated offer of this field to the United States government during World War II. Born 1903 in Dallas, H. L. Curtis was educated at the

University of Dallas, Southern Methodist University, and Texas A. & M. He married (1929) Marjorie McCall of Brady and moved here after business successes in Dallas. Served on city council 1936 to 1940 and as mayor 1940 to 1944. In 1940 Mayor Curtis obtained designation of Brady Airfield as a national defense airport, with funding for enlargement and hard-surfacing. Small old field was relinquished and this larger tract provided. City paid about $40,000; Federal grant was $141,631. Brady's clear skies, dry climate, and freedom from commercial air traffic made it a favored site. A contract school moved here from Love Field, Dallas, on March 16, 1941, and became Brady Aviation School. Ltd. Mayor Curtis led the city to grant free use of the field for ten years, with one dollar a year charged for utilities. Over 10,000 cadets trained here before the school closed in Aug. 1944. This was final duty for a few: 21 cadets, six instructors, a personnel officer lost their lives in accidents. This was one of 17 Texas civilian fields training military pilots during World War II.   (1972)

BRADY (McCulloch Co.) *US 190, 6 mi. NE*
Onion Creek Indian Fight (Battleground 1 mi. NE of Marker)
One night in 1866, five men from Richland Springs (about 25 mi. NE) recovered stolen horses from Indians camped near here. A metal arrow hit a Mr. Lafferty, slid halfway around his skull, was cut out with a pocket knife, and Lafferty survived. The grave of an Indian casualty is about 300 yards north.   (1973)

BRADY (McCulloch Co.) *North Bridge St. (US 190/377) at Walker St.*
Union Passenger Depot
The Fort Worth and Rio Grande Railway built the first rail line into Brady in 1903. Eight years later the Gulf, Colorado & Santa Fe Railroad constructed a second line into town. This depot, built in 1911, was designed for passenger use for freight service. Prominent features of the depot include the corbeled brickwork, segmented arches, the red tile roof, and a parapet over the observation bay.   (1984)

BRADY (McCulloch Co.) *US 87/377 at US 190, courthouse*
McCulloch County
Created Aug. 27, 1856. One of 128 counties formed from Bexar County that extended from the Rio Grande to the Panhandle, and as far west as El Paso. Named for Texas hero, Ben McCulloch, who fought in Texas Revolution, Indian, Mexican and Civil Wars. Indian and frontier hazards made growth slow and 20 years passed before buffalo were hunted off and ranches established. Organized Aug. 4, 1876 with Brady, county seat. Became ranch, farm, recreation center. Site of geographical center of Texas and 1831 Calf Creek Battle, where James Bowie, Alamo hero, defeated 100 Indians.   (1936)

BRADY (McCulloch Co.) *US 87/377 at US 190, courthouse*
McCulloch County Courthouse
County organized 1876, with Brady as county seat; first courthouse built 1879. Present courthouse (second and on same site) completed 1900; Martin and Moodie, contractors, for "turn key" construction. Local labor and materials were used as far as practical. Native sandstone from local quarries. Modified Roman architecture employing arch vault. Victorian cupola; pine woodwork, flooring, at time of construction.   (1967)

BRADY (McCulloch Co.) *US 87 at US 190, courthouse*
General Ben McCulloch, C.S.A. (1811–1862)
Distinguished ranger, frontier surveyor, Indian fighter, lawman, statesman and military commander. Born in Tennessee. Followed David Crockett to Texas to fight in war for independence. Commanded one of the "Twin Sisters" cannons in the Battle of San Jacinto, April 21, 1836. Served in the Congress of the Republic of Texas. In 1846, during war with Mexico, led Ranger company in successful scouting mission 100 miles behind enemy lines. During 1849 California Gold Rush was sheriff of Sacramento County. Home again in 1852, became U.S. Marshal, Eastern District of Texas. Led Texas volunteers in San Antonio Feb. 16, 1861, when U.S. arsenal was surrounded and its surrender demanded—an encounter in a charged atmosphere that could have become the first armed conflict of the Civil War, although it ended without the firing of a shot, and with U.S. troops leaving the state. President Jefferson Davis offered him first general staff commission in the Civil

War. Made a brigadier general on May 14, 1861, he had charge of troops, in Arkansas and Indian territory. Was the Confederate commander in victory at Wilson Creek, Mo., 1861. Was killed in Battle of Pea Ridge, Ark.

BRADY (McCulloch Co.)   *SH 71, 13 mi. SE at San Saba River*
Voca Waterwheel Mill (¼ mi. E)
Built 1876, by H. A. Chadwick and Sons, William and Milam, who constructed other mills in the region. Water was diverted from river by a still-visible, 1300-yard millrace. Originally used to grind wheat and corn; a saw was soon added to provide "rawhide" lumber. First cotton gin in the county, powered by this wheel and producing 3 bales per day, was constructed in early 1880s. A store operated near the mill for a short time, but moved to Voca after landlord refused to allow the sale of bitters. Mill operated until washed away by flood, June 1899.   (1972)

BRANDON (Hill Co.)   *SH 22 at FM 1243, in front of old schoolhouse*
Old Brandon Mill (1.5 mi. SW)
One of earliest grist mills in Hill County. Built (1868) by Dr. Jas. T. Harrington, who also founded town of Brandon. Corn meal, basic to settlers' diet, was ground here. Dr. Harrington built a dam on White Rock Creek near here as a water source for power in the millhouse. His grist mill served a wide area for nearly 50 years. A grist mill was primary need in every early community. Where bread could be made, settlements thrived. A good water supply and a grist mill were essential to a successful town. Today only store foundations of old Brandon mill remain.   (1967)

BRAZORIA (Brazoria Co.)   *SH 332, .9 mi. E of SH 36*
Brazoria Bridge
The town of Brazoria began in 1828 as a port and trading center in Stephen F. Austin's colony. Partially burned in 1836 during the Texas Revolution, it rebuilt and served as county seat until 1897. To escape floods and to enjoy a better life, the townspeople moved to "new town" near the St. Louis, Brownsville, and Mexico Railway in 1912. This town became "old town." The first traffic bridge, built across the Brazos River in this historic region in 1912, provided a vital link between eastern and western Brazoria County. Falling victim to the elements and lack of maintenance, the wood-decked bridge fell into the river in the 1930s. Built in 1939, during the great depression, using local labor, county bond money, and funds from the public works administration, this Brazoria Bridge sustains the historic transportation route. Nicknamed "The Bridge That Goes to Nowhere" before the soil embankments were built, this 1124' concrete and steel bridge has three Parker through truss spans. It is supported by concrete-filled caisson and concrete piling, and approaches composed of 14 concrete-supported I-beams with steel guard rails. An important example of its style, this Brazoria Bridge is a significant part of Brazoria County history.   (1991)

BRECKENRIDGE (Stephens Co.)   *SH 67, 15 mi. N*
South Prairie Cemetery
Founded in 1880, this cemetery was the community burial ground for South Prairie, a settlement which once included homes, a post office, blacksmith shop, mercantile, and school. The community gradually declined in favor of the nearby towns of Ivan and Eliasville. The oldest burial in the cemetery is that of six-month-old Birddie G. Norton. Among the graves here are those of area pioneers and veterans of the Civil War, World War I, and World War II. Maintained by a cemetery association, the graveyard is the last visible reminder of South Prairie.   (1990)

BRECKENRIDGE (Stephens Co.)   *US 183, 20 mi. NW in roadside park*
Stephens County, C.S.A.
Created as Buchanan County, 1858; organized 1860; renamed 1861 to honor Alexander H. Stephens, Vice-President Confederate States of America. Crossed in 1850s by Fort Belknap-Austin Military Road, gained a few settlers of the boldest type; John R. Baylor, Indian agent, Civil War general, Confederate congressman; and Peter Gunsolus, a doctor whose 7 marriages gave him 51 children. During the Civil War, the few residents "forted up." County men were on Confederate frontier defense line from Red River to Rio Grande, patrolling this area. Until they were subdued in 1875, hostile Indians harassed the settlers and hindered county development. Reorganized 1876, with Breckenridge as county seat. Growth was aided by sawmill for rawhide lumber (cut from local wood and used green, before it had time to warp and get too tough to be nailed). An 1878 visit

by train robber Sam Bass and gang excited the area. But so few prisoners ever occupied the early jail that it was used for storage of cotton. The 1919 oil boom brought a railroad. Region became center of petroleum production, processing, well servicing and supply. Also has farming, ranching, industrial and recreation facilities. (1965)

BRECKENRIDGE (Stephens Co.)
US 183, 1 mi. N
Picketville (0.5 mi. E)
One of Stephens County's first white settlements, Picketville was founded before the Civil War (1861–1865) on Gunsolus Creek. Without military defense during the war, families "forted up" here for protection against hostile Indian attacks. The name probably came from picket construction in which tree limbs were placed on end and chinked with mud. Picketville served as the county seat until Breckenridge was settled in 1876. Then the town began to decline, leaving only a cemetery. After many graves were accidentally destroyed, Boy Scout troops restored and fenced the site. (1975)

BRECKENRIDGE (Stephens Co.)
US 180, 5 mi. E
Stephens County
Created as Buchanan County January 22, 1858. Organized September 20, 1860. Name changed to Stephens December 17, 1861. Named in honor of Alexander H. Stephens, 1812–1883, Vice-President of the Confederate States. Breckenridge, the county seat. (1936)

BRECKENRIDGE (Stephens Co.)
200 W. Walker St. (US 180)
Walter Prescott Webb Formative Years
Noted historian Walter Prescott Webb (1888–1963) came with his family to Stephens County at the age of four. Over the next seventeen years, Webb received an education in frontier life that formed the basis of his intellectual development and his theories on the role of the Great Plains in American history. Webb's father, Casner, was a rural schoolteacher and farmer. As he moved to different teaching assignments, the family moved with him. W. P. Webb thus was exposed to the physical geographical variety within the county that was so important to his western thesis. His neighbors were prime sources of frontier lore. Although Webb's public school experiences were infrequent, it was during these formative years in Stephens County that he developed his love of books and his desire to attend college. Also during this time, Webb was contacted by William Hinds of New York, who was to become his benefactor and a great source of encouragement for the young scholar. In 1906 Walter P. Webb received his teaching certificate and spent the next three years as a rural educator. In 1909, at the age of 21, Webb left his home in Stephens County to pursue his college education at the University of Texas in Austin. (1985)

BRECKENRIDGE (Stephens Co.)
US 183 at Brown Branch Creek
B. T. Brown House
One of the oldest structures in Breckenridge, this ranch house was erected by Benjamin Tarver Brown (1831–1905), a Confederate Army captain who came to Stephens County in 1866. He built this house in 1876, the year Breckenridge was founded as county seat. Limestone blocks were cut nearby for the 18-inch thick walls, and other building materials were hauled by wagon from Fort Worth. The structure was restored by Mr. and Mrs. H. C. Kelley, who purchased it in 1941.(1975)

BREMOND (Robertson Co.)
SH 6 at FM 1373, 2.5 mi. W
Wootan Wells
Famous early health spa and resort. First well was dug 1878 by landowner Francis Wootan. Water tasted good, but turned dishes yellow and clothes red. Even so, it seemed to possess amazing curative properties. Wootan soon built a hotel and in 1879 a resort town made its debut. He formed promotion company with T. W. Wade and more hotels, a bottling works, dance pavilion, and school sprang up. Leading socialites came for miles to "take the waters." Disaster struck in 1915 when fire swept the town. In 1921 the last buildings also burned. (1969)

BRENHAM (Washington Co.)
US 290, 11 mi. SE in roadside park
Early Texas River Steamers
River-shipping efforts in pioneer Texas by steamboat were centered primarily on the Brazos (about 2 mi. E.); and Washington-on-the Brazos (about 15 mi. N.) was an important distribution

point for commercial interests. The Brazos flowed through most productive cotton and sugar region in Texas; steamers greatly aided shipment of these items to markets in New Orleans. The first steamer reached Washington in 1840; by 1849 its docks were busy with steamboats making regular river trips. Between 1820–1840 settlers made journey to Texas on the Red River in steamers if the river was high enough and there were no obstructions. Buffalo Bayou, extending from Houston to Galveston Bay, was waterway traveled most often by steamers, and took over trade from Brazos River because it had a better outlet to the sea. Navigation of the Trinity, Colorado, and Sabine Rivers also increased inland growth and development. While rivers in Texas seemed to offer possibilities for steamboat travel, the story of river navigation is largely one of disappointment. Most meandering rivers were too shallow, often flooded, needed clearing; many were choked with driftwood. These hazards greatly retarded economic and social development of the state. By 1865 the importance of river steamers was gone. (1967)

BRENHAM (Washington Co.) US 290 at US 290 Bus., SE
Brenham
Founded 1843. Named for Richard Fox Brenham (1810–1843), Republic of Texas patriot. Railhead and supply center in Civil War. Blinn Memorial College founded here, 1883. Center for farming, trade and manufacturing. Home of famous annual Maifest, colorful folk tradition. Historical sites marked.

BRENHAM (Washington Co.) 1101 S. Blue Bell Rd.
Blue Bell Creameries
In August 1907, the Brenham Creamery Company formed to purchase excess dairy products from farmers and produce butter for local sales. In 1911, the creamery began making ice cream, producing a maximum of two gallons each day. E. F. Kruse, who managed the creamery from 1919 to 1951, changed the company's name to Blue Bell Creameries in 1930. During the company's early years, management set the tone for careful business practices and respect for tradition. Under the Kruse family's leadership, business expanded into markets outside of Brenham. Blue Bell has become one of the nation's most successful ice cream brands with a focus on its "country" origins, quality ingredients and friendly service. (2007)

BRENHAM (Washington Co.) SH 36, 5 mi. N to CR 51, then 1 mi. W
Thomas Affleck
Born and educated in Scotland, Thomas Affleck (1812–1868) emigrated in 1832 to the United States, where he became one of the most well-known agriculturalists of his time. A prolific writer, Affleck was associated with several agricultural and horticultural publications. An early advocate of scientific farming, he wrote and theorized on topics such as forage, erosion control, hedging, livestock improvements, and plantation management. His publication, "Affleck's Southern Rural Almanac and Plantation and Garden Calendar," was published yearly from 1845 to 1861. During the late 1850s, Thomas Affleck and his wife, Anna (Dunbar) Smith, came to Texas and established their Washington County plantation, which included what is now the Gay Hill Community. The Affleck Plantation, known as "Glenblythe," was extensive and highly organized. It included a wagon factory, where wagons and ambulances were made for the Confederacy. After the end of the Civil War, Thomas Affleck was active in developing plans for Texas' economic recovery. He traveled to England and Scotland, encouraging investment and emigration. Upon his death at the age of 56, Affleck was buried near this site in the graveyard he established on the grounds of "Glenblythe." (1985)

BRENHAM (Washington Co.) SH 36, 6.1 mi. N
Robert Starke Armistead (November 5, 1800–June 14, 1866)
A native of North Carolina, Robert Starke Armistead moved with his family to Alabama in 1818. He married Ann Sylvesta Carney in 1826 and they came to Texas in 1835. Armistead served in the Republic of Texas Army in 1836 and with forces defending San Antonio during the Vasquez Invasion in 1842. He was a charter trustee of Baylor University in 1845. Settling in Washington County, the Armisteads operated a large agricultural enterprise and in 1863 adopted a daughter, Sallie. Robert and Ann are buried nearby in a family cemetery on land once a part of their farm. (1990)

59

BRENHAM (Washington Co.)   *SH 36 at FM 390, 7 mi. N*
La Bahia Road
One of the first overland routes used by European explorers of Texas, La Bahia road was originally an east-west Indian trail in southeastern Texas and Louisiana. Earlier it may have been animal trail. Although not as famous, or long, as El Camino Real (The San Antonio Road), La Bahia is probably older and it figured quite importantly in the movement of explorers, soldiers, traders, and settlers across Texas. Possibly the first European to set foot on the road was La Salle, who explored for France in this area during 1685–1687. Almost certainly it was traveled by the Spaniard Alonso de Leon, who searched for the French intruders in 1689. From 1812 on, the trail and its westernmost town, La Bahia (now Goliad), served agents of both war and peace. The Gutierrez-Magee Expedition, part of Mexico's revolt against Spain, used the road in 1812–1813. In 1821 the first Anglo-American colonists in Texas, the vanguard of the "Old 300," came down La Bahia into this area. During the 1836 Texas Revolution, the road found use by troops of the Texan Army; Col. James Fannin and his 400 men were massacred near the road—in Goliad. In the 20th century, La Bahia's route helped surveyors map modern Texas highways.   (1971)

BRENHAM (Washington Co.)   *SH 36, 10 mi. N to FM 390, then W 1 mi.*
Glenblythe Plantation, Home of Thomas Affleck
In the 19th century, one of the world's foremost researcher-writers on agriculture and horticulture. Lived 1858–1868 on his 3,500-acre plantation 2 mi. S of here, developing famous "Central Texas Nurseries" and experimental fields for new plant varieties. On this property gained recognition as one of earliest promoters and developers of conservation farming. Born 1812 in Scotland; came to the United States in 1832, soon starting in Mississippi one of the South's finest nurseries; gained wide fame as scientist and writer on agriculture. Before moving here, landscaped state capitol grounds for both Louisiana and Texas. Surrounded Glenblythe Mansion and guest houses (2 mi. S) with ornamental gardens and greenhouses, vegetable garden, orchard, a church, hospital, day nursery, store, homes, workshop, stock pens, flour and lumber mills. During Civil War (1861–1865) built ambulances, wagons; fed Waul's Legion in training camp near here. After the war, was key figure in rehabilitation of farming of Texas; made a trip to Europe to recruit settlers. Died 1868, and was buried near his home. Writings, especially "Affleck's Southern Rural Almanac," were influential for years. His "Report on Agricultural Grasses" was a senate executive document of 1879.   (1967)

BRIDGE CITY (Orange Co.)   *SH 87, 3 mi. S at Neches River*
Rainbow Bridge
The rapid growth of the petrochemical industry in Orange and Jefferson Counties in the early 20th century led to increased population in this area. In order to serve the transportation needs of workers and others in this vicinity, the Dryden Ferry was established in 1926. It soon proved inadequate for the volume of traffic, however, and plans began for the construction of a bridge to span the Neches River. Jefferson County, the State of Texas, and the federal government (through the public works administration) all provided funding for the bridge's construction. While the citizens of Orange County also supported the project, the county's economic situation did not permit monetary assistance. Construction of the bridge began in 1936, and was not completed until over two years later. Measuring 176 feet in height and 7,760 feet in length, it was the largest bridge ever built by the state of Texas up to that time. Dedication ceremonies were held on Sept. 8, 1938, attracting a crowd of approximately 20,000. Among the activities were a boat regatta on the river and a stunt diver's plunge from the top of the bridge into the water below. The structure was officially named "Rainbow Bridge" in a 1957 contest.   (1990)

BRIDGEPORT (Wise Co.)   *FM 920, near Trinity River*
Toll Bridge and Old Bridgeport
When Butterfield Overland Mail traversed this area (1858–1861) on St. Louis to San Francisco route, a crossing over west fork of the Trinity was a necessity. Col. W. H. Hunt on Feb. 11, 1860, obtained a charter and built a toll bridge here (50 yd. W). The Overland Mail ceased operating as Civil War began. The bridge soon collapsed. However, a settlement had begun here, and in 1873 Charles Cates, a Decatur merchant, spanned the river with an iron bridge. When the Rock Island Railroad built to this point in 1893, town moved but retained historic name.   (1972)

BRIGGS (Burnet Co.) US 183
The Community of Briggs
Pioneers mainly from the old south settled here on the Aaron Boyce land grant in the 1860s and 70s. They had a school, and held church services, at Gum Springs in the 1880s. In 1888 a post office opened at Taylor's Gin Store; this was renamed in 1898 for Mrs. Henry D. Briggs, an early settler. On April 12, 1906, a tornado destroyed much of the village. Afterward Briggs was rebuilt on a platted townsite: it thrived from 1906 to 1920, but began declining after a 1928 fire. Many of the townspeople have worked since 1950 at Fort Hood, in neighboring Bell County. (1977)

BRIGGS (Burnet Co.) US 183, 3.2 mi. S
Prairie View Cemetery
Pioneer settlers in this vicinity met together for worship services in the Gum Springs School-house until 1892, when Stephen Taylor deeded land at this site for church and cemetery purposes. This historic cemetery began in the churchyard of the First Methodist Episcopal Church, south, (also known as Prairie View Church) in the early 1890s. The earliest documented grave in the cemetery is that of Scottish native James Smith (1836–1892), who immigrated to Texas in 1884. Those interred here include pioneer settlers; a number of infants and small children; and veterans of the Civil War, World War I, World War II, and Korea. The Prairie View Church moved to Briggs in 1906 and became the Briggs Methodist Church. The congregation later was dissolved, and the members attended worship services in neighboring communities, and the church building was moved to Lampasas in 1951 and converted into a parsonage. The Prairie View Cemetery serves as a physical reminder of the area's pioneer heritage. The Prairie View Cemetery Association, organized in 1977, provides maintenance for the historic graveyards. (1991)

BRONTE (Coke Co.) US 277, 12 mi. NE
Fort Chadbourne
Established by the United States Army, October 28, 1852, as a protection to frontier settlers against Indians. Named in honor of Lieutenant T. L. Chadbourne, killed at Resaca de La Palma, May 9, 1846. Occupied by Federal troops, 1852–1861, 1865–1867. An important station on the Butterfield Overland stage route, 1858–1861. (Fort Chadbourne, Coke County)

BRONTE (Coke Co.) US 227, 11 mi. NE in roadside park
Southern Overland Mail, 1858–1861 (Butterfield Stage)
One mile southeast to Fort Chadbourne, a station on the Butterfield mail and stage line, which linked St. Louis and San Francisco, 1858–1861. The fort was established in 1852, occupied until its surrender to state forces in 1861, and garrisoned at times after the Civil War. (1936)

BRONTE (Coke Co.) SH 70 at US 277, 8 mi. N
Indian Rock Shelters
Throughout this area during the last several centuries, rock ledges gave protection to Lipan, Kickapoo, Comanche, and Kiowa Indians. In one typical shelter archeologists found evidence of 3 periods of occupation, plus numerous intricate petroglyphs (rock carvings). River shells, turkey and deer bones, flint knives, scrapers, and points lay about the area. One of several hearths (2' 3' in size) consisted of small pieces of sandstone lining a natural rock trough. On the highest level was found green bottle glass from nearby Fort Chadbourne (1852–1867). (1970)

BRONTE (Coke Co.) US 277 at SH 158
Bronte
Eastern gateway to Permian Basin, in Coke County. Called Oso and Broncho in early 1800s. Formally named for English novelist Charlotte Bronte, in 1890. Incorporated 1907. Basic agricultural economy, predominantly ranching. Site of major oil and gas development since 1948. (1964)

BRONTE (Coke Co.) SH 158 W (West Main St.)
Bronte Depot
Built by local stonemason James C. Lammers (1874–1942), this depot was completed in 1911, two years after the first train arrived in Bronte. Built of locally quarried materials, the depot features stone lintels and window sills and a red tile roof. Originally owned by the Kansas City, Mexico, & Orient Railway, the Bronte depot was sold in 1928 to the Atchison, Topeka, & Santa Fe Railway Company, which discontinued operations here in 1967. (Recorded Texas Historic Landmark—1989)

BROOKSHIRE (Waller Co.)
FM 1489 at Old US 90
Kellner Townsite (In NE Part, Stephen F. Austin Grant to Wm. Cooper)
First town in area. Platted 1893 by John G. Kellner (1846–1933), donor, Missouri, Kansas & Texas Railroad right of way and station site. Kellner's rich Brazos River watershed farm and ranch lands produced rice, cattle, peanuts, pecans, and (later) natural gas. His old home is nearby. Town was renamed Brookshire.

BROWNFIELD (Terry Co.)
US 380, 14 mi. W
Tokio School
Early classes in the Tokio area were held in the ranch house of the J Cross Ranch near the turn of the century. In 1911, a school building was constructed near the center of town (about 300 feet N), and classes were relocated. Larger school buildings later were erected, once due to fire and twice due to changing space needs. The school facilities continued to serve the community's educational as well as religious and civic needs until 1941, when Tokio School was consolidated with the Brownfield Independent School District. (1991)

BROWNFIELD (Terry Co.)
US 380, 6 mi. W
Gomez Baptist Church
On August 3, 1903, nine worshipers gathered together under a wagon sheet tent to organize a Baptist church. Led by the Rev. J. R. Miller, the congregation met once a month in the Gomez schoolhouse. A one-room sanctuary, erected in 1909, was moved three-quarters of a mile northwest when Gomez was relocated due to highway construction. A larger church building was erected in 1936, and by 1942 the church had its first full-time pastor. The Gomez School, converted for church use in 1953, was destroyed by fire in 1960 and was replaced by a new structure. (1988)

BROWNFIELD (Terry Co.)
US 380, 4.4 mi. W
½ mi. S of this Marker Stood Town of Gomez
In 1903, owners of land here in center of then-unorganized Terry County platted this town, secured a post office named for Spanish-American patriot Maximo Gomez, drilled a public water well, and induced merchants and citizens to move here. This was the first inhabited townsite in the county. Its promoters hoped it would be the county seat, but that honor went to Brownfield (4.4 mi. E) in 1904 when the county was organized. Gomez had a post office until 1926, school until 1941. A church, some businesses (.75 mi. NW), and the old cemetery retain the name. (1974)

BROWNFIELD (Terry Co.)
US 380, 10 mi. E in roadside park
Terry County
Formed from Young and Bexar Territories. Created August 21, 1876, organized June 28, 1904. Named in honor of Colonel Benjamin Franklin Terry (1821–1861). Leader of the famous Terry's Texas Rangers. Brownfield, county seat. Primarily a farming area.

BROWNFIELD (Terry Co.)
US 62/82 at US 385
Site of Joe T. and Laura Hamilton Home
In 1885, Joseph Thomas Hamilton (1856–1932) married Laura Letha Franklin (1867–1936) in Franklin County, Texas. Natives of southern U.S. states, the couple moved west with their first three children and settled here in 1902, before Terry County was organized. In 1907, they established a home near this site. Joe was a stock farmer, carpenter, mail carrier and livery worker, and he was one of three men contracted to build the county's first courthouse. Laura, in addition to managing a large household, often assisted neighbors as nurse and midwife. Today, this site is a link to the early pioneers who built Brownfield and surrounding communities. (2005)

BROWNFIELD (Terry Co.)
US 62 at US 82, N edge of city
The Oak Grove
Landmark for pioneers, freighters, these "shin oakes" are unusual for growing spontaneously on treeless high plains.

BROWNFIELD (Terry Co.)
SH 137, 13.7 mi. SE
Mail Relay Station (500 yds. W)
W. J. French (1859–1930) settled here in 1903, and built two-story house. Site became regular water stop for freighters and drovers. In 1905, French obtained the mail contract between Lamesa

and Gomez, via Brownfield. Five-passenger "hacks" started each day from Lamesa and Gomez, and met at this half-way point at noon to exchange mail and passengers and change horses. After riders were served a hot meal, cooked by Mrs. French, "hacks" returned to starting points, completing a 40-mile round trip. Service was discontinued in 1910, when mail was rerouted.   (1973)

BROWNSBORO (Henderson Co.)   *SH 31E at FM 314*
Site of Old Normandy (0.5 mi. SE)
First Norwegian colony in Texas. Founded in 1845 by Johan Reinert Reierson (1810–1864) and Ole Reierson, of Holt, Norway. In "Christianssandsposten," J. R. Reierson urged Norwegians to find "A Rich Life" by migrating to Texas. His associate editor, Elise Tvede (1815–1895), also came to Texas and continued writing for publications in Norway. She married Wilhelm Warenskjold, lived in this area, and opened home to Norwegian newcomers. By 1853 a Norwegian-Lutheran church and cemetery had been established here. Normandy was later renamed Brownsboro.(1970)

BROWNSBORO (Henderson Co.)   *SH 31E at FM 314*
Brownsboro Norwegian Lutheran Cemetery
After migrating from Norway in 1845, Ole Reierson bought the land that included this cemetery site (1.1 mi. ESE). He chose the spot for his burial and carved several of the plain brown gravestones before he died in 1852. The cemetery's 24 marked and 81 unmarked graves are mostly those of Norwegian immigrants. A Lutheran church, built nearby in 1889, served as a cemetery chapel until the 1920s. Will Tergerson tended the site for many years. An association formed in 1974 by descendants of early settlers now maintains it.   (1976)

BROWNSVILLE (Cameron Co.)   *US 281, 22 mi. NW in roadside park*
Thornton Skirmish
The spot where "American blood was shed on American soil" April 25, 1846. Here Captain Seth B. Thornton and 62 dragoons were attacked by Mexican troops.

BROWNSVILLE (Cameron Co.)   *US 281, 20 mi. NW*
Las Rucias
Here Colonel John S. Ford of the Confederate Army defeated the Union Forces June 25, 1864.

BROWNSVILLE (Cameron Co.)   *US 281, 8.5 mi. NW*
Esparza Cemetery
This graveyard was named for Carlos Villarreal Esparza (1828–1885), whose family's occupation of the surrounding ranch land began in the early 19th century. According to family records, the original Esparza Cemetery was established south of this site in the mid-1800s. In 1888, Carlos' widow Francisca Garcia Esparza moved his grave and those of other family members because of flooding and other problems at the old cemetery. It is believed that Carlos' parents, Pedro and Felicidad Villarreal Esparza, are interred here. The cemetery is the resting place of family members who served in World Wars I and II, local civic and political leaders, officers in law enforcement and the Texas Rangers. A record of the area's Mexican American pioneers, it continues to serve the community.   (1999)

BROWNSVILLE (Cameron Co.)   *US 281, 4 mi. NW*
Sabas Cavazos Cemetery
Established in 1878 with the burial of rancher and businessman Sabas Cavazos, this small cemetery has served the Cavazos and related families for more than a century. It is located within the Potrero de Don Sabas Cavazos, a portion of the Espíritu Santo Land Grant conveyed to José Salvador de la Garza by the King of Spain in 1781. Born December 4, 1809, in Camargo, Nuevo Santander, Mexico, Sabas Cavazos was the son of José María Francisco Cavazos and Estefana Goseascochea, and a great-grandson of José Salvador de la Garza. Encompassing more than one-quarter million acres of land, the Espíritu Santo Grant included the future sites of Fort Brown and the city of Brownsville. The De la Garza family established Rancho Viejo, the first settlement in the Brownsville area. The communities of San Pedro, El Carmen, La Gloria, and La Puerta were established by Doña Estefana. Although in use since 1878, the cemetery was not officially recorded in deed records until 1947. Among those buried here are members of the extended Cavazos family, their relatives, and members of the San Pedro community. The site is maintained by descendants of persons buried here.   (1995)

BROWNSVILLE (Cameron Co.) *US 77, 4.8 mi. N*
"Rancho Viejo"
Here Jose Salvador de la Garza built his ranch El Espiritu Santo in 1771, first European settlement in Cameron County.

BROWNSVILLE (Cameron Co.) *US 77/83 at FM 802*
Brownsville, C.S.A.
A major center of activity for Confederacy, chief depot for war material and supplies imported from Europe through neutral port of Bagdad, Mexico. Terminus of cotton road. Point of entry and departure for important personages of South in intercourse with outside world. Occupied by large Federal expeditionary force Nov. 6, 1863 after Confederates had destroyed Ft. Brown, cotton, commissary stores and supplies and had withdrawn. Became temporary seat of Union State Government with Texan A. J. Hamilton Military Governor. Back Side:

Brownsville, C.S.A.
When Confederate forces reoccupied Brownsville July 30, 1864 it resumed its importance as South's supply source and terminus of cotton road. Cotton export through Brownsville and other Rio Grande points means of survival of Confederacy west of the Mississippi. Imports from Europe and Mexico formed almost entire supply for military and civilians. Gen. Magruder, Gen. Bee, Col. "Rip" Ford and other prominent Confederate officers headquarters here. Center of international intrigue throughout war. (1963)

BROWNSVILLE (Cameron Co.) *US 77/83 at FM 802*
Cameron County
Created February 12, 1848 from Nueces County; organized August 7, 1848. Named in honor of Ewen Cameron, 1811–1843. Captain in the Mier Expedition, shot at Queretaro. County seat, Santa Rita, 1848–1849. Brownsville, since. The earliest battles of the Mexican War and the last battle of the Civil War were fought in this county.

BROWNSVILLE (Cameron Co.) *FM 511 at SH 48, at Navigation*
District Admin. Building Port of Brownsville
The first serious attempt to study the possibility of construction of a deep-water seaport in this part of South Texas was undertaken in 1854 when a survey was conducted by United States Army engineers. At that time, the only natural harbor in the area was located at Brazos de Santiago Pass near Point Isabel (16 mi. NE). Shipping through that pass dated to the 16th century, but the presence of shifting sandbars prevented large vessels from anchoring at that point. In 1906, Louis Cobolini, a commercial fisherman in Point Isabel, took on the cause for a deep-water port. He compiled data that convinced U.S. Army engineers that such an undertaking was practical and deserved federal economic support. During the next 20 years, various attempts at dredging channels and eliminating the sandbars were made without much success. Recognizing the need for deep-water transportation to assure sound economic growth, the citizens of Brownsville created a navigation district in 1929 to provide local support for the federal government to build a deep-water port. Between 1934 and 1936, this ship channel, linking Brownsville and the Gulf of Mexico, was dredged. The port facilities were formally dedicated in May 1936. (Texas Sesquicentennial 1836–1986)

BROWNSVILLE (Cameron Co.) *SH 4, 20.3 mi. NE at Boca Chica*
Palmetto Pilings
These palmetto pilings are the remains of the Boca Chica crossing of the railroad from Boca Chica inlet to White's ranch on the Rio Grande. Begun by General Francis H. Herron, U.S.A., in 1864 and completed in 1865 by General Philip H. Sheridan for the transportation of military supplies. The cypress piling, 1,000 feet north are what remain of a floating bridge constructed across Boca Chica inlet by General Zachary Taylor in 1846 as a part of the road from Brazos Santiago to the White ranch landing and Clarksville on the Rio Grande, for transportation of military supplies.

BROWNSVILLE (Cameron Co.) *SH 4, 16 mi. NE*
Site of Camp Belknap
In May 1846, when war was declared against Mexico, the U.S. Congress authorized the raising of 50,000 volunteer troops to supplement the regular U.S. Army. General Zachary Taylor was quickly inundated with volunteer soldiers arriving at Brazos Santiago, and was forced to place them in tem-

porary encampments. Camp Belknap, located on this site, was established in the summer of 1846. The camp was located on a long narrow rise of land, measuring about 2 miles in length and one-half mile at its widest point. It was the first high ground encountered after leaving the Gulf Coast. Thought to be the largest encampment for volunteer soldiers, troop estimates total 7,000–8,000 men including several regiments from eight states. Soldiers suffered exposure to the elements, unsanitary living conditions, overcrowding, biting insects, thorny plants, and disease. Many died a premature death, often resulting in one to two funerals daily. No enemy attacks took place despite one false alarm. During August and September most of the volunteers were moved upriver either to camps nearer Matamoros, or farther to Camargo. The camp was completely empty by December 1846. (1996)

BROWNSVILLE (Cameron Co.) *SH 4, 12 mi. NE*
Battle of Palmito Ranch
The last land engagement of the Civil War was fought near this site on May 12–13, 1865, thirty-four days after Robert E. Lee surrendered at Appomattox. Col. Theodore H. Barrett commanded Federal troops on Brazos Island 12 miles to the east. The Confederates occupied Fort Brown 12 miles to the west, commanded by Gen. James E. Slaughter and Col. John S. (Rip) Ford, whose troops had captured Fort Brown from the Federals in 1864. Ordered to recapture the fort, Lt. Col. David Branson and 300 men advanced from Brazos Island. They won a skirmish with Confederate pickets on May 12. Barrett reinforced Branson's troops with 200 men on May 13 and renewed the march to Fort Brown. Confederate cavalry held the Federals in check until Ford arrived with reinforcements that afternoon. Ford's artillery advanced and fired on the northern end of the Federal line while the cavalry charged. The Confederate right charged the southern end of the Federal line and captured part of the Union infantry. Barrett ordered a retreat toward the U.S. position on Brazos Island. While the Confederates reported no fatalities in the Battle of Palmito Ranch, the Union forces reported 4 officers and 111 men killed, wounded, or missing. (1963, 1990)

BROWNSVILLE (Cameron Co.) *E. Elizabeth St. at International Blvd.*
The Chisholm Trail
Iberian range cattle, progenitors of the Texas Longhorn, were brought into Texas by Spain in the 1600s and 1700s. The cattle thrived on the area's rich grasslands and roamed throughout Texas. At the time of the Texas Revolution (1835–1836) vast Mexican ranchos with their illustrious vaqueros (Spanish for cowboys) were an established tradition in the Rio Grande Valley. By 1860, cattle ranching dominated land use in the region. Demand for beef rose dramatically after the Civil War. Longhorn cattle worth $2 and $3 in Texas sold for $30 and $40 in midwestern railroad centers such as Kansas City and Chicago. Area ranchers, aware of the longhorn's stamina, united to drive their cattle to frontier railroad terminals in Abilene and Dodge City. The Rio Grande was the southernmost point at which cattle were gathered for the drive north through Austin, Fort Worth, Red River Station, and into Oklahoma. There the trail joined the original 220-mile Chisholm Trail into Kansas established by Indian trader/guide Jesse Chisholm in 1865. The entire route and its feeder trails soon became widely known as the Chisholm Trail. An estimated 10 million cattle were driven north along the Chisholm Trail by the late 1870s when use of the trail was drastically curtailed by quarantines. (1994)

BROWNSVILLE (Cameron Co.) *1300 Mexico Blvd.*
Brownsville-Matamoros Bridge
The St. Louis, Brownsville and Mexico Railroad arrived in Brownsville in 1904. The Rio Grande separated the U. S. railway from the Mexican National Railway line. Congressman John Nance Garner (1868–1967), later vice president of the United States, introduced a bill into Congress in 1908 providing for the construction of a bridge spanning the river and connecting the two railways. The Brownsville-Matamoros Bridge Company, owned equally by the St. Louis, Brownsville and Mexico Railway and the Mexican National Railway, was incorporated in 1909 to handle bridge operations. In 1909 St. Louis, Brownsville and Mexico Railway magnate Benjamin F. Yoakum (1859–1929) met with representatives of the Mexican National Railway. An agreement was reached, and Yoakum hired the Foundation Company of New York to build the concrete foundations and the Wisconsin Bridge Company of Milwaukee to erect the steel spans. Work on the structure began in April 1909. The entire structure, a swing bridge of riveted construction, was completed in summer 1910. It was swung open in July of that year for inspection and was photographed by Robert

Runyon. By that time, river traffic in the area had ceased, and the swing function was unnecessary. The approximate cost of the bridge, which totaled 227 feet in length, was $225,000. The bridge was renovated for heavier automobile traffic in 1953 and 1992. Although the Brownsville-Matamoros Bridge Company erected an adjacent bridge in 1997 for automobile traffic, the original bridge continues to be used for rail and truck traffic.   (1999)

BROWNWOOD (Brown Co.)   *SH 279, 24 mi. NW*
Cross Cut Cemetery
Settlement began in this area of Brown County after the Civil War when several families from southern states moved here. They formed a community, initially known as Cross Out. It became Cross Cut in 1897 when an error was made on a post office application. Caroline Pentecost Elsberry was the first person buried in this community cemetery in July 1879. The two-acre plot of land dedicated as a graveyard is believed to have been donated by Mark and Sarah Pentecost. Oil was discovered in 1923 in the Cross Cut sand formation. The small town quickly swelled to accommodate the increase in population and several new businesses were added. By 1940 the population of the town was exceeded by the number of burials in the cemetery. In 1954 the Cross Cut School consolidated with Cross Plains Schools, and the town declined thereafter. Only a few buildings and the cemetery remain. Among those buried here are early settlers and their descendants, and veterans of conflicts from the Civil War through the Vietnam War. A cemetery association was formed in 1976, and a perpetual care trust was established. The site continues to serve the area.   (1997)

BROWNWOOD (Brown Co.)   *US 67/377, E city limits in roadside park*
Brown County
Created August 27, 1856; organized March 21, 1857. Named for Capt. Henry S. Brown. Came to Texas in 1824. Indian trader and fighter. Commanded a company at the Battle of Velasco, member of the convention of 1832. County seat, Brownwood, 1856. Moved to new site of same name, 1867.

BROWNWOOD (Brown Co.)   *US 67, at city limits in roadside park*
City of Brownwood (First Site 1 mi. E; Second, 5 mi. SE, Present Location)
Settled 1857. Acquired a post office 1858. An oil vein ruined 1860s water well of townsite donor Greenleaf Fisk. Wagon-yard keeper Martin Meinsinger sold medicinal oil from 1878 well. Commercial drilling began 1889. Farming, cotton sales, business town since 1880s; was reached by Santa Fe Railroad, 1880; Frisco, 1890. Two colleges—Daniel Baker and Howard Payne—were situated here in 1889. Camp Bowie, World War II military post, operated in Brownwood from 1940 to 1946. Center for agriculture-retail sales-industry. Has a coliseum, parks, 110 miles of lake shore.   (1968)

BROWNWOOD (Brown Co.)   *Center Ave. at Broadway,*
                                                              off US 377, at courthouse
Greenleaf Fisk (1807–1888) "Father of Brownwood"
Donor of present townsite of Brownwood, Fisk was noted as a soldier, public servant, surveyor, and businessman. The son of English parents, he was born in New York. As a boy he was so studious that he voluntarily gave up recess periods to read. In 1834 he abandoned his preparation for the Presbyterian ministry and, with a friend, embarked down the Ohio River on a skiff to brave the Texas frontier. Settling at Mina (present Bastrop), he fought in the Battle of San Jacinto in 1836. He later served in various county offices in Bastrop and Williamson Counties and was a senator in the Republic of Texas. As a government surveyor in this period, he mapped this region and liked it so well he determined to settle here. Having received in 1846, for his service in the Texas Revolution, a large land grant in this vicinity, he moved here in 1860. Besides teaching, he also served as county judge and in other offices. When difficulties arose over the location of the county seat, he donated 60 acres for the town and 100 acres for county purposes. He then persuaded many citizens to move here from the old townsite. At his death in 1888, Fisk was buried in Greenleaf cemetery. He married twice and had 15 children.   (1968)

BROWNWOOD (Brown Co.)   *2701 US 377 S*
Dr. Mollie W. Armstrong
(January 23, 1875–May 23, 1964)
Mary Elizabeth (Mollie) Wright Armstrong was instrumental in establishing optometry as a profession in Texas during the first half of the 20th century. A native of Bell County, she briefly

66

attended Baylor Female College in Belton, where she met her future husband, Walter David (W.D.) Armstrong. They married in 1892 and moved to Brownwood. W.D., a watchmaker, opened a store in partnership with his brother and, as was the business custom at the time, the store inventory included eyeglasses. Mollie's interest in optometry began when a traveling optical salesman fitted her with glasses, curing her chronic headaches. Studying on her own, she completed a Kellum and Moore School of Optometry correspondence course. She excelled in her studies and finished her degree in Refraction at the Atlanta, Ga. Campus in 1899. She returned to Brownwood and opened and optical department in the family store, becoming the first woman optometrist in Texas. She earned her Doctorate of Optics from Northern Illinois School of Optometry in 1905. A leader in her profession, Dr. Armstrong was a charter member of the Texas Optometric Association, which she served as the first woman president in 1923. Gov. Miriam A. Ferguson, a Bell County childhood friend, appointed her to the Texas State Board of Examiners in Optometry. Dr. Armstrong later worked on national issues as a board member of the American Optometric Association. She was also a Brownwood civic leader, supporting libraries and parks, serving on the Chamber of Commerce, and founding the local Business and Professional Women's Association.   (2006)

BROWNWOOD (Brown Co.)   *SH 377, Greenleaf Cemetery*
Robert E. Howard (January 24, 1906–June 11, 1936)
Born in Parker County, Robert Ervin Howard grew up in the Brown and Callahan County communities of Cross Cut, Cross Plains, and Brownwood. He attended Brownwood High School and Howard Payne College, and published his first works of fiction in school newspapers. He later wrote poetry and short stories for popular magazines. His main interest was in science fiction and fantasy. In 1932, he created the character Conan the Barbarian. Howard committed suicide at age 30. His Conan character has become known worldwide through books, magazines, and movies.   (1991)

BROWNWOOD (Brown Co.)   *SH 377, 6 mi. W at sign pointing*
                                                             to Indian Creek Cemetery
Katherine Anne Porter (May 15, 1890–September 18, 1980)
Born Callie Russell Porter in Indian Creek, Katherine Anne Porter moved to Hays County with her family following her mother's death in 1892. She left Texas in 1915 and worked as an actress, teacher, reporter and publicist in such places as Chicago, Denver, Mexico, and New York. Her first book of short stories was published in 1930. Her acclaimed 1962 novel, "Ship of Fools", was followed by the Pulitzer prizewinning "The Collected Stories of Katherine Anne Porter" in 1965. Upon her death in 1980, her ashes were buried next to her mother's grave in Indian Creek Cemetery.   (1990)

BRUCEVILLE (McLennan Co.)   *IH 35N, rest stop*
Martin Irons
A native of Scotland, Martin Irons (1833–1990) came to the United States at the age of fourteen as a machinist's apprentice. After learning the trade, he lived and worked in numerous places throughout the country. By 1884, he was employed as a machinist in the Missouri Pacific Railway shop in Sedalia, Missouri. A firm believer in organization as a means by which individuals could improve their lives, Irons became an active participant in groups such as the Knights of Pythias and the Grange. While working in Sedalia, he became interested in an early union society known as the Knights of Labor and was instrumental in organizing workers employed by Jay Gould's Network of Southwestern Railroad Lines. The railroad union, known as District Assembly 101, went on strike in 1886. Irons, then chairman of the executive committee, came into prominence as its leader. The strike was marked by violence, and when it ended, Irons was blacklisted. He retired in nearby Bruceville but remained active in social reform movements until his death. Irons' grave in the Bruceville Cemetery is marked by a monument, placed in 1911 by the Missouri Federation of Labor.   (1984)

BRYAN (Brazos Co.)   *SH 6 at E 26th St.*
Brazos County
Created from Robertson and Washington Counties in 1841. First called Navasota, changed 1842 to Brazos after two rivers on county's boundaries. Organized in 1843, with Booneville as county seat; Bryan, county seat since 1866. Area originally included in Stephen F. Austin's second colony, 1828. Became a part of the Washington municipality, 1837, under the Mexican government. First railroad reached Millican in 1860. A. & M. University opened, 1876. Economy based on agricultural, industrial and educational activities.   (1966)

BRYAN (Brazos Co.)
300 E. 26th St., 1 blk. W of SH 6 Bus.
William Joel Bryan
Native of Missouri. Member of prominent family who were Texas statesmen, planters, developers. Grandson of Moses Austin, who obtained from Mexico charter for American Colony in Texas, but died before making settlement. Nephew of Stephen F. Austin, "Father of Texas", who actually established the colony. Came to Texas with his mother, Emily Austin Bryan Perry, in 1831. During Texas Revolution, fought in Battle of Bexar, 1835. For 71 years was a planter on land near Peach Point, where the bachelor Stephen F. Austin had a room reserved for him in Perry Home. As eldest nephew, inherited family leadership when Stephen F. Austin died in 1836. Backed his brothers' careers, especially in the case of Guy M. Bryan, U.S. Congressman 1858–1860, and for many years a leader in Texas government. During the Civil War, cared for business interests of his 4 sons in the Confederate Army. At his own expense fed Confederate troops stationed near his plantation to defend the Texas coast. Backed construction of Deep Water Harbor at mouth of the Brazos. During building of Houston & Texas Central Railroad, donated site for Bryan, which in 1866 became county seat of Brazos County. (1965)

BRYAN (Brazos Co.)
SH 21, 8 mi. SW
Route of El Camino Real
(Also known as Old San Antonio Road and Old Spanish Road)
Great thoroughfare of pioneer Texas, stretching 1,000 miles from Saltillo, Mexico, to present Louisiana. The general route followed ancient Indian and buffalo trails, but the oldest marked portion, known as "Trail of the Padres," was blazed in 1691 under Domingo Teran de Los Rios, first governor of Texas. This part joined Monclova, then capital of the province, to the Spanish missions of East Texas. San Antonio, military nerve center of the region, was a major stop. Over the centuries, explorers, traders, smugglers, armed men, and civilians traversed this road. In 1820 Moses Austin traveled it to San Antonio to request a land grant from Spanish officials. The colonizing venture he started later brought thousands of Anglo-Americans over the road to help settle Texas. In 1915 the Texas legislature appropriated $5,000 to survey and mark the route. The Daughters of the American Revolution and other patriotic groups sponsored and endorsed the project, and V. N. Zivley was commissioned to make the survey. In 1918, the State and D. A. R. placed granite markers approximately every five miles along the Texas section of the road. Today many modern highways, particularly State 21, follow the original route of El Camino Real. (1973)

BRYSON (Jack Co.)
E. Dempsey St. (US 380)
Bryson
Jack County Petroleum Capital. Founder, Henry E. Bryson (September 1, 1839–October 25, 1909), a Civil War veteran, farmer and stockraiser, built first log cabin here in 1878. After Bryson post office was established in 1882, the town developed as a center for the growing of cotton and grain. Rock Island Railroad reached here in 1902. The first oil well was drilled 1925; town in 1920s and 30s had a gasoline plant; from 1935 until late 1954 an oil refinery was in operation here. Churches, schools, social and civic clubs and Masonic bodies have contributed to growth. (1968)

BUCKHOLTS (Milam Co.)
US 190, 6 mi. W
Major Bryant's Home
Major Bryant's home and trading post stood six miles southeast of this marker.

BUCKHOLTS (Milam Co.)
US 190, 6 mi. W
Bryant Station
Pioneer village of Milam County established as an Indian trading post by Major Benjamin F. Bryant, frontiersman who had commanded a company in the Battle of San Jacinto. Appointed Indian Agent in 1842 by Sam Houston, President of the Republic of Texas. Little River Crossing on trail and stage routes. U. S. Post Office, 1848–1874. (1936)

BUDA (Hays Co.)
Main St. (Old N. Loop 4) at Ash St.
Buda
Originally known as Du Pre, Buda was founded along a line of the International and Great Northern Railroad. Cornelia A. Trimble gave land for the townsite in 1881. The name "Buda" was adopted in the late 1880s, although its origin is unclear. According to popular legends, it was either related to

Budapest, Hungary, or evolved from the Spanish word for widow, "viuda," and honored the women who cooked in one of the local hotels. Buda was once the site of a variety of businesses, including a theater, skating rink, newspaper, and two banks. The town was incorporated in 1948. (1981)

BUFFALO (Leon Co.)
US 79, 2 mi. S in picnic area
Colonel Robert Simonton Gould (1826–1904)
Born in North Carolina. Educated at University of Alabama. Came to Texas in 1850. Practiced law in Centerville. Served as the first district attorney, then as judge in the old 13th Judicial District. Represented Leon County as member of secession convention, 1861. Afterward, as this county voted 534 to 82 in favor of secession, raised locally troops which as Co. B. became nucleus for 6th Texas Cavalry or (Gould's Battalion), in the Confederate Army. First as major, then as colonel, Gould led battalion for 4 years in Louisiana and Texas. Saw duty in Red River campaign to prevent invasions of Texas, fighting in the 1864 repulses of Federals at Mansfield and Pleasant Hill. At Jenkins Ferry, Ark., Col. Gould had his horse killed under him. After the war he was reelected judge of the old 13th District, but was removed in 1867 by military authorities in charge of reconstruction in Texas. Appointed Assistant Justice of Texas Supreme Court in 1874, he was afterward elected, and served until Dec. 31, 1882 (being Chief Justice in 1880–1882). Was named, along with Governor O. M. Roberts, as one of two first professors of law at the University of Texas, holding tenure 1883–1889. Died in Austin. (1965)

BUFFALO SPRINGS (Clay Co.)
FM 174 at FM 3077
Buffalo Springs
A landmark as early as 1849. Watering place for buffalo hunters. Site of a proposed permanent United States Army post, July, 1867. Abandoned due to lack of water and timber, November 19, 1867, and Fort Richardson on Lost Creek was established instead, November 26, 1867. Served as a stage stand and camp ground between that post and Fort Sill. Scene of battle, July 12, 1874, between Indians and George W. Stevens, captain of Texas Rangers.

BUFFALO SPRINGS (Clay Co.)
FM 174 at FM 3077
Buffalo Springs, C.S.A.
On line of sentry forts along Red River and far frontiers of North Texas, 1861–1865. Used at intervals by cavalry, especially at such times as 1863 massing of 3,000 Federals to the north, in Indian territory. Soldiers here saw little of war's glory, had large share of fighting and shortages of guns, ammunition, food, clothing and horses. Site of "forting up" of families wishing to stay, with goods and stock, near frontier homes. Lived in picket houses in fortified square, placing guards on water or wood gathering parties; in 1862 left during water famine. (1965)

BULLARD (Cherokee Co.)
US 69, .25 mi. S
The Burning Bush Colony
From 1913 until 1919 a religious community operated in this vicinity, on the former Joseph Pickens Douglas Plantation. The colony was established by the Metropolitan Church Association, commonly called the Burning Bush Society, an evangelical organization founded in Chicago about 1900. This 400-member Burning Bush Colony was set up to be a self-sustaining agricultural community. It operated its own school, sawmill, power plant, water system, and sewage disposal facility. Unable to pay its debts, the colony disbanded after the close of World War I. (1984)

BURKBURNETT (Wichita Co.)
SH 240, 14 mi. W
Tenth Cavalry Creek
First called Getty's Creek, this stream was renamed by cowboys and settlers who found near its mouth, on Red River, remains of a military outpost garrisoned by the U.S. Tenth Cavalry from 1873 to 1875. Most of the Negro soldiers and white officers stationed there had previously served in the Federal Army during the Civil War (1861–1865) and at Fort Sill, in Indian territory. This staked timber outpost was attacked by Indians; legend says that all the officers, men and horses killed in the battle were buried in a common grave somewhere along this creek.

BURKBURNETT (Wichita Co.)
SH 240, 7.1 mi. W
Ghost Town of Clara
Herman Specht migrated in 1870 to Galveston from Germany. In 1884, he married Clara M. Vogel Lange (1853–1912), a wealthy widow. Adding to earlier property holdings in Galveston, he

began buying extensive tracts of land in northern Wichita County, which eventually totaled 21,000 acres. In 1886, he platted the town of Clara which he named for his wife. The streets were named for Texas heroes. He donated this site for the Trinity Lutheran Church. Specht advertised for German colonists from other states to settle here. Specht built his home in Iowa Park in 1890 and ran a ranch at Clara where he grew wheat. North of the church site, he had a large experimental nursery for unusual plants. The 1891 drought wiped out the nursery and Specht's crops. The 1900 Galveston storm destroyed the remainder of their vast holdings. Clara included a church, schools, store, garage and post office. Hampered by an inadequate water supply, the town began to decline with the consolidation of the school with the Burkburnett schools. During the oil boom of the 1920s, many residents moved to Wichita Falls. Good roads and cars made it possible to shop elsewhere. The town finally vanished except for the church, rectory, and cemetery. (1978)

BURKBURNETT (Wichita Co.) SH 240, 6 mi. W
The Receiver Bridge
A natural border of the Louisiana Territory when it was acquired by the United States in 1803, the Red River later served as a boundary between the states of Texas and Oklahoma. The exact location for the line of separation was challenged in 1920 soon after an extension of the Burkburnett oil field led to increased drilling activity in the area, including the banks and the bed of the stream. Since the Red River meandered, causing wide flood plains, the state of Oklahoma initiated a suit to determine ownership of the land. By authority of the United States Supreme Court, the disputed land was temporarily placed under the jurisdiction of the federal government. Frederick A. Delano, whose nephew Franklin Delano Roosevelt later became President of the United States, was named as the receiver in charge of the property. As part of his plan of supervision, he had a one-lane wooden bridge (2.5 mi. N) built to the center of the river, providing access to the drilling sites. The boundary between the two states was set as the south bank of the Red River in 1923. It was not until four years later that a special commission completed the actual survey work. The bridge was partially destroyed later during a 1935 flood. (1981)

BURKBURNETT (Wichita Co.) SH 240, 5 mi. W
Bridgetown
When the northwest extension of the Burkburnett oil field opened in 1919, prospectors thronged this area. Bridgetown sprang up at the Texas end of a mile-long Red River toll bridge built for oil field traffic. It became the largest and wealthiest of 12 communities that mushroomed in this area during rivalry among major oil companies and independent producers. Lease values rose from $10 to $20,000 an acre. A city of tents, shanties and a few substantial structures, Bridgetown had a long main street with a Mission church at one end and a saloon at the other. Its post office opened July 15, 1920. The population in the early 1920s was estimated at 3,500 to 10,000. Litigation over riverbed oil rights caused the U.S. Supreme Court to station a receiver in the town. He was Frederick A. Delano, uncle of future president Franklin D. Roosevelt. With aid from Texas Rangers, Delano and other leaders invoked law and order. In a few years oil yields diminished, and the jail, theaters, dance halls, and gambling houses vanished. By 1929 only 100 inhabitants remained. By 1931 the bridge was down. The post office closed in 1935. Afterward the site of the makeshift oil "capital" reverted to range and agricultural uses. (1977)

BURKBURNETT (Wichita Co.) SH 240 at FM 368, 3 mi. W
Northwest Extension Oilfield
Oil exploration and production in this area was minimal until April 17, 1919, when the Bob Waggoner Well No. 1 blew in at 4,800 barrels per day. It was the first well in what became known as the Northwest Extension Oilfield, comprised of approximately 27 square miles on the former S. Burk Burnett Wild Horse Ranch. R. M. "Bob" Waggoner's well led to a boom, and the area was suddenly thick with oil derricks. The hastily organized tent cities of Thrift, Springtown, Morgan City, Waggoner City, Bridgetown and Bradley's Corner supported the industry. Today, sparsely sited pump jacks continue to draw oil, but in far smaller quantities than the early wells of Wichita County. (2006)

BURKBURNETT (Wichita Co.) Loop 267 W of IH 44
Burkburnett ("Boomtown, U.S.A.," 1 mi. SW)
One of the most famous Texas boom towns. Name was given to post office at request of President T. R. Roosevelt after his 1905 wolf hunt with rancher Burk Burnett in this area. Townsite was laid

out in 1907 by Joseph A. Kemp and Frank Kell, surveyors and promoters of Wichita Falls & Northwestern Railroad. First oil discovery was Chris Schmoker No. 1, in 1912. A 2200-barrel gusher was brought in on S. L. Fowler farm about a mile from this site, July 29, 1918, by a company formed by Fowler, his brother, W. D. Cline, and J. I. Staley. In 3 months 200 wells had been completed in Burkburnett townsite—a forest of derricks. Money and oil flowed freely. A bank capitalized at $25,000 got monthly revenue of $10,000 from a well drilled at its back door. The town's population jumped from 1500 to 15,000 in a year. Boom area was extended by finds on properties of Burk-Waggoner Company and by Kelly-Allen operations to the southwest. Town was made world famous in 1941 by the movie "Boomtown," filmed from a popular story entitled "Lady Comes to Burkburnett." Economy is dependent on agriculture and oil. An important neighbor is Sheppard Air Force Base.   (1966)

BURKBURNETT (Wichita Co.)   *Loop 267 at IH 44*
The Red River
Named for the red soil across which it flows; the main stream is 1,360 miles long, and for 440 miles the river forms the Texas-Oklahoma boundary. For years this was an international boundary. The 1819 treaty with Spain established the course of the Red River to the 100th meridian as part of the boundary between the United States and New Spain. Until after the 1845 annexation of Texas, this river did not lie entirely within the United States. During the colonial period, the waterway and the crossing here became a main gateway into Texas. In the mid-19th century, brisk steamer traffic went on at eastern end of the river. A military expedition under Capt. Randolph B. Marcy in 1852 explored the Red to its upper reaches in land held by wild Indians. In 1921, the Burkburnett oil boom here led to a dispute between Texas and Oklahoma over ownership of the valuable river bed. The Supreme Court in 1921 and 1923 upheld the south bank as the Texas border. This site is 25 miles west of important old Fort Sill crossing on the major military road that once linked the Oklahoma fort to outposts on the Texas frontier. The bridge here, opened to traffic in 1927, is the second free bridge to span the Red River.   (1968)

BURKE (Angelina Co.)   *US 59 at CR 59D*
Burke Methodist Church
Founded in 1889 by a small group of Methodists, this church has played an integral role in the history of the community. H. and Nannie Belote donated land to the congregation in 1894, and the first church building was completed in 1901. It was moved to another section of church property in 1920 and was remodeled in 1940 to serve the needs of the growing membership. A new brick sanctuary and educational building were completed in 1957. Burke Methodist Church has served the community with a variety of worship, educational, and outreach programs.   (1991)

BURKEVILLE (Newton Co.)   *SH 87, 8 mi. NW*
The Old Beef Road
Early 19th century trade routes across the Sabine River were few, and served all travelers and traders. The Beef Road, which replaced earlier "Zavala Road," was an important route by 1840, crossing this area. Named for cattle trade, it began in Huntsville and Liberty regions, and ran through Zavala, Jasper, and into present Newton County, where it forked near this site, forming three routes. The northern fork, to Natchitoches, crossed the Sabine at Bevil's Ferry (later Haddon's); the middle route, to Alexandria, led to Hickman's Ferry (later Burr's). The southern branch, to Opelousas, crossed at New Columbia. The cattle were corraled at night in "Beef Pens," located at points along the trails, including Weeks' Chapel and Toledo. During Civil War, the Beef Road was an important supply artery to the Confederate states, until the Federal Army gained control of the Mississippi River in July 1863. This halted the eastern cattle drives. Sabine River crossings were fortified against attack, as the roads would be a necessity for an invading force, but the expected invasion never came. Railroad expansion into Kansas, in the later 1860s, diverted the cattle drives to the north, and led to decline of Beef Road as a major cattle trade route.   (1973)

BURKEVILLE (Newton County)   *SH 87, 7 mi. N*
The Survey Community
William Williams, an early 1800s Sabine Valley pioneer, obtained a large land grant in 1834 from the Republic of Mexico. His surveyed land attracted settlers, who called the location "The Survey."

In 1847, Wade H. Mattox (1800–1863) built the first frame house in the settlement, using lumber hauled from Alexandria, La., by a neighbor, Ezekiel Cobb (1825–1864). By the 1850s, The Survey had settlers named Booker, Bush, Dade, Clark, Collins, Conner, Droddy, Garlington, Hardy, Joiner, Jones, McGee, Mitchell, Smith, Trotti, and Weeks. The economy was based on farming and (later) lumbering. At least 16 Survey community residents fought for the Confederacy in the Civil War (1861–1865). In 1889, the Methodists built a church on land given by Mr. and Mrs. J. W. Mattox. The building was also used for school purposes. Surveyville post office, opened in 1903, was soon renamed "Mayflower." Population shifts starting in the 1940s caused the school to consolidate with Burkeville (1949), the post office to close (1951), and the church to disband (1961). Public facilities, including the church building, Mattox cemetery, and several other burial grounds, are now maintained by the Survey Cemetery Association. (1975)

BURKEVILLE (Newton Co.) *SH 63, 11 mi. NE near Sabine River Bridge*
Site of Old Burr's Ferry (At Highway Bridge)
An important communications point between Texas and the United States, especially during settlement era of early 1800s. Named for Dr. Timothy Burr (1790–1852), second cousin of U.S. Vice President Aaron Burr. Dr. Burr is said to have come to the Sabine area in 1809, but moved his family down from Ohio in 1820s. He practiced medicine from home plantation on the Sabine. Family operated the ferry in the 1840s. Town of Burr's Ferry grew up on east side of the river. This crossing (earlier called Hickman's Ferry) gave pioneers the means to enter Texas with their stock, household goods, and other property. It was one of four main points of entry on Texas-Louisiana border. Besides the famous El Camino Real (King's Highway) from Natchitoches, other entry roads were the "upper" route, from present-day Shreveport; "lower" route, from Opelousas; and this one, called "The Old Beef Trail" because it was used to drive thousands of cattle from Texas to Alexandria for shipment to such cities as New Orleans, as early as the 1820s and '30s. This crossing was considered strategic in 1860s, during the Civil War. Breastworks were built on east bank, and timber cleared here on west bank in effort to guard against Federal invasions. (1968)

BURKEVILLE (Newton Co.) *SH 63 W of SH 87*
Blum Male and Female College (200 ft. NW)
Chartered February 26, 1880, by 36 incorporators; named for Leon Blum, Galveston merchant, largest holder in $20,000 capital stock—$5 per share. First directors were: R. J. Brailsford, H. J. Casey, W. W. Downs, W. A. Droddy, T. W. Ford, M. D. Hines; first president was Joseph Syler. Pupils ranged in age from 5 to 50 years; those under 12 met in downstairs of 2-story building; older pupils and adults met upstairs. Average enrollment per term was 100 resident and boarding pupils. School "took up" at 8 a.m.; closed at 4:30 p.m. Students entered and left school by lining up—boys on one side and girls on the other—a division which continued inside the school room. Lessons were recited on a recitation bench; all tests were oral, often an occasion for community gathering. Subjects offered besides the 3 r's were: philosophy, Latin, grammar, algebra, history, geometry, rhetoric, and geography. Friday afternoons were devoted to spelling matches, recitations. A well in school yard furnished water; most students brought lunch from home in a tin bucket which was covered with a lid ventilated by nail holes. Soon was called Burkeville School, and after expiration of college charter on February 20, 1905, the building served that purpose until torn down in 1912.

BURKEVILLE (Newton Co.) *SH 63 at SH 87, 1 mi. S*
First Courthouse of Newton County
County organized in 1846; Seat of Justice not established until two years later by public subscription. A building was erected here in 1848 on land donated by John R. Burke for whom the town received its name. Newton became the county seat in 1853. (1936)

BURNET (Burnet Co.) *US 281, 1.7 mi. N*
Burnet County
Formed from portions of Travis, Williamson and Bell counties. Created Feb. 5, 1852; organized August 28, 1852. Named in honor of David G. Burnet (1788–1870), president of the Provisional Government of the Republic of Texas in 1836. County seat, Burnet, famous for its granite mountains. (1936)

BURNET (Burnet Co.) *US 281, 1 mi. S*
Magill Family Cemetery
Surrounded by a rock wall, the small pioneer family cemetery just west of this site is located on land that was once part of the William H. Magill homestead. Magill, a veteran of the Battle of San Jacinto, moved his family to Burnet County in 1850. He established this graveyard with the burial of his 15-year-old son, John, in 1863. The remaining four marked graves include William H. Magill (1813–1878); his second wife, Elizabeth (1831–1914); and his parents, Nancy (1792–1865) and Samuel (1783–1865) Magill. At least one unmarked grave is known to exist. (1985)

BURNET (Burnet Co.) *PR 4, 5 mi. W of US 281S*
Longhorn Caverns
Rich in history and folklore, a young geologic formation only a few million years old. Bones of elephant, bison, bear, are found here. When white men came to area in 1840s, Indians knew the caverns: Rangers once found and rescued a kidnapped girl from Indians in the "Council Room." During the Civil War (1861–1865), gunpowder was manufactured and stored here. In 1870s outlaws, including the Sam Bass Gang, sometimes lived in the cavern. It was the site of a night club in the 1920s and has many unique features. It was opened to the public in 1932. (1967)

BURNET (Burnet Co.) *SH 29, approx. 1 mi. E*
Airy Mount Barn
Kentucky native Adam Rankin Johnson (1834–1922) came to Texas in 1854. After attaining the rank of brigadier general in the Confederate Army, Johnson later settled in Burnet County where he was active in business and civic affairs. In 1882, he donated land for the railroad that carried Burnet County granite for the Texas State Capitol. This stone barn, on the homestead he called "Airy Mount," was built in the early 1880s and remained in the Johnson family until 1915. (1986)

BURNET (Burnet Co.) *SH 29, .2 mi. W*
Site of Fort Croghan
Established by Lieut. C. H. Tyler, United States Second Dragoons, by order of the War Department, March 18, 1849, as protection to frontier settlers against hostile Indians. Abandoned in December, 1853 as the settlements had extended farther west. (1964)

BUSHLAND (Potter Co.) *IH 40, 1 mi. E in roadside park*
Tecovas Springs
Located 6 miles northwest of this marker. Favorite campsite of prehistoric Indians, and of later traders, military parties and hunters, from time of 18th century Spanish explorations. Meeting place of 19th century Plains Indians with traders, smugglers and the renegade peddlers called comancheros. Summer range home ground of Mexican shepherds before the cowmen came in the 1870s. Since 1881, location of the headquarters of the Frying Pan, ranch started by J. F. Glidden and Henry S. Sanborn, inventors and promoters of barbed wire. (1964)

BUTLER (Freestone Co.) *US 84 at FM 489, 1.7 mi. E*
Butler Soldiers' Homes, C.S.A.
Commissioners courts in Texas usually furnished to soldiers enlisting in the Civil War their uniforms, guns, blankets—and sometimes even their horses. The county courts also aided dependents, war orphans and widows. Further, they recognized local people who had "soldiers' homes," and reimbursed them for meals given men en route to and from the army on furloughs and special missions. Freestone County had at least 11 soldiers' homes. Near this site, one of 2 in Butler was run by Hillary Manning, a plantation owner. A soldiers' home usually was set up as an act of neighborliness. The Rev. Thomas Castleton, who lived near Houston, organized many homes. Also he commended the people of Butler, Fairfield, Goliad and Hillsboro for setting up soldiers' homes of their own accord. At Christmas in 1864, Rev. Castleton received for the benefit of the soldiers donations of $4100 in gold, 3 beef animals and 2 milk cows, gifts of private citizens supporting the work. He also was given a 3-story brick hotel to be used as a soldiers' home. Other soldiers' homes were at Columbus, Crockett, Palestine and Richmond (Fort Bend County) like many other productive activities carried on voluntarily. These homes showed the concern of Texas for her men. (1965)

BYNUM (Hill Co.)   *SH 171 at school grounds*
Bynum School
The first school in Old Bynum Community began in 1880 before the settlement had a name. After a store and a post office were built, the area adopted its name from a nearby creek. The school was moved to the new townsite on the railroad in 1905, and an independent school district was organized. Over the years, the following schools consolidated with Bynum: Davis, GroveCreek, part of Honest Ridge, Pecan, Pierce (1905–1914); Watson (1931); Massey, McMurry (1938); Brandon (1953); and Irene (1958). The school now is a historic reminder of the region's heritage. (1984)

CADDO (Stephens Co.)   *US 180 at FM 717*
Caddo
The 1860 census reported fewer than 200 residents in Stephens County. That year, Joe Schoolcraft settled on Caddo Creek, 15 miles south of a Caddo Indian village. He built his home on the north bank of Caddo Creek at Elm Creek. The town grew during the next decade, and in 1876, local ranchers began recording their brands at the courthouse. Early settlers included Jere Hart, C.J. Johnson, A.W. Corbett, Tom Thompson, W.B. Richardson, William Copeland, John Robinson and Josephus Knott, as well as the Graceys, Swensons, McMeens, Lees and Winstons. Perry K. Taylor opened a store in 1875. Shortly thereafter, R.Q. Lee and the Butlers opened "the Big Red Store," which became Sandidge, Lee & Co. in 1906. The Caddo post office opened in 1877. In 1883, the town hired Dora Mandy as the first schoolteacher. A two-story structure was built in 1890 and was used for school, church and Masonic lodge meetings; it burned in 1910, and residents then built a red brick and rock schoolhouse on Caddo Creek. The first physician came in 1886, and the town's early doctors included a woman named Dr. Evans. Local churches organized in the 1890s; the Baptist congregation built its sanctuary in 1894. Early settler Tom Lay hauled water to local residents, who also had access to telephone service in 1898. Cattle, horses, sheep and cotton were the mainstay of the town until 1916, when the first oil well came in. In 1919, Caddo led the state in oil production. The boom, which attracted thousands of new residents and numerous businesses, lasted until the early 1920s. By World War II, the population had declined. The last class of maroon and white Caddo Cougars graduated in 1945; the town consolidated its school with Breckenridge. Highway construction bypassed the town in the 1950s, and Caddo's population continued to decrease. Fewer than 50 people lived in the town in 2000, most relying on agriculture and oil.
(2002)

CALDWELL (Burleson Co.)   *SH 21, 10 mi. NE between FM 50*
                                                                and Brazos River Bridge
Moseley's Ferry
Situated where the Old San Antonio Road crossed the Brazos River, this public ferry was begun by Michael Boren (1806–1875) about 1846. The ferry and a settlement nearby were named for Daniel Moseley (1787–1856), who took over the service in 1849 and whose family ran it until 1868. Other ferrymen continued to transport travelers, livestock, and freight across the river until 1912, when the Houston & Texas Central (now the Southern Pacific) constructed a railroad bridge at this location. Today a highway bridge spans the Brazos where Moseley's Ferry once operated.
(1975)

CALDWELL (Burleson Co.)   *SH 21, 5 mi. E in roadside park*
"Dream Capital of Texas" Fort Tenoxtitlan
(Site about 8 mi. NE)
Founded by Mexico as a bulwark against Anglo-American immigration, this fort and its nearby city were twice proposed for the capital of Texas. Alarmed by the influx of Anglo settlers into Texas, Mexico in 1830 sought to erect a line of forts to keep out the intruders. The ancient Aztec name for Mexico City (originally pronounced "Ten-Ox-Teet-Lan") was given this site; it means "Prickly Pear Place." So hopeful of the fort's success was the military commandant of the region that he envisioned it as the capital of Texas. But Anglo immigration did not cease. Instead it thrived on the friendship of the local soldiers and incoming pioneers. The colonizer Sterling C. Robertson introduced scores of settlers. In 1832, the soldiers were withdrawn and the fort finally defaulted to the Anglos. Subsequently it was a supply center and mustering point for expeditions against the Indians. During its brief life many Texas patriots lived here, including 5 signers of the Texas Dec-

laration of Independence, a martyr of the Alamo siege, and 7 soldiers of the Battle of San Jacinto. Tenoxtitlan was again suggested for the capital of Texas during the Republic, but Austin won out. In 1841, after many Indian raids, the site was abandoned. (1970)

CALDWELL (Burleson Co.)
SH 21, 5 mi. E in roadside park
One Mile North to Site of Elizabeth Chapel Methodist Church
First Methodist church in the county. Began as Sunday school in home of Isaac Addison, early settler. Later moved to home of Mrs. Elizabeth Scott. Organized about 1839 by Robt. Alexander, famous pioneer minister. Soon a small, hand-hewn frame building was erected and named for Mrs. Scott. Land containing both the church and cemetery was given to Methodist Episcopal Church, south, by Mrs. Scott's son, Philip, in 1878. Membership reached peak of 165 in 1885. Church merged with the Cooks Point Church about 1907. (1970)

CALDWELL (Burleson Co.)
SH 21, 5 mi. E
Cooks Point United Methodist Church
This congregation began in 1881 to serve the German speaking population in the area. Organized largely through the efforts of Anna Duewall, who had come to Burleson County with her family in 1880, the fellowship originally was known as the German Methodist Church, Caldwell. The Rev. Jacob Ott served as first pastor. Worship services were held in the members' homes until a sanctuary was built in 1883. The congregation adopted the name Cooks Point in the 1940s and continues to play an important role in the surrounding rural area. (1984)

CALDWELL (Burleson Co.)
SH 21, 4 mi. E
Duewall House
Rudolph and Anna Duewall established a family farm here in the 1880s upon moving to Burleson County. Their son Edward (1885–1944) and his wife, Lizzie (Herrmann) (1890–1947), continued the farm operations. In 1928, they built this house on the site of the original Duewall House to accommodate their family of six children. Carpenter Otto Berndt used materials from the first farmhouse and from the second Burleson County courthouse in the home's construction. The vernacular farmhouse features exposed rafters and a cross-gabled roof. (2001)

CALDWELL (Burleson Co.)
SH 21 E just outside city limits
City of Caldwell
Founded 1840 by Lewis L. Chiles, a veteran of Battle of San Jacinto. Named for Mathew "Old Paint" Caldwell, Indian fighter and signer of the Texas Declaration of Independence. This was county seat, Milam County, in 1845; since 1846 county seat of Burleson County. Home, Burleson County Fair. (1967)

CALDWELL (Burleson Co.)
SH 21 at SH 36
Burleson County
Farmed early as 1744 by Indians under guidance of Spanish missionaries. In 1830, Ft. Tenoxtitlan, guarding Brazos crossing, San Antonio Road, attracted Anglo-Texans, who lived off wild game in early years. County created and organized in 1846. Named for Gen. Edward Burleson (1798–1851), veteran of Battle of San Jacinto; Indian fighter; Republic of Texas vice-president and senator; later a state senator. County seat, Caldwell (named for Mathew Caldwell, signer of Declaration of Independence). During the Civil War, furnished troops, cotton and food to Confederate Texas. (1965)

CALDWELL (Burleson Co.)
SH 21, 8 mi. SW in roadside park
John Mitchell
Born in Tennessee c. 1836–37, John Mitchell came to Texas in 1846. He began purchasing land in this area in 1870, the same year he married Viney Cox. As a member of both the 12th and 14th Legislatures, Mitchell championed increased educational opportunities for African Americans. Elected as a delegate to the 1875 Constitutional Convention, he defended the policies of Gov. Davis and was one of 11 members to vote against adoption of the new constitution, which ultimately marked the end of reconstruction in Texas. John Mitchell returned to Burleson County as a farmer and rancher, and donated land for a church and school that bore his name. Upon his death in 1921, he was buried in a family graveyard. (2002)

CALDWELL (Burleson Co.)
SH 21, 8 mi. W
An Arm of the Chisholm Cattle Trail
The Chisholm Trail, which was developed following the Civil War, allowed Texas cattle to be driven to railheads in Kansas for shipment to eastern markets. An arm of the celebrated route, reaching from Matagorda County to the main trail near present McGregor, passed through this area. With the establishment of James L. Dean's store, later the site of Deanville, and the White Inn, the trail became a significant commercial road. Vital to the development of Burleson County's cattle industry, it declined in use after rail lines reached the area in the late 1870s.   (1981)

CALDWELL (Burleson Co.)
SH 21, 9.4 mi. SW at rest area
Site of El Camino Real (The Old San Antonio Road)
Great thoroughfare of early Texas. Following ancient Indian and buffalo paths, sometimes on same course as 1691 "Trail of the Padres," stretches 1,000 miles from Saltillo, Mexico, to present Louisiana. Highway for explorers, traders, smugglers, adventurers, settlers, armies. Was surveyed about 1800 and given name of "King's Highway." Here, as in some other areas, the modern highway follows historic El Camino Real. Also, in this particular area, El Camino Real marked boundary between the major early 19th century colonies of Stephen F. Austin and Sterling C. Robertson.   (1968)

CALLIHAM (McMullen Co.)
SH 72, in Choke Canyon Lake Park
First Producing Gas Well in McMullen County and
First Gas Pipeline to San Antonio
(South of Frio River, 1 mi. NE)
Thirty years before the first producing gas well was drilled in this county, traces of salt water, sulphur, gas, and oil in water wells gave hints of the presence of petroleum here. For years wildcat drilling went on, but with only moderate success. Then in 1908, a well on Charles Byrne's land began to blow warm sulphur water and gas 120 feet into the air every 8 days, arousing much interest. After this discovery, Byrne, a promoter, set out to locate capitalists to develop his petroleum deposits. Armed with a picture of the gusher and a bottle of area oil, he attracted the attention of W. M. "Bee" Stephenson, his sons Light and Donald, and others. The well they drilled here in 1917–1918, on the Tom Brown tract, blew in at 816 feet with 62,000,000 cubic feet of natural gas a day, but for 3 months it spewed out of control because of the intense subsurface pressure and inadequate equipment. After other producers were drilled, W. M. Stephenson arranged to pipe gas to San Antonio, 68 miles north, in 1922. Among those joining this enterprise was H. A. Pagenkopf, a Wichita Falls oil man. Thus, petroleum took a leading role in the economy of McMullen County.   (1970)

CALVERT (Robertson Co.)
SH 6, 6 mi. N
Site of Extinct Town of Hammond
Dr. Ben F. Hammond moved here from Alabama in 1853 and built a plantation home about a mile to the west. Neighbors included James Love and Robert S. McCall. Hammond depot and post office were opened at this point on the Houston & Texas Central Railroad after the doctor granted right-of-way through his land in 1869. Near the depot, used by planters for their shipping, were a few stores. As the railroad declined, the town had vanished by 1950. Area residents are mostly the descendants of persons given land at emancipation (1865) by Dr. Hammond and other planters.   (1976)

CALVERT (Robertson Co.)
SH 6, 5 mi. N
Site of Harvey Massacre (1 mi. W)
At this site one Sunday night in November 1836, the family of John Harvey was attacked by an Indian raiding party. Harvey, his wife, and son were all killed, Mrs. Harvey's blood staining the open pages of the family Bible. Their daughter Ann, aged 5, and a servant girl were taken captive, later to be sold as slaves. The price of Ann was a few blankets. After four years in Mexico, Ann was recovered by her uncle, James Talbot of Alabama. In 1848 she wed Sanders Briggs and in 1853 they moved to Texas, where they built a home—ironically—near the site of the massacre. (1972)

CALVERT (Robertson Co.)
Main St. (SH 6) at Hanna St.
Home Area of Chinese Farmers
Imported from Asia about 1874 to help in cotton fields, these exotic workers wore queues and attracted much notice. At least 24 families were brought here; many became permanent residents, respected for their good work. Over 25 ethnic groups settled in Texas—many having preceded the

Chinese. Other than American Indians, first permanent Texas settlers were cattle raisers from the Canary Islands. Other migrant groups included Cuban cigar makers and European lace makers. Given new opportunities, their descendants now are in industry, business, professions.   (1968)

CAMERON (Milam Co.)   *US 77, 1.8 mi. N*
Milam County
A part of Robertson's Colony in 1834, a part of the Municipality of Viesca, 1835. Name changed to Milam December 21, 1835 in honor of Benjamin Rush Milam, 1788–1835, who fell at San Antonio. After Burleson and Robertson Counties were cut off, Nashville became the county seat in 1837. The later creation of Williamson, Bell, McLennan and Falls, reduced Milam County to its present size. Cameron, the county seat since 1846.

CAMERON (Milam Co.)   *US 190/77, 1.6 mi. E*
Steamboat *Washington* Landed Here
In the winter of 1850–1851 with Captain Basil M. Hatfield, Commander, the steamboat *Washington* landed here with a shipment of merchandise from Washington-on-the-Brazos to J. W. McCown and Co., merchants at Cameron. The first, last and only steamboat to navigate Little River.

CAMERON (Milam Co.)   *US 190 at Lamar in city park*
Site of First Home in Cameron
Boyhood home of L. S. "Sul" Ross (1838–1898), Texas governor from 1887 to 1891. His father Shapley P. Ross, Indian agent and Ranger, built the house after moving here about 1841; he chose this site because it had a good spring. L. S. Ross, who was a Confederate general, served as president of Texas A.&M. College after holding office as governor. In 1890 this pavilion was erected to accommodate band concerts, meetings, and rallies. It was the scene in 1892 of a landmark debate between two gubernatorial candidates: Gov. James S. Hogg and George Clark.   (1969)

CAMP VERDE (Kerr Co.)   *SH 173 at FM 480*
Camp Verde General Store and Post Office
Mercantile business opened 1857 as Williams Community Store, serving trade around Camp Verde Army Post (site of U.S. War Department's 1857–1869 camel experiment). Post office opened in 1887.   (1971)

CAMP WOOD (Real Co.)   *SH 55, 4 mi. N*
Private Frank Marshall, C.S.A.
Buried here, 3/10 mi. from Camp Wood. A 29-year-old Harrison Countian, symbolizes Texans who died for the Confederacy in the Arizona-New Mexico campaign. Served from April 19, 1861, till death June 16, in W. P. Lane Rangers in second front stretched from San Antonio to Santa Fe. Frontier posts at Camp Wood, Ft. Inge, Ft. Clark, Camp Hudson, Howard Spring and Ft. Lancaster supported the 1861–1862 campaign to make the Confederacy an ocean-to-ocean nation. Combat forces included such Texans as Tom Green, Wm. R. Scurry, W. P. Hardeman and Wm. Steele, all later to be generals in the Confederate Army. Green and Scurry commanded troops that won battle of Valverde in Feb. 1862. This victory and others enabled the Confederacy to occupy Arizona and New Mexico and hope to gain California. However, Texas troops found their lines too long and supplies an impossible problem. With scanty food, no blankets, no means of transportation, the army limped back to Texas. On reaching San Antonio, troops hid near the Menger Hotel, pooled their rags to dress one man, then sent out for clothes to cover them so they could go home. Yet these same men re-grouped and won many victories later in the Civil War.   (1965)

CAMP WOOD (Real Co.)   *SH 55, .5 mi. N*
Site of Camp Wood
Established May 20, 1857, as a means of preventing Indian raids on the San Antonio–El Paso route and the Rio Grande Valley. Abandoned March 15, 1861, when Federal troops were withdrawn from Texas.

CAMP WOOD (Real Co.)   *SH 55, .3 mi. N*
Site of the Mission San Lorenzo de la Santa Cruz
Founded by Franciscan missionaries among Lipan Apache Indians in 1762. Abandoned in 1769.   (1936)

CAMP WOOD (Real Co.)   *SH 55, Lindbergh Park*
Charles A. Lindbergh in Texas
Texas was important in the career of Charles A. Lindbergh (1902–1974). When he bought his first W. W. I surplus Jenny in Georgia, he flew it to Texarkana in 1923 so he could say he had flown in Texas, the ambition of every barnstormer. With Leon Klink, in March 1924 he landed Klink's Canuck in Camp Wood while trying to fly to California. Next day in attempting to take off, he accidentally crashed into Warren Pruett's store. No one was hurt and his offer to pay for the damage was rejected. Then called "Slim," Lindbergh made many friends here. Two weeks after visiting Camp Wood, he became a U.S. Air Service Cadet at Brooks Field, San Antonio. He completed advanced flight training at Kelly Field in 1925. On May 20–21, 1927, he made the first solo flight from New York to Paris, to world acclaim. Later in 1927, he returned to Texas, surveying the first commercial transcontinental air-route through Amarillo; in 1929 he inaugurated U.S.-Mexico air mail in Brownsville. A great aviation pioneer, he drew up and proved many major air routes. He flew combat in World War II, collaborated in medical research, helped organize the Berlin Airlift, and remained a hero to the people of Camp Wood, Texas.

CANADIAN (Hemphill Co.)   *US 60/83, 1.7 mi. NE*
Site of Old Springer's Road Ranch (12.2 mi. E)
First post office in Hemphill County. Unique for tunnel from dugout home-store to corral. On 1870s trail from Ft. Elliott (35 mi. SW) to Ft. Supply, Ind. Terr., to Ft. Dodge, Kans. Established by A. G. Springer; besides running 300 head of cattle, Springer's was a stagecoach stand, tavern; store (mainly for teamster, hunters) had liquor, canned goods, hunting equipment. Poker-expert Springer was frequent host to soldiers seeking entertainment in tavern. In 1877, he and Tom Ledbetter, his partner, were killed in gun battle with angered soldiers, and were buried at the ranch.   (1967)

CANADIAN (Hemphill Co.)   *SH 60/83 just N of Washita River*
Gen. Nelson Miles' Expedition
(Headquarters Dugout, 2.3 Mi. W, on Washita River)
Indian raids brought Miles' men to Texas from north in 1874 as part of U.S. Army pincers' tactic operating from a dugout post. The 12 infantry and cavalry units had supply camps on the Canadian, Red and Washita Rivers. On Nov. 8, 1874, Miles' troops recovered three captive German sisters; fought 8 Indian battles during winter. At this post Gen. Miles nominated for medal of honor several of his men—among them renowned Panhandle settler, Billy Dixon. In 1875, Ft. Elliott was opened at Old Mobeetie to continue frontier protection.   (1967)

CANADIAN (Hemphill Co.)   *US 60/83, .25 mi. N in roadside park*
Hemphill County
Formed from Young and Bexar Territories. Created August 21, 1876; organized July 5, 1886. Named in honor of John Hemphill, 1809–1862, First Chief Justice of the Supreme Court of the State of Texas, Adjutant General of the Somervell Expedition, Member of the first State Constitutional Convention, Member of the United States Congress. Canadian, the county seat.   (1936)

CANADIAN (Hemphill Co.)   *US 60/83, .25 mi. N in roadside park*
Canadian River Trail
Trade, exploration and hunting trails along the Canadian are older than recorded history—old when used 1541 by Spaniard Coronado hunting Golden Cities of Cibola. Route in 1840 for Josiah Gregg and 34 Missouri men with goods worth $25,000 headed for trade in Santa Fe. Used by 1849 parties escorted by U.S. Army Captain R. B. Marcy on way to California Gold Rush. Hunters, cattlemen, settlers used Canadian River trails in 1870s and '80s, as Panhandle was opened to civilization. River's name, "Canadian," came from Spanish for "boxed-in."   (1966)

CANADIAN (Hemphill Co.)   *US 60/83, .25 mi. N at roadside park*
Robert R. Young (February 14, 1897–January 25, 1958)
A leader in America's finance and transportation. Born here, in house built by lawyer Temple Houston, son of Republic of Texas President Sam Houston. His grandfather was traildriver, pioneer rancher; his father, president of the first bank in Canadian. Educated at old Canadian Academy, Culver Military Academy (where he won highest honors), University of Virginia. Married, 1916, Anita O'Keeffe, sister of the famous painter Georgia O'Keeffe. Had a daughter. One of close friends was

King Edward VIII of England. Assistant to treasurer of General Motors, 1920s. Made fortune in stock market in 1929. After years on Wall Street, won acclaim of financial world in a proxy battle to gain control of and modernize New York Central Railroad. In this fight, enlisted aid of Texas friends Clint Murchison and Sid Richardson. Until 1939, retained banking interests in Canadian. Was a lifelong member of Presbyterian Church here. Remembered native state with gifts of rare papers to University of Texas. Restored an historic local burial ground, naming it "Edith Ford Cemetery," to honor an aunt who reared him after early death of his mother. Maintained close ties (in visits, hunting trips, correspondence) with people known in boyhood.

CANADIAN (Hemphill Co.)
US 60/83, 6.5 mi. S
58 yds. W to Routes of Historic Trails
During the mass slaughter of buffaloes in the Panhandle, 2 trails arose to meet the needs of the hunters and their ever-hungry markets. Started about 1876, both moved vast convoys of wagons across the plains. Charles Rath—transporting gun powder, lead, tobacco, whiskey and food staples—blazed a road from Dodge City to the Double Mountains. In 2 years, however, the best hunting was over and the route fell into disuse. Ed Jones and Joe Plummer forged a trail from Kansas to Ft. Elliot. Their route became a freight road and finally a cattle trail. (1969)

CANADIAN (Hemphill Co.)
US 60/83, 7.9 mi. S
Route of Marcy Trail
This overland route, blazed in 1849 by energetic and efficient army Captain R. B. Marcy, was best known as part of the California Gold Trail. Starting in Oklahoma, Marcy led an expedition across the Texas Panhandle and back through Central West Texas. Both of the wagon roads he laid out served the emigrant traffic. In 1853 this section was planned as part of the route for the first transcontinental railroad in America, but the Civil War shifted sentiment to northern routes. Its importance declined after the railroad came through this county, 1887. (1969)

CANADIAN (Hemphill Co.)
SH 33, 10 mi. E of US 60/83, 7 mi. S
Site of Lyman's Wagon Train Battle (2.5 mi. S, 1.7 mi. E)
During the U.S. Army campaigns in 1874 against marauding Indians, Capt. Wyllys Lyman led a wagon train to Camp Supply, Okla., for rations for Gen. Nelson A. Miles' troops on duty in Texas. On the way, Indians attacked, and the longest Indian battle in Panhandle history ensued. Fighting from a wagon corral Sept. 9 to 14 Lyman and 95 soldiers held off about 400 Comanche and Kiowa Indians. A scout escaped and reached Camp Supply for help. Company K, 6th Cavalry, traveled 80 miles without rest in a raging rainstorm to aid the wagon train. On its arrival, the Indians fled. (1967)

CANADIAN (Hemphill Co.)
US 60, 17 mi. SW
Fossil Beds (3 mi. SE)
Cited as one of most prolific fossil fields of Lower Pliocene Age at time of discovery, these beds are about 13,000,000 years old. Geologists of Rio Bravo Oil Company found them in 1928 on C. C. Coffee ranch, and their reports brought specialists from several major institutions to the area. The fossil bones buried here included (among others) those of a prehistoric camel, a kind of antelope, horse, bone-crushing dog, mastodon, and wild pig. Further studies led scientists in 1941 to adopt "Hemphillian" as the name for the geologic age represented by these fossils. (1970)

CANTON (Van Zandt Co.)
SH 64 at county courthouse
Cadwell Walton Raines (September 18, 1839–August 2, 1906)
Born in Georgia, Raines came to Texas in 1858. After serving in Gen. R. M. Gano's Texas Cavalry Regiment in the Civil War, he was a teacher in New Braunfels and a lawyer in Canton. Van Zandt County judge from 1876 to 1878, he played a major role in the infamous County Seat War of 1877. He published newspapers at Wills Point, Mineola, and Quitman, where he became Wood County judge and was appointed state librarian in 1891 by his friend Governor James Stephen Hogg. Raines rebuilt the neglected State Library and began its invaluable collection of Texana in 1895. (1998)

CANTON (Van Zandt Co.)
SH 64 at courthouse
Oran Milo Roberts (July 9, 1815–May 19, 1898)
A South Carolina-born Alabama legislator, Oran M. Roberts came to San Augustine, Texas in 1841. He served in district and state judicial positions, including the First District Court in Canton

in 1850, and was president of the Secession Convention in 1861. After service as a colonel in the 11th Regiment, Texas Infantry, his postwar career included a second turn as a state supreme court judge; he made the 1877 ruling that ended the Van Zandt County Seat War. Roberts was elected governor of Texas in 1878. He was a law professor at the new University of Texas until 1893. Roberts helped form the Texas State Historical Association in 1895.   (1998)

CANTON (Van Zandt Co.)   *City Lake Dr., 1 mi. E in City Park*
Dipping Vat
Before discovery of a dip (1894) and vaccine (1898), the American cattle industry faced ruin, as it lost $40 million annually from cattle tick fever. In 1918, tick eradication began in East Texas, with colorful, exciting "dipping days" enforced every two weeks from spring to fall. Sometimes citizens resented the compulsory dipping, and dynamited vats or held shootouts with authorities. This dipping vat is typical of 50 built in Van Zandt County. It was on property of G. M. Hilliard (1856–1931), pioneer rancher and merchant. His estate in 1968 sold this park site to city of Canton.   (1973)

CANTON (Van Zandt Co.)   *SH 64, 1 mi. SE*
Van Zandt County
A portion of the original Mercer Grant, created from Henderson County 1848. Named in honor of the illustrious statesman Isaac Van Zandt. Born in Tennessee, July 10, 1813. Delegate to the Annexation Convention in 1845. Died in Texas, October 10, 1847. Canton the county seat; Van, the oil field center; Grand Saline, famed for its salt industry.

CANTON (Van Zandt Co.)   *SH 19 at SH 64, 2 blks. N*
Hillcrest Cemetery
Located within the original 1850 town plat of Canton, this cemetery has served citizens of this area for well over a century. The oldest documented burial is that of Ann Calhoon (1807–1860). Among those buried here in marked and unmarked graves are Van Zandt County pioneers; veterans of the Civil War, World War I, and World War II; and business and community leaders. Serving as a reminder of Canton's pioneer heritage, the Hillcrest Cemetery is a reflection of the history of the town and its citizens.   (1990)

CANTON (Smith Co.)   *CR 4923, 2.5 mi. N of SH 64, 19 mi. SE*
On this Site the Cherokee Chief Bowles Was Killed
On July 16, 1839 while leading 800 Indians of various tribes in battle against 500 Texans. The last engagement between Cherokees and whites in Texas.

CANTON (Van Zandt Co.)   *SH 243, 8 mi E*
Shelby Expedition through Van Zandt County
Gen. Joseph O. Shelby's command refused to surrender at the close of the Civil War. Shelby's men, the First Missouri Cavalry of the Confederate States of America, marched via Clarksville to Van Zandt County, proceeding through Grand Saline to Canton and on to Stone Point soon after learning of Gen. Robert E. Lee's surrender. From about April 22 to May 29, 1865, Shelby's troops camped at Stone Point while their leader attended a Confederate conference at Marshall, Texas. Determined to continue the war, Shelby's men journeyed to Mexico, stopping where they were needed to enforce the peace in a ravaged postwar Texas.   (1998)

CANYON (Randall Co.)   *US 60/87, 1.5 mi. N on access road*
Randall County
Created 1876; named for Confederate General Horace Randall. Settled 1877 by rancher Leigh Dyer, brother-in-law of Chas. Goodnight, man who brought first cattle to Panhandle. Organized in 1889. County seat: Canyon, home of West Texas State University, Panhandle-Plains Historical Museum, Palo Duro State Park, Buffalo Lake.   (1965)

CANYON (Randall Co.)   *US 60/87, 1 mi. N*
Col. John I. Gregg 1872 Battle Site
The decade after 1865 was a time of transition for the U.S. Many citizens moved west, coming into conflict with Native American tribes living on the Great Plains. Settlers demanded the U.S. Army provide their protection. The Army responded by conducting campaigns against the Southern Plains Indians. In 1872, one such campaign included troops of the Eighth Cavalry commanded by

Colonel John I. Gregg, who departed from New Mexico into West Texas to locate Native American raiders. On August 16, his troops skirmished here with Kiowas, killing or injuring twelve while suffering one wounded. This and the Red River War (1874–75) led to the subjugation of Plains Indians and their confinement to reservations. (2006)

CANYON (Randall Co.) *SH 217, 12 mi. E at Palo Duro Canyon State Park*
The Battle of Palo Duro Canyon, September 28, 1874
One of the most significant battles of 1874–1875 Indian campaign; columns of troops converging from five directions harassed Indians on the Panhandle Plains for over six months. The 4th Cavalry under Col. Ranald S. Mackenzie, moving north from Fort Concho, tracked a large band of Indians to their secret canyon camp. Moving silently at dawn down a perilous path on the south rim, the first troops reached the floor of the canyon before the aroused camp fled. Some of the warriors took up positions on the canyon walls from which they fired on the troops, seeking to give their families time to escape. Realizing his tactical disadvantage, Mackenzie ordered the Indian camp and supplies burned and withdrew, taking along 1,400 captured horses (1,000 of which he later destroyed). The cavalry suffered no casualties in the fight and only four Indian dead were counted. Having lost half their horses as well as all their supplies and shelter, the Indians drifted back to their reservations at Fort Sill and Fort Reno. (1967)

CANYON (Randall Co.) *SH 217, 4 mi. E*
Francisco Vásquez De Coronado on the Texas Plains
On April 22, 1540, Francisco Vásquez de Coronado (1510–1554) set out from Culiacan (in present Sinaloa, Mexico) with an expedition of 1500 men to search for seven golden cities reported far to the north. Coronado entered the present United States in Arizona and proceeded northeast to the Rio Grande pueblos in New Mexico, where he spent the winter of 1540–1541. On April 23, 1541, Coronado left the Rio Grande, traveling eastward to seek the golden city of Quivira. A native guide called "El Turco" led the conquistadores aimlessly across the arid plains in an attempt to get them lost. On May 29, 1541, with supplies depleted, Coronado entered Palo Duro Canyon, where wild fruit and water abounded. While in the canyon, Coronado discovered the guide's betrayal. On June 2, Coronado selected 30 men and started northward in quest of Quivira. The rest of the expedition, under command of Tristan de Arellano, remained in the canyon for 2 weeks before returning to the Rio Grande. According to legend, Fray Juan de Padilla conducted a feast of thanksgiving for the group while in Palo Duro Canyon. In 1542, after failing to find the Seven Cities of Gold, Coronado returned to Mexico a broken man. (1973)

CANYON (Randall Co.) *SH 217, 4 mi. E*
Los Ciboleros (New Mexican Buffalo Hunters)
For centuries Pueblo Indians of present New Mexico trekked to the plains to hunt buffalo to supplement their diet of beans and corn. After acquiring horses from the Spanish in the 17th century, the annual trips were made more easily and with greater success. By the 19th century, the ciboleros (from "Cibolo"—Spanish for buffalo) became very important, providing food for the growing New Mexican population and hides for the rich Santa Fe-Chihuahua trade. Cibolero expeditions often included as many as 150 people. The daring cazadores (hunters), picturesque in leather jackets and flat straw hats, rode into the herds armed only with lances, killing 8 to 25 bison each in one foray, and depending on the speed, ability, and skill of their horses for safety. Others, including occasional women and children, cut meat into strip for drying and cured the hides for tanning. With their carts laden with fruits of the hunt, the ciboleros returned to New Mexico and a hero's welcome. The Plains Indians, protecting their hunting grounds, maintained constant warfare against the ciboleros throughout the 19th century, but the colorful lancers survived until Anglo-American hunters decimated the great buffalo herd in the late 1870s. (1973)

CANYON (Randall Co.) *SH 217, 1 mi. E of courthouse*
Site of an Early Barbed Wire Fence in the Panhandle
In the latter 1800s, when fencing was needed in the treeless Texas Panhandle, the solution proved to be barbed wire. Joseph F. Glidden of Illinois devised and by 1876 was manufacturing (with I. L. Ellwood) the first really practical barbed wire on the market. H. B. Sanborn was sent to Texas as their agent, and remained to become a builder of the Panhandle. Wanting free access to water and grass, ranchers at first resisted fencing. Cowboys disliked it, as fewer range riders were

needed on fenced lands. The old-timers grew bitter, because of blocked trails—herds had to be hauled rather than driven to market. Yet newcomers wanted fencing, in order to have use of land purchased for ranching. Merchants and city-builders wanted fences, to assure settlement. The T-Anchor, owned by Jot Gunter and Wm. B. Munson, real estate investors of Grayson County, built a line fence on this site in 1881, enclosing a 240,000-acre horse pasture. Also built in this area, by popular subscription, was a "drift" fence to hold cattle back from wandering south in blue northers and blizzards. Barbed wire gradually came into general use. It saved the cattle industry, because improvements in breeding and feeding were possible on fenced ranges.

CANYON (Randall Co.)   *4th Ave. (SH 217) at 25th St.*
Panhandle-Plains Museum
In 1932 the State of Texas matched $25,000 of private funds to construct the original unit. Since 1935 the museum, through Works Progress Administration projects, has increased its archeological and paleontological materials beyond the facilities of the building. An allocation of $25,000 was used to construct and equip a basement addition designed by Rittenberry and Carder, Architects, to provide ten thousand square feet of additional floor space. The museum is located on the campus of the West Texas State College and is operated by the Panhandle-Plains Historical Society.

CANYON (Randall Co.)   *E 4th Ave. (SH 217) at Panhandle-Plains Museum*
The Charles Goodnight Memorial Trail
The highway from this museum to the Palo Duro State Park (12 mi. E) approximates course used by Charles Goodnight, outstanding Texas cowman and trail blazer, when he trailed 1600 cattle from Colorado to found first ranch on the Staked Plains of Texas in 1876. He entered precipitous Palo Duro Canyon by way of Old Comanche Indian Trail; drove thousands of buffalo from what is now park area; established his home ranch a few miles farther down canyon. Goodnight was born in Illinois, March 5, 1836. At age of 9 he rode bareback to Texas behind covered wagon driven by his parents; he hunted with Caddo Indians beyond the frontier at 14; guided Texas Rangers fighting Comanche and Kiowas at 25; blazed cattle trails about 2,000 mi. long with Oliver Loving at 30. In partnership with John G. Adair, he expanded his original Palo Duro ranch into the giant JA and other holdings of more than a million acres and 100,000 cattle. He preserved the buffalo, founded a college, encouraged the settlement of the plains and led in a long fight for law and order. This foremost plainsman died March 12, 1929, and is buried at Goodnight, Texas.   (1968)

CANYON (Randall Co.)   *2401 4th Ave. at Panhandle Plains Museum*
T Anchor Ranch
In fall 1877, Leigh and Walter Dyer and Samuel Coleman drove about 400 cattle to Spring Draw and built a two-room log cabin. The firm of Gunter, Munson & Summerfield bought their claim, and in 1880–81, cowboys built line camps and corrals and fenced 240,000 acres—the area's first use of barbed wire. In 1882, sixteen cowboys and 125 horses herded more than 10,600 cattle in the largest drive on record. The T Anchor weathered a cowboy strike (1883), drought (1885) and blizzard (1886). British-based Cedar Valley Land and Cattle Co. bought the ranch in 1885. When Randall County organized in 1889, six of the first officers were T Anchor employees. Foreman Lee John Hutson operated remaining lands until 1902, when the land was divided into smaller ranches and farms.   (2011)

CANYON (Randall Co.)   *300 Blk. 4th Ave. (SH 217)*
Company F, 2nd Battalion, 142nd Infantry,
36th Division, Texas National Guard
The 36th Division of the U.S. Army served with distinction in World War II. When mobilized, Company F of the Division's 142nd Infantry consisted primarily of Randall County soldiers, including ten sets of brothers, as well as a father and son. The unit deployed for Italy in 1943 and was among those landing at Salerno. The men actively served in the European theater of operation, spending 400 days in combat, participating in two assault landings and receiving seven campaign streamers. During the war, eight local men lost their lives and two received the Distinguished Service Cross. From 1951 to 1968, when it disbanded, the company trained at a National Guard Armory at this site.   (2005)

CANYON (Randall Co.)   *26500 23rd St. (US 87)*
Dreamland Cemetery
Originally named Canyon City Cemetery, this burial ground has served the nearby community since early in Canyon's history. In 1891, S. W. Kelley deeded property to Randall County for cemetery use. That same year, the first burials occurred, for William E. McElroy and for Jerry Adams, an African American cowboy who died during a cattle drive. The Civic Improvement League changed the cemetery's name to Dreamland in 1901, and additional acreage was added to the property in 1932 and 1963. Many early pioneers of Randall County, who were mostly farmers and ranchers, are buried here. A number of noted county figures are also interred, including L. G. Conner, the founder of the Canyon City (now Canyon) and prominent financier L. T. Lester. Other prominent early Randall County residents buried here include Judge Burney Slack, E. D. Harrell, John and Margaret Knight, C. R. Burrow and Clyde Warwick. More recent burials include J. A. Hill and J. P. Cornette, West Texas A&M Presidents; Hattie Anderson, Panhandle Plains Historical Museum founder; Margaret Harper, creator of the Palo Duro Canyon outdoor drama "Texas"; and musician Buddy Knox. Others represented here include veterans of conflicts dating to the Civil War. Randall County maintained the property until 1957, transferring operations to concerned citizens who formed the Dreamland Cemetery Association. Today, the association continues to care for the historic Dreamland Cemetery, which still serves the residents of Randall County and remains as a testament to the early settlers of Canyon.   (2007)

CANYON (Randall Co.)   *US 87, 14 mi. S, 1 mi. N of Happy*
Site of Old Happy
The Hugh Currie family home, "Happy Hollow" (built 1891, near this site), was for many years only house of Amarillo-Tulia freight and stage lines. Settlers got mail and freight here. The U.S. Postal Department cut name to "Happy" for the post office. The town moved (2 mi. W) to Santa Fe Line, 1906.   (1973)

CARLSBAD (Tom Green Co.)   *US 87*
Anti-Tuberculosis Colony No. 1
(McKnight State Tuberculosis Hospital)
In 1911 the Texas Legislature passed a law calling for the establishment of state institutions for the treatment of tuberculosis. Founded across the highway in 1912, the Anti-Tuberculosis Colony No. 1 opened with facilities for 57 patients on a 330-acre tract of land. The Tuberculosis Nursing School was founded here in 1915, and by 1961 had graduated 500 male and female nurses. The colony developed into a self-sustaining community with an average population of 2,000. Housed in 36 buildings on 992 acres of land, the institution included a post office, library, public school, power plant, dairy, vegetable garden, bakery and butcher shops. It was renamed the State Sanatorium in 1919. Most patients were in residence for nine months. At its height the Sanatorium proved a treatment capacity for 950 adults and 250 children. The institution was renamed McKnight State Tuberculosis Hospital in 1955 in honor of Dr. J. B. McKnight, superintendent from 1914 to 1950. The advent of anti-tubercular drugs and thoracic surgery altered the treatment of tuberculosis and eventually the institution closed in 1971. Fifty thousand adults and 5,000 children received treatment here.   (1997)

CARRIZO SPRINGS (Dimmit Co.)   *US 83, 3.7 mi. N*
Dimmit County
Created February 1, 1858. Organized November 2, 1880. Named in honor of Philip Dimmitt, a pioneer trader and captain in the Texas Army who died in 1841. Carrizo Springs, the County Seat.

CARRIZO SPRINGS (Dimmit Co.)   *US 277, 4 mi. NW*
Burleson Cemetery
Among the earliest settlers in the area later named Dimmit County, the Burleson family settled near Carrizo Springs between 1865 and 1870. James A. (1869–1895), Joseph E. (1870–1895), and Samuel (1877–1895) Burleson died suddenly, probably of food poisoning. The following July, Marion M. Burleson (1853–1895) succumbed to heat stroke and was buried on family land with his brothers and a Burleson child. As time passed, the graves on this site became a mystery. Investigations at the end of the twentieth century by the Texas Department of Transportation found it to be the final resting place of the Burleson family.   (1998)

CARRIZO SPRINGS (Dimmit Co.)   *103 N. 5th St. (US 277)*
Dimmit County Courthouse

Named for one of the framers of the Texas Declaration of Independence, Dimmit County was created from four other counties in 1858. The county was formally organized in 1880, and Carrizo Springs was chosen as the county seat. On November 12, 1883, the County Commissioners Court chose noted architect Alfred Giles to design a permanent courthouse for Dimmit County. Later that month, on November 26, the court reversed its decision and selected J. C. Breeding & Sons of San Antonio to act as both architects and builders. Probably working from Giles' initial plans, they erected a structure which featured a double gallery porch. The building's cubical form and Italianate detailing resemble Giles' designs for other Texas courthouses erected about the same time. By the 1920s, the thriving Dimmit County needed a larger government facility. The Commissioners Court called in Henry T. Phelps to design an expansion. At Phelps' instruction, the San Antonio Construction Company demolished the north second story wall, removing exterior rock from the lower north and south walls and adding new, longer wings on each end. As was his custom, Phelps worked along a Classical Revival plan, requiring a symmetrical façade. He relocated the main entrance to the west side of the building, highlighting it with four massive columns and a recessed porch. The 19th century windows were widened, and Phelps changed the Second Empire roofline to an elaborate cornice. The architectural character of the Dimmit County courthouse was transformed from a simplified Italianate style of the late 1880s to the restrained Classicism popular in the 1920s.   (2000)

CARTHAGE (Panola Co.)   *US 79, 24 mi. NE*
Site of Bethany

A thriving town of the fifties. Through it passed the Shreveport Road, over which many emigrants entered Texas.

CARTHAGE (Panola Co.)   *US 79, 18 mi. NE*
Mt. Zion Cemetery

This site was originally part of a tract owned by pioneer area settlers Richard and Polly Golden. They later gave it to their daughter Elizabeth and her husband Cornelius Crenshaw, who buried a son here in the 1840s. They deeded the property to trustees of the Mt. Zion Methodist Church and Cemetery in 1850. Additional land, conveyed to the local farmers' Grange in 1875, was included when the group disbanded. Still in use, the burial ground contains the graves of many early leaders of Panola County and veterans of American military service.   (1981)

CARTHAGE (Panola Co.)   *US 79, 4.5 mi. E*
The Respess Family and Respess Creek

In the 1870s Richard Ormand Respess (1839–1906) and his wife Nannie Lois Williams moved here from Harrison County. Respess gave the land and taught at the first school built in the Frog Pond community, known later as Liberty Chapel. His oldest son Charlie O. (1859–1917) lived near this site and operated a general store. During the years that the family allowed free access for perch and cat fishing, the stream became known as "Respess Creek." It is the only reminder of the pioneer family who lived here.   (1979)

CARTHAGE (Panola Co.)   *US 79 at US 59 Bus., Anderson Park*
Margie Neal (1875–1971)

A native of Panola County, Margie Elizabeth Neal began her career as a teacher in 1893. She became editor and owner of the *East Texas Register* newspaper in 1904. A respected educator and leader in the woman suffrage movement, she was the first woman appointed to the State Normal School Board of Regents in 1921. Five years later she made history as the first woman elected to the Texas Senate. After serving in several federal positions in Washington, she returned to Carthage in 1945 and was active in civic affairs for many years.   (1988)

CARTHAGE (Panola Co.)   *Panola St. (US 79 Bus.) at US 59F*
Jonathan Anderson

Kentucky native Jonathan "Old Shelby" Anderson, a grandson of American Revolution veteran Bailey Anderson, settled in this area when Texas was part of Mexico. He served in the Texas Revolution and fought at the Battle of San Jacinto. In 1848 he donated 100 acres here for the formation of Carthage, the new seat of government for Panola County, which was organized two years earlier from Shelby County. He later served as sheriff and tax assessor-collector. This park, the site of the former Carthage courthouse square, was named for Anderson in 1956. (1980)

CARTHAGE (Panola Co.) *109 W. Panola St. (US 79)*
The Panola *Watchman*
Tom M. Bowers (1837–1916) printed the first issue of *The Watchman* on July 2, 1873. He had published the *Carthage Banner* here from 1859 until he left about 1861 to serve in the Confederate Army. Type was handset, and news items came from other publications and letters to the editor. Following Bowers' ownership, the paper was headed by three state representatives—T. E. Boren, Jasper Collins, and O. P. Carswell—between 1884 and 1906. R. M. Park added a Linotype machine in 1915. In 1971, the publishers converted to offset, sending printing to Marshall. In 1984, the first offset press was installed. (Texas Sesquicentennial 1836–1986)

CASTROVILLE (Medina Co.) *Houston Square*
Alsatians of Texas
In 1842, empresario Henry Castro brought his first colonists to Texas to settle land west of the Medina River. Most of the immigrants were from the Rhine River area of Europe. Many claimed the province of Alsace, on the border of France and Germany, as their homeland. The Alsatian colonists brought with them their combined French and German heritage, which has left a distinctive mark on this area of the state. In 1844, Castro laid out a townsite, which the settlers chose to name Castroville. It became the center of Alsatian culture in Texas. The houses, European in style, are primarily single-story dwellings of cut limestone, mortared with adobe, and white-washed. Over the years, farming has been the major occupation of people in the area, as it was in Alsace. The Alsatian immigrants and their descendants have made a distinct impression on area politics, holiday customs, cuisine, and religion. Winemaking, using grapes grown along the Medina River, is another early tradition that has continued over the years. The history of Alsatians in Texas is a reflection of ethnic and cultural diversity in the state's rich heritage. (1985)

CASTROVILLE (Medina Co.) *US 90 at Alamo St. in September Square*
Henri Castro
Henri Castro, a native of Bayonne, France, and the descendant of Portuguese nobility, served briefly in Napoleon's French Army. In 1813 he married Marie Amelia Mathias. He later immigrated to the United States and in 1827 became a naturalized U.S. citizen. He returned to France in 1838 and joined the banking house of Lafitte and Company. While there he helped negotiate a loan for the Republic of Texas for which a grateful President Sam Houston later appointed him Texas' General Consul in Paris. Between 1843 and 1847 Castro administered, as Empresario, the settlement of at least 2,134 European colonists in this area. Castro eventually exhausted his own personal wealth to sustain his colonial effort. His extraordinary dedication to his colonists has led many to compare him favorably to the legendary Stephen F. Austin. Henri and Marie lived in Castroville with their four foster children. By 1860, however, the family was living in San Antonio. Henri and his son, Lorrenzo, traveled to Eagle Pass to run a family mercantile business. On his way to France in 1865, Castro was diverted to Monterrey, Mexico, where he became ill and died. He was buried in Monterrey in 1865. In 1876 the newly created Castro County, Texas, was named for Henri Castro. (1994)

CASTROVILLE (Medina Co.) *E US 90 at Florence St.*
Landmark Inn
Built as a one story home and store, about 1844 by French settler Caesar Monad. Later became Vance Inn, after top floor and bath house were added to accommodate travelers. Civil War bullets were made of the lead lining peeled off a room of the bath house in 1860s. After 1927, Jordan T. Lawler and his sister Ruth Lawler, natives of New Orleans, La., owned and restored inn.

CASTROVILLE (Medina Co.) *US 90 W, Moye Retreat Center*
Moye
Named for the Rev. John Martin Moye, founder (1762) of the Sisters of Divine Providence, religious order that opened school in Castroville in 1868, and built first part of this structure in 1873: first mother house of the order in the United States. Occupants since 1900 have been Providence Industrial School, St. Philip's Seminary, refuge for persecution victims, and several other endeavors.

Repurchased 1939 by Sisters of Divine Providence and used as military academy for boys. Now used as training center for religious life. (1972)

CASTROVILLE (Medina Co.)   *Angelo St., 1 block N of US 90*
St. Louis Church
Built by Alsatian settlers of Castro Colony, in Republic of Texas. Dedicated by Rt. Rev. John Odin, C. M. First Catholic Bishop of Texas, on November 9, 1846. Claude Dubuis, 1847 pastor, was later Bishop of Texas. Here in 1868 Sisters of Divine Providence opened their first permanent school in Texas. First Mother House of Order in Texas. Marked 100th anniversary of founding of the Sister of Divine Providence in Texas.

CATARINA (Dimmit Co.)   *19290 S US 83*
Catarina Hotel
Catarina grew around headquarters of the Sinton-Taft Ranch, later called Taft-Catarina Ranch. Kansas businessmen C. H. Kearny, J. E. Jarrett and H. V. Wheeler bought the ranch in the 1920s for development, attracting many buyers. By 1928, the town had approximately 2,500 residents and many businesses, including this hotel. In 1925–26, C. H. Kearny and Lee Peters designed and built the hotel in the Spanish eclectic style, with features including tile roofs and mission elements, cast stone detailing, and a U-shaped plan with courtyard and fish pond. The building, which once also housed a bank, café, shops and offices, is a reminder of the town's boom era. (2002)

CEDAR HILL (Dallas Co.)   *102 S US 67 at Belt Line Rd.*
City of Cedar Hill
Prospective settlers who traveled to this area during the 19th century were attracted to its high prairie hill and established a community here known as Cedar Hill in the late 1840s. Its early economy was based on providing support services for the surrounding farm communities. Cedar Hill was struck by a disastrous tornado in 1856, which slowed growth until the railroad came through in 1882. The town experienced a transition from rural to urban development during the late 20th century. It remains one of Dallas County's oldest settlements. (1985)

CELESTE (Hunt Co.)   *US 69 at Kingston St.*
Audie Murphy
Most decorated soldier in World War II. Born 4.5 miles south, June 20, 1924, sixth of nine children of tenant farmers Emmett and Josie Killian Murphy. Living on various farms, Audie Murphy went to school through the 8th grade in Celeste—considered the family's home town. He had to quit school to help support the family, acquiring marksmanship skills by hunting to provide food. On his 18th birthday, after being rejected by the Marines because of his size (5 feet, 7 inches; 130 pounds), he enlisted in the Army while working in Greenville. For unusual courage and bravery, he received 24 decorations, including the U.S. Congressional Medal of Honor; the French Legion of Honor, Chevalier; the Distinguished Service Cross; and a Silver Star. After the war he became a successful actor, his most prominent role portraying himself in the film "To Hell and Back," his war career autobiography. Following his untimely death in a plane crash in Virginia, May 28, 1971, and burial in Arlington National Cemetery, the U.S. Congress paid him a final tribute, dedicating a new veterans' hospital in San Antonio to the memory of this American hero. Survived by widow Pamela, sons Terry and James. (1973)

CENTER (Shelby Co.)   *US 84, 1.5 mi. E of Paxton Switch*
Site of 1870s–1900 Town of Spivey
Founded by Civil War veteran James Jackson Spivey; brothers Elisha P. and George W. Spivey lived nearby. In early days mail arrived by wagon. Houston East & West Texas Railroad crossed the founder's land, building Spivey Station, 1886. During late 1880s Hicks Lumber Mill and workers' houses were erected. U.S. post office was established in 1891, with Isaac W. Spivey, postmaster. Friendship Baptist Church was organized in 1890s with James M. Spivey, pastor. After 1900, town gradually moved over to Paxton Switch. Friendship Cemetery, with 33 graves, marks the old site. (1971)

CENTER POINT (Kerr Co.)   *SH 27, .5 mi. E of FM 480*
Site of Zanzenberg
Home of Dr. Charles de Ganahl (1824–1883), a signer of the Texas Articles of Secession in 1861 and army surgeon for the Confederate States of America. The home was erected in 1856 and named

after Dr. Ganahl's ancestral home in the Austrian Tyrol of Europe. Here the first post office in Kerr County was established in 1857 with his wife Virginia (1834–1895) as the first postmaster.   (1968)

CENTERVILLE (Henderson Co.) — *CR 2927, 6 mi. NW of Eustace*
Site of Centerville
Replaced Buffalo as county seat, 1848, due to central location in county; on land donated by James Harper Starr (1809–1890), Texas statesman. Clerk's records were kept in a log cabin courthouse. When county was reduced in area, 1850, county seat was moved to Athens, and Centerville died.   (1973)

CHANDLER (Henderson Co.) — *811 W. SH 31*
Cherokee Exodus from Texas
Driven from eastern states by white settlers, Cherokee Indians migrated to the East Texas area, becoming established by 1820. In 1822, they unsuccessfully sought title to their land from Mexico. The years following were ones of an increasingly uneasy truce for both Texans and Cherokees. In 1839, Mirabeau B. Lamar, Republic of Texas president, sent orders for the tribe to leave Texas. In July 15–16 battle northwest of here two Texans and eighteen Indians, including Chief Bowles (aged 81), were killed. The remaining Indians retreated into what is now Oklahoma.   (1969)

CHANDLER (Henderson Co.) — *SH 31W at CR 3302*
John Crane
In 1830, John Crane applied to be a part of Joseph Vehlein's Colony. Reportedly from Virginia, he was a veteran of the War of 1812. He moved his wife and seven children to what is now Walker County, Texas, in 1834. There, he organized men and became a part of the Texas Revolution. He fought at the Siege of Bexar in December 1835. The next year, he was involved in the Runaway Scrape and also served in the Texas Army in John M. Wade's Cavalry Company. Following the Texas Revolution, Crane remained with the army. While Republic of Texas Sam Houston encouraged settlers to coexist with Native American tribes, Mirabeau B. Lamar's subsequent administration took steps to remove the Indians from the land. The resulting conflicts became known as the Cherokee War. It culminated in the 1839 Battle of the Neches, fought in Henderson and Van Zandt counties. Communication had broken down between representatives of the Republic and Chief Bowles (or Duwali) of the Cherokee tribe. Companies under the leadership of Kelsey H. Douglass, Edward Burleson and Gen. Thomas J. Rusk engaged Bowles' forces on July 15, 1839, on what is today known as Battle Creek. John Crane and a Doctor Rogers were both killed. The fighting continued the following day, when Chief Bowles was also killed. His death led to the eventual expulsion of his people from Texas. Crane and Rogers are believed to be buried in unmarked graves outside of Chandler on part of the battlefield (now private property). Although some elements of Crane's military service are unknown, including his military rank, he remains an important figure in Texas history. Today, he is remembered as a patriot and early Texas settler, a pioneer in the Republic of Texas.   (2004)

CHANNING (Hartley Co.) — *517 Railroad Ave. 2 blks. W of US 385*
XIT General Office
Built in 1898–99 to house the general offices of the 3,000,000-acre XIT Ranch, this building also served as the residence of the ranch's general manager. Five railroad cars of bricks were brought in to construct the house, which features Victorian-era detailing in its decorative brackets and turned wood columns. Designed to impress visitors to the ranch, the building's Victorian elements distinguished it from the surrounding ranching environment.   (1964)

CHANNING (Hartley Co.) — *9th St. and Railroad at courthouse*
Hartley County Courthouse
Hartley County was created in January 1891, and an election held that year designated the town of Hartley as county seat. A frame courthouse was built on the town square. In October 1896, largely due to XIT Ranch interests, a second election was held which resulted in the removal of the county seat to Channing. The frame courthouse was dismantled and moved to the new county seat, where it was reconstructed. In May 1905, the commissioners court approved the construction of a new courthouse. Contracts were awarded to Solan & Wickens, Contractors, and O. G. Roquemore, architect. The two-story structure was completed in October 1906 at a cost of $10,525. The Beaux

Arts style building features a triumphal arch on the front facade, native sandstone base, and Roman Ionic paired columns. When completed, the top story provided a courtroom and two offices, and there were five offices and a lobby on the first floor. At the time of construction, the building was served by its own water well and lighting system. A vault was added to the county clerk's office in 1927. A second vault and jury dormitories were built in 1935.

(Recorded Texas Historic Landmark—1987)

CHAPPELL HILL (Washington Co.)   *US 290 at FM 1155*
Chappell Hill
Founded 1847. Named for Robert Chappell, an 1841 settler. Early education center, with Chappell Hill Male and Female Institute, 1852, and Soule University, 1850. Male students marched away to Civil War in 1861. C.S.A. Quartermaster Depot located here. Many early Texas landmarks in vicinity.

CHEROKEE (San Saba Co.)   *SH 16 at site of school*
Site of Old Behrns West Texas Normal and Business College
Opened 1895 by noted educator Francis Marion Behrns. A 3-story native blue marble main hall and frame dormitory were built by interested local citizens. Courses included mathematics, natural sciences, Latin, oratory, commercial subjects, literature, psychology, music and painting. Character building was stressed. Its graduates led in teaching and other professions. After the Behrns school closed in 1903, buildings were used by Cherokee Junior College; after 1921, by public schools. In 1945, fire destroyed old main hall. (1966)

CHERRY SPRINGS (Gillespie Co.)   *US 87, 2.5 mi. S in roadside park*
John O. Meusebach (1812–1897)
To be a Texan, Meusebach gave up title of baron in 1845. As commissioner-general, German Emigration Company, he founded Fredericksburg in 1846 as gateway to Fisher-Miller Land Grant, hunting ground of the Comanche. By emptying his fire-arms, he won trust of Indians and made treaty to provide for unmolested settlement. Indians called him "El Sol Colorado" (The Red Sun). State senator, 1851. In 1854 issued colonists' headrights. To his family motto, he added "Texas Forever." Lived in Loyal Valley. Grave near Cherry Spring. (1964)

CHESTER (Tyler Co.)   *FM 2097, 2.5 mi. N*
Alabama-Coushattas of Texas
Two tribes, welded into one in their wanderings, visited Texas briefly in 1816, at Peach Tree Village, Tyler County, before swinging back into Louisiana. Seeking land to call their own, however, returned and made first home in Texas on this site, from 1836 to 1844, under leadership of First Chief Colabe Sylestine and Second Chief Antone Sylestine. Tribe built log cabins for chiefs and lean-tos of bark and wood for rest of the people. Settlement locations had to be carefully selected. As place for important tribal gatherings, an open field of deep sand had to be situated at center of every village. Here were held tribal pow-wows and ceremonial dancing, but the field's really popular function was as the ball park. Ball playing among the Alabama-Coushattas was a form of lacrosse, in which a long-handled racquet was used to catch, carry or throw a hard ball past the goalee. Women of the tribe, when they played, used no racquet—only their hands. Known as migrants, rather than agricultural Indians, the Alabama-Coushattas nevertheless were Texas settlers who contributed to the culture of the state. (1964)

CHESTER (Tyler Co.)   *FM 2097, 2.5 mi. N*
Site of Old Peach Tree Village
In the early 19th century, the Alabama Indians—then a large tribe—made their headquarters on this site, and called their village "Ta-Ku-La," which meant "Peach Tree." Two trails blazed by early pioneers crossed here. A north-south trail came from Anahuac on the Gulf of Mexico, over the Neches River, leading onward to Nacogdoches; the other ran east-west from Opelousas, Louisiana, through what is now Moscow, to present Huntsville, then west to San Antonio. Other trails diverged from this: to the Galveston Bay area, San Felipe de Austin, and Goliad. The crossing of the trails made this a trading center of importance. With the coming of white settlers, the Alabama Indians withdrew, and the remnant of that tribe is now located about 15 miles south—occupying

the only Indian reservation in Texas. In old Peach Tree Village, some historic homes are marked. It is also site of the Kirby Museum, founded by John Henry Kirby (1860–1940), who was born here, and whose career included service as a legislator, as well as leadership in lumbering, banking, oil development and railroad building. (1966)

CHICO (Wise Co.) FM 1810, 2 mi. E
Indian Captives Dot and Bianca Babb (Captured 2 mi. S; This Town on Getaway Route)
Two of Texas history's best-known Indian captives, 13-year-old T. A. "Dot" Babb (1852–1936) and his 9-year-old sister Bianca (1855?–1950) were stolen by Comanches from their home near here in September of 1865. While at play one day, the children were surprised by a raiding party of 35 to 40 Indians. Mrs. Babb was killed and Dot, Bianca, and a Mrs. Luster (a visitor) were taken to Indian Territory (present Oklahoma). After helping Mrs. Luster escape on the way, Dot was very nearly executed, but so stoic was he in facing death that the Indians admiringly spared his life. For the next two years Dot and Bianca lived, in different tribes, as adopted Comanches. Bianca later recalled that the Indians held a feast—with coffee, a luxury—upon her arrival and that they colored her blonde hair with charcoal and buffalo tallow. Dot, after a winter as the squaws' flunky, asserted his male rights and thereafter spent his time taming horses. He was taken on raids against other tribes and showed signs of becoming a fine warrior. After two years, the children's father ransomed them and a joyful reunion occurred. Both Dot and Bianca spoke with sympathy, however, of many Indian customs and of kind treatment during captivity. (1971)

CHILDRESS (Childress Co.) US 83 at FM 1034, 20 mi. N
On Old Shoenail Ranch Land, Community of Loco (2 mi. E)
Named for weed found here in 1880s by early settlers—the families of Dick Brown, Walter Campbell, and Bobby Payne. The Browns survived the last Indian battle of Buck Creek in 1887. Soil-based local economy moved from mule-power to tractors with lugs, to rubber-tire tractors, to irrigation farming. The Loco Post Office was established in 1892. Town at its height had 4 churches, a high school, a garage, 2 cotton gins, 3 stores, barber shop, blacksmith shop, cafe, and a golf course. Little now remains except the school's storm cellar. The post office closed in 1964. (1970)

CHILDRESS (Childress Co.) 100 Ave. E NE, 1blk S of US 287 at courthouse
Colonel Wm. Edgar Hughes of the Mill Iron
Born 1840. Came from Illinois to Texas, 1859. During Civil War rose from private, 1st Texas Artillery, to colonel in 16th Cavalry. Was in bloody battles of Shiloh, Chickamauga, Nashville, Richmond. After war, when "didn't have 2 pairs of pants," taught school and read law in Weatherford. As lawyer, took many land cases. In 7 years became organizer and president, City Bank of Dallas (now 1st National, Dallas). Later an officer in Exchange Bank, Dallas; Union Trust Co., St. Louis; Continental Trust Co., Denver. In 1880 bought half interest in Mill Iron Ranch. Purchased small holdings from Pease to Red River—Bridle Bits, DV'S, Diamond D's and others. Range lay in Childress, Cottle, Hall, Motley Counties. In 1885 added windmills, wells, to run larger herds— up to 50,000. In early years used dugouts, chuckwagons for headquarters. First small ranchhouse was built at windmill 62, near Estelline. Bought out Rocking Chair Ranch, Collingsworth County, 1896. Until 1898 ran only longhorns. Was said to have had the largest men, most practical jokers, longest cattle drives, biggest horses in Texas. He sold off the last Mill Iron herd in 1918—year of his death. (1965)

CHILDRESS (Childress Co.) 100 Ave. E NE, 1 blk. S of US 287 at courthouse
Childress County
Formed from Young and Bexar Territories. Created August 21, 1876. Organized April 11, 1887. Named in honor of George Campbell Childress 1804–1841. A member of the Convention in 1836. Co-author of the Texas Declaration of Independence. Childress, the county seat. (1936)

CHILDRESS (Childress Co.) RR 401 at Fair Park
Goodnight Trail
In hostile Indian years of 1866–71, route of great cattle drives from Texas to U.S. forts in Colorado and New Mexico. Col. Charles Goodnight, trailblazer, drove thousands of cattle to water here. Site later (1886) became Childress. Cattle watering hole is now lake in Fair Park. (1964)

CHILLICOTHE (Hardeman Co.)
301 Avenue J South (US 287)
Chillicothe First Methodist Church
Originally organized in 1886 in the Jackson Springs community, this church was first served by circuit riders C. T. Neese and J. T. Hosmer. Shortly after the Fort Worth and Denver City Railway came through Chillicothe in 1887, the Jackson Springs Church moved into town. This edifice was erected at the church's second Chillicothe location. Designed by prominent area architect Rockwell Henry Stuckey (1855–1936) in 1916, the structure features classical columns, cornice and eaves. Notable elements include the ornate stained glass windows and octagonal dome, a feature often associated with Stuckey's work. The original stained glass windows were crafted in Germany during World War I and crossed the Atlantic three times before being accepted at New York and shipped to Chillicothe by train.
(1998)

CHILTON (Falls Co.)
US 77, 6 mi. N
Site of North Prairie School
On June 8, 1896, the citizens of North Prairie petitioned the Falls County Commissioners Court for a community school district, and North Prairie School District No. 65 was created. In 1910 a 2-room school housed two teachers and about 20 students. By 1926 the North Prairie School had grown to include about 30 students with three teachers providing instruction in nine grades. World War II called away many of North Prairie's young people. The community declined in population as did many community schools of the era, and in 1946 the North Prairie School District was consolidated with nearby Chilton schools. The North Prairie schoolhouse was razed within a few years, but remains a significant part of local history.
(1999)

CHIRENO (Nacogdoches Co.)
SH 21, 3 mi. NW
Half Way House—Old Stage Coach Inn Built 1850
Pre-Texas Revolution stage stop on King's Highway from San Antonio Nacogdoches-San Augustine-Natchitoches; also a post office under the Republic; overnight accommodations to progenitors of Texas Revolution.

CHIRENO (Nacogdoches Co.)
Main St. (SH 34) between Easy St.
and Gingerbread Ln.
Camp Chireno, World War II Prisoner of War Camp
During World War II, the Frost Lumber Co. (Nacogdoches) and the Angelina Lumber Co. (Lufkin) requested that the War Manpower Commission (WMC) establish Camp Chireno as a "permanent" branch of Camp Fannin (Smith County). The WMC leased private land and built the 30-acre compound west of here along Camp Road. Located in an area devastated by the January 1944 ice storm, this camp benefited from Chireno's established railroad facilities. The site first received prisoners of war (POWs) in May 1944. The camp's 300 POWs spent their time cutting and salvaging timber and pulpwood. The camp closed in March 1945, near the end of the war.
(2008)

CHRIESMAN (Burleson Co.)
SH 36, 7.5 mi. NW of Caldwell
Alexander Thomson (August 29, 1785–June 1, 1863)
A leader in colonizing Texas. Born in St. Matthews Parish, S. C.; lived also in Georgia, then in Tennessee where in 1830 he became partner of the Empresario in development of the Sterling C. Robertson Colony. Conducting a number of families who had signed agreements to settle in the Robertson Colony, he crossed into Texas and came to Nacogdoches three days after Mexican officials there received notice of 1830 law requiring passports of immigrants. After Thomson tried unsuccessfully to have rule waived for hardship reasons, the party bypassed Nacogdoches, making a new trail often used afterward and known as the Tennesseans' Road. Thomson lived for a time in Austin's Colony, representing District of Hidalgo (now Washington County) at Texas Convention of 1832. By 1835, when he was consultation delegate from Viesca (later Milam Municipality), he was living and serving as official surveyor in Robertson's Colony. Still a leader, he was Robertson's executor in 1842. Married twice, father of 13, he was ancestor of many noted Texans, including Thaddeus A. Thomson, United States envoy to Colombia and signer of the Thomson-Urrutia Treaty in 1914. Alexander Thomson is buried in Thomson Family Cemetery one mile to the northeast.

CHRIESMAN (Burleson Co.)
SH 36 at FM 1363
Chriesman
Chriesman (originally "Yellow Prairie," 0.5 miles east). Settled by Alexander Thomson, Jr., early Texas patriot and partner of the colonizer Sterling C. Robertson. When railroad came through in 1880, the settlers moved to tracks. Renamed, 1884, after Capt. H. C. Chriesman, surveyor for Stephen F. Austin. Now serves surrounding ranches.

CHRISTOVAL (Tom Green Co.)
Loop 110, off US 277
Christoval
Frontiersmen began to immigrate into the south Concho Valley in 1870s, locating along the "Toe Nail" Trail from Fort McKavett to Fort Concho. By mid-1880s the settlement began to develop and a union church was organized. The South Concho Irrigation Co. was established in 1885, and built a dam and 3 miles of canals to furnish water to dry farmland. Christopher C. Doty (1857–1944), who had arrived in Texas in 1879, opened a store and applied for a post office in 1888. After rejection of application for "Alice," due to another office of that name, Doty suggested "Christobal" (Spanish for Christopher). Confirmation of establishment of the office and Doty's appointment as postmaster arrived in Jan. 1889, but the spelling of the name had been changed to Christoval. After flood in Aug. 1906, a tract of bottomland was purchased for a city park, which became popular Baptist campground and site of Confederate reunions, both attended by thousands of regional residents. A bath house, built in 1915 at nearby Mineral Wells, was first of several local health facilities. Arrival of the Panhandle & Santa Fe Railroad, in 1930, made Christoval a shipping point for area sheep, wool, and cattle industries. (1973)

CIBOLO (Guadalupe Co.)
FM 78 at city park
Cibolo
A town began to grow here after the Galveston, Harrisburg and San Antonio Railroad built a line through western Guadalupe County in 1875. A general store, operated by George Schlather and Ernst Jenull, was opened the following year to serve the predominantly German population. A post office was established in 1876, and the town was named Cibolo from an Indian word for buffalo. The community was also known as Fromme's Store after Charles Fromme purchased the general store in 1882. Cibolo was officially incorporated in 1965.
(Texas Sesquicentennial 1836–1986)

CLAIRETTE (Erath Co.)
SH 6, 7 mi. N of Hico
Clairette Cemetery
Joseph and Elizabeth Salmon and their children moved to the Republic of Texas in 1839. They settled in this area in 1854. When their 15-year-old son, Albert, died in 1858, he was buried at his favorite campsite in a grove of oak trees on the family land. Albert's brother, Joseph Salmon, Jr., deeded the acre of land surrounding the grave site for use as a community cemetery in 1876. Additional land acquisitions over the years have increased the size of the cemetery. The diverse styles of gravestones found here serve as reflections of the area's pioneer heritage. (1991)

CLAIREMONT (Kent Co.)
US 380 at SH 208
Old Kent County Jail
Built 1894, of red sandstone quarried nearby. Horse and cattle thieves, murderers, moonshiners most common prisoners. One of most difficult West Texas jails from which to escape. No attempted break successful. (1965)

CLARENDON (Donley Co.)
SH 70, 20 mi. NW
Boydstun Cemetery (3.7 mi. SW)
Pioneer area settler Henry S. Boydstun (1858–1942), a native of Illinois, moved his family to this area in 1890. That year, his infant son, Eddie, died and was buried in the southwest corner of the family farm. In 1898, Boydstun deeded two acres at the site for use as a public burial ground. A small farming community that developed near there included a school and, from 1891 to 1940, a post office (listed as Boydston). Although Boydstun deeded land for the cemetery, he and his wife, Mary (d. 1950), were interred in the nearby town of Groom. (1988)

CLARENDON (Donley Co.)

SH 70, 16.5 mi. N

Jericho Cemetery (1 mile west)

Settlement of this area of Donley County began in the late 19th century, before the town of Jericho was founded as a station on the Chicago, Rock Island and Gulf rail line about 1902. Early community burials took place in the pasture near this site, and the graveyard eventually was set aside in the county deed records. The first documented burial is that of Mattie Ray (1850–1895), and the second is that of seven-month-old Garil Prest Schaffer, who died in 1897. Others buried in the Jericho Cemetery include victims of smallpox and influenza epidemics, military veterans and area pioneers. (2001)

CLARENDON (Donley Co.)

SH 70, 5 mi. N

Clarendon Cemetery

In this first cemetery of Donley County, sixteen rods west lie the first dead of Old Clarendon. Here white civilization sank its roots in sadness, and from the graves in this sacred acre strong pioneer spirits turned to face the future with greater love for the land and a firmer determination to build for a tomorrow which we know today. To those of the Old Clarendon Colony who first found rest on this bold promontory and to their survivors, this stone of imperishable Texas granite is loyally and lovingly dedicated. Erected by the State of Texas, July 4, 1938.

CLARENDON (Donley Co.)

SH 70, 5 mi. N

Replica of First Donley County Courthouse (Originally about 6 mi. NW)

Soon after founding in 1878 of Clarendon Colony by the Rev. Lewis H. Carhart, workers were brought from Vermont to quarry local stone and erect 2-story structure for hotel, stagecoach stand, and public meeting hall. With organization of Donley County, April 11, 1882, Clarendon was named county seat. The hotel became (and remained for years) the first courthouse—and third courthouse in entire Panhandle of Texas. It served settlers in an 8,000-square mile area, since eight unorganized counties were for years attached for judicial purposes to Donley County. (1967)

CLARENDON (Donley Co.)

SH 70, 4 mi. N of Salt Fork

Old Mobeetie Trail (To Early Town, About 40 mi. NE)

A road older than recorded history, carved out in centuries of wintertime travel to the south, spring migration to the north, by millions of bison and by Indians who lived by hunting these large animals. Important in era of Texas Panhandle settlement. Used in 1873–1874, when first lifelong residents put dugout dwellings in the Panhandle and began to hunt buffalo to fill demand for hides and meat. Fort Elliott, established 1875 to regulate Indians resisting white settlement, soon had as a neighbor the town of Mobeetie, which for some years was the county seat for 28 counties and a place to go for medical aid, supplies and access to stage travel. In 1876 Kansans came this way south for better hunting, calling this "Rath Trail," for their leader. Also in 1876 cattlemen began to bring herds here. By 1880 this ancient path was a southern arm of Jones and Plummer Trail, over which cowboys moved longhorns to railroads and northern cattle markets. Beginning about 1887 the Mobeetie Trail was used by "nesters" taking up farm lands alongside the old great ranches. Those it served founded and expanded agricultural-commercial economy of the Panhandle. (1966)

CLARENDON (Donley Co.)

US 287 at SH 70 in roadside park

Donley County

Formed from Young and Bexar Territories. Created August 21, 1876; organized March 22, 1882. Named in honor of Stockton P. Donley 1821–1871, a Confederate officer elected to the Texas Supreme Bench in 1866. Clarendon, the county seat. (1964)

CLARKSVILLE (Red River Co.)

US 82, 1 mi. W

A House of the William Becknell Family

William Becknell (1788–1856) of Missouri is renowned for opening the Santa Fe Trail from the United States into Spain's new world empire in 1821. He and his wife Mary settled in 1835 near here, on Becknell's prairie, with a daughter and two sons. On the way to the Alamo, David Crockett visited them. Becknell himself fought in 1836 in the Texas War for Independence. After milled lumber became available, he or his family built the earliest portion of this house. It was later enlarged and relocated. (1978)

CLARKSVILLE (Red River Co.) US 82, 1 mi. W
City of Clarksville
Incorporated December 29, 1837. Named in honor of James Clark who settled here in 1834.

CLARKSVILLE CITY (Gregg Co.) US 82 at municipal bldg.
Point Pleasant
From about 1850 until 1871, a post office, which served the Point Pleasant community, operated near this site. The area was known as Gilead under the first postmaster, L. B. Camp, who earlier had established a ferry crossing the Sabine River (2 mi. W). When the name Point Pleasant was adopted in 1852, J. K. Armstrong (d. 1860) was named postmaster. Other postmasters who served Point Pleasant were William W. Walters (d. 1885), who operated the stage stop where the post office was located, Claiborn Halbert, and Joshua W. Monk. Elisha A. Mackey was Point Pleasant's last official postmaster. During its 21 years of existence the Point Pleasant Post Office served approximately 48 families including those of Jarret Dean, James Hendrick, Mason Moseley, Augustus Moseley, A. H. Abney, A. C. Williams, Jacob M. Lacy, A. G. Rogers, and A. T. Wright. The Point Pleasant School (called Possom Trot and still operating in 1908 with Trustees R. A. Hendrix, E. W. Clements, and Mr. Phillips) and Moseley Cemetery also served these pioneers. When the railroad came through in 1873, the new towns of Gladewater and Longview drew residents away from the Point Pleasant area. Clarksville City, created by the 1931 East Texas oil boom, later developed at the site of the Point Pleasant community. Incise on back: In memory of our mother Minnie Clements Phillips (1892–1973). (1984)

CLARKSVILLE (Red River Co.) US 82, town square
The Rev. William Stevenson (October 4, 1768–March 5, 1857)
Frontier minister; friend of Stephen F. Austin, Father of Texas. A circuit rider in Missouri Conference, Methodist Church, Mr. Stevenson in 1815 made a pastoral trip to Pecan Point, home of Claiborne Wright, member of newly-arrived Anglo-American colony on Texas side of the Red River. Records indicate that his preaching to Wright and friends in 1815 constituted the first Protestant sermons ever given in Texas, then part of Catholic "New Spain." He thus established a beachhead for religious freedom in Texas at this point of entry. (1972)

CLARKSVILLE (Red River Co.) SH 37, 3.5 mi. SW
Site of McKenzie College
An outstanding school in the Southwest before the Civil War. Established in 1841 by the Reverend John W. P. McKenzie (1806–1877), pioneer missionary of the Choctaws, circuit rider in Texas in 1838. Opened in a log cabin, it expanded to four large buildings on 900 acres. Chartered January 10, 1854. Enrolled 300 boarding pupils annually. Closed in 1869.

CLARKSVILLE (Red River Co.) SH 37 near CR 1280, 6 mi. SW
J. D. Tippit
Slain in the line of duty while on alert for President John F. Kennedy's assassin, J. D. Tippit (1924–1963) grew up on his family's farm near this site. He served as a paratrooper in the 17th Airborne Division during World War II and received the Bronze Star. J. D. married his high school sweetheart in 1946 and started a family in Red River County. He joined the Dallas Police Department in 1952 and later was honored for his quick thinking and outstanding judgment. On November 22, 1963, Tippit was working a beat in central Oak Cliff when he stopped Lee Harvey Oswald for questioning. Oswald shot and killed him. J. D. Tippit, who left a wife and three children, is buried at Laurel Land Memorial Park in Dallas. (2001)

CLAUDE (Armstrong Co.) US 287 at FM 2250, 15 mi. W, frontal road in Washburn
Town of Washburn
Planned by R. E. Montgomery, son-in-law of Fort Worth & Denver City Railway Builder-President Gen. G. M. Dodge. Named for family friend. Promoted 1887, Washburn for a time was F. W. & D. C. Line's terminus. It had first newspaper of plains—"Armstrong County Record." Also had general store, lumber yard, 2 hotels, 2 saloons. Became junction point, branch line connecting F. W. & D. C. with Santa Fe Railway at Panhandle. Remaining as town dwindled: Judge Jas. Logue, donor cemetery site and founder Washburn State Bank, 1908; H. E. White, owner of store, lumber yard and elevators. (1970)

CLAUDE (Armstrong Co.)   US 287 at Trice St.
Route of Coronado Expedition
Led by Francisco Vazquez de Coronado, this trail-blazing expedition set out from Mexico City in 1541 in search of Cibola, fabled 7 Cities of Gold. Finding only Indian pueblos, Coronado changed his course for Quivira, a supposedly wealthy Indian kingdom. This quest brought the entourage across the Panhandle plains to present Tule Canyon. Then with 30 men, Coronado went north by "Needle Point"—a route taking in Palo Duro Canyon and present Armstrong County, via Claude. He next continued into Kansas, but failing to find riches, returned to Mexico in 1542.   (1969)

CLAUDE (Armstrong Co.)   US 287 at Trice St.
The Great Panhandle Indian Scare of 1891
Although most Indians had left the Panhandle plains by the 1880s, fear of Indian attacks was still prevalent among settlers who arrived in the next decade. On Jan. 29, 1891, rumors of approaching Indians spread throughout the entire region. For three days settlers hastily prepared to defend themselves by fleeing or barricading their homes and replenishing their weapon and ammunition supplies. Later it was discovered that the rumored Indian war cries and smoke signals were actually ranchers in pursuit of a steer they finally caught and cooked over an open fire.   (1983)

CLAUDE (Armstrong Co.)   US 287 at Trice St.
Armstrong County
Created 1876. Name honors several Texas pioneers named Armstrong. Ranching became the chief industry when huge JA Ranch was established here in 1876. Farming was introduced after the railroad came through, 1887. County was organized in 1890. Present courthouse was built 1912.
        (1969)

CLAUDE (Armstrong Co.)   US 287, one block W of town square
Armstrong County Jail
Erected in 1953, this building is constructed of stone used to build the first masonry jail in Armstrong County, 1894. Stone for the structure (which replaced a primitive, frame "calaboose") was quarried 14 miles south at Dripping Springs in Palo Duro Canyon and then hauled here in wagons driven by local citizens. The rock was cut at this site. The 1894 building had two stories, topped by a dome, and 20-inch walls. So sturdy was it that dangerous convicts from other counties were kept here. Old-timers remember that only three prisoners ever escaped.   (1969)

CLAUDE (Armstrong Co.)   SH 207, 17.5 mi. S
The S. P. Hamblen Family
Pioneered at this site, in dugout to the west. S. P. Hamblen (1846–1930) and wife Virginia Ann (1861–1950) settled in Lakeview area (9 mi. S. of Claude) in 1889. Hamblen helped establish Lakeview School, 1890. He engaged in farming and stockraising, and also dealt in cedar posts cut in Palo Duro Canyon and sold in Amarillo at 3¢ each. Hauls over the Old Indian Trail were made with such great effort that W. H. Hamblen (oldest son, who helped his father) longed for good roads and later was designer of Hamblen Drive. Mrs. Hamblen, at home with her children, tended the ranch, courageously protecting family from the prevalent rattlesnakes, and repulsing vicious lobo wolves that attacked the young cattle. The Hamblens lived at this site, known as Mesquite Flat, in 1901–1902. The father and older sons, W. H., David and Claude, put up corrals and a barn, and then built the rockwalled 24 x 36-foot dugout. The tenth child of the family, Luther Ray Hamblen, was born in the Mesquite Flat dugout on March 3, 1902. Moving from this place, the Hamblens sought the best location for educating their children, who in the tradition of their parents became respected citizens of the West.   (1970)

CLAUDE (Armstrong Co.)   SH 207, 26 mi. S in roadside park
First Battle of the Palo Duro (Aug. 30, 1874)
Opening fight in 1874–75. U.S. action against tribes supposedly on Indian Territory Reservations (present Oklahoma), but actually occupying the Texas Panhandle. South from Fort Dodge, Kans., marched 750 soldiers under Gen. Nelson A. Miles, who on Aug. 28 had to leave guards with his stalled supply train. Attacked on Aug. 30 in rugged terrain by superior numbers of Cheyennes, Comanches, and Kiowas, Miles won victory in 5-hour fight at Battle Creek (10 mi. E. of here)—first of 14 fights in Red River War that broke the Indians' power in Texas Panhandle.   (1971)

CLEBURNE (Johnson Co.)　　　　　　　　　　*US 67, 50 yds. W of city limits*
Site of Wardville (¼ mi. S of marker)
First county seat of Johnson County, chosen in Aug. 1855, and located on an 80-acre donation from William O'Neal. Named for Thomas William Ward (1807–1872), a Republic of Texas soldier and second commissioner of General Land Office of Texas. The first courthouse, 16 feet square, was built by O'Neal of logs overlaid with clapboards, at cost of $49. When Wardville was found to violate Texas Constitution's requirement that a county seat be within 5 miles of center of county, it was abandoned (1856). Ironically, later county line changes made it near the center.　　(1972)

CLEBURNE (Johnson Co.)　　　　　　　　　　　　*SH 171S at city limits*
Riggs Pennington Home
Heart pine and cypress wood, square nails. Carpenters' wages were $87, a cow and a horse. Pennington (1845–1921), born in the Republic of Texas, was a Confederate soldier, farmer, banker, business man.　　(1965)

CLEBURNE (Johnson Co.)　　　　　　　*2 N. Main St. (SH 171/174) at courthouse*
Cleburne Town Square
Traces its beginning to 1854 when first house, a log cabin, was built here near a good spring. County seat was bodily moved by wagon to this place (then called Camp Henderson) in 1867, and renamed to honor Patrick Cleburne, a Confederate general under whom many local Civil War veterans had served. Cleburne's growth has been rapid, particularly in the field of commerce, since · 1876. The Gulf, Colorado and Santa Fe Railroad line from Galveston to Fort Worth passed through Cleburne in 1881. A short time later, new branches connected the town with Dallas and Weatherford. In 1898, the railroad's workshops were located here and development of Cleburne as an industrial center began. By 1950, Cleburne boasted a steel foundry, milk processing plants, ladies' garment factory, lime plant, chair factory, battery plant and the state's largest railroad construction and repair shops. Typical of other American towns, outward expansion found the original business district taking on a neglected appearance. In 1968, a group called "Our Town, Inc." became concerned with this deterioration and enlisted citizens' aid to help reverse the trend and restore the downtown district.　　(1970)

CLEBURNE (Johnson Co.)　　　　　　　*2 N. Main St. (SH 171/174) at courthouse*
Colonel Middleton T. Johnson and
General Patrick R. Cleburne
County named for Texas Confederate—Colonel Middleton T. Johnson, 1810–1866, South Carolinian; Legislator Alabama; came to Texas 1840. Member Republic of Texas Congress. Cavalryman in U.S. War with Mexico. Texas Ranger surveyor of early railroads. As colonel raised 14th Texas Cavalry regiment, taking them to Little Rock 1862 for induction C.S.A. service. Buried Mill Creek Cemetery, Arlington, Texas. Johnson County voted 500-50 for secession 1861. Soon raised 9 companies for C.S.A. service. 12th Texas Cavalry Regt. which served in Arkansas, Louisiana, on Texas coast to prevent invasion Texas. Remaining eligible men western part county placed in state militia late 1863 to protect frontier. City named for Confederate—General Patrick R. Cleburne 1828–1864. Born near Cork, Ireland; came to U.S. 1849. Drug clerk in Ohio, became lawyer in Arkansas. Recruited 1st Arkansas Regt. for Confederacy. Elected colonel. Promoted brigadier general March 1862, made major general Dec. 1862. Rapidly earned reputation as a superb combat officer on numerous fields with army of Tennessee Eight. Texas regiments of Granbury's Brigade were under Cleburne, and in 1864 Atlanta campaign he said, "The piles of the (Union) dead were silent but sufficient eulogy upon Granbury and his noble Texans." On Nov. 30, 1864 Cleburne, a savage fighter, met death six paces from the Federal lines in battle of Franklin, Tenn. Became known as "Stonewall Jackson of the West."　　(1963)

CLEVELAND (Liberty Co.)　　　　　　　　　　　　*SH 321, 9 mi. SE*
Old Wells' Store
Center section built about 1875 by D. D. Proctor & Company; later operated by L. L. Wells. This structure and earlier one on same site each served as general mercantile store. This building was center for visits and exchange of local news at "Tarkington's Prairie" community. Building has been used as post office, wagon stop, credit house, and voting place. Was located on old Nacogdoches-Lynchburg Trail, a 19th century thoroughfare.　　(1968)

CLEVELAND (Liberty Co.)   *SH 321, 5.5 mi. SE*
Burton B. Tarkington
Burton B. Tarkington (1790–1861) and his wife Sarah Berry Tarkington migrated with their family from Indiana in the mid-1820s to the Mexican state of Coahuila. They settled west of the Trinity River in present northwest Liberty County, and began ranching and raising crops. The area around their farm became known as Tarkington's Prairie, and a creek in the area is called Tarkington Bayou. According to family legend, the Tarkingtons and other early settlers had to vacate their property in 1836 when Santa Anna's forces advanced prior to the Battle of San Jacinto. Apparently, Tarkington did not have a land grant from the Mexican government for the land he claimed, but when Texas gained independence from Mexico in 1836, he received a headright land grant of one league and one labor (4,605 acres). The grant was patented in 1847 by the new state of Texas and became known as the Tarkington Survey. Tarkington became a leader in the community. He served in the Texas Militia in 1842, and was elected Liberty County commissioner for three terms beginning in 1854. He received recognition for his service from Governor H. R. Runnel. Tarkington died Feb. 2, 1861, and is buried in the McGinnis Cemetery (.25 mi. W).   (1996)

CLEVELAND (Liberty Co.)   *SH 105/321 at San Jacinto Ave.*
City of Cleveland
The town of Cleveland traces its beginnings to 1878, when local attorney and politician Charles Lander Cleveland (1824–1892) deeded land to the Houston East and West Texas Railroad, stipulating the building of a railway depot and the establishment of a town to be named Cleveland. By 1879 the settlement boasted a sawmill, two boarding houses, railroad interests, and a number of homes. Churches and schools were established and the town continued to grow, with an economy based on timber and railroad industries. The city was officially incorporated in 1935.   (1986)

CLIFTON (Bosque Co.)   *SH 6, 4 mi. S at reunion grounds*
Election Oak
One of three polling places in first election held after Bosque County was organized in 1854. Of 21 votes cast on that occasion (Aug. 7, 1854) in county, 17 were polled under this tree. J. K. Helton was election judge. Officials elected were L. H. Scrutchfield, judge; P. Bryant, sheriff; Jasper N. Mabray, clerk; Isaac Gary, assessor-collector; Archibald Kell, treasurer. In later years, Bosque County Old Settlers Association used this site for reunions, by the courtesy of Tom M. Pool, owner of the land. Site was known locally as Pool Park.   (1970)

CLIFTON (Bosque Co.)   *FM 182 at FM 219, 7 mi. W*
Norwegian Settlements in Bosque County
Though never as numerous as some national groups emigrating from Europe, Norwegians left an imprint on rural life in Texas. Hundreds sailed to the United States beginning in the 1830s. For those who settled in Texas, Bosque County had great appeal, because with its woods, hills and steep, sloping streams, it resembled parts of Norway. In 1854 Ole Canuteson started here what became Texas' largest Norse settlement. Until past the turn of the century, the Gary Creek Valley settlers spoke mainly Norwegian and retained many customs of their homeland.   (1969)

CLIFTON (Bosque Co.)   *FM 219, 8.5 mi. W*
Cleng Peerson (May 17, 1782–Dec. 16, 1865)
Called the "Father of Norwegian immigration to America," Cleng Peerson migrated to the United States from his native Norway in 1821. He traveled extensively and encouraged his countrymen to settle on land he selected in the East and Midwest. Coming to Texas in 1849, Peerson discovered Norwegian families living near Dallas and located sites where others might move. In 1853, he led a group to Bosque County, beginning the large Norwegian settlement in this area. Peerson lived on the O. Colwick farm (.5 mi. S) until his death. He is buried in the church cemetery at Norse. (1975)

CLINE (Uvalde Co.)   *US 90, in Cline*
Cline Community (½ mi. S of this site)
First settler, Celeste Pingenot came to this area in 1870. He built first house on south bank of Turkey Creek, 1871. Established stagecoach stand, store and inn; named it Wallace. He was first postmaster, commissioned, 1878. Community protected from Indians by small detachment of soldiers billeted at "The Spring," nearby. August Cline was employed by Pingenot to operate store

and stagecoach stand. When railroad came in 1883, built rock house and post office on north bank. Became postmaster. Renamed community, Cline.   (1967)

COLDSPRING (San Jacinto Co.)   *SH 150, .5 mi. E*
San Jacinto County
Eighteenth century Spanish explorers gave to the hyacinth-choked stream the name of Saint Hyacinth. Anglo-Americans settled here after 1820. Formed from portions of Polk, Montgomery, Liberty and Walker Counties. Created January 5, 1869; recreated August 13, 1870; organized December 1, 1870. County seat, Cold Springs, 1870; later, Coldspring.

COLDSPRING (San Jacinto Co.)   *1 Byrd Ave. (SH 150) at courthouse*
San Jacinto County Courthouse
A fire in 1915 destroyed the San Jacinto County courthouse. Landowners donated land at this site and relocated the center of county government to "new town" Coldspring. The county hired builders Price and Williamson to construct the new courthouse based on plans by the Houston firm of Lane and Dabney. It was constructed in 1916–17 of brick fired locally from local clay. Merchants and citizens followed the courthouse to the new location, and by 1925, "old town" Coldspring was deserted. Repairs in 1936 modified its appearance somewhat, but the courthouse retains elements of its original Italian Renaissance design in its arched doors and windows on the east and west elevations.   (2000)

COLDSPRING (San Jacinto Co.)   *1 Byrd Ave. (SH 150) at courthouse*
Townsite of Coldspring
Before founding of town, this land lay in Mexican grant made to Col. Robt. Rankin, veteran of American Revolution. Post office here bore name "Coonskin" (1847), then "Fireman's Hill," and finally "Cold Springs" (1850). Spelling later became "Coldspring." Original town plat contained 14 blocks. First courthouse, of wood, burned 1915. Present stone building replaced it in 1918. By 1923 most of town had moved up the hill to present site. Early schools included an 1847 academy, the 1880 "Male and Female Institute," and Mrs. India Grace's private school of 1880s.   (1970)

COLDSPRING (San Jacinto Co.)   *SH 150, 1 mi. SW in rest area*
The Big Thicket, C.S.A.
In early Texas, a paradise for settlers liking solitude. During the Civil War, became notorious as haunt of army deserters or men avoiding conscript officers and living off the country. The thicket was so hard to penetrate that it was the despair of commanding officers. Soldiers who remained loyal were somewhat demoralized by seeing that men camping in the big thicket were safe from punishment for desertion. On at least two occasions, however, the men were discovered. Once a fire was set in a circle around them, and smoked them out. A later camp was located by a veteran hunter whose pack of bear dogs brought out the deserters. Before they were hunted out, the deserters found thicket life good. They feasted on game and wild honey. Their wives, living nearby, would visit the men occasionally. Except when conscript officers were in the locality, the wives would visit caches established by the men and remove meat, hides or honey to be marketed for the support of the family. These people felt justified in deserting. Many were foreign-born and had sworn allegiance to the U.S. only 5 to 10 years earlier. Confused by the onset of war, they had fled from their homes.   (1965)

COLDSPRING (San Jacinto Co.)   *SH 150, 13.8 mi. W*
Old Waverly
Early center of culture for this part of Texas. Settled 1835–1850's, mainly by people from Alabama. Community was named for the Waverly novels of Sir Walter Scott, then very popular. To provide education equal to any, Waverly Institute was founded in 1854, with separate departments for boys and girls. Plantation system prevailed until 1860s. During Civil War, Federal troops camped in heart of Waverly, on Soldier's Hill. Of three early churches, only the Presbyterian (organized in 1860) still exists; its present building was erected in 1904.   (1969)

COLEMAN (Coleman Co.)   *US 84, .6 mi. N*
Coleman County
In early Texas this area had Apache, Comanche, Kiowa camps and mountain lookouts. A white settlement began at Camp Colorado, U.S. 2nd Cavalry Post on Jim Ned Creek, 1857. The county

was created Feb. 1, 1858 and named for Robert M. Coleman (1799–1837), a signer of Texas Declaration of Independence and a hero of the Battle of San Jacinto. To south part of county, 1862, came John Chisum, to raise cattle to be furnished to Confederate troops fighting Civil War. The county was organized Oct. 6, 1864, and courts first met at Camp Colorado. Coleman was approved as county seat April 28, 1876. (1965)

COLEMAN (Coleman Co.) *Walnut (SH 206) at courthouse*
County Named in 1857 for Robert M. Coleman (1799–1837)
Born in Kentucky. Came to Texas in 1832. Commanded company of volunteers at siege of Bexar (San Antonio), Dec. 5–10, 1835. Delegate to Constitutional Convention where he signed Texas Declaration of Independence, 1836. Aide-de-camp to Gen. Sam Houston at Battle of San Jacinto, 1836. Later fought Indians as a Texas Ranger. (1966)

COLFAX (Van Zandt Co.) *IH 20, 5 mi. E in roadside park*
Battle of the Neches (Site 15 mi. SE)
Main engagement of Cherokee war fought July 15 and 16, 1839, between 800 Indians (including Delawares and Shawnees) and 500 troops of the Republic of Texas. An extraordinary fact is that David G. Burnet, Vice President of the Republic; Albert Sidney Johnston, Secretary of War; and two other high officials took active parts in the fighting. When killed, Chief Bowles, aged Cherokee leader, carried a sword given him by Gen. Sam Houston. After the defeat of the tribes, they scattered, thus virtually ending Indian troubles in the settled eastern part of Texas. (1968)

COLLEGE STATION (Brazos Co.) *FM 60, 6 mi. W*
The Brazos River
Largest river between the Red and the Rio Grande, the 840-mile Brazos rises in 3 forks: The Salt, Clear and Double Mountain Forks. According to legend, this river saved Coronado's expedition of 1540–1542 from dying of thirst, so the men thankfully named it "Los Brazos de Dios" (Arms of God). On its banks were founded historic San Felipe, capital of Stephen F. Austin's colony, and Washington where in 1836 Texas' Declaration of Independence was signed. Vast plantations thrived in the fertile Brazos Valley, making cotton "king" in Texas until the Civil War. (1969)

COLLEGE STATION (Brazos Co.) *SH 6 Bus. off Texas Ave. at*
Main entrance, A&M Campus
Texas A&M University
The State Legislature authorized the Agricultural and Mechanical College of Texas April 17, 1871, under terms of the Federal Morrill Act. Constitutionally a part of a chartered, yet-unorganized state university, A&M gained its own directorate in 1875 with Governor Richard Coke as board president. Brazos Countians provided its 2,416-acre site. Committed to "teach . . . branches of learning" . . . related to agriculture and mechanic arts . . . to promote liberal and practical education," A&M opened Oct. 4, 1876, as the first state institution of higher learning actually operating in Texas. Thomas S. Gathright was president. Its original six students in seven academic departments grew to 28,038 students in eleven academic colleges by 1976. Initially an all-male, all-white school, it was desegregated as to color in 1963 and made fully coeducational in 1971. The Legislature recognized its diversified programs and international leadership in education and research by awarding the new name, Texas A&M University, on Aug. 23, 1963. On Sept. 17, 1971, the U.S. Congress made this one of America's first four Sea Grant colleges. National defense has drawn from Texas A&M thousands of ROTC men, including 29 general officers for World War II. (1978)

COLMESNEIL (Tyler Co.) *US 69N*
Zion Hill Missionary Baptist Church
Zion Hill Missionary Baptist Church is one of the earliest churches to serve this area's African American community. In the early 1880s, a freedmen's colony grew here in response to the availability of jobs at a newly opened sawmill. The Rev. George Durden and his congregation, with the assistance of the Rev. A. Venerable, moderator of the Trinity Valley Baptist Association, officially organized Zion Hill Missionary Baptist Church in 1881. It was the first black church congregation in Colmesneil. Worship services were held in a log cabin built by the congregation until the early 1900s. The church has occupied several locations and has served not only as a

place of worship, but also as a school for black children. In the early 1900s Zion Hill Missionary Baptist Church was moved to a site east of the Southern Pacific Railroad tracks adjacent to the Odd Fellows Hall. In 1933, the church was rebuilt at this site six blocks southwest of its original location. For over one hundred years Zion Hill Missionary Baptist Church has served the community with a variety of worship and educational programs and maintained a leadership role in civic activities. (1991)

COLMESNEIL (Tyler Co.)   *FM 1745, 4 mi. W*
Site of One of Earliest Tyler County Landmarks, Enloe Mill (1 mi. S.)
A major contributor to county and state history. Built about 1840 on Billums Creek, where the swift current made by inflow of Belts Creek would turn a water-wheel, to generate power. Mill took name from owner Benjamin Enloe, an 1837 settler who bought this property in 1849. Enloe, his son David and grandson George were known to several generations as mill operators. From this mill came lumber for the first frame courthouse in Woodville, built in 1852 while David Enloe was county sheriff. Since people came from wide area to this mill, there grew up one of area's main roads (later known as Boone's Ferry Road), connecting Fort Teran with the Old Spanish Trail from Liberty to Nacogdoches and crossing present road at this point. Enloe's Mill, one of 27 in Tyler County by 1857, produced essentials of life for settlers: cornmeal for their bread and lumber for erecting homes and other buildings. This mill also ginned cotton, their "money" product. Although long known for its raw materials rather than manufactured goods, Texas gained self-reliance from early landmarks such as Enloe's Mill. (1968)

COLORADO CITY (Mitchell Co.)   *SH 163, 4 mi. S*
Plainview Baptist Church
Begun as a mission of the Spade Community's Liberty Baptist Church, this fellowship met as early as 1906 in the Plainview Community Schoolhouse. On May 16, 1908, an organizational meeting was held to establish an independent congregation that became known as Plainview Baptist Church. Several members of the Liberty Baptist Church joined the new church at Plainview to provide leadership during its early years. Throughout its history, Plainview Baptist Church has maintained an active fellowship and has played an important role in the community's development. (1983)

COLORADO CITY (Mitchell Co.)   *SH 208, E city limits*
Colorado City Standpipe
In response to the need for a water supply system for Colorado, as this town was then known, the city's governing body issued waterwork bonds in 1884. The bond money was used to build this standpipe and to lay mains through which the city's water supply could run. The 90-foot steel standpipe was erected in 1884 by Riter and Conley of Pittsburgh, Pennsylvania, and continues in use as a storage facility for emergency water needs. The development of the city's water services was a major factor in the town's survival in the dry West Texas area. (1985)

COLORADO CITY (Mitchell Co.)   *SH 208, 6 mi. S*
Seven Wells (Site Located 1 mi. S)
This area, now covered by Lake Champion, was once the site of springs that originated from underground water which also supplied Champion Creek. They were called "wells" because the seven spring basins closely resembled man-made wells. Buffalo tracks cut deep into the creek banks of soft sandstone indicated this was a watering place for great herds of bison. At least four trails crisscrossed the area where North and South Champion Creeks converged. For hundreds of years Indians also camped here, and in the 1880s a small, early Mitchell County settlement grew up near the wells. The place remains today one of scenic beauty. (1968)

COLORADO CITY (Mitchell Co.)   *SH 208, 6 mi. S*
Union Methodist Church
Organized March, 1891, by Rev. J. W. Montgomery. First church built by J. M. Dorn and neighbors. All faiths worshipped here. Was also used as schoolhouse and community meeting place. Present church built 1905, and renamed Dorn Chapel. Planks over nail kegs were early pews. (1967)

COLUMBUS (Colorado Co.) *SH 71 at S end of Colorado River Bridge*
Site of Robson's Castle and Columbus, Texas, Meat & Ice Company
Robert Robson (1804–1878), one of many Scotsmen seeking fortune in North America, came to the Texas Republic in 1839. On land he owned at this site, he built a concrete "castle," using native lime and gravel. It had running water, pumped from the Colorado into a tank on the roof, then through wooden pipes to its many rooms. It also had a roof garden and an encircling moat, with drawbridge. From Bastrop to Matagorda, it drew guests to champagne suppers, card parties, and balls. Undermined by an 1869 flood, it became a ruin and was razed when site was put to new use in 1880s. Columbus, Texas, Meat & Ice Company built its 3-story plant on this site in 1884. It was then one of three packing houses in Texas. Established to process at place of origin, the plant could handle 125 cattle a day. Some of its beef went to Queen Victoria's London. Robert E. Stafford (1834–1890), a wealthy trail driver and rancher, veteran of Civil War service with famous Hood's Texas Brigade, owner of a private bank and extensive Colorado County properties, was president and major stockholder in the packing house. In the early 1890s, after Stafford died, the plant closed. (1973)

COLUMBUS (Colorado Co.) *SH 71, 1.5 mi. NW*
Colorado County
A part of Stephen F. Austin's first colony; created March 17, 1836; organized in 1837. The river traversing the region was called "Colorado" (Red) by Spanish explorers who mistook it for the reddish Brazos. From the river, the county took its name, Columbus, the county seat. (1964)

COLUMBUS (Colorado Co.) *US 90, 2 mi. W*
Site of the Camp
March 20–26, of one division of General Santa Anna's army under the command of General Joaquin Ramirez y Sesma. It crossed the Colorado at Atascosita Ford, eight miles below Columbus. (1964)

COLUMBUS (Colorado Co.) *US 90, .3 mi. E*
Benjamin Beason's Crossing of the Colorado River
Site of the camp, March 19–26, 1836, of the Texas Army under General Sam Houston, who directed the retreat from Gonzales to the San Jacinto. (1964)

COLUMBUS (Colorado Co.) *400 Spring St., courthouse*
The Rangers of Austin's Colony
By March 1822, Stephen F. Austin had attracted 150 colonists to Texas. The pioneers faced many hardships, including concern for their protection from Indians along the Colorado and Brazos Rivers. In December of that year, Trespalacios, the Mexican governor, divided the colony into two districts, each having an alcalde to preside over matters of local administration and a captain to handle protection of the colonists. In 1823, after several Indian attacks on members of Austin's Colony, Captain Robert Kuykendall and Alcalde John Tumlinson of the Colorado district requested permission from Trespalacios to raise a company to protect the colonists. Ten men were recruited to serve under the command of Moses Morrison. When Stephen F. Austin returned from Mexico City in August 1823, he found the colony still plagued by Indian disturbances and announced that he would employ ten additional men, at his own expense, to serve as "rangers" for the common defense. Although the law enforcement group known as the Texas Rangers was not formally organized until 1835, the "rangers" of Austin's Colony are the earliest recorded force of this type raised in Texas and served as a model for the later formation of the Texas Rangers.
(Texas Sesquicentennial 1836–1986)

COMANCHE (Comanche Co.) *US 67/337, 5 mi. E*
Hasse Community
Began as "Cordwood Junction," a siding on the Fort Worth & Rio Grande Railroad. Flatcars loaded wood here to be shipped over a wide area. As demand for the fuel increased, the railroad built a station house at site. It was named in 1892 for O. H. Hasse, thought to have been the local railway agent, 1890s. Cotton and cattle brought more business to town. A cotton gin, stock pens, and lumber yard were built. With the advent of automobiles, migration to urban centers, and highways, however, Hasse began to dwindle. Today only a few buildings remain. (1970)

COMANCHE (Comanche Co.)   US 67/377 at SH 36W
Comanche County
First settled in 1854 by five families, the county, created and organized 1856, was named for Comanche Indians, Lords of Texas frontier, who were losing hunting grounds to settlers. First county seat was Cora. Comanche has been county seat since July 18, 1859. Indians harassed settlers, stealing cattle and horses, and keeping farmers out of fields. Food from neighboring Bell County kept people here from starvation in 1862. By 1879 a stage line crossed county; the Texas Central Railroad came through in 1880; Fort Worth & Rio Grande Railroad in 1890. An oil boom occurred in 1918–1920. Agriculture has long been major industry. (1967)
   1936 Text: Created January 25, 1856; organized May 17, 1856; named for the Comanche Indians, nomads of the Plains; successful hunters, superb horsemen, and courageous warriors; the terror of Texas frontier settlers, who dispossessed them of their hunting grounds. County Seat Troy (changed to Cora), 1856; Comanche, since July 18, 1859   (1936)

COMANCHE (Comanche Co.)   US 67/377 at SH 36W
Old Corn Trail
Surveyed in 1850 by army engineers. This was the first wagon road to penetrate this area. Point of origin was San Antonio, site of U.S. Army District Headquarters after annexation of Texas in 1846. This segment of road extended from Fort Gates (in Coryell County) to Fort Griffin (Shackelford County) and Fort Belknap (Young County). Although used for communications and troop movements, most common traffic was in supplies—especially feed for army horses and mules. Hence the name "Corn Trail." Presence of the road and its traffic from fort to fort encouraged settlement. In 1851 John A. and J. M. McGuire moved to a site near here on Indian Creek. James H. Neel settled on Resley's Creek in 1852; in 1854 James Mercer and Capt. Frank Collier pitched tents on Mercer Creek, soon to be joined by their families and the Holmsleys and Tuggles. Collier put up first log house; Holmsley plowed first furrow. By Christmas of 1855 there were enough citizens here to petition for a county, and Comanche County was created by the Texas Legislature Jan. 25, 1856. The Corn Trail was a main civilian thoroughfare, and continued to serve its original purpose as a route for frontier troops and supplies.   (1967)

COMANCHE (Comanche Co.)   101 W. Central Ave. (US 87/SH 36) at courthouse
General Ashbel Smith, C.S.A. (1805–1886)
Born in Connecticut. Graduated at 19 from Yale. Studied medicine in France, where friends were Revolutionary War hero Lafayette and inventor Samuel F. B. Morse. As a North Carolina doctor he later took interest in politics and government. Came to Texas 1837. Was made Surgeon-General of Army. As headright (settler's land bounty) and pay for Army service, obtained in 1839 Comanche County tract on South Leon River, near this site. Was sent to England and France, 1842, as Texas Charge D'Affaires. In Cabinet of President Anson Jones, was last Secretary of State of Republic of Texas. Served in U.S. Army in Mexican War. As member of Texas Legislature, 1855–1857, worked on behalf of schools and railroads. Won Civil War citations for bravery. Commanded 2nd Texas Infantry. Built defenses and helped to save Texas Coast from Federal invasion. In 1865, at the end of the war, served as one of Commissioners empowered to negotiate peace terms for Texas. Was elected to Legislature in 1865 and in 1877. Serving as first Chairman of Board of Regents of University of Texas, set ideals of scholarship.   (1965)

COMANCHE (Comanche Co.)   101 W. Central Ave. (US 87/SH 36) at courthouse
Robert Thomas Hill
Robert Thomas Hill began life on August 11, 1858, in the aristocratic comforts of his parents' Nashville, Tennessee, home. His family, however, suffered tragic losses during the Civil War and by 1864 young Robert was an orphan living in his grandmother's Nashville home. He left Nashville in 1874 for Comanche County, Texas, to join his brother, Joe, as an employee of a local newspaper known as the "Comanche Chief." Hill's interest in the area's geology inspired him in 1882 to enter Cornell University where he graduated with honors in geology in 1887. In 1888 he became assistant professor of geology at the University of Texas. He participated in the State Geological Survey and identified and named the Balcones Escarpment. In 1891 Hill became president of the prestigious Cosmos Club, a society of the nation's most distinguished scientists. In the 1890s and early 1900s Hill studied the aquifers of Texas, New Mexico, and the Indian territory, and explored the geology of the trans-Pecos, Southwest U.S., West Indies, Mexico, and Central America. Hill's

publications represent one of the most distinguished geological studies produced by one individual. He died on July 28, 1941. He was cremated and his ashes scattered over Round Mountain, a butte near Comanche. (1995)

COMANCHE (Comanche Co.) *SH 16, 12 mi. S*
Captain James Cunningham, 1855
Capt. Jas. Cunningham home, 1855. Lumber hauled from Waco by ox wagon. Local stone, place of county's first wedding. (1965)

COMFORT (Kendall Co.) *US 87, 6 mi. N*
Stieler Ranch House
Designed and built 1890–1892 by Hermann Stieler, German rock mason and local sheep rancher. He came from Germany; hauled freight for Charles Schreiner Company and to Camp Verde. Made this place a shearing station for fellow ranchers. Coaches from nearby stage line often stopped for food, repairs. Style is typical of era. Each floor has two rooms on either side of central "dog trot" hall. Interior was remodeled in 1937. Has Medallion Plate. (1970)

COMFORT (Kendall Co.) *SH 27 at Cypress Creek*
Hanisch House
Using trees growing on nearby Cypress Creek, log portion of this house was built 1857 by Emil Serger and Paul Hanisch. Housed first pharmacy in Comfort. West wing and "Sunday House" were built in 1870, 1885. Restoration by Mr. and Mrs. J. C. Rice, 1947. Medallion Plate. (1965)

COMFORT (Kendall Co.) *952 High St.*
Meyer Hotel Complex
German native Frederich Christian Meyer (1828–89) came to Comfort in 1862. A wheelwright, Meyer also ran a stage stop and weigh station at this site. He later purchased the property, which included a small log cabin he enlarged by adding a second story. In 1869 he constructed a two-story stone residence here for his wife Ernestine (Mueller) (d. 1910), a midwife. A separate wooden structure was built for her work, south of the original log cabin in 1872. The building housed maternity rooms for use by the women of the surrounding area ranches. In 1887, when rail lines were completed through the area, Comfort began showing promise as a resort community. That same year, the Meyers constructed a two-story frame building south of their residence to serve as a hotel. The upper floor of the structure was used for guests and the ground floor housed a large kitchen and a dining room. With the help of their 8 children, Ernestine continued to operate the hotel after her husband's death in 1889, despite a fire which damaged the family home. A second guest house was added east of the first hotel in 1920 by a daughter Julia (Meyer) Ellenberger, who operated the business until her death in 1956. (1981)

COMFORT (Kendall Co.) *High St. between 2nd and 3rd Sts.*
"Treue Der Union" (Loyalty to the Union)
This German language monument, erected 1866, houses the memory of 68 men (mostly Germans) from this region who were loyal to the Union during the Civil War. Trying desperately to reach U.S. Federal troops by way of Mexico, about 40 of the men were killed by vengeful Confederates bent on annihilating them, in the Battle of the Nueces (on Aug. 10, 1862) and a later fight (Oct. 18). The bodies of the slain and those who drowned swimming the Rio Grande were left unburied. A group of Germans gathered the bones of their friends and buried them at this site in 1865.

COMFORT (Kendall Co.) *Broadway St., .5 blk. E of SH 27*
Freidenker (Nineteenth Century Freethinkers)
From 1845 to 1861, a number of German Freidenker ("Freethinkers") immigrated to the Texas hill country. Freethinkers were German intellectuals who advocated reason and democracy over religious and political authoritarianism. Many had participated in the 1848 German revolution and sought freedom in America. The Freidenker helped establish Bettina, Castell, Cypress Mill, Luckenbach, Sisterdale, Tusculum (Boerne) and Comfort. Laid out in 1854, Comfort soon was home to about half the population of hill country Freethinkers. Freethinkers valued their newfound freedoms of speech, assembly and religion. Their settlements, where a knowledge of Latin was considered essential for a cultured intellectual society, became known as "Latin Colonies." They

strongly supported secular education and generally did not adhere to any formal religious doctrines. They applied themselves to the crafts of physical labor and divided their time between farming and intellectual pursuits. Freethinkers advocated universal equal rights, and their moral values were dominated by their respect for life. They actively supported such social issues as the abolition of slavery and the rejection of secession. Their loyalty to the Union during the Civil War cost many their freedoms and their lives. Following the war, many Freethinkers relocated to nearby urban areas, while others returned to Germany. (2000)

COMMERCE (Hunt Co.) *1501 Monroe Street, 1blk. off SH 224*
Site of Birthplace of Maj. Gen. Claire L. Chennault (1890–1958)
Organizer-Commander of the famous "Flying Tigers" of the China-Burma-India Theater in World War II. An outstanding air strategist, Chennault had retired from a pioneer flying career when, in 1937, he was asked by Gen. Chiang Kai-Shek to help China develop an air force to combat threatening raids by Japan. Four years later, with World War II spreading, he received permission from the U.S. to seek a corps of American airmen to help train the Chinese. A total of 252 men—87 pilots and 165 ground personnel—joined the "American Volunteer Group." Its popular name resulted from a misunderstanding of the sharks' teeth painted on the noses of the aircraft. The Tigers formed three squadrons—"Adam and Eve," "Panda Bears," and "Hell's Angels"—supported by the expert pilots of the China National Aviation Corps, a daring supply transport group. So effectively had Chennault studied Japanese air tactics that his tiny band officially destroyed 539 enemy aircraft while losing only 90 itself. During 1941–1942, they checked Japan's invasion of China, then joined regular units. Jack Cornelius, also a native of Commerce and a close friend of Chennault's, was a member of the first pursuit squadron of the Tigers. (1968)

COMSTOCK (Val Verde Co.) *SH 163, 11 mi. N*
Dead Man's Pass
This narrow canyon marks a remote and perilous section of a road traveled from San Antonio to El Paso and on to California following the Gold Rush of the 1840s. Adding to the hardships of a journey that took several weeks, this particular area was notorious for wild animal attacks and raids by Native Americans and highwaymen. Also known as Dead Man's Run, the feature was named by 1849; an ambush on a Dr. Lyon's wagon train that ended with two teamsters and an unknown number of Indians dead. In 1850, a group met a similar fate when they turned back from Beaver Lake (25 mi. N) and passed through here en route to San Antonio for supplies. Four teamsters were killed in the encounter. The U.S. Army attempted to protect travelers on the hazardous road. When forts Clark (60 mi. SE) and Inge (90 mi. SE) proved to be too remote, the army established Camp Hudson on the Devils River 10 miles north of here in 1857. However, dangerous conditions continued for many years. In A Texas Pioneer, freighter August Santleben (1845–1911) enumerated several dozen civilians and soldiers killed along the trail, including five members of the Amlung family and seven others who perished here one day in 1858. The pass was considered dangerous as late as the early 1880s. Santleben chronicled several deaths in the area over a 40-year period, totaling nearly 400 in southwest Texas. Two similar topographic names nearby recall the risks of 19th century travel. Dead Man's Creek rises two miles southwest of this site and flows southeast to the Devils River, while Dead Man's Canyon begins a mile to the northeast and runs west to the Pecos. This path that later became a stage route to Ozona and then State Highway 163 is today remembered as a treacherous frontier road. (2007)

COMSTOCK (Val Verde Co.) *US 90, 16 mi. W at roadside park*
Railroad Bridges Over the Pecos
A major tributary of the Rio Grande, the Pecos River was long a barrier to transportation, particularly across the deep gorge that once marked its joining with the Rio Grande. Construction of the first railroad bridge over the Pecos took place in 1882 as part of the transcontinental route of the Southern Pacific Railroad across the lower portion of the United States. Access to the bridge, which was then deep in the canyon, was by means of a circuitous route and two tunnels. In 1890, Southern Pacific officials began planning for a new bridge, one that would cut directly across the ravine by means of a high-line viaduct that would save miles and straighten the route. Work began in late 1891 and was completed within three months at a cost of more than $250,000. Supported by 24 towers, the bridge was the highest in North America and the third highest in the world at the

time of its completion. Passenger trains slowed to six miles per hour before crossing it and stopped while on the bridge to afford travelers a view. During World War II, the Pecos High Bridge became essential to the transportation of war materials. In response to heavier trains and the war demand, a new bridge was built in 1944, with special permission from the War Production Board to use "critical materials" in its construction. The 1944 Pecos High Bridge remains in use, although the gorge is not so deep as it once was, due to the rising of the river with the construction of Amistad Reservoir. (2002)

COMSTOCK (Val Verde Co.) *US 90, 16 mi. W at roadside park*
Site of Vinegarroon
Crossing the Pecos River Canyon was the last major obstacle the Southern Pacific Railroad faced in completing its southern transcontinental route linking New Orleans and San Francisco. As "Tunnel No. 2" was excavated on the west side of the canyon in 1882, a camp for the railroad workers was established near the site. Named Vinegarroon for a type of scorpion found in the area, the camp served as a temporary home for thousands of primarily Chinese laborers. Roy Bean had a saloon and served as Justice of the Peace in Vinegarroon until it was abandoned after the rail line was complete in 1883. (2001)

COMSTOCK (Val Verde Co.) *US 90, 16 mi. W at roadside park*
Near Site, Southern Pacific Ceremony of Silver Spike
Marked completion of Southern Pacific Railway. Eastern part originated in Texas in 1850s; then was rechartered 1870 by Texas Legislature as Galveston, Harrisburg & San Antonio Rwy., designed to join Houston and San Antonio to the Rio Grande. T. W. Peirce of Boston gained control in 1874. Meantime, C. P. Huntington of California was building the Southern Pacific eastward; he wanted a Texas line to join his tracks, and reached agreement with Peirce. On Jan. 12, 1883, the two railroads met near the Pecos High Bridge, and were joined by a silver spike. (1967)

COMSTOCK (Val Verde Co.) *US 90, 11 mi. W at Pecos River overlook*
Medal of Honor Fight, 1875
In the 1870s, the U.S. Army relied on Black Seminole (Seminole-Negro) Indian scouts in campaigns against raiding Native Americans along the Texas-Mexico border. In April 1875, Lt. John L. Bullis and three scouts—Sergeant John Ward, Private Pompey Factor and Trumpeter Isaac Payne—left Fort Clark to scout for raiders in this area. After four days, they found a fresh trail and on April 25, within a half-mile of this site, they engaged a party of about 30 Comanche Indians with dozens of horses. Outgunned and outnumbered, the scouts withdrew, but Bullis' horse bolted, stranding him. Factor and Payne provided cover fire, and Ward rescued his Lieutenant. The three Seminole scouts later received Medals of Honor for their gallantry. (2006)

COMSTOCK (Val Verde Co.) *US 90, 11 mi. W at Pecos River overlook*
The Pecos River in Literature and Folklore
Noted for mineral-thick waters and sudden floods, the Pecos River snakes through Texas on its way to the Rio Grande. Historian J. Evetts Haley and folklorist J. Frank Dobie, who called it "a strange river," and a "barricade," are among many who have immortalized the Pecos in writing. Zane Grey wrote, "Rising clear and cold in the mountains of northern New Mexico, its pure waters cut through rough country that changed its flood to turbid red." Storytellers have likened the river and the arid land along it to hell, death and violence. A natural border for several counties, the Pecos is where the mythic Wild West begins, the land that produced the legendary Judge Roy Bean and fabled Pecos Bill. (2005)

COMSTOCK (Val Verde Co.) *US 90, 11 mi. W at Pecos River overlook*
Pecos River High Bridge
High canyon walls dominate the last 60 miles of the Pecos River before it enters the Rio Grande. The Southern Pacific Railroad built the first high bridge across the Pecos River in 1891. The first highway bridge to span the river was built one mile downriver from here in 1923. Just 50 feet above water, the 1923 bridge was destroyed by floodwaters in 1954. Two temporary low-water bridges built nearby in 1954 and 1955 also were destroyed by floodwaters. A new 1,310-feet long bridge was completed here in 1957. At 273 feet above the river it is the highest highway bridge in Texas.
(Sesquicentennial of Texas Statehood 1845–1995)

CONCAN (Uvalde Co.)   *SH 127 W at US 83*
C.S.A. Saltpetre Mine
Important to Texas in waging the Civil War. Site of natural deposits of bat guano, worked in the 1860s to obtain the chief ingredient for gunpowder. Cave inhabited by bats, source of the guano, extends about 23 miles. One room in the great bat den is 585' x 325', and has a 45' ceiling. A narrow gauge railway with mule drawn cars was used in the digging. Corrals for the mules occupied one chamber of the cave. Putrefied and dried bat guano, mixed with smaller parts of sulphur and charcoal, gave firepower to Civil War guns.   (1965)

CONCAN (Uvalde Co.)   *US 127 at US 83*
Silver Mine Pass (2 mi. W)
Named for silver mine opened near pass by Spaniards in 1700s or earlier. Ore was inferior, and mine was abandoned; but 14 shafts (some interconnecting) remain. Near the mine are remnants of a fortification made by 30 men under leadership of James Bowie, later (1836) a hero of the siege to the Alamo. In 1831, while at work at this mine, Bowie's men repulsed a Comanche attack in a fierce, all-day battle. Hero of the fight was Bowie's slave, "Black Jim Bowie," who risked his life by leaving the fortification to bring water to the besieged.   (1968)

CONE (Crosby Co.)   *US 62, at site*
Village of Cone
Named in 1903 for S. E. Cone, who helped carry mail here from the nearby town of Emma. Post office was established same year in general store of R. E. Chapman, who became the first postmaster. Town once had a school, stores, and churches. Now center of irrigated section, which produces cotton, sorghum grains, and wheat.   (1969)

CONROE (Montgomery Co.)   *FM 3083, Four Corners*
Conroe Oil Field
One of the great petroleum areas of the Texas Coastal Region. Opened Dec. 13, 1931, by the discovery well of George Strake (No. 1 South Texas Development Co.), about 1.4 miles west of here. Initial daily flow: 15,000,000 cubic feet of gas, along with white gasoline. Strake's Second Well, a 900-barrel-a-day producer, and the Heep Oil Corp.-No. 1 Freeman (both coming in during June 1932) proved existence of a large field. Fast-paced drilling ensued. In Jan. 1933 Madeley No. 1, of Kansas Standard, came in as a wild well and on fire. TNT charges and tons of earth did not smother the fire; it burned about three months. Cratering spread to Harrison and Abercrombie well nearby, and that gushed out of control. In Jan. 1934 a driller for Humble "killed the blowout," by using directional drilling for first time in coastal Texas. This saved the field. (The crater is 600 feet deep.) The Conroe Field was the first in Texas to adopt 20-acre spacing, before this was mandatory under conservation rules. It has yielded over 400,000,000 barrels of oil; now produces at the yearly rate of 5,300,000 barrels. After the dramatic discovery here, Montgomery County developed 11 other oil fields, and has vast reserves for continuing production.   (1967)

CONROE (Montgomery Co.)   *SH 105, 7.5 mi. W near Lake Conroe dam site*
West Fork of the San Jacinto River
Patiri and other Indians lived here in Archaic and Neo-American Periods. When Spanish incursions began in the 1700s, the river was named either for hyacinths or for the saint on whose day it was discovered. Pioneers from the United States settled on the San Jacinto before Stephen F. Austin founded his colony to the west in 1821. Upon their wish to join him, he took this area into his colony in 1824. The San Jacinto won world fame when beside its lower channel Mexican Dictator Santa Anna with 1700 troops was defeated on April 21, 1836, by General Sam Houston and Texas volunteers fighting for freedom. Riverside farms became plantations, often shipping cotton by keelboat down the San Jacinto, in 1845–1861. Until woodlands vanished during the years 1880–1930, sandhill cranes and bear abounded. Reforestation, begun in 1936, brought back timber industries and small game. The lake now makes this a residential and recreational paradise, but covers such landmarks as Grandma Ed'ards Fishing Hole, Indian Camp Creek, and the White Sugar Sand Crossing. Downriver, after this fork and the East Fork unite, the San Jacinto forms part of the Houston Ship Channel, the link between Port of Houston, the Gulf, and the High Seas.   (1975)

COOKS POINT (Burleson Co.)   *SH 21 near FM 1362*
Cooks Point
Founded about 1840 where colonial road from southeast crossed San Antonio Road. Settler Gabriel Jackson had two story log cabin–trading post here. Community was named for Silas L. Cooke, who surveyed much land in this vicinity. It is now a thriving rural village.   (1969)

COOKS POINT (Burleson Co.)   *SH 21 at FM 1362*
Near Homesite of Judge Andrew S. Broaddus (1810–1891)
Noted pioneer leader. Member Virginia House of Delegates (1844–1845). Piloted to Texas (1854) a mile-long wagon train of 200 people, who built Salem Baptist Church—reminder of their Virginia home. Broaddus debated the Hon. Sam Houston at Waugh Campground (8 mi. W), 1857. He served in 1861 in Texas Secession Convention; 9th (1861–1863) Texas Legislature; 13th Texas Legislature (1873); also on commission to locate and build Texas Agricultural & Mechanical College (now University); Judge, 32nd District (1874–1875; 1879–1880). Married twice, had 13 children.
(1971)

COOKS POINT (Burleson Co.)   *FM 50, 2 mi. E of SH 21*
Brazos River Levee
Destructive Brazos River floods have often plagued residents of Burleson County. In 1899, a 30-inch rain killed 35 and caused about $9 million in property damage. Again in 1900, 1902, and 1908 Brazos River bottom inhabitants endured serious flooding. In 1909, W. S. Mial and 49 other citizens asked the commissioners of Burleson County to build levees along the Brazos to protect the valuable farm land. In July 1909, voters unanimously approved the issuance of bonds and the higher taxes to pay off the debt. Contractors Roach and Stansell built the 8-foot levee which extended south for 30 miles. Its test came in December 1913, with a storm far worse than the 1899 flood. Residents of this area, depending on the levee for safety, did not flee until the water had risen dangerously. Too late, they discovered the levee trapped water and then broke, unleashing a wall of destruction from which there was no escape. Victims rode out the flood on roofs and in treetops. There were 180 deaths and $8 million property loss. Still convinced of the value of the levees, voters in 1914 approved reconstruction bonds. The indebtedness was not retired until 1963, long after modern flood control methods made the area safe.   (1978)

COOKVILLE (Titus Co.)   *US 67, 7 mi. E of Mt. Pleasant*
W. A. Keith House
Oldest house in Cookville. Erected in 1880 by W. A. "Doc" Keith (1850–1930), farmer, county attorney (1895), postmaster. Built of rough-milled, hand-planed pine with hand-hewn oak sills. Originally had three rooms and hall. Has been remodeled slightly. Has Medallion Plate.   (1970)

COOL (Parker Co.)   *US 180, 2.8 mi. W*
Weatherford, Mineral Wells and Northwestern Railway
In 1852, years before the nation's first transcontinental rail line was completed in 1869, the Texas Legislature chartered what would become the Texas & Pacific Railway Company. The Civil War halted progress, but in 1888 the line reached Weatherford in its advance westward to the Pacific coast. The tracks then turned south to avoid the Palo Pinto Hills. This left northwestern Parker County and most of Palo Pinto County without rail support. In the 1880s, Mineral Wells became a resort. A stage line connected it to the railroad at Millsap, but the town's popularity called for a rail connection. Several men, led by W. A. Stone of Missouri, received a charter for the Weatherford, Mineral Wells & Northwestern Railway Company in 1889. The line linked Mineral Wells to Weatherford, which by then was served by the T&P and Santa Fe railroads. The WMW&NWRR established a depot, offices and repair shop in Weatherford. The new line, built largely on land obtained from the Franco-Texan Land Company, included stops at Lemley, Franco, Garner and Rock Creek. On January 1, 1891, a crowd in Mineral Wells greeted the first train's arrival, and by 1899 approximately 33,000 passengers made the trip each year from Weatherford to Mineral Wells. The line also supported freight shipments. T&P eventually acquired the line and extended it to Salesville, Oran and Graford. By the beginning of the 1940s, after decades of highway expansion, the rail line was no longer productive. The advent of World War II and the training of troops at nearby Camp Wolters resurrected the line briefly. It became part of the Missouri Pacific system in 1988 and closed in 1992.   (2006)

COOPER (Delta Co.)   *SH 24, 4.5 mi. NE*
Erected in the Centennial Year, to Commemorate Founding of Delta County
Named for shape, resembling Greek letter, and for evident origin of its land—sedimentation at fork of North and South Sulphur Rivers. The first (1820–1830) political activity here was oversight by the Sulphur Forks Indian Commission (of the United States) of the Caddo, Delaware, Quapaw, and Seminole inhabitants. After Texas Independence in 1836, the Delta came under jurisdictions of Red River, Lamar, and Hopkins Counties. Families and wagon trains from Kentucky, Tennessee, and other states—and from other parts of Texas—settled here as early as the 1830s. The people of the Delta in 1868 petitioned for creation of the county; in 1870 the Legislature of Texas complied. The county seat, a new town to be in the geographic center, was named for Leroy Cooper, chairman of the House Committee on Counties and Boundaries. Gov. E. J. Davis named as commissioners to organize the county: Joel Blackwell, John P. Boyd, James Hamilton, J. W. Iglehart, and Thomas J. Lane. To supervise sales of lots in Cooper, Erastus Blackwell was appointed sheriff. The organizing election was held on Oct. 6, 1870, naming Charles S. Nidever as chief justice. Commissioners elected were John P. Boyd, J. F. Alexander, Alfred Allen, and J. M. Bledsoe.   (1970)

COOPER (Delta Co.)   *SH 19/154, 6 mi. SE*
DeSpain Bridge (Site 4.2 mi. SW)
Located where the Bonham-Jefferson Road crossed the South Sulphur River, this pioneer bridge served the area's rich cotton trade for some 20 years. It was constructed before 1850 by landowner Brig DeSpain and his neighbors to provide access to the county seat—Tarrant—in Hopkins County. The land was originally awarded to the family of Randolph DeSpain, a Texas Revolutionary soldier who was killed in the massacre at Goliad in 1836. Strongly built of native oak and bois d'arc wood, the bridge withstood heavy traffic of ox-wagons and horse-drawn vehicles. The narrow ridge of land where it was situated was known as "Granny's Neck," for Mrs. Mary Sinclair, who lived in the vicinity. Until cotton and corn became important crops, the South Sulphur River ran clear. Afterward, eroded dirt from plowed fields muddied its waters. Shortly after 1870—the year Delta County was organized—heavy rains washed out the bridge. The state of Texas built a new one, which took the name of G. W. Harper, toll keeper. Later Hopkins and Delta Counties assumed maintenance of this new bridge, which continued to channel cotton and corn wagons between the two regions for several decades.   (1970)

COOPER (Delta Co.)   *SH 154, 3 mi. E*
Hiram Rattan (Homesite .3 mi., Grave .4 mi. N)
Delta County pioneer, born 1805. Settled in Texas, 1835, on brother Larkin Rattan's 1,000-acre land grant; later became site for city of Paris. Both Rattan families moved to Delta County in 1839. Hiram obtained two third-class land grants for producing grain and livestock. Larkin later joined the California Gold Rush, then returned to his native Illinois. Four Rattan relatives were massacred by Texas Indians. Civil War and politics divided family but never their devotion to Texas. Descendants include educators, military and political leaders.   (1967)

COOPER (Delta Co.)   *SH 154S at FM 1529*
Delta County
Formed from Lamar and Hopkins counties; created July 29, 1870. The name describes its position and triangular shape. Cooper, the county seat. Named for shape, resembling Greek letter (triangle), and for evident origin of its land—sedimentation at fork of North and South Sulphur Rivers. The first (1820–30) political activity here was oversight by the Sulphur Forks Indian Commission (of the United States) of the Caddo, Delaware, Quapaw, and Seminole inhabitants. After Texas Independence in 1836, the delta came under jurisdictions of Red River, Lamar, and Hopkins counties. Families and wagon trains from Kentucky, Tennessee, and other states—and from other parts of Texas—settled here as early as the 1830s. The people of the delta in 1868 petitioned for creation of the county; in 1870 the Legislature of Texas complied. The county seat, a new town to be in the geographic center, was named for Leroy Cooper, chairman of the House Committee on Counties and Boundaries. Gov. E. J. Davis named as commissioners to organize the county: Joel Blackwell, John P. Boyd, James Hamilton, J. W. Iglehart, and Thomas J. Lane. To supervise sales of lots in Cooper, Erastus Blackwell was appointed sheriff. The organizing election was held on Oct. 6, 1870, naming Charles S. Nidever as Chief Justice. Commissioners elected were John P. Boyd, J. F. Alexander, Alfred Allen, and J. M. Bledsoe.   (1936)

COOPER (Delta Co.)   *FM 64, 3.5 mi. W*
The Pioneer Smith Brothers
Tall, strong men who helped to carve Delta County out of Texas frontier. Benjamin, Charles, Gilford and Mira J. Smith came to Texas from Arkansas before or during the 1840s. They obtained from heirs title to the Moses Williams Land Grant, patented 1849, and surveyed by Major George W. Stell. After 1853 several generations of the Smith family lived here. The brothers were each 6 feet, 4 inches or taller and weighed over 250 pounds. They cut logs and built their cabins with puncheon (split-log) floors, riven-board roofs, and homemade furniture. Instead of nails wooden pegs were used; instead of glass windows, board shutters. Chimneys were of black clay mud plastered over sticks. Bear meat was the main food, obtained by hunting with flintlock rifles in such dangerous places as Jernigan Thicket, 2 miles west. Charles H. Smith kept bees, and was known as "Honey." Mira J. Smith was a key man in settling of Delta County, because he was an early blacksmith. His first son, Moses, became a tanner; the second son, Henry, a blacksmith. The women of the four families carded cotton and wool, and spun, wove, and sewed clothing. Young Moses Smith also made men's buckskin suits. Grant has produced over $1,000,000 worth of cotton.   (1968)

COPPERAS COVE (Coryell Co.)   *US 190, 1 mi. S*
Ogletree Stagestop and Post Office (.5 mi. W)
After Marsden Ogletree (1819–1896) and his family migrated from Georgia, he received a land grant in 1878. Inscriptions on two stones in this house indicate the structure was erected the same year. It served as the family home, grain store, and stopping place for the Lampasas to Belton stagecoach. Since the mail arrived by stage, a post office was opened here in 1879 with Ogletree as postmaster. Legend says that the settlement received the name "Coperas Cove" from a copperas-tasting spring in the cove of a nearby mountain. Samuel Gilmore served as the second postmaster. In 1881, Gilmore's father-in-law Jesse M. Clements (1822–1900) and his wife Charley deeded land for the right-of-way to the Gulf, Colorado & Santa Fe Railroad. The following year the railroad laid out the new townsite of Coperas Cove. Soon the center of the community, including the post office, moved over to the railroad. Later the town corrected the spelling of its name to "Copperas Cove." In 1891, Clements bought this house and used it as the headquarters for his large ranching operations. The old stone stagestop remains a visible link with the community's pioneer heritage.   (1979)

CORPUS CHRISTI (Nueces Co.)   *IH-37, frontage road at Mountain Trail*
Calallen
The rural Nueces County settlement of Calallen was established by the Calvin Townsite Company on August 18, 1910. The president of the firm was the prominent local cattleman Calvin J. Allen (1859–1922), for whom the town was named. The area's abundant water supply and the settlement's location on the St. Louis, Brownsville and Mexico Rail Line resulted in Calallen's development as an important agricultural center of the region. Calallen's greatest period of growth occurred from the 1920s to the 1940s. During that time it was the site of a hotel, funeral home, lumberyard, post office, doctor's office, bank, churches, a variety of stores and a school district, formed in 1914. Major employers here included a Corpus Christi water plant and the vegetable packing firm of C. E. Coleman. Residents of the community included some of the prominent cattlemen and business leaders of South Texas. Calallen's decline began as new roads resulted in dramatic growth for Corpus Christi. Although the Calallen school remained in operation, the rural town was annexed by Corpus Christi in 1970. Today the area serves as a reminder of the early residents who were vital to the growth of Nueces County.   (1982)

CORPUS CHRISTI (Nueces Co.)   *IH 37, Violet Rd. exit, on frontage rd.*
Nuecestown (4 mi. N)
Henry L. Kinney (b. 1814), who founded Corpus Christi, established Nuecestown in 1852 at the location of the first ferry crossing on the Nueces River west of Corpus Christi. He sent agents to Europe, primarily England and Germany, to promote his new settlement. Each immigrant purchased 100 acres of land, a town lot, and 10 head of cattle. Nuecestown, known locally as "The Motts" because of several clusters of trees, grew to have, in addition to the ferry, a hotel, packery, and one of the county's first cotton gins. A post office opened in 1859. After the Civil War it was a gathering place for cattle drovers in the area herding longhorns to be driven to northern railheads. On Good Friday, March 26, 1875, Mexican bandits entered the region on a raid, causing many

Corpus Christi residents to flee. After plundering the Frank store (3 mi. E), the raiders turned on Nuecestown, looting and burning T. J. Noakes' store and post office, killing one man, and capturing several hostages. A party of citizens pursued the attackers unsuccessfully, and another man was killed. When bypassed by the St. Louis, Brownsville, & Mexico Railway about 1905, Nuecestown began to decline. The post office closed in 1927. (1973)

CORPUS CHRISTI (Nueces Co.) IH-37 at courthouse
Nueces County
Named for Rio Nueces (River of Nuts), its northern border. In 1519, Pineda, one of the first Spanish explorers, paused briefly in this area. Spain founded Fort Lipantitlan nearby in 1531. Post, named for an Indian village, fell into Anglo-American hands in 1835 during Texas Revolution. Strategic value of this area (with its outlet to the sea) was recognized in 1845 when U.S. Army forces camped here en route to battlefronts in Mexican War. County was created in 1846 and organized in 1847 with Corpus Christi as the county seat. (1970)

CORPUS CHRISTI (Nueces Co.) US 181 at end of Mesquite St.
near Harbor Bridge
Early History of the Port of Corpus Christi
Protected by offshore islands, the shallow waters of Corpus Christi Bay were a haven for smugglers before the Texas Revolution (1836). Commercial activity began when Henry L. Kinney (1814–1860s) opened a trading post here about 1838. After the Mexican War (1846–1848), Corpus Christi became a departure point for the California Gold Rush (1849) and a main stop on the route between San Antonio and the Rio Grande Valley. In 1854 the city authorized dredging operations to make the harbor accessible to deep water vessels. In 1857 a circuitous 32-mile long channel was opened from Corpus Christi Bay to Aransas Pass. Blockaded by Federal ships during the Civil War (1861–1865), Corpus Christi remained a major port for Confederate trade with Mexico until the harbor was captured in 1864. The ship channel was widened and deepened in 1874. Elihu Harrison Ropes of New Jersey came to Corpus Christi in 1890 with ambitious plans for development of the city and port. Using a steam dredge, he began digging a 14-mile long, 15-foot deep pass across Mustang Island. The "Ropes Boom" collapsed in the Panic of 1893, but Ropes' efforts laid a foundation for the opening of the Port of Corpus Christi of Sept. 15, 1926, and its success as one of the nation's largest seaports. (1977)

CORPUS CHRISTI (Nueces Co.) Ocean Drive at Cole Park
Alonzo Álvarez de Pineda
In 1519, the Spanish government commissioned Alonzo Álvarez de Pineda (1494–1519) to explore the coast of the Gulf of Mexico in the hope of finding a water passage from the Gulf to the Orient. Ships, men, and money for the expedition were provided by the Governor of Jamaica, Francisco de Garay, who had been on Christopher Columbus' second voyage to the New World. Pineda followed the coast from what is now western Florida to present-day Vera Cruz, Mexico. During his 9-month expedition he mapped nearly 800 miles of shoreline, including the rivers and bays that emptied into the Gulf. He arrived in Vera Cruz in August 1519 to find that another explorer, Hernán Cortés, already had claimed the land. After escaping from Cortés, who had attempted to capture him, Pineda sailed north, stopping briefly near a river that was probably the Rio Grande. He may have died of wounds received in an Indian fight there, since his return to Jamaica never was confirmed. Pineda's report and detailed map were forwarded to Governor Garay and then to King Charles I of Spain. Although Pineda's expedition was a failure in that he found no passage to the Orient, it did encourage further exploration along the Gulf Coast that led to colonization by Spaniards and other Europeans. (1983)

CORPUS CHRISTI (Nueces Co.) Ocean Dr. at SH 3
Karankawa Indians
Among the first Indians encountered in Texas by 16th and 17th century European explorers were the nomadic Karankawas, who lived along the coast from Galveston Bay to the Corpus Christi area. A primitive tribe, the Karankawas fished and gathered roots and cactus fruit for food. The men were usually tall and wore their hair long or braided with colorful bits of flannel and rattlesnake rattles. The women were shorter and stouter. The Indians often smeared their bodies with alligator grease and dirt to repel mosquitoes. At first friendly to Europeans, they later gained a reputation

109

for savagery. Persistent reports that the Karankawas were cannibals may be traced to occasional ritualistic practices. Attempts by Spanish Franciscans to found missions for this coastal tribe were not successful. Never large in numbers, the Karankawa population dwindled as a result of diseases contracted from Europeans. During the 19th century, many of the Indians were killed in warfare with Jean Lafitte's pirates and with Anglo-American colonists. Remaining members of the tribe fled to Mexico about 1843. Annihilation of that remnant about 1858 marked the disappearance of the Karankawa Indians. (1976)

CORPUS CHRISTI (Nueces Co.)   *SH 358 near Laguna Shores Rd.*
Flour Bluff
In the spring of 1838 France blockaded the coast of Mexico during the Pastry War, so-called because of the mistreatment of French citizens, including pastry chefs, living in Mexico. The strategic location of Corpus Christi Bay led to the revival of smuggling in this area. Supplies were carried overland across the Rio Grande, and the illicit trade flourished as Mexico bought sorely needed goods in Texas. Although President Sam Houston did not wish to antagonize Mexico, Mexican patrols at Corpus Christi offended many Texans. In July, 1838, authorities at Texana heard reports of Mexican activity near the bay. A captured Mexican sea captain said that his government had declared Corpus Christi a port of entry and had dispatched about 400 men to protect it. A summons was issued, calling Texans to rally at Texana, Aug. 7, to drive the invaders from the Republic's boundaries. By the time the volunteers reached the area, some of the Mexicans had landed their supplies near the tip of Corpus Christi Bay and returned to Matamoros. The rest scattered, leaving about 100 barrels of flour and parts of a steam engine. The Texans confiscated the usable flour, and other contraband, and the site became known as Flour Bluff. (1976)

CORPUS CHRISTI (Nueces Co.)   *SH 358 to JFK Causeway to 2 mi. onto PR 22*
Padre Island and Padre Nicolás Ballí
First called Corpus Christi Island or Isla Santiago, Padre Island was named for Padre Jose Nicolás Ballí (177?–1829). His family migrated from Spain in 1569 and became large landowners in the lower Rio Grande Valley, influential in military and governmental affairs. Ordained about 1790, Padre Ballí applied to Spain's King Charles IV in 1800 for 11 1/2 leagues of land on the island. Padre Ballí had the land surveyed and in 1804 started the first settlement, Rancho Santa Cruz, about 26 miles from the southern tip. He began the island's first mission for the settlers and to Christianize the Karankawa Indians. With help from a nephew, Juan José Ballí, as "Mayordomo" or Foreman, Padre Ballí started ranching, bringing in large herds of cattle, horses, and sheep. Padre Ballí served as missionary and the collector of finances for all churches in the Rio Grande Valley. With financial aid from his mother Doña Rosa María de Hinojosa, he opened the first mission in present Cameron County and began a church and the first school at present Matamoros, Mexico. Padre Ballí's ministry influenced the lives of early settlers in south Texas. He was buried near Matamoros. (1979)

CORPUS CHRISTI (Nueces Co.)   *Park Road 22, N of SH 361 on Padre Island*
The Pat Dunn Ranch
Patrick Francis Dunn, the son of Irish immigrants Thomas and Catherine H. Dunn, was born Oct. 10, 1858, in Corpus Christi. He married Clara J. Jones Aug. 30, 1883. In Dec. 1883, Pat Dunn entered a partnership with his mother and brother, Thomas, to graze cattle on Padre Island, and as manager moved to the island in Jan. 1884, settling 20 miles down the coast. Laguna Madre and the Gulf of Mexico served as natural fences; during roundup, ranch hands drove stock into several corrals scattered along the 110-mile island. When his children reached school age, Dunn moved back to Corpus Christi and established headquarters at the north end of the island. In 1907, after buying his brother's interest, he built a 2-story house on Corpus Christi Pass (0.5 mi. E.), using lumber washed ashore from shipwrecks. Much of the house and corrals were constructed of fine mahogany. The house was destroyed in the hurricane of 1916, the year of his mother's death, which left Dunn as sole owner of the ranch. Pat Dunn sold his Padre Island interests in 1926, retaining grazing rights, which he used until his death March 25, 1937. His son, Burton Dunn, continued ranching operations until his death Sept. 8, 1970, after which the last cattle were removed from Padre Island. (1973)

CORPUS CHRISTI (Nueces Co.)   *SH 286 at FM 70, 12 mi. S at Chapman Ranch*
Chapman Ranch
In Jan. 1919, Philip Alexander Chapman (1847–1924) purchased 34,631 acres of the Laureles Division of the King Ranch for development as farm lands similar to others he owned in East Texas and Oklahoma. He sent his son, J. O. Chapman (1883–1953), to supervise operations. Arriving in Sept. 1919, J. O. Chapman began dividing "Nueces Farms" into 160-acre tracts and leasing them to tenants. In 1924, the name was changed to Chapman Ranch. The town, founded in 1925, had a hospital, cotton gin, 2 schools, its own power plant, and "The Commissary," which housed grocery, hardware, and mercantile stores, a barber shop, soda fountain, automobile agency, service station, post office, and ranch headquarters offices. In 1926, over 20,000 acres were in cultivation. The ranch contracted with manufacturers to test modern farm equipment. Several implements were invented here. In the late 1920s, Chapman Ranch was advertised as the world's largest mechanized farm. During the 1930s, the ranch conducted extensive crop experiments, and developed a superior strain of long-staple cotton, the seed of which was marketed worldwide. By 1941, the town had dwindled away, and the land was partitioned among P. A. Chapman's children, whose heirs continue to operate the ranch.   (1973)

CORRIGAN (Polk Co.)   *N. Home St. (US 59) at Ben Franklin St.*
Town of Corrigan
Located in piney woods of east Texas. Founded about 1860 by landowner and settler James B. Hendry, who donated property for original townsite. When the Texas & New Orleans Railroad was built through area in the early 1880s, a prosperous timber-based economy developed here. The town was named for T. & N. O. official, Pat Corrigan. In 1884 the Trinity & Sabine Timber Company platted town, and soon a hotel, blacksmith shop, several stores, and a 10-pin (bowling) alley appeared. Today lumber, ranching, and farming undergird economy.   (1970)

CORSICANA (Navarro Co.)   *IH 45 Bus., 2.2 mi. N in roadside park*
Navarro County
Formed from Robertson County. Created April 25, 1846; organized July 13, 1846. Named in honor of Jose Antonio Navarro 1795–1871. Soldier, patriot and statesman, signer of the Texas Declaration of Independence, member of the Texas Congress 1838, Commissioner on the Santa Fe Expedition, delegate in 1845 to the Constitutional Convention. County seat Corsicana.

CORSICANA (Navarro Co.)   *401 W. 7th St. (SH 31)*
Collin Street Bakery
Immigrant baker from Wiesbaden, Germany, and W. T. McElwee, a local cotton buyer. Combining the talents of a baker whose pride and joy was baking a better cake with the flare of a man whose business ability had a touch of the sensational was a move that resulted in a most unusual and successful business enterprise. One of Weidmann's few assets was an unknown cake recipe. This was to become the famous original "deluxe fruitcake," today shipped to every state in the United States and to many foreign countries. McElwee, a lover of sports and the theatre, built a rooming house over the bakery in 1906, and invited visiting baseball players, circus performers and vaudeville troupes to stay there. Soon guests were having fruitcakes shipped to friends in remote places. Employees at the bakery during this era recall visits from Will Rogers, Enrico Caruso, John J. McGraw, "Gentlemen Jim" Corbett and many other celebrities. They also recall the day the great circus showman, John Ringling, and many of his famous performers stopped in and ordered Christmas cakes sent to their many friends in distant lands.   (1967)

CORSICANA (Navarro Co.)   *1465 W 2nd (SH 22) at 24th St.*
James Clinton Neill
Born in 1790 in North Carolina, James Clinton Neill came to Texas in 1831 with Stephen F. Austin's third colony. He settled in Milam County and represented his neighbors at the Convention of 1833. On September 28, 1835, Neill entered the Texas Army as captain of artillery, and was promoted to Lt. Colonel in December. He was in charge of artillery at the Siege of Bexar, and soon thereafter was appointed by Sam Houston to the Commandancy of San Antonio and the Bexar District, including the fortifications at the Alamo. When he received word in February of illness in his family, Neill left the Alamo in the command of William B. Travis, and so was not among the

defenders who lost their lives on March 6. In charge of an artillery unit with Sam Houston's army in April, Neill was wounded in a skirmish on April 20, one day before the Battle of San Jacinto. He was appointed Indian commissioner in 1844. Neill was living in present Navarro County when it was created from Robertson County in 1846. He and two partners donated land for the county seat. James Clinton Neill and his wife, Margaret Harriet were the parents of three children. Neill died in March 1848, and is buried in Grimes County.   (Texas Sesquicentennial 1836–1986)

CORSICANA (Navarro Co.)   *300 W 3rd St. at courthouse*
José Antonio Navarro
Lover of liberty. Foe of despotism. Born in San Antonio, Texas, February 27, 1795. Died January 13, 1871 and buried there. Member of the Legislature of Coahuila and Texas, 1821; land commissioner of De Witt's colony 1831 and of Bexar District, 1834–1835; signer of the Texas Declaration of Independence, 1836; member of the Congress of the Republic of Texas, 1838–1839; a commissioner of the Santa Fe Expedition, 1841; member of the Constitutional Convention of 1845; senator in the Legislature of Texas, 1846–1849. Navarro County gratefully bears his name. Corsicana was named by him for the isle of his father's birth—Corsica.   (1936)

CORSICANA (Navarro Co.)   *SH 22 W, Collins Catholic School*
James L. Collins
Born in Weston, West Virginia, James Lawrence Collins (1883–1953) began his career in the petroleum industry at age fourteen. New oil discoveries in Texas brought him to the Corsicana area about 1923. He soon formed a partnership with two brothers, John and Robert Wheelock, and founded the Wheelock & Collins Oil Co. Collins' business was instrumental in the development of the Corsicana field, the East Texas field, and other oil fields around the country. His success and expertise were widely recognized throughout the industry and led him into positions of leadership in several national petroleum associations. Never married, Collins provided upon his death that his $13 million estate be divided among four organizations. These included Dallas' Scottish Rite Hospital for Crippled Children and St. Joseph's Orphanage. Part of the estate went to his local Roman Catholic parish, which used the money to build and operate the school at this site. The remainder of his estate went to create scholarships for graduates of Corsicana High School. Collins' contributions as a businessman and civic leader played an important role in the development and history of the Corsicana area.   (1983)

CORSICANA (Navarro Co.)   *US 287, 6 mi. S*
Air Activities of Texas
Prior to the United States entry into World War II, the U.S. Government contracted with a number of civilian flying schools to assist in training military pilots for the Army Air Corps. In December 1940 the Air Activities of Texas, Corsicana Field, was authorized to provide primary flight training, the second phase of a three-level process. Construction of the facility on a 400-acre tract of land began here in February 1941, and employed more than 250 laborers. In addition to a landing strip, they built hangars, barracks, offices, maintenance buildings, and a mess hall/kitchen. In March, 51 cadets arrived to complete 10 weeks of intense training. By 1943, each class contained more than 300 cadets. By 1944 8,480 cadets received flight instruction in 37 training classes. The flight school employed more than 550 civilians by January 1944, and provided a significant impact on the local economy. As the war drew to a close, the need for the flight school became unnecessary, and it closed. Post-war use of the property began in 1946 with the opening of Navarro Junior College, which occupied the site until 1951. The City of Corsicana purchased the site in 1963 for a municipal airport.   (1996)

COST (Gonzales Co.)   *Spur 95, 1 mi. N of SH 97*
Site of Cost School
In the 1890s, children of families living in the Cost community, originally known as Oso, attended area schools that were part of the White School District No. 38 and the County School District No. 38-1/2 to the east. By 1903, the county built the Cost Community School, although some students attended Oso School about two miles west of Cost. In 1915, officials created the Cost Common School District No. 22. Trustees R. N. Hester, B. L. Dikes, Otto Luescher, Ernst Schieberle and Samuel Lester hired noted architect Henry T. Phelps to design a new building to

house grades one through ten at this site on land given and sold to the district by Schieberle and Dikes. Gonzales resident Fred Meisenhelder won the contract for construction, and the two-story brick schoolhouse opened its doors to 125 students on October 2, 1916. In May 1918, the first students graduated from the school. During the next several years, the school curriculum expanded from basic subjects to include music, homemaking, manual training (shop) and athletics. The district added a wood-frame lunchroom facility in 1948. The next year, the Cost District was annexed into the Gonzales Independent School District, and students began making the transition to Gonzales schools. Cost School closed its doors in May 1959, and the next year a local property owner bought it and used the bricks to construct a home across the road. For many years, community groups continued to use the former lunchroom for meetings, but today the Cost School is only a memory.   (2006)

COTULLA (La Salle Co.)   *IH 35, .5 mi. S beyond Nueces River Bridge*
The Nueces River at Texas Boundary
Until 1836 this river formed the undisputed western boundary of Texas. By the Treaty of Guadalupe Hidalgo, signed in February 1848, the boundary line between Mexico and the United States was fixed at the Rio Grande.

COTULLA (La Salle Co.)   *448 S IH 35*
Cotulla Ranch
Polish immigrant Joseph Cotulla (1844–1922) came to America in 1856, traveling with his family by ship and oxcart. He worked on area ranches and registered his own brand, the BAR JF, in 1863. Joseph enlisted in the First Texas Cavalry of the Union Army and served for two years during the Civil War. He drove cattle from the Nueces River to Kansas for several years. He started an area ranch with four other men in 1869 before establishing his own ranch in 1874. Cotulla continued to buy land and amassed more than 30,000 acres in La Salle, Dimmit and Webb counties. He donated 120 acres of the ranch to the railroad in 1881 to develop a townsite, which bears his name and became La Salle county seat. The original ranch land remains in the family today.   (2009)

COTULLA (La Salle Co.)   *SH 97 at N. Stewart St., courthouse*
La Salle County
The Presidio Rio Grande brought travel to this area for centuries. In 1852, the U.S. Army built Fort Ewell, to protect the region. William A. Waugh, the first settler, established a ranch in 1856 near Cibolo Crossing on the Spanish road. On Feb. 1, 1858, the county was created but not organized. It was named for Robert Cavalier, Sieur De La Salle (1643–1687), first French explorer of Texas. The county's first post office opened in 1871 at the Guajuco Crossing. County government was organized at Crarey's Rancho on Nov. 2, 1880. Offices were at temporary sites until 1884, when Cotulla was made the County Seat.

COVE (Chambers Co.)   *Cedar Point Rd. (FM 2354) S*
Site of Home of General Sam Houston
Constructed about 1860. Occupied by him as a residence during part of 1861 and a part of 1862.

CRANDALL (Kaufman Co.)   *Gleason and South Main (US Bus. 175)*
Crandall
Named for The Rev. C. F. Crandall (1827–1906), Methodist minister who came here from Indiana, 1877, and bought 1800 acres of land. When Texas Trunk Line Railroad built east from Dallas in 1880, he gave bonus for rail service and was first postmaster when post office was created in 1881. Baptists, Disciples of Christ, and Methodists built churches. Townsite plat was recorded in 1889. The city school system was established in 1901. By the early 1900s, town had a lumber yard, several stores, 3 physicians, 3 banks. It remains a center for agriculture and recreation.   (1971)

CRANE (Crane Co.)   *US 385 NW of McCamey*
Castle Mountain (2 mi. E)
About 3000 ft. elevation. Since 17th century, a landmark in travel from Texas points to Mexico and California. According to tradition, named by Spaniards for resemblance to ancient castles. Has association with stories of lost trains of gold and other treasures.

CRANE (Crane Co.)   *US 385, 5 mi. N in roadside park*
Crane County
Formed from Tom Green County. Created February 26, 1887; organized September 3, 1927. Named in honor of William Carey Crane (1816–1885), a Baptist minister, president of Baylor University (1863–1885). Crane, County Seat.

CRANE (Crane Co.)   *US 385, 5 mi. N in roadside park*
Church & Fields Oil Discovery Well (Drilling site 2.25 mi. SE)
Since 1839, Texas has set aside her public lands to finance education. The University of Texas at Austin acquired the land at this site in 1883, after the first owner, a railroad company, returned it to the state as worthless. For years McElroy Ranch grazed cattle here. On similar terrain 70 miles to the southeast the Santa Rita gusher blew in during 1923, and soon other university lands were being explored for oil. Church & Fields Exploration Company, composed of George M. Church and Robert Fields of San Angelo, obtained a permit late in 1925 to drill in Section 34, Block 30, in university land on McElroy Ranch. On Dec. 28, 1925, contractor Burton F. Weekley and driller John Garlin started the Church & Fields well, 2.25 miles southeast of this spot. In March 1926 this became Crane County's first oil producer, opening a new major field for West Texas. Soon other wells were drilled and local population rose from 27 to about 4,500. In Sept. 1927, county government was organized as a result of the oil field activity. Until 1955, the discovery well continued to produce. Since the day it proved successful and an asset to education and energy production, over a billion barrels of oil have come from University of Texas lands.   (1978)

CRANE (Crane Co.)   *201 W. 6th St. (SH 329) at courthouse*
Crane, William Carey (County Named For)
Noted church leader, educator. A Virginian. Received B. A. and M. A., George Washington University. Taught in Georgia, 1837–39; was ordained Baptist minister, 1838. Was pastor of various leading churches; president of 2 church colleges in Mississippi, 1851–60. Came to Confederate Texas, 1863, as president, Baylor University—position held 22 years. His work and use of his personal funds kept Baylor open while many of state's 25 colleges were closed. First president, 1871, of Texas State Teachers Association and chairman, committee to study public school reorganization.   (1965)

CRANE (Crane Co.)   *US 385, 23 mi. SE*
Horsehead Crossing, C.S.A.
One of the most important sites in the old west. Named for skulls pointing toward crossing. Only ford for many miles where animals could enter, drink and leave Pecos River safely. Elsewhere deep banks would trap them. Ford mapped 1849 by Capt. R. B. Marcy, head of army escort for parties on way to California gold rush. Used in 1850's by frontiersman Henry Skillman, contractor for first mail route from San Antonio to El Paso. As change station, echoed with brass bugle call of Butterfield coach carrying mail from St. Louis to San Francisco, in first stage service to span continent, 1858–1861. During the Civil War, 1861–1865, used by wagons hauling highly valuable salt scooped from bed of nearby Juan Cordona Lake, to meet Texas scarcities. Also scene of spying and counter spying of Federal and Confederates watching Overland Trail. Federals, operating out of El Paso, feared invasion by way of Horsehead. Confederates several times threw back armies that sought to enter the state in order to deploy along the old Overland Trail and conquer north and west Texas. Later this became important crossing for cattle on Goodnight-Loving trail, mapped in 1866.   (1965)

CRAWFORD (McLennan Co.)   *9162 Cedar Rock Parkway (FM 185)*
Crawford
Located in an area of McLennan County once inhabited by Tonkawa Indians, the community of Crawford grew slowly from an 1850s settlement centered around Tonk Crossing (two miles northeast). The first townsite was at the crossroads of the Waco to Gatesville and Belton to Fort Graham trade routes. The exact source for the town's name is unknown, but possibilities include Coryell city resident William Nelson Crawford, who graded the Tonk Creek Crossing, A. C. Crawford of Galveston, a director of the Gulf, Colorado & Santa Fe Railroad, or Texas Ranger George Crawford, who was stationed here. Development increased following the Civil War, and the post

office opened in 1871. By the latter part of that decade, the town included several stores, a tavern, a blacksmith shop and a school with an enrollment of about 100. In 1881, the Gulf, Colorado & Santa Fe Railroad, building north from Temple to Fort Worth, bypassed the original townsite, and residents began moving here along the new line. Crawford experienced economic growth as a result, and there were soon four churches, a cotton gin and a grain mill. Incorporated in 1897, the town remained an important agricultural center throughout the twentieth century, at times boasting more than 700 residents, two banks and dozens of local businesses. In July 1999, Texas Governor George W. Bush and his family bought the former Englebrecht Ranch (Prairie Chapel Ranch) west of town. His election as President of the United States in 2000 turned the ranch into the "Western White House," the site of gatherings for U.S. officials and foreign Heads of State. Crawford gained international media attention and served as the official voting place for President Bush and First Lady Laura Bush.   (2004)

CRESSON (Parker Co.)   *US 377, 3.5 mi. N, Pate Museum of Transportation*
Sunshine Special's, Ellsmere

One of the most elegant private cars in the world when it was built in 1914 for the personal use of Dr. W. S. Webb, president of Wagner Palace Car Company. When New York Central's "20th Century Limited" express broke New York–Chicago rail passenger speed record 1932, this was the rear car. Owned 1920–1961 by T & P Railway. Presented in 1962 to Fort Worth Children's Museum.

CRESSON (Parker Co.)   *US 377, 6 mi. W Cresson*
Elizabeth Crockett

Three miles south to the grave of Elizabeth Crockett, wife of hero of the Alamo. Died March 2, 1860, age 74.

CROCKETT (Houston Co.)   *SH 21 near FM 227 intersection, 19.5 mi. NE*
Site of the Daniel McLean Claim

Daniel McLean (1784–1837) first came to Texas in 1813 with the Gutierrez-Magee expedition, and was one of 93 survivors of the fateful Battle of the Medina. Returning with his wife Hannah (Sheridan) in the original Austin Colony, he settled this league in 1821 and became first permanent resident of area now in Houston County. McLean and his brother-in-law John Sheridan were killed by Indians May 10, 1837, near site of present town of Elkhart, Texas. Daniel and Hannah McLean are buried near this marker. Because of their pioneering spirit, this has been McLean land since 1821.   (1972)

CROCKETT (Houston Co.)   *SH 21, 17.7 mi. NE*
Glover School

Established in 1881, the Glover School served residents of the rural Glover community. Under the direction of teacher James Breeze, a one-room schoolhouse was built on A. E. Sloan's land, now the site of the old Glover cemetery. A consolidated school district was formed in 1936 and the third schoolhouse was built at this site soon after. Destroyed by fire in 1938, it was rebuilt the next year. The school merged with the Kennard district in 1967, but community identity and pride provided by the early school are reflected in biennial reunions of ex-students and teachers.   (1981)

CROCKETT (Houston Co.)   *SH 21, 14 mi. NE*
Pine Springs Campground

A favorite campsite of Tejas Indians in the years before European settlers arrived, this location was used in turn by explorers, Spanish missionaries, traders, and armies. Travelers were attracted by abundant game, including deer and wild turkey, and fresh water which flowed from springs 300 feet from El Camino Real (The King's Highway). Nineteenth-century pioneers ringed their wagons in the grove and rested en route to settlements. Hunting parties later camped at Pine Springs for weeks at a time.   (1972)

CROCKETT (Houston Co.)   *SH 21, 4 mi. E*
Stage Coach Inn

Built as a home by Joseph D. Rice, Sr., who came to Texas in 1828. In 1838 it was designated as a stopping place for the stage coach from Nacogdoches to Crockett.

CROCKETT (Houston Co.)   *SH 21, 4 mi. E*
Original Site of the Joseph R. Rice Log Cabin
Joseph Redmond Rice (1805–1866) and his wife, Willie Masters Rice (1809–1881), natives of Tennessee and Kentucky, built a one-room log cabin on this site in 1828. Rice's brothers and his father-in-law, Jacob Masters, probably helped with the building. The men cut the logs in the woods, and Willie Rice drove a team that snaked them to the clearing for the house-raising. Menaced by hostile Indians, the Rices fled to Louisiana, but returned in the 1830s. Over ensuing years, they enlarged the cabin and increased their family to eleven children. Their dwelling became known in the Republic of Texas as a place to lodge or take meals on the San Antonio Road, between the towns of Nacogdoches and Crockett. After Joseph and Willie Rice died, descendants lived in the log house until 1919, when a grandson shifted it some 300 feet and built a new frame house on the original site. The historic house was then used to store grain and shelter farm implements and the family automobile. The Rice homesite was commemorated in 1936 by the Texas Centennial Commission, and in 1973 the old log house was given to the state. Relocated in Tejas Mission Park (16 mi. NE), it has been restored and is on exhibition as a relic of frontier days.   (1976)

CROCKETT (Houston Co.)   *SH 21, 1.5 mi. E*
A. E. Gossett Home
House on typical southern plan, with separate kitchen in back yard. Built 1835 by A. E. Gossett, owner of large land grant from Mexico. An early 1836 visitor was former Tennessee neighbor, Col. David Crockett, on his way to the Alamo, and camping with his company for a night at the spring nearby. Has Medallion Plate.   (1964)

CROCKETT (Houston Co.)   *SH 7, 12 mi. E*
Randolph Community (1 mi. N)
Settled 1838, by Cyrus Halbert Randolph (1817–1889) on the San Felipe de Austin–Nacogdoches mail route. Randolph was member of Snively Expedition, county justice of peace, coroner, chief justice, and sheriff; state legislator and treasurer. School was opened about 1850, and post office established June 30, 1858. Had 2 stores, blacksmith shop, saloon, and barber shop in 1860, when it tried to wrest the county seat from Crockett, after which Randolph slowly began to decline in population. Demise of the settlement was marked by the closing of the post office September 29, 1881.   (1973)

CROCKETT (Houston Co.)   *SH 19, .8 mi. N*
Houston County
Houston County, created from Nacogdoches County, June 12, 1837; organized the same year; named in honor of Sam Houston 1793–1863, Commander-in-Chief of the Texan Army at San Jacinto, President of the Republic and Governor of the State of Texas, Senator in the United States Congress, 1846–1859. Crockett, the County Seat.

CROCKETT (Houston Co.)   *US 287 at FM 2160, 3 mi. N*
John Wortham
A pioneer area landowner and farmer, John Wortham (1804–1867) was a petitioner for the creation of Houston County in 1837. He later served as captain of an independent Ranger company, as Major in the Republic of Texas Army, and as Quartermaster of the Texas Militia. In addition to his military service, he was a trustee of Trinity College and was appointed to the first Board of Land Commissioners for the Texas Republic. He also owned a local sawmill and gristmill. Twice married, Wortham was the father of 12 children. He was buried on his land (2.3 mi. SW).   (1982)

CROCKETT (Houston Co.)   *401 E. Houston (SH 21) at courthouse*
Crockett
Founded 1837. Named for David Crockett, who had visited here on way to the Alamo, 1836. Old fortified log courthouse was often the refuge for settlers during Indian wars. During Civil War had camp of instruction. Telegraph and stagecoach station for South. Forestry, farming and livestock center.   (1964)

CROCKETT (Houston Co.)   *707 E. Houston St. (SH 21)*
Monroe-Crook House
Built 1854 by A. T. Monroe, prominent merchant and grandnephew of U.S. President James Monroe. Style is Greek revival. Bricks between the inner and outer walls provide insulation and

strength. Attorney George W. Crook bought the house in 1911. It is now owned and preserved by his daughter. (1969)

CROCKETT (Houston Co.) *SH 21 at Loop 304, .5 mi. W*
Smith Brothers
Houston County natives Francis Albert (1875–1949) and James Henry (Jim) (1878–1930) Smith formed a business partnership in 1904 called Smith Brothers. Among their early business enterprises were a livery stable, family farms, and real estate. Following the advent of the automobile industry, they also sold cars and became interested in road construction. Using their own funds, the Smith Brothers constructed a 6.9-mile section of Old State Highway 21 west of Crockett in 1923. It was the first paved highway in the area. The company also paved roads in the city, including brick paving on the courthouse square. The brothers' business grew to include projects in California, Kansas, Florida, Illinois, North Carolina, Oklahoma, Louisiana, Tennessee, and New Mexico. Other Smith Brothers companies, formed in Dallas and San Antonio, included contracting and cement operations, as well as real estate development and investments in hotels in San Antonio, Corpus Christi, and Crockett. They also owned ranches in Houston and Concho Counties. Following Jim Smith's death in 1930, many of the company's assets were liquidated. The partnership was finally dissolved in 1937. (1989)

CROCKETT (Houston Co.) *SH 21 at FM 1280, 14 mi. SW at Austonio*
Site of Old Block House
Established before 1836; used by Elisha Clapp and neighboring settlers as a place of defense against Indians. Abandoned about 1844. (1936)

CROCKETT (Houston Co.) *SH 7, 6.6 mi. W*
Oakland
Named for the oak trees in the vicinity, Oakland was a rural settlement in the late 19th and early 20th centuries. A townsite was never platted, and the community was composed of scattered homes between the Trinity River and Crockett. A church, cotton gin, and school were in operation for a brief time. Among the early settlers of the area were Wilson E. Hail, who later served as Houston County sheriff, and Z. S. Thompson. The settlement began to decline by the 1930s. Some descendants of early settlers remain in the area. (1988)

CROCKETT (Houston Co.) *SH 19, 3 mi. S*
Givens Homesite
Solomon George Givens and his wife Lula (Burleson), both born in Houston County in 1871, were the children of former slaves. They were married in Crockett in 1891, and in 1892 they bought 34 acres of land here. Their farm proved a success and in 1893 they built a large 8-room house at this site. The Givenses were noted for their charity and as leaders in the development of a nearby school and Baptist church; baptism services took place in a tank on their land. For many years their home was the center of an African American farming community known as "Givens Hill." (1994)

CROCKETT (Houston Co.) *US 287 right-of-way, 7 mi. SE*
Hopewell Community and Gudeblye School
The Hopewell Community began as a freedmen's town in the 1870s. At its height it included homes, farms, small businesses, a church, and a school. Established on land once owned by an Anglo teacher named Good Blye (Bly), the school's name evolved into Gudeblye over the years. In 1925, it became a part of Houston County's Agricultural Training School program, and by 1949 it was annexed to the Crockett School System. Descendants of the early settlers and alumni of the school still reside in the area. (1990)

CROCKETT (Houston Co.) *US 287, 15 mi. SE*
Albert Holley House
In 1857, Albert Holley (b. 1828), his mother and two brothers, migrated to Houston County from Alabama. While the others journeyed to Texas by boat, he brought the family's supplies overland by wagon with 137 slaves. By 1860, he and his wife Julia (Russell) (1840–1897) had begun homesteading this land. After serving in the Civil War, where he was a prisoner of war, Albert continued to farm here. In 1867, he constructed a new home for his family at this site. He died in 1907, but his land remained in the ownership of Holley family members until 1976. (1983)

117

CROSBY (Harris Co.) *US 90E, 2 mi. SW*
Harrison Barrett (ca. 1845–1917)
Born into slavery, Harrison Barrett was the son of Simon and Eliza Barrett, who had come to Texas from Louisiana. In addition to Harrison, the couple had two other sons and two daughters. Following the emancipation of Texas slaves in 1865, Harrison Barrett spent several years gathering his family together. He eventually found all except one sister, and they settled on land east of the San Jacinto River. He purchased this land in 1889 and began a community which would later be known as Barrett's Settlement. Beginning with seven houses, the community grew to include additional homes, farms, and businesses. Considered the leader of the community, Barrett established a school, church, and cemetery. After a post office substation was opened here in 1947, the area became known as Barrett Station. Married to the former Annie Jones soon after his emancipation, Barrett was the father of twelve children. His homestead, twice rebuilt by descendants, still stands on its original location. Harrison and Annie Barrett, along with four other family members, are interred in the nearby family cemetery, named Journey's End by descendants in 1985. (1988)

CROSBY (Harris Co.) *US 90 Bus. at San Jacinto River, 1 mi. SW*
Humphrey Jackson (November 24, 1784–January 18, 1833)
Educated in law, Humphrey Jackson left his native Ireland in 1808, during a period of political conflict. He migrated to the United States and settled on a sugar plantation in Louisiana. While there, he served in the 1815 Battle of New Orleans. Unable to manage his plantation without the use of slavery, which he opposed, Jackson sold his land and came to Texas in 1823 to join Stephen F. Austin's colony. Not realizing he was locating outside the colony's boundaries, he settled on land at this site. When the error was discovered, he joined other area settlers in successfully petitioning the Mexican government to form the San Jacinto District under control of the Austin Colony. Jackson was elected to serve as alcalde of the new district. One of the pioneer settlers in present Harris County, Jackson was active in the early local government. His efforts on behalf of the surrounding settlement and his ability to mediate disputes impartially led to further development of the area. In 1833, Jackson was killed by a falling tree while clearing his land. Twice married, he was the father of four children. His descendants include prominent business, professional, and political leaders. (1982)

CROSBYTON (Crosby Co.) *US 82 at FM 651, Pioneer Memorial Museum*
High Plains Pioneer Henry Clay Smith (1836–1912)
First to set up a post office and farm in Crosby County; first to break land and build a water well on High Plains. At the start of the Civil War, he was a miner at Pinos Altos, New Mexico, and joined in moves to take over gold and silver mines for the South. But Indian raids closed mines. When the Confederate Army withdrew from Arizona and Mexico in 1861, Smith along with others joined the South's cause. He served four years in Texas and spent rest of his life here. A replica of the old rock house he built near here in 1877 is now shown in the museum at Crosbyton. (1965)

CROSBYTON (Crosby Co.) *US 82/SH 114 at FM 651*
Crosby County
Formed from Young and Bexar Territories. Created August 21, 1876. Organized September 20, 1986. Named in honor of Stephen Crosby 1800–1869. Came to Texas in 1845. Commissioner of the General Land Office. County seat, Estacado, 1886, Emma 1890. Crosbyton, since 1911.
(1936)

CROSBYTON (Crosby Co.) *US 82/SH 114 at FM 2591, 4 mi. E*
Old Dewey Lake
Once an important landmark for early surveys of this area, Dewey Lake got its name after surveyors returned from here to headquarters and found, to their embarrassment, they had not yet named this site. Gallantly, they decided to call it after land office employee Miss Dewey. Lake shore was site of Texas Ranger Camp "Roberts" (1879–1882) and the "Stag House," barracks for the cowboys of the Two-Buckle Ranch. Surveyors often camped here too. The lake disappeared in the 1880s after two creeks eroded its banks, forming a new channel which drained the lake basin. (1967)

CROSBYTON (Crosby Co.)   *US 82/SH 114 at FM 2591, 4 mi. E*
Two-Buckle Ranch Headquarters,
Kentucky Cattle Raising Company
Headquarters for the Two-Buckle Ranch was built near this site, at Silver Falls, in 1884 by the Kentucky Cattle Raising Company, which had been founded two years earlier by a group of Louisville, Kentucky, distillers. Claude Tilford was hired by the company to manage the 145,240-acre ranch. A variety of grain and hay crops were grown. The ranch's cattle operation featured cross breeding and separation of breeding stock. In 1901, the C. B. Livestock Company bought 90,000 acres of the land and used the established headquarters for its -N- ranching and plains land development operations. A dipping vat was built in 1912 and was used by all area cattlemen to combat Texas cattle fever. Since the 1915 breakup of the C. B. Livestock Company, succeeding owners have continued to add to and preserve the original headquarters site. A barn, garage, concrete storage tank, as well as a dam across White River were added during the 1920s. Over the years, this land has been home for a number of families who have contributed to Crosby County's ranching heritage. The Two-Buckle Ranch headquarters is a historic reminder of this early West Texas industry.   (1984)

CROSBYTON (Crosby Co.)   *US 82/SH 114 at FM 2591, 4 mi. E*
Main Supply Camp on Historic Mackenzie Trail (3 mi. SE)
Trail followed by Gen. Ranald Mackenzie, U.S. 4th Cavalry in 1871 frontier campaign. He camped at Dewey Lake after brush with Indians. In 1872, he was again ordered to ferret out the Comanches. From his main supply camp on Brazos River Freshwater Fork (now White River) he launched a drive against Quanah Parker. Ended with fights in Palo Duro and Tule Canyons, last battles between Indians and Cavalry in this area: Opened the plains to white settlement.   (1966)

CROSBYTON (Crosby Co.)   *SH 82/SH 114 at FM 2591, 4 mi. E*
Texas Ranger Campsite (1 mi. N)
Law and order for plains area began here in 1879 with creation of Camp Roberts, first ranger station in Panhandle. Company C of the newly formed Frontier Battalion of Texas Rangers was located here and commanded by Capt. G. W. Arrington, Civil War veteran, hard-fighting ranger, later a Panhandle sheriff and rancher. Battalion commander was Maj. John B. Jones. Frontier Battalion was created to protect settlers from marauding Indians and outlaws; rowdy cowboys also needed disciplining. Capt. Arrington's C Company was to have 75 men to meet these duties—he never had more than 28. A large territory and few men to cover it meant scouting parties always on the move. Living conditions on the vast, arid plains, scouting trips, encounters with violence, long watches over dangerous captives made a Ranger's life hard. Each man was self-supporting, furnishing his own saddle, ropes, guns, clothing, horse, bedding; he received small salary, ammunition and food from the state. Shooting matches provided much of his off-duty entertainment. By 1881 local Indian menace was removed; rangers went to new frontier, 1882. Remnants of Camp Roberts today are foundations of three sod buildings around an old well used by the Rangers.   (1967)

CROSBYTON (Crosby Co.)   *US 82 at FM 836, 10.3 mi. E*
Near Site of Pansy Baptist Church
The Pansy Baptist Church was organized in 1905 by J. V. Leatherwood, John Holt, P. H. Leatherwood, Snow Loyd, and J. M. Leatherwood to serve the residents of the Pansy community, and church services were conducted in the school building until 1916 when the congregation constructed its first sanctuary. An arbor was built on the church grounds for revival services. Church building was moved two miles south in 1946 for the convenience of the membership. A parsonage was erected in 1947 for the congregation's first full-time pastor and a new sanctuary was built and was dedicated on July 16, 1950. The church building burned in August 1965, and services were held in a church member's barn until December, when a new structure was completed. The church supported a strong mission outreach program. Through the years population dwindled in the rural community of Pansy. In 1995, the remaining members of the Pansy Baptist Church voted to disband. The church building was donated to the Mt. Zion Baptist Church, an African American congregation in Floydada. The building was moved 32 miles by 140 volunteers from Crosbyton, Pansy, Floydada, and Wiley.   (1996)

CROSS PLAINS (Eastland Co.)   *SH 36, 5.1 mi. E*
Pioneer Cemetery
Tradition holds that Captain A. M. Curry suggested the name for the Pioneer community, established in 1883. Bill Smith became its first postmaster in 1885. The burial here of Mrs. S. A. Briggs (believed to be Catherine P. Owsley Briggs) in 1879, however, predates the community development. Landowners William L. and Mary Ann (Hampton) Browning formally deeded the site in 1906 for use as a burial ground for the largely agricultural settlement. An oil boom in the 1920s brought thousands of new residents. By the 1940s, oil production waned, and the railroad, as well as the majority of settlers and businesses, left the area. Over the years, additional land donations have enlarged the cemetery. Pioneer Quilting Club members served as long-time caretakers, raising funds for cleaning and for a war memorial placed in 1948 to commemorate area soldiers killed in World Wars I and II. Among the others buried here is Catherine Martin O'Neal Lovett, a Cherokee survivor of the Trail of Tears march of 1838. Today, an association maintains the burial ground, which is a link to the early settlement of Pioneer.   (2004)

CROSS PLAINS (Callahan Co.)   *SH 36 W, in Treadway Park*
1 mi. E to Fort Mason—
Camp Cooper Military Road
Route for U.S. 2nd Cavalry and supplies from San Antonio to Fort Mason (about 100 mi. S of here) to Camp Cooper (about 65 mi. N.) in campaigns of 1851–1861 against Plains Indians. Great military men of American history traveled this road, including Robt. E. Lee (later a commanding general, C.S.A.) and Geo. T. Thomas, "Rock of Chickamauga."

CROWELL (Foard Co.)   *SH 6, 8 mi. NE*
Pease River Battlefield
In 1860, at the Battle of Pease River, Indian captive Cynthia Ann Parker and her daughter, Prairie Flower, were rescued by Texas Rangers under Captain L. S. Ross (later Governor of Texas). Cynthia Ann, most celebrated of all Comanche captives, had been taken at age 9 in a raid on Fort Parker, May 19, 1836. Traders who saw her later said she had taken the name "Naduah" and wished to remain among her adopted people. She married Chief Peta Nocona, by whom she had 2 sons, Pecos and Quanah Parker. Although she was returned to her uncle's family, she was never completely happy and tried to escape several times. She died 1864.   (1968)

CROWELL (Foard Co.)   *SH 6, 4.5 mi. N*
Site of Old Pease City
Founded in 1880 by Benjamin E. Lower, John Wesley and wife, first settlers. Lower became the first postmaster, 1880; Mrs. Wesley was second, 1882. Place was named for Pease River and E. M. Pease, Texas governor (1853–1857 and 1867–1869). Second group of settlers was family of W. T. Dunn. Stone post office–trading post served 3,500 square miles of sparsely settled country. Mail delivery was by stage or horse. The post office was abolished 1885 when Margaret became seat of Hardeman County. In 1891 site of Old Pease City and Margaret became part of Foard County.   (1967)

CROWELL (Foard Co.)   *SH 6, 2 mi. N*
Foard County
Formed from Hardeman, King, Cottle and Knox counties. Created March 3, 1891; organized April 27, 1891. Named in honor of Robert L. Foard 1831–1898. A Confederate officer. Prominent lawyer of Columbus, Texas. Crowell, the county seat. Traversed by a railroad in 1908.

CROWELL (Foard co.)   *SH 6 at courthouse*
Robert L. Foard, Star and Wreath
County named honor Texas Confederate officer (1836–1898). Came to Texas from Maryland, 1853. Prominent pioneer lawyer and citizen. Lt. Columbus Grays Texas Militia Co. 1861. Confederate major 13th Texas Infantry Regiment, which successfully guarded portion Texas coast against raiding parties from Union blockading vessels. 13th stationed 7 weeks, 1863, Brashear City, LA., as part campaign to prevent split of South by loss of Mississippi River. Returned to coast duty until war's end. A memorial to Texans who served the Confederacy.   (1963)

CRYSTAL CITY (Zavala Co.)   US 83, 1.9 mi N
Zavala County
In 1832 land grant of Mexico to John Charles Beales. Lake Espantosa was campsite on road from Mexico to San Antonio. County created from Uvalde and Maverick, 1858. During the Civil War, especially in 1863–1864, was crossed by Cotton Road to Eagle Pass, entry point of Confederate goods, including guns, powder, medicines. Organized 1884. Named in honor of Lorenzo de Zavala (1788–1836), signer of the Texas Declaration of Independence; first vice president to serve Republic of Texas. Original county seat was Batesville. Since 1927 it has been Crystal City.   (1965)

CRYSTAL CITY (Zavala Co.)   FM 65 near US 83 in city
Zavala County
Explored as early as 1691 by the expedition of Domingo Teran de Los Rios, Spanish governor of Texas. The historic San Antonio Road crossed this region from southwest to northeast and was used by most of the Spanish explorers and travelers of the 18th century. French-American explorer St. Denis used it in 1714, as did the Canary Islanders, who made one of the first civil settlements in San Antonio, in 1718. The county was created in 1858 from Uvalde and Maverick Counties and named for Texas patriot and statesman Lorenzo de Zavala. Not until 1884, however, did enough people reside here to permit it to be organized. The first county seat was Bates City, later renamed Batesville. First judge was J. M. Downs and commissioners were W. C. Mangum, E. P. Waller, V. M. West and G. B. Kenney. Before 1884 was out, a school election had been held in Palo Blanco, and a $7,500 contract had been let for a courthouse and jail. When the county seat moved to Crystal City (1928) courthouse and jail were built here. New courthouse erected 1969 at cost of $475,000 was commissioned by 1968–1969 county courts: Irl Taylor, judge; Cecil Davis, Jr.; F. D. Keller, Jr.; H. R. Reynolds; E. B. Ross; Jesus Rodriguez; and Henry Volz, Jr., commissioners.   (1969)

CRYSTAL CITY (Zavala Co.)   1400–1500 blks. of 7th Ave. S of US 83
Crystal City Family Internment Camp, World War II
When the U.S. entered the war in 1941, an immediate fear was the possibility of enemy agents in the country and the Western Hemisphere. As one response, thousands of Japanese-Americans were moved away from the West Coast. Lesser-known was an internment camp system operated by the Immigration and Naturalization Service. The government built these camps to hold Japanese, German and Italian nationals arrested in the U.S. and Hawaii, and in Peru and other Latin American countries until they could be exchanged for American detainees. Three of these camps were in Texas at Kenedy, Seagoville and Crystal City. The Crystal City camp, converted from an existing migratory labor camp, was the largest internment facility in the U.S. and the only one built exclusively for families. The original 200-acre camp later expanded to almost 500 acres, with agricultural areas and support facilities. The primary living area was a 100-acre compound enclosed by a 10-foot barbed wire fence, complete with guard towers and spotlights. Like a small town, the compound had 700 buildings and included family housing, schools, a hospital, shops, warehouses, markets and recreation areas. Although intended for Japanese, the Crystal City camp also held Germans and a few Italians. The population averaged 2800 throughout the war. It reached a peak of almost 3400 in December 1944, two-thirds of whom were Japanese. At the end of the war, the government paroled internees throughout the U.S. or sent them to their home countries. The Crystal City camp was the only one still in operation by June 1946. It officially closed February 27, 1948, and the property transferred to the city and school district. Texas in World War II.   (2005)

CUERO (DeWitt Co.)   US 183, 10 mi. N
¼ mi. E to Site of Concrete College (1865–1881)
One of most respected schools in Texas in its day. Founded by the Rev. John Van Epps Covey (1821–1898), noted educator and minister. Embraced primary through collegiate levels, accepting only students over 12 years old for college work. Broad course offerings included classical and modern languages, penmanship, music (piano, guitar, violin, flute), plus homemaking and etiquette for girls. A well-attended business school taught bookkeeping, banking, commercial law, and letter-writing. Enrollment, including boarding and day students, averaged 100; peaked at 250 in 1873. On weekdays pupils rose at 5 A.M., took a brisk walk before breakfast, heard devotional services, and went to classes. Nights were reserved for study and discussion, with "lights out" at 9 P.M. Gambling, liquor, smoking, and profanity were strictly forbidden. Students wrote their lessons on slates, as

paper was expensive, then recited them to the instructor. June graduation was the ceremonious occasion of public speeches and oral examinations. In 1881 the college closed after epidemics broke out and the railroad bypassed town of Concrete. Years later rock walls of main building were crushed and used to surface roads. Only rubble marks site today.

CUERO (DeWitt Co.) *US 183, 7 mi. N*
Dr. William Watt White (1829–1914)
Surgeon of Waul's Legion, Confederate Army. Came to Texas about 1850. In 1856 got M.D. Degree in Philadelphia. During Civil War, saved many lives, but took typhoid, which contributed to loss of his eyesight. After blindness, practiced rest of his life. Was local educational and civic leader, this county. Confederate doctors had many problems with drug supply, surgical tools, horse-drawn ambulances, and hospitals. Instruments had to be bought in Europe (shipped through naval blockade) or captured from the foe. Drugs came in by blockade-runner or were brought from north by ladies who hid them in their pompadours, bustles, petticoats. Scarcities led to use of dogwood, willow and poplar bark tea as substitute for quinine. Mullein and other wild herbs were also medical substitutes. Garden poppies were milked for opium. Sutures were made of horse-hair softened by boiling, or by raveling silk cloth. Female nurses were used for first time in army hospitals. This was first war to use anesthetics. Amputations left severed limbs stacked like wood around the field hospitals. Ambulances seemed never at hand for casualties; many died awaiting aid. Till the atom bomb, the Civil War was history's bloodiest. (1965)

CUERO (DeWitt Co.) *US 183 right-of-way, 5.5 mi. N*
George Washington Davis
Pennsylvania native George Washington Davis (1797–1853) brought his family to Texas in 1831. He selected a league of land near present-day Cuero in the Green DeWitt Colony and became an active participant in the movement toward Texas Independence, serving as a delegate to the second Convention of Texas in 1833 and as a delegate to the Consultation at San Felipe in 1835. After the revolution, Davis held a number of local public offices. He and his wife, Rebecca (d. 1846), are buried 1.8 miles west of this site. (Texas Sesquicentennial 1836–1986)

CUERO (DeWitt Co.) *US 183 at US 77A, 4 mi. N*
Site of Friar-Cardwell Stage Stand
In 1839 or 1840 at the junction of the La Grange-La Bahia and Victoria-Gonzales Roads (.5 mi. E), Daniel Boone Friar (1800–1858) built a home and store that served as a social, political, transportation, and trade center for early DeWitt County. In 1841 the two-story frame structure became an overnight stop on stagecoach lines between San Antonio and coastal towns. It was designed as a temporary courthouse for the short-lived judicial county of DeWitt in 1842. When the county was actually organized in 1846, the court met at Friar's place for several months. It was also the county's first post office, established on May 22, 1846, and named Cuero, with Friar as postmaster. In 1849 Friar sold the building to Crockett Cardwell (1812–1891), who continued to operate it as a stage stand, store, post office, and community meeting place. The county's first Masonic Lodge, Cameron Lodge No. 76, A. F. & A. M., was organized in an upstairs room in Nov. 1850 and met there until Jan. 1853. When the Gulf, Western Texas, and Pacific Railroad located the town of Cuero four miles south of the Cardwell Stand in 1873, the post office was moved to that site. As the town along the railroad grew, other activities at the old stage stand ended. It was torn down in 1916. (1974)

CUERO (DeWitt Co.) *US 183 at US 77A, 4 mi. N*
Old Chisholm Trail
From site near here, 1800 longhorns were moved out April 1, 1866, on first trail drive from this area to northern markets. Crockett Cardwell, owner of cattle bed ground, had gathered the herd. The trail boss was Thornton Chisholm, a native of DeWitt County. Indian Scout Jesse Chisholm in 1865 had marked the upper trail from the North Canadian to the Arkansas River. Road here became a prong of the famous Chisholm Trail, going past Gonzales, San Marcos, Austin, Round Rock, Georgetown, Gatesville, Glen Rose and Red River Station, into Indian Territory. The 30 men of this 1866 drive to St. Joseph, Mo., were gone 7 months, 10 days. The cook and many of the men made numerous later drives; but Thornton Chisholm died in 1868. 260,000 cattle—accumulated in Texas in 4 years of Civil War—went in 1866 up the Chisholm Trail, a flood channel from a vast reservoir

of beef. Sold in northern markets or to the U. S. Government to feed Indians on reservations or soldiers in forts, the trailed cattle helped Texas recover from the war. From 1866–1895 at least 10,000,000 cattle were driven up the Chisholm Trail by courageous Texas cowboys—the greatest movement of animals under the control of men in all history. (1966)

CUERO (DeWitt Co.)   *US 77/183 near NE city limit*
DeWitt County
Included in the colonial grant in 1825 to Green De Witt, Texas Empresario, settled until 1840 largely by Anglo Americans. Created a county of the State of Texas March 24, 1846. Its area being taken from Gonzales, Victoria and Goliad counties. Organized July 13, 1846, with Cameron as the county seat, named in honor of its original grantee Green De Witt 1787–1835. By 1860 half its population was of German birth. Clinton served as county seat, 1849–1877. Cuero, incorporated April 23, 1873, was made county seat in 1876, in memory of Arthur Burns. First settler in De Witt County, 1826, Columbus Burns, first Anglo-American child born in the county, 1829. George Washington Davis, delegate to the Second Convention of Texas, 1833. George W. Davis, participant in the Battle of Gonzales, 1835. George W. Davis, delegate to the Consultation, 1835. Captain John York, Captain David Murphree, James M. Bell, Albrecht Von Roeder, Louis Von Roeder, Squire Burns, John F. Pettus, participants in the capture of San Antonio, 1835. Thomas R. Miller, William Dearduff, martyrs of the Alamo, 1836. J. L. Allen a messenger from the Alamo, 1836. O. H. Perry Davis of Fannin's command who escaped the Refugio Massacre 1836. Captain David Murphree, John F. Pettus, James Bell, Joseph Kent Berry Doolittle, Allen Caruthers, Robert J. Kleberg, John McCrabb, James J. Tumlinson, Louis Von Roder, heroes of San Jacinto. Creed Taylor, Squire Burns, Josiah Taylor, Chas. A. Ogsbury, George W. Davis, soldiers in the Texas Army 1836; James Norman Smith, first school teacher in De Witt County 1840. Captain Daniel B. Friar, Miles S. Bennet, James J. Tumlinson, Josiah Taylor, Creed Taylor, participants in the Battle of Salado Creek, Bexar County, 1842. George Lord, Alfred A. Allee members of the Mier Expedition 1842 and all other pioneers of the Republic of Texas who resided in De Witt County prior to or after the Revolution. (1936)

CUERO (DeWitt Co.)   *US 87E, near city limit*
Cuero
Founded 1873 with arrival of Gulf, Western, Texas & Pacific Railroad. County seat moved here from Clinton, 1876. Population grew after coastal storms of 1875 and 1886 destroyed Indianola and refugees from there made a new start here. Home of Turkey Trot, begun in 1912. Farming, ranching, oil and gas center. (1968)

CUERO (DeWitt Co.)   *US 87, 5 mi. SE*
Burns Station Cemetery
Reminder of DeWitt County's earliest settlement, Irish Creek, begun in 1826 when Arthur Burns (1780–1856) migrated from Missouri and Iowa to Texas. He joined colony of Green DeWitt and built a 2-story log home near here. Used as a refuge during Indian raids, the house was also visited by General Sam Houston, 1836. On Dec. 19, 1837, President Houston appointed Burns to Board of Land Commissioners, Victoria County (which then encompassed this portion of DeWitt County). Area's first grist mill (operated 1856–1869 by Moses Rankin) was established by Burns. Near it clustered the Sherman & Thomas General Store, Charlie White's Blacksmith Shop, and Warn Hardware. The Irish Creek settlement became known as Burns Station, as it was a stage stop on the Victoria-Gonzales Road. Cemetery site, donated 1853 by Ardelia Burns Cook, daughter of Arthur Burns, adjoined the Irish Creek Methodist Church. In oldest marked grave lies Joseph Allen (1812–1853), born in Ireland. Here also is buried Sarah, Arthur Burns' widow. (Burns is buried in Iowa.) In 1870s, Burns Station lost business to Thomaston and Cuero, but was a stop on the Gulf, West Texas & Pacific Railroad until the name was changed in 1902 to "Verhelle," honoring a railroad official. (1970)

CUERO (DeWitt Co.)   *US 183, 3 mi. S*
Clinton (0.6 mi. E)
Created in 1846, DeWitt County was named for empresario Green DeWitt. The county seat, originally at Cameron, was moved in 1848 to the pioneer town of Clinton, named for DeWitt's son. County government returned briefly to Cameron, but Clinton again served as the county seat from

1850 until 1876, when Cuero was named the seat of government. Courthouses here included a log cabin and two frame buildings. A cemetery and well remain at the site of Clinton, evidence of the once-thriving community that was the home of many prominent area pioneers.   (1967)

CUERO (DeWitt Co.)   *US 183, 7 mi. S*
Hopkinsville Community—A Colony of Freedmen
Members of the Hopkins family came to DeWitt County in 1854 as slaves of Judge Henry Clay Pleasants (d. 1899). They worked for a time on a Gonzales County plantation and returned to this area after the Civil War as freedmen. In 1872, Henry Hopkins bought 42 acres of land and established the Hopkinsville Community (1 mi. W). Residents of the settlement organized the Antioch Baptist Church in 1873 and began a school about ten years later. Although the school closed in 1956, members of the Antioch Baptist Church continue to worship near Hopkinsville.   (1983)

CUMBY (Hopkins Co.)   *SH 11, 6 mi. N*
Mt. Zion Churches and Cemetery
Mt. Zion Methodist Episcopal Church organized here before creation of Hopkins County, 1846. Also at Mt. Zion, 1849, Harmony Cumberland Presbyterian Church was organized, with 13 members, by the Rev. Anthony Travelstead. After years of worship in oak groves, brush arbors and homes, church edifice was built jointly 1861. Site given by David Findley, Nicholas Harlow. More land given 1904 by J. A. Rains, Chas. E. Brown. In 1901 Harmony Cumberland Presbyterian Church became Mt. Zion Cumberland Presbyterian Church; continued to function. Methodists moved away in 1914.   (1967)

CUNEY (Cherokee Co.)   *US 175 at CR 3327*
Cuney
The earliest area settlers were Andrew "Andy" Bragg and Nelson Sneed, black farmers who moved here in 1870. Former slaves, they were later joined by other freedmen farmers, landowners and tradesmen. The settlement that resulted was known as Andy. In 1916 former Palestine banker H. L. Price moved to the community. Encouraged by the area's potential as a commercial and agricultural center for blacks, he directed formation of the Andy Real Estate Company. He was joined in the operation by his son Cuney Price, W. D. Thomas, J. Z. Thomas, W. A. Hall, and John Bragg. The firm renamed the town Cuney for Price's son, who was named for the prominent black business and state political leader Norris Wright Cuney. Statewide promotion of the town resulted in rapid growth for Cuney, which soon included churches, stores, gins, sawmills, a railroad station, a hotel and a baseball team. Nelson Sneed donated land for the establishment of community schools. Cuney declined after World War I as agricultural prices decreased and area residents moved to other towns for work. Today it serves as a reminder of the area's pioneers and the significant contribution they made to the heritage of Texas' black community.   (1982)

DAINGERFIELD (Morris Co.)   *US 259 N, 6 mi. N*
Rocky Branch
The abundance of creeks attracted travelers to this area, settled as early as the 1820s, and local tradition holds the community was named for the rocky beds of the creeks. The Rocky Branch Community grew throughout the 19th century; the earliest church, Spring Hill Primitive Baptist, was built in the 1850s. Over the years, the settlement boasted businesses, including lumber, grist and syrup mills, cotton gin, broom factory and general store. It also had a rodeo arena and baseball team, as well as a precinct courthouse, post office (1890–1904), community center and a Woodmen of the World band. Families made mattresses and canned foods at the community's school (1879–1943), which consolidated with the Paul H. Pewitt and Daingerfield districts in 1951.   (2002)

DAINGERFIELD (Morris Co.)   *SH 11/49 N, at entrance to*
                                                          Daingerfield State Park, 3 mi. E
Caddo Trace (1 mi. N)
Hunting and trade route for area between Arkansas and Red Rivers; used by Caddo Indians, who occupied the northeast corner of Texas and adjacent states. Like many Indian trails, it was later usurped by whites; after 1840, it became part of stage and mail routes. Teamsters used it transporting goods to market; soldiers marched along it to and from several wars. The Trace follows or

crosses in places 3 other early trails: Cherokee, Choctaw, and Trammel's. Today State Highways 11 and 49 (Hughes Springs to Daingerfield) follow the same general route.   (1967)

DAINGERFIELD (Morris Co.)   *US 259 at Coffey St.*
Daingerfield, C.S.A.
Civil War center for manufacturing, supply and travel. Place of enrollment of several Confederate Army units. Local industries supporting the war effort included 3 tanyards—sidelines of the beef slaughtering trade that helped feed troops and civilians. The tanyards made leather for soldiers' boots and shoes and for cavalry saddles, bridles, and harnesses. On nearby rivers or ponds were 3 sawmills, one grist (corn meal) mill, and a distillery. Foundries in the area were predecessors of the 20th century Lone Star Steel Company. An "old" town before the Civil War. Founded about 1830 at a spring where Capt. London Daingerfield was killed by Indians. The square was laid off in 1841 when this was designated seat of justice for judicial county of Paschal. Courts continued to he held here, though Paschal was abolished in 1842. One noted 1842 trial was for a group that included Stephen Peters (one of the men who had platted the town square), accused of murdering Robert Potter. Potter, formerly Secretary of the Navy and one of the authors of the Constitution of the Republic of Texas, had been killed in the Regulator-Moderator Feud, a political power struggle in East Texas.   (1964)

DALHART (Dallam Co.)   *US 87, 1 mi. NW*
Dallam County
Formed from Young and Bexar Territories. Created August 21, 1876; organized July 28, 1891. Named in honor of James W. Dallam 1818–1847. Compiler of digest of decisions of Supreme Court of the Republic of Texas, 1845. County seat, Texline, 1891–1903. Dalhart, since. This area was once part of XIT Ranch.   (1964)

DALHART (Dallam Co.)   *US 87 at US 385, at "Empty Saddle" monument*
Mrs. Cordia Sloan Duke (Jan. 10, 1887–July 23, 1966)
Chronicler of a unique era in the history of the Southwest. Born in Belton, Mo. At 17, taught school in Indian Territory (Okla.). In 1907 she married Robert L. Duke, a ranch hand who had risen to division manager of the XIT Ranch (then world's largest). In addition to her own family, she "looked after" the 150 cowboys who worked the 3,000,000-acre spread. Kept a diary of everyday events in ranch life around here and successfully encouraged 81 others to do likewise. Thus was preserved an authentic account of a passing phase of American life—the cowboy and his work.   (1969)

DALHART (Dallam Co.)   *US 87 at US 385*
Heartland of Old XIT Ranch
Great Texas ranch of international fame. Payment made in an 1882 contract for the construction of granite capitol building in Austin. As contractors, some out-of-state investors (headed by the wealthy Chicago merchants, John V. and Senator C. B. Farwell) built the largest state capitol in North America and received in payment 3,000,000 acres of land. The grant, 200 miles long and of varying widths (enclosed later by a 6,000-mile barbed wire fence), extended from near site of present Lubbock to the Oklahoma line 40 miles north of here. It included land in counties of Bailey, Castro, Cochran, Dallam, Deaf Smith, Hartley, Hockley, Lamb, Oldham and Parmer. Trail Boss Abner Blocker delivered first herd to Buffalo Springs in 1885 and scratched the "XIT" in corral dust with boot heel to design famous brand. Although its land was parcelled and sold, the XIT lives in Texas memories—especially here, 32 miles south of its Buffalo Springs headquarters. Dalhart holds an annual XIT reunion with rodeo and parade featuring a horse with an empty saddle, in honor of range riders of the past. Permanent tribute of XIT cowboys is this "empty saddle" monument, designed by western artist Bobby Dycke, dedicated in 1940.   (1968)

DALHART (Dallam Co.)   *US 54 at 5th St.*
Dallam County Courthouse
Created in 1876 and organized in 1891, Dallam County was named for Republic of Texas Attorney James W. Dallam (1818–1847). Texline, located on the line of the Fort Worth and Denver City Railroad and the only town in the county when it was organized, served as first county seat. A courthouse was built in 1891. Ten years later, when the Rock Island Railroad built a line through the

county, the new town of Dalhart was established where the Rock Island and Fort Worth and Denver City rail lines crossed. The county commissioners court voted to move the county seat to Dalhart in 1903, and in May that year an election was held to approve bonds for a courthouse. County government soon outgrew the 1903 building, and in 1922 the voters approved more bonds for a new courthouse. Designed by the Amarillo architectural firm of Smith & Townes, this Classical Revival structure was completed in 1923. Built of brick with cast stone detailing, the building rises from a rusticated ground floor to more finely detailed upper stories, and features Ionic columns, curvilinear parapets, and denticulated cornice. A fine example of its style, the courthouse continues to serve the citizens of Dalhart and Dallam County. (1991)

DALLAS (Dallas Co.)   *Elm, Market and Main Sts., Dallas County Historical Plaza*
Dallas County
After Texas became a republic in 1836, the Trinity River separated Robertson County to the west and Nacogdoches County to the east. This area, called "Three Forks" for the confluence of three branches of the Trinity, was settled mainly by Peters colonists after 1841. A town named Dallas was on this site by 1842. Its founder, John Neely Bryan, led efforts to create Dallas County in 1846, which included the settlements of Dallas, Cedar Springs, Farmers Branch, and Hord's Ridge. The legislature possibly named the county for George Mifflin Dallas (1792–1864), then Vice-President of the United States. The town of Dallas was confirmed as county seat by election in 1850. The 1850 census showed 2,743 settlers in the county, most of whom were farmers. Railroads came in the 1870s and the population leaped in 1880 to 33,488, one-third living in the city of Dallas. In 1885, farmland sold for $15 per acre; by 1920, with cotton prices briefly soaring, farmland was worth $300 per acre. Railroads, interurban lines, and highways aided the urbanization of the county, which accelerated during the 1930s depression. After World War II the county became primarily urban. In 1980, the county population was 1,556,549, less than two percent rural.
(Texas Sesquicentennial 1836–1986)

DALLAS (Dallas Co.)   *100 S. Houston near IH 35*
Women's Suffrage in Dallas County
The first organized effort on behalf of women's suffrage in Texas occurred in May 1893, when the Texas Equal Rights Association (T.E.R.A.), later known as the League of Women Voters of Texas, was formed at a convention held at Dallas' Windsor Hotel. Of the forty-eight charter members of the organization, fourteen were Dallasites. In October of that year, T.E.R.A. leaders helped to organize the Texas Woman's Congress, which met at the State Fair in Dallas. During this period, a weekly suffrage column, entitled "Women in Public" was published in the *Dallas Morning News*. Suffrage advocates continued their work into the 20th century. On March 13, 1913, forty-three Dallas women gathered to establish the Dallas Equal Suffrage Association (D.E.S.A.), which became the League of Women Voters of Dallas in October 1919. Many of the women had participated in previous suffrage organizations; younger members were eager to contribute to the cause. The group elected Margaret Bell Houston Kaufman, granddaughter of Sam Houston, as its first president. During World War I, D.E.S.A. officers served as leaders in local wartime organizations while continuing to advocate the cause of women's suffrage. During the 1918 Texas gubernatorial campaign, members of D.E.S.A. procured signatures of over 10,000 Dallas County women on a petition backing a primary suffrage bill. The bill passed, enabling Texas women to vote in primary elections. Dallas county suffragists registered over 16,000 women to vote in the July 1918 primary election. The Nineteenth Amendment to the U.S. Constitution allowed women to vote on August 26, 1920. This act was the culmination of years of struggle and effort put forth by the suffragists of Dallas County and the nation. (2009)

DALLAS (Dallas Co.)   *411 Elm Street*
Formerly the Texas School Book Depository Building
This site was originally owned by John Neely Bryan, the founder of Dallas. During the 1880s, French native Maxime Guillot operated a wagon shop here. In 1894, the land was purchased by Phil L. Mitchell, president and director of the Rock Island Plow Company of Illinois. An office building for the firm's Texas division, known as the Southern Rock Island Plow Company, was completed here four years later. In 1901, the five-story structure was destroyed by fire. That same year, under supervision of the company vice president and general manager F. B. Jones, work was completed on this structure. Built to resemble the earlier edifice, it features characteristics of the commercial

126

Romanesque Revival style. In 1937, the Carraway Byrd Corporation purchased the property. Later, under the direction of D. H. Byrd, the building was leased to a variety of businesses, including the Texas School Book Depository. On November 22, 1963, the building gained national notoriety when Lee Harvey Oswald allegedly shot and killed President John F. Kennedy from a sixth floor window as the Presidential motorcade passed the site. (1980)

DALLAS (Dallas Co.)   *Elm, Main, and Commerce Sts. in Dealey Plaza*
Kennedy Memorial Area
John Fitzgerald Kennedy 35th President of the United States was mortally wounded on November 22, 1963, feet to the right of this marker as the Presidential car was headed toward the underpass to the west on Dallas' Elm Street. Firing from the window on the extreme right of the sixth floor of the building immediately northeast of this spot, the assassin also wounded critically, but not fatally, Governor John Connally of Texas, riding with the President. From this spot, the President was rushed to Parkland Hospital where he died. This marker commemorates the tragic loss of a great American, mourned by the nation he served.

DALLAS (Dallas Co.)   *2628 Elm St., 1 blk. off US 75*
Original Site of the Coca-Cola Bottling Company
One of the first companies in the nation granted franchise rights for the distribution of Coca-Cola in bottles, the Coca-Cola Bottling Company of Dallas produced the city's first bottle of Coca-Cola on this site on June 10, 1902. J. T. Lupton of Chattanooga, Tennessee, was the principal owner, with an initial investment of $5,000. Three employees handled the entire operation. They were: R. D. Twinam, company manager; Mr. Dixon, the bookkeeper; and Fred Welsh, who operated the bottling machine. The employees sold 37 cases on the first day of production and delivered them in a one-horse wagon. In the bottling process, glass Coca-Cola bottles were filled by using a hand-operated, foot-powered machine that held two bottles, one beneath the syrup and the other under the filling head for the carbonated water, where the bottles also were capped. Bottles were reused and had to be hand-washed by putting cleaning fluid and steel pellets, similar to gunshot, into the bottles and shaking them vigorously. By 1905, sales of Coca-Cola had increased such that the company moved the bottling plant to 1800 Wood Street. From its small beginnings here in Deep Ellum, the Coca-Cola Bottling Company of Dallas, later renamed the Coca-Cola Bottling Company of North Texas, grew to more than 2,600 employees in 19 locations by its centennial in Dallas in 2002. (2002)

DALLAS (Dallas Co.)   *Young St., City Hall Plaza*
City of Dallas
Pioneer John Neely Bryan (1810–1877) settled on the banks of the Trinity River just west of this site in 1841. A town he called Dallas grew up around his cabin. Chosen as county seat four years after the creation of Dallas County in 1846, the city of Dallas was incorporated in 1856, with Dr. Sam B. Pryor serving as first mayor. Although John Neely Bryan had anticipated that river navigation would lead to growth for the city, it was the arrival of the Houston and Texas Central Railroad in 1872 and the Texas and Pacific Rail Line the following year that helped to establish Dallas as a major commercial center. By 1890, Dallas was the state's most populous city. Wheat and cotton production provided impetus for continued growth. Insurance and banking also contributed to the city's prosperity, and its selection as the site for a regional Federal Reserve Bank in 1914 was an economic milestone. Following the discovery of oil in East Texas in 1930, Dallas banks concentrated on providing financial services for that industry. Noted throughout its history for aggressive civic leaders, Dallas won the right to host the Texas Centennial Exposition in 1936.
(Texas Sesquicentennial 1836–1986)

DALLAS (Dallas Co.)   *Houston St. Viaduct*
Navigation of the Upper Trinity River
Since the founding of Dallas, many of the city's leaders have dreamed of navigation on the upper Trinity River, but none of their attempts achieved lasting success. Fluctuating water levels and massive snags in the river below Dallas hindered early navigation. In 1866, the Trinity River Slack Water Navigation Co. proposed dams and locks for the waterway. Capt. James H. McGarvey and Confederate hero Dick Dowling piloted Job Boat No. 1 from Galveston to Dallas, but the trip took over a year. In 1868, the Dallas-built Sallie Haynes began to carry cargo southward. Rising railroad freight charges spurred new interest in river shipping in the 1890s. The Trinity River Navigation Co.,

formed in 1892, operated Snag Puller Dallas and the H. A. Harvey, Jr., which carried 150 passengers. The Harvey made daily runs to McCommas Bluff, 13 miles downstream from Dallas, where a dam, dance pavilion, and picnic grounds created a popular recreation spot. In 1900–1915, the U.S. government spent $2 million on river improvements, including a series of dams and locks, before World War I halted work. A critical 1921 corps of engineers report ended further federal investment. Despite sporadic interest in later years, the dream of Dallas as an inland port remains unrealized.   (1985)

DALLAS (Dallas Co.)   *2807 Harry Hines Blvd.*
Pike Park
The city of Dallas purchased this site in 1912–1913 for a neighborhood park. Developed as Summit Play Park, it served a predominantly Mexican-American community by the 1920s. The park name was changed in 1927 to honor a former park member, Edgar L. Pike. During World War II, Pike Park was an important gathering place for Mexican-American servicemen, both residents of "Little Mexico" and those visiting the city. It has become the focal point of the community's cultural, recreational, and political interests. Annual festivities, including Cinco de Mayo and Diez y Seis de Septiembre, reflect a proud heritage.   (1981)

DALLAS (Dallas Co.)   *SH 289, University Park at Park Cities YMCA*
Preston Road
Named for Ft. Preston, built 1841 at best ford on upper Red River (N of here). Followed pre-Columbian Indian trail. Republic of Texas staked out road to fort from Austin. "Preston Road" later served as cattle trail from ford of Trinity River at Dallas to Oklahoma border.   (1968)

DALLAS (Dallas Co.)   *10600 Preston Rd. (SH 289)*
St. Mark's School of Texas
St. Mark's School has its foundation in three 20th-century preparatory schools, each of which contributed to its high standards and national reputation for academic excellence. Founded in 1906 by educators Menter and Ada Terrill, the Terrill School opened in a Swiss Avenue home with 42 students. The Terrills were strict disciplinarians and demanded high levels of scholastic competence. The school attracted the sons of many of Dallas' prominent families. By the late 1920s, athletics had begun to replace academics as the primary focus, and in response, several Dallas families began the Texas Country Day School for Boys to provide a strong academic preparatory education for their sons. When it opened with ten students and four faculty members in September 1933, Texas Country Day School was located two miles north of the Dallas city limits. With the post–World War II economic boom, this area became an affluent suburban neighborhood, and many of its youth attended Texas Country Day School. Meanwhile, the Cathedral School for Boys opened under the auspices of the Episcopal diocese of Dallas after the Terrill School closed in 1946. In 1949, negotiations to merge the Cathedral School and Texas Country Day School resulted in the formation of St. Mark's School of Texas, which held its first classes in September 1950 on the former Texas Country Day School campus. In the last half of the 20th century, St. Mark's School solidified its place in Texas' educational history as a significant college preparatory institution through expanded facilities and exemplary faculty, which led to increased enrollment and solid financial support.   (2002)

DALLAS (Dallas Co.)   *5200 N. Buckner Blvd. (Loop 12)*
Buckner Baptist Children's Home
Founded out of concern for dependent, orphaned children, this institution opened in 1879 under the guidance of the Rev. Robert Cooke Buckner (d. 1919). Originally known as Buckner Orphan's Home, the first structure on this site was built in 1880 and housed six children. By 1910, the orphanage was caring for 600 children. Supported by the Baptist General Convention of Texas since 1914 and later renamed Buckner Baptist Children's Home, the facility now primarily cares for children from broken homes. For more than 100 years, the Buckner Home has been a leader in Texas child care.   (1983)

DALLAS (Dallas Co.)   *13500 N. Central Expy. (US 75)*
Demonstration of the First Working Integrated Circuit
The twentieth-century age of electronics can trace its roots to the 1906 invention of the triode vacuum tube, which marked the birth of modern radio. The invention of the transistor after World War II ushered in a new era of solid-state electronics. As engineers designed increasingly complex

128

equipment, the difficulty of interconnecting large numbers of individual transistors and other components to form electronic circuits was a barrier to further progress. The need arose for a reliable, cost-effective way to produce and interconnect the components. Technical research groups in the United States and abroad began work on the problem. In 1958, Jack St. Clair Kilby, an engineer at Texas Instruments (TI) in Dallas, designed and built an integrated circuit with all the components formed in a single piece of semiconductor material. On September 12, 1958, he demonstrated this first working integrated circuit to TI personnel in the semiconductor building on this site. This conceptual breakthrough and work elsewhere led to development of the microchips that are at the core of modern electronic products, including a broad range of consumer electronics, digital computers, defense systems, and global communications networks. (1988)

DALLAS (Dallas Co.)   *Garland Rd. (SH 78) at Highland Rd.*
White Rock Dam, Reservoir and Park
Early Dallas residents relied on natural springs, Artesian wells and the Trinity River for their water. By the early 1900s, these sources began to prove inadequate for the growing city. In 1909, under Mayor Stephen J. Hay, the city began acquiring 2,292 acres of land to build a reservoir on White Rock Creek. The Fred A. Jones Co. began construction in January 1910, and the new dam and pump house were finished in 1911. Due to ongoing drought conditions, the lake did not fill until April 1914. Beginning in 1917, the city permitted fishing on the lake. Within 10 years, sailing and boating were popular activities. In 1929, the land around the lake became a city park. The next year, the city built a picnic shelter and tables, and the firm of Carsey and Linskie designed an Art Deco bathhouse and boathouse. The city also developed a sandy swimmers' beach. Until 1935, the city administered a prison farm at the lake, and from 1935 to 1942, a Civilian Conservation Corps (CO. 2896) camp operated, building many facilities. During this time, the Works Progress Administration provided for many other improvements. In the 1930s and 1940s, more than a half million people visited the lake each summer. During World War II, the former CCC camp became a U.S. Army Air Corps center and the site of a camp for German prisoners of war. A drought in 1953 caused the city to ban swimming and temporarily use the lake as a water source. In 1958, the city passed an ordinance banning large outboard motors; this drove outboard enthusiasts to other lakes. The number of park visitors declined in the ensuing years, but revitalization efforts have led to increased park usage and a movement to preserve the park and its history. (2006)

DALLAS (Dallas Co.)   *US 75 at Pacific Ave*
Junction of the Texas & Pacific and
Houston & Texas Central Railroads
The city of Dallas secured its role as the economic, communication and transportation center of North Texas with the completion of the junction of the Texas & Pacific and Houston & Texas Central Railroads in 1873. In 1871, as railroads began to approach Dallas, county and city leaders paid the Houston & Texas Central $5,000 to shift the proposed route seven miles to the west, so that its north-south tracks would run approximately one mile from the court house. One year later, when leaders could not convince the Texas & Pacific to shift their proposed route by payment, they devised a way to force the shift. State Representative John V. Lane secured a rider amendment stating that the proposed east to west railroad extension cross the Houston and Texas Central line within one half mile of Browder's Springs, which was the town's public water supply. The legislators did not know that the springs were also located one mile from the Dallas County Courthouse. Angered by the amendment's passage, the Texas & Pacific Railroad still planned to build the tracks one mile south of Browder's Springs. However, the gift of right-of-way for the line along Burleson Avenue (which was changed to "Pacific Avenue" in honor of the rail company), $100,000 in bonds, and additional right-of-way at the intersection with the Houston & Central rail line for a depot finally convinced the Texas and Pacific to move the tracks to follow Pacific Avenue, downtown. The resulting intersection became one of the first rail crossroads in Texas. (2008)

DALLAS (Dallas Co.)   *SH 352, State Fair Park*
State Fair of Texas
Founded in 1886, the State Fair of Texas now ranks as the most largely attended state fair in the U.S. It was begun as a private, nonprofit corporation for civic purposes by Capt. W. H. Gaston and other pioneer business and civic leaders of Dallas. Since 1904, the fair grounds have been owned by the city, which maintains them as a public park except during the annual two-week fair. The fair

suspended operations for two years in order to permit the central exposition of the Texas Centennial Celebration to be held here in 1936. In 1937, the Pan American Exposition used the grounds. Over the years great names have appeared here, including wild west showman Buffalo Bill, Harry Houdini the magician, silver-tongued orator William Jennings Bryan, and Comanche War Chief Quanah Parker. Federal, state, and city governments have erected a series of permanent buildings on the fair grounds, including the Hall of State, five other museums, music hall, livestock coliseum, and "Cotton Bowl." Originally 80 acres in size, the grounds have been successively enlarged to include the present 250 acres. Over 100,000,000 persons have entered its gates during annual expositions.   (1969)

DALLAS (Dallas Co.)   *SH 352, State Fair Park at Hall of State*
Texas Centennial Exposition
As plans began to take shape for the centennial celebration of Texas Independence, a group of Dallas businessmen led by R. L. Thornton, Sr., Fred Florence, and Nathan Adams, joined together to promote the city as the host of the major centennial event. The Centennial Exposition Corporation, formed in 1935, took temporary control of the State Fair grounds, and a team of over 100 architects, artists, and craftsmen soon began designing the exposition complex. Employing thousands of people in the midst of the great depression, the project resulted in the creation of impressive structures, works of art, and landscaping. Officially opened by Gov. James Allred on June 6, 1936, activities of the exposition included a spectacular parade through downtown Dallas, guest speakers, and nationwide news coverage. In his speech to the crowd, U.S. Secretary of Commerce Daniel Roper declared, "America, here is Texas!" President and Mrs. Franklin D. Roosevelt visited the exposition on June 12. The exposition ran for 178 days, entertaining over six million people. It was a turning point in the development of the city of Dallas and left a legacy of art, history, architecture, and culture to generations of Texans.   (1988)

DALLAS (Dallas Co.)   *Belle Starr Dr. & Scyene Road (SH 352)*
Site of the Scyene Meeting Place
In the 1840s, settlers held public meetings under a tree at this site. Beginning in the 1850s, several successive 2-story frame buildings stood here and housed Masonic Lodge, church, elections, and social activities. Scyene Meeting Place housed one of the first public school sessions in Dallas County. In her girlhood, outlaw Belle Starr was a pupil in that school. In 1872, Texas & Pacific Railroad bypassed Scyene and the town dwindled. Yet the Woodmen of the World and other groups continued to meet in the community building, and school was held here until 1927.   (1976)

DALTON (Cass Co.)   *SH 77W, just E of CR 2729*
Trammel's Trace
Many prominent Texas pioneers traveled past this site as they entered Texas via the historic Texas route known as Trammel's Trace, which crosses this field. Near here, Trammel's Trace joined the Spanish or Mexican Trace connecting early settlements on the Red River with the El Camino Real near Nacogdoches. In 1813, horse trader and smuggler Nicholas Trammell established the road which bears his name, widening it for wagon use in 1824. By beginning at Fulton, Arkansas, on the great bend of the Red River, Trammell extended the great Southwest Immigration Road from St. Louis (Missouri) into Texas. The trace entered Texas north of Texarkana (Bowie Co.) and crossed the Sulphur River into Cass County at Epperson's Ferry. It headed past this point and joined the pre-existing Spanish Trace (1 mi. southwest). Trammell then improved the Spanish Trace southward to Nacogdoches. Trammell likely reused some trails that were worn down by centuries of travel by game animals, Native Americans and the Spanish. By the 1850s, other roads from the distant communities of Monterey, Daingerfield, Boston, Naples and Clarksville also converged on the junction, and a community developed near this hub of early roads. The site would become known as Old Unionville when residents moved the town north after the Civil War. Although the community no longer exists, archeological research has located the former settlement and documented the convergence of early roads at the site. Today, few vestiges of Trammel's Trace remain, but continued use of this section into the 20th century as a county road preserved this portion of the important immigration route. (2008)

DANEVANG (Wharton Co.)   *SH 71 at FM 441*
Danevang ("Danish Meadow")
The first successful Danish community in Texas. Established in 1894 on a portion of 25,000 acres secured through option by Danish Folk Society from Texas Land and Cattle Company. Most im-

migrants came first to the northern United States, where other Danes had settled, and then to Texas, desiring to preserve their national culture, language, and religion. A Lutheran church was erected in 1895. Hardships included disease, insects, poorly drained land, and primitive transportation: but hard work, farming ability, and cooperation brought success. (1970)

DAWN (Deaf Smith Co.)
US 60 E access road, at Dawn Community Park
Town of Dawn
Had second post office in county, in 1889. Named by pioneers who saw here the "dawning of a new country." Santa Fe Railroad station house (a box car) was first building on site, 1905. Town was developed by W. E. Neal and Sons in 1914, with lumber yard, hotel, bank, and store, Now center of farming industry. (1970)

DAWSON (Navarro Co.)
SH 31, 2 mi. W
Battle Creek Burial Ground
A surveying party of 25 Texans ran into about 300 Kickapoo Indians on a buffalo hunt; failing to heed warning to leave, the Texans were ambushed on Oct. 8, 1838. Only seven survived, and four of these were wounded. After the escape, they came back to bury their comrades in a common grave. (1966)

DAYTON (Liberty Co.)
US 90, in Dayton
The Runaway Scrape
Famous flight of Texians to escape Santa Anna's invading Mexican Army. Tales of the Alamo butchery on March 6, 1836, and the continuing retreat of Gen. Sam Houston's army prompted colonists to abandon homes and property and seek refuge in East Texas. Families left beds unmade, breakfast uneaten, and ran for their lives, traveling in wagons, carts, sleds, on foot, or by horseback, dropping gear as they went. Many Liberty Countians remained at home until mid-April, helping refugees struggle toward the Sabine in order to cross to safety in the United States. Terrible hardships plagued the runaways trying to ferry the swollen Trinity River. In rain-soaked camps many children died of measles and other ills. Wading through flooded bottomlands, the wayfarers came with relief to the prairie and the Samaritans in Liberty. After resting a few days, tending the sick, and burying the dead, most of the wanderers moved on toward Louisiana. East of Liberty stragglers heard the cannonading at the Battle of San Jacinto on April 21, 1836. Fearing that Santa Anna's legions had whipped the ragged Texian forces, they hurried on, but shortly heard joyful news: "Turn back, turn back." Freedom had been won for them by Sam Houston's Army. (1972)

DAYTON (Liberty Co.)
US 90 right-of-way, 2.5 mi. W
Stilson
The community of Stilson traces its origins to the arrival in the 1890s of the Texas and New Orleans Railroad. Out-of-state developers O. H. Stilson and Rodney Hill bought land in 1896 and immediately began planning a town. They advertised the new community to farmers in Iowa, and a number of families came here to begin new lives. Among those who came to build homes and establish farms were many Swedish immigrants, including C. F. Seaberg and C. D. Nelson. By the late 1890s the town boasted a fourteen-room hotel, a general store, a gin, a blacksmith shop, a rice mill, a warehouse, a barber shop, a post office, a railroad depot, and a school. The one-room Stilson School served students in all grades, taught by one teacher. The school was closed in 1918 when area children began attending classes in Dayton. The Stilson post office was established in 1898 and was located in the general store operated by C. S. Brown. The post office was discontinued in 1925, and rural mail delivery from Dayton began in 1926. Stilson began to decline when the population gradually shifted to nearby Dayton. Descendants of many early settlers still reside in the area. (Texas Sesquicentennial 1836–1986)

DE KALB (Bowie Co.)
US 82, at city limits
De Kalb
Named for Maj. Gen. Johann de Kalb—a hero of the American Revolution—upon suggestion (1836) of David Crockett, a visitor on his way to fight in Texas War for Independence. Other Texas heroes traveling through here were James B. Fannin and Wm. B. Travis. Settled by 1831, when land was given for a public school by Dr. W. H. Boyce, Wm. L. Browning, D. M. Chisholm, Clement R. John and Judge (and Dr.) James W. Smith. Site of first college in Bowie County, founded in 1839

and of ninth Masonic Lodge in Texas, organized 1840. Served as county seat, 1840–1841. On two early stagelines. A stopover for U.S. immigrants to Texas Republic, and 49'ers on way to California Gold Rush. In 1870s hideouts of train robbers Sam Bass, Jesse James, other notorious characters were nearby. Texas & Pacific Railroad reached here 1876. Site in 1889 of P. S. Ramseur's sawmill which shipped high quality lumber all over United States; to get logs to mill, he built a railroad, traces of which still exist. Although in 1896 and 1923 most of businesses were destroyed by fires, city prospers today. Center of ranching, truck farming, and pulpwood production. Known as "The Pride of East Texas." (1966)

DE LEON (Comanche Co.)   *303 N. Texas Street (SH 16)*
De Leon Peanut Company
Cotton was the major cash crop for farmers in Comanche County until the early 20th century. The combined effects of disastrous weather conditions in 1908–1809, a national economic downturn, and a major infestation of the Mexican boll weevil in 1914 caused many Comanche County farmers to abandon their decades-long reliance on cotton and turn to the more lucrative prospect of peanut farming. Because shipping peanuts to Fort Worth for processing reduced local farmers' profits, N. T. Haskins organized the De Leon Peanut Company in 1912. Its first board of directors included R. W. Higginbotham, W. H. Williams, B. T. Higginbotham, Jr., J. B. Wilson, A. E. Hampton, and W. E. Lowe. By 1914, peanuts were the leading cash crop in the county, and the company enlarged its operations to meet growing demand. A six-story main building was completed in 1917; soon the plant was processing up to ten railroad carloads of peanuts per day. The business survived an economic crisis in the 1920s and remained a strong force in the local community, which has been called "the peanut capital of the world." Acquired by a national company in 1967, the De Leon Peanut Company has played a vital role in Comanche County history. (1994)

DE LEON (Comanche Co.)   *302 N. Texas Street (SH 16)*
Texas Central Railroad
Railroad construction in Texas, interrupted by the Civil War and by the national economic depression of the early 1870s, began a period of recovery in the late 1870s and early 1880s. Chartered on May 31, 1879, the Texas Central Railway was owned by the Houston & Texas Central Railway and was in competition with the Texas Pacific to build a line westward through North Central Texas. Extending from Ross Station near Waco in 1879, the Texas Central reached the Erath-Comanche County line in 1880. The Texas Central laid out the town of De Leon on April 10, 1881, and railroad official Robert M. Elgin conducted the sale of town lots from the back of a flatcar on July 7. Although the initial sale of lots was slow, the town soon developed and attracted new settlers from the southeastern United States. Railroad offices, shops, and a roundhouse were built here, and De Leon became the area's primary shipping point for cotton and, later, peanuts and other products. Acquired by the Missouri-Kansas-Texas (Katy) Railroad in 1910, the line continued to operate until 1967, when local backers purchased part of the line and continued to provide shipping service to customers along "the peanut line" connecting Dublin, De Leon, and Gorman. (1994)

DE LEON (Comanche Co.)   *SH 6*
Frances Marie Sparks Brown (October 17, 1849–January 1, 1934)
Frances Marie Sparks, a native of North Carolina and daughter of Daniel and Kezziah Sparks, married Thomas Brown in 1865. They lived in Grayson County, Texas, before moving to a 410-acre farm near here about 1876. During the 1880s and 1890s, Frances served as a midwife and lay doctor for families in the area. Known as "Aunt Fanny," she often rode 6–8 miles by horseback at night to deliver a baby. Despite her husband's death in 1912 Frances skillfully managed her farm and reared 12 children while continuing to nurse many of her neighbors back to health. (1993)

DECATUR (Wise Co.)   *US 380, 10 mi. E*
Cattle Trail Crossing (Located ¼ mile S, on Denton Creek)
Near this site ran one of the many "feeder" branches of the famous Chisholm Trail, best-known of all the cattle trails that once linked the vast grasslands of Texas with the meat-hungry markets of the North. The original trail, which stretched from the North Canadian to the Arkansas River, was blazed in 1865 by Jesse Chisholm, a half-Scottish and half-Cherokee trader. The 220-mile route, soon taken up by drovers, was extended north and south. Branches all the way from the Rio Grande gradually snaked up to join the main trail at the Red River. Although unpredictable Texas weather

and hostile Indians sometimes prevented the drovers from keeping to the main route, certain points were fixed. One of these was the Trinity River Ford at Fort Worth, just south of here, where cattle might have to wait for weeks to cross if the river had recently flooded. In 1895, the fenced range, railroad, and quarantines against the fever tick had reduced to a trickle the flood of cattle leaving Texas on the hoof; but by this time, the trail had helped restore the economy of Texas (wrecked by the Civil War) and it had left a legacy in folksong and legend of cowboy days on the untamed Texas frontier. (1968)

DECATUR (Wise Co.) *US 380, 5 mi. E*
Old Campsite of Jesse and Frank James (Approximately 1 mi. S)
Famous western frontier outlaws, who had many Texas hide-outs along a line from the Rio Grande to the Red River. The camps—extending into Missouri, their home state—were used for hiding stolen horses until posses could be thrown off the trail. The campsites were sometimes known to scattered settlers, who feared or befriended the bandits. Also friendly with the James Brothers (and also operating sometimes in Texas) were fellow Missouri outlaws Cole Younger and "bandit queen" Belle Starr. This was an era of widespread lawlessness in Texas. Billy the Kid roamed into West Texas. The Daltons, John Wesley Hardin, Cullen Baker, Bill Longley, Sam Bass and many others found it easy to kill and rob and then hide in wild areas where they were beyond the reach of local officers, and food was plentiful. After reconstruction ended in 1874, Texas Rangers were reorganized, to restore respect for the law. Given special powers, in 1889–1890 they arrested 579 wanted men (including 76 alleged murderers). Jesse James and some other notorious badmen by then were dead. Frank, reformed, worked as a salesman in Dallas, Paris, and other Texas towns. (1967)

DECATUR (Wise Co.) *US 380, 5 mi. E*
Dr. William Renshaw (1822–1887)
Born in Illinois, William Renshaw studied medicine and set up practice in Sparta, Tennessee. His wife Sarah received from the Mexican Government a grant of land in Texas, where her father Samuel Worthington lost his life in a colonization attempt in 1828. Dr. Renshaw traveled to Texas in 1853 to locate this headright, which encompassed many acres of Wise County north of this marker site. Dr. Renshaw returned to Sparta and served two terms in the Tennessee Legislature before moving his family to Texas in 1859. The first doctor to settle permanently in Wise County, Dr. Renshaw was often away from home for long periods, with a practice extending from Denton to Jacksboro. The Renshaws organized one of the county's earliest schools, taught by J. D. White, for their own and neighbor children. After the Civil War, the family moved to Decatur, where Dr. Renshaw and his son Lute opened a drugstore. They were devout Baptists and supported Decatur Baptist College. Dr. Renshaw died in 1887 and was buried at Oak Lawn Cemetery in Decatur. As his 10 children married, each received a portion of the Worthington Survey. Two family members still own part of the property. A number of descendants became doctors. (1976)

DECATUR (Wise Co.) *US 81/287, N city limits*
Butterfield Overland Stage Line
Through Decatur passed the Butterfield Overland Mail Line connecting St. Louis and San Francisco with semi-weekly stage and mail service, 1858–1861. The length of the route, 2795 miles and the superior service maintained made this a pioneer enterprise of the first magnitude.

DECATUR (Wise Co.) *Main St. at US 380/287/81 at courthouse*
Randolph Vesey (1832–1908)
Respected Negro citizen and homeowner. Champion pioneer fiddler, popular at Forts Belknap, Griffin and Richardson and Over County. Once when he was an Indian captive, held in Kansas, Texans sent ponies to ransom him. He is buried in Oaklawn, Decatur. Born in Georgia. He served during the Civil War as body servant and voluntary battle aide to Gen. W. L. Cabell of the Confederate Army. Vesey's courage and loyalty were typical. Hundreds of slaves went to war with masters. Many operated farms and ranches of soldiers away at war, producing cotton and food for the Confederacy. Others did work for hire, with wages supporting the master's family. On patrol duty they protected homes from Indians, bandits, outlaws. During war years, 1861–1865, some 30,000 to 50,000 Negroes—free and slaves—aided Confederate armies. They served with the nitre and mining bureau and departments of medicine, engineers, quartermaster general, ordnance and commissary

general. They built fortifications on coasts from Brownsville, Texas, to Norfolk, Virginia, and its inland points. Many were army teamsters, wheelwrights, blacksmiths, butchers, shoemakers, cooks and nurses. Texas and other states later provided land grants and pensions for many.   (1965)

DECATUR (Wise Co.)   *Main St.at US 380/287/81 at courthouse*
Charles Vernon Terrell (May 2, 1861–November 17, 1959)
A leading public man in Texas, 1896–1939. Born in Wise County to early (1854) settlers. After two years at Texas A. & M., read law and began practice in 1886. Served 1888–1892 as Decatur city attorney; 1892–1896 as county attorney; 1896–1901 and 1909–1913 from Denton-Montague-Wise Counties, in Texas Senate. There he sponsored act creating North Texas State University. He was State Treasurer of Texas from 1921 to 1924. Appointed in 1924 to the Texas Railroad Commission (chairman 2 terms), he served during landmark years when Texas was catapulted into role of a major world energy supplier. Through regulation of oil and gas shipping, the Railroad Commission became the agency for making production rules. When East Texas in the 1930s began to produce oil in volumes such as the world had never known, and the state invoked martial law to quell strife there, Commissioner Terrell and associates pioneered in conservation without the sacrifice of industrial leadership. After his retirement in 1939, his native county had an oil discovery at Park Springs, in 1942. The Chico Field came in with larger yields in 1947. C. V. and Etta (May) Terrell were parents of Tully Vernon, John Preston, and Margaret (Mrs. F. T. Ward).   (1972)

DECATUR (Wise Co.)   *900–904 US 81/287 S*
Texas Tourist Camp Complex
Local businessman E. F. Boydston (1888–1945) purchased this site, a former feed lot, in 1927 for $400. Recognizing a potential business opportunity in offering services to the traveling public, he built a wooden shed and gas station in 1927. Travelers were allowed to build camp fires during overnight stays, and by 1931 Boydston added three wooden cabins with garages to the camp complex. The buildings later were faced with rock, and more cabins and garages were added in 1935. The original wooden gas station was covered with petrified wood in 1935 when the highway was widened and remained in operation by the Boydston family until 1988. The Texas Lunchroom, a one-room frame building, was built in 1929. Renamed the Texas Cafe in 1935 and faced with stone to match other buildings in the complex, it was enlarged to provide second-floor living quarters. Popular with local high school and college students, as well as families and the traveling public, it was closed in the 1960s after a highway bypass built west of town diverted traffic from this area. The cafe reopened in 1993. One of the few intact examples of tourist camps built throughout Texas in the mid-20th century, this property is significant for its association with the early development of automobile tourism.   (1995)

DEL RIO (Val Verde Co.)   *US 90, 8 mi. E*
Site of Chihuahua Road (Crossing at West End of Bridge)
In the 19th century, a life line that connected Chihuahua, Mexico, with the Texas port of Indianola. Opened to exploit rich trade in Mexican silver and gold, the road eventually carried every type of goods (including, in 1860, 27 camels), adventurers, settlers, soldiers, and "Forty-Niners" bound for the California Gold Rush. All sorts of vehicles used the Chihuahua Road: stagecoaches, wagons, ox-carts, and traveling ambulances, which were light carriages with 4-foot wheels. Not until the railroad came to San Antonio, 1877, did this road lose its commercial importance.   (1967)

DEL RIO (Val Verde Co.)   *US 90, 6 mi. E at Laughlin AFB main gate*
Military Aviation in Val Verde County
In 1911, eight years after the Wright Brothers' historic flight at Kitty Hawk, North Carolina, Galbraith Perry Rodgers landed his plane at Del Rio while on the first transcontinental flight across the United States. The arrival of a plane in Del Rio was a major event then, but it became a common sight in later years. During World War I, the town was the center of aerial patrols along the United States–Mexico border. In 1919, planes were dispatched to the area in reaction to Pancho Villa's border raids. One pilot stationed here to fly border patrols was Lt. James H. Doolittle, who later gained international attention in World War II. In the 1940s, Del Rio was chosen as the site of an air base because of the flat terrain and the mild climate. Opened as the first B-26 bombardier school, Laughlin Air Force Base was named in honor of Lt. Jack T. Laughlin, the first pilot from Del Rio killed in action in World War II. Later a pilot training school, it closed after the war. In 1952,

through the efforts of local residents, it was reopened. Laughlin has been utilized for astronaut training, Strategic Air Command U-2 reconnaissance missions, the development of Air Training Command's undergraduate pilot training mission, and other important innovations.   (1981)

DEL RIO (Val Verde Co.)   *US 90, 6 mi. E at Laughlin AFB main gate*
Laughlin Army Air Field
With the need to train more pilots for military service during World War II, the U.S. Army established an air field east of Del Rio in 1942. The region's year-round good weather and vast areas of open ground offered near ideal flight training conditions. On July 2 of that year, the Army activated the field as what the local press called a "jaw-shattering title": The Army Air Forces Transition Flying School, Medium Bombardment. Lt. Col. E. W. Suarez oversaw construction of the base, which was accessible by U.S. Highway 90 and by the Southern Pacific rail line. Col. George W. Mundy became the base's commanding officer on December 26, 1942. Earlier in 1942, Del Rio native and Army pilot Lt. Jack Thomas Laughlin died in military action, becoming the first pilot from the community killed in World War II. He was shot down over the Java Sea while flying a B-17. Local citizens and U.S. Congressman Charles L. South petitioned the Army to name the base for Laughlin, which the Army agreed to in 1943. Laughlin's widow and the young daughter he never met attended the field's dedication that year, and Maj. Gen. Gerald C. Brant delivered a dedicatory speech. Instructors at the field trained experienced pilots on the Martin B-26 medium bomber, which was also known as the Marauder, the Widow Maker and the Flying Prostitute. Laughlin pilots went on to fly missions in both the European and Pacific theaters of the war. The Army closed the base at the end of the war but reopened it as Laughlin Air Force Base in 1952.   (2006)

DEL RIO (Val Verde Co.)   *US 90, 6 mi. E at Laughlin AFB main gate*
Lt. Jack T. Laughlin
Born in Del Rio on Sept. 17, 1914, Jack Thomas Laughlin graduated from Del Rio high School and earned a degree from the University of Texas. In 1940, he joined the Army Air Corps and the following year received his pilot's wings at Stockton, CA. On Jan. 29, 1942, during World War II, his B-17 Flying Fortress was shot down over the Java Sea in the Indonesian Islands. The U.S. Army established an airfield in Del Rio that year, and citizens and officials requested it be named for Laughlin, the first Del Rio born pilot killed in the war. Despite the official policy for naming bases, the idea prevailed, and in March 1943 Laughlin Field was dedicated with the pilot's widow and daughter in attendance.   (2006)

DEL RIO (Val Verde Co.)   *US 90, 6 mi. E at Laughlin AFB main gate*
Rudolph Anderson, Jr.
U.S. Air Force pilot Rudolf Anderson was the only American airman shot down during the Cuban Missile Crisis. Born in 1927 in South Carolina, Anderson joined the military in 1951 and soon began flying reconnaissance missions during the Korean Conflict. Stationed at Laughlin Air Force Base by 1957, he was here when the Cuban Missile Crisis developed in October 1962. On October 27, while piloting a U-2 plane over Cuba to provide surveillance of a medium range ballistic missile site under construction, antiaircraft fire hit his plane, killing him. The Air Force decorated Anderson posthumously and in 2001 renamed Laughlin's operation building Anderson Hall. He is buried in South Carolina.   (2006)

DEL RIO (Val Verde Co.)   *US 90, just E of N Bedell Ave.*
Val Verde County
Formed from Crockett, Kinney and Pecos Counties. Created March 24, 1885; organized March 31, 1885. Named in honor of the battle fought at Val Verde near Fort Craig, New Mexico, February 19, 1862. Del Rio, the county seat.

DEL RIO (Val Verde Co.)   *608 Griner St., 2 blks. S of US 277*
Canal System of Del Rio
Crude irrigation systems, drawing water from San Felipe Springs and Creek, were first devised by Indian and Spanish inhabitants of this area. Anglo-American settlers also saw the need for irrigation in this arid region, and about 1869 a group of landowners formed the San Felipe Agricultural, Manufacturing & Irrigation Company. Among early stockholders were W. D. Adams, Donald Jackson, Joseph Ney, Randolph Pafford, James H. Taylor, and A. O. Strickland. They dammed San

Felipe Creek just below the Springs, and by 1871 had built canals diverting water to 1,500 acres of land. Under the 1875 irrigation law, the company received a 99-year state charter authorizing the digging of two canals: five-mile long "Madre Ditch" and mile-long "San Felipe Ditch"—plus lateral canals. In 1876 the state inspector reported that the San Felipe Company had irrigated about 3,000 acres. Land grant provisions of an 1876 law awarded the company 5,000 acres of state land for the total mileage of its canals. In addition to promoting agricultural development the work of the San Felipe Company stimulated the growth of Del Rio, since the irrigation canals provided water to the city as well. Today this vital water supply system is still in operation.

DENISON (Grayson Co.)   *SH 91/FM 1310 in overlook area*
Lake Texoma
Completed 1944. Texoma is today the second largest lake in Texas and the eleventh largest reservoir in capacity in the United States. Its main purposes are flood control, power generation and recreation. Lake Texoma was promoted largely through the efforts of Sam Rayburn (1882–1961), noted Speaker of the House who represented District 4 in Congress for 49 years. In normal operation, lake shoreline covers 550 miles, with the Red River arm (45 miles) in Texas and the Washita arm (30 miles) in Oklahoma covering 93,080 acres. The waters are impounded by Denison Dam. When Texoma was created, it caused the relocation of railroads, highways, utilities and cemeteries. The site of Preston, historically the Red River crossing for the Butterfield Stage, was submerged, as were the sites of Hagerman and part of Cedar Mills, Texas. In 1966 numerous areas on Texoma drew 8,500,000 tourists who could also visit Eisenhower State Park at the southeast end of the lake. The park was named in honor of Dwight D. Eisenhower, the thirty-fourth president of the United States. Texoma is one of more than 200 major inland lakes and reservoirs in Texas which contribute greatly to the economic and industrial growth of the state.

DENISON (Grayson Co.)   *US 75, 5 mi. N*
Colbert's Ferry
Established about 1853 by Benjamin F. Colbert. Across it came thousands of immigrants into Texas in the fifties. The stages of the Southern Overland Mail Line, which provided mail and passenger service between St. Louis and San Francisco, crossed there, 1858 to 1861. Abandoned in 1931 when a highway bridge spanned the Red River.

DENISON (Grayson Co.)   *US 69/75, 1 mi. S of the Red River*
at Texas Travel Information Center
1931 Free Bridge Controversy
As a result of late 1920s legislation in Texas and Oklahoma, the two states cooperated on a project to build free highway bridges spanning the Red River to accommodate rapidly increasing highway traffic. One of these bridges was near Colbert Bridge, a toll bridge descended from the mid-19th century Colbert's Ferry. When the free bridge was ready to open in early July 1931, the Red River Bridge Company, operators of Colbert Bridge, obtained a federal restraining order against the opening of the free bridge until contractual payments had been made to compensate the company for their anticipated loss. Texas Governor Ross Sterling complied, but Oklahoma Governor William Murray, who was not a party to the contract between the Texas Highway Commission and the Red River Bridge Company, asked Governor Sterling to join him in protesting the injunction. Sterling refused. Murray ordered the removal of barricades erected by the Texas Highway Commission. For twelve hours, traffic flowed freely across the bridge. By July 17, Texas Rangers guarded the southern side. Oklahoma highway crews rerouted traffic from Colbert Bridge to Preston Bridge several miles away and dismantled the approach to the Colbert Bridge from Oklahoma. As tensions came close to breaking in the summer heat, the injunction was suspended; the Texas Rangers opened the bridge on July 25. The new bridge was officially opened on Labor Day, 1931. It served until 1995, when it was replaced by a new structure. A portion of the free bridge was placed in a park in Colbert, Oklahoma, about two miles north.   (1998)

DENISON (Grayson Co.)   *R. C. Vaughan Rd., off US 75*
near entrance to Loy Lake Park
The Civilian Conservation Corps at Loy Park
Grayson County officials became aware of a growing need for a public recreation facility for the area's approximately 65,500 residents in 1930. Three years later the federal government agreed

to create a small lake on land provided by the county. The county commissioners court purchased a site 2.5 miles southwest of Denison in October 1933 and secured the services of the Civilian Conservation Corps (CCC), a federal public works program, to construct the dam and build a recreational park. In early November, 200 men from Wisconsin who comprised CCC Company 857 arrived in Grayson County to begin construction. Many men returned home in April 1934 at the end of the six-month CCC contract. Though it was unusual to employ CCC workers in their own areas, 48 Grayson County men were enlisted to replenish the supply of workers in Company 857. By 1934 the CCC men had created a recreation center with a lake, a roadway, 13 culvert bridges, 6 "battleship" picnic units, a baseball diamond, and a partially completed central tower of native stone. Initially called Grayson County Park, the facility was renamed Judge Jake L. Loy State Park in 1934 in an effort to secure state assistance in completing the park. The commissioners court retrieved custody of the park in 1937 after no state maintenance had occurred. Under the supervision of the county commissioners court, the facility created by the depression-era Civilian Conservation Corps program continues to be enjoyed by area citizens. (1998)

DENISON (Grayson Co.) *Old Settlers' Village in Loy Lake Park off US 75*
Old Bass Home (Originally at 215 W Houston, Sherman)
Oldest extant house in city. Erected in 1850s by Dr. R. L. Bullock. Built around typical "dog run," or entry hall. Had first window glass in county. Family home of Confederate Col. T. C. Bass since 1867. His daughter Nettie, born here 1868, lived in home 97 years. (1968)

DENISON (Grayson Co.) *Off US 75 in Loy Lake Park*
Sand Springs (About 100 yds. N)
A noted watering place on pioneer trails, known as early as 1840 to settlers and prospectors who camped near the strong currents of water boiling up at the foot of a rocky bluff. The sandstone of the bluff's face became an inscription rock, in which travelers carved names or initials and dates of their visits, sometimes to assure friends or relatives who were to follow later over the same trail. The campsite for prospectors, including California-bound gold seekers passing this way, 1849–1850s, the spot was mapped in 1857 as a watering spot for the Southern Overland Mail coaches of John Butterfield, racing from Saint Louis to San Francisco. After the Civil War (1861–1865), many cattle herds passed this way for water while being driven north to market. When Missouri, Kansas & Texas Railroad was built to Denison townsite in 1872, Sand Springs gained new importance, feeding Waterloo Lake, built in late 1800s and used for many years (prior to 1908) as city's main water supply. But the old campsites were inundated. Other steps in man's progress reduced flow of the water. The area remained a popular picnic ground for years. Its history is revealed by the weathered carvings still visible on the inscription rocks. (1972)

DENISON (Grayson Co.) *Lamar Avenue and Day Street, 2 blks. off US 69*
Birthplace of Dwight D. Eisenhower
Thirty-fourth President of the United States; born here Oct. 14, 1890, third son of David J. and Ida Elizabeth Stover Eisenhower. Dwight Eisenhower graduated from the U.S. Military Academy, 1915; in 1943, during World War II, was appointed Commanding General of Allied Forces in Europe; served as president of Columbia University, 1948–1952; was President of U.S., 1952–1960; active elder statesman later. (1968)

DENTON (Denton Co.) *Elm (US 77/377) at Hickory St.*
Denton County
Created April 11, 1846 from Fannin County; organized July 13, 1846 with Denton as county seat. Both town and county are named in honor of John B. Denton 1806–1841. Pioneer preacher, lawyer and Indian fighter. First county seat designated as Pinckneyville. 1846. Site selected in 1848 called Alton. Permanently located at Denton in 1857. (1964)

DENTON (Denton Co.) *Elm (US 77/377) at Hickory St.*
John B. Denton
Born in Tennessee July 26, 1806, came to Texas in January, 1836. As a Methodist circuit rider killed in the Village Creek Indian fight May 24, 1841 in what is now Tarrant County. Named for Gen. Edward H. Tarrant who commanded the volunteers. Denton city and county were named for the pioneer lawyer, preacher, soldier of that name. (1936)

DENTON (Denton Co.) *Elm (US 77/377) at Hickory St.*

The City of Denton

Pioneers settled this locality in the 1840's. In 1846 the Texas Legislature created Denton county—one of several carved from the Peters Colony grant. After trying other sites, the voters in 1856 accepted for county seat this tract donated by Hiram Cisco, William Loving, and William Woodruff. The city and county were named for John B. Denton (1806–41), a minister killed while defending frontier settlers. Woodruff, fellow surveyor C. C. Lacy, and attorney Otis Welch platted the townsite. In 1857 city lots were auctioned, the post office opened, and a church was founded. J. M. Blount, Joseph A. Carroll, W. F. Egan, and I. D. Ferguson were pioneer leaders. A cotton gin and plants for making bricks, corn meal, flour and ice soon developed. The "Monitor," a newspaper, began its career in 1868. Sam Bass (1851–78), legendary western outlaw, trained and raced "The Denton Mare" while living and working as a local farm hand. North Texas State University originated here as Texas Normal College in 1890, and Texas Woman's University opened in 1903 as the College of Industrial Arts. Agriculture-related businesses, education, and small factories sustain the economy. The city grew from 1,194 in its first census (1880) to 39,874 by 1970. (1977)

DENVER CITY (Yoakum Co.) *SH 214, 4.5 mi. N, Yoakum County Park*

Discovery Well in the Wasson Field

L. P. and Ruth Bennett moved to Yoakum County in 1916 to take over the ranching operation they had inherited from Ruth's father Dr. J. R. Smith of Munday. In 1927, they leased part of the ranch to the Texas Pacific Coal and Oil Company for the drilling of exploratory oil wells. By the mid-1930s the Bennett's cattle business was declining as a result of the economic depression and a severe area drought. They were in danger of losing their property through foreclosure when oil was discovered on the ranch. The find was made on October 10, 1935 at the Ruth Bennett No. 1-678 (6 mi. NE), a well supervised by Fort Worth wildcatter Red Davidson and crews of the Honolulu Oil Company. With the discovery, the Bennetts were able to pay all claims against their land. Increased drilling activity in the area created a "boom town" atmosphere and led to the founding of Denver City (6 mi. S) in 1939. Petroleum remains the major industry in Yoakum County, a national leader in the production of crude oil. In 1964, Gene H. Bennett, the youngest son of L. P. and Ruth Bennett, donated this portion of the Bennett ranch to the county for use as a park. (1981)

DESDEMONA (Eastland Co.) *SH 16, city limits*

Fort Blair, C.S.A.

A few miles to the southwest. Largest far western "family fort" used throughout Civil War. Started by C. C. Blair, 1857 settler. 1861–1865 occupants were Wm. Arthur, Blair, J. M. Ellison; Jasper, Jim and Tom Gilbert; W. C. McGough, W. H. Mansker and sometimes others. The fort had 12 log cabins, 14 ft. square, 14 ft. apart in two parallel rows. Pickets walled spaces between cabins. Ammunition and supplies could be bought only by making long, dangerous trips to the Brazos settlements or to the south. Men were hard to spare for a trip, from the fort's defenders against Indians. Candles, soap, soda, food, clothing were made in the fort, by use of rat renderings, beeswax, wood ashes, wild herbs, bark, roots, berries, animal skins. Families had to promote education for their children. Other area forts included Allen's Ranch, also in Eastland County; Lynch and Green ranches, Shackelford County; Buffalo Springs, Clay County; Bragg's and Murray's Forts, Young County; Picketville, Fort Davis, Owls Head and Mugginsville, Stephens County. After the war, Desdemona was established as a stop on the Old Waco-Ft. Griffin Road. It boomed to fame when oil was discovered in 1918. Its call for help to end lawlessness added new glory to Texas Rangers. (1965)

DESDEMONA (Eastland Co.) *SH 16, 1 mi. S*

Desdemona Cemetery

The town of Desdemona was a well established frontier community by the 1870s; a post office opened there in 1877. J. S. and Rosa Jones deeded one acre from the D. W. Funderburgh land survey for a "public graveyard" in 1880. The earliest marked grave is that of William E. Wright (1815–1878). It is likely that older unmarked burials exist among the oak trees here. Native rocks incised with initials or dates mark some early graves. Those buried here include pioneer settlers and their descendants; frontier matriarch Mrs. Kate (Kizzie) Shuler; veterans of the Civil War, World War I and World War II; Capt. A. J. O'Rear, a county commissioner and postmaster; S. E. Snodgrass, a physician who served the area for 50 years; local citizens who profited from the 1918 oil boom: Joe and Almeda Duke, owners of the site of the first oil gusher; and many young children. In 1918–1819 oil discoveries surrounded the cemetery with flowing wells and oil derricks. H. H. Williams' estate donated two acres of land in 1965. The Desdemona Cemetery Association manages and maintains the site. The cemetery continues to serve the area as it has for more than a century. (1996)

DEVINE (Medina Co.) *SH 173, 3 mi. N*
Spanish Exploration in Medina County
By 1531, Spain ruled present Mexico, Central America, the Caribbean, half of South America, and much of the United States. The desire to claim new lands north of the Rio Grande led to continuous Spanish expeditions through present Texas during the 16th, 17th, and 18th centuries. The expedition of Alvar Nuñez Cabeza de Vaca traveled through Texas between 1526 and 1537, exploring and mapping the unknown territory. Later Spanish expeditions, which established missions, presidios (forts), and townships, included those led by Alonso de Leon; Father Manuel de la Cruz; Father Juan LaRios and Fernando del Bosque; Domingo Teran de los Rios; and Father Isidro de Espinosa. At least twenty Spanish expeditions led by soldiers, missionaries, and settlers crossed present Medina County before 1844. Detailed descriptions of the area appear in the official accounts of many of the expeditions. Many of the county's geographical features retain the names given them by Spanish explorers of the 16th, 17th, and 18th centuries. Spanish names associated with early settlements, sites, rivers, and streams serve as reminders of the rich Spanish heritage of the area now known as Medina County. (1989)

DEVINE (Medina Co.) *SH 132 at SH 173*
Judge Thomas J. Devine (1820–1890)
Born in Nova Scotia. Came to Texas in 1843. Became district judge, 1851. On the powerful Public Safety Committee of the Texas Secession Convention, 1861. Named with Samuel A. Maverick and Philip N. Luckett to take possession of the Federal property in Texas. Backed by Col. Ben McCulloch and 1,200 Minute Men, forced surrender of 3,000 troops with arms, ammunition, supplies and $30,000 cash. Served throughout the Civil War as one of two Confederate judges in Texas. Tried cases of persons accused of Union sympathies; dispositions of goods owned by northern enemy; and maritime disputes arising from the coastal blockade and shipwrecks. In 1864 was made special commissioner to settle disputes among foreign merchants handling cotton (South's only medium of trade for vital supplies) across the Mexican boundary. At war's end, left with other Texas leaders hoping to continue fight from Mexico. On his return became only southerner besides President Jefferson Davis to be twice indicted for treason. Was pardoned in June 1867 by President Andrew Johnson. On Texas Supreme Court and University of Texas Board of Regents. This town named for him in 1882.

DEWEYVILLE (Newton Co.) *SH 12, on Texas side of Sabine River Bridge*
Deweyville
Original site, called "Possum Bluff," was purchased with a team of oxen by Pierre Lavine from Bill Morrison, 1886. Town was renamed for Admiral George Dewey during Spanish-American War. Leading industry, sawmill, was built by Sabine Tram Co., 1897; and was owned 1919–1943 by Peavy-Moore Lumber Co. (1967)

D'HANIS (Medina Co.) *US 90, 1.5 mi. E in Old D'Hanis*
Site of Saint Dominic Catholic Church and Cemetery
Congregation formed in 1847 with founding of D'Hanis Colony by settlers from Alsace, France. In 1853, when town became a mission parish, limestone church was built, using timber hauled by ox-wagon from Medina River. Sandstone extension was built in 1868 upon arrival of first resident pastor but abandoned after 1914 when new church was built in "New" D'Hanis (1½ miles west). Cemetery, dating from burial of child of colonists in 1847, was used until 1893, when new cemetery was started following diphtheria epidemic. (1972)

D'HANIS (Medina Co.) *Main St. (US 90) at Lindsay Ave.*
D'Hanis
In 1847 Henri Castro established D'Hanis, his fourth colony, 1.5 miles east of this site, named for a Castro Company official. Alsatian immigrants endured great hardship to build a community that thrived for over 30 years. In 1881, when the railroad bypassed the town, D'Hanis moved with

139

it. Aided by the railroad, new D'Hanis flourished, sending cattle, cotton, and brick to markets. From 1900 a strong Mexican-American community grew in the town, contributing to its fortune. The new area survived despite crop failures and the Great Depression, becoming known simply as D'Hanis. (1997)

DIANA (Upshur Co.) US 259, 1 mi. S
Two Early Railroads (Crossing, 400 yds. E)
The Marshall & East Texas Railroad, chartered 1908 was part of a line built 1882. Operated a passenger train nicknamed the "Misery & Eternal Torment," and ran a logging train until 1917. The Port Bolivar & Iron Ore Line was founded 1911 to haul ore from Upshur County to the Texas coast, but never built farther than Longview, 30 miles south. It ceased operations in 1929. The history of these lines is that of many "special interest" railroads. They thrived during the early days of Texas industry, but today have been abandoned or incorporated into larger lines. (1967)

DIBOLL (Angelina Co.) US 59, 3 mi. S
Site of Clark's Ferry and Clark's Ferry Cemetery
Established by I. D. Clark in 1856, this ferry provided an important crossing on the Neches River between Angelina and Polk counties. When Clark died in 1859, his widow, Ann, operated the ferry with the help of two slaves until her own death in 1863. Ownership of the land remained in the Clark family. In 1881, W. B. Clark was issued a license to operate the ferry. A town was platted at the ferry crossing and named Clark's Station, also known as Miami. In 1860, a community cemetery was established north of the town. The ferry was phased out after modern highways were built. (1996)

DIBOLL (Angelina Co.) 400 Kenley at Temple St. (US 59)
Diboll
A sawmill established here in 1894 by T. L. L. Temple gave rise to a town that by 1900 contained a commissary, post office, churches, homes, and schools run by the Southern Pine Lumber Company. The town was named for the Diboll family of New Orleans from whom Temple initially purchased timber rights. Diboll remained a company town until Southern Pine Lumber Company began promoting private ownership of homes and businesses in the 1950s. Diboll was incorporated in 1962 and today boasts a multi-ethnic citizenry which supports numerous community activities. (1994)

DICKENS (Dickens Co.) US 82, 17 mi. E
Pitchfork Ranch
Irish-born Jerry Savage established an open range ranch at this site about 1879. In 1881, St. Louis businessman Eugene F. Williams and Texas cattleman Dan B. Gardner purchased the ranch and in 1883 joined forces with landholder Sam Lazarus to form the Pitchfork Land and Cattle Co., Inc. Williams' heirs later acquired controlling interest of the cattle empire. The first structures here were dugouts in the river bank, while the present buildings date from 1902. Pitchfork Ranch has doubled its original size to 165,000 acres and now operates ranches in Kansas and Wyoming. (1983)

DICKENS (Dickens Co.) Dickens Springs Park on US 82
Dickens Springs
At one time, water covered this area. Sandstone, the prominent rock around this site, is porous, causing exposed strata at canyon rims to form a natural drainage outlet for upland aquifers, making possible the existence of these springs. Situated at the head of a canyon ravine immediately below the upper prairie region of the rolling plains, the ancient springs have been a favored human habitat since the earliest human occupation in this region. Many nomadic tribes have used the site, leaving behind a wealth of archeological evidence. John A. Askins and his family settled near these springs in late 1883, and it became known to pioneers as Askins Springs. A traveling real estate developer called Dr. M. S. Crow arrived here in 1891 and was a driving force in the organization of the town of Dickens about a half-mile west of the Askins land. In 1891 he gave a speech proclaiming his intent to give ten acres around "Crow Springs," as he called them, to the town of Dickens. The new city park became known as Dickens Springs. Generations of Dickens citizens and tourists, attracted by the rugged and colorful scenery and the unique collection of plants, have visited this site for picnics and social gatherings. In 1978 the Departments of Anthropology and of Park Management at Texas Tech University made an intensive survey of the land surrounding Dickens Springs. Though

140

many artifacts were lost to souvenir hunters, the university workers uncovered a variety of ancient tools, rarely of local origin. In the 21st century, Dickens Springs continues to provide water and beauty to the area for modern visitors as it did for the nomadic peoples of the past.   (2000)

DICKENS (Dickens Co.)   *SH 114, .5 mi. E*
Dickens Cemetery
The only cemetery to serve the town of Dickens, this graveyard began in 1891, the same year the town was founded. Mrs. C. F. Jones, wife of pioneer settler and town barber C. F. Jones, died in 1891 and was buried by her husband at the foot of a hill overlooking the Croton Breaks. The owner of the property, M. S. Crow, at the suggestion of his attorney W. C. Ballard, donated five acres of land surrounding the grave site for a community cemetery. W. C. Ballard, considered by many to be the "Father of Dickens," died in 1913 and was buried here, as well. Many early settlers and city and county officials are interred in this graveyard. Also buried here are veterans of the Civil War, the Spanish-American War, World War I, World War II, the Korean War, and the Vietnam War. Through the years, the size of the Dickens Cemetery has increased through additional land donations. Fence was erected in 1919, and in 1948 local citizens formed a cemetery association to care for the grounds and monument. Now encompassing more than eighteen acres, the cemetery serves as a reflection of area history.   (1994)

DICKINSON (Galveston Co.)   *SH 3, school admin. bldg.*
Townsite of Dickinson
Oldest mainland settlement in Galveston County, named for John Dickinson, one of "Old 300" settlers in original colony (opened in 1821) of Stephen F. Austin. Townsite is on Dickinson Bayou land grant of James F. and Emily Austin Perry (brother-in-law and sister of Austin), surveyed in April 1830 by Austin and his friend Seth Ingram. Early settlers here included Alexander Farmer, who in 1831 obtained a land grant where he built home after Texas War for Independence ended in 1836; and Herman Benson, whose mid-1840s dog trot cabin still stands. Gen. E. B. Nichols, merchant, statesman, and leader in Houston-Galveston area in 1857 built summer home still standing in Dickinson. Colonial era economy was based on agriculture and cattle raising. Toward end of 19th century produce was shipped by eight trains a day; for a time area was known as "Strawberry Capital of the World." The Coast County Fair was held here 1895–1896. Picnic and fairgrounds with exhibit building stood alongside Galveston, Houston & Henderson Railway tracks. Community's first church (Methodist) was organized in 1876, and served by circuit riders. Dickinson post office was opened in March 1890; first tax-funded school, in 1892. Town remains a coastal beauty spot.   (1972)

DIME BOX (Lee Co.)   *SH 21, 5 mi. NW*
County's Second Oldest Community, Old Dime Box
Located in Texas, founder Stephen F. Austin's "Old Three Hundred" colony. First known as Browne's Mills. Present name derived from practice of leaving dimes in box at Joseph S. Browne's Mill so that postman John W. Ratliff would bring items from Giddings to community members.   (1968)

DIME BOX (Lee Co.)   *FM 141 at Stayton Avenue on NW side*
Dime Box
Founded 1913. Name derived from the practice of leaving dimes in community mailbox on old San Antonio Road in return for items from Giddings. Nation's first town to contribute one hundred per cent to "March of Dimes" program, 1945. Official national program opening held here in 1946.   (1968)

DIMMITT (Castro Co.)   *SH 86, 5.8 mi. E*
Summerfield-Dameron Corner
In 1876, English native John Summerfield (1853–1918) began his work locating and surveying millions of acres of land in present-day Randall, Deaf Smith, Castro, and Swisher Counties. One of the earth monuments he erected that year was located near this site and became a starting point for surveys in many Panhandle counties. In 1925, a group of Castro County citizens placed a concrete monument at the site, which has become known as Dameron's Corner after a local landowner. The monument was buried in 1958 when a road was cut through the area.   (1985)

DIMMITT (Castro Co.)   *Jones St., 1 blk. S of SH 86 at courthouse*
Shoot-out on Jones Street
At an 1891 meeting to discuss the selection of a Castro County seat, words were exchanged between Ira Aten, a retired Texas Ranger speaking on behalf of Castro City, and Andrew McClelland, a spokesman for Dimmitt. The inflammatory remarks led to a gunfight between the two men on Dec. 23, five days after Dimmitt was chosen county seat. In an exchange of shots in the middle of Jones Street, Aten wounded Andrew McClelland and his brother Hugh. Aten was acquitted of the assault charges and a short time later was appointed Castro County sheriff.   (1983)

DIMMITT (Castro Co.)   *SH 194 at US 385, in roadside park at city limits*
Castro County
Formed from Young and Bexar Territories. Created August 21, 1876; organized December 8, 1891. Named in honor of Henri Castro, 1786–1861, a distinguished pioneer and colonizer of Texas. Founder of the towns of Castroville, Quihi, Vandenburg, and D'Hanis, in Medina County. Dimmitt, the county seat.   (1964)

DIMMITT (Castro Co.)   *FM 145 and FM 1055, 18 mi. S via US 385*
The J. W. Carter Family and the 7-UP Ranch
The first permanent settlers in Castro County, the James W. Carter family moved to this area in 1884. A tent and dugout served as home until a house was constructed (100 yds. W). Their cattle, which they brought with them, were marked with the 7-UP brand. Their daughter Lizzie (b. 1886) was the first white child born to a permanent settler in the area. James Carter (1845–1916) was instrumental in the organization of the Castro County government in 1891 and served on the first commissioners court. Carter and his wife Ellen (1855–1942) later opened a hotel in Dimmitt.   (1981)

DINERO (Live Oak Co.)   *FM 534 at post office*
Town of Dinero
Settled about 1838 by farmers and ranchers. First named "Barlow" after the local ferry operator. Townspeople were instrumental in organizing Live Oak County, 1856; started a school by 1858. About 1872, rumors of money ("Dinero" in Spanish) buried here led town to change of name. A post office was established in 1885. Town buildings were moved a mile west, 1913, to be on new rail line. In 1925 Dinero piped first natural gas to Houston. Oil, gas continue to bolster economy. Local landmark is hanging tree. Famous resident was J. Frank Dobie (1888–1964), Texas author.   (1970)

DONNA (Hidalgo Co.)   *US 83 Bus. at S 8th St.*
Donna
Two East Texas men, T. J. Hooks and A. F. Hester, began developing this area for settlement in the late 1890s. Through formation of the La Blanca Agricultural Company, they set up farms and irrigation systems and advertised the area's favorable climate and resources. In 1904, when a rail line was built here, they founded the town of Donna, named for T. J. Hooks' daughter. Ed Ruthven opened the first store and, in 1908, the town incorporated with R. P. Boeye as mayor. Since the earliest days of the 20th century, Donna has developed as one of the leading cities of the Rio Grande Valley.   (Texas Sesquicentennial 1836–1986)

DONNA (Hidalgo Co.)   *US 281 at FM 493, 7 mi. S*
Run
This area in the mid-1800s was part of the Asadores Ranch owned by Salvador and San Juana Cavazos. In 1898, east Texas rice farmers A. F. Hester, Sr. and T. J. Hooks bought land in the vicinity. They and others began La Blanca Agricultural Company and the Arroyo Canal Company to build an irrigation system. They also helped usher the railroad into the area. Ed and George Ruthven moved to the area by 1904. Ed established a store and was postmaster for the community of Run (a contraction of his surname), and George built irrigation pumps. Andrew Champion also owned a general store. A school opened in 1905, but many area residents began moving to Donna following a devastating flood four years later.   (2006)

DONNA (Hidalgo Co.)   *US 281, .5 mi. W of FM 493*
Donna Public Schools
The present school system for the town of Donna can be traced to a 1904 school in the Run community (6 mi. S). Classes were first held in the home of A. F. Hester, a founder of Donna. The

earliest school for the new town opened in 1908. Teachers held classes in a one-room structure and a store building until completion of the first schoolhouse in 1911. The Donna School District was set up in 1919. Since then, several early area schools, including Run in 1972, have merged with Donna. It is now one of Hidalgo County's leading educational systems. (1986)

DONNA (Hidalgo Co.) *US 281, 2.7 mi E of FM 493*
Balli Cemetery
Juan Jose Hinojosa (1700–1789) was granted land including this site posthumously in 1790. His great-grandson Antonio Balli Cavazos (1813–1887), was the first to live on the land, which he named the Balli San Antonio del Esterito Ranch in 1839. He established the family cemetery. The earliest marked grave is that of Atilano Pina (d. 1874), the husband of Francisca Natividad Balli Rubalcaba. Antonio Balli Cavazos was laid to rest with his wife Manuela Rubalcaba in 1887. The last burial was that of Apolonio Balli Salazar in 1956. There are 17 marked and at least 16 unmarked graves in the Balli Cemetery. The graveyard is all that remains of a 7,000-acre cattle ranch that dominated this part of the Valley for 120 years. (1998)

DOUGLASSVILLE (Cass Co.) *SH 8*
Douglassville Cemetery
Williamson Petty (1820–1861), Sulphur River ferryman, donated land for this cemetery from a claim which he settled in 1850. Col. John C. Douglass (1818–1863), from Georgia, bought in 1855 all of the Petty claim not previously reserved for school and church. The cemetery took its name from his town of Douglassville. The earliest legible stone (1859) marks the grave site of Mrs. Henrietta Cook and her infant twins. Additional land was acquired in 1928 and 1939. The cemetery has about 400 graves and a governing association. (1976)

DRISCOLL (Nueces Co.) *US 77 just N of FM 665*
Site of Santa Petronila Ranch
Appointed in 1764 by the Governor of the Spanish colony of Nuevo Santander, Captain Blas Maria de la Garza Falcon (1717–1767) established an outpost and way station (8 mi. E), the first in present-day Nueces County. He was commissioned to explore the coast and establish a mission for Christianizing the Indians. By 1766, he had moved his family, friends and herds of livestock to what was called Rancho de Don Blas or Santa Petronila Ranch. Until 1836, many colonists came from the Rio Grande area. The ranch served as headquarters for expeditions including those led by Falcon and his son Alferez Don Joseph Antonio de la Garza who explored the islands along the Gulf Coast. Falcon probably named Santa Gertrudis Creek after his only daughter, Gertrudis de la Garza. He played an important role in settling towns along the Rio Grande and Nueces River and Padre, Mustang and St. Joseph's Islands. Soldiers at the garrison patrolled the region against the fierce Karankawa Indians and foreign invasion. Many colonists returned to the Rio Grande settlements because of Indian raids and the Texas War for Independence (1836). After the war they reestablished homes here. Many of their descendants still live in the area. (1978)

DUBLIN (Erath Co.) *105 E. Elm St.*
Dublin Dr Pepper Bottling Company
Sam Houston Prim (1863–1946) arrived in Dublin in 1891 with $680 worth of bottling equipment, purchasing property at the southeast corner of Patrick and Elm streets to house his bottling works. Prim bottled Dr Pepper, along with other products, under an informal agreement until 1925, when he formally chose as a Dr Pepper distribution territory a 44-mile radius centered on Dublin—an area that remains as the company's territory today. At the time of Prim's death, Dr Pepper executives noted that he had bottled the soft drink longer than any other individual. The company has remained in operation since that time, making it the oldest Dr Pepper bottler in the world. (2009)

DUBLIN (Erath Co.) *206 W. Blackjack St. (SH 6)*
Lt. Col. George A. Davis, Jr.
One of six sons who served in the military, George A. Davis, Jr. was born in Dublin in 1920 to Pearl (Love) and George Davis. He enlisted as an aviation cadet at Lubbock in Mar. 1942. Davis was among the first P-47 Thunderbolt pilots, flying hundreds of missions during World War II. In

the Korean War, he was a leading Ace in the 334th Fighter Interceptor Squadron. On Feb. 10, 1952, Davis led an F-86 SabreJet Combat Aerial Patrol near the Manchurian border. He shot down two attacking MIG-15s before his plane took a direct hit and crashed south of the Yalu River. Already highly decorated, Davis posthumously received the Congressional Medal of Honor and promotion to Lt. Colonel for his final heroic actions. (2008)

DUMAS (Moore Co.) *SH 152, 12 mi. E*
Route of Tascosa-Dodge City Trail
As ranchers and merchants settled in this part of Texas during the 1870s, the need for a direct supply line became evident. This trail was established in 1877 for cattle drives and freight hauls from Tascosa (38 mi. SW) to markets in Dodge City, Kansas. It also served as a stagecoach and mail route. The town of Tascosa received a post office in 1878 and was the Oldham County seat from 1880 until 1915. The coming of the railroad in 1887 led to the decline of the town and to the abandonment of the Tascosa-Dodge City Trail. (1966)

DUMAS (Moore Co.) *US 87/287, S city limits*
Geological Riches of Moore County
Have proved beneficial from earliest times when prehistoric man developed first industry in Texas by mining flint deposits along the Canadian River. Items made from these quarries have been found over a large portion of the western United States. Slabs of dolomite from area were used to build sturdy, warm homes; interiors were coated with mixture of sand, clay and caliche—an advance uncommon in prehistoric North America. Modern man has established 31 industries based on oil and gas, to take advantage of geological riches untapped by ancient man. (1970)

DUMAS (Moore Co.) *US 87/287, S city limits*
Site of Historic Drift Fence
Until the mid-1880s, no range fences existed in the Texas Panhandle. Thus when winter blizzards came, cattle drifted from Oklahoma, Colorado and Kansas to the Texas ranches of ("T Box T"—Dominion Cattle Co. Ltd.), K ("Seven K"—York, Parker & Draper), CC ("Bar C's"—Creswell Land & Cattle Co.), ("Turkey Tract"—Hansford Land & Cattle Co.), LX (Bates & Beal), LIT (Littlefield) and LE (Lee & Reynolds). The influx caused these ranches in the Canadian River breaks to be overgrazed, for by spring roundup there were as many northern as local cattle in the herds. To prevent the costly and time-consuming job of separating the cattle, each Texas rancher agreed to construct a fence along his north boundary line. The resulting fence was 200 miles long and ran from the northeast corner of the Panhandle southwest to near the site where Dumas was later founded, then west about 35 miles into New Mexico. It was a 4-strand, 4-bar fence with posts 30 feet apart and a gate every 3 miles. The materials amounted to about 65 carloads of wire and posts hauled from Dodge City. In 1890, however, to comply with an 1889 state law prohibiting any fence from crossing or enclosing public property, most of the fence was removed. (1969)

DUMAS (Moore Co.) *US 87/287 at courthouse*
Moore County Courthouse
Land for this courthouse square was donated by Louis Dumas, who laid out the townsite in 1891. One year later, Moore County was formally organized as a government, and in 1893 the county's first courthouse was built. The original courthouse was replaced by the current structure, built by C. S. Lambie and Company at a cost of $155,000. The brick building was occupied by county officials during the first week of August 1931. Both courthouses have held all county records and have served as focal points for the community and for the entire county. (1984)

DUMAS (Moore Co.) *715 S. Dumas Ave. (US 287)*
City of Dumas
In 1891, Louis Dumas and J. R. Wheat formed the Panhandle Townsite Company to develop and promote a community they named Dumas. A post office was established the same year, and in 1892 Dumas was elected the seat of Moore County government. A mercantile store opened in 1894, and the First State Bank was organized in 1908. The dry, arid land surrounding Dumas attracted few newcomers, and the population remained sparse until oil was discovered in 1927. The town's history is a good reflection of life in the Texas Panhandle. (1986)

DUMAS (Moore Co.)   *US 87/287, 7 mi. S*
Moore County
Created 1876 from Bexar Land District. Named in honor of Edwin W. Moore (1810–1865), Commodore of the Navy, Republic of Texas. County was organized July 5, 1892, with Dumas (named for promoter of the townsite) as county seat. Stagecoach and freighters furnished transportation in early days. The county was thinly settled; ranching was the main industry prior to discoveries of oil and gas in 1926. A zinc smelter was built in 1936. Economy is now based on petrochemicals, helium, oil, gas, cattle feeding, ranching, grains, soybeans, sugar beets and castor beans.   (1969)

DUMAS (Moore Co.)   *US 87/287, 7 mi. S*
Route of Old Tascosa-Dodge City Trail
Founded 1877 for cattle drives and freight hauls from Tascosa (38 mi. SW) to market in Dodge City, Kans. A mail route. The first stagecoach stop out of Tascosa was 3 mi. SW of here. Tascosa had a post office, 1878; was county seat, Oldham County, 1880; declined after 1887.   (1966)

DUMAS (Moore Co.)   *FM 1913 at Plum Creek Rd., 24.8 mi. SE*
Exploration Route of Lt. James W. Abert
(Campsites: 5 mi. SW and 3 mi. NE of Marker)
The United States government had the Canadian River explored in 1845, just before Texas joined the Union. Topographical engineer James W. Abert (1820–1897), a West Point graduate, had charge of a 33-man party, and spent two or more days in the vicinity of this marker. Near here he was visited by Kiowa Indians, who said that they were at war with Texans. Abert was made welcome after he proved to be an American. His map of the river and notes on geography and the Indians proved valuable to Texas and the nation.   (1976)

DUNDEE (Archer Co.)   *US 82/277, 1 mi. E*
Alex Albright (September 22, 1861–April 8, 1937)
A pioneer American Karakul breeder. Born in Nebraska; grew up in cattle business. In 1890, came to Dundee; opened a general store. Built Elm Lodge Ranch (1,400 acres on Holliday Creek, 4 mi. SE). At first raised purebred Lincoln sheep. In 1910, with help of U.S. ex-President Theodore Roosevelt and the Czar of Russia, he imported valuable Karakul sheep from Asia. Later his upbred flock of 1,200 took prizes all over the world. Albright's first wife, Dorothy Jane Duncan, died in 1900. Second wife, Marie Sahores, assisted him in ranching business. Daughters were Zella, Ester, and Marie.   (1971)

DUNN (Scurry Co.)   *SH 208 at post office*
Dunn
Started as change station for teams hauling goods north after T.&P. Railway reached Colorado City in 1881. Freighters camped here beside creek. A blacksmith shop and store were started to supply them. In time a town developed. Mail was dropped at home of Mr. and Mrs. A. T. Dunn. Post office, granted 1890, was given their name; Mr. Dunn was first postmaster. In 1890, the first school was built. A well, windmill and trough were added for travelers and town. Because it was in middle of the road, well was covered when highway was paved in 1938.   (1966)

EAGLE LAKE (Colorado Co.)   *US 90A 2 mi. W*
Navigation of the Colorado River
Because overland travel in early Texas was an enterprise often fraught with hardship, frustration, and danger, many individuals looked to rivers for a solution to the problem. From 1829 to the Civil War, optimistic Texans attempted to ply the area's long meandering rivers, but met repeated disappointment. The most serious drawback to navigation of the Colorado was "The Raft." This was a series of timber masses—some floating, some sunken—choking off the river about 10–15 miles above its mouth. The length was variously given as 3–8 miles. In spite of this, the keelboat David Crockett became the first boat to navigate the river, in 1838. After that, flatboats brought cotton, hides, lumber, and pecans down as far as the raft, but there goods had to be taken off and hauled laboriously by wagon to Matagorda. The Republic of Texas incorporated 2 companies to clear the river and the state authorized the construction of a new channel around the raft, but the obstruction remained an impediment and hazard. Although shallow-draft boats managed occasional trips, the more efficient railroads eventually took away much business. After the Civil War, Texas rivers ceased to be an important factor in transportation.   (1969)

EAGLE PASS (Maverick Co.)   *US 57, 8 mi. NE*
Dead Man's Hill (¾ mi. E)
A knoll by which the old Uvalde road passed. Hill acquired name in 1877 when three traders from Guerrero, bound for San Antonio, were killed here by a party of Lipan-Apaches. The victims' mutilated bodies were found hanging from the wheels of their carts.   (1968)

EAGLE PASS (Maverick Co.)   *US 277, 2 mi. N*
Eagle Pass Coal Mines
Although the Indian, Spanish, and early Anglo-American inhabitants knew of this area's large bituminous coal deposits, commercial mining did not begin until 1885, when F. H. Hartz opened a hillside mine near the Rio Grande. For a time, it was the largest producing mine in Texas, but damage from an 1892 fire caused it to close several years later. Hartz then started another mine for the Maverick County Coal Co., which evolved into the Olmos Coal, Coke, and Oil Co. Under the direction of Pasquale and Rocco DeBona, this company reached a production peak of 1,200 tons a day. Another mining operation was the Eagle Pass Coal and Coke Co., formed in 1893 by Louis Dolch, J. B. Dibrell, and Emil Moshiem. Their mines (.25 mi. S) supplied fuel for Southern Pacific Railroad locomotives until 1902. The town of Dolchburg, now called Seco Mines, was built in 1905, with housing for 90 workers. After Dolch's death in 1907, the International Coal Mine Co. took over the operation. By 1910, this firm employed 350 men and produced about 1,000 tons of coal a day. Competition from oil, natural gas, and other fuels caused the mines to decline. The main Olmos Co. shafts closed in 1912, but Olmos' Lamar Mine (3.5 mi. NE) and the International Co. Mines were operating as late as 1925.   (1975)

EAGLE PASS (Maverick Co.)   *Quarry St. at Madison, at courthouse,*
2 blks. W of US 277
Maverick County
Created Feb. 2, 1856, from Kinney County. Organized July 13, 1871. Named for Texas Revolution veteran, signer of Declaration of Independence, Texas Legislator Samuel A. Maverick (1803–1870). The county centers in an area of dairies, farming, ranching. Hard-traveled El Camino Real (path into Texas history for Louis St. Denis, Spanish missionaries, Moses Austin and countless troops and settlers) crossed the Rio Grande near Eagle Pass, the county seat. Site of Spanish mission ruins, military posts. Fort Duncan, now a military park, housed both U.S. and Confederate troops.   (1965)

EAGLE PASS (Maverick Co.)   *400 E Garrison St (US 57)*
Camp Rabb and Fort Duncan, C.S.A.
Camp Rabb, 15 miles northeast, was one of 18 Confederate outposts placed a day's horseback ride apart, from Red River to Rio Grande, to prevent Indian attacks and Federal invasion. Named for captain in Frontier Regiment, Texas Cavalry; guarded ford on the Cotton Road, used as major Southern supply line. Fort Duncan, at this site, a former U.S. outpost, protected Civil War trade of cotton for vital supplies and arms. Fort served the counter threat from Federals in upriver El Paso and the Davis Mountains.   (1964)

EAGLE PASS (Maverick Co.)   *off US 57 at Fort Duncan*
Fort Duncan
Established March 27, 1849, by Capt. Sidney Burbank with companies A, B, and F, First U.S. Infantry. Name honors Col. James Duncan, a hero of the Mexican War. Fort served as frontier outpost near trail of California emigrants; base of operations against hostile Lipan Apache Indians. In 1851, it became the headquarters of the First Infantry. By 1856, Garrison included units of Mounted Rifles and First Artillery. Abandoned May 1859, post was regarrisoned in March 1860 because of border assaults by Juan N. Cortina, desperado of the area. At outbreak of the Civil War, 1861, fort was again abandoned, only to be occupied later as "Rio Grande Station," by Confederate forces. In 1868, Fort Duncan was regarrisoned by the 9th Infantry and Headquarters Company of 41st Infantry, under Col. William R. Shafter. Seminole-Negro scouts, organized here Aug. 16, 1870, played a large part in ridding Western Texas of Indians. After 1883, post declined in importance; known as Camp Eagle Pass, it was abandoned about 1900. Mexican border troubles in 1916 again brought reoccupation; its use as a training camp continued during World War I. In 1938, the fort property was purchased by city of Eagle Pass, for use as park and recreation area.   (1970)

EARTH (Lamb Co.)
US 70, 5.2 mi. W
Spring Lake
Indian camp and watering place extensively used in hunting buffalo. Became cattle territory in 1882 when Tom Lynch drove his herds from New Mexico. After acquisition by the Capitol Syndicate, this became headquarters of largest division of the XIT Ranch.

EARTH (Lamb Co.)
E Main St. (US 70)
Earth
Before white men entered this region in late 19th century, nomadic Apache, Comanche, and Kiowa Indians followed the buffalo from water hole to water hole. A favorite Indian camp was at a spring (5 miles west), near which the Springlake headquarters of the XIT Ranch were located in the 1890s. William Electious Halsell (1850–1934) purchased Springlake Division in 1901. Halsell and his son, Ewing Halsell (1877–1965), established the 300,000-acre Mashed O Ranch in 1902. When the economic base of the High Plains began to shift from ranching to farming, and other large ranches were being sold for the plow, the Halsells, in 1923, offered a portion of their land for sale to new settlers. Sale of fertile rangelands attracted many farmers from the Midwest, where land prices were soaring. The Halsell family selected this site for a new settlement in August 1924, built a hotel, cotton gin, and school, and named it, "Fairlawn". When the post office opened in 1925, the names "Fairlawn" and "Tulsa" were rejected, and "Earth" chosen. Marshall Kelley was appointed first postmaster. Earth soon had several churches and business enterprises. Earth was incorporated in 1946, and continues to serve an area rich in agricultural diversification.   (1973)

EAST COLUMBIA (Brazoria Co.)
SH 35, 8 mi. E in roadside park
James Britton "Brit" Bailey (1779–1833)
Pioneer Texan noted for his courage, integrity, and eccentric behavior. Came to Texas in 1818 with wife and six children. He settled on what came to be "Bailey's Prairie." Joined Stephen F. Austin's colony, 1824. Bailey became a captain in the local militia. Fought in battles preceding 1836 Texas Revolution. At his request he was buried standing up, facing west, gun at side so no one could look down on him, even in death.   (1970)

EASTLAND (Eastland Co.)
IH 20, 2 mi. E
Hargus Farm
North Carolina native Larry Hargus (1810–1887) and his wife Mary (Corder) (1824–1910) came to Eastland County in 1879. In 1881, they bought the original tract of their farm at this site from C. U. Connellee, a founder of Eastland. Members of the Hargus family were active in the development of a local Methodist Church and a son, James, was a Texas Ranger and a Civil War veteran. The family farm was later inherited by Larry Hargus' son Barry, who lived here with his wife Mackie (Gilbert) and eight children. This land has remained in the family for over 100 years.   (1982)

EASTLAND (Eastland Co.)
IH 20, .6 mi. E
Eastland County
Formed from Young and Bexar Territories. Created February 1, 1858. Organized December 2, 1873. Named in honor of Captain William Mosby Eastland, 1806–1843. Hero of San Jacinto. Member of the Mier Expedition he drew the first black bean at Salado, Mexico, and was executed, on March 25, 1843. Eastland, county seat.

EDEN (Concho Co.)
US 83 at town square
Eden
Founded 1882. Incorporated 1910. Named for Frederic Eden, native of England and pioneer ranchman on whose land the town was located, and who donated land for this public square. Farming and ranching area. Wool and mohair marketing center. Elevation 2,052 feet. Location of Concho County Hospital.

EDEN (Concho Co.)
US 83 at W. Blanchard St.
General Ira C. Eaker
Ira Clarence Eaker was born April 13, 1896, in Field Creek, Llano County, Texas. In 1906, his parents, Young Yancy and Ladonia (Graham) Eaker, moved the family to the Eden area, where he and his brothers attended school. Eaker enlisted in the army on April 7, 1917, one day after the U.S. declared war on Germany. He was recruited into the army's early aviation program and continued

his pilot training through the war, after which he commanded a squadron in the Philippines. There he helped devise an aircraft level instrument, which was further developed by the Air Corps Material Division. In 1926–27, Eaker served as a pilot in the Pan American Goodwill tour. He also conceived and tested innovative flight procedures. During the 1930s, he earned a journalism degree and graduated from the Army Command and General Staff School in Kansas. At the outbreak of World War II, Eaker was sent to England to organize and oversee the U.S. 8th Army Air Force Bomber Command, coordinating efforts with the Royal Air Force in round-the-clock bombing of Germany's war works. He sometimes accompanied his men, believing a commander should know what his troops face in combat. He commanded the 8th Army Air Force and later the Mediterranean Allied Air Forces. Near war's end, he served at the Pentagon as Deputy Commanding General of the Army Air Forces. Eaker retired in 1947 and worked for Howard Hughes and then for Douglas Aircraft Company, from which he retired in 1961. He launched a newspaper column a few years later and involved himself in military commentary for the rest of his life. Remembering his foundation in Eden and his Eden classmates, he returned here often for family and community events. The recipient of more than 50 awards and decorations, including knighthood in England and a U.S. Congressional Gold Medal as "aviation pioneer and air power leader," he died August 6, 1987.   (2003)

EDINBURG (Hidalgo Co.)   *100 N Closner St. (US 281), Hidalgo Plaza*
Padre Miguel Hidalgo y Costilla
Miguel Hidalgo y Costilla (1753–1811), for whom the county of Hidalgo is named, was born near Guanajuato, Mexico, while the country was still under Spanish rule. After being ordained a priest in 1779, he served churches in Colima, San Felipe, and Dolores, where he emerged as a champion of human rights who feared the colonial system would never allow independence and justice for all citizens. A firm believer in economic independence from the mother country, Hidalgo worked toward that goal by teaching farming methods and industrial techniques to Indians and others in his parish. In 1810, Padre Hidalgo, along with military leader Ignacio de Allende, conspired to overthrow the royalist government. Warned that officials suspected their plot, Hidalgo gathered sympathizers in Dolores. Following early mass on the morning of Sept. 16, 1810, Hidalgo made his famous "Grito de Dolores," a call to arms which in effect began the revolt that led to Mexican Independence from Spain in 1821. During a battle on the bridge of Calderon, Padre Hidalgo was captured and later was unfrocked and shot. Considered "the father of Mexican Independence," Padre Hidalgo continues to be honored for his leadership throughout Mexico and the Southwest.   (1983)

EDINBURG (Hidalgo Co.)   *100 N. Closner Blvd. (US 281 Bus.), at courthouse*
El Sal del Rey, C.S.A.
Large salt lake located 26 miles northeast was principal source of salt in South Texas during the Civil War. Put under state guard and agent 1862. Salt sold to families, Texas Military Board, Army of Confederacy and wagons returning north on cotton road—vital trade route for South thru Mexico. Due to military and domestic importance, Union forces periodically wrecked the salt works from November 1863 until war's end. It was also a Texas Confederate base for the 1864 recapture of Brownsville. A memorial to Texas who served the Confederacy; erected by the State of Texas 1963. Back side:

El Sal del Rey, C.S.A.
Salting or smoking were only ways to preserve meat at time of Civil War. When South levied a meat tithe, salt necessary to cure bacon and beef for military. Salt was a must for horses and mules used by cavalry, artillery and supply wagons. Hides were preserved with it to make leather for shoes and harness. Other wartime salt works were operated along coast and in 7 counties in central, east and west Texas. El Sal del Rey, Spanish for "Salt for the King" also played a significant role in the history of Texas mineral law. A legal controversy raged for years over its ownership. Under Spain, mineral rights belonged to crown. Mexico retained the principle of the state ownership of minerals. Texas, as Republic and State, kept minerals in the public domain. Private possession of the lake began with the 1866 Texas Constitutional Convention which relinquished all minerals to landowners. The principle of private ownership was readopted in the Constitutions of 1869 and 1876.   (1963)

EDINBURG (Hidalgo Co.)   *100 N. Closner Blvd. (US 281 Bus.), at courthouse*
Hidalgo County
Formed from Starr and Cameron counties. Created January 24, 1842. Organized April 7, 1854. Named in Honor of Miguel Hidalgo y Costilla—1753–1811 Mexican Patriot. County Seat, 1852,

Edinburgh, name changed February 7, 1861, to Hidalgo. Moved to present site, then called Chapin, October 12, 1908. Name changed to Edinburg, February 3, 1911. (1936)

EDINBURG (Hidalgo Co.) *200 N. Closner Blvd. (US 281 Bus.), at Hidalgo County Museum*
John Closner Home
Built 1887, enlarged 1888. Social center. Had county's only piano. While pioneering in farming and irrigation, Closner also brought law and order to the outlaw-plagued county. After 1884–1890 service as deputy, was elected sheriff in 1890—the ninth in 7 years. Without using six-gun or killing a man, tamed gangs of rustlers and bandits. When he retired in 1912, he had enforced six-shooter law (no guns worn)—a border first. (1966)

EDNA (Jackson Co.) *SH 111, 12 mi. NW in Morales*
Old Morales Store
Originally built in early 1860s of rough pine. Local gathering place then—as now. Exterior appearance is same. Awarded Medallion Plate. (1967)

EDNA (Jackson Co.) *SH 111, 7 mi. N*
Enon Cemetery
In 1856 the Rev. Joseph I. Loudermilk (1816–1880) came to Jackson County and organized Enon Baptist Church—the first church of that faith in the county. He was pastor from that time until his death, and was buried here. A five-acre site was given by John and Clarissa Andrews on Oct. 23, 1858, for the church and cemetery. The first interment (1862) was Isaac J. Sheppard. There are now 65 graves and cemetery is still open for burials. Site of the church is partially enclosed by cemetery fence. (1972)

EDNA (Jackson Co.) *401 Wells St. (SH 111) at Texana Museum*
The Famous Lavaca-Navidad Meeting of 1835
At the cotton gin of William Millican, near here, on July 17, 1835, occurred the significant Lavaca-Navidad meeting, held by pioneers living near the two rivers. James Kerr, the founder of Gonzales, was chairman and the Rev. S. C. A. Rogers, secretary. The meeting adopted resolutions protesting mistreatment of Texas colonists by the government of Mexico. This early formal public protest was a forerunner of the Declaration of Independence on March 2, 1836, and the constituting of the Republic of Texas. (1974)

EDNA (Jackson Co.) *201 Bois d'Arc, off SH 111 at St. Agnes Catholic Church*
Mission Nuestra Señora del Espíritu Santo de Zúñiga
Situated in the present county of Jackson. Was the Mission Nuestra Señora del Espiritu Santo de Zuniga. Established by Joseph de Azlor, Marquis of Aguayo, and Father Fray Agustin Patron, O.F.M. in 1722 for civilizing and Christianizing of the Karankawa, Cujane, Coco, Copane, and other Indian tribes. Under the protection of the Presidio de Nuestra Señora de Loreto. Both moved to Mission Valley on the Guadalupe River in 1726. Moved finally to Santa Dorotea, now Goliad near the San Antonio River in 1749.

EDNA (Jackson Co.) *403 N. Wells St. (SH 111)*
Brackenridge Cemetery
Among family members buried there: John A. Brackenridge (1800–62), a Warrick County, Ind., neighbor from whom young Abraham Lincoln borrowed law books, 1855 founder of Texana Presbyterian Church; his son, George W. Brackenridge (1832–1902), emissary to Benito Juarez in Mexico from President Lincoln in 1860s, founder (1866) San Antonio National Bank, donor San Antonio's Brackenridge Park, member first board of regents, the University of Texas, serving 30 years, philanthropist; daughter Mary Eleanor Brackenridge (1837–1924), on first board of regents, CIA (Texas Woman's University). (1972)

EDNA (Jackson Co.) *115 W. Main St. (US 59/SH 521), courthouse*
Jackson County, C.S.A.
In 1861, voted for secession 147 to 77. With its beef and cotton, helped supply South. Furnished salt from beds near Cox's creek; hides and tallow from a plant between Port Lavaca and Texana; lead from Navidad mine (now a "lost mine"). Homefolk molded bullets and sent them to fighting

men, along with clothes woven, sewed or knitted by the family. Couriers operated along a line that skirted blockaded coast from mouth of Caney Creek to Brownsville. Home guard kept enemy ships off the shores. A Confederate gunboat, chased from Lavaca Bay, sank in the Navidad.   (1965)

EDNA (Jackson Co.)   *115 W. Main St. (US 59/SH 521), courthouse*
Jackson County
Home of the Karankawa Indians granted in part to Stephen F. Austin and to Martín de León. Settled 1824–1835 by colonists largely from Alabama, Louisiana, Kentucky, Tennessee and west of the Lavaca, Mexico. Organized as a municipality December 5, 1835. Named in honor of Andrew Jackson, president of the United States. Created a county March 17, 1836, organized in 1836 with Texana, formerly Santa Anna, county seat; Edna, county seat since 1883. In memory of John McHenry, Francis M. White, James Kerr, F. F. Wells, early settlers. William Menefee, Elijah Stapp, signers of the Texas Declaration of Independence. William Sutherland, martyr of the Alamo; George Sutherland, John S. Menefee, James A. Sylvester, heroes of San Jacinto. Clark L. Owen, colonel in the Confederate army, and other pioneers who resided in this county before or directly after the Texas Revolution. Jackson County: average altitude 75 feet, annual rainfall 37 inches. Soil: black hogwallow, sandy loams, alluvial. Crops and products: cotton, livestock, corn, dairying, vegetables, poultry, pecans, oil and gas.   (1936)

EL PASO (El Paso Co.)   *IH 10 W, at tourist bureau in Anthony at state line*
El Paso
Largest U.S. city on the Mexican border. Named for the mountain pass: Historic gateway for Indians, priests, gold-seekers, traders, stages. Federal troops occupied this area longer than any other in Texas during the Civil War. Agricultural, industrial and military center. Texas Western College (now University of Texas at El Paso), Spanish missions.   (1991)

EL PASO (El Paso Co.)   *IH 10 access rd. between N. Stevens and N. Bowie*
Concordia Cemetery
Known as Concordia during the 1840s, this area was the home of Chihuahua trader Hugh Stephenson. In 1856 his wife, Juana (Ascarate), was buried in what is now part of Concordia Cemetery. The graveyard gained widespread use in the 1880s when El Pasoans drove three miles to Concordia to bury their dead. By 1890 various sections had been purchased by different groups and were designated Catholic, Masonic, Jewish, Black, Chinese, Military, Jesuit, city, and county. Buried here are gunfighter John Wesley Hardin, and numerous civic leaders, pioneers, and war veterans. (1984) Concordia Cemetery Established 1856.   (2005)

EL PASO (El Paso Co.)   *US 62 (Paisano Dr.) and East Wald Kip Way*
The Pass of the North
Historically a major trade and travel artery for North America because it is the northernmost Rocky Mountain pass that stays snow-free throughout the year. Indians used pass long before Spaniard Cabeza de Vaca, thought to be first white man in area, crossed it about 1536. Juan de Onate brought first cattle into U.S. through the pass in 1598. Route was heavily traveled during California gold rush, 1849, and in later years important stage lines and railroads crossed Rockies here. Today the pass lies on one of three major travel routes across the continent.   (1968)

EL PASO (El Paso Co.)   *4001 E. Paisano Dr. (US 62) at entrance to El Paso Zoo*
Franklin Canal
For centuries, the Rio Grande has been molded and shaped by the humans living along its banks. Informal irrigation systems have existed along the life-sustaining river from the Spanish Colonial period. As early as the 1840s, area farmers began more modern improvements on these systems. By 1889 El Paso developers needed a means to efficiently provide water to farmers in the El Paso Valley. The El Paso Irrigation Company began construction on the Franklin Canal the following year. A dispute between the U. S. and Mexico over water rights led to the International Treaty of 1906, in which it was agreed that the U. S. would deliver 60,000 acre feet of water to Mexico via the Franklin Canal. Completed in 1912, the canal began at the international dam and extended five miles, paralleling the Rio Grande on its north bank and continuing through downtown El Paso. It was intended to deliver water thirty miles into the El Paso Valley. Demands on the canal increased as the area's population grew. Upgrades began in 1914 and continued into the 1930s. The American Dam

was created in 1938 to hinder the efforts of Mexican citizens to siphon water from the Rio Grande. Modifications have been made to Franklin Canal throughout the 20th century. It is an important element in the history of water control along the U.S.-Mexico border. Essential to irrigation on both sides of the Rio Grande, the canal continues to affect development in both countries.   (1998)

EL PASO (El Paso Co.)   *Loop 375 E at mile marker 17.4*
Fusselman Canyon
Below is Fusselman Canyon, which follows the Fusselman Canyon Fault, a major natural cut into the Franklin Mountains. For centuries it has served as a natural corridor for the movement of people, goods and livestock between the river valley to the west and the desert basin to the east. The canyon also served as a source of seasonal water, plants and animals for the many Native Americans who inhabited this region. It is named in honor of Charles H. Fusselman (1866–1890), Texas Ranger and U.S. Deputy Marshal. In the late 19th century, El Paso was a booming town, but outlying areas were still plagued by frontier conditions. On April 17, 1890, local rancher John Barnes reported that his horses and cattle had been stolen. Later that day, Charles Fusselman was deputized and led Barnes and city policeman George Herold into the Franklin Mountains to chase the rustlers. The thieves intended to drive the horses and cattle through the canyon (along the path of today's Woodrow Bean Trans Mountain Road), through Smuggler's Gap at the top of the canyon, and then into the Rio Grande Bosque near Canutillo, Texas. Fusselman's party captured one of the rustlers before encountering the outlaws' camp. There they were met with a barrage of gunfire, and Fusselman was shot and killed. The outlaws escaped after the outnumbered Barnes and Herold left their prisoner and fled the scene. Fusselman's body was later recovered and taken to Lagarto, Texas, where he was buried. For the next ten years, lawmen pursued the rustlers. Geronimo Parra, the outlaw leader, was finally arrested, tried and found guilty of Fusselman's murder. He was legally hanged in January 1900 in El Paso. The canyon became known as Fusselman Canyon in honor of the slain deputy and ranger.   (2002)

EL PASO (El Paso Co.)   *FM 258, entrance to Socorro Mission*
The Camino Real
For more than 200 years the Camino Real, or Royal Road, was the major route for transporting commercial goods from Mexico City and Chihuahua to Santa Fe and Taos. First traveled by Juan de Oñate during his 1598 expedition to New Mexico, the Camino Real followed the San Elizario, Socorro, and Ysleta road, crossed the Rio Grande west of present downtown El Paso, and continued north into New Mexico. When the Rio Grande was established as the U.S.-Mexico boundary in 1848, this section of the old Camino Real became part of the United States.   (1983)

ELDORADO (Schleicher Co.)   *US 277, 15.4 mi. N*
Site of Mark Fury Ranch Stage Stand
Originally part of the Mark Fury Ranch, this site was used as a stagecoach stop from 1894 to 1909. Theodore Jackson Savell (1872–1954) owned and operated the line between San Angelo and Sonora. Six mornings each week a horn was blown to announce the arrival of the stage. In emergencies on the road, help was prompt because the line served as a thread of life for this remote area. The Savell stages were instrumental in the early development of the region, providing passenger, mail, and express service.   (1980)

ELDORADO (Schleicher Co.)   *US 277, 15 mi. N*
Christopher Columbus Doty (April 16, 1857–October 26, 1944)
First permanent citizen of Schleicher County. Came to Texas from Missouri, 1879. Soon bought headquarters at Ten-Mile Water Hole (½ mi. East). Drilled first water well in county 1882 and erected first windmill south of Concho River, thus establishing area's agricultural industry. The organization of this county in 1901 included his property, and he was elected first tax assessor-collector. Later was justice of the peace, a rancher, active Methodist and a Mason. He married Alice Pancoast on June 3, 1887, and they had one daughter, Annie Marie.   (1968)

ELDORADO (Schleicher Co.)   *US 277, 5 mi. N*
Site of Verand
First town in present Schleicher County. Named for the Vermont Cattle Company, on whose land it was situated. Post office established 1892; closed 1895. 49er's crossed this area on way to gold fields of California. Site of Comanche and Apache Indian raids in 1870s, 1880s.   (1968)

ELDORADO (Schleicher Co.)
US 277, 2.5 mi. N at picnic area
Schleicher County
Formed from Crockett County. Created April 1, 1887. Organized July 9, 1901. Named in honor of Gustav Schleicher, 1823–1879. Pioneer German settler, member of the Texas Legislature, member of the United States Congress. County seat, Eldorado. First bale of cotton, 1904. (1936)

ELDORADO (Schleicher Co.)
US 277, 10 mi. S
Site of J. D. Earnest Ranch Stage Stand
During the ownership of rancher J. D. Earnest, this site was used as a rest stop on the stage line between San Angelo and Sonora. Owned and managed by Theodore Jackson Savell (1872–1954), the operation began providing mail and passenger service to the area in 1894. Each weekday two stages pulled by four horses made the 75-mile run. On rare rainy occasions the passengers helped push the stagecoach up muddy hills. The Savell Line remained in operation until 1909, when mail was first delivered to the county by automobile. (1980)

ELECTRA (Wichita Co.)
SH 25, 14 mi. S
The Kadane Discovery Well (About 700 ft. SW)
Oil development in this part of Wichita County began in 1919 from shallow depths in the KMA field. As the original wells went dry, and a severe national depression blighted the country in the 1930s, the oil industry sought new production. The Mangold family, owners of land at this site, offered liberal terms for deeper exploration, but at first found no driller willing to take the risk on the scant capital then available. Finally, veteran operator George K. Kadane (1881–1945) and sons Edward, Jack, and Mike had the courage to drill in this area of negative geologic readings. On Nov. 11, 1937, they struck oil at a depth of 3,800 feet, bringing in Mangold No. 1 as a gusher. The discovery effected an extension of the KMA Field. This spot was labeled "Kadane Corner" on local maps. Other operators rushed in, starting a new Wichita County boom. Along with a rapid rise in population came new housing construction, new industries, new jobs, and an era of financial growth. In 1942, a test well on the Griffin ranch came in at 4,300 feet. Final development of the field resulted in more than 2,000 producing wells in an area of 75,000 acres. Over a 40-year period, the field has yielded 250 million barrels of oil. (1978)

ELECTRA (Wichita Co.)
SH 25, 12 mi. S
The Old Buffalo Road (About 100 yds. W)
Named for its traffic in buffalo hides and bones, this North Texas road gave subsistence to pioneers while aiding in mass "harvest" of the American bison. As long as buffalo survived (providing food, shelter and clothing) the Indians were lords of the plains. Recognizing this, the authorities encouraged hunting. Harvested hides were taken to market over this road. The buffalo and Indians gone, permanent settlers arrived. In adverse years (while a man tried to get a start at farming, ranching or storekeeping), bones were salvaged and sold for grocery or seed money. This old road was route of hundreds of wagons taking buffalo hides to market before 1878 and hundreds of wagons taking bones to Wichita Falls and Henrietta before 1890. The road came east from the Plains, near south line of Foard and Wilbarger Counties to Guide Mound; then three miles east (near this marker) and south to Wichita River bridge; then to the county line three miles west of Holliday. Next it passed the north edge of Holliday, and south of Lake Wichita, then crossed at the old Van Dorn Crossing five miles south of Jolly. Pioneers also called it "Great North" Road or "Good Creek" Road. It proved invaluable to economy and mapping of area. (1970)

ELGIN (Bastrop Co.)
SH 95, 8 mi. S
Camp Swift
Named for Major General Eben Swift (1854–1935) Camp Swift, established primarily for infantry division training, was a major military training facility for 300,000 men and women during World War II. The camp was active from May 1942 until July 1946, and covered nearly 56,000 acres. Shaped like a triangle, the reservation was like a self-contained city and included 2,750 buildings. The camp had the capacity to house and train 45,000 people. The 95th, the 97th, and the 102nd Infantry Divisions and the 10th Mountain Division trained here during the war. The 2nd Infantry Division was processed through the camp after the war. More than 32,000 casualties were suffered by these 5 divisions. The camp also provided training for more than 100 separate nondivisional combat and other support units, and the only nurses combat training program in Texas.

About 4,800 German prisoners of war were also held at Swift. At the end of World War II the camp shifted from war time training to processing more than 12,400 officers and enlisted personnel from the service to civilian life. On June 30, 1946, the camp became inactive, and utilization was transferred from the U.S. Army to the State of Texas in December 1948. (1996)

ELGIN (Bastrop Co.)
N. Main St. (State Loop 109) at SH 95
City of Elgin
After Houston & Texas Central Railroad built through this area in 1871, town was platted (1872) and named for Robert M. Elgin (1825–1913), H. & T. C. land commissioner. Brick and tile, for which Elgin is widely known, have been chief products here since 1882 when Thomas O'Connor (1846–1937) made hand-molded, sun-dried brick. Other manufacturing and agricultural products bolster the economy. Settlers of six ethnic origins have made the city a center of cultural richness, with good homes, churches and schools. (1972)

ELKHART (Anderson Co.)
SH 294 at CR 130, 4.8 mi. NW
Site of Henry High School
Despite adverse conditions, African Americans in Texas in the late 19th century worked hard to provide their children with an education. Students in this area attended Mt. Moriah, Boxes Creek, Beulah, Washington Chapel, Union Hope and New Mt. Zion schools. The abbreviated school year allowed the children to help their parents during planting and harvest seasons, and most students focused only on the basics of reading, writing and arithmetic. In the 1930s, Hattie Jamerson, of the Mt. Moriah community, urged local residents to build a high school to serve the rural area's African American students. John Henry Sims, born and educated in Mt. Moriah, returned here in 1932 after earning a teaching certificate in Kansas. Inspired by Jamerson's efforts, he met with Julian P. Greer of the Elkhart Independent School District, and the school board selected a six-acre site here for a school building. Community residents razed the old school buildings and brought the lumber to use in the new construction, which began in 1937. The school was named for its first principal, George H. Henry, and it opened in January 1938. Students in grades 7–11 met at one end, and the other side housed elementary grades. Students could take basic classes, as well as science, history, homemaking, farming and shop. After Henry retired in 1946, H. J. Hurt served as principal. In 1939, the first five students graduated from Henry High School, which remained open until 1963, when it merged into Green Bay High School in Tucker. Elementary classes remained until integration with Elkhart schools in 1967. Since 1980, former Henry High students have met biennially to celebrate their educational roots and the community's historic efforts in providing for its children. (2004)

ELKHART (Anderson Co.)
SH 294, .5 mi. W
Pilgrim Predestinarian Regular Baptist Church
Organized in Crawford County, Illinois by Elder Daniel Parker in 1833 with the following charter members: Daniel Parker, Pheby Parker, Patsey Parker, Julious Christy, John Parker, Rachel Christy, Salley Brown. The first Baptist church in Texas. First meeting held in Stephen F. Austin's Colony January 20, 1834. First log church built in 1839. Pilgrim Baptist Church grounds. (1964)

EMORY (Rains Co.)
US 69, 3 mi. E
Site of Fraser Brick Company
Here in 1905 Walter B. Fraser (1877–1968) built a pioneer Texas factory which produced bricks and hollow clay building tile. This was the first industrial plant in Rains County and it employed about 40 men. When, in 1909, a post office was established near here, its name "Ginger" was taken from the distinctive color of the burnt clay bricks made at the plant. Operations ceased when this clay supply neared exhaustion in the 1940s. Walter B. Fraser retired in 1944. The business prospered at its other Texas locations until sold in 1961. (1968)

EMORY (Rains Co.)
Quitman St. at Texas St. (SH 19) at courthouse
Rains County
One of the earliest areas of Texas to be settled. J. H. Hooker, first known settler, built a grist mill on the Sabine River here in the 1840s. Emigrants from the Old South came in after 1840 although the county was not created until 1870. The name honors pioneer Emory Rains (1800–1878). He served as senator in 8th Legislature from district out of which this county was later carved and had

a long public service career. Rains County is known as the birthplace of the Farmers Cooperative and Educational Union of America, founded in 1904. (1970)

EMORY (Rains Co.)   *167 Quitman St. (CR 2795)*
Rains County Courthouse
The community of Emory was once called Springville, part of Wood County. In 1870, the Texas Legislature created Rains County from portions of four other counties. Named for early Texas patriot Emory Rains, the county chose Springville as its center of government, renaming it Emory and choosing an existing public square for the site of the county courthouse. The first courthouse, a temporary log structure, served the county for nearly two years, when a two-room building was constructed. It and all the records housed within it burned in 1879, and the county returned to the log structure until a two-story, red brick courthouse was completed in 1884. It was gutted by fire in 1908, but the steel vault containing county records survived the fire. The Bryan Architectural Company of St. Louis, Missouri was selected to design a new courthouse, built around the steel vault still in its original location. Crushed brick from the 1884 building was used in the foundation. The Falls City Construction Company of Louisville, Kentucky served as builder, and the new facility opened in 1909. The courthouse exhibits a unique cruciform plan with projecting wings. The exterior is of ginger brick, produced at the Fraser Brick Co. in Ginger (3 mi. East); both the town and brick were named for the distinctive clay color. Designed in the Classical Revival style, the structure features pilasters and pediment-capped entries, as well as a central dome, reportedly not part of the original design. The courthouse square has long served as a social gathering place. Notable speakers on the square have included U.S. Speaker of the House Sam Rayburn and former president Lyndon Johnson. The site of community fairs, festivals, celebrations and parades, the square continues to be a focal point for Emory and Rains County. (2002)

ENCINO (Brooks Co.)   *US 281, 6.5 mi. N*
Falfurrias to Encino Road
Visible from this site is a small section of roadway that dates from the earliest efforts of the State Highway Program to oversee road construction. In 1918, one year after the establishment of the Texas Highway Department, plans were drawn for the Brooks County segment of what would become U.S. 281. That portion of the road constructed in 1918 was a soft sand thoroughfare terminating at Encino (6.5 mi. S). A caliche surface was applied in 1920, and the concrete paving now in evidence was laid in 1928. The remaining portion of the Falfurrias to Encino Road is a reminder of early road construction methods and transportation networks into the Rio Grande Valley. (2002)

ENCINO (Brooks Co.)   *US 281, 1 mi. S*
El Encino del Poso (The Oak in the Hole)
In this vicinity once stood a magnificent live oak tree that was an early landmark on the South Texas Plains for many years. Noted for its size and its wide canopy, it was located in a large hollow created by livestock that gathered beneath its branches and by winds that eroded the exposed soil. El Encino del Poso was a landmark for early trails and land grants. It also served as the location of a stagecoach station and as the basis for naming Encino (1 mi. N). The tree died in the 1890s, before the formation of Brooks County, the victim of an extended drought.
(Texas Sesquicentennial 1836–1986)

ENNIS (Ellis Co.)   *US 287, 5 mi. W*
Thomas C. Neel (1825–1863)
Georgia native Thomas C. Neel married Willia E. Latimer in 1848. The couple moved their family to Texas in 1854 and to Ellis County in 1855. They established a cotton and wheat plantation near what would become Ennis. Neel called his wife "Will" and the plantation became known as Will's Town, which later was shortened to "Wilton." A post office opened on the plantation in 1857; it served under both the United States and Confederate governments. In 1861 Neel was appointed a delegate to the Secession Convention. Later that year, he was elected to represent the 42nd District in the House of Representatives in the 9th Legislature. Shortly after that term ended, he was elected state senator from the 19th District, but he became ill and died before he was able to serve in the 10th Legislature. (2000)

154

ENNIS (Ellis Co.)   *US 287 at Main St.*
Town of Ennis
Founded 1872 as market town on Houston & Texas Central Railway; named for an H.&T.C. official, Cornelius Ennis (1813–1899). Cumberland Presbyterians built first church, 1872; first school session opened 1873. Czechs settled here 1874, adding a new segment to Anglo-French-Mexican-Texans employed in cattle and cotton economy. In 1892, banker Joseph Baldridge and associates secured H.&T.C. division shops for the town. In 1911, St. John's School was established here. In 20th century, local industry, recreation areas, and municipal services spur continuing growth. (1972)

ENNIS (Ellis Co.)   *US 287 at Main St.*
Railroads in Ennis
The Houston and Texas Central Railroad built tracks through Corsicana en route to Dallas in 1871. In 1872 the town of Ennis was platted along this line on 647 acres selected by Captain W. G. Veale. The town was named for railroad official Colonel Cornelius Ennis. The Houston and Texas Central (H&TC) began an extension from nearby Garrett to the town of Paris in 1882. Railroad magnate Hetty Green purchased the line in 1892. The line was extended to Ennis in 1894, and the railroad was named the Texas Midland Railroad. As a result of high community involvement, Ennis became a division point. The H&TC established a roundhouse, machine shops and its northern division headquarters here with the agreement that the shops would never be moved while Ennis could supply water for them. Two lakes were built for this purpose in 1891 and 1895. The Southern Traction Company was chartered on March 12, 1912, and operated an interurban line from Dallas to Corsicana via Ennis beginning October 20, 1913. The interurban line in Ennis ran along McKinney Street, turned onto Baylor Street, continued east one block and then proceeded south on Dallas Street. In Dallas, the interurban connected to Southern Traction's line to Waco. Southern Traction merged with Texas Traction in 1917. The interurban railway was abandoned in February 1941. The rail line to Paris was abandoned between Ennis and Kaufman in 1942, and all Texas Midland lines were closed by 1975. At the dawn of the 21st century, the Houston and Texas Central Railroad line that established Ennis was owned and operated by the Union Pacific Railroad. (2000)

ENNIS (Ellis Co.)   *501 W. Ennis Ave. (US 287) at Ennis Public Library*
Jack Lummus (October 22, 1915–March 8, 1945)
Born on an Ellis County farm, Jack Lummus attended school at Alma and Ennis, and Baylor University on an athletics scholarship. He played minor league baseball in Texas and football for the New York Giants. He joined the U. S. Marines in 1942 and on February 19, 1945, landed with the Fifth Marine Division in the first wave of assault troops on Iwo Jima. On March 8, after fighting without respite for two days and nights, Lummus and his rifle platoon slowly advanced toward a complex of pillboxes before being halted by Japanese forces. Despite injuries from two grenade explosions, Lummus single-handedly destroyed three enemy emplacements before stepping on a land mine, sustaining fatal wounds. His Congressional Medal of Honor celebrates his "conspicuous gallantry and tenacious perseverance in the face of overwhelming odds." (1999)

ENOCHS (Bailey Co.)   *SH 214, 2.69 mi. N*
La Pista de Vida Aqua
La Pista de Vida Agua (Trail of Living Water) crossed the Llano Estacado, linking several lakes in the region. Three lakes in Bailey County lie along the trail: Coyote Lake, where the MacKenzie Expedition camped; Monument Lake; and White Lake in Muleshoe National Wildlife Refuge. By the late 1700s, a trading route, known as the Comanchero Trail, developed along the road. In the late 1800s, the Ft. Sumner Wagon Road, leading from Colorado City (Mitchell Co.) to Ft. Sumner, New Mexico, where it turned north to join the Santa Fe Trail, overlapped La Pista de Vida Agua. By 1881, a mail route followed the trail. Today, the lakes, which had been used since prehistoric times, no longer provide water, as there is only seepage from springs that once flowed freely. (2008)

EULESS (Tarrant Co.)   *SH 360, E side near SH 183*
Founder of World-Famous Cattle Trail, Jesse Chisholm (1806–1868)
Represented the Republic of Texas and President Sam Houston in many negotiations with Indians. Half Scotsman, half Cherokee; a scout, hunter, trader, and trailblazer. Spoke 40 Indian languages and dialects, and was a respected influence among Southwestern tribes, including the

wild Kiowas and Comanches. In 1843, near here at Bird's Fort on the Trinity, was interpreter for a peace conference; in 1849, was in negotiations at Grapevine Springs, to the north. He is best known for marking the Chisholm Trail across Oklahoma and Kansas. Cowboys driving cattle north to seek favorable markets used his direct route which avoided deep rivers and lay in grassy, watered land. He thus helped rebuild Texas economy that had been wrecked in 1861–1865 by the Civil War. Cattle had increased greatly in wartime. Texas had no market; drives were necessary, so $5 Longhorns could go to northern markets to bring $30 or more per head. In 1867, the Chisholm Trail was extended to Abilene, Kansas, where cattle loading pens and railroad shipping cars were provided. This was the best known of several cattle trails from Texas over which some 10,000,000 beeves were driven from the state during the years 1866–1884. (1967)

EUREKA (Navarro Co.) US 287, .5 mi. W
Home of Whitney Montgomery, Poet (1877–1966)
Born in Navarro County in white-columned house across pasture south of this site. Began to write poetry when he was 15 years old. Author of more than 500 published poems which appeared in many major magazines; won numerous poetry prizes. Moved to Dallas, 1927. Was editor and publisher of "Kaleidograph" magazine and press. Helped to organize and was vice president of the poetry society of Texas.

His home was honored in this poem, entitled "I Own a Home":
I can not boast of a broad estate,
But I own a home with a rose at the gate.
I hold the title, and I keep the keys,
And in and out I can go as I please.
My home is not grand, but I live content,
For no man sends me a bill for rent.
And no man comes with a brush and a pail
To paint a sign on my door, "FOR SALE."
I can not boast of a broad estate,
But I own a home with a rose at the gate. (1967)

EUSTACE (Henderson Co.) US 90 just S of FM 316
Payne Springs Methodist Church and Cemetery
For over a century, this church and cemetery have served the community of Payne Springs, originally known as Mallard Prairie. By 1880, the church already had a large membership and met in a log structure. The church building served as a gathering place for elections and political rallies. Summer revivals were held under a brush arbor on the church grounds. The revivals often lasted two weeks and were social as well as religious events. Local tradition indicates the cemetery was started when a child from a family traveling west was buried by a small cedar tree in the church-yard. The first marked grave was that of a mother and daughter who were buried on the other side of the cedar. Elenor Reynolds (1812–1880) and her daughter, Mary Ann Davis (1829–1880), died within a day of each other. The Mallard Prairie school once stood near the church and cemetery. It later moved across the road, and the growth of the cemetery took in land where the school and early church buildings stood. The burial ground now contains over 1,000 graves. An annual July 4th workday evolved into a fund raising event for the cemetery's upkeep. (1984)

EVANT (Coryell Co.) US 281 in town square
Evant
The town of Evant traces its history to an earlier settlement in this area. Langford Cove, founded in 1855 by Asa Langford (1820–1970), was located adjacent to and partly within the south bound-ary of the present town of Evant. A United States Post Office was authorized in 1876 under the name Cove. Evan T. Brooks and his family arrived in the area in 1876. In 1881 Brooks platted a townsite which was filed in Hamilton County records as Brooksville. The same plat appeared in Coryell County records in 1884 as Evant, so named from a combination of Brooks' first name and middle initial. Streets and blocks were carefully planned, including a town square. The Cove post office was transferred to Evant and renamed in 1885. In 1878 a one-room plank schoolhouse was erected on land donated by Asa Langford in 1875. It was replaced in 1888 by a stone structure which, with additions and modifications, served Evant Independent School District until 1976.

Over the years, businesses were established and churches and community groups were organized. The citizens of Evant voted to incorporate in an election held in December 1976. (1986)

FAIRFIELD (Freestone Co.) *US 84, Wm. L. Moody Reunion Grounds*
Colonel Wm. L. Moody (1828–1920)
Came to Texas from Virginia, 1852. Organized and was captain of Co. G, 7th Texas Infantry, the first Freestone County unit to go into battle in the Civil War. Captured at Fort Donelson, Tenn., Feb. 1862. Exchanged, soon won promotion to colonel for bravery on battlefield. Commended for personally leading and rallying men in hand-to-hand combat in thick woods. Wounded and returned to Texas, where he served till war ended. In 1866 moved to Galveston. Became leader in financial, business, philanthropic and civic affairs.

FAIRFIELD (Freestone Co.) *IH 45N, 7 mi. NW*
Homesite and Burial Place of General Joseph Burton Johnson
(April 7, 1816–January 18, 1874)
Planter, soldier, civic leader. Born in Georgia. Commissioned a captain in U. S. Army in Florida in 1837; a major, 1846. Came to Freestone County in 1854. For headquarters on his 10,550-acre plantation, built (1860) at this site a 12-room stone mansion. Served as brigadier general of Texas State Troops in Civil War. A county commissioner; first master of Texas State Grange; a Royal Arch Mason. Made gifts to worthy causes and to minorities. He married Patience Ponder; had 5 children. Descendants include lawyers, merchants, doctors, law officers, printers, teachers. (1971)

FALCON (Zapata Co.) *4th St. at Ramiro St., off US 83*
Old Falcón
In 1745, Col. José de Escandón was commissioned by the Viceroy of New Spain to lead the colonization of this area. The first settlers arrived 3 years later and were assigned land on which to build their homes. A survey conducted in 1767 resulted in the allocation of individual land grants to the settlers, which marked the start of private property ownership in the area. About 1800, José Eugenio Ramírez established a ranch on the north bank of the Rio Grande and named his headquarters Ramireño. The settlement that grew up around his home was plagued throughout the 19th century with Indian raids, particularly when military protection was withdrawn during the years of the Mexican Revolution (1810–1832). In the early 1900s, Ildefonso Ramírez opened a general store, and, when a post office was established in 1915, the name of the village was changed to Falcón in honor of José Eugenio's wife, María Rita de la Garza Falcón. After Falcón Dam was completed in 1952, the town was flooded, and residents were forced to relocate to this site. The history of Old Falcón, however, with its ties to 18th-century Spanish colonialism, remains an important part of their heritage. (1983)

FALFURRIAS (Brooks Co.) *SH 285, 4.2 mi. E*
.5 mi. S is Site of Town of Flowella
On 1831 "Loma Blanca" grant and 1873 land of Perez family, who in 1898 sold "Parrita" (Little Grape Vine) to Mrs. King of King Ranch. Flowella was founded 1909 by E. O. Burton and A. H. Danforth as trade town for a projected farm colony, and named for a flowing well in middle of townsite. The Calahan family opened hotel in 1909, store and post office, 1910. School building, also erected in 1910, provided a social-cultural center for some 100 residents. In adverse seasons, closings began: the store, 1911; hotel, 1915; post office, 1923; school, 1928. None of the original buildings remain. (1973)

FALFURRIAS (Brooks Co.) *US 281 at FM 1418, .5 mi. N*
Site of Los Olmos
The first permanent settlement in Brooks County, Los Olmos was located at the southwest corner of El Paisano Land Grant, given to Ramon de la Garza about 1830 by the Mexican State of Tamaulipas. Situated near the main route to the Rio Grande, the village served a region settled originally by ranchers from Northern Mexico. By 1880, it had a post office, stores and a school, which operated until 1945. The schoolhouse was the site of services conducted by traveling priests. As the town of Falfurrias grew, Los Olmos began to decline. Descendants of its founders still reside in this area. (1976)

FALFURRIAS (Brooks Co.)
US 281 at SH 285, at Pioneer Park
Falfurrias
Founded as a cattle shipping point by Edward C. Lasater in 1904, the town bears the name of a village on land he purchased in 1893. When the San Antonio & Aransas Pass Railroad extended its lines, Lasater (1860–1930) platted present townsite, built a hotel, general store, water and power plants, and cotton gin. He opened the area to truck, citrus, and dairy farms. He founded South Texas' first creamery—now widely recognized. A post office, newspaper, churches, and schools were opened. A citrus packing plant was built in 1914. Still later the city became an oil and gas production center. (1971)

FALFURRIAS (Brooks Co.)
US 281, 10 mi. S in state roadside park
Brooks County
Formed from Hidalgo, Starr and Zapata Counties, created March 11, 1911; organized September 2, 1911. Named in honor of James Abijah Brooks, Captain of Texas Rangers, 1882–1906, Member of Texas Legislature, County Judge, Brooks County since 1911. Falfurrias, county seat. (1964)

FANNIN (Goliad Co.)
FM 2987, 1 mi. N of US 59
Site of Battle of El Perdido
During 1810–1819 efforts to expel Spain from Texas, a bloody clash occurred here on June 19, 1817, between the forces of Col. Antonio Martinez, last Spanish Governor of Texas, and a Mexican Republican Army of Invasion that was on its way to attack and capture La Bahía. Republicans had 42 men under Col. Henry Perry and Maj. James H. Gordon, former U.S. officers, veterans of the 1815 Battle of New Orleans. Outnumbered 3-to-1, Perry and Gordon refused offer of safe surrender, saying they would die first. Along with 24 of their men, both were killed. (1967)

FANNIN (Goliad Co.)
FM 2508, 1 mi. S at Fannin State Park
Battle of Coleto and Goliad Massacre
After the fall of the Alamo, March 6, 1836, Colonel James Walker Fannin, with about 400 soldiers, mostly volunteers from the United States in the Texas War for Independence, was ordered by Texas General Sam Houston to retreat from Goliad to Victoria. March 19, the heavy Mexican force of General Urrea surrounded the withdrawing Texas contingent near Coleto Creek, and bitter fighting ensued. Fannin's volunteers hurled back the assaults of the Mexican force. On the following day, faced with several times their number, the Texans surrendered in the belief they would be treated as prisoners of war of a civilized nation. After removal to Goliad, the Fannin men were marched out and massacred on Palm Sunday under orders of Santa Anna, the General of the Mexican Armies. Thus Dictator Santa Anna added another infamy to that of the Alamo and gave to the men who saved Texas at San Jacinto their battle cry, "Remember the Alamo, Remember Goliad." The memorial to Fannin and his men is near Goliad. (1974)

FARMERSVILLE (Collin Co.)
SH 78 at McKinney St.
Farmersville
Originated 1849 as a settlement on the Jefferson-McKinney Road, and near Republic of Texas National Road. Named by pioneers for their chief occupation. After 1854, the Yearys and their neighbors of Sugar Hill (2 mi. NE) began relocating here. Dr. H. M. Markham, practicing here by 1855, is said to have been Collin County's earliest physician. The First Methodist Church was organized in 1856. William Gotcher on March 4, 1859, donated land for the public square. A school was operating as early as the 1860s. The First Baptist Church was organized on May 14, 1865. The town was incorporated on June 2, 1973. First mayor: John S. Rike. Aldermen: James Church, Ben King, John Murchison, Tom Tatum, John P. Utt. Marshall: Jeff Hines. Institutions of the 1880s still in operation include Farmersville Times and the First National Bank. As town became a trade center, agriculture kept pace. Farmersville in 1930s was known as the "Onion Capital of North Texas," annually shipping over 1,000 carloads of onions. Along with some small industry, cattle, cotton, and maize crops remain important. Audie Murphy, the most decorated American hero of World War II, had been a resident of Farmersville before he entered the United States Army. (1973)

FARMERSVILLE (Collin Co.)
200 blk. McKinney St.
Audie Murphy's Homecoming, June 15, 1945
With Allied victory in World War II Europe secured, Farmersville celebrated the return of the area's most famous citizen soldier. On his 18th birthday, Audie Murphy enlisted in the U.S. Army

at the Greenville Post Office. In more than two years of combat, he fought in North Africa, Sicily, Italy and France and earned every Army citation for valor, including the Congressional Medal of Honor. His homecoming drew an audience of several thousand to the town square. *Life* magazine's July 16, 1945 issue made the Farmersville ceremony and Murphy's family reunion its cover story, commemorating the efforts of a grateful nation and hometown. (2008)

FARWELL (Parmer Co.)   *US 70, .5 mi. E*
Martin Parmer
Formed from Young and Bexar Territories. Created August 21, 1876; organized May 7, 1907. Named in honor of Martin Parmer. Came to Texas in 1825 and located at Mound Prairie. A leader in the Fredonian War in 1826. Signer of the Texas Declaration of Independence. Died in 1850. County seat Parmerton, 1907. Farwell, since 1909.

FARWELL (Parmer Co.)   *US 84, .5 mi. SE in roadside park*
Near Route of Coronado Expedition
One of first explorations of North America by Spain. Began in Mexico, crossing into Texas at or near present Parmer County. The party, led by Francisco Vazquez de Coronado, was sent to investigate reports of great wealth among the Indians. In one city, Quivira, the ruler reputedly ate from gold plates. After entering Texas, Coronado and 36 men separated from the main group and continued north. In August, 1541, on the present Kansas-Nebraska line, he found Quivira—an ordinary Indian village. After the winter of 1541–1542, he returned to Mexico. (1969)

FARWELL (Parmer Co.)   *401 3rd St. at courthouse*
Parmer County
Created Aug. 21, 1876, from Bexar County. Named for Martin Parmer ("The Ringtailed Panther"), signer of Texas Declaration of Independence. Organized May 7, 1907. The XIT Ranch, extending across nine counties, initially owned most of Parmer. The Capitol Syndicate, which built Texas' capitol, received in payment 3,050,000 acres of land and established the XIT in 1885. By 1890, population of the county was only 70. But with syndicate land sales, buyers came on the new railroad in 1904. Brisk settlement began, with many small farms. Farwell is the county seat. (1965)

FAYETTEVILLE (Fayette Co.)   *SH 159 at FM 955*
The Sladek-Hillman House
F. J. Sladek, a Bohemian immigrant, built this home about 1896. In 1899, ownership was transferred to Anna Hillman, the widow of Ludwig Hillman, one of the early settlers of the Fayetteville area. She lived in the house until her death in 1923. The interior of the Victorian cottage features 12-foot ceilings and millwork carvings of intricate detail. The front porch columns are bracketed and the bay window is decorated with fish scale siding. (1979)

FERRIS (Ellis Co.)   *FM 983 at Main*
City of Ferris
Site was occupied in 1851 by the Ephraim Andrews family and their in-laws, the McKnights, settling a purchased land grant. The Duffs, Greens, McDaniels, and Orrs also pioneered here. The Cumberland Presbyterian Church was founded in 1858. The Andrews family (1874) deeded 100-acre townsite, named for Judge J. W. Ferris (1823–1899), to the Houston & Texas Central Railway. Post office opened June 22, 1874, in store of the first postmaster, Jackson J. Straw. First cotton gin opened in 1880; first newspaper in 1889. The Ferris Institute was operated 1892–1907. City has been a brick-making center since 1895. (1974)

FIELDTON (Lamb Co.)   *FM 1072, .75 mi. S*
One of the Trails of Ranald Mackenzie
Col. Ranald S. Mackenzie (1840–1889) of the United States Army was ordered in the 1870s to conquer Indians on Texas frontiers. He led 240 enlisted men and eight officers in an expedition along the draw here. Heading toward New Mexico, he hoped to break up a ring of traders paying Indians to steal cattle and horses. He marched past this point about August 1, 1872; in a swift, secret move against the traders. The path beaten out by his men was serviceable later to scouts and settlers. Its traces are still known as Mackenzie's Trail. (1977)

FLORESVILLE (Wilson Co.)   *US 181 Bus., 3 mi. NW*
Casa Blanca
Home of Don Erasmo Seguin who died here in 1857. By appointment of the Spanish Governor he inducted Stephen F. Austin into Texas, 1821. Texas Deputy to the Mexican Congress, 1824. On October 13, 1834 in a convention in Bexar he made the first effort to organize a provisional government in Texas.

FLORESVILLE (Wilson Co.)   *US 181, .25 mi. NW*
Cemetery of Canary Islanders
Cemetery of Canary Islanders predates church built 1732 by colonists who arrived 1731, led by Juan Leal Goras. They farmed and raised stock. Their villa, San Fernando, was first municipality in Texas. Among unmarked graves is that of flamboyant Doña Maria Cavillo. Site now county-owned.   (1967)

FLORESVILLE (Wilson Co.)   *1420 3rd St. (US 181)*
Wilson County
Wilson County created February 13, 1860; organized August 6, 1860; named in honor of James Charles Wilson 1816–1861; member of the Mier Expedition; district clerk of Brazoria County, 1844; Senator from Matagorda County; Floresville, the county seat.   (1936)

FLORESVILLE (Wilson Co.)   *SH 97, 2 mi. S*
Mission de las Cabras ("Mission of the Goats")
A fortified visita of Mission Espada, founded 1731 in San Antonio. Situated near Paso de las Mujeres ("Crossing of the Women"), an important ford on the San Antonio River, known to most parties obliged to travel between Mexico and San Antonio. Meadowland along the river and near the crossing was used to pasture cattle owned by Mission Espada. Indians under Espada's protection were kept here to herd the cattle. For the care of souls of the herdsmen, a chapel was built. The 1895 guide, "San Antonio at a Glance," described the Old Cabras site as a 2-acre, diamond-shaped lot with bastions at each end. After secularization of the missions in 1794, lands here were owned by one of the descendants of Spain's colonists from the Canary Islands, Ignacio Calvillo. In turn, the Cabras site was inherited by Calvillo's flamboyant daughter, Doña María Del Carmen (born in 1765). Noted for her independent spirit, she forsook her husband, Gavino Delgado, and personally managed the ranch, her long black hair flying in the wind as she rode a great white horse. She kept down Indian troubles by paying tribute in beef. In her time and for a century afterward Old Mission Cabras remained in use for rites of the church.   (1970)

FLOYDADA (Floyd Co.)   *SH 207 at FM 786 intersection, 5 mi. N*
Della Plain
A severe drought in the mid-1880s brought Baylor County rancher T. H. Braidfoot to this area in search of better conditions for his cattle. In 1887, with the support of J. R. McLain of Seymour, he founded the settlement of Della Plain at this site. Other early contributors to the town's development included Seymour residents I. R. Darnell and Dr. L. T. Wilson. Named for J. S. McLain's daughter Della and for the surrounding terrain, it was hoped the town would become the county seat when Floyd County was formally organized. Della Plain became an early agricultural center for the region and was soon the site of a school, church, post office, stores and a newspaper, the Della Plain Review. Growth, however, was limited by an inadequate water supply and by the establishment of the nearby towns of Lockney (1889) and Floydada (1890). Rapid decline began after Floydada was named the seat of Floyd County in 1890. Four years later the community cemetery was all that remained of Della Plain. Despite its brief history, the pioneer town had a dramatic impact on the region. Its residents led in the later development of the county and nearby cities. Their descendants still live in the area.   (1982)

FLOYDADA (Floyd Co.)   *US 62, 5 mi. S*
Floyd County
Formed from Young and Bexar Territories. Created August 21, 1876; organized May 28, 1890. Named in honor of Dolphin Ward Floyd, a captain who died at the Alamo. County seat, Floyd City, 1890. Floydada, since 1892.   (1965)

FLOYDADA (Floyd Co.)   *US 62, 8 mi. S*
Coronado in Blanco Canyon
From 1540 to 1542, Francisco Vazquez de Coronado led the first organized European exploration of the southwest in search of the fabled "cities of gold." With a company of more than
a thousand men and women and thousands of horses and mules, cattle and sheep, Coronado
trekked north from Culiacan, Mexico, through land that became Arizona, New Mexico, Texas,
Oklahoma and Kansas. The exact route along which their Indian guides led the Spaniards between Pecos Pueblo in New Mexico and the Arkansas River in Kansas has long been a subject
of debate among historians. Surviving documents are brief, vague and occasionally contradic-
tory. Twice in the spring of 1541, the company camped long enough to have created detectable
archeological evidence; the first time, they chose the site of a Teya Indian camp. A hailstorm
struck, destroying most, if not all, of their pottery. They occupied a second camp for two weeks
in a canyon that was described as being "a league wide." In the 1950s and 1960s, two pieces of
chain mail were discovered by local ranchers in and near Blanco Canyon. Since 1993, a series of
other objects, both European and from other parts of the southwest, have been found in the same
area. They include projectile points similar to those used on crossbow arrows. Crossbows were
obsolete after this expedition and are unlikely to have been used by any other group of significant
size. In the late 1990s, archeologists began the task of confirming this area as the location of
one of Coronado's camps. Evidence and artifacts recovered supported the theory that Coronado
passed through Blanco Canyon.   (2000)

FLOYDADA (Floyd Co.)   *US 62, 8 mi. S*
Roots of the Catholic Faith in West Texas
Spaniards first introduced the Catholic faith into this region when conquistador Francisco
Vásquez de Coronado passed through in a 1540s expedition to conquer the fabled cities of gold.
He and his men rested at a campsite in Blanco Canyon, southeast of present-day Floydada. The
South Plains would come under the care of the Mexican Diocese of Linares. Once a United States
territory, this area came under the jurisdiction of an American bishop who extended direct pastoral
care. In 1890, the Catholic Church created the Dallas Diocese, which attended to this region. By the
early 1900s, Father David H. Dunn ministered to area Catholics, many of whom were immigrants
responding to the availability of land in West Texas; other Catholics arrived from Mexico during
the Mexican Revolution. By 1908, the first Catholic church in the future Diocese of Lubbock was
built in Hermleigh. Soon, circuit-riding priests ministered in the area. In 1926, the Catholic Church
established the Diocese of Amarillo and church growth continued in the following decades. The
1950s was the most productive decade of area church building, partially attributed to the Bracero
program, in which hundreds of thousands of workers emigrated from Mexico into the U.S. each
year. Church building continued at a high rate into the 1970s. In 1983, the Vatican established the
Diocese of Lubbock, formed from 20 counties of the Diocese of Amarillo and five from the Diocese
of San Angelo, which was created in 1961. Today, the Diocese of Lubbock continues to serve the
spiritual needs of Catholics in the region.   (2008)

FOLLETT (Lipscomb Co.)   *SH 15, 8 mi. E*
Northeast Corner of Texas (3.56 mi. N)
Established by law in 1850 as intersection of 100° longitude and 36° 30' latitude, this point
remained in dispute 70 years. Of some nine surveys made to locate corner of ground, almost none
coincided. Even so, three blocks were annexed to Texas from Oklahoma (1903–1929)—to confu-
sion of landowners. One man claimed he went to bed in Oklahoma and awoke in Texas. In 1929
U.S. Supreme Court had a final survey run. Some people with land formerly in Oklahoma could
not afford to repurchase it in Texas, but exact site of corner was at last determined.   (1970)

FOLLETT (Lipscomb Co.)   *E. Ivanhoe (SH 15)*
Follett
A gateway to Texas Panhandle's "Golden Spread." Founded as "Ivanhoe," on a site across state
line, in Oklahoma. Town moved twice to locate on a railroad. Situated here in 1917, and renamed
for Horace Follett, railroad surveyor. Economy based on wheat, cattle, grain sorghums and (since
1950s) oil and gas production.   (1967)

161

FORESTBURG (Montague Co.)   *FM 455, 5 mi. S*
Butterfield Overland Stage Line Crossing
This is the crossing used by the Southern Overland Mail Line connecting St. Louis and San Francisco with semi-weekly stage and mail service, 1858–1861. The length of the route, 2795 miles, and the superior service maintained made this a pioneer enterprise of the first magnitude.

FORNEY (Kaufman Co.)   *IH 20 access road E of FM 740*
Brooklyn Lodge No. 386, A.F. & A.M.
Following the arrival of the Texas and Pacific Railroad in the village of Brooklyn in 1873, the town name was changed to Forney in honor of John Wein Forney, a director of the railroad. The local Masonic Lodge was organized the same year, using the original town name. The lodge first met in a building shared with the local school and union church. Over the years, lodge members have contributed to the community with projects such as laying the cornerstone of Lewis High School in 1922. A new lodge was completed in 1966.   (1988)

FORRESTON (Ellis Co.)   *US 77, 1 mi. S*
Chambers' Creek
Named in honor of Thomas Jefferson Chambers, (1802–1865), to whom the first land grant within present Ellis County was made in 1834 by the Mexican Government. Also known as Howe's Settlement in honor of William R. Howe, first settler in the region in 1843. An early post office in Robertson County. First county seat of Navarro County, 1846–1848.   (1964)

FORT DAVIS (Jeff Davis Co.)   *SH 17, 12 mi. NE*
Wild Rose Pass
In early days the Indian trail through these mountains followed the gorge below, known as Limpia Canyon. To avoid the floods, travelers over the San Antonio-El Paso road, emigrants, U.S. Troops, supply trains and the mail chose this higher pass famed for its wealth of wild roses.

FORT DAVIS (Jeff Davis Co.)   *SH 17, 2 mi. NE*
Barry Scobee Mountain (1 mi. N 6,300 ft. elev.)
Camp grounds and lookout post (1850s–1880s) for military, mail coaches, freighters, travelers, emigrants. Site of area's last Indian raid, 1881. Part of John G. Prude Ranch. Named by Gov. John Connally Dec. 21, 1964, to honor Barry Scobee, whose efforts were largely responsible for the preservation of Old Fort Davis. He was born 1885, in Missouri. Served in U.S. Army in Philippines and later on merchant ship in World War II. Was editor, reporter, printer, publisher. Came to Fort Davis in 1917 and became an authority and writer on Trans-Pecos history.   (1965)

FORT DAVIS (Jeff Davis Co.)   *SH 17, 1 mi. NE*
Fort Davis
Established by Lieut. Colonel Washington Seawell with six companies of the U.S. Infantry on October 7, 1854 for the purpose of protecting Presidio del Norte from Indian raids. Named in honor of Jefferson Davis, then Secretary of War. Evacuated by Federal Troops April 13, 1861. Permanent buildings were erected when reoccupied in 1867. Abandoned as a military post in 1891 after the country had been cleared of Indians and bandits.

FORT DAVIS (Jeff Davis Co.)   *109 State St. (SH 17/118)*
Old Fort Davis, C.S.A.
Confederate supply point and frontier outpost on great military road from San Antonio to El Paso 1861–62. After surrendered by U. S. Army, occupied by detachment 2nd Texas Mounted Rifles. Apaches ambushed patrol from fort under Lt. Mays in Big Bend area August 1861. Used by Texas Confederate troops en route to and from New Mexico–Arizona campaign to stop flow of Gold to North and gain access to Pacific. Two cannons buried nearby on return have never been found. Occupied briefly California Union Cavalry, August 1862. A memorial to Texans who served the Confederacy.   (1963)

FORT DAVIS (Jeff Davis Co.)   *SH 17/118*
St. Joseph Catholic Church
Catholic clergy began serving residents of the Fort Davis area about 1872. Father Joseph Hoban was appointed pastor in 1876 and the First St. Joseph Catholic Church building was erected in

1879. Father Hoban was followed by circuit-riding priest who regarded St. Joseph's as the central church of the region. Father Brocardus Eeken came to Fort Davis in 1892. He and fellow Carmelite friars traveled thousands of miles each year, ministering to the 18 churches and mission stations in the Trans-Pecos and Big Bend. A new church was consecrated in 1899. Many parishes, including those in Alpine and Marfa, were created from this parish. Father Brocardus retired in 1935. St. Joseph Catholic Church continues to serve a large and diverse congregation.   (1999)

FORT DAVIS (Jeff Davis Co.)   SH 17 at SH 118
Jeff Davis County Courthouse
Designed by the architectural firm of L. L. Thurman and Co. of Dallas, this building was erected in 1910–1911 and replaced the original 1880 adobe courthouse. This concrete and stone Classical Revival edifice, erected by the Falls City Construction Company of Louisville, Kentucky, is dominated by a massive portico supported by Doric columns. Other distinctive design elements include the alternating horizontal bands of pink rusticated stone made of locally quarried materials and the Beaux Arts style clock tower, which features a Seth Thomas timepiece. The courthouse continues as the seat of local government.   (2000)

FORT DAVIS (Jeff Davis Co.)   SH 17, 1 blk. S of courthouse
Jeff Davis County
Formed from Presidio County. Created March 15, 1887. Organized May 16, 1887. Named in honor of Jefferson Davis, 1860–1868, president of the Confederate States. Fort Davis, County Seat. Presidio County, 1875. County Seat, Jeff Davis County, since 1887.

FORT DAVIS (Jeff Davis Co.)   Third St. at Fort St., 2 blks. off SH 17/118
San Antonio–El Paso Road
Westward expeditions opened trails from San Antonio to El Paso in the late 1840s. Two routes, called the Upper and Lower Roads, converged at the Pecos River to traverse the Davis Mountains. Henry Skillman (1814–1864) began a courier service along the road in 1850 and was awarded a U.S. government contract to carry the mail. He formed a partnership with George H. Giddings (1823–1902) in 1854, and they established relay stations along the route, including one at the new U.S. Army post at Fort Davis. During the Civil War, control of the area passed to the Confederates, and Giddings continued mail service for the new government. By 1867, Fort Davis was occupied by four companies of the 9th U.S. Cavalry. After Federal reoccupation, stage and courier routes were more frequently utilized, with travelers often accompanied by army escorts from Fort Davis and other posts. After the arrival of railroads in West Texas in the 1880s, use of overland roads declined sharply, though the trails did provide access to new settlers and were still used by the army as links between forts. Vestiges of the Old San Antonio–El Paso Overland Road can still be seen in Fort Davis and surrounding areas.   (Texas Sesquicentennial 1836–1986)

FORT DAVIS (Jeff Davis Co.)   SH 118, 12 mi. SE
First Rural School West of Pecos River (240 ft. S)
Built 1881 of adobe brick by settlers P. H. Pruett, Cal Nations, James Dawson, Joe Dorsey. At the same time Pruett built home a half-mile west. A Texas Rangers' camp in area gave protection from Indians. Mrs. Pruett once made a midnight ride to alert Rangers to approach of Apaches. Pruett sold home, 1883, to Fort Davis Commandant B. H. Grierson, and founded "Lone Cottonwood" ranch 4 miles north. School was closed after he moved. In 1912 Pruett sold "Cottonwood" to H. L. Kokernot; now several Kokernot ranches use it as headquarters.   (1967)

FORT DAVIS (Jeff Davis Co.)   SH 118, 6 mi. W
Prude Ranch
Andrew Prude purchased three sections of land here in 1897 from J. F. Taylor, and established the A. G. Prude Ranch. Soon he moved his wife Ora to a small log house on their property on Limpia Creek. In 1900 he completed a wooden frame house for their family, and in 1902 he added 1257 acres to the ranch. In 1911 a large 2-story ranch house was built of adobe bricks cast in a nearby stock tank, and was called the "Big House." By 1920 Andrew Prude had expanded his ranch to 40 sections of land. In 1921 the Prudes started a guest ranch to share the beauty of the land and cool summer months with city dwellers. Early guests arrived on the Southern Pacific Railroad. When a severe drought and the Depression of the 1930s forced Andrew Prude to sell his cattle and most of

his land, the Prudes decided to operate the guest ranch full time. Soon a new highway was built, and guests traveled here from many locales. New guest houses were built, and a coaching school and rodeo were added, followed by summer camps for boys and girls, and educational programs. The facilities have expanded over the years to accommodate a wide variety of activities. Prude Ranch continues to be a popular tourist destination. (1996)

FORT DAVIS (Jeff Davis Co.) *SH 118, 14 mi. NW to Mt. Locke*
McDonald Observatory of the University of Texas
Original unit in complex forming one of the great observatory centers of the world. Built in the 1930's under terms of legacy from William Johnson McDonald (1844–1926), a Paris (Texas) banker interested in the stars. A well-educated man, McDonald lived frugally. As a hobby, he read science books and viewed planets through a small telescope. His will granted to the University of Texas $800,000: "To build an observatory and promote the study of astronomy." This site was selected because of its high ratio of clear nights, its 6,800-foot altitude, its distance from artificially-lighted cities, and its quite low latitude that permits observation of southern skies. The observatory was operated for its first 25 years mainly by astronomers from the University of Chicago, more recently primarily from the University of Texas. Until 1948, its 82-inch telescope was second largest in the world. Its fine work and site have resulted in the addition of other telescopes, including a 107-inch instrument sponsored jointly by the National Aeronautics and Space Administration, the National Science Foundation, and the University of Texas. Discoveries made here have included interstellar polarization and the satellites of several planets. (1968)

FORT DAVIS (Jeff Davis Co.) *SH 166, 17 mi. SW*
Bloys Camp Meeting
Held each year since 1890. Founded by Rev. W. B. Bloys, a Presbyterian. His camp pulpit was an Arbuckle coffee crate. First campers, 48 people from remote ranches and towns, slept in tents, wagons. Family groups had chuck-box meals, sharing with guests. Some 1,500 attend mid-August meetings today. Still nothing is ever sold in camp. Baptists, disciples of Christ, Methodists and Presbyterians incorporated the Cowboys' Camp Meeting in 1902. Site, Skillman Grove, has been a camp ground since the 1850s. Elevation is about 6,000 feet. (1965)

FORT HANCOCK (Hudspeth Co.) *SH 148 Spur at railroad tracks*
Fort Hancock Mercantile
Established when the town of Fort Hancock was founded in 1883, this general store is the oldest in Hudspeth County. Started by a Mr. Ross, later the first area postmaster, it was sold in 1916 to Q. A. Hare and his wife. In 1960, they transferred the business to their daughter Mrs. Bob Sims and her husband. It has remained in continuous operation, serving the Mexican border area with modern supplies as well as items like horse collars and coffee mills. (1967)

FORT HOOD (Bell Co.) *US 190, at 2nd Armored Division Museum*
Gen. Patton's "Hell on Wheels"
The 2d Armored Division, United States Army
Formed to meet 20th Century challenges, this force includes Battery A, 1st Battalion, 3rd Field Artillery, which has been in service since 1778. That battery and other veteran units have found new capabilities in this age of mechanized combat involving lightning mobility and massive firepower. In 1940, as German Panzers overran France, the United States Congress created the 1st and 2nd American Armored Divisions. The 2nd was organized July 15, 1940, at Fort Benning, GA., by Gen. Charles L. Scott, and received its "Hell on Wheels" name in 1941 from Gen. George S. Patton, Jr. First U.S. Armored Force in combat in World War II, "Hell on Wheels" landed in North Africa on Nov. 8, 1942. It won great victories at Safi and Casablanca, in the assault on Sicily, the 1944 Normandy Invasion, the Battle of the Bulge, and other campaigns. Along 11,702 miles of combat advance, the 2nd won 7 French Croix de Guerres, 19 distinguished unit citations, and was first foreign division ever given the Fourragere of Belgium. The 2nd provided honor guard for President Harry S. Truman at the Potsdam Peace Conference. Since 1945, Fort Hood has been 2nd's permanent base. (1975)

FORT McKAVETT (Menard Co.)

US 190, 17 mi. W of Menard,
then 6 mi. SW on FM 864

Site of Fort McKavett

Established March 14, 1852 by the United States War Department as a protection to frontier settlers against hostile Indians. Named in honor of Captain Henry McKavett, who fell at the Battle of Monterrey, September 21, 1846. Evacuated by Federal Troops, March 22, 1859. Reoccupied April 1, 1868. Abandoned June 30, 1883.

FORT STOCKTON (Pecos Co.)

US 67, 15 mi. NE

Pecos County Camptosaur Tracks

In the arroyo southwest of this site are dinosaur tracks made 120 million years ago when area was part of sea that extended north from the Gulf of Mexico. These tracks, embedded in rocks of the Comanchean Cretaceous Period, were left by a Camptosaurus Dinosaur, ancestor to the better known duck-billed Trachodon. According to research, this plant-eating animal was about 20 feet long and ten feet tall. His hind legs were strong and longer than his arms which were used to grasp and tear food. His neck was short; head small; the tail long, perhaps equal in length to the body. Measurement of the exposed tracks (17½ in. wide and 21 in. long) determine that this Camptosaur's stride was 5 ft. 10 in. from toe to heel; his pace, 11 ft. 8 in. The shallow sea in which this dinosaur (and other forms of animal and plant life) lived and died was gradually covered by deposits of mineral-laden earth. As this area rose and settled through hundreds of centuries, the buried organic matter was gradually converted through chemical changes to vast resources of petroleum, natural gas and sulphur. This Camptosaur's tracks remain to remind mankind of the Prehistoric Age in which the oil industry had its infant beginnings. (1968)

FORT STOCKTON (Pecos Co.)

IH 10, 8 mi. W

Pioneer Stagecoach Stand Operators Mr. and Mrs. Isaac J. Rude

On their way to California from Tennessee in the 1850s, Isaac J. and Sarah Isabella Rude settled in West Texas. In the Davis Mountains, Rude built and operated a station for the Butterfield Overland Stage; here passengers had meals while mules were unharnessed and exchanged for a fresh team. Soon Butterfield—the pioneer passenger and mail service (1858–1861) from St. Louis to California—had Rude move here to Ft. Stockton and build another stand. In 1859, when a stop was added at Leon Water Hole, 5 mi. west of Ft. Stockton, Rude built and ran the stand there. The food there was the best on the route, said a journalist. Sarah Rude (1834–1916) carried a pistol under her apron to protect her children. When Indians attacked the Davis Mountains stand, the men loaded guns and handed them to Mrs. Rude, a calm, sure marksman. Just over 5 ft. tall, she butchered and skinned beeves to feed her family when her husband was away. After stages stopped operating in 1861, Isaac Rude, like others associated with the Overland Mail, joined the Confederate Army. Later he became a prosperous businessman in McKinney. Born in 1829, he died in 1902. (1967)

FORT STOCKTON (Pecos Co.)

US 385, just S of IH 10

Pecos County

Formed from Presidio County. Created May 3, 1871. Organized March 9, 1875. On March 9, 1875, the following county officers were elected: George M. Frazer, Chief Justice; Cesario Torres, Commissioner; Francis Rooney, Commissioner; Hipolito Carrasco, Commissioner; Martin Hufmann, Commissioner. Fort Stockton, County Seat. Oil was discovered in the Yates Field in 1926.

FORT STOCKTON (Pecos Co.)

1000 E. Railroad St.,
S of intersection with IH 10/US 67

Oil and Gas Industry in Pecos County

Located in the petroleum-rich Permian Basin, Pecos is one of the most prolific oil- and gas-producing counties in Texas. The petroleum business here began about 1900 with the drilling of the Turney well near an ancient "seep", a traditional local source of oil for lubricating and medicinal purposes. A short-lived boom in 1921 caused by the discovery of the "Miracle Well" heralded the arrival of the fabulous Yates oil field (1926), indicating the area's great potential oil wealth. Since that year over 710 million barrels of oil have been produced from the Yates, Fort Stockton and other county fields. The presence of natural gas, known for years, was slow to be exploited because gas was considered an undesirable by-product of the oil business. The first commercial use of gas here was inspired after it was found by workers drilling a water well, in 1925. The discovery, about 1948, of Santa Rosa field spurred exploration that brought in the Puckett field in 1952. Subsequent deep drilling tapped many extensive pools, including in 1963 the prolific Gomez Field, which had produced over 478 billion cubic feet of gas as of 1970. Today petroleum is the single most important economic asset of Pecos County.   (1973)

FORT WORTH (Tarrant Co.)   *800 Main, General Worth Square*
General William Jenkins Worth (1794–1849)
William Jenkins Worth, a native of Hudson, New York, was severely wounded at Lundy's Lane during the War of 1812. In 1820, he became instructor of infantry tactics and soldierly discipline at the United States Military Academy at West Point. He was appointed the first commandant of cadets in 1825. When Worth was reassigned in 1828, Robert E. Lee was serving as cadet adjutant. Worth was involved in defenses along the Canadian border in the 1830s, and in 1841–1842 led an expedition against the Florida Seminole Indians. He was awarded a commendation from the Florida Territorial Legislature and was promoted to brigadier general. During the Mexican War, Worth fought at the Battle of Monterrey. He received a Sword of Honor from the U.S. Congress and a promotion to major general. While serving as commander of the Texas and New Mexico military districts, Worth died of cholera in San Antonio in 1849. Fort Worth, a frontier post established after his death, was named in his honor. Worth was buried in New York City. His grave, at Broadway and Fifth Avenue, is marked by a fifty-foot monument and is surrounded by a fence of cast iron swords, copies of his New York State Sword of Honor.   (1987)

FORT WORTH (Tarrant Co.)   *W. Weatherford (Spur 347) at Main St.*
Tarrant County Courthouse
Designed by firm of Gunn & Curtis and built by the Probst Construction Company of Chicago, 1893–1895. This red Texas granite building, in Renaissance Revival style, closely resembles the Texas State Capitol with the exception of the clock tower. The cost was $408,840 and citizens considered it such a public extravagance that a new County Commissioners' Court was elected in 1894.   (1969)

FORT WORTH (Tarrant Co.)   *108 W Bluff St., Heritage Park*
Fort Worth–Yuma Mail (Star Post Route No. 31454)
By the 1870s remote areas of the frontier not served by the railroads needed mail delivery routes. In response the U.S. Post Office Department, in 1873, began establishing Star Post Routes. On Aug. 15, 1878, Star Route No. 31454 was opened between Fort Worth and Yuma, Arizona Terr., under contract to J. T. Chidester. Stagecoaches carried the mail along much the same route used by the Butterfield Overland Mail in the late 1850s. Fort Worth to Yuma mail was discontinued after completion of the Southern Transcontinental Railroad in 1881.   (1976)

FORT WORTH (Tarrant Co.)   *200 W Belknap at US 287, NW of courthouse*
Fort Worth, "Where the West Begins"
Founded June 6, 1849, as frontier post of Co. F, 2nd Dragoons, 8th Dept., U.S. Army. The Commander, Maj. Ripley Arnold, named the camp for his former superior officer, Maj. Gen. William Jenkins Worth. In 4 years of operations, the post had but one serious Indian encounter. A town grew up alongside the fort, as center for supply stores and stagecoach routes. In 1856, Fort Worth became county seat of Tarrant County. A boom started after 1867 when millions of Longhorns were driven through town en route to Red River Crossing and Chisholm Trail. Herds forded the Trinity below Courthouse Bluff, one block north of this site. Cowboys got supplies for the long uptrail drive and caroused in taverns and dance halls. After railroad arrived in 1876, increased cattle traffic won city the nickname of "Cowtown." By 1900, Fort Worth was one of the world's largest cattle markets. Population tripled between 1900 and 1910. Growth continued, based on varied multimillion-dollar industries of meat packing, flour milling, grain storage, oil, aircraft plants and military bases. Fort Worth also has developed as a center of culture, with universities, museums, art galleries, theatres and a botanic garden.   (1969)

FORT WORTH (Tarrant Co.)   *US 287 at 9th St.*
Ephraim Merrill Daggett
Canadian born Ephraim Merrill Daggett was reared on a farm in Indiana. He traded with the Indians at Fort Dearborn (Chicago) in the early 1830s then moved to Shelby County, Republic of

Texas, in 1838. There he and his family became involved in the East Texas Regulator-Moderator feud (1839–1844). He later served as a Captain in the Mexican War of 1846. While serving as State Legislator from Shelby County (1851–53), he established a mercantile business and a hotel in the frontier town of Fort Worth. In 1854 he moved his family here and soon thereafter began purchasing large tracts of Tarrant County real estate. Daggett used his influence as a former legislator to help secure Fort Worth's selection as County Seat in 1860. After serving as Brigadier General during the Civil War, he engaged in the mercantile and cattle business in Fort Worth. In 1873 Daggett's likeness was chosen to adorn the City's first seal. His role in bringing the Texas & Pacific Railroad here in 1876, developing a downtown district, and in helping transform Fort Worth from an abandoned military post to a center of commerce earned Daggett renown as "The Father of Fort Worth." He is buried in the City's Pioneer's Cemetery. (1993)

FORT WORTH (Tarrant Co.)   *100 Commerce St. (US 287) at park*
Eastern Cattle Trail
This native stone, dug from the Trinity River Valley, marks the route of the Eastern Cattle Trail, where cattle were driven north on Rusk Street, now Commerce Street, through the City of Fort Worth, Texas, to the bluff and then across the Trinity River to the broad valley below, where they rested before continuing their long drive north. From the end of the Civil War to the bringing of the railroad in 1876, great herds of cattle passed this way to Abilene, Kansas. The Eastern Trail, also called the McCoy Trail, became the Chisholm Trail when it reached the Red River. Fort Worth, the last place for provisions before Indian Country, received its name, "Cow Town" and it first major industry, from this period. (1983)

FORT WORTH (Tarrant Co.)   *100 blk. of E Exchange Ave., off US 287*
Fort Worth Stock Yards Entrance
Spanning Exchange Avenue, this gateway to the Fort Worth Stock Yards was completed in 1910. Constructed by the Topeka Bridge & Land Co. for the Fort Worth Stock Yards Co., it was a significant feat of concrete work for that era. The columns are 22 feet high and 13 feet in circumference. The sign is 36 feet long and 4 feet high. The entrance is a significant landmark in this historic area of Fort Worth. (1985)

FORT WORTH (Tarrant Co.)   *131 E Exchange Ave., off US 287*
The Fort Worth Stock Yards Company
The Fort Worth Stock Yards Company was created in 1893, when Boston capitalist Greenlief W. Simpson led a group of investors in purchasing the Fort Worth Union Stock Yards. Under Simpson's leadership, the company earned the support of the Texas Cattle Raisers Association and lured the prominent meatpacking companies of Armour and Swift to open plants here. Publicity through the company's market newspaper and annual fat stock show, both begun in 1896, resulted in a significant increase in the number of animals brought to market. The Stock Yards Co. built the area's livestock-related facilities and had controlling interest in many north Fort Worth businesses and properties. The first five decades of the 20th century were the most successful for the Fort Worth Stock Yards Co. During World War I, foreign governments purchased draft animals, making Fort Worth the largest horse and mule market in the world. In 1917, overall livestock market receipts reached 3,500,000 and in 1944, sales exceeded 5,000,000 head of livestock. However, by the 1950s, local auctions were drawing sellers away from this central market. Today the Fort Worth Stock Yards Co. continues as a significant part of the city's unique heritage. (Texas Sesquicentennial 1836–1986)

FORT WORTH (Tarrant Co.)   *3419 E. Belknap (US 377)*
Riverside Methodist Church
According to local oral tradition, Riverside Methodist Episcopal Church, South, began in March 1888, when the Rev. C. F. Vance and ten people held Sunday school in an abandoned saloon at East First and Sylvania Streets. After organizing a congregation, the members bought land at the corner of East First and Ross Avenue (now Retta) in 1893 and built a frame sanctuary. In its early years, the congregation was served by visiting ministers and by students at Polytechnic College (Now Texas Wesleyan University). The church building was moved to the southeast corner of Noble Street and Frey Avenue (now Riverside Drive) in 1907. It continued in use until 1925, when it was replaced by a basement for a new structure and the name of the church was changed in 1924 to Sylvania Heights Methodist Episcopal Church, South, but in 1935 it reverted to its original name when Frey Avenue

was renamed Riverside Drive. A sanctuary was completed over the 1925 basement in 1937, and a new facility was built on adjacent lots in 1951. Highway construction and changing neighborhood dynamics led to the church's relocation to this site in 1982. After a denominational name change in 1968, it became known as Riverside United Methodist Church. (1991)

FRANKLIN (Robertson Co.) *US 79, 1.3 mi. E*
Robertson County
Settled by people from Tennessee under an 1822 contract held by Sterling Clack Robertson (1785–1842), who later signed the Texas Declaration of Independence. Colony and county were named for him. County was created Dec. 14, 1837; organized March 1838. County Seats: "Old Franklin," 1838–1850; Wheelock, 1850–1855; Owensville, 1855–1869; Calvert, 1870–1879; Franklin since 1879. Sent 5 troop companies into Confederate service in Civil War. Established mill to make flour, cotton and wool cloth. Furnished cotton cards, medicines, flour, bacon and salt to soldiers' families. (1965)

FRANKSTON (Anderson Co.) *SH 155 in Frankston*
Frankston Railroad Depot
In 1900 the Texas & New Orleans Railroad, now part of the Southern Pacific Line, platted the town of Frankston. The station was first called Frankfort and the post office Ayres. Both were renamed Frankston in 1902 for Miss Frankie Miller, who gave land for a city park. In 1906 this frame depot was built. The railroad connected local farmers with distant markets and provided passenger service from 1903 to 1964. The depot was restored in 1976 as a museum. (1977)

FRANKSTON (Anderson Co.) *SH 155 at Main St.*
Frankston City Park
In 1900 the Texas & New Orleans Railroad built a line through this area and plotted a townsite here on land owned by Frankie Miller. The town was named for "Miss Frankie" who donated this site, known as the Town Square, for a city park. By 1908 a city park existed here, and a post office and many of the town's earliest businesses had opened around the park square. A gazebo, built about 1920, replaced a small bandstand and became the site of various local festivities and social events. The park square continues to serve as the town's social and business center. (1995)

FREDERICKSBURG (Gillespie Co.) *FM 965, 18 mi. N*
Enchanted Rock
From its summit, in the fall of 1841, Captain John C. Hays, while surrounded by Comanche Indians who cut him off from his Ranging Company, repulsed the whole band and inflicted upon them such heavy losses that they fled. (1965)

FREDERICKSBURG (Gillespie Co.) *Milam St. (RR 965) 1 mi. N, then W on Cross Mountain Dr.*
Cross Mountain
This marl and limestone hill, elevation 915 feet, was an Indian signal point, advancing news of the intrusions of white settlers. The hill was first recorded and described by the German geologist, Dr. Ferdinand Roemer in 1847. A timber cross found on the hilltop the same year suggests that Spanish missionaries recognized it as a landmark on the path from San Antonio to Mission San Saba. John Christian Durst (1825–1898), arriving with his family in 1847 from Germany, received a town lot and 10 acres of land, including this hill. On finding the cross, he named it "Kreuzberb," or Cross Mountain. The Easter fires on Cross Mountain and the surrounding hills recall a German tradition of burning the old growth to make way for the new, and also commemorate the 1847 Treaty made by John O. Meusebach and the settlers to establish peace with the Comanche Nation. In 1849, a Bohemian priest, Father George Menzel, erected a more substantial cross as a symbol of redemption and civilization. Easter sunrise services were held on the mountain for many years prior to 1941. In 1946 the Very Rev. F. X. Wolf threw the switch to illuminate the permanent cross of metal and concrete built by St. Mary's Catholic Church. (1976)

FREDERICKSBURG (Gillespie Co.) *US 290, 4.4 mi. W*
Philipp Hartmann Family Cemetery
Philipp Hartmann and Elisabeth Crenwelge were married in their homeland of Bruchweiler, Prussia in 1853. They and their two children immigrated to Texas in 1855, arriving at the Port of

Galveston. They settled in the Live Oak area near Fredericksburg, where Philipp became a farmer and butcher. Nine more children were born to the family; the four who died in infancy and early childhood are a testament to the hard conditions of 19th century life. The family established this cemetery 100 yards north of their homestead in 1859. Elisabeth died in 1877 and Philipp remarried the following year. His new wife, Rosina Hildebrand, bore four children; two died young. Philipp died in 1911 and Rosina died in 1913, leaving a large and prosperous family. The Hartmann Cemetery remains a fine example of a German immigrant family graveyard.   (1999)

FREDERICKSBURG (Gillespie Co.)   *315 W Main St. (US 290)*
Sunday Houses
Small townhouses built by German settlers who lived in distant rural areas. Used over weekends by families while they traded or attended church. A typical early Sunday House had one room with a lean-to kitchen and a half-story above, which was reached by outside stairway or ladder. Built during 1890s–1920s. Most Sunday Houses were frame but some were rock. Homes found use during school sessions, periods of religious instruction or serious illness. Some of the large ones made comfortable retirement homes for elderly German farmers.   (1970)

FREDERICKSBURG (Gillespie Co.)   *Main St. (US 290), Pioneer Plaza*
Vereins Kirche
Church for all denominations, school and community hall. Built, summer 1847, after the Comanche Peace Treaty made by John O. Meusebach, commissioner, German Emigration Company. Located in Main Street between courthouse and Market Square of early Fredericksburg. Razed after the celebration of fiftieth anniversary of the arrival of first settlers, 1896. Replica, first used as museum, and library, constructed 1934–1935.   (1967)

FREDERICKSBURG (Gillespie Co.)   *Main St. (US 290) at Washington St.*
Nimitz Hotel
This property was purchased by Charles Henry Nimitz, Sr., in 1855. By 1860, the Nimitz Hotel was established, hosting frontier travelers and providing a home for the large Nimitz family. Expanded in the 1870s to feature a steamboat shaped facade, the hotel was a center for community activities. It was sold by the family in 1926 and underwent major alterations. In 1964, it became a museum honoring fleet Admiral Chester W. Nimitz and those who served with him in World War II. The steamboat facade was later rebuilt and remains a local landmark.   (1989)

FREDERICKSBURG (Gillespie Co.)   *247 E. Main St. (US 290)*
Birthplace of Fleet Admiral Chester W. Nimitz, USN
Typical early Fredericksburg home built 1866 by Carl Basse. Property of the Henke family since 1873. Heinrich Henke, early settler, Confederate freighter, had butcher counter on front porch; meat processing was done in back yard; there the horses that pulled meat vending cart were stabled. Shop later built on foundation of stone walls surrounding lot. He and his wife Dorothea (nee Weirich) added the long dining room and kitchen with sloped roof to accommodate their twelve children. Many of their furnishings are preserved by Udo Henke, a descendant. In small room to rear of front bedroom, on Feb. 24, 1885, their daughter, Anna Henke Nimitz, gave birth to Chester William Nimitz, destined to command the greatest naval armada in history. A 1905 honor graduate of the U.S. Naval Academy, Nimitz was Chief of Staff to Commander, Atlantic Submarine Fleet, W.W. I. Installed first naval ROTC unit in U.S. Navy, 1926; selected Commander in Chief Pacific Fleet after attack on Pearl Harbor; appointed Fleet Admiral, U.S. Navy, 1944. As representative of the U.S. he signed Japanese surrender documents on his flagship, USS Missouri, Sept. 2, 1945 in Tokyo Bay. Admiral Nimitz died in San Francisco on Feb. 20, 1966.

FREDERICKSBURG (Gillespie Co.)   *US 290, 2 mi. E*
Site of Fort Martin Scott
Established by the United States Army December 5, 1848 as a protection to travelers and settlers against Indian attack. Named in honor of Major Martin Scott, Brevet Lieutenant Colonel, 5th United States Infantry, killed at Molino del Ray, September 8, 1847. Its garrison participated in many Indian skirmishes. Occupied intermittently after 1852. Held by the Confederates, 1861–1865. Permanently abandoned in December, 1866.

FREDERICKSBURG (Gillespie Co.)   *US 290, 2 mi. E*
The Pinta Trail
Origin of the Pinta Trail is attributed to nomadic plains Indian tribes. Early Spanish and Mexican expeditions followed the general route of the trail, which extended from San Antonio de Bexar to the San Saba River near present Menard. A survey by German immigrants in 1845 provided a wagon road over part of the trail, and, after the discovery of gold in California in 1849, the trail was utilized by U.S. military companies seeking to open new routes to the western States. Use of the trail declined with the advent of railroads in the late 1800s and early 1900s.
(Texas Sesquicentennial 1836–1986)

FREDERICKSBURG (Gillespie Co.)   *US 290, 3.3 mi. E*
The Easter Fires
Blazing on the hills around Fredericksburg each Easter Eve, combined with a local pageant, these fires recall an old tale. In March 1847, when Comanches and whites signed a major peace treaty, the Indians lighted huge signal fires on these hills. To calm her children's fears, one mother—recalling Easter fires in her native Germany—told them the smoke came from pots in which the Easter Bunny was dying eggs with flowers. As the tale spread and pioneers kindled the fires in each year of peace with the Indians, the local yearly celebration arose.   (1968)

FREDERICKSBURG (Gillespie Co.)   *US 290, 10 mi. E in roadside park*
Texas Rancher General E. Kirby Smith, C.S.A. (1824–1893)
Born in Florida. Graduated from West Point. Fought in Mexican War. On the Texas frontier in the 1850s, commanded Camps Belknap, Cooper and Colorado. In 1860 and many years afterwards was a partner of J. M. Hunter of Fredericksburg in a Texas ranch. Resigned from U.S. Army, 1861, to serve Confederacy. Was appointed 1863, to command all the area west of the Mississippi. At that time Federals held the river, all of Missouri, much of Arkansas, Louisiana and Indian Territory, and were trying to take Texas and her supplies of food, cotton and horses. The Trans-Mississippi Dept. had many problems. The French under Maximilian were approaching from Mexico. Indians and bandits constantly raided frontiers. Freighters and blockade runners had to be employed for exporting cotton—the only product the south had for trading to get guns, ammunition and goods. Texas was chief source of the cotton Gen. Smith used for financing his army. It was place of safety to which he sent his wife and children. It gave him ovations as he went to Mexico after the war ended. Young Texans studied, 1875–1893, in his mathematics classes at the University of the South, Sewanee, Tenn.   (1965)

FREDERICKSBURG (Gillespie Co.)   *SH 16 right of way, 2 miles S*
Guenther's Live Oak Mill
By 1848, Carl Hilmar Guenther (1826–1902), master millwright, had completed his apprenticeship in Germany and immigrated to the U.S. In search of opportunities and a good gristmill site, he journeyed south from Wisconsin to New Orleans, and then west to Texas. In 1851 he bought land and water rights on Live Oak Creek near Fredericksburg. After six months of construction, his mill was operational, but a flood destroyed the first dam. One month after the flood the mill was working again. Ox drawn wagons loaded with harvested crops converged on the mill in the mornings, and after the farmers' business was completed the men remained to visit with each other. The mill became a center of social life in the hill country community. Guenther was granted U.S. citizenship in Gillespie County in 1854. He married Dorothea Pape in 1855. They lived in a home near the mill and were eventually the parents of seven children. In 1859, Guenther chose a site about one mile from the center of San Antonio as a new site for his mill operation. Guenther Mills soon became the Pioneer Flour Mills, an enterprise which became a flourishing business in Texas and the Southwest.   (1991)

FREDERICKSBURG (Gillespie Co.)   *SH 16, 7 mi. S*
Pedernales Rural School
The Pedernales community, established here by German immigrant farmers in the 1840s, was joined with the Live Oak community to form a school district in 1854. Sometime prior to 1875 a native stone schoolhouse was built at this site. State funds and tuition supported the 1-teacher, 7-grade school. Picnics on "schulpruefung" (final exam day), plays, Christmas programs, and music practices became traditional activities at the school. Falling student enrollment during World

War II led to the school's closing in 1945. The school building was converted to residential use in the 1980s. (1993)

FREDERICKSBURG (Gillespie Co.)   *SH 16, 7 mi. SW in roadside park*
Gillespie County
The trails of roving Indians crossed these hills, settled by German pioneers, in 1846. A group of Mormons settled at Zodiac in 1847. Created February 23, 1848. Organized June 5, 1848. Named for Richard Addison Gillespie, a Texan from 1837, a defender of the Texas Frontier, Captain in the Mexican War, who fell at Monterrey, September 22, 1846. Fredericksburg, the County Seat.
(1965)

FREEPORT (Brazoria Co.)   *SH 36, 10 mi. W*
Old Oakland Plantation
Founded 1828 by Henry Wm. Munson, who bought site from Stephen F. Austin, Father of Texas. This land joined Peach Point Plantation, Austin's home. Munson, one of Texans in uprising over injustices at Anahuac and Velasco in 1832, died in yellow fever epidemic in 1833. (1965)

FREEPORT (Brazoria Co.)   *SH 36, 9 mi. W on Peach Point Rd. in Jones Creek*
Major Guy M. Bryan, C.S.A. (1821–1901)
Born in Missouri. Rode a mule to Texas in 1831 to join his uncle, Stephen F. Austin, Father of Texas. A private of Texas War for Independence. Legislator, Congressman, Member of Texas Secession Convention. Enlisted as a private in the Civil War. But his administrative ability, diplomacy and political understanding soon cast him in the role of trouble-shooter and liaison man between State and Confederate Governments and the military. Convinced C.S.A. leaders of need to leave enough troops in Texas to guard coastline and prevent Indian attacks. Arranged 1862 Conference of Governors of Missouri, Arkansas, Louisiana and Texas, and delivered their request to President Jefferson Davis for creation of a strong military department west of the Mississippi River. Helped reorganize armed forces in east Texas. Served as confidential adjutant to both Pres. Davis and Trans-Mississippi Commanding General. Settled dispute among military, state of Texas and Confederacy on acquisition and sale of cotton—lifeblood of the South. Took part in battles in April 1864 to prevent Federal invasion of Texas. Arranged Governors' Conferences in 1863 and 1865. Buried in State Cemetery in Austin.

FREEPORT (Brazoria Co.)   *SH 36, 9 mi. W at Peach Point Rd. in Jones Creek*
Battle of Jones Creek
Fought by Texan Army of 23 men under Capt. Randal Jones (1786–1873), sent out 1824 by Stephen F. Austin to the lower Brazos to fight cannibal Karankawa Indians. Scouts found the camp here. Attack at dawn found Indians ready with spears. Jones' guns got 15 Indians, dispersed the rest. (1965)

FREEPORT (Brazoria Co.)   *SH 36, 8 mi. W*
⅛ mi. S to Peach Point
Home of Mrs. Emily M. Perry, 1795–1851, only sister of Stephen F. Austin, who regarded the place as his home after the burning of San Felipe on March 29, 1836. (1964)

FREEPORT (Brazoria Co.)   *SH 36, 1 mi. W*
Stringfellow Ranch
Born at Old Brazoria, Robert Edward Lee Stringfellow (1866–1941) began his career on a cattle ranch at the age of 14. Soon he acquired his own herd. He opened a Velasco meat market in 1890 and provided beef for workers building jetties at the mouth of the Brazos River. Stringfellow's ranch holdings here in southern Brazoria County increased to 20,000 acres. A philanthropist and civic leader, Stringfellow was an early builder and investor in Freeport townsite. After he was injured in the 1932 hurricane, his wife Nannie (Maddox) (d. 1971) operated the ranch and Freeport interests. (1980)

FREEPORT (Brazoria Co.)   *SH 332, 1 blk. S of Intracoastal Waterway*
Gulf Intracoastal Waterway
This complex of barge canals and natural channels—most valuable waterway in America—stretches 1,116 mi. from Brownsville, Texas, to St. Mark's, Florida. Is longer and carries more

tonnage than Suez and Panama Canals. Is a vital link in economy of Texas and has been one of main causes of rapid development of Gulf Coast area. The Canal system was begun in 1854 when a short canal was built from Galveston Bay to mouth of Brazos River as aid to Texas trade; it was 50 ft. wide 3½ ft. deep and dug by hand-labor and mule teams. Later projects widened, lengthened canal along the coast. Most important period in growth of the waterway system was result of determined efforts by two Texas businessmen, Clarence S. E. Holland and Roy Miller. In 1905–1907 these men organized the initial financial support, arranged construction and won congressional backing for canal improvements. By 1966 annual total tonnage on the waterway exceeded 78,500,000 tons. Hundreds of companies now have plants or warehouses along the canal; its impact on growth of Gulf Coast has been immense. Several inland cities have become seaports; canal helped to make Houston nation's third largest port. Low shipping costs created by waterway have brought prosperity to entire Texas Gulf Coast.   (1967)

FREEPORT (Brazoria Co.)   *SH 332, 1 block S of Intracoastal Waterway*
Velasco
Four miles southeast to the original town of Velasco, landing place of the "Lively," first vessel bringing immigrants to Austin's Colony in 1821. There the Battle of Velasco, between Texas Colonists and Mexican Troops, was fought June 26, 1832. A treaty of peace between Texas and Mexico was signed there May 14, 1836, by Presidents David G. Burnet and Antonio Lopez de Santa Anna but was never ratified by Mexico.   (1964)

FREEPORT (Brazoria Co.)   *SH 332, 1 block S of Intracoastal Waterway, 5 mi. E*
Old Velasco, C.S.A.
Historic and key Texas port of entry located near here. During the Civil War was fortified by troops and 8 gun batteries at the mouth of the Brazos River to provide shelter and landing facilities for blockade runners, to protect rich farmlands, and to prevent Federal invasion. The South exchanged cotton for European guns, ammunition, milled goods and medicines for army and home use. Velasco was one of the busiest ports. Federal vessels attempted to stop vital trade, and constantly fired upon runners as well as the shore defenses and patrols. The runners would approach the port on dark nights when the waters were smooth, and by the use of sounding lines could determine nearness to shore and avoid blockaders. Boilers would be kept well fired with hard coal that burned with a minimum of smoke, in case it became necessary to outrun Federal patrol ships. Union ships had to go to New Orleans for drinking water, food and fuel, because Texas Marines on rafts or dredgeboats or Texas Cavalry and Infantry units kept them off the shores. The raw courage of the Texas coastal defenders made this a most dramatic story in the history of the Confederacy.

FREEPORT (Brazoria Co.)   *Ave. B and Skinner St. in Velasco*
4 mi. SE to the Original Town of Velasco
Landing place of the "Lively," first vessel bringing immigrants to Austin's Colony in 1821. There the Battle of Velasco, between Texas Colonists and Mexican Troops, was fought June 26, 1832. A treaty of peace between Texas and Mexico was signed there May 14, 1836, by Presidents David G. Burnet and Antonio Lopez de Santa Anna but was never ratified by Mexico.   (1964)

FREER (Duval Co.)   *US 59 SW in roadside park*
John C. Duval (1816–1897)
First Texas man of letters. Wrote history not as a visitor, but a participant, and wrote to entertain and inspire. His "Early times in Texas" tells of days when, by bringing news of the outside world to the lonely settlers, a man could travel from the Sabine to the Rio Grande and spend not a cent for board. It also gives a personal account of Palm Sunday 1836 at Goliad, when Santa Anna's men shot down disarmed Texas prisoners of War—a massacre from which Duval himself escaped, though an older brother was killed. His books, including "Early Times," "Bigfoot Wallace" and "Young Explorers," were not widely distributed at the time of publication, but made history live. As a young Austin citizen, the renowned O. Henry was influenced by Duval's work; so was J. Frank Dobie, dean of 20th century Texas writers. Duval was born in Kentucky; son of a territorial governor of Florida. Graduate of the University of Virginia. Civil engineer. First came to Texas in 1835. Fought in the Texas Revolution. Was a Texas Ranger and made a career of surveying frontier lands. Fought in the Mexican War and in the Civil War. This county was named for him and for two of his distinguished brothers.   (1965)

FREER (Duval Co.)   *SH 16, 27 mi. S*
Barroneña Ranch
The Barroneña Ranch is an important reminder of early South Texas ranching. Named for a creek (now called Los Machos) which traverses the property, the ranch was part of a larger tract owned by Diego Hinojosa, who received a grant of five leagues from the Republic of Mexico. In 1856, Hinojosa received a state of Texas patent for 2,237 acres of this land. James O. Luby (1846–1932) later owned a part of the ranch. A native of England and a confederate veteran of the Civil War, Luby became the first county judge of Duval County in 1876. Barroneña Ranch was purchased by J. M. Bennett (1831–1920) in 1905 and has remained in the Bennett family since that time. The nucleus of the ranch is a 19th century adobe house, reportedly a stage stop between Goliad and Laredo. Other structures include a native rock water trough and storage tank; a native rock wall more than one mile long; remains of a dipping vat and smokehouse; and rock foundations of other buildings, including a blacksmith shop. Richard King, grandson of the founder of the King Ranch, leased the Barroneña Ranch in the 1920s. Santa Gertrudis cattle, developed by the King Ranch, were introduced here following World War II.   (1989)

FRIENDSWOOD (Galveston Co.)   *502 S Friendswood*
Friendswood
This community was founded in 1895 by a group of Friends (Quakers) led by F. J. Brown and T. H. Lewis. They acquired the land from J. C. League and named the settlement Friendswood. From the very beginning, church and school were central to the life of this community. In 1900 an academy building was built on this site, with lumber from huge pine trees felled by the 1900 hurricane. The Friends Church, which until 1958 was the only church in the community, used the academy building for both worship and education. In the early years it provided the only secondary educational facilities for the surrounding area. The last school term was held in 1938, but the building continued to be used for worship until 1949 when it was replaced by a more modern structure. The heritage of this community, received from its founders, is based on Christ's words: "Ye are my friends, if ye do whatsoever I command you." John 15:14

FRIONA (Parmer Co.)   *700 S. Main St. (SH 214) in park*
Friona
When established by the XIT Ranch in 1898, this community was originally called Frio, after Frio (Cold) Draw, and it served as a shipping point on the recently built Pecos & Northern Railroad. In 1906, the George G. Wright Land Co. took options on area lands and initiated a colonization project, promising fertile land and a healthful climate to attract prospective settlers from Ohio to Kansas. The company erected a hotel, livery stable and a bank. The town's name changed to Friona when the post office opened March 16, 1907. Sarah D. Olson served as the community's first postmaster. That same year, Parmer County organized, and the Union Congregational Church became Friona's first church. A school opened the following year. A controversy between Friona and Farwell over the location of the county seat led to an election in 1913. Voters chose Farwell and Friona residents contested the results, but a court ruled in 1916 in favor of Farwell. That year, S. A. Harris began publishing a local newspaper, the Friona Sentinel; it became the Friona Star in 1925. Residents voted to incorporate the city in 1928, electing John W. White as mayor. In the latter part of the 20th century, Friona served as a regional marketing center for agricultural and beef products, and claimed the distinction of "Grain Sorghum Capital of the World." A June 1995 tornado destroyed the original historical marker for the community, and during the town's centennial year, 2006, citizens dedicated this replacement marker in City Park, across the street from the old Syndicate Hotel.   (2006)

FRISCO (Collin Co.)   *SH 289, 4 mi. S in Lebanon*
The Shawnee Trail
In 1838, the Republic of Texas Congress appropriated money for construction of a north-south road opening the Northern Texas area to trade. The project leader, Colonel William G. Cooke, followed an existing Indian trail which reached from the Red River to Austin. A supply fort established on the river near the trading post of Holland Coffee was named for Captain William G. Preston, a veteran of the Texas Revolution, who was in charge of troops stationed there in 1840. The part of the road running south from the Red River to the Trinity River crossing was known as the Preston Road. At the Trinity crossing in 1841 John Neely Bryan began the settlement of Dallas. By the

1850s, the road was known as the Shawnee Trail and was used by immigrants coming to Texas. It also served as a cattle trail, leading to northern markets. The number of cattle drives decreased as new trails were opened to serve the growing Texas Cattle Industry. Further decline occurred when rail lines were completed to the area in the 1870s. Lebanon served as an assembly point for cattle drives on the Shawnee Trail. Bypassed by the Frisco Railroad in 1902, the town declined. The post office, opened in 1860, closed in 1905. (1980)

FRISCO (Collin Co.)   *SH 289, NW corner of Gaylord and Preston Rd.*
Site of Lebanon
Settlers traveling to this area of Texas after it opened for settlement as part of the Peters Colony found free land, clear spring water and plenty of timber. Those who decided to stay named it Lebanon and began to establish homes and farms. On March 1, 1860, the U.S. Postal Service granted a post office to Lebanon, with Phillip Huffman serving as first postmaster. Although a general store begun by Z. T. Rainey in 1858 closed during the Civil War, other businesses soon were established. Located on the route of the historic Preston Road/Shawnee Trail, Lebanon was a popular stopping place for cattle drivers who used that road as their north-south route. Primarily a farming community, the town grew in the 1880s and 1890s to include a blacksmith shop, dry goods store, a saddlery, churches, doctors' offices, a hotel, tavern and other businesses. A two-story union school was built in 1885 to serve the schoolchildren in the community. In 1902, the St. Louis and San Francisco Railroad bypassed Lebanon, which resulted in an exodus of residents and businesses to the new railroad town of Frisco. The school closed in 1947, and by 1959 there were fewer than a dozen homes remaining in Lebanon. As the 21st century dawned, only three buildings stood from the original townsite, but the history of Lebanon remains as a part of the urban and suburban development in this part of Collin County. (2002)

GAIL (Borden Co.)   *US 180 at courthouse*
Borden County
Originally a part of Bexar District. Created August 21, 1876. Organized March 11, 1891. Named in honor of Gail Borden 1801–1874. Pioneer surveyor, newspaper editor, and inventor of the process of condensing milk. Gail, county seat.

GAIL (BordenCo.)   *US 180 at courthouse*
Borden County Jail
Built of hand-hewn native stone from Gail Mountain, this jail planned for maximum security. Is one of the oldest jails in use in West Texas. Diebold Safe and Lock Co. was awarded the $4,500 contract in 1896. Behind two-foot thick outside walls, the cell walls and floor are of ⅓ inch case hardened steel plates, impervious to hack saw blades. Doors fastened with huge hasps and padlocks opened by six-inch key. (1967)

GAIL (Borden Co.)   *FM 669 at US 180 at museum*
1902–1904 Land Rushes
Cowboys and settlers fought here in early days for right to claim lands placed in public domain in 1902 by Texas courts. To keep land they were using, ranchers sent their men, wearing blue ribbon arm bands, to file claims at office of county clerk. Nesters, with red ribbons, rushed for same land. To avoid bloodshed, sheriff W. K. Clark disarmed them. For three days prior to deadlines, the cowboys and nesters had knockdown dragout fights at the filing window. Later nesters starved out, because of droughts: land they took up reverted to grazing. (1970)

GAINESVILLE (Cooke Co.)   *US 82, 5 mi. E at roadside park*
Gainesville
Founded 1850. Named for Gen. Edmund P. Gaines, who in 1836 aided Republic of Texas. Military supply headquarters during Civil War. Important in defense against Indian attacks and invasion. Center for agriculture, industry, oil. Home of famed Gainesville Community Circus. (1964)

GAINESVILLE (Cooke Co.)   *US 82, 5 mi. E in roadside park*
The Cross Timbers
Two long, narrow strips of timber extending parallel to each other from Oklahoma to Central Texas form a marked contrast to adjacent prairie. The more fertile East Cross timbers begin here in Cooke County. Area was famous pioneer landmark as well as obstacle to travel because of its dense

growth. It divided the hunting grounds of the Plains and East Texas Indians. Until 1870s it marked boundary of settlement, for Plains Indians avoided the timber. Forests' most important function was (and is) causing soil to retain water. (1970)

GAINESVILLE (Cooke Co.) *off IH 35, 1 mi. W at Elm Creek*
Cooke County
Created March 20, 1848. Organized March 10, 1849. Named in honor of William G. Cooke, 1808–1847, captain of the "New Orleans Greys," 1835; assistant inspector general at San Jacinto, 1836; member of the Santa Fe Expedition, 1841; Secretary of War and Marine, 1845; adjutant general, 1846–1847. County seat, Gainesville. (1964)

GAINESVILLE (Cooke Co.) *California St., off IH 35 at Elm Creek Bridge*
Cooke County, C.S.A.
Military, defense center in Civil War. Cooke voted 221 to 137 anti-secession, yet nine military units served Confederacy from here. In constant danger of Federal or Indian attack, Col. Wm. C. Young of Cooke, with 1,000 men took Indian territory forts from Federals April–May 1861. Commissioners set up regular patrols, forted a home as refuge for dependents, and gave $4,000 for munitions and wool cards to make cloth. Cotton gin, grist mill, gunsmiths, blacksmiths made war goods. C.S.A. was furnished epsom salts from Indian Creek. Corn, beef, pork, wheat, other produce fed the military, home front. County swapped 25 steers for salt for dependent families. People worked hard, sacrificed much, protected homes of fighting men of Confederacy.

2nd Frontier Regiment
Organized Oct. 1863 with Gainesville as headquarters, the Second Frontier Regiment, Texas Cavalry C.S.A. guarded counties along Red River to keep down outlaws, Indians, deserters. Col. James Bourland (1803–1868) was appointed commander and it became known as "Bourland's Border Regiment." Union invasion from north of Red River was constantly threatened. These mounted troops patrolled, maintained posts along river and in Indian territory. Confederate Seminole troops served with the unit. Famous Confederate Indian Gen. Stand Watie and his Cherokee Brigade shared duty along perilous border. Bourland also worked with frontier regiment, state troops, that maintained line posts 100 mi. west, a day's horseback ride apart, from Red to Rio Grande Rivers, and with a state militia line 30 mi. to the west. (1963)

GAINESVILLE (Cooke Co.) *California St., off IH 35 at Leonard Park*
The Great Hanging at Gainesville, 1862
Facing the threat of invasion from the North and fearing a Unionist uprising in their midst, the people of North Texas lived in constant dread during the Civil War. Word of a "Peace Party" of Union sympathizers, sworn to destroy their government, kill their leaders, and bring in Federal troops caused great alarm in Cooke and neighboring counties. Spies joined the "Peace Party," discovered its members and details of their plans. Under the leadership of Colonels James Bourland, Daniel Montague, and others, citizens loyal to the Confederacy determined to destroy the order; and on the morning of October 1, 1862, there were widespread arrests "by authority of the people of Cooke County." Fear of rescue by "Peace Party" members brought troops and militia to Gainesville, where the prisoners were assembled, and hastened action by the citizens committee. At a meeting of Cooke County citizens, with Colonel W. C. Young presiding, it was unanimously resolved to establish a citizens court and to have the chairman choose a committee to select a jury. Sixty-eight men were brought speedily before the court. Thirty-nine of them were found guilty of conspiracy and insurrection, sentenced, and immediately hanged. Three other prisoners who were members of military units were allowed trial by court martial at their request and were subsequently hanged by its order. Two others broke from their guard and were shot and killed. The Texas Legislature appropriated $4,500 for rations, forage used by state troops here during the unrest. (1963)

GAINESVILLE (Cooke Co.) *1003 W. California St. (FM 51)*
Moffett Park
The owner of 90 acres in this vicinity, Missouri native Ned Moffett, Sr., (1842–1924) wed Mary Stone on April 19, 1866. The couple had nine children, and early census records listed the family as Mulatto. The Moffetts permitted use of this property along Elm Creek for celebrations by local African American citizens, and in 1943 the City of Gainesville bought the land from heirs to form Moffett Park. The first large social event in the new park was the 1944 Juneteenth celebration.

175

Recreational facilities eventually included playground equipment and a pool. Following integration of nearby Leonard Park in the mid-1960s, the site declined in use, but it remains an important reminder of the city's past. (2005)

GALVESTON (Galveston Co.)   *IH 45 at north end of Galveston Causeway*
Civil War Fortifications at Virginia Point
The site of an important railroad bridge which provided the only connection between the Texas mainland and Galveston Island in the mid-19th century, played an integral role in the Confederate defense of Galveston during the Civil War. A convoy of Union ships began a blockade off Galveston Island on July 2, 1861. Confederate Brig. Gen. Paul O. Hebert, commander of the Military Department of Texas, established the Military District of Galveston in October that year. Under the command of Col. John C. Moore, the district included Galveston Island, Virginia Point, the adjacent coast, and Bolivar Peninsula. Moore ordered fortifications built at Virginia Point at the head of the railroad bridge. When Federal troops captured Galveston Island, Gen. John B. Magruder, who had succeeded Hebert, ordered Confederate land forces to this strategic point. Moving over the railroad bridge to the island under cover of darkness on December 31, southern forces attacked the Federals just before dawn on New Year's Day 1863 and recaptured Galveston Island. At the end of the war in 1865, Galveston was the larger of only two southern ports remaining in Confederate hands. Incise on reverse: Researched by Ft. Virginia Point Chapter, United Daughters of the Confederacy. (1991)

GALVESTON (Galveston Co.)   *IH 45, north end of Galveston Causeway*
Site of Landmark Campbell's Bayou (1 mi. E)
Settled 1821 by Privateer James Campbell (1791–1856), U.S. Navy veteran, War of 1812, who after discharge was lieutenant and close friend of Buccaneer Jean Lafitte, operating out of Galveston (then called Campeche). In Karankawa Indian rituals about 1817, Mary Sabinal (1795–1884) became Campbell's bride. When Lafitte left Texas in 1821, Campbell pleased his wife by settling here as a rancher. Community remained until its second destruction by hurricane, 1915. Graves of the Campbells and many other early Texans are in cemetery at Campbell's Bayou. (1968)

GALVESTON (Galveston Co.)   *1417 Harborside Dr. (SH 275)*
Jean Lafitte
Notorious pirate. Settled here in 1817 with his buccaneers and ships; under Mexican flag, continued his forays against Spanish shipping in the Gulf. On this site, he built his home, Maison Rouge (Red House), which was part of his fort; and upper story was pierced for cannon. It was luxuriously furnished with booty from captured ships. Leaving Galveston in 1821, upon demand of the United States, he burned his home, fort and whole village; then sailed to Yucatan. In 1870, present structure was built over old cellars and foundations of Maison Rouge. (1965)

GALVESTON (Galveston Co.)   *2219 Market St.*
William Lewis Moody, Jr. (January 25, 1865–July 21, 1954)
Famed for a long career of dynamic leadership in Galveston business, civic affairs, and philanthropy. Born in Freestone County; son of William Lewis and Pherabe Elizabeth Bradley Moody. Educated at Virginia Military Institute, he later traveled and studied abroad before joining his father's cotton firm in Galveston in 1886. He organized in 1889 W. L. Moody and Co., a private bank (still operating). He founded American National Insurance Co. (1905); City National Bank, later called the Moody National Bank; National Hotel Co. (1930); and other firms. He owned *Galveston News* (Texas' oldest newspaper), *Galveston Tribune*, *Texas City Sun*, 11 ranches, and many other interests. He took active part in relief and reconstruction after the disastrous Galveston hurricane of 1900. He married Libbie Rice Shearn in 1890. Their children were Mary Elizabeth (Mrs. E. C. Northen), W. L., III, Shearn, and Libbie (Mrs. Clark W. Thompson). Known as one of the ten richest men in America, W. L. Moody, Jr., in his lifetime gave the state a school for cerebral palsied children. With his wife he set up (1942) the Moody Foundation, which has since given millions of dollars for charitable, scientific, educational and religious purposes throughout Texas. (1971)

GALVESTON (Galveston Co.)   *2618 Broadway (SH 87)*
The Moody Home
Family residence, W. L. Moody, Jr. Built about 1894, and for many years home of Mr. Moody, prominent financier and philanthropist who established the Moody Foundation. Late Victorian

176

architecture. Said to have been first Texas residence built on steel frame. Has magnificent stained glass windows, ornate ceilings, rare handcarved woodwork. A large handsome home, famed for its hospitality. (1967)

GALVESTON (Galveston Co.) *1403 Broadway (US 87)*
Powhatan and Mattie Wren House
In 1873, Edward Sylvester paid W.C. Crookshank to build a side-gabled cottage with galleries that ran the length of the north and south sides of the house. Originally, there was a small building at the back of the lot most likely used as a kitchen. Sylvester and his wife Lydia lived in the house for several years before they sold it to Powhatan and Mattie (Campbell) Wren. Powhatan Wren was born in Powhatan County, Virginia in 1842 and moved to Galveston by 1867. He worked for the Galveston, Houston & Harrisburg Railroad as a freight agent, and later as a city clerk and county clerk, and as chief clerk of the U.S. Customs House. To make his home large enough for his family, which included six children, Wren hired Robert B. Garrett in 1885 to enlarge, remodel and update the house with Victorian details to its present form. The house has kept its appearance since that time. The 1900 hurricane obliterated most of the neighborhoods between Broadway and the Gulf of Mexico, but this house survived. After the city completed construction on the first section of the seawall in 1904, workers raised the house so fill could be pumped under the structure. The house remained in the family until 1921, then passed through a series of owners and divided into a duplex in the 1930s, when leaseholders began to open businesses in the lower level. The structure remained rental property through many of the subsequent years. Located in Galveston's historic East End, the eclectic styled house features a side-gabled roof, shiplap wood siding, a gallery porch and central door with sidelights. (2007)

GALVESTON (Galveston Co.) *1402 Broadway (SH 87)*
The Bishop's Palace
Built, 1886–1893, by Col. Walter Gresham, civic leader and U.S. congressman. Nicholas J. Clayton was architect. One of the most lavish and massive homes in U.S. House is a Victorian adaptation of Renaissance style. Silver and onyx mantel in music room won first prize, 1886, at New Orleans Exposition. Mrs. Gresham painted murals, ceilings. Catholic Diocese bought home, 1923, made one room into chapel with stained glass windows. (1967)

GALVESTON (Galveston Co.) *1114 Broadway (SH 87)*
Boddeker House
The son of German immigrants, Joseph Boddeker came to Galveston with his parents about 1850. After service in the Civil War, he worked as a riverboat pilot and purchased this lot for his family home in the 1870s. When the original Boddeker House was destroyed in the 1900 storm, Capt. Boddeker purchased and relocated this 1893 house from 12th and Sealy. His son James (1875–1940), who lived here with his wife, Elizabeth, was a successful businessman and civic leader, serving as county commissioner from 1912 until 1940. Upon his death, Elizabeth completed his term as commissioner, becoming the first woman in Galveston County to hold that post. (2001)

GALVESTON (Galveston Co.) *SH 87 at Galveston Ferry Landing*
Galveston Island
Few spots have played a more exciting role in the life of Texas than Galveston Island. Cabeza de Vaca, the Spanish explorer, wrote of the cannibalistic Karankawa Indians when he was shipwrecked here in 1528. The island became headquarters for Jean Lafitte and other adventurers between 1815 and 1821. Importance of the harbor was recognized as early as 1825 when Stephen F. Austin petitioned the Mexican government to establish a port. Galveston became temporary capital of the Republic in April, 1836, when President David G. Burnet fled here at the approach of Mexican Gen. Santa Anna. After the revolution Galveston's place as first city of the Republic became fixed. Immigrants poured through the port. The Texas Navy was berthed here. With statehood in 1845 came continued growth; Texas first telegraph (1854), first national bank (1865), first electric lights (1888). Capture and recapture of Galveston were principal Texas engagements of the Civil War. The port fell to blockading Union troops Oct. 4, 1862. It was retaken Jan. 1, 1863, by Gen. John B. Magruder and remained in Confederate hands. Galveston was again on the nation's lips Sept. 8, 1900, when a hurricane packing winds of 120 mph swept a vast tidal wave across the island, killing 5,000. No other American disaster has taken a greater toll. The storm had two immediate results—

construction of a protective seawall 17 feet high and 7½ miles long and creation of a commission form of city government, an innovation that spread to other American municipalities. The port remains one of the state's most important, handling more sulphur than any in the world. Important to sightseers and motorists are the toll-free ferries operated by the Texas Highway Department across the 2½-mile strait between the island and Port Bolivar. (1967)

GALVESTON (Galveston Co.) *2100 block of Seawall Blvd.*
Hotel Galvez
Built at a cost of $1,000,000, this hotel was financed by local businessmen and public subscribers to help the economy of Galveston following the 1900 hurricane. Completed in 1911, it was designed by the St. Louis firm of Mauran and Russell. The Spanish colonial revival styling includes a red tile roof and white stuccoed brick walls. The hotel and city are named in honor of Count Bernardo de Galvez (1746–1786), Spanish Governor of Louisiana and Viceroy of Mexico. (1980)

GALVESTON (Galveston Co.) *2100 block, Seawall Blvd.*
The Original Galveston Seawall
On Sept. 8, 1900 a devastating hurricane and tidal wave destroyed much of Galveston and left 6,000 persons dead. After the tragedy, the city appointed a board of three engineers, Brig. Gen. (Ret.) Henry M. Robert (1837–1923), author of Robert's Rules of Order, Alfred Noble, and H. C. Ripley, to devise protection from future storms. Work on their proposal, to be financed jointly by city, county, and state governments, was started in 1902. To prevent flood damage, buildings were jacked up and the surface of the entire city upgraded, increasing the elevation to a maximum of 12 feet above sea level. As a shield against high waves, a solid concrete wall was built along the gulf shore of the island. The original section of the seawall, begun in Oct. 1902, stretched 3.3 miles. Founded on wooden pilings, the 17-foot high barrier was backed by a sand embankment and protected in front by stone riprap. The Gulf side of the wall curved outward to prevent water from washing over the top. Finished in July 1904, the seawall proved its value in 1915, when a hurricane more severe than the storm 15 years earlier did far less damage. Since then, the wall has been periodically lengthened. Freed from the threat of further destruction, Galveston has grown into a modern and prosperous city. (1975)

GALVESTON (Galveston Co.) *2106 Seawall Blvd., Moody Civic Center*
Galveston: Gateway to Texas
From the days of European conquest, the Gulf of Mexico was the main road to Texas. Some settlers of the 1820s even came by keelboat, going ashore along the way to kill game, in the same way an overland party would live off the country while traveling. Planters from the old South and some farmers from the mid-continent came by land. But roads, wet and rough, had too many rivers crossed only by costly, ill-tended ferries; and cutthroats haunted many of them. Galveston in the 19th century was chief port of entry. It was sister city to New Orleans, so well organized was passage from one to the other. Texas ports of entry included Velasco, Quintana, Lavaca, Indianola, Matagorda, Point Isabel, Houston, and Corpus Christi. Yet Galveston—with the best natural harbor between Pensacola and Vera Cruz—dominated travel into Texas. This port welcomed statesmen, speculators, teachers, soldiers, clergymen, doctors, merchants, craftsmen, tourists, European immigration. Col. Wm. Lewis Moody (1828–1920), a Virginian, landed here in 1852, entered business world, courageously led unit in the Civil War, founded a fortune. Gifts of his family to Texas for educational and humane purposes have included facilities at this site. (1965)

GALVESTON (Galveston Co.) *5600 Seawall Blvd.*
Peter Leroy Colombo
Born in Galveston, Peter Leroy Colombo overcame disabilities to become a highly accomplished lifeguard. Born in 1905, Colombo lost his hearing, speech and use of his legs at the age of seven, due to meningitis. His brothers took him to the Texas coast where he swam, regaining use of his legs, though his hearing never returned. In 1915, Colombo began to attend the Texas School for the Deaf in Austin, where he learned to read lips and communicate in sign language, and where he also continued to train in swimming. He returned to Galveston in 1921 and soon joined the Surf Toboggan Club, a group of volunteer lifeguards. Colombo became a hired lifeguard at the age of 18. In a time of segregation, he would go on to save hundreds from drowning, regardless of race, over a career spanning approximately 50 years. In addition, Colombo set many endurance and speed

records in swimming matches, often participating in races that were up to 30 miles long. He was also a pioneer surfer on the Galveston beaches. Colombo officially retired in 1967, but continued to swim and serve as a lifeguard when he was able. When Peter Leroy Colombo died in 1974, he was recognized with a moment of silence by the Texas State Legislature. He had officially saved over 900 people from drowning, with many other rescues going unrecorded. In 2005, the natatorium at the Texas School for the Deaf was named in his honor. Today, Peter Leroy Colombo is remembered as an individual who did not allow disabilities to limit him, risking his life to rescue hundreds along the beaches of Galveston.   (2008)

GALVESTON (Galveston Co.)   *Park at intersection of 13-mile Road and Termini Road*

West Galveston Island

First known to world history in 16th century, from report of Spanish soldier Cabeza de Vaca, who was shipwrecked on this island in 1528. Area was also visited by French explorer La Salle in 1685. Second known Caucasian to live here was the buccaneer Jean Lafitte, who had to fight Karankawa Indians for site he chose as operating base for his pirate fleet in 1815 or 1816. In the 1820s, a debarkation point for illegal slave ships developed on West Island. Humane and civilized traffic afterward found its way here. Stagecoach service was established in the 1850s from Galveston to Old Velasco (now Freeport) on a west beach road, with a ferry at San Luis Pass. An important lace manufacturing concern was located here, and by 1885 the Galveston & Western Railway carried visitors by the hundreds to a race track near the center of the island. Since 1957, West Island has rapidly become a major recreational and resort area, with leisure homes fronting the Gulf, the canals, and the bay. There is still enough wilderness to attract migratory shore birds; more than 95 percent of the known species in America annually spend some time on this island.   (1967)

GANADO (Jackson Co.)   *2nd St. at E. Putnam Ave.*

Ganado

Established in 1882 as a shipping point on New York, Texas & Mexican Railroad. Named Ganado (Spanish for "herd") by railroad official. Became a boomtown in 1891–92 when Scandinavian immigrants settled area. Today a farm, oil and shipping center.   (1967)

GARDEN CITY (Glasscock Co.)   *SH 158 at Main St., courthouse*

Glasscock County

Created in 1887. Organized in 1893 with Garden City county seat. Named for George W. Glasscock (1810–1868), flatboating partner of Abraham Lincoln in Illinois. Came to Texas 1834 and fought 1835–1836 in the War of Independence from Mexico. Built first Central Texas flour mill, Williamson County. Georgetown was named for him. Was in Texas legislature 1864–1868. Of the 254 counties, 42 bear Indian, French, Spanish names. Ten honor such colonizers as Stephen F. Austin, "Father of Texas." 12 were named for Washington, Clay and other American patriots. 96 were named for men like Glasscock who fought in the Texas War of Independence at the Alamo (15 dying at the Alamo), signed the Declaration of Independence or served as statesmen in the Republic of Texas. 23 have the names of frontiersmen and pioneers. 11 honor American statesmen who worked for the annexation of Texas; 10, leaders in Texas since statehood, including jurists, ministers, educators, historians, statesmen, and 36, men prominent in the Confederacy during the Civil War. Midland and 8 others have geographical names. San Jacinto and Val Verde were named for battles, Live Oak and Orange, for trees, and Mason for a fort.   (1964)

GARDEN CITY (Glasscock Co.)   *SH 158 at Main St., courthouse*

Glasscock County Courthouse and Jail

On May 9, 1893, a little over one month from the date of Glasscock County's formal organization, the first county commissioner's court issued bonds to erect a combination courthouse/jail building. L. T. Noyes of Houston, with the assistance of plasterer William T. Lovell, completed the structure on February 12, 1894. Originally, the ground floor of the building was used for court sessions and the second floor used as the jail. The 2-story stone building, later used only as a jail, features subtle Classical influences, including corner pilasters and a tall corbelled cornice. County bonds issued through the First State Bank of Garden City in 1909 were used to employ Mutual Construction Company, Inc. of Louisville, Kentucky, and architects Edward C. Hasford & Co., of Dallas, to build a new courthouse. The 2 ½ story Classical Revival structure, constructed of 3-foot thick native stone from a local ranch owned by Steve Calverley, was completed on August 27, 1910. It features colossal Doric columns supporting its open pediment and a horizontal belt course which follows its 2nd floor window sills. The current Glasscock County Courthouse has been in continuous use since 1910. The original courthouse/jail structure was replaced by a new jail in 1980.   (1962)

GARFIELD (Travis Co.)   *SH 71 E*
Haynie Chapel Methodist Church
Founded 1839 in the Republic of Texas by Rev. John Haynie (1786–1860). First church was of logs, and located a mile north on land of Andrew Deavers Houston. This building, the third, was put up in 1907. Plaque erected by Houston descendants, Mr. and Mrs. E. W. (Nellie Houston) Schuhmann. History given by Rev. Olin W. Nail, present pastor. Awarded Medallion Plate. (1964)

GARLAND (Dallas Co.)   *SH 78 at DeWitt Rd., 1 mi. NE*
William Sachse Cemetery
William Sachse, a native of Prussia, arrived in nearby Collin County in 1845 as a Peters colonist. He became a successful businessman, rancher, and trader, and participated in several cattle drives to Kansas. His business successes over time allowed him to acquire more than 5000 acres of land in Collin and Dallas Counties. In 1886, Sachse gave some of this land to the Gulf, Colorado & Santa Fe Railroad for a railway line and townsite. The community that grew up around the railroad was named Sachse in his honor. Sachse moved his family to the new town and soon set aside two acres of land for a church and this cemetery. The graveyard has been used throughout its history as a public burial ground. The oldest marked grave, that of William Sachse, is dated 1899. Sachse's second wife, Martha (Frost), a number of their descendants, as well as many early settlers and their descendants also are buried here. Some of the family names recorded here are Salmon, Herring, Ingram, House, Harper, and Brand. The William Sachse cemetery, with its ties to early settlement in this part of the state, is an important reminder of the area's heritage.   (1985)

GARLAND (Dallas Co.)   *SH 78 at W. Miller Rd.*
Pioneer Cemetery
The final resting place for many Dallas County pioneers, this cemetery began in the churchyard of Duck Creek Methodist Church, a congregation organized in the 1850s. The graveyard includes sections established by the Duck Creek Masonic Lodge (1883) and the Knights of Pythias Lodge (1900). The oldest marked burials date from the 1870s, although earlier death dates appear on graves relocated here from another cemetery. Interred here are local, state, and national elected officials, victims of a 1927 tornado, and veterans of conflicts from the War of 1812 to Vietnam.   (1986)

GARWOOD (Colorado Co.)   *SH 71 at FM 333, 2 mi. N*
First Producing Gas Well in Colorado County
(12 mi. W)
Completed on July 17, 1932, as Nelson No. 1 Well, at a depth of 4,052 ft.; was drilled by Coyle-Concord Oil Company, owner of 30,000 acres of block leases in area. Many other wells were soon drilled as a result of success here. Site called Garwood Field. In 1932 no market was found for this gas. Two extensions of the field were later located and commercial outlets obtained. Gas production has contributed to prosperity of the county. Texas reserves of natural gas are nearly 119 trillion cu. ft., or 42.3% of United States reserves.   (1967)

GATESVILLE (Coryell Co.)   *US 84, 4.5 mi. E*
Site of Fort Gates
First settlement in Coryell County. Established by Brevet Colonel W. R. Montgomery, 8th U.S. Infantry, October 26, 1849, on the Military Post Road between Austin and Fort Graham as a protection of the frontier against hostile Indians. Named in honor of Collinson R. Gates, gallant officer in the Mexican War. Abandoned in March, 1852, as the frontier line had advanced further westward. Used as a place of defense by settlers during Indian raids. First seat of Coryell county February 4–May 27, 1854, when Gatesville was established.

GATESVILLE (Coryell Co.)   *US 84, 2 mi. E*
Coryell County
Formed from Bell County. Created February 4, 1854. Organized March 4, 1854. Named in honor of James Coryell, born in Tennessee in 1796. A member of the Bowie Expedition to the old San

Saba silver mines in 1831. A Texas Ranger. Killed by Indians near Fort Milam, May 27, 1837. County seat, Fort Gates, 1854. Gatesville since.

GATESVILLE (Coryell Co.)   *600 E. Main St. (US 84)*
Coryell County Courthouse
An outstanding example of Second Empire Victorian style, often seen in Texas Courthouse design. Erected in 1897 on land donated by early settler R. G. Grant. Architect for this third Coryell Courthouse was W. C. Dodson; builder, Tom Lovell. Limestone and red sandstone blocks were precut to the exact size at quarry, then hauled here by horse-drawn wagons. At each entrance are columns in Roman Corinthian style; and over the east entrance is builder's mark of an owl. Statues on the roof represent "Justice." Noted trials have been held in this building.   (1969)

GAUSE (Milam Co.)   *US 79, 5 mi. NE*
Site of Town of Nashville
Surveyed in the fall of 1835 as the capital of Robertson's colony. Named for Nashville Tennessee, where Sterling C. Robertson and many of his colonists had formerly lived. Seat of Justice Milam Municipality 1836; Milam County, 1837. First home in Texas of George C. Childress, chairman of the committee who drafted the Texas Declaration of Independence.

GAUSE (Milam Co.)   *US 79*
The Town of Gause
William J. Gause (1829–1914), born in Alabama, moved to Texas in 1849, to the Brazos region in 1856, and to this locality in 1872. Buying lumber in Montgomery, he gave his friend Dan Fowler half in return for hauling it here. The two built the first homes in this settlement. In 1873, Gause gave right of way and 100 acres of land to the International & Great Northern Railroad, and the town was platted. Gause post office opened in 1874, with James S. Reynolds as postmaster. The I.G.N. freighted out great quantities of cotton, and the town thrived. Cotton gins, stores, blacksmith shops, a lumber yard, a bank, hotels, livery stables, a newspaper and other businesses were established. Besides W. J. Gause, civic leaders included Dr. J. E. Brown, Richard Cox, Dr. James Dollar, Lafayette Ely, Bill Faubian, Dan Fowler, J. C. Lister, C. C. Moore, Dr. John Porter, Frank Thomas, and T. L. Watts. Churches were organized and a Masonic Lodge chartered. The county's first independent school was established in Gause. Good highways, mechanized farming, and decline of railroading halted commerce in the town of Gause. It survives, however, as a residential site chosen by descendants of the pioneers and by commuters to industrial plants and businesses in this vicinity.   (1974)

GENEVA (Sabine Co.)   *SH 21, near post office*
El Lobanillo
Pueblo of Gil Ybarbo (1729–1809), where his ill mother and other refugees remained when Spain evacuated colonists from western Louisiana and East Texas in 1773. Granted 1794 to Juan Ignacio Pifermo, and inherited in early 1800s by John Maximillian (1778?–1866), this is now known as oldest continuously occupied site in East Texas.   (1972)

GEORGE WEST (Live Oak Co.)   *US 281, 4.2 mi. N*
Near Crossing of Old Ox-Cart Road
From the early days of Spanish Colonial Texas well into statehood, the only "Highways" in the area were private dirt roads. Although many had names, others were simply called "Oxcart roads" for the sturdy Mexican carts so frequently seen on them. In the 19th century this site was a junction for two of these roads, one extending from Brownsville to San Antonio, the other from Laredo to Goliad, then over to Indianola on to the Gulf. This strategic location helped Oakville grow into a thriving town and become county seat of Live Oak County in 1856. Ox-carts were unique in being constructed entirely of wood, fastened by wooden pins and rawhide thongs. The two wheels stood taller than a man and the bed was usually fifteen feet long, covered by a thatched roof. To stop the deafening squeak of the wheels, drivers greased the hubs with prickly pear leaves. Pulled by several yoke of oxen, the carts usually traveled in groups. Their arrival meant fresh coffee beans, salt, and sugar for isolated settlers. Although gradually replaced by wagons, carts were for two centuries almost the only freight vehicles in Texas. Reminders of their former importance long remained in the names of these two old roads.   (1968)

GEORGE WEST (Live Oak Co.)   *US 59 Bus. at Guadalupe St.*
City of George West
Founded 1913 by George Washington West, rancher and civic leader, who secured railroad route through Live Oak County and provided several municipal buildings and plots for others. Became county seat in 1919. Market and shipping point for cattle and cotton.   (1967)

GEORGE WEST (Live Oak Co.)   *US 281, 1.4 mi. S*
Live Oak County
Created by legislature Feb. 2, 1856, and organized August 4 with Oakville as county seat. Formed from San Patricio and Nueces Counties. Named for its Live Oak trees. County seat moved, 1919, to George West on railroad. Center for ranching, farming, petroleum production and processing. Recreation areas include Tips State Park and Lake Corpus Christi. Historic sites are Fort Ramirez, first settlement; Fort Merrill, built 1850 to protect early settlers; Brownsville-San Antonio Oxcart Road, used by general Santa Anna on the way to the Alamo. Other sites marked.   (1936)

GEORGE WEST (Live Oak Co.)   *US 281, 23 mi. S*
Fort Ramirez
As late as 1920 dilapidated rock walls stood on this site known as Fort Ramirez. Treasure hunters pulled them down and workmen on the pipe-line passing near hauled them to the hollow below. Erected at an unknown date by two brothers named Ramirez, from whom Ramirena Creek derived its name. The structure is believed to be the first in what is now Live Oak County. It was combined ranch dwelling and fort. The owners were run off or killed by Indians in 1813. A full account of the fort and its traditions is given in "Coronado's Children" by J. Frank Dobie.

GEORGETOWN (Williamson Co.)   *SH 195, 5 mi. N in Berry's Creek*
James B. Williams 1821–1891
James B. Williams and his wife, Sarah Coffey, were born in Kentucky. Soon after their marriage, he led a wagon train headed for Texas. They reached Berry's Creek, Dec. 24, 1848, the same year that Williamson County was organized. In a few years, they moved to San Saba County where he served as sergeant in the 2nd Co. of Texas Rangers under his uncle, Capt. John Williams, the famous Indian Scout. After Capt. John was scalped by the Indians in 1862, James B. moved his family back to Glasscock Valley in Williamson County. They raised 10 children, most of whom raised large families and they in turn played an influential part in shaping the destiny of the fledgling Williamson County.   (1973)

GEORGETOWN (Williamson Co.)   *SH 29, 9.5 mi. E*
Jonah Cemetery
Jonah Cemetery was established in 1902 when community leaders J. M. Barrington, W. S. McMakins, C. Brady, A. J. McDonald, and R. H. Northcutt purchased two acres near the San Gabriel River to be used as a cemetery. Burials were free to area residents. The earliest marked grave is that of George N. Northcutt. Other graves of interest are those of Confederate veterans Isiah S. Hicks and M. G. Walton. Twin sisters Sarah E. (Yoes) Robbins and Margaret (Yoes) Barrington are interred here near many of their 22 children. One of the last physical remnants of a once-thriving rural community, the Jonah Cemetery continues to serve the area.   (1998)

GEORGETOWN (Williamson Co.)   *SH 29, 7 mi. E*
Jonah
On 1820s land grant to Nashville Colony, settled 1851 by wagon train from Arkansas, and called Water Valley. In 1884, repeated ill-luck in selecting an acceptable name for post office led to renaming the town Jonah. This was site of famous grist mill, 1865–1912.   (1970)

GEORGETOWN (Williamson Co.)   *SH 29, 5 mi. E in roadside park*
Texan Santa Fe Expedition
A dramatic chapter in administration (1838–1841) of Republic of Texas President Mirabeau B. Lamar. Aware of United States-Mexico commerce crossing Texas by the Santa Fe Trail near the Canadian River, President Lamar sought similar trade advantages for Texas. He initiated the Texan Santa Fe Expedition early in 1841, with Dr. Richard F. Brenham, Col. Wm. G. Cooke and Jose Antonio Navarro as commissioners. Cooke began recruiting in April, forming an artillery and five infantry companies. Remainder of 321 members included merchants (with $200,000 worth of

goods), teamsters, guides and others. George W. Kendall, of the New Orleans "Picayune," joined to write classic book on the venture. Travel was by 21 slow ox-wagons. First day's march, June 19, 1841, ended on the San Gabriel, and expedition's campsite is near here. Before reaching the Santa Fe Trail some 600 miles north, the men were to have torturing experiences with drouth and unknown terrain. Ill from hardships, the group was betrayed into the hands of Mexican authorities and sent as prisoners to Mexico City. However, this penetration of upper Texas gave the republic stronger claims to her northern lands. (1970)

GEORGETOWN (Williamson Co.) SH 29, 3 mi. E at San Gabriel River Bridge
Mankins Crossing (100 yards W)
This historic crossing on the San Gabriel River was named for pioneer settler Samuel Mankins, who purchased land along the river in 1849. The limestone bed in the river provided a convenient crossing for area farmers. A nearby community included a school, church, and cotton gin. A 1914 concrete and gravel causeway was replaced by a state highway department concrete bridge in 1931. After the highway department built a new bridge on higher ground at Highway 29 in 1958, the Mankins Crossing Bridge became a popular recreational site for area residents. (1990)

GEORGETOWN (Williamson Co.) SH 29, 3 mi. E
The Double File Trail
Laid out about 1828 by Delaware Indians, "The Double File Trail" got its name because two horsemen could ride it side by side. The Delawares carved this trace migrating ahead of expanding white settlements. They moved from what they called "The Redlands" in East Texas to Mexico near present Nuevo Laredo. Of the 200 to 250 families reported in East Texas in the 1820s, only about 150 remained after the move. Early sites in Williamson County were settled where this trail crossed waterways. Texas Rangers and the Sante Fe Expedition also traveled the track. (1978)

GEORGETOWN (Williamson Co.) 921 W. University (SH 29)
Old Dimmitt Home
Built in 1866 by John Jones Dimmitt; of native limestone hauled in by ox drawn wagons. Home of prominent citizens in Georgetown over 100 years. Dimmitt—a surveyor, lawyer, mathematician, linguist, one time county attorney, and partner in building of Georgetown Railroad—was civic leader; instrumental in getting Southwestern University moved to Georgetown. Awarded Medallion Plate. (1967)

GEORGETOWN (Williamson Co.) IH 35, N of FM 2243 (Leander Rd.) exit
Page-Decrow-Weir House
Built in 1903, this house was owned by a succession of area ranchers. J. M. Page had the home built for his family, but sold it to his brother-in-law Thomas Decrow in 1903. The home was purchased in 1920 by Horace M. Weir, and in the 1930s a polo training center was operated on the property. A Georgetown landmark, the Queen Anne style home features an octagonal tower, two-tiered wraparound porch, and a two-story bay window. (1988)

GEORGETOWN (Williamson Co.) IH 35, 1 mi. S at cave entrance
Inner Space Cavern (Laubach Cave)
Discovered in May 1963 on land of W. W. Laubach by core-drilling team, Texas Highway Department. Exploration began in November 1963 and continues to present. Carved by water from Edwards limestone, cave lies along the Balcones Fault and is estimated to be 100 million years old. 95 percent of formations are still growing. Cave was apparently open during late Pleistocene (20,000–45,000 years ago), for bones of many extinct mammals have been found in debris cones filling former natural entrances. Remains of sabre-toothed cats and mammoths are represented. (1973)

GERONIMO (Guadalupe Co.) SH 123, 1 mi. S
José Antonio Navarro Ranch
Born in San Antonio, José Antonio Navarro (1795–1871) held several offices in the Mexican government before becoming an active participant in the movement for Texas independence. Navarro possessed numerous landholdings in this part of the state. In 1832, he purchased land along Geronimo Creek (approx. 1.2 mi. E) for farming and ranching activities. The ranch house served as a haven for his family during his captivity by the Mexican militia in 1841 until his return to

the ranch in 1845. A signer of Texas Declaration of Independence, Navarro owned the ranch until 1853.   (1985)

GERONIMO (Guadalupe Co.)   *SH 123, .25 mi. S*
Navarro School
The original Navarro School, named for early Texas leader Jose Antonio Navarro, was a one-room building located about one-half mile northeast of this site in 1889. A second structure was added in the early 1900s. In 1912, the Navarro Agricultural High School was built on land purchased from L. H. Heinemeyer. It was replaced in 1953 by new elementary and high school facilities on this site. Sports and other extra-curricular activities were established as the school grew. For over a century Navarro School has served students in the Geronimo area.   (1989)

GIDDINGS (Lee Co.)   *Main St. (US 77) at E. Hempstead, courthouse*
Lee County
Located on Old San Antonio Road, on land surveyed in 1821 as part of the original colony of Moses and Stephen F. Austin. In 1854 became site of major settlement by Wends, from Northern Europe, under the leadership of Pastor Johann Kilian. Had only school in the U.S. that taught in the Latin-like Wendish language. County created from parts of Washington, Fayette, Bastrop and Burleson. Organized in 1874. Named for Robert E. Lee (1807–1870), General of the Army of Northern Virginia in the Southern Confederacy, 1862–1865. Giddings is the county seat.   (1965)

GIDDINGS (Lee Co.)   *Main St. (US 77) at E. Richmond, courthouse*
City of Giddings
County seat of Lee County. Named for Jabez D. Giddings (1814–1878), of Washington County, one of four brothers from Pennsylvania who were Texas transportation pioneers and business leaders. The town was established as a shipping point when Houston & Texas Central Railroad (in which J. D. Giddings was a stockholder) reached here in 1871. A second and third railroad (San Antonio & Aransas Pass, 1889, and Hearne & Brazos Valley, 1913) increased city's prestige. Commission form government was adopted in 1913. A diversified economy developed.   (1971)

GIDDINGS (Lee Co.)   *200 S. Main St. (US 77)*
Lee County Courthouse
Designed by J. R. Gordon along lines similar to New York State Capitol and several buildings at Harvard University. Classified as Richardsonian Romanesque style, after the famous Louisiana-born architect Henry H. Richardson. Built by Sonnefield, Emmins and Abright of San Antonio, 1899. Replaced first courthouse, which burned 1897. Located on crest of divide separating the Colorado and Brazos River basins.   (1968)

GIDDINGS (Lee Co.)   *SH 21 at border of Lee and Bastrop counties*
King's Highway—El Camino Real—Old San Antonio Road
First opened by Louis de St. Denis, 1715, route from Mexico to Louisiana.   (1918)

GILMER (Upshur Co.)   *SH 155, 14 mi. NE*
Tarver's Ferry (Site 6/10 mi. E)
Once located at a strategic crossing of Big Cypress Creek, this pioneer ferry transported settlers moving west into Texas through populous Jefferson, on Big Cypress Bayou. Those going to the interior of Texas often came by horse or oxen, stopping for provisions at nearby town of Coffeeville. The ferry operator probably was James L. Tarver, who lived on Coffeeville Road, 1860s. Many years before, the Caddo Indians forded stream at this same point in their travels. By 1867 a bridge was built at the crossing and the ferry was no longer needed.   (1968)

GILMER (Upshur Co.)   *SH 155, 13 mi. NE*
Old Coffeeville, C.S.A.
Ferry Point near this site, on Big Cypress. Important town of 1850s, with an academy, 2 dry goods stores, 2 groceries, drug store, 3 doctors, Methodist and Presbyterian churches, a hotel and Masonic lodge. During Civil War, lived up to its name, selling coffee when other towns had none. Had a Confederate camp of instruction, one of three in Upshur County, established in response to June 8, 1861, call of Governor Edward Clark for such camps to be set up at expense of local citizens. Trained infantry and cavalry.   (1965)

GILMER (Upshur Co.) *SH 155, 13 mi. NE*
C.S.A. Camp Talley
Camp of instruction. Set up near Old Coffeeville soon after governor's June 8, 1861, proclamation requesting voluntary popular support for troop training. Merchants were to give goods; farmers, food; laborers, their work; camp officers, leadership. Trainees received no pay until mustered into the Confederate Army. (1964)

GILMER (Upshur Co.) *US 271, 5 mi. N*
Ben Phillips Place
Built 1872 with square nails, broadax hewn boards. Center for talk of politics and news. "A stranger never passed this home." Many marriages performed here by Ben F. Phillips (1845–1927), Church of Christ minister, student of politics, philosopher, Confederate veteran. He represented Upshur-Camp Counties, 1890–94, in Texas legislature. Married Mattie Fambrough (1856–1937) and had nine daughters. Awarded Medallion Plate. (1964)

GILMER (Upshur Co.) *SH 154, 5.5 mi. SE*
Indian Rock Village
An ancient Indian people, their name unknown, located this rock suited to their need and caused it to serve them in preparing food. Without tools but with great patience and skill, they fashioned these Stone Age mortars in which to grind their corn. Their successors in the land the Texans of 1936, salute the industry and skill of these original inhabitants.

GILMER (Upshur Co.) *SH 154, E city limits*
Meshack Roberts
A faithful slave. Came to Gilmer with his master, O. E. Roberts before 1850. While Mr. Roberts was away in the Civil War, ran the farm and looked after the family. To get money to finance farm costs, shod horses for soldiers and others, baked and sold ginger cakes. Was example of the sincere loyalty found over the South. At war's end, master gave him freedom, land and material to build a home. Later, moved to Marshall, where served in the Texas Legislature. In 1882, helped establish Wiley College for Negroes.

GILMER (Upshur Co.) *US 271, S of intersection with SH 300*
Site of the Pioneer Dickson Orphanage
Only home in Texas for Negro orphans for thirty years, 1900–1929. Founded by W. L. Dickson, Negro Baptist minister, only superintendent home ever had. Orphans remained here until they reached 21, unless adopted or indentured by good families. A choir of children made good-will trips to raise funds. In Aug., 1929, home was deeded to the State, together with 700 acres of land and 27 buildings. Name was then changed to the Gilmer State Orphanage for Negroes, which ran until 1943, when the children (about 180) moved to State Home in Austin. (1968)

GILMER (Upshur Co.) *US 271, S city limits*
Gilmer
Founded 1846. Named for Thomas W. Gilmer, U.S. Secretary of the Navy and ardent champion of annexation for Texas. Supply, training, production and educational center during the Civil War. Farming, lumbering and oil hub. Home of famous annual yamboree, Sweet Potato Festival.

GILMER (Upshur Co.) *US 271 right-of-way, 8 mi. S*
West Mountain Cemetery
Part of a Republic of Texas land grant formerly occupied by Caddo and Cherokee Indians, this cemetery was established in the mid-1850s by plantation owner Alpha Phillips. The first grave, that of his father, William, is marked with a stone cairn. The family cemetery came to be used by neighbors, West Mountain Community residents, and transients. A volunteer association was begun in the 1920s to maintain the grounds, and its members have added acreage to the graveyard over the years. Originally known as Old Phillips Cemetery, it has been called West Mountain Cemetery since 1933. (1985)

GILMER (Upshur Co.) *SH 155, south edge of town*
Gilgal Baptist Church
In 1865, the Rev. John Baptist led the founding of this congregation. The members built a brush arbor here and chose the name "Gilgal" after the site of the Israelites' first encampment in the

Promised Land. Tom Littlepage gave two acres for the church grounds and for a black school. Later, three acres were purchased from Judge J. R. Warren. The first frame church building was erected here in 1872 during the ministry of the Rev. J. H. Hill. In 1900, after serving this fellowship, the Rev. W. L. Dickson founded an orphanage, fulfilling his lifelong dream. The Dickson Colored Orphans Home, near Gilmer, operated for years before the state government took charge and moved the facility to Austin. The Rev. S. H. Howard served longer and baptized more members than any other pastor of this congregation. About 1905, during Rev. Howard's ministry, this structure was completed. The building was veneered with brick during the pastorate of an evangelist, the Rev. H. W. Gray. The first fulltime minister, the Rev. Floyd D. Harris, led in the building of the educational annex. A parsonage was constructed during the pastorate of the Rev. U. L. Sanders. (1979)

GILMER (Upshur Co.)   SH 155, 9.5 mi. SW
New Hope Missionary Baptist Church
Organized September 22, 1855, with 15 charter members, in New Hope community (4 mi. NW). Monthly meetings were held in a one-room log school. The building, with 2 acres of land, was given to the church in 1872. A new sanctuary erected in 1883 was torn down and rebuilt at Crossroads community (2 mi. NW), 1914. In 1950 the church purchased an acre of land at the present site. A new building was erected, again using lumber from the old structure. Many present members are descendants of people who composed original congregation. (1970)

GILMER (Upshur Co.)   SH 155, 12 mi. SW
Upshur County
Named in honor of Abel Pucker Upshur, 1790–1844. Distinguished debater and orator as Secretary of State under President John Tyler. He began negotiations in 1843 for the annexation of Texas. Gilmer, the county seat.

GILMER (Upshur Co.)   SH 154 at FM 1002, 11 mi. W
Town of Rhonesboro
Founded 1902; named for W. M. Rhone, only sawmill operator in area until 1901, when arrival of Marshall & East Texas Railroad created a town which grew to have 15 sawmills, 10 stores, 2 churches, a school, hotel, bank, gin, and cotton yard. Mill operators were Connally; Barton and Smith; McWhorter; Cone and Watkins; Whitter; Dacus; Waterman; Nolan; James; Swann; Beavers and Meek; P. K. Williams; M. C. and F. C. Florence; Roger and J. O. Schrum. After pine forest here was depleted (1917), the mills moved and the railroad was abandoned. (1967)

GIRVIN (Pecos Co.)   FM 11, 11 mi. NW
Horse Head Crossing (2 Miles NE)
Famed ford of the Pecos River, named for abundance of horse and mule skulls lining the banks in the 19th century. Many water-starved animals, stolen in Mexico by Indians and driven along the Comanche War Trail, died after drinking too deeply from the river. After the California gold strike in 1848, Horse Head Crossing became a major landmark on the trail west, as it provided the first water for about 75 miles on the route from the East. Emigrants arriving here either turned northwest along the river or crossed and continued southwest to Comanche Springs at Fort Stockton. In 1858, the crossing became an important stop on the Butterfield Overland Mail Route from St. Louis to San Francisco. An adobe stage stand was built and a ferry put into operation, but both were abandoned in 1861, when mail service was terminated. In late 1862, during the Civil War, Federal forces kept a close watch at the crossing in reaction to a threatened Confederate invasion. Cattle began to be trailed across the Pecos in 1864, and in 1866, Charles Goodnight and Oliver Loving blazed their famous trail, which came to this point and turned upriver. Completion of two railroads across West Texas in the early 1880s caused abandonment of the crossing. (1974)

GLADEWATER (Gregg Co.)   US 80, 1 mi. W
Gladewater
Founded as St. Clair, about 3 miles east. Moved to present site on Glade Creek and T & P Railway, 1872. Population grew from 500 to 7000 after oil was discovered in 1931. It became hub of production and refining operations. Manufacturing, clothing, medical, farming and dairy center. Home of annual East Texas Quarter Horse Show. Has world's richest self-supporting cemetery.

Round-Up Association sponsors June rodeo, nationally known, in unique arena—an abandoned crude oil storage pit. (1965)

GLADEWATER (Gregg Co.) *200 N. Main St. (US 271) at Quitman St.*
John Ben Shepperd (October 19, 1915–March 8, 1990)
A native of Gladewater, John Ben Shepperd began a law practice in Longview soon after his graduation from the University of Texas Law School in 1941. After service in World War II, he gained prominence as national president of the Jaycees. His public service career began in 1946, when he was appointed to fill his father's unexpired term as county commissioner. Governor Allan Shivers appointed Shepperd secretary of state in 1950. He was elected attorney general in 1952 and was reelected in 1954. As attorney general, he attacked political corruption in Duval County and the misuse of state veterans land funds. After retiring from public office in 1957, Shepperd moved to Odessa where he practiced law and supported numerous civic and charitable endeavors. He was appointed to a number of state and national boards and commissions, including the Texas State Historical Survey Committee (now Texas Historical Commission). He was the driving force in the growth and development of the Historical Marker Program, which became nationally recognized during his term as chairman. He renovated his Gladewater boyhood home and farm after his retirement. He is buried in the family cemetery south of town. (1992)

GLEN ROSE (Somervell Co.) *SH 144, 4 mi. N*
Squaw Creek Indian Fight, 1864
Civil War frontier victory, near this site. About 25 raiding Indians jumped a fox hunter, Rigman Bryant, killed him, shot his dog, stole his horse. That afternoon the Indians and stolen horses were seen by a minister, Silas Scarborough, W. C. Walters and a Negro bringing home a turn of meal from the gristmill. Scarborough and Walters headed into a cedar brake. The Indians urged the Negro to join them, shot him full of arrows when he refused. In a few hours the Cavalry attacked the Indians, recovered the horses, killed one Indian, chased the others away. One settler was shot. In a week the wounded Negro died. Many of the 1848–1861 settlers on the Paluxy and Squaw Creek were away in the Confederate Army. Very young boys and elderly men joined defense forces. Some drew military duty for 10 days, were off 10 days to look after mills, cattle, horses and farms. For safety, women dressed as men while their sons, husbands and fathers were away. At times 50 to 100 tents were used in hasty "forting up" of families. During the war, Alex McCammant established county's first tannery, using cedar leaves in processing hides. For cloth making, county's first cotton was grown. (1965)

GLEN ROSE (Somervell Co.) *US 67, 8 mi. E*
Barnard's Trading Post No. 2
The Torrey brothers of Connecticut and their childhood friend George Barnard, with President Sam Houston as a partner, contracted to build a series of trading posts along the Brazos River in 1843. Barnard's friendly manner made the Indians his friends, paving the way for more peaceful frontier settlement. In 1846, George ransomed a young girl, Juana Cavasos, from a group of Comanches at the post on Tehuacana Creek near Waco for $300. By 1847, she had married his brother Charles. In 1849, Charles and George established a post within this valley where Charles and Juana would live. In view of Comanche Peak in modern-day Hood County, the second post was four miles north of this site and near a Shawnee-Delaware village, trading goods from a bulletproof "dog-run" log house, the brothers did an excellent business, and Juana's influence on the region equaled theirs. Two Anglo communities sprang up in the area: George's Creek and Fort Spunky. The government relocated the area's Indian population to Oklahoma in 1859; the need for a trading post dwindled. 1860 found Charles and Juana beginning a community on the Paluxy River, where he built a large stone gristmill. The town that grew around the mill was called Barnard's Mill, later renamed Glen Rose. (1998)

GLEN ROSE (Somervell Co.) *US 67, 2 mi. W*
Booker Home
This home was built in the early 1870s by William G. McCamant, who came to Texas about 1856. McCamant, who had worked for the creation of Somervell County, was appointed one of the county's first commissioners. The house was sold to Civil War veteran George L. Booker in 1896, during his 36-year tenure as county surveyor. The house features 18-inch thick walls made of limestone that was quarried nearby. The chimneys on either end are typical of 1870s frontier homes. (1963)

GLEN ROSE (Somervell Co.)

107 Vernon St. at SH 144, courthouse

Dinosaur Tracks

Formed 100,000,000 years ago, tracks of 3 kinds of dinosaurs are preserved in the limestone below Paluxy River. Types include Acrocanthosaurus (a meat-eater), Camptosaurus (plant-eater who left 3-toed bird-like tracks), and Pleurocoelus (a plant-eater who made huge 5-toed prints). For years following their discovery (about 1910), the tracks remained a novelty. When Paluxy River ran low, farmers caught catfish stranded in them. Excavations by a prominent museum and several universities in 1938 brought the tracks to the attention of the world.   (1970)

GLIDDEN (Colorado Co.)

US 90 at 8th St.

Glidden

Before the railroad came to Colorado County, this area was the origin of several cattle drives to northern markets. Early settlers in the region were area gravel industry pioneer J. N. Mahon; John Turnbough, a contractor who came in 1877; rancher J. L. Townsend, who purchased land in 1879 and later served as Colorado County sheriff; T. J. Oakes, A. A. Oakes, and A. J. Folts, founders of a mercantile business that remained in operation for more than 100 years; and the L. H. Schulenburg family, who developed the first addition to Glidden. In 1882, T. J. Oakes sold land to the Galveston, Harrisburg & San Antonio Railway Company. A switchyard, depot, roundhouse, turntable, water well, and section house were built. H. T. Youens was station agent in 1885. The townsite of Glidden, named for railroad engineer F. G. Glidden, was platted that year and quickly developed as a rail center for the surrounding area. Many Scotch-Irish and English railroad workers were attracted to Glidden during its early years. In 1888, the post office was established, and by 1897 a school had opened. Although Glidden has continued as a railroad town, many changes have taken place in the rail industry and in the community. The history of Glidden is an important part of Colorado County's heritage.   (1985)

GOLDSMITH (Ector Co.)

SH 158, at city limits

North Cowden

Site of Ector County's second big oil strike. Named for ranching family of John M. Cowden, an 1885 Permian Basin settler. One of 4 brothers, ranching community leaders on Texas frontier. Oil and gas development began here with the L. No. 1 discovery. Post office granted 1947. Town continues as a Permian Basin petroleum source. (Only the site now remains.)

GOLDTHWAITE (Mills Co.)

US 84, 8.5 mi. E

Center City Cemetery

The Center City Cemetery began with the burials in 1874 of Julia M. Bishop and M. E. Hughes, the adult and infant daughters of W. C. and Caroline Hughes, early settlers of this area. Judge L. E. Patterson purchased 2.5 acres containing the Hughes burials in 1905 for use as a community graveyard. Concern for its upkeep prompted the establishment of a cemetery committee in 1951. A $1000 gift to the cemetery in J. M. Dalton's will in 1967 helped establish a maintenance fund. The more than 500 burials recorded here include those of many of this area's earliest settlers.   (1993)

GOLDTHWAITE (Mills Co.)

US 183 right-of-way, 7 mi. S in
Lady Bird Johnson Roadside Park

The San Saba Peak

Rising to an altitude of 1,712 feet, San Saba Peak is an oblong promontory with rimrock edges on the north and west sides. The Spanish governor of Texas, Don Juan Antonio Bustillo y Cevallos, named the ancient landmark in 1732. Tales of lost silver mines have centered on the surrounding area for centuries. Inhabited by early Indians, San Saba Peak has been a landmark for pioneers, surveyors, and cowboys; the site of battles between Indians and early settlers; a signpost on the Fort Phantom Hill supply road; a register for Western travelers; and a setting for Easter services.

(Texas Sesquicentennial 1836–1986)

GOLDTHWAITE (Mills Co.)

US 183, at courthouse

Mills County

Formed from Brown, Comanche, Hamilton and Lampasas Counties. Created March 15, 1887. Organized August 30, 1887. Named in honor of John T. Mills, 1817–1871. Judge of the Third and Seventh Judicial Districts in the Republic of Texas. Goldthwaite, county seat.

GOLDTHWAITE (Mills Co.)   *US 183 at courthouse*
Mills County Jail, 1888
First structure built by newly organized county, before county seat was chosen. Awarded Medallion Plate.   (1965)

GOLDTHWAITE (Mills Co.)   *FM 574 at CR 433, 18.5 mi. W*
The Regency Suspension Bridge (Near Extinct Town of Regency, 22 mi. SW)
This area's first Colorado River bridge was at Regency, on Mills–San Saba County line. Built 1903, it served ranchers and farmers for going to market, but fell in 1924, killing a boy, a horse, and some cattle. Its successor was demolished by a 1936 flood. With 90 percent of the work done by hand labor, the Regency suspension bridge was erected in 1939. It became the pride of the locality, and youths gathered there in the 1940s to picnic, dance, and sing. Bypassed by paved farm roads, it now (1976) survives as one of the last suspension bridges in Texas.   (1976)

GOLDTHWAITE (Mills Co.)   *SH 16, 1 mi. S*
Goldthwaite Memorial Cemetery
In 1888, three local men bought land for use as a cemetery; the first burial was that of Houston Roberts. The Odd Fellows Lodge bought the grounds in 1894, adding land over the years. Watson Whittaker was killed during an 1898 train robbery and made headlines as a funeral train brought him to Mills County for burial here. The lodge sold the cemetery in 1943 to the city, and it became Goldthwaite Memorial Cemetery. Local groups made improvements and placed memorials to honor the sacrifice of area veterans buried here. Today, the cemetery provides a link to area history.   (2003)

GOLIAD (Goliad Co.)   *US 183/77A, 14 mi. N*
Weser
Many German and Polish immigrants came to Texas in the 19th century on a ship named "Weser." Arriving at the Port of Galveston, a number of the pioneer settlers made their way overland to this area, establishing a community in the 1850s and 1860s. By 1881, when a post office was granted, it was officially named Weser for the ship that had brought the immigrants to America. By 1900 the settlement included, in addition to the post office, a general merchandise store, a steam grist mill, a cotton gin, a school, a blacksmith shop, a Western Union Telegraph office, a saloon, a Sons of Hermann Lodge hall and a dance hall. A community brass band entertained residents and played for local celebrations. The population of Weser consisted primarily of farmers and ranchers and their families. The school they established for their children served as a focal point and gathering place for area residents. Early facilities were replaced with a new building erected by volunteers in 1903. It continued to serve students in the Weser area until 1943, when it closed its doors. The building was later sold and moved out of the community. The highest population figure recorded for the town was 153 in 1904. It remained steady until the 1920s, when new generations began moving away to larger cities for greater economic opportunities. By the 1930s only two businesses remained in Weser, and the population had dropped to 50, a figure that remained steady for the remainder of the 20th century. Although smaller in number now, the Weser community represents a typical rural settlement in Goliad County.   (1999)

GOLIAD (Goliad Co.)   *US 59, 4 mi. E*
Site of September 1824 Indian Treaty
After finding bones of 2 men eaten by Karankawa Indians, Stephen F. Austin and 100 Texans met near here with a priest and men of La Bahía, where the Indians had taken refuge. The Indians were pledged to keep away from Texas colony. Breaking of the treaty caused tribe later to be driven from Texas.   (1967)

GOLIAD (Goliad Co.)   *US 59, 4.5 mi. W in roadside park*
Goliad County
First known to Spanish settlers as Nuestra Señora de Loreto, later called La Bahía del Espíritu Santo. Established as a mission in 1749. Became a strategic fort under Spanish, Mexican, Texas occupancy, 1810–1821, 1835–1836. Name changed to Goliad and created a Mexican municipality in 1829. Scene of massacre of Fannin and his command in 1836. Organized as a county, 1836, with town of Goliad as the county seat. Home of Confederate General Hamilton P. Bee. From population of 3,384, county sent several army companies to the Civil War.   (1965)

GOLIAD (Goliad Co.) *US 59, 4 mi. W*
Mission Nuestra Señora del Rosario
(Mission Our Lady of the Rosary)
Founded in 1754 for the Cujane Indians. Capt. Manuel Ramirez de la Piseina, commander of nearby Presidio la Bahía, named this mission for his parish church in Spain, and Fray Juan Dios Camberos ministered to the first converts here. The Indians were taught crop-raising. In the years following, much livestock, including 30,000 head of cattle, belonged to Rosario. But these, along with Indian land at the mission, had to be surrendered later to the Spanish crown. In 1807 Rosario was permanently abandoned and its lands were distributed to Spanish settlers. (1969)

GOLIAD (Goliad Co.) *Market St. at courthouse*
Santa Anna's Surrender Ratified
Gen. Vicente Filasola, second in command of Mexican armies in Texas War for Independence, fled from area of his nation's defeat at San Jacinto, April 21, 1836. Filasola's aim was to go back to Mexico with his army. After he had passed through Goliad, he was overtaken at Mujerero Creek (12 mi. SW) by Texan army couriers, Col. Ben Fort Smith and Capt. Henry Teal. Signing the ratification of peace at Mujerero, May 26, 1836, were Gen. Filasola, Gen. Eugene Tolsa, Col. Augustine Amat, Col. Smith, and Capt. Teal. (1970)

GOLIAD (Goliad Co.) *US 77A/183 .25 mi. S, Goliad State Park and Historic Site*
Mission Nuestra Señora del Espíritu Santo de Zuñiga
(Mission of Our Lady of the Holy Spirit of Zuñiga)
Founded in 1722 by the Aguayo Expedition on "La Bahía del Espiritu Santo" (the Bay of the Holy Spirit), present Lavaca Bay. This mission reflects its former site in the popular name, "La Bahía." Its formal name (in part) honored Baltasar de Zuniga, Viceroy of New Spain. Because of threats from the French and the Indians, Spain founded this mission and its auxiliary fort, Presidio Nuestra Señora de Loreto de La Bahía (now ¼ mi. SE) to defend its territory and convert the natives. Difficulties, however, caused both to be moved, in only four years, to the Guadalupe River, and again in 1749 to this site on the San Antonio River. At its peak of success the mission possessed huge herds of cattle and supplied settlements in Mexico, as well as missions in present Texas. In 1758 about 180 persons resided at the mission and fort. All about were Indian "Jacales," crude clayplastered brush huts thatched with grass. Spacious grazing lands and fertile fields surrounded the area, where colonists had formed a small community. After a general decline caused the mission to be secularized in 1830, it fell into ruin. In 1932, this land was deeded to the state by Goliad County. The mission complex was partially restored, 1936–1939. (1969)

Cattle Drive from La Bahia
After Spain joined the American colonists in declaring war on England in 1779, Spanish soldier Bernardo de Galvez traveled to New Orleans to raise an army. Aware of the great number of wild cattle in Texas from his time spent stationed in the region, Galvez asked the Spanish governor of Texas to send cattle to feed his troops. As a result, about 10,000 head of cattle from Texas missions and ranches were assembled at Presidio La Bahia. Between 1779 and 1782, in what is believed to be the first major Texas cattle drive, cattle were herded from La Bahia to Spanish soldiers preparing to fight in the American Revolution along the Gulf Coast. (1999)

Judge James Arthur White and the
Civilian Conservation Corps at Goliad State Park
Mississippi native and Goliad County Judge James Arthur White (1878–1953) possessed a fervent interest in Texas history, notably that of his adopted city of Goliad. He began in 1928 to organize support for a state park to protect Goliad's many significant historic sites. Judge White drafted a bill in 1931 to create the park and a state-funded bridge and highway (later U.S. 183). Despite the bleak financial prospects of the Depression era, Judge White secured funding and labor from the Federal Civil Works Administration in 1933. When funds were expended by 1934, White applied to the Civilian Conservation Corps (CCC) program. Preliminary study of the site began in March 1935. Forty cottages, each to house six men, were constructed in May. The first CCC enrollees to arrive were veterans of the Spanish American War, the Boxer Rebellion in China and World War I. They had their own newspaper, "The Goliad Veteran," and their evening schedules included an extensive educational program. Historians and architects traveled the U.S. and Mexico

researching Spanish Colonial Mission architecture. Supervised by National Park Service architects and local craftsmen, the CCC workers ultimately reconstructed a school-workshop, church and granary at Mission Espiritu Santo and also erected maintenance and shop buildings, a latrine, custodian's lodge, museum and administration building and developed a state park road and picnic facilities. Judge White served on the Texas Centennial Commission, and through his influence Goliad received $100,000 in state and federal funds for Memorial Auditorium (1937) and a burial monument for Col. J. W. Fannin and his men (1939). The CCC camp was closed by June 1941 due to the threat of World War II. (2000)

Aranama College
Named for 18th century Indian converts of mission Espiritu Santo de Zuniga. A men's college. Founded 1852 by Western Presbytery of Texas. Used buildings of old mission plus funds given by Goliad. Taught Latin, Greek, geography, surveying, bookkeeping, writing, reading, elementary and higher mathematics, English grammar and orthography. Closed like most of Texas 25 colleges after the Civil War began (1861) and most students joined the Confederate Army. Had its buildings wrecked by the great storm of 1886. (1965)

GOLIAD (Goliad Co.) US 77A/183, 1 mi. S, Presidio La Bahia
La Bahía Mission
The Mission of Espíritu Santo de Zuñiga or La Bahía was established as an Indian school in 1749 and that of Rosario de los Cujanes 1754. A non-mission school for the families of soldiers and settlers was begun by Juan Manuel Zambrano with Jose Galan as teacher in 1818. The buildings of the old mission were leased by Rev. John Hillyer for a girls' school in 1848 and were used by the Presbytery of Western Texas for more than 20 years as Aranama College. Beginning in 1852 Payne Female Institute was conducted in Goliad, 1852–1885.

Presidio de Nuestra Señora de Loreto de la Bahía
(Fort of Our Lady of Loreto of the Bay)
One of the most historic Spanish forts in Texas. Popularly called Presidio la Bahía, it was founded on Espiritu Santo (present Lavaca) Bay in 1722. Twice moved, it was re-established here in 1749 to protect Espiritu Santo Mission (¼ mi. NW). In the chapel is the statue of Our Lady of Loreto placed here in 1749. The turbulent history of this fort has often rung with the sound of revolution. Between 1812 and 1820 several irregular "filibustering" forces, including the Gutierrez-Magee Expedition and others led by James Long and Henry Perry, occupied or assailed the fort for various idealistic and profiteering motives. Here, too, 92 Texas citizens and soldiers drew up and signed Texas' first formal Declaration of Independence on December 20, 1835. In the ensuing War for Texas Independence, Col. James Fannin and 341 prisoners of war were held here and, on Palm Sunday, 1836, were massacred in and around the fort by their Mexican captors. When the fort was authentically restored, 1936–1967, by the Kathryn O'Connor Foundation, nine "levels of occupancy" were uncovered. Church services are now held in the chapel. The presidio has been named a registered national historic landmark. (1969)

General Ignacio Zaragoza (January 14, 1829–September 8, 1862)
Nacio en este lugar cuando se llamaba "Bahía del Espiritu Santo." En 1855, al mando de un ejercito de voluntarios Mexicanos, contribuya a la derrota del Dictador Santa Anna. Siempre fue caudillo en la defensa de su patria, el 5 de Mayo de 1862, durante la invasion de las fuerzas Francesas de Napoleon III y Maximiliano, en la Batalla de Puebla y al mando de 4,000 soldados mal armados, derroto a 8,000 Zuavos veteranos Franceses. Esta heroica victoria dio a Mexico su gran fiesta patriotica nacional "El Cinco de Mayo." Born on this site when it was called "Bahía del Espiritu Santo." In 1855, at the head of an army of Mexican volunteers, contributed to the defeat of Dictator Santa Anna. Always a leader in the defense of his country, on May 5, 1862, during the invasion of the French forces of Napoleon III and Maximilian, in the Battle of Puebla, he led 4,000 poorly armed soldiers to defeat 8,000 veteran French Zouaves. This heroic victory gave Mexico its great national patriotic anniversary, "El Cinco de Mayo." (1967)

Manuel Becerra
Born at Presidio La Bahía del Espíritu Santo in 1762, Manuel Becerra played a significant role in the settlement and politics of the region. Becerra and his wife, Juana María Cadena, and their two daughters, María Josefa and Gertrudis, were leading citizens of La Bahía. In 1820, Antonio María

Martínez, the last Spanish governor of Texas, called for the formation of the ayuntamiento of La Bahía as required in the Spanish Constitution of 1812. The ayuntamiento, or town council, included Manuel Becerra, who was elected its first secretary. Becerra's involvement with colonization efforts came the following year, as he was selected to accompany Stephen F. Austin to the Colorado River to find a suitable site for Austin's first colony. His friendship with empresario Martín de León led to his eventual responsibility within de León's Guadalupe Colony in 1827, when de León placed Becerra in charge of the colony's political and business affairs. The same year, Becerra helped negotiate a treaty with the Coco and Karankawa tribes to enhance peace and stability in the region. In 1832, Becerra received a land grant of 8,856 acres in what is now Refugio County and later assisted colonizer James Power in the colonization of the Power Colony at Villa de Refugio. As a citizen under the flags of Spain, Mexico, the Republic of Texas and the United States, Manuel Becerra bore witness to many of the formative events in Texas history and played a significant role in colonization efforts. He died in what is now Refugio County about 1849.   (2001)

Angel of Goliad
Amid the cruelties of the Texas War for Independence, one notable woman committed acts of bravery and compassion. Francisca Alavez (also known by similar names) accompanied Mexican Army Capt. Telesforo Alavez to Texas in March 1836. In seven incidents between March and April, she intervened with Mexican troops under command of Gen. José de Urrea to help captured Texian prisoners at Agua Dulce, Copano, La Bahia, Victoria and Matamoros. On Mar. 20, Maj. William P. Miller and 75 men of his Nashville Battalion were captured as they unloaded their ship at Copano Bay. Alavez insisted that binding cords which cut off circulation be removed and food and water provided. The men were moved to Presidio La Bahia at Goliad, where hundreds of Col. James Fannin's troops were already held after their capture at Coleto Creek. At least 342 men were taken out of the fort on Mar. 27 and shot under orders of Gen. Santa Anna in what was termed the Goliad Massacre. Alavez helped save the lives of many men, including 16-year-old Benjamin Hughes. Another survivor, Dr. J. H. Barnard, recalled that she pleaded for their lives, helped sneak out some troops at night and hid some of the men. Her humanitarian acts included tending to wounds and sending messages and provisions to those still imprisoned. The Texas Centennial of 1936 revived interest in Alavez with articles, a play, and a bronze bust and historical mural for Goliad's Memorial Auditorium. Additional commemorations, such as a resolution from the Texas Legislature in 2001, have helped confirm Dr. Barnard's assertion that "her name deserves to be recorded in letters of gold among those angels who have from time to time been commissioned by an overruling and beneficent power to relieve the sorrows and cheer the hearts of men."   (2009)

Replica of Texas Independence Flagpole
Displays a replica of banner unfurled Dec. 20, 1835, at signing of Declaration of Independence of Texas from tyranny of Santa Anna's regime in Mexico. That declaration, drafted by staunch early patriots Philip Dimmitt and Ira Ingram, and signed by 92 citizens and soldiers, was later suppressed as premature, but it forecast coming events. A battle flag used 11 weeks earlier (and sometimes called "First Flag of Texas") lacked the support of a formal declaration of independence. The Goliad flag also waved over an army—one in possession of fort at La Bahía.   (1968)

Grave of Col. J. W. Fannin and His Men
After Battle of Coleto (March 19–20, 1836), where a Texas army under Col. James Walker Fannin met defeat by Mexicans in superior numbers, the Texas soldiers were held in Presidio la Bahia, supposedly as war prisoners. However, by order of Mexican Gen. Antonio Lopez de Santa Anna, approximately 400 of Fannin's men were marched out and massacred on Palm Sunday, March 27, 1836. The wounded were shot one by one in the fort compound. Col. Fannin was the last to die. Because of their profession, Drs. J. H. Barnard, J. E. Field and Jack Shackelford were spared; about 25 men were saved by a Mexican woman, "The Angel of Goliad." Approximately 30 escaped by feigning death or by swimming the San Antonio River. The Texans' corpses were stripped and partly burned, but left unburied. This atrocity three weeks after the fall of the Alamo gave Texans part of the battle cry—"Remember the Alamo! Remember la Bahía!"—under which decisive victory was won at San Jacinto on April 21, 1836. Gen. Thomas J. Rusk and the Texan army afterwards marched here and gathered the bones of Fannin's men from the terrain. From Presidio la Bahía, the remains were carried in procession to the grave, and there given a military funeral and burial on June 3, 1836.

GOLIAD (Goliad Co.) *SH 239 and Pettus Lane, 13 mi. W*
Pettus Cemetery
Virginia native John Freeman Pettus (b. 1808) came to Texas in the early 1820s as a member of Stephen F. Austin's first colony. During the Texas Revolution he served with Ben Milam in the siege of Bexar and participated in the Battle of San Jacinto. Soon after moving his family to Goliad County about 1876, he chose this site near his home as the family burial ground. Pettus died in 1878 and was the first buried here. Graves include those of 3 other Austin colonists: Elizabeth Pettus, Sarah Pettus, and Phoebe Scott; and a San Jacinto veteran, James Austin Clements.   (1981)

GONZALES (Gonzales Co.) *US 90A, 2 mi. NW*
Duncan Ferry (Site 1 mi. S)
Started about 1834 by Benj. Duncan (1793–1866), a Scotchman. According to tradition, Mrs. Almaron Dickinson stopped first at Duncan's home on her way to tell people of Gonzales of fall of the Alamo. She was one of few survivors of this bloody Battle of Texas Revolution in which many Gonzales men died. Upon hearing news, General Sam Houston ordered retreat of the Texas Army (camped in Gonzales) and on night of March 13, 1836, he had town and ferry burned to keep them from enemy hands. Duncan later rebuilt ferry, which was operated until 1866.   (1971)

GONZALES (Gonzales Co.) *US 90A, 1.2 mi. W past San Marcos River bridge*
James Hodges, Sr.
James Hodges, Sr., came to Gonzales in April 1835. Soon after his arrival, he purchased four leagues (17,721 acres) of land at the forks of the San Marcos and Guadalupe Rivers for $3,000 in silver. On September 26, 1835, in an election held under the auspices of the Gonzales Committee of Public Safety, Hodges was elected one of six delegates to the Consultation of 1835. Convened in San Felipe de Austin on November 3, delegates to the Consultation created a provisional government and organized an army under the command of Sam Houston. Returning to Gonzales after the Consultation, Hodges provided supplies for the Texas Army in 1836. He and his family left the area during the Runaway Scrape, but later returned to Gonzales County. In 1838, Hodges served on the county's Board of Land Commissioners. Twice married, James Hodges was the father of eight children. He and his family continued to live on their land on the San Marcos and Guadalupe Rivers. After his death on December 24, 1846, Hodges was buried on the family farm in a plot which became known as the Hodges Family Cemetery (about one mile southeast).   (1990)

GONZALES (Gonzales Co.) *US 183 right-of-way at US 90A, .25 mi. N*
Fort Waul
Named for Confederate General Thomas N. Waul, Fort Waul was built to defend inland Texas from possible Federal advances up the Guadalupe River from the Gulf of Mexico, as well as to provide protection for military supply trains. Construction of the earthen fortification was overseen by Col. Albert Miller Lea, Confederate Army engineer. Begun in late 1863, the fort was partly built by slave labor and measured approximately 250 by 750 feet. Surviving records do not indicate whether the fort was ever actually completed.   (1988)

GONZALES (Gonzales Co.) *Sarah Dewitt Dr. (US 90/SH 97) at FM 794*
Site of Confederate Fort
Surveyed 1864 by Lt. Col. Albert M. Lea. Built to fortify Gonzales against attack by Federal gun boats. Constructed from stones of male building of Gonzales College. Marker placed by Texas Society, Children of the American Revolution, 1961.   (1964)

GONZALES (Gonzales Co.) *US 90A, 10 mi. E*
⅛ mi. N is Sam Houston Oak
⅛ mile north is where General Sam Houston established his headquarters camp, March 13, 1836, after burning the town of Gonzales. Under this oak his small army was joined by many volunteers from the eastern settlements, who went with him to San Jacinto.   (1965)

GONZALES (Gonzales Co.) *US 90A, 6 mi. E*
2 mi. N to Site of Maurin Quarry
In operation 1883–1908, this quarry supplied sandstone for buildings in Gonzales, Shiner, Moulton, Flatonia, Hallettsville. Stone was first dynamited, then cut by hand. It was shipped by wagon until railroad was built. The founder was Firmin Maurin, from Marseilles, France. (1969)

GONZALES (Gonzales Co.)   *US 90A, 2 mi. E on Spur 146*
Route of Old Chisholm Trail
Blazed by trail boss Thornton Chisholm on an 1866 drive from Cardwell's Flat, near Cuero, to Austin (Texas) and Missouri, this section of the famous trail was used until 1869. Over it thundered thousands of cattle headed for northern markets, where sale of beef meant cash to Texas cattlemen and economic growth during the post–Civil War period. Until the railroad was built from Texas to Dodge City, trails such as this were also the only supply line for U.S. forts, Indian reservations and large Kansas-centered markets.   (1967)

GONZALES (Gonzales Co.)   *US 90A, 2 mi. E near Ken Creek*
David Burkett (1798–1845)
Progressive patriot and citizen soldier in Texas War for Independence. A member of Green DeWitt's colony. Came to Texas with his family, 1830. Served as a guard for women and children fleeing Gonzales before the approach of Santa Anna, 1836. Is buried on his 4,428-acre land grant extending south from this site.   (1966)

GONZALES (Gonzales Co.)   *Spur 146, Kerr Creek*
Kerr's Creek
Commissioned to found a capital for colony of Green DeWitt, ex-Missouri state Senator James Kerr settled here. He and six other men built homes on this stream—known ever since as Kerr's Creek. After a destructive Indian raid in 1826, the settlement was abandoned.   (1966)

GONZALES (Gonzales Co.)   *1200 blk. of St. Louis St.*
Route of Gen. Sam Houston to San Jacinto
Stricken with news of the fall of the Alamo and threatened by a massive Mexican army, Sam Houston gathered the nucleus of a Texan army here, issued orders to burn this town (to hinder the Mexicans) and marched east, March 13, 1836. He won victory at San Jacinto, April 21.   (1969)

GONZALES (Gonzales Co.)   *off US 183, St. Louis at St. Joseph Sts.*
Battle of Gonzales
The first battle of the Texas Revolution, fought on the west side of the Guadalupe River about four miles above Gonzales on October 2, 1835, came to be known as the Lexington of Texas. The incident grew out of Col. Domingo de Ugartechea's demand late in September for a cannon given to the settlement for defense against Indians. When the colonists refused to deliver the cannon, Ugartechea sent 150 dragoons to demand the weapon. Alcalde Andrew Ponton, in the meantime, sent word to other colonists that he had refused to surrender the cannon, which on September 29 was buried in George W. Davis' peach orchard. From September 30 to October 2 the number of defenders at Gonzales had grown from 18 to about 160. Under command of John H. Moore and J. W. E. Wallace they dug up the cannon, mounted it on ox-cart wheels, filled it with chains and scrap iron, crossed the river and marched toward the enemy. When the Texan scouts discovered the Mexican force early October 2, they fired their pieces and retired with the Mexicans in pursuit. A discharge from the six-pounder caused the latter to retreat. When the Texans opened with their artillery and charged the enemy his force was driven back in the direction of San Antonio.

GONZALES (Gonzales Co.)   *200 block of St. Louis St.*
First Shot of the Texas Revolution
On this site September 29, 1835 the Gonzales cannon was buried from the 150 Mexican dragoons sent to demand it. Three days later it was mounted on ox-cart wheels, loaded with chains and scrap iron, and fired at the Mexican army, the first shot of the revolution. This location was known as George W. Davis peach orchard.   (1965)

GONZALES (Gonzales Co.)   *US 183, 1 mi. S at Guadalupe River Bridge*
Old Eighteen
On this site, September 29, 1835, began the strategy of the 18 Texians who by advising with Alcalde Andrew Ponton, held for two days 150 Mexican dragoons sent to demand the Gonzales cannon, allowing colonists time to mass recruits for the Battle of Gonzales.
The Old Eighteen
Captain Albert Martin, Almond Cottle, Jacob C. Darst, Ezekiel Williams, Winslow Turner, Simeon Bateman, Wm. W. Arrington, Joseph D. Clements, Gravis Fulcher, Almaron Dickerson,

George W. Davis, Benjamin Fuqua, John Sowell, Valentine Bennet, James B. Hinds, Charles Mason, Thomas R. Miller, Thomas Jackson. (1965)

GONZALES (Gonzales Co.) *US 183, 1 mi. S*
Site of Gonzales Cannon Dispute
On this site September 29, 1835, the Mexican government troops demanded the return of the Gonzales cannon. After two days delay, awaiting recruits, the colonists answered, "Come and Take It." (1965)

GONZALES (Gonzales Co.) *US 183, 1.7 mi. S*
Santa Anna Mound
Extending from this point one-quarter mile west is Santa Anna Mound, formerly De Witt Mound, now site De Witt family cemetery. Here Mexican troops camped between September 29 and October 1, 1835, awaiting delivery of the Gonzales cannon. Colonists refusing to surrender cannon, the Mexicans retreated toward Bexar, where on October 2, five miles west, the Texians overtook them. The Battle of Gonzales ensued with Texians as victors. (1965)

GONZALES (Gonzales Co.) *SH 97, 3 mi. SW*
Site of the First Shot of the Texas Revolution Near Gonzales
Near here on October 2, 1835 was fired the first shot of the Texas Revolution of 1835–1836, the shot heard round the world. At Gonzales the Texians defied the Mexican government and refused their demand for the Gonzales cannon with the "Come and Take It" challenge until reinforcements arrived from other parts of De Witt's colony and from the colonies on the Colorado and Brazos. They then pursued the Mexicans from Gonzales to near this point and fired upon them with this cannon, driving them back to Bexar. This shot started the revolution and was directly responsible for adding more territory to the United States than was acquired by the freeing of the original thirteen colonies from England.

GONZALES (Gonzales Co.) *SH 97, 6.5 mi. SW*
The First Shot of the Texas Revolution
(Erected by the school children of Gonzales)
This is the site of the first battle of the Texas Revolution and the monument marks the exact spot where the first shot of the Texas fight for freedom was fired. Here, over the Texas forces commanded by Col. J. H. Moore and Lt. Col. J. W. E. Wallace, waved the famous battle flag inscribed "Come and Take It." When the cannon was fired, the Mexican forces broke rank and fled in terror, leaving one dead on the battlefield.

GONZALES (Gonzales Co.) *SH 97, 7 mi. SW*
The First Shot of the Texas Revolution
One and one-half miles from here the first shot of the Texas Revolution was fired from a small cannon by Texans under the command of Col. John H. Moore, October 2, 1835. (1965)

GONZALES (Gonzales Co.) *US 97, 7 mi. SW*
Memorial Monument—First Shot Texas Revolution
The monument in this roadside park was erected by the State of Texas in recognition of the fact that the first shot of the Texas Revolution was fired near here on October 2, 1835. Bronze and granite, designed and cast by Waldine Tauch, world famous sculptress.

GONZALES (Gonzales Co.) *SH 80, 1.6 mi. N of Nixon*
Ghost Town of Dewville (Site 7 mi. NW)
Small farming community. Started in 1850s. Named for Frank Dew (1862–1940), early settler. The main buildings were a store, Masonic lodge hall, gin, Sandies Chapel (Methodist, founded 1897), a school (1898). Post office was established in 1901. After populace dwindled, post office closed, 1955. (1971)

GOODNIGHT (Armstrong Co.) *US 287 and FM 294, 1 mi. E*
Site of Old Goodnight Ranch
First ranch in the Texas Panhandle. Established in 1876 by Charles Goodnight, 1836–1929. Noted scout, Indian fighter, trail blazer and rancher, the Burbank of the range. (1964)

GOODNIGHT (Armstrong Co.) *FM 294 near US 287 at community center*
Town of Goodnight
Named in honor of Charles Goodnight, 1836–1929. Noted scout, Indian fighter and trailblazer, who established the first ranch in the Texas Panhandle in 1876 and is also known as the "Burbank of the Range."

GOODNIGHT (Armstrong Co.) *US 287 near Goodnight home*
Charles Goodnight (1836–1929)
Texas Ranger, Indian fighter. At age 19, on way to California gold fields, saw ranching possibilities, settled and started ranch in Palo Pinto County, 230 miles southeast of here. In Civil War, scout, guide and hunter for frontier regiment Texas Cavalry, protecting settlers from Indian raids and federal invasion. With Oliver Loving, moved cattle herds across arid West Texas and New Mexico lands dominated by Comanche Indians, establishing Goodnight-Loving Trail northeast to U.S. forts. Founded old Goodnight College.

GRAFORD (Palo Pinto Co.) *SH 254, 3 mi. E in roadside park*
Simpson Crawford
A native of Kentucky, Simpson Crawford (1824–1908) served in the Mexican War (1846–1848) at Vera Cruz and Mexico City. Following the war he returned to Kentucky and married Elizabeth Evans. In 1852, they moved to Texas, settling first in Titus County. In 1854, they came to Palo Pinto County and built a home (¾ mi. NW) in the Keechi Valley area of Peters Colony. A successful rancher owning 3,100 acres, Crawford also served in the Texas Rangers. His first wife died in 1858 and he married Mary Brown four years later. He is buried in Crawford Cemetery (1.5 mi. N). (1980)

GRAFORD (Palo Pinto Co.) *SH 254, 2 mi. E*
Alfred Lane (March 7, 1827–July 15, 1864)
Remembered as a "splendid brave man" by his brother-in-law, cattleman Charles Goodnight, Tennessee native Alfred Lane moved to Texas with his family in 1836 and settled in Robertson's Colony on the Brazos River. Following his marriage to Elizabeth Annie Goodnight in 1851, Lane moved to the Black Springs area of Palo Pinto County in 1856, where he raised horses on the open range of the Keechi Valley. He scouted with the Texas Rangers frontier regiment during the Civil War. After helping Goodnight drive cattle west of Fort Belknap, Lane was killed by Indians as he returned home. He is buried nearby in Crawford Cemetery along with his wife, Elizabeth (2 mi. NE). (1997)

GRAFORD (Palo Pinto Co.) *SH 254, 2 mi. E*
The George Rice Bevers Homesite
On the Fort Worth–Fort Belknap Road, near Flat Rock Crossing of Keechi Creek. Occupied 1854 when such travelers as Indian agent Robert S. Neighbors were fed or housed overnight by Bevers. First Palo Pinto County school opened in vicinity in 1856, on a path smoothed by oxen pulling a log. In Bevers cemetery lies a victim of 1860s Indian raids that sent settlers to refuges as remote as the courthouse in Fort Worth. Bevers (1825–1904), his wife, Lucinda Jane Tacker (1825–1873), and children lived near Curetons, Goodnights, Slaughters, other noted pioneers. (1971)

GRAFORD (Palo Pinto Co.) *SH 337 E of junction with SH 16*
Comanche Trail through Palo Pinto County
Plains Indians of the 18th century blazed a trail to a Taovaya village on the Red River from raids on settlements in northern New Spain. The trail linked watering holes and natural provisions crucial to survival for Comanches, Kiowas and allied tribes. At the Taovaya camp, Indians traded for goods brought upriver by French traders. For generations, Native Americans, Spanish military, trade and treaty expeditions, American explorers, and early settlers used the trail. The Comanche Trail entered western Palo Pinto County at the Brazos River near the mouth of Caddo Creek, turning northeast at McAdams Peak and crossing Dillingham Prairie. Part of the historic trail now lies beneath Possum Kingdom Lake. (2007)

GRAFORD (Palo Pinto Co.) *FM 2353, .5 mi. S, 15 mi. SW, Observation Point*
Morris Sheppard Dam and Possum Kingdom Lake—
A Project of the Brazos River Authority
Built in response to disastrous Brazos River flooding, Morris Sheppard Dam and Possum Kingdom Reservoir were early attempts at water conservation and flood control in Texas. The U.S.

Government funded $4,500,000 of the three-year, $8,500,000 project through the Works Progress Administration, a Depression era recovery agency. Named for U.S. Senator Morris Sheppard and completed in 1941, the dam is 2,740 feet long and 190 feet high. Nine spillway gates allow for the passage of flood waters and drift material. Power generating facilities consist of two 11,250-kilowatt units which serve much of the surrounding area. The creation of Possum Kingdom Lake from the impounded waters of Morris Sheppard Dam sent bridges, roads, and an entire town underwater. Recovery was initially slow, but quickly picked up after World War II with the establishment of major fishing lodges, camping areas, and other recreational facilities. The growth and success of the area is a tribute to the spirit of the surrounding communities which continue to benefit from the project's original purposes of water conservation and supply, and hydroelectric power generation. (1983)

GRAHAM (Young Co.)   SH 16, 20 mi. NW
Markley Cemetery Decoration Day
Cemetery was begun in 1881, with interment of M. C. Norfleet, adjacent to the old Plum Grove School. By 1890, the burial ground had fallen to neglect. A group of men from the surrounding rural community, including J. C. Calvin, J. W. Cox, R. E. Currie, S. G. Dean, Nelson Owen, M. A. Stewart, Andy and Ike Tinney, J. M. Wallace, and W. M. Watson, organized an annual "Graveyard Working Day", to be held on the first Saturday in May. In the early years, people came by wagon and horseback, some camping overnight. After the cleaning work had been completed bouquets of wildflowers were placed on the graves. About 1900, the settlement was named "Markley", in honor of A. C. Markley, an area landowner who had served in the frontier army during the Indian wars. In 1925, the observation was changed to the first Sunday in May. Although a perpetual care program has been initiated, decoration ceremonies have persisted as an annual social event, preserving a heritage of community cohesiveness and participation. Among the graves decorated each year are those of thirteen Confederate veterans of the Civil War: John F. Bussey, J. C. Butler, Jessie Byrd, R. E. Currie, George J. Lucas, J. D. Mankins, J. L. McDaniel, J. L. Norfleet, Nelson Owen, J.C. Stanley, James Stinnett, Cates Thompson, and David White. (1975)

GRAHAM (Young Co.)   SH 16, 8 mi. NE
Warren Wagon Train Massacre
On Salt Creek Prairie (1.5 mi. W), on May 18, 1871, Kiowas and Comanches from the Fort Sill Reservation, in present Oklahoma, attacked a train of 12 wagons owned by Capt. Henry Warren, a contractor of supplies of U.S. forts in this frontier region. Seven teamsters were killed. The chiefs who led the raid were soon arrested. In a nationally spotlighted trial at Jacksboro, Satanta spoke with great eloquence on behalf of his people. Texas' governor, E. J. Davis, later commuted the death sentences given by the court. Satanta committed suicide. (1977)

GRAHAM (Young Co.)   SH 16, in Shawnee Park
Brazos River Indian Reservation
In February 1854 the Texas legislature designated 12 Spanish leagues (or 53,136 acres) of land to be maintained as Indian reservations by the federal government. In August 1854, Major Robert S. Neighbors, United States supervising Indian agent, and Captain Randolph B. Marcy, of the United States Army, made surveys in both Spanish and American measurements; American dimensions were platted, totaling 69,120 acres. In the 8-league tract here in Young County—on either side of the Brazos River—were placed tribes of Anadarko, Caddo, Tehuacana, Tonkawa, Waco and others, together with splinter groups of the Cherokees, Choctaws, Delawares, Shawnees and some other remnants. The southern Comanches had their 4-league reservation about 45 miles to the west. Under the guidance of United States agents, the Indians of the Brazos River Reservation made much progress in agriculture, stock raising and other arts of civilization. Drouth and other adversities, however, led to closing of the reservations. Emptied in 1859 when the Indians were removed to vicinity of present Anadarko, Oklahoma, lands of the reservation reverted to the state, and were opened to the pre-emption of Texas citizens in 1873. (1970)

GRAHAM (Young Co.)   SH 67, off hwy. between 5th & 6th Sts.
Graham Salt Works
Saline residue found along the banks of Salt Creek attracted settlers to this area in the 1850s. The first person to undertake commercial production of salt here was Martin V. Bowers, who arrived

in the area prior to the Civil War. A farmer and local politician, he later sold his business to A. B. Gant and moved to Parker County. Gant, a Confederate veteran, operated the salt works until 1871, when he was elected to the Texas Legislature. He sold the operation to Gustavus A. (1836–1906) and Edwin S. (1831–1899) Graham, brothers who had come to Texas with the Texas Emigration and Land Company. The Grahams improved the salt works by adding new equipment in 1872. With a capacity of producing 2,500 pounds of salt per day, the Graham Salt Works was in operation for only two years. The salt, sold to merchants in nearby towns, cost more to transport than to produce, and the operation was discontinued. Although short in duration, the Graham Salt Works played a vital role in local development. The Graham brothers donated land for a town, named for their family, as well as for Oak Grove Cemetery, where both brothers were later buried.   (1987)

GRAHAM (Young Co.)
SH 67, 5 mi. SW

The Tonk Valley Community

Earliest known attempt at permanent settlement in this valley was made in 1851 by Elijah Skidmore, who was killed after a few months on the frontier. Locality takes its historic name from the Tonkawa nation, known in its own language as "the most human of people." In 1855 the Tonkawa were placed in this valley on a reservation provided by an act of the Texas legislature; but in 1859 the tribe was removed to Indian Territory (now Oklahoma). After the Civil War ended in 1865, and especially after the Indian reserve was opened to settlers in 1873, pioneers established livestock farms here. Their children went to school in a log cabin with dirt floor and homemade split log benches. Schoolmistress Addie McNabb accepted as salary a gray plow pony and a small amount of cash. In 1877 Baptists organized a church with the Rev. G. W. Black as pastor; also in 1877 Methodists founded Monk's Chapel, with the Rev. B. H. Johnson as pastor. The first building strictly for church use was erected 1909. School consolidations (1922) enlarged community and (1948) saw local children transported into Graham. Community life is centered in the churches.   (1972)

GRANBURY (Hood Co.)
SH 144 near FM 51

Wright-Henderson-Duncan House

The three principal owners of this home each served terms as sheriff of Hood County. A. J. Wright (1819–1889) began the limestone structure about 1873 as a one-story dogtrot dwelling. James F. Henderson, who acquired the house in 1881, added the second floor and Victorian galleries. Charles M. Duncan (1878–1957) and his wife Emma (Wade), owners for a long period in the 20th century, helped preserve the residence.   (1977)

GRANBURY (Hood Co.)
100 Blk. Pearl St. at courthouse

County Named for Famous Confederate General John Bell Hood

Born Kentucky. West Point graduate. Army service on Texas frontier led Hood to adopt the Lone Star State. Resigned U.S. Army 1861 to serve South. Commanded 4th Texas Infantry. Led "Hood's Texas," most renowned Confederate Brigade. Rose rapidly to Lieutenant General. Known as "The Fighting General" for leadership in the Army of Northern Virginia. Although lost leg Battle Chickamauga, became commander Army of Tennessee. A memorial to Texans who served the Confederacy.   (1963)

GRANBURY (Hood Co.)
100 Blk. Pearl St. at courthouse

Hood County Courthouse

Fifth courthouse on this site. Erected 1890–1891, this handsome building is a Texas version of the French second empire style. First courthouse (1867) was a 1-room log cabin housing county records, lawyers and land agents' offices, and mail station. It was succeeded by 3 stone structures. Contractors Moodie and Ellis and Architect W.C. Dodson built this native stone edifice. The clock tower, added after completion, was reinforced with steel in 1969.   (1970)

GRANBURY (Hood Co.)
SH 144, 3.5 mi. S

Comanche Peak

Prominent Indian and pioneer landmark. Actually a mesa, the peak rises 1,229 feet (above sea level). May have had ceremonial value for local tribes or have been a lookout point for game and enemies. A Comanche trail crossed county in this vicinity. In 1846, whites and Indians en route to the so-called "peak" for a meeting also failed to find it because of its flat top. Later settlers held dances here and students from Add-Ran College (about 10 miles N) had picnics at the peak. Boys also hunted wolves and rattlesnakes among caves and rocks on the top. (1969)

GRANBURY (Hood Co.)   *US 377, 4 mi. W*
The Colony Cemetery
Residents of the community known as The Colony came to Hood County with their white southern owners as early as the 1850s. After emancipation they began to settle in this area, and many acquired land under a state law which provided settlers with the opportunity to live on land for as many as seven years before securing a patent for the property. "Doc" Foster and Simon and Hettie Hightower were such landowners. The Colony grew rapidly in the last years of the nineteenth century. A church called Mt. Zion, which also served as a temporary school was established. The earliest marked grave in the Colony Cemetery is that of Mary Edwards, who died in 1876. The Colony residents played important roles in the development of Hood County. They helped clear land for the courthouse site, executed their masonry skills on the buildings on the Granbury square, and worked on area farms. Church fundraising events and celebrations such as Juneteenth, the celebration of Texas' notification of the end of slavery, were an important part of the Colony's community life. By the end of the Depression era of the 1930s, most of the adult residents had left the Colony for nearby towns, and many of the community's youth left the area completely, though they often chose to be returned to the Colony Cemetery for burial. The last three residents of the Colony left in the 1940s. The Colony Cemetery is an important chronicle of the history of Hood County and particularly of the generation of African Americans who were born in slavery and who forged new lives after emancipation, paving the road of freedom for their descendants. (2000)

GRAND SALINE (Van Zandt Co.)   *Garland St. (US 80) at Main St. (SH 17)*
Wiley Hardeman Post (1898–1935)
Pioneer aviator Wiley Hardeman Post was born on November 22, 1898, in the community of Corinth in Van Zandt County, to William Francis and Mae Laine Post, who moved to Oklahoma when Wiley was a boy. Wiley was inspired as a youth to learn to fly. In the late 1920s, he obtained flight training, made his first solo flight, and acquired an air transport license. Despite the loss of one eye in an oil-field accident, Post worked as a barnstormer, commercial pilot, and flight instructor. Post set many flight records and won the national air races in 1930. He and Harold Gatty circled the world, flying 15,474 miles in less than 9 days in 1931. Post soloed around the world in less than 8 days in 1933. Post invented and developed the first pressurized flight suit, explored stratospheric flight, and used an early Sperry autopilot mechanism. He worked with the U.S. Army Air Corps on an experimental automatic direction finding (ADF) radio compass, and was a pioneer in the use of liquid oxygen for high-altitude flight. Post and humorist Will Rogers died in a plane crash on a trip to Alaska in 1935. His plane the "Winnie Mae" is in the Smithsonian Institution's Air and Space Museum in Washington, D.C. (1996)

GRANDFALLS (Ward Co.)   *SH 18, 1.5 mi. S*
Butterfield Overland Stage Line
One of the longest stage routes ever established, the Southern Overland mail line (Butterfield Route), which provided semi-weekly service, St. Louis to San Francisco, 1858–1861. Followed substantially the route of this highway through Ward County.

GRAPEVINE (Tarrant Co.)   *SH 121, S of Sandy Lake Rd.*
The Missouri Colony
In 1844, related families from Platte County, Missouri, settled in this area. James Gibson, one of the earliest settlers in Tarrant County, owned this site. In 1845, more relatives and friends arrived. They became known as the "Missouri Colony." The pioneers raised cattle and grain. John A. Freeman taught school and preached to the settlers at Lonesome Dove. Some original colonists moved to pioneer other frontier regions. Others remained to help build the northeastern section of Tarrant County, the first permanently settled area in the county. (1979)

GRAPEVINE (Tarrant Co.)   *SH 26, .25 mi. SW of Bethel Road*
Morgan Hood Survey Pioneer Cemetery
Originally part of the Morgan Hood Survey, this small cemetery (75 ft. SE) has been abandoned for over a century. Its one visible grave is marked with portions of a sandstone burial cairn, a

common method of marking graves in this area in the 1850s–1870s. The subject of speculation since no written records remain, the graves may be those of members of the Peters Colony, early pioneers who entered the Grapevine area in 1844. Although nearly all traces of the cemetery are gone, it serves as a reminder of Tarrant County's early days of settlement. (1983)

GRAPEVINE (Tarrant Co.)   *off SH 26, .1 mi. E of Mustang Dr.*
The Peters Colony in Tarrant County
In 1841, W. S. Peters of Kentucky and associates contracted with the Republic of Texas to bring immigrants to this area. By 1848, Peters Colony land covered nearly 2 million acres in North Central Texas, including all of Tarrant County. Speculation in unlocated land certificates was rampant. About 150 colonists and their families, most of whom were American-born farmers of meager means, settled in Tarrant County. As the most extensive empresario enterprise undertaken by the Republic, the Peters Colony helped open this area of Texas to settlement. (1990)

GRAPEVINE (Tarrant Co.)   *211 S. Main St. (Spur 103)*
Grapevine
Wild mustang grapes growing profusely in this area inspired the name "Grapevine" for this community. Ambrose Foster (1794?–1847) and his wife Susannah Medlin (1796–1876) were among the first settlers in 1845, from Platte County, Missouri. The Fosters, their daughters and sons-in-law acquired land that became the heart of Grapevine. Within the first year worship services and school classes were conducted. Cattle raising was the major enterprise prior to the Civil War. Beef cattle were sold to Camp Worth (present Fort Worth) by Archibald Leonard, Fosters' son-in-law, who owned a mercantile store. In 1858 a Federal Post Office was established and run by Solon Dunn. During the 1870s the village was also known as "Dunnville". In 1914 the name became "Grapevine". After the Cotton Belt Railroad line opened in 1888, the town thrived as a shipping center for cotton, grain, truck crops and dairy products. In 1907 Grapevine incorporated. By 1934 two major paved roads leading to Dallas and Fort Worth were constructed. A dam built in 1942 on Denton Creek formed Lake Grapevine. It serves as a water supply, flood control measure, and a recreational area. In 1974 the Dallas–Fort Worth Airport opened within the city limits. (1979)

GREENVILLE (Hunt Co.)   *SH 34, 13 mi. N*
Old National Road Crossing
One mile northeast below junction of Short Creek and Sulphur River. The Central National Road of Texas (Republic) was created by act of Texas Congress, 1844, with intent to give the new nation a unified transportation route. From present Dallas to the head of navigation on the Red River, northwest of Clarksville, road linked to Northeast Texas the military routes of West and Central Texas; connected with routes east at Jonesborough and Paris. It failed to gain international status congress hoped for, due to population shifts, coming of railroads and development of other routes. (1967)

GREENVILLE (Hunt Co.)   *US 69, 6 mi. N in Kellogg Community*
Central National Road of the Republic of Texas
Surveyed and established by virtue of an act of the Congress of the Republic of Texas in 1844, running from the Trinity River to the Red River. It crossed the highway near this point. "An Old Road is the Soul of the Past." (1926)

GREENVILLE (Hunt Co.)   *US 69, 2.3 mi. NW of Celeste*
Headwaters of the Sabine River
A half mile to the west rises the Sabine River, lower channel of which separated new world empires of France and Spain and in 1836 became Republic of Texas–United States border. Fork here is called Cow Leach, for Indian chief who lived in the area. This marker is on a 3-way watershed. Flow to the north goes into the Sulphur and to the Mississippi; the west drains to the Trinity; south goes into the Sabine, which forms Texas-Louisiana boundary and pours more water into Gulf of Mexico than any other Texas river (6,400,000 acre feet annually). (1971)

GREENVILLE (Hunt Co.)   *2821 Washington St.*
Greenville
In 1846, the Texas legislature created Hunt County and specified that Greenville would be the name of the county seat, honoring Texas War for Independence veteran Thomas J. Green. Voters ul-

timately selected this location, on land donated by Tennessee surveyor McQuinney Howell Wright, for the new community of Greenville. The townsite was platted in May 1846 and the first lots were sold at auction the following January, although Wright did not file the deed officially conveying his land until March 22, 1850. Albert G. Hamilton served as first mayor after the town incorporated in 1852. Unlike most north central Texas counties, Hunt County voted in favor of secession during the national crisis in the 1860s. Economic hardship, occasions of violence, and occupation by federal troops characterized the Civil War and Reconstruction period in Greenville. The arrival of the Missouri, Kansas and Texas railroad in October 1880 was a watershed in Greenville's history. The railroad provided cotton farmers with easier shipping access, and cotton production and processing became major economic activities. New businesses and service industries, including banks, hotels, street cars, and the state's first municipally owned electric utility, developed to serve the growing community. Greenville was home to Majors Army Air Field and three colleges in the 20th century. Its location at the crossroads of major state and national highways helped Greenville develop over the years to become an industrial and trade center in northeast Texas.   (2001)

GREENVILLE (Hunt Co.)   *US 380, 2 mi. W*
Route of Old Colony Line Road
Early travel artery. Followed the north boundary line of the Chas. F. Mercer colony, a 6,500 square-mile tract granted to Mercer in 1844 by Sam Houston (President of the Republic of Texas) for purpose of bringing colonists into Texas. Southern half of Hunt County once lay in this pioneer colony. Over the road came ox-wagons from Jefferson to supply stores in Greenville, McKinney, Dallas, Fort Worth and the frontier. Settlers from the old south traveled it in a steady stream of covered wagons. Highway 24 today traces part of the road.   (1968)

GREENVILLE (Hunt Co.)   *SH 276 at Golf Dr., 25 mi. S*
Lake Tawakoni
One of the largest lakes wholly within Texas. Completed 1960, it covers 36,700 acres. Impounded by 5.5-mile-long iron bridge/dam on Sabine River, it has a shoreline of 200 miles. Constructed and owned by the Sabine River Authority of Texas. Financed by city of Dallas under terms of a water supply contract. Other towns also by lake's water. Prehistoric animal bones and remains of a Tawakoni Indian village were discovered here. Lake is operated under Iron Bridge Division, S.R.A. of Texas. It embraces Wind Point Park, a public recreational resort.   (1970)

GRIT (Mason Co.)   *US 83, Grit Cemetery*
John Bate Berry (1813–1891)
Forefathers resisting America's foes on many frontiers inspired John Bate Berry, who came to Texas from Kentucky in 1826. He fought (1835–1836) in the Texas War for Independence and in the 1842 Mier Expedition to stop Mexican raids on the Republic of Texas. Captured, imprisoned, then freed in 1844, he scouted for the American Army in 1846, during the Mexican War. Later he married, lived in this locality, and fought to make frontiers safe for settlement.   (1977)

GROESBECK (Limestone Co.)   *SH 14, 4 mi. N at Fort Parker State Park*
Fort Parker
Built 1834 for protection from Indians. Named for leaders who brought first Predestinarian Baptist church body to Texas: elder Daniel Parker; his father, elder John; brothers Jas. W., Benjamin, Silas, John. Also here were Kellogg, Frost, Nixon, Duty and Plummer families. On May 18, 1836, raiding Comanches killed Benjamin, John and Silas Parker; Samuel and Robert Frost and others; captured Elizabeth Kellogg, Rachel Plummer and son James, and Silas' children, John and Cynthia Ann. In captivity, Cynthia Ann married Chief Peta Nocona; her son, Quanah, was last Comanche chief. With her baby, Prairie Flower, in 1860 she was captured by Texas Rangers. She, the baby and Quanah are buried at Fort Sill.   (1965)

GROESBECK (Limestone Co.)   *SH 14, 4 mi. N at Fort Parker State Park*
Civilian Conservation Corps at Fort Parker State Park
In August 1935, construction of a state park began here on the former town site of Springfield under the direction of the Civilian Conservation Corps. The group assigned to build Fort Parker State Park was Company 3807(C), an African American CCC Camp. From 1935 to 1942, the park company constructed park buildings, roads and facilities, erected a dam across the Navasota River,

and reconstructed old Fort Parker. Located nearby, old Fort Parker was rebuilt in preparation for a Texas Centennial observance in 1936, and was the first of the CCC projects completed. The dam that created Lake Fort Parker was concluded by 1938 and required breaking and hauling rock for cement, digging out the dam footings, spillway, and wing walks, and pouring cement for the dam. Creating the park facilities included clearing and building five miles of roads, constructing an activity center/bath house, drinking fountains, and cement picnic tables. Former Texas Governor Pat Neff dedicated Fort Parker State Park in May 1941, and declared it open to the public. Company 3807(C) was transferred out of the area in 1942 after completing several complex tasks over a span of almost seven years. (1997)

GROESBECK (Limestone Co.)
SH 14, 4 mi. N at Fort Parker
Memorial Park Cemetery
Fort Parker Memorial Park
Site of the grave of victims of the massacre at Fort Parker by Comanche and Kiowa Indians on May 19, 1836, in which Cynthia Ann Parker and others were captured. The trunk of the oak tree under which they were buried still stands, and the grave is marked by a granite slab. Also site of state monument to the Pioneers, erected in 1922, and the graves of other old settlers and veterans of the Texas War of Independence.

GROESBECK (Limestone Co.)
SH 14, 5 mi. N
Old Springfield
Named for the large spring on townsite donated Jan. 6, 1838, by Moses Herrin, who gave 4 lots to any person agreeing to settle in the town. Twelve families later in 1838 were forced out by Indian hostility. Post office was established in 1846. When Limestone County was created April 11, 1846, Springfield—its only town of any size—became county seat. First courthouse was built 1848 near Navasota River; new 2-story brick courthouse in 1856 on the hill. Home of Springfield District of Methodist Church—from which stemmed the Northwest Texas Conference. Also had active Baptist and Disciples of Christ churches. Springfield College was established, but closed during the Civil War. The Navasota Stock Raisers Association was organized here. When Houston & Texas Central Railroad was built some miles to the east in 1870, population dwindled. In 1873 there were 2 great fires in the town—one burning the courthouse. Surviving buildings were moved away. Groesbeck became the county seat. The old cemetery and Springfield Lake, both in Fort Parker State Park, retain the historic name of the once important town. Lake Springfield provides recreation, irrigation and municipal water.

GROESBECK (Limestone Co.)
SH 164, 10 mi. W
Lost Prairie Cemetery and Church
Established by volunteers in 1846; sponsoring group formed about 1900. According to legend, a man lost in the surrounding woods named the site when he stumbled onto the prairie. The graves of many early settlers include Azariah G. Moore, a soldier in the Texas War for Independence. First officials of the cemetery association were Jeff Rambo, chairman, and Beulah Holloway, secretary. Successors include Dan Dove, Jake Hudson, W. C. Jackson, Bill Kennedy, I. M. Kennedy, Joe Lansford, Cliff Sims and J. B. Sims. Others helping in preservation of site were R. L. Dossey, J. A. Easterling, W. K. Hardison, W. L. Henderson, A. B. Sims, E. E. Sims, J. J. Sims, J. L. Sims and R. A. Sims. Others have served as caretakers since the grounds were opened; among them George Henry, J. N. Henry and Bill Sims. Baptist church was situated here about 1850. Present building is fourth structure to serve as a church. First pastor was Rev. William Clark. Founding members included the Beavers, Browns, Easterlings, Gregorys, Henrys, Kennedys, Lansfords, Mortons, Rambos, Sandifers, Shugarts, Sims, Summers, Thompsons and Waylands. One early church member, A. J. Rogers, was named a deacon after returning from the Civil War. (1967)

GROVETON (Sumpter Co.)
US 287, 4.6 mi. E
Site of the Town of Sumpter
The legislature of the State of Texas created Trinity County out of Houston County in 1850. A group of seven commissioners was appointed to locate and survey a site for the seat of government. The town of Sumpter was founded in this area, near the geographic center of the county. Trinity County's first seat of justice grew slowly. Early settler Solomon Adams operated a small general store, and his log home also served as a hotel. The courthouse was a small frame building located

on the plaza, near which a log schoolhouse was erected. When Goodwin Woodson and R.D. Crow opened a saw and grist mill four miles south of Sumpter in 1857, the town began to develop rapidly and was incorporated five years later. As the population increased, a larger courthouse was built. An influx of businesses, such as drugstores and saloons, appeared around the courthouse square. A number of plantations flourished in the area until the coming of the Civil War. In 1872, the courthouse at Sumpter burned, and a rail line was built through the town of Trinity. Sumpter was gradually abandoned, and the nearby cemetery is all that remains of the once-thriving community.

GROVETON (Trinity Co.)   US 287 at courthouse
Groveton
Named for a grove of black jack oak trees, Groveton resulted from the establishment of the Trinity County Lumber Company sawmill in 1882. After the Trinity and Sabine Railroad Company built a sixty-five mile branch line through area forests, the Trinity County Lumber Company bought about 29,000 acres of land from the Trinity and Sabine Timber Company, leaving acreage on either side of the railroad tracks for a town. The county seat was moved from Pennington to Groveton in 1882. By 1884 the first permanent courthouse was completed and the town included a barber shop, grocery store, drug store, hotel, boarding house, several saloons, homes, and a school. The city was incorporated on September 29, 1919 and officials were elected. By 1930 all the timber for miles around had been cut; consequently, the sawmill closed December 31, 1930. The once prosperous town of Groveton went into decline. The Civilian Conservation Corps was responsible for road construction and a reforestation program in the 1930s. Through the years Groveton has seen economic booms and hard times, but as the county seat, it has survived to leave a rich heritage.   (1991)

GROVETON (Trinity Co.)   US 287 at courthouse
Trinity County Courthouse
The Trinity County and Sabine Pass Land and Railway Company laid out the new town of Groveton in 1881, when the I&GN Railroad came through the area. The following year, Trinity County voters chose it as their seat of government. The company constructed a temporary courthouse for the county, and the frame structure, located at what is now Main at First streets, served the county until 1884. That year, the government moved into a brick building at this site. The construction was not solid, though, and by the early 1900s, county commissioners were concerned for the safety of county records. They hired W.A. Norris to build a records vault exactly like the one L. S. Green had designed for Polk County. They paid Green for the use of his plans, and the county moved its records to the building in 1908. In late 1913, the county commissioners hired C. H. Page and Bros. of Austin to design a new courts building that would incorporate the 1908 records vault. Accepted in July the next year, the structure was rectilinear in plan, stretching to connect almost seamlessly to the records vault built on the east side of the courthouse square. Classical Revival features include a full-height portico with paired Tuscan columns, as well as brick parapet, denticulation, corbelled window surrounds and stepped wings. Today, the courthouse remains a center of county life. The site of parades, rallies and festivals, the structure is a symbol of justice and a unified citizenry. Within its walls, births, marriages and deaths are recorded, and fates are decided. It remains a link to the promise the future held for early-20th century residents of Trinity County, and to the efforts and dedication of those who have since worked to preserve the county's heritage.   (2004)

GRUVER (Hansford Co.)   SH 136, 9 mi. S
Site of Cator Buffalo Camp
Established by James H. and Bob Cator in the spring of 1872. While hunting buffalo in the fall of 1875 the camp became a trading post known as Zulu.   (1965)

GRUVER (Hansford Co.)   SH 15, 2 mi. SE
Old Farwell
Established 1886 about ½ mile northeast of this site. Intended to be county seat of Hansford County, created 1876, organized in 1889. Lost election to town of Hansford, which served till 1928 but is also now non-existent. Named for early surveyor John V. Farwell and members of his family, Chicago department store executives who operated XIT Ranch in this and 9 other counties—their fee in payment for the building of the Texas state capitol, 1882–1886. Stones here are from the casing of a 200 foot well dug by hand to supply water to the town.   (1964)

GUSTINE (Comanche Co.)

SH 36 near Main St. in roadside park

Cora

Founded 1854, as Troy. Later renamed in honor of a Miss Beeman of Bell County. In 1856 organization of Comanche County—then extending farther south and east than today's boundaries—Cora became county seat. A log cabin residence in Cora was the first Comanche County courthouse, serving until the county seat was relocated in 1859 in new town of Comanche. That first courthouse and all the other buildings are gone from site of Old Cora. Only a cemetery—the oldest in Comanche County—remains. Thus Cora is an example of the many early, important towns no longer existent in Texas. In the 254 counties of Texas, there have been 126 cases of redesignation of county seats. (Two counties have had five county seats each.) Boundary changes (as in Comanche County), shifts in travel routes (as when railroads were built), changes from agrarian to industrial economy have caused counties to move their county seats to new locations. Old courthouses have found later usefulness as ranch headquarters, municipal buildings, or private homes. The first log cabin courthouse of Comanche County reverted to use as a residence, but later was restored and used—as are many former courthouses —as part of a museum. (1967)

GUSTINE (Comanche Co.)

SH 36 at Main St.

Gustine

Settlers began arriving in this area of Comanche County in the 1870s. Among the pioneers were members of the Blankenship family, who inherited land granted to brothers Christopher and A. K. Clark for Republic of Texas military service. The first settlement, located about three-fourths of a mile northeast of this site, was named Evergreen. It included homes, a store, blacksmith shop, cotton gin, and school. In the 1880s, when a new road opened between Comanche and Hamilton, the citizens of Evergreen moved their town to this site to be on the route of the new road. A U.S. post office opened in January 1888, and was named for postmaster Samuel Gustine. By the early 20th century, the town of Gustine boasted homes, churches, and businesses, including two cotton gins, three poultry companies, a grist mill, retail stores, telephone and electric utilities, a newspaper, and a bank. The Cotton Belt Railway built a line through the area in 1910, causing an economic boom until it was discontinued in the 1930s. State Highway 36 was built on the railroad right-of-way, however, maintaining the town's most important transportation route. (1992)

GUTHRIE (King Co.)

US 82, 2.4 mi. W in roadside park

King County

Created Aug. 21, 1876, from Bexar County, whose diamond-shaped boundaries extended from the Rio Grande to the Panhandle to El Paso. Named for William King, who died at the Alamo. Chief industry, ranching, is reflected in its famous brands: "6666," "Pitchfork," "JY," "SMS," and "MATADOR." A population of only 173 in 1890 was aided in formal organization by petitions signed by itinerants. Names of favorite horses were also added. Organization came on June 25, 1891. In establishing county seat, cowboys voted for Guthrie, which won over Ashville, choice of the ranchers. (1965)

HALE CENTER (Hale Co.)

IH 27, 7.5 mi. S

Stant Rhea Stage Stand

Early settlers in this area kept in touch with the world by picking up their mail at railheads. Federal mail delivery to post offices began when W. L. Tharp took a route from the new railroad town of Amarillo to Plainview and Estacado in July and August, 1888. There were no roads; the round trip took six days. About 1889, W. H. Fuqua of Amarillo, who had a new U.S. mail contract, used a compass and laid off a route with several stations—one of Plainview. He soon added passenger service, but then disposed of the line, which about 1890 fell into the hands of Stant Rhea and Robert Montgomery. Buying out Montgomery, Rhea carried the mail for 19 years. Sidney Stanton "Stant" Rhea (1862–1922) was a small, red-haired man who drove wild Spanish mules hitched to a buckboard (or carriage). He made the 240-mile round trip from Amarillo to this area three times a week. With later route changes and better roads, he came this way daily. Six miles east of this spot he had a mule corral and a dugout. Stage passengers and mail patrons used the dugout as a waiting room. Until railroads outmoded his service, Stant Rhea's route and stage stand were important in the development of the South Plains. (1976)

HALE CENTER (Hale Co.)   *IH 27, .5 mi. S*
Ranching and Farming in Hale County
Pioneer ranchers began to settle Hale County in the early 1880s. Land was plentiful and cheap, but life was hard. Many settlers lived in dugouts. Supplies were freighted from Colorado City until the railroad reached Amarillo. Cattle roamed the free grazing land until roundup time, when they were separated according to brands. Ranchers earned extra income by selling buffalo bones for fertilizer, working on the railroad, or hiring out to larger ranches. Many worked at the Circle Ranch of Col. C. C. Slaughter, which covered land in four counties. Other significant ranches included the Callahan, Barton, and Norfleet ranches. When the public land was gone and free grazing ended, the larger ranches were divided into smaller tracts. The transition from ranching to farming was difficult. By the early 20th century, wheat farming and dairy production began to replace ranching operations. The dust bowl and depression of the 1930s brought new hardships. Soon after World War II, however, a high percentage of the cultivated acreage in Hale County was under irrigation. This allowed for crop diversification with high yields of grain sorghum, corn, soybeans, wheat, vegetables, and livestock production. Cotton has become the leading cash crop.   (1985)

HALLETTSVILLE (Lavaca Co.)   *US 90A, 9 mi. E at Navidad River Bridge*
The Wild Man of the Navidad
A mysterious runaway Negro slave who alternately terrified and aroused pity of settlers in this region for about 15 years. The mysterious exile, at first with a companion, appeared along the Navidad bottoms about 1836. Hiding in trees during day, he stole into kitchens at night for food, but always left half. He also took tools, returning them later, brightly polished. Slaves called him "The Thing That Comes," fearing a ghost. Captured in 1851, the wild man proved to be an African chief's son. Resold into slavery, he died peacefully as "Old Jimbo" in 1884.   (1970)

HALLETTSVILLE (Lavaca Co.)   *US 90A, 5 mi. E*
Rabb Switch
Edward M. Rabb (1855–1908) a native of La Grange, Fayette County, Texas, was the son of William and Prudence Smalley Rabb. In the 1880s Dr. Edward M. Rabb settled in this area and purchased 2089 acres of land from S. W. Campbell. At his death, Dr. Rabb left a will with instructions calling for a wood and water switch to serve the railroad to be built on a portion of his land. The San Antonio and Aransas Pass Railroad was built across the Navidad River in 1887. The switch was constructed and local residents cut and loaded firewood for shipment to Houston. The land that was cleared of firewood was used to farm cotton and corn, the primary source of income for farmers in the area. Two stores opened at Rabb Switch, and a school built in the 1800s was moved to the community in 1919 and served 30–35 students. The railroad ceased operations during the 1950s, at the same time that U.S. Highway 90-A was improved. When the school was closed in 1953, students were transferred five miles west to the Hallettsville Independent School District, and the population declined thereafter as businesses closed.   (1997)

HALLETTSVILLE (Lavaca Co.)   *US 77, S. La Grange St.*
Hallettsville
Founded 1833 when John Hallet erected a log cabin near Lavaca River. Town was named for his widow, Margaret, who gave the land when town became county seat in 1852. Farming, livestock, poultry processing, and cotton marketing center. State championship high school rodeo held annually in June.   (1968)

HALLETSVILLE (Lavaca Co.)   *US 77, 1 mi. S*
William Smothers (1760–1837)
A veteran of the American Revolution, a native of Virginia, William Smothers was orphaned at 12 when Indians killed his father, and his mother died of shock. In the American Revolution, he fought at King's Mountain, Guilford courthouse, Camden, and Eutaw Springs. He moved to Kentucky in 1781, built two forts near present Hartford, originally called "Smothers Station," and in 1798 founded an Ohio River port that later became Owensboro. He was a leader in civil affairs in early Kentucky, was a militia captain, and commanded troops in the War of 1812. Smothers Park in Owensboro is named in his honor. Smothers scouted in Texas before 1820, returned in 1821 with the exploring party of Stephen F. Austin, and helped build Fort Bend for the safety of the "old 300"

settlers. In 1824 Mexico gave him a land grant; in 1826 he and two sons helped settle DeWitt's colony, receiving land grants in the vicinity of this marker. Fearless and a skillful guide, he often hunted with his friend Jim Bowie. Reputedly he tomahawked bears in hand combat. Married twice, he was ancestor of many leading Texans. He died in 1837, after seeing a son and three grandsons help to win the Texas War for Independence. (1977)

HALLETTSVILLE (Lavaca Co.)   *US 77, 5.5 mi. S*
John Himes Livergood
(September 10, 1815–October 3, 1893)
A native of Pennsylvania, John Himes Livergood came to Texas in 1837 and received 640 acres of land on Peach Creek near Gonzales. From that time until Texas' annexation to the United States nearly ten years later, Livergood played an integral role in the defense of frontier settlements and in several major events during the Republic period. In 1840, Livergood joined Capt. Adam Zumwalt to pursue an Indian party that had attacked his neighbors. The chase ended with a decisive victory at the Battle of Plum Creek. Later he served in several scouting expeditions, including the Spy Company of the Texas Rangers under John (Jack) Coffee Hays. He took part in the Battle of Salado Creek and the Somervell Expedition in 1842. As a member of the doomed Mier Expedition to invade Mexico, he was a survivor of the Black Bean Episode and was finally released from Perote prison in 1844. While visiting family in Missouri in 1847, John H. Livergood met Sarah Ann Elizabeth Perkins (1828–1909). They married in 1847 and established a home (eventually with 13 children) on the Lavaca River. The Livergoods helped found Mossy Grove Methodist Church and were active leaders there. A farmer and rancher, Livergood also entered the political life of Lavaca County, serving as Chief Justice (County Judge) from 1850 to 1852 and later as Justice of the Peace. In his final military service, Livergood served in the Lone Star Guard, the Texas State Troops and the Confederate Army during the Civil War. Both he and Sarah Ann Livergood are buried at Mossy Grove Cemetery. (2001)

HALLETTSVILLE (Lavaca Co.)   *US 77, 9 mi. W in roadside park*
Route of the Texas Army
In Texas Revolution, Gen. Sam Houston and his Texas Army crossed Rocky Creek near this spot, March 15, 1836, retreating eastward from town of Gonzales. Their victory 5 weeks later over Santa Anna's Mexican army, in Battle of San Jacinto, brought freedom to Texas, April 21. (1969)

HALLSVILLE (Harrison Co.)   *200 W. Main St. (US 80)*
Hallsville
Formerly Hallville. Successor to Fort Crawford and Ash Springs, pioneer settlements of 1840s. Hallsville was founded when Texas & Pacific Railway was built. First train arrived Aug. 17, 1869. Western terminus for a time, and site (1870–73) of T. & P. shops, town attracted ox-wagon freighting in wool, cotton and buffalo hides from the West. Hallsville, named for Kentuckians Elijah and Volney Hall, received charter Aug. 13, 1870. Volney Hall was a vice president of the old Southern Pacific Railway, which was rechartered as the T. & P. Acquired Sub-Courthouse, 1965. (1973)

HAMILTON (Hamilton Co.)   *US 281, 11 mi. N*
Olin Baptist Church
Founded in 1878 by five charter members, this church originally was named Kings Chapel. It was also known as Pleasant Hill Missionary Baptist Church and as Dry Fork Church. The church deacons purchased land at this site in 1899, and when a post office for the community was granted under the name Olin, the church was renamed Olin Baptist Church. Serving the community for well over a century, this church has offered a variety of worship and educational programs and has supported both domestic and foreign missionary endeavors.

HAMILTON (Hamilton Co.)   *US 281, 6.5 mi. N in roadside park*
Hamilton County, C.S.A.
Created and organized in 1858. By 1860 had 489 people in 78 families from 15 states. Vote in 1861 was 86–1 in favor of secession. 60 farmers were organized as Hamilton County Minute Men, a unit of part-time soldiers. Others joined Confederate regiments and fought at Vicksburg, Shiloh and other memorable battles. During the Civil War travel was on horseback and hauling

by ox wagon. Homes were of logs split from timber along creeks and rivers. About half an acre a day was farmed, with homemade wooden tools. Corn and wheat were raised. On burned-over ground each family grew its own tobacco, hanging the leaves inside the living room to dry. Diet was mostly beef, cornbread and coffee substitutes. Homes were lighted by wicks stuck into tallow-filled eggshells. With few men on hand to brand and herd, feuds rose over thefts and straying cattle. In differences over war issues, 2 men fled to Mexico to join Federals. Later they returned, trying to recruit neighbors into a unit disloyal to Texas to welcome planned Federal invasion. Further trouble came from many Confederate deserters who took refuge along the streams and lived by theft and violence.

(1965)

HAMILTON (Hamilton Co.) *US 281, 1 mi. N*
Hamilton County
Created February 2, 1842, from Montgomery and Houston Counties. Recreated January 22, 1858. Organized August 2, 1858. Named in honor of General James Hamilton, 1786–1857, lawyer and Governor of South Carolina. Appointed diplomatic agent to Europe by President Lamar. Hamilton, the county seat.

(1965)

HAMILTON (Hamilton Co.) *US 281 at Francis Marion Rd.*
Ann Whitney
Elizabeth (Ann) Whitney, a native of Missouri, accepted a teaching position at a newly erected rural school located about seven miles north of present day Hamilton in 1867. This school, called the Leon River School, was situated on a rise overlooking the Warlene Valley. On a hot summer afternoon in 1867 Ann and her students were suddenly attacked by Comanche Indians. According to local tradition Ann was repeatedly struck by arrows fired through cracks in the schoolhouse walls. Although fatally injured she nevertheless bravely aided the escape of all but one of her young students.

(1992)

HAMILTON (Hamilton Co.) *121 S. Rice Avenue (US 281)*
Manning-Gordon-Henderson House
Local contractor Louis V. Manning built this house between 1880 and 1885 on land inherited from his father, pioneer Ezekiel Manning, and lived here until 1904. The John H. and Abbie Gordon family owned the house from 1907 to 1936 and the Oliver Dow and Minta Henderson family took up residence here in 1936. A simple example of a cross-gabled roof Queen Anne house, its distinguishing details include fish-scale textured gables, cutaway bay windows, and a front entry porch with ornamental posts and brackets and a jigsawn frieze. Also of interest is the unusual siding flanking the entry door.

(1999)

HAMLIN (Jones Co.) *South Central Ave. (US 83) between 2nd and 3rd Sts.*
Hamlin
Early settler R. D. Moore conveyed 320 acres of land to the International Construction Co. (also called the Orient Land Co.) of Kansas City, Missouri, for a town site along the Panhandle Gulf Railway in September 1902. Probably named for Orient executive W. H. Hamlin, the Hamlin community was organized in 1905, the same year it received its first post office. The Kansas City, Mexico and Orient Railway reached Hamlin in 1906 and a newspaper, the Hamlin Herald, was first printed that same year. Hamlin was incorporated as a town and a school system was established in 1907. By autumn 1908, Hamlin had grown to more than one thousand citizens as more railroads reached the area. Hamlin quickly became a major shipping point, with its economy based on agriculture and the railroad. Among the town's business operations were cotton compresses, a cotton oil mill, an ice plant, a cement and plaster plant, a grain elevator, several cotton gins, an electric generating plant, an ice cream factory and bottling works, and a telephone company. Churches formed in Hamlin's early days included Church of Christ, Baptist, Methodist and Church of the Nazarene. A movie theatre opened in 1907. Central Nazarene College was established in 1909. The Oscar Depriest School System for African American students began operation in 1925. Oil was discovered near Hamlin in 1928, broadening the area's economic growth with oil and gas exploration. In 1950, the town's population was 3,564. The school system was integrated in 1965. The population of Hamlin in 1990 was 2,791. At the dawn of the 21st century, Hamlin remains a center for farming and varied manufacturing.

(2000)

HAPPY (Swisher Co.) US 87, N city limits
Harman-Toles Elevator (¼ mi W)
Holland E. Toles (1894–1941) opened a grain elevator in this area in 1926, and was joined by Vernon Harman in 1938. After Toles' death, Harman formed a new partnership with John F. and Holl Ed Toles. World War II, increased irrigation, and a Federal grain program created a need for larger storage facilities. On March 1, 1945, construction was begun on this six-unit concrete elevator. Labor was provided by the U.S. government, utilizing 50 Italian prisoners of war from a camp near Hereford, under Geneva Convention provisions. The project was completed on July 10, 1945. (1974)

HARLETON (Harrison Co.) SH 154, Centennial Park
Harleton
Although settlement in this area between the forks of Big and Little Cypress Creeks began in the 1830s, notable growth did not occur until the arrival of a railroad here in 1891. The railroad was a vital part of a venture financed by John H. Inman, organized by Edwin J. Fry, and executed by brothers Robert H. and James W. Harle, to exploit the area's virgin forests. Organized as the Hope Lumber Company, they constructed a depot and large commissary, installed a band sawmill, and extended a tram road into the Eagle Creek area. The nearby village of Grady was unable to compete against the Harles' well-stocked store and dance hall and soon faded. Its post office, renamed Harleton after the Harle brothers, was relocated to the Harle Store. Harleton's economy boomed as timber production led to increased farm activity, and local merchants such as D. C. Webb and Son, Dreyfus-Little Mercantile Co., J. P. Craver and Son, and R. W. Taylor General Merchandise increased stocks to meet a growing demand for wares. By the late 1890s, however, Hope Lumber Company had processed the area's available timber and closed its mill. The railroad later joined with the Marshall & East Texas Railroad. Harleton continued, supported by agriculture and other timber operations in the area. (1993)

HARPER (Gillespie Co.) US 290 at FM 783
Harper Presbyterian Church
Organized in 1881 as the Barnett Spring Presbyterian Church, this congregation originally met in a schoolhouse. The fellowship moved to Harper in 1901 and erected this frame church on land donated by Arch Austin. Sale of property given by R. W. Crosley helped finance the construction. In 1903 a bell was purchased for the belfry. This structure housed the Harper school in 1906 and again in the 1940s. It also served as a worship site for other denominations. (1976)

HARPER (Gillespie Co.) US 290 at FM 783, 300 ft. S
Site of the McDonald Massacre
Pioneer preacher Matthew Taylor and the families of his daughter and two sons moved here in 1863 from their homestead on the Llano River. They built a cabin on this site near the source of the Pedernales River. In August 1864, Matthew and his son Jim returned to the Llano for a load of hay, leaving in charge Eli McDonald, husband of Matthew's daughter Caroline. On August 8, 1864, at a nearby spring, Jim Taylor's wife, Gill, was surprised by a band of Kiowas and wounded by an arrow. Before she died, she warned the others, who took refuge in the cabin. After a brief fight, the Indians killed Eli McDonald. They captured his wife, Caroline, and daughters, Mahala and Becky Jane; and Alice, James, and Dorcas, children of Matthew's son Zed. Matthew's wife, "Aunt Hannah," escaped and hid in a cave in what is now Harper Community Park. Matthew and Jim Taylor discovered the tragedy the next day and sought help from Eli McDonald's nephew Monroe. The two victims of the massacre were buried near Spring Creek, twelve miles east of Harper. "Aunt Hannah" was found and reunited with her husband. The captives wandered as far north as Oklahoma with the Kiowa tribe before they were located and ransomed by the U.S. government. (1976)

HARPER (Gillespie Co.) FM 290 at US 783
First Baptist Church of Harper
Organized in 1887 with nine members, the First Baptist Church congregation initially met in the local school building and a brush arbor. A wooden sanctuary and parsonage were built in 1897. The congregation has been involved in community activities and mission work for many years. Harper High School held classes in the church building in 1921 and 1941–1942. A native stone structure was erected in 1944, consisting of a sanctuary and Sunday School rooms. A fellowship

hall annex was added in 1971. This church has been part of Harper history for over one hundred years.

(1987)

HARTLEY (Hartley Co.)
US 87, 1.8 mi. SE
Hartley County
Formed from Young and Bexar Territories. Created August 21, 1876. Organized February 5, 1891. Named in honor of two brothers, Oliver Cromwell and Rufus Hartley, distinguished members of the Texas bar. Hartley, county seat.

HASKELL (Haskell Co.)
US 277, at courthouse
Haskell County
Created February 1, 1858. Recreated August 21, 1876. Organized January 13, 1885. Named in honor of Charles Ready Haskell, 1817–1836, a Tennessean who was shot with Fannin in the massacre at Goliad. Haskell, the county seat. Crossed by Capt. R. B. Marcy in surveying a route to California in 1849. First settlement at Haskell, 1882.

HASKELL (Haskell Co.)
US 277 at SH 283, 15 mi. S
The Mackenzie Trail Historical Marker, Located 1 mi. N Stamford
This is the largest such marker between Vicksburg, Miss. and the Pacific. Erected by descendants of Open Range Ranchers. The MacKenzie Trail was the only way west between T. P. and F. W. & D. Rwys for decades. MacKenzie Trail Memorial Assoc.

HAWKINS (Wood Co.)
US 80, 1 mi. E
Jarvis Christian College
In 1904 the Texas Negro Disciples of Christ joined with the Christian Women's Board of Missions (CWBM) to establish a school for black youth. A campus, consisting of a 456-acre tract donated by Ida and J. J. Jarvis of Fort Worth in 1910 and 182 adjoining acres purchased by the CWBM, was created here in 1912. Jarvis Christian Institute opened in 1913 with 12 elementary students. It added courses for high school in 1914, junior college in 1927, senior college in 1937, and gained full accreditation in 1950. It remains affiliated with the Christian Church (Disciples of Christ).

(1993)

HEBBRONVILLE (Jim Hogg Co.)
205 N. Smith St. (SH 16)
Hotel Viggo
The original part of this hotel was built by C. F. Luque in 1915 for the owner, Viggo Kohler, to accommodate businessmen and area travelers. Soon after it opened, Hotel Viggo served as a fortress when area ranchers feared an attack by Pancho Villa's men. As a result of the town's oil boom, a south wing was added in 1924. The Mission Revival hotel has been a landmark on the Jim Hogg County courthouse square since Hebbronville's early days.

(1983)

HEBBRONVILLE (Jim Hogg Co.)
N. Smith (SH 16/359) at courthouse
Jim Hogg County
Formed from Brooks and Duval counties; created March 31, 1913; organized August 11, 1913. Named in honor of James Stephen Hogg, 1851–1906, first native Texan to serve as Governor; father of the Railroad Commission. Hebbronville, the county seat.

(1936)

HELENA (Karnes Co.)
FM 81 at SH 80
Helena
Founded in 1852 on San Antonio River by Thomas Ruckman, a graduate of Princeton, and Lewis Owings, later first governor of Arizona Territory. Town was named in honor of Owings' wife, Helen. Situated on branch of famed Chihuahua Trail (running from Indianola to San Antonio to Northern Mexico), Helena was to experience quick growth. Much traffic of wagon freight and gold bullion travelled trail. Four-horse stages daily passed through town. Helena was designated county seat when Karnes County was created and organized in 1854. First election of county officials was held on gallery of Ruckman-Owings store. During Civil War, Karnes County mustered six companies, including Helena guards, for service. Helena was a confederate post office and issued its own stamps. Much Confederate cotton destined for Mexican ports passed through Helena. During its heyday, Helena had a courthouse, jail, newspaper, academy, drugstore, blacksmith shop, two hotels,

and several saloons and general stores. Bypassed by the S.A. & A.P. Railroad in 1886, town died. County seat was moved to Karnes City in 1894 after hotly contested election.

HELENA (Karnes Co.)
FM 81, Old Helena Courthouse
Ox-Cart Road (Section of Chihuahua Road)
After centuries of use by buffalo and Indians, this trail from San Antonio to the Texas coast gained importance when opened to colonial travel by the Alarcon Expedition in 1718. Spanish conquistadores and priests, the Gutierrez-Magee Expedition (which invaded Spanish Texas in 1812), Stephen F. Austin, Alamo heroes, Santa Anna's messenger ordering the death of prisoners at Goliad, Polish and German settlers of Texas—all traveled the road. Rich trade in gold, silver, and leather with Mexico and the West was conducted along the road from San Antonio to Powderhorn. The U.S. 2nd Cavalry forts, established to protect the Texas frontier, moved men and supplies over it. Materials were transported in two-wheeled ox-carts, prairie schooners, Wells-Fargo wagons drawn by sixteen mules, and by pack animals. In 1852, Helena was founded on the road as a midway point between San Antonio and Goliad; Lewis S. Owings operated a daily stage line here, 1854. Major incidents of the bizarre Cart War of 1857 between Texan and Mexican teamsters occurred near Helena. Herds of longhorns from South Texas crossed the road here enroute to market. After the railroad came through county in 1886 the Ox-Cart Road was abandoned.

HELOTES (Bexar Co.)
14464 Old Bandera Rd. off SH 16
Helotes
According to archeologists, human occupation of the Helotes area dates to about 7000 years before present, when small bands of nomadic Indians who migrated seasonally in search of food and game camped in this vicinity. Early Texas Pioneer John M. Ross acquired title to the land here in 1836, purchasing rights to a Republic of Texas land grant from Almazon Huston, Quartermaster General of the Republic of Texas Army. In 1852 Ross sold the property to Thomas Devine and Francis Giraud, who formed a partnership to survey the land and sell it in smaller plots. In 1858 Dr. George Frederick Marnoch purchased the land which later became the townsite of Helotes. The town of Helotes developed around the home and Mercantile Store of Arnold Gugger, who purchased property from Marnoch's heirs in 1880. Gugger became postmaster in 1888, and in 1908 sold his land to Bert Hielman, who opened the town's first dance hall. Many farms and cattle and sheep ranches were established in the area. Helotes became a popular stop for cowboys driving cattle to auction in San Antonio. Many descendants of early settlers still live in the area. (1992)

HEMPHILL (Sabine Co.)
SH 87 right-of-way, 4.5 mi. N
Matthew Arnold Parker
(May 17, 1801–March 19, 1862)
First chief justice of Sabine County, Republic of Texas. Parker was born in Georgia. He came here from Louisiana in 1822, settling at this site which was on land later included in his headright grant from the Republic. In 1836 he served in the defensive Sabine Volunteers. President Sam Houston appointed him chief justice (or county judge) in Dec. 1836, and he was on a commission to detect fraudulent land claims in 1840. After his wife, Mary (Isaacs), died (1845), he married Elizabeth Lowe. He was father of 16 children. He died in DeWitt county, and was buried near Nordheim.
(1974)

HEMPHILL (Sabine Co.)
201 SH 184 (Main St.)
Hemphill
In 1858, Sabine County organized the community of Hemphill, named for Texas Supreme Court Justice John Hemphill (1803–1862). An election determined that the county seat would be moved from Milam to this new settlement in the center of Sabine County. Earl Percy Beddoe surveyed and laid out the town site on an 80-acre tract owned by Richard Fendall Slaughter and his wife, Anna (Holman). A post office was established in Hemphill in 1859. Builders constructed the first courthouse in Hemphill shortly after the community's establishment; it was replaced in 1864 by another building, which burned down in 1875. Builder completed another courthouse in 1877, which was eventually replaced by the current structure in 1906. Other significant early institutions included Sabine Valley University, established in 1879, and First National Bank, which opened in 1907 and closed during the Great Depression. Hemphill Common School District No. 1 organized in the late

1800s, and by 1890 listed three trustees, two teachers and eighty-eight students. The population of Hemphill increased steadily between 1850 and 1930, due in great part to the presence of the Knox Sawmill in the western part of town. Temple Lumber Company later bought the mill, which burned in 1937. Combined with post–World War II rural-to-urban migration trends and the lack of major thoroughfares in the town, the closing of the sawmill promoted a decline in the community's population. Today, Hemphill remains the seat of the Sabine County government, and is home to several national, state and local offices, remaining a community of vital importance in the state of Texas. (2008)

HEMPSTEAD (Waller Co.) — SH 6, 1 mi. N
Waller County
Created from Austin and Grimes Counties, April 28, and organized Aug. 16, 1873. Named for Edwin Waller (1800–1861), a signer of the Texas Declaration of Independence, 1836; Postmaster General, Texas Republic; first mayor of Austin. Site of rich 1831–1874 Groce plantations, later home of sculptress Elisabet Ney. Hempstead, founded 1857 during building of Houston & Texas Central Railroad, an important transportation center, is the county seat. Since 1878, county has been site of Prairie View Agricultural & Mechanical College. Economy is based on industry, diversified agriculture, and oil production. (1967)

HEMPSTEAD (Waller Co.) — SH 159, 1.5 mi. SW
The Camp Site of the Texas Army
Five miles southeast to the camp site of the Texas Army March 31 to April 13, 1836, when it crossed the Brazos on the steamboat Yellowstone and began its march toward Harrisburg.

HEMPSTEAD (Waller Co.) — US 290, 3.5 mi. E in roadside park
Clear Creek Confederate War Camps
Although no physical evidence has been found of the Confederate camp sites in this area, historical accounts have established that this part of Waller County was the location of several Civil War encampments. The close proximity of Clear Creek, the railroad, and the city of Hempstead made this area a logical site for training soldiers and for holding Federal prisoners. Although Camp Groce and Camp Herbert were the most widely known, other camps were known to have been established as the need existed and were abandoned when no longer necessary. (1985)

HEMPSTEAD (Waller Co.) — US 290, 3.3 mi. E, rest area, near entrance to Liendo Plantation
Groce Family Plantations
Pioneers in this Texas area. Had early cotton gin and ferry. Founder of family was Jared E. Groce (1782–1836), who came to Texas in 1822. His large wagon train brought elaborate plantation equipment. Groce built "Bernardo" and "Groce's Retreat." Heirs built "Pleasant Hill," "Eagle Island" and "Liendo" (the only surviving Groce mansion, 2 mi. NW of here). A contribution of the family to the cause of Texas freedom was providing rations and ferry service to army of Gen. Houston on eve of San Jacinto victory. Descendants have contributed leadership to the state. (1970)

HEMPSTEAD (Waller Co.) — FM 529, 14.8 mi. S
Norris Wright Cuney (May 12, 1846–March 3, 1898)
Born in the slave quarters of Sunnyside plantation (3.2 miles SE), Cuney displayed such intelligence as a boy that in 1859 he was sent to Wiley Street School for Negroes in Pittsburgh, Pa. On returning to Texas after the Civil War, he studied law and began operating a wharf contracting company in Galveston. Cuney soon became an active member of the Texas Union League, which urged black political activity and Republican Party loyalty. In 1870 he organized the Negro Longshoremen's Association. In later years he served Galveston as a city alderman, school board member, and U.S. customs collector, and ran twice without success for the state legislature. On July 5, 1871, he married Adelina Dowdie; they had two children. After 1872 he emerged as leader of the Republican Party in Texas, attending national party conventions as chairman of the Texas delegation. He served on the Republican National Executive Committee in 1891–1892. The party broke his power in Texas in 1896 by refusing to seat his delegation, an action which deprived blacks of a voice in Texas politics until the 1960s. Cuney, one of the most prominent blacks in Texas history, died in San Antonio, where he had moved for his health. He was buried in Galveston. (1973)

HENDERSON (Rusk Co.)   *SH 43, 8 mi. NE*
New Prospect Baptist Church and Cemetery
Located on part of the Hansel Wright Survey, this congregation and cemetery were established in the 1850s. Many early church members, including organizers Thomas Ballenger (1811–1882) and B. F. Montgomery (1810–1900), migrated to the area from Spartanburg County, South Carolina. This site was named in honor of a church in their home state. The first property here was obtained in 1855 from Miles Yandle, the son-in-law of Hansel Wright. The burial ground contains the graves of many pioneer settlers and members of the fellowship.   (1980)

HENDERSON (Rusk Co.)   *SH 323, 6 mi. W*
Pleasant Hill Cemetery
Located on land donated in 1845 by Captain Robert W. Smith (1814–1851), a veteran of the Texas Revolution, this cemetery first served the members of Pleasant Hill Cumberland Presbyterian Church. The earliest marked grave is that of DeWitt Smith, who died in 1850. Also buried here are 112 victims of the March 18, 1937, explosion which destroyed the school at New London (4 mi. NW) and killed 293 students and teachers. Annual Pleasant Hill homecoming activities, including a memorial service and dinner on the grounds, are conducted here each July.   (1980)

HENDERSON (Rusk Co.)   *US 79 at FM 1793, 13 mi. E*
Trammel's Trace
An early Indian trail later named for Nicholas Trammel who surveyed it in 1813 for the U.S. Used in describing most of the boundary between Rusk and Panola counties. Portions of the trace are incorporated into the county line road 7/10 of a mile south of this marker. It passes through Tatum, placing the town site in both counties. The trace extended from Red River to Nacogdoches and brought in great numbers of pioneers, including many who became Texas heroes.

HENDERSON (Rusk Co.)   *SH 64, 6 mi. W in roadside park*
East Texas Oil Field Discovery Well,
the Joiner No. 3 Daisy Bradford
Discovery genius was C. M. (Dad) Joiner, 70 year old Oklahoman, who for years had believed there was oil in Rusk county. Driller was E. C. Laster. Final crew: Dennis May, Dave Cherry, Glenn Pool, Jim Lambert and Dave Hughes. Two previous attempts had been made by Joiner on the Miller farm, both ending in mechanical failure. A bit jammed in the first hole, and the second was abandoned on the advice of Laster because the drill pipe was stuck. Rig was skidded 300 feet down slope (derrick had a broken sill). "This is as good a place as any," said Laster, and the Joiner no. 3 Daisy Bradford was spudded in on May 8, 1929. Equipment consisted of an old rotary rig powered by one single cylinder engine, one 45 hp boiler and one old cotton gin boiler fired with soggy oak and pine chunks by Dan Tanner, roustabout. The depression was on and money hard to raise. The crew often went without pay and Dad Joiner sacrificed much of his 10,000 acre block of leases to keep the venture going. Finally on Sept. 5, 1930, a drill stem test logged at 3536 feet into the Woodbine formation showed oil. A better rig had to be brought in to complete the well. Casing was set at 3400 feet and on October 3, 1930, the well blew in and oil went over the crown block. The news spread like wildfire. Cars were bumper to bumper on all roads leading to the well, and the boom was on. Derricks rose in all directions. In its first 30 years, this great field produced in excess of 3½ billion barrels of oil. It now covers some 200 square miles, largest in the world.

HENDERSON (Rusk Co.)   *SH 64, 6 mi. W*
Gaston Public School Complex
An oil boom here in the early 1930s prompted the formal organization of the Gaston Independent School District in 1931 to cope with the community's rapidly expanding student population. The district chose Dallas architects Emory White and Howard DeFee to design both an elementary and a 2-story high school building. These brick structures were completed at this site, along with a football field, in 1932. The district added a wooden gymnasium and brick auditorium in 1936, home economics cottage in 1938, brick cafeteria in 1939 and shop building in 1940. Linked by arcades, the structures exhibit classically articulated features and sophisticated cast-stone and window details. The rustic style landscaping, which includes walls made of native stone from the nearby Hardy farm, was completed by the Works Progress Administration in 1936–1940. Students at this institution earned county, district and regional championships in football, basketball, and track, as

well as awards in journalism, band, debate and other literary areas, including a Rhodes Scholarship, during the 1940s and 1950s. Gaston schools merged with the London School System in 1965 to form the West Rusk County Independent School District. (1993)

HENDERSON (Rusk Co.)
US 79 Bus. at 1st. St.
Henderson
Founded as the county seat for the newly created county of Rusk in 1843, Henderson was named for Republic of Texas pioneer and statesman James Pinckney Henderson, who would later become the first governor of the state of Texas. Land for the town was donated by W. B. Ochiltree, who stipulated that it be named for his friend Henderson, and by Republic of Texas General James Smith, who is known as the "Father of Henderson." Town lots were sold soon after the city was established, with land set aside for both churches and schools. A wooden courthouse was built in the center of town in 1849, and the town grew steadily as homes and businesses were constructed. A disastrous fire destroyed much of the central business district in 1860. Following the Civil War and the arrival of the railroads in this area in the 1870s, a large number of brick structures were built in the downtown area. The discovery of the vast East Texas oil field in 1930 caused an economic boom in Henderson. The population increased from 2,000 to 10,000 within a matter of months. The town continues to serve as a center of commerce and civic activities. (1989)

HENDERSON (Rusk Co.)
S. Main Street (US 79) at Howard St.
Howard-Dickenson House
First brick home in county. Built 1855 by brothers, David P. and Jas. Logan Howard, settlers from Richmond, Va. The Howards made bricks with mud mill and later with a patented machine and kiln on the premises. (Howard bricks and carpentry went into the old courthouse on square—and most of city's major construction in later 1800s.) Structure is iron-reinforced; has hand-wrought woodwork and oldest plastered walls in city. A frequent visitor in early years to this house was Texas statesman Sam Houston, a cousin of Martha Ann (Mrs. Dave) Howard. The home was bought in 1905 by Mrs. M. C. Dickenson, the daughter of Dr. Alfred Graham, a pioneer physician of Rusk County. To the original house, the Dickensons added a frame wing at the rear. Purchased in 1950 by Mr. and Mrs. Homer L. Bryce, and given by the Bryces in 1964 to the Rusk County Heritage Association, the house was restored in 1967 by work of Friends of Texas History. (1968)

HENDERSON (Rusk Co.)
S. Main (US 79) at Jacksonville Dr.
Park Named for General James Smith
(Sept. 10, 1792–Dec. 25, 1855)
On this hill, as he wished for burial in sight of courthouse, is grave of General James Smith, co-founder of Henderson. A South Carolina native, he fought for the U.S. in War of 1812. Moved to Texas 1835. Returned to U.S. to raise troops for Texas War of Independence. Later he fought in Republic's Indian Wars; Regulator-Moderator uprising in 1840s in East Texas; and in Mexican War. He was first Judge, East Texas District; a legislator; honored in naming of nearby Smith County. His wife, Hannah Parker Smith, is buried beside him in this park. They had ten children. (1968)

HENDERSON (Rusk Co.)
US 79, 11 mi. SW
Pleasant Grove Methodist Episcopal Church South Cemetery
The East Texas farming community of Pleasant Grove, also known as "Shake Rag," was established during the 1850s by southern planters. Among the first settlers were Judge Stephen Decatur Morris (1819–1898) and his wife, Mary (Bradford) (1823–1906), on whose plantation early Methodist worship services in the area were held. About 1853, a sanctuary for the Pleasant Grove Methodist Episcopal Church, South, was built. The Methodist Cemetery was established here in 1873, with the burial of James Bradford Morris (b. 1856). He was the son of Stephen and Mary Morris. Others buried here include Dr. Richard H. C. Shelton, an eminent southwestern surgeon; other friends and relatives of Stephen and Mary Morris; and pioneer settlers. Church trustees Seaton Moore, Simpson Moore, and G. D. Boatwright purchased this land for the church and cemetery in 1877. The Pleasant Grove Church eventually disbanded, with the remaining members joining St. Paul's Methodist Church in Henderson (11 mi. NE). By 1929, the year of the last burial in this graveyard, most Methodist families were using the city cemetery in Henderson. The Pleasant Grove Cemetery remains an important part of the record of early settlement in this part of Rusk County.

(Texas Sesquicentennial 1836–1986)

HENRIETTA (Clay Co.)   *US 82 at US 287, east city limits*
Clay County
Formed from Cooke County. Created December 24, 1857. Organized August 6, 1860. Disorganized in 1862 because of Indian raids. Reorganized August 4, 1873. Henrietta, headquarters for buffalo hunters until 1878. The first Hereford cattle in Texas were brought to Clay County 1875 from Beecher, Illinois by William S. Ikard. Original county seat Cambridge moved to Henrietta 1874.   (1964)

HEREFORD (Deaf Smith Co.)   *US 60, 5.5 mi. N*
Site of Great Cowboy Strike (3 mi. E)
Began in spring of 1883 when range hands from LS, LX, LIT and other large ranches organized a strike for better wages; was a reaction to loss of privileges given earlier and to attitude of big land owners toward cowboys. Several hired hands gathered at Alamocitos, headquarters of LS, to protest. Men on every ranch soon asked for higher pay, but strike failed due to surplus of cowboys and no means to enforce demands. Strike gave force to little men opposing cattle barons and three years later erupted in Tascosa into one of the bloodiest gun fights the West had ever seen.   (1967)

HEREFORD (Deaf Smith Co.)   *4th St. at courthouse*
Deaf Smith County
Formed from Young and Bexar Territories. Created August 21, 1876. Organized October 3, 1890. Named in honor of Erastus "Deaf" Smith 1787–1837. Came to Texas in 1821. Rendered valuable service as a scout and spy during the Texas Revolution and was conspicuous for his bravery in the Battle of San Jacinto. County seat, La Plata, frequently called Grenada, 1890–1898. Hereford, since 1899.   (1964)

HEREFORD (Deaf Smith Co.)   *US 60 at Main St.*
Pioneer Windmill
A wind-driven machine for pumping water. Its use made gardening easier and led to irrigated farming on arid High Plains. With barbed wire, it enabled settlers and stockmen to penetrate region in 1870s. Town had name "Windmill City" because of some 400 towers once on landscape.
                                                                                                    (1970)

HEREFORD (Deaf Smith Co.)   *W 4th Street at Bennett, in city park on US 385*
Town without a Toothache
Hereford's "miracle water" was brought to national fame in 1941 when Dr. Edward Taylor, state dental officer, told the American Dental Association that tooth decay was almost unknown here. This ideal situation had been discovered by a local dentist, Dr. George Heard, originally from Alabama. In a cross-section survey, dentists found that few local people had dental cavities. Hereford's mineral-rich water and soil are thought to prevent tooth decay. Demand arose for Hereford water to be shipped all over the U.S. and to foreign nations.   (1967)

HEREFORD (Deaf Smith Co.)   *US 60 at US 385*
Mackenzie Trail
Along this lonely, arid trail Gen. Ranald S. Mackenzie led his troops on scouting forays in the 1870s. Known for bravery and skill as a Civil War officer, he was sent to Texas and quickly adjusted to dangers and problems of frontier fighting. He fought against Comanches at Blanco and Tule Canyons. On Sept. 28, 1874, in Palo Duro Canyon, he led his men in one of the last major Indian battles in Texas where he slew more than 1,000 horses to cripple Indian action; thus he helped bring peace to the Texas Panhandle, making it safe for settlers.   (1965)

HEREFORD (Deaf Smith Co.)   *US 60, 1 mi. SW*
Prisoner of War Camp Chapel (3.5 mi. S)
A prisoner of war camp, used primarily for Italian soldiers, was in operation near this site during World War II. Known as the Hereford Military Reservation and Reception Center, it was first used in 1943 for prisoners captured in an invasion of North Africa. Many of the approximately 7,000 Italian soldiers imprisoned here became friends with local residents and with American troops. Since the war, some have returned for visits and others have settled in the region. The camp chapel, constructed by the prisoners, is the only building remaining at the site.   (1982)

HEREFORD (Deaf Smith Co.)   *US 60, 4 mi. SW in roadside park*
Ghost Towns of Deaf Smith County
Here as in many Texas counties, ghost towns and ghost post offices outnumber living ones. La Plata (formerly Grenada) thrived as county seat and was a major stop of New Mexico-Amarillo Road, 1880s and '90s. Its 28 houses and businesses were removed to Hereford with the county government in 1898. Ayr, which lost county seat to La Plata, 1890, had an early post office and a few frame buildings. Other nonexistent post offices include Escarbada (on XIT ranch), 1889; Dean, 1892–1899; Mirage (probably on LS ranch), 1891–1894; Kelso, 1907–1908.   (1969)

HEREFORD (Deaf Smith Co.)   *US 385, 4.5 mi. S in Castro County*
Prisoner of War Camp
Near this site during World War II the Hereford Military Reservation and Reception Center, a prisoner of war camp, was established. During nearly three years of operation, approximately 7000 Italian soldiers were imprisoned. Through their work on area farms and such projects as the painting of religious murals in St. Mary's Catholic Church at Umbarger (25 miles northeast), many of the soldiers made lasting friendships with local residents and with American troops at the camp. The center's chapel, constructed by the prisoners, is the only building remaining at the site.   (1982)

HERMLEIGH (Scurry Co.)   *US 84, S*
St. John's Catholic Church
This area was settled in the early 1900s by a number of farm families from South Texas. Catholic services were first conducted by priests from Abilene in the homes of Albert J. Kuss, Sr. (1863–1945) and other settlers. The Church of Francis Xavier was built in 1908 on land donated by Robert Herm (1874–1927) in the new town of Hermleigh. In 1936, the name of the church was changed when funds were given to the congregation with the stipulation that its name be St. John's. Included in the new diocese of Lubbock in 1983, St. John's is the oldest parish in the diocese.   (1988)

HICO (Erath Co.)   *SH 6, 7 mi. NW*
Clairette Schoolhouse
The first Clairette schoolhouse was a one-room log structure built as early as 1871. This two-story building was constructed in 1912, one year after the creation of the Clairette Independent School District. It served until 1949, when the rural school was closed. The native stone building was then used for various community functions. The old Clairette schoolhouse features a one-story porch with Tuscan columns at the entryway.   (1985)

HICO (Hamilton Co.)   *US 281 at 1 St.*
First United Methodist Church of Hico
In 1881, the Rev. John W. Hearn and Elder L.B. Hickman led 29 members in a newly organized Methodist church in Hico. The congregation held its early services in the Hico schoolhouse, and charter members included the L.T. Dillashaw, J.B. Hillyer, George D. Autrey and D.G. Barrow families. During a 10-day revival in winter 1884–85, evangelist R.R. Raymond helped raise money for a church sanctuary. Texas Central Railway donated land in 1886 for the use of the Methodist Episcopal Church, South, congregation of Hico. A sanctuary was completed in spring 1887 at this site. The structure served the congregation, which had grown to more than 300 members, until 1902–03, when the current sanctuary was built of wood with handcrafted benches and pulpit. The church held an open house and homecoming in 1954, showing to former members and pastors a new education building and remodeled sanctuary, with an enclosed bell tower and new tan brick façade over the original wood cladding. The congregation's numbers grew during the 20th century as other area churches merged their memberships into Hico's. These churches represented the communities of Carlton, Clairette, Duffau, Fairy and Pleasant Hill. During its years as a congregation, the church has contributed to area communities through its many services, including Boy and Girl Scout programs, community dinners, and clothes and food pantry, as well as its youth, music and education programs, missionary funding, study and worship.   (2002)

HIDALGO (Hidalgo Co.)   *US 281 Spur, terminus at the Rio Grande River*
Hidalgo-Reynosa Bridges
At the time of the formation of Hidalgo County in 1852, the village located here, originally named Edinburgh, became the new county seat. A ferry service was operating between the village

and Reynosa, Mexico. By 1861, the town's name was changed to Hidalgo, and regular ferry service was inaugurated in 1910 by Crisoforo Vela (1856–1932). First using rowboats and, later, raft-like conveyances, the ferry continued in operation until Joe Pate erected a bridge here in 1926. The 1926 suspension bridge was damaged by floods in 1933. Although rebuilt and strengthened, it fell into the river and was destroyed in 1939 after cable anchors on the U.S. side failed to hold. A second suspension bridge was erected the following year and was purchased by the city of McAllen in 1960. A four-lane prestressed concrete bridge was opened to traffic on June 1, 1967. The suspension bridge was removed for salvage in 1971. Construction of an additional four-lane bridge was completed in 1988. For over six decades, the Hidalgo-Reynosa bridges, operated jointly by McAllen, Hidalgo, and Mexican interests since 1960, have facilitated transportation and fostered international cooperation and friendship between Texas and Mexico. (1989)

HIGGINS (Lipscomb Co.)   *US 60, 1 mi. E*
Lipscomb County
Formed from Young and Bexar Territories. Created August 21, 1876. Organized June 6, 1887. Named in honor of Abner S. Lipscomb, 1789–1856. Secretary of State in President Lamar's Cabinet. Member of the Constitutional Convention, 1845. Associate Justice of the first Supreme Court of Texas. Lipscomb, the county seat.

HIGGINS (Lipscomb Co.)   *US 60, W in city park*
Higgins
Town platted, post office opened and first train arrived, 1887. Named for G. H. Higgins, wealthy railroad stockholder. Early cattle shipping point. Devastating tornado struck April 9, 1947. An estimated 45 were killed, 140 injured. Ranching, farming and oil are chief area industries. Oil drilling was begun in 1957. (1967)

HIGGINS (Lipscomb Co.)   *US 60, W in city park*
Will Rogers (Nov. 4, 1879–Aug. 15, 1935)
One of America's best loved humorists, whose stage act, gently mocking man's foibles, was highlighted by rope tricks learned here in his youth. Born in Oklahoma. In 1898, threatened with discipline for pranks, he left school and came to Texas. He became a cowboy on the Little Robe ranch near Higgins and made a lifelong friend of young Frank Ewing, son of his employer. In 1902 he joined a Wild West show; was famous by 1918. Rogers died in a crash during a globe-circling pioneer flight with aviator Wiley Post, 1935. (1967)

HIGH ISLAND (Galveston Co.)   *SH 124 between 9th St. and Pierce St.*
High Island
The coastal community of High Island sits atop a salt dome at the east end of Bolivar Peninsula. It was named High Island because the hill sits about 45 feet above sea, the only dry land visible during storms and flooding. Settled by Anglos in the early 1800s, nearly all of High Island lies within the Martin Dunman Survey, granted in 1837. The pioneers were mostly farmers, though George E. Smith gained fame from his patented bottled water from natural springs on his land. The town expanded in 1886 when the Gulf and Interstate Railroad began operations in the area. A depot was built, along with many new businesses. In 1897 C. T. Cade constructed the Sea View Hotel on the hill overlooking the Gulf of Mexico. The hotel became a place of refuge in 1900 and 1915 when hurricanes struck the Texas Coast, causing flooding over the peninsula. Oil was discovered on High Island, with successful drilling beginning in 1916. Petroleum deposits found at the perimeter of the salt dome in 1931 started an oil boom, and provided employment for the region. High Island has become recognized internationally as an important habitat for migratory birds, bringing crowds of bird-watchers annually to the area. (1996)

HILLSBORO (Hill Co.)   *SH 171, 6 mi. NW*
The Lackawanna Ranch
Dr. John S. Scofield (1826–1901) chose the Indian name "Lackawanna" for the 2500 acre tract of land he bought here in 1858. After moving with his family from Kentucky, he served Hill County as a doctor and county judge. Later he was a director and vice-president of Sturgis National Bank. Dr. Scofield introduced shorthorn cattle to this area. His son, Frank (1887–1974), who inherited this part of the ranch in 1901, raised prize-winning shorthorns. After the first house on this site burned,

the present structure was built in 1917. The Lackawanna ranch was purchased in 1945 by E. G. Murphree.
(1975)

HILLSBORO (Hill Co.)   *SH 81/171 at Franklin St.*
Hill County
Created February 7, 1853. Organized May 14, 1853. Named in honor of Dr. George W. Hill, 1814–1860. Member of the Texas Congress and Legislature. Secretary of War of the Republic of Texas, 1843–1845. Lexington, first village 1853. Hillsboro, county seat since.
(1936)

HILLSBORO (Hill Co.)   *SH 81/171 at Franklin St.*
Hill County Courthouse
The fourth courthouse for Hill County (organized in 1853) and the third one located in Hillsboro, this impressive landmark replaced a brick court building erected in 1874. Contractors Lovell, Miller and Hood of Brownsville built this rusticated limestone structure in 1890. Waco architect W. C. Dodson, who designed a number of public buildings, planned the modified French Second Empire styling. The three-story courthouse is topped by a seven-story clock tower.
(1964)

HILLSBORO (Hill Co.)   *118 S. Waco St. (SH 81/171)*
City of Hillsboro
In 1853, the Texas Legislature carved Hill County out of Navarro County. Named for physician and Republic of Texas Secretary of War Dr. George Washington Hill, the new county had only recently attracted Anglo settlement, following the establishment in 1848 of Fort Graham. County commissioners selected Hillsboro, originally spelled Hillsborough, as county seat. They established the town on land donated by Thomas Steiner, John Caruthers and Jonathan Newby, and the community soon had a school and post office, as well as a wood-frame courthouse. Cotton became the mainstay of Hillsboro's late 19th-century economy. The city experienced rapid growth after the Missouri, Kansas & Texas Railroad and other lines came to the town in the early 1880s. In addition to bringing new settlers and giving access to shipping and transportation, railroads provided many new jobs. The city continued to grow and incorporated in 1881. The cotton industry produced a building boom between 1890 and 1910, as evidenced by the numerous Queen Anne homes still intact today, as well as the noted 1890 Hill County Courthouse. In 1923, the community established the Hillsboro Junior College, which over the years has become Hill College. Many Texas political leaders have come from Hillsboro, including U.S. Congressman Joseph Abbott and Texas Lt. Governor Bob Bullock, as well as Thomas Slater Smith, Robert Lee Bobbitt, Robert W. Calvert, Crawford C. Martin, Nelson Phillips and Sam Johnson. In 1981, Hillsboro became one of the Texas Historical Commission's five original Texas Main Street Cities. The growing city continues to provide leadership, as well as natural, cultural and educational resources.
(2004)

HILLSBORO (Hill Co.)   *SH 81/171 at courthouse*
Site of Old Lexington Village (1 mi. S)
Founded about 1851 on Jack's Branch. Was Hill County's first settlement and only polling place when county organized on May 14, 1853. For 4 months two log homes functioned as a courthouse until a special election put the county seat at Hillsboro.
(1965)

HILLSBORO (Hill Co.)   *IH 35/US 77 at Old Brandon Rd. in city park*
Abbott's Grove
In the early days of Hillsboro, a grove of pecan, hackberry, elm and other trees grew along the banks of Hackberry Creek. Hillsboro residents came to the grove for community celebrations and festivities. They called it Abbott's Grove in honor of one of the city's popular leaders, Joseph Abbott (1840–1908). He and his wife, Rowena (Sturgis), built their family home on the land south of the creek. Two of their five children owned adjacent property. Jo Abbott was a distinguished lawyer, judge, Texas legislator and U.S. Congressman. He and brother-in-law George F. Sturgis operated what would become the Sturgis National Bank. An avid anti-prohibitionist, Abbott was often a speaker at rallies and barbecues held in the 1880s and 1890s in the grove near his home. Other events at the grove included community and holiday picnics, concerts, ball games, and reunions for groups like the Old Settlers and Confederate Veterans Associations. At Abbott's death in 1908, prominent businessman and banker George Carmichael (1855–1924) purchased the Abbott home and property, and donated $1,000 in 1921 to designate the grove as a city park. The newly

organized Hillsboro Rotary Club got behind the effort, and after a few months of raising funds the Rotarians were successful in their campaign. The new municipal park continued the name of Abbott's Grove. Use of the park at Abbott's Grove fluctuated over the years, but after a period of underutilization the park is once again a source of community pride, and a place for birthday parties, end-of-school events and other celebrations. Hillsboro citizens enjoy the scenic setting and the many amenities found in historic Abbott's Grove. (2004)

HILLSBORO (Hill Co.) *SH 22 at Walnut Ave. opposite Hill Junior College*
Confederate Veterans and Old Settlers Reunion Grounds (1 mi. S)
Formed in 1901, the Confederate Veterans and Old Settlers Association of Hill County acquired 73 acres of wooded land as a site for its summer reunion. The 3–5 day encampment, held annually from 1902 to 1924, was an important social and recreational event in this locality. Many families traveled by wagon and camped at the site. Special trains from Hillsboro brought other visitors, and a gravel auto road was completed in 1909. The reunion usually attracted a crowd of several thousand persons. Activities included speeches, musical programs, baseball games, and, on one occasion, a carnival midway show. Located on the grounds were a spring-fed lake, large pavilion, and baseball park. Some families leased their camp lots and built summer cottages. The Fraternal Picnic Associations's July 4th picnic, 1908–1914, and other meetings and social events were also held here. With the reopening (1916) of the Hill County Fair and a decrease in numbers of veterans and old settlers, reunion attendance dropped sharply at the end of World War I (1918). The association deeded its property to the state in 1924 to be developed as Jefferson Davis State Park, but those plans were never realized. (1977)

HITCHCOCK (Galveston Co.) *SH 6 at FM 2004*
Hitchcock
In region held before 1820s, by Karankawa Indians, and afterwards by cattle raisers. The Gulf, Colorado & Santa Fe Railway built through the area in 1870s, naming station for Galveston civic leader and late landowner, Lent Munson Hitchcock (1810–1869). On the railway, George Henckel in 1880s opened a produce commission house. Leaders among fruit and vegetable growers included Emil and Hypolite Perthius, H. M. Stringfellow, and Jacques Tacquard. Stores, a butcher shop, bakery, hotel, and saloons were established. The townsite was platted and public school opened 1894. Churches were active. St. Mary's (later Our Lady of Lourdes) Catholic Parish had first house of worship. A building for Protestants, soon a Methodist church, was erected 1894. Other faiths arrived later. After 1920, truck farming declined; packing houses closed. In 1930s, local men found work in Texas City. A coast auxiliary army replacement center opened here in 1940; it later became Camp Wallace, an anti-aircraft training center. A blimp base was operated 1941–1945, for surveillance against enemy submarines. Hitchcock remains a center of small business and industry, with modern homes on garden acreage owned and occupied by urban and industrial workers. (1973)

HITCHCOCK (Galveston Co.) *SH 6, at entrance to Jack Brooks Park*
U.S. Naval Air Station (Blimp Base) (7/10 mi. S)
In an effort to defend U.S. coasts and shipping lanes against German submarine activity during World War II, the U.S. Navy established bases to house huge lighter-than-air (LTA) craft, also known as blimps. With the ability to hover above a target, the blimps were uniquely qualified for coastal defense and observation. Because of its site on the flat Texas Coastal Plain, Hitchcock was chosen as the location for one of the nine new blimp bases. Construction began in 1942, and the facility was commissioned on May 22, 1943. The resulting military personnel build-up caused an economic boom in the community. The Hitchcock base consisted of forty-seven buildings, including a massive hangar to house six blimps, administration buildings, warehouses, living quarters, and recreational facilities. Aircraft from the base, in addition to their regular patrolling duties, were also used to assist with hurricane relief efforts and war bond drives. In 1944, after the blimps were no longer needed, the Hitchcock base was redesignated for other purposes. Following the war some of the buildings were used by private interests, and after hurricane damage in 1961 the blimp hangar was razed. (1989)

HITCHCOCK (Galveston Co.) *SH 6, .5 mi. W of entrance to Jack Brooks Park*
Camp Wallace
Named for World War I Army Colonel Elmer J. Wallace, Camp Wallace was established as a training facility for military personnel during World War II. The U.S. government acquired more

than 3,300 acres of land between the towns of Hitchcock and Alta Loma on State Highway 6 for placement of the facility. Construction began in November 1940. Before the erection of structures, 17 miles of access roads were built, 29 miles of electrical lines were installed, and a 3.9-mile spur rail track from the main rail line were laid. The site contained a total of 399 structures. Some buildings were constructed at Galveston's Fort Crockett and transported to the site, including a cold storage depot, bakery, laundry, and morgue. The camp contained a medical facility, 161 barracks, and a service club. By May 1941, the camp accommodated 10,250 people, including officers, enlisted personnel, and civilian staff and training continued through World War II. The site also housed German prisoners of war. In April 1945, Camp Wallace was transferred to naval supervision, and later served as a distribution center releasing veterans back into civilian life. The site was used by the Red Cross in 1947 following the explosions at Texas City. The camp was declared surplus by the U.S. government in 1947.

(1996)

HITCHCOCK (Galveston Co.)   7902 SH 6
Stringfellow Orchards
Nationally and internationally recognized horticulturist Henry Martyn Stringfellow (1839–1922) started an experimental garden and orchard at this location in 1883. In 1890, he published a treatise containing innovative organic gardening methods that were adopted by Japanese, German, and many American fruit and vegetable growers. Silver medals garnered at two world fairs and world-wide acclaim for additional publications solidified his stature as a premier experimental horticulturist of his time, vestiges of his handiwork were evident here over 100 years later.

(1992)

HOCHHEIM (DeWitt Co.)   US 183, 1.7 mi. S
Stagecoach Inn (.15 mi. W)
Built of hand-quarried native stone in 1856 by V. Hoch, a settler. Served as an inn on the Austin-Indianola Stage Road. While drivers changed four-horse teams, the passengers welcomed the chance to enjoy the inn's food and hospitality.

(1965)

HOCHHEIM (DeWitt Co.)   US 183
Hochheim (Hoch's Home)
Founded near home and stage stand of Valentine Hoch on old Austin-Indianola road, 1856. In 1864 German Methodist Church was built; post office opened 1869. County's first protestant church (organized 1841 on Cuero Creek by J. M. Baker and James N. Smith) moved here in 1882 as Hochheim Presbyterian Church. The Baptist church was founded later (1923). Concrete Lodge No 182, AF & AM (chartered 1856 with F. J. Lynch first Worshipful Master), became Hochheim Lodge, 1884, buying 1885 upper story of school house for lodge hall. In 1921 bought lower story, housing school until 1938.

HOCHHEIM (DeWitt Co.)   US 183, on bluff near Guadalupe River
Cuero I Archeological District
Extending 45 miles along the Guadalupe River Basin, Cuero I Archeological District was created to define and preserve cultural resources threatened by a proposed reservoir. Archeological investigation in 1972–73 revealed 352 significant prehistoric and historic sites spanning 9,000 years of human occupancy. The remains include the camps of prehistoric nomads and of historic Indians such as Tonkawas and Comanches. Other sites mark early Anglo-American settlement, which began with the colonizing efforts of Green DeWitt in the 1820s and '30s.

(1979)

HOLLIDAY (Archer Co.)   US 82, 1 mi. N
Captain John Holliday (Dec. 8, 1811–Aug. 19, 1842)
Born Hollidaysburg, Pennsylvania; came to Texas about 1835. Joined Texian Army, and was one of 24 survivors of the Goliad Massacre, March 27, 1836. Joined Texian-Santa Fe Expedition, and en route to New Mexico, Aug. 4, 1841, carved his name on a tree in this vicinity. After reaching Santa Fe, the party was arrested and marched to Perote Prison near Mexico City. In Aug. 1842, Holliday was released, but he died of yellow fever aboard ship two days from Galveston, and was buried at sea. Nearby Holliday Creek and the town of Holliday were named for the carving on the tree.

(1973)

HONDO (Medina Co.)
US 90, 3.5 mi. E
Medina County
Formed from Bexar County. Created February 12, 1848. Organized August 7, 1848. Named for river which traverses the county. County seat, Castroville, 1848–1892. Hondo, since. Primarily a farming and ranching area.

HONDO (Medina Co.)
1600 Ave. M, 3 blks. N of US 90
Hondo
Spanish explorers passed this way several times in the centuries preceding Anglo settlement of the area. The original village that would become Hondo was situated on "El Arroyo Hondo" named by the Spanish. Permanent settlers to the area began arriving with Henri Castro in the 1840s. The Galveston, Harrisburg and San Antonio (GH & SA) Railroad began to consider the busy village on Hondo Creek for the location of a depot in the late 19th century. They ultimately chose 188 acres 5 miles west of the town. The first deeds were executed in 1881. A post office for Hondo City was approved in 1882. Knowing that the county seat might be moved from Castroville to a more central location, the GH & SA donated land for a courthouse in 1883. The county seat was relocated to Hondo City in 1892. In the early 20th century the town, by then known simply as Hondo, developed as a trade center and cotton shipping point. Oil was discovered in the area in the 1920s. The population grew steadily with commerce; by 1940 it reached 2,500. The town's population exploded in 1942 when an Army Air Corps base was built to the northwest. Hondo was incorporated that year and the federal government provided educational funds and installed a sewage system to accommodate the boom. At its peak Hondo had an estimated population of 12,000. The base was closed in 1946, but continued to operate as a civilian pilot training center through the 1950s. Hondo grew steadily in the late 20th century. Its population in 1998 was more than 8,000. The community continues to thrive.
(1999)

HONDO (Medina Co.)
SH 173, 4 mi. N
Vandenburg
Located on the banks of Verde Creek (Arroyo Verde), Vandenburg, founded in 1846, was one of the colonies established by Empresario Henri Castro. Immigrants settled nearby and began farming. They dug a trench eight feet wide by six feet deep to protect them and keep their cattle nearby. Worship services conducted by visiting ministers were held in homes or under an arbor. Drought in 1847–49 caused crops to fail. Many settlers died from cholera. Most families moved to other communities by the 1860s. Two cemeteries are among the few physical remnants of Vandenburg.
(1996)

HONEY GROVE (Fannin Co.)
US 56, 3 mi. W
Wheeler House
First Classic Revival house in area. Has unusual stairway. Built 1852–1854, with slave labor. Fifth house on Bonham-Paris Stagecoach Road. Chimney stones and lumber hand-hewn. Joists were pegged rather than nailed. Sold in 1884 by Wiley Halsey, builder, to Confederate veteran Peyton Wheeler and wife, Martha Jane Hamil. Their descendants have erected this marker. Awarded Medallion Plate.
(1965)

HOOKS (Bowie Co.)
IH 30 near Hooks
Pecan Point Signers of the Texas Declaration of Independence
Five of the most prominent delegates to the Constitutional Convention of Texas, held March, 1836, hailed from Pecan Point, in this vicinity. Richard Ellis (an attorney and judge) was chosen president of the meeting and later served four terms in the Senate of the Republic. Collin McKinney (a magistrate) helped draft the Declaration and served three terms in the House. A. H. Latimer (an attorney) served two terms. Samuel Price Carson (attorney) became Texas' Secretary of State and with Robert Hamilton (financier) was an agent to the United States.
(1969)

HOOKS (Bowie Co.)
US 82 at west city limits
Hooks
Established about 1848 as a supply center for 5,000-acre plantation of Warren Hooks; 1841–1860 post office for area was Myrtle Springs, home of Hooks' son, Col. Robert W. Hooks, 11th Texas Cavalry, Confederate Army. Post office placed here 1884 was named for Warren Hooks. Farming

continued until 1942, when Hooks "boomed" suddenly. Population soared from 400 to 3,000 with opening of Lone Star and Red River Ordnance plants. Economy is diversified, with cotton and soybean production. A religious town, Hooks has sixteen churches. (1969)

HORSESHOE BAY (Llano Co.) — SH 71 at FM 2147

Charles Haynes (September 12, 1814–December 29, 1868)

Born in Vermont, Charles Haynes came to Texas in 1836 with the "Buckeye Rangers" of Ohio to fight for independence. He settled at Lockhart, operated a blacksmith shop, was a member of the first county commissioners' court, a justice of the peace, and a leader in Masonic work. About 1859 he moved with his family to Llano County. At Comanche schoolhouse in 1860, he organized Llano Lodge No. 242, A. F. & A. M. Twice married, he was father of eight children. (1974)

HOUSTON (Harris Co.) — Independence Pkwy, N of SH 225 at San Jacinto Battleground State Historic Site

Battle of San Jacinto

At mid-afternoon April 21, 1836, two miles to the north, General Sam Houston with about 1,000 Texans in 18 minutes annihilated the 1,400-man army of Antonio Lopez de Santa Anna, President of Mexico. Screened by trees and rising ground, Houston's men formed with Edward Burleson's regiment at center, Sidney Sherman's on the left wing, artillery under George W. Hockley on Burleson's right, the infantry under Henry Millard on the right of the artillery. Under M. B. Lamar, a future President of Texas, the cavalry took the extreme right, to cut off possible flight of Mexican troops. Their 4-piece band playing a popular love song, "Will You Come to the Bower," the Texans attacked at a run, crying, "Remember the Alamo! Remember Goliad!" Such was their fury that 630 of the enemy were killed, 730 captured. Enemy lead shattered Gen. Houston's ankle, but he lost only 9 men killed or mortally wounded and 30 wounded less seriously. San Jacinto stands as one of the world's greatest victories. It gave Texas independence, and with her annexation 9 years later brought into the Union all or parts of Arizona, California, Colorado, Kansas, New Mexico, Nevada, Oklahoma, Utah, and Wyoming.

Site of Battle of San Jacinto

Near here on the afternoon of April 21, 1836, the Army of the Republic of Texas commanded by General Sam Houston was drawn up to attack an invading Mexican Army commanded by General Antonio Lopez de Santa Anna (3.5 mi. S San Jacinto State Park, State Hwy. 134). The Texas Army attacked in four divisions: the cavalry on the right, commanded by Mirabeau B. Lamar, next, the infantry under Lieutenant Colonel Henry Millard; the "Twin Sisters" cannon under Colonel George W. Hockley; the 1st regiment in the center under Colonel Edward Burleson; the 2nd regiment, the left wing, under Colonel Sidney Sherman (3 mi. S San Jacinto State Park, State Hwy. 134). Within a few minutes the Battle of San Jacinto was over. According to General Houston's report 630 Mexicans lay dead on the field. 208 were wounded and 730 were taken prisoners. Money, arms and equipment were captured. The Texans had 9 killed and 30 wounded (1.4 mi. S San Jacinto State Park, State Hwy. 134). The Mexican cavalry was on the left wing; infantry and artillery in the center behind a fortification of boxes and baggage; while the extreme right was far extended (2.5 mi. S San Jacinto State Park, State Hwy. 134). To the tune of "Will You Come to the Bower" the Texans advanced; "Remember the Alamo! Remember Goliad" was their cry. With cannons and gunshot, clubs and Bowie knives they fought; no quarter was given; the rout was complete—the slaughter terrific.

Mexican Cavalry, Battle of San Jacinto

The Mexican cavalry was on the left wing, infantry and artillery in the center behind a fortification of boxes and baggage, while the extreme right was far extended. (1936)

1 mi. NE to Site of Lynch's Ferry

A pioneer ferry of Texas under Mexico and the Republic. Established at the confluence of Buffalo Bayou and the San Jacinto River, 1822, by Nathaniel Lynch, one of Stephen F. Austin's "Old Three Hundred" colonists. Usual charges at ferries like this were man and horse, 25 cents; cattle, 4 cents a head. But rates could be raised for risky high-water service. Lynch, from Missouri, was an active Texas merchant and judge. After a small settlement grew up near his ferry, he platted the town of "Lynchburg" about 1835, but few shared his enthusiasm for the spot. In March and April, 1836, as Texan settlers fled the Mexican Army during the War for Independence, hundreds crossed the San

Jacinto at Lynch's Ferry. By April 2 the prairie was covered with wagons, horses, mules, tents, and baggage; but 19 days later at the Battle of San Jacinto, the Mexican General Santa Anna, hoping to cut off a Texan retreat at the ferry, was himself defeated near the site. In later years Lynchburg became a steamboat stop for the picturesque stern-wheelers plying Buffalo Bayou, as eastbound freight was transferred there. Today the modern, motor-driven "Lynchburg Ferry." (1969)

HOUSTON (Harris Co.) *531 Crockett Dr. in Channelview, off IH 10*
Lorenzo de Zavala (1788–1836)
Three miles east is homesite and grave of a signer of the Texas Declaration of Independence and first Vice-President of the Republic of Texas—an illustrious statesman of two nations. He was born in Mexico. De Zavala, an ardent liberal and earnest advocate of democratic reforms, served his native country as representative in the Spanish Cortes, Madrid; Minister of the Treasury; President of Chamber of Deputies; Governor of State of Mexico and Ambassador to France. De Zavala tired of Santa Anna's tyranny, resigned his ambassadorship and moved here in 1835. When Mexican officials learned of his taking refuge in Texas and ordered his arrest, he became a strong leader in cause of Texas Independence. Voters in Harrisburg sent him in 1835 to the Consultation at San Felipe de Austin and later to the Independence Convention at Washington-on-the-Brazos. The De Zavala home, a plank-covered log house across from San Jacinto Battleground, served as a hospital for both sides after the battle. An observer on the scene described de Zavala as "the most interesting man in Texas"—He was a leading author, learned publicist, philosopher, historian, economist and constant lover of liberty. (1968)

HOUSTON (Harris Co.) *off US 90 near Clinton Dr. at Houston Ship Channel*
Constitution Bend
Now Houston's famous ship-turning basin, this bend in Buffalo Bayou was named for the *Constitution*, first steamboat to turn around here, in June 1837. At the time, Houston was less than a year old. It was serving as temporary capital of the Republic of Texas, which was itself barely more than a year old. According to one story, the town's founders, John and Augustus Allen (brothers), paid the captain of the boat $1,000 to make the trip as a publicity measure. The trading vessel was approximately 150 x 24 x 8 feet in size, with one deck, no mast, a round stern, male figurehead, and a cabin on the deck. The *Constitution*'s trip up Buffalo Bayou was not easy. Lines were run from it to trees and the boat was laboriously hauled forward by windlass. It ran aground twice. At one grounding, famous passenger Thomas Jefferson Chambers (patriot of the Republic) had enough time to visit a friend on shore. Upon their arrival at Houston, 35 of the 150 passengers memorialized the captain for his landmark voyage. The exit of the *Constitution* was no more graceful than her entrance: she had to back down the narrow bayou until she reached a spot wide enough to turn around. The name of this bend records that event. (1970)

HOUSTON (Harris Co.) *Milam St. and Congress Ave., S of IH 10/US 90*
Old Market Square
Platted 1836 by surveyors Gail Borden, Jr., and Moses Lapham as "Congress Square." It was intention of city fathers Augustus C. and John K. Allen to have permanent Capitol of Republic of Texas located here. However, this was never realized and almost immediately it became center of commerce for the flourishing city. Residents, farmers, peddlers and Indians all crowded here daily with wagon loads of goods to trade. Soon merchants were vying for permanent sites for stores. One early observer noted "reason for its popularity was that the municipal government was conducted in Kesler's Arcade, a saloon only a half block away." In 1840 Houston's first municipal market house was built here. Before it was completed, city officials voted to enlarge and include a city hall also. For 30 years building served dual role—the market overflowing till it reached the streets. Many items, including household and farm goods, were sold here. It was here that Houston Independent Light Guard mobilized after Texas decided to invade Mexico, 1842. Several municipal buildings occupied the site following original market-city hall. However, the seat of city government was eventually moved to a new location and this became a park. (1969)

HOUSTON (Harris Co.) *400 blk. McKinney, off IH 45, Sam Houston Heritage Park*
Houston City, Republic of Texas
By vote of Congress, Nov. 30, 1836, chosen temporary capital for new Republic of Texas. At the time a small townsite at the head of Buffalo Bayou navigation. Into a "Houston City" of mud, tents,

cabins on April 1, 1837, came President Sam Houston and his government. Finding its quarters unfinished, Congress postponed its opening session until May 1. The capitol building was a 2-story plantation style house, with columned porches. It was scene of many important Indian treaties, diplomatic negotiations, legislative functions. As no church yet graced the city, it also was used for religious services. That muddy April saw the city hold its first big social event—the anniversary celebration of the San Jacinto victory, with parade, reception, and ball. On Dec. 5, 1837, some war heroes and other leaders founded in the capital the Texas Philosophical Society, the Republic's first learning organization. In a powdered wig, and dressed to resemble George Washington, President Houston made a 3-hour farewell address, after which Mirabeau Buonaparte Lamar was inaugurated his successor on Dec. 10, 1838. In 1839, removed to Austin, the capital returned here, but only briefly, 1842, during the Mexican invasion. (1965)

HOUSTON (Harris Co.)
Bagby St. at Rusk St.
Democratic National Convention, 1928
Due to the efforts of businessman Jesse H. Jones, the Democratic National Committee chose Houston as the site of the 1928 Democratic National Convention. Located on this site, the 20,000-seat Sam Houston Hall was completed in 64 days at a cost of $200,000. The convention met from June 26 to 29. Major issues addressed included the enforcement of prohibition and the plight of America's farmers. One senator remarked that the 1928 delegates constituted the most disorderly orderly crowd he had ever seen. On June 28 New York Governor Alfred E. Smith (1873–1944) was nominated for president on the first ballot. An anti-prohibitionist, Smith was the first Roman Catholic to be nominated for the U.S. presidency by a major political party. Senate Majority Leader Joseph T. Robinson, a Southerner and supporter of prohibition, received the nomination for vice president on June 29. Smith, who did not attend the convention, later read a formal acceptance speech in Albany, New York. On November 6, Republican candidate Herbert Hoover won the national election by a wide margin. Though Alfred E. Smith had been nominated for the nation's highest office at the Houston convention, he did not carry Texas in the November general election. (1988)

HOUSTON (Harris Co.)
620 Crawford St., 4 blks. W of US 59
Daughters of the Republic of Texas
On November 6, 1891, seventeen women met at the home of Mrs. Andrew Briscoe at this site to organize an auxiliary to the Texas Veterans Association. Mrs. Anson Jones was elected president of the new organization, Daughters of the Lone Star Republic. Goals set for the group included preserving the memories of Texas Revolution heroes, instilling Texas patriotism in the state's school children, preservation of historic sites, and promoting statewide celebrations of Texas Independence Day (March 2) and San Jacinto Day (April 21). The first annual meeting of the organization was held in Lampasas on April 21, 1892. A resolution was passed to change the group's name to the Daughters of the Republic of Texas. By 1892 the first two chapters had been formed, one in Galveston and one in Houston. The D.R.T. has been in the forefront of many historic preservation projects throughout the state. Clara Driscoll, on behalf of the D. R. T., wrote personal checks to save the Alamo from demolition. The organization also led efforts to preserve and commemorate the San Jacinto Battlefield site, and maintains the old General Land Office and French Legation buildings in Austin as museums. (Texas Sesquicentennial 1836–1986)

HOUSTON (Harris Co.)
W. Dallas Ave. at Heiner St., near IH 45 S access rd.
Origins of Freedman's Town
Located in Houston's Fourth Ward, the original Freedman's Town settlement was founded soon after the emancipation of enslaved blacks on June 19, 1865, at the end of the Civil War in Texas. Positioned west of downtown and directly south of Buffalo Bayou, the community gradually expanded to the south and west during the late 19th and early 20th centuries. Freedman's Town quickly became the economic and cultural center of Houston's African American population, growing throughout the 1880s and 1890s. The neighborhood stretched from Buffalo Bayou south to Sutton Street, and west from Milam and Travis streets to Taft Street. A streetcar line was built west along what is now W. Dallas Street, and another line ran along Andrews to present Wilson Street, and north to Robin Street. Portions of the district, which included farmland, remained sparsely settled for several decades. The neighborhood changed as residents built many small wood-frame cottages, as well as a number of larger T-plan and L-plan houses. Commercial structures included

223

several corner grocery stores and restaurants, as well as apartment buildings and boardinghouses. Historic churches such as Antioch Missionary Baptist, Good Hope Missionary Baptist, Shiloh Missionary Baptist, St. James United Methodist and Bethel Baptist played important roles in the community. Clergymen from the churches were among the most prominent early leaders in Freedman's Town and included the Revs. Jack Yates, Ned P. Pullum and Jeremiah Smith. Cultural institutions included a high school, hospital and Carnegie Library. City growth and urban renewal later in the 20th century changed the boundaries and the character of Freedman's Town. (2005)

HOUSTON (Harris Co.) San Jacinto St., East lawn of old Harris Co. courthouse
Harris County

Inhabited during the 17th century by Karankawa and Orcoquiza Indians, and considered in 1756 by Spain for site of Presidio de San Agustin de Ahumada, this region was settled permanently in 1822 by the colonists of Stephen F. Austin. In 1824, John R. Harris (1790–1829) received title to 4,428 acres of land in Buffalo Bayou–Braes Bayou junction area, and started village named for his family and for Harrisburg, Pa., founded by his grandfather. Colonial settlements in the vicinity were Cedar Bayou, Lynchburg, Midway, Morgan's Point, New Kentucky, and Stafford's Point. First step toward local government was taken when Stephen F. Austin and the Baron de Bastrop met (1824) with colonists at the house of William Scott, Midway, to explain colonization laws. Harrisburg, a town by 1826, was one of the original and most influential colonial municipalities, with a major role in Texas War for Independence, which won freedom in 1836. The county of Harrisburg (later Harris) was created Dec. 30, 1836. The capital of the Texas Republic was within its boundaries for several years. In the Civil War, it was a command and ordnance center (1863–1865), of Trans-Mississippi Department, Confederate Army. It has since grown into a center for world commerce. (1972)

HOUSTON (Harris Co.) 4100 blk. Alameda Rd., S of US 59
Houston's First Sit-In

From 1896 until the 1960s in the southern United States, Jim Crow laws effectively banned African Americans from using public facilities and basic services that were used by whites. In March 1960, thirteen students from Texas Southern University (TSU) started a non-violent movement protesting these laws and changed Houston forever. These young architects of change formed the Progressive Youth Association (PYA), meeting at the South Central YMCA or in their apartments to plan strategies. These "war room" meetings are where they organized Houston's first sit-in. On March 4, 1960, the thirteen students met at a flagpole on TSU's campus and marched in pairs one mile to Weingarten's Supermarket (4110 Alameda Road) with the objective of being served at the lunch counter. Dozens more joined them as they marched, singing black spirituals. Though white employees refused to serve the students and patrons hurled insults at them, they sat there silently for hours, occupying all 30 counter stools in shifts. More sit-ins occurred over the following days and weeks. The sit-in at Weingarten's Supermarket was the first in a series of non-violent demonstrations leading to the peaceful end of segregation in public places. Houston's lunch counters quietly desegregated on August 25, 1960. Department stores, hotels and restaurants soon followed, and Houston's Astrodome opened in 1965 as an integrated facility. The sit-ins ended with the signing of the 1964 Civil Rights Act. Today, these thirteen unsung heroes are remembered for starting a movement that advanced civil rights and equality in Houston. (2009)

HOUSTON (Harris Co.) 1700 blk. MacGregor Dr., Dick Dowling statue,
Hermann Park
Major Richard William (Dick) Dowling, C. S. A.
(January 14, 1837–September 23, 1867)

Born in 1837 near Tuam, County Galway, Ireland, Richard Dowling emigrated to New Orleans in 1846 during the Irish potato famine. In 1857, Dick married Elizabeth Anne Odlum in Houston. By 1860 he had owned 3 bars, installed Houston's first gas lighting in his home and business, and was a charter member of Houston Hook and Ladder Company No. 1. During the Civil War, Dick was First Lieutenant, Company F, Cook's Regiment, First Texas Heavy Artillery. He was in command at Fort Griffin in 1863. On September 8 he held fast with only 6 cannons and 47 men inside the fort despite rumors of a Federal invasion and orders to retreat. Twenty-seven ships carrying Maj. Gen. William B. Franklin and 5,000 Union troops sailed into Sabine Pass; Dowling and "The Irish Davis Guards" shot so accurately that Franklin's forces surrendered in 45 minutes. The Confederate

Congress called the Battle of Sabine Pass "one of the most brilliant . . . achievements . . . of this war." Discharged as a major in 1865, Dick reopened his most famous bar, "The Bank of Bacchus." In 1866 he formed the first oil company in Houston. By 1867, he owned more than 22 square blocks of downtown Houston and vast lands across Texas. Dick Dowling died of yellow fever at age 30 and is buried in Houston's St. Vincent's Cemetery. (1998)

HOUSTON (Harris Co.)   *7401 Katy Freeway (IH 10)*
First Baptist Church of Houston
In February 1841, the Rev. James Huckins visited the fledgling city of Houston, where a small group of Baptists had been meeting informally since 1838. Under Huckins' leadership, a congregation was organized on April 10, 1841, with 16 charter members. Noted Texas minister William E. Tryon became the Houston church's first resident pastor in 1845. His first concerns were the erection of a church building and increasing the membership. The new structure, located at the corner of Travis Street and Texas Avenue, was dedicated in May 1847, and membership increased dramatically. Pastor Tryon succumbed to yellow fever in 1847. Under the leadership of his successor, Dr. Rufus C. Burleson, membership grew to 140 by 1852. Membership declined during the Civil War and Reconstruction, reaching 100 again in 1871. The church began a mission in nearby Richmond in the 1870s, followed by two mission chapels north of Buffalo Bayou and Tuam Mission in South Houston in the 1890s. These and other missions sponsored by the First Baptist Church became self-supporting Baptist churches. In 1907 the church joined with others in establishing the Star of Hope Mission and the Baptist Sanitarium (later Baptist Memorial Hospital). The congregation persevered during the Depression and World War II. The congregation experienced unprecedented growth in the early 1970s, and on April 3, 1977, relocated to this site from 1010 Lamar in downtown Houston. Membership increased to 21,000 by the year 2000. In addition to evangelism, discipleship and missions, the church became known for other specialized ministries, including music and pageantry, programs for the deaf, community service and support to smaller churches. (2001)

HOUSTON (Harris Co.)   *7934 SH 6*
Heritage Presbyterian Church
Originally constructed near the banks of Little Cypress Creek (11 mi. NW) in 1916, this chapel served the congregation of St. John Lutheran Church. Designed with Gothic detailing, it was built by German craftsmen. When the fellowship grew too large for the sanctuary, it was purchased by the members of Windwood Presbyterian Church and moved to Grant Road (8 mi. NE). Heritage Presbyterian Church relocated it here in 1980. (1980)

HOUSTON (Harris Co.)   *SH 6 at Groschke Rd.*
Bear Creek Methodist Church and Cemetery
German immigrants settled in the area surrounding the junction of Langham and Bear Creeks in the 1840s. Settlers traveled to nearby churches for Sunday services until about 1879, when 7 charter members established the Bear Creek German Methodist Church. The congregation initially met in members' homes. The church was subsequently made a mission of the Rose Hill Methodist Church near Tomball. In 1890, a small church building was erected near the Hillendahl family cemetery. The site proved to be poorly drained and often inaccessible, and in 1902 the congregation moved the sanctuary here on 3 acres donated by Fred and Katherine Brandt. A part of the acreage was laid out as a cemetery. Christine Backen's burial in 1904 was the first recorded here. The cemetery is still active and is maintained by the Addicks Bear Creek Cemetery Association. A summer storm destroyed the sanctuary in 1915, but by the end of that year a new church building had been erected. Area flooding in 1935 resulted in the construction of the nearby Addicks Reservoir in 1940 and the subsequent removal of the church to another site about 1.7 miles south of here. The congregation changed its name to Addicks United Methodist Church in 1968. (1994)

HOWE (Grayson Co.)   *Denny St. (SH 5) between O'Connel and Haning*
Mame Roberts (Aug. 19, 1883–Dec. 24, 1976)
The daughter of James M. and Martha Sue (Baxter) Roberts, Mame Roberts lived her entire life in or near the community of Howe. Largely self-taught, she worked as a substitute teacher in the lower grades at the Howe Public Schools in the early 1900s before turning to her life's work—promoting civic improvements and beautification. As the writer of a weekly column in the Howe Messenger, Mame Roberts promoted her hometown and encouraged its beautification. Her campaign to make

Howe the "prettiest little town in Texas" motivated other small Texas towns to take similar action. A series of articles in the Dallas Morning News provided step-by-step instructions for carrying out beautification efforts, and she was in great demand as a speaker at garden club gatherings throughout this part of the state. Mame's work attracted the attention of Life magazine and Reader's Digest, and she was named "Woman of the Day" on May 14, 1949, on Eleanor and Anna Roosevelt's national radio program. Her leadership positions included: president of the Grayson County Federation of Women's Clubs; president of the Texoma Redbud Association, which urged the planting of redbuds along highways in Texas and Oklahoma; and founder and president of the Howe Sesame Club. Her work, which spanned the decades before and after World War II, is a significant part of the civic history of Howe and of all the towns that put her lessons into action.   (2002)

HUBBARD (Hill Co.)   SH 171 at 2nd St.
Hubbard
Founded 1881, as a shopping and supply point on the St. Louis and Southwestern Railroad. Named for Richard B. Hubbard (1832–1901), colonel in 22nd Texas Infantry during the Civil War, Texas governor (1876–1878), United States minister to Japan (1885–1889). Banking & market town. Has mineral waters.   (1964)

HUBBARD (Hill Co.)   SH 171 at 2nd St.
Hometown of Tris Speaker (1888–1958)
A legend in his own time, Tris Speaker was born, educated and buried here. Known as the Grey Eagle, he was the first Texan named to National Baseball Hall of Fame. First man elevated to Texas Sports Hall of Fame. Was on Boston's 1912 and 1915 World Series winning teams. Managed Cleveland Indians in their first pennant win, 1920. At 18 began professional play at $50 a month. Became a smart, able business man. Never wasted big money of playing career. Always "came home" to Hubbard. Here he was lifetime member of volunteer fire department.   (1964)

HUMBLE (Harris Co.)   110 W Main St., off Eastex Fwy. (IH 69/US 59)
City of Humble
A pioneer oil boom town. Originated as crossroads community named for settler Pleasant Smith Humble (1835?–1912), who lived here before 1889, hewing his timber into railroad ties, mining gravel from his land, keeping store, and serving as justice of the peace. Neighbors included the Bender, Durdin, Isaacks, Lee, Slaughter, and Williams families. Economic bases were farms and saw-mills. The post office opened 1902. In 1904, C. E. Barrett (1866–1926) drilled for oil in this area, securing small production on Moonshine Hill. On Jan. 7, 1905, he brought in the No. 2 Beaty well which yielded 8,500 barrels a day, opening the great boom. From a village of 700, Humble grew at once into a town of 20,000. Field production—the largest in Texas for the year 1905—was 15,594,923 barrels of oil. The field was named for the town. A group of its operators, including Ross S. Sterling, later (1931–1933) Governor of Texas, in 1911 incorporated a new oil company named for the field, thus spreading into the annals of world commerce the town's name. Production from several strata here exceeded the total for fabulous Spindletop by 1946. Known as the greatest salt dome field, Humble still produces and the town for which it was named continues to thrive.   (1972)

HUNGERFORD (Wharton Co.)   SH 60 in traffic triangle at Colorado St.
Site of Post West Bernard Station (3.5 mi. NW)
In the summer of 1837, Post West Bernard Station was established as an ordnance depot of the army of the Republic of Texas. Its location on the West Bernard River was strategic in protecting Houston, then capital of Texas, from possible invasion by Mexico. Cannons, rifles, muskets, powder, and shot were stored at the station. Troops under Lt. H. L. Grush and later Capt. Martin K. Snell maintained the post despite harsh living conditions. In 1838–1839, this station transferred its inventory of ordnance to the newly completed Houston arsenal.   (1985)

HUNGERFORD (Wharton Co.)   SH 60 in traffic triangle at Colorado St.
Site of Quinan Community (¼ mi. W)
The village of Quinan was established about 1872 on the Wharton-Richmond road. It was named for Judge George E. Quinan (1819–1893), who lived south of here on Peach Creek. A native of Ireland, Quinan served in the Texas Senate and on the State Court of Civil Appeals. He

was one of the founders of the State Bar of Texas. The community named for him had a school, Methodist church, and a post office located in John C. Habermacher's store. The Quinan community declined after the founding of Hungerford in 1882. The post office and businesses were relocated here later.

(1985)

HUNGERFORD (Wharton Co.)   *SH 60 in traffic triangle at Colorado St.*
New York, Texas & Mexican Railroad and the Community of Hungerford
Attracted by the State of Texas' offer of free land to railroad developers, a charter for the New York, Texas & Mexican Railroad was secured in 1880. Its major investor, John W. MacKay, made his fortune in the Nevada silver mines. His brother-in-law, Count Joseph Telfener of Lombardy, Italy, arranged for the construction. Work began in 1880 on the 91-mile stretch of railroad track between Rosenberg and Victoria. The pasta diet of many of the Italian laborers lent itself to the railroad's nickname, the "Macaroni Line." Telfener and MacKay established six stations along the line—Inez, Louise, Edna, Hungerford, Telfener, and MacKay—and named them for themselves and family members. The community of Hungerford was named for their father-in-law Daniel E. Hungerford, who served as vice-president of the New York, Texas & Mexican Railroad. Not the successful business venture they had envisioned, the company was sold to Southern Pacific Railway in 1885. With an economy based on farming and ranching, the community of Hungerford has continued to flourish over the years. Its origin is a reflection of the varied history of the railroad in Texas.

(Texas Sesquicentennial 1836–1986)

HUNGERFORD (Wharton Co.)   *SH 60 in traffic triangle at Colorado St.*
J. D. Hudgins Ranch
Joel Hudgins (1800–1873) of North Carolina came to the Republic of Texas in 1839 and settled in the Hungerford area. He married Rachel Ann Northington McKenzie (d. 1903) in 1847. He was elected county commissioner in 1854. After Joel's death, Rachel and their four sons began to buy more land and expand the ranching operation. Josiah Dawson (J. D.) Hudgins (d. 1928) headed the family's interests. He also owned a store, cotton gin, sawmill, and grew rice. In 1897, the four brothers divided the family property and operated independently. In 1915, J. D. and his children purchased their first purebred Brahman cows, descendants of the herd brought from India by A. P. Borden in 1906. J. D.'s son Walter Hudgins (d. 1943) helped organize the American Brahman Breeders Association in 1924. The Hudgins Ranch acquired the bull "Manso" in 1933. Manso's descendants are the cornerstone stock from which the ranch's American Gray Brahman herd was developed, now one of the largest registered American Gray Brahman herds in the world. Cattle from this ranch have been exported to over 42 countries and 34 states in the U.S. In 1962, the ranching partnership was reorganized into five separate entities, with each division operated by descendants of J. D. Hudgins.

(1985)

HUNT (Kerr Co.)   *SH 39, 1 mi. E, east of river bridge*
Schumacher Crossing on the Guadalupe River
Christian Schumacher emigrated with his family from Germany to Texas in 1845, the year he was born. He came to Kerr County in 1860, later marrying Sarah Brazeal Sublett and moving to land along the Guadalupe River, near the site of an antebellum sawmill operation built by Gustav and Fredrich Tegener. In the 1920s, son John Randolph Schumacher built a series of dams across the river, providing security from raging floodwaters for a stream crossing and new road to Hunt. Today the dams remain and an improved highway bridge crosses the stream. Schumacher Crossing is still enjoyed for its scenery and access to the river.

(2003)

HUNT (Kerr Co.)   *1580 SH 39*
Hunt
Farmers and ranchers settled along the North and South Forks of the Guadalupe River in the late 1850s, forming the Japonica and Pebble communities. In 1912, Alva and Lizzie Joy bought land at the confluence and named the central settlement that developed there in honor of Robert Hunt, the prior landowner. Alva Joy established a post office in 1913, and an independent school district formed in the 1930s. By the 1930s, the area began attracting artists, including the acclaimed E. M. Schiwetz. During the next decades, Hunt became a center for summer camps, exotic game ranches, and religious and corporate retreat facilities, but retained its identity as a small, rural community.

(2005)

HUNTSVILLE (Walker Co.)

SH 19, 8.2 mi. NE

Akin Hill (3 mi. SE)

A landmark on the "Old Colony Road" between Huntsville and Ryan's Ferry on the Trinity River. Named for Thomas Akin (1828–1878), a native of Mississippi, who came to Texas in 1853 with his wife, Ruth Leakey Akin, whom he met and married in Bienville Parish, La., along the way. Akin, a horse trader, farmer, and singing teacher, came to this area in 1854, settled in the rural community of McGuire, and built a cabin at the base of the hill. While Akin served in the Civil War as a courier for Confederate Gen. John B. Hood, Mrs. Akin moved the family a few miles to the east. The couple had 7 children. (1974)

HUNTSVILLE (Walker Co.)

SH 19, 8 mi. NE

Camp Huntsville, World War II Prisoner of War Camp

Camp Huntsville, completed here in 1942, was one of the first prisoner of war (POW) camps built in the U.S. during World War II. Designed to house 3,000 POWs, it had more than 400 buildings, as well as eight branch camps. The first POWs, part of Germany's Afrika Corps, arrived in spring 1943, and by fall the population peaked at 4840. Late in the war the camp became a branch of Camp Hearne (Robertson Co.). In Sept. 1945, Camp Huntsville sent its German POWs to Camp Hearne in preparation for the arrival of Japanese POWs at this site. The camp closed on Jan. 5, 1946, and the government transferred more than 800 acres, including buildings, to Sam Houston State Teachers College for use as a country campus. Texas in World War II—2006. (2006)

HUNTSVILLE (Walker Co.)

SH 75, 12 mi. N

Harmony Cemetery

According to oral history, the first person buried here was Vincent Herlock, who appeared in the 1850 census of Walker County with his wife and four sons. Herlock died in January 1851, and the cemetery was known for a time as Herlock Cemetery. Other 1860s and 1870s burials included those of members of the Murray and Goolsby families, and the graveyard was known by the Goolsby name as well. In 1906 the Harmony Missionary Baptist Church, formerly of the Sion community (4 miles north), was reestablished on this site. After the church was disbanded in the 1930s, the cemetery fell into disrepair. A cemetery association was formed in the 1970s to care for the site. The cemetery remains a chronicle of the pioneer settlers of Walker County. (2000)

HUNTSVILLE (Walker Co.)

US 75, 7 mi. N

Cook Springs Baptist Church

Baptists organized here in 1901 and held services at the Guinea Glade school (about 2 mi. NW). Brother Elisha E. Day (1848–1936), pastor of the Woodville Church (about 10 mi. SW), helped establish the congregation and conducted its first services. Charter members included Mr. and Mrs. Jim Cauthen, Mr. and Mrs. W. H. Hill, Mr. and Mrs. Jesse Petree, Mr. and Mrs. John L. Petree, Mrs. Mary Petree, Mr. and Mrs. Peter Petree, Mr. and Mrs. E. H. Tharp, and Miss Ruth Tharp. Mrs. Sarah Brown Gaines, wife of Toliver L. Gaines, organized the Sunday school. In 1903, Mrs. Scisely Wells Cook Rose (1830–1912), also a charter member, gave this spring-fed site for a church building. She asked that the church be named for her late husband, John William Cook, who died in 1864 in the Civil War. Records date from 1907, when deacon Edwin Harris Tharp (1849–1922) was church clerk and C. W. Matthews was the first called pastor listed. By 1912, a wooden sanctuary was completed. Services were held one weekend per month, Saturday night and Sunday morning. A new building was dedicated in 1945, assembled and furnished largely by the labors of the congregation. Many additions indicate the growth of the church, yet the original spring survives, occupying a revered site. (Texas Sesquicentennial 1836–1986)

HUNTSVILLE (Walker Co.)

SH 75, 2 mi. NW of intersection with IH 45

Hillary Mercer Crabb (1804–1876)

Georgia native Hillary Mercer Crabb, a veteran of the militia in his home state, moved his family to the Mexican state of Texas in 1830. While awaiting a land grant they settled in the Sabine District. From there Crabb joined the Texas Militia and served in such action as the 1832 Battle of Nacogdoches. In 1835, he was granted property at this site. The rural community that developed around his homesite (400 yds. W) became known as Crabb's Prairie. Crabb was instrumental in the early development of Huntsville and Walker County. A leader in civic and social activities, he became the first probate judge when the county was created in 1846. He also served as a justice of the peace and chief justice (county judge). In 1852, he was elected to serve the unexpired term of State Representative F. L. Hatch. Among Crabb's accomplishments as a legislator was the introduction of a bill to create Madison County. Opposed to secession, Crabb moved to Lavaca County at the outbreak of the Civil War. He later moved to Madison County, where he served as sheriff. His influence as a prominent landowner, church leader, Mason and public servant had a dramatic impact on the early growth of this area. (1982)

HUNTSVILLE (Walker Co.)   *IH 45 frontage road at FM 1696, 7 mi. N*
Near Gravesite of Veteran of American Revolution Mark Manning (1750–1850)
Served in American Revolution from Halifax district of North Carolina, his native state. Later lived in South Carolina and in Conecuh County, Ala., coming to Texas at 97 to live with sons who had large land grants and helped to settle Walker County. Some 20 or 30 veterans of the American Revolution followed the nation's westward movement to Texas, perpetuating here their devotion to freedom and liberty. Manning's sons fought in the Texas Revolution before he came to the new Republic. Manning is buried in family cemetery (2 mi. NE). (1972)

HUNTSVILLE (Walker Co.)   *1000 University Ave., 1 blk. N of US 190*
Walker County
The earliest known inhabitants of this area were the Cenis and Bidai (Bedias) Indians. Spanish explorers began to arrive in 1542, followed by the French in 1687. The area was thinly populated by Spanish and Mexican settlers until the early 1830s when colonists came from the United States. Brothers Pleasant and Ephraim Gray established a trading post near this site about 1835 or 1836, naming it for their home in Huntsville, Alabama. The region was included in neighboring counties until Walker County was created by the First Legislature of the State of Texas in 1846; it was named for U. S. Senator Robert J. Walker, who introduced legislation for Texas' annexation. The state penitentiary was established at Huntsville in 1849. Agricultural products, primarily cotton, were shipped out by steamboat from the late 1840s. When the Civil War began, R. J. Walker declined to support the Confederacy. The Texas Legislature renamed the county in 1863 for Texas Ranger Samuel H. Walker. Martial law was declared in the county for 60 days in 1871 because of Reconstruction-era racial violence. With the arrival of the railroads in the 1870s, depot towns flourished. Huntsville narrowly avoided the fate of other towns bypassed by the railroads when residents hurriedly raised funds to build a spur. Cotton never regained its pre–Civil War stature, and lumber and livestock became important businesses in the 20th century. The heritage of Walker County, from Native Americans to frontier settlers and U. S. Citizens, is one of independent spirit and determination. (1999)

HUNTSVILLE (Walker Co.)   *9th St. at Ave. I, 2 blks. N of US 190*
Sam Houston
Born March 2, 1793, in Rockbridge County, Va.; son of Samuel and Elizabeth Houston. Moved to Tennessee in 1807 with widowed mother and her family. In 1813 joined U.S. Army under Gen. Andrew Jackson, with whom he formed lifetime friendship and political ties. In Tennessee, taught school, kept a store, served in U.S. Congress, was state governor. In 1829, after his young bride left him, resigned as governor and went westward. Settling in 1833 in Nacogdoches, became a leader in cause of Texas independence from Mexico. Elected March 4, 1836, to command the Army of the Republic, engineered retrograde movement that led to victory of San Jacinto, which won Texas independence. President of the Republic, 1836–1838 and 1841–1844, he was senator after annexation. In 1859 he was elected governor, and served until secession. In 1861 he declined to take oath of office in Confederacy, retiring instead after a quarter-century of service to his state. However, he did not oppose Confederate army enlistment of his young son, Sam Houston, Jr. While the Civil War continued, he died on July 26, 1863, at his home, "Steamboat House," Huntsville. With him was his family, to hear his last words to his wife: "Texas—, Margaret, Texas—".

HUNTSVILLE (Walker Co.)   *SH 30, 5 mi. W at Williams Road*
Sam Houston Industrial and Training School
Legislated after the close of the Civil War, the Texas Constitution of 1866 provided for a public school system supported by funds derived from property taxes; monies collected from African Americans would go to schools for their children. Although the law continued to change during the next decades, the primary providers of African American education were the Freedmen's Bureau,

churches, missionary associations and philanthropists. Samuel W. Houston (1864–1945) was born in Huntsville to Joshua and Sylvester Houston. His father was a slave and personal bodyguard of former Texas President Sam Houston. His family believed strongly in education, and he earned degrees from the Hampton Institute in Virginia, Atlanta University in Georgia and Howard University in Washington, D.C. He returned to Huntsville in 1900 and established a newspaper. He then taught in Grimes County and at the Huntsville Community School before establishing a school circa 1906 near here in what was the Galilee community. The Sam Houston Industrial and Training School began in the Galilee Methodist Church, which Houston rented for the classes. He soon added teachers and programs, offering vocational curriculum as well as the arts and humanities. Trustees built the first schoolhouse in 1914 and continued to add facilities, including dormitories and workshops. By 1930, the school served hundreds of students from around the state. That year, the Sam Houston school merged into the Huntsville Colored School, which became Sam Houston High School. It closed in 1968 due to integration. The foundation set by Houston and other early educators ensured the education of generations of African American students in the 20th century. (2005)

HURST (Tarrant Co.)
1300 blk. Cardinal Rd., off SH 10 and Loop 820
Parker Cemetery
Land for cemetery donated by Isaac Duke Parker, Jan. 14, 1901. He was son of Isaac Parker, pioneer politician for whom Parker County was named and who was the uncle of Cynthia Ann Parker, white girl captured by Comanche Indians in 1836 and reared as an Indian. She was the wife of Comanche Peta Nocona and mother of Quanah Parker, the last great Comanche war chief. Both Isaac Parker and Isaac Duke Parker served as members of the Texas legislature. Isaac Duke Parker is buried here. Cemetery also contains a public burial section. (1968)

HUTCHINS (Dallas Co.)
Dawdy Ferry Rd., 1.3 mi. E of IH 45
Dawdy's Ferry
Illinois Native Alanson Dawdy (1826–1901) came to Dallas County in 1847. In 1854, he was granted a license to operate a ferry at this site on the Trinity River, the southernmost crossing at the time. An important route for citizens living on both sides of the river, the ferry continued in operation until about 1876. Ferry charges included one dollar for a wagon with four or more animals, ten cents for a man and horse, and five cents for a person on foot. The first permanent bridge was installed at this site in 1888. Dawdy was a veteran of the Mexican and Civil Wars.
(Texas Sesquicentennial 1836–1986)

HUTTO (Williamson Co.)
US 79 at FM 1660
Hutto
Located near Shiloh, one of the earliest villages in Williamson County, this area was settled in 1855 by J. E. Hutto (1824–1914) and Adam Orgain, a former slave. Hutto sold land for this townsite to the International & Great Northern Railroad in 1876. A post office was established in 1877 with Hutto as postmaster. By 1882, the town had a school and a Baptist church. By 1898, there were six churches, a Masonic lodge, newspaper, hotel, bank, two gins, and several stores. Hutto grew rapidly after Swedish immigrants turned nearby farms to cotton production. The town was incorporated in 1911. (1976)

HYE (Blanco Co.)
US 290
Hye Post Office
Named for Hiram ("Hye") Brown, founder of store, in 1880. Post office established 1886. Present store with Bavarian metalwork built in 1904. Owned by Deike family since 1923. At age four, Lyndon B. Johnson, future U.S. President, mailed a letter here—a postal customer for first time in his life. Postmaster General Lawrence F. O'Brien was sworn into cabinet of President Johnson at this post office in 1965. Awarded Medallion Plate.

IDALOU (Lubbock Co.)
US 62/82, 2 mi. E
Idalou Cemetery
John William Turner, Jr. and his wife, Mary Alice, deeded two acres of their farm as a burial ground in January 1921. The first burial was for their infant nephew, Weldon Fred Turner, whose grave is indicated by a homemade marker. In May of that year, C. J. and Mary Hallmark buried their infant son C. J., and 13-year-old Mable Gladis Andrews was interred in July. By 1928, when

the Turners and Selma Graves donated more land to the burial ground, area residents had formed the Idalou Cemetery Association, with E. T. Daniell, W. M. Weaver and H. W. Lasater serving as the original board members. Over the next decades, the association accepted additional land donations, which increased the cemetery to its present size. Volunteers and families have attended workdays to help maintain the site. Today, the cemetery's features include curbed plots and numerous upright shoulder stones typical of 20th-century grave marker designs, and the open prairie landscape highlights native plantings. The cemetery is a link to the many generations who have contributed to the history of Idalou.

(2002)

INDEPENDENCE (Washington Co.)   *FM 390 E of intersection with FM 50*
Independence
Local legend tells of Dr. Asa Hoxey who, celebrating the Texas Declaration of Independence in 1836, moved to change the name of Coles settlement to Independence. Actual county records show an 1835 origin for the town of Independence, with C. Baker, J. G. W. Pierson, A. F. Burchard, and R. Stevenson, proprietors. The still-strong Independence Baptist Church was established in 1839 with Pastor T. W. Cox. Local resident Sam Houston was baptized in Little Rocky Creek in 1854. The wealthiest town in Texas by 1845, Independence won the bid for Baylor University, newly chartered by the Republic of Texas. J. B. Root became its first U. S. Postmaster in 1846. By the 1850s Independence had a hotel, jail, stagecoach depot, Masonic lodge, cemetery, and small commercial district. Both the city leaders and Baylor administrators refused to grant right-of-way to the Santa Fe Railroad. By the 1880s, trade was going to competing towns and Independence began to decline. Baylor University moved its schools to Waco and Belton in 1886. By the 1990s, Independence was a rural community with a population of 140. Remaining attractions include the Baptist church and numerous historical sites in the area.

(1997)

INDEPENDENCE (Washington Co.)   *FM 390 at FM 50*
Margaret Moffette Lea Houston Wife of Gen. Sam Houston
April 11, 1819–Dec. 3, 1867 and her mother Nancy Moffette Lea,
May 1, 1780–Feb. 7, 1864
Women of character, culture and staunch devotion to their families and church, each in her own way greatly influenced the career of Sam Houston and the course of Texas history. A daughter, Madora Cole McCrocklin, gave the site. Many statesmen, educators, physicians, lawyers, war veterans and other "old Texians" are buried here.

(1970)

INDEPENDENCE (Washington Co.)   *FM 390, 1 blk. E of FM 50*
Hood's Texas Brigade, C.S.A.
Co. I, Fifth Texas Infantry Regt., Army of Northern Virginia, was raised here Aug. 1861, as "The Texas Aides" by Capt. J. B. Robertson. Unit fought in many battles of Civil War—Gaines Mill, Second Manassas, Antietam, Gettysburg, Chickamauga and the Wilderness. Robertson became brigadier general and succeeded Hood as Commander Oct. 1862. Replaced by Brigadier General John Gregg, Jan. 1864. Col. R. M. Powell later held post until end of the war. The brigade surrendered at Appomattox, April 12, 1865, with 12% enlistees surviving. "Defeat could not dim their record."

INDEPENDENCE (Washington Co,)   *FM 390, .3 mi. E of FM 50*
Margaret Lea Houston House
Margaret Lea Houston, Gen. Sam Houston's widow, lived here with their 8 children, 1863–1867. House built in 1830s.

(1965)

INDEPENDENCE (Washington Co.)   *FM 390, 3 blks. W of FM 50*
Old Baylor Park
Under a charter issued in 1845 by the Republic of Texas, Baylor University was established on this site and operated here until its removal to Waco and Belton in 1886. Afterward the site was bought by John Thomas Hairston (1835–1918), a church leader in Independence for over 40 years. Passed to his son, the land was returned in 1933 to Baylor by Dr. Thomas Coke Hairston (1875–1954), a grandson of Albert Gallitan Haynes, an original trustee of Baylor University who served on the board for 25 years. In 1965 the park became part of Texas Baptist Historical Center.

INDIANOLA (Calhoun Co.)
SH 316, 15 mi. SE of Port Lavaca
Site of the Town of Indianola (1844–1886)
First called by German immigrants Karlshaven, an important port of Texas. Cargoes of ships were hauled to and from points in Texas and Mexico by carts until 1860 when the San Antonio and Mexican Gulf Railroad and the Indianola Railroad were completed to Victoria. The town was partly destroyed with great loss of life by a hurricane, September 17, 1875. It was rebuilt but completely destroyed by another hurricane, August 20, 1886. (1964)

INDIANOLA (Calhoun Co.)
SH 316 Terminus
Indianola
Many currents of the mainsteam of Texas history flow in this onetime port. Pineda explored the coast in 1519 and LaSalle planted a settlement near here in 1685. Once an Indian trading point, it was a major seaport from 1844 to 1875. Texas colonists, including Germans led by Prince Carl of Solms-Braunfels, entered through Indianola. "Forty-niners," supplies for frontier forts, and experimental army camels were landed here. During the Civil War Indianola and Fort Esperanza, which controlled the gateway to Indianola through Pass Cavallo, were objectives of Federal blockading vessels. Pass Cavalo, ten miles south, was one of several entrances to the inside waterway created by Matagorda Peninsula and the offshore islands extending to the Rio Grande. To deny Confederate use of this waterway for commerce through Mexico, the Federals had to seize control of these entrances. Before Confederate defenses at Fort Esperanza were completed, two Federal steamers slipped through Pass Cavallo to Indianola and on October 31, 1862, demanded the surrender of Lavaca (now Port Lavaca) to the northwest. The Confederate command refused, stood off the naval guns with land batteries, and forced the withdrawal of the Federal ships. Federal forces attacked Fort Esperanza November 22, 1863. The Confederates withstood the assault of naval and land forces for six days then spiked their guns, destroyed their magazines, and withdrew to the mainland. Indianola then fell December 23. On Christmas Eve, Federal and Confederate forces clashed at Norris Bridge, eight miles north. Two days later Lavaca was occupied and the entire Matagorda–Lavaca Bay area remained in Federal control until war's end. Indianola was partially destroyed by a hurricane in 1875 and completely destroyed by another in 1886.

INDIANOLA (Calhoun Co.)
SH 316 Terminus
Rene Robert Cavelier Sieur de la Salle
Born in Rouen, France, November 22, 1643. Came to Canada in 1666. Founded a first settlement near Montreal, led several expeditions on the Great Lakes and the Ohio and Illinois Rivers. Completed the exploration of the Mississippi 1682. On July 24, 1684 La Salle sailed from France to establish a colony at the mouth of the Mississippi. Landed at Matagorda Bay February 15, 1685. There established Fort St. Louis. While on his way to Canada he was murdered near the Trinity River, March 19, 1687. A gentleman but not a courtier. A proud independent yet timid nature. An explorer of bold vision and untiring energy. La Salle's colony on Matagorda Bay gave the United States its first claim to Texas as a part of the Louisiana Purchase. "America owes him an enduring memory, for, in this masculine figure, she sees the pioneer who guided her to the possession of her richest heritage." Francis Parkman. (1964)

INDUSTRY (Austin Co.)
FM 1457 at FM 389, 8 mi. NW
Town of Shelby
Named for 1822 settler David Shelby, this town grew up at the mill of German pioneer Otto Von Roeder. The Ohlendorfs, Vogelsangs, Rothermels, and Vanderwerths arrived in 1845; other Germans came in ensuing years. The post office opened 1846 with Shelby as postmaster. A school (1854), an agricultural society, a singing society and a band were started. Mission work, begun in 1876, led to founding of Peace Lutheran and St. Paul Lutheran Churches. By 1900 there were at least a dozen businesses here. Decline of farming led residents to live on ancestral land and work in cities. (1974)

INDUSTRY (Austin Co.)
SH 159, 2 mi. W in roadside park
Charles Fordtran (May 7, 1801–Nov. 1, 1900)
In Jan. 1831 Charles Fordtran, a German of Huguenot descent, joined the colony of Stephen F. Austin. His first work was to survey land for Austin's partner, Samuel May Williams. He was given a league (4,428.4 acres) as his fee. Soon he brought in two families of settlers who worked for him for a time, then obtained their own land in present Fayette County. On July 4, 1834, he married

Almeida Brookfield (1817–1887), daughter of a noted Indian-fighting family. Fordtran also fought Indians who stole livestock and kidnapped the wives and children of colonists. In the Texas War for Independence, he joined the "Spy Rangers" under Capt. John Bird, defending civilians who were fleeing to escape the Mexican invaders. Charles Fordtran was one of the first Teutonic settlers in Texas—arriving some years before the main tide of German immigration. Music and good living abounded in his home. He and his wife had 14 children, with nine living to adulthood. Of four sons in the Confederate Army during the Civil War (1861–1865) two survived. His descendants have made contributions to Texas history as industrialists, engineers, lawyers, physicians, and teachers. This marker stands on land he received in 1831.   (1976)

INEZ (Victoria Co.)   US 59 at FM 444
Fort St. Louis
Thirteen miles southeast of Inez is located the site of Fort St. Louis, first French settlement in Texas, attempted by Rene Robert Cavelier Sieur de La Salle in 1685. Devastated by the Karankawa Indians. Burned by members of the Alonso de Leon Expedition in 1689. On its remains the Spaniards constructed Presidio de Nuestra Señora de la Bahía del Espiritu Santo. Established by Joseph de Azlor Marquis of Aguayo and Father Fray Augustin Patron, F. M., in 1722 as a protection for the Mission of Nuestra Señora del Espiritu Santo de Zuniga for civilizing and Christianizing of the Indian tribes of the vicinity. Moved to Mission Valley on the Guadalupe River near present Victoria in 1726. Moved finally to Santa Dorotea, now Goliad, near the San Antonio River.

INGRAM (Kerr Co.)   SH 27, 8.5 mi. NW
The Dowdy Tragedy of 1878
The pioneer family of Susan (1830–1913) and James Dowdy (1818–1900) moved from Goliad to Kerr County in 1878 and settled on Johnson Creek. Shortly after the family arrived, four of the Dowdy children, Alice, Martha, Susan, and James, were killed by Indians while tending sheep near their home. The attack occurred on Oct. 5, 1878, at a site about 3.5 miles northwest of present Ingram. The victims were buried the following day at Sunset Cemetery, northwest of Ingram. This incident was one of the last Indian raids in Kerr County.   (1979)

INGRAM (Kerr Co.)   SH 27, 2 mi. NW at Henderson Branch Rd.
Henderson Cemetery (2 Mi. N)
Howard Henderson (1842–1908) came to Texas in 1857. He was a survivor of the Civil War Battle of the Nueces in 1862, in which he and other Unionists were ambushed by a Confederate force near the Nueces River. He later served as a Texas Ranger. Henderson married Narcissa Turknett in 1866 and they settled near this site. In 1870, upon the deaths of their infant twin sons Thomas and Philip, they began a family burial ground which became known as Henderson Cemetery. Other family members and neighbors were also buried in the graveyard.   (1990)

INGRAM (Kerr Co.)   SH 27, 1 mi. E
Nichols Cemetery
Born about 1805, Rowland Nichols settled in Kerr County where he served as county commissioner. Upon his death at the hands of Indians, Nichols was buried, as he wished, under a live oak tree on his farm on April 11, 1859. This site became a community burial ground and the burial place of many area pioneers, including J. C. W. Ingram (1829–1902), for whom the town of Ingram was named. Additional property was later purchased from Lafayette Nichols to enlarge the cemetery. For over a century Nichols Cemetery has served the residents of this part of Kerr County. (1982)

INGRAM (Kerr Co.)   SH 39, 2 mi. W
Site of Sherman's Mill
A pioneer Kerr County water-powered mill located near Kelly Creek-Guadalupe River confluence. It ground corn, sawed lumber, ginned cotton. Built in 1870s by John Sherman, it was in use until destroyed by flood in 1932. Sherman, his wife, and 8 children lived in house still standing nearby.   (1972)

IRA (Scurry Co.)   SH 350, 4 mi. SW
Campsite of the Marcy Expedition
At a grove of mesquite and wild china trees by a creek near here, Capt. R. B. Marcy's expedition camped Oct. 7, 1849. While blazing the famous Marcy Trail, they saw nothing deadlier than

quail and wild turkeys in the area, but the next day tragedy struck. Lt. Montgomery Pike Harrison (1826–1849)—grandson of President Wm. Henry Harrison and older brother of later President Benjamin Harrison—left camp alone to scout a ravine. When he did not return by dark, the company fired a Howitzer to signal him, but received no answer. Searchers the next day found signs that Harrison, always friendly to the Indians, had stopped and smoked with two Indians, believed to be Kiowas. He was disarmed, however, taken one mile south and then shot with his own rifle. The Indians scalped and stripped the body and threw it into a ravine on Canyon Creek, They were pursued, but never captured. Marcy later reported that when his men heard of Harrison's death, many hid their faces "to conceal their tears." The body was packed in charcoal and taken in a coffin made from a wagon bed to Ft. Smith for burial. Despite this tragedy, Marcy's trail became a major wagon road, taking gold seekers to California and troops and supplies across the West Texas frontier.   (1967)

IRA (Scurry Co.)   *SH 350 at FM 1606*
J. J. Moore No. 1 Oil Well (1.4 mi. S)
First producing oil well in Scurry county; opened a major West Texas petroleum area. Drilled February to October 1923 by E. I. (Tommy) Thompson, W. W. Lechner and E. E. (Buddy) Fogelson of Loutex Corp. W. A. Reiter located the well. Leon English was field geologist. Drillers were Jesse Thomas, Begossa Murphy, Tom Mann, Charlie Dodson, Sim Taylor. The tool dresser, James O. Jarmon, was the only man working the well from top to bottom. Pat and Mike Moore, the young sons of the landowner, helped to fire the steam boiler. The drill struck a pressurized reservoir of "cold air" (nitrogen and helium), unique in Texas at that time. It blew mud and water 60 feet above the well head. Soon harnessed, it replaced steam to operate the drilling. It also refrigerated food and water. Completed to 3575 feet and plugged back to 1800 feet in the San Andres formation, the J. J. Moore No. 1 has yielded over 500,000 barrels of oil; is still producing. Several "dusters" were drilled nearby in 1924. Exploration was further discouraged in the 20s by low prices. Eventually, however, here in the Sharon Ridge Field over 2200 wells have been brought in. In 1948 deep wells began to tap the canyon reef in Scurry. The county now has over 4,000 oil wells.   (1966)

IRA (Scurry Co.)   *SH 350 at FM 1606*
Ira
Named for Ira Green, who had a crossroads store near this site. First homes and school were half-dugouts (cellars with windows set above ground level). Post office established 1896. On opening of block 97 to settlers, 1899, area became active farm and ranch community. Oil production since 1923.   (1966)

IRAAN (Pecos Co.)   *SH 349, 11 mi. NW at rest area*
Camp Melvin and the Pontoon Crossing of the Pecos River
As it winds its way across Texas, the Pecos River can often be swift and dangerous. Historically, frequent flooding made even the best crossings unusable. In May 1684, Spanish explorer Juan Domínguez de Mendoza and his expedition team camped at a site south of here, now on private land, where they could safely cross the river. They named the location San Pantaleon. In 1840, trader Dr. Henry Connelly used the same crossing, and over the years it came to be known by various names, including Connelly's, as well as Fennelly, Camp Melvin, Camp Melbourne, Ficklin, Pecos and Pecos Mail Station. By the 1860s, the two main routes through the region bypassed the crossing here, as other fords presented fewer obstacles or appeared more secure. The northern route's Horsehead Crossing, however, was a target for Comanche attacks, and the southern route near Fort Lancaster failed to provide a convenient connection between Forts Concho and Stockton. As a result, Capt. F.S. Dodge of Fort Stockton sought a new crossing in 1868, and he chose the one previously used by Domínguez and Connelly. Designing a means to allow travelers a safe and reliable crossing of the Pecos was difficult, as the river's width often varied greatly. In partnership with stage line operator Ben Ficklin, the U.S. Army built a floating pontoon bridge near here. Landings on either bank could be moved closer or farther apart to accommodate changes in stream width. To protect travelers, the Army established Camp Melvin (Melbourne, Milvin) nearby, and a mail station also operated in the vicinity. By 1920, however, only parts of the pontoon bridge and nearby buildings remained. Increased settlement and improved transportation relegated the pontoon crossing and Camp Melvin to history.   (2006)

IRAAN (Pecos Co.)
US 190/SH 349, west city limits
Marathon Oil Company Discovery Well
Opening one of the greatest fields in the world, Marathon Oil Company (then Ohio Oil Company) brought in the I. G. Yates "A" No. 1 Well on October 29, 1926. It was a gusher from a shallow depth of 1,004 feet. Previously oil men had said, "You won't find any oil west of the Pecos." This did not stop the work of Marathon Oil Company's predecessor firm and its partners in many ventures, the veteran wildcatters Michael L. Benedum and Joseph C. Trees, of Pittsburgh, Pennsylvania. Their strike was sensational. Within a year, the Yates field had more than 100 wells—two with even higher yields than Yates No. 1. Under the 20,000-acre Ira G. Yates ranch lay one of the largest oil reserves in the world. The many developers voluntarily adopted proration. Their plans for allocating and restricting Yates Field production were approved in 1928 by the Railroad Commission of Texas. This was the first complete proration of an oil field in the state—and an important milestone in petroleum conservation. The discovery well has since been deepened to 1,283 feet. It still has a potential daily flow of 77,760 barrels. The Yates Field now has 607 wells.　(1966)

IRAAN (Pecos Co.)
US 190/SH 349 at Farr St.
Iraan
In 1922 three local businessmen, O. W. Parker, George Thompson, and I. G. Yates, leased the drilling rights on twenty sections of ranch land to Transcontinental Oil Company. After two dry holes were drilled the I. G. Yates well No. 1 blew in on October 28, 1926. The area around ranch headquarters became a boom town. Because it was isolated, support of the increased population became difficult. Yates converted a barn into a hotel and the area became known as Red Barn Community. In April 1927 Yates commissioned H. L. George of San Angelo to survey a townsite at this location, 3 miles north of Red Barn. A contest was held to choose a name for the new town. The winner was "Iraan", submitted by C. R. Hallmark who combined the names of Ira Yates and his wife Ann. His prize was a city lot. The first business to operate in Iraan was a service station run by K. P. Looney. A Post Office was opened in 1928. A nondenominational chapel known as union church was set up from contributions by Yates and Mid-Kansas Oil Company. During the boom days of Iraan, V. T. Hamlin worked as a free-lance writer. It was here that he created the comic strip "Alley Oop." A park honoring his cartoon characters is located in the city.　(1980)

IRAAN (Pecos Co.)
W on US 190 at Long Loop Rd.
Giddings' Pecos Station
In the mid-19th century, stagecoach lines were a primary means of moving people, mail and supplies through the region. The U.S. government contracted with Henry Skillman for the San Antonio–El Paso Stage line in 1951. In this area, the route ran along the historic Chihuahua Trail, also known as the Lower Road, which was designed to carry U.S. mail. The service soon added passenger and freight delivery. Skillman and William "Bigfoot" Wallace were two of the better known drivers. In 1854, George H. Giddings took over the San Antonio to El Paso line and created a series of stage stations in the area. In 1858, he established one near the "S" crossing of the Pecos River. It had two structures built of adobe, limestone and wood. Teamsters used the larger building as a kitchen and dining room and the smaller structure as sleeping quarters. An adobe or high pole corral with a wide gate stood behind the buildings, housing dozens of horses and mules. Water came from a nearby hand-dug well, formerly an existing spring. In early 1862, a driver of the stage to Fort Lancaster reported Indians had destroyed Pecos Station, and the site was abandoned. Lt. Col. Thomas B. Hunt led a detachment past the ruins in 1869, giving the position as the west bank of the Pecos, 2.5 miles from Camp Melbourne. The exact location of the remote post, however, remained in doubt over the years until archeological investigations in the early 21st century. Stone foundations and cultural artifacts from the 1850s, along with evidence of earlier Native American occupation, helped identify this isolated scene of frontier life.　(2007)

IRVING (Dallas Co.)
200 block S Main
City of Irving
Permanent settlement in this part of Dallas County began before the Civil War with the establishment of small farming communities and supply centers. In the early years of the 20th century, while working on the construction of the Rock Island railroad extension from Fort Worth to Dallas, two members of the survey party—its chief, J. O. Schulze, and a surveyor, Otis Brown—purchased just

over 80 acres of land from pioneer farmer H. W. Britain. Soon they had platted a townsite, which they named Irving. On December 19, 1903, Schulze and Brown held a barbecue and auction for the sale of town lots. The first issue of the Irving "Index" was distributed to those in attendance. Approximately 40 lots were sold, and construction of buildings soon began. The post office, which had been located at Kit, moved to Irving in 1904. Co-founder Otis Brown served as Irving's first mayor after the town was incorporated in 1914. Over the years Irving grew to be a modest suburb of Dallas. With the construction of the Dallas-Fort Worth airport, Texas Stadium, and the Las Colinas Business Park, Irving experienced major economic growth during the last quarter of the 20th century.   (Texas Sesquicentennial 1836–1986)

ITALY (Ellis Co.)   *SH 34 at Couch St.*
General Edward H. Tarrant
Veteran of the War of 1812, member of the Texas Congress and a courageous Indian fighter. Born in North Carolina, 1796, died in Parker County, Texas, August 2, 1858. Reburied in Ellis County near his former plantation, 1859. His remains removed to the county named in his honor in 1928 and reinterred in Fort Worth.   (1936)

JACKSBORO (Jack Co.)   *US 281/SH 114, 12 mi. N*
Lost Valley
Marked by "Seven Blue Hills" in distance. To right is Spy Knob—a lookout during pioneer days. Noted atrocity site: In 1857, the Cambren and Mason families, settlers, were victims of white renegades and Indians. On May 18, 1871, on western rim, teamsters of Warren Wagon Train were killed soon after General W. T. Sherman of the U.S. Army had traveled safely through this valley. On July 12, 1874, the escort part of Major John B. Jones, Commander of the Frontier Battalion, Texas Rangers, was ambushed here, with two men killed. In later years, this has been peaceful farm-ranch area.   (1970)

JACKSBORO (Jack Co.)   *US 281, city limits near depot*
Butterfield Stage Line
Here ran the Southern Overland Mail Line connecting St. Louis and San Francisco with semi-weekly stage and mail service, 1858–1861. The length of the route, 2795 miles, and the superior service maintained made this a pioneer enterprise of first magnitude.

JACKSBORO (Jack Co.)   *US 281, .5 mi. S*
Fort Richardson
Established November 26, 1867 by the United States Army to defend the frontier against the Indians. A mail station on the Butterfield Overland Stage Line 1858–1861. Abandoned as a military post May 23, 1878.

JACKSBORO (Jack Co.)   *US 281, S near bridge*
Sewell Park
This site became Jacksboro's first park after tract here on Lost Creek was donated to city on June 25, 1921, by pioneer teacher-lumberman-rancher-public benefactor Dan Roland Sewell (1872–1957). City's first waterworks were installed during Sewell's service as mayor, Feb. 17, 1913 to April 11, 1921.   (1972)

JACKSONVILLE (Cherokee Co.)   *US 175, 2 mi. NW*
Old Neches Saline Road (Crosses Highway 175 Here)
Originally an Indian trail. Used in 1765 by the Spanish priest Calahorra on an Indian peace mission. Gained importance, 1820s, for use in hauling salt from Neches Saline to Nacogdoches. Survivors of the Killough family massacre of 1838 fled via the road to Fort Lacy. The Texas Army used it en route to fight Mexican rebel Cordova in 1838 and in Cherokee War, 1839. Some of Kentucky volunteers went this way to the Mexican War, 1846. After Indian wars, road brought in many settlers. Jacksonville, Dialville, and Larissa grew up along its path.   (1970)

JACKSONVILLE (Cherokee Co.)   *US 69, 4 mi. N in park*
Love's Lookout
On this nine-mile-long ridge there are two historic lookout points which command a view of 30 to 35 miles. Between this site, with an elevation of 713 ft., and Point Lookout (¼ mi. NW), lies a

narrow valley. An Indian trail and later a pioneer road crossed this valley. The pass became known as McKee's Gap in 1846, after Thomas McKee led a group of Presbyterians here from Tennessee and began the town of Larissa (3.5 mi. NW). Named by McKee's son the Rev. T. N. McKee, the village flourished as the location of Larissa College from the 1850s until the 1870s. Point Lookout was a popular recreational area for citizens of Larissa until the railroad bypassed the town and it declined. Around the turn of the century, John Wesley Love (1858–1925) bought this land and developed a 600-acre peach orchard. Known as Love's Lookout, the scenic point was used for outings by area residents. After Love's death, his family gave 22.22 acres, including the lookout site, to the state for a park. The city of Jacksonville bought 25 adjoining acres and developed both tracts as a WPA project. J. L. Brown (1866–1944) and Jewel Newton Brown (1873–1966), former Larissa residents, gave the city 122 acres next to the park in 1940 in tribute to pioneers of Larissa. (1978)

JACKSONVILLE (Cherokee Co.) — US 79, 8 mi. W
Texas Civil War Iron Works
To make farm and kitchen tools need in wartime, Chapel Hill Manufacturing Co. in 1863 set up plant on this site, processing native iron; used Cherokee limestone to purify the ore. Nearby hardwood supplied charcoal. Crew included 100 Louisiana slaves. Ore from hilltop fed through smokestack into furnaces on lower ground. Slag caught in furnace grates. Melted iron fell through and was cast into molds. Plant had associated sawmills, brickyards and commissary—freighting goods from Mexico. By the 1880s, at least 16 iron works operated in East Texas. (1965)

JACKSONVILLE (Cherokee Co.) — 301 W Larissa (1 blk. off US 79)
Larissa House
Oldest home in Jacksonville. Begun in Texas colonial style, 1857. W. A. Brown (1841–1933), veteran of Gen. N. B. Forrest's confederate cavalry, built main structure, 1874. Victorian additions in 1890s. Lumber, hand-sawn heart pine, cut nearby. Square nails. Brick of local iron ore clay. While making fine walnut staircase, craftsman lived with family. Reared here was J. L. "Lem" Brown, merchant, author of Larissa, a history of this area. (1965)

JACKSONVILLE (Cherokee Co.) — US 69 at FM 22, 4 mi. S
Town of Craft
Known first as Independence, the town of Craft grew up in the 1890s on the railroad. When a post office was established in 1891, the name Craft was chosen to honor Thomas J. Craft, first postmaster and community leader. In 1896, C. D. and S. H. Jarratt and W. R. Stout began commercial tomato growing and production here. By 1917, 90 percent of Texas' tomatoes were shipped from this area. The town declined in the 1930s but is important for its early role in the East Texas tomato growing and shipping industry. (1985)

JARRELL (Williamson Co.) — IH 35, 2 mi. S, northbound access road
Corn Hill Community
Settled primarily by settlers from Texas and southern states, Corn Hill was one of the earliest communities in Williamson County. John E. King, county judge from 1858 to 1860, named it for the home he built on a hill and nearby cornfield in 1852. The dispersed agricultural community was the first stop on the stage line running from Georgetown to Fort Gates (Coryell County). A post office opened in 1855 and by the 1860s, an influx of new residents settled here. In 1878, George G. Grant established Corn Hill Academy Male and Female School, built on land donated by Judge King. It thrived and in 1886 moved to a new two-story building with four classrooms, a bell tower and an auditorium, which provided meeting space for local church services. By 1893, a public school opened as part of Corn Hill Independent School District. By the end of the 19th century, Corn Hill had a saddle club, several churches, two local cotton gins, Corn Hill College, fraternal lodges and school organizations. By the early 1900s, community residents became active in Populist politics and in the Farmers' Union. Industrial activity of the early 1900s included the Corn Hill and Gravis Telephone Company and a waterworks; a planned interurban to Bartlett never materialized. The settlement began to decline in 1909 when the Bartlett Western Railway bypassed two miles to the north, establishing the town of Jarrell. Steam engines helped move homes and businesses to the new townsite, and other moved to the village of New Corn Hill, but many residents chose to remain here. Today, the dispersed Corn Hill settlement survives as a reminder of the area's early agrarian heritage. (2007)

JASPER (Jasper Co.) *SH 63, 4 mi. W*
Bevilport
Important river shipping and trading point; was made seat of Bevil municipality, 1834. Named for John Bevil, Texas Ranger, a delegate (1835) to Consultation on Texas Independence, chief justice of Jasper County (1839), farmer. On Angelina River, Bevilport shipped cotton, hides and other East Texas products to markets in New Orleans. Its docks were busy with flatboats, keelboats—its stores packed with travelers. Texas rivers flowing to Gulf of Mexico were favorite areas for settlement; Bevil and others prospered on rich "bottom" lands, using river as road to market. (1967)

JASPER (Jasper Co.) *FM 2799 at Main St.*
Jasper County, C.S.A.
Communication, transportation, supply and military center in Civil War Texas. Voted 315 to 25 in favor of secession. Crossed by Texas troops in the 1862–64 Louisiana campaigns to prevent split of the South and invasion of Texas. Confederate Army ran Houston-to-Alexandria, La., military horseback courier route through here. In last years of the war, Abel Adams, a local 14-year-old, rode this in a high lope, for Gen. John B. Magruder, commander of the Department of Texas. Beef was driven to troops in the Old South by way of 1823 trail across the county. Had a Confederate Quartermaster Depot and 9-county headquarters, 2nd Brigade, Texas State Troops, under Gen. W. M. Neyland, local citizen. County men in service on various war fronts of the South included Co. G, 13th Texas Cavalry; Co. C, 25th Texas Cavalry, Dismounted; Co. E, 27th Texas Cavalry, in Whitfield's Legion. In 1865, as survivors were returning home, Union occupation troops bivouacked in the Jasper Town Square. Commander was Gen. George Custer, later to go down in history for his "last stand" at the Little Big Horn, 1876. Driving her beautiful horse and carriage, his young bride called on the Jasper ladies. (1964)

JASPER (Jasper Co.) *US 96 at Brewster Rd.*
Stephen Williams (May 9, 1760–ca. 1839)
Was born in 1760 in North Carolina. In 1778, he enlisted in the first of what would be many times in the armed forces. Enlisting three times in the Revolutionary War army, Williams fought in battles including Briar Creek, Camden, and Eutaw Springs. Following the Revolutionary War, he moved to St. Helena parish, Louisiana. When the War of 1812 broke out, he volunteered for service and at age fifty-two served as a sentry. About 1830, shortly after the death of his wife, Williams relocated to Bevil's settlement in Jasper County, Texas and received a Mexican land grant. In November 1835 as the Siege of Bexar began, the 75-year-old veteran went armed with his rifle to participate. He served with four grandsons and one son-in-law in Captain Cheshire's Company and became first sergeant, ultimately receiving a Republic of Texas land grant for his service. Williams returned to Bevil's settlement, where he died about 1839. He was buried on his homesite, and his grave was marked with a Texas Centennial Marker in 1936. Williams' body was later reburied in the State Cemetery in Austin, and the Centennial marker was relocated to this site. (1991)

JAYTON (Kent Co.) *SH 70, 3 mi. N in roadside park*
Putoff Canyon (East of Here)
Named for a Mr. Putoff, early settler. In region of salt water, canyon was noted for its freshwater spring "strong enough to swim a horse". Area was a resort, 1900–1914, for many artists. Western writer Zane Grey used region as setting for his novel The Thundering Herd. (1969)

JAYTON (Kent Co.) *SH 70 at courthouse*
Kent County
Formed from Young and Bexar territories; created August 21, 1876; organized November 8, 1892. Named in honor of Andrew Kent who fell at the Alamo. Clairmont, the county seat, 1892; Jayton, since 1952. (1936)

JAYTON (Kent Co.) *402 Donoho St., 1 blk. W of Main St. (SH 70)*
First National Bank Building
An excellent example of early 20th century classical revival style, the First National Bank of Jayton was erected about 1912 by descendants of early Kent County pioneers. Classical features of the edifice, such as the polished granite Ionic columns, bull's eye windows, quoins, and the unusual recessed entry portico, are typical of the favored imagery of stability and order among banks of the

period. The domed skylight is a device often employed by the building's architect, Rockwell H. Stuckey (1855–1936). The bank closed in the 1930s; the building continues to serve the community as a financial institution, many of its personnel descendants of bank founders. (1998)

JEFFERSON (Marion Co.) *SH 49, 1 mi. NE*
Jefferson
Founded 1836. Named for President Thomas Jefferson. Chief river port of Texas, 1846–1870. This prosperous ante-bellum city became a Confederate Quartermaster Depot; produced boots, shoes, iron goods, preserved meats for army. Nearby oil field discovered in 1939. Many fine old homes and other landmarks. (1964)

JEFFERSON (Marion Co.) *SH 49, 5 mi. W*
Kellyville
Named for George Addison Kelly. Died in 1909. Proprietor of an early foundry which cast cowbells widely used by ox-team freighters. After 1860 his factory turned out the first modern plows used in Texas.

JEFFERSON (Marion Co.) *SH 49 at FM 729, 4 mi. W*
Site of Early Bell Foundry
From a log blacksmith shop in 1854 grew a bell foundry owned by G. A. Kelly which manufactured cowbells widely used by pioneer ox-team freighter. Later the Kelly plow, one of the first modern plows made in Texas, was manufactured here. (1936)

JEFFERSON (Marion Co.) *SH 49, 2 mi. W*
Site of First Ice Factory in Texas
Established by Boyle and Scott about 1875. Sold ice at ten cents per pound. B. T. Benefield delivered it. The plant was later moved to Harrisburg.

JEFFERSON (Marion Co.) *SH 49, 1 mi. W*
Freeman Plantation
This Greek revival plantation home was built about 1850 by Williamson M. (1807–66) and Drucilla (1812–65) Freeman for their children. A cotton and sugar cane planter, Freeman also operated a river freighting business. Materials used in construction of the house include hand-hewn timbers and brick made on the site. In the 1870s the residence was sold to R. E. Rowell (1826–1900), a former Confederate doctor, who later served as county treasurer. A rear wing was added to the home during the ownership of oilman L. S. Flannery (d. 1961), who purchased the property in 1937. (1980)

JEFFERSON (Marion Co.) *Broadway (SH 49) at Friou St.*
T. J. Taylor, Jr. Home
On an original land grant of the Republic of Texas. Built about 1852 by Berry Hodge, prominent surveyor, using slave labor. Among later owners was a civic leader who published the "Jefferson Jimplecute." Restored in 1950 by the now deceased T. J. Taylor, Jr., brother of U.S. First Lady, Mrs. Lyndon B. Johnson. Awarded Medallion Plate. (1964)

JEFFERSON (Marion Co.) *N. Walnut St. (SH 49)*
Civil War Meat Packing Plant
About 2 miles to the southwest, the meat plant of J. B. Dunn dressed, packed and shipped beef, pork and mutton to the Confederate Army. In 1861 began by packing 150 beeves a day. Well located, on the cypress bayou shipping route, with cattle in trailing distance, in East and North Texas. Herds were bought at $20 to $40 a head. Used 42-gallon wooden barrels. Filled these with meat and brine. Obtained salt from New Iberia, La., and elsewhere through the Confederate government. Yet even with use of preservative salt, bloody water was sometimes found in the packed meat. The army complained it was made to accept this, though regular customers would have rejected it. The greater portion of cattle went out of Texas on the hoof, to be served as fresh meat after being slaughtered in the army camp. So much beef, pork, mutton, grain, sugar, salt, peas, beans, flour and corn meal was shipped away that Texas became known as the breadbasket of the Confederacy. Supplying food was only one part of the Texas war effort, which included yielding her cotton crops as currency to buy guns and ammunition and other goods, and sending her men and horses into the fight. (1964)

239

JEFFERSON (Marion Co.)   *S. Polk St., north side of bridge*
Jefferson Turn Basin
Wide, deep lagoon in Cypress Bayou, used for turning around ships in Gulf-Red River trade. First steamer to reach here was the Lama in 1844, by way of Red River, which for 200 miles above Shreveport was clogged by a "raft" of debris that had begun forming about 1529. Cypress Bayou thus was best travel route into Oklahoma, Western Arkansas, and North Texas. Until federal government in 1873 removed the raft, Jefferson was Southwest's greatest inland port, with this basin its business center. Last steamer operated here in 1903.   (1964)

JEFFERSON (Marion Co.)   *US 59, 1 mi. S on east side N of bridge*
Trammel's Trace
Traces began as foot paths used by the Indians to mark their trails through wilderness areas. They later were used by surveyors in mapping early land grants. In 1824, Nicholas Trammel (1780–1852), a government scout, began opening up the trace that now bears his name. Trammel's Trace was, for many years, an important route of immigration into Texas. Approximately 180 miles long, it began at Fulton, Arkansas, and continued to Nacogdoches, Texas. Trammel's Trace entered Marion County on its northern boundary and left the county about 3.5 miles south of Jefferson.   (1984)

JEFFERSON (Marion Co.)   *US 59, 2 mi S*
Jefferson
Home to the Caddo Indians for centuries, this area of Texas attracted Anglo-American colonists to settle here in the early 1800s. Founded in 1839, Jefferson developed along a double-grid pattern. Daniel Nelson Alley platted the townsite in a true North-South and East-West pattern, while Allen Urquhart drew a plan with streets leading diagonally to and from Big Cypress Bayou. Jefferson was a center of commerce and an important shipping point on the Red River system. Riverboats arrived at the wharves daily, making it a major inland port of entry for Texas pioneers. It was the seat of Cass County from 1846 to 1852, and was named seat of the new county of Marion in 1860. During the Civil War, Jefferson served as a major supply center for the Confederacy. The late 1860s saw the imposition of martial law by Federal reconstruction troops, and a devastating fire in 1868 destroyed much of the central business district. Destruction of a massive logjam on the Red River in November 1873 diverted the river's flow and lowered the water in Big Cypress Bayou. The decline of Jefferson's economy due to the loss of its port continued until 20th-century tourism began to revive the town.   (1990)

JERMYN (Jack Co.)   *SH 114, about 3 mi. W, 300 yds. S of site*
Site of Loving Ranch House
Built 1872 by J. C. Loving, the son of pioneer trail driver Oliver Loving. J. C. Loving was an organizer and first secretary of Texas and Southwestern Cattle Raisers Association. Organization's first office was at the ranch, which was later operated by Loving's son, Oliver II.   (1968)

JERMYN (Jack Co.)   *SH 114, 1 mi. E*
Community of Jermyn
Located on the western edge of Lost Valley, a 20-square-mile area of Jack County, Jermyn was founded in 1909 as site of the roundhouse, depot, and office building for the Gulf, Texas & Western Railroad. It was named for J. J. Jermyn (1852–1928), line's president. Land for the town was donated by Oliver Loving II (grandson of "Dean of Texas Trail Drivers") and W. P. Stewart. Many lots were sold and the town embarked on two decades of prosperity and progress. A school was built about 1912 and Jermyn came to have numerous businesses, including a hotel, garage, bank, two general stores, blacksmith shop, land office, cotton gin and warehouse, restaurant, drugstore, ice house, lumber yard, confectionary, U.S Post Office, and a newspaper—The "Enterprise"— succeeded by the "News". With the sale of the G.T. & W. Railroad to the Frisco system in 1930, however, a gradual decline set in. By 1936 the line curtailed passenger service, then all service. Highway construction hastened the railroad's—and the town's—economic demise as citizens moved to the cities to find work, and businesses closed. Today the post office, two churches, and a general store still function and part of the school serves as a civic center. Current economic base is ranching.   (1972)

JOAQUIN (Shelby Co.)
On Bell St. (US 84)
B. F. Morris and the Town of Joaquin
Alabama-born Benjamin Franklin Morris (1827–1900) came to Texas in 1838 and settled in the area that became the pioneer village of Sarat. A prosperous farmer and rancher, he gave right of way through 500 acres of his land to the Houston, East & West Texas Railroad in 1884. He also provided a 100-acre townsite to be named for his grandson Joaquin (1878–1898), requesting that a depot be built here and that passenger trains stop daily. Morris, a Confederate veteran, later donated a building site for the First Baptist Church of Joaquin. (1977)

JOHNSON CITY (Blanco Co.)
US 281, 11 mi. NE in roadside park
Home County of Pioneer Leader Joseph Wilson Baines (1846–1906)
Born in Louisiana; in 1850 came to Texas, where his father, Rev. Geo. W. Baines, founded a church newspaper and was president of Baylor University. Served in the Williamson cadets, in Civil War. Lived in Collin County, 1867–1883. Married Ruth A. Huffman. Was a teacher, lawyer; founder and publisher of McKinney "Advocate." Served 1883–1887 as Secretary of State for Texas. Practiced law in Blanco, 1888–1903. Died in Fredericksburg. His daughter Rebecca (Mrs. Sam Ealy Johnson) became the mother of Lyndon Baines Johnson, 36th President of the United States. (1965)

JOHNSON CITY (Blanco Co.)
US 290 at entrance to
Johnson Ranch Headquarters
Blanco County Trail Drivers
From this headquarters site in the 1870s, the brothers J. T. and Sam Ealy Johnson started thousands of cattle up trails to Kansas and other shipping or market points. To the west, at Williamson's Creek, and at Deer Creek (southeast) the Johnsons had gathering and processing pens. They had largest individual trail driving outfit in Blanco and six nearby counties, sending north several herds of 2,500 to 3,000 each season. Sam Ealy, the younger Johnson brother, is known to history as grandfather of 36th President of the United States, Lyndon Baines Johnson. (1969)

JOHNSON CITY (Blanco Co.)
W. Pecan Dr., 1 blk. N of US 290 at courthouse
Blanco County
Formed from Burnet, Hays, Gillespie and Comal Counties. Created February 12, 1858. Organized April 12, 1858. Named for the stream which traverses the region. County seat, Blanco City, 1858–1890. Johnson City, since. (1964)

JOHNSON CITY (Blanco Co.)
7th at G St., 1 blk. N of US 290 at courthouse
Blanco County Courthouse
Designed by San Antonio architect Henry T. Phelps, the 1916 Blanco County Courthouse was the first permanent courthouse built after the seat of government moved from Blanco to Johnson City in 1890. Serving as contractor for the project was stonemason James Waterston, who had come from Scotland to Texas in 1883 to aid in the construction of the state Capitol. The Classical Revival limestone structure features Doric columns and a domed cupola. (1983)

JOHNSON CITY (Blanco Co.)
N. Nugent (Loop 356), adjacent to courthouse
Dr. James Odiorne, 1816–1887
Prominent pioneer physician, civic leader. Practiced medicine in Illinois and Kentucky before settling in Texas in 1857, moved to Blanco County in 1860. He was Civil War surgeon at Fort Mason, Texas. Served as commissioner and chief justice of Blanco County, 1860. Owned a newspaper, 1885–1887. As doctor, he went by horseback or gig, regardless of weather. Scarcity of drugs led him to use native herbs for medication; for a sedative (opium), grew and milked garden poppies. He died of burns when alcohol exploded during the compounding of medicine in his drugstore near this site. (1972)

JOHNSON CITY (Blanco Co.)
Elm St. at Ave. G, 1 blk. S of US 290
L.B.J. Boyhood Home
Sam Ealy Johnson Jr. (1877–1937) and his wife Rebekah Baines Johnson (1881–1958) bought this residence in 1913. Sam, an educator and six-term Texas legislator, and Rebekah, an educator and journalist, raised five children here. The frame house was built in 1901, with simple Clas-

241

sical details and decorative bargeboards of milled wood. Each wing is one room deep for light and ventilation. Various porches, open and enclosed, indicate additions over the years. In 1937, the Johnson's eldest son, Lyndon (1908–1973), launched his first campaign for Congress, and his ascent to the U.S. presidency, from the east porch. (1965)

JOSHUA (Johnson Co.) *SH 174, 4 mi. N*
Sam Bass Holdup
Along with two partners, Sam Bass, daring Texas outlaw, stopped a Fort Worth–Cleburne stage near here Dec. 20, 1877. Without firing a shot, they disarmed the driver, robbed passengers of $11.25. One outlaw, shot by a witness, was left by Bass to die. Less than a year later, Bass too was slain. (1966)

JOURDANTON (Atascosa Co.) *1 Courthouse Circle Dr., 1 blk. N of SH 97*
Atascosa County
As early as 1722 El Camino Real (the King's Highway) from the Rio Grande to San Antonio was well established in this area. The Spanish word "Atascosa," denoting boggy ground that hindered travel, gave region its name. The county was created in 1856 from land formerly in Bexar County. Jose Antonio Navarro, whose 1831 claim was the first grant recorded in area, gave land in 1857 for first county seat, Navatasco. County seat moved to Pleasanton in 1858, to Jourdanton in 1911. Livestock, oil, gas and strawberries are well-known products of the county. (1969)

JOURDANTON (Atascosa Co.) *1604 E. Oak St. (SH 97)*
Jourdanton
In 1909, Jourdan Campbell (1867–1938) and Theodore H. Zanderson (1854–1927) established the Jourdanton community, named for Campbell, on the eastern edge of their Toby Ranch property. Jourdan Campbell was born in Atascosa County, and was a merchant and county commissioner. He first met Zanderson, a Dane whose significant business interests centered on wool and mohair, in San Antonio. The two entrepreneurs convinced Dr. Charles Franklin Simmons, a land speculator who had previously worked with Campbell, to lay rail through the new townsite; the first train came through Jourdanton on September 4, 1909. Jourdanton soon had utilities, a bank, a newspaper (The Atascosa Monitor), a post office and several businesses. The community also had a school, several churches and a cemetery. Residents, encouraged by the settlement's rapid growth, and led by newspaper owner Ralph Roy "Railroad" Smith, began to promote the idea of Jourdanton becoming county seat. In 1910, Atascosa County residents voted that the county seat be moved from Pleasanton to Jourdanton. In 1911, the town incorporated, and by 1914, it had two railroads and the population had doubled. Many residents were farmers or ranchers. By the 1940s, oil and natural gas reserves were discovered nearby, which led to another period of growth; later, the discovery and mining of lignite to the south also helped sustain Jourdanton's economy. The town grew further with the additions of the Smith Village and Atascosa Estates developments. Although the railroads stopped running by the 1960s, Jourdanton continued to grow, and remains a community rich in culture, heritage and diversity. (2009)

JOURDANTON (Atascosa Co.) *1604 E. Oak St. (SH 97)*
Ralph Roy Smith
R. R. "Railroad" Smith (1880–1944) was born in Gonzales County to Alexander Frohock and Mary McGill (Mathews) Smith. Around 1907, Smith moved to Atascosa County where he opened up a law practice and entered into the newspaper business with a cousin. Smith successfully ran for the Texas House of Representatives in 1908, and during the Thirty-First Legislative session he solely sponsored a bill creating the Texas State Library and Historical Commission. Smith served later terms in 1911 and 1921. Smith moved his newspaper from Pleasanton to Jourdanton in 1909 and was also a strong advocate of moving the county seat from Pleasanton to Jourdanton in 1910. (2009)

JOURDANTON (Atascosa Co.) *1604 E. Oak St. (SH 97)*
Jourdan Campbell
Jourdan Campbell (1867–1938) and his family moved to Atascosa County by 1870; his father John Campbell founded Campbellton. Jourdan married Alice Louise Marr in 1897 and the couple had eight children. Jourdan became county commissioner in the 1890s, and in 1907 with Col. T. H. Zanderson bought the 33,760 acre Tobey Ranch, part of which would become Jourdanton. Once the

town was formed, Campbell was vice president of the bank and lobbied for a railroad. Jourdanton became Atascosa County seat in 1910. Campbell also supported a 65-mile hardtop highway project linking Jourdanton to the principal communities of Atascosa County. Jourdan Campbell was the driving force behind Jourdanton's creation, prosperity and growth. (2011)

JOURDANTON (Atascosa Co.) 200 Zanderson (SH 16)
Jourdanton Independent School District
From a tiny school to an official, recognized single-campus concept, the Jourdanton Independent School District has remained dedicated to education and community. In the early 20th century, county schools such as the Hilburn School northwest of Jourdanton served the area. Soon the growing enrollment and need for teachers prompted the community to appeal to the legislature. In 1911, the state legislature authorized the creation of the Jourdanton Independent School District, the first in Atascosa County. Residents quickly passed a bond election to build a school and park system. A three-story brick building was erected in the center of Jourdanton. A football field and high school building were added on adjoining lots. In 1938, a gymnasium was completed with assistance from the Works Progress Administration. To accommodate a growing district, a new campus was constructed on the southern edge of town in 1953 where it remains today. Over the decades, Jourdanton Independent School District overcame many obstacles. With the outbreak of World War I and II, the school lost educators and administrators to military service and assisted the war effort by holding war bond drives on campus. Many students from the district attended colleges and then returned to teach the next generation of students. Other graduates have gone on to become chefs, lawyers, researchers, writers, and athletes. Through commitment to education and achievement, Jourdanton Independent School District has cemented its reputation for excellence for a vibrant and growing community. (2011)

JUNCTION (Kimble Co.) Loop 291 off IH 10, 18 mi. W
Ft. McKavett–Ft. Clark Military Road
From nearby Ft. Terrett, this road in 1852 led south to Ft. Clark and north to Ft. McKavett. Selected mainly because it had water available, it served as route for freight and mail, 1868, when forts were reactivated. Over it went troops, supplies, a few immigrants and pioneer ranchers. It was noted also for passage of forays of Col. Ranald Mackenzie against the hostile Indians to the northwest. After forts were abandoned in 1883, ranchers drove cattle to market over parts of the road. (1966)

JUNCTION (Kimble Co.) IH 10, 7.8 mi. SE at Segovia exit
Near Route of Old Military Road
Supply line from U.S. Army headquarters in San Antonio to Fort Terrett, 1852–1854. In the 1850s two-thirds of Texas was held by Comanches or threatened by raids. Posts such as Fort Terrett stood from Red River to the Rio Grande, for protection. The Fort Terrett road paralleled Johnson (Elm) Fork of the Llano, and crossed the main Llano near Junction. The army closed Fort Terrett in 1854, but settlers used the route as their main road to San Antonio. It appeared on Kimble County maps until 1930. Parts of the road are still visible. (1966)

JUNCTION (Kimble Co.) US 377, 8 mi. NE
Teacup Mountain
Named for its peculiar formation. Probably used as a lookout post by both whites and Indians in pioneer days. Near here occurred the Indian killing of pioneer James Bradberry, Sr., 1872; and the capture of a wanted man by Lt. N. O. Reynolds and four fellow Texas Rangers in 1878. (1967)

JUNCTION (Kimble Co.) US 377/83, 1.5 mi. N
First Court in Kimble County
(Site: ½ mi. NW, on Main Llano River)
Held in spring of 1876, under a live oak tree that had a hive of wild bees in its trunk. The site, "Old Kimbleville," had been suggested as the county seat. District Judge W. A. Blackburn, of Burnet, arrived by horseback. District attorney was Frank Wilks. The jury was seated on two logs. Another log was the judge's bench, and a piece of gnarled live oak limb the gavel. Prisoners awaiting trial were chained to nearby trees. Major trials were for horse thefts. Texas Rangers were on hand to testify and to guard court, as this was during lawless era. (1967)

JUNCTION (Kimble Co.)
US 377, 1.5 mi. N
The Killing of Sam Speer (⁹⁄₁₀ mi. W, Hwy. 290; and 200 yds. S)
On Dec. 24, 1876, a band of Indians killed Sam Speer, only 17 years of age, who was driving horses near here. A 50-caliber gun his brother was using failed to fire. This was the last Indian murder in Kimble County. Speer is buried in the North Llano cemetery.   (1967)

JUNCTION (Kimble Co.)
Main St. (Loop 481) at 5th St.
Kimble County
Jumano and Apache Indians inhabited region when Spanish explorers traveled across it in the 17th and 18th centuries, and were displaced by the Comanche tribe by the mid-19th century. Area was under military jurisdiction of Forts Terrett (1852–1854) and McKavett (1852–1859, 1868–1883), which were aided in defense by the Texas Rangers. County was created from Bexar County, 1858, named for George C. Kimble (1801–1836), who died defending the Alamo. Organized in 1876, with the county seat first at Kimbleville, then Junction in 1877. Haven for lawless element until the Rangers restored peace in 1880s. Ranching is primary industry, producing wool and mohair.   (1973)

JUNCTION (Kimble Co.)
US 377, 1.7 mi. SW
Vicinity of Bradbury Settlement
(2 mi. above forks of N. and S. Llano rivers)
One of earliest Kimble County communities. Opened by James Bradbury, Sr., a frontiersman. Between 1850 and 1864 he moved here from Williamson County with six children, after death of his wife. He erected several picket or log buildings, and had blacksmith shop for repairing guns and tools. Main business was ranching. Diet included fish, game, honey and bear meat cured as bacon. Five other men (some with families) lived nearby. Bradbury was killed in 1872 in an Indian fight. In 1875 his land was bought and occupied by Dr. E. K. Kountz and family.   (1970)

JUNCTION (Kimble Co.)
US 377, 2 mi. SW of courthouse
Isaac Kountz
Killed on this spot by Indians on Christmas Eve, 1876. He was 16 years old, and herding sheep for his father, Dr. E. K. Kountz. A brother, Sebastian, aged 11, escaped. A posse and Texas Rangers chased the Indians to the Guadalupe River. Young Kountz was buried in Junction cemetery.   (1967)

JUNCTION (Kimble Co.)
US 377, 3 mi. SW
John James Smith (March 4, 1822–April 22, 1924)
Illinois native John James Smith came to Texas shortly before enlisting for service in the Mexican War, 1846–1848. He later served as a Texas Ranger, helping protect frontier areas from attacks by hostile Indians. During the Civil War, Smith joined the Confederate Army and served for four years. Following his discharge from the military, he served as city marshall of Greenville, Texas, for two years. Smith moved to Kimble County in 1881, where he was a farmer and a respected citizen. He lived at his nearby farm home (300 yds. SE) until his death at the age of 102.   (1981)

JUNCTION (Kimble Co.)
US 377, 4 mi. SW
Site of Four Mile Dam (100 yds. S)
Built under an 1896 charter, obtained for the Junction City Irrigation and Power Ditches, to furnish power for mills and mining, supply city mains, water extensive lands and livestock. At first under engineering supervision of G. W. Ragsdill, a local man, then of R. J. Hand, San Antonio, project was sold 1903 to Jay E. Adams, San Antonio, and A. C. Green, of Palestine, Texas. Dam was of native stone and cypress wood; ditches were 4 ft. deep, 20 ft. at top, 12 at bottom. Big ditch carried water late as 1925; but was unprofitable. Charter was forfeited in 1950.   (1967)

JUNCTION (Kimble Co.)
US 377, 8 mi. SW
R. M. Turner Family
On April 28, 1879, R. M. Turner (1858–1928) entered Kimble County with bride, Emma (Scarborough), (1863–1945), from DeWitt County. They settled near this site, on the north bank of the South Llano River, where Turner soon became a prominent cattle and sheep rancher. Of ten children born to the Turners, eight reached adulthood. Most of them remained in the county to become leading citizens. Most noted was Jack Turner, conductor of the first Angora doe sale in Texas, and

one of the organizers of National Angora Goat Breeders Association, in 1925, serving as the first secretary, then president.

(1973)

JUNCTION (Kimble Co.)
US 377, 9.5 mi. SW
Doom of the Outlaws of Pegleg Station

Here the climax of a western track-down occurred on Jan. 18, 1878, when Texas Rangers killed suspected murderer Dick Dublin, member of a gang of outlaws. Although a friend yelled for him to run, Dublin was shot (150 yds. S) as the intrepid James B. Gillett and 3 other Rangers rushed his hide-out (60 yds. E). Dick's brothers (Role and Dell), Mack Potter, and Rube Boyce were captured after a partner of the gang turned informer. Three of them (plus two others) were convicted Aug. 23–24, 1880, of the 1877 robbery of the U.S. mail at Pegleg Station.

(1968)

JUNCTION (Kimble Co.)
US 377, 10.5 mi. SW
Wooten Cemetery

Typical of burial sites chosen by early Texas Hill Country pioneers, Wooten Cemetery was established by April 1880 when one-year-old Cornelius Clay Jackson was buried. His headstone is the earliest grave marker in the cemetery. His mother, P. Jane Jackson, died in 1881 and is interred nearby. Other notable graves include a family group believed to be tuberculosis victims. The plot of the Allsup family is also prominent, as is the grave of Civil War veteran Simon Lee Wooten (1830–1896), for whom the cemetery is named, who came to Texas from Georgia upon the death of the Old South.

(1997)

JUNO (Val Verde Co.)
FM 189 at SH 163, 2 mi. N
Hood's Devil's River Fight

The men of Company G, a small unit of the U.S. 2nd Cavalry, left Fort Mason on July 5, 1857, under the command of Lt. John Bell Hood (1831–1879), in pursuit of Comanche Indians in the vicinity. Traveling northwest, they discovered a fresh Indian trail leading southward toward Mexico. Crossing bluffs near the Devil's River on July 20, the men encountered an Indian camp on a ridge about two miles from the stream, marked by a white flag. Suspecting an ambush, Hood proceeded cautiously toward the ridge. A small band of Indians advanced to meet Hood's party. Then, throwing down the flag to signal their concealed allies, the Indians attacked. Outnumbered, and hampered by brush fires set by Indian women, the soldiers were forced into fierce hand-to-hand combat. The Company fell back to reload their weapons, only to hear the loud cries of Comanche women through the smoke and dust, indicating an Indian retreat. Two cavalrymen, William Barry and Thomas Ryan, were killed, and five others, including Hood, were wounded. Later reports revealed that nineteen Indians were killed, and many more wounded. Hood and his men were later cited for valor in army reports.

(1987)

JUSTICEBURG (Garza Co.)
US 84, NW of post office
Garza County's First Oil Well (3½ mi. E)

After several unsuccessful ventures from 1911 to 1919, the first oil producer in the county was completed on J. M. Boren property at Justiceburg in 1926. The well was begun in 1924 by Phelps, Caldwell and Blackwell Oil Company. It produced a total of 1,641 barrels before it was abandoned in 1932. In 1932 four producing wells were completed south of Post. A refinery was built near city. Garza County has a number of fields, and its 1,500 wells have produced more than 85,000,000 barrels of oil.

KARNACK (Harrison Co.)
FM 134 at Spur 449
Home Town of Mrs. Lyndon B. Johnson
(Wife of 36th President of the United States)

On December 22, 1912, in the family home 2.7 miles south, was born Claudia Alta Taylor. She was third child (only daughter) of Thomas Jefferson and Minnie Pattillo Taylor. Her father had a general store in Karnack for many years. Young "Lady Bird" (a pet name originated by her nurse, Alice Tittle) attended public schools in Fern community, near here, and in Jefferson and Marshall, and earned Bachelor of Arts and Journalism Degrees at the University of Texas. On November 17, 1934, she married Lyndon Baines Johnson, congressional staff member who became head of National Youth Administration in Texas in 1935. The Johnsons are parents of two daughters, Lynda Bird and Luci Baines. During her husband's rise to world leadership—as United States

Congressman, Senator, Senate Majority Leader, Vice President, and President—Mrs. Johnson added to role of wife and mother that of hostess to many of the greatest statesmen of the world. As First Lady of the United States, she is true to her East Texas heritage of love for gardens, trees, unspoiled natural scenery, and historic sites. She sponsors vital natural programs of conservation, beautification, and historical preservation. (1967)

KARNACK (Harrison Co.)
PR 2 at FM 134, entrance to Caddo State Park

Old Town of Port Caddo
(Site located in and around Caddo State Park)

Ancestral home of Texas Caddo Indians, this region gained a distinctive character in the 19th century. From 1806 to 1845 it lay in an area disputed by various countries and designated, from 1819, as the "neutral ground." Settlers living here were far from neutral, however. They became independent and resisted paying taxes levied by any "outside" authority. Port Caddo, founded 1838 on Caddo Lake, soon grew to importance, and its rowdy reputation grew, too, as ship's crews, gamblers, and Indians filled its streets. Meanwhile, new towns and roads sprung up nearby. Continuing upheaval led to the assassination of the tax collector in 1840 and townsmen joined in the factional "Regulator-Moderator War" from 1840 to 1844. When Texas proposed to join the Union in 1845, Port Caddoans saw a chance to end their problems and voted strongly in favor of statehood. From 1845 to the 1850s Port Caddo thrived, growing to 500, but then declined as the port of Jefferson and the county seat of Marshall drew away business. With the end of the great plantations after the Civil War, falling of the water level in Caddo Lake, and coming of the railroad to nearby Karnack (1900), Port Caddo gradually faded out of existence. (1968)

KARNES CITY (Karnes Co.)
US 181 at Esplanade

Karnes City

Seat of Karnes County; was founded in Christmas season, 1890, when a partnership headed by Otto Buchel bought 1,000 acres of land from J. L. Calvert for $5 an acre. The tract was near the geographic center of the county and adjoined the right-of-way of the San Antonio & Aransas Pass Railroad. The young town was first named Karnes in honor of Henry W. Karnes (1812–1840), Texas Ranger hero. Although a small, mild-mannered man, Karnes was conspicuous for his cool courage in battle. Red-headed, he was once besieged by a group of Comanche women who attempted to wash the "berry juice" out of his hair. When the first Karnes post office was established April 1, 1891, "City" was added to the name. The new town grew so fast that within three years citizens petitioned for an election to remove the county seat from Helena to Karnes City. The voters favored Karnes City two-to-one and the move was made January, 1894. Having grown steadily since 1891, Karnes City has had seven newspapers, four banks, and many businesses. During the railroad boom, when a train was the most exciting way to travel, six passenger trains per day came through town. The economy of the area has been based on ranching, farming, uranium, oil, and gas. (1967)

KAUFMAN (Kaufman Co.)
SH 34, 1.5 mi. S

Kaufman County Poor Farm

As did many Texas counties of the era, Kaufman County created a poor farm in 1883 in order to provide the indigent residents and families of the area with food, shelter, and medicine. This work program replaced earlier relief efforts. All able-bodied persons were required to work, including resident guards and county inmates convicted of minor crimes who were originally brought from the jail daily for labor; by 1893 they were housed on the farm. In the 1930s the farm was used to demonstrate new agricultural techniques. Usually filled to capacity, the farm operated until the 1970s. By 1997, a cemetery and a few buildings remained. (1997)

KAUFMAN (Kaufman Co.)
100 W. Mulberry St. and Grove St. (SH 243) at courthouse

Kaufman County

Created February 26, 1848; organized August 7, 1848; named in honor of David Spangler Kaufman 1812–1851; came to Texas in 1837 and located at Nacogdoches; member of the Texas Congress 1839–1845; Member of the United States Congress. Kaufman, the County Seat. (1936)

KELLER (Tarrant Co.)
US 377 at Bear Creek Rd.
Keller
After Texas and Pacific Railroad came through this area, H. W. Wood, a druggist, set aside 40 acres on July 19, 1881, for this townsite. He named the new village "Athol." Within a year, the name became "Keller," honoring John C. Keller, railroad construction crew foreman. Many businesses grew up to meet the needs of the surrounding farms. In 1886, the post office was established. There were two hotels, three doctors, a newspaper, and a school. The Baptist, Methodist, and Presbyterian congregations erected a union church building in 1886. Keller was incorporated in 1958.   (1980)

KEMAH (Galveston Co.)
SH 146 at Bel Rd.
Kemah
Michael Gouldrich, one of Stephen F. Austin's original three hundred colonists, received a Mexican land grant here in 1824. Elizabeth S. Justice acquired a part of the property in 1853. By the early 1890s Abraham and Elizabeth (Justice) Kipp, their daughter Jane, and her husband, James Bradford, had acquired the balance of the original Gouldrich Mexican land grant. In 1898 the Texas & New Orleans Railroad extended a track through the area which prompted the Kipp and Bradford families to establish a townsite here named Evergreen. Despite its destruction by a storm in 1900, the village was rebuilt after the Kipps and Bradfords erected large family homes here in 1901. The name of the town was changed to Kemah with the granting of a post office in 1907. Gulf-related businesses such as boat building, commercial fishing, and tourism helped Kemah grow into a town of 1,300 people by 1922. Kemah was connected with Seabrook by bridge in 1929. A large shrimp fleet located here after the Clear Creek Channel opened in the 1950s. Kemah sustained major storm damage in 1961 but recovered and was formally incorporated in 1965. Marine storage facilities built in this area in the 1970s and 1980s continued to boost the local economy.   (1993)

KEMPNER (Lampasas Co.)
US 190, W city limits
Kempner
Founded 1882. Named for Texas philanthropist, banker, railroad magnate Harris Kempner (1837–1894). An immigrant from Poland, Kempner joined Parsons' Brigade, Confederate Army. Wounded in Red River campaign, he was left on the battlefield for dead, but recovered and served to the war's end. Then he helped to rebuild Texas.

KENDALIA (Kendall Co.)
FM 473, city limits
George Wilkins Kendall, 1809–1867
A molder of world opinion. His theme: Greatness of Texas. Born in New Hampshire, learned printing and worked in New York, Boston and Washington, D.C. With Francis A. Lumsden, in 1837 founded New Orleans "Picayune." Joined the Texan–Santa Fe Expedition, 1841, as a reporter. Was imprisoned along with other ill fated members. Wrote a book on the expedition. During Mexican War, 1846–1848, often rode with the Texas Rangers, in world's first war coverage by a foreign correspondent. Filed his news by Pony Express. In 1847 settled on Texas sheep range, at Post Oak Springs. Continuing news columns brought him in a single mail 300 letters from far away as Sandwich Islands, inquiring about Texas. During the Civil War, produced wool for Confederate uniforms, blankets. Proposed a weaving mill on Comal River, for making cloth near the flocks. Received no government response. To keep producing wool, had to fight Comanches, range fires, freezing disasters. When roaming vandals threatened to kill sheepherders, he and his teenage son tended flocks themselves. To end of his life, his regular dispatches to the "Picayune" continued to praise good life in Texas.   (1965)

KENDLETON (Fort Bend Co.)
Loop 541 at Lum Rd.
Kendleton
The site on which Kendleton now stands was originally a Mexican land grant to settler Elizabeth Powell, whose house was an early-day stage stop. During the Texas Revolution, in 1836, Santa Anna's Mexican Army camped near here. Later the settlements of Oak Hill and Humbolt existed briefly. Kendleton began during Civil War reconstruction when Wm. E. Kendall sold land, for as little as 50 cents an acre, to assist freed Negroes in starting their own farms. The rural village was named in his honor when the railroad came through, 1884.   (1969)

KENEDY (Karnes Co.)   *300 Main St. (SH 72)*
Kenedy
The town of Kenedy occupies a site that once was part of a royal Spanish land grant to Don Carlos Martinez. American settlement in the area began after the Texas War for Independence (1836). Land for a townsite was purchased in 1886 by railroad promoter Mifflin Kenedy, for whom the community was named, and a post office was established the following year. Kenedy's early growth was attributed to its position as a major stop on the San Antonio and Aransas Pass Railroad. Early buildings in Kenedy included a church, store, and cotton gin. By 1906, businesses in the town included newspaper offices, a bank, livery and feed stables, and one of the largest cotton compresses in the state. Incorporated in 1910, Kenedy gained a reputation for gun fighting that earned it the name "Six Shooter Junction." In 1915, hot mineral water was discovered near the depot, and the Hot Wells Hotel and Bath House was a thriving business for nearly 25 years. An alien detention camp was located on the outskirts of town during World War II. Although passenger train service no longer runs through Kenedy, this historic town remains an economic center for the surrounding agricultural area.   (1986)

KENNARD (Houston Co.)   *SH 7, 1.4 mi. E*
Community of Coltharp (1.2 mi. SE)
By the 1850s, Eli Coltharp lived beside Cochina Bayou. He opened a store and post office at his home on the stage route west of Nacogdoches. The farm area called Coltharp Hill boasted a gin, gristmill, blacksmith, and millinery shops. A school building housed Coltharp Masonic Lodge No. 419, now in Kennard. When the railroad bypassed Coltharp and a sawmill opened nearby in 1901, residents worked at the mill and farming declined. The post office closed in 1909 and Coltharp school consolidated with Kennard in 1925. Many descendants of early settlers remain in the area.   (1979)

KENNARD (Houston Co.)   *SH 7, 1.2 mi. E*
Hagerville Community (5 mi. SE)
Kentuckian James Murphy Hager (1822–1879) and his wife Naoma (Clark) came to Texas in the 1840s. Hager, a farmer and cabinet maker, opened a blacksmith shop and mill in Houston County. The Nacogdoches-to-Navasota stage and mail road ran beside his log home. Hager's son James Polk began a post office in 1891 and named the area "Hagerville." Another son W. J. (Bill) donated land for a schoolhouse that was used for worship. Many residents moved closer to the sawmills and the post office closed in 1905. Business declined but the community retains its identity.   (1979)

KENNARD (Houston Co.)   *SH 7 at Main St. (FM 357)*
Kennard
The town of Kennard was founded in 1903 by the Louisiana and Texas Lumber Company and platted on 160 acres. Land agent Alexander McTavish also acted as Kennard's first postmaster. The town served as a terminus for the Eastern Texas Railroad, a line established to transport timber to Angelina County. Many businesses and citizens from earlier settlements nearby moved to Kennard when the rail line located here. Schools were built nearby as early as 1864 and served the area until Kennard school opened in 1903. Religious observances began with tent meetings conducted by traveling ministers. Permanent churches were soon organized. Early establishments included a bank, hotel, drug store, general merchandise stores, cafe, meat shop and Woodmen of the World Lodge. In the 1920s and 1930s the timber industry and farming grew while other businesses came to town including a cottonseed mill, cotton gins, syrup mills, a blacksmith shop, gas stations, and a boardinghouse. In 1933, State Highway 7 was built through Main Street, shifting the town's business center there. Incorporated as a city in 1969, Kennard continues as an active and involved community located in the heart of the Davy Crockett National Forest.   (1996)

KENNARD (Houston Co.)   *SH 7, near school campus*
A Former Rosenwald School
(Now "The Little Red Schoolhouse")
A symbol of black America's pride in education, plus crusade of Julius Rosenwald (1862–1932), a Chicagoan who in 1913 began to fund school buildings for Negroes. By 1920, when this one-teacher structure was built at Ratcliff (4 miles East), Rosenwald's grants had to be matched—in this case, by Houston County funds. Alfred Foy (1865–1944), a veteran of brush arbor and log cabin

classrooms, taught in this building at Ratcliff 1920–1923 and 1924–1927; Miss Detroit Denman, 1923–1924; Mrs. Evola Colbert Dorn, 1927–1955. Their pupils' playground equipment consisted of a baseball diamond, basketball goal, mulberry tree and swing. Yet patrons—true to zeal that helped obtain the building—brought in food and saw that the children had hot lunches. Sessions ceased in 1955 when the Ratcliff school was consolidated with Kennard Common School District No. 75. The Ratcliff building was used 1955–1968 as the community center for socials and public meetings. In 1968 the "Old Rosenwald School" was moved to Kennard for use by Headstart and related programs. Texas had a total of 518 school buildings funded in part by the Rosenwald Foundation—22 of them in Houston County—providing classrooms for thousands. (1973)

KENNEY (Austin Co.)   *Old SH 36 right-of-way, 2.5 mi. S*
James Bradford Pier (Nov. 23, 1813–Feb. 5, 1888)
A native of Circleville, Ohio, J. B. Pier came to Texas in 1835 with his wife, Lucy (Merry). The Piers settled in this area near the site of the early Texas town of Travis. Pier served as a member of the Texas Army during the War for Independence. He was detailed as a rear guard at the camp opposite Harrisburg during the Battle of San Jacinto. In later years, he was a farmer, stock raiser, teacher, and merchant. He served as justice of the peace of Austin County and was the first postmaster of the Travis community. Pier is buried in the nearby Travis Cemetery. (1985)

KENNEY (Austin Co.)   *SH 36 at Hall Rd.*
John Wesley Kenney (1799–1865)
One of great pioneer Methodist ministers of Texas. Pennsylvania-born, he began preaching at age 19. In 1833 he came to Texas and soon settled in this county. Unkempt in appearance, Kenney redeemed his eccentricity with an eloquent style of preaching. In Texas—then part of Mexico and Catholic by law—he helped found Methodist societies and, in 1834, served a vast circuit covering all of present state west of Trinity River. In 1836 he took part in Texas War for Independence. His lifetime saw Methodism become one of the major denominations in state. (1972)

KERMIT (Winkler Co.)   *SH 18, 10 mi. N at state line*
Texas Territorial Compromise of 1850
Four miles east of this site is an official corner post marking agreement of Texas to give up some of the land won in her 1836 War for Independence. It also marks New Mexico's southeast corner. When Texas was annexed to the United States, 1846, her territory included 98,300 square miles now in the states of Colorado, Kansas, New Mexico, Oklahoma and Wyoming. After the Mexican War (fought 1846–1848, over the annexation), anti-slavery forces in the U.S. sought to trim the size of Texas, a slave state. To raise money and establish a definite boundary, Texas accepted the compromise of 1850 and agreed to give up a third of her area in return for payment of $10,000,000. The money paid debts of the former Republic of Texas, set up a $2,000,000 public school fund, and erected state buildings, including a new capitol (which subsequently burned in 1881). By the 1850 compromise, the western boundary of Texas follows the 103rd Meridian south from 36°30'; near here intersects the 32nd Parallel, then goes west along the parallel to the Rio Grande. The corner marks not only a peaceable boundary pact, but also shows an unbroken stretch of Permian Basin lands, unified in geography and common goals. (1966)

KERMIT (Winkler Co.)   *SH 115 at FM 874, 8 mi. NE*
Winkler County
Formed from Tom Green County. Created February 26, 1887. Organized April 5, 1910. Named in honor of C. M. Winkler, 1821–1882, statesman, soldier and jurist. Kermit, the county seat. A petroleum producing and cattle raising area.

KERMIT (Winkler Co.)   *SH 115 at FM 874, 8 mi. NE*
The Sand Hills
Mapped by U.S. government, 1849, for gold seekers and settlers. Known earlier to Indians and many Spanish explorers, a 100-mi. belt of sand in Winkler and 4 other Texas Counties and in New Mexico. Width varies from 3 to 20 mi. Outer dunes are held by dwarf oaks. Water at 2' depth supports willows, cottonwoods, and a plum thicket. (The plums gave food to early settlers.) Many dunes more than 70' high. Heavy, shifting sands a natural barrier to travel. Campsite and game reservation for Indians. Now part of expansive cattle ranges and rich oil fields. (1967)

KERMIT (Winkler Co.)   *SH 302, 17 mi. E*
Blue Mountain
Winkler County's highest point (3500 Ft.), Blue Mountain has long served as a lookout and landmark on the west Texas plains. Here Indians found fuel, sheltering caves, and water. They left artifacts in the caves and pictographs on the cave walls that boasted their prowess as horse wranglers, hunters, and fishermen. A directional sign told of a water hole nine days by trail to the northeast. Pictographs also told the story of a fight between two lizards. The pass is called Avary Gap for John Avary, who first settled the area in 1880.   (1964)

KERMIT (Winkler Co.)   *SH 302, 1.5 mi. W city limits*
Old Duval Townsite
First post office in Winkler (then part of Tom Green) County opened near here (1908) on John Howe ranch. Mail came in twice weekly to serve 300 persons. Duval townsite, promoted all over the United States by the Pueblo Investment Co., opened on March 19, 1910, with free lots, a picnic, and cowboy tournament. In April, Kermit became seat of Winkler County; post office moved there in October. Duval failed to develop and townsite rights were canceled after 1928 oil discovery here. Ownership of many valuable lots sold in 1910 is still unclear today.   (1968)

KERMIT (Winkler Co.)   *SH 302, E. city limits*
Kermit
County seat of Winkler County. Organized in 1910. Incorporated in 1938. Named for Kermit Roosevelt, son of President Theodore Roosevelt, who had visited a local ranch. One of the top oil and gas producing counties in state. Ranch center. Gateway to New Mexico.

KERMIT (Winkler Co.)   *SH 18, 12 mi. S*
Willow Springs
6.6 miles east in Sand Hills. Water hole vital to Comanche, explorer. "Judge" A. Hayes found charred remains of 40-wagon train massacre in 1901. Ox bows, human bones, flintlocks, other relics of the ill-fated and unidentified group in Sul Ross State College museum at Alpine.   (1964)

KERRVILLE (Kerr Co.)   *SH 27, 1.3 mi. E of Spur 100*
Kerr County
Formed from Bexar County. Created January 26, 1856. Organized March 22, 1856. Named in honor of James Kerr, 1790–1850. The first American settler on the Guadalupe River. General manager of Dewitt's colony. Signer of the Declaration of Independence. Member of the Third Texas Congress. County seat, Kerrsville, afterwards Kerrville (1856 to 1860). Comfort 1860–1862. Kerrville, since.

KERRVILLE (Kerr Co.)   *800 Junction Hwy (SH 27)*
Kerrville
Kerr County was formally created on January 26, 1856, and named for Republic of Texas soldier and pioneer James Kerr. Among the first settlers in the area was Joshua D. Brown, a veteran of the Battle of San Jacinto. Brown was instrumental in naming the county for his friend James Kerr. The new county seat was named Kerrsville in May 1856 when Brown donated four acres of land for a public square. (The "S" was later dropped.) Early Kerrville settlers included Anglo-American pioneers and German immigrants. The area became an important cattle raising and shipping point in the 1870s. In an election held on September 7, 1889, the citizens of Kerrville voted to incorporate the city, and a mayor and five aldermen were elected later that month. Joseph A. Tivy served as first mayor. The town continued to grow. A city marshal was soon hired and a volunteer fire department was established in 1891. Also in the 1890s city water works and electric service were instituted. By the mid-20th century agriculture, medical services, and tourism had become the major economic concerns of the city.   (1989)

KERRVILLE (Kerr Co.)   *Sidney Baker St. (SH 16) at Main (SH 27) at courthouse*
Camp Verde, C.S.A.
Texas Frontier Regiment Outpost was established 1862, southeast and near old U.S. Post Camp Verde. Part of Red River–Rio Grande line of posts a day's horseback ride apart. The troops furnished own guns, mounts, but often lacked food, clothing, supplies. Still, scouting parties, patrols effectively curbed Indian raids until war's end. Kerr County population was 585. County voted

76–57 for secession 1861. 75 men served in Confederate and state forces. Some sent to protect Texas coast from Union invasion, some helped to defend frontier in this region, others fought on distant battlefields. 19 men from county served in Texas Union Forces. Old U.S. Post Camp Verde was taken by C.S.A. troops Feb. 1861. The Confederates captured 80 camels and two Egyptian drivers with other U.S. property. These camels were used to haul cotton—life's blood of South—to Mexico to swap for vital supplies, including salt from lakes north of Brownsville. During post dances ladies rode a camel "Old Major" around the parade grounds. 600 Union soldiers captured leaving Texas early in Civil War were confined in prison canyon southwest of the camp. 3 cliffs, described as "very difficult to ascend" surrounded the prison area. Prisoners, held from Aug. 1861 until sometime in 1862, were allowed to build shacks and get adequate exercise with little risk of escape. One Union prisoner performed as ventriloquist at post dance, scaring ladies with unseen pig sounds.

(1963)

KERRVILLE (Kerr Co.) — 700 Main St. (SH 27) at courthouse
James Kerr (1790–1850)

Kentucky native James Kerr, the son of a Baptist minister, was reared in Missouri. Kerr fought in the War of 1812 and was later sheriff of St. Charles County, Missouri. He married Angeline Caldwell in 1818 and served in the Missouri Senate and House of Representatives. Kerr was appointed Surveyor General of the Texas colony of Green DeWitt in 1825. With his wife, three children and several slaves, he joined Stephen F. Austin's "Old Three Hundred" colony in Brazoria. In August 1825 he set out to select a site for the DeWitt Colony. Kerr named the community Gonzales in honor of the Governor of Coahuila, Mexico. By this time, Angeline Kerr and two of the children had passed away. Kerr was active in area politics and law enforcement during the formative years of the Republic of Texas. He acted as attorney and surveyor for Benjamin Rush Milam in 1827. He negotiated for peace before the Fredonian Rebellion, signed a treaty with the Karankawa Indians and fought other tribes. He was the Lavaca delegate at the Convention at San Felipe de Austin in 1832 and served as a member of the Second and Third Conventions. Two years later, he married Sarah Fulton. He became a major in the Texas Rangers in 1835 and in the Republic of Texas army in 1836. He was elected to the Third Texas Congress in 1838. Kerr's later years were spent practicing medicine in Jackson County. In 1856, pioneer Joshua Brown gave the land around this site in order that Kerr County be named for his longtime friend, Texas frontiersman and patriot James Kerr.

(2000)

KERRVILLE (Kerr Co.) — 2100 Memorial Blvd (SH 27)
Schreiner College (Schreiner Institute)

Kerrville leaders began to envision a college in the early days of the 20th century. Negotiations with the Presbyterian Synod of Texas were pursued from 1904, when plans were made for an annual camp meeting that might one day evolve into a boys' school. In 1914, local businessman Charles Schreiner (1838–1927) announced his plan to donate 140 acres of land and at least $100,000 to the Synod of Texas to fund the Charles Schreiner Institute for Boys. The plan was delayed by World War I. Finally, on September 18, 1923, the school's opening ceremonies were held, with James J. Delaney (1879–1959) as president. Ninety-five students were enrolled in the first year. The school stressed military discipline and religious instruction as a backdrop for general education. In 1932, girls were admitted as day students. Many students and younger faculty left Schreiner for military service and defense work during World War II, and a naval flight school was established at the institute for the war's duration. Sixty-six alumni lost their lives in World War II. Military training became optional in 1957. In 1971, the board of trustees voted to discontinue military training. Female boarding students were enrolled, and the recruitment of minority and disadvantaged students was instituted. The last high school class graduated in 1976. In 1984 the school became a four-year baccalaureate college. Schreiner College continues to evolve as one of Texas' leading private institutions.

(1998)

KILGORE (Gregg Co.) — SH 135, 1 mi. N of IH20
Liberty City

Historic rural community in oil-rich Gregg County. Settled before Civil War. Has also been known as Sabine, Mount Moriah, McCrary's Chapel, Goforth and Hog Eye (for an early settler with an "eye" for hogs). Present name adopted in early days of famous East Texas oil boom. Area served by Sabine School District, established 1893; an example of excellent schools in county. Also crossed by great system of improved, all weather county roads—finest in state. Center of farming, livestock raising. Has fine churches, park and community meeting places.   (1965)

KILGORE (Gregg Co.)   *US 259 at Kilgore St.*
"Oil City of the World," Kilgore
Founded 1872 with coming of the I.G.N. Railroad. Named for site donor, a Confederate colonel, Constantine B. Kilgore, state senator and U.S. congressman. Geographical center of huge East Texas oil field. World's greatest concentration of steel derricks. Petroleum production, service, supply, processing hub. Commercial, industrial, farm, education and medical center. Home of Kilgore College and its famous "Rangerettes," women's precision drill team; and of Van Cliburn, international concert pianist.   (1965)

KILGORE (Gregg Co.)   *Main and Commerce Sts.*
World's Richest Acre
Part of fabulous East Texas oil field discovered in 1930. This 1.195-acre tract had first production on June 17, 1937, when the Mrs. Bess Johnson-Adams & Hale No. 1 Well was brought in. Developed before well-spacing rules, this block is the most densely drilled tract in the world, with 24 wells on 10 lots owned by six different operators. This acre has produced over two and a half million barrels of crude oil. Selling at $1.10 to $3.25 a barrel, it has brought more than five and a half million dollars. A forest of steel derricks for many years stood over the more than 1,000 wells in downtown Kilgore, marking the greatest concentration of oil wells in the history of the world. Dozens of these derricks still dot city's internationally famous skyline. Since 1930, the East Texas oil field has produced nearly four billion barrels of oil. It now has more than 17,000 producing wells, and geologists predict a future of at least 45 years for this "granddaddy of oil fields." Its development has attracted to the area many diversified industries and a progressive citizenship with a high degree of civic pride.

KILLEEN (Bell Co.)   *US 190 Bus. at Conder in park*
City of Killeen
When the tracks of the Gulf, Colorado and Santa Fe Railroad were extended from Temple to Lampasas in the early 1880s, a switching station was installed near the midway point. The settlement that grew up around the site became the town of Killeen, named for Frank P. Killeen, a native of Ireland and a senior official of the rail company. The first train arrived on May 15, 1882, marking the beginning of the town. Many early residents of Killeen came from the nearby pioneer communities of Sugar Loaf (6 mi. N) and Palo Alto (3.5 mi. NE). Town lots were sold by the GC&SF Railroad and one of the earliest structures built was a wooden community school, which opened in the fall of 1882. By the following year, Killeen was the site of two gristmills and a cotton gin. The town was incorporated in 1893, and W. E. Hudson was elected to serve as the first mayor. In the early years of Killeen's development, the town was primarily an agricultural center for the production of cotton, grain, wool, and cattle. In 1942, it became the home of Camp Hood, now Fort Hood. The federal installation's growth as a major military base has had a dramatic impact on the city, making it one of the fastest growing towns in Texas.   (1982)

KILLEEN (Bell Co.)   *2201 E. US 190 Bus.*
John Blackburn Log House
John Churchill Gaines Blackburn (1832–1912) was born in Tennessee and came to Texas in 1853. He and his wife Mary Ann Chambers Blackburn (1831–1908) first stopped with other family members in Williamson County, then moved to Bell County in 1854. Blackburn's father, John Porter Blackburn (1786–1855) had previously established claims in Texas, including land in this county near the Palo Alto community (then about 4 mi. NE). There John C. G. Blackburn established a 30-acre farm. He enlisted in the Confederate State Militia in 1861 when the Civil War began. Blackburn built this oak-log structure in 1863, according to family tradition, just before enlisting in the Confederate cavalry. He was then assigned to frontier duty along the Rio Grande for the duration of the war. The Blackburns built a larger house at Palo Alto in 1883. This structure survived at its original site until 1954, when a Fort Hood expansion prompted its removal to Westcliff Road in Killeen (2 mi. NE). It remained there until 1976, when the cabin was moved here and rebuilt as an artifact of frontier life in Bell County. John C. G. and Mary Ann Blackburn are

buried at the Blackburn cemetery near their homestead on old Schwald Road (about 4 mi. NE on Fort Hood property). *(Texas Sesquicentennial 1836–1986)*

KINGSLAND (Llano Co.)
FM 1431, overlooking the lake
Lake Lyndon B. Johnson
This lake, originally Granite Shoals, was renamed for the President of the United States on April 22, 1965, by the board of directors, Lower Colorado River Authority (LCRA); in gratitude for his work as U.S. Congressman and Senator toward the development of the project. Mr. Johnson devoted much time and skill to the completion of LCRA programs creating flood control, water conservation and low cost electric power for the people of the Highland Lakes country. A native of this hill country, Mr. Johnson maintained a home on the lake and used it often as a place for relaxation and the entertainment of guests. It is near his ranch and boyhood home. The body of water impounded by the Alvin J. Wirtz Dam has 6,200 surface acres and 138,000 acre-feet. Construction was begun on the dam in 1949 and since its completion the lake has primarily been a source of hydroelectric energy from the overflow of Lake Buchanan to the north. It is also one of Texas' most outstanding boating and fishing areas. This lake, some 20 miles long, is one of seven in the LCRA which extend 100 miles up the Colorado from Austin. Together they form the largest hydroelectric system in the state.
(1967)

KINGSTON (Hunt Co.)
US 69, 1.5 mi. S
Audie Murphy
Most decorated soldier in World War II. Born 4.5 miles south, June 20, 1924, sixth of nine children of tenant farmers Emmett and Josie Killian Murphy. Living on various farms, Audie Murphy went to school through the 8th grade in Celeste—considered the family's home town. He had to quit school to help support the family, acquiring marksmanship skills by hunting to provide food. On his 18th birthday, after being rejected by the marines because of his size (5 feet, 7 inches; 130 pounds), he enlisted in the army while working in Greenville. For unusual courage and bravery, he received 24 decorations, including the U.S. Congressional Medal of Honor, the French Legion of Honor, Chevalier, the Distinguished Service Cross, and a silver star. After the war he became a successful actor, his most prominent role portraying himself in the film To Hell and Back, his war career autobiography. Following his untimely death in a plane crash in Virginia, May 28, 1971, and burial in Arlington National Cemetery, the U.S. Congress paid him a final tribute, dedicating a new veterans' hospital in San Antonio to the memory of this American hero. Survived by widow Pamela, sons Terry and James.
(1973)

KINGSTON (Hunt Co.)
US 69, 1.5 mi. S
Birthplace of Audie Murphy
Most decorated soldier in World War II. Born June 20, 1924, to Emmett and Josie K. Murphy, 400 yards east on the W. F. Boles farm. Enlisted in the Army on his 18th birthday while working in Greenville. He was awarded 24 citations for bravery in action, including Congressional Medal of Honor and French Legion of Honor, Chevalier. After the war, he became a successful actor, with his most prominent role portraying himself in the war film, "To Hell and Back." Died May 28, 1971, in a Virginia plane crash and was buried in Arlington National Cemetery.
(1973)

KINGSTON (Hunt Co.)
US 69, .9 mi. S
Harrell Camp Ground (⅒ mi. W)
One of first religious sites in Hunt County. Influential for 50 years. Cabins and brush arbor built in 1850's by early settler Richard Harrell (1813–1895). Methodist gospel services drew people here from many counties in summers while crops grew and work was slack. With milch cows, cook stoves, bedding, wash tubs, water barrels, families forded Sabine River to camp for weeks. Children and adults sang hymns, studied scriptures, listened to sermons—diversions in hard and lonely lives. In months between camp meetings, passing travelers often were sheltered in camp.
(1965)

KINGSVILLE (Kleberg Co.)
SH 141, 5.5. mi. W
Near Site of Hide and Tallow Plant (King Ranch, 1866–1869)
Business founded by Capt. Richard King to advance economic recovery after the Civil War had ended in 1865. The King ranch beef herds were "money on the hoof," but cull animals also had

value if by-products (hides for leather, tallow as a soap ingredient, etc.) could be salvaged from them. A slaughtering plant was built on Santa Gertrudis Creek, about two miles west of ranch headquarters and north of this marker. Baled, cured hides and barreled tallow were hauled by oxcarts to ships on the bay, then sent to market. The tallow was rendered in round iron vats about 18 feet long and six feet in diameter. In service only a short time (plant closed within four years), two of these remained at the old site for 50 years. One of the two was later moved to the Kingsville oil field for use as a storage tank. When it proved unsatisfactory, it was returned and placed at Sillo Barro pens for water storage. Second vat was cut up for scrap iron during World War II. Site of the old plant is still called "matanza" (slaughter) pasture. Descendants of the hide and tallow plant employees are working a century later as King Ranch cowboys. (1971)

KINGSVILLE (Kleberg Co.)   *SH 141 W, at entrance to King Ranch*
King Ranch, C.S.A.

A major South Texas way-station on Cotton Road, lifeline of southern states in the Civil War. Had water, food, mules, oxen and bunks for drivers of wagons hauling cotton to trade for war goods. Also bivouacked Confederate troops in war marches. Founded 1853 by Capt. Richard King, who by 1861 had—in partnership with Mifflin Kenedy and James Walworth—20,000 cattle and 3,000 horses. Walworth was a delegate to Texas Secession Convention. In wartime, King managed ranch and salt works on coast to benefit Texas and the Confederacy. Kenedy ran the partnership's 22 boats from gulf to Rio Grande City; ferried cotton from Texas to Matamoros, Mex., where it was exchanged for guns, factory goods, ammunition, medicines and coffee, scarce in the Confederacy; and took cotton from Bagdad, Mex., out to ocean vessels riding high seas to dodge the Federal blockade. King and partners were supply agents for the Rio Grande military sub-district. With concentration of goods here, ranch tempted bandits and was target of Federals seeking to break up Cotton Road activity and get beef, cotton and horses for their planned Texas conquest. After Federal raids, was patrolled by the Confederate cavalry of Col. John S. (Rip) Ford. (1965)

KINGSVILLE (Kleberg Co.)   *SH 141 W, at visitors center*
The King Ranch

Richard King (1824–1885), a Rio Grande steamboat captain, bought two Spanish land grants on Santa Gertrudis Creek and founded the legendary King Ranch in 1853. He brought longhorn cattle from Mexico and battled droughts and cattle thieves to build a profitable ranch. Operating first in partnership with G. K. ("Legs") Lewis and later with Mifflin Kenedy and James Walworth, King became sole owner in the late 1860s. During the Civil War (1861–1865), The King ranch was a way-station for Confederate cotton going to Mexico. Herds carrying King's famous "Running W" brand followed the cattle trails to northern markets in the 1870s. After King died, his widow, Henrietta (Chamberlain) (1832–1925), named as ranch manager Robert Justus Kleberg (1853–1932), who later married her daughter Alice Gertrudis King (1862–1944). The ranch became less isolated in the early 1900s, when the railroad arrived and the town of Kingsville was settled. Constant improvement of herds by King-Kleberg descendants produced a new breed of cattle, the Santa Gertrudis, and fine quarter horses and thoroughbreds. Petroleum was discovered on ranch property in the 1930s. Today the King ranch has grown to almost one million acres in South Texas, plus holdings in other states and nations. (1977)

KINGSVILLE (Kleberg Co.)   *SH 141 W, on private property*
Santa Gertrudis, Headquarters of the King Ranch

On this site, part of the De la Garza Santa Gertrudis Land Grant purchased by Captain Richard King in 1853, has stood each of the King Ranch headquarters. The first, an adobe jacal, was replaced by a frame cottage which later burned. Under the direction of Robert J. Kleberg, Sr., this house was designed by Carlton W. Adams for Mrs. Henrietta King. Completed in 1915, it is the family home of Captain King's descendants who are owners of the King Ranch. (1980)

KINGSVILLE (Kleberg Co.)   *SH 141, W in roadside park*
Kleberg County

Formed from Nueces County. Created February 27, 1913. Organized June 27, 1913. Named in honor of Robert Justus Kleberg, 1803–1888, a pioneer German settler in Texas. A veteran of San Jacinto. Kingsville, county seat.

KINGSVILLE (Kleberg Co.)

SH 141 W at roadside park

Plaque dedicated to memory General Joseph Dorst Patch
Camp Kingsville, U.S.A. (1915–1917)

Established in September 1915 by Lt. Joseph Dorst Patch, acting under orders of the United States Army during the troubles on the Mexican border. This camp served as the operational base for companies K, L, and M of the 26th Infantry, U.S. Army. These units were detailed to defend the Armstrong, Kenedy and King ranches and the rail line from San Antonio to Norias against raids by Mexican insurgents striking north of the Rio Grande. Early in 1917, this camp was visited by the U.S. border commander, Gen. John J. Pershing, who later that year chose men of the 26th Infantry to become a vanguard regiment of the now famous First Division, American Expeditionary Forces in World War I. With departure of the chosen troops, bound for France, Camp Kingsville was closed. Joseph Dorst Patch, born December 8, 1885, at Fort Huachuca, Ariz., enlisted in 1909 and was commissioned in 1911. He married Minerva King of Agua Dulce. He served in two world wars, and was awarded the Purple Heart, the Distinguished Service Cross, the Croix de Guerre with bronze star, and the Order of the Bath (British). Retired in 1945 as a major general, he turned to writing as a vocation. His home was in Corpus Christi, where he died November 21, 1966. (1971)

KINGSVILLE (Kleberg Co.)

SH 141, 1.4 mi. W at park area

Mexican Activities at Santa Gertrudis in the 1830s

As a favored camp, important in Mexico's relations with early Texas. Visited June 1832 by Matamoros citizens on their way to compliment Irish settlers with a feast at Banquete Lake, 25 miles to the north. Gen. Juan Urrea camped here Feb. 25, 1836, with his unit of Santa Anna's invading army. With him were several persons who became agents of mercy to the Texans—a famous Mexican woman known as "The Angel of Goliad," Col. Francisco Garay, and Lt. Col. Juan Holsinger. But also with Urrea was Lt. Col. Jose de la Portilla, who under orders from Gen. Santa Anna carried out the 1836 Palm Sunday massacre at Goliad. The Mexicans left Santa Gertrudis to fight Texans at San Patricio, Agua Dulce, Refugio, and Coleto. Santa Gertrudis soon afterward saw Mexican armies in retreat. Gen. Urrea returned here in May, heading south. Gen. Vicente Filisola and other officers also returned here June 11, as aftermath of defeat of the Mexican Army at San Jacinto. With them were 4,500 soldiers, throngs of camp followers, numerous fleeing Negro slaves, thousands of draft and cavalry horses, and even herds of captured range cattle. The camp at Santa Gertrudis was used often after 1830s by soldiers of Texas and the United States. (1967)

KINGSVILLE (Kleberg Co.)

US 77 Bus., 3 mi. N at San Fernando Creek

Camp San Fernando (1862–1864)

Military post on San Fernando Creek, near this site. Guarded the lifeline of the Confederacy, the Cotton Road, export-import route that ran from the Sabine River in East Texas to the Rio Grande. Manned 1862 by 32nd Texas Cavalry flying Bonnie Blue flag; in 1863, a banner lettered: "We Fight for Our Rights." Temporarily occupied, Nov. 1863, by Gen. H. P. Bee. In Feb. 1864 a strong complement arrived under Col. J. S. (Rip) Ford. Col. Matt Nolan reported to Ford a victory over Federals under Capt. C. Balerio 50 mi. southwest of Banquete. Winning troops were under Capt. Thomas Cater, Wm. Tate Taylor, and A. J. Ware, plus home guard under Capt. Santiago Richardson. (Capt. Richard King, of King Ranch, also served in the home guard.) Col. Ford's "Cavalry of the West" included Maj. Felix A. Von Blucher, chief of staff; Capts. H. C. Merritt and J. Littleton, commissaries; Col. Albert Walthersdorff, technician; Capt. W. G. M. Samuels, ordnance. On March 30, 1864, the Arizona companies of Lt. Col. Daniel Showalter reached camp San Fernando. In April Col. Ford and Col. Santos Benavides attacked the Federals in the Rio Grande Valley. Cols. Nolan and B. F. Fry continued to watch over the Cotton Road and "keep an eye" on Corpus Christi. (1966)

KINGSVILLE (Kleberg Co.)

US 77 Bus., 3 mi. N

Historic Cattle Dipping Vat

In 1894 this vat—believed to be the first in the world—was built to stop the spread of tick fever, which was destroying thousands of U.S. beef cattle. By the 1880s, the disease had become widespread, and official and "shotgun" quarantines prevented cattle from moving across the affected area, bounded by a line from the Rio Grande to the Atlantic. Although the mortality rate from tick fever (also called "Texas" and "splenetic" fever) sometimes reached 90 percent, longhorns and other native southwestern cattle were immune. They did, however, carry the insect, which could infect other animals. Efforts to eradicate the tick (Margaropus annulatus) centered here, headed by officials from Texas A. & M. College and the U.S. Bureau of Animal Industry. Manager of the King Ranch, R. J. Kleberg, allowed the vat to be built, and 25,000 tick-infested cattle from the ranch were dipped. An effective formula of oil and sulphur was found here. In October 1898, the U.S. quarantine was lifted for cattle treated in the dip. This eradication program not only introduced a new weapon for controlling cattle diseases, but also freed the industry from restrictive quarantines, thus increasing the value of cattle throughout the U.S. (1967)

KINGSVILLE (Kleberg Co.)
Kleberg Ave. at 3rd St.
Henrietta M. King High School
Completed in 1909, this school building originally housed all grades of the Kingsville school system. The site and funds for construction were donated by school benefactor Henrietta M. King (d. 1925), the widow of King Ranch founder Capt. Richard King. The structure reflects influences of the Alamo, Concepcion, and San Jose missions of San Antonio. Rebuilt after an interior fire in 1925 and named for Mrs. King, it remains in use as a public school. (1981)

KINGSVILLE (Kleberg Co)
US 77 Bus. S, between Gen. Cavazos Blvd. and Trant
Taylor Camp Site, 1846
In 1846 Zachary Taylor's army marched from Corpus Christi to the Rio Grande. On March 10, 11, 12, 13, the four regiments in succession camped at this spot on Santa Gertrudis Creek. War with Mexico over the boundary of Texas began soon. The first battles—Palo Alto and Resaca de la Palma—occurred near present Brownsville. General Mariano Arista led the Mexican army. The results of the war: The boundary of Texas was fixed at the Rio Grande; the Treaty of Guadalupe Hidalgo gave the United States New Mexico, Arizona, Nevada, and California; a notable group of men got training for later public service. Of the 251 officers camped here, many rose to national fame.

The Honor Roll
Twelve leaders in the Texas battles gave name to United States forts in Texas: Wm. G. Belknap, Jacob Brown, J. E. Blake, W. W. S. Bliss, Theodore L. Chadbourne, James Duncan, Clinton R. Gates, Zebulon P. M. Inge, George T. Mason, J. B. McIntosh, Samuel Ringgold, William Jenkins Worth. Many who camped here became commanders of great armies in the Civil War. Among them: Augur, Bee, Bragg, Kirby Smith, Longstreet, Meade, Pemberton, Reynolds, Twiggs, Whistler. Two of them—Zachary Taylor and Ulysses Simpson Grant—became President of the United States.

KINGSVILLE (Kleberg Co.)
US 77, 3 mi. S
First Producing Gas Well in Kleberg County (3.3 mi. E)
Natural gas was first encountered in 1912 by Frank House while drilling for water on the Oscar Rosse farm. Other efforts to obtain fresh water resulted in more gas pockets or water contaminated with salt or oil. An unsuccessful attempt was made in 1915 to develop gas production. In Oct. 1919, the Kleberg County Oil & Gas Company was formed in Kingsville by lumber and hardware merchants Charles H. Flato and his son, Charles, Jr.; oil sales manager H. C. Dennett; grocer J. J. Ivey; postmaster Marcus Phillips; Kingsville mayor J. C. Nolan; and retail merchants Sam Sellers, Ben F. Wilson, and C. M. Allen. The company leased the Rosse farm on Oct. 30, 1919, and contracted Hammill & Bess Drilling Company of Bay City to drill a well. The Rosse No. 1 was completed on Jan. 16, 1920, at a depth of 3,000 feet. Pipelines were soon laid into Kingsville to supply businesses and residences with gas. Another well, the Rosse No. 2 completed in March 1920, was the first producing oil well in the county. The discovery of gas and oil in the county provided a foundation for economic growth through development of petrochemical and refining industries. (1974)

KNIPPA (Uvalde Co.)
US 90, E city limits
Town of Knippa
Served by the Texas & New Orleans Railroad since 1882, this area was settled in 1887 by George Knippa. A freighter who worked between East Texas and Mexico, Knippa also encouraged many friends to move to the fertile land of this county. In 1899 gold-mining was tried here by an aged, white-bearded stranger known as Wilson. In 1900 the community acquired a post office and in 1909 a town was laid out. Previously called Chatfield, it was renamed Knippa. The Trap Rock mine, a stone and gravel business which started in 1913, is still in operation. (1969)

KNIPPA (Uvalde Co.)

US 90W at entrance to Vulcan Materials Co.

Knippa Trap Rock Plant

Volcanic lava deposited here more than 60 million years ago cooled and hardened over time to form basalt, a dark igneous rock also known as trap rock. M. B. (Pete) Walcott purchased acreage here about 1904 and in 1907 formed the Genevieve Mining Co. to search for gold. Although little gold was found, substantial quantities of high quality trap rock were discovered. The Texas Trap Rock Company established a quarry about 1911 and shipments of rock began in 1912. A large highly-visible screening house was completed in 1914. By 1919, Knippa's trap rock plant, the largest in Texas at that time, was capable of producing about 100,000 tons of trap rock per year. The company transported the trap rock by spur line to the Southern Pacific Railroad in nearby Knippa. The company and its employees became an integral part of the community. Knippa High School named its football team the "Rockcrushers" in 1946. The trap rock operation, purchased by White's Mine Company in 1968, was acquired by Vulcan Materials Company in 1987. Trap rock has been applied to various uses such as railroad ballast, decorative stone, and as insulation material. Its historic and primary use, however, has been as a road paving material.   (1994)

KOSSE (Limestone Co.)

SH 14, 1.5 mi. N

Brown Family Cemetery

The Brown Family Cemetery traces its origin to the settlement of North Carolina native Ervin Brown (1801–1875) and his wife Matilda (1807–1871) in Washington County, Texas, in 1846. Ervin and Matilda moved their family to a 1600-acre farm in Limestone County near the community of Eutaw in 1857. Ervin was a charter member of the Eutaw Masonic Lodge in 1859. Ervin and Matilda are both buried in this cemetery. Their son, Thomas Jefferson (T. J.), served as a Confederate captain in the Civil War and later as Chief Justice of the Supreme Court of Texas from 1911 to 1915. The earliest documented burial here was that of Mary Ann Brown, who died on April 26, 1865. She was the wife of Ervin's son James Petty (J. P.) Brown. A captain in the Confederate Army during the Civil War, J. P. was elected to the Texas House of Representatives in 1879. J. P. and Mary's son Gibson A. Brown became a prominent figure in Texas and Oklahoma. In 1896 he successfully argued for legislation to protect property owners affected by the U.S. Supreme Court decision marking the South Fork of the Red River the official boundary between the two states. Neither T. J. Brown nor Gibson Brown are buried here, however. The cemetery remains in use by Brown descendants.   (1993)

KOSSE (Limestone Co.)

SH 7, 8.3 mi. E

Kimik Kiln

Limestone County historically supported numerous pottery producing kilns. This industry succeeded near area outcroppings of kaolin, or potter's clay, within the Wilcox geologic formation. Alberry Johnson began the first county pottery in 1859 near Dooley Creek. Like most other regional potteries, Johnson's kiln was of the groundhog variety, a subterranean design with a doorway leading to a long underground passage lined with brick or rock. At the end of the corridor, a chimney rose out of the ground, drawing heat from a firebox outside the door which baked pottery within the passageway. William Curtis Knox later moved Johnson's operation and established the town of Pottersville (8 mi. NE). The pottery was one of the largest in Texas, remaining active until 1912; today, Pottershop Cemetery marks the site. Several other kilns in the area provided work and income to supplement residents' farming efforts. Near this site, German immigrant Lee Kimik built a kiln active in the 1870s and 1880s. Records indicate that the business remained in fulltime operation eight months of the year. The kiln, similar to other groundhog examples, had longer and deeper sidewalls, possibly indicating European design influences. Unlike other area potters who marketed their work collectively, Kimik sold his wares directly to the community of Headsville (1.5 mi. S). He also marked his pottery, a rare feature among his Texas peers. In 1984, archeologists documented the Kimik Kiln site (41LT198), reviving the story of Lee Kimik through archival research and archeological investigation. The historic site has made significant contributions to understanding the industry and artistry of 19th-century Texas.   (2007)

KOSSE (Limestone Co.)

SH 7, 1 mi. E

Eutaw (Site of Extinct Town is .3 mi. N)

Settled in 1840s. On Franklin-Springfield, Waco-Marlin stage routes. Post office opened 1856 with Nathan Gilbert postmaster. Eutaw Lodge No. 233, A. F. & A. M., was chartered 1859. Among early settlers were Henry Fox, Allen McDaniel, Charles C., Frank and Wesley McKinley, and T. A. Polk. Town had churches, school, stores, blacksmith shop, wagon yard. The "Eutaw Blues" (Co. K, 12th Tex. Cav., C.S.A.) fought in Civil War, 1860s. Officers: Capt. A. F. Moss, 1st Lt. A. H. McDaniel, 2nd Lt. J. P. Brown. Bypassed in 1870 by Houston & Texas Central Railroad, town died. Salem Baptist Church marks site. (1973)

KOUNTZE (Hardin Co.) *US 69, 7 mi. S*
Hardin-Concord Road (In use 1859–1900)
One of oldest landmarks in area. Formed by wagon and horseback travel from early settlements on Pine Island Bayou (to the SE) to Hardin, first county seat of this county (to the NW). Much of old road can be traced today. The highway crosses its course here. (1971)

KOUNTZE (Hardin Co.) *SH 326, 3 mi. SW*
"Old" Hardin
Founded 1859 as first county seat of Hardin County, created in 1858. Prospered until bypassed by Sabine & East Texas Railroad in 1881. A fire of suspicious origin razed the courthouse here on Aug. 8, 1886. In an 1887 election, Kountze, on the railroad, was named the county seat. (1970)

KOUNTZE (Hardin Co.) *300 W. Monroe St. (SH 326) at courthouse*
General Braxton Bragg, C.S.A. (1817–1876)
American military leader honored in this county in name of an early town (12 mi. W). Born in North Carolina, Bragg was in Texas in 1840s with army of General Zachary Taylor, to fight in Mexican War. Made a brigadier general of the Confederacy, 1861, he won renown by capturing many guns and prisoners at Shiloh (1862), and for Southern victory in Battle of Chickamauga (1863). He was respected as a strong disciplinarian, a devoted patriot, and a man with a stern sense of duty. Serving as military advisor (1863–1865) to President Jefferson Davis, he traveled with President Davis after Confederate surrender on a suggested escape route, but was captured by Federals and paroled in Georgia in May 1865. After an 1866–1870 term as Alabama commissioner of public works, he moved to Galveston. There he was chief engineer in charge of construction of Gulf, Colorado & Santa Fe Railway, chartered May 28, 1873. When the G. C. & S. F. built into this area, a junction point on the line was named for General Bragg. The 1901–1934 town of Bragg (now a ghost site) had many facilities serving the Saratoga Oil Field. This was one of many towns (and counties) in Texas named for statesmen, military leaders and soldiers. (1969)

KOUNTZE (Hardin Co.) *SH 326 at Redwood St.*
Courthouses of Hardin County
Hardin County was created in 1858. The first official Hardin County building was probably a two-story log building that burned about 1886. Early county records were destroyed in the conflagration. In 1887, architect Frank Smith of Beaumont designed a two-story frame structure built in Kountze by local contractor W. B. Pedigo. A safe was positioned inside the structure and the walls were built around it. The building was replaced in 1905. J. B. Hooks moved the old courthouse across the street to become the J. B. Hooks Abstract Company. A new masonry courthouse was erected in 1905. It was designed by Andrew P. Bryan and built by M. J. Lewman and Company. Domed in the tradition of the nation's capitol and the Texas State Capitol, the edifice was built of native stone from the Pecos area of West Texas. Salmon-colored brick was imported from the Hydraulic Press Brick Company of St. Louis, and the columns and bases were crafted by Bedford Stone Company. A carbide lighting system was installed in 1918. A three-story colonial-style sandstone building was erected with four 24-foot two-story columns front and back and 16 smaller columns supporting the dome. This building served until 1958. A modern facility was planned by Dickson-Dickson and Associates and built by Lumbeck Construction Company in 1958. The 1905 edifice was destroyed in 1960. At the end of the 20th century, the 1958 courthouse was still in service and the 1887 building continued to stand, now the home of law offices, near the courthouse square. (2000)

KYLE (Hays Co.) *IH 35, 3 mi. S in rest area (Mile Marker 211)*
Beef for the Confederacy
Throughout Hays County, 1861–1865, as in the rest of Texas, beef production for the Confederacy was a major patriotic service. Leading ranchers, called government stockraisers, had the duty

of supplying the commissary department of the army. Hays County, with its well-established cattle industry, had several men designated as C.S.A. beef raisers. These included James M. ("Doc") Day, John W. Day, Wm. H. Day, and their brothers-in-law, Jesse L. Driskill; Wm. Washington Moon; and Ezekiel Nance. These men had hazardous work. They had either to fight or detour around Indians, rustlers and enemy patrols. Herds had to swim flooded streams, some with quicksand beds. Wm. H. Day once was almost drowned while swimming a herd across the flooding Brazos. At least two of the Day brothers were in military service as well as supply duty. Moon, a veteran of the Mexican War, and founder of the City of San Marcos, not only was a stockraiser but also joined the 32nd Texas Cavalry. He donated beef to soldiers' families and furnished leather and horse feed to his cavalry company. Besides supplying beef to the quartermasters, Nance manufactured cotton cloth for the Confederacy.   (1965)

KYLE (Hays Co.)   *FM 150 off IH 35*
Katherine Anne Porter (May 15, 1890–September 18, 1980)
Katherine Anne Porter, one of America's most distinguished writers of fiction, was born Callie Russell Porter in Indian Creek, Brown County, Texas. Her mother, Mary Alice Jones Porter, died in 1892, and her father, Harrison Boone Porter (1858–1942) returned with the children to his native Hays County to live with his mother, Catherine Ann Skaggs Porter (1826–1901). Porter spent her childhood in Kyle and attended the public schools here. Following a brief failed marriage, she left Texas in 1915. She went to Chicago and, using the name she adopted from her grandmother, became a journalist. She traveled throughout the world and began her writing career. Porter's first book of short stories, "Flowering Judas and Other Stories," was published in 1930. Considered a preeminent writer of short stories, she published another collection, "Pale Horse, Pale Rider" in 1939. Her acclaimed 1962 novel "Ship of Fools" was followed by the Pulitzer prize-winning "The Collected Stories of Katherine Anne Porter" in 1965. Porter returned to Texas to visit her former homes in her later years and, according to her request, upon her death her ashes were interred next to her mother's grave in the Indian Creek Cemetery.   (1990)

LA GRANGE (Fayette Co.)   *SH 71, 12 mi. W at roadside park*
First Roadside Park in Texas
Established fall 1933, when a local state highway official built tables and benches (since then replaced) here to encourage motorists to stop and rest. Texas was one of the first states to sponsor building of roadside parks, which provided work for many of the unemployed during the 1930's depression. Early highway beautification efforts also started here. Today areas along Texas highways are noted for their landscaping and abundance of native wildflowers. Texas roadside parks, many of which have restrooms and cookout areas, totaled 1,008 in 1967.   (1968)

LA GRANGE (Fayette Co.)   *US 77, 4.5 mi. N*
Rabb's Prairie
This portion of Fayette County is named for William Rabb (1770–1831), a prosperous miller from Pennsylvania who came to Texas in 1821 with members of his family. Rabb claimed a site on the east side of the Colorado River he had selected during an exploratory trip in 1819. He was a member of Stephen F. Austin's first colony in Texas, and recipient of one of the earliest and largest land grants of more than 22,000 acres, of which 13,285 acres comprised Rabb's Prairie. Part of Rabb's agreement with Austin was to build a gristmill for future settlers of the colony. Two grinding stones for the mill weighing about one ton each were imported from Scotland and unloaded at the mouth of the Colorado River on the Gulf of Mexico. In order to transport the heavy stones to the site of the gristmill, Rabb constructed a wooden axle and attached a round stone on both ends to serve as wheels. He then hitched oxen to the vehicle and pulled it about 100 miles overland to his mill. Rabb and his sons completed the mill in 1831; Rabb died shortly afterward. Through the years his descendants played significant roles in the development of Texas. The community of Rabb's Prairie was named for this pioneer family.   (1996)

LA GRANGE (Fayette Co.)   *SH 159, 5.3 mi. NE of Fayetteville*
Breeding Family Cemetery (300 yds. NW, across the highway)
David and Sarah Davis Breeding came to Texas from Kentucky and settled here in 1833 with sons John, Richard L., Napoleon B., Fidelio S., and Benjamin W.; John, Napoleon, and Fidelio Breeding fought in Texas army during the War for Independence, participating in the victory at

San Jacinto on April 21, 1836. In 1838 David Breeding was a member of the board of land commissioners of Fayette County. John was the first county sheriff, also taking office in 1838. Family cemetery was opened with burial of David Breeding, 1843. Sarah and John Breeding also lie here.

First School in Fayette County
In a log house on Breeding's land, the first known school session in Fayette County was taught in 1834 by a Mr. Rutland. Attending were Edward, George, Gus, and James Breeding, orphan nephews of David Breeding; Lyman Alexander, Patsie Dougherty, Marian and Sally York, and Emily Alexander (later Mrs. Joel Robison, wife of one of the captors of Santa Anna), whose father Sam Alexander kept four students as boarders. Capt. Jesse Burnham (or Burnam) brought his children 15 miles and built a shed tent with a long bedstead for the girls; the boys slept under the trees.

LA GRANGE (Fayette Co.)   *SH 159, 4.8 mi. NE*
Rutersville
Founded in 1838 upon the recommendation of Dr. Martin Ruter (1785–1838), as a site for an institution of higher learning. Named in honor of Dr. Ruter, a pioneer Methodist missionary who entered Texas on Nov. 21, 1837, and weakened by his travels, died on May 16, 1838. Later in the year of his death, a company of ten Methodists bought a tract of land, platted the townsite, and began to build Rutersville. In 1840, Rutersville College was chartered by the fourth congress of the Republic of Texas as the republic's first Protestant college. The legislation specified the school should not be exclusively for the benefit of Methodists, and it was patronized by families of various faiths. Rutersville students were noted for their loyalty to neighbors, sometimes spending days away from class, pursuing Indians. The Rev. Chauncey Richardson, A. M. (1802–1852), whose grave is nearby, was first president of the college. The campus was half a mile southeast of this marker. After the Civil War ended in 1865, the original inhabitants of Rutersville sold their property. It was later purchased by German immigrants, whose descendants now live here in large numbers. (1972)

LA GRANGE (Fayette Co.)   *SH 159, 4.8 mi. N in Rutersville*
Asa Hill of Rutersville (1788–1844)
Born in Martin County, N. C. Married Elizabeth Barksdale in Georgia, Oct. 6, 1808. Came to Texas 1835. In army in 1836, was sent by Gen. Houston to warn people in enemy's path. Settled here 1839. In 1840, enrolled eight children in Rutersville College. With sons Jeffrey and John C. C., joined the 1842 expedition to Mier, Mex. Captured, he drew a white bean—thus escaped death, but was in prison until Aug. 1843. Jeffrey was wounded, captured, likewise imprisoned. John C. C., then 14, was adopted by Gen. Santa Anna. Asa Hill died here; was buried on Cedar Creek, off SH 159. (1973)

LA GRANGE (Fayette Co.)   *N. College St. at E. Travis St. (SH 71)*
Fayette County
Formed from Colorado and Bastrop counties. Created December 14, 1837. Organized January 1, 1838. Named in honor of Marquis de Lafayette. 1757–1834. Nobleman and republican friend of Washington and of the United States. County Seat, La Grange. (1936)

LA GRANGE (Fayette Co.)   *Travis St. (SH 71) at College St.*
Fayette County, C.S.A.
Although voted 600 against to 580 for secession, began Confederate recruiting in June 1861. La Grange was headquarters for 22nd Brigade, Texas state troops, Brig. Gen. Wm. G. Webb commanding, of which 18 companies (1,238 men) and 72 officers were from Fayette. Special county war taxes provided relief for soldiers' families. Funds were also raised by the famous "Cow Order" for seizure of strays. Censors here banned exchanges of mail with the U.S. Confederate cotton gathered in and stored at La Grange and Round Top was freighted to Mexico by local men hauling 5 or more bales on each 3-months-long trip. In 1863 a dozen teamsters lost outfits and barely saved themselves when bandits struck near Roma, on the Mexican border. Gen. Webb and Cols. John C. and Wm. F. Upton were Fayette County men. Local C.S.A. units were commanded by Capts. Ira G. Killough and Ben Shropshire, who fought in the Arizona–New Mexico campaign. Gen. Tom Green, first county surveyor, an Indian fighter and hero of San Jacinto and the Mexican War, had a part in such Confederate victories as the recapture of Galveston and the Battle of Mansfield, La.

LA GRANGE (Fayette Co.) *N. Washington St. at Colorado St.*
The Dawson Expedition / Historic Oak
It was under this historic oak when the men of Capt. Nicholas Mosby Dawson's company assembled on September 15, 1842 and went to the relief of San Antonio to repel the invasion of Texas by the Mexican Army under Gen. Adrian Woll. In the fight near Salado Creek, September 18, Dawson and 35 of his men were killed, 15 captured and imprisoned in Castle Perote in Mexico, and 3 escaped. Here on the courthouse square, the scarred remains of what was once a mighty oak marks the spot from which La Grange has on every occasion sent its sons to battle. In fights with the Indians, the struggle with Mexico, in the War Between the States, the Spanish American War, and in two World Wars, sons of Fayette County were first marshalled under this tree. Wives, mothers, sweethearts here bade farewell and sent their men to battle, each time to win acclaim as true patriots.
(1963)

LA GRANGE (Fayette Co.) *SH 71 at FM 955, 10 mi. SE*
James J. Ross
Born in South Carolina in about 1787, James Jeffres Ross was a member of the "Old Three Hundred." He arrived in Stephen F. Austin's colony in late 1822 or early 1823, moving onto the league granted him near Eagle Lake in Colorado County. In 1828, he moved to the S. A. Anderson league and built a home about one mile southwest of this site. Col. Ross, as he was known, soon assumed a position of leadership as captain of the militia of the Colorado district. He was a delegate to the second convention at San Felipe in 1833 and was one of those appointed in 1834 to help obtain Austin's release from imprisonment in Mexico. He helped establish a stage line and a stop that became the town of Fayetteville. An important figure during the early years of settlement in this part of the state, Ross was a successful farmer, rancher, trader, and merchant. Ross Prairie and Ross Creek, both in this vicinity, bear his name. He was killed by angry neighbors in January 1835 for sheltering Indians at his home and was buried in nearby Ross Cemetery. His home, which came to be known as the Ross/Martinek House, was owned by Czech immigrant Joseph Martinek and his descendants for nearly seventy years.

LA GRANGE (Fayette Co.) *US 77, 4 mi. S*
The Oldest Czech Settlement in Texas
Was established at Hostyn when in November, 1856, the families of Josef Janda, Valintin Kolibal, Frantisek Koza arrived here from Czechoslovakia.
(1964)

LA GRANGE (Fayette Co.) *State Loop 92 at Monument Hill State Park, off US 77, 2 mi. S*
Monument Hill Tomb
In September 1848, the remains of Texans killed in the 1842 Dawson Massacre and the 1843 "Black Bean Death Lottery" were reburied at this site in a sandstone vault. The Kreische family did its best to care for the grave during their ownership of the property, but it suffered from lack of formal oversight. In 1905, the state authorized acquisition of .36 acres here, and the Daughters of the Republic of Texas raised funds for a new cover for the tomb in 1933. During the 1936 Texas Centennial celebration, the 48-foot shellstone shaft with a stylized, Art Deco-influenced mural was erected to mark the mass grave more prominently. Local citizens purchased 3.54 acres as a donation to the state for parkland in 1957.
(2002)

LA JOYA (Hidalgo Co.) *US 83, 2.7 mi. W*
Hidalgo County's First Oil Well
John M. Lawrence No. 1 oil well was brought in Sept. 18, 1934, near this site by veteran driller Otto C. Woods. Well flowed 1,000 or more barrels a day. At first the oil formed a lake beside the well. County has produced 20 million barrels of oil.
(1967)

LA JOYA (Hidalgo Co.) *US 83, 1.8 mi. W, Havana Cemetery*
Havana
Located on land known as Porcion 46, ceded by the crown of Spain to Don Jose Matias Tijerina in 1767, the community of Havana was named for Havana, Cuba, where Tijerina had stopped on his journey from Europe. Among the early settlers here were the families of Josefa de la Garza Salinas and Civil War Union soldier Patricio Perez. A frame church was built in 1891 and named for St.

Joseph. Descendants of early settlers still live in the area. Many Havana pioneers are buried here in the Havana Cemetery. (1988)

LA PRYOR (Zavala Co.)   *US 83, roadside park at Nueces River*
The Bosque-Larios Expedition (April 30–June 12, 1675)

In the 16th century, Northern Mexico was torn by strife as the Indian inhabitants resisted Spanish efforts to enslave them. A century later, wealthy humanitarian Antonio Balcarcel set out to invoke justice and help missionaries Christianize the land. In the spring of 1675, Balcarcel sent out an armed expedition under Fernando del Bosque to accompany Fray Juan de Larios on a mission north of the Rio Grande. Also in the party was Fray Dionisio de San Buenventura, an army chaplain. Entering Texas at a site near present Eagle Pass, the expedition marched almost to the present site of San Antonio. Three days after entering Texas, when they were in camp on the Nueces, about nine miles southwest of present Uvalde, they set up a portable altar. The expeditionaries gathered with some 1,172 Indians to hear Fray Larios chant the mass. Later Fray Larios baptized 55 infants and instructed the adult Indians so that they might be baptized at a future time. The celebration at the Nueces on May 16, 1675, is known as the earliest recorded occasion of a high (sung) Mass in Texas. Missionary activity that began on that day eventually brought about the founding of the Texas mission system. (1975)

LA PRYOR (Zavala Co.)   *US 83, 8 mi. N in roadside park*
Camp Nueces, C.S.A.

Founded April 1862 near this site, to guard vital traffic as it crossed the Nueces on the San Antonio–Eagle Pass road. A post of the Confederacy's frontier regiment, under Col. James M. Norris. Its duty was to see that cotton got through to Mexico and munitions, medicines and factory goods came north to supply the Confederacy. One of the chain of posts a day's horseback ride apart, on line from Red River to Rio Grande. Never able to relax, in constant danger of Indian raids; short of food, horses and guns, Nueces (like other frontier camps) had none of war's glory and more than its share of hardships. Located in Zavala County, created in 1858 and named for Lorenzo de Zavala. This is one of 10 counties to commemorate colonizers. Of the 254 counties, 42 have Indian, French or Spanish names. 12 honor Washington and other American patriots. 96 were named for 1836–1846 heroes of the Republic of Texas (including 15 who died in the Alamo). 23 have names of other early statesmen. 11 honor U.S. leaders in the campaign to annex Texas. 10 honor state jurists, ministers, educators, statesmen, historians. 36 are named for leading men of the southern Confederacy. 14 have names from local geography. (1965)

LA VERNIA (Wilson Co.)   *US 87 in La Vernia*
Old Chihuahua Road

Mexican cart road from central Mexico to Texas coast at Indianola. Route of marauding Indians as well as Alsatian, German, Polish, Irish immigrants seeking freedom in new world. After 1835 was important in gold and silver exporting; in 1850s for army travel. (1967)

LA VERNIA (Wilson Co.)   *US 87 at city hall*
La Vernia

Established about 1846 or 1847 by Claiborne Rector, who built a stage stop and blacksmith shop here to serve travelers on the Chihuahua Road, a major trail in early Texas. Main Street today follows route of the old road. Settlement was called "Post Oak" until mail service started, 1856. Name was then changed to Spanish "La Verdear" because of many green oaks in area. English speakers called it "La Vernia". Like much of Texas, this area was settled by southerners in search of fertile land. In Civil War, La Vernia was a recruiting and officer training center. (1968)

LA VERNIA (Wilson Co.)   *624 W. US 87*
Applewhite Homestead

The family of Henry Applewhite (1630–1704), who sailed from England to Jamestown, Virginia, in 1656, remained in Virginia for several generations. Applewhite's descendant, Thomas Applewhite, was born in North Carolina in 1791 and served as a sergeant in the War of 1812. In 1842 Thomas married his second wife, Elizabeth Oglesby (1820–1898). The Applewhites, accompanied by 8 slaves, moved to this area of Texas in 1853. They purchased 214 acres of farmland here in 1854 and by 1860 the Applewhites owned 9 slaves, some of whom had taken the Applewhite name.

According to local oral tradition, at one time the Applewhites' homestead may also have served as a brief stop for stagecoaches traversing the area along an alternate route of that part of the Chihuahua Road extending from Indianola to San Antonio. Thomas (d.1864) and Elizabeth Applewhite are buried in LaVernia in concrete cemetery. A number of Applewhite families, the descendants of African Americans who established homes here during the 1860s, remained in the area for many generations. Thomas and Elizabeth Applewhite's original stone house was mostly destroyed during highway construction in the 1950s. (Sesquicentennial of Texas Statehood 1845–1995)

LADONIA (Fannin Co.)   *W. Main St. (SH 50) at Town Plaza*
Ladonia
Settled about 1840 by James McFarland and Daniel Davis, this community was first called McCownville after early settler Frank McCown. The town's first merchant, James H. Cole, a carpenter who moved to the county in 1855, planned and staked out the town site and included wide streets. According to local legend McCown changed the town name in 1857 to honor Ladonna Millsay, a traveler on a wagon train from Tennessee who entertained residents with her singing. By 1858 the settlement had a post office named Ladonia. The town grew rapidly after 1860 because of its fertile farming area. The community incorporated in 1885 and had a population of 700, two cotton gins, a bank, a flour mill, a school, and several churches. The arrival of the Gulf, Colorado and Santa Fe Railway in 1887 made Ladonia an agricultural marketing town for cotton, corn, oats and wheat and resulted in a business boom. The population had increased to 2,000 by 1897 and the town included 100 businesses. The town declined slowly as agricultural goods were shipped over improved roads and citizens moved to larger cities. By 1936 Ladonia had 1,119 citizens and 39 businesses. By 1990 the population was 658.
(1997)

LAKE JACKSON (Brazoria Co.)   *SH 332, 1 mi. W, Lake Jackson Wilderness Park*
Joseph H. Hawkins
Native Virginian Joseph H. Hawkins practiced law in Kentucky, where he served as State legislator and U.S. congressman before moving to New Orleans. There he befriended Stephen F. Austin, who was broke and reluctant to complete his father's colonization plans on his own. Hawkins encouraged him to continue, offering him a job and, later, capital for the project. In 1821, the two men formalized an agreement in which Austin acknowledged receipt of $4,000 and agreed to divide equally the lands he would receive as colonizer, or empresario. Hawkins sent boats of supplies and colonists to meet Austin in Texas but died in 1823, leaving his wife, George Ann (Nicholas), and five children deeply in debt. She returned with the children to her native Kentucky to be near her family and Hawkins' brother, Littleberry. She appointed Nathaniel Cox to help settle her husband's estate. In 1824, the Mexican government gave Austin, as empresario, almost 100,000 acres, but law required a person to reach majority age and live in Texas to own land, so the Hawkins children could not immediately claim their share. Austin worked with Cox to find a suitable agreement and, in 1833, conveyed to the Hawkins heirs some 42,000 acres of land in and around Brazoria County. Each of Hawkins' children lived briefly in Texas. Edmund St. John (d. 1836) was the first, followed by Norbourne, who died at Goliad in 1836, George (d. 1837), and then Joseph Thomas (d. 1850). Mary Jane came in 1839 but, after her husband died, returned to Kentucky, where she stayed. Although none of his heirs persevered in Texas, Hawkins' legacy in Texas is apparent in the success of Austin's first colony and all that sprang from the early Texas settlement. (2002)

LAMESA (Dawson Co.)   *US 87, 1.5 mi. S at US 180 at picnic area*
Dawson County
· Created February 1, 1858. Recreated August 21, 1876 from Bexar Territory organized February 13, 1905 named in honor of Nicholas Mosby Dawson 1808–1842 who fought at the Battle of San Jacinto and fell at Dawson's Massacre. Lamesa, County Seat. (1936)

LAMESA (Dawson Co.)   *N. 22nd St. (FM 2592) at Chicago St.*
Site of Chicago
W. C. Bishop of Chicago, Ill., and wealthy lumberman George N. Fletcher established the OTO (later Bar TO) ranch about 1887 on Fletcher's extensive landholdings in Dawson County. A post office was opened at the ranch headquarters on May 15, 1889, and named Chicago, both in honor of Bishop's home town and in humorous reference to the sparse population of the area. The postal facility served other large ranches in this vicinity, such as C. C. Slaughter's Long S. In the 1890s,

Fletcher left the ranching venture, and A. F. Crowley and W. H. Godair became Bishop's partners. By that time, a village had begun to grow up around the post office. A. B. Oden served as OTO ranch foreman and postmaster of Chicago from 1894 to 1903. When Walter Stemmons replaced him in both positions in 1904, the settlement was renamed Stemmons. The same year, a post office was established in the new town of Lamesa, two miles south of Chicago. Dawson County was organized in 1905, and both towns entered the contest for county seat. When Lamesa won, residents of Chicago quickly relocated their homes and businesses there. The school and Baptist and Methodist churches also moved to Lamesa. Within days, the community of Chicago had disappeared. (1977)

LAMKIN (Comanche Co.)   SH 36
Lamkin
Originally established in 1870, one-half mile north on banks of the Leon River. Named for George Lamkin, donor of land for the townsite. Business firms included general store, blacksmith shop, gin, post office, and drugstore. Despite several floods and fires, pioneer merchants gamely rebuilt. Only after the flood of 1908 destroyed old Lamkin was town moved to present site. Two years later with the coming of the Cotton Belt Railroad, Lamkin developed into a shipping center for farmers and ranchers. By 1920, the town had 2 gins, a hotel, bank, produce house, lumberyard, blacksmith shop, 3 general stores, post office, 4 churches, telephone exchange and drugstore. Consolidated public school had an average attendance of over 200. Basketball team was county champion for 4 consecutive years. Annual attraction was horse and mule show. In 1922, fire destroyed a major portion of business firms. Lamkin rebuilt but failed after railroad discontinued, 1936. An often-related pioneer story was of 1869 Indian raid 2 miles east of here on Resley's creek. The home of Mrs. Elizabeth Ewell was ransacked by 19 renegade Indians. The widow and her 2 sons were not at home but on their return were greeted by clouds of feathers from ripped mattresses. A posse drove the Indians away.   (1967)

LAMPASAS (Lampasas Co.)   US 281 at FM 1690, 12 mi. N
2.5 mi. E is Birthplace of Stanley Walker (1898–1962)
Noted Texas journalist and editor. Began his career in Austin and Dallas. From 1920 to 1935 was with New York Herald-Tribune, where as city editor, he trained many writers. Also was on staff of Philadelphia Ledger. He wrote The Night Club Era, Mr. Astor's Horse, 5 other books, many articles. Spent last years here.   (1966)

LAMPASAS (Lampasas Co.)   US 281, 3 mi. N in roadside park
Indian Culture Sites
Scattered throughout this area, campsites, flint quarries, and rock paintings testify that primitive tribes lived here for centuries. Tonkawas, Comanches, and Lipan Apaches were the main inhabitants in the early 1800s. Typical of the sites was a burial found near a river. The shallow grave contained the tightly flexed skeleton of a man aged about 60 at his death. Pitted bones (indicating disease), a broken arm, and worn teeth suggested the difficulty of his life. A pebble painted with black lines, probably an offering, was also found near the burial.   (1969)

LAMPASAS (Lampasas Co.)   US 190, 9 mi. NW
Pleasant Valley Farmers' Alliance No. 1
First chapter of the farmers' alliance in Texas. Founded 1877, it became one of the strongest arms of the national agrarian reform movement of the era. The group was begun by John R. Allen on Donaldson Creek (1 mi. S) in a "rawhide" (rough) lumber school. Its main purpose was to improve ruinous farm living and economic conditions. Missing livestock were traced by 2 secret officers known as "Grand Smokies." In 1887 the 3,000 sub-alliances merged with the "farmers' union," then helped spark the Populist Party Drive of the 1890s; but by 1900 they had died out.   (1969)

LAMPASAS (Lampasas Co.)   US 190, 3.8 mi. E
Battle Branch
This branch of Sulphur Creek was named for an event in the Horrell-Higgins feud. On the morning of March 26, 1877, Tom and Mart Horrell were going to Lampasas to attend district court. En route they were ambushed by gunmen hiding in the brush near this location. The Horrells returned fire and the attackers rode away. Mart took his wounded brother to a nearby residence and continued to town for help. He led a squad of Texas Rangers to the site, but officers never caught the

attackers. Many believed a Higgins faction had set up the ambush. The feud would continue with additional gunfighting for several more months.   (2003)

LAMPASAS (Lampasas Co.)   *US 190, 1 mi. E*
Hughes Springs
One of the Lampasas sulphur springs named in honor of first settler in the vicinity in 1833, Moses Hughes, whose wife regained health through its waters.

LAMPASAS (Lampasas Co.)   *US 190E at Alexander*
First United Methodist Church of Lampasas
Methodists in Lampasas were holding church services as early as 1866. The Rev. William F. Cummins is the first known pastor to have served the Methodist circuit in this area. Although the exact details of the organization of the First United Methodist Church of Lampasas are unclear, it is known that a sanctuary was built on Fourth Street in 1880, during the pastorate of the Rev. E. F. Kahle. Four years later, the congregation sponsored the opening of Centenary College. The Christian boarding and preparatory school was located in Lampasas and was in operation for about ten years. In 1900, under the leadership of the Rev. J. S. Braswell, the fellowship moved to a new church home on Key Avenue. The congregation relocated to Highway 190 East and Alexander Drive (1 mi. N) in 1966. Mergers with the Black Methodist congregation known as Alice Chapel and a rural Methodist church at Ogles have strengthened the membership. With ties to the reconstruction era in Texas history, the First United Methodist Church of Lampasas has played a long and distinguished role in the leadership of this community. Descendants of some of the earliest known members still worship with the congregation.   (Texas Sesquicentennial 1836–1986)

LAMPASAS (Lampasas Co.)   *S. Live Oak at 4th St., courthouse*
Lampasas County, C.S.A.
Organized 1856; had 1028 people in 1860; favored secession by 85 to 75 vote in 1861. Sent 2 units to serve in Texas state troops, 2nd frontier District; one unit to 17th Texas infantry; 2 units to 27th Brigade, Texas militia. Also had 48 minute men in 6 patrols to guard home front and property of men away at war. After a week of duty, each unit returned home to aid women and children tending cattle, crops. Helped supply frontier troops and miners in Longhorn Caverns. Indians still roamed here during Civil War, stealing horses, killing hunters and others.   (1965)

LAMPASAS (Lampasas Co.)   *409 S. Pecan St. N of SH 257*
Lampasas County
Formed from Travis and Bell counties; created February 1, 1856; organized March 10, 1856; The name Lampazos, first given to the river by the Spaniards, was suggested by the many cockle-burs in the region. First settlements about 1850; first railroad, 1882; county seat, Burleson, after 1856, called Lampasas.   (1936)

LAMPASAS (Lampasas Co.)   *Plum St. E of US 281 at Brook Park*
The 1957 Flood
The area around Lampasas drains to the Sulphur Creek basin, and the stream flows across the town from the southwestern edge to the east side, intersecting with Burleson Creek and other branches along the way. Floods have struck the town throughout its history, and notable early ones occurred in 1873, 1936 and 1944. Following the 1944 rise, city officials took measures to address the problem, dredging the creek and constructing earthen levees. Such work, however, failed to prepare the town for what would occur in the next decade. 1957 was a year of heavy rainfall in Texas, following a long period of drought. On May 12 of that year, only two weeks after an earlier rise, sustained downpours in the area caused water to begin collecting along upper reaches of the Sulphur Creek headwaters, and as it quickly joined up with downstream tributaries it began to spill over the banks. Through the night of Mothers Day, May 12, 1957, floodwaters raged through the middle of town, slamming into stores and houses with dramatic force, and washing away cars and other property. Flat tops of buildings around the square became islands of safety for those trapped by the water, and residents fought to save themselves and their families. Tragically, five people died in the incident. Following the devastating flood, the citizens of Lampasas regrouped and rebuilt, and businesses reopened within months. The tremendous loss of life and property caused by the Mothers Day flood of 1957 spurred city officials to action, and new flood control measures soon

followed. The 1957 flood thus proved to be a turning point in city planning and development, as well as the history of Lampasas. (2005)

LAMPASAS (Lampasas Co.) US 281, Hancock Park
Hancock Springs
First white settlers in 1850s found Indians using curative waters here. Town was quickly developed around the springs. Stage and freight routes and many cattle drives came this way. The springs took the name of landowner, John Hancock. On a hill to the north about 1882, promoters of the Santa Fe Railway built the 200-room Park Hotel, with boardwalk to the springs, bathhouses, many other luxuries. It gained wide fame as south's finest health resort. Closed in a few years as a hotel, it later housed Centenary College, until it burned in 1895. Area is now a city park. (1966)

LANCASTER (Dallas Co.) SH 342 at Lancaster Hutchins Rd.
The Rawlins Homestead
In 1845, Roderick Rawlins the elder settled this area. His son Roderick A. Rawlins (1833–1910) married his teacher, Virginia Bledsoe, daughter of the founder of Lancaster. They started this house in 1855. After serving as a Confederate officer during the Civil War (1861–1865), Capt. Rawlins rebuilt his home in the popular Greek Revival style. It stood halfway between Waxahachie and Dallas. Travelers obtained water and sometimes camped at its well. (1964)

LANGTRY (Val Verde Co.) US 90 at RR 1865, 15 mi. W
Pumpville
In 1882, the Galveston, Harrisburg & San Antonio Railway created a water stop for steam engines on a new line through this area. Two and a half miles north of this site, the company built a pump house, depot and other facilities. A community first known as Samuels and later renamed Pumpville developed around the rail amenities. Residents worked for the rail company or area ranches, which used the stop as a way to get livestock to market. With the advent of the diesel engine, which did not require water, the railroad removed its structures, and only the ranching community remained. The townsite, which once boasted a post office, schools and general store, remains a focal point for the local population. (2005)

LANGTRY (Val Verde Co.) Loop 25 off US 90 across from visitors center
Langtry
Langtry was created in 1882, when the Galveston, Harrisburg & San Antonio Railroad, later known as Southern Pacific, signed a deed with the Torres family, who owned the land. The town, which provided water for locomotives, developed from a tent town to a bustling settlement after the rail line was completed. The town was most likely named for George Langtry, who led an area rail building crew. Lore, though, links the town's most famous inhabitant to its naming; Roy Bean, who owned a local saloon and served as Justice of the Peace, became known as "The Law West of the Pecos." He was enamored of Lillie Langtry, a popular British actress, and although she was probably not the town's namesake, she did visit here in the early 20th century. In addition to the infamous Bean, other local men and women contributed to the town's western ambience. J.P. Torres, part of the town's founding family, also served as Justice of the Peace and operated a store and saloon. He, like many of the area residents, also raised livestock, most often sheep or goats. Accessibility to the trains attracted many ranchers, who supported local businesses. Langtry supported other industries, including a rock crushing plant created for the railroad. The town also attracted tuberculosis patients who came in hopes of regaining their health. During the Mexican Revolution, soldiers came to Langtry for goods, guns and munitions. The rail line was rerouted in the 1920s, and Langtry's population declined, today existing primarily as a tourist site. The landscape and the remaining buildings still speak to what once was a bustling West Texas town. (2003)

LANGTRY (Val Verde Co.) Loop 25 off US 90 across from visitors center
Law West of the Pecos
Judge Roy Bean lived a life in which fiction became so intermingled with fact that he became a legend within his lifetime. Basis for his renown were the decisions which he reached in this building as the Law West of the Pecos. Court was held as frequently on the porch, spectators grouped about on horseback, as within the building. Nor was Bean above breaking off proceedings long enough to serve customers seeking services dispensed by the other businesses carried on in his

courtroom-home. The judge's "law library" consisted of a single volume, an 1879 copy of the Revised Statutes of Texas. He seldom consulted it, however, calling instead on his own ideas about the brand of justice which should apply. This he effectively dispensed together with liberal quantities of bluff and bluster. Since Langtry had no jail, all offenses were deemed finable with Bean pocketing the fines. Drunken prisoners often were chained to mesquite trees in front of the building until they sobered up enough to stand trial. Bean reached a peak of notoriety when, on February 21, 1896, he staged the banned Fitzsimmons-Maher heavyweight title fight on a sand bar in the Rio Grande River, a stone's throw from his front porch. By holding it on Mexican territory he outwitted Texas Rangers sent to stop the match—and turned a handsome profit for his shrewdness. This building was named the "Jersey Lilly" for the famous English actress Lillie Langtry whom Bean admired and for whom he claimed to have named the town. His lamp frequently burned into the night as he composed letters to her. But he never saw her since her only visit to Langtry occurred in 1904, less than a year after Bean died.

LAREDO (Webb Co.)
US 83, NW Laredo
Población de Dolores
Oldest Spanish settlement on north bank of the Rio Grande. Founded August 22, 1750 by Jose Vasquez Borrego, Lieutenant of Jose de Escandon.

LAREDO (Webb Co.)
Santa Maria Ave. at IH 35 and W. Del Mar Blvd.
Webb County
Formed from Nueces County. Created January 29, 1848. Organized March 16, 1848. Named in honor of James Webb 1792–1856, Attorney General and Secretary of State of the Republic of Texas, 1838–1841. Laredo, the county seat, founded in 1755 by Tomas Sanchez.

LAREDO (Webb Co.)
2400 San Bernardo Ave. (IH 35 access rd.)
San Bernardo Avenue
San Bernardo Avenue, which began as a commercial road in Laredo, became known as the San Antonio Highway by 1938, replacing the earlier route along Santa Maria Avenue. Due to the anticipated increase in tourism, San Bernardo Avenue property started to be developed even earlier for travel-related businesses, including motor courts and filling stations. The city marketed itself as a gateway to Mexico, and San Bernardo Avenue soon provided the most accessible route. Other tourism-related businesses also grew in correlation with the strip's increasing importance. Many entrepreneurs opened motels, restaurants and other businesses along the strip to serve visitors. These modern structures along the path often featured architectural detailing representing earlier Western and Spanish themes, which sometimes differed considerably from other building designs within Laredo. The exaggerated designs catered to out of town visitors and their concepts of the region. Advertising along the highway also reflected these themes. The new businesses and emphasis on tourist attractions were vital for Laredo's early commercial growth and development, helping to expand the city's economy. Today, the San Bernardo commercial strip is still a vibrant part of the city as Laredo continues to be a popular tourist destination. Its architecture evokes an era of early auto tourism, an integral part of the area's history in the twentieth century. (2006)

LAREDO (Webb Co.)
500 Flores Ave., 1 blk. E of IH 35A
Laredo's Washington's Birthday Celebration
In 1897, Laredo's local lodge of the Great Council of Texas of the Improved Order of Red Men decided to organize a celebration of George Washington's birthday. On February 21, 1898, the Red Men held a two-day festival featuring a mock battle, parade, concert, reproduction of the Boston Tea Party and fireworks. The lodge held the next celebration two years later in 1900, beginning the annual observance of this tradition. In 1902, the City of Laredo and the Chamber of Commerce became involved. In 1923, the Washington's Birthday Celebration Association of Laredo formed and began overseeing the festival. Several events have become an annual part of the celebration, including galas, parades, luncheons and a bridge ceremony whose purpose is to unite the cultures of Mexico and the United States in festivity. Started in 1900 with the meeting of the mayors of Laredo and Nuevo Laredo, the bridge ceremony has grown more elaborate as time has passed. It has often included important political officials, such as Texas governors, U.S. Senators and Representatives, and Cabinet members. Other events added through the years have also sought to promote a positive relationship between the United States and Mexico. Today, the celebration continues to grow

in scope and influence, lasting as long as three to four weeks each year and bringing millions of dollars into the city. It remains a vital part of Laredo's tradition and economy. (2006)

LAREDO (Webb Co.)
1005 Zaragoza St., 2 blks. E of IH 35A
Republic of the Rio Grande
In January 1840 Senor Antonio Canales and other Federalists met near Guerrero to found the Republic of the Rio Grande. Canales and friends were loyal to the Mexican constitution of 1824, which had been set aside by Centralists in Mexico City. The Republic was to govern northern Mexico and the part of Texas south of the Nueces. Jesus Cardenas was president; Francisco Vidaurri y Villasenor, vice president; and Juan Francisco Farias, secretary. The capitol was established at 1000 Zaragoza Street, on this plaza in Laredo. Centralist General Manuel Arista brought an army here to crush the Republic. In March he took Laredo without a fight; then after a battle at Morelos, he captured and killed Federalist leader Antonio Zapata. Mexican and Anglo-Texan Federalists counterattacked, and recaptured Laredo and several other towns; but confronted by a large Centralist force at Saltillo, the Anglo-Texans found themselves and some Carrizo Indians making a lone stand. Many comrades had fled. After a bloody battle, the Indians and Texans escaped to the north of the Rio Grande. Canales, deserted by his army, surrendered to Arista near Camargo, and in a few days Cardenas gave up Laredo. The Republic of the Rio Grande had lasted 283 days. (1994)

LATEXO (Houston Co.)
FM 2663, .3 mi. E
Town of Latexo
Early community called Oldham, near Bethel Church and school, was renamed Starks' Switch when International & Great Northern Railroad in 1872 laid sidetrack to serve Starks' sawmill (2 mi. W). Latexo post office opened in 1907, after the Louisiana Texas Orchard Company platted 3,000 acres of fruit land and a town here. Lumbering later stripped timber from area, but permanent settlers grew fruit and cotton. About 1915 Latexo became first Houston County school to teach agriculture. Ranches sprang up, 1960s. Unincorporated, town has fire squad, other civic services. (1972)

LATEXO (Houston Co.)
SH 19/US 287 at FM 2663
Latexo Baptist Church
The community of Stark Switch, originally known as Oldham, was the home of Protestant worship for early settlers from the mid-19th century. Stark Switch Baptist Church of Christ was organized on July 19, 1900, with 27 charter members. The Louisiana Texas Orchard Company became the community's major employer in the early 1900s. The community name changed to Latexo in the company's honor, and the Baptist church name changed to Latexo Baptist Church in 1905. The congregation moved into the local schoolhouse in 1905 and purchased the building from the county in 1912. After 1930 the community gradually moved east with the new main highway, and Latexo Baptist Church followed in 1945. The church thrived in its new location, building new facilities to meet the needs of its members and programs. Celebrating a century of service in the year 2000, the church continues in the traditions of its founders. (2000)

LAVON (Collin Co.)
SH 78, 2 mi. N
Thompson Cemetery
Collin county pioneer Abner Thompson came to this area about 1850 and settled on land that was originally part of the Silvester Williams Survey, deeding a portion of it to be used as a cemetery. The first burial, that of Thompson himself, took place in 1852. His grave is marked with two large square stones which have deteriorated through time and have become nearly illegible. Tall posts of Bois d'Arc, which mark the nearby grave of one of Thompson's employees, have stood the effects of weathering for more than one hundred years. Also buried here are Miles and Emily J. Graves who, in 1862, donated over an acre of land to the Mount Pleasant Baptist Church, which was organized five years earlier. When the congregation divided in the early 1880s, that land was given to the Thompson Cemetery, which was enlarged several more times in later years. A Memorial Day service has been held at the Thompson Cemetery each year since the early 1950s, bringing together people from the nearby communities of Lavon and Copeville. There are over 800 graves here which are given perpetual care by the Thompson Cemetery Association. (2005)

LEAKEY (Real Co.)   US 83, 1 mi. NE
Real County
Located on the Edwards Plateau, Real County is in an area of rolling terrain broken by the canyons of the Frio River. Because of raids by Comanche, Apache, and Lipan-Apache Indians, white settlement was hindered until after 1881. Mission San Lorenzo de la Santa Cruz was founded by the Spanish in 1762 near present Camp Wood. The county was created on April 3, 1913, from Edwards, Kerr, and Bandera Counties. Organized on July 26, 1913, it was named in honor of Julius Real (1860–1944), a prominent businessman and state senator, 1909–1914 and 1924–1928. Leakey, the county seat, was established by John Leakey (1824–1900), a pioneer settler in the region.   (1968)

LEAKEY (Real Co.)   US 83, at courthouse
John Leakey
Tennessee native John Leakey (1824–1900) came to Texas in 1847, settling for a time in Henderson County where he was a brickmason and rancher. He and his wife Nancy (Patterson) moved to Uvalde County in 1852 near present day Sabinal. A desire to pursue other endeavors took him to the Frio Canyon where there was an abundance of cypress timber. Despite constant threats of Indian attacks, Leakey settled his family and started a cypress shingle business. He served the Confederacy as a freighter during the Civil War, hauling provisions for the troops. Leakey returned to his home after the war to establish a steam sawmill and to attend to his ranching interests. He also began a school for the children of the community, and his home often served as a resting place for itinerant preachers. The town, situated on the Bandera-Edwards county line, was laid out in 1833 and named in honor of the resourceful pioneer who donated land for this plaza, a church, school, and cemetery. Leakey served as county seat of Edwards County until 1891, and became county seat of Real County when it was organized in 1913. A successful businessman, Indian fighter and pioneer, John Leakey's contributions and leadership were vital to the early growth of the area.   (1983)

LEAKEY (Real Co.)   US 83 at courthouse
Real County Courthouse
Leakey was the county seat of Edwards County from 1883 to 1891 when a vote moved the seat to Rocksprings. Real County, named for businessman and State Senator Julius Real, was organized from parts of Edwards, Kerr and Bandera counties in April 1913. Leakey was named the county seat and a temporary building was erected on the square. Controversy over the site of the county seat continued for several years, so Judge D. D. Thompson began planning for a permanent courthouse upon his election in 1917. Voters approved bonds to finance a permanent structure. The bonds were financed through Hanover National Bank of New York. Architect H. A. Reuter designed the 1918 courthouse, and the firm of McCreary and Schott served as contractors. According to oral history, a local builder known as "Scotty" Archibald made a significant contribution, as well. E. F. Vanderbilt was construction superintendent. Using native limestone quarried from Tucker Hollow near the site, workers erected Reuter's vision of a Classical Revival edifice with a fortress-like façade. The rusticated limestone bands were laid in regular courses with quicklime bonding to create the building's texture and solid feel. A stone pediment with simple cornice topped by a standing seam metal roof contributes to the building's character. Renovations and additions made in 1978 transformed the original doors into large central windows with flat arch and transoms. The fine structure retains its original flavor and distinctive features and remains the center of Real County government.   (2000)

LEAKEY (Real Co.)   US 83, 5.2 mi. S
Near Route of Famous Cattle Trail
One of many "feeder trails" in Texas that converged with the legendary Chisholm Trail above the Red River, this route directed thousands of longhorns to northern markets during the first years after the Civil War. Many local settlers took part in the drives, which lasted for months, and their tales are full of stampedes and Indian raids. At times, the trail was used by herds of 200–300 hogs being driven 40 miles to local markets. The cattle industry and trails such as this helped save Texas' economy—torn by the Civil War—and enriched pioneer folklore.   (1968)

269

LEANDER (Williamson Co.)   US 183 at RR 2243
Webster Massacre
1½ miles east to the grave of the victims of the Webster massacre, which occurred August 27, 1839, when John Webster and a party of about thirty, en route to a land grant in Burnet County, were attacked by a band of Comanche Indians. After attempting to flee under cover of darkness, they were trapped on an open prairie. Mrs. Webster and her two children were made prisoners. All others were killed. In death they rest together in one grave.   (1936)

LEANDER (Williamson Co.)   US 183, S of W. South St.
Leanderthal Lady
On Dec. 29, 1982, Texas Highway Department archeologists uncovered the skeleton of a prehistoric human female at the Wilson-Leonard Brushy Creek site (approx. 6 mi. SE). Because of the proximity of the grave site to the town of Leander, the skeleton became known as the Leanderthal Lady. Carbon testing indicates the woman lived 10–13,000 years ago. She was about 30 years old at the time of death and measured 5'3" in height. As one of the earliest intact burials uncovered in the United States, the site is a valuable source of information on the nation's prehistoric past.   (1985)

LEANDER (Williamson Co.)   US 183 in city
Leander
Leander grew from the once thriving town of Bagdad, founded in 1854 (1 mi. W). When the Austin & Northwestern Railroad bypassed Bagdad in 1882, a new town was surveyed and named for railroad official Leander Brown (1817–89). Homes and businesses from the older community quickly moved to the new site along the rail line. The post office was brought here from Bagdad in 1882. The school started here in 1893 has grown into the largest school district in Williamson County. Originally in a rural area, Leander had boomed in recent years due to Highland Lakes development.

LEESVILLE (Gonzales Co.)   SH 80 at FM 1682, ¾ mi. E
Leesville Baptist Church
The first meeting place of this congregation, organized in 1875, was destroyed by a storm in 1886. The membership then moved across O'Neal Creek to this site, purchased from pioneer settler N. H. Guinn, and erected this simple frame church in 1887–1888. The steeple which once topped the building was removed in 1924. After a disastrous flood in 1936, Leesville was relocated along the state highway (¾ mi. W). This church is one of the structures that mark the old townsite.   (1976)

LEFORS (Gray Co.)   SH 273, 10 mi. SE
Battle of North Fork of Red River
On Sept. 29, 1872, Col. Ranald S. Mackenzie (1840–1889) found on this site a 262-tepee village of Comanches defying treaties that sought to confine them on Indian Territory reservations. Mackenzie's 231 U.S. Cavalry and Infantrymen captured the village in half an hour and routed Chief Mow-Way's warriors, who made a desperate resistance from sheltering creek banks. That night the Indians succeeded in recapturing their horses from an army guard detail. This taught Mackenzie a lesson that led to his eventual victory in the 1874 campaign to subdue the Indians.   (1972)

LEFORS (Gray Co.)   SH 273 at Spur 398
Captives Rescued
Ten miles southwest of here Lieutenant Frank D. Baldwin, commanding two companies of United States troops, attacked a large band of Cheyenne Indians and rescued two white girl captives, November 8, 1874.   (1965)

LEON VALLEY (Bexar Co.)   6613 Bandera Rd. (SH 16)
Huebner-Onion Homestead and Stagecoach Stop
This site was home to two important area families, as well as a stagecoach stop in the 1800s. Development here began in 1858 when Joseph Huebner and his family, who arrived from Austria five years earlier, bought acreage surrounding what is now Huebner Creek and Huebner Road. A successful San Antonio businessman, he soon erected three limestone buildings here and began to acquire herds of horses, mules and cattle. He also opened a stagecoach stop at the family's homestead ranch on the San Antonio to Bandera Stage Line Route. The stop included blacksmith services, change of stock and overnight accommodations if travelers were unable to pass over

the flooded creek. Joseph Huebner died in 1882 and was buried on the homestead property. After Huebner's death, and well into the early 20th century, the family continued to operate the ranch, watering hole and livery service on this land. In 1930, Judge John F. Onion and his wife Harriet acquired a section of the Huebner property that included the homestead site. John (d. 1955) began a family legal tradition, working as a lawyer and later serving as a San Antonio municipal judge, Bexar County Justice of the Peace and Bexar County District Judge. Harriet (d. 1983) was a school-teacher in Leon Valley. Due to metropolitan growth, the homestead was in danger of disappearing, but grassroots efforts led by the historical society of Leon Valley, along with corporate donations and the purchase of land, helped save this historic property. Today, it serves as a natural area and educational site.

(2007)

LEONA (Leon Co.) *IH 45, 3 mi. N in rest area*
Fort Boggy
Pioneers who settled in this area about 1840 included members of the Middleton, Byrns, Staley, Erwin, Jones, Capp, Bloodworth, Philpott, Easton, Howell, and Hinton families. Nearby Kichai and Kickapoo Indian camps afforded these early settlers little sense of security. On February 5, 1840, Christopher C. Staley was ambushed and killed by a group of Indians while out hunting near his home. This incident led to the building of Fort Boggy for the protection and safety of the settlers. Named for its proximity to Boggy Creek, the fort consisted of two blockhouses with eleven dwell-ings inside an area of about 5,000 square feet. A military company, authorized by Texas President Mirabeau B. Lamar, was formed under the leadership of Capt. Thomas Greer to protect the fort. According to one account, 77 people moved into the fort upon its completion. Illness proved to be a major problem for them. In 1841, while leading a scouting party beyond the fort, Captain Greer was killed in an Indian attack. Soon after, the threat of raids lessened, and the need for Fort Boggy no longer was vital. For many years, however, a community church and school retained the name "Boggy." As an early aid in the settlement of this area, Fort Boggy remains significant to the history of Leon County.

(1985)

LEONA (Leon Co.) *US 75, 1 mi. N*
Leon County
Formed from Robertson County, created March 17, 1846. Organized July 13, 1846. Named in honor of Martin de Leon, 1765–1833, a Texas empresario, founder of Victoria. County seat, Leona 1846. Centerville, since 1850.

(1936)

LEONARD (Fannin Co.) *SH 78, 3 mi. E*
Savage
William Hamilton "Uncle Billy" Savage (1822–1909) and his wife Elizabeth (Henson) moved to this area in 1869. Due to bad road conditions, they often stocked extra supplies and sold them to their neighbors. Their store became the center of Savage community (2.5 mi. E). The village had a doctor, blacksmith, cotton gin, stores, school, church, and a post office established in 1891. Savage began to decline after World War I (1917–1918) when it was bypassed by construction of new roads in the area. Annual reunion activities are held in Leonard (3 mi. SW).

(1980)

LEONARD (Fannin Co.) *SH 78, 6 mi. W*
Indian Creek Baptist Church and Cemetery
The oldest readable gravestone in this burial ground bears the date 1870, four years before the founding of the Indian Creek Baptist Church. Worship services were first held in a schoolhouse ¼ mile south of this site. Dock Holcomb donated this property adjacent to the cemetery, and a church building was completed in 1882 using lumber hauled by wagon from Jefferson. For over a century the burial ground was under the direct care of the congregation. An annual cemetery decoration day was begun in 1900.

(1982)

LEVELLAND (Hockley Co.) *FM 597, 21 mi. NW at White Ranch Hdqts.*
Casas Amarillas (Yellow Houses)
Most famous landmark on the South Plains. Ancient Indian camp ground visited in the 17th century by Spanish missionaries. Here the whites recovered, through trade, property stolen by Indians. Camp site for buffalo hunters, freighters and cattlemen. Acquired by XIT syndicate, 1882; by George W. Littlefield, 1901.

(1936)

LEVELLAND (Hockley Co.)　　　　　*US 385, 4.2 mi. N in roadside park*
Hockley County
Formed from Young and Bexar Territories. Created August 21, 1876. Organized February 21, 1921. Named in honor of George W. Hockley, commander of the artillery San Jacinto. Secretary of War of the Republic of Texas. Died in 1851. Levelland—called Hockley City until 1912—county seat. 　　　　　　　　　　　　　　　　　　　　　　　　　　　　　　　　　(1936)

LEVELLAND (Hockley Co.)　　　　　*SH 114, 2.4 mi. W of Smyer*
The Spade Ranch
Founded by Isaac L. Ellwood (1833–1910), inventor who made a fortune in barbed wire, and bought (1889) from veteran cattlemen D. H. and J. W. Snyder an 8 x 25-mile range (128,000 acres) in Hale, Hockley, Lamb and Lubbock Counties. This range was used for Spade-branded calves from Renderbrook Spring, his southmost ranch, in Mitchell County. He continued buying South Plains land until Spade range was 54 miles long. Headquarters (originally in Lamb County) was moved to South Camp (3/10 mi. N of here) after farm-land sales in 1920s. Ellwood's descendants still own and operate the Spade. 　　　　　　　　　　　　　　　　　　　　　　　　(1972)

LEWISVILLE (Denton Co.)　　　　　*1197 W. Main (FM 1171)*
Within Area Encompassed by the Peters Colony
A reservation of land made under an empresario contract by the Republic of Texas, 1841. Its purpose was to introduce colonists into this area. Under the first of four contracts, W. S. Peters and 19 partners agreed to introduce 600 families in three years, to furnish each with seed, shot, and a cabin, and also to survey the land. Each family was to receive 640 acres of land free and each single man, 320 acres; of this, the company could take half for its services. Three later contracts altered terms somewhat, and although the land company underwent several internal upheavals, by 1848 there were approximately 1,800 colonists and their families in the area. Resentment over the company's share of land climaxed in 1852 when settlers drove out the unpopular agent, Henry O. Hedgcoxe, in the so-called "Hedgcoxe War." Because of its success in opening a large area of the frontier and its later effect on Texas land and immigration policy, the law establishing this colony was one of the most important in the republic. In spite of unusual tumult and hardship, the final Peters Colony Area today extends over five counties and encompasses one-fourth of the state's population, including its largest combined metropolitan area. 　　　　　　　　　(1969)

LEWISVILLE (Denton Co.)　　　　　*900 blk. Lakeside Cir. off Hebron Pkwy.*
Texas International Pop Festival
The Texas International Pop Festival took place near this site during Labor Day weekend, 1969. It was held two weeks after the Woodstock Music and Art Fair introduced much of mainstream America to the "hippie" culture by way of news reports of the chaos that occurred there in part due to rainy weather and lax security. The Texas festival brought as many as 150,000 hippies, bikers and music lovers to Lewisville, which at the time had a population of approximately 9,000 citizens. The Dallas International Motor Speedway, situated along Interstate Highway 35 south of town, was chosen as the location for the event. Twenty-five musical acts, representing the genres of soul, blues and rock and roll performed during the three days of the festival. Acts included Janis Joplin, Sly & The Family Stone, Grand Funk Railroad, Chicago Transit Authority, Herbie Mann and a relatively unknown United Kingdom band called Led Zeppelin. On the north side of Lewisville, a public campground situated on the shores of Lewisville Lake served the thousands of festival attendees. A small "free stage" was constructed at the campground and local bands were brought in to perform for the campers. The skinny-dipping in Lake Lewisville that resulted from the lack of shower facilities and the late-summer heat drew much attention. Many locals demanded that the festival be shut down because of the threat of violence and unsavory activity, but there were no acts of violence reported at the festival. However, area citizens were introduced to a culture that had previously been foreign to them and many who attended look back on the festival as a life-changing event. 　　　　　　　　　　　　　　　　　　　　　　　(2010)

LEWISVILLE (Denton Co.)　　　　　*Lewisville Lake Park, Lake Park Rd., off IH 35E*
Lewisville Prehistoric Site (1.5 mi. SE)
During the construction of Lewisville Dam in 1950, a number of aboriginal artifacts were unearthed. Archeologists conducted several excavations (1952–1957) before the waters of Garza-

Little Elm Reservoir covered the site. The excavations revealed 21 hearths, vegetable matter, animal bone fragments and lignite (coal) which was used for fuel. Scientific radiocarbon dating techniques indicate the organic material is approximately 12,000 years old. The Lewisville discoveries are similar in age and content to findings at the Clovis site in New Mexico. (1980)

LEXINGTON (Lee Co.)
US 77, near S city limits at roadside park
Indian Camp Branch
Located along an old buffalo trail, this creek was once fed by a spring and was a favorite camping place for Indian hunting parties. It was named Indian Camp Branch by James Shaw (1808–1879), a veteran of the Battle of San Jacinto (April 21, 1836), to honor the hospitality of a band of friendly Tonkawa Indians he encountered near this site in 1837. Shaw built a cabin in this area and was soon joined by other Anglo-American settlers. A teacher, surveyor, and postmaster, Shaw also served as a senator and representative in congresses of the Republic and State of Texas. (1976)

LIBERTY (Liberty Co.)
SH 146, 23 mi. N
Site of the Town of Grand Cane
Here General Sam Houston built a home in 1843 and in it resided until 1845. A post office was established May 22, 1846, with Vernon B. Lea as postmaster. It was discontinued October 25, 1868, and reestablished April 26, 1869. The name of the town was changed to Ironwood August 26, 1869. The post office was discontinued March 15, 1900.

LIBERTY (Liberty Co.)
SH 146 at FM 1011
Atascosito
1756—Liberty Bicentennial, observance 1956 Atascosito, established Indian village prior to 1690. Established as district on Atascosito Road by Spanish government in 1857 to prevent French trade with Indians. Bill Daniel, director general; W. D. Partlow, chairman, historical marker committee.

LIBERTY (Liberty Co.)
SH 146 at FM 1011
Homesite of George Orr
George Orr first came to Texas in 1813 as a member of the Gutierrez-Magee Expedition. He returned in 1821 with his family and established a home at this site on the Old Atascosito Road. The Orr home was an important stopping place for travelers. Orr served several terms as alcalde of the Atascosito District and participated in the dedication of Fort Anahuac in 1831. He died in 1835, prior to Texas Independence, but his contributions to the settlement of this area helped pave the way for future colonization. The Orr home was razed about 1882. (1990)

LIBERTY (Liberty Co.)
1923 Sam Houston St., 1 blk. W of SH 227
Casa Consistatorial (Courthouse Square)
Originally one of five squares platted for public use in 1831 by J. Francisco Madero, General Land Commissioner of Texas (under Mexican government), in accordance with the provisions of 1825 Law of Colonization-Article 34. Madero changed name of site from Atascosito, meaning boggy, to Liberty to reflect his hopes for the future of Texas. The first courthouse was built on this square, 1831; a second in 1857; a third in 1877; a fourth in 1895–1896; and the present one in 1930–1931. Many Texas statesmen including Sam Houston and David G. Burnet practiced law here. (1968)

LIBERTY (Liberty Co.)
SH 227 at Sam Houston St.
Liberty County
A trail across this region traveled and described by Alonso de Leon in 1690 became the "La Bahia" or "Lower Road" in the 18th century. First settlement, Atascocita, established in 1757. The town established May 5, 1831 as the "Villa de la Santisima Trinity de la Libertad" (City of the Blessed Trinity of Liberty) became the county seat and gave the county its name when created and organized in 1836. (1936)

LIBERTY (Liberty Co.)
SH 227 at Sam Houston St.
Sam Houston in Liberty County
Pioneer, lawyer, statesman, and leader of the Texas victory over Mexico at San Jacinto, General Sam Houston began a relationship with Liberty County in 1833 that was based on land ownership

which continued until his death in 1863. During those years he concluded nine land transactions involving nearly 20,000 acres. He established family homes at Cedar Point (now part of Chambers County) in 1840 and at Grand Cane (22 mi. N) in 1842. From 1838 to 1855, Sam Houston practiced law in Liberty, maintaining an office on this site across from the Courthouse Square. Houston's other activities in Liberty County included his attendance at worship services of the Concord Baptist Church (Grand Cane), of which his wife, Margaret Lea Houston, was one of the founders in 1845. Sam Houston's activities in Liberty County took place while he was serving in various leadership roles for Texas, including President of the Republic of Texas (1836–1838, 1841–1844) and as the first United States Senator for the newly-annexed state of Texas (1846–1859). He has been honored in Liberty County by the naming of Sam Houston Avenue and the Sam Houston Regional Library and Research Center. (1967)

LIBERTY (Liberty Co.) *2315 US 90E*
Mexican Hill
Following the decisive battle of San Jacinto in the Texas War for Independence, most of the Mexicans captured in the battle were taken to Galveston. Problems concerning a lack of provisions and the threat of attack persuaded Texas President David G. Burnet to transfer some of the prisoners to Liberty. In August 1836, some 60 Mexicans were transported by schooner to Anahuac, where they were met by William Hardin, who took them on to Liberty. Georgia native William Hardin (1801–1839) had come to Liberty from Tennessee in 1825. During the years before the Texas Revolution, he served as commissioner of police and Alcalde of Liberty. Hardin was elected a delegate to the convention of 1833 at San Felipe and later served as an election judge in Nacogdoches and as a primary judge in Liberty. The Mexican prisoners stayed on Hardin's property near this site, which has come to be called Mexican Hill. Among the men were General Martin Perfecto de Cós and Ten. Colonel Pedro Delgado, who wrote an account of his time in Liberty. According to Delgado, the Mexicans were treated well and given the best care available during their stay, which lasted until the government of Texas released them on April 25, 1837. (1985)

LIBERTY (Liberty Co.) *US 90 at Trinity River*
The Trinity River
Longest river lying entirely within Texas. The watershed of the Trinity covers 17,969 square miles, an area larger than any one of the nine smallest states of the union. More than 20 percent of the people in Texas reside in this area—more people than in any one of the 24 least populous states. The first recorded exclusive navigation rights to the Trinity were given by Mexico in 1833 to district commissioner J. Francisco Madero, but before he could exercise his rights, the Texas Revolution intervened. As early as 1838, during the Republic of Texas, steamboat navigation had begun on the Trinity. The famous steamer Ellen Frankland plied it regularly. In 1852 a survey authorized by the U.S. Congress reported that "the Trinity River is the deepest and least obstructed river in Texas." The river played a vital role in the Civil War, when a company of Alabama-Coushatta Indians transported key military supplies and boats from Anderson County to waiting Confederate officials in Liberty. Until 1874 steamers chugged from Galveston to as far north as Porter's Bluff in Ellis County. Under the River and Harbor Act of 1965, Congress authorized the comprehensive development of the Trinity basin's water resources. (1970)

LIBERTY (Liberty Co.) *US 90 at Trinity River*
Early Meat-Packing Plant
Probably first commercial meat-packing plant in Texas. In the early 1840s, English firm of Jones & Co. established a beef-preserving plant at Liberty Landing. British gold bought beef on hoof at four cents a pound. In processing, barrels of meat were put in iron cylinders and air was expelled, causing a vacuum. Brine was then added. When beef was removed, it was packed in salt and shipped to Galveston by steamer and on to West Indies in English sailing vessels. Firm also made candles, tallow, neat's-foot oil and glue. A flood destroyed the factory in 1844. (1969)

LIBERTY HILL (Williamson Co.) *SH 29, 2 mi. NW*
Liberty Hill Cemetery
Weathered gravestones show use of this spot for burials since 1852, when the earliest settlers were establishing homes in area. The first formal grant of land here as a community burial ground

was made by John T. and Amelia Edwards Bryson in 1875, when three and one-half acres were deeded to the Liberty Hill cemetery trustees: T. N. Bryson, C. C. Chance, W. H. Poole, J. B. Roddy, and T. S. Snyder. This acreage was protected by a stone fence built with their own hands by the Brysons and their neighbors. Additions to original plot include land formerly owned by John T. Bryson and donated by Dr. and Mrs. H. L. Fowler. Royal Arch Masons in 1932 established an adjacent three-acre Masonic cemetery, later transferring title to the Liberty Hill Lodge No. 432, A. F. & A. M., which gave it in 1959 to the Liberty Hill Cemetery Association. By later land purchases, the cemetery now contains more than twenty acres. Funds have come by bequests from Walter Gardner, Arthur Gray, and T. L. McDaniel. Many other persons have also contributed to funds for the cemetery. In 1953 the Liberty Hill Cemetery Association was incorporated, with Dr. J. Gordon Bryson as president; C. L. Chance, vice president; C. F. Hickman, treasurer; and Mrs. Letitia Russell, secretary.

(1971)

LIBERTY HILL (Williamson Co.) *SH 29, 1 mi. NW*
Bryson Stagecoach Stop
John T. Bryson (d. 1894) and his wife Amelia (d. 1897), prominent early settlers of the Liberty Hill community, constructed this home in the 1850s. Built on a frame of notched and fitted hewn cedar logs and featuring chimneys of native stone, the original open dog-trot construction is typical of pioneer Texas houses. The Bryson residence also served as a stop on the stagecoach route between Austin and Fort Croghan, near present Burnet.

(1981)

LINDALE (Smith Co.) *US 69 at CR 431, 7 mi. N*
Camp of the Army of the Republic of Texas,
Last Cherokee War
Gen. Kelsey H. Douglass, Gen. Thomas J. Rusk, Gen. Edward Burleson, and Col. Willis H. Landrum. Texas Secretary of War Albert Sidney Johnston ordered the army mustered out after its decisive victory in Battle of the Neches against Chief Bowles of the Cherokees and associated tribes on July 16, 1839, in Van Zandt County. From the Burleson Lake Camp, the soldiers departed for their homes on July 15, 1839.

(1975)

LINDALE (Smith Co.) *US 69, 4 mi. N*
Milburn-Gary House
Anglo settlement of the Gum Springs area in Smith County was underway when the community name changed to Starrville in 1852, in honor of pioneer Russel Julius Starr. Located on the Dallas-Shreveport freight route, Starrville included a post office, school, Masonic Lodge and Bethel Baptist Church. The Rev. Williamson Milburn was appointed pastor of the Baptist Church in 1854. The Rev. Mr. Milburn bought land from Benjamin Harry in 1853 that was part of the A. J. LaGrone survey patented in 1850. This home was built by the Rev. Mr. Milburn in 1855. The structure was built with hand-picked knot-free lumber on a foundation put together with wooden pegs, and featured solid oak walls. Its wide doors and floor plan are indicative of a 19th-century house. Business owners W. D. and W. V. Hyer purchased the home and sold it to Jesse B. Gary, a local farmer, in 1880. John Henry Gary, Sr., bought the property from his father in 1900, and moved the house 400 yards north of its original location to access a better water supply. The home remained in the Gary family until 1964. The home was uninhabited for many years. It was moved to this site in 1995.

(1996)

LINDEN (Cass Co.) *US 59, 9 mi. S in roadside park*
Texas Confederate Legislator Dr. M. D. K. Taylor (1818–1897)
Alabama physician. Came to Texas, 1847. Served Cass County in Texas House and Senate for 24 years. Was called the ablest parliamentarian of his time. Served as one of the speakers of Texas House of Representatives in critical Civil War years, 1861–1865. Legislators passed laws to raise, equip and supply 90,000 Texas soldiers who fought on all fronts and provided for defense of state's 2000 mile frontier and coast against Indians, enemy troops and ships. As naval blockade reduced imports, the legislature established plants to make guns, powder, cloth, salt. Contracts, subsidies and land grants were provided to encourage private industry to help meet heavy wartime demands for arms, supplies, clothing, food. Taylor and the other lawmakers taxed property and business and required farmers to turn in tithes of produce to meet the crisis. Funds were voted to buy cotton for

state exchange for goods in Mexico to aid soldiers' dependents and to provide hospitals and medical care for troops—in and out of state. The legislature was in almost continuous session. Poor pay and inflated Confederate money caused many members to live in tents and covered wagons on the capital grounds and cook over campfires. (1965)

LINDEN (Cass Co.)
US 59, 7 mi. NE in roadside park
Cass County
Formed from Bowie County land. Created April 25, 1846; organized July 13, 1846. Named in honor of Gen. Lewis Cass (1782–1866), United States soldier and statesman, a strong advocate of annexation of Texas. Important river port city of Jefferson was county seat until Marion County was carved out of Cass in 1860; Linden, near center of county, then became county seat. During wave of sectional patriotism in 1861, the name "Cass" was changed to "Davis," in honor of Jefferson Davis, President of the Confederate states. The original name was restored in 1871. (1971)

LINDSAY (Cooke Co.)
US 82, 2.3 mi. W in roadside park
First Cooke County Surveyor Daniel Montague (1798–1876)
Born in Massachusetts. Moved to Texas 1836. Accepted post of surveyor, Fannin Land District, helping settlers locate claims and fight Indians. Joined Snively expedition to capture Mexican traders trespassing in Republic of Texas, 1843. Captain of company in Mexican War, 1846. When Cooke County was created, 1848, Montague was named county surveyor. Like most surveyors, took land as pay for duty that called for constant risk of life. Rifles to stand off Indians were in field kits. Like surveyor-Senator John H. Reagan, Montague was honored in having a county named for him. (1968)

LINN (Hidalgo Co.)
SH 186, 4 mi. E
El Sal Del Rey, C.S.A.
Large salt lake located 26 miles NE was principal source of salt in South Texas during the Civil War. Put under state guard and agent 1862. Salt sold to families, Texas military board, army of Confederacy and wagons returning north on Cotton Road—vital trade route for South thru Mexico. Due to military and domestic importance, Union Forces periodically wrecked the salt works from November 1863 until war's end. It was also a Texas Confederate base for the 1864 recapture of Brownsville. Back Side:
Salting or smoking were only ways to preserve meat at time of Civil War. When South levied a meat tithe, salt was necessary to cure bacon and beef for military. Salt was a must for horses and mules used by cavalry, artillery and supply wagons. Hides were preserved with it to make leather for shoes and harness. Other wartime salt works were operated along coast and in 7 counties in Central, East and West Texas. El Sal del Rey, Spanish for "salt for the king" also played a significant role in the history of Texas mineral law. A legal controversy raged for years over its ownership. Under Spain, mineral rights belonged to crown. Mexico retained the principle of the state ownership of minerals. Texas, as republic and state, kept minerals in the public domain. Private possession of the lake began with the 1866 Texas Constitutional Convention which relinquished all minerals to landowners. The principle of private ownership was readopted in the constitutions of 1869 and 1876. (1963)

LINN (Hidalgo Co.)
US 281 right-of-way, .5 mi. S
La Noria Cardeneña
Parts of present Hidalgo, Cameron, Willacy, and Kenedy Counties were once included in two Spanish land grants, San Juan de Carricitos and San Salvador del Tule. The original grantee of the Carricitos grant was José Narciso Cavazos. After his death, ownership of the land passed to his heirs. The Tule lands were granted to Juan José Ballí in 1798. Ballí obtained a business loan from Antonio Cárdenas of Reynosa, Mexico. Following Ballí's death and subsequent litigation over the loan, the lands reverted to Cárdenas heirs in 1828. The Cárdenas family established La Noria Cardeneña Ranch in 1829, so named because of the fresh water wells (norias) found in the region. Gradually, the Cárdenas and Cavazos families were joined by a number of marriages, which also combined property interests. Although the families endured many hardships, including years of Indian and bandit attacks, they continued to run a strong ranching operation. Still in existence on

part of the ranch is a small cemetery, begun in 1835 and named Niño Jesús de Praga in 1863. Also surviving are the mid-19th century main ranch house and a church built next to the cemetery in 1944.

(1988)

LIPSCOMB (Lipscomb Co.)   SH 305 at Spur 188
Lipscomb, Texas
Established 1886, by settlers hoping to benefit from proposed Santa Fe Railroad in Panhandle. Post office was opened in 1886; Lipscomb Town Company sold land for $3 an acre in 1887. In first month, seven businesses started. When county was organized in 1887, Lipscomb became seat, named for A. S. Lipscomb, Secretary of State in Republic of Texas and Justice of State Supreme Court. Hotel from undeveloped town of Dominion moved here, 1887. First courthouse was built in 1887. The first school—in a church—had 25 pupils, 1888. A new courthouse was erected in 1916.

(1967)

LIPSCOMB (Lipscomb Co.)   Main St. (Spur 188)
Lipscomb County Courthouse
Established in 1886 and organized the following year with Lipscomb as county seat, Lipscomb County was named for Abner S. Lipscomb, an associate justice of the Texas Supreme Court in the 1840s–1850s. A one-story wood frame building served as the first county courthouse. During the first decade of the 20th century, the number of farms and ranches in the county more than doubled, and the population more than tripled that of the 1900 census. In 1915, county voters approved the issuance of bonds for a new, larger courthouse to serve the governmental functions of a growing county. The Commissioners Court selected William M. Rice of Amarillo as both architect and general contractor for the project. Edward S. Altmiller, who had been the contractor for the 1910 Lipscomb County jail, served as construction superintendent. Rice designed the courthouse in the Classical Revival style, with style-defining features such as the arched doorway and the triangular pediment supported by Doric order columns over the entrance. Design and construction took place primarily during 1916, with final details completed in early 1917. Despite its status as the smallest town in the county, largely the result of being bypassed by the railroad, Lipscomb retains its designation as county seat. The Lipscomb County courthouse, which dominates the town site, continues to function as the center of government and politics for county residents.   (2000)

LITTLEFIELD (Lamb Co.)   US 385 right-of-way, 12 mi. N
Rocky Ford Crossing and Community
(The Ford was .5 mi. W)
The 840-mile Brazos River was both friend and foe to settlers. Here near the source of Double Mountain Fork, after XIT ranch was sold to smaller operators about 1912, the river that had attracted settlers was found to obstruct wet-weather travel. In 1926, the settlers built a gyprock road across the valley and lined the river bed with rock to make a passable road. They also built a tabernacle for church, elections, and other gatherings. New roads bypass Rocky Ford, yet the community still thrives.

(1976)

LITTLEFIELD (Lamb Co.)   US 84 at Delano Street
Replica of XIT's Giant Windmill
Yellowhouse division of the 3,050,000-acre XIT Ranch built (1887) a 132-foot windmill southwest of here. Set in a canyon, it had to be tall to catch breezes and pump water. It was known as the world's tallest windmill until it was toppled by winds in 1926. This replica was erected May 27, 1969.

(1970)

LITTLEFIELD (Lamb Co.)   US 84, NW city limits
Major George W. Littlefield (1842–1920)
Came to Texas 1850. In Civil War, with Terry's Texas Rangers, fought at Shiloh, Chickamauga, Lookout Mountain and other bloody battles. Helped open South Plains, the Panhandle and New Mexico to ranching. His "LIT" and "LFD" herds were famed all over the West and in Canada. Became Austin banker, devoted friend and benefactor to the University of Texas. Financed studies, donated property and established the Littlefield Grant for Southern History. Founded town of Littlefield.

LITTLEFIELD (Lamb Co.)
FM 54, 8 mi. W
Comanchero Trail
One of several routes used by traders dealing with Indians, primarily Comanches (hence name). Weapons, whiskey and trade goods were swapped for stolen Texas cattle, horses and captives. Pursuit apparently began in the 1760s when Mexican hunters ventured out on "Staked Plains" (Indian domain) to hunt buffalo for New Mexico meat markets. Early explorers Zebulon Pike (1807), Josiah Gregg (1830), and Capt. R. B. Marcy (1848) told of finding Comanchero campsites and wagon trails on the plains. The Comancheros ceased to operate in the mid-1870s. (1970)

LIVINGSTON (Polk Co.)
US 190, 16 mi. E at entrance to reservation
Village of Alabama-Coushatta Indians
Who came into Texas early in the 19th century and have always been friendly with the whites.

LIVINGSTON (Polk Co.)
Reservation, US 190, 16 mi. E
Confederate Service of Alabama and Coushatta Indians
Alabama and Coushatta Indians of Polk County were trained as cavalrymen in 1861 by Indian agent Robert R. Neyland as the War Between the States advanced. In April 1862, nineteen Alabama and Coushatta, including Chief John Scott, enlisted in the Confederate Army as members of Company G, 24th Texas Cavalry. They trained in Hempstead, Texas, and in Arkansas, where their commander, General Thomas C. Hindman, converted them to infantrymen. After voicing displeasure with the change from cavalry to infantry duties, they were permitted to return to their Polk County homes to await further orders. Following brief service in the Confederate Navy under Galveston Bay Commander W. W. Hunter, they were reorganized as a cavalry company in the 6th Brigade, 2nd Texas Infantry Division. In 1864 the company roster listed 132 men. Their primary job was to build and operate flat-bottomed boats (scows) to transport farm produce and other supplies needed by the confederacy down the Trinity River to the port at Liberty, Texas. Official correspondence of wartime Texas Governors Francis R. Lubbock and Pendleton Murrah refer to the Alabama and Coushatta Indians' loyalty in their role as Confederate infantry, cavalry, and navy servicemen. (1994)

LIVINGSTON (Polk Co.)
US 59, N city limits
Polk County
Created from Liberty County March 30, 1846. Organized July 13, 1846 with Livingston as county seat. Named for James Knox Polk, 1795–1849, President of the United States who favored the annexation of Texas. Early settlements were Drew's Landing, Mariana, Swartwout. On 1,280 acres granted by the State in 1854, the descendants of the Alabama Indians still live. (1936)

LIVINGSTON (Polk Co.)
1502 US 59 North Loop
Greenfield Cemetery
In 1846, local officials designated a block in the central part of Livingston for use as a cemetery for local African Americans. Originally called Livingston Colored Cemetery, the burial ground was bounded by Feagin, Tyler, Sherman and Houston streets. As the railroad brought new residents to the city in the 1880s, cemetery space became limited. In the 1890s, leaders from the black community sought the advice of County Judge Arthur B. Green, and he offered to give the citizens three acres of land for a new cemetery. Trustees of the cemetery accepted the gift on October 24, 1896. They moved the graves from the original location to the new site and changed the cemetery name to Greenfield to reflect the judge's generosity. In 1910, cemetery trustees bought additional land from Green's widow and children. The cemetery's earliest marked grave dates to 1906, but dozens of earlier graves exist. The military service and fraternal organization markers found throughout the burial ground reflect the contributions, efforts and work of generations of the area's African American residents. (2003)

LIVINGSTON (Polk Co.)
101 W. Church Street (US 190 at US 59 Bus.)
Polk County Courthouse
Completed in 1924, this is the fifth courthouse to serve Polk County. Citing "lack of space and modern conveniences," the Commissioners Court hired the Houston architectural firm of McLelland & Fink to design their new building. Contractor Isaac Young completed demolition of the 1884 courthouse by July 1923, and the first court meetings were held in this building by the fall of 1924. Designed to include an auditorium, library, American Legion hall and post office, which were

replaced in later years by administrative and judicial offices, the Polk County Courthouse features Classical Revival styling with Beaux Arts influences. It stands as a significant part of Livingston's architectural heritage. (2001)

LIVINGSTON (Polk Co.)   *W. Church St. (US 190) at N. Drew St.*
Early Indian Trails
From 1830 to 1840 five Indian trails (some several centuries old) crossed Polk County. The Coushatta and Alabama tribes started two trails and also traveled Long King's, Kickapoo, and Battise traces. These routes helped settlers map roads; modern highways follow the trails in places. (1967)

LIVINGSTON (Polk Co.)   *819 W. Church St. (US 190)*
Education in Livingston
Education has been integral to life in Livingston since the town's inception in the 1840s. Moses Choate's 100-acre donation for the townsite included land for a school. Trinity Masonic Lodge No. 14, A.F. & A.M. financed a free academy that began in 1849 and operated for 31 years. Classes were held on the first floor of the Masonic lodge, located on the southwest corner of what is now Old City Cemetery. In 1888, the Livingston Free School Corporation built a frame schoolhouse on Jackson Avenue, dedicated as Livingston Graded School. Trustees added ninth and tenth grades in 1906 under principal J. F. Stevens, creating Livingston High School. Classes were on the second floor, and the first graduating class in 1908 had three students. That summer, the schools offered an institute for African American teachers; the first African American school was on West Street. A 1910 bond issue paid for a two-story brick building on Jackson Avenue designed by the noted architectural firm of C. H. Page & Son of Austin. The district divided the previous schoolhouse into a new African American school and a residence. Trustees added an eleventh grade to Livingston High School in 1913, allowing graduates to meet college entrance requirements. In the 1930s, the district built Dunbar High School for African Americans and a new Livingston High School for Anglo students. This campus later expanded with a football field, auditorium and an additional classroom building. Trustees added a twelfth grade in 1941. A Freedom of Choice program began the integration process in 1965, and three years later all students attended classes together. The high school moved to new facilities in 1977. In 2006, the centennial year for Livingston High, the graduating class had nearly 300 students. (2007)

LIVINGSTON (Polk Co.)   *FM 1988, 6 mi. SW, Lake Livingston Viewing Area*
Early Roads in Polk County
Travel was of great importance in Polk County's early days. Civilized Indians—particularly Creeks, Alabamas, Coushattas, and Kickapoos—were numerous and had many trails for inter-communication. Long King's Trace (named for a chief) led from Alabama villages through site of present Livingston, past site of this marker. The Coushatta Trace began in Louisiana, wound through what is now Polk County, joining (more than 100 miles west) an ancient road into Mexico. The Alabama Trace branched off El Camino Real (The King's Highway) east of Nacogdoches and came to the site of present Alabama-Coushatta reservation. Indians started many other local roads. A Mexican-Indian trail became the Nacogdoches–Liberty Stagecoach Road, after white settlement began in 1820s. Settlers brought in goods by Trinity River boats, establishing 20 landings (or wharves) on the 72 miles of Polk County riverfront. Roads led to the interior from the landings; boats handled shipping of county produce for many years. Northeast of Livingston is the "Old Israel Road"—named for a religious colony whose buildings have disappeared. As with many of the Indians, memory of these people is preserved only in the road's name. (1970)

LLANO (Llano Co.)   *SH 71, 12 mi. NW*
Community of Valley Spring
O. C. J. Phillips, first settler, arrived in 1853. Whistleville combined with Bugscuffle to form Valley Spring, with post office established 1878. This was birthplace of James Field Smathers (1888–1967), inventor of electric typewriter. (1970)

LLANO (Llano Co.)   *SH 29 at CR 261, 16 mi. E*
C.S.A. Salt Works
Located between Tow Valley and old Bluffton, 15 miles NE. Since 1935 under Lake Buchanan. During Civil War made salt for table, curing meat, and hides, feeding cavalry horses. A day's boiling

279

in 100 iron, 250-gallon kettles produced 20 to 30 bushels of salt. Cooled, sacked and hauled out, this met Texas wartime shortages. First Llano County district court was held at Salt Works. Stage coach stop was nearby. Brine here was Cambrian Sea waters trapped 500 million years ago in sand and strata. Indians led first settler here.

LLANO (Llano Co.) — *601 Bessemer (SH 16)*
Badu House
Built in 1891 during the city's iron production boom days, this structure originally housed the First National Bank of Llano. In 1898 it was purchased by French native N. J. "Professor" Badu, a noted local mineralogist, for use as a residence. Designed by the Austin firm of Larramour and Watson, it features Renaissance Revival detailing and a distinctive band of native granite in a checkerboard pattern. Badu's descendants lived here for many years. (1981)

LLANO (Llano Co.) — *801 Ford St. (SH 71)*
Llano County Courthouse
Designed by Austin architect A. O. Watson, this building is the fourth courthouse for Llano County. Work on the structure began in 1892 and was completed one year later. The contractors were J. A. and G. H. Wilson of Sulphur Springs. The courthouse was later surrounded by an iron fence, but only the stone foundations remain. Exterior styling of the building features detailing of sandstone, marble, and granite. Fires damaged the interior in 1932 and 1952. (1980)

LLANO (Llano Co.) — *SH 71, in park S side of Llano River Bridge*
Llano County Granite Industry
Llano County's granite industry can be traced to 1888 when J. K. Finlay first polished a stone from his mill site and David Stewart opened a quarry south of Llano. Prominent sculptor Frank Teich leased a quarry from Stewart and established Teich Monument Works in 1900. Thirteen varieties of granite were found in Llano County. Noted mineralogist N. J. Badu discovered in the county a form of granite called "Opalene" or "Llanite," which contains opalite flakes. Although difficult to cut, the excellent quality of Llano granite made it suitable for buildings and monuments.

LLANO (Llano Co.) — *SH 71, 15 mi. SE near Honey Creek*
Early Explorers in Llano County
By commission of the governor of Spanish Texas, Bernardo de Miranda in 1756 examined Cerro del Almagre, a red ochre hill supposedly rich in silver. His party of 23 from San Antonio struck Honey Creek near here, then went to the junction of the Llano and Colorado Rivers. Three pounds of ore from Cerro del Almagre assayed only ten ounces of silver to 100 pounds of ore. Plans for further explorations were therefore abandoned as such low yield, coupled with transport problems and Indian threats, made mining seem unattractive. (1971)

LLANO (Llano Co.) — *SH 71, 15.2 mi. SE*
Packsaddle Mountain
Two and one half miles east on the Packsaddle Mountain, in a battle fought August 4, 1873, Captain J. R. Moss, Stephen Moss, William B. Moss, Eli Lloyd, Arch Martin, Pink Ayers, E. D. Harrington, and Robert Brown routed a band of Indians thrice their number. The last Indian battle in this region. (1936)

LLANO (Llano Co.) — *SH 16, 9 mi. N*
Baby Head Cemetery
According to local oral tradition, the name "Babyhead" was given to the mountain in this area in the 1850s, when a small child was killed by Indians and its remains left on the mountain. A local creek also carried the name, and a pioneer community founded in the 1870s became known as Baby Head. The oldest documented grave here is that of another child, Jodie May McKneely, who died on New Year's Day 1884. The cemetery is the last physical reminder of the Baby Head community, which once boasted numerous homes, farms, and businesses. (1991)

LLANO (Llano Co.) — *SH 16, 10 mi. S*
Oxford Cemetery (¼ mi. E)
The Oxford Community was founded in 1880 when Confederate veteran A. J. Johnson came to Llano County and laid out the townsite. In 1881, a burial ground was established near this site for

the use of the families of Oxford. Burials date from 1883, although some of the graves that were moved from a neighboring cemetery bear earlier death dates. Among those interred there are the town's founder, A. J. Johnson (1832–1912); and James R. Moss (1843–1924), who captained the Packsaddle Mountain fight, an 1873 battle that drove raiding Indians out of Llano County. (1985)

LLANO (Llano Co.)   *SH 16 at FM 965, 15 mi. S*
Enchanted Rock
Nine miles west is Enchanted Rock. From its summit, in the fall of 1841, Captain John C. Hays, while surrounded by Comanche Indians who cut him off from his ranging company, repulsed the whole band and inflicted upon them such heavy loss that they fled. (1936)

LOCKHART (Caldwell Co.)   *US 183, 3 mi. N in roadside park*
Dr. D. Port Smythe (1824–1889)
Pioneer Lockhart physician, from Alabama. Studied medicine, University of Pennsylvania. Was Civil War surgeon, Texas Mounted Rifles and Cavalry, on Texas frontier and in Louisiana, Arkansas and Indian Territory. Typical of Texas Confederates, his letters home show concern for wife and children: contain instructions on teaching child to read, crops, plowing, animal care, fences, debt collection. Professor of Chemistry, 1871, Galveston Medical College. A & M College physician, 1879–1882. First to serve full time in any Texas college or university. (1965)

LOCKHART (Caldwell Co.)   *US 183, Lions Club City Park*
Battle of Plum Creek
The harsh anti-Indian policies of President Mirabeau B. Lamar and Mexican efforts to weaken the Republic of Texas stirred Indian hostilities. Hatred increased after the Council House fight in San Antonio, March 19, 1840, where 12 Comanche chiefs were killed. After regrouping and making plans for revenge, 600 Comanches and Kiowas, including women and children, moved across Central Texas in early August. They raided Victoria and Linnville (120 mi. SE), a prosperous seaport. About 200 Texans met at Good's Crossing on Plum Creek under Major-General Felix Huston (1800–1857) to stop the Indians. Adorned with their plunder from Linnville, the war party stretched for miles across the prairie. The Battle of Plum Creek, August 12, 1840, began on Comanche Flats (5.5 mi. SE) and proceeded to Kelley Springs (2.5 mi. SW), with skirmishes as far as present San Marcos and Kyle. Mathew Caldwell (1798–1842), for whom Caldwell County was named, was injured in the Council House Fight but took part in this battle. Volunteers under Edward Burleson (1793–1851) included 13 Tonkawa Indians, marked as Texan allies by white armbands. Texas casualties were light while the Indians lost over 80 chiefs and warriors. This battle ended the Comanche penetration of settled portions of Texas. (1978)

LOCKHART (Caldwell Co.)   *110 S. Main St., 1 blk. W of US 183*
Caldwell County Courthouse
The first Caldwell County Courthouse was erected on this site in 1848, when the county was organized and named for Mathew Caldwell, a Texas Ranger and signer of the Texas Declaration of Independence. It was replaced in 1858 by a 2-story limestone edifice, measuring 65 feet by 40 feet, with six offices and two rooms for storing records. By 1893, that building had become too small for a growing county. In April 1893, Judge George W. Kyser and commissioners J. H. Jolley, G. A. McGee, C. R. Smith, and R. A. Tiller approved plans for the present courthouse. The cornerstone was laid by Lockhart Lodge No. 690, A. F. & A. M., on August 15, 1893. Contractors Martin, Byrne, and Johnston completed the building on March 19, 1894. The 3-story structure is built of sandstone with red sandstone trim. It displays the fine workmanship and elaborate detail common to architecture of the period. The mansard roof is characteristic of the second empire style that was often used for public buildings. The courthouse is topped by a central clock tower, with additional towers at each corner and flanking the north and south entrances. When it was built, the structure was equipped with the latest conveniences of the day, including electricity. (1976)

LOCKHART (Caldwell Co.)   *110 S. Main St., 1 blk. W of US 183*
Caldwell County
A part of De Witt's Colony, 1825–1836. A part of Gonzales County to 1848. First settlements were on Plum Creek and the San Marcos River. Created March 6, 1848; organized August 7, 1848. Named in honor of Mathew Caldwell, "Old Paint," 1798–1842, soldier-statesman. Signer of

the Texas Declaration of Independence, Commander of the Texas Rangers. Lockhart, the county seat. (1936)

LOCKHART (Caldwell Co.) 308 W. San Antonio St. (SH 142)
Susanna Dickinson Hannig—Messenger of the Alamo
At this site once stood the home of Susanna Dickinson Hannig (1814–1883), who came to Texas from Tennessee in 1831 with her husband Almeron Dickinson. He died at the Battle of the Alamo on March 6, 1836. Susanna, with her daughter Angelina, was among the survivors. She carried news of the Alamo's capture to Gen. Sam Houston, commander of the Texas Army. Susanna settled in Lockhart in 1855 and bought this property. She married Joseph William Hannig, who had a cabinet shop here. In 1858 they moved to Austin, where Susanna died and is buried. (1978)

LOEB (Hardin Co.) US 69
Former Townsite of Concord
First town in Hardin County. Established in 1858 at a strategic crossing from Beaumont to points north. Original name was Benton. Rapidly became a thriving steamboat port and reached a population of about 300, but declined in the 1880s with coming of the railroad. (1970)

LOMETA (Lampasas Co.) US 183, 1.5 mi. NW
Site of Lometa Reservoir
Remains of facilities at the site of Lometa Reservoir (Santa Fe Lake) are evidence of the role the Santa Fe Railway Co. played in area development. Lometa was established as a railroad town in the mid-1880s. When a second rail line came through in 1909, the railroads needed a water supply for steam locomotives. Completed in 1911–12, a dam backed waters of Emory and Salt Creeks, and the resulting lake provided water for the trains and became a recreation area. The need for water declined as diesel engines replaced steam locomotives in the 20th century. The reservoir was taken out of service in the 1970s, but a new dam and lake were later built. (2005)

LOMETA (Lampasas Co.) US 190, 9 mi. W
Chadwick's Mill (Site 3 mi. N)
Famous pioneer sawmill, flour mill, and cotton gin. Built 1874 by Henry A. Chadwick and son, Milam. A sturdy oak dam across river supplied power. A millrace chiseled in sandstone channeled water to millstones. Mill and gin house were also sandstone. A fish trap in millrace offered food and sport to customers, who often had to wait several days for a turn at the mill. This scenic spot grew to be a popular resort around 1900, with hotel and dance platform. Attracted hundreds of campers. Change in course of river, 1915, forced mill to be abandoned. (1970)

LOMETA (Lampasas Co.) US 190 at US 183, .5 mi. W
C.S.A. Salt Works
Located between Tow Valley and Old Bluffton, 15 miles NE. Since 1935 under Lake Buchanan. During Civil War made salt for table, curing meat and hides, feeding cavalry horses. A day's boiling in 100 iron, 250-gallon kettles produced 20 to 30 bushels of salt. Cooled, sacked and hauled out, this met Texas' wartime shortages. First Llano County district court was held at salt works. Stagecoach stop was nearby. Brine here was from Cambrian sea waters trapped 500 million years ago in sand and strata. Indians led first settler here. (1964)

LOMETA (Lampasas Co.) US 190, 2 mi. W
Phantom Hill Road
In 1851–1852, in a major reorganization of the frontier defense system, the U.S. Army built a line of 7 forts between the Red River and the Rio Grande to protect the scattered remote settlements and travel routes to California. On Nov. 14, 1851, Fort Phantom Hill was established near present Abilene (120 miles NW) by Col. J. J. Abercrombie and the 5th Infantry. The Phantom Hill Road, the vital transportation and communication link between the fort and military headquarters at Austin (80 miles SE), was the first road in Lampasas County, and crossed at this site. Supply trains of up to 24 wagons drawn by mules, horses, and oxen passed along this route to the frontier fort. The road was used primarily by the military until the abandonment of Fort Phantom Hill on April 6, 1854, but also served as a thoroughfare for early settlers entering the region and continued in that capacity until after the Civil War. About 1870, traffic passing through the area was diverted to the Senterfitt Stage Station (1.5 miles SW), and this section of the road abandoned. Several isolated

segments of the Phantom Hill Road remain in use in the county, and physical evidence of the Emy's Creek Crossing (200 yards S) still exists. (1974)

LOMETA (Lampasas Co.) *US 190, S at city limits*
Scholten Railroad (Owned by the "Scholten Brothers Cedar Company")
A 25-mile narrow gauge railroad that operated about 1912–1920 from Lometa to San Saba County. Constructed by Edward and Alfred Scholten (from Holland). Line hauled cedar posts and piling to Santa Fe line at Lometa to be distributed to fast-growing West Texas. Employees totaled 500. Headquarters were located 100 yards west. (1968)

LOMETA (Lampasas Co.) *US 190 S to Lometa Regional Park*
Operation Longhorn
The close of World War II brought new tensions to America that led to the Cold War. Under fear of communism and nuclear assault, the U.S. Army and Air Force simulated a war in one of the largest maneuvers ever to be staged on American soil. Called Operation Longhorn, the simulation included thwarting an invasion and recovering from an atomic attack. To carry out the mock war, which began in late March 1952, ranchers between Waco and San Angelo signed easements to their land. Several Lometa-area ranches became sites of battles and campgrounds as more than 115,000 troops came to Texas for maneuvers. The town's population grew from 900 to 22,000, and the troops and supporting civilian staff members faced life in a small town. Local residents cooperated and participated by rationing and trading with troops, offering facilities for a mock U.S.O. (United Service Organizations) facility and attending programs and presentations given by soldiers. Such programs included an airdrop of 2,500 troops, as well as weapons, equipment and rations, in a training maneuver that pitted the 31st Infantry, 47th Infantry, and 1st Armored Division against the 82nd Airborne Division out of Fort Bragg, North Carolina. In a nationally publicized event, aggressor forces captured and occupied Lampasas (17 mi. SE), establishing mock control of media and setting curfews. The city was liberated near the end of the simulation on April 9, 1952. The $3,300,000 exercise left local residents with damaged ranch land, outbuildings, fences and gates, as well as spooked livestock, but also gave them an opportunity to experience war in their own community. (2004)

LONDON (Kimble Co.) *US 377, 1.5 mi. SW*
Reichenau Gap
For more than 100 years, travelers followed the road from Mason to Junction through this pass. Named for Adolph A. Reichenau, a German emigrant who settled near pass in 1860 as an early landholder in nearby Big Saline Valley. He moved in 1866 because of Indian depredations. (1966)

LONDON (Kimble Co.) *US 377*
London Town Square
Planned as a court square of proposed county. Platted about 1878 by Postmaster Len L. Lewis, whose town name choice, "Betty Lewis" (for his wife), was vetoed by postal authorities. "London" is thought to have been proposed by the Pearl family, for their old Kentucky home town. On the western cattle trail, London had trail drivers as residents and sold supplies to crews passing with longhorn herds. Businesses in early days: blacksmith shop, stores, cotton gin. Also there were 3 churches and a school. Coke R. Stevenson, 1941–47 Texas Governor, lived here as a child. (1971)

LONE STAR (Morris Co.) *US 259 S near Big Cypress Bridge*
Site of Old Spearman's Ferry (1 mi. W)
Operated along with a mill by E. B. Smith during the Republic of Texas. Bought by John Spearman in 1850. At this site in 1870 the state authorized a toll bridge. Fees ranged from 2¢ for a sheep to $1 for an 8-horse team and loaded wagon. This was at Big Cypress Bayou on Pittsburg-Jefferson Stage Road. (1966)

LONE STAR (Morris Co.) *Main St. (US 259) at FM 250*
Iron Bluff Cemetery
Livingston Skinner (1795–1874) came to this part of Texas from Georgia in the early 1840s with his wife, Hedidah "Jodie" (Hughes) (1806–1881), and their children. The Iron Bluff Cemetery began as a family cemetery at the northwest corner of their property. The first marked burial in the graveyard dates to 1853 and is that of the Skinners' daughter E. F. (Emily). They buried her sister

N. E. A. (Amanda) here the following year. Other family members interred here include son William Moses Skinner (1832–1907), a Confederate veteran, and daughter Sarah Ann and her husband Joseph D. Lilly (1816–1860), who was a Texas Ranger as well as the first sheriff of Titus County. Residents of Lone Star began using the burial ground, which once was also the site of the Iron Bluff Schoolhouse. Among those buried here are numerous veterans of the Civil War, and landowner Livingston Skinner, a veteran of the War of 1812 and the Creek Indian Wars of 1813–14, as well as veterans of World War II, the Korean Conflict and Vietnam. Iron Bluff Cemetery serves as an important link to these veterans and to generations of other area residents who played important roles in the area's history. (2005)

LONGVIEW (Gregg Co.) *US 80 at FM 3272, 7 mi. W*
Cherokee Trace
In 1821 near this site, Cherokee Indians blazed a trail from near Nacogdoches, Texas, to their home reservation at White River, Ark. They slashed trees, cleared path, planted "Cherokee" roses, and established camps at springs. Used by Sam Houston, friend of the Cherokees, on his move to Texas; by David Crockett, other soldiers of the Texas Revolution, and thousands of immigrants. After June 1839, when Texas settlers drove the Cherokees out of the state, the Indians departed over this trail; others traveled it for years thereafter. (1967)

LONGVIEW (Gregg Co.) *US 80 at Fisher Rd., 3 mi. W*
Longview
Named for "long view" from rock hill when in 1870 surveyors laid off townsite. Incorporated June 24, 1871. Became county seat of Gregg County, and railroad, agricultural and lumber center. Early home of Governors Thos. M. Campbell and James S. Hogg. Since nearby 1931 Lathrop Well discovery extended East Texas oil field—world's largest—has become oil, financial, industrial, medical, cultural, religious hub. Home of Letourneau College, combination technical school and industrial plant, producing some of the world's largest equipment. (1965)

LONGVIEW (Gregg Co.) *US 80, 2 mi. W*
Rockwall Farm
Large colonial home built 50 yards north, 1854. Overnight stop on Wm. T. Brooks' stagecoach line from Monroe, La., to Tyler. From here, mail went to Earpville, a site now in Longview. Slaves hewed lumber, made the chimney blocks from trees and clay on the place. The first floor partitions folded away to make big ballroom. The black walnut coffin built for house owner John Harris was favored table for poker upstairs. Last owners, J. Roy Sparkman and Jack Castleberry families, restored, opened to visitors. House burned in 1952. (1964)

LONGVIEW (Gregg Co.) *US 80 at North High*
Gregg County
Formed from Rusk and Upshur Counties. Created April 12, 1873. Organized June 28, 1873. Named in honor of General John Gregg (1828–1864), delegate to Secession Convention and to the Provisional Congress of the Southern Confederacy. A Confederate officer. Longview, the county seat. (1965)

LONGVIEW (Gregg Co.) *IH 20 at FM 2087, .6 mi. W*
Old Fredonia Townsite
The community of Fredonia was founded by Haden Edwards, a land grantee who contracted in 1825 with the Mexican government to establish 800 families of settlers in East Texas. A later misunderstanding with Mexico caused him to organize the famous Fredonian Rebellion and flee to the U.S. in 1827 in failure. The town of Fredonia prospered, though, as an important ferry crossing and river port. The numerous structures built by residents included a brick kiln, homes and warehouses, mainly for cotton. After the Civil War, the population declined and the post office closed. Residents abandoned the town after it was bypassed by the railroad circa 1870. (2005)

LOPEÑO (Zapata Co.) *US 83 right-of-way in Lopeño*
Old Lopeño
Development of this area began about 1749 when Col. José de Escandón began bringing colonists to establish permanent settlements along Mexico's northern frontier. When parcels of land were granted to the colonists by the Spanish government in 1767, Ysabel María Sanchez, widow of

early settler and rancher Joseph López, was allotted more than 6,000 acres. The village of Lopeño that later developed on part of the land was named in honor of the López family. During the early 1800s, part of the López land passed to the ownership of the Ramírez family, founders of the nearby village of Falcón. In 1821, Benito Ramírez built a combination home, fort, and chapel that later came to be called Fort Lopeño. Federal troops briefly occupied the fort during 1856 while in the area helping to ease border disturbances. The general store established in Lopeño in the early 1900s by Seraffin Benavides served as the area's only supply point at the time. A post office was established in 1920, and in 1934 oil and gas wells were successfully drilled just outside the village. When Falcon Reservoir was created in 1952, residents relocated their village to this site. (1984)

LOTT (Falls Co.)
SH 320, 9 mi. S
Homesite of Theodore Rabroker, Founder of Westphalia Community
In 1866, Theodore Rabroker (1835–1905) and his wife Mary Ann (Brucktrops) (1836–1886) immigrated from Westphalia Province, Germany. They lived for a time in Pennsylvania and Iowa. In 1877, while moving to Frelsburg, Colorado County, Rabroker saw the fertile land in this area and visualized a German-Catholic community here. In 1879, he and his wife and three children became the first settlers. In 1881, Rabroker purchased 271 acres from William Neyland and became Neyland's land agent, encouraging Frelsburg families to come here. Rabroker provided a place for prospective residents to live until they bought property. Only German-Catholics were invited to settle within a five-mile radius; this resulted in strong community traditions. The Rev. John Lauth celebrated the first mass in 1882 in the Rabroker home (400 yds. W). The residence served as the center for village religious and civic activities until a church building was completed in February 1884. After a storm destroyed the structure in May, Rabroker led efforts to erect a new church edifice, completed in July 1884. After his first wife died, Rabroker married Theresa Halfman (1854–1932) and they had six children. The Rabroker home was destroyed by fire in 1975. (1979)

LOTT (Falls Co.)
SH 320 & Judge R. W. Bailey Dr.
Lott
Located on a straight line from Cameron to Waco, this site was the natural choice for development of a new town along the San Antonio and Aransas Pass Railroad in 1889. The Texas Townsite Company bought land from area pioneers Captain and Mrs. George H. Gassaway, who had purchased 7,000 acres in 1871. The railroad was given a right-of-way, and development began on a town, named in honor of railroad president Uriah Lott (1842–1915). As the construction crew worked to complete the rail line, businesses sprang to life in the new town. A post office was established, and the city was incorporated in a November 1890 election. City officers were elected in December, and Albert B. Hemphill became the first mayor. The Texas Townsite Company donated land to the town for a school and churches. The first school opened in 1890, followed by churches of several denominations. Fraternal organizations were established, and the Lott volunteer fire department was organized in 1895. Following the completion of the railroad, Lott experienced a time of rapid growth. Although the railroad route closed in 1949, (the town flourished.
(Texas Sesquicentennial 1836–1986)

LOVELADY (Houston Co.)
SH 19, 3 mi. N
Houston–Leon County Coal Company
The Houston County Coal and Manufacturing Company was formed in 1900 for the purpose of mining lignite. Near this site, a slope mine was opened and a company town named Wooters was established. Company founders were A. H. Wooters, D. A. Nunn, G. Q. King, and Eli Elkins; John LeGory joined as a principal partner in 1906. The early years of the company were difficult, as a market had to be found for lignite, a substance between peat and bituminous coal. Lignite was sold to power plants, gins and other facilities in East Texas. In 1907 land was purchased in Leon, Limestone and Freestone Counties, and additional mines were established in Evansville in Leon county. To reflect this expansion, the company name was changed to the Houston–Leon County Coal Company. During its peak years from 1916 to 1925, the company employed about 200 people. The miners represented a diverse mixture of cultures; some were recruited as they arrived on foreign vessels in Galveston. In 1932 the company was dissolved when natural gas changed the fuel market in Texas, though stockholders maintained diverse real estate holdings in the area. The lignite rights were retained by the owners, many of whom are descendants of the original stockholders. (1996)

285

LOVELADY (Houston Co.)   *SH 19, at park*
Town of Lovelady
Founded by Houston & Great Northern Railroad investors as line was built through grant of Cyrus Lovelady, near communities of Nevil's Prairie, Pennington, and Weldon. Post office opened on Nov. 8, 1872. Town soon had livery stables, stores, blacksmith shop, and hotels, prospering as market and shipping point. By 1876 day school and Sunday School were held in a log house. A two-story structure was shared 1881–1888 by Baptists and Lovelady Lodge No. 539, A. F. & A. M. Churches of other faiths were built later. The town, incorporated 1927, is now center for ranching, pulpwood production.   (1972)

LUBBOCK (Lubbock Co.)   *US 84, NW city limits*
Lubbock
Founded 1891. Named for Col. Thomas S. Lubbock, Texas Republic soldier and Civil War hero. Incorporated 1909. Commercial-marketing-processing heart of a mechanized-irrigated cotton, grain and cattle area. Home of Texas Tech, Lubbock Christian College, West Texas Museum, Mackenzie State Park.

LUBBOCK (Lubbock Co.)   *US 84, .5. mi. NW of Loop 289 overpass*
Lubbock Lake Site
This bend in the Yellowhouse Canyon has seen the passing of many from the time of the prehistoric mammoth-hunting Llano culture of 12,000 years ago. An archeological site of great importance lies in the bottom of this valley; here is recorded the evidence of periodic visits by nomadic hunting groups and Plains Indians. Springs and water holes made this spot a favored hunting and camping site in prehistoric and early historic times, but it is noted mainly for providing the first radio-carbon date on the Folsom Culture of 10,000 years ago and the association of man-made artifacts with bones of extinct mammoths, horses, bison, and camels. Some historians think Coronado passed here in 1541 and Spanish expeditions coming from Santa Fe to the Concho River looking for fresh-water pearls passed this way in the middle 1600s. Later visitors were buffalo hunters and Indian fighters in the 1870s. A general store—first commercial building in the area—was built here about 1880 by George W. Singer. Patronized by ranchers, cowboys, and dwindling numbers of buffalo hunters and friendly Indians, Singer's became a post office in 1884 and a widely known landmark by 1885. The first building burned, 1886.   (1970)

LUBBOCK (Lubbock Co.)   *IH 27/US 87, 1 mi. N of Loop 289*
Site of Old Lubbock
A predecessor of present Lubbock, this area was, in 1890, a subject of heated dispute by three factions (led by W. D. Crump, W. E. Rayner, and Frank Wheelock) that vied in the founding of the county seat. Unlike most county seat debaters in Texas, though, these men had no long-established town to support. Their main interest was in organizing the county. In the course of the rivalry, the groups founded two settlements. The Crump faction, later joined by the Wheelock group and several financial backers, started "Old Lubbock" at this site. Called "North Town" because it was located north of Yellow House Canyon, the site took in section 7, Block A, bounded by the present streets of Quirt, Ash, Erskine, and Kent. The site soon attained a population of about 50 and boasted a reported 37 buildings, including the most historic one in the county: the Nicolett Hotel. Rayner's rival settlement south of the canyon was named "Monterey" and was popularly called "South Town." Surprisingly, though, the factions did not reach the permanent hostility common to such disputes. On December 19, 1890, they united in a compromise unique in West Texas history; and as a result, the city of Lubbock was founded on the site where it now stands.   (1968)

LUBBOCK (Lubbock Co.)   *IH 27 frontage rd. at Municipal Dr.,*
                                                            Mackenzie Park
General Ranald Slidell Mackenzie
Born in New York City on July 24, 1840, Mackenzie attained the rank of major general during the Civil War. On February 25, 1871, at Fort Concho, Texas, he assumed command as colonel of the 4th Cavalry, which soon became the finest regiment in the army. He commanded three expeditions into this region against the Indians. The first, in 1871 against the Comanches, was unsuccessful; but in 1872 he found two feasible routes across the vast, hitherto unexplored Llano Estacado; and

on September 29, he defeated the Comanches on the north fork of the Red River. After a successful raid into Mexico in 1873, he commanded three of five columns of army troops in a final campaign against the Comanches, Kiowas, and southern Cheyennes; and on September 28, 1874, he surprised and destroyed three of their villages in the depths of Palo Duro Canyon, also capturing 1,424 horses and mules in the engagement. Left without food, shelter, supplies and horses, the Southern Plains tribes then submitted to life on the reservation, thereby opening Western Texas to white settlement. Later promoted to brigadier general, Mackenzie died in New York, January 19, 1889, and was buried in West Point Cemetery. This park is named in his honor. (1968)

LUBBOCK (Lubbock Co.)

3121 4th St., Ranching Heritage Center, Texas Tech Campus

The Free Range Era of Ranching, Northwest Texas, 1878–1885

After Indians and buffalo were removed in 1870s, several hundred cattlemen with small herds came to rolling plains near site of later Lubbock, to graze free range. Vital natural water sources were found east of the caprock, where springs and streams were fed from the Ogallala formation of the High Plains. Here, with good years and rising prices, the free rangers prospered until 1884, when syndicates began purchasing land and enclosing large blocks with barbed wire. Free range men had to sell their herds to the syndicates or move farther west. The Spur Ranch alone acquired over 500,000 acres of land and bought cattle and brands from 37 of the free rangers. Similar ranches were developed by the Curry Comb, Ioa, Jumbo, Long S, Magnolia, Matador, Pitchfork, Square and Compass, T Bar and Two Buckle interests. By 1885, all free range operations were transformed into large, enclosed ranches. Some free rangers exchanged cattle for stock in syndicates, others were employed by syndicates, and a few moved to Arizona, New Mexico or Wyoming. A few—including the Edwards, Long, and Slaughter families—acquired land and became sizable operators. (1970)

LUBBOCK (Lubbock Co.)

1st St. at Ave. K

Migrant Labor Camps of Lubbock County

Early Hispanic residents of frontier Lubbock County included ranch hands in the 1880s. Railroad lines brought many workers to the South Plains, the majority recruited from El Paso. Rail companies built row houses near construction sites, and Lubbock's rail labor camps became ethnic enclaves for Hispanic workers. One of the early settlements southwest of town was called Shipley's Railroad Camp. Cotton raising, which began as a side crop on area ranches, also attracted temporary labor as production increased. One field labor camp developed near the Slaton roundhouse. Cotton pickers from South Texas and Mexico arrived in a seasonal migration, although some found year-round ranch work. While on the migration circuit, Hispanic citizens lived in large labor camps throughout the county and along every major highway into Lubbock. In the city, a *barrio* called "Mexican Town" or the "Chihuahua District" developed in this locale. Standard homes were tents or simple structures, and the neighborhood was poverty-ridden and overcrowded. The Great Depression worsened living conditions for most residents but especially for the working poor. Mexican migrants and Hispanic citizens also faced segregated facilities including schools, theaters and restaurants. In 1948 the city council paid for a corrugated metal building at the largest camp as a labor recruiting site. In May 1970, a tornado destroyed much of the neighborhood, and of the twenty-six people killed nearly half were *barrio* residents. By 2000, Hispanics made up about one-third of the city population and one-half of the public school enrollment. Lubbock also boasted dozens of Hispanic organizations advocating for business, civil rights, leadership, families, the arts, youth and education. Aztlan Park is the site of the former migrant labor camp. (2008)

LUBBOCK (Lubbock Co.)

2004 W. 19th St. (US 82)

Lubbock High School

The city of Lubbock experienced a significant increase in population during the 1920s as it became the agricultural, educational, service, and trade center of the South Plains. This high school was built out of the need for providing an education for the young people of the rapidly growing community. Designed by the Lubbock architectural firm of Peters, Strange and Bradshaw, the original building consists of two- and three-story classroom wings, offices, a gymnasium, and an auditorium, all constructed around two open courtyards. Over the years, as Lubbock's population increased, the facilities were expanded several times to meet the need. The richly ornamented, North Italian Romanesque style high school was completed in 1931, despite the beginnings of economic hardship resulting from the onset of the Great Depression. The building features decorative brickwork, terra cotta ornamentation, and a campanile, or bell tower. Lubbock High stands as a significant example of institutional architecture in Texas, as well as a local landmark known for its many students who became Lubbock's outstanding civic and community leaders. (1984)

LUBBOCK (Lubbock Co.) — 6105 W. 19th St. (US 82)
Bledsoe Santa Fe Depot

A relic from one of America's last frontiers. Built in 1925 on range land of newly organized Cochran County, at Bledsoe, this structure not only served its purpose as a railroad station, but was a meeting hall for churches and social groups. Sheepherders and cowboys would bed down on its floor when detained at the station in shipping season. Phased out of service by 1966, structure was moved 70 miles to be preserved by Gene Hemmle. (1973)

LUBBOCK (Lubbock Co.) — SH 114, W of Loop 289
Carlisle Cemetery

The pioneer Carlisle community was named for W. Augustus "Uncle Gus" Carlisle (1849–1920), who settled here with his wife Lizzie (Spikes) (d. 1914) in 1890. A cattleman and a prominent land-owner, Carlisle made significant contributions to the development of the area, including a donation of land for a school. In 1918, he set aside this part of his property for use as a public cemetery. It was first used for the burial of George W. Wood (b. 1879), a victim of the 1920 influenza epidemic. Other graves include those of pioneers, area settlers and early leaders of Carlisle. (1983)

LUFKIN (Angelina Co.) — US 59, 9 mi. N near Angelina River Bridge
Don Joaquín Crossing on Bedias Trail

Used by Indians, explorers, traders, and missionaries, this trail ran from Bedias Indian camps on the lower Trinity River to Spanish missions near Nacogdoches. Don Joaquín de Orobio y Basterra, captain of the presidio at La Bahia (present Goliad), led reconnaissance troops along trail in 1746 and gave his name to the Angelina River Crossing. Italian born trader Vincente Michiuli owned a large ranch near the crossing before 1800. Bedias Trail was important in Angelina County's development. Railroads and major highways later followed the trail's route. (1979)

LUFKIN (Angelina Co.) — US 59 at CR 110, 4 mi. N
Redland Baptist Church

Liberty Baptist Church, established in the Redland community in 1859, became Redland Baptist Church after reorganizing in 1895. Worship services were held in a local schoolhouse until 1924 when the congregation built its first sanctuary. A new church building was erected in 1939, and in 1942 the first full-time pastor was called. Growth in church membership resulted in the construction of new facilities in 1960 and a larger sanctuary at this site in 1976. Redland Baptist serves the community with a variety of programs and supports a wide range of missionary work. (1994)

LUFKIN (Angelina Co.) — SH 103, 17 mi. E
Ewing

The boom town of Ewing stood for two decades on the west bank of the Angelina River. Named for plantation owner James A. Ewing, the town was located near a rail line and virgin hardwood forests. In 1919, H. G. Bohlssen purchased a 100-acre tract of land and built a sawmill. A company town, Ewing grew rapidly and at its peak contained a post office, commissary, church/school, boarding house, and a population of 850. After many men left to serve in World War II, or in war related industries, the mill closed in December 1944. (1997)

LUFKIN (Angelina Co.) — SH 103, 3 mi. E
Southland Paper Mills, Inc.

First plant to turn southern pines into newsprint, mill here revolutionized paper industry in the Southern United States. Seeking local paper rather than foreign supplies, Southland was incorporated in 1938 and began operations, 1940. Its mills made possible use of southern pine (earlier rejected for newsprint because of its high resin content). In 1942, additional facilities were built to supply bleached pulp. Success of this pioneer complex gave Texas an avenue for aiding world in supply of vital paper. (1968)

LUFKIN (Angelina Co.)　　　　　　　　　2221 N. Raguet St. (SH 339)
German POWs in the East Texas Timber Industry
The U.S. Army began building POW camps in the United States in early 1942 for captured Axis prisoners. During World War II, the Army shipped almost 425,000 military prisoners to 511 camps in the U.S. Approximately 50,000 of those POWs, primarily Germans, were housed in 70 Texas facilities ranging from 9000-prisoner base camps to small branch camps for 250. The POWs filled American labor shortages brought on by the war's strain on available stateside man power. In Texas almost half of the camps provided agricultural workers for rice and cotton fields. Texas businessmen requested another 12 camps for help in the timber industry. Most of these were set up to salvage lumber and pulpwood from a severe ice storm in January 1944. The headquarters for the salvage work was Lufkin, the only Texas town to have two POW camps during the war. The original POW camp, known as Camp Number 1 was located just north of the city on U.S. Hwy 69. Southland Paper Mills, led by Ernest Kurth, S. W. Henderson and Arthur Temple, leased an abandoned CCC camp from the U.S. Forest Service. Construction of the camp began in November 1943 and it officially opened on February 15, 1944. The camp's 300 German prisoners produced pulpwood until it closed in 1946. Southland's success with POW labor encouraged other lumber companies to follow suit. Southland established Camp Number 2 in late April 1944 at the county fairgrounds, one mile southeast of town, where the Lufkin school district later established schools. It operated briefly in 1944 to provide labor for salvaging ice-damaged timber. The Army housed the 500 prisoners at the camp in cement and wood dorms. Camp Number 2 closed in September 1944.
(2006)

LUFKIN (Angelina Co.)　　　　　　　　　　　　SH 94 at Ellis Ave.
Lufkin CCC Camp
Created by President Franklin Roosevelt and approved by an Act of Congress in 1933, the Civilian Conservation Corps (CCC) provided youth employment programs during the Great Depression. The Lufkin CCC Camp, located near this site from 1933 until 1942, was administered by the Texas Forest Service. Young men helped to build roads and bridges, string telephone lines, and plant trees. The Lufkin CCC Camp proved to be instrumental in relieving unemployment but also helped revive the East Texas forest industry through its use of progressive forestry techniques.
(1984)

LUFKIN (Angelina Co.)　　　　　　　　First St. and Frank Ave. (SH 94)
Lufkin Telephone Exchange
Telephone service in Lufkin began in 1898 when Dr. Alexander Madison Denman and his friend Judge Edwin James Mantooth strung telephone wires between their offices. The system was so popular that the pair soon formed the Lufkin Telephone Exchange with partner Eli Wiener, operating from offices on this site. In 1908 they contracted with the Southwestern Telegraph and Telephone Company to provide long distance service. The company grew as rapidly as telephone technology itself, eventually acquiring the telephone exchanges of a large portion of East Texas. In 1985 the corporation was reorganized as the Lufkin-Conroe Telephone Exchange.
(1998)

LUFKIN (Angelina Co.)　　　　　　　　　US 59S Bus. at Tulane St.
City of Lufkin
Founded 1882. Soon became a thriving sawmill community. Named for E. P. Lufkin, chief of crew that surveyed railroad through town. Has been county seat of Angelina County since 1892. Now a regional manufacturing and commerce center. Products include paper and wood products, oilfield pumps, trailers, and foundry castings.
(1970)

LUFKIN (Angelina Co.)　　　　　　　　805 E. Denman Ave. (SH 278)
First United Methodist Church of Lufkin
Margaret (Fullerton) Abney, born in Alabama in 1829, joined the Methodist Church with her family at a camp meeting held at nearby McKendree Campground in 1863. Because the nearest Methodist church was ten miles away, Mrs. Abney held Bible study meetings in her home on Sunday afternoons. This group of Abney family and friends formed the nucleus of the membership of the Methodist Episcopal Church, South, when it organized a Lufkin congregation in 1882. One of eight churches in the Homer circuit, the congregation met once a month in a local school building to hear the sermons of the Reverend H. H. Vaughan. In 1884 a 200-seat frame church building was erected in downtown Lufkin on land donated by the railroad. The building was shared with local

Presbyterians and Baptists. By 1891, membership had grown to 100 and the pastor held services twice a month. Ten years later, the membership numbered 286 and the pastor was serving full-time. Completed in 1905 at a cost of $14,750, a new sanctuary seated more than 800 people. The church prospered, requiring an educational building by 1928. Despite the difficult times of the Depression era and World War II, the congregation continued to grow, and the church was relocated to Denman Avenue in 1959. By 1978, when the congregation celebrated the 100 years since Mrs. Abney began her Sunday School, the church complex included six buildings. The First United Methodist Church of Lufkin continues an active tradition of community and missionary service.   (1998)

LUFKIN (Angelina Co.)   US 69, .5 mi. SE
Angelina County
Created and organized in 1846. Originally a part of Nacogdoches county. Bears the name of the river traversing the region. The following towns have served as the county seat: Marion, 1846–1854; Jonesville, 1854–1858; Homer, Feb. 3–May 17, 1858; when its name was changed to Angelina, 1858–1890; Lufkin, 1890.   (1963)

LUFKIN (Angelina Co.)   US 69, 12 mi. SE
Site of the Town of Jonesville
Second county seat of Angelina County, August 22, 1854–May 19, 1858.   (1964)

LULING (Guadalupe Co.)   US 90 right-of-way, 3 mi. W
San Marcos Primitive Baptist Church
The San Marcos Primitive Baptist Church, so named because of its proximity to the San Marcos River, was organized in 1853 at the home of George Daniels, who also served as the congregation's first pastor. The five charter members of the church were William Baker, Vashti Baker, Hannah Daniels, I. D. Owen, and Sylvanna Daniels. George Daniels served as pastor until 1862, when James Milton Baker (1831–1910) began his 48-year service as minister of the San Marcos Church. A native of Alabama, Baker was the son of charter members William and Vashti Baker. The family had come from Alabama to Texas in 1852 and had settled in this area during the following year. The first church building and early records of the church were destroyed in a flash flood that probably occurred in 1869 or 1870, but the congregation continued to meet. In 1886, J. M. Baker deeded land at this site for the church and cemetery. In 1930, the San Marcos Primitive Baptist Church moved to Luling (3 mi. E) but continued to meet here occasionally until 1970. This historic site serves as a reminder of the heritage of the Luling congregation.   (1985)

LULING (Caldwell Co.)   US 183 at E. Austin St.
Edgar B. Davis, Oil Pioneer-Philanthropist
(Feb. 2, 1872–Oct. 14, 1951)
One of the great benefactors of Texas. Born in Brockton, Mass. Had business careers in shoe manufacture and rubber planting. On retirement, came here and in wildcat operation brought in Luling Oil Field, 1922. By 1926 had 215 producing wells. Gave employees $2,500,000 in bonuses, then endowed Luling Foundation, for advancement of agriculture and human opportunity in area. Result has been conservation of land, upbreeding of crops and livestock and introduction and marketing of superior products. Davis remained in this area and is buried near Luling.   (1969)

LULING (Caldwell Co.)   US 183N at Blanche Square
William Johnson Cabin
The Rev. William Johnson (1822–1889), farmer and Baptist minister who came to Texas in 1833, built this shotgun-style cabin near Tenney Creek (11 mi. NE of Luling) in 1870s. Family included five children. His son, W. E. (Billie) became a physician in Tilmon. Since 1893 the Jeff Connolly family has owned Johnson's land. T. B. Coopwood, M.D., used cabin as office in late 1890s. Mr. and Mrs. Jeff Connolly donated structure in 1972 to be relocated here.   (1973)

LUTIE (Collingsworth Co.)   US 83, 3 mi. N
Nicholson School
Once the center of a thriving agricultural community, Nicholson school was named for county judge Arthur Clyde Nicholson, during whose term the school was opened in 1915. As Nicholson school increased in enrollment, reaching a peak of 150 students in 1929, additional teachers and classrooms were added. Consolidation with other rural schools began in 1934 and was completed

in 1937, when the last classes at Nicholson school were held. A concrete cellar near this site is all that remains of the original school property. (1984)

LUTIE (Collingsworth Co.)   FM 1439 at US 83
Site of Lutie School
The community of Lutie, named for early settler Lutie Gresham Templeton, traces its history to 1909. Two years previously, local citizens had formed the Pleasant Valley School about one mile northeast of the town site. Community leaders moved the school to Lutie in 1912, renamed it and added a room. A third room was added in 1929, and the school continued to serve area children until 1937, when it consolidated with the school in Samnorwood (4 mi. NW). Land where the school was located reverted back to the family of the original donor, John Henry Young, Sr. (1874–1950). (1992)

LYONS (Burleson Co.)   SH 36, north edge of town
Lyons
An 1878 railway work camp; in 1880 became town of Lyon's Station, named for site donor, W. A. Lyon. Soon had 3 cotton gins, an oil mill, many businesses. In 1894 hosted first auto ever seen in this county, with rides for the daring. Now gateway to Lake Somerville Recreation Area.(1968)

MABANK (Kaufman Co.)   US 175 Bus. at W Market St.
Mabank
Originally part of the George T. Walters Survey, this acreage in the 1840s and '50s belonged to many absentee landowners including Sam Houston. In 1887 John R. Jones, a merchant from nearby Goshen, and his wife Joella platted and developed a town called "Lawn City" (1 mi. NE). Soon a post office was established and the name changed to "Lawndale". When the Texas & New Orleans Railroad bypassed Lawndale in 1900 on its route from Kemp to Athens, it ran through the northern part of the Mason-Eubank Ranch. The owners, Thomas H. Eubank (1859–1952) and rancher-banker G. W. ("Dodge") Mason (1858–1917), set aside one square mile of their holdings for a town. The name "Mabank" was formed by combining the names of the two landowners. Lawndale families and merchants began moving to Mabank. The town grew rapidly, boasting a park, depot, and stock loading pens. There was a gin, post office, cafe, hotel, and several mercantile businesses. Later, church lots were set aside for Baptist, Methodist and Presbyterian congregations. The Baptist church erected a building for a community house and school. The economy of the area depended first on farming and later on ranching. The 1966 development of Cedar Creek Lake strengthened the community. (1979)

MADISONVILLE (Madison Co.)   SH 21, 1 mi. SW of courthouse
CCC Camp Site
A part of the National Civilian Conservation Corps program of the New Deal era, Camp Sam Houston in Madisonville was a soil conservation camp. Begun in July 1935 and occupied by workers one month later, the camp provided jobs for 196 men. Members of the camp worked with area farmers and ranchers, demonstrating techniques of soil erosion control and pasture management. Covering a radius of 21 miles, CCC improvement projects included all of Madison County, as well as portions of Grimes, Leon, and Walker Counties. The camp was closed in 1941. (1988)

MADISONVILLE (Madison Co.)   901 N May (SH 75)
Madison County
Formed from Grimes, Walker and Leon counties. Created January 27, 1853. Organized April 4, 1853. Named in honor of James Madison (1751–1836), "Father of the Constitution," fourth President of the United States. County seat, Madisonville.

MADISONVILLE (Madison Co.)   SH 90 right-of-way, 3 mi. S at Ranch Lane
Site of Bullard Community (3 miles east)
Alabama native Calvin Cullee Bullard (1824–1882) brought his family to this area from Hunt County, Texas, in 1867 and settled on 160 acres of land between Bedias Creek and Caney Creek. In their new home, he and his second wife, Zillah (Woodbury), reared three of Bullard's children from his first marriage and six of their own. Calvin Bullard had a blacksmith shop in the community that bears his name, and several of his descendants followed in his footsteps. The Bullards were also farmers, as were other families in the area, raising cotton as their primary cash crop. Active beyond

their community, Calvin E. Bullard served a term as county tax assessor-collector and Rube Bullard was a justice of the peace and five-term Madison County commissioner. A one-room schoolhouse was built in the Bullard community to address the educational needs of the neighboring children. It operated from 1890 until 1923. Worship services were held in the schoolhouse, as well as in an outdoor brush arbor when the weather permitted. Calvin and Zillah Bullard and many of their descendants are buried in the Bethel Cemetery in nearby Grimes County. Their contributions to Madison County history as early settlers and the founders of a community reflect the settlement patterns in this part of Texas and remain an important part of the area's history. (2001)

MALONE (Hill Co.)
SH 171 at FM 308
German Settlers in Hill County
Germans first came to Texas in 1821, immigrated by the hundreds in the 1840s, and in the 1880s began to move into Hill County. Here land was made available by such earlier settlers as G. W. McNeese, the Savage family, A. D. Walling, the Whites, the Worleys. First to arrive (1882) were Fritz Lentz and Alex Radke. Later came families named Degner, Dietz, Gehrels, Gehring, Geltmeier, Hodde, Huse, Kaddatz, Kelm, Klein, Klinert, Krueger, Kunkel, Maas, Manske, Manthei, Meyer, Neumann, Piel, Reinke, Schronk, Schulz, Sonnenberg, Schmidt, Steffer, Strauch, and Zettler. Pastor J. C. Rieger came from West (16 mi. SW) and held church services in settlers' homes. Salem Lutheran congregation was organized with 15 charter members on June 6, 1886, and erected a church building three months later. St. Peter's Lutheran Church was founded July 1, 1906, at Walling with nine charter members. Religious leaders (some of whom also taught in the parochial school) have included Pastors Bartel, Finke, Gaertner, Heinmeier, Hodde, Hopmann, Kramer, Liefer, Manchina, Oertel, Seils, Walters, and Wunderlich. By diligence and thrift, these people made garden spots of their farms; and with love of God, of family, and of music, they created a goodly heritage. (1974)

MANKINS (Archer Co.)
US 82 in Mankins
The D. S. Dudley Show
Founded in late 19th or early 20th century as a Wild West circus, the D. S. Dudley Show has been chief industry in Mankins for over half a century. Dick "Cheyenne" Dudley (born in 1896), a prize-winning bronco rider, bought the show in 1914, interrupted his career to serve overseas in the U.S. Army in World War I, came back and married Ruth Wolf of Mankins. Together they toured the Southwest with the show 8 months of the year, employing as many as 250 people, wintering here with their exotic animals. Younger generations of their family continue with the show. (1974)

MANOR (Travis Co.)
Loop 212 in Manor
City of Manor
In area first settled by James Manor (1804–1881), who came from Tennessee with Sam Houston in 1832, later returning for his family and a sister and brother. Until 1852, area was subject to Indian raids. Other pioneers included A. F., W. M., and James Boyce, Sterling Chamberlain, Dave Eppright, J. I. Haynes, Ed Harrington, A. C. and W. H. Hill, W. B. Howse, N. A. Rector, W. L. Shipp, E. D. Townes, and Joe, Bill, Sam, and Walter Vaughan. In 1854, a boys' school was opened and a Methodist church organized. Isaac Wilbahn (1857) gave site, and Parsons Female Academy (named for a leading contributor) was established, to become one of the celebrated schools of 19th century Texas. Its teachers included the Rev. and Mrs. D. H. Bittle, and T. C. Bittle; its students, T. B. Wheeler (1840–1913), Mayor of Austin (1872–1877), Judge of 12th District (1880–1886), Lieutenant Governor of Texas (1887–1891); and John C. Townes (1852–1923), Judge of 33rd District (1882–1885), 26th District (1888), and Dean of the University of Texas Law School (1901–1902, 1907–1923). In 1871, James Manor donated right of way for the Houston & Texas Central Railroad. The town founded and named for him in 1872 was incorporated in 1913. Cotton, king here for years, has been supplanted by cattle raising as base for the local economy. (1972)

MARATHON (Brewster Co.)
US 90 at US 385, 1 mi. E at roadside park
Denuded Ouachita Rock Belt
In highway cuts toward the east are excellent exposures of almost vertical rock layers—part of the Ouachita Fold Belt, a northeasterly trending, folded and faulted mountainous range which was uplifted about 275 to 290 million years ago. The deformation is comparable in age to the uplift that formed the Appalachian Range of the Eastern United States. The term "Ouachita" for

this earth formation comes from the Ouachita Mountains of Arkansas and Oklahoma. (These were named by the Indians, whose words were rendered into written language by 16th century French explorers.) In the hillside toward the northeast, the highly deformed strata are overlaid by almost horizontal layers of "younger" rock—formed about 135 million years ago. Erosion wore down the old mountains; and when the area was again covered by the sea, the horizontal layers were deposited on the sea floor. Later uplifting earth movement comparable in age to the forming of the Rocky Mountain Range gently elevated this area, exposing it to erosional forces which have shaped the topography seen today. This region abounds in vivid lessons in geology, and is under constant study by scientists. (1970)

MARATHON (Brewster Co.) US 90, 1 mi. E
Marathon
Fort Pena Colorado, the last active fort in this area, on the Old Comanche Trail, about 4 miles to the southwest was established in 1879. Marathon was founded in 1881. Named by an old sea captain, A. E. Shepard, for the Plain of Marathon, in Greece, of which the hills here reminded him. Cradle of West Texas cattle industry. Among the first noted ranchers here were Mayer M. Halff and brother, owners of the famous Circle Dot brand. Original gateway to the Big Bend National Park. (1965)

MARATHON (Brewster Co.) US 385 at US 90 E
Colonel Lewis Given Harman (1818–1902)
Typical of those who served the South and then moved into new counties of western Texas. Surveyor, Indian agent, soldier, legislator, justice of the peace. Born in Tennessee. Moved to Texas 1838. Fought in Mexican War. Though 43 when Civil War began, immediately joined 11th Texas Cavalry, in swift 1861 campaign to place Confederate Forts in Indian Territory. Was post commander, Fort Arbuckle, I. T., June to August 1861. Civic leader in Marathon after its founding in 1882. Had town's first Masonic funeral. (1964)

MARATHON (Brewster Co.) 102 NW 1st St. (US 90W)
The Gage Hotel
This brick hotel building, designed by the El Paso firm of Trost and Trost, was constructed in 1926–1927 for Vermont native Alfred S. Gage. A cattleman, Gage founded the largest ranching operation in the Trans-Pecos, consisting of over 600 sections of land. After moving to San Antonio, where he became a successful businessman and banker, the hotel served as his Marathon residence and as the headquarters for his local cattle and banking interests. (1981)

MARATHON (Brewster Co.) US 385, 12 mi. S
Los Caballos (In Core of the Ouachita Structural Belt)
Highly deformed rocks in the Ouachita Fold Belt, a northeasterly trending range, uplifted about 275 to 290 million years ago. The intricate folding is shown by whitish rock bands—called caballos (the Spanish word for horses)—exposed on both sides of this highway. The Ouachita Fold is comparable in age to the uplift that formed the Appalachians in the eastern part of the United States. The northwesterly trending Del Norte-Santiago Range (southmost extension of the Rocky Mountains) forms the southwestern skyline. The rocks of this range were deposited in a sea that covered the Ouachita Fold Belt after erosion had reduced the highlands and a later submergence lowered the area. Santiago Peak (named for a local man who was killed by Indians and buried beneath the peak) is the high, flat-topped mountain to the southwest. It was once a mass of molten magma that cooled and hardened underneath the earth's surface and was uncovered by later erosion. The Del Norte-Santiago Range, uplifted and folded 40 to 60 million years ago, is not half the age of the Ouachita Fold. This is a remarkable fusion of "old" and "young" mountains—and is unmatched at any other site in North America. (1976)

MARATHON (Brewster Co.) US 385, 35 mi. S on Maravillas Creek
Double Mills
A natural watering place in prehistoric times, as evidenced by artifacts found here. Used later by Indians and Spaniards on road from Northern Mexico. As Maravillas Creek developed from a draw into water channel, old water hole vanished. About 1900 an early rancher, George Miller, dug two wells and put up twin windmills. After that, site was called Double Mills. Became campsite for

ranchers driving cattle and horses from Mexico or the Chisos Mountains to railroad at Marathon. Also for wagon trains of ore; and for U.S. troops on border duty.   (1967)

MARATHON (Brewster Co.)   *US 385, 38 mi. S at Stillwell-Heath turnoff*
Black Gap Wildlife Management Area
Black Gap, a natural cleft in the basalt ridge northeast of the Sierra del Carmen, frames the headquarters site of the Black Gap Wildlife Management Area. Established in 1948, the "Gap" contains approximately 100,000 acres representative of the rugged Big Bend country—the typical arid, mountainous Southwest. Owned by the people of Texas and operated by the Game and Fish Commission, the area is the scene of research and developmental work dedicated to the conservation and restoration of wildlife species indigenous to the region. Mule deer, javelina, prong-horned antelope and scaled quail are among the principal game species managed. Work is in process to restore the bighorn sheep which, by the 1960s, were all but eliminated from Texas. Scientific land use practices, designed to increase the yield of natural foods for wildlife, have been instituted by the commission. Water retention and utilization is accomplished by the construction of water impoundments, diversion dams and "push ups" seeded with native vegetation. Research findings, through demonstrations and educational extension programs conducted on this Federal-State cooperative project, are available to surrounding landowners and others who are interested. Game surpluses produced on the Black Gap are harvested periodically by hunters under a controlled public hunt program.

MARATHON (Brewster Co.)   *US 385, 42 mi. S near entrance of*
Big Bend Nat'l Pk.
Comanche Trail
You are now traveling the Comanche Trail, blazed by Comanche Indians, en route from the Western Plains to Mexico, and traveled later by emigrants and soldiers. It extended south from the Horse Head Crossing of the Pecos by Comanche Springs (Fort Stockton) to the Rio Grande.

MARBLE FALLS (Burnet Co.)   *FM 1431, 1 mi. W*
Granite Mountain
This 866-foot dome of solid pink granite, covering 180 acres, contains the largest quarry of its kind in the United States. This mountain, like all granite formations, was once melted rock similar to lava. As the molten rock cooled thousands of feet below the earth's surface, it hardened into large crystals of quartz, feldspar, and several dark-colored minerals. Wherever strength, durability and beauty of finish are required, granite is a favored building stone. The mountain was part of a grant made to Texas colonist William Slaughter. The site became famous commercially when a dispute arose in the 1880s over the type of stone to be used in the Capitol in Austin. The issue was settled in 1885 when Governor John Ireland resisted demands to use non-native limestone. Following this decision, a special track was built to haul the granite to the rail line in Burnet. The stone was generously donated to the state by quarry owners G. W. Lacy, N. L. Norton, and W. H. Westfall. Today, granite from the quarry here is shipped to all parts of Texas, the U.S. and foreign countries for use in monuments, shafts, jetties, and buildings. It has been used in the Galveston Sea Wall and in new state office buildings near the Capitol in Austin.   (1979)

MARBLE FALLS (Burnet Co.)   *801 US 281, visitor center*
Marble Falls Depot
The town of Marble Falls was laid out in 1887. Texas Mining & Improvement Co. deeded land for a depot to Austin & Northwestern Railroad. This building was erected in 1893 and then Southern Pacific Railroad bought the line and property. Area residents gathered at the depot to visit and watch for the train. Excursions were offered and passenger service provided. Hogs, horses, cattle, cedar posts, cotton, pecans, and hides were shipped to market from here. In 1937, passenger service was discontinued and the depot was closed in 1968. It was moved to this site in 1976.   (1979)

MARBLE FALLS (Burnet Co.)   *819 7th St. at US 281*
Governor O. M. Roberts' House
President of the 1861 Secession Convention and a Confederate officer, Oran M. Roberts (1815–1898) served as Governor of Texas from 1879 to 1883. After leaving office, he became a

law professor at the University of Texas. He built this cottage at Third and Main Street and settled there after his retirement in 1893. Mr. and Mrs. H. E. Faubian bought the house in 1901 and moved it to this site. They altered the front porch and roofline, adding Victorian touches.　(1978)

MARBLE FALLS (Burnet Co.)　　US 281 at Third St.
The Roper Hotel
George C. and Elizabeth Roper constructed this double-galleried hotel building about 1888. In the growing town of Marble Falls, the Roper Hotel became a popular stop for visiting businessmen and dignitaries. It was purchased by W. F. Smith in 1926 and later operated as the Central Hotel and the Francis House. His son R. O. Smith, who became manager in the 1930s, later served as mayor of Marble Falls. The hotel remained in the Smith family until 1963.　(1981)

MARBLE FALLS (Burnet Co.)　　US 281, N of Colorado River Bridge
Marble Falls Factory Site
The potential of water power on the Colorado River led town developer Gen. Adam R. Johnson and Farmers Alliance members to build a cotton mill on this site in the 1890s. The two-story stone factory, 300 ft. long and 100 ft. wide, was erected for the Marble Falls Cotton and Woolen Co., formed in 1892. New machinery run by hydroelectric power was installed by the Marble Falls Textile Mills Co. in the 1920s. Woolen goods, surgical gauze, and air conditioners were made here before the factory was gutted by fire in 1964 and razed in 1971.　(1977)

MARFA (Presidio Co.)　　US 67/90, 13 mi. E
Paisano Pass
Legend recounts that two Spaniards meeting here greeted each other as "Mi Paisano" (My Countryman). First known to history when Juan Dominguez de Mendoza camped here on January 3, 1684. Well known after 1850 as a point on the Chihuahua Trail, an emigrant road to California.

MARFA (Presidio Co.)　　US 67/90, 8 mi. E
Site of Marfa Army Air Field
During World War II, the U.S. Army Air Forces (USAAF) established a significant number of training airfields across the state of Texas. The USAAF Western Flying Training Command selected Marfa as the site for an advanced multi-engine flying school in 1942. Due to an initial lack of supplies and properly trained personnel, the USAAF struggled at first to establish the command effectively and to provide adequate housing for those who served here. The airfield had four hangars, five runways and a unique angled parking apron. There were seven auxiliary fields in the area. Support personnel here included a Women's Army Corps unit established in 1943 and African American troops, assigned primarily to motor pool duties. Trainees included allied Chinese flying cadets, the first class arriving in September 1944. After Germany surrendered in May 1945, the USAAF considered deactivating Marfa Army Air Field and placed the installation on standby status. However, the need for additional transport aircraft in the Pacific campaign temporarily extended the mission of the airfield. In June 1945, the USAAF placed the airfield in the Troop Carrier Command as home of the 818th Army Air Forces Base. The USAAF formally deactivated the base in September 1945, and the gradual exodus of the military had a devastating impact on Marfa. The military sold off buildings, many later used for civilian purposes in Marfa, Alpine and other locales. Today, all that remains of the once impressive site are foundations, runways and the memories of those who proudly supported the airfield during the war.　(2007)

MARFA (Presidio Co.)　　US 67/90, 5 mi. E
Marfa Lights
The Marfa Lights, mysterious and unexplained lights that have been reported in the area for over one hundred years, have been the subject of many theories. The first recorded sighting of the lights was by rancher Robert Ellison in 1883. Variously explained as campfires, phosphorescent minerals, swamp gas, static electricity, St. Elmo's Fire, and "ghost lights," the lights reportedly change colors, move about, and change in intensity. Scholars have reported over seventy-five local folk tales dealing with the unexplained phenomenon.　(1988)

MARFA (Presidio Co.)   *US 67/90, .7 mi. E*
Presidio County
Formed from Bexar County. Created January 3, 1850. Organized March 13, 1875. So named for the early "Fortress Garrisoned by Soldiers." Erected for the protection of the Big Bend Missions. County seat: Fort Davis, 1875; Marfa since 1885.

MARFA (Presidio Co.)   *US 67, .7 mi. E*
Presidio
Oldest town in Americas. At confluence of Concho and Rio Grande rivers. A settlement for over 10,000 years. Site of first recorded wagon train crossing into Texas December 10, 1862 (?–date not legible). Headed by Antonio de Espejo. Marker placed jointly by Texas Society Children of the American Revolution, Texas Society Daughters of the American Colonists.   (1961)

MARLIN (Falls Co.)   *SH 6, 5 mi. SE in roadside park*
C.S.A. General Thomas Harrison (1823–1891)
Youngest of only trio of Texas brothers who all gained rank of General in Confederate Army. Lived in Falls County in 1850s. Veteran of Mexican War and of Texas Frontier Defense. Rose in Civil War to command of Terry's Texas Rangers. Rode with cavalry of Gen. N. B. Forrest, who got "Thar fustest with the mostest." Fought at Shiloh, Murfreesboro, Ft. Donelson, Knoxville, Atlanta. Was wounded 3 times and had 5 horses shot from under him. Elected district judge in 1866, was removed by reconstruction regime. Served as trustee of Waco University.   (1965)

MARLIN (Falls Co.)   *SH 6, 5 mi. SE at roadside park*
Site of Colonial Capital Sarahville de Viesca (1 mi. SW)
Founded 1834 by Sterling C. Robertson, colonizer of a 100 by 200-mile area embracing all or part of 30 later Texas counties. Situated near falls of Brazos River, where over a stony ford passed much traffic between east and southwest Texas, this was Robertson colony capital. An important Sarahville site was land office, where settlers applied for their titles. Town was named for Robertson's mother, and for Agustin Viesca, governor of the province of Coahuila and Texas. Target of Indian hostilities, Sarahville was abandoned, 1836.   (1970)

MARLIN (Falls Co.)   *SH 6, 4.5 mi. S*
Falls County
Created Jan. 28, 1850, from Limestone and Milam Counties. Organized Aug. 5, 1850. Named for falls on the Brazos River which flows through the center of the county. White colonization in the area pre-dates the Texas Revolution, but colonists fled on news of Santa Anna's assault, 1836. John Marlin, for whom county seat was named, returned and settled near present city. Growth was steady and the first railroad reached the county in 1870. A center for farming, manufacturing and dairying. Curative artesian water gives Marlin recognition as a health spa.   (1965)

MARLIN (Falls Co.)   *SH 6, 4.5 mi. S*
Indian Battlefield
At this site, near the pioneer home of George Morgan, a battle took place, January 16, 1839, between settlers in this region and Indians under Chief Jose Maria in which the colonists were defeated. A treaty with these Indians made soon after brought comparative peace to this region.   (1964)

MARLIN (Falls Co.)   *FM 712, 5 mi. SW, E bank of Brazos at site of falls*
Falls of the Brazos River
When Anglo-Americans began to settle in Texas, the falls of the Brazos were located 2 miles southwest of here. At that time, the water fell about 10 feet over a rocky ledge. The falls served the Indians and early settlers as a trail landmark, meeting point, and campsite. In 1834 colonizer Sterling C. Robertson (1785–1842) established the town of Sarahville de Viesca at the fall line on the west bank of the Brazos, but it was abandoned in 1836 because of Indian hostilities. Later renamed Ft. Milam, the settlement lasted only a few more years. It was followed by the town of Bucksnort, begun in the 1840s on the east side of the river. The falls also formed a natural fording place for frontier travel; the rocky stream bed was the only hard-bottom crossing of the Brazos within 200 miles of the coast. The rapids marked the limit of the river's 19th century steamboat traffic as well. Organized in 1850, Falls County was named for this distinctive landmark. Marlin became the county seat in 1851, and Bucksnort soon disappeared. The Brazos River changed course in 1866,

moving the fall line to the present site and lowering the rapids to about 2 feet. Today a county park is located along both sides of the river at the falls.

(1975)

MARSHALL (Harrison Co.)   *SH 43, 5.5 mi. NE at Pine Bluff Rd.*
Marshall-Shreveport Stagecoach Road
Before the Civil War (1861–1865), the stage road was the main transportation artery between Marshall and Shreveport, providing a link with New Orleans and distant markets. Extending northeast from Marshall, the stage road paralleled the later route of State Highway 43 and passed about 2.5 miles north of this site. Merging with the route from Jefferson, it turned southeast toward Waskom. In some areas, iron-rimmed wheels and horses' hooves trampled the narrow roadbed as much as 12 feet below the surrounding terrain. Travel over the dirt road was uncomfortable in dry weather and often impossible in rainy seasons. Regular stage service was established by 1850, with three arrivals and three departures weekly from Marshall. Arrival of the stage was a major event. At the sound of the driver's bugle, townspeople rushed to meet the incoming coach. By 1860, Marshall had several stagecoach lines and a network of roads. The Marshall to Shreveport line was operated by plantation owner William Bradfield and his son John. The stage continued to run during the Civil War, despite the shortage of drivers and horses. Use of the stage road declined after the war, when the Southern Pacific completed a rail line to Shreveport.

(1979)

MARSHALL (Harrison Co.)   *US 59, 5 mi. N*
John Barry Henderson Home
Rear wing built before 1861. Way station on route of Shreveport-to-Daingerfield stage. Main part built 1868–1871 by Henderson, who during Civil War had furnished beef to the Confederate Army. Thick ground floor walls are of hand-cut local iron-ore rock (only 19th century native stone home in county). Frame second story has narrow cantilevered porch with ornamental railing. Still in family of Henderson. Awarded Medallion Plate.

(1965)

MARSHALL (Harrison Co.)   *US 80, 6 mi. E of US 59 in roadside park*
Harrison County
Formed from Shelby County. Created January 28, 1839. Organized June 12, 1842. Named in honor of Jonas Harrison, a pioneer statesman of New Jersey who came to Texas in 1820. A member of the first convention of Texas held at San Felipe in 1832. Died in 1836. Marshall, the county seat. Named in honor of John Marshall, Chief Justice of the United States Supreme Court.

MARSHALL (Harrison Co.)   *E. Grand Ave. (US 80) at N. Columbus St.*
Marshall Cemetery
Incorporated Dec. 12, 1849. Resting place of many early Texas leaders and patriots: Edward Clark (1815–80), Governor of Texas, 1861; Colonel, C.S.A., Walter P. Lane (1817–92) veteran of Texas Revolution and Mexican war; Brigadier General, C.S.A., John T. Mills (1817–71), Associate Justice Supreme Court, Republic of Texas, District Judge in the state. A county is named for him. Horace Randal (1833–64), Brigadier General, C.S.A.; also honored by naming of county in his memory. Unknown soldiers who died in local hospitals, honored by an obelisk erected by the United Daughters of the Confederacy.

(1966)

MARSHALL (Harrison Co.)   *201 W. Grand Ave. (US 80)*
Site of Confederate Hat Factory in Marshall, C.S.A.
Texas had very few factories in 1861 when she joined the Confederate States of America and went to war on the issue of states' rights. Some of the manufacturing plants necessary to supply military goods were thereupon established in and around Marshall, which later (1863) became headquarters for Confederate operations west of the Mississippi River. At the site of this marker, there was operated in the basement of a dwelling house a factory which brought high quality fur felt from a plant situated on Young's Mill Pond near Hallsville (13 mi. W). and made military hats to outfit Texas soldiers and other troops fighting for the Confederacy. Some 40 men were employed here in blocking and finishing hats and in making blankets and saddle blankets. Successive generations of the Edmund Key family owned and occupied the house where the Confederate Hat Factory had been operated during the Civil War. After the structure burned in 1962 the Key family tendered (in 1975) the site to the Harrison County Conservation Society as a park dedicated in memory of civic leaders Edmund and Rae Lyttleton Key.

(1976)

MARSHALL (Harrison Co.)   *US 59, S of Loop 390*
Marshall
Founded 1839. Named for John Marshall, Chief Justice of U.S. Supreme Court. Supply, ordnance, medical, telegraph and military headquarters during Civil War. The Confederate capital of Missouri was located here. Trade, industry, rail and historical center.

MASON (Mason Co.)   *US 87, 1.3 mi. N*
Crosby Cemetery
The first burial ground for the citizens of Mason and Koocksville, this cemetery traces its history to the 1850s. The oldest documented burial is that of Kate Lemburg, who died in 1856. Also interred here is Mason County's first sheriff, Thomas Milligan (1810–1860). The Crosby family purchased the property surrounding the cemetery in 1866, and it has been known as Crosby Cemetery since that time. Those buried in the cemetery include members of the Crosby and other pioneer families. It stands as a reflection of the area's heritage.   (1988)

MASON (Mason Co.)   *US 87 at US 377, 1 mi. N in roadside park*
Old Fort Mason
Situated near a spring long used by Indians; built of stone quarried from Post Hill, fort helped protect Texas frontier from Indians. Colonel Robert E. Lee, stationed in Texas 2 years, commanded Fort Mason from Feb. 1860 to Feb. 1861. Here he made his decision as to his part in the Civil War, saying: "If the union is dissolved, . . . I shall return to my native state and . . . save in defense . . . draw my sword on none." He left Fort Mason Feb. 13, 1861. In wartime he remembered "the enemy never sees the backs of Texans."   (1965)

MASON (Mason Co.)   *US 87, .5 mi. N*
Two Sheriffs of Mason County
A native of Kentucky, Thomas S. Milligan (1810–1860) moved to this area in 1855 and operated a change station for the stage line. He was also a rancher and supplied beef to the soldiers at Fort Mason. Shortly after Mason County was organized in 1858 he became the first elected sheriff. Two years later he was killed by hostile Indians near his home (1.6 mi. NW). His grandson Allen Thomas Murray (1880–1929) became county sheriff in 1924 and like his grandfather died in the line of duty. He was killed by a bootlegger near this site in 1929.   (1980)

MASON (Mason Co.)   *San Antonio St. (US 87) at courthouse*
Fort Mason and Camp Llano, C.S.A.
Fort Mason, located 5 blocks south, was headquarters for the first regiment Texas Mounted Rifles 1861–62. These Confederate troops occupied the line of old U. S. forts to give protection against Indians. 215 prisoners-of-war were confined here. In spring 1862, the line of frontier defense was tightened and Camp Llano was established 9 miles east. Texas Frontier Regiment occupied this post, part of a line a day's ride apart on horseback from the Red River to the Rio Grande. Settlers then used Fort Mason for protection. Scouting parties and patrols of Confederate and state troops visited the post in aggressive warfare to keep Indians near their camps and away from settlements. Upon secession Mason County men joined regional, state and Confederate troops to protect the frontier. They usually had to supply their own guns, mounts and sustenance. Although large-scale raids had been checked, Indians roamed this area, stealing horses, attacking isolated farms, burning buildings, kidnapping women and children. However, an old Mason pioneer operated a one-mule stage route between Camp Colorado, Mason and Fredericksburg. Hiding from Indians at night, he and his mule made the trip every two weeks carrying the mail without mishap.   (1964)

MASON (Mason Co.)   *San Antonio St. (US 87) at courthouse*
Mason County Courthouse
Constructed in 1909, this is the third courthouse to serve the people of Mason County. Commissioners Court probably met in other locations until the first courthouse was built in 1872. It burned in 1877 and was replaced that year by a second red sandstone building. Designed by E. C. Hosford and built at a cost of $39,796, this Beaux Arts style courthouse features a center dome and clock tower, gable front porticoes with two-story Doric columns, and rusticated stonework with contrasting stone lintels.   (1988)

MASON (Mason Co.)
SH 29 at Live Oak
Mason House Hotel & Stage Station
Built in 1869–70 by S. F. (Lace) Bridges, the Mason House was a hotel and stagecoach stop on the San Antonio to El Paso Road. It was a popular stopping place, providing respite for many weary travelers and hearty meals for local residents. A tragic fire in 1900 resulted in the death of 23-year-old Annie Medlock. Eventually the building was converted into apartments, and some alterations occurred in the 1930s, including the addition of an exterior stairway. A number of historic features still remain on the property, including the original kitchen cistern and stone fences. (1999)

MASON (Mason Co.)
224 Broad St., N of US 87
Methodism in Mason County
When Mason County organized in 1858, a number of Methodists lived in this area, served by English and German speaking circuit preachers. In the town of Mason, four different conferences (North and South for both English and German) met separately in the community schoolhouse. Together in 1877 they built a sanctuary, which was shared until the membership outgrew the building. Services were also held in the county courthouse before new facilities were built in the 1890s. By 1939, all the conferences had united. Methodists in Mason County have a long history in raising up pastors for ministry, as well as training interns from Southern Methodist University. They have also given extensively to charities, missions, orphanages and hospitals. (2008)

MASON (Mason Co.)
Broad St. at Comanche Creek
Broad Street Bridge
In 1914, citizens of Mason petitioned the County Commissioners Court for a reliable means of crossing Comanche Creek, which separated north and south Mason. Initial construction bids were deemed too high and a second petition was presented in 1917. Because Mason had no railroad to transport large pre-fabricated building materials, the Alamo Construction Company crafted the bridge of reinforced concrete on site in 1918. Perhaps the last concrete truss bridge to remain in Texas, the Broad Street Bridge continued to support vehicular and pedestrian traffic in Mason in 1998. (1998)

MASON (Mason Co.)
916 San Antonio St. (US 87)
Rudolph and Therese Runge House
In the 1880s and 1890s, stonemason Thomas Broad built several homes in Mason similar to this one, owned by E. J. and Louise Broad from 1891 until they sold it in 1895 to Therese (Marschall) Runge (1855–1946). Her husband, Rudolph Runge (1849–1914), was a German native who became a noted local attorney. The couple's sons, Carl and Roscoe, became prominent lawyers and politicians. The family sold the home in 1946, and subsequent owners have maintained the building's Victorian elements, many of which are common in Thomas Broad's work. These include turned posts and the use of random ashlar stone with unique pointing treatment and articulated quoins. (2003)

MASON (Mason Co.)
US 87, 2 mi. S at rest area
Mason County
Created January 22, 1858, and organized August 2, 1858, this county was named for its most important settlement, Fort Mason. Garrisoned intermittently from July 6, 1851, to March 23, 1869, Fort Mason was named for Lt. G. T. Mason of the United States 2nd Dragoons, killed in Mexican War action on April 25, 1846, near Brownsville. Fort Mason was one of a chain of posts situated a day's horseback ride apart, from Red River to the Rio Grande, for protecting frontier against Apaches, Comanches, other Indians. (1971)

MASON (Mason Co.)
US 87, 18 mi. SE
Homesite of John O. Meusebach, 1812–1897 (14 mi. SE, in Loyal Valley)
By 1848, German colonization reached area under direction of John O. Meusebach, who succeeded Prince Carl of Solms-Braunfels as colony leader and who signed treaty with Comanches allowing peaceful settlement of the land between the Llano and San Saba Rivers. He later retired here to a 640-acre farm where he died. His colonists have influenced Texas through their ingenuity, thrift, and enterprise. They came seeking political and personal freedom and remained to create a unique culture through their blending of German custom with American necessity. (1969)

MATADOR (Motley Co.)   *US 62/70, 10 mi. E in roadside park*
Tee Pee City
At the junction of the Middle Pease River and Tee Pee Creek (8 mi. NNE), is the site of Tee Pee City. In the 1870s, traders established an outpost there to take advantage of the area's buffalo hide trade. The small community of picket houses and tents derived its name from abandoned tipi (tee pee) poles found along the creek. Charles Rath, an important figure in West Texas history, was among the partners in the original operation that resulted in the formation of the settlement, bringing in wagons, cattle, mules and dance hall equipment. Rath then continued south to establish his headquarters on the Double Mountain Fork of the Brazos, leaving management of the Tee Pee City camp to others. An 1877 account of the settlement identified one or two saloons, a dance hall, gambling hall and two-room hotel, as well as other businesses. The 1880 census listed 12 residents. The R.V. Fields and A.B. Cooper families arrived in 1879, the same year Tee Pee City's post office opened. By then, few buffalo remained in the area. Hunters had killed thousands, nearly depleting the southern herd. Cooper freighted supplies and ran a general store out of a dugout. The community supported a post office (1879–1900), as well as a school (1895–1902), but Tee Pee City was best known for its rowdiness, brawls and shootings, which warranted the attention of G.W. Arrington's Texas Rangers. In 1904, the Matador Land and Cattle Company bought the land and closed down the saloon, which had been off limits to Matador employees due to its wild reputation. A 1936 state monument placed at the townsite was moved here in 2002. Little remains at the original site, now on private land.   (2002)

MATADOR (Motley Co.)   *US 62/70, E city limits*
The Motley County Railroad
Pioneer carrier for cattle and farm goods. Chartered June 20, 1913, by 92 people of Motley and nearby counties. One man is said to have invested $50,000. Matador Land & Cattle Company also provided bonus funds. Original directors were J. C. Burleson, A. B. Echols, J. N. Gaines, T. E. Leckie, I. E. Martin, R. P. Moore, J. D. Morriss, J. E. Russell, and A. C. Traweek. Trains used cattle sweepers, as 8-mile track ran through unfenced ranches. Line joined Quanah, Acme & Pacific tracks near Roaring Springs. The M. C. R. R. ceased to operate in 1936.   (1970)

MATADOR (Motley Co.)   *US 70, 12 mi. W*
Henry H. Campbell (1840–1911)
A native of North Carolina, Henry Harrison Campbell arrived in Texas with his family in 1854. Following his service in the Confederate Army, he worked as a cattle drover. In 1879, with four other investors, he founded the Matador Ranch at Ballard Springs (ten miles southeast). Campbell's wife, Elizabeth Bundy, joined him at the ranch in 1880. Refusing to live underground in a dugout, she insisted on camping in a tent until lumber could be hauled in for a two-room house. She served as hostess and nurse at the ranch, and later was post-mistress at Matador. In its first three years, the Matador Ranch holdings grew to include 40,000 head of cattle on 100,000 acres of land, with an additional 1.5 million acres of free range rights. In 1882, the ranch was bought by a Scottish syndicate, the Matador Land and Cattle Company, Ltd. Campbell continued his association with the ranch, serving as ranch superintendent until 1890. Henry H. Campbell led efforts to create Motley County in 1891. After serving two terms as county judge, he retired to concentrate on his ranch interests on Dutchman Creek. He died in Matador on May 23, 1911.   (1988)

MATADOR (Motley Co.)   *SH 70, .5 mi. S in Virginia Walton Pk.*
Motley County
Formed from Young and Bexar Territories. Created August 21, 1876. Organized February 5, 1891. Named in honor of Dr. Junius William Mottley, 1812–1836. Signer of the Texas Declaration of Independence. Aide to General Rusk at the Battle of San Jacinto where he was mortally wounded. Matador, the county seat.

MATADOR (Motley Co.)   *SH 70, .5 mi. S near ranch headquarters*
Matador Ranch
The Matador Cattle Company began as an open range ranch in 1879 when Henry H. Campbell, A. M. Britton, and three others bought range rights in this area. In 1882 the ranch was purchased by Scottish investors, who formed the Matador Land and Cattle Co., Ltd. The ranch utilized one

and one half million acres of owned and leased range in Motley, Floyd, Dickens, and Cottle Counties. In 1902, the ranch acquired the 210,000-acre Alamocitas Ranch in Oldham County. Additional pastures were leased in the Dakotas, Montana, and Canada. At its height the ranch owned 90,000 cattle and title to 879,000 acres of Texas land. In 1913, the Quanah, Acme, and Pacific Railroad was built through the ranch in Motley County and the town of Roaring Springs was established. General managers of the ranch were Britton (1879–1890), Murdo Mackenzie (1890–1911, 1923–1937), John MacBain (1912–1922), and John Mackenzie (1937–1951). The general manager's office was located first in Fort Worth and later in Trinidad and Denver, Colorado. Corporate offices were maintained in Scotland from 1882 until the ranch's liquidation in 1951. The ranch headquarters was purchased by Koch Industries, Inc. and became the Matador Cattle Co.

(Texas Sesquicentennial 1836–1986)

MATAGORDA (Matagorda Co.)
SH 60 at Catalpa
Dale-Rugeley-Sisk Home ca. 1830
Has withstood many hurricanes. A cultural, social, political center. Home of A.C. Horton, 1st Lieutenant-Governor of Texas and governor 7 months; Rev. Caleb Ives, 1st rector of 1st Episcopal Church in Texas; W. L. Sartwell, partner in Ives-Sartwell-Academy; a leading churchwoman, Mrs. S. M. Dale; F. L. Rugeley, son of a Confederate leader; Robt. J. Sisk, pioneer in rice, oil and land development. Awarded Medallion Plate.
(1964)

MAUD (Bowie Co.)
US 67, 1 mi. NE
Site of Epperson's Ferry
At this crossing, constructed by nature and used by Caddo Indians, early French and Spanish explorers, and travelers over Trammel's trace, Mark Epperson before 1837 established a ferry used until the construction of a wooden bridge antedating the modern structure erected in 1924.

MAVERICK (Runnels Co.)
SH 158, E city limits
Maverick
Founded in the 1870s. Named for Samuel A. Maverick (1803–1870), who came to Texas 1835. Fought in the Texas War for Independence. In secession convention, 1861, he was made one of the commissioners to negotiate surrender of United States troops in San Antonio. In 1853 he had land in this important ranching area.

MAY (Brown Co.)
US 183 right-of-way
The May Community
Originally part of a Mexican land grant given to Empresario John Cameron in 1827, May developed in the 1870s when several pioneer families settled here. Baptists and Methodists quickly organized churches. A one-room school known as Old Swayback provided the first formal education for the children. Nathan L. May built a trading post in 1879 and became the town's first postmaster in 1881. By 1907, the village had a blacksmith shop, general store, newspaper, and bank. The early history of May climaxed in 1911 with the coming of the railroad.
(1981)

MAY (Brown Co.)
18001 US 183 N
May United Methodist Church
Methodists in this area were initially served by circuit-riding preachers. First to come to the region in the 1860s was the Rev. Hugh M. Childress, and worship services were held in private homes. In 1882, the Rev. Peter Gravis organized Mt. Zion Methodist Church, which later merged with the congregation at Byrds. Both of these communities, along with Bethel, Brooks, Clio, Gap Creek, Green's Chapel, Holder, Pleasant Valley, Rocky, Shrum, Verbena, Williams, Windham and Wolf Valley became part of the May charge. Brush arbor revivals were held each summer. The May Methodist Church was formally organized in 1886. Members gathered for services in nearby Verbena until 1890, when they began meeting in the newly constructed May schoolhouse. Four years later, members built their own one-room church, which served until they constructed a new brick building with memorial stained glass windows in 1929–30. After 70 years of service, the church building was destroyed by fire in January 2000. Throughout its history, the May United Methodist Church has upheld the ideals and traditions of its pioneer founders. Despite the Depression, droughts, floods, wars and fire, the church has served its members and the May community for more than 100 years.
(2001)

MAYDELLE (Cherokee Co.)   US 84, 1 mi. N
Pleasant Grove Missionary Baptist Church
This congregation was organized in 1854 and represents one of Cherokee County's oldest Baptist churches. The Rev. G. W. Slover served as first pastor. The first church building, erected here on land donated by Green B. Hill, was replaced with a frame sanctuary after the Civil War. Sunday School and other church facilities have been added over the years. Several early church members and their descendants are buried in the nearby Pleasant Grove Cemetery. The church, whose past membership has included several area civic leaders, continues to provide spiritual guidance for the area.   (1994)

MAYDELLE (Cherokee Co.)   US 84, in front of the Texas State Railroad depot
Maydelle
In 1906, the Texas State Railroad built to this area for timber to fuel iron manufacturing at the penitentiary in Rusk. The branch prison established at the railhead was called Camp Wright. When Rusk native Thomas Campbell became governor, he persuaded the legislature to extend the line to Palestine, where it met the I&GN Railway. The line brought new settlement to the Camp Wright area, and in 1910, residents platted the new town of Maydelle, named for the governor's daughter, who sang at the townsite's dedication. The town was an early center for cotton, timber and tomato production, but its population, like in other rural Texas towns, declined by the latter part of the 20th century.   (2003)

MAYDELLE (Cherokee Co.)   US 84 right-of-way at FM 747, 4 mi. W
Mewshaw State Sawmill and Maydelle CCC Camp
In operation from 1908 to 1912, the Mewshaw State Sawmill at this site produced 35,000 board feet of lumber daily and was staffed by convict laborers from the nearby Rusk Penitentiary. The village of Maydelle later developed on the rail line which ran between Rusk and Palestine, and in 1933 a forest conservation camp under the auspices of the Federal Civilian Conservation Corps (CCC) was established here. The camp was closed in 1937, but the benefits of its programs are still evident in the I. D. Fairchild State Forest, now a wildlife sanctuary.   (1991)

MAYDELLE (Cherokee Co.)   US 84 right-of-way, 6 mi. W at the Neches River
Ben Cannon Ferry
Native Americans and early Anglo settlers in this region forded the Neches River at this site called Duty Crossing for early settler Richard Duty. A significant link in the history of transportation across the river, the Ben Cannon Ferry is first documented in Cherokee County commissioners court records in 1848. Pioneer settler Ben Cannon operated the ferry until 1851. A toll bridge operated north of the ferry site from 1854 to 1924. The route of the Texas State Railroad crosses the Neches just north of the ferry site.   (1991)

McADOO (Dickens Co.)   FM 264 at US 82, 3 mi. S
Marshall Clinton Formby, Jr.
(April 12, 1911–December 27, 1984)
Born in Hopkins County in East Texas, Marshall Clinton Formby, Jr., moved with his family to McAdoo (3 mi. N) when he was five years old and spent his adult life working for the betterment of this part of the state. Educated at Texas Technological College (now Texas Tech University), the University of Texas and Baylor University school of law, Formby used his talents in a variety of business and public service opportunities. Marshall Formby maintained extensive farming interests in West Texas in addition to oil ventures and radio, newspaper and cable television enterprises. He served as Dickens County Judge from 1936 to 1940 and was elected to the Texas Senate, although his participation as a U.S. Army captain in the European theatre of World War II kept him away from the state capitol for much of his term. Formby continued his statewide public service as a governor-appointed member of the Texas Highway Commission in 1953–59, including two years as chair. During his tenure, he worked for the paving of Farm-to-Market roads and for the implementation of the Interstate Highway System in Texas. A member of the Texas Tech Board of Regents, he also served 12 years on the state's College Coordinating Board. Active in the Baptist church and in numerous civic organizations, Marshall Formby received many awards and honors for his service to his community, region and state. He died at his home in Plainview in 1984 and is buried in the McAdoo cemetery.   (2002)

McCAMEY (Upton Co.)
US 385, 12 mi. NW
Castle Mountain
About 3,000 ft. elevation.
Since 17th century, a landmark in travel from Texas points to Mexico and California. According to tradition, named by Spaniards for resemblance to ancient castles. Has associations with stories of lost trains of gold and other treasures.
(1966)

McCAMEY (Upton Co.)
US 385, 3 mi. NW
King Mountain
Probably named for Guy King, rancher who drilled first water well on top of mountain about 1900. Elevation is 3,000 feet. Part of an uplift in southern Permian Basin; associated with county oil fields. Many Indian relics have been found along the rim rock.
(1968)

McCAMEY (Upton Co.)
US 385, 3 mi. NW
McCamey
Founded 1926. Had 10,000 people in 1927. Named for Geo. B. McCamey, driller of discovery well that by 1964 had led way to opening of 31 oil and gas fields in Upton County. (Discovery well is 2.3 miles north of town.) Center for horse, sheep, goat ranching. Has 5 parks. Home of Mendoza Trail Museum.
(1964)

McCAMEY (Upton Co.)
US 67, 10 mi. E
Rodman-Noel Oil Field
Discovered 1953. Initial well, about 2½ miles south of this spot, was drilled by E. G. Rodman and W. D. Noel as No. 1 Radford Grocery. It was completed January 13, 1953, for a natural flowing potential of 960 barrels in 24 hours, from Grayburg formation and at total depth of 1744 feet. It is located 1980 feet from the south and west lines of section 1 of the Gulf, Colorado and Santa Fe survey in Railroad Commission District 7C. The field has a number of wells completed for natural potentials in excess of 3,000 barrels a day. The drillers Rodman and Noel were oil business veterans at the time they brought in this Upton County field. Already experienced in various phases of petroleum development, E. G. Rodman became an independent producer in Texas in 1938. W. D. Noel became an independent producer in Texas in 1940. Their interests extend into international exploration and other phases of oil development, including manufacture of petrochemicals. Their opening of this field—which contributed substantially to the 1925–1960 Upton County total of 272,628,476 barrels of production—was made 28 years later than the great boom in McCamey.
(1964)

McCAMEY (Upton Co.)
US 67, 10 mi. E
Rattlesnake Butte
Named for wildlife seen here 1910 by University of Texas geology team of students and professors mapping county resources. A meandering formation, 2,600 Ft. elevation, this is part of an uplift in southern Permian Basin; associated with uplift are county's oil fields.
(Recorded Texas Historic Landmark, 1967)

McCAMEY (Upton Co.)
US 67, 8 mi. E
Table Top Mountain
Round, flat-topped mesa rising 475 feet above its base; part of an uplift in Permian Basin, which was once a prehistoric sea. The limestone-topped buttes and mesas in this area are remnants of rock that covered county 115 million years ago, but has now been mostly eroded.
(1967)

McCAMEY (Upton Co.)
US 67, 7.5 mi. E
Square Top Mountain
Named 1919 by students and professors making a geological survey for the University of Texas. The peak rises 450 feet above its base and may be part of King Mountain, 1.5 mi. W. This pioneer landmark contains fossil shells 450 million years old from a prehistoric sea.
(1967)

McCAMEY (Upton Co.)
US 67, 5 mi. E
Castle Gap
Castle Gap, famous early pass for southwestern trails, lies 14 miles northwest along the Upton-Crane County line. Through this mile-long gap between Castle and King mountains flowed the

full panorama of Texas history—Indian, Spaniard, Stage and Trail Herd Driver, Settler, '49er. In prehistoric time Castle Gap was a landmark for nomadic Indian tribes and later guided the Comanches on their war trail into Mexico. The first white man to discover the pass was probably the Spanish explorer Felipe Rabago y Teran in 1761. Then came the '49ers in their frenzied rush to the California gold fields, to be followed by other, more permanent settlers. From 1858 to 1861 the famed Butterfield Overland Mail coaches rumbled through the pass on their 24-day journey from St. Louis to San Francisco, pausing briefly at the adobe-walled Castle Gap station for fresh teams. Then they were off again, fording into the sunset. By 1866 the Goodnight-Loving cattle trail was firmly established at the gap, funneling tens of thousands of bawling longhorn cattle to the northern markets. During this same period, legend holds that a treasure-laden aide of Emperor Maximilian of Mexico, fleeing the country when the regime collapsed, buried gold and jewels in the area. Dust of the pioneers settled long ago. Today Castle Gap slumbers peacefully, disturbed only by visitors, occasional treasure hunters and those who probe for ruins of the Butterfield station and the rapidly fading ruts of coach and wagon. (1962)

McCAMEY (Upton Co.)

SH 67, E edge of city

Early Humble Camp in Permian Basin

The world's largest complex of oil wells in the 1920s was developed in this area. Key to success of this vast petroleum field lay in finding ways to convey oil to growing fuel markets. First efficient transportation came in 1925 with the laying of the Humble pipeline from Kemper station, near Big Lake, to Comyn station (a distance of about 500 miles), to connect with existing Comyn-Baytown system. Early camp for pipeline construction crews was built here 1926 when Humble extended its line west from Big Lake field. Camp's site led to growth of McCamey and building of a refinery. McCamey became important center of oil production and operation. A constant flow of oil went through Humble's pipeline on its long journey to the Gulf Coast. Even with use of pipeline and railroad tank cars, more oil was produced than could be marketed. New practices had to be used to prevent overproduction and waste. Thus Humble pipeline became involved in the first voluntary proration in Texas, when in 1928 producing capacity of local wells was reduced to a level consistent with transportation facilities. Today in Texas, Humble has 15,000 oil and gas wells; 9,545 miles of pipeline; and one refinery. (1967)

McDADE (Bastrop Co.)

US 290 at Loop 223

McDade

Laid out 1871; named for James McDade, Brenham lawyer. Became a thriving town, important freight center and early day stage stop. School-church built 1872. Vigilantes (organized 1883) lynched 3 men on Christmas Eve, causing a shoot-out next day at the Rock Saloon (now a museum). (1968)

McKINNEY (Collin Co.)

US 75 access rd., 7.7 mi. N,
Throckmorton Rd. Exit

Governor James Webb Throckmorton
(February 1, 1825–April 21, 1894)

A doctor's son, James W. Throckmorton was born in Tennessee. He migrated with his parents to the Texas frontier in 1841 and settled near this site. At age 17, he became hunter and scout for his pioneer neighbors. He served in the Mexican War (1846–1848). In 1848, he married Annie Rattan (1828–1895) and built a home near McKinney. Trained as a physician, Throckmorton disliked medicine and in 1851 entered law and politics. He served 1851–1857 in the Texas Legislature, where he promoted railroad building. Later he became attorney for Texas & Pacific Railroad. He was state senator, 1857–1861 and 1863–1865. Although he upheld the right of secession, he was one of seven men who voted against Texas leaving the union at the Feb. 1861 Secession Convention. During the Civil War (1861–1865), he fought in the Confederate Army. Elected governor in the summer of 1866, he grappled with postwar problems of frontier defense and Federal military occupation. In July 1867, Gen. Philip H. Sheridan, commander of the 5th Military District to which Texas was assigned, removed Throckmorton from office as "an impediment to reconstruction" and named E. M. Pease provisional governor. Throckmorton continued his political career in the U.S. Congress, serving his North Texas district in 1875–1879 and 1883–1887. (1977)

McKINNEY (Collin Co.)   *US 75, N city limits*
McKinney
Founded 1845 by Collin McKinney, a signer of the Texas Declaration of Independence. In Civil War, Gen. J. W. Throckmorton (later a governor of Texas) organized McKinney's Co. K, 6th Texas Cavalry, an outstanding Confederate fighting unit. Manufacturing, trade and hospital center.

McKINNEY (Collin Co.)   *SH 380, 3 mi. W*
Site of Buckner
John (Jack) and Polly McGarrah and family came to this site from Tennessee in 1842. The third settler in present Collin County, McGarrah opened a trading post to barter for hides and furs. While in the act of building a family fort, he and his men had to defend themselves from roaming hostile Indians. The Texas Legislature created Collin County on April 3, 1846, directing that its county seat, to be named "Buckner," would be no more than three miles from the geographic center. Buckner townsite was soon laid out here in McGarrah's settlement. On the Fourth of July, citizens met here and elected their first county officials. They also raised a military company for the Mexican War. On Sept. 21 there was an auction of Buckner town lots; on Nov. 25, 1846, the post office opened, with McGarrah as postmaster. By 1848, it was noticed that Buckner townsite was outside the legal limits for the county seat. The legislature ordered another election and named the new county seat "McKinney," honoring early settler Collin McKinney, a signer of the Texas Declaration of Independence. Residents moved their homes and other buildings to McKinney (3 mi. E), and Buckner townsite reverted to agricultural land uses.
(1978)

McKINNEY (Collin Co.)   *US 380, 3 mi. W*
Buckner Cemetery
The land surrounding this historic cemetery was part of a grant obtained by John McGarrah, a member of the Peters Colony who arrived in this area in 1843. McGarrah founded a trading post near this site, and soon the Fort Buckner settlement was established. It would later become the first county seat of Collin County. David William O'Brien (1808–1885) came to Collin County with his family in 1857. He eventually acquired the part of the McGarrah Land which included this site. The Buckner Cemetery, which was established on the O'Brien Land, has also been referred to as O'Brien Cemetery over the years. Although there may be earlier unmarked graves, the oldest documented burial is that of Franklin O'Brien (1851–1870). Many early pioneers of Collin County are interred here, including victims of a smallpox epidemic in the 1870s. According to local tradition, a Kiowa Indian named Spotted Tail also lies here in an unmarked grave. The only physical remnant of the Buckner community, this cemetery serves as a reminder of the early history of Collin County.
(1988)

McKINNEY (Collin Co.)   *411 S. Chestnut, 1 blk. W of SH 5*
Birthplace of Rebekah Baines Johnson
Joseph Wilson Baines (1846–1906), son of minister-editor-Baylor University President George W. Baines, settled in Collin County in 1867. He taught school and in 1869 married Ruth Huffman, daughter of a physician of the Peters Colony. Baines read law under ex-governor James W. Throckmorton, began his practice, edited the McKinney "Advocate", and helped organize and build the city's first Baptist church. He and his wife lived at this site when their child Rebekah was born. Baines served 1883 to 1887 as Texas Secretary of State, later practiced law in Blanco and Fredericksburg, and was a legislator in 1903–1904. Rebekah Baines (1881–1958) studied at Baylor College in Belton and became a teacher and journalist. In 1907 she married Sam Early Johnson, Jr. (1877–1937), a rancher and former schoolteacher who also served in the Texas Legislature from 1905 through 1908 and from 1917 through 1923. The couple continued to ranch in the Hill Country, published the Johnson City "Record-Courier", and were parents of five children. Their eldest, Lyndon Baines Johnson (1908–1973), after a long career in the national Congress, served as the 36th president of the United States.
(1976)

McKINNEY (Collin Co.)   *Kentucky St. at Louisiana St. (Spur 359)*
Collin County
Formed from Fannin County. Created April 3, 1846. Organized July 13, 1846. Named in honor of Collin McKinney, 1766–1861 land surveyor, signer of the Texas Declaration of Independence,

member of Congress, Republic of Texas, member of the Texas Legislature. County seat, Buckner, 1846–1848. McKinney, since.

McKINNEY (Collin Co.)   *N. Tennessee at Virginia St. (Spur 359)*
1927 Collin County Courthouse

Collin County was formed in 1846 and its only town, Buckner, was automatically selected as the county seat. To comply with state law, an election was held to relocate the county seat to the center of the county. Only eleven people participated due to inclement weather, and when the vote was tallied McKinney was established as the county seat in 1848. The first courthouses in McKinney were modest wooden structures. A third courthouse was erected on this site during 1874–1875, and was opened for use in 1876. The 2-story Victorian structure was made of native limestone blocks with a steep mansard roof and a main entrance that faced east. The building's architect, often mistakenly identified as Charles Wheeler, was Charles Wheelock of Sherman. The much-celebrated courthouse on the square became a backdrop for parades and other events. The structure was overcrowded and in poor condition by the mid-1920s. Extensive exterior and interior renovations included the removal of the mansard roof and tower caps, as well as the addition of a third story and basement. Overseen by W. A. Peters of the Paris, Texas, architectural firm of Sparger and Peters, the work resulted in a Classical Revival edifice completed in 1927. Original features included tripartite windows with flanking double classical columns on the north and south façades. The new structure was commonly known as the "Temple of Justice," and continued to be the center of activity for city and county functions. It remained in service as a courthouse until 1979. The structure remains a fine example of 20th century Classical Revival design and a monument to Collin County history.   (1998)

McKINNEY (Collin Co.)   *N. Tennessee at Virginia St. (Spur 359)*
Old Collin County Courthouse

Collin County was created from Fannin County in 1846. It was named for pioneer area settler Collin McKinney (1766–1861), a signer of the Texas Declaration of Independence. The first county seat was established at Buckner (2 mi. NW). In 1848 William and Margaret Davis conveyed 120 acres of land at this site for a more central seat of government, which became the community of McKinney. The first two courthouses in the new town were built of wood. In 1874 county commissioners approved plans for a more substantial courthouse on this site. Sherman architect Charles Wheeler designed the building and O.J. King served as general contractor. Constructed of stone from a local quarry (3.5 mi. NE), it was completed in 1876. A grand ball was held in the courthouse to celebrate the event. By the 1920s the courthouse was inadequate to meet the needs of a growing county. Extensive changes, including the addition of a basement and a third floor, were made in 1926–27 under the direction of architect W.A. Peters of Paris, Texas. The site of many political speeches and events, the building was used as a courthouse until 1979. It now serves as a historic reminder of the county's early development.   (1982)

McKINNEY (Collin Co.)   *US 75/SH 121 at Wilmeth Rd.*
Site of Wilmeth-McKinney Homestead

Joseph Brice (J.B.) Wilmeth (b.1807) and Nancy Ferguson (b.1807) were married in Tennessee in 1826. They settled here on 320 acres of virgin prairie in 1846. They began to farm their land and soon built a grand two-story family home at this site. Elder J.B. Wilmeth, along with pioneer settler Collin McKinney, established Collin County's First Christian Church at Liberty in 1846. J.B. organized McKinney's First Christian Church in 1848, and early worship services were held in his home. Between 1848 and 1887, the Wilmeth home also was the site of a free school taught by J.B. and his children. J.B. served on the commission that selected the Collin County seat and later served as district clerk and county judge, and in 1850 the Wilmeths' daughter, Martha, married Daniel L. McKinney, grandson of Collin McKinney. Following the deaths of J.B. and Nancy in 1892, Martha and Daniel lived in the Wilmeth home until Daniel's death in 1906. The homestead was next occupied by Martha and Daniel's son, John Brice, and his wife, Annie (Magers), until their deaths in 1968. Materials from the original Wilmeth home were used to build a new house here in 1941. The property continues to be recognized as an important site in early Collin County history.   (1994)

McKINNEY (Collin Co.)
SH 5 at SH 121
Pecan Grove Memorial Park
This park is situated on property granted by the Republic of Texas to Samuel McFarland in 1845, only four years after the first permanent settlement in this area was begun by a pioneer from Tennessee, Dr. William E. Throckmorton (1795–1843), and his family. By the 1850s, when the first known burials occurred, R. A. Davis owned the land. The name of the spot was derived from a handsome stand of trees. Ownership by the public began in 1870 with the purchase of a 21.3-acre tract by Isaac F. Graves, I. D. Newsome, G. A. Foote, E. R. Stiff, and Thomas J. Brown. The original charter was issued in 1889 to Pecan Grove Cemetery Association, Inc., a private corporation. Additional land was purchased in 1892 and 1960. The name "Pecan Grove Memorial Park," granted in a new charter in 1964, commemorates the courageous and compassionate pioneer men and women of this vicinity. One of these, Dr. James Webb Throckmorton (1825–1894), was a Texas legislator in the 1850s; became a Confederate brigadier general during the Civil War; was governor of Texas in 1866–1867; and was in the United States Congress intermittently from 1875 to 1888. Pecan Grove Decoration Day is held every spring.
(1976)

MEADOW (Terry Co.)
US 62/82, 2.5 mi. SW of Meadow
Route of Nolan Expedition
Army and civilian effort in 1877 to halt raiding of chief "Old Black Horse's" Comanches. In group were 60 Negro troops of Co. A, 10th U.S. Cavalry, and 22 buffalo hunters known as "The Forlorn Hope." Troops departed Fort Concho in early July, led by Capt. Nicholas Nolan. Eluded by Indians and finding water holes dry, on July 27 men were thirst-crazed. By drinking horse blood and urine, soldiers lived 86 parched hours; finally reached old supply base. Hunters left group; found water alone. All but 4 soldiers survived this heroic test of endurance.
(1972)

MEDINA (Bandera Co.)
SH 16 at E. city limits
Old Standard Home
On land owned by John James, surveyor of Bandera and Castroville townsites, and by Confederate General John Bell Hood. Hostile Indians prevented construction until 1878, two years prior to founding of Medina. Owned by Standard family since 1889.
(1965)

MEGARGEL (Archer Co.)
SH 114, at city park
On Route of the Comanche Exodus
After living 1854–1858 on the reservation set aside by State of Texas near camp Cooper (30 mi. SW), the Comanche Indians with their goods were removed to Oklahoma. Near this spot on a head branch of Kickapoo Creek (so named, 1830) the Exodus camped on Aug. 3, 1859, with its escort, a company of 1st United States Infantry under Capt. C. C. Gilbert, along with the Indian agent Matthew Leeper. At same time (25 mi. E), Maj. George H. Thomas escorted the supervising Indian agent, Maj. R. S. Neighbors, and 1059 lower Brazos reserve Indians to Oklahoma Reservation. Megargel was founded here, 1910.
(1971)

MELVIN (McCulloch Co.)
US 87 at FM 503, 1.5 mi. NW
"1870's Cowboy-Indian Fight"
(Battleground 1 mi. N of Marker)
Near here in 1874 or 1875, 18 Indians attacked W. B. Brown and two comrades, spooking one horse and capturing bedrolls and grub, but sparing the men, who thankfully escaped. In the 1870s, when they were being driven off the range, capture of supplies meant victory to the Indians.

MEMPHIS (Hall Co.)
SH 256, 12 mi. W
Shoe Bar Ranch Headquarters
On first ranch in Hall County, started in 1880s by pioneer cattlemen T. S. Bugbee and O. H. Nelson. This residence was built about 1884. A nearsighted owner, J. K. Zimmerman of Kansas City, was wary of surprise visitors, and put in only one outer door. Adobe building bricks were made nearby. The tamped clay walls are 24 inches thick. At this headquarters, citizens met on May 4, 1890, and organized Hall County's local government. Awarded Medallion Plate.
(1962)

MEMPHIS (Hall Co.)   *Heritage Hall, Main and 6th St.*
Hall County
Formed from Young and Bexar Territories. Created August 21, 1876. Organized June 23, 1890. Named in honor of Warren D. C. Hall 1788–1867. Member of the San Felipe Convention in 1832. Second in command of the Texans at Anahuac, 1832. Memphis the County Seat.

MENARD (Menard Co.)   *US 83, 3.4 mi. N in roadside park*
Menard County
Formed from Bexar County. Created Jan. 22, 1856. Organized June 25, 1866. Named in honor of Michael Branaman Menard, 1805–1856. Signer of the Texas Declaration of Independence, member of the Texas Congress, founder of Galveston. Menard, county seat.

MENARD (Menard Co.)   *US 83 at US 190*
Paso de la Santa Cruz (Holy Cross Ford)
Spot where in 1753 Juan Galvan, Spanish explorer, put up a huge cross, to show his choice of site for Mission San Saba. Indians gathered at the cross, remaining to participate in the first known Christian worship service in this area. The mission, 2 miles east, and the river ford were both named for the cross.   (1964)

MENARD (Menard Co.)   *US 83 at US 190*
Frisco Depot
Seeking a rail line to speed marketing of their livestock, residents of this area in 1909 asked the Fort Worth–Rio Grande Railroad, a branch of the Frisco System, to extend track from Brady (40 mi. NE) to Menardville. Ranchers donated right of way, while townspeople erected this depot and shortened the town's name to "Menard." Celebrations marked the arrival of the first train, Feb. 10, 1911 and completion of this Mission Revival station, July 4, 1911. The Santa Fe System later acquired the line. After rail service ended in 1972, this building became a historical building.   (1978)

MENARD (Menard Co.)   *US 83 at Canal Street*
"The Ditch"
The Vaughn Agricultural and Mechanical Canal Company was chartered in 1874 by William J. Vaughn, president; William Tipton, director; and James H. Comstock, director and secretary. Major H. M. Holmes was appointed attorney. Irrigation for 2,000 acres of valley land and power for grist mills are furnished by gravity flow from San Saba River. Use of "the ditch," running from 5 miles above town to 5 below, began in 1876. Vaughn sold his controlling interest to Gus Noyes in 1886. Since 1905 "the ditch" has been operated by Menard Irrigation Company, using the original dam.

MENARD (Menard Co.)   *US 83 at W. 1st St.*
Pioneer Rest Cemetery
Burial plot was begun by Adam Bradford, who buried his father, Jack Bradford, here in 1863. As the town and cemetery grew, the city bought the tract from Mrs. Gustav E. Schleicher in 1904. Fence surrounding cemetery was built of stone from the old courthouse and jail, razed in 1931, and reputed to have been in the original structure of nearby San Luis de Las Amarillas (built by the Spanish in 1757). Final resting place for many area pioneers, including soldiers, cowboys, gamblers, preachers, civil war veterans, Indian fighters, and Texas Rangers.   (1973)

MENARD (Menard Co.)   *US 83, 1mi. S in roadside park*
Puerto de Baluartes (Haven of the Strong Points)
In this pass between the hills—location of present day Menard—a site for an important spanish mission to the Apaches was chosen in 1754 by Don Pedro de Rabago y Teran, second explorer sent on the assignment by the viceroy of New Spain. Suitable to be fortified and farmed, this pass had its mission built in 1757.   (1964)

MENARD (Menard Co.)   *US 190, 1 mi. W, Celery Creek*
Arroyo de Juan Lorenzo
Name used by Spaniards of Presidio de San Saba (in existence from 1757 to 1770) for this stream now called Celery Creek. Stone to build Presidio was quarried from bluffs along the creek and deep banks let hostile Indians approach undiscovered to attack the Presidio, half a mile to the southwest.

MENARD (Menard Co.)   *SH 29, 10 mi. SE at roadside park*
Pegleg Crossing on the San Saba; about 1 mi. NE
An hourglass-shaped pass through the hills where McDougal Creek joins San Saba River. For years a favored Indian campground, it entered written history, 1732, as site of Spanish-Apache battle. Saw passage of adventurers, mustang hunters, Indian fighters, German settlers, gold-seekers. Probably named by landowner Wilhelm Harlen for one-legged land commissioner T. W. Ward. Crossing became station on stage line. Gained notoriety for many hold-ups that occurred at "robbers' roost" (1 mi. W). Pegleg served in later era as crossing on Great Western cattle trail. (1970)

MENTONE (Loving Co.)   *SH 302, .5 mi. SW*
Goodnight-Loving Trail
Blazed from the Fort Griffin–Dodge City trail through New Mexico, to Colorado about 1860 by Oliver Loving, 1812–1867, first cattle trail driver from Texas.

MENTONE (Loving Co.)   *SH 302, .5 mi. SW in roadside park*
Route of Old Butterfield Stagecoach Road
Over these tracks passed the Butterfield Stage, 1858–1861, providing for first time in history a combined passenger and mail service from Atlantic to Pacific Coast. Operating westward from St. Louis and Memphis, John Butterfield's company used 1,350 mules and horses and 90 concord coaches and wagons. Stages traveled rapidly, despite lack of real roads. A signal given approaching a station would assure food on table for travelers, and fresh horses ready. Stations were 12 to 113 miles apart. Route changes were often made to obtain water. The passengers and crew wore guns. Indians liked horses, so to reduce the danger of Indian attacks, mules were used West of Ft. Belknap. Trip one way took 25 days—7 consumed in crossing Texas, from near Preston (now under Lake Texoma) to Jacksboro, Ft. Belknap, Ft. Chadbourne, and El Paso. One-way fare for the 2,700 miles was $200. This marks a 113-mile span, from Emigrants' Crossing (82 mi. S) to Pope's Crossing (31 mi. N), that on inaugural trip, Sept. 16–Oct. 12, 1858, had no team-change. Route ran parallel to Pecos River. By November there were 3 change stations in this area, one being Skillman's Stop (6 mi. N). Route was shortened in 1860, going by Forts Stockton, Davis and Quitman, west of the Pecos. (1968)

MENTONE (Loving Co.)   *SH 302 at courthouse*
Loving County
Formed from Tom Green County. Created February 26, 1887. Organized July 8, 1893. Named in honor of Oliver Loving, 1812–1867, farmer, rancher and an early trail-driver. Mentone, county seat.

MENTONE (Loving Co.)   *SH 302 at courthouse*
Oliver Loving C.S.A. (1812–1867)
Only Texan instrumental in mapping 3 major cattle trails: Shawnee, Western and Goodnight-Loving Trails. Born in Kentucky. Came to Texas 1845, to farm, haul freight, deal in cattle. Started large Palo Pinto County ranch. In 1858, drove herd to Chicago—first time in history Texas cattle trailed to northern market. In 1859 drove to Denver. When Civil War broke out, 1861, was Confederate beef contractor, furnishing meat to army commissaries. Served on 24-hour patrol squad against Indians in frontier town of Weatherford. Mapped an 1862 expedition by 300 or more Texans to wipe out depredating Indians on the home grounds in Colorado, but failed to get necessary men to put this plan into action. After the war, with Charles Goodnight, drove cattle from Palo Pinto to Horse Head Crossing on the Pecos, then up the river to Indian reservations and forts in New Mexico. In 1867 on this trail, was shot by Comanches: crawled 5 miles, chewing an old kid glove for food. Hauled at price of $250 to Fort Sumner by Mexican traders, he had wounds treated, but died of gangrene. Partner packed corpse in charcoal, hauled him to Weatherford for burial, fulfilling last wish. Loving County was named for him in 1887. (1965)

MENTONE (Loving Co.)   *US 302 at courthouse*
Smallest County Seat in Texas, Mentone
Only town in Loving County—last organized, most sparsely populated (both in total and per square mile) county in Texas. Established 1931 and named for an earlier town (10 miles north) which legend says was named by a French surveyor-prospector after his home on the Riviera. With population of 42, Mentone has no water system. (Water is hauled in.) Nor does it have a bank,

doctor, hospital, newspaper, lawyer, civic club, or cemetery. There are only two recorded graves in county; some Indian skeletons, artifacts are found. Oil, farming, cattle country.   (1967)

MENTONE (Loving Co.)   *SH 302, 3 blks. N of courthouse*
Mentone Community Church
Built 1910 in Porterville, a town abandoned after Pecos River flood of 1930. Moved here for school and social center. Also used by various church groups and for non-denominational worship. Oldest building in Loving County. Awarded Medallion Plate.   (1964)

MERCEDES (Hidalgo Co.)   *US 281, .5 mi. E of intersection with FM 491*
El Horcon Tract and Río Rico
The Treaty of Guadalupe Hidalgo which ended the Mexican War (1846–48) designated the main channel of the Rio Grande as the Mexico-U.S. boundary. Disputes arising from frequent changes in the river's course led to the Treaty of 1884 which recognized only those river diversions resulting from natural occurrences. The International Boundary Commission was established in 1889 to administer the Treaty of 1884. In 1906 the American Rio Grande Land and Irrigation Company dug an unauthorized canal about two miles south of here which altered the natural course of the Rio Grande. As a result, a 419-acre section of U.S. property called El Horcon tract was isolated south of the river. Although still U.S. territory according to the Treaty of 1884, the tract and the popular gambling and resort community of Río Rico which flourished there during the 1920s and 1930s became increasingly subject to Mexican administration and jurisdiction. After the U.S. granted Mexico territorial rights over El Horcon tract and Río Rico in 1970, a native of Río Rico sued the U.S. government to guarantee his U.S. citizenship. This lawsuit began an eight-year legal battle that eventually led to U.S. citizenship for about 200 people born in Río Rico prior to 1970.   (1994)

MERCEDES (Hidalgo Co.)   *US 281, 1.2 mi. W of intersection with FM 491*
Relampago Ranch
Originally part of a Spanish land grant, Relampago (Lightning) Ranch community lay along the stage and military route from Rio Grande City to Brownsville. In 1852, Thaddeus Rhodes (1828–1904) acquired acreage here when he came as Hidalgo County clerk. Later he served as commissioner and judge. He and Jose Maria Mora (1824–1884), who bought adjoining land about 1856, helped bring economic and social stability. Mora and later his son Melchor, a deputy sheriff and Texas Ranger, farmed, ranched, and had the only general store in the area. Descendants still live on the property.   (1980)

MERCEDES (Hidalgo Co.)   *US 83 at intersection Mile 3 Rd. W*
The Rev. Pierre Yves Keralum "The Lost Missionary" (1817–1872)
Architect Pierre Yves Keralum was ordained an oblate priest at Marseilles, France, in 1852. That same year he came to South Texas as a member of the Missionary Oblates of Mary Immaculate (O.M.I.). Evidence of his architectural skill can be seen at Our Lady of Refuge Church in Roma and the cathedral in Brownsville. As a missionary, Keralum covered a large area of South Texas, ministering to thousands of people. He disappeared while traveling in this area in 1872. His remains were not discovered until ten years later.   (1989)

MERCEDES (Hidalgo Co.)   *US 281, 4 mi. S at roadside park*
Military Highway of the Lower Rio Grande Valley
Plains Indians made trails near the banks of the Rio Grande that were used by Spanish explorers in the 18th century. Early settlers built a road close to the river bank connecting their ranches. Later called the Military Road, it ran from Brownsville to Laredo, linking frontier forts and stagecoach and mail lines. An inland route for cotton shipping during the Civil War, parts of it also were used for cattle drives. It served as the military telegraph road between Forts Brown and McIntosh in the 1870s. Paved by the 1940s, the highway is a significant part of the region's history.   (1997)

MERIDIAN (Bosque Co.)   *SH 144, 1 mi. NW in roadside park*
¼ Mile West to Boyhood Home of John A. Lomax (1867–1948)
Only a log kitchen now marks the homesite of John Lomax, one of the foremost collectors of American folksongs. Here, on part of the Chisholm Trail, young Lomax heard cowboys crooning and yodeling to restless herds; Negro servants taught him jig tunes, chants, work songs, and calls; and on winter nights his family sang songs and swapped stories around a blazing fire. Lomax began

to write down this music while still a boy; and when he left Bosque County at age 20, he carried with him a roll of cowboy ballads—the nucleus of his lifelong work. (1970)

MERIDIAN (Bosque Co.)
SH 22, .7 mi. W
Bosque County
Named for the Bosque (Spanish for "woods") River. The territory now part of this county was traversed in 1841 by the Texan-Santa Fe Expedition. Maj. George B. Erath, noted surveyor and soldier, explored the region prior to its settlement. The first colonists established homes in 1850–1851. Among the national groups who immigrated here were the English (at Kent), Norwegians (at Norse and elsewhere), and the Germans (in eastern part of county). Formally created and organized in 1854, Bosque County had traditionally had farming-ranching economy. The Chisholm Cattle Trail crossed the area in the 1870s. (1973)

MERTENS (Hill Co.)
SH 22 at Stroud St.
Mertens Baptist Church
On June 14, 1884, a small group of Baptists, led by W. J. Priddy, D. P. Sanders, and J. C. Osborne, met to organize a Baptist church. Originally known as Richland Baptist Church, the congregation worshiped in the Richland school until 1892, when they moved a few miles northwest to the town of Mertens. Now known as Mertens Baptist Church, the membership has grown and expanded its facilities over the years. Throughout its history the congregation has provided significant service and leadership to the residents of this part of Hill County. (1984)

MERTZON (Irion Co.)
US 67, 2 mi. W
Irion County
Created March 7, 1889. Organized April 16, 1889. Named in honor of Robert Anderson Irion, 1806–1860. Came to Texas, 1833, and located at Nacogdoches. Member of the First Texas Congress, secretary of state in the cabinet of President Houston, 1837–1838. Sherwood the county seat, later moved to Mertzon.

MERTZON (Irion Co.)
Sherwood Ave. at Parkview St., off US 67, courthouse
Dove Creek Battle
On January 8, 1865 eight miles east of here Confederate troops and Texas militiamen engaged a large party of Kickapoo Indians. The Indians, formerly hostile to the South, had entered Texas without authority and were making their way to Mexico. The troops attacked them and following five hours of desperate fighting, withdrew, having suffering the loss of 22 killed and 19 wounded. Indian losses from the encounter were probably less. Later raids by the Kickapoos were traced to the Dove Creek fight.

Texas Civil War Indian Trouble
War brought turmoil to Indians living in Kansas and the Indian Territory, with unfortunate results for Texans on the frontier. Most Cherokees, Choctaws, Creeks and Seminoles aided the South, while others adhered to the North. Few Comanches made a treaty with the South; but a great majority with their allies, the Kiowas, held aloof from either side and plundered the frontier at will. Apaches and Kickapoos did the same from Mexico. Texas and Confederate troops, despite poor arms and mounts, held defense lines until war's end.

MESQUITE (Dallas Co.)
18680 IH 635
Site of Galloway Farmstead
Confederate veteran Benjamin Franklin Galloway (1833–1912) and his wife Eliza (Fletcher) (1852–1883) came to Texas from Tennessee in 1872. Their son Bedford Forest is said to have been born in a covered wagon at Duck Creek (Garland) in 1873. They purchased 101 acres in 1874 and Benjamin Galloway erected a cabin where they lived while a two-room house was built. A farmer, he also raised horses, mules and cattle. A second son, Nathan Lemmon, was born in 1876. Twin sons were born in 1883, but they lived only a day, and Eliza Galloway died soon after. Her niece, Clara Gentry, came to live with the family that year. At that time Benjamin had a Blackland Prairie hay company. Dallas clients included Tennessee Dairy, Caruth Farm and Ringling Brothers Circus. Benjamin Galloway married Amanda Jane Miller (1848–1938) of Tennessee in 1887 and built a 1½ story addition onto the home place. The structure eventually featured an entrance hall, bedroom, parlor, and a kitchen on the first level, with children's rooms upstairs. A son was born in 1888, but

died at birth. Bedford returned home after attending college in Waco and New Orleans and made his living farming, baling hay and ginning cotton. He and his first wife, Nannie Lawrence, had four children. After her death in 1915, he married Bertha Dakan in 1917 and they had two daughters. Bedford was a city alderman, a member of the school board, and served as mayor of Mesquite from 1927 to 1940. A Galloway descendant restored the house between 1949 and 1950 and built another addition in 1955. Designated a Recorded Texas Historic Landmark in 1973, the Galloway Home Place was moved from this site to a more rural location in Sunnyvale in an effort to protect it from encroaching urban development. (2000)

MESQUITE (Dallas Co.) 209 W. Main St. (SH 52)
City of Mesquite
In May 1873, Texas & Pacific Railroad engineer A. R. Alcott platted a new depot town named Mesquite. The post office opened the following year. The community developed along the rail line, with businesses initially facing Front Street. As the town grew, business owners turned their front doors to Main Street in an effort to create a Town Square. Voters incorporated Mesquite in 1887. In 1903, following a legal challenge, the city re-incorporated with new boundaries. Mesquite, which began with an agrarian economy, grew rapidly in the second half of the 20th century as a Dallas suburb. The school district, established in 1901, is a draw for new residents, and the city continues to grow. (2004)

MESQUITE (Dallas Co.) 200 blk. W. Main St. (SH352)
Sam Bass Train Robbery
Sam Bass, with Seab Barnes, Hank Underwood, "Arkansas" Johnson, and Frank Jackson—held up a Texas & Pacific train here, April 10, 1878. They took $152, but missed hidden shipment of $30,000. In planning a bank robbery 3 months later, Bass was fatally shot by rangers. (1968)

MEXIA (Limestone Co.) Comanche Crossing Road (US 84), 9 mi. W at entry to Booker T. Washington Park
Booker T. Washington Park
(Near the Historic Comanche Crossing of the Navasota River)
Set aside by deed in 1898 as a permanent site for celebrating June 19th—the anniversary of the 1865 Emancipation of Slaves in Texas. It was 2.5 miles south of this site that slaves of this area first heard their freedom announced. Limestone County in the 1860s—era of initial celebrations here—had many able Negro leaders. It sent to the Texas Constitutional Convention of 1866 one of its Negro citizens, Ralph Long. From among people who lived in this locality at the time of emancipation came Negro legislators Giles Cotton, Dave Medlock and Sheppard Mullins. Even before land was dedicated for the park here, this was site of annual celebrations of June 19th. For many years the Honorable Ralph Long was the featured orator, speaking at times from bed of a wagon parked in the shade. As many as 20,000 often gathered for the occasion. On July 7, 1912, the 19th of June organization was chartered, to administer the park and perpetuate regional history. The Negro people of Texas have shown outstanding initiative in fields of civic leadership, education, culture and business. In 1860 they numbered 187,921; in 1960 there were 1,187,125 Negroes in the state.

MEXIA (Limestone Co.) SH 171, 2.5 mi. NW
Joseph W. Stubenrauch (February 7, 1852–September 21, 1938)
Argricultural genius, born in Ruelzheim, Rhenish Bavaria, of a family of horticulturists. Educated in Germany. Migrated to New York in 1871 and to Texas 1876. In Limestone County (surrounding this marker site) lay 100 acres of open prairie land which he purchased. He discovered that fruit varieties then being grown here were unsuited to the climate. By cross-pollination, budding and grafting, he developed some 100 new varieties of peaches. More than 20 which were propagated for commercial purposes included "Anna," "Barbara," "Carman," "Frank," "Fredericka," "Katie," "Liberty," "Lizzie," "Miss Lola," and "Tena." In 1882, his younger brother, Jacob, also came and settled nearby. Both men were outstanding citizens. Joseph W. Stubenrauch shared his findings through his writings for *Farm and Ranch*, *Rural New Yorker* and *Holland's Magazine*. He practiced and advocated terracing, crop rotation and diversification, soil testing, fertilization and irrigation. Many of his ideas of conservation farming and agricultural education were incorporated into U.S. Government programs. He was nationally recognized for his contributions to American agriculture. (1970)

MEXIA (Limestone Co.)

SH 14, S edge of town

Mexia Oil Boom

One of great free-wheeling oil booms of America—before proration was enforced. Population in Mexia increased from 4,000 to 50,000 within days after oil discovery in 1920 at Rogers No. 1 Well, located 1.6 miles west of this marker, just off FM road 1633. Earlier (in 1912), Blake Smith and other Mexia men had brought in a gas field. Believing oil also could be found here, they interested a veteran operator—flamboyant wildcatter A. E. Humphreys—who struck oil at 3,105 feet. By May, 1921 gushers were flowing. Humphreys had 2,000 men; did a $4,000,000 business. His fortune later was estimated at $37,000,000. The boom was on. Other companies were formed. A second renowned wildcatter, J. K. Hughes, shared the leadership in developing the field to capacity. Millionaires, merchants, operators and workers swarmed to Mexia for a share in the "black gold." Many undesirables came, also, and one day were ousted by the thousands by Texas Rangers. In 1920–1921, first boom year, $5,000,000 went into construction; tanks for over 30 million barrels of oil were built; but even so storage area was inadequate for output. A park and clubhouse developed near this site by Col. Humphreys—mementos of boom—are still in use.   (1967)

MIAMI (Roberts Co.)

US 60, 4.5 mi. NE

Fossil Beds

Cited as one of most prolific fossil fields of lower Pliocene age at time of discovery, these beds are about 13,000,000 years old. Geologists of Rio Bravo Oil Company found them in 1928 on C. C. Coffee Ranch, and their reports brought specialists from several major institutions to the area. The fossil bones buried here included (among others) those of a prehistoric camel, a kind of antelope, horse, and wild pig. Further studies led scientists in 1941 to adopt "Hemphillian" as the name for the geologic age represented by these fossils.   (1970)

MIAMI (Roberts Co.)

US 60, 3 mi. N in roadside park

Roberts County

Formed from Young and Bexar Territories. Created August 21, 1876. Organized January 10, 1889. Named in honor of John S. Roberts, a signer of the Texas Declaration of Independence, and Oran Milo Roberts, governor of Texas, 1878–1882. County seat, Miami, to October, 1889. Parnell, to August 1, 1898. Miami, since.

MIAMI (Roberts Co.)

US 60 at S Mobeetie St.

Miami Railroad Depot

When the Southern Kansas Railway Company of Texas built a line through Roberts County in 1887, Miami developed at the end of the track as a campsite for workers. The crew set up a kitchen and a tent hotel. Soon the railroad built a public water well and telegraph lines to nearby Fort Elliott. Passengers and supplies for the post and nearby town of Mobeetie began arriving by rail. This depot was erected in 1888 between North Main and Birge Street. The Santa Fe Railroad bought the line in 1899 and this structure remained in service until 1978.   (1979)

MIAMI (Roberts Co.)

111 W. Commercial St. (US 60)

Cottage Hotel

The prominent Lard family helped Lizzie Lard build the Cottage Hotel to support her two daughters after she was widowed 1893; it was completed in 1895. As Miami became the county seat and a regional trade center, the hotel prospered. Its parlor was popular as a meeting site for local businessmen and a social gathering place for young people. Dr. Pryor Lee Shelton bought the property in 1906, renaming it the Commercial Hotel. In 1914, Tom Graham, manager of the competing Fitch Hotel, bought the Commercial Hotel and called it the Survant for his wife, Eva Survant. They operated the establishment for fifty years, holding banquets, reunions and other social events in the dining room until 1964. From 1973 to 1993 the building served as a residence, but in the early 1990s it was restored to its original function as an inn.   (2000)

MIAMI (Roberts Co.)

301 Commercial (US 60)

Roberts County Courthouse

Prominently sited atop a grassy slope overlooking the town of Miami, the Roberts County Courthouse was built in 1913, during a time of regional economic development spurred by the oil and ranching industries. One of six Texas courthouses designed by architect Elmer George Withers of

Stamford, the Roberts County Courthouse features Beaux Arts styling with simple Classical features. As the center of social and governmental activity for this rural county, the building has played an important role in the county's history. (2000)

MICO (Medina Co.)   CR 271, dam walkover in Mico
Medina Dam
Henri Castro, who colonized this area in the 1840s, envisioned irrigated farms along the Medina River. The project was delayed, however, until after the turn of the century, when Dr. Fred Stark Pearson, an internationally known engineer, persuaded British investors to finance construction of a dam at this site. Completed in 1912, Medina Dam was hailed as the largest in Texas and the fourth largest in the United States. Limestone boulders from a nearby quarry added bulk to the massive concrete structure. Four miles downstream, a small diversion dam conducted water into a system of irrigation canals. Gravitational force delivered the water to fields. The outbreak of World War 1 (1914) disrupted ties with British investors. Seeking new capital, Dr. Pearson and his wife left for England in 1915 on the Lusitania and were killed when a German submarine torpedoed the ship. The irrigation network created by Medina Dam brought new prosperity to this region. Vegetables raised in irrigated fields became a valuable crop. Water and electricity were made available to rural residents. In 1925, voters established the Bexar-Medina-Atascosa Counties Water Improvement District No. 1 to manage the project. (1978)

MIDLAND (Midland Co.)   IH 20, 4.8 mi. E in roadside park
Marcy Trail
Platted in 1849 by a U.S. Army surveying expedition under Capt. Randolph B. Marcy. Guided by Manuel, a Comanche Indian, Marcy crossed the dreaded Staked Plains of West Texas, proving their feasibility for travel, and opening a new and shorter road west. Marcy's trail from Dona Ana, N.M., to Fort Smith, Ark., became a major road to the California gold fields. Later the Overland Stage followed it for about 125 miles and in 1881, Texas and Pacific Railroad built along part of the route.

MIDLAND (Midland Co.)   SH 158, 6 mi. NW
Site of Old Roadbed Midland & Northwestern Railroad
Standard gauge 66 mile line built by David Fasken, Sr., to carry cattle, ranch supplies, passengers. Operated 1916 to 1920—critical era of World War I and world starvation aftermath. Linked towns of Fasken, Florey, and Seminole with Texas & Pacific Railway at Midland. At first, operated with locomotive borrowed from T. & P. Train had to stop for pasture gates to be opened. Crew shot coyotes and rattlesnakes. In a breakdown, the passengers were fed, sheltered at Fasken. Work crew slept on the prairie. Flooded out in 1920, M. & N. R. was abandoned. Roadbed still is visible. (1967)

MIDLAND (Midland Co.)   N. Colorado St. at Wall St. at courthouse
Midland County (Created and Organized, March, 1885)
First known as the junction of many trails and site of the last Comanche raid into Texas. In 1881 the Texas and Pacific Railroad was built; equidistant between El Paso and Fort Worth, this became known as Midland. First settler was a sheepman in 1882. Cattlemen came with Herefords in 1888. Water wells and windmills lured small farmers. Became headquarters for 1928 Permian Basin Oil Discovery. In 1945 its first well came in. The "Midland Man," oldest skeletal remains in North America (18,500 B.C.), was found in 1954. (1965)

MIDLAND (Midland Co.)   N. Colorado St. at Wall St. at courthouse
Midland Man
Oldest human remains in new world. Found 1953 on ranch near here by pipeline welder Keith Glasscock. Fossilized skull, rib and hand bones had been exposed by weather conditions. Tests indicated these were bones of a woman who lived as long ago as 9000–9500 B. C.; nearby were bones of extinct species of horse, camel, mammoth, peccary, wolf, sloth; with weapons, tools and signs of ancient campfires. Drs. Fred Wendorf and Alex D. Kreiger, archaeologists; Claude C. Albritton, geologist; T. D. Stewart, physician and anthropologist, made studies of the discovery. (1966)

MIDLAND (Midland Co.)   Texas Ave. at Baird St., 1 blk. off Spur 546
John Valentine Pliska
Mechanical genius who made and flew first locally-owned aircraft. Born in Austria, Pliska came with parents to Texas, and after 1903 followed blacksmith trade in Midland. He built (1912) and

314

flew at intervals up to 15 minutes an aeroplane of his own invention. (Plane now in museum at Midland-Odessa air terminal.) Pliska was a master smith. Gen. John J. Pershing had U. S. Army horses shod here during border trouble prior to World War I. Branding irons for a large West Texas area were also made here. Pliska married Louise Hundle. They had seven children.   (1970)

MIDLAND (Midland Co.)
SH 158, 10 mi. SE
Midland County's First Producing Oil Well
The discovery of oil in the Permian Basin during the 1920s helped sustain the area economy during the Great Depression, and many oil and gas companies established headquarters in Midland. Not until the 1940s, though, did Midland County begin seeing its own productive oil wells. Geologist H. L. Beckman worked with the Rowan Drilling Company to stake out Humble Oil and Refining Company's No. 1 Mrs. O. P. Buchanan Well at this site. They spudded the well on September 14, 1944 and completed in on November 6, 1945 at a total depth of 12,574 feet. The well produced 332 barrels of oil in 29 hours and became Midland County's first producing oil well. It was plugged on August 1, 1947.
(2005)

MIDWAY (Madison Co.)
SH 21, 4.5 mi. NE
Nuestra Señora del Pilar de Bucareli
In this vicinity, at Paso Tomas on the Trinity, was the Spanish Town Nuestra Señora del Pilar de Bucareli (1774–1779). Indian troubles had caused Spain to move Louisiana colonists to Bexar (San Antonio). These people, however, pled to return to East Texas, and secured the consent of Viceroy Antonio Maria Bucareli. Led by Gil Ybarbo (1729–1809), they built at the Trinity crossing a church, plaza, and wooden houses, and grew to a town of 345 people. But ill luck with crops, a few Comanche raids, and river floods sent the settlers farther east. Again led by Ybarbo, they rebuilt the old town of Nacogdoches, 1779.
(1972)

MIDWAY (Madison Co.)
SH 21, 4 mi. NE, W of Trinity Bridge
Robbins Ferry
First known as Paso Tomas (Thomas Ford) at the crossing of the San Antonio and La Bahia roads over the Trinity. Ferry established about 1821 by Joel Leakey. Named in honor of Nathaniel Robbins, who operated it many years. Acquired about 1852 by Elisha Clapp, whose descendants operated it until 1930 when Clapps Ferry Bridge was constructed.

MIDWAY (Madison Co.)
SH 21 at Antioch Rd., 3.7 mi. NE
Antioch Church of Christ
Believed to be among the oldest independent African American churches in Texas, this congregation was established on the Hayes Plantation and named Antioch after a biblical passage. The church moved from the plantation in 1865 and relocated in Midway, where trustees acquired property. The church building also served as a school until a bungalow schoolhouse was erected in 1915. In 1917 a second Church of Christ was formed in the area. The two congregations merged in 1924 and the school was replaced as a Rosenwald School the next year. New church structures were erected in 1937 and again in 1990. The active congregation continues to serve the community with a variety of outreach and worship programs.
(1999)

MIDWAY (Madison Co.)
SH 21, 3.5 mi. NE
Site of Trinidad
A fort and town as early as 1805. Captured by the McGee-Guitierrez Expedition in October, 1812. Near here the survivors of the Battle of the Medina were executed in 1813. Inhabitants of the town were butchered by order of the Spanish Commander and the town desolated.

MIDWAY (Madison Co.)
SH 21, 2 mi. SW
James and Calpernia Mitchell
James (1795–1870) and Calpernia (Franklin) (1805–1865) Mitchell came to Texas from Virginia in 1833 and received a Mexican land grant. In 1837, James served as a member of the commission to locate the seat of the newly formed Montgomery County; in 1846, when Walker County was formed, he became one of the first county commissioners. The Mitchell house and inn on the old San Antonio road provided rest for weary travelers and served as an area post office from about 1840 to 1850. The parents of Edwin, Thomas, James, Nathan, and Anthony Wayne, Calpernia and James are interred in the family cemetery near this site.
(1998)

MILAM (Sabine Co.)   *SH 21 at SH 87*
Milam
Founded in 1828 as Red Mound. Named in 1835 for Benjamin Rush Milam. Seat of Justice of Sabine Municipality, 1835; of Sabine County, 1837–58. Incorporated December 29, 1837. Internal Revenue Post during the Republic Headquarters of the Quartermaster's Department C.S.A. for Sabine County, 1861–1865. First home in Texas of John S. Roberts, a signer of the Texas Declaration of Independence. Home of John C. Hale, martyr of San Jacinto.

MILAM (Sabine Co.)   *SH 87 at SH 21*
John C. Hale
John C. Hale, one of nine patriots killed at the Battle of San Jacinto, was born in Scott County, Virginia on April 3, 1806. He married Barshaba Miller in his home state in 1830, and by 1835 moved with his wife and children to Sabine County. They were living in Milam when John joined the war effort against Mexico as a first lieutenant. At the age of 30, he died in combat in the final military conflict of the revolution on April 21, 1836, and was buried with seven other battle casualties at the site of the Texan campground. For Hale's service, his heirs received 960 acres of land. In addition, the Legislature named Hale County in West Texas in honor of his patriotism and service during the Texas Revolution.   (2006)

MILAM (Sabine Co.)   *SH 21 at Las Boregas Creek*
Las Boregas Camp Site
Las Boregas Creek formed the eastern boundary of the 1794 Spanish land grant to Juan Ignacio Pifermo, making this grant the oldest in Sabine County. *El Camino de los Tejas*, a portion of *El Camino Real*—the main road into Spanish Texas—crossed the creek near this point. During the Spanish colonial period, a well-known campsite developed near the creek. A Spanish army post was also established upstream to protect settlers and travel c. 1800. The name of the creek is possibly a misspelling of *borregas*, meaning "lambs less than a year old." According to his journal, Empresario Stephen F. Austin, "The Father of Texas," spent his first night in Texas on "Boreg Creek" on July 16, 1821.   (2008)

MILAM (Sabine Co.)   *SH 21, .25 mi. E*
The Milam Masonic Institute
Many pioneers belonged to the Ancient, Free and Accepted Masons, an order active in education. Among Masons settling in this area by 1845 were Republic of Texas leaders William Clark, James Gaines, D. S. Kaufman, Willis H. Landrum, and F. M. Weatherred. The Rev. Littleton Fowler (1803), a Mason, opened in 1845 in this county the Midway Institute, which was soon absorbed by Red Mound Seminary. Set to work at Red Mound (Milam), 1847, was Jackson Lodge No. 35, A. F. & A. M., with John Boyd, G. A. Norford, A. D. Oliphint, O. J. Polley, and J. T. Scruggs as officers. The Lodge soon operated the Milam Masonic Institute, successor to the earlier schools. On the charter application (1853) M. M. I. was listed as already "a flourishing school." Later, Sexton Lodge No. 251, A. F. & A. M., operated M. M. I., a great contributor to East Texas culture until tax-funded education became universal in the 1870s. Among supporters of M. M. I. were Masons with the family names Anderson, Causey, Davis, Deweese, Dorsey, Elliott, Gellately, Halbert, Harper, Harris, Jacks, Low, McCloskey, McGown, McMahan, Mason, Nethery, Noble, Pratt, Reeves, Renfro, Sanders, Slaughter, Smith, Speights, Sweet, Tucker, Vickers, Watson, White, Whittlesey, Williams, and Yeiser.   (1974)

MINEOLA (Wood Co.)   *300 US 69N (Greenville Hwy)*
Mineola Fire Department
In the 1870s, the Texas & Pacific and International & Great Northern railroads built lines through this area, with the town of Mineola serving as the eventual juncture of the two. Fire was one of many challenges faced by early local inhabitants of the new town; on a single night in the 1880s, a reported eighteen downtown buildings burned, including houses, businesses and a Masonic temple. Residents built new brick structures, but the threat of fire remained. In 1906, officials installed a fire gong at the city well to use as an alarm, and the city council began discussing the formation of a hook and ladder company. The next year, several men organized the Mineola Fire Company, a volunteer group with no connection to the city government, which received its first firefighting equipment in 1908. The volunteer company continued to grow over the next several years, adding

chemical and hose trucks, and developing membership requirements. The city adopted the fire company as an official department in 1924 and purchased an American La France fire engine. Between that year and 1928, the city experienced several disastrous fires, including one in 1926 that required assistance from Tyler and Winnsboro firefighters. R. D. Adrian received the contract to build a fire station, completed in 1932. It provided fire equipment storage space, a meeting room and a jail. By the mid-1940s, the city paid insurance on all firemen, who remained volunteers. In 1954, the city hired its first paid firefighters. Ten years later, the department began holding annual rodeos for the community. Over the past several decades, the city has expanded the department and sent its workers to training in firefighting and other emergency and rescue procedures.   (2005)

MINEOLA (Wood Co.)   *101 E. Broad St. (US 80) at Johnson St.*
Site of Public Mineral Water Well
Mineola settlers chose this area, nicknamed "the Forks of the River," for its abundance of water. The town's first water service was administered by A. W. Front, who made daily deliveries to his 50 clients. A water well was located on this site as early as 1885; workmen drilling for salt between 1889 and 1890 discovered mineral water. In 1896 a 60-foot windmill tower with a 3,000-gallon cypress wood tank was constructed and a mineral well dug to 150 feet by Henry L. Beaird. This became the town's main water source. A 1913 analysis of the water revealed more than 12 minerals associated with healing properties. In 1906, an electric motor replaced the windmill. The well was capped in 1924 when the street was bricked over. The exact site of the public mineral water well was the center of the intersection of Highway 80 and Johnson Street.   (1998)

MINEOLA (Wood Co.)   *US 69 at Front St.*
Railroads in Mineola
This city's fortunes have been tied historically to railroads. Mineola was born in the summer of 1873, as the Houston and Great Northern (later International and Great Northern) and Texas and Pacific lines raced to a predetermined crossing point. The company arriving first would secure ownership of rail facilities, so construction crews worked day and night, with the I&GN building northwest from near Tyler and the T&P extending westward from Longview. The two lines neared this spot on the same day and the crews were within sight of each other that morning. Accounts differ on which railroad won the competition, with disagreement over the exact surveyed location and whether being first meant the first tracks or first train to arrive. The City of Mineola incorporated in 1877 and its rail success continued as the Missouri, Kansas and Texas line extended to Greenville in 1881. This connected the growing trade center with major cities—Dallas, Sherman, Shreveport and Houston—in all directions. The railroads also brought new settlers to Mineola, and a new depot opened in 1905. The T&P moved its terminal here from Longview in 1929, bringing about 200 employees and making a significant economic impact on the city. Its presence sustained Mineola while other towns suffered through the Great Depression. In the following years, a new fire department, post office and schools were in operation. The city became a shipping center for agriculture, notably watermelons, sweet potatoes and cotton. The T&P dedicated a new passenger depot in 1951, but rail connections to Greenville and Lindale were later abandoned. Passenger service, suspended in Mineola's centennial year of 1973, returned in 1996.   (2007)

MINEOLA (Wood Co.)   *205 N. Johnson St., 1 blk. N of US 80*
Gov. James Stephen Hogg and Wood County
James Stephen Hogg lived in Wood County from 1868 to 1882, formative years of his political career. When he became Governor, he appointed several Wood County friends to public offices. They included: Sarah Rosalie Patten Buchanan, who became a professor at Sam Houston State Normal College; William Jesse McDonald, a city deputy appointed Ranger captain; Cadwell Walton Raines, a newspaperman and county judge who became State Librarian; and former City Marshal George Reeves, who became a penitentiary agent. Friendships Gov. Hogg made in his Wood County years had an important impact on the county and on the State of Texas.   (2006)

MINEOLA (Wood Co.)   *US 69S at S. Johnson St.*
Mineola Black Spiders
In the 1800s and into the first half of the twentieth century, African-American baseball teams played separately from white teams. The community of Mineola, though small in population, had both white and black baseball teams. The Mineola Black Spiders was composed of African-American men and

youth from the town. The ballplayers wore solid gray uniforms and played at Epperson Park in south Mineola, in addition to traveling to games in Dallas, Commerce, Shreveport (Louisiana), and other places. Home games sometimes attracted around 200 spectators. Vernon Klingaman, who moved to Texas in the late 1920s, settling in Mineola, soon became involved with the team. He expanded the roster, opening it to non-residents, and changed the name to the Texas Black Spiders. In 1932, the players departed Mineola for the Midwest, becoming a barnstorming team, staging exhibition games in various locations. That year, the team underwent a name change, becoming the Mason City Black Bats. They headquartered in Iowa, though most members would return to the Spiders' squad, while others moved back to Texas. The Black Spiders gained a reputation as being one of the fastest teams from the South. They were also very successful; in 1936, the Spiders' record was 34–1. However, by 1937, there was a substantial turnover in team personnel. The Black Spiders fielded a team in 1938, but disbanded afterward. Today, the team is mostly forgotten in Mineola. However, the Black Spiders remain a significant part of the community's history as a black baseball team that became a success locally and in the Midwestern United States. (2010)

MINEOLA (Wood Co.) *114 N. Pacific St. (US 69)*
Government Projects in Mineola
During the Great Depression (1929–41), Mineola residents were aided by federal and local government initiatives. Federal programs such as the Works Progress Administration (WPA) and Civil Works Administration (CWA) employed workers; provided funds for civic improvement, including street paving and the construction of a federal building; opened government aid offices; and commissioned artist Bernard Zakheim to paint a mural in the city post office. Municipal authorities also helped residents in need, made sewer and water extension improvements, and conducted a malaria control program. These government efforts combined to protect Mineola residents in a tumultuous time in U.S. history. (2009)

MINERAL WELLS (Palo Pinto Co.) *100 Blk. S, Oak St. (US 281)*
Mineral Wells
A town built on water. Founded 1877 by J. A. Lynch, a settler who miraculously recovered from rheumatism after drinking the foul-tasting, but apparently healthful, water in this well. As the news spread, hundreds converged to "take" the waters, and a boom town sprang up. Its commercial slogan "crazy" arose from a deputed cure of insanity at the "crazy woman well". Although the water's curative value is likely due to dissolved Epsom and Glauber salts, amazing powers were attributed to it. For years Mineral Wells was Texas' leading health spa. (1969)

MISSION (Hidalgo Co.) *US 83 Bus. at Conway Ave.*
The Border Theater
A fine example of a mid-20th century motion picture theater with regional stylistic influences, the Border Theater was completed in 1942. Dallas architect William J. Moore designed the structure, which was built by contractor George Holliday. The theater was large enough for 740 patrons and housed the office of owners Mr. and Mrs. R. N. Smith. Changes to the edifice's exterior include a raised marquee and the addition of a tile canopy. The Border Theater remains a monument to Mission's architectural and cinematic history. (Recorded Texas Historic Landmark 1997)

MOBEETIE (Wheeler Co.) *SH 152, 1 mi. W*
Site of Fort Elliott
Established June 5, 1875. One of the last forts established in Texas for the purpose of clearing the region of Indians. Around it Mobeetie, rendezvous of buffalo hunters and traders, grew up. The post was abandoned in 1889.

MOBEETIE (Wheeler Co.) *SH 152 at FM 48*
Mobeetie
Oldest town in Texas Panhandle. Originally a trading post, 2 mi. south, 1874; moved nearer Fort Elliott, 1875. Earlier called Sweetwater, was renamed in 1879. Courthouse was completed by Mark Huselby, first county tax assessor, and other citizens. Popular with hunters, cowboys, gamblers—town in 1881 became judicial center of 35th District. Temple Houston, son of the hero, Sam Houston, was district attorney and the first state senator for this district. After bypass by the Santa Fe Railroad (1888) and a destructive 1898 tornado, Mobeetie declined. (1967)

MONAHANS (Ward Co.)
IH 20 in roadside park
Ward County
Formed from Tom Green County. Created February 26, 1887. Organized March 29, 1892. Named in honor of Thomas William Ward, 1807–1872, at the storming of Bexar, December, 1835; commissioner of the General Land Office, 1841–1848; United States Consul at Panama, 1853–1856.

MONAHANS (Ward Co.)
IH 20/US 80, 6 mi. E
Monahans Sandhills State Park and Museum
In these shifting seas of sand, rich in stone evidences of primitive men, today's visitors find flint points, sandstone metates and manos of peoples who were here as early as 10,000 years ago and late as the 1870s. Bones of great mammoths and gigantic bison prove that this desert was in post-glacial times a land of lakes and tall grasses. Cabeza de Vaca in 1535 and Antonio de Espejo in 1583 encountered Jumanos, historic tribe which hunted here. In 1590 Castano de Sosa found a tribe he called Vaqueros because they lived by hunting cows (buffalo)—the tribe later called Apaches. For more than 100 years at this stop on Great Comanche War Trail extending into Mexico, Apache fought Comanche for pools of water and acorns of dwarf shinnery oak. The California or Emigrant Trail through the Sand Hills started with the gold rush, was first mapped in September 1849 by Capt. Randolph B. Marcy, U.S. Topographical Engineers, and in 1854 by Capt. John Pope, who explored a railroad route toward the Pacific Ocean. 3,840 acres of sand hills were designated in 1957 as a state park, after acquisition and construction of museum by Ward County. Has picnic facilities.

MONAHANS (Ward Co.)
400 Museum Blvd.
Million Barrel Tank
A project of the Shell Oil Company, the construction of this oil storage tank in 1928 was the result of an oil boom in the area. Built to accommodate crude oil until it could be shipped to refineries, the tank was constructed by crews working on a 24-hour schedule using hand operated and horse-drawn equipment. Covering eight acres of land, the tank was able to hold over one million barrels of oil. It was filled to capacity only once. Efforts to convert it into a water-filled recreation center in the 1950s were unsuccessful, and it became a museum in 1986. (1988)

MONROE CITY (Chambers Co.)
SH 65 at entrance to Exxon Refinery
Anahuac Oil and Gas Field
Although oil production of major value began in Chambers County in 1916, this prolific Anahuac Field was discovered on March 3, 1935, with completion of Humble Oil & Refining Company's A. D. Middleton No. 1 (1.8 mi. SE). The camp which housed Humble crews who developed the field was adjacent to this site. The field encompasses some 14,000 acres of prime rice and grazing land and produces from 21 zones in a highly faulted domal structure. Producing depths range from 6,600 feet to 8,600 feet. Peak production was reached in World War II, when in 1944 annual total was 11,916,137 barrels. Discovery well had an original potential of 144 barrels a day from depth of 7,050 feet. It was deepened to 7,088 feet and recompleted March 14, 1935, with a new potential of 518 barrels. Through 1966, A. D. Middleton No. 1 has produced in excess of 390,000 barrels of oil. Over 177 million barrels of oil and 268 billion cubic feet of gas have been produced from the field. (In Chambers County, a pioneer oil producing area, over 475 million barrels of oil have been produced since 1916.) At present, there are 408 wells in the Anahuac Field, and it is expected that production will continue into the 21st century. (1967)

MONT BELVIEU (Chambers Co.)
IH 10 at FM 565, 6 mi. E
Cove
In 1824, Joseph Lawrence of New York, a reputed member of Jean Lafitte's privateering band, settled on a nearby marshland ridge. Known as Lawrence's Island, it became the nucleus of later settlement, which included James Haney and members of the Dugat, Mackey, Stubbs, and Wilburn families. In 1827, A. B. J. Winfree came here from Louisiana and settled on a land grant. The wide-spread community around his property soon became known as Winfree's Cove and later simply as Cove. The economy of the Cove community was originally based on cattle, but later included farming, fishing, and fur trapping. Several businesses were located here, including ferries, a shipyard, and general stores. The settlement also included a post office from 1885 to the 1940s, a

319

school which was established in the 1870s and consolidated with the Barbers Hill District in 1937, and churches. In order to avoid annexation, Cove was incorporated as a municipality in 1973. An important agricultural center for Chambers County and the upper Texas coastal region, the town of Cove has maintained a form of local government that reflects the residents' values, independence and rich heritage. (1982)

MONTALBA (Anderson Co.) SH 19, 3.5 mi. N
Old Montalba

In area known as Beaver Valley, settled about 1853—the year that pioneer P. G. Oldham built his home a half-mile northwest of this marker. This was on the Palestine-Athens Road, the route taken by mail hacks in early days. To the east was a campground where travelers often spent the night, and where later inhabitants of the area used to gather for seasonal religious camp meetings. Near the Oldham home was the Beaver Valley Primitive Baptist Church. Mr. Oldham donated land for a cemetery adjoining the church. Nearby stood a noted early school, Beaver Academy. The church was later known by name "Holly Springs." The first local physician, Dr. T. J. Adams, built his homestead in the woods of Beaver Valley in 1859, and conducted a wide practice until he was past 80. During the Civil War, while the young men of the area were away in the army, an iron foundry in this valley made arms and bullets for the Confederacy. In 1880 a post office was granted under the name Montalba—suggested by early settler Tobe Hamlett, inspired by snowclad mountain on the horizon. Mrs. Mollie Hamlett was the first postmaster. In later years Montalba settlement was moved southward, and now thrives as a market and supply point for valley. (1970)

MONTELL (Uvalde Co.) US 55, 20 miles NW of Uvalde
Church of the Ascension

Bishop W. P. Elliott held first Episcopal rites in Montell, 1890. Church was built with donations from friends throughout the world, under the leadership of the Rev. Richard Galbraith, who came from Ireland in 1883. The first service was held in this edifice Christmas Day, 1890. Services of Consecration by the Right Rev. J. S. Johnston, Bishop of West Texas, 1891. (1965)

MONTELL (Uvalde Co.) SH 55, behind Church of the Ascension
Montell Methodist Church

A Methodist Church mission was established in the community of Montell in 1889. Served by missionary N. W. Keith, the congregation met in a number of locations, including a brush arbor in the summer months. A Union Sunday School was organized by 1895. A permanent church building was dedicated on June 1, 1908. Services were held once a month except for a period during World War II when they were temporarily suspended. Since 1948 the congregation has met for worship on alternating Sundays. Descendants of pioneer members remain active in the church.
(Texas Sesquicentennial 1836–1986)

MONTELL (Uvalde Co.) SH 55 in Montell
General John R. Baylor

Born in Kentucky. Came to Texas Republic 1839. Colorful Indian fighter. In war against Cherokees 1840. Member Texas Legislature 1853. Comanche agent 1855–57. Delegate from Weatherford, Secession Convention. Commanding detachment of Second Regiment Texas Mounted Rifles occupied, took over supplies, Ft. Bliss, June 1861—during campaign to extend Confederacy westward to the Pacific. Repulsed Federals, Mesilla, N. Mex., July 25. With 200 men took 700 Federals, their transports, arms, ammunition, 200 horses, 270 beeves, four cannon at San Augustin Springs, July 27. With Capitol at Mesilla, organized government, proclaimed Confederate control of Arizona, Aug. 1. Baylor became military, civil governor. Sent C.S.A. Treasury $9,500 captured at Ft. Fillmore. Supervised gold, silver mining for C.S.A. Order to kill instead of capture troublesome Apaches incensed authorities against him, had Baylor recalled to Texas, stripped of rank. As private "served guns in hottest of the fight" to recapture Galveston, Jan. 1, 1863. Salvaged U.S. warship parts to make cannon light enough to go into battle on back of mule. 1863–65 in Confederate Congress. Given new command. Made Brigadier-General 1865. Raised, led troops in frontier defense. Fear of his moves pinned down thousands of Federals in California, Arizona. Climaxed war service on Northwest Texas border. Post-war lived in San Antonio. Farmed, ranched Uvalde County. Buried in Montell. (1963)

MONTELL (Uvalde Co.)

SH 55 in Montell

Near Site of Nuestra Señora de la Candelaria Mission

Third mission under this name founded in Texas. Established near here on the Nueces River in 1762 by Franciscan missionaries for the conversion of the Indians and protection of Spanish lands. Typical of many Spanish missions in Texas, Candelaria had twice moved closer to centers of civilization since its first founding in 1749 on the San Gabriel River. Beset with friction between friars and soldiers, the first Candelaria was abandoned in 1755 and then moved to the San Marcos River. Soon, however, the friars found that the Indians were more concerned with protection than with Christianity. In 1757 the mission was again discontinued. In 1762 Candelaria was re-established here, and about 100 Lipan-Apaches quickly volunteered to live within its walls. A chapel, large thatched building, a house, and possibly other structures were erected. But once more, difficulties arose—scarcity of meat, unrest and insincerity among the mission Indians, inadequate defense, devastating raids by Comanches and Apaches. About 1767 the mission was abandoned for the last time. Little remains of it today, for the smooth building stones were taken by Anglo settlers in the 1800s to build their houses.

(1968)

MONTGOMERY (Montgomery Co.)

SH 105, 1.5 E

Former Homesite of Joseph L. Bennett

Joseph L. Bennett, who came to Texas in 1834 and settled in this area, joined the Texas army in early 1836. As captain of a company of local volunteers, he left this area about March 1, 1836, to lead his troops to aid Texan forces at the Alamo. Upon reaching the Colorado River he learned of the fall of the Alamo, and so discontinued the mission. He soon joined with Sam Houston's main army and in April was elected Lt. Colonel of the 2nd Regiment of Volunteers, the company he commanded at the Battle of San Jacinto. Bennett received land grants in payment for his military service, and in 1837 President Sam Houston appointed him to command a frontier defense unit. Elected by Montgomery County voters to the Republic of Texas Congress, he served for two terms, 1838–1840. He briefly resumed military service in 1842 as a member of the Somervell Expedition against Mexico. Bennett also was active in local civic affairs, serving as mail carrier from Houston to Montgomery, county commissioner and supporter of area schools. He moved his family to his headright land grant in present Navarro and Freestone counties in 1848. He died later that year and was buried in a family graveyard near Streetman.

MONTGOMERY (Montgomery Co.)

SH 105, 1.3 mi. E

Site of the Home of Charles B. Stewart (1806–1885)

Member of the Consultation, 1835. First Secretary of State. Signer of the Texas Declaration of Independence. Delegate from Montgomery County to the Constitutional Convention of 1845. Member of the Texas Legislature.

MONTGOMERY (Montgomery Co.)

SH 105 at Pond St.

Reuben Jonathan Palmer (January 18, 1829–March 20, 1868)

Born in Appomattox County, Va., son of Reuben DeJarnette and Martha P. (Christian) Palmer; he was educated at Randolph-Macon College. Moved to Texas in 1856. A Montgomery lawyer; served in 9th Legislature, State of Texas, and in Secession Convention, 1861. Married Frances Winifred, the daughter of Robert G. and Agnes (Wood) Branch. Had three children: Robert Guerrant, Cora Christian (later Blanding), and Edward Gray.

(1972)

MONTGOMERY (Montgomery Co.)

SH 105 at Pond St.

The Old Methodist Churchyard

In Jan. 1839, the Rev. Isaac Strickland organized a Methodist Church whose members soon built a log meetinghouse on this site donated by founders of the town of Montgomery. The churchyard came into use for burials during the 1840s. When Pastor G. W. Rabb was dying in 1851, he requested burial beneath the altar of the frame church then being built to replace the log cabin. His grave and a monument commemorating pioneer circuit riders now (1976) mark the original Methodist Church site. The church and the nearby parsonage, which is said to have been the first Methodist parsonage built in Texas, were relocated in 1908. A tabernacle later erected beside the cemetery has also been demolished. A stone in this cemetery commemorates a soldier of the American Revolution who helped settle this county and died here. Churchyard burials included veterans of the War of 1812, the Texas War for Independence, Mexican War, and Civil War, as well as many other pioneers, state and county officials, merchants, ministers, and physicians. In some of the unmarked graves are travelers who died here among strangers. Although a new cemetery opened in 1868, this one was also used until no space remained. (1976)

MONTGOMERY (Montgomery Co.)   N. Liberty St. (FM 149) near Clepper Dr.
Montgomery County, C.S.A.
A wealthy farm area in 1861. In Civil War, supported Texas with goods, funds and men. 2 companies from here were in famed Hood's Texas Brigade—with only 9 men in one living to return. Young boys, old men and the partially disabled formed 5 Home Guard and State Companies. The county clothed its own soldiers. The courthouse then on this site had a sewing room for that work. Cooperating were homefolk using looms and cotton cards. People ate sparingly, had few new clothes. By 1864, so much was given to war effort that not a store was open in Montgomery. (1965)

MORAN (Shackelford Co.)   SH 6 at FM 576
Cottle No. 1 First Natural Gas Well in Shackelford County (2 mi. NE)
The appearance in 1908 of oil and gas in water wells in this vicinity prompted the Texas Company (later Texaco, Inc.) in June, 1909, to begin leasing large tracts of land. After a surface geological survey, a wooden derrick complete with cable tools and steam engine was erected by contractor F. J. Winston on a prospective location on the Jim Cottle Ranch and on Sept. 23, 1909, drilling operations began. Equipment breakdowns were frequent and sometimes lengthy, but finally, on Nov. 9, 1910, after 13 months of drilling, the Cottle No. 1 struck natural gas at a depth of 2660 feet. This discovery opened the Moran Field, and was the first commercial gas well completed in this vast West Texas area. In the spring of 1911, gas was piped to Moran for residential and business use. Within two years (in 1913) the cities of Albany, Cisco, and Abilene were supplied for the first time with natural gas. By Oct. 1913, with five producing gas wells, the Moran field won recognition as one of the most important sources of fossil fuels in Texas. Although the Cottle No. 1 was plugged years ago, Moran Field continues to be an economic mainstay in this area. (1974)

MORAN (Shackelford Co.)   SH 6 at FM 576
Moran
Pioneers came to this area as early as the 1860s. During the Civil War (1861–1865), they built the temporary fortress settlement of Mugginsville on Deep Creek. At one time, a branch of the Western Cattle Trail passed nearby. Population increased after the arrival of the Texas Central Railroad in 1881. The town of Moran was established by Swope Hull, who opened a grocery store at the rail crossing on Deep Creek in 1883. He was postmaster of the community's first post office, called "Hulltown," which opened August 29, 1883. Hull bought 160 acres between Post Oak and Deep Creek and platted a townsite in March 1884. Most of the property was bought by I. B. (Ben) Scott, who sold his interests in 1890 to M. D. Bray (1845–1926), a prominent local merchant and landowner. The town's name was changed in 1890 to "Hicks" and in 1892 to "Moran" for Texas Central Railroad president John J. Moran. By the 1890s, the community had a school and Baptist, Church of Christ, Cumberland Presbyterian, and Methodist congregations. A newspaper was begun in 1895 and bank in 1902. Incorporated in 1919, Moran was a shipping point for drilling supplies during the oil and gas boom of 1910–1930. Today the area's economy is based on farming, ranching, and oil and gas production. (1976)

MORGAN (Bosque Co.)   SH 174, 10 mi. E in Kimball Bend Park
Chisholm Trail Kimball Crossing
Kimball, one of the first towns in Bosque County, was established at this site in the early 1850s. One of the westward wagon routes forded the river at this crossing until a ferry was built in 1865. The famous Chisholm Trail made its major crossing of the Brazos here. During the 1870s tens of thousands of Texas Longhorn cattle forded the river and were driven to Northern markets. Building of barbed wire fences and railroads in the 1880s caused abandonment of the Chisholm Trail. Kimball, with no railroad and loss of the cattle trail, became a ghost town by the middle 1900s.

MORGAN (Bosque Co.)   SH 174, 4.5 mi. N
Union Hill School
Started before 1879, the Union Hill School was one of several rural schools that served the early settlers of Bosque County. A two-room 1888 schoolhouse, located across the road, was used until

1914, when a two-story building was constructed at this site. A nearby stable housed the students' horses during the school day. Enlarged by the 1926 merger with the Auburn Hill District, Union Hill became part of the Kopperl District in 1939. Former students, which include many area business, professional, and agricultural leaders, still meet for a biennial school reunion.   (1981)

MORTON (Cochran Co.)   *SH 24 at courthouse*
Cochran County
Created August 21, 1876, from Bexar County. Named for a native of New Jersey, Robert Cochran, a private who died for Texas Independence in the siege of the Alamo. Indian hostilities and the distance to market and supplies made settlement slow. The 1900 census listed 25 cowboys. In 1910 there were 75 persons; then 67 in 1920. Organized May 6, 1924, with Morton as county seat. Oil discovery and development of irrigation caused rapid growth, and made it a farm and petroleum center. Site of Silver Lake, a saline known to early Spanish explorers as Laguna Quemado. (1965)

MOSCOW (Polk Co.)   *Loop 177 at Sambo Rd. at Hobby Park*
Texas Statesman William Pettus Hobby (1878–1964)
Businessman and politician William Pettus Hobby was born near this Moscow site, the son of Eudora Adeline (Pettus) and Edwin E. Hobby, a state senator and judge. At age 17, William joined the staff of the Houston *Post* and rose to managing editor at 23. He was named publisher of the Beaumont *Enterprise* in 1907. Texas voters elected William P. Hobby Lieutenant Governor in 1914 and 1916. He became Governor with the impeachment of James E. Ferguson in 1917. In 1918, Hobby was elected to his own full term (1919–1921). In 1924, he served on the first board of regents of Texas Technological College (Texas Tech). Hobby was also president of the Houston *Post* from 1924 until his death in 1964. In 1931, Hobby married Oveta Culp, parliamentarian of the Texas House and daughter of Elizabeth (Hoover) and former state representative Ike W. Culp. For the next quarter century, William and Oveta shared editorial administration of the Post, except four years during World War II when Oveta served as commander of the Women's Army Corps of the United States military forces, and from 1953 to 1955, when she served in the administration of President Dwight D. Eisenhower as the first Secretary of the Housing, Education and Welfare Department. William and Oveta had two children: William Pettus, Jr. and Jessica. Hobby's highlights as Governor included initiation of a free schoolbook program, compulsory school attendance law, state government budget system and state drought relief. His leadership was vital to Texas' participation in World War I and the effecting of woman's suffrage in the state and nation.   (1964)

MOSS HILL (Liberty Co.)   *SH 146, N of SH 105 in roadside park*
Kalita, Chief of the Coushatta Indians
Friend of the Pioneers.

MOULTON (Lavaca Co.)   *SH 95 at Nelson St.*
Moulton
Founded (about 2 mi. NW) in early 1850s. Moved to this site after 1887 when the San Antonio & Aransas Pass Railroad extended its line from Yoakum to Waco, placing a station at this point. Sam and Will Moore, brothers, took lead in building an outstanding school here in 1901. Town remains an agricultural and shipping center.   (1970)

MOUNT CALM (Hill Co.)   *SH 31 at CR 3272, 2.4 mi. SW*
Col. Leonard Williams (1798–1854)
Heroic frontiersman and soldier. Was made colonel by his friend, President Sam Houston. After being a Comanche captive, was a diplomat and Indian agent. Settled near here, 1845. Built area's first tank, using scraper of cowhide. Wife was Nancy Isaacs. They had six children.   (1967)

MOUNT ENTERPRISE (Rusk Co.)   *SH 315, 6 mi. N*
Shiloh Cemetery
This cemetery dates from the 1853 burial of Maranda Gilbreath. Four years later, the land was officially set aside by early settler Josiah Johnson for use as a public burial ground. Many of the unidentified graves are thought to be those of slaves. The cemetery contains the burial sites of pioneers, community leaders, and war veterans. A traditional Fourth of July cemetery cleaning began in 1876. One of the older burial grounds in Rusk County, Shiloh Cemetery is located beside Trammel's Trace, an early East Texas roadway.   (2005)

MOUNT PLEASANT (Titus Co.)
US 67, 1 mi. E in roadside park

Titus County
Formed from Red River and Bowie Counties. Created May 11, 1846. Organized July 13, 1846. Named in honor of Andrew J. Titus, 1814–1855; pioneer of Northwest Texas; soldier in the Mexican War; member of the Texas Legislature. County Seat, Mt. Pleasant.

MOUNT PLEASANT (Titus Co.)
SH 49 in Dellwood Park

Dellwood Park
Before 1830, Caddo Indians had campgrounds here around mineral springs flowing red, white, and blue waters. First home at future Mount Pleasant was built here in 1830s by Benjamin Gooch. A health-recreational resort by 1895, springs area was site (1909–1916), of the lavish Dellwood Hotel, built by the Red Mineral Springs Development Co., headed by Dr. T. M. Fleming. These steps are from Dellwood Hotel, which burned. Favorite spot for Confederate conventions, political rallies, and other meetings, the site was acquired 1951 by City of Mount Pleasant, as Dellwood Park. (1973)

MOUNT PLEASANT (Titus Co.)
SH 49, 7 mi SE

Caddo Indian Communities in the Cypress Drainage
Comprised of various groups with distinct dialects and customs, the people known today as the Caddo once occupied a region that included parts of present Louisiana, Arkansas, Oklahoma and Texas as early as A.D. 800. By the 16th century, the Caddo developed complex, hierarchical societies with civic and ceremonial centers, as well as advanced agricultural practices. Early Spanish and French accounts provided historic records of the Caddo and their customs. Despite successful trade with the Europeans, especially the French, the Caddo eventually faced a rapidly declining population due to exposure to Old World diseases, as well as the arrival of other Native American groups from the eastern United States. Anglo-American settlement in Texas further threatened and limited the Caddo homeland, and by the late 1850s they were forced to relocate to Indian Territory (present Oklahoma). Today, the Caddo nation headquarters is in Binger, Oklahoma, where members of the tribe maintain cultural traditions through pottery, song, dance and language. As an ancestral homeland, this area is an important part of the Caddo's rich heritage. Archeologists utilize records, artifacts and landscape features to learn more about the tribe's history. Pottery styles, mound construction, cemetery types and farming methods reveal much about the Caddo and provide insight on settlement patterns, the family unit, interregional trade and other elements of tribal life. Research at community sites in the area drained by Cypress Creek reveal elements of Caddo occupation dating from as early as A.D. 800 to 1680, an era that included cultural contact with Europeans and Southeastern Indian groups. (2004)

MOUNT VERNON (Franklin Co.)
IH 30, 6 mi. E

Gray Rock Cemetery
Unmarked graves here may date from the 1840s, when the nearby town of Gray Rock was settled along a frontier highway. Of the 411 marked graves, the oldest is that of an infant, Lula Smith, who died Feb. 15, 1872. Although the land was deeded to two deacons of the Baptist church in 1887, it has always served as a community cemetery. An 1899–1900 epidemic of typhoid fever accounts for some of the burials. The town of Gray Rock vanished after the railroad bypassed it, but the cemetery is still in use. Gray Rock Cemetery Committee, organized in 1906, now maintains the site. (1975)

MOUNT VERNON (Franklin Co.)
US 67, 4 mi. E at Ripley Creek Crossing

Ripley Massacre
Ambrose Ripley and his wife Rachel (Wood) brought their family to Texas in 1837, settling near here in what was then Red River County. They established their home near the Nacogdoches Road (Cherokee Trace) and a stream now known as Ripley Creek. On April 10, 1841, while Ripley was away, a band of Indians attacked his farmstead, killing first his eldest son who was plowing in the field. Mrs. Ripley and five children were killed trying to reach a canebreak and one infant died when the house was burned. Two of Ripley's daughters eluded the Indians and made it to a neighboring farm. Charles Black and Charles S. Stewart led a group of settlers north in pursuit of the band. Near the Sulphur River they encountered Indians, who may or may not have been involved

in the massacre, and attacked them, killing several. The Ripley family massacre was an isolated incident in this area, but it proved to be a rallying point for increased frontier defenses and for support of the anti-Indian policies of Texas president Mirabeau B. Lamar. The attack also influenced the formation of a militia unit under the leadership of Gen. Edward H. Tarrant and Cols. James Bourland and William C. Young to rid the area of Indians. (Texas Sesquicentennial 1836–1986)

MOUNT VERNON (Franklin Co.)
US 67 at SH 37
Franklin County
Formed from Titus County. Created March 8, 1875. Organized April 30, 1875. Named in honor of Benjamin C. Franklin, 1805–1873, hero of San Jacinto, district judge of the Republic of Texas. Member of the legislature. Mt. Vernon, county seat.

MOUNTAIN HOME (Kerr Co.)
SH 41, 16 mi. W at entrance to ranch
Y. O. Ranch
Charles Armand Schreiner (1836–1927), a native of Alsace-Lorraine, immigrated to Texas with his family in 1852. He joined the Texas Rangers at age fifteen, and in 1857 entered the cattle business at Turtle Creek in Kerr County. He left to serve in the Third Texas Infantry during the Civil War, and returned to Kerr County in 1865. Moving to Kerrville in 1869, he opened a successful mercantile business. The threat of Indian raids in the area soon prompted the formation of the Kerrville Mounted Rifles, and Schreiner was appointed captain by Governor Richard Coke in 1875. In 1880, he bought the Taylor-Clements ranch and its Y. O. Brand. Texas Longhorn cattle became Captain Schreiner's primary concern, and over 300,000 head were driven from this area to Kansas railheads. Because of Schreiner's venture in raising sheep and goats, Kerrville was known as the "mohair center of the world." The last cattle drive from the ranch was held in 1941, the stock being moved to Kerrville for shipment to Fort Worth. The Y. O. Ranch has also become known throughout the world for its Texas Longhorn cattle and its native and exotic wildlife conservation programs. (Texas Sesquicentennial 1836–1986)

MUENSTER (Cooke Co.)
US 82 near City Park
Muenster
In 1889, brothers Anton, August, and Emil Flusche contracted to sell 22,000 acres of this land along the Missouri, Kansas & Texas Railroad. Jot Gunter gave 25 acres for a school, church, cemetery, and park. The first mass, celebrated Dec. 8, 1889, marked the official beginning of this German Catholic town. Despite drought, typhoid fever, and tornadoes destroying the first two church buildings, the area grew and farming and dairy business increased. Farmers established an insurance company and a marketing group for buying products in bulk. An oil boom in 1926 added to the prosperity. (1979)

MULESHOE (Bailey Co.)
SH 214, 2.5 mi. N
.5 mi. W to Townsite of Old Hurley
First town in Bailey County. Promoted in 1907 by land company of Stevens A. Coldren (d. 1924). He had a townsite surveyed and named it for Patrick J. Hurley (1883–1963), New Mexico political leader. Company built a general store, hotel, and livery stable. Wide plowed furrows indicated future streets. In August 1907 a post office was established. Settlers came in and a church and school were begun. In 1913, however, the railroad bypassed town. Efforts to start "New Hurley"—on the rail line—failed. After Muleshoe became county seat, 1918, Hurley expired. (1970)

MULESHOE (Bailey Co.)
US 70/84, .5 mi NW in roadside park
Bailey County
A part of Bexar Territory, 1836–1876. Created August 21, 1876. Organized November 5, 1918. Named in honor of Peter James Bailey, 1812–1836, a Kentucky lawyer killed in defending the Alamo. Muleshoe, the county seat. (1964)

MULESHOE (Bailey Co.)
SH 214, 2 mi. S
The XIT Ranch South Line (About 100 ft. S of This Marker)
One of most famous boundaries in Texas. Marked edge of XIT—Ranch empire bartered away by Texas for its capitol building. The 16th Legislature in 1879 designated a 3,000,000-acre tract

to be used in payment for the capitol. The grant extended 200 miles north from line here. Besides portion in this county, it included land in counties of Castro, Cochran, Dallam, Deaf Smith, Hartley, Hockley, Lamb, Oldham, and Parmer. Heading the investors who built the capitol were wealthy Chicago merchants John V. and C. B. Farwell. Their surveying was begun in 1886.   (1970)

MULESHOE (Bailey Co.)   *SH 214, 20 mi. S on refuge entrance road*
Muleshoe National Wildlife Refuge
Founded in 1935 as a wintering area for migratory waterfowl, Muleshoe Wildlife Refuge is on the "central flyway" in a chain of refuges from Mexico to Canada. Migrating birds begin arriving in August and remain until April. The largest wintering concentration of sandhill cranes in North America is most noticeable here from October through March. The site, covering over 5,000 acres, provides habitat for many other species of birds and wildlife. Muleshoe is one of several National Wildlife Refuges in Texas that protect migratory water-fowl, endangered wildlife species, or unique natural habitats.   (1985)

MULESHOE (Bailey Co.)   *FM 746, 15 mi. SW via SH 214*
Coyote Lake
One of numerous natural, salt lakes in the Texas Panhandle; its waters, although brackish, have been welcome enough at various times to Indians, buffalo hunters, and thirsty cattle on hot, dry days. The lake, having a shoreline of over six and a half miles and a bed area of 829 acres, is one of the largest of the many saline lakes in the region. In early days, the Comanches were masters of this area, but after the 1874 Battle of Adobe Walls, they no longer hindered settlement of the Staked Plains. Today, artifacts found near the lake shore show that this was once a favorite Comanche camp site. Even while the Indians were still a menace, buffalo hunters swarmed into the Panhandle, and they, too, often camped on Coyote Lake. Until 1877, they killed so many of the huge, shaggy beasts that the southern herd, once numbering millions, nearly became extinct. From 1885 to about 1910, Coyote Lake served as a watering spot for cattle on the huge (3,050,000 acres) XIT Ranch, which blanketed the western Panhandle. In 1898, when the Pecos & Northern Texas Railroad built through Bovina (30 miles north), the lake watered thousands of cattle en route from southern ranches to the railhead, and from there to Northern markets.   (1968)

MULLIN (Mills Co.)   *US 84/183 near RR 573*
The Settlement of Williams Ranch
Once a prominent frontier town, Williams Ranch grew up around the homestead of cattleman John Williams (1804–1871), who came to this area in 1855. The community flourished during the Civil War (1861–1865) because of trade with Mexico and by 1874 had stores, saloons, a hotel, mill, and blacksmith shop. In 1875 Henry Ford and J. M. Parks bought most of the land in the village and platted a townsite. They proposed the name "Parksford" but "Williams Ranch" prevailed when the post office opened in 1877. The community was a stagestop and a roundup point on the Western Cattle Trail. It claimed the first hotel, newspaper, telegraph, and public school in Brown and Mills Counties. In 1881 it was one of the towns considered as a site for the University of Texas. Williams Ranch reached its peak of activity in the early 1880s, with a population of over 250. The settlement began to decline when the railroad bypassed it in 1885. An outbreak of mob violence was quelled by the Texas Rangers in 1887. By 1892 the post office and all businesses had closed. Today the site is marked by the natural springs that attracted the original settlers and by Williams Ranch Cemetery, burial place of many pioneers and their descendants.   (1976)

MYRTLE SPRINGS (Van Zandt Co.)   *SH 64, 3 mi. SW*
Hayden Baptist Church
The organizational meeting for this congregation was held in October 1878. Led by Dr. George D. Staton, who also served as first pastor, the fourteen charter members adopted the name Myrtle Springs Baptist Church and agreed to meet monthly. A church building, constructed in 1889, served the congregation until 1900, when the meeting place was moved to the Cow Prairie Schoolhouse, which was located near this site. Four years later, the fellowship built a new sanctuary and adopted the name Hayden Baptist Church. The pioneer church continues to serve the surrounding rural area.   (1985)

NACOGDOCHES (Nacogdoches Co.)

US 59, 5 mi. N at Millard's Crossing

The Millard-Lee House

Built about 1837 by Nacogdoches merchant-deputy postmaster-road overseer Robert F. Millard (1803–1847) as family home that sometimes was also a boardinghouse. In 1859 David Lee, a blacksmith-merchant-county official, bought the house, then situated near public square in Nacogdoches (5 mi. S). It remained until 1960 the Lee family home. In 1970, Mrs. Albert (Lera Millard) Thomas bought, moved, and restored it here at Millard's Crossing, named for the builder's family. (1974)

NACOGDOCHES (Nacogdoches Co.)

US 59 Bus., 5 mi. N at Millard's Crossing

Burrows-Millard House

Confederate veteran Elijah M. Burrows (1844–1893) built the rear portion of this pioneer farmhouse before he married Mary Josephine (Molly) Millard (1848–1901) in 1867. Between 1869 and 1874, he added the rooms and porch across the front. Members of the Burrows family occupied the structure until 1972, when George Van Burrows gave it to Lera Millard (Mrs. Albert) Thomas, descendant of the builder. She moved it ½ mile north to this site and restored it. (1976)

NACOGDOCHES (Nacogdoches Co.)

US 59, 3 mi. N

Nacogdoches County

Home of the Nacogdoches Indians in the 17th century. Spanish settlements, 1716, alternately settled and abandoned in 18th century due to French encroachments. Scene of the Fredonian Rebellion in 1827. Organized a municipality, 1832, under the Mexican government. Created a county March 24, 1837. Nacogdoches, established 1779, became the county seat in 1836.

NACOGDOCHES (Nacogdoches Co.)

4800 blk. North St. (US 59 Bus.)

Nacogdoches

Home of the Nacogdoches Indians in the 17th century. Spanish settlements, 1716, alternately settled and abandoned in 18th century due to French encroachments. Scene of the Fredonian Rebellion in 1827. Organized a municipality, 1839 under the Mexican government. Created a county March 17, 1836; organized May 24, 1837. Nacogdoches, established 1779, became the county seat in 1836.

(1936)

NACOGDOCHES (Nacogdoches Co.)

SH 21, 8 mi. E

Site of El Atascoso

In the 1778 return to East Texas of settlers removed in 1772–1773, this Atascoso Bayou-to-Puentesuellos segment of El Camino Real was site of many camps, and here Jose Mora established Rancho "El Atascoso." Others settled nearby, joining him for protection against the original Indian inhabitants.

(1973)

NACOGDOCHES (Nacogdoches Co.)

SH 21, 3.5 mi. E

Sam P. Smith Place

A good example of an East Texas farm home, this house originally had five rooms, four porches, and an enclosed dog trot. It was built in 1880 for Samuel Pharr and Mary Spencer Smith by Smith's brother-in-law Andrew B. Ireson. A local cabinetmaker and carpenter, Ireson also designed the woodwork and some of the furniture. Sam Smith, who grew up in Nacogdoches County, was a farmer. He and Mary had 12 children and lived here until their deaths in 1941. (1985)

NACOGDOCHES (Nacogdoches Co.)

SH 21, 4 mi. E

Fairview Church Cemetery

According to tradition, a small group of Nacogdoches-area Methodists came together before 1860 to organize a church, which they named Pine Grove. In the late 1870s, congregation members moved their small log building to a site in front of this cemetery. A. J. Muckleroy, in 1878, had donated two acres of land to the Methodist Episcopal Church, South. When the Pine Grove Church moved to the Muckleroy land, the congregation changed its name to Fairview Church. The earliest marked grave at the Fairview Church Cemetery is that of Elijah Muckleroy and dates to 1851, although earlier graves may exist. For decades, families of those buried in the graveyard maintained the grounds and grave sites. In 1941, the families established an annual homecoming Sunday, and by 1964 the Fairview Cemetery Association had organized to oversee care of the cemetery. Today, encompassing approximately 12 acres and more than 1,500 marked graves, the cemetery features stone cairns and curbed plots. It serves as a link to the early rural community and the history of its settlement. (2003)

NACOGDOCHES (Nacogdoches Co.) 101 W. Main St. (SH 21)
William ("Bill") Goyens
Born a slave in South Carolina, 1794; escaped to Texas in 1821. Rendered valuable assistance to the Army of Texas, 1836. Interpreter for the Houston-Forbes Treaty with the Cherokees, 1836. Acquired wealth and was noted for his charity. Died at his home on Goyens' Hill 1856. His skin was black His heart, true blue. (1936)

NACOGDOCHES (Nacogdoches Co.) Fredonia at El Camino Real (Main)
The Battle of Nacogdoches (August 2, 1832)
One of the opening actions of the Texas War for Independence, this battle occurred soon after settlers drove out the Mexican garrisons at Anahuac and Velasco. In 1832, Col. Jose de las Piedras, in command of over 300 soldiers, ordered the residents to surrender all firearms. Citizens of Nacogdoches and other East Texas towns resisted by forming the "National Militia," commanded by James W. Bullock. When Piedras refused to support the constitution of 1824, the militia marched toward the Mexicans on the square and the Mexicans opened fire. In hand-to-hand combat, the militia took the stone fort and several nearby structures, but the Mexicans continued to hold Piedras' headquarters in the Red House. Adolphus Sterne showed San Augustine "Redlanders" how to outflank the Mexicans. Piedras' men fled during the night and were captured August 3 by militiamen near Loco Creek. Fighting ended after the Mexicans arrested their leader at John Durst's home. A peace treaty was signed on August 6. Piedras lost 47 men. Four Texans died, including the Alcalde of Nacogdoches, Encarnacion Chireno. Because of this incident, Mexican troops were never again stationed in East Texas, leaving settlers free to meet and air their grievances. (1979)

NACOGDOCHES (Nacogdoches Co.) North St. (US 59 Bus.) at Powers St.
La Calle Real del Norte
An 18th-century trail connecting the Indian villages of the Nacogdoche and Nasoni Indians. Travelled by Spanish missionaries, soldiers and settlers, French traders and American filibusters before Anglo-American colonists came to make Texas their home. (1936)

NACOGDOCHES (Nacogdoches Co.) Corner of North (US 59 Bus.) at Rusk St.
Homesite of Thomas J. Rusk (1803–1857)
Soldier-statesman of the Republic of Texas. A hero of San Jacinto. Commander in chief of the army 1836. Chief justice of the Supreme Court 1839. President of the Constitutional Convention, 1845. United States Senator, 1846. He called Nacogdoches his home from 1835 to 1857. (1936)

NACOGDOCHES (Nacogdoches Co.) 1936 North St. (US 59 Bus.) at SFASU
Campus between Austin & Rusk buildings
Pioneering Higher Education in East Texas
The absence of an institution of higher learning to train teachers in East Texas became obvious in the early 20th century. "Normal institutes" or ad hoc college courses were important statewide attempts to supplement the educational level of the teachers in rural school systems. The Legislature's decision in 1909 to abolish the community school system in favor of public school systems further increased demand for trained teachers. To address the needs of the East Texas region, the Legislature in 1915 authorized the placement of a normal college east of the 96th meridian. Legislative, sectional, and political difficulties delayed the charters until 1917. By the time the schools were funded in 1921, the state had passed the compulsory education law for children and the certification law for teachers, creating a huge demand for educated instructors in Texas. In the rural districts of Texas, 24% of public school teachers had not completed high school, 22% had normal college training, and 13% were graduates of other college and university programs. Stephen F. Austin State Teachers College opened in 1923. The faculty consisted of 24 instructors selected by President Alton W. Birdwell. The majority of the educators' degrees came from Texas universities, but other major national institutions were represented. The vast majority of students came from East Texas, particularly the counties surrounding Nacogdoches. The early faculty, staff,

and students of Stephen F. Austin State Teachers College transformed teaching into a profession in East Texas while making education an attainable goal in the region. These men and women laid the foundation for public education in East Texas.   (1999)

NACOGDOCHES (Nacogdoches Co.)   *1936 North St. (US 59 Bus.), SFASU campus between Austin & Rusk buildings*
The University Tradition in Nacogdoches

The Spanish friars who built the Mission of Our Lady of Nacogdoches passed to the townspeople a sense of scholarship and educational responsibility. Prominent citizens such as Sam Houston and Thomas J. Rusk were well known for their attention to education. Town citizens pursued the establishment of a university in the 1840s. The Republic of Texas granted a charter for a school in February 1845. Nacogdoches University was a preparatory school with some college subjects included in the curriculum. Townspeople gave money, materials, land and labor to support the school and secure for their children the best education possible. The school moved into its permanent home on Washington Square in 1858. Hard times began with the Civil War; later, several entities operated the institution, including the Catholic Church, local Masons, and Keachi College of Louisiana. In 1904, the trustees deeded the campus to the newly created public school district of Nacogdoches. Citizens began a movement in 1906 to lobby for the formation of a new college. This culminated in the first, although ultimately unsuccessful, attempt to establish an East Texas normal school in 1915. When legislation in 1917 called for a college "east of the 96th meridian," Nacogdoches organized a citizens' committee. A pamphlet entitled "Twenty-three reasons why Stephen F. Austin State Normal College ought to be located at Nacogdoches . . ." stated their case. As they had 70 years earlier, the people of Nacogdoches lobbied heavily for the new college, pledging 208 acres of land, 250 students, paved streets, and free electricity to the institution. When the opening was postponed from the summer of 1923 to the fall, the town recruited students from all of East Texas and even supplied a temporary home for a year—Washington Square.   (1999)

NACOGDOCHES (Nacogdoches Co.)   *1936 North St. (US 59), in front of Rusk Bldg., SFASU campus*
Alton W. Birdwell (1870–1954)

Born near Elkhart in Anderson County, Alton W. Birdwell was reared in the Piney Woods of East Texas. His early education was provided through home schooling; he earned money for later study by hand-molding clay bricks and hewing railroad ties. Birdwell attended classes at the University of Texas, the University of Missouri, and the University of Chicago. His first teaching position was at Pleasant Retreat in Smith County in 1892. Birdwell served as principal in Tyler, superintendent of schools in Troup, and superintendent of Smith County schools. He became a professor of history at Southwest Texas State University (SWT) in 1910, and married fellow teacher Maude Margaret Shipe in 1914. He took courses in normal school administration at Peabody College in Nashville, Tennessee, where he was acclaimed for his work in education theory. He earned a master's degree from Peabody in 1916 and returned to SWT as dean of the faculty. Birdwell was appointed president of the newly-created Stephen F. Austin State Normal School in 1917. Because World War I delayed the opening of the school, he remained at SWT, serving the war effort in various defense groups. In August 1922, Birdwell and his family arrived in Nacogdoches. Delays in construction of the Austin building forced him to postpone the opening of the college in 1923; he nevertheless opened the institution in borrowed facilities. Birdwell selected the faculty, taught history, and worked with area schools to support the college. He was equally resourceful in expanding the school in the 1920s and in protecting the college from collapsing enrollment and legislative cuts during the Great Depression. After his retirement in 1942, Birdwell remained on the faculty and served as president emeritus until his death.   (1999)

NACOGDOCHES (Nacogdoches Co.)   *US 59 Bus., on SFASU campus at end of Vista Dr.*
Stephen Fuller Austin (November 3, 1793–December 37, 1836)

Republics often point to one person whose vision and leadership led to their creation. For the Republic of Texas (1836–1845) that person is Stephen Fuller Austin. Austin, the son of Moses and Maria Brown Austin, was born on the Virginia frontier. He attended schools in Kentucky and Connecticut before opting to work in his father's mercantile business in Missouri. He served as a judge in Arkansas prior to moving to New Orleans where he worked at a newspaper and studied law. In 1821 Moses Austin was granted permission by Spain to settle 300 families in Texas. His untimely death while in Louisiana recruiting settlers left the completion of his ambitious project to his son Stephen. Although a series of Mexican leaders subsequently rejected his father's original grant, Austin persevered and successfully lobbied for the grant's continuance. He astutely governed every facet of the original 300 families' settlement in southeast Texas (1821–1825) and those of another 900 families in the area by 1832. Austin was imprisoned in Mexico after requesting separate statehood for Texas in 1833. He returned to Texas in 1835 and helped it gain independence from Mexico. Austin, chosen as the new Republic's first secretary of state, is known as the father of Texas. (Stephen F. Austin Bicentennial 1793–1993)

NACOGDOCHES (Nacogdoches Co.)

Griffith Blvd at Clark Blvd, off US 59 Bus. on SFA campus

Stone Fort Museum

Opening in 1936, the Stone Fort Museum has interpreted the history of East Texas and of the Old Stone Fort while also elevating the local historic preservation ethic. The Old Stone Fort, built in the late 18th century, was an integral part in a wide array of historic changes occurring in East Texas. The razing of the original building in 1902 caused consternation throughout the state and encouraged organizations to preserve other historic structures. In 1908, the Cum Concilio Club, a local women's organization, opened a memorial building dedicated to the razed structure. By the 1930s, the Texas Centennial Advisory Board of Nacogdoches, along with the Nacogdoches Historical Society, proposed that the monument be replaced by a structure that more closely replicated the original building. A renewed interest in history, spurred by the upcoming centennial of Texas independence, aided the realization of the project. The Texas Centennial Commission approved the construction of the building on the campus of Stephen F. Austin State Teachers College (now Stephen F. Austin State University). Architect Hal B. Tucker designed the structure, and construction was completed by October 1936. Since then, museum staff have worked to interpret the history of the Old Stone Fort and of East Texas, with particular emphasis on the periods of Spanish and Mexican rule. In 1992, work was completed on renovations to the museum building, meant to restore a higher degree of authenticity. Today, the Stone Fort Museum continues to serve Texas by interpreting East Texas history though exhibits, programs, and its housing in a replica of an important early Texas structure. (2008)

NADA (Colorado Co.)

SH 71 in front of post office

Nada Post Office

The post office in Nada was established in 1894 when William J. Engbrock, Jr., was appointed the first postmaster. The post office was located in the general store owned by his father, William Engbrock, Sr., until 1898. Subsequent locations of the post office changed several times over the years, depending on the profession of the succeeding postmasters. Twice it was housed in the medical office and pharmacy of Dr. Francis Daehne, appointed in 1898, and Dr. John A. Halamicek, appointed in 1915. The post office returned to the general store during the terms of Joseph H. Labay, named in 1900, and Joseph J. Patter (Potter), appointed in 1903. Adolph Hruzek became postmaster in 1911 and moved the post office to his general store across the street. Appointed in 1921, Antone Lichnovsky moved the office in 1935 to his general store built near the newly constructed State Highway 71. His daughter, appointed in 1946, also served from her store. In 1953, the post office moved to the site of the postmaster's new service station and garage, where it remained for thirty years. In 1987, a new post office facility was built here on land purchased from the Braden family. (1996)

NAPLES (Morris Co.)

US 67 E in roadside park

Morris County

Created and organized in 1875, with Daingerfield as county seat. Named for William W. Morris (1805–1883), who came to Texas in 1849. When the Civil War began in 1861, was in 8th Legislature that armed the state, enacted soldiers' families' relief laws and set up 2,000 mile frontier and coastline defenses. Also in 13th Legislature, 1873–1875. Of the 254 Texas counties, 42 bear Indian, French or Spanish names. 10 honor such colonizers as Stephen F. Austin, "Father of Texas." 12 were named for Washington, Clay and other American patriots. 96 were named for men who fought in the Texas War for Independence (15 dying at the Alamo), signed the Declaration of Independence from Mexico, or served as statesmen in the Republic of Texas. 23 have the name of frontiersmen and pioneers. 11 honor American statesmen who worked for the annexation of Texas;

330

10, leaders in Texas since statehood, including jurists, ministers, educators, historians, statesmen; and 36, men like Morris prominent in the Confederacy during the Civil War. Delta and 8 others have geographical names. San Jacinto and Val Verde were named for battles; Live Oak and Orange, for trees; and Mason for a fort.

(1964)

NAPLES (Morris Co.)

US 67 at Walnut Ave.

Naples

When railroad by-passed prosperous town of Wheatville (3 mi. N), this rival town emerged at railroad. Post office moved here Jan. 1882, and was called Station Belden. Name was changed to Naples by U.S. Post Office Department, Feb. 1895. With depletion of hardwood forests, economy returned to cattle and agriculture.

(1967)

NAPLES (Morris Co.)

US 67 right-of-way at Baker St.

Home Town of United States Senator Morris Sheppard (1875–1941)

One of great lawmakers of the United States. Born near Naples, son of John L. and Alice Eddins Sheppard. Attended local schools. Received degrees of B.A. and LL.B., University of Texas; LL.M., Yale; LL.D., Southern Methodist University. Entered law practice in 1898. Served in United States Congress 1902–1913; United States Senate, 1913–1941. Active in legislation for agriculture, waterways, topographical and geological surveys, development of helium and potash deposits, construction and improvement of federal buildings (including national archives), federal insurance for bank deposits, and air mail service. Author in senate of Federal Credit Union Act, the Federal Maternity and Infancy Act, and the 18th (Prohibition) Amendment. He supported the 19th (Women's Suffrage) Amendment. One of creators of World War I aircraft board, he continued to champion military aviation, even when air power was discredited during 1920s and '30s. His leadership prevented disastrous curtailment of air power and helped prepare nation's air defenses in World War II. He was chairman Senate Military Affairs Committee, 1933–1941. Sheppard Air Force Base, Wichita Falls, was named in his honor in 1942. He married Lucile Sanderson; they had 3 daughters.

(1968)

NASH (Bowie Co.)

US 82 at S. Pecan

Town of Nash

Begun about 1873; first named "T. C. Junction" for its location on transcontinental division of Texas & Pacific Railroad. In 1884 post office was established and named "Park," after Dr. J. N. Parker, the first postmaster. First school started 1885 in single room. New buildings have been erected in 1904, 1924, 1967. In 1906 the town was named in honor of Martin Manny Nash, division superintendent of Texas & Pacific. Noted resident was Dr. Joseph Abner Dodd (1871–1944), who served 6 terms in Texas House of Representatives. Present town population stands at 2,000.

(1970)

NATALIA (Medina Co.)

IH 35, 1.9 mi. NE in rest area

Robert Lee Bobbitt (Jan. 24, 1888–Sept. 14, 1972)

Robert Lee Bobbitt was born near Hillsboro, Texas, the son of Joseph A. and Laura Duff Bobbitt. He graduated from North Texas Normal College in 1911, and from the University of Texas Law School in 1915. After opening a law practice in Laredo, Bobbitt married Mary B. Westbrook on April 20, 1918, while an officer in the 90th Infantry Division during World War I. Bobbitt was elected to the Texas Legislature in 1923, served three two-year terms, the last as speaker of the House of Representatives, and was appointed attorney general in 1929. He returned to private practice in San Antonio in 1931, and served on the board of directors of the Texas College of Arts and Industries. In 1935, he was selected as an associate justice of the San Antonio Court of Civil Appeals, a post from which he resigned in 1937 to receive an appointment as the chairman of the Texas Highway Commission. During Bobbitt's six-year term, the Texas Highway Department made great strides toward a goal of a connected system of paved roads in the state. In 1944, Bobbitt was a presidential elector, and, in 1958, was appointed to last public service post, as member of the board of regents of North Texas State College, his alma mater.

(1974)

NAVASOTA (Grimes Co.)

SH 6, 11 mi. S in roadside park

Primus Kelly

A faithful Negro slave. Came to nearby Courtney, Grimes County in 1851 with his master, John W. S. West from North Carolina. West was a prominent and wealthy pioneer planter and landowner.

At the outbreak of the Civil War, West sent Kelly "to take care" of his three sons—Robert M., Richard and John Haywood—who joined the famous Terry's Texas Rangers, where they served with distinction. Kelly was not content "to wait on" his charges but joined them in battle, firing his own musket and cap and ball pistol. Twice Kelly brought to Texas the wounded Richard, twice took him to the front again. After war, bought a small farm near "Marse Robert," raised a large family and prospered. Died in 1890s. The courage and loyalty of Kelly was typical of most Texas Negro slaves. Hundreds "went to war" with their masters. Many operated the farms and ranches of soldiers away at war, producing food, livestock, cotton and clothing for the Confederacy. Others did outside work to support their master's families. They protected homes from Indians, bandits and deserters and did community guard and patrol duty. At war's end, most slaves, like Primus Kelly, became useful and productive citizens of Texas. (1965)

NAVASOTA (Grimes Co.) *SH 90, 2 mi. E*
R. B. S. Foster Home
Early Texas plantation home in architectural style of the Atlantic States. Malcolm Camp, wealthy cotton planter, built this structure in 1859, with lumber hauled from East Texas sawmills. High-ceiling rooms are very large. Formal dining room in sandstone-lined cellar was unique. Had detached kitchen. Purchased 1883 by a leading local citizen, R. B. S. Foster (1848–1889), this was birthplace of his three children—Georgia, Robert F. and Nettie Rose. So stable is this locality that home was continuously occupied until 1966 by Fosters or their agents. (1968)

NAVASOTA (Grimes Co.) *SH 6 Bus. at Brule Dr.*
La Bahía Trail
Originally an Indian trail through Southern Texas and Louisiana; known to Spanish explorers as early as 1690, when the De Leon Expedition passed this site on the way from Mexico to East Texas. With 115 men, 721 horses, 82 loads of flour, and other supplies, Alonso de León, Governor of Coahuila, and Father Massanet, a Franciscan priest, entered the wilds of Texas. The purpose of the expedition was to discourage French encroachment from the north, as well as to explore, colonize, and Christianize the Indians. They followed the rugged trail from the present town of Refugio to Goliad and continued northeast to Navasota, probably following Cedar Creek through this town. Then they journeyed north until reaching the Neches River, where (near present Weches) they founded the Mission of San Francisco de Los Tejas. The church was called after the Tejas, or "Friendly" Indians, whose name was eventually given to the entire state. Although De León's party went no farther on the western section of the trail, known as Atascosito Road, the eastern section extended into Louisiana. In nineteenth century, the route gained importance as a cattle trail, the Opelousas Road, that moved Texas herds to market in the north and east. (1967)

NEEDVILLE (Fort Bend Co.) *SH 36, 250 ft. N of junction with FM 1236*
Town of Needville
Had beginning in 1892 when settler August Schendel opened general store here, on his land. Blacksmith shop, cotton gin, and room for post office had been added by 1894, when Schendel was appointed first postmaster. He suggested naming place "Needmore" because it needed more of everything, but another town already had that name. Slowly village became trade center. First church service was held 1891; school opened by 1897. Early economy, based on stock-raising and farming, was altered radically with discovery of oil, natural gas, and sulphur, 1920–1930s. (1971)

NELSONVILLE (Austin Co.) *SH 159, 1 mi. E of junction with FM 2502*
First Czech Immigrants in Texas
People from Czechoslovakia began to come to America for liberty as early as 1633. First known Czech in Texas was Jiri Rybar (George Fisher), customs officer in Galveston in 1829. Others arrived individually for years before letters sent home by the Rev. Josef Arnost Bergman, an 1849 Czech settler at Cat Spring (9 mi. S), inspired immigrations in large numbers. Josef Lidumil Lesikar (1806–1887) was instrumental in forming the first two large migrations, 1851 and 1853, with names of family parties listed on ship logs as Silar (Shiller), 69; Lesikar (Leshikar), 16; Mares (Maresh), 10; Pecacek (Pechacek), 9; Rypl (Ripple), 7; Coufal, 6; Rosler (Roesler), 6; Motl, 5; Jezek, 4; Cermak, 3; Janecek, 3; Jirasek, 3; Kroulik, 2; Tauber, 2; Marek, 1; Pavlicek, 1. With pastor Bergman's counsel, many of the Czechs began to farm in Austin County. Other immigrations occurred in the 1850s, and became even heavier in the 1870s. Czechs eventually spread throughout the state, gaining recogni-

tion for industry, thrift, and cultural attainments. To preserve their heritage they succeeded in having a chair of Slavic languages established (1915) at the University of Texas, and later at other schools. Their ethnic festivals have been held in various cities for many years. (1974)

NELSONVILLE (Austin Co.)
SH 159, 2 mi. W
The Old Roesler Place
August Roesler (1836–1933), who migrated to Texas from Germany during the 1850s, built a simple frame dwelling at this site in 1873. Near a busy public road, it was a frequent stopping place for travelers. In 1892, after the Roesler family had moved to a larger residence on the property, their first home burned. With help from his neighbors, Roesler then constructed this board and batten farmhouse, a replica of the earlier structure. (1977)

NEW BOSTON (Bowie Co.)
SH 8, 7 mi. N in roadside park
Site of the Texas Home of Richard Ellis
A Virginian by birth and education, jurist and statesman of Alabama, 1813–1825. Came to Texas, 1825. President of the Constitutional Convention, March 1836, and member of the Congress of the Republic of Texas. Born February 14, 1781. Died here December 20, 1846. (1964)

NEW BOSTON (Bowie Co.)
SH 8, 7 mi. N in roadside park
Harvey C. Sanders, C.S.A. (1837–1925)
Native of Kentucky. In Civil War, fought at Shiloh, Chickamauga and other battles. After being wounded twice, became a guard at Confederate White House. When Richmond fell on April 3, 1865, was placed in escort for the departing president. Rode 5 weeks toward Florida, where President Jefferson Davis was planning to sail for Mexico to join many other Confederate leaders. (These southerners intended to regroup an army, march north to Texas and continue their fight for states' rights.) President Davis and his guards were followed by thieves trying to steal the Confederate treasury, the horses and the wagons. The assassination of Abraham Lincoln on April 14 and the offer of a reward of $100,000 caused many adventurers to hunt for President Davis. Just before dawn of May 10, near Irwinsville, Ga., federals captured him and his party, including 2 Texans, Postmaster-General John H. Reagan and Presidential Aide F. R. Lubbock, a former governor of Texas. Mrs. Davis and children were soon freed, but all the men were imprisoned. Sanders was released in a year. Later he came to Texas and lived near this site after 1887—honored for years as the last man of the Davis bodyguard. (1965)

NEW BOSTON (Bowie Co.)
US 82 N in city parking lot
New Boston
Established as shipping point when Texas & Pacific Railroad was built across Bowie County in 1870s. Drawing business from original town of Boston (4 mi. S). New Boston townsite was platted in 1876; its post office opened Jan. 26, 1877, with L. C. Demorse as postmaster. Baptists organized church here in 1880; Methodists, 1883; Church of Christ, 1943. The first building designated as a school was erected in 1886. New Boston men who have served in the Texas Legislature: Blair McGee (1889); Norman L. Dalby (1909–1910); R. M. Hubbard (1929, 1931), and Joseph White, Jr. (1939). (1971)

NEW BOSTON (Bowie Co.)
James Bowie Dr., off IH 30 at courthouse
Bowie County
In 1836 a part of Red River County. Created December 17, 1840. Organized February 1, 1841. Named in honor of James Bowie, 1785–1836; member of Long's expedition; defender of Texas liberty; a martyr of the Alamo. Old Boston, 1841, Texarkana and New Boston have served as county seat.

NEW BOSTON (Bowie Co.)
IH 30, 20 mi. SW in rest area, SE of Sulphur River Bridge
Early Protestant Preaching
The Rev. William Stevenson (Oct. 4, 1768–March 5, 1857), a Missourian, friend of Stephen F. Austin, preached in 1815 at Pecan Point on the Red River, north of here. Records indicate that his were the first Protestant sermons ever given in Texas, then part of Catholic "New Spain." Many settlers also entered Texas through Red River County. (1970)

NEW BRAUNFELS (Comal Co.)   *FM 306, 12 mi. NE at N lookout on Canyon Dam*
German Pioneers in Texas

In this area, now covered by Canyon Lake, German emigrants were the first settlers. A society of nobles (Mainzer Adelsverein) sponsored the emigration of 7,380 Germans to Texas from 1844 to 1847. They founded New Braunfels in 1845. Moving west, they established Fredericksburg in 1846. Their Comanche Indian treaty opened 3,800,000 acres between the Llano and Colorado Rivers to peaceful settlement. Farmers and artisans, scholars and scientists, they triumphed over epidemic and privation to help build Texas and the West.   (1968)

NEW BRAUNFELS (Comal Co.)   *FM 1863, 15 mi. NW via SH 46*
Natural Bridge Caverns

Discovered March 27, 1960, by four students of St. Mary's University, San Antonio. Named for the rock bridge that marks entrance. Dedicated on August 5, 1964 by Governor John Connally. Of early cretaceous age; still forming. Site of artifacts from 5,000 B.C., and human remains at least 8,000 years old; also Indian campsites.   (1967)

NEW BRAUNFELS (Comal Co.)   *Bus. IH 35, N of intersection with SH 46*
Comal County

Formed from Travis and Bexar land districts. Created March 24, 1846. Organized July 13, 1846. Named for the river so called from the pancake shape of the islands formed by its springs. New Braunfels, county seat established March 21, 1845. Named in honor of the founder, Prince Carl of Solms-Braunfels.   (1964)

NEW BRAUNFELS (Comal Co.)   *S. Seguin Ave. (SH 46) at Main Plaza*
Main Plaza Bandstand

Following a petition by local residents, the City of New Braunfels built its Main Plaza Bandstand in 1905. Neo-classical in design, it originally served as a stage for summer evening concerts by the Waldschmidt Fire Department Band. In 1926, with funding provided by the Women's Civic Improvement Club, workers raised the pavilion on a limestone base so a ladies restroom could be constructed with windows for light and ventilation. Today, the bandstand is a focal point in the city's landscape, symbolizing the central role music and community events played in the history of New Braunfels.   (2003)

NEW BRAUNFELS (Comal Co.)   *S. Seguin Ave. (SH 46) at Main Plaza*
Site of Nuestra Señora de Guadalupe Mission
(Our Lady of Guadalupe Mission)

Established in 1756 on the Guadalupe River at or near present New Braunfels as an extension of the ill-fated Mission San Francisco Xavier de Horcasitas (1746–1755). Earlier located 100 miles northeast, San Francisco Xavier had been shaken by attacks, disease and strife between friars and soldiers, which had climaxed in the murder of a friar in 1752. Although most of the personnel and Indian converts (Neophytes) fled, the mission continued until 1755. After that time it moved to the Guadalupe River to gather its scattered Mayeye Indians, who refused to enter Valero Mission (the Alamo) in San Antonio. Like the other three San Xavier Missions, San Francisco Xavier was short-lived. Good features at this site included five springs, fertile fields, timber, meadows and the nearby river. Two friars ran the small mission, with a citizen guard, so as to avoid friction. Four Spanish families and 41 Indians (27 of them baptized) comprised the inhabitants of the mission as of January, 1757. Never a strong mission, Guadalupe continued only until March, 1758. At this time the church withdrew its staff because of increasingly dangerous raids by Comanches and other northern tribes.   (1968)

NEW BRAUNFELS (Comal Co.)   *150 N. Seguin Ave. (SH 46)*
New Braunfels: County Seat of Comal County

Early inhabitants of this area included Karankawa, Lipan, Tonkawa and Waco Indians. Between 1844 and 1846, the Verein Zum Schutze Deutscher Einwanderer in Texas (Society for the Protection of German Immigrants in Texas) sent more than 7,000 German settlers. Several hundred of them arrived in this area in 1845. Led by Prince Carl of Solms-Braunfels, they founded a community here on Good Friday, March 21, of that year. Rafael L. and Maria Antonia Veramendi Garza sold the colonization society more than 1,200 acres of land for the settlers, who held a drawing for lots shortly after arriving. Briefly referred to as Comal Springs, the community was named New Braunfels for the German town of Braunfels on the Lahn River. On May 11, 1846, the Texas Legislature incorporated the city, although the charter was not ratified until the following year. By 1850, New Braunfels was reportedly the fourth largest city in Texas. Because of its temperate climate and abundant natural resources, agriculture and industry thrived. Early craftsmen included bakers, blacksmiths, butchers, button and fringe makers, cabinetmakers, carpenters, coppersmiths, locksmiths, machinists, saddlers, tailors, shoemakers, tanners, tinsmiths, turners and wagon makers. Industries included brick kilns, cotton gins, a door and blind factory, flour and grist mills, breweries, a sawmill, a soap and candle house, and a woolen mill. The city's settlers were undaunted by early hardships. Many old-world customs survive among descendants of the original colonists, and the city's heritage is reflected in its buildings, street names and institutions. (2005)

NEW BRAUNFELS (Comal Co.)

Landa St. (SH 46) at Landa Park near Founders Oak

Landa Park

Joseph Landa purchased the land that now encompasses this park in 1859. The Comal Springs, the largest group of springs in the American Southwest, are the focus of the park. Landa used the Comal River to power gristmills, cotton and woolen factories, an ice plant and a brewery. During the Civil War, a saltpeter processing plant was also located on the site. Joseph's son Harry Landa opened Landa's Park as a tourist site in 1898, when the International and Great Northern Railroad built a spur to the site. By 1900, both the I&GN and the Missouri-Kansas-Texas (Katy) railroads ran weekend excursion trains to the park, where visitors enjoyed picnics, dancing and steamboat excursions on Landa Lake. Landa later sold the park to a San Antonio investment group, who operated it until financial problems caused the park's closure in 1933. In 1936, concerned citizens led by Erhard P. Nowotny petitioned the City of New Braunfels to purchase the park, and city residents voted three to one in favor of the move. The park has remained open to the public since that time. Throughout the years the park has grown in acreage, and many improvements have been made. In the 1930s, Works Progress Administration (WPA) employees built concession stands, restrooms, parking areas, and retaining walls. Later improvements have included a miniature golf course, playgrounds and nature trails. Wurstfest, an annual celebration of food and music, has been held in the park each November since the early 1960s. Today, Landa Park continues to serve the public as a leisure destination both for the citizens of New Braunfels and for area travelers. (2009)

NEW BRAUNFELS (Comal Co.)

SH 46, entrance to Wurstfest Assn. Grounds

First Patented Wire Fence

Virginia native William H. Meriwether (b. 1800), an early Comal County plantation owner, ran a sawmill, cotton gin, and gristmill at this site. As an agriculturalist, he was aware of the need for an economical and practical source of fencing material. His interest led to the development of a smooth wire and board fence that effectively resisted the temperature changes that had been so damaging to earlier wire fences. His invention, known as snake wire fencing, was awarded patent No. 10211 on November 8, 1853. It was the first patent for a wire fence issued in the United States.

Although not widely accepted, Meriwether's fence was an important step in the development of an economical fencing material. It also played a role in later wire fence patent disputes. Meriwether sold his mill site to German native Joseph Landa in 1859 and moved to Tennessee, where he died in 1861. (1982)

NEW BRAUNFELS (Comal Co.)

SH 46 N, .5 mi. N of Loop 337

Mission Nuestra Señora de Guadalupe

Established by Franciscan missionaries in 1757 for the purpose of civilizing and Christianizing the Tonkawas, Mayeyes, and their associates. Formerly at Mission San Francisco Xavier on the San Gabriel River. Abandoned in 1758. (1936)

NEW CANEY (Montgomery Co.)

US 59 S, between frontage road and courthouse annex

New Caney

Permanent settlement in what is now New Caney began in the 1860s. The area was first called Presswood for the pioneer family of Austin and Sarah (Waters) Presswood. The Presswoods came to Texas in 1862, purchased land in the area, and raised cattle on the open ranges. The family of

John Wesley Robinson (1819–1903) also settled here in the 1860s and began farming, cattle raising, and cotton ginning operations. When the Houston, East and West Texas Railway Line was laid through Montgomery County in the 1870s, the community became a shipping point for livestock. It was then known for many years as Caney Station, named for the dense cane brakes growing along nearby creeks. In 1882, when a post office was established, the name New Caney was adopted. Early industries in New Caney were confined chiefly to those that were necessary to carry on farming and cattle raising. As the timber industry began to flourish, however, mining props, used to support the earth along the side and roof of mining tunnels, were shipped out of New Caney. The settlement and early history of New Caney are important reminders of the rich heritage of this part of East Texas and Montgomery County. (1984)

NEW CANEY (Montgomery Co.)
US 59 at Reinhardt Rd.
Reinhardt Homestead
Conrad Reinhardt (1886–1969) bought this property in 1918 and established this homestead where he and his wife, Lillie Bell Freeman (1894–1970), raised a family and lived until their deaths. Built about 1920 of heart of pine and magnolia lumber cut from the property's trees, the house reflects the bungalow style in its hipped roof and three-bay porch with tapered columns on brick piers. A garage, two barns, and three shed structures complete the complex. (1991)

NEW LONDON (Rusk Co.)
SH 42, south steps of cenotaph
New London School Explosion
On March 18, 1937, a massive explosion destroyed the New London Junior-Senior High School, instantly killing an estimated 296 students and teachers. The subsequent deaths of victims from injuries sustained that day brought the final death count to 311. The explosion was blamed on a natural gas leak beneath the school building. Within weeks of the disaster the Texas Legislature passed a law requiring an odor to be added to natural gas, which previously was odorless and therefore undetectable. This memorial to victims of the explosion was erected in 1939. (1989)

NEW LONDON (Rusk Co.)
SH 42 at Phillips St.
London Baptist Church
London Baptist Church traces its history to 1856. By 1857, church members shared meeting facilities with the Odd Fellows Lodge in a jointly owned building located on the stagecoach route from Henderson to Waco. The structure was destroyed by fire in 1877. In 1897, a new building was constructed near the same location. When oil was discovered in the area in 1930, London became a boomtown and the church prospered, as well. Throughout its history, London Baptist Church has served the community with a variety of worship, educational and outreach programs. (1991)

NEW SUMMERFIELD (Cherokee Co.)
SH 110, 4 mi. N, Blackjack Community
Samuel Smith Homesite
Samuel Smith (1800–1873), a native of Switzerland, came to Knox County, Tennessee, at the age of 19. In 1823, he married Oney Karnes and received his United States citizenship four years later. In 1849, the Smiths joined a group of immigrants from North Carolina and Tennessee who journeyed to Texas and founded the town of Knoxville in northeast Cherokee County. Samuel and Oney Smith brought six of their seven children with them to Texas. They purchased land three miles southwest of Knoxville in the Blackjack community. Smith built a farmhouse at this site in 1859, and the homestead remained in the family until 1874. As the patriarch of a family that made significant contributions to the rural Blackjack community, Samuel Smith is an important figure in the context of northeastern Cherokee County history. Members of the Smith family deeded land for the church and cemetery, operated the first blacksmith shop in the settlement, and were associated with the International & Great Northern Railroad when it came through the area in 1872.
(Texas Sesquicentennial 1836–1986)

NEW SUMMERFIELD (Cherokee Co.)
SH 110, 4 mi. N
Site of Griffin
Founded by settlers who came here from Griffin, Georgia. In the early 1850s became a flourishing town. Birthplace of John Benjamin Kendrick (1857–1933), Texas cowboy who settled in Wyoming in 1879 after going up the trail for years with herds of cattle. He served in Wyoming State Senate, 1910–1914; as governor, 1914–1916; then as U.S. senator, 1916–1933. Town of Grif-

fin gradually lost people and businesses to railroad towns after 1872. Last store here was closed, 1930.

(1965)

NEW SUMMERFIELD (Cherokee Co.)   SH 110
New Summerfield Methodist Church
Founded about 1878 in the Union Chapel community (approximately ¼ mi. SE of this site), this congregation has been in continuous existence since that time. Built on land donated by Dr. and Mrs. G. F. Fullerton, the Methodist Episcopal Church, South, was used as a union church, providing a place of worship for all denominations in the community. Public school classes were held in the building during the week. A new community built up about the turn of the century at this location. Named Summerfield after the pioneer Summers family, it gradually replaced the Union Chapel community. The Methodist church relocated to the new town and became known as Summerfield Methodist Episcopal Church, South. The congregation moved into a new building in 1919. It continued to occupy that facility until 1931, when a new brick structure was completed. When the town was renamed New Summerfield in 1938, the church's name changed once again. After the merger of the Methodist and Evangelical United Brethren denominations in 1968, it became known as New Summerfield United Methodist Church. A part of Cherokee County history for over a century, the church continues to serve its community.

(1989)

NEW SUMMERFIELD (Cherokee Co.)   SH 110, 1 mi. S
McDonald Cemetery
Located on the original homestead of William and Clarissa Johnson and their family, this community cemetery began in the 1850s. Although there may have been earlier interments (possibly including William Johnson) the earliest documented burials, those of two young daughters of Dr. and Mrs. J. C. Privett, took place in 1856. Dr. Privett died in 1857 and was buried next to his daughters. After Clarissa Johnson married Thomas McDonald in 1858, her homestead became known as the McDonald Farm. By 1870 the small graveyard on Clarissa's farm had become a community burial ground known as McDonald Cemetery, although it was not formally designated as such in deed records until 1930. Among those buried in the McDonald Cemetery are members of the Johnson and McDonald families. There are over 550 documented burials, as well as a number of unmarked graves. The original one-acre plot of land set aside for the graveyard was enlarged in later years by additional land acquisitions. For well over a century, the McDonald Cemetery has served as a reminder of Cherokee County's pioneer heritage. It remains one of the area's important cultural resources.

(1990)

NEW WAVERLY (Walker Co.)   SH 75, 2.6 mi. N
Minnie Fisher Cunningham
(March 19, 1882–December 9, 1964)
A native of Walker County, Minnie Fisher earned a pharmacy degree at the University of Texas Medical Branch in Galveston in 1901. She worked in a Huntsville drugstore and married attorney B. J. Cunningham in 1902. They moved to Galveston in 1907, and she later lived in Austin and Washington, D.C. A leader in woman suffrage organizations, she was president of the Texas Equal Suffrage Association and helped found the National League of Women Voters. In 1928 she became the first Texas woman to run for the U.S. Senate. Her campaign was unsuccessful, and the year also was marred by the death of her husband. Her career turned toward public relations for government agencies, including the Texas Agricultural Extension Service and the U.S. Department of Agriculture. An activist in the National Democratic Party, she counted President Franklin D. Roosevelt among the many friends who fondly called her by her nickname, "Minnie Fish". In 1944 she ran for Governor of Texas against Coke Stevenson, placing second among nine candidates in the primary. She built a home near this site in 1946 and continued to work in Democratic Party politics until her death at age 82.

(1990)

NEWCASTLE (Young Co.)   SH 251, S city limits
Site of Camp Van Camp
Established April 30, 1859, by the United States Army. Named in honor of Cornelius Van Camp, 2nd lieutenant, Second U.S. Cavalry, killed in action at the Wichita Village, October 1, 1858. Abandoned August 28, 1859.

NEWCASTLE (Young Co.)

FM 61, 3 mi. S at Fort Belknap

Fort Belknap

Established in 1851. The largest military post in northern Texas until the Civil War. The first county seat of Young County. A station on the Southern Overland Mail Line connecting St. Louis and San Francisco. (1858–1861)

Butterfield Overland Stages

The Butterfield Overland Stages connecting St. Louis and San Francisco with semi-weekly service, 1858–1861, traversed this county, with a station at Fort Belknap. (1936)

Tonkawa Scouts, C.S.A.

By the time of the Civil War, 1861–1865, Texans knew the horrors of Indian warfare. Hostile tribes made a business of stealing horses, cattle, women and children. The paths they followed in the "bright Comanche moons" were marked by fires and ruin. The Tonkawa tribe, by contrast, sought friendship with Texans. They became valued allies in the Civil War, scouting against hostile Indians and watching for signs of Federal invasion. Old Texas Indian fighters, who once had fought Tonkawas along with others, in wartime asked for Tonkawa scouts. Along the frontier defense line from Red River to the Rio Grande, commanders valued them so much they fed them at personal expense when necessary to obtain their help. A few Tonkawa scouts were more useful than two or three companies of regular soldiers. They could stalk enemies better than bloodhounds. They paid for their Confederate loyalty. On Oct. 25, 1862, near present Anadarko, Okla. Hostile Indians attacked the Tonkawa camp, killing 137 men, women and children out of 300. When later their Chief Castile requested a tribal home in Texas, they were located at Fort Griffin, where they remained until 1884, and then were removed to Oklahoma.

Major Robert S. Neighbors

As Indian agent, forceful peacemaker and humanist, Maj. Neighbors had more influence over Texas' Indians than any other man of his era; came to Texas in 1836. He served as quartermaster in Texas Army, 1839–1841. While on Texas Ranger duty in San Antonio, 1842, he was taken as a prisoner of war to Mexico by Gen. Adrian Woll and spent 18 months in Perote Prison. Began his service to the Indians in 1845. As agent for Lipan-Apache and Tonkawa tribes, he used field system of control, visiting Indian homes, learning a red man's way of life, improving living conditions, helping them to trade. He ably defended their rights, was counselor and friend, and sought new homes for them, never faltering in commitment to their safety. As a Texas commissioner in 1850 he organized El Paso County; he was also a state representative, 1851–1852, and a presidential elector in 1852. Major Neighbors later became the supervising agent for all of the Indians in Texas. Frontier civilians and soldiers failed to support his Indian policies. Many became hostile. On Sept. 14, 1859, he was murdered near here by a white man as he was returning after safely removing all reservation Indians from Texas. He was buried in Belknap Cemetery (½ mi. E of town). (1967)

NEWCASTLE (Young Co.)

US 380, 2.5 mi. SW

Joseph Alfred Woolfolk

A native of Kentucky, Joseph Alfred Woolfolk (1836–1918) earned a law degree from the University of Louisville in 1856. He moved to Belknap, Texas, in 1858 and was hired by the Texas Emigration and Land Company to survey land grants in the Peters Colony. Licensed to practice law by the First District Court in Young County, he served as county attorney and county clerk. At the outbreak of the Civil War, Woolfolk joined a home guard Texas Rangers unit, and in late 1862 transferred into the regular Confederate Army. Captured by Union Troops in West Virginia in July 1863, he spent the remainder of the war in a prison camp in Ohio. Upon his release in 1865 he returned to his native Kentucky, where he married Elizabeth J. Lewis (1846–1922). They became the parents of 9 children. The Woolfolks returned to Texas in 1867 and settled in Weatherford. In 1871, Woolfolk gained notoriety when he was appointed by the court to defend Satanta and Big Tree, Kiowa Indians on trial for murder in the infamous Salt Creek Massacre near Jacksboro. Woolfolk moved his family to a ranch in Young County in the late 1870s. He again served as county attorney in 1881. He and Elizabeth are buried in a private family cemetery near this site. (1994)

NEWCASTLE (Young Co.)

US 380, 8 mi. SW

Indian Raid on Elm Creek, C.S.A.

Indian troubles continually plagued the Texas frontier in the Civil War, with great loss in lives and property. One of the most serious raids occurred near here on Oct. 13, 1864, at Fitzpatrick Ranch. Comanches killed seven ranch people and five Confederate soldiers. Six women and children were kidnapped. 10,000 cattle were stolen. Brit Johnson, Negro slave who that day lost his whole family, later "joined" the Comanches, got their confidence, and freed his people. Later Indians punished him with mutilation and death.

NEWCASTLE (Young Co.)

US 380, 8 mi. SW

Proffitt Cemetery

Members of the Robert Smith Proffitt family came to this area about 1862 and established homes. A son, John Proffitt (1846–1925), amassed large land-holdings and built a gin and other businesses. The developing community was named Proffitt. At its height it boasted homes, a post office, school, retail businesses, a Methodist church, and Baptist church. On July 17, 1867, three young men were killed in an Indian raid near this site. They were buried in a common grave on John Proffitt's land about one mile south of town. Theirs was the first burial in the community graveyard which became known as the Proffitt Cemetery. The cemetery contains both marked and unmarked graves of area pioneers. The numerous interments of infants and children illustrate the often harsh conditions of frontier life. The largest number of burials occurred in the years between 1910 and 1920, and include many victims of the World War I–era influenza epidemic. Also buried here are veterans of the Civil War, World War I, and World War II. Maintained by a cemetery association, this historic graveyard stands as a memorial to Young County Pioneers. (1990)

NEWCASTLE (Young Co.)

US 380, 8 mi. SW at roadside area

Carlton-Johnson-Proffitt Grave

In memory of Patrick Euell Proffitt, Rice Carlton, and Rueben Johnson, three 19 year old boys killed in one of the Elm Creek Indian raids, July 17, 1867. (1964)

NEWCASTLE (Young Co.)

US 380, 5 mi. E

Harmonson Rancho

Kentucky native Peter Harmonson (1797–1865) came to Texas in 1845 as a settler in the Peters Colony. The following year he helped form Denton County, where he served as the first sheriff. In 1854, he brought his family here and established a ranch near this site known as Harmonson Rancho. An organizer of Young County, he served as its first chief justice. He died from a wound received in an Indian raid on the Elm Creek community. In 1869, after it was sold, his ranchsite and his son Z. J. "Jack" Harmonson figured in a skirmish between Indians and local cattlemen. (1982)

NEWTON (Newton Co.)

US 190, 3 mi. SE in roadside park

Newton County

Formed from Jasper County. Created April 22, 1846. Organized July 13, 1846. Named in honor of Sergeant John Newton, 1752–1807, hero of the American Revolution. County seat, Newton, 1846; Burkeville, 1848; Newton since 1853.

NEWTON (Newton Co.)

US 190, 3 mi. SE in roadside park

Newton County, C.S.A.

Supply and military center in the Civil War. Target area for Federals trying to move up the Sabine or across Louisiana and take Texas. Confederates built breastworks and maintained arsenal at Burkeville. Major supply route, "The Old Beef Trail," begun 1823 through area later Newton County, was road taken by thousands of cattle being sent from Texas to feed armies and civilians as far eastward as Mobile, Ala. Sabine ferries were equipped with cattle pens; also ferrymen kept oxen trained to lead herds swimming across the river. Some local beef went eastward, too. Farrsville, a town founded about 1850 on Cow Creek, had a military campground and corrals furnishing fresh stagecoach teams. Its tanning vats and shops made boots and shoes for the Confederacy. Its water mills ground corn for bread, sawed lumber, ginned cotton-products used in supplying the South. The commissioners court made appropriations to outfit military units (buying horses for men unable to furnish their own), aid dependent families, and supply the people with cotton cards to turn the lint into batts for spinning, weaving and knitting. The county, which had voted 178 to 3 for secession, sent about 400 soldiers into the Confederate Army. (1965)

NEWTON (Newton Co.)
305 N. Rusk St. (US 190)
Newton County Pre-War Maneuvers
By 1941, the U.S. military was painfully aware of its unpreparedness to combat the modern mechanized armies in Europe. To increase its combat effectiveness, the U.S. Army conducted the Louisiana maneuvers, which included 3,400 square miles of Texas. The maneuvers involved nearly half a million men and 19 divisions. Many Newton County citizens allowed the U.S. Army access to their lands for training. Troops, horses, tanks, mechanized vehicles and airplanes (utilized for spotting and 'flour' bombing raids) came from various Texas posts. Newton County residents supported these critical military maneuvers (1941–1944), that effectively phased out the horse cavalry and provided valuable lessons as the U.S. Army learned how to fight and win a mechanized war. (2010)

NOCONA (Montague Co.)
US 82, 6 mi. W
Red River Station, C.S.A.
Established nine miles northwest 1861 as Civil War outpost near major buffalo and Indian crossing. Local soldiers, determined to guard edge of settlement against Indian raids, Union invasion from Indian territory, joined by Texas frontier regiment cavalry company. Families of settlers, cattlemen built log cabins within post stockade. Poorly fed, clothed and short on horses and ammunition Confederates patrolled area effectively. Comanche, Kiowa raid at Illinois Bend 15 miles east Jan. 1863. Major cattle crossing after war.

Texas Civil War Frontier Defense 1861–1865
Texas made an all-out effort for the Confederacy after voting over 3 to 1 for secession. 90,000 troops, noted for mobility and heroic daring, fought on every battlefront. An important source of supply and gateway to foreign trade thru Mexico, Texas was the storehouse of the South. Red River station and other posts on this line were backed by patrols of State Rangers, organized militia, and citizens' posses scouting from nearby "family forts." This was part of a 2000 mile frontier and coastline successfully defended by Texans. (1963)

NOCONA (Montague Co.)
FM 103, 10 mi. N
North Nocona Oil Field, Montague County Oil Discovery, 1922
Pennsylvania oil man George Williams, backed by Cad McCall, drilled for oil intermittently, 1918–22, beginning at Eagle Point (4.5 mi. SE). Leasing by individuals and major companies—including, Phil Lesh, A. E. Humphrey, and the Texas Co.—kept rigs working. Gas blew in at 800-foot depth on J. W. Maddox-J. E. Lemons land, one well yielding over 100,000,000 cubic feet daily. The gas was piped to Nocona and rural homes. Oil was discovered in 1922 on Maddox site, at about 1,000 feet. Production continued at 1,000–2,000 feet, there and elsewhere. The gas caused trouble: A capped well blew mud from prairie dog holes and gas from water well a quarter-mile away. In 1925, a gas well on W. W. Jones land (2 mi. W) blew out a gigantic crater. Another well (.75 mi. W) caught fire, burned its rig, and was finally doused by nationally-famed oil well fire fighter Tex Thornton. With an estimated 100,000,000 barrel total on record, this 12,295-acre field still produces. (1972)

NOME (Jefferson Co.)
US 90 W
Opelousas Trail
Named for one of several Atakapan-speaking Native American tribes originally connected by this trail, the Opelousas Trail ran from La Bahia (later Goliad) to the Mississippi River in Louisiana. Evidence of cultural interchange between tribes indicates the presence of such a trail for hundreds of years. Spanish explorers, soldiers, and vaqueros employed this route. By the 1750s, French traders had been traveling the trail for about twenty years. After 1820 settlers began to arrive from Louisiana and other southern states. Don Martin de Leon and anglo cattlemen such as James Taylor White and William B. Duncan herded large droves of cattle, mules, and horses to market in New Orleans. A post route was established along the Opelousas in early 1836. That spring, Texas pioneers fled along this path during the "Runaway Scrape." Later, Santa Anna was led down the trail toward New Orleans and ultimately to Washington, D.C., as a prisoner of war. A stage and mail

route followed the trail after 1850; the Confederate Army used the road to move troops during the Civil War. Use of the route continued throughout the 20th century. Many segments of the trail were incorporated into U.S. Highway 90 from Liberty to Orange. (1998)

NORMANGEE (Leon Co.) *Old Spanish Road, W of junction with FM 39*
El Camino Real—The Old San Antonio Road
First blazed in 1691 by Captain Don Domingo Teran de los Rios, first provisional governor of Texas, in an expedition officially directed by Father Fray Damian Massanet, O.F.M. Apostolic missionary and explorer in Texas. The general route was northeast from the Rio Grande to the San Antonio River, thence across the Guadalupe, San Marcos, Colorado, Brazos and Trinity Rivers to the missions in East Texas. Other expeditions taking the same route: Espinosa, Olivares Aguirre in 1709; St. Denis in 1714; Ramon in 1716; Alarcon in 1718; Marquis of Aguayo in 1720; Moses Austin in 1820. The Republic of Texas officially made this road a boundary between a number of Emperarial Land Grants. Normangee home of the old San Antonio Road Association.

NORMANNA (Bee Co.) *US 181, on S edge of town near Medio Creek crossing*
Community of Normanna
Settlement dates from about 1850. First town, two miles west, was called San Domingo for its location near junction of San Domingo and dry Medio Creeks. After railroad was built, 1886, citizens moved to Walton (new flag station) to be on line. Name honored Sheriff D. A. T. Walton. When Norwegians settled area, 1890s, Walton became Normanna. Word originally suggested the qualities of old Norse heroes, but through local usage came to mean "Home of the Norseman." Town thrived for years; then declined after series of fires and advent of the automobile. (1969)

NORTH COWDEN (Ector Co.) *SH 158, N city limits*
North Cowden
Site of Ector County's second big oil strike. Named for ranching family of John M. Cowden, an 1885 Permian Basin settler; one of four brothers, ranching community leaders on Texas frontiers. Oil and gas development began here with the 1930 discovery. Post office granted 1947. Town continues as a Permian Basin petroleum source. (1965)

NOTREES (Ector Co.) *SH 302 in Notrees*
Town of Notrees
Post Office established 1944 in drug store of C. J. Brown, Jr., who named it in response to title suitable to locality. Residents have since made history by planting shade trees. Now production hub of Permian Basin; center of gas processing industry, and home of Otto's Boys Ranch. (1965)

NURSERY (Victoria Co.) *US 87 in Nursery*
Murphy Home
Built 1897 combining Southern plantation and New England saltbox styles of architecture. Home of prominent Nursery citizens R. S. Fowler, John M. Horton, E. S. Jennings, Louie Carpenter, and for many years, W. M. Murphy, Sr. Has Medallion Plate. (1966)

O'DONNELL (Lynn Co.) *US 87 Bus. at city plaza*
O'Donnell
Named for Tom J. O'Donnell, promoter of South Plains railroads, including 60 miles of Santa Fe line from Slaton to Lamesa. On this new railroad (important as freight hauler) town of O'Donnell was founded in 1909 by H. E. Baldridge and Charles H. Doak—two of the organizers and first officials of Lynn County. Doak built a hotel in projected town of O'Donnell in 1909. L. G. Phillips established the first store. On July 4, 1910, a big picnic was held to celebrate arrival of first Santa Fe train. Old "Central" post office (previously on Dee W. Harris Ranch, 5.5 mi. NW) was moved to new town in 1910 and was officially renamed O'Donnell on Feb. 7, 1911. W. R. Standefer was employed to survey townsite in 1911. H. E. Baldridge offered free building lots to churches. A Methodist church was organized in 1911; Church of Christ and Presbyterian churches in 1912; First Baptist in 1914. Town was incorporated in 1923, with W. R. Sanderson as first mayor. School, improved dramatically since its early wooden building, serves a large area. A graduate was actor Dan Blocker ("Hoss" Cartwright). Now a dryland farming center, O'Donnell in 1961 had what was then largest cotton gin in the world, ginning 21,000 bales of cotton during that year. (1969)

OAKHURST (San Jacinto Co.) *FM 946, 3 mi. SE (2 mi. off road)*
Site of Raven Hill
Plantation home of General Sam Houston, who was called "The Raven" by the Cherokee Indians. Built in 1844. Sold before 1860.

OAKVILLE (Live Oak Co.) *IH 37 at FM 1358*
Oakville
So named from its Live Oak trees. County seat from 1856 to 1919 of Live Oak County, which was created February 2, and organized August 4, 1856. (1936)

OAKVILLE (Live Oak Co.) *IH 37 access road in Oakville*
Oakville Post Office
Irish immigrants settled this area as part of the John McMullen and James McGloin Mexican Land Grant. Located on the Sulphur tributary of the Nueces River, this site was known as "On the Sulphur." Live Oak County was organized in 1856 and Oakville was named county seat. Thomas Wilson gave 640 acres for the townsite stipulating that separate squares be marked as public, graveyard, church, and school squares. Oakville grew as stores, two hotels, a livery stable, a school, and two churches were established. The Oakville post office was established May 11, 1857, with Joshua Hinton as the first postmaster. The mail came four times a week on stagecoaches traveling from San Antonio to Corpus Christi and on to Brownsville. By 1879, the San Antonio–Corpus Christi stage left both ends of the line six days a week. Stage travel became less popular with the arrival of the railroad. When the San Antonio, Uvalde & Gulf Railroad bypassed Oakville in 1913, the town began to decline. The county seat was relocated in 1919 at George West. In 1966, the Oakville post office was designated as a rural branch of the Three Rivers post office and continues to serve the community. (1979)

ODEM (San Patricio Co.) *US 77, 4.5 mi. S*
Sharpsburg and Borden's Ferry
Named for an early area sheep rancher, the town of Sharpsburg grew into a regional trade center in the 1870's when Sidney Gail Borden (d. 1908) operated a general store, cotton gin, grist mill, and grape vineyards; bought a meat packery; and expanded an existing ferry business on the Nueces River. Flat bottomed sailing vessels allowed goods to be shipped on the Shallow River to markets including Corpus Christi. With processing and transportation facilities in place, Borden platted the town of Sharpsburg and sold lots, attracting several hundred settlers. Stores, a post office, a school, and a boardinghouse were also established. Farmers from towns as far away as twenty-five miles came to Sharpsburg to process their goods and ship them to area markets. Sharpsburg's growth peaked in the 1890's. Bypassed by the railroads, its population declined steadily. In 1912 Sharpsburg's school was consolidated with the Odem school district and closed, and in 1913 a bridge was constructed at the Ferry site. Though the town is no longer in existence and its site is again part of an area ranch, Sharpsburg and Borden's ferry remain an important part of early San Patricio County history. (1991)

ODEM (San Patricio Co.) *US 77, 4 mi. S*
Angelita ("Littlest Angel")
Angelita was one of several rural communities which grew up in San Patricio County after the Civil War. A schoolhouse was erected in the 1880s and was the center of community life. After the arrival of the St. Louis, Brownsville, and Mexico Railroad in 1904, a town was platted and businesses were established. The railroad station at Angelita provided a shipping point for agricultural products and cattle from nearby farms and ranches. The relocation of the post office and school to Odem in 1916 caused the town of Angelita to decline and eventually vanish. (1988)

ODESSA (Ector Co.) *US 385, 12.5 mi. N*
Near Site of Baker Ranch School
Since there were no public schools in rural Ector County, R. W. Smith and Teague Baker in 1906 erected an 8' x 10' school building in Baker's pasture. They hired a teacher at $15 a month, plus room and board, which each furnished on alternate months. Ranch schools like this one taught not only children of ranchers, but also those of cowboys and nesters—small farmers coming west to homestead or to buy land at nominal prices. Baker Community later had a public school. Till the Permian Basin had good roads and buses, ranch schools served it well. (1965)

ODESSA (Ector Co.)   *US 385 at SH 158, 12.5 mi. N*
LeGrande Survey of 1833 (SE Corner 18 mi. E of This Site)
Made in era of Mexican rule in Texas for John Beales, who through partnership, acquired 70,000,000 acres of land and gained the title of "Texas' Largest Land King." Alexander LeGrande's survey covered about 2,000 miles in West Texas, Oklahoma Panhandle and Eastern New Mexico— then south to the 32nd parallel. Hardship and tragedy plagued LeGrande's party. Attacked by Indians, he abandoned survey. First exploration here is usually credited to Capt. R. B. Marcy, U. S. Army. LeGrande's work was years earlier.   (1967)

ODESSA (Ector Co.)   *US 385, 4.6 mi. N*
Emigrant Trail, Gateway to the West
Road of stubborn seekers of 1849 California gold fields and better life. Bringing the old, infant, the yet unborn and all worldly goods, family wagons entered Texas at Preston, on Red River, to go southwest via springs (including some now in Monahans Sandhills Park) to Emigrants' Crossing on the Pecos, then upriver and west through Guadalupe Pass to El Paso. Old wagon parts by the trail tell of some disasters. Capt. R. B. Marcy in 1849 and Capt. John Pope in 1854 made army surveys of the trail. It passed near this spot.   (1964)

ODESSA (Ector Co.)   *US 385 at 42nd St., Ector County Coliseum*
El Paso Natural Gas Company's
First Compressor Transmission Engine
A landmark tool in man's conquest of energy. This compressor went into use in Culberson County, Tex., on Oct. 1, 1931, and served until 1969, aiding in the rise of the Southwest as an industrial empire. This was the first compressor transmission engine at the number one transmission station of El Paso Natural Gas Company, founded in 1928 by Paul Kayser, a Houston attorney. The pioneer transmission station of the El Paso Natural Gas Company was one of the earliest in the Permian Basin. A Cooper-Bessemer Type 19, this machine is an 800-horsepower horizontal tandem reciprocating compressor engine. Equipped with two 10¼-inch by 24-inch gas compressor cylinders, it weighs about 173,000 pounds. It served under load for 152,064 hours, compressing more than 144 billion cubic feet of natural gas in its working lifetime. It conveyed production from fields at Jal, N. M., and in Winkler County, Tex., to city of El Paso and southern New Mexico and Arizona. It was the first machine of its kind in a system that expanded into 22,000 miles of forwarding lines furnishing low-cost energy for industries and households in eleven western states.   (1970)

ODESSA (Ector Co.)   *US 385 at 42nd St., Ector County Coliseum*
The Permian Basin
One of the two richest oil fields in the world. Discovery began in 1920 at a Mitchell County well. Next came the 1923 Big Lake strike, then the wild 1925 boom in Upton County, followed by production in Andrews, Crane, Ector, Martin, Midland, Pecos, Ward, Winkler and 24 other counties. In some years new wells averaged 38 a week. Fortunes were made, lost, then regained—all within months. So great were yields that oil brought 50 cents a barrel, while drillers paid $5.00 a barrel for drinking water. Area is 88,610 square miles, with center here at Odessa. Extends across a deeply buried prehistoric sea that more than 250 million years ago contained much fish and reptile life, including dinosaurs. Shores and islands later grew giant vegetation, until earth changes buried animals and plants in pockets that turned hydrocarbons into petroleum. In 40 years from its discovery, the Permian Basin was producing 53% of total oil in Texas and 20% of U.S. crude oil. It is one of the world's largest producers of channel carbon black. Other by-products are sulphur, asphalt, synthetic rubber ingredients and petrochemicals.   (1964)

ODESSA (Ector Co.)   *2500 blk. of Andrews Hwy. (US 385)*
Site of Odessa College, 1889–1891
Established through efforts of Odessa Townsite Co., which gave $12,000; a Northern Methodist group matched this fund in 1888. Rev. M. A. Daugherty, Pittsburgh, Pa., was placed in charge, and a 20-acre plot was allotted to the college. Erection of a two-story building began in 1890. In 1891 classes for 14 students were taught by Miss Alice Wright, of Maine. A "mystery" fire destroyed the college after one session. This church-sponsored college was never rebuilt. In 1946, the new Odessa College was founded to fulfill aims of leadership in education.   (1967)

ODESSA (Ector Co.)   *US 385 at 3rd St.*
Ector County Land Rush
Here in 1904 a fight involved almost every man in Ector County, over filing a claim for 4 sections of public land. Elias Dawson and Charlie Lewis each brought friends to help him file. Before courthouse doors opened, several men had clothes or boots torn off, in foes' efforts to find filing papers. When the doors opened, a man was boosted over the heads of the crowd, and Lewis won the 4 sections of land. Texas as a republic owned over 200,000,000 acres of public land. She used land to attract settlers, pay her soldiers, set up school funds. At annexation, she retained her public lands—the only state to do so. In a boundary dispute she ceded 63,552,144 acres; used land to pay for railroads, harbors and canals; compensated Civil War soldiers or widows with land; traded 3,000,000 acres for a state capitol. By 1883 her lands were over-committed. Free grazing had to be stopped. Terminations of leases and the corrections of surveys later made available some land for filing. This led to the 1904 rush. In one courthouse a man hid overnight to be first in line. Cattle chutes to a clerk's window would be lined for months with men hoping to file. Cowboys and farmers battled. Filing was a challenge.   (1965)

ODESSA (Ector Co.)   *US 385 at 3rd St.*
General Matthew D. Ector
Enlisted 1861. Lieutenant 3rd Texas Cavalry. Fought Arkansas, Missouri and Indian Territory. As colonel led 14th Texas Cavalry Kentucky invasion. Made brigadier general 1862 to command famed Ector's brigade in Tennessee and Mississippi battles. Wounded four times without leaving Chickamauga field. Under constant fire 70 days in Georgia. Lost leg in Atlanta 1864. Assigned to defense of Mobile, Alabama. A memorial to Texans who served the Confederacy, erected by the State of Texas.   (1963)

ODESSA (Ector Co.)   *SH 191 at Loop 338*
Emmet V. Headlee, M.D.
Emmet V. Headlee was a fourth-generation physician; his great-grandfather, Elisha Headlee, was a Civil War surgeon. His grandfather and father practiced medicine in Teague (Freestone Co.), and Emmet was born there in 1900. At age thirteen, he saved a friend from drowning, an act which earned him a stipend from the Carnegie Hero Fund which helped pay for his college courses. He earned a Bachelor's degree from the University of Texas in 1922 and his Doctor of Medicine degree from Baylor University College of Medicine in 1926. While interning at St. Paul's Sanitarium in Dallas, Dr. Headlee met and married Marie Sprusil (b. 1900), a native of Cleveland, Ohio, and a registered nurse and certified nurse-anesthetist. The young couple arrived in Odessa in Nov. 1926, and Dr. Headlee became the only doctor in a town which then numbered about 450 people. His first office was in the back of a drugstore, and the front rooms of the Headlees' first home were examination and operating rooms. Dr. Headlee became Ector County Health Officer and also served patients from throughout the region. He opened a seven-bed hospital in 1934, which expanded before 1949, when Medical Center Hospital opened with Dr. Headlee on staff. Near this site, the Headlees bought land for the animals which Dr. Headlee accepted as payment in lieu of cash during the Great Depression. In 1949, the couple built a house here. In 1957, in recognition of her long years of dedicated service in church and charitable work, Marie Headlee was named "First Lady of Odessa." The civic-minded Dr. Headlee was active in community, school and medical organizations until his death in 1965. Emmet and Marie Headlee provided great leadership to Odessa, which has become a major medical center in West Texas.   (2011)

ODESSA (Ector Co.)   *IH 20 Bus., E of Loop 338*
Ector County
Created February 26, 1887 from Tom Green County. Organized January 15, 1891. Named in honor of Matthew Duncan Ector, 1822–1879, member of the Texas Legislature, a Confederate officer, and outstanding jurist. Odessa, the county seat.   (1964)

ODESSA (Ector Co.)   *IH 20 Bus., E of Loop 338*
Comanche War Trail
A barbed, bristling flying wedge—the Comanches—rode into 18th century Texas, driving the Wichitas and Caddoes east, the Apaches west, becoming lords of the South Plains. Harassed the

344

Spanish and Anglo-Americans along frontier from Corpus Christi on the Gulf up to the Red River. Wrote their name in blood clear down to Zacatecas, Mexico. Captured women, children and horses along their road of blood, tears and agony. Many roads converged into the Great Comanche War Trail, which passed about 20 miles southeast of this marker.

ODESSA (Ector Co.)
IH 20, 10 mi. W
Odessa Meteor Crater
The Odessa Meteor Crater, second largest in the United States and sixth in the world, was formed some 20,000 years ago when an iron meteorite believed to weigh 1,000 tons crashed into the earth near this site. Impact was so great that 4.3 million cubic feet of rock was expelled or shifted, forming a cone-shaped crater 500 feet wide and nearly 100 feet deep. Action of wind and water during subsequent centuries filled the cavity with silt so that today its concave surface is only five to six feet below the level of the surrounding plain. It retains its original broad diameter, surrounded by a low, rock-buttressed rim created when limestone formations were shattered and forced to the surface by the burrowing mass. Fragments of the meteorite collected around the crater indicate that it was 90 percent iron, with small amounts of cobalt, copper, carbon, phosphorus, sulphur and chromium. Although the main mass has never been found, it is believed to lie embedded 179 feet below the surface. In addition to the principal crater, scientific investigation has revealed the presence of two smaller adjoining depressions, formed by less massive bodies that fell in the same meteor shower which sent the large mass to earth. Although not now discernible, they were from 15 to 50 feet wide, and from seven to 17 feet deep. Neither penetrated deeply enough to encounter solid rock but was formed primarily in clay-like deposits. Meteors are believed to have been formed by the breaking-up of a planet similar in size and composition to the earth. The body is thought to have been part of the solar system . . . perhaps the mythical planet between Mars and Jupiter whose disruption must have created the asteroids.

ODESSA (Ector Co.)
IH 20, 13 mi. W in rest area
The Caprock
A range of flat-topped ridges and cliffs stretching from Texas Panhandle to 20 miles south of this point and extending into New Mexico. The name also refers to tough limestone that caps ridges, rising sharply 200 to 1,000 ft. above plains. This section, Concho Bluffs, marks western edge of caprock escarpment, called the "break of the plains" because it divides the Staked Plains from the North Central Plains of Texas. Observed by Coronado's Expedition, 1540–1541. Provided shelter in storms, but delayed entrance of settlers to Staked Plains. Herds of stampeding cattle at times plunged over its edge. In this area, the caprock blocked eastbound wagons, including some from California gold fields in 1850s. Because of scarce surface water, Staked Plains were too dry for farming or ranching until wells were drilled and windmills installed. Ridges and canyons here hindered railroad building. In 1881 workmen earned $2.50 a day—highest wages ever paid until then on a Texas railroad job—at "Colt's big rock cut" (the mile-wide, 17-ft. chasm visible here). A tragic accident with dynamite injured several of Colt's men and killed three. Their graves, known to the pioneers around Odessa, were on a hill northeast of the tracks, but cannot now be found.
(1967)

ODESSA (Ector Co.)
IH 20, 14 mi. W at roadside park
Odessa
Founded 1881. Legend says name came from an Indian princess who wandered into camp of Texas & Pacific Railroad construction gang. Others say it was for Odessa on Russian plains—area West Texas resembles. County seat ever since Ector was organized, 1891. Has had great growth since 1926 oil strike. Center for one of the two largest oil fields in the world. Has largest inland petrochemical complex in United States, alone with many other diversified industries. It is also the oilfield supply capital of the world. Odessa College has served area since 1946. City has 143 churches; a symphony orchestra; clubs for sports, service, culture. Recreational attractions include nation's second largest meteor crater; exact replica of Shakespeare's 16th century Globe Theatre; 4 museums; a planetarium; industrial tours; "Permian Playhouse"; "Prairie Dog Pete" park; world's largest jackrabbit statue; and 21 playground-parks. Unique "Presidential Room" depicts lives of U.S. Presidents in art, documents, and memorabilia. Sandhills Hereford and Quarterhorse Show opens annual rodeo season for entire Southwest. World famous Permian Basin Oil Show is held biennially.
(1967)

345

OLDENBURG (Fayette Co.)

Oldenburg

The land in this area was included in a Mexican land grant awarded to Nathaniel Townsend in 1838. Portions of the grant were sold to a succession of different people over the years, and in 1885 August Heintze and Gus Steenken purchased about eighteen acres. Heintze and Steenken, both natives of Oldenburg, Germany, founded a community and named it after their hometown. The majority of the settlers in this area were immigrants from Germany and Bohemia. At its height Oldenburg boasted homes, farms, and a number of businesses and institutions, including stores, saloons, a cotton gin, tin shop, doctors' office, blacksmith shop, post office, church, dance halls (festplatz), and schools. The first school in the community was known as the German and Bohemian Oldenburg School. Founded in 1898, it was succeeded in 1922 by Oldenburg Common School District No. 5. A separate school for black students opened about 1930. By 1944, both schools were consolidated with the Fayetteville school district. Descendants of early German and Bohemian settlers continue to reside in this vicinity.

(1990)

OLIVIA (Calhoun Co.)

SH 172 at city limits

Olivia

Established in 1892, the community of Olivia was named for Olivia Haterius, wife of the Rev. Carl J. E. Haterius, a Swedish Lutheran minister who bought land in the area and advertised a new settlement to other Swedish immigrants in the midwest. Twelve Swedish families responded to the initial advertisement and moved to Olivia with others following in a few years. By 1900, a number of non-Swedish families had settled here, as well. The first public building in Olivia was a one-room schoolhouse where children were taught during the day and parents attended classes at night to learn English. The Eden Lutheran Church held services in the schoolhouse until 1910, when a sanctuary was built. John Lind built the first store in the community on Carancahua Bay in 1894. The post office was housed in Lind's store and mail was delivered once a week. Lind moved his store to the center of the townsite in 1900. In 1906, Edward Wilson, another Swedish immigrant, bought the Olivia store and was appointed postmaster. Other businesses included a hotel doctor's office, grocery store, blacksmith shop, and cotton gin. Since 1900, the thriving community has changed and grown, but retains its proud Swedish heritage.

(1992)

OLIVIA (Calhoun Co.)

SH 172 at CR 317

Olivia Cemetery

In 1892, the Rev. Carl J. E. Haterius of Galesburg, Illinois, acquired land at this site with the intention of establishing a community for Swedish settlers. He named the settlement for his wife, Olivia. When the townsite was laid out in 1893, land was set aside for this burial ground in association with the Swedish Lutheran Eden Church. The earliest marked grave is that of Anna Berardino Wilson, who died in 1902. Swedes and non-Swedes together contributed to the early development of Olivia, and the community cemetery serves as a reminder of their contributions.

(Texas Sesquicentennial 1836–1986)

OLNEY (Young Co.)

SH 79, 3 mi. N in Archer Co.

The Confluence of the Brazos, Trinity, and Red River Watersheds

The Trinity, a major Texas river, rises 250 yards west of this 1250-foot mound. South of this site water drains to the Brazos, and north and west to the Red. This high point has been important in Texas history. It guided Capt. Diego Parilla to battle Indians on the Red in 1759 and aided Capt. R. B. Marcy in mapping a California trail in 1849. Marcy and Maj. R. S. Neighbors used it as a beacon point in finding a site for an Indian reservation in 1854. It also was on U.S. Cavalry maps for 1870s Indian campaigns.

(1976)

OLNEY (Young Co.)

SH 114, 9 mi. SE

Site of Cottonwood Spring

19th century oasis around a lone cottonwood tree and a good spring. Wagon ruts from heavy traffic attracted here are still visible on hill to the southwest. In 1849, Capt. Randolph B. Marcy, U.S. Army, camped with his soldiers at this spring as they mapped a gold-seekers' road to California. Capt. Marcy was to return as escort (1851) for Col. W. F. Belknap, en route to establish Fort Belknap (15 mi. SW), and with Maj. Robert S. Neighbors (1854), exploring for Indian reservation sites. Maj. Enoch Steen of the 2nd U.S. Dragoons was here in 1855, platting a route to Fort Riley,

Kan. The Leach Wagon Train camped here in 1857 while opening the Butterfield Overland Mail Route, along the Preston Road to Red River. Riding to the north of Red River to fight wild Comanche raiders, two expeditions camped here in 1858: Capt. John S. ("Rip") Ford with Rangers, in April; Maj. Earl Van Dorn with U.S. Cavalry in the fall. Maj. Neighbors in Aug. 1859, escorting Texas Indians to reservations in present Oklahoma, found the spring dry. Water returned, however. Cattlemen used the spring for generations, until in mid-20th century, the water table dropped permanently and the cottonwood died.

(1974)

OLNEY (Young Co.)   *SH 114, 6 mi. SE*
Little Salt Creek Indian Fight
(Battleground about a Mile to the North)
Duel between a cattle roundup crew and Indians, on May 16, 1869. Cowboys attacked at their work were Shapley Carter, Bill Crow, and Henry Harrison, all of Palo Pinto County; crew captain Ira E. Graves, J. W. Gray, W. C. Kutch, and Jason McClain, of Jack County; Joe Woody, Parker County; George and John Lemley and Rube Seachrist, Young County; Dick, the cook, from Tarrant County. All day the crew held at bay 57 Comanches, who left that night. Nine cowboys were wounded—Carter, Crow, and John Lemley died. Texans never forgot the unprovoked attack.

(1971)

OLTON (Lamb Co.)   *US 70, 1.5 mi. E in roadside park*
Lamb County
Formed from Young and Bexar territories. Created August 21, 1876. Organized June 20, 1908. Named in honor of George A. Lamb, 1814–1836, a second lieutenant who fell in the first charge at the Battle of San Jacinto. Olton, county seat.

OMAHA (Morris Co.)   *US 259, 6 mi. N city limits*
Omaha
On Seidicum Line, the old Bowie–Red River Counties boundary surveyed in 1840. Thompson Morris laid out "Morristown" in 1880, but post office was "Gravett." To arbitrate, a drawing from a hat suggested "Omaha," for old home of a settler from Alabama. Town is now a shipping center for plants and farm products.

(1966)

ORAN (Palo Pinto Co.)   *FM 52 in Oran, 2 mi. N of SH 254*
Charles Goodnight
Here at Black Springs in the Keechi Valley in 1857, the celebrated pioneer open range cowman and trail driver Charles Goodnight (1836–1929) located his first ranch on the extreme Indian frontier of Texas. From here he took part in the 1860 Pease River fight when Cynthia Ann Parker was recaptured from Comanches. He served as scout and guide for the Texas Rangers during the Civil War and in 1866 he laid out the Goodnight-Loving Cattle Trail, over which thousands of longhorns were driven to market in New Mexico. In 1867, at Fort Sumner, New Mexico, his partner Oliver Loving died from wounds suffered in an Indian attack. Without the aid of an undertaker, Goodnight carried the body by wagon through hostile Indian territory for burial at Weatherford (24 mi. SE). Goodnight extended his cattle trails to Wyoming and to Colorado, where he started a ranch near Pueblo. In 1876, he established the first cattle ranch in the vast Texas Panhandle, which became the internationally known JA Ranch. Involved in the preservation of the area's native buffalo, he also bred the first herd of cattalo by crossing buffalo with range cattle. Goodnight's pioneer efforts led to the development of the frontier and the Texas cattle industry.

(1982)

ORANGE (Orange Co.)   *7925 IH 10E*
Old First Orange Baptist Church
Old First Orange Baptist Church was organized on September 20, 1857, and is the earliest known religious establishment in Orange County. Charter members were Mr. and Mrs. Hollingsworth, Mr. and Mrs. Harvey Finch, Mr. and Mrs. Fietus Finch, Josh Harmon, Aion Ashworth, Henry Humble and F.A. Burton. David D. Foreman (Forman) of the Louisiana Baptist Association helped with the organization and served as the congregation's first pastor. The church originally met at a small schoolhouse located near 37th and South Streets, but an 1865 hurricane destroyed the structure. F.A. Burton helped direct construction of a new sanctuary, among a grove of sweet gum trees near what later became U.S. Highway 90. This structure was torn down and reconstructed at the church's present site circa 1892, when an acre of land was deeded to the church by Joshua Cole.

347

F.A. Burton was a member of the congregation from its inception until his death in 1925, a total of sixty-eight years. Records show that he served as pastor 1869–1971 and again from 1880 until 1887. Additional acreage was added to the church property through the years, and structures on the site have been added and modified. In September of 2005 Hurricane Rita swept through the area, and for the second time in its existence, the congregation lost its sanctuary to a hurricane. Another structure, completed in May of 2007, was constructed on the same site. Mission and community outreach projects are important to the church, including the construction of churches in seventeen states, and the repair of area homes after hurricanes.   (2008)

ORANGE (Orange Co.)   *Green Ave. at Simmons Dr. (US 90)*
Levingston Shipbuilding Company and Edward T. Malloy
In 1859, three brothers, Samuel, David and John Levingston, arrived in Orange from Ireland and purchased an existing shipyard, where they built wooden ships for more than thirty years. The son of Samuel Levingston, "Captain" George Levingston, established his own shipbuilding business in 1919–1920. In 1930, Levingston purchased five acres at Front and Mill Streets in Orange, enlarging his operation, and Levingston Shipbuilding Company operated from this location for the remainder of its existence. Incorporation in 1933 sustained the company during the slow economic times of the 1930s. Edward T. Malloy was hired in 1939 as a general manager, and stayed with the company for thirty-seven years, becoming president of the company when he bought the controlling interest in 1945. World War II brought a vast influx of business—the company had begun construction of military vessels before the United States entered the war, and continued to be a major supplier for the Army and Navy during the duration. Levingston Shipbuilding delivered its first vessel for the war effort, a 530-ton steel tugboat named Tuscarora on December 13, 1941. Between 1941 and 1945, Levingston built and delivered a total of 160 vessels for the U.S. Navy and U.S. Army including tugs, tankers, barges and ocean going rescue tugs. After World War II, Levingston Shipbuilding changed with the economic times and became a worldwide leader in the design, engineering and construction of off-shore drilling rigs, jack-up platforms, and self-propelled drilling ships. Levingston Shipbuilding was the only U.S. builder of all five types of offshore drilling rigs until it ceased operations in 1985.   (2008)

ORANGE (Orange Co.)   *Green Ave. at Simmons Dr. (US 90)*
Office of the Supervisor of Shipbuilding
and Consolidated Steel Corporation
Orange's location at a bend in the Sabine River, adjacent to the immense virgin pine forests of southeast Texas, made it an ideal site for shipbuilding. However, by 1930 all of the easily obtainable timber was exhausted, and the associated sawmills closed. The Depression of the 1930s also weighed heavily on the population of Orange. In July 1940, Congressman Martin Dies and Vice-President John Nance Garner attached an amendment to a large general appropriations bill to build twenty-four surf-landing crafts and twelve destroyers in Orange. The Office of Supervisor of Shipbuilding, USN, Orange, Texas, was established at this time, with CDR E.B. Perry as the first supervisor. The supervisor was responsible for directing the construction of the thirty-six crafts, and also the establishment of a shipyard in Orange to support the endeavor. The facility was built on sixty-five acres at a bend in the Sabine River. Levingston Shipbuilding's tugboat and barge shipyard occupied a small portion of the west side, and the remainder was occupied by Consolidated Steel Corporation's steel fabricating plant, where the Office of the Supervisor was also located. On May 14, 1941, construction began at Consolidated Steel on the Destroyers USS Aulick and USS Charles Ausburne, the first two warships constructed on the gulf coast for the U.S. government. In total, thirty-nine destroyers and 100 destroyer escorts were built at the Consolidated Steel Corporation yard during World War II. After the war, the naval facility prepared ships for storage in the Naval Reserve Fleet as the United States Naval Inactive Ship Maintenance Facility.   (2008)

ORANGE (Orange Co.)   *US 90, 4 mi. W at Womack Rd.*
Site of World War II P. O. W. Camp
During World War II, over 50,000 German prisoners of war were interned in over 70 Texas P. O. W. camps. Base camps were established at military bases throughout the state. The base camps operated a number of branch camps in their respective areas. Detailed from a base camp at Huntsville, about 140 German prisoners were housed in a U. S. Army tent camp near this site in 1944. Located on land owned by the Lutcher Moore Lumber Company, the camp was built with

construction materials and labor provided by the Orange County Farm Labor Committee of the U. S. Agricultural Extension Service. Transported to their work details by army trucks each day, the German prisoners worked as laborers in area rice fields, helping to bring in the harvest of farmers whose employees had gone to war. The work of the prisoners became a crucial element in the area's wartime food production, and many of the prisoners enjoyed good working relationships with their employers. Although the original prison camp operated for only a short time in 1944, prisoners transported from camps in China, Texas, and Edgerly, Louisiana, were once again employed on Orange County farms in 1945.

(1991)

ORANGE (Orange Co.)
US 90, 3 mi. W
Orange County
Formed from Jefferson County. Created February 5, 1852. Organized March 20, 1852. Named for the fruit grown in this district since the earliest settlements near the mouth of the Sabine River. County seat, Madison, 1852. Name changed to Orange, February 6, 1858.

ORANGE (Orange Co.)
Front and 4th St., Riverwalk Park
Atakapan Indians of Orange County
The Atakapan Indians, a tribe associated with southeastern U.S. bands, lived in this area for centuries. Studies have suggested their presence covered a large region of Southeast Texas. Their name comes from the Choctaw Indians, and means "man-eaters." It is believed that Indians encountered by Spanish explorer Cabeza de Vaca in 1528 along the Gulf Coast may have been Atakapas. The first documented contact with the tribe was by French sailor Simars de Bellisle in 1719. Put ashore with four others to collect fresh water, the men were abandoned, and de Bellisle, after the deaths of his companions, was made a captive of the Indian tribe for a time. Later contact with the Atakapans included trade with French and Spanish explorers. The tribe was evidently a fairly loose confederacy of small, scattered bands. Archaeological evidence suggests they subsisted mainly on small game, fish, and wild plants, and evidently were not farmers. Shell middens found indicate the existence of Atakapan campsites in this vicinity. The tribe disappeared from Texas in the early 19th century, either becoming extinct or integrating into other tribes.

(Texas Sesquicentennial 1836–1986)

ORANGE (Orange Co.)
Civic Plaza
William Henry Stark
A native of San Augustine County, William Henry Stark (1851–1936) lived in Burkeville and Newton before moving to Orange in 1870. Here he worked in the early area sawmills and became acquainted with every phase of the lumber industry. In 1881, Stark married Miriam Melissa Lutcher (1859–1936), the daughter of Henry Jacob Lutcher, a partner in the Lutcher and Moore Lumber Company. Stark joined his father-in-law's firm and, because of his knowledge of milling operations, was soon placed in charge of two mills in Louisiana. Stark's success in the lumber industry led him to invest in other businesses, including iron and coal production, real estate, and ranching. His progressive ideas, including deep water ports on the Sabine River and an irrigation system that provided stimulus for the region's rice industry, led to increased growth for the city of Orange. Stark also served as a regent for the University of Texas, 1911–1915, an office later held by his son Lutcher Stark, who became Chairman of the University Board. The many contributions W. H. Stark made to Orange are reflected in the city's steady growth, industrial strength, and community pride.

(1982)

ORANGE (Orange Co.)
IH 10W, 1 mi. E of FM 1442
Peyton Bland
Born in 1815 in Vermilion Parish, Louisiana, Peyton Bland became a vital figure in Orange County. He migrated to Texas as a young man and at Orange in 1835 enrolled to serve in the Texas Revolution. Bland participated in the Grass Fight and the Battle of San Antonio before being discharged. Later reenlisting, he performed guard duty during the Battle of San Jacinto, among other responsibilities. Bland married Susan (Susannah) Harmon in Beaumont in 1838. The couple moved and settled on an Orange County farm, raising 13 children. Bland built his home on Cow Bayou, north of here, where in addition to farming he ran a local store. Bland also took part in the thriving Texas cattle industry, driving cattle to market in New Orleans. A local resident, later describing Bland, remembered "When he entered the room, he filled the door. He was huge,

with pistols on his hips—he scared us kids to death." Bland once again joined the military when he enrolled in the Orange County Coast Guard in 1862, during the Civil War. This company was attached to the Second Regiment, First Brigade of Texas militia. After the war, he served briefly as an Orange County commissioner. In 1873, Bland died of pneumonia, and his family buried him in a now unknown site near the San Bernard River in Wharton County. Today, Peyton Bland is remembered not only as an important contributor to Orange County and Texas, but also as a pioneer who worked in farming, business and cattle in times of peace and as a military man when called on during times of war. (2007)

ORANGE (Orange Co.) *IH 10, 10 mi. W at Claiborne West Park*
Claiborne West (1800–1866)
Born in Franklin County, Tennessee, Claiborne West moved as a young man to Louisiana. He married Anna Garner in 1824 and they had nine children. His family immigrated to this area in 1825 and received a land grant in the Cow Bayou settlement. Soon West joined in the struggle for independence from Mexico. As one of the representatives from Liberty Municipality, he attended the 1832 convention and the 1835 consultation at San Felipe de Austin. West was responsible for the designation of Cow Bayou as Jefferson Municipality, the forerunner of Jefferson and later Orange County. He served as a representative from the municipality to the general council and acted as local postmaster. At the general convention at Washington-on-the-Brazos on March 2, 1836, West was one of 58 signers of the Texas Declaration of Independence. He helped draft the Republic of Texas Constitution. From July to October, 1836, West served in Franklin Hardin's company of volunteers. He then served in the first Congress of the Republic of Texas. West moved from here to Montgomery County and later settled in Seguin. He was buried in the Riverside Cemetery at Seguin. (1979)

ORLA (Reeves Co.) *US 285, 6 mi. NW*
Pope's Crossing
Crossing site was 4.9 miles northeast, in Loving County. Now under Red Bluff Lake. (1964)

ORLA (Reeves Co.) *US 285, 3 mi. NW*
Red Bluff Dam (3 mi. NE)
Constructed for irrigation and electrical power purposes during 1934–1936, dam is located on Pecos River 8 miles south of Texas–New Mexico state line. It impounds an 11,700-acre lake occupying parts of Reeves and Loving Counties, Tex., and Eddy County, N.M. Floods first filled the reservoir in June, 1937. Capacity is 310,000 acre feet of water. Main embankment—9,230 feet long—rises 105 feet above stream bed at highest point. Dam has top width of 25 feet. These waters irrigate about 140,000 acres, which extend for 100 miles along the Pecos River. (1972)

ORLA (Reeves Co.) *US 285 in Orla*
Orla
Gateway to Red Bluff Lake, Guadalupe Mountains, Carlsbad Caverns recreational areas. Established 1890 on Pecos Valley Railroad. Developed during land promotions. Had school, general stores, hotel, livery stable. In 1931 remaining merchant and postmaster Hal Olds moved ¼ mi. west to new highway. (1965)

OZONA (Crockett Co.) *SH 137 at US 190, 22 mi. NW*
Crockett County's First Producing Oil Well
In 1923 World Oil Co., owned by Chester R. Bunker, Ft. Worth publisher and printer, began drilling on the L. P. Powell ranch. Work progressed slowly, depending on the availability of money, under the direction of superintendent Mickey Green and the tool pusher known only as "Dangerous Dan." The wildcat operation proved successful in the spring of 1925, when the first well (10 mi. NW) came in at a depth of 2647 feet and began producing 25 barrels of oil a day. The strike opened up the World pool, more commonly known as the Powell Field, which is still yielding oil. Eventually 180 wells were drilled by a number of companies on Powell's 9260-acre ranch. Bunker, a New York-born World War I veteran, sold his rights to Humble and Marland Oil Co. after the strike, but Powell's heirs still own the land. Powell No. 1 has produced continuously since 1925 and now, under the operation of Petro-Lewis, yields 10 barrels a day. Powell No. 1 was the beginning of a vital new industry for Crockett County, before 1925 primarily a ranching area. The next important

strike occurred in the Crockett Field in 1938. There are currently over 2000 producing oil and gas wells in the county.

(1975)

OZONA (Crockett Co.)
SH 163, about 9 mi. N at roadside park

High Lonesome Stage Stand (Site 11 mi. NE)

First station after leaving Ozona on the San Angelo-Ozona mail line. Here, at the 20-mile point of an 86-mile run, fresh horses awaited. The stand, built in 1902, served one of Texas' last commercial stage lines. Ten horses were kept here, as at the three other stations: Shoeingstand (where the horses were re-shod each six weeks), Sherwood and Knickerbocker. Frequent riders were whiskey drummers (peddlers), lightning rod salesmen and preachers. Automobiles (1908) and finally the railroad (1910) put the "hacks" on this line out of business.

(1969)

OZONA (Crockett Co.)
SH 163 right-of-way, 7 mi. N

Ozona-Barnhart Trap Company

By the 1920s, many ranchers in Crockett County had fenced their land, preventing their neighbors from driving sheep and cattle to the railroad shipping point in Barnhart (23 mi. N of here). A solution to the problem was offered by the Ozona-Barnhart Trap Co., which was organized in Ozona in 1924. By buying or leasing land for trails, traps (small pastures), pens, and water wells, the company established a corridor through which ranchers could drive their livestock to the railroad without crossing their neighbors' fences or destroying his grass supply. The main trail extended about 34 miles, from south of Ozona to Barnhart, with branch lines throughout the county. The McNutt traps (2 mi. NW), with 1340 acres of pasture, were the hub of the trail. Sale of stock to area ranchmen financed the enterprise, and operating expenses were handled by a charge per head of livestock for services used. The O. B. Trap Co. saved the ranching industry at a time when it was the only important business in Crockett County. The need for the trail dwindled with the rise of truck transportation in the 1930s, but drives were still held until the 1950s. The O. B. Trap Co. now leases its land for grazing or gas production.

(1974)

OZONA (Crockett Co.)
11th St. (Loop 466) at Ave. D, off IH 10 at courthouse

Crockett County

Formed from Bexar Territory. Created January 22, 1875. Organized July 7, 1891. Named in honor of David Crockett, 1786–1836, member of the United States Congress from Tennessee. Killed at the Alamo. Ozona, county seat.

(1964)

OZONA (Crockett Co.)
11th St. (Loop 466) at Ave. D., off IH 10 at courthouse

Fort Lancaster, C.S.A.

Site 33 miles west on U.S. 290. Upon U.S. surrender Texas forts start Civil War, made part Confederate far western frontier line. Occupied by 2nd Texas Cavalry. On supply line to and from Arizona–New Mexico campaign 1861–1862. Intended to make Confederacy an ocean to ocean nation. When regular patrols to guard supply trains and check Indian activities grew dull, life spiced by camp newspaper and nightly sport of shooting pesky coyotes.

(1963)

OZONA (Crockett Co.)
US 290, 9 mi. SE of Sheffield at Fort Lancaster

Ruins of Fort Lancaster

Established in 1855 by the United States government as a protection to travelers and mail on the Overland route from San Antonio to San Diego. Abandoned in 1861. Reoccupied in 1868 for a short time.

(1964)

OZONA (Crockett Co.)
US 290, 9 mi. SE of Sheffield at Fort Lancaster

Howard's Well (19 mi. to the SE)

First known to civilized men in the 18th century, when, according to legend, Franciscan Padre Alvarez prayed for water to ease his thirst, put down his staff, and saw a spring gush forth from the ground, this landmark of western travel was named for its rediscoverer, Richard A. Howard of San Antonio, an ex-Texas Ranger. Howard and other men, along with 15 Delaware Indian guides, made up an expedition sent out in 1848 under Col. John Coffee Hays to map a wagon road from San Antonio to El Paso. Although aided by the discovery of the well, the expedition failed, turning back in a state of near-starvation. In 1849 the U.S. Army made its maps of the route, with Howard along as a guide. Many forty-niners went this way to the California gold rush. In 1853 the first regular San Antonio-to-El Paso mail line was routed by way of the well. So were many later ventures. Although

white travelers seldom caught sight of them, Indians frequented the well. There, on April 20, 1872, Comanches and Kiowas surprised a large wagon train led by a man named Gonzales, and killed 16 persons. This was one of the events that led to the U.S. Government's cancellation of hunting permits for reservation Indians.
(1976)

OZONA (Crockett Co.)   *US 290, 30.5 mi. W via IH 10, Lancaster Hill roadside park*
Old Government Road
Route of march and troop supply on Texas frontier. Followed in part pre-Columbian Indian trails and "Old Chihuahua Trail" that ran from San Antonio to El Paso and Mexico. In 1840s this was extended to Gulf Coast Port of Indianola, where imported goods arrived from the United States and Europe, and were freighted out to be exchanged in Chihuahua for ore of silver and gold, leather goods, and other products. In 1848 water holes and camp sites were marked as this road was re-charted for use of U.S. troops sent to protect Texas frontiers from Indian invasions. Army posts were built along this road: Fort Clark, between San Antonio and Del Rio, 1852; Fort Davis, in the Davis Mountains, 1854; Camp Lancaster, at this site, became Fort Lancaster in 1856. Camp Hudson and Fort Stockton were founded in 1857 and 1859. With all the army traffic, trail won new name of "Government Road." Pioneer settlers, adventurers, California-bound gold seekers—even camel trains in government service—traveled this road in spite of frequent encounters with Comanches, Apaches, Kiowas, and other Indians. The army finally stationed troops in continuous picket line from San Antonio to El Paso. However, it was not until 1870 that relatively safe passage was assured.
(1968)

OZONA (Crockett Co.)   *SH 163, 20 mi. S*
Site of Comstock-Ozona Stage Stand
(Flagstone ruins nearby mark)
Site of early 1900s stage stand. First stop on passenger and mail line connecting Ozona with Southern Pacific railhead at Comstock—80 miles distant. When stage pulled in about 8:30 A.M. (having left Ozona at 5:00) agent had fresh horses in harness for next 20-mile run. Agent's family lived in tent with a flagstone floor. Other structures here were rock pens for a pig and cow and probably a corral for horses. Automobile replaced stage about 1914, but wagon ruts are still visible.
(1972)

PADUCAH (Cottle Co.)   *US 70 at US 62, E*
Cottle County
Created in 1876, organized in 1892, in area where the Pease and Little Wichita Rivers break level terrain. Named for George Washington Cottle (1798–1836), an 1832 settler in Dewitt's colony, who after fighting in 1835 Battle of Gonzales entered the Alamo March 1, 1836, and died there defending Texas. Of the 254 counties, 42 bear Indian, French or Spanish names. 10 honor such colonizers as Stephen F. Austin, "Father of Texas." 12 were named for Washington, Clay and other American patriots. 96 were named for men who fought in the Texas War for Independence (15, including Cottle, dying at the Alamo), signed the Declaration of Independence or served as statesmen in the Republic of Texas. 23 have names of frontiersmen and pioneers. 11 honor American statesmen who worked for the annexation of Texas; 10, leaders in Texas since statehood, including jurists, ministers, educators, historians, statesmen; and 36, men prominent in the Confederacy during the Civil War. 8 have geographical names. 2 were named for battles, 2 for trees, one for a fort. Cottle is noted for fine farms and ranches, with Paducah the principal market and shipping point.
(1964)

PADUCAH (Cottle Co.)   *811 9th St. (US 62/83)*
Cottle County Courthouse
The Texas Legislature created Cottle County in 1876 and named it for George Washington Cottle, who died defending the Alamo forty years earlier. Stage routes connected early ranches, including the OX, SMS, and Matador, to established towns in other counties. In late 1891, settlers petitioned for the county to be organized, and an election in January 1892 formalized Cottle County's boundaries. A geographically central site was selected as county seat and named for Paducah, Kentucky, hometown of settler Richard Potts. County business was conducted in existing homes until a permanent courthouse, a small one-story frame building, was finished in May 1892. That was replaced in November 1894 with a two-story brick building, with a prominent bell tower, designed by J. A.

White. The Cottle County economy flourished, and in April 1929, county commissioners awarded a contract for a new courthouse to architect C. H. Leinbach. Four days later, they rescinded that order and the citizens voted on $150,000 in courthouse bonds, a measure that failed outside Paducah but passed in the city and carried overall. The county gave a new contract to the Wichita Falls firm of Voelcker and Dixon, designers of 11 courthouses across Texas. In the fall of 1929, work began here on one of the premier Art Deco style courthouses in the state, a four-story brick and terra cotta building that looms over the square. Stepped blocks project from a central mass, with carved eagles, stylized figures of justice and liberty, and inscriptions above each of four entries. The unusual design, which has drawn comparison to an Egyptian temple, makes it one of the most distinctive public buildings in the region. (2005)

PADUCAH (Cottle Co.)
811 9th St. (US 62/83)
The Gray and The Blue
Into the western part of Texas, about 1885 came Civil War veterans of the Gray and the Blue, to tame the wilderness. They grazed cattle where drought parched the grass. Lived in dugouts. Found daily existence a siege that reminded them of war hardships. On occasional trips into town, verbally refought the war on the Courthouse Square, but lived peacefully together to build a great country. In Cottle County, 85 per cent of the early pioneers had worn the Gray. One out of 3 had been in Texas units. Others were from Alabama, Arkansas, Tennessee and Virginia. Of the great early brands, most were owned by Confederate veterans, but one in Cottle was run by a strong pro-Unionist. 8,722 Union veterans lived in Texas in 1890. One example in Cottle County at this time was Union veteran, William Frederick Liedtke (1836–1914), who had migrated to the U.S. from Prussia in 1856. He served as a county official and then as state auditor of Nebraska before settling in Paducah. He was legal advisor, abstractor and Justice of the Peace here. Gray or Blue in the 1860s, the 1890 uniform tended to be cowman's regalia on an American looking to the future rather than at the past. (1964)

PAINT ROCK (Concho Co.)
US 83, 4 mi. N
Confederate Beef Contractor John S. Chisum (1824–1884)
On this site during the Civil War and later, grazed by tens of thousands the longhorns of cattle baron John S. Chisum. Ranch headquarters were 10 miles east. Here in 1863–1865, Chisum not only ranched but also was buyer of cattle to feed Confederate armies stationed west of the Mississippi River. Born in Tennessee, he came to the Republic of Texas in 1837. After a term as Lamar County Clerk, started ranching in 1853. For room to expand, moved his well known "Jingle-Bob" herds to the Concho in 1863. Though he was not the man who gave the name to the famed northbound trail (this was Jesse Chisolm) John S. Chisum's drives were heroic. Herds bound in wartime for Louisiana army camps had to by-pass or to fight Indians, rustlers and occasionally a federal patrol. Concho cattle had to swim across the deep, cold Brazos River. Here cowboys would prod a heavy, wild bull till he was angry; then he would turn on men and horses. Or the Brazos itself killed men and horses. Still, beef went through to the Confederates. After the war, Chisum developed ranches in New Mexico and was a bystander in the Lincoln County Wars of Billy the Kid and other desperados. (1965)

PALACIOS (Matagorda Co.)
SH 35 Bus., 1.5 mi. W
Site of Camp Hulen
Camp Palacios was established on this site in 1925 as the summer training camp for the 36th Infantry of the Texas National Guard. Located on the Turtle and Tres Palacios bays, the land was donated by Palacios area citizens. Over 6,000 guardsmen arrived in July of 1926 for the first training session. Renamed for Major General John A. Hulen (1871–1957) in 1930, the new camp supported the largest concentration of troops for field training in the United States military. In 1940, the War Department leased Camp Hulen; first to undergo anti-aircraft training were National Guard units from several states. By 1941, the city of Palacios suffered a housing shortage that was alleviated by government housing near Camp Hulen. After extensive development the camp had facilities for 12,000 military personnel. Basic training continued until early 1944 when U.S. soldiers were removed. German prisoners of war, guarded by a small contingent of U.S. personnel, were housed here from 1943 to 1945. In 1946, the War Department returned Camp Hulen to the National Guard, for whom it had become too small. Buildings were slowly dismantled and sold. In 1965, the property was sold jointly to a group of Palacios citizens and a development company. (1997)

Correction: 36th Infantry should read 36th Division. Formed during World War I, it was re-designated 36th Infantry Division during World War II. The division trained here each summer, 1926–1937 and 1939.
(1998)

PALACIOS (Matagorda Co.)
Spur 141 W, off SH 35 Bus.
General John Augustus Hulen
Missourian John Augustus Hulen (1871–1957), citizen soldier and railroad executive, came to Texas with his family in the 1870s. He later attended Virginia's Staunton Military Academy and returned to Texas. He joined a militia unit and later served in the Spanish-American War and then in the Philippines. There he earned a Silver Star and a Congressional Citation. In World War I, he earned a French Croix de Guerre and a U.S. Distinguished Service Medal. After the war, he was instrumental in establishing Camp Palacios in 1925, renamed Camp Hulen in 1930 in his honor. In 1935, he retired from service a Lieutenant General, the highest rank in the militia.
(2002)

PALACIOS (Matagorda Co.)
208 Main St. (SH 35)
Pybus-Koerber House
In 1915, builder Joseph Pybus erected this home, designed by C. F. Emmons. James L. and Ina Mae (Perryman) Koerber bought it from the Pybus family in 1924. Owner of the Palacios Garage and Auto Co., J. L. also served as mayor, 1948–52. Other business interests included a canning operation and travel court on this site. The travel court, along with rooms in the house, provided space for military personnel and families from Camp Hulen. The bungalow cottage features a pyramidal roof, central hipped dormer, three-bay porch and textured concrete blocks with oyster shell aggregate.
(2004)

PALESTINE (Anderson Co.)
SH 155 at FM 321, 7 mi. N
C.S.A. Iron Works
Near old towns of Plenitude and Mound Prairie, John Billups, native of Georgia, as early as 1847 used Anderson County ore for iron to manufacture grist mills and cotton gins. In the Civil War, with partner D. D. Hassell, made Confederate rifles—some with bayonets. As part of program to increase wartime production of arms, the state exempted men and gave subsidies to the plant. Texas also made pistols, percussion caps, gunpowder. Plants were at Lancaster, Austin, Bastrop, Fredericksburg, Rusk, Tyler.

PALESTINE (Anderson Co.)
SH 155 right-of-way at Brushy Creek Rd.
Site of Northeast Texas Christian Theological
and Industrial College (about 1 mi. N)
Led by the Rev. A. J. Hurdle, the Northeast Texas Christian Missionary Convention of the Christian Church (Disciples of Christ) was formed in Daingerfield in 1900. Established to serve black members of the denomination, its primary purpose was the creation of a college. The Christian College Building Association was formed by a group of women within the organization, and by 1904 enough funds had been raised to purchase forty-nine acres of land near Palestine, Texas. Contractor J. L. Randolph was hired in 1910, and on May 26, 1911, the cornerstone was laid for the main college structure. Opening with seven students in January 1912, the Northeast Texas Christian Theological and Industrial College consisted of several large frame buildings and had a faculty of four. D. T. Cleaver served as the first president and was succeeded by I. Q. Hurdle. In addition to their classroom studies, the students farmed the college lands and raised livestock. After the main college building was destroyed by fire about 1920, the school closed. The remaining buildings were later razed, leaving no visible reminders of the institution that once provided an education to students from several states.
(1989)

PALESTINE (Anderson Co.)
5300 N. Loop 256
Alonzo Marion Story
Alonzo Marion Story (1882–1966) was born in New Orleans to parents John and Mary Story. He attended public schools and graduated from Louisiana's Leland College before doing post-graduate work in Texas and Colorado. Story came to Texas at the age of 21 and taught mathematics in Midway. He also served as a mail clerk before moving in 1912 to Palestine, where he taught math at Lincoln High School, the school for African American students. He taught there until 1917, when he moved to Austin to be principal of the state's Deaf, Dumb and Blind Institute for African Ameri-

cans. In 1924, Story was offered a job as principal in Dallas. Instead, he returned to Palestine's Lincoln High School, where he taught math and served as principal. Beloved and respected, Story stayed until retiring in 1949, teaching his last years with no eyesight. After retirement, he tutored from his home. In 1953, the school district opened a new facility and named it Alonzo Marion Story High School in honor of the revered educator. After desegregation, the school became a junior high and then an elementary school before being destroyed by a tornado in 1987. In 1990, the district built a new school named for him. Story dedicated his life to education. In addition to his roles as teacher and principal, he was director of religious education at West Union Baptist Church and served on the executive committee of the Texas State Teachers Association and as vice president of the East Texas Teachers Association. His immeasurable contributions to Palestine are reflected in the community's commemoration of his life. (2002)

PALESTINE (Anderson Co.)
US 79, 4.7 mi. NE
Anderson County
Created March 24, 1846, from Houston County. Organized July 13, 1846 with Palestine as the county seat. Named in honor of Kenneth Lewis Anderson, vice-president of the Republic of Texas 1844–1845.
(1964)

PALESTINE (Anderson Co.)
US 84, 11 mi. E
Fields Chapel Methodist Church and Cemetery
Pioneer settlement began in this vicinity in the late 1830s and early 1840s, this area was the location of several camp revival meetings. The Rev. John W. Fields organized the Methodist Episcopal Church in 1852 and the church was named for him. Trustees elected were W. R. Anglin, J. J. O'Quinn, E. W. Hassell, Joseph Shaver, A. J. Killion, L. D. Fulton, and A. K. W. Jones. Adrian Anglin donated land to this congregation and property deeds were signed on June 23, 1853. The church members built a church that also served as a school. That structure was in use until the late 1940s, when a white brick sanctuary was erected. The cemetery may have been in use prior to the date of the church organization, as there is evidence of more than 100 unmarked graves identified only by iron ore rock, native to the area. The oldest marked grave, dating to November 8, 1858, is that of Arminda Florence Langston, infant daughter of Willis B. and Amarillo Anglin Langston. The burials include many pioneer settlers and their descendants and veterans of the Civil War. The community has gathered for homecoming, a social event held annually on these grounds. The church and cemetery continue to serve this area of Anderson County. (1996)

PALESTINE (Anderson Co.)
US 84, 2 mi. E
Texas State Railroad
The Texas Prison System built a short rail line from the Rusk State Penitentiary to hardwood timber stands where charcoal was made for firing the prison's iron ore furnaces. The rail line became the foundation of the Texas State Railway, organized in 1896 to make the prison self-supporting and to develop the region's economy. Built by prisoners and supervised by the state penitentiary system, the line was completed in 1909 to Palestine (30 mi. W) where it connected with existing route. Financial woes and the closing of the furnaces led to the line being leased to the Texas & New Orleans Railroad and later the Texas & Southeastern Railroad, which operated the line until 1969. Control of the line was transferred to the Texas Parks and Wildlife Department in 1972 for development as a state park. Restoration of the tracks between Rusk and Palestine was accomplished by Texas Department of Corrections inmates. New depots and parks were built at each terminus. Vintage steam locomotives and rail cars were purchased to provide tourist passenger service from Palestine to Rusk. The park has become one of the most popular tourist attractions in the state. (1997)

PALESTINE (Anderson Co.)
US 79 at FM 1990 near Ft. Houston
Fort Houston (Site ¼ mi. S)
A stockade and blockhouse of The Republic of Texas. Built in 1835–1836 to protect settlers who founded Houston, a pioneer town, now in Anderson County. Friendly Indians would come to trade at the site, but wary settlers often slept inside the 25-foot-square blockhouse, built of heavy logs. Trappers bought supplies there and men from Houston formed one of the first Ranger units in Texas. The fort defended a large area of the frontier, 1836–1839, but it was abandoned about 1841. The site later became part of home of John H. Reagan, Texas statesman. (1969)

PALESTINE (Anderson Co.)
US 79, 2.7 mi. SW
Home of John H. Reagan, Fort Houston
A fort and stockade built about 1836 on the public square of the Town of Houston (then in Houston County), as a protection against the Indians, by order of General Sam Houston, commander-in-chief of the Texan Armies. The town was abandoned in 1846 for Palestine, the new seat of Anderson County, the fort about 1841. The site is now a part of the historic home of John H. Reagan, which is called Fort Houston. (1964)

PALESTINE (Anderson Co.)
US 287 at CR 499, 20 mi. NW
Early Settlement of Northwestern Anderson County
Early Texas settlements were often centered around institutions such as churches and schools. Even those that were short-lived played significant roles in the historical development of the state. When Anderson County organized in 1846, the area west of Catfish Creek was only sparsely populated. Community development began in the 1840s on land owned by Georgia-native Charles Gilmore (1796–1880). His house served as first polling place, first school and location for early meetings of the Gilmore's Chapel Methodist Church, the first area church. He then donated land for its cemetery and sanctuary. In 1854, local Baptists met there and organized Judson Baptist Church, moving later to a nearby site (1 mi. N) and then to Cayuga (3 mi. NW). Wild Cat Bluff (7.5 mi. NW), near the confluence of Wildcat Creek and the Trinity River, was also settled in the 1840s. It was an important ferry crossing and flourished until after the Civil War, when the river became unnavigable. Just over in Henderson County, settlers came as early as 1846 and founded a Masonic lodge. In 1852, Bethel Post Office, the first in the area, opened with Gilmore as postmaster. Soon the center of activity moved near the present-day community of Bethel (2.5 mi. SE), and Gilmore's Chapel Community disappeared. Although some of these communities and institutions did not survive, their stories demonstrate early settlement patterns and reflect the goals and needs of area pioneers, who established schools, churches and businesses, relying on mutual support and effort to develop Anderson County. (2002)

PALESTINE (Anderson Co.)
US 287 NW, .5 mi. W of intersection with SH 19
Lone Pine Baptist Church
This congregation traces its history to a small group of worshipers who gathered together in the early 1890s to hold services in a small schoolhouse near this site known as Rocky Point. A plot of land was purchased by the church in 1903, and a one-room frame structure was built for school and church purposes. The one pine tree on the property gave the church its name: Lone Pine Baptist Church. Although the congregation met regularly before then, the church was formally organized on July 8, 1908, with thirty-four charter members. The Rev. A. M. Thompson was called as first pastor, a position he held until his death in 1911. In 1916, a larger building was erected for the combination church and school. About one year later the two institutions were divided and a church structure was built in June 1920. Called the Tabernacle, it had permanent walls and a roof, but the interior floor was of dirt. Continued growth over the years enabled the congregation to improve the Tabernacle and build additional facilities. A new church auditorium was dedicated in 1957. The church continues to serve the community as it has for over eight decades. (1989)

PALESTINE (Anderson Co.)
US 287, 6 mi. S
Campbell Cemetery
Typical of a number of small family cemeteries located throughout the state of Texas, this graveyard was established by the Campbell family, who moved to the Mound Prairie community in this area in 1844. Albert Gallatin Campbell (1808–1876), his wife Jenny Elvira, and their children John Bartlett, Isadore, and James, established a farm. Soon the family grew with the addition of another daughter, Jettie, and another son, Alexander. John Bartlett Campbell (1834–1915) returned home after service in the Civil War and worked in a hardware store to earn money to purchase his own farm. He eventually purchased 270 acres and built a large home, where he and his wife Mary Elizabeth (1853–1927) reared their twelve children. John Bartlett Campbell set aside one acre of land on his farm for a family burial ground, and in 1876 his father, Albert Gallatin Campbell, became the first person buried here. Albert's was the only burial in the graveyard for twenty-four years, until his grandson, 23-year-old John Bartlett Campbell, Jr., died in 1900 of scarlet fever. The cemetery is still in use by Campbell family descendants. (1994)

PALESTINE (Anderson Co.)   US 287, 6.5 mi. S
John Starr House
Home of 1848 settler Starr and wife Susannah (sister of religious leader Daniel Parker, aunt of famed Indian captive, Cynthia Ann Parker). Late Greek revival style. Built in 1856, fireplaces are of handcut native sandstones. Awarded Medallion Plate.   (1968)

PALESTINE (Anderson Co.)   FM 1990, 11 mi. SW at SH 294
Site of Old Magnolia (one-half mi. S)
Founded in 1840s as a ferrying point on the Caddo Trace; later became a major landing for flatboats and steamers on the Trinity River, where cotton and other products were shipped by a four-day trip to Galveston to be exchanged for flour, salt, and sugar. Magnolia—named for a huge tree in center of town—reached its zenith in 1863, when it had several hundred people and eight major stores. Focus of social life then was Haygood's Magnolia Tavern, where board and lodging for a man and two horses cost $2 a day. Haygood's was the scene of many gala parties feting riverboat passengers, for when a deep-throated steamer whistle blew a few miles from port, it signaled a rush of people from miles around eager to greet arrivals and collect long-awaited parcels. Growing river traffic spawned many towns like this, and from 1830 to 1880, Texas waterways were dotted with boats. From the first, though, the state's rivers were unsuited for extensive trade, because even the largest were shallow, winding, and often choked with debris. After 1880, trains replaced riverboats. An irony of the transition was that one of the last steamers to pass Magnolia, in 1872, carried rails for the tracks being laid through nearby Palestine.   (1967)

PALO PINTO (Palo Pinto Co.)   US 180, 12 mi. W
Brad Cemetery
According to local tradition, a young girl died as her family traveled past Thomas Lindsey's land in the 1870s. A short time later, Lindsey buried his sister near the girl's grave. The earliest marked grave is that of Tump Mapes (June–October 1877). The Lindsey Cemetery was deeded to William and Ada Graves in 1911, shortly after the site became known as Ioni Cemetery. In 1929, the land was conveyed to trustees Cozby, Fitzgerald, and Slemmons; it became known as Brad Cemetery in the 1940s. The cemetery association was incorporated in 1973. With more than 400 graves, the cemetery continues to serve the people of the area.   (1998)

PALO PINTO (Palo Pinto Co.)   US 180, 2 mi. W at rest area
Palo Pinto County
Created Aug. 27, 1856, from Navarro and Bosque Counties; organized in 1857. Spanish name Palo Pinto refers to spotted oak, a common regional tree having bark with a mottled appearance. Good hunting and abundant water made area a favored Indian locality. The first Anglo-American settlers arrived in 1850s, including Texas cattlemen and trail-blazers Charles Goodnight and Oliver Loving. The discovery, in 1880, of mineral water and arrival of Texas & Pacific Railroad brought an influx of settlers and helped establish a strong economy. The county seat, first named Golconda in 1856, was renamed Palo Pinto in 1858.   (1973)

PALO PINTO (Palo Pinto Co.)   520 Oak St., 1 blk. S of US 180
Courthouses of Palo Pinto County
Palo Pinto County was created in 1856 and named for a creek south of here that was perhaps named by Spanish explorers of the Brazos River Valley. The county seat of 320 acres was surveyed at its geographical center and was originally named Golconda. A court session in 1857 called for the first courthouse to be built of wood frame construction, with two doors and three windows. The contract was awarded to a bid of $300. Shortly after, in 1859, the town name was changed to Palo Pinto. In 1882, just after the Texas Legislature allowed counties to issue bonds for new courthouses, a large sandstone structure was built. It cost $35,000 and exhibited Second Empire styling with a central clock tower. A two story sandstone annex was added in 1906 and connected to the courthouse by an iron bridge. Sandstone for the buildings was quarried south of the city. In 1940 these buildings were demolished and a new courthouse was erected by Work Projects Administration workers. The reinforced-concrete structure featured subtle classical detail and was clad with some of the sandstone from the old buildings. It was completed in 1942 at a cost of $250,000.   (1986)

PALO PINTO (Palo Pinto Co.)
US 180 at courthouse
Jonathan Hamilton Baker (July 13, 1832–October 18, 1918)
Virginia native Jonathan Hamilton "Ham" Baker came to Texas in 1858 with his brother G. W. Baker and his uncle Eli Young. Stricken by malaria while a teacher in Fort Worth, he later moved to Palo Pinto County where his uncle Frank Baker was homesteading. Here he opened a school, believed to be the first regularly organized school in Palo Pinto, and soon after helped establish the town's first Methodist church. In 1859, Baker was chosen to lead a company of local men organized to defend the area against Indian attacks. He first served under Capt. J. R. Baylor and later participated with Capt. Lawrence Sullivan Ross in the recovery of Cynthia Ann Parker, the white woman seized by Comanches in 1836. During the Civil War he served as the leader of the home guard. Baker was also an open range cattleman, and in 1869 he began driving his herds to Kansas railheads. Active in local government, he served as deputy sheriff, justice of the peace, deputy postmaster, and clerk of the county and district. In 1890, he moved to Granbury, where he became a successful nurseryman. For over 60 years Baker kept a detailed diary, which now provides a thorough account of his distinguished life and the frontier of Texas. (1983)

PAMPA (Gray Co.)
US 60, 2 mi. E
Gray County
Formed from Young and Bexar territories. Created August 21, 1876. Organized May 27, 1902. Named in honor of Peter W. Gray 1819–1874, member of the First Legislature of Texas. Member of the Confederate Congress. Appointed to the Texas Supreme Bench in 1874. County seat, Lefors, 1902. Pampa, since 1928. (1965)

PAMPA (Gray Co.)
SH 152 at FM 3302, 11 mi. E
Site of Pampa Army Air Force Base
In the early 1940s, Pampa Mayor Fred Thompson and a delegation from the city's chamber of commerce traveled to Washington, D.C. to promote this area as a possible site for a military base. Attracted by the terrain, climatic history, available land, and community response, army officials chose this site for the establishment of an installation to train pilots and support personnel for World War II. Construction of the Pampa Army Air Force Base began in June 1942, under the direction of the Tulsa, Oklahoma office of the Corps of Engineers. Overseeing the initial stages of the operation was Col. Norman B. Olsen. Temporary offices were set up in the Rose Motor Company and Culberson-Smalling buildings in town. Col. Daniel S. Campbell became the commanding officer in September 1942, and within two months the first planes and aviation cadets had arrived. The Pampa Army Air Force Base closed September 30, 1945, after just three years of operation. During that time 6,292 aviation cadets and 3,500 mechanics were trained. The base's safety record was one of the best in the U.S. training command during World War II. Despite a brief history, the base had a dramatic impact on the development of the Pampa area. (1982)

PAMPA (Gray Co.)
SH 70, 6 mi. S
The Red River Expedition of 1852
In 1852, U.S. Army captain and explorer of the Southwest Randolph B. Marcy and George B. McClellan, later Democratic candidate for President against Abraham Lincoln, led Company D, 5th Infantry into the Texas Panhandle to locate the headwaters of the Red River. Their findings had great impact on the determination of Texas' border with the state of Oklahoma. Until the 1852 journey, it was not known that there are two large branches of the Red River that intersect the 100th meridian, which forms the eastern boundary of the Texas Panhandle. On June 16th, the company discovered the headwaters of the north fork (approx. 1 mi. SE). On July 1st, they found the source of the southern, or Prairie Dog Town, fork in Palo Duro Canyon. Marcy's report to Congress is one of the earliest known written records of Gray County. Since several early treaties had used the Red River as a boundary and since there was an extensive area of land between the two branches, the question arose as to which fork was in the minds of the contracting parties when the boundary was first defined. Marcy testified before a Congressional committee that the south fork should be the boundary, and an 1896 Supreme Court decision confirmed his findings. (1984)

PAMPA (Gray Co.)
320 S. Cuyler St.
Woody Guthrie
American folk musician Woodrow Wilson "Woody" Guthrie (1912–1967) moved to Pampa from his native Oklahoma at age 17. Here he learned to play the guitar and joined with other musicians

to perform for area events. Guthrie briefly attended Pampa High School and, from 1930 until 1935, worked as a soda jerk at this site, home of the former Harris Drug Store. He also spent much time reading books in the Pampa city library, preparing him for his most productive years as a poet-lyricist and folk balladeer during the 1940s and early 1950s. He left Pampa for California in 1937 and in 1940 went to New York City, where he was recognized for his writings and performances. He died there in 1967.

(2002)

PANHANDLE (Carson Co.) *SH 207, 18.8 mi. N*
First Rotary Drilling Rig Used in Texas Panhandle (2.5 mi. SE)
In October 1923, W. T. Willis, J. E. Trigg, and H. D. Lewis, partners in one of Texas' largest drilling firms, broke ground at the S. B. Burnett 6666 Ranch with the first rotary drilling rig used in the Texas Panhandle. Success of this drilling method was a major event in this region. Drilling equipment included a $25,000 rotary rig; a 6-inch diameter drill pipe; a derrick; 3 steam boilers; 2 mud pumps; and other tools. Rotary rigs began to replace cable tool rigs on the Texas Gulf Coast about 1900, but the lack of a rotary drill bit capable of piercing rock delayed its use here. (1993)

PANHANDLE (Carson Co.) *SH 207, 18.8 mi. N*
Gulf Burnett No. 2 (1 mi. SE)
(Carson County Oil Discovery Well)
The Panhandle's first oil well, Gulf Burnett No. 2, was struck by the Gulf Production Company on May 2, 1921, on the 6666 Ranch of S. B. Burnett. The prediction of oil in this area by U.S. geologists in 1904 and the discovery of natural gas nearby in 1918 induced Amarillo businessmen to finance Burnett No. 2. Though the first oil was of poor quality, major oil discoveries in the nearby Borger and South Pampa fields in 1926 spurred a regional oil boom and established the Panhandle as one of Texas' richest petroleum areas. Carson County has produced 150 million barrels of oil since 1921.

(1993)

PANHANDLE (Carson Co.) *SH 207, 18.8 mi. N*
3.5 mi. SE to site of No. 2 Burnett,
Carson County Oil Discovery Well
First oil well in the entire Panhandle. Brought in May 2, 1921, by Gulf Production Company on the 6666 Ranch of Captain S. B. Burnett. The first oil was of poor grade and transportation facilities were inadequate but interest grew, for the area was to become one of the world's largest producing gas fields. The discovery of the prolific Borger and South Pampa Fields (1926) caused great excitement and established the Panhandle as one of Texas' richest petroleum areas. Since 1921, Carson County has produced over 140,000,000 barrels of oil.

(1970)

PANHANDLE (Carson Co.) *SH 207, 14 mi. N*
6666 Dixon Creek Ranch
Takes name from creek where noted buffalo hunter and scout Billy Dixon established first dug-out home of High Plains, 1874. Ranch founded, 1882, by Francklyn Land and Cattle Co., English firm backed by Cunard Steamship Co. Fenced, 1884, with barbed wire hauled here from railroad at Dodge City; posts were of Palo Duro Canyon cedars. Purchased in 1903 by S. Burk Burnett (1849–1922), trail driver, rancher; an organizer and for 45 years on executive board, Texas Cattle Raisers Association. Host during 1905 wolf hunt to U.S. President Theodore Roosevelt. (Ranch not open to public.)

(1965)

PANHANDLE (Carson Co.) *4th St. at Main, 1 blk. W of SH 207 at library*
Carson County
Formed from Young and Bexar territories. Created August 21, 1876. Organized June 29, 1888. Named in honor of Samuel P. Carson, 1798–1840, statesman of the United States and the Republic of Texas. Wheat, oil and gas contribute to its wealth. Panhandle, county seat.

(1964)

PANHANDLE (Carson Co.) *405 Elsie (SH 207)*
Conway Community Church
Residents of Conway, established 9 miles south of here in 1905, attended non-denominational services in a relocated school house until this Union Church building was completed in 1912. It became an important gathering place for the Conway community and housed regular worship services until 1968. Membership in the congregation dwindled and the building fell into disrepair.

Former church members and area volunteers devoted thousands of hours to restore this structure to its historic condition and relocate it here to the Square House Museum complex in 1991.   (1993)

PANHANDLE (Carson Co.)   *SH 207 at 5th St., Square House Museum*
Square House
Built 1887–1888 for official of Southern Kansas Railway when terminal track was laid from Kiowa, Kansas to Panhandle, Texas. This pioneer cottage was home of famous Panhandle pioneers: banker-judge James Christopher Paul; rancher-judge J. L. Harrison; innkeeper James B. Wilks; and Sheriff Oscar L. Thorp. Was oldest house in Panhandle when purchased in 1965 for restoration as Carson County Museum. Awarded Medallion Plate.   (1966)

PANHANDLE (Carson Co.)   *SH 207 at 5th St., Square House Museum*
Last Great Panhandle Cattle Drive to Montana
Each spring and summer after 1880, many Texas herds went up the trail to Northern states for fattening. For the cowboys, trail drives meant hard work. They had to turn stampedes, ford rivers and quicksand streams, and fight Indians and cattle thieves. They endured hunger, thirst, and other physical hardships. The Last Great Texas Panhandle Drive was organized here at N Bar N (N - N) Headquarters. Ranch manager was J. L. Harrison; trail boss, T. L. (Tom) Coffee. 100 cowboys drove 10 herds, each with 2500 cattle, or a total of 25,000 beeves, to Montana from April to September 1892. The cattle belonged to Niedringhaus Brothers, German tinsmiths of St. Louis, who put into ranching a fortune made in enamel granite household wares. From 1882 to 1886, N Bar N leased range in Carson and neighboring counties from the Francklyn Land & Cattle Company, a British syndicate backed by Cunard Steamship Line. Afterward this range belonged to White Deer Land Company. The N Bar N outfit left here because White Deer Land Company wanted the range cleared of large herds. By 1907 the 650,000 acres of its land was offered for sale to small ranchers and farmers. It was fenced and the steam plow introduced to turn the rich, grassy sod.   (1965)

PANHANDLE (Carson Co.)   *SH 207 at 5th St., Square House Museum*
Pioneer Dugout
In the 1874–1888 era, the High Plains (a sea of grass) had no native timber, stone, or adobe building materials. Homes were dugout or, if settlers, wagons went some 300 miles for lumber, half-dugouts. Dugouts were warm in winter, cool in summer. Some were carpeted and cloth-lined. Some had an extra room for the schoolteacher or other guests. The cooking and heating stoves burned buffalo chips, cow chips. This exact replica of a Carson County half-dugout was donated by Opal Purvines to honor her parents, the John F. Weatherlys, and other pioneer families. (1967)

PANHANDLE (Carson Co.)   *US 60, at E city limits*
Terminus of the Santa Fe Railroad, Panhandle, Texas
Originally "Carson City," town name was changed 1887 when this site appeared to be the future metropolis of the Panhandle: it was to be at the junction of Santa Fe (under name "Southern Kansas") and Fort Worth & Denver City Railroads. Plans changed, however, and the F. W. & D. C. took a route 16 mi. south, bypassing Panhandle. (Amarillo was soon founded on the F. W. & D. C.) Even so, Panhandle became a major shipping center. During great ranching era and again in 1926 oil boom, it moved more freight than any other town on Santa Fe Line except Chicago.   (1968)

PANHANDLE (Carson Co.)   *US 60, 4.5 mi. SW*
First Tree Texas High Plains
Set in front of dugout home by Thomas Cree, 1888. Good luck symbol of settlers through drought, blizzard and heat. Note: This tree, which had survived nature's worst, was killed a few years back by a cropduster's poison, which was being sprayed on a nearby field. Cree's Bois D'Arc tree died in the 1970s. County residents planted a new tree here in 1990 as a memorial to the area's early pioneers.

PANHANDLE (Carson Co.)   *US 60, 4.5 mi. SW*
Thomas Cree Homesite
After serving as a teamster in the Civil War (1861–1865), Thadium (Thomas) B. Cree worked for the Union Pacific Railroad. In 1888, he and his wife came to the High Plains. They acquired this land and, with no trees for lumber, they build a dugout home. Cree traveled 35 miles at his wife's request to find a sapling and planted it here. He watered it from a nearby lake that he dug from a

360

buffalo wallow. The tree never grew but lived many years despite blizzard, heat, and drought. Gov. John Connally dedicated a historical marker in 1963 to the first tree in the Panhandle.   (1980)

PANNA MARIA (Karnes Co.)   *Main St., FM 81*
Town of Panna Maria
Oldest Polish settlement in Texas. Established December 24, 1854 by The Reverend Leopold Moczygemba, O.F.M., who was instrumental in bringing from Poland about 100 Polish peasant families. Within a few months, the majority sought homes in other localities in Texas.

PANNA MARIA (Karnes Co.)   *Main St., FM 81*
Oldest Permanent Polish Colony in America
Settled by 100 Polish families who came to Texas to gain economic, political and religious freedom. Led by Father Leopold Moczygemba, O. F. M. Conv., they made a contract in 1854 with John Twohig, a San Antonio banker and merchant, for land at this site. The colonists, natives of upper Silesia and Krakow, landed at Galveston after a hard voyage of nine weeks on a sailing ship. They hired Mexican carts to haul their farm implements, featherbeds, and the cross from their parish church in Poland. The 800 men, women and children walked—some in boots, others barefoot—the 200 miles inland to their new home. Babies were born on the way, and some of the people died. All suffered from hunger and exposure. On Dec. 24, 1854, they reached this site. They named it Panna Maria (Virgin Mary) placing it under the patronage of the immaculate conception. Beneath a large oak they offered their first midnight mass of Thanksgiving and petition for strength and courage. They camped out until they could put up huts of mud, straw or wood, later building in stone. In spite of hardships, they founded a stable community, aided in settling other frontiers, pioneered in education and gave Texas many patriotic, dedicated citizens.

PANNA MARIA (Karnes Co.)   *FM 81, .75 mi. E of SH 123*
Immaculate Conception Church
Oldest Polish parish in America. Offered its first mass on Dec. 24, 1854 (altar under an oak tree). First building erected 1855. This church with 100-foot tower built 1877; remodeled 1937. Awarded Medallion Plate.
                                                                                  (1966)

PARIS (Lamar Co.)   *Entrance #5, off US 271, 9 mi. N*
Camp Maxey
Recognizing in 1940 that hosting peacetime draftees might revive the county's economy, the city of Paris sent a request for the army to build a training camp here. The local American Legion acquired land options. Delegations from the Chamber of Commerce of Lamar County received initial support, but Congressman Lyndon Johnson moved the planned camp to his district at Bastrop. In response U. S. Senator Tom Connally and army officials ensured a camp for Paris, confirmed in July 1941. The 70,000 acre site was being surveyed when the U. S. entered World War II in December. Camp Maxey, named for C. S. A. General and U. S. Senator Sam Bell Maxey from Paris, was activated on July 15, 1942. Its main entrance was "Gate 5" marked by stone portals at this site. Two infantry divisions, the 102nd "Ozark" and 99th "Checkerboard," trained here with the 250th Field Artillery and other army units. A regional hospital and a prisoner of war camp hosting 7,000 Germans were part of the reservation. Local women formed the "Maxey Command" to host dances for the total of 194,800 soldiers stationed here. Area residents housed thousands of dependents and filled 10,300 civilian jobs on base. The camp was closed when the P. O. W. stockade was vacated in early 1946.
                                                                                  (1992)

PARIS (Lamar Co.)   *US 82 at FM 38, 8 mi. W*
Tridens Prairie
In 1841, when Zacharia Westfall was granted 1280 acres of land in this area, much of the northeastern region of Texas was covered with natural prairies. Over the years most of them have been plowed or destroyed. Tridens Prairie, which covers 97 acres of Westfall's original grant, is an undisturbed remnant of the blackland prairie that now is under preservation management. Tridens Prairie is part of a natural grassland that extends from Texas through the midwestern United States and into southern Canada. Its name is derived from the native, perennial bunch grass known as long-spiked tridens. Over 150 species of grasses and wildflowers have been identified in Tridens Prairie. Dominant grasses of the prairie include Sporobolus silveanus (silveanus dropseed), Tridens

strictus (long-spiked tridens), Paspalum floridanum (Florida paspalum), and Tripsacum dactyloides (eastern gama). One of the few remaining native grasslands in the state and once part of a large hay-producing region, Tridens Prairie is an important part of Texas' natural history. It is being preserved by the Texas Nature Conservancy and Texas Garden Clubs, Inc. (1985)

PARIS (Lamar Co.) — US 82, 5.5 mi. W
Smiley-Woodfin Native Prairie Grassland
This meadow, approximately 2,100 acres, is the largest section of native grassland existing in Texas. It was originally part of a prairie system that stretched throughout the midwestern United States and into Canada. Since the earliest settlers arrived in this area in the 1830s, when Texas was part of Mexico, this grassland has remained uncultivated, providing an annual harvest of native grasses. A lack of fuel and surface water made this area unsuitable for pioneer farmers. Although similar land nearby was tilled and planted, often resulting in erosion of overworked soil, this site was saved by the owner M. L. Smiley (1872–1953). A native of Lamar County, he used the meadow for cattle grazing and for hay production. Early harvests consisted of cutting and stacking the grasses for drying, or transporting the hay to nearby steam-powered presses. The process was later simplified by the use of gasoline-powered machines that harvested and baled the hay on the site. After Smiley's death, the meadow was inherited by brothers George S. and Gene M. Woodfin. Today the Smiley-Woodfin prairie grassland is the largest supplier of native hay in the state. (1981)

PARIS (Lamar Co.) — US 82, W city limits in roadside park
Lamar County
Created December 17, 1840, from Red River County. Organized in 1841. Named in honor of Mirabeau B. Lamar, 1798–1859. Father of Texas education. President of the Republic of Texas, 1838–1841. Lafayette, 1841; Mount Vernon, 1843; Paris, originally called Pinhook 1844; have served as county seat.

PARIS (Lamar Co.) — US 82, W city limits in roadside park
Central National Road of the Republic of Texas
Designed as a military highway, intended to make linkage with United States military road built to the north of the Red River in the 1820s. This was part of the national effort of Republic of Texas to open a good road system. Congress in 1839 passed a bill for a road east from Washington-on-the-Brazos to the Sabine River; 1841 legislation called for a road from the Nueces to the Red River and another from Austin to Santa Fe, New Mexico. The Central National Road was created in 1844, to reach from mouth of Elm Fork on the Trinity to Kiomatia Crossing on the Red. It went down a main street in Paris, which was founded in 1844; near its south end was the 1841 John Neely Bryan home, around which the City of Dallas originated. Major George W. Stell surveyed the 130-mile route. Plans called for a road 30 feet wide and clear of tree stumps over 12 inches high. For each mile of road built (including bridges), grants of 160 acres of public lands were offered. Commissioners were Roland W. Box, Harrison County; James Bradshaw, Nacogdoches County; William M. Williams and Jason Wilson, Lamar County; John Yeary, Fannin County. The route is roughly followed by later roads. (1968)

PARIS (Lamar Co.) — US 82, W side of city plaza
John James Culbertson (March 16, 1853–September 27, 1932)
Born in Cincinnati, Ohio, John James Culbertson grew up in large northeastern cities. He married Emily Lou Lee of New Jersey in 1882 and soon became a salesman for a cotton product company based in Alabama. During his southern travels, Culbertson saw the potential for profit from cottonseed oil. He moved to Paris and was instrumental in building the first Paris cotton mill about 1884. The company, Paris Oil Works, was sold to American Cotton Oil Trust in 1887, and Culbertson moved to Arkansas to manage a southern oil company plant. Four years later the Culbertsons returned to Paris, where he built a small cottonseed oil empire through the Paris Oil and Cotton Company, later known as Southland Cotton Oil Company. Culbertson was asked to participate in a master plan for the growth of Paris in 1913. As an influential Texas financier, he was appointed to the Board of Directors of the Federal Reserve Bank in Dallas when it was formed in 1914. His nationwide reputation as a cotton producer led President Woodrow Wilson to appoint him to the board that organized a bureau to oversee cotton and cottonseed products for the U. S. Food Administration in 1917. After Paris was ravaged by fire in 1916, John and Emily Culbertson

were among leading citizens who rebuilt the city. Held in high esteem by the people of Paris, the Culbertsons gave many public spaces, monuments and works of art to the city and several local institutions, including the Paris Public Library and the fountain of imported Carrara marble on the city's central plaza.

(1999)

PASADENA (Harris Co.)
SH 225 in Memorial Park
City of Pasadena
This area has progressed from Indian territory to pioneer ranch land to space-age Pasadena. Known at one time for its strawberry patches, it is now acclaimed for its oil and chemical industries. The Vince Brothers, members of Stephen F. Austin's original 300 settlers, developed area as ranch land. The armies of both Sam Houston and Santa Anna traveled through what is now Pasadena in 1836 to San Jacinto to decide the future of Texas. "Deaf" Smith destroyed a bridge on the Vince Ranch to block possible escape by the Mexican Army. After the brief battle, Santa Anna eluded the victorious Texas Army on a horse stolen from Allen Vince. He was captured approximately one mile from this marker. Site of the bridge and capture may be seen by following signs to the north. In 1850, surveyors of the Galveston, Harrisburg and San Antonio Railroad called the area "Land of Flowers." Col. J. H. Burnet, a land developer from Galveston, founded Pasadena in 1895. He said, "Pasadena will be the hub of a vast, rich agricultural area." The area fully justified his vision for, by 1908, "delicious strawberries, figs, oranges and vegetables" were the boast of Pasadena. (1967)

PASADENA (Harris Co.)
SH 225 near Allen–Genoa Rd.
Allen Ranch
This busy commercial area was once part of the Allen Ranch, one of the oldest and largest ranches in Southeast Texas. A portion of the land was granted to Morris Callahan in 1824 by Mexico and inherited by his niece, Rebecca Jane Thomas (d. 1919), who married Samuel William Allen (1826–1888) in 1844. Allen bought additional land, including a 1300-acre tract belonging to his friend, Governor Francis R. Lubbock, and began operation of a prosperous cattle ranch. He helped organize the firm of Allen & Poole to ship cattle to eastern and foreign markets. Samuel Ezekiel Allen (1848–1913) took over operation of the ranch from his father in 1881. He and his wife Rosa Lum (d. 1931) built a large home near the junction of Buffalo Bayou and Sims Bayou (1 mi. N). Allen was a leading Houston businessman as well as a cattleman. At the time he died, Allen's property included 13,000 acres in Harris County and 10,000 acres in Brazoria County. In 1917, Rosa Allen sold 700 acres to the Sinclair Oil Company (now Atlantic Richfield Corporation) as a refinery site. The remaining land was later divided for industrial, commercial, and residential use. The ranch house was moved to Galveston Bay, where it became Camp Allen of the Episcopal Diocese of Texas.

(1976)

PATTISON (Waller Co.)
FM 362 in Pattison
James Tarrant Pattison Homesite
Located at important junction of Atascosito Road and the San Felipe Trail, this homesite was established by James Tarrant and Sarah Smith Pattison on their Republic of Texas land grant and became a stage coach stop. Their plantation of 5,000 acres had its own grist mill and cotton gin. The first church and school in the community were founded through the efforts of Pattison. Town developed here before 1854 was named by a son, George Madison, for the original settler, James Tarrant Pattison (1810–1872). Heirs still live here.

PATTISON (Waller Co.)
FM 1458, 2 mi. W
Judge Edwin Waller (March 16, 1800–January 3, 1881)
Virginia native Edwin Waller migrated to Texas from Missouri in 1831 as part of Stephen F. Austin's third colony. An active participant in the earliest stages of Texas' struggle for independence, Waller participated in the 1832 Battle of Velasco, served as Alcalde of Brazoria, and represented the town of Columbia in the Consultation of 1835 at San Felipe. A framer of Texas' Declaration of Independence and Constitution, Waller also served in the army during the 1836 Texas Revolution. After the war he became postmaster general and later a land commissioner for the new republic. In 1839, as a government agent, he platted the townsite of Austin, the new capital of Texas. The next year he became the first mayor of the city. Resigning during his first term, he moved to his plantation home, just north of this site. The Waller plantation was the center of a large rural area. Here Waller opened a post office and store and provided for a school and church. For many years he also

served as Austin County Judge. In 1873, a new county, which included this area, was formed from Austin and Grimes Counties and named in his honor. Buried on his plantation, his body was later reinterred in the State Cemetery at Austin. (1982)

PEARLAND (Brazoria Co.)
SH 35 at Halik Rd.
Old Settler's Cemetery (0.2 mi. W)
Settlement of this area began as a result of railroad development through north Brazoria County in 1882. First known as Mark Belt, the townsite was platted in 1894 and named Pearland because of the abundance of pear orchards in the vicinity. An advertising campaign featuring favorable farm conditions brought many settlers to the area in the 1890s. Although some were discouraged by storm and freeze damage to their homes and crops in the early years, many remained and established permanent homes. A community graveyard was begun with the burial of pioneer Echolean C. Ackerly, who died August 11, 1894. Four years later her burial plot and the surrounding land was officially dedicated as a cemetery. Six Civil War veterans are interred in the graveyard. The cemetery contains many types of burials. The early practice of scraping the earth over graves was followed by cement paving, gravel cover, and bricking. Styles of gravestones range from simple stone markers to tombstones featuring elaborately carved decorations. Old Settler's Cemetery remained the primary community burial ground until 1936. It continues to serve as a reminder of Pearland's early history. (1988)

PEARSALL (Frio Co.)
2 blks. E of US 35E at courthouse
Frio County (Created 1858, Organized 1871)
Home of Pachal Indians before Spaniards arrived in Mexico (1519). First area explorer was Alonso de Leon, 1690, searching for Fort St. Louis founded by La Salle. Upper Presidio Road—artery of travel from Saltillo, Mexico, to East Texas—crossed Frio River and became a King's Highway, 1720. Frio Town, first county seat, was located on the road, over which Santa Anna marched to destroy defenders of the Alamo in 1836. County took name from Frio (a Spanish word which means "cold") River. The county seat moved to Pearsall, 1883. Jail, built 1884, is the oldest building in town. (1968)

PECOS (Reeves Co.)
US 285 at N city limits
Vicinity of Significant Neighbors-Ford Trail
First wagon road to El Paso from Austin. Opened 1849 by Maj. Robert S. Neighbors and Dr. John S. "Rip" Ford, Texas Rangers and leading statesmen. With Indian guides Jim Shaw (a Delaware) and Guadalupe (a Comanche), they left the Pecos, followed Toyah Creek to Davis Mountains, then went west to the Rio Grande. On the return past Guadalupe Peak, Pecos River and Horsehead Crossing, rations gave out and they ate roasted mescal roots, panther and horse meat. Their route had water and wood and became a great stage, military and emigrant road. (1966)

PECOS (Reeves Co.)
US 285 at 1st St., West of the Pecos Museum
Reeves County—Pecos, Texas
Flat, arid, grassy land with a moderate water supply from the Pecos River and springs in Toyah Valley. Yuma Indians are thought to have done irrigated farming here in 16th century. Mexicans later raised vegetables, grain. Cattlemen moved in during the 1870s. Texas & Pacific Railway opened route to El Paso in 1882. Farmers, merchants, mechanics settled in Pecos City and Toyah. County was organized in 1884. Modern irrigated agriculture began about 1900. Only dam on Pecos River in Texas was built in this county 1935. Privately owned deep wells are also used. (1967)

The Pecos Cantaloupe
Nationally famed melon, originated in this city. Residents from 1880s grew melons in gardens, noting sun and soil imparted a distinctive flavor. Madison L. Todd (March 22, 1875–Sept. 10, 1967) and wife Julia (Jan. 30, 1880–Feb. 5, 1969) came here from East Texas and New Mexico. In 1917, Todd and partner, D. T. McKee, grew eight acres of melons, selling part of crop to dining cars of Texas & Pacific Railway, where Pecos cantaloupes first became popular and in wide demand. McKee soon quit business, but Todd remained a leader for 41 years. Famed lecturer Helen Keller, Presidents Eisenhower and Johnson, and many other distinguished persons have ordered and appreciated Pecos cantaloupes. Exclusive clubs in New York, Chicago, St. Louis, and other cities are regular clients of Pecos growers. Genuine Pecos cantaloupes begin ripening in July and continue

on the market until late October. The varieties are the same as those grown in other areas. Climate, soil, and special cultivation methods account for the distinctiveness of Pecos melons. 2,000 acres are now planted annually. M. L. Todd was known in his later years as father of the industry. He and his wife and family were leaders in civic and religious enterprises. (1970)

Emigrants' Crossing (20 mi. SE)
One of the few spots where pioneer travelers could cross the Pecos River by fording. At Emigrants' Crossing, the deep, treacherous river flows over exposed rock. It is one of only three fords in a 60-mile segment of the stream, and was the one favored by parties migrating in 1849 from the eastern United States to West Coast Gold Fields. Often called the California Emigrants' Crossing, or the Red River Trail Crossing, it was also the one used in 1858 by coaches of Butterfield Overland Mail, which had an adobe station and a high-walled adobe corral there. (1972)

Spanish Explorers
Antonio de Espejo in 1583, after exploring among Pueblos in New Mexico, reached the Pecos River southeast of Santa Fe. He named it Rio de Las Vacas (River of Cows), for the abundance of buffalo. On his return route to Mexico, he went down the river to near the present town of Pecos. Jumano Indians led his party to their camp on Toyah Lake. He then went down Toyah Creek and through the Big Bend. While Espejo was first to explore the Pecos, Castano de Sosa, on his way into New Mexico in 1590, was the first European to travel its full length. (1966)

PECOS (Reeves Co.)
US 285 at Walthall St., rodeo grounds
World's First Rodeo
Held a block south of Pecos courthouse, July 4, 1883. Started with claims of cattle outfits—NA, Lazy Y, and W Ranches—that each had fastest steer ropers. Settlers in town for Fourth of July picnic were spectators. The prizes were blue ribbons cut by pocket knife from new dress of a 4-year-old girl in the crowd. Best roper was Morg Livingston of the NA; second, Trav Windham, Lazy Y. Others entered: Howard Collier, Fate Beard, Jim Mannin, George Brookshire, John Chalk, Jeff Chism, Jim Livingston, Jim and Henry Slack, Brawley Oates, Henry Miller, E. P. Stuckler. (1965)

PENNINGTON (Trinity Co.)
US 287 at FM 2781
Steele's Academy
Site of Steele's Academny, named in honor of its founder and principal D.W. Steele of New Hampshire Academy. Attended by students from many counties. (1936)

PENWELL (Ector Co.)
IH 20, 2.5 mi. W on east access road
Ector County Discovery Well (2 mi. S)
The discovery of oil in Ector County December 28, 1926, marked the beginning of a new economic era for this region. The first well, "J. S. Cosden No. 1–A W. E. Connell," was named for the driller and owner of land. Its meager initial output of 38 barrels per day did not cause much excitement, but experts insisted that vast oil deposits lay under area (Permian Basin). In 1929, Robert Penn's gusher catapulted Odessa to boom-town fame. Oil has sustained the area economy since then, although the discovery well was plugged and abandoned in 1940. (1967)

PENWELL (Ector Co.)
IH 20, W city limits
Penwell
Birthplace of Ector County's oil boom. First civic development here was wide-open town, "Derrick City," platted March, 1927, after Dec. 28, 1926, oil discovery by driller Josh Cosden on land of W. E. Connell, near the old farming and cattle station, Judkins. However, when Connell well began pumping only 20 barrels a day, the boom crowd moved away. The city was abandoned. As nearby counties off the railroad struck oil that had to be shipped by the Texas & Pacific to refineries, Ector County in 1927 had a "truck drivers boom"—a foretaste of the leadership in supply and servicing that was to develop progressively. Then on Oct. 14, 1929, on Robert Penn's land here, a 375-barrel per day well came in. With that showing, exploration continued, soon followed by the Penn Well, the 600 to 700-barrel a day gusher. In a busy, bustling and prosperous tent city, the Penwell post office was established June 30, 1930. This has remained a central distributing and shipping point for numerous fields in several Permian Basin counties, thereby establishing an earned reputation as "the crossroads of the oil patch." (1965)

PERRY (Falls Co.)
Judge Albert G. and Harriet Elizabeth Grimes Perry
SH 6 right-of-way

Tennessee native Albert G. Perry (1807–1874) began the study of law at age sixteen in his brother's Alabama law office. He became a successful attorney, but in 1831 left for Texas, settling in Washington, where he opened a law office. The following year, on January 8, he married Harriet Elizabeth Grimes (1816–1888), the daughter of pioneer Jesse Grimes (1788–1866), signer of the Texas Declaration of Independence. In 1826, Harriet had arrived in Texas with her father and eight siblings, one of whom, Albert Calvin Grimes, later died at the Alamo. In late 1833 or early 1834, Perry became secretary to the alcalde at Sarahville de Viesca in Robertson's Colony (in present Falls County), and in 1835 was First Lt. of a frontier defense ranger company. He was a member of the Viesca Committee of Safety, and was a delegate to the Consultation of 1835. The Perrys lived in Washington from 1836 to 1843, when they moved to Anderson in present Grimes County. In 1852, they moved to Falls County, where they farmed, and he was county and district judge. In 1883, when the railroad bypassed the community of Peyton, a new settlement developed along the rail line and was named Perry in honor of Albert G. Perry. (Texas Sesquicentennial 1836–1986)

PERRYTON (Ochiltree Co.)
Ochiltree County
US 83, 2 mi N

Formed from Young & Bexar territories: Created, August 21, 1876 Organized, February 21, 1889. Named in honor of William Beck Ochiltree, 1811–1867, Associate Justice, Supreme Court of Texas, 1842, Secretary of the Treasury, 1844, the last Attorney General of the Republic of Texas, member of the Texas Legislature, 1855; delegate to the Secession Convention of 1861, colonel in the Confederate army. County Seat Ochiltree, 1889; Perryton, since 1920. (1936)

PERRYTON (Ochiltree Co.)
Colonel William B. Ochiltree
US 83 at courthouse

Secretary treasury and last attorney general Republic of Texas. Secession Convention delegate 1861. Influential member Provisional Congress which drafted Confederate Constitution, mobilized manpower, set up financial structure, elected political leaders. Resigned to raise 18th Texas Infantry. Led troops to Arkansas in 1862 when regiment called in campaign to repel Union forces from state. A memorial to Texans who served the Confederacy, erected by the State of Texas 1963. (1963)

PERRYTON (Ochiltree Co.)
George Morgan Perry
22 SE 5th Ave.

A native of Iowa, George Morgan Perry (1862–1944) moved to the Texas panhandle town of Ochiltree in 1886. Active in the formal organization of the county, he served as county clerk, district clerk, and county judge. A supporter of railroad building in the panhandle, he was honored by the Santa Fe Railroad when the town of Perrytown was established on the rail line and named for him in 1919. He served as first president of the Chamber of Commerce and continued to promote settlement and business development in the city until his death in 1944. (1994)

PERRYTON (Ochiltree Co.)
Ochiltree Townsite (Bordering This Highway)
SH 70, 8 mi. S

This county was created in 1876 and named for noted Texas Jurist William Beck Ochiltree (1811–1867). In 1876 it was attached for judicial purposes to Clay and later to Wheeler County. In 1886, pioneers began to settle in dugouts here on the prairies near Wolf Creek, saying they lived "in Ochiltree." For convenience in making land and tax transactions, and establishing law and order, they organized the county in 1889, making their village the county seat. First elected officials were William J. Todd, county judge; Dave C. Kettell, sheriff and tax collector; George M. Perry, county clerk; Myrtle L. Daily, treasurer. In 1891 a 2-story courthouse was built (100 yds. E) of lumber freighted from Dodge City, Kans. This also served as church, schoolhouse, and social hall for the town. By 1903, Ochiltree had 600 people, churches, a high school, a newspaper, bank, flour mill, and other facilities. In 1919, the Santa Fe Railway founded a new town between Ochiltree and Gray, Okla., and induced people from both places to relocate by offering free lots. In 1919 steam engines and heavy equipment hauled the improvements from Ochiltree to the new site (8 mi. N), called Perryton, in honor of veteran county official George M. Perry. (1976)

PERRYTON (Ochiltree Co.)

SH 70, 9 mi. S

Ochiltree Cemetery

In 1902, Jim McLarty and J. V. Stump fenced off 90 acres for a cemetery in the town of Ochiltree. Soon afterwards, Jim was thrown from his horse and killed, and at age 21 became the first person buried in the cemetery. In 1927, the county acquired the deed from Mr. J. M. Blasingame; in 1930, a cemetery association was formed. During the depression of the 1930s, an entry gate was built with help from the Works Progress Administration. Veterans of the Civil and Spanish American Wars, World Wars I and II, and the conflicts in Korea and Vietnam are among the citizens buried here.   (1997)

PETTUS (Bee Co.)

US 181, 3 mi. N at roadside park

Town of Pettus (Located 3 mi. S)

Oil capital of Bee County, Pettus was settled in the 1850's when John Freeman Pettus (1808–1878) set up his sprawling ranch about 4 miles south of here. The son of one of Stephen F. Austin's first 300 colonists, Pettus was an extensive cattle and horse breeder. The town, previously called "Dry Medio" for a nearby creek, was named for him during the Civil War. The community was in the vicinity of two important Indian skirmishes in Bee County in 1859 and the 1870's; but the town slept until 1886, when the tracks of the San Antonio & Aransas Pass Railroad reached this site. It then awoke to become the cattle shipping center for the area. In the same year, John S. Hodges, a pioneer citizen, laid out the townsite and donated land to be used for streets and S. A. & A. P. right-of-way. For years the railroad stockyards and depot were places of bustling activity as freight trains came for loading and wood-burning steam engines took on water. In 1909 the presidential train of Wm. H. Taft stopped at the Pettus water tank. The tank—a final monument to steam railroading here—was razed, 1965. In 1929 the Houston Oil Co. brought in its well "No. 1–Maggie Ray McKinney" and from that time Pettus has played a continuing useful role in Texas economy.   (1968)

PETTUS (Bee Co.)

US 181, 2 mi. N

Bee County

Named for Col. Barnard E. Bee (1787–1853), who served Republic of Texas as Secretary of War, Secretary of State, and Minister to the United States. County was created by legislative act on Dec. 8, 1857; organized Jan. 25, 1858, from land earlier in Goliad, Karnes, Live Oak, Refugio, and San Patricio Counties. County seat in 1858 was on Medio Creek; since 1860 at present Beeville. A cattle region since Spanish times, Bee County became important beef producer in 1865. San Antonio & Aransas Pass Railroad provided first modern transportation in 1886. Oil was discovered here in 1929.
      (1971)

PFLUGERVILLE (Travis Co.)

FM 1825, Pecan & 3rd St.

Pflugerville

Henry Pfluger (1803–67), who migrated from Germany to Texas in 1849–1850, moved his large family here in 1853. Other settlers joined them, and in 1872 a school was begun on Henry Lisso's farm. Immanuel Lutheran Church was founded in 1874. Primarily a farming settlement, Pflugerville had no commercial businesses until 1890, when Louis Bohls built a general store. A post office was opened there in 1893 with Bohls as postmaster. In 1891, two community organizations were formed: the German-American Mutual Assurance Association, to insure townspeople against natural disasters; and "Pflugerville Schuetzen and Kegel Verein," a shooting and bowling club. The village began to grow when the Missouri, Kansas & Texas Railroad arrived in 1904. George Pfluger (1834–1910) and his son Albert (1878–1969) platted the townsite, and George donated land for a train depot and a school. Early businesses included drugstores, groceries, a hotel, grist mill, cotton gin, ice factory, and a blacksmith. In 1907, La Rue Noton and Archie Ward started a telephone system. Farmers State Bank, chartered in 1906, became First State Bank in 1933. A newspaper, The Pflugerville Press, was published from 1907 until 1942. In 1958–1962, the Pflugerville High School football team gained national fame by winning 55 consecutive games.   (1976)

PHARR (Hidalgo Co.)

US 281, 7.25 mi. S

Jackson Ranch Church

This fellowship was founded in 1874 by the Rev. Alexander H. Sutherland (1848–1911), an early Methodist missionary, on Juan Manuel de la Vina's El Capote Ranch. In 1883, the congregation began meeting near this site on the Jackson Ranch when owner Martin Jackson donated the land.

He later built a small chapel for their use. In 1910, most of the church members moved to the new city of McAllen, and only a few families continued to worship here. As one of the first Protestant congregations in Hidalgo County, this church has continued to serve area residents. (1983)

PHARR (Hidalgo Co.)
US 281, S at Pharr-Reynosa International Bridge
Louisiana–Rio Grande Canal Company
Wisconsin native John Closner established the first steam-powered irrigation system in the lower Rio Grande Valley in 1895. Closner successfully grew sugar cane and entered a sample for judging at the St. Louis World's Fair of 1904. The award-winning sugar cane and Closner's promotion of the lower Rio Grande convinced a number of financiers and agriculturists to invest in the region's irrigation and development possibilities. In 1909 H. N. Pharr, J. C. Kelly, John C. Conway, and A. W. Roth formed the Louisiana-Rio Grande (LRG) Canal Company to transform about 40,000 acres of arid land in Hidalgo County into productive farmland. To do this the company built two pumping stations to divert water from the Rio Grande through an elaborate irrigation system to a planned community of small farmsteads. The agricultural success of the LRG Canal Company, its successor the Hidalgo County Water Improvement District #2, and other similar operations in the region resulted in an influx of Anglo farmers and settlers from the Midwestern U.S. into this mainly Hispanic region of Texas. The bountiful harvests propelled the Rio Grande Valley to the forefront of Texas agriculture by the mid-20th century and earned the region a reputation as the "winter garden" of Texas. (1995)

PIERCE (Wharton Co.)
US 59 bypass
Site of Pierce Hotel
Here, in the 1890s, the celebrated Texas cattleman A. H. "Shanghai" Pierce (1834–1900) platted the townsite of Pierce, which he hoped would become the Wharton County seat. Its proximity to his ranch headquarters in the central part of the county was a major factor in his choice of location for the town. He laid out a public square, courthouse square, academy square, and a cemetery. He built several structures in the town, including a three-story hotel located at this site. The Pierce Hotel was designed to accommodate cattle buyers, traveling salesmen, and others attracted to the area by the railroad and Pierce's ranching interests. Located near the Southern Pacific Railroad depot and across from the present Pierce ranch entrance, the hotel was designed as the center of the town's planned growth, which did not develop. Although never opened to the public as a hotel, the building was used for various purposes by several long-term tenants. A landmark on the Texas coastal prairie for more than eighty years, the Pierce Hotel was razed in 1980. Still at this site of the hotel is its Widow's Walk, which was preserved as a symbol of the structure's historical significance. (1984)

PILOT POINT (Denton Co.)
Main St. at Washington St. (US 377)
City of Pilot Point
Attracted by fertile land and abundant water and game, pioneers began to settle at this site near the edge of the Cross Timbers region in the late 1840s. The village, first known as Pilot's Point, was named for a high point of timber that served travelers as a landmark. Near an early immigrant trail, Pilot Point was also a stop on the Butterfield Stage Route. A townsite was platted in 1854 on land originally granted to Charles Smith. Dr. R. W. Edleman (1825–1904) of Missouri came here to launch a medical practice and open a drugstore. James D. Walcott ran the earliest general store and became the first postmaster in 1855. Alphius Knight, a settler from New York, built and conducted the first school in the town. Established by three local residents in 1872, Pilot Point Seminary was later renamed Franklin College and operated here for almost 30 years. In 1878 the town's first newspaper was published and in 1884 a bank opened. A marketing center for farmers and stock raisers, Pilot Point had a grist mill and a cotton gin. The arrival of two railroads, the Texas and Pacific and the Missouri, Kansas and Texas, boosted the local economy in the 1880s. Agriculture and light industry form the base of the town's economy in the 1970s. (1978) Incise on back: Marker sponsored by Chamber of Commerce. Researched by: Mavis Burton, Norma Cole, Clifton Irick, Judy Lewellen, Estelle Whitley. (1978)

PITTSBURG (Camp Co.)
US 271, 3.5 mi. N
Camp County
Formed from Upshur County. Created April 6, 1874. Organized June 20, 1874. Named in honor of John La Fayette Camp, 1828–1891, soldier-lawyer-statesman, member of the Constitutional Convention, 1866, state senator in 1874. Pittsburg, the county seat. (1964)

PITTSBURG (Camp Co.)

US 271, 3.5 mi. N

Colonel John L. Camp (1828–1891)

Came to Texas from Alabama in 1849. Practiced law and taught school in Gilmer. In Civil War, organized and was elected captain of Co. E, 14th Texas Cavalry (dismounted), unit in famed Gen. M. D. Ector's Brigade. In thick of fight, in Tennessee and Georgia, was wounded twice, captured twice. Was in prison camp at the war's end. Elected to Congress in 1866, was denied his seat because of Confederate service. Served as district judge and state senator. Campaigned for adoption of constitution of 1876, to end reconstruction in Texas. (1964)

PITTSBURG (Camp Co.)

FM 21, 6 mi. NW via SH 11

Cherokee Trace

This Indian trading route to Arkansas and Oklahoma was laid out by Cherokees. A tribesman with a keen sense of direction pulled buffalo hides behind his horse to press down the tall grass. Groups of Indians followed blazing the trail, removing logs and underbrush, and marking fords. Others located springs and good camping places. After the road was established the Cherokees planted roses and honeysuckle which still mark the old trace. After the Indians were driven out, settlers came into Texas by this route. The first residents in Camp County lived on the trail.(1979)

PITTSBURG (Camp Co.)

140 Quitman St. (SH 11) at Market St.

Pittsburg

Anglo settlement of this area began in the 1850s. The W. H. Pitts (1815–1898) family arrived from Georgia in 1854, and soon were joined by more settlers from the southern United States. Pitts donated land for a townsite, which was named in his honor. In 1874, when Camp County was created from Upshur County, Pittsburg became county seat. Two railroad lines were built through the area by 1880, and in 1891 the citizens voted to incorporate their town. Pittsburg continues to serve as a transportation, business, marketing, and cultural center for the county. (1991)

PITTSBURG (Camp Co.)

SH 11 at FM 1519, 7 mi. W

Leesburg Cemetery

Dwight Hays Townsend (1834–1906) donated land for this cemetery about 1870. The graves of two children which were relocated here from the Leesburg schoolyard are thought to be the earliest burials on the site. The oldest marked grave is that of Tapley Wylie (1836–1870). This cemetery is the primary burial ground for the rural community of Leesburg. Those interred here include pioneer settlers, community leaders, a large number of infants and children and veterans of the Civil War, World Wars I and II, Korea, and Vietnam. (1992)

PLAINS (Yoakum Co.)

US 82/380 at courthouse

Yoakum County

Created August 21, 1876, from Bexar County. Named for Henderson Yoakum, who wrote a classic on early Texas history. Only Texas county named for an author. Indian activity and frontier hazards made growth slow. Only itinerant buffalo hunters and scattered ranchers here until after 1900. County organized September 7, 1907. By 1910 population reached 602 as result of sale of state lands. Discovery of oil in 1935 brought industry and more people. A "Bonus Shack" typical of cabins used by homesteaders is used as a historical museum in Plains, the county seat. (1965)

PLAINVIEW (Hale Co.)

US 70 at FM 179, 14 mi. W

Halfway

Settlers came to this area seeking abundant grass, fertile soil, and water. This site, acquired by R. L. Hooper (1872–1952) and his wife Ada Mae (Huguley) (1880–1955) in the 1890s, received its name because it stood "halfway" between Olton and Plainview. It made a good rest stop for ranchers, with a windmill for water and overnight camping. Early pioneers raised enough grain for their stock. Arrival of the railroad in Plainview in 1906 and use of irrigation systems developed a vast agricultural region. In 1908, Hooper provided six acres and helped build a schoolhouse for his seven and the neighbors' children. Hooper donated land in 1910 for Edgar Howard to build the first store where he ran a post office and wagon yard. Methodist and Baptist congregations met in the school building until they erected sanctuaries. The post office closed in 1914 but the settlement boasted a blacksmith shop and a cotton gin. In 1917, Hooper gave one acre for a burial ground. Although population decline caused the Halfway school to consolidate with Plainview in 1952, the community is still prospering. Located here is the High Plains Research Foundation to aid farmers in the surrounding 19-county area. (1979)

PLAINVIEW (Hale Co.)   *US 70, 5 mi. W*
The Slaton Well (.5 mi. N)
The Plainview Commercial Club, led by President J. O. Wyckoff, saw the potential of irrigation during a 1910 visit to wells in New Mexico. Local banker and farmer J. H. Slaton agreed to bear cost of a test well sunk on his land if it succeeded. G. E. Green and J. N. McNaughton completed the well in Jan., 1911. At 130 feet, using a nine-inch centrifugal pump, it yielded 1,700 gallons of water a minute. The success of the Slaton Well led to extensive irrigation. It transformed this semi-arid area of West Texas into one of the most productive food crop regions in the world. (1976)

PLAINVIEW (Hale Co.)   *5th St. (US 70) at Joliet St. in city park*
Plainview Point
The first of this distinctive type of early man dart point was found by 15 year old Val Keene Whitacre in 1941, in a caliche quarry on Running Water Draw. In 1944, quarry workers uncovered a fossil bone deposit, which was noted by scientists surveying the geology of the Plains. The next year a team of archeologists from the University of Texas, including Dr. E. H. Sellards and Dr. Alex D. Krieger, excavated the site and found 26 man-made artifacts, including several of the points, in association with the remains of about 100 extinct bison (Bison Talori), about twice the size of modern species. The bone bed probably resulted from the primitive hunting method of stampeding bison over a cliff, and butchering of the dead and crippled animals for food. The cliff eroded away, and covered the bones with 12 to 14 feet of silt. When exposed, the bone bed was 62 feet long, up to 10 feet wide, and 1.5 feet thick. Radiocarbon dating indicates that this site is 8,000 to 9,000 years old. The Plainview Point is found most commonly in the Great Plains Region of North America, but has been located also in Alaska and Mexico. (1973)

PLAINVIEW (Hale Co.)   *IH 27 Bus. at 5th St. (US 70)*
Colonel C. C. Slaughter
First native-born cattle king of Texas. Eldest of several rancher brothers. At age 12 "made a hand" on East Texas ranch of father, Rev. Geo. W. Slaughter. By 17 made his own trades in lumber, wheat, cattle. In 1856 moved his cattle to Palo Pinto County, on his first West Texas ranch. During the Civil War, he supplied beef to Confederacy and served in frontier regiment, to prevent Indian attacks. After the war he led cattlemen in aiding economy of bankrupt Texas by securing cattle markets. A fat steer bought for $6–8 in Texas by middleman was sold for $30–40 at shipping point. In 1867 he sold 300 head at record $35 and led the way to rancher marketing. Kept his love for trailing, even after he became millionaire. He also pioneered improvement of Texas Longhorns by use of champion Shorthorn and Hereford bulls. In Eastern speeches, he advocated beef on daily diet. To curb rustlers and establish efficient roundups, he helped organize first cattle raisers association. His 89,000-acre "Running Water" spread in Hale and Lamb counties was part of 1,000,000 acres ranched. He was a banker, active churchman, philanthropist. His descendants have erected a memorial center bearing his name on the campus of Wayland College here. (1965)

PLAINVIEW (Hale Co.)   *IH 27 Bus. at 5th St. (US 70)*
The Old Mackenzie Trail
General Ranald Slidell Mackenzie. The Old Mackenzie Trail by "Larry" Chittendon. Stretching onward toward the sunset, o'er prairie, hill and vale, far beyond the double mountains winds the Old Mackenzie Trail. Ah, what thoughts and border memories does that dreaming trail suggest, thoughts of travelers gone forever to the twilight realms of rest. Where are now the scouts and soldiers, and those wagon trains of care, those grim men and haggard women and the echoes whisper—where? Ah, what tales of joy and sorrows could that silent trail relate: tales of loss, and wrecked ambitions, tales of hope, of love, and hate: Tales of hunger, thirst, and anguish; tales of skulking Indian braves, tales of fear, and death, and danger, tales of lonely prairie graves. Where are now that trail's processions, winding westward sure and slow? Lost: ah, yes, destroyed by progress, gone to realms of long ago. Nevermore shall bold Mackenzie, with his brave and dauntless band, guide the restless, roving settlers through the Texas borderland. Yes, that soldier's work is over, and the dim trail rests at last, but his name and trail still lead us through the borders of the past. The

Mackenzie Trail first crossed by General Ranald Slidell Mackenzie, 4th United States Cavalry, in 1871 in quest of warring bands of Indians. Erected by the state of Texas with funds appropriated by Federal government to commemorate one hundred years of Texas independence. (1836–1936)

PLAINVIEW (Hale Co.)
IH 27/US 87 Bus.,
1 mi. S at city limits in roadside park
Hale County
Formed from Young and Bexar territories. Created August 21, 1876. Organized August 13, 1888. Named in honor of John C. Hale, a lieutenant who fell at San Jacinto. Plainview, county seat.
(1965)

PLAINVIEW (Hale Co.)
US 87, 4 mi. N
Liberty Community and Finney Switch
In 1887, Joseph B. Leach and his brothers, John and Dee, immigrated to this area from Liberty, Kentucky. Joseph filed on a 160-acre homestead and built a half dugout and sod house and a windmill. The Leach brothers often hauled freight for Plainview merchants. More families arrived in this five-mile square area. By 1892, there were enough children for a schoolhouse to be erected. Methodist and Baptist services and community activities were held in the building. The settlement was called "Liberty" for Joseph Leach's Kentucky home. William R. Finney and his family settled nearby in the early 1900s. When the Santa Fe Railroad from Amarillo to Plainview located a switch in 1906 on Finney's land, the site became "Finney Switch." Soon irrigation wells improved agriculture and dairy farming began. Liberty schoolhouse was moved in 1912 and in 1920 a four-room brick building was erected south of Finney. About 1925 the first business, a store, opened. The Baptist and Methodist congregations built sanctuaries by 1940. With the consolidation of the Liberty and Plainview schools in 1948 and changes in farming, the population decreased. (1979)

PLAINVIEW (Hale Co.)
SH 194, 7.5 mi. NW
Running Water Community (2 mi. S)
Attracted by abundant water from Running Water Draw, J. W. and T. W. Morrison established a ranch in 1881 with headquarters about ten miles west of here. Most of the early settlers in this region worked for the ranch. Later, several partners joined the operation, including wealthy cattleman C. C. Slaughter. In 1884, Dennis and Martha S. Rice purchased several sections of land along the draw south of this site. Rice hoped to start a town and lure the railroad across his land. He began Wadsworth post office in his dugout in 1890. It was renamed Running Water in 1891. Rice organized the Running Water Townsite and Investment Company and staged a picnic and barbecue, July 4, 1892, for the purpose of selling town lots. Soon the community had a blacksmith shop, grist mill, a two-story store building, several residences and churches. The early one-room schoolhouse was later replaced by a brick structure. Although the Fort Worth & Denver Railroad bypassed Running Water in 1928, it remained a thriving village for several years. In 1935, the post office moved to Edmondson switch on the railroad and many residents relocated here. In 1937, the name of this settlement was changed to Edmondson. (1978)

PLEASANTON (Atascosa Co.)
IH 37 right-of-way, 2 mi. N of SH 97
Site of San Augustine Church
Between 1850 and 1860, Manuel, Enrique, and Francisco Esparza brought their families to settle in what is now Atascosa County. The brothers, along with their sister and mother, were within the walls of the Alamo when it fell to the Mexicans in March 1836. Their father, Gregorio, died in that battle. The Esparza brothers farmed and ranched the open land near this site. Almost immediately after arriving, Enrique and Manuel constructed a small chapel for family worship. In 1869, Enrique and his wife, Gertrudes, donated five acres of their land to the Roman Catholic Church. About the same time, the Esparzas constructed a larger church building of native stone. The small mission church was named San Augustine. A storm damaged the church building in 1940 and services were discontinued, although San Augustine was not formally closed until 1942. By the late 1960s, only three exterior rock walls remained, and these were later razed. Many settlements in Texas sprang from the activities of mission churches such as San Augustine that were located at river crossings or ranch headquarters. Although many have disappeared or have been forgotten, they are an important part of the state's heritage.
(Texas Sesquicentennial 1836–1986)

PLEASANTON (Atascosa Co.)

Main St. (US 281) at Goodwin St.

Pleasanton (Founded 1858)

Named for early Texas settler John Pleasants, by John Bowen (d. 1867), San Antonio's first Anglo-American postmaster. Bowen, assisted financially by associate Henry L. Radaz, in Sept. 1858 founded this town at the juncture of Atascosa River and Bonita Creek as the county seat of Atascosa County. The first courthouse in Pleasanton (second in county) stood on this site. Men from this and surrounding counties met here in Civil War (1862) to form Co. E, 32nd Texas Volunteer Cavalry, Confederate Army, under Captain Lewis Maverick. In an area thick with longhorns since Spanish and Indian days, Pleasanton became a cattlemen's capital. Beginning in 1860s, the Stock Raisers' Association of Western Texas often convened here. This was place of publication of "Western Stock Journal," founded 1873. Here gathered the hardiest and most skillful cowboys, including those driving herds from Mexican border to shipping points in Kansas. In spring of 1873 they drove 43,000 Atascosa County cattle up the trail. Pleasanton was county seat until 1911, and still grows. In 1961 it absorbed North Pleasanton (founded 1912 as site for San Antonio, Uvalde and Gulf Railroad shops). County's largest town, it is famous for live oak trees, and commerce in beef, peanuts, and petroleum. (1973)

POINT BLANK (San Jacinto Co.)

SH 156 near entrance to Robinson Cemetery

Governor George Tyler Wood (1795–1858)

Born in Georgia and married there in 1837 to Martha Evans Gindrat (1809–1863), a widow with 3 children, George T. Wood came to Texas with his family in 1839 and settled along the Trinity River near Point Blank. Wood studied law and was elected to the 6th Republic of Texas Congress, 1841–1842, and the Annexation Convention of 1845. As a state senator in 1846, he sponsored a bill creating Tyler County. Woodville, the county seat, was named for him, as was Wood County, created in 1850. Wood left the senate in 1846 to fight in the Mexican War (1846–1848). His military heroics helped make him the popular choice for governor in 1847. Under Gov. Wood, the recently-organized state government faced the problems of recurring Indian hostilities and a boundary dispute in Santa Fe County (now part of New Mexico). Gov. Wood urged sale of public lands to pay the large public debt. His administration saw the establishment of a state library and a penitentiary. Mrs. Wood, who raised silkworms and made her own silk cloth, did not accompany her husband to the state capital at Austin, then a rough frontier town without an official governor's residence. After failing to win a second term in 1849, Gov. Wood returned to his home at Point Blank. He died at age 63 and was buried nearby. (1976)

POINT BLANK (San Jacinto Co.)

SH 156, .75 mi. S

The Robert Tod Robinson House

Adjacent to property of Governor George T. Wood, and on high ground near juncture of waterways and land trails important in early Texas, this was originally a log house with wide front verandas on the two floors. It was built in 1857 by Point Blank planter Robert Tod Robinson (1826–1878), copying style from his native state of Alabama. He brought up a large family; his descendants include soldiers, statemen, and civic leaders. The log house was covered with siding in 1919, and facade was modified in 1970s. A descendant owns and preserves it. (1975)

POINT COMFORT (Calhoun Co.)

SH 35, 6 mi. NE of Port Lavaca

Site of Cox's Point

An early landing place of supplies for the interior. Captain Jack Shackelford's "Red Rovers" of Alabama disembarked at this point. A town established here in 1836 was burned by Indians in 1840. (1964)

POLLOK (Angelina Co.)

7483 N. US 69

Gann Memorial Cemetery

This burial ground, which contains over 3,000 graves, has served area residents since the mid-1800s. In 1860, Nathan W. Gann, who came to Texas with his family in 1836, donated this property and a church building he constructed to Williams Chapel Methodist Church. The first known burial on this land was of Jacob J. Gann in 1861. In 1893, the church disbanded and this property reverted to Nathan Gann, who then deeded it to the Missionary Baptist Church, which is now known as O'Quinn Baptist Church. Many early Angelina County pioneers used this property as a burial ground. As the area's lumber and agricultural industries developed, a number of rural communities organized. The former Lufkin U.S. Air Force Radar Base (later the site of Lufkin State School) was also located nearby. Gann Memorial Cemetery became the primary burial ground for residents of the area, which became known as the Central-Pollok community. Among those interred here are at least five county officials, over 200 veterans of conflicts dating to the Civil War and numerous members of various fraternal associations. Over the years, family members of the interred cared for the cemetery, which grew due to the generosity of local landowners. In 1978, the Gann Memorial Cemetery Association began to maintain it. The cemetery features curbing, false crypts, vertical stones and obelisks. Today, Gann Memorial Cemetery continues to serve local families and provides a reminder of the early pioneers of the Central and Pollok communities.

(Historic Texas Cemetery—2007)

POLLOK (Angelina Co.)
7622 US 69N, 3.8 mi. SE
Central Consolidated School
This school traces its origin to five small schools in the Pollok-Central area: Union, Durant, Pollok, Clawson and Allentown. An effort to solve the problem of inadequate funding for each of these rural schools led to their consolidation in 1929 as the Central Consolidated Common School District. A new brick building at this site greeted approximately 200 students in grades one through eleven when it opened in September 1929. With J. W. Dunn presiding as superintendent, Central Consolidated boasted nine teachers and had eight students in its first graduating class. Over the years, Central Consolidated became the focal point of the community. Its growth led to the construction of separate buildings for primary, elementary, junior high and high school classes, three gymnasiums, a cafetorium, and technology and agricultural buildings. Additional schools, including Cordaway Springs and Simpson, merged with Central Consolidated in 1939–40. In 1955, Central converted from a common school district to an independent school district. Providing a strong educational foundation and extracurricular activities for students in the northwestern part of Angelina County, Central Consolidated has played a significant role in the county's educational history.

(2002)

POLLOK (Angelina Co.)
Paul Townsend Rd. (CR 4A) at SH 7
Pollok Baptist Church
Founded as Warren Chapel Baptist Church in 1891, this congregation became known as Pollok Baptist Church in 1896. The first meeting place was shared by the Methodist and Presbyterian churches. Land acquired in 1906 by the Baptists was the site of the first church building. Early baptisms were performed in the Angelina River. Services were held once or twice monthly until 1945 when the first full time pastor was called. Fire destroyed three church buildings in 1932, 1955, and 1960; the congregation rebuilt each time, and continues to serve the area. (1996)

PONTOTOC (Mason Co.)
off SH 71 in Pontotoc
Pontotoc and San Fernando Academy
(Site of academy is 100 yd. N)
Pontotoc, settled about 1859, was named by first merchant, M. R. Kidd, for his former home town in Mississippi. Post office was opened 1878 in B. J. Willis home, with Mrs. Willis post master. Founded by interested citizens, San Fernando Academy (probably named for nearby creek) opened 1883. Pupils (200 during academy's career) took regular subjects or courses leading toward teacher certificates. Principals were K. T. Hamilton and W. C. Roaten. After academy failed site was sold by W. J. and B. J. Willis and used by the public school until 1927. (1972)

PORT ARANSAS (Nueces Co.)
SH 361 at ferry landing, Roberts Point Park
Aransas Pass, C.S.A.
Aransas Pass, 5 miles to the southeast, a gap between Texas coastal islands, was strategic in the Civil War because it let in friends, kept out foes. Admitted goods to be hauled on the overland road from the coast to San Antonio. A haven to blockade runners, who came to Corpus Christi, Copano or Aransas Bays with ammunition, guns, medicines, steel, rope, crockery, cloth, trenching tools, shoes, bar iron or other goods. They took out 50 to 250 bales of cotton a trip. Holds and decks were so full that men had to walk on cotton to work the sails. Behind the island chain which Aransas Pass helped to guard, mail and goods traveled along a 300-mile inlet from Bagdad and Matamoros in neutral Mexico up to Matagorda. The islands, inlet and passes were fortified by Confederate infantry, cavalry and marines manning dredgeboats, rafts or prize ships. Confederates won victories

at Aransas Pass on Feb. 22 and April 22, 1862. With 1,900 Federal troops, Gen. N. P. Banks took the 100-man Aransas garrison on Nov. 17, 1863, but failed to hold the mainland behind the pass. In June 1864, the Federals withdrew. To the war's end, blockade runners fed vital goods into the Confederacy by way of Aransas Pass.

PORT ARANSAS (Nueces Co.)
101 E. Brundrett St., off SH 361
Mustang Island

Port Aransas is located on Mustang Island, one of seven Texas barrier islands. It is named for the wild horses that came here from shipwrecks and Spanish expeditions, and which once populated the island. The earliest humans here were members of nomadic groups collectively known as the Karankawas; they stayed on or about the islands in winter and fall, before moving inland during spring and summer. Robert Ainsworth Mercer (1799–1875) was Mustang Island's first settler; he came here in 1855 with his wife Agnes and children Mary Agnes, John and Edward. The Mercers built a house and a complex they named *El Mar Rancho* (Sea Ranch). Other settlers soon joined them, forming a small community; however, the new settlement was abandoned during the Civil War, when the USS *Arthur* took station off Mustang Island to blockade the Aransas Pass. The Federal sailors lived off the land, prompting six settlers to fire on them on February 11, 1862. The USS *Arthur* bombarded the island and a landing party further damaged property, leading to the islanders' flight from the island. Settlers returned here after the war, with many engaging in the booming cattle industry. By the 1880s, when the industry declined, islanders found markets for turtles and wild ducks. Many also offered goods and services, including guidance to hunting and fishing grounds, to workers constructing the Aransas Pass Jetties. Sportsmen began to visit the island, and by the 1920s tourism became the basis for its economy. By 1929, two roadways and a ferry service allowed for easier access to the island and further development of the tourist industry. Today, Mustang Island continues to be a popular destination for visitors, while also serving as home to increasing numbers of Texans.
(2009)

PORT ARTHUR (Jefferson Co.)
SH 93 at 60th St.
Spindletop to Port Arthur Oil Pipeline Corridor

On January 10, 1901, the landscape of Texas changed forever. On that day, the Lucas Gusher came through at the Spindletop oilfield, discovered on a salt dome formation near Beaumont. Flowing at an estimated 100,000 barrels a day, the Lucas Gusher marked the beginning of a Texas oil boom that would last for decades. Many of the nation's biggest oil companies, including the Texas Company (Texaco), Gulf Oil Corporation, Sun Oil Corporation, Magnolia Petroleum Company and Humble (Exxon company), began at Spindletop. Capitalizing on the vast new oilfield, the Port Arthur Townsite and Land Company, which had been creating infrastructure for a railroad and shipping terminal city, deeded an oil pipeline right-of-way to James M. Guffey and John H. Galey. The line transported oil from the Spindletop oilfield to Guffey's refinery, which became the Gulf Refining Company of Texas. Within three years, more than 500 miles of oil pipelines had been constructed in southeast Texas. Further expansion by Guffey's company linked Port Arthur to oilfields in Oklahoma, and his refinery became one of the largest in the U.S. Area oil pipelines boosted both the Texas and U.S. economies with new businesses, technology and other advances. The pipelines enabled companies to collect and refine Texas oil reserves, and Port Arthur's location allowed product to be delivered quickly around the country. The Texas petroleum industry played a large role in U.S. involvement in both world wars and helped establish the nation as a 20th-century superpower.
(2004)

PORT ARTHUR (Jefferson Co.)
SH 87, 2 blks. S of SH 82
The Port Arthur Refinery

The eruption of the Lucas Gusher at the Spindletop Oil Field in January 1901 established Texas as a major oil source and signaled the beginning of a significant economic boom to the state. The new town of Port Arthur benefited tremendously from its proximity to the oil field. In early 1901, a consortium of men from Pittsburgh, Pennsylvania, formed the J. M. Guffey Petroleum Company to finance and develop an industry for the oil from its Spindletop leases. In need of refining facilities and a sales organization, the consortium chartered the Gulf Refining Company on November 10, 1901, and built a refinery at Port Arthur for the purpose of making the crude oil into a usable commodity. Early products of the refining company included gasoline, kerosene and engine oil. In 1907, assets of the J. M. Guffey Petroleum and Gulf Refining companies were merged into the Gulf Oil Corporation. At the end of 1910, Port Arthur was the company's lone refinery until a second was built in Fort Worth the following year. Innovative production, refining and retailing techniques after World War I kept the company on solid economic footing. Expansion continued after World War II, and by 1955, Gulf Oil was the nation's largest producer of ethylene. By 1960, the Port Arthur facility was refining 270,000 barrels of crude oil per day into 600 different products. Gulf Oil became part of Chevron in 1984. In 1995, Clark Refining took ownership of the Port Arthur plant, and in 2000, Clark's name was changed to Premcor. Upholding an excellent safety record, the Port Arthur refinery has been a significant factor in the city's development as a major petrochemical center.   (2001)

PORT ARTHUR (Jefferson Co.)   *SH 87, .25 mi. S of Taylor's Bayou Bridge*
Early Oil Tanker Service
Part of the huge transportation complex that moves petroleum to world markets. Traffic in oil tankers and barges in Texas mushroomed two months after the state's first oil gusher, "Spindletop," roared in. On March 11, 1901, the first boat to transport the Spindletop product, the Atlas, left Sabine Pass with about 3,000 barrels of crude oil. Port Arthur exported one of the earliest large shipments of oil about April or May, 1901, on the Atlas and two other vessels. The cargo was bound for the refineries of Standard Oil Company of Philadelphia to be tested for "illuminating" purposes. Many persons then scoffed at the idea of using oil as a fuel. One year after Spindletop, Texas commerce, formerly based on cattle and cotton, had been vastly changed by petroleum. More than half of all ships entering Sabine Pass and Port Arthur were connected with the oil industry. By April of 1902, shipments had already exceeded the 1,750,000 barrels exported in 1901. By 1902, steamers were burning Texas oil as fuel and the Guffey Petroleum Company had begun to build Texas' first tanker fleet—five ships. Today the value to Texas' economy of crude oil alone totals more than three billion dollars yearly.
(1968)

PORT ARTHUR (Jefferson Co.)   *SH 87 at Neches River*
Rainbow Bridge
The rapid growth of the petrochemical industry in Jefferson and Orange Counties in the early 20th century led to increased population in this area. In order to serve escalating transportation needs, plans began in the 1920s for the construction of a bridge to span the Neches River. Due to the depressed economy and differences of opinion among business leaders, the campaign to build the bridge (led by the Port Arthur News and American Legion Post No. 7) lasted for seven years. In 1934, Gov. Miriam A. Ferguson signed a special law to enable county bond and federal public works administration funds to pay for state highway and bridge construction. The project engineer, G. G. Wickline, used innovative techniques to design a bridge that would cross 7,742 feet of marshy terrain and river bottom. The bridge's 680-foot central span, designed to clear a navy ship carrying a moored dirigible, was, at 176 feet, the world's highest elevated roadbed over tidal waters. The final cost of the bridge was $2,750,000. Its dedication on September 8, 1938, drew huge crowds and was a major local event. In a 1957 contest sponsored by the North Port Arthur Lions Club, it was named "Rainbow Bridge."
(1990)

PORT BOLIVAR (Galveston Co.)   *US 87 at Bolivar Ferry landing*
Bolivar Point
In 1815 Colonel Henry Perry established a military camp here as part of a plan to invade Spanish Texas. In 1816 Galveston-based privateer Louis-Michel de Aury forced shiploads of captured African slaves to walk from this point to New Orleans along old Indian trails. Aury is credited with naming the point after South American liberator Simon Bolivar. While commanding a filibuster to win Texas independence, James Long established Fort Las Casas on Bolivar Point in 1820–21. His wife, Jane Herbert (Wilkinson), gave birth to a daughter, Mary James, in December 1821 at the fort. Mary James Long is often referred to as the first Anglo child born in Texas. A lighthouse, erected here by the Federal government in 1852 and later dismantled by Confederate soldiers during the Civil War, was rebuilt after the war. Many area residents sought shelter within the lighthouse during the damaging storms of 1900 and 1915. The Gulf and Interstate Railroad was completed from Beaumont to Bolivar Point in 1896. A boon to peninsula farmers, the railroad was destroyed in the 1900 storm, then rebuilt in 1903. Ferry service, purchased by the Texas Highway Department in 1933, continues to provide free public access to Galveston Island.
(1995)

PORT ISABEL (Cameron Co.)
Maxan St. at Yturria St., at library
Point Isabel, C.S.A.
After Texas seceded and joined the Confederacy, the Federal navy in later 1861 blockaded this port with the U.S. "Santiago de Cuba." Commerce stoppage caused removal of customs offices to Brownsville and some civilians to neutral Bagdad, Mexico. The Confederates ceased to use the lighthouse, and it became a watchtower for blockade runners, and thus Laguna Madre their haven. Boats from the U.S.S. "Brooklyn," in May 1863, attacked vessels in port and a Confederate unit near the lighthouse. The Confederates tried to blow up the tower—a defense measure—but only succeeded in damaging fixtures. The French, supporting Maximilian in Mexico, prohibited the landing of war material at Bagdad. Defying both the French and U.S. naval patrols, Mexican lighters from the Rio Grande landed here in Sept. 1863 with a large cargo of C.S.A. arms. In Nov. 1863, U.S. forces from the expedition of Gen. N. P. Banks occupied Point Isabel. The blockade was lifted and the port reactivated. In Aug. 1864, the Confederates drove the Federals across the bay to Brazos Island. The next March, Federal Gen. Lew Wallace (later author of "Ben Hur") met Confederate officers here to talk peace. (1964)

PORT ISABEL (Cameron Co.)
421 E. Queen Isabella Blvd. (SH 100)
Old Point Isabel Lighthouse
The beacon for the commerce of the Rio Grande. Erected by the United States government in 1852. Extinguished during Civil War. Discontinued, 1888–1895. Permanently discontinued, 1905.

PORT ISABEL (Cameron Co.)
S. Garcia St. at SH 100
Port Isabel (Old "Point" Isabel)
An historic haven for gulf shipping. Visited 1520 and named for Queen Isabella (1451–1504) of Spain by map-maker Alonso Alvarez de Pineda. In early eras, when cargo was loaded and unloaded by small boats, ocean vessels would anchor beyond Brazos Santiago Pass and have goods ferried across shallow Laguna Madre to this place, a site of civilized habitation ever since a village was established here in 1786. From here, freight went to the Rio Grande and from there to places far inland in northern Mexico. Point Isabel, however, had a grave access problem: Adjacent lowlands hampered the oxcarts that moved freight to and from the port. Charters were issued for railways in 1850 and 1853, but the roads were never built, although by 1859 some $4,000,000 worth of imports and exports passed this way annually. In 1866, Mifflin Kenedy, Capt. Richard King of the King Ranch, and other powerful businessmen got a charter but built no road. Finally in 1871 the Rio Grande Railroad Company built and put into use 22 miles of track, from Brownsville to a terminus here (200 ft. N of this site). Although often damaged by storms, this railroad served until 1933, when shipping was diverted to the new deepwater port in Brownsville. (1970)

PORT ISABEL (Cameron Co.)
SH 100, 3 mi. E at approach to Padre Island
Padre J. Nicolas Balli
Padre Island, off the South Texas Coast, is named for Padre Jose Nicolas Balli (177?–1829), whose family migrated from Spain in 1569 and became large landowners in the Lower Rio Grande Valley. In 1800, Balli applied to King Charles IV of Spain for 11½ leagues of land on the island, and in 1804 started its first settlement, Rancho Santa Cruz. Padre Balli served as collector of finances for all the churches in the Rio Grande Valley and founded the first mission in present Cameron County. Padre Balli's ministry was a great influence on the lives of early South Texas settlers. (1983)

PORT LAVACA (Calhoun Co.)
US 87, 6 mi. W
Moses Johnson, M.D. (1808–1853)
Born in Virginia, Dr. Moses Johnson settled in Port Lavaca about 1837. After moving to Austin in 1840 to practice medicine, he was elected city alderman and then mayor. An active Mason, he served as Grand Marshal of the Grand Lodge of Texas, A. F. & A. M. in 1844. When Anson Jones was elected president of the Republic in 1844, he named his friend Johnson treasurer. In 1845 Johnson's Austin home and the treasury records were destroyed by fire. He moved his family back to Port Lavaca the next year. He died in a yellow fever epidemic there on Oct. 2, 1853 and is buried ¼ mile west of this site. (1975)

PORT LAVACA (Calhoun Co.)   *SH 35 right-of-way, 12 mi. SW*
Green Lake
Named for the nearby tidal lake of the same name, the community of Green Lake began to develop in the late 1840s, although records indicate there were some settlers in the area before that time. A group of wealthy planters from Kentucky migrated to the area about 1849, along with their families and many slaves. They established extensive cotton plantations and built large and impressive homes. Early in its history, in 1851, a tornado struck the settlement, but miraculously caused little property damage and no injuries. A private school was established in 1852 and served children of the Green Lake and surrounding communities. The outbreak of the Civil War caused many changes in Green Lake. Following the U.S. surrender by General David Twiggs in 1861, Federal troops camped near here awaiting transport ships. With its agricultural economy based largely upon slave labor, Green Lake declined following the war when landowners, facing a labor shortage, began to leave the area. By 1875 most of the original settlers were gone. Although in existence a relatively short period of time, Green Lake contributed to the history of Calhoun County.   (1988)

PORT LAVACA (Calhoun Co.)   *SH 316, 12 mi. SE via SH 238*
Mrs. Angelina Bell Peyton Eberly (About 1800–March 15, 1860)
A Tennessean, Angelina Peyton came to Texas in 1822. With her husband, J. C. Peyton, she operated an inn in San Felipe, capital of the Austin Colony. Peyton died in 1834; in 1836 the widow married Jacob Eberly. She and Eberly had a hotel in Austin by 1842, when Angelina Eberly discovered men secretly removing records from the capital. Firing a cannon, she started the "Archives War," and rescued the original records of the Republic of Texas. Later she lived at Indianola. Her burial place and marker (¾ mi. NW) were destroyed in a flood in 1875.   (1978)

PORT LAVACA (Calhoun Co.)   *200 S. Ann St. at courthouse*
Calhoun County Hurricanes
Severe storms with high winds, heavy rains and tidal surges, hurricanes have played a significant role in events that shaped Calhoun County's history. Entire towns, including Indianola (a key Gulf seaport and Calhoun County seat) and Saluria (Republic-era port on Matagorda Island) were destroyed by 19th-century storms. Over the centuries, residents have dealt with wind and water damage to property, and lives have been lost during hurricanes. Stories of survival and rebuilding in the aftermath of these torrential storms also figure prominently in Calhoun County history.   (2001)

PORT LAVACA (Calhoun Co.)   *300 block S. Commerce St. (SH 238)*
Alsatian Immigration through Lavaca Bay
Texas land empresario Henri Castro contracted to bring colonists of various European nationalities to Texas beginning in 1842. The first of these were Alsatians, most of whom spoke German and held German sympathies. They arrived at Galveston, their official port of entry, with 114 passengers from France in early 1843; most then sailed for Lavaca (later Port Lavaca). They waited here before beginning their overland journey to what became Medina County, to establish the town of Castroville. Another, largely Alsatian, group of 129 arrived at Galveston January 1, 1844. About 40 continued to Lavaca, landing on the 10th. Conditions were difficult, and many immigrants succumbed to various coastal fevers. Other ships followed in 1845 and 1846. Castro's contract expired in 1847, after he had transported more than 2,000 colonists to Texas, most through Lavaca Bay.   (1999)

PORT LAVACA (Calhoun Co.)   *200 blk. of S. Commerce St. (SH 238)*
Civil War Bombardment of Port Lavaca
As part of the U.S. Naval initiative to control Texas Confederate ports, the gunboats Clifton and Westfield turned to the town then known as Lavaca after easily taking Galveston and Indianola. On October 31, 1862, under a flag of truce, Commander Willliam B. Renshaw demanded the surrender of Lavaca. Maj. Gen. Daniel D. Shea refused. After an evacuation period of merely 90 minutes, Renshaw's ships attacked the town. The city garrison returned the fire. Partially disabled, the Union boats fell back, but rained a steady barrage upon the town until night came. They resumed shelling the following morning, then retreated. The city streets were ravaged by gunfire, but Port Lavaca remained in Confederate hands until December 1863.   (1998)

PORT LAVACA (Calhoun Co.)   *2300 SH 35 at Bauer Community Center*
Port Lavaca
Founded in the aftermath of a Comanche raid on the nearby settlement of Linnville, the town of Lavaca ("the cow") was established in 1840. The busiest port in the Matagorda Bay area and a major center for overland export of cattle and other goods, Lavaca was an able successor to Linnville. Lavaca was the first Calhoun County seat from 1846 to 1852, when Indianola assumed the role. The county seat was returned to Lavaca briefly during the Civil War, when the town withstood fire from federal gunboats, then returned to Indianola. In 1886, Indianola was ravaged by a Hurricane and Lavaca was again county seat. With railroad expansion in Texas, Lavaca moved away from cattle and turned to seafood. Called Port Lavaca from the late 1880s, the village boomed. Tourism and the population increased; several factories were opened; the town became a general law city in 1909. The Gulf Intracoastal Waterway was connected to Port Lavaca in 1913 and a seawall was completed in 1920. Shrimp and frozen seafood became major items for export. Natural gas and oil were discovered in 1934 and 1935. From the late 1940s major manufacturing began to contribute to Port Lavaca's growth. Port Lavaca became a home rule chartered city in 1956, and a deep water port was located here in 1965. Port Lavaca celebrated 150 years of rich history in 1990.   (1998)

PORT LAVACA (Calhoun Co.)   *SH 35, west end of causeway*
Half Moon Reef Lighthouse
Constructed in 1858, this three-story hexagonal lighthouse was originally located in Matagorda Bay, at the southern tip of Half Moon Reef. The beacon served as an aid to ships trading in Port Lavaca and the nearby town of Indianola (14 mi. SE). During the Civil War the light was disabled by Confederate troops in an attempt to disrupt Federal efforts to capture Southern blockade runners. The lighthouse was restored to full operation in 1868 and remained in service until 1943 when it was moved to Point Comfort (7 mi. NE). It was relocated here in 1979.   (1980)

PORTLAND (San Patricio Co.)   *US 181 access rd. at N end of bridge*
Site of Indian Point Mass Grave of 1919 Hurricane Victims
In the early morning hours of Sunday, September 14, 1919, a hurricane made landfall in Corpus Christi after gathering strength in the Gulf of Mexico for two weeks. Crowds packed the North Beach area for their last weekend of the summer season, most continuing to ignore the last-minute evacuation warnings of police officers, firefighters and soldiers from Fort Brown. The rapidly rising water blocked vacationers from escaping to higher ground. As the water rose, people climbed to their rooftops and tied ropes to themselves and their children so that they might not be lost. A giant wave of water carrying oil from ruptured tanks on Harbor Island, timber from Port Aransas and cotton bales from a dock in Corpus Christi crashed down on North Beach, sweeping its victims into the black waters of Nueces Bay. On Monday morning the sun rose on a scene of terrible destruction. Though the official death toll was 284, estimates place the actual number, including those lost at sea, at one thousand. In the ensuing days, the survivors worked together to rebuild their homes, rescue the injured and bury the dead in mass graves, some containing more than fifty bodies, using farm implements as undertaking tools. A month later the bodies were removed to Rose Hill Cemetery in Corpus Christi and other sites as requested by friends and family members. Property damage and crop losses were estimated at twenty million dollars. The great storm of 1919 was the worst disaster to hit Corpus Christi in the twentieth century. The mass graves at Indian Point were about one hundred yards east of this site.   (2000)

PORTLAND (San Patricio Co.)   *US 181 access rd. at N end of bridge*
Reef Road
Early settlers in the eastern and central areas of San Patricio County faced difficulty traveling across Corpus Christi Bay to Corpus Christi, the main center for trade. The Reef Road, which according to local tradition was discovered by Indians, was the shortest and most favored route. Consisting of oyster shell reefs close to the water's surface, the road was passable only at low tide. Construction of the railroad (1887) and first causeway (1915) across the bay signaled a decline in usage of the road, but it remains an important part of the county's history.   (1989)

POST (Garza Co.)   *SH 207, 11 mi. N*
Duffy's Peak (3 mi. E)
Height so prominent it was Garza County's earliest bench mark, designated by peg-legged surveyor Jasper Hays, who in 1877–1878 was marking bounds of Llano Ranch, first property to be

occupied by settlers in county. Hays began at a corner established for the Houston & Great Northern Railroad Company near the White River in Crosby County, and shot west toward this peak. Tradition has it that a member of Hays' crew died and was buried near this peak which was afterward named for him. Local heights named for natural wonders include "The Ice Cream Cones," "Cow Head Mesa," "Indian Head Point" and "The Chimneys." Other interesting uplands are "Two Bush Hill," "The Devil's Breakfast Table," "Needlepoint Peak" and "Buffalo Point." Two balanced rocks known to early settlers have now disappeared because of wind and weather erosion. Duffy's Peak, like most of the scenic formations, is of sandstone, clay and sand. It still figures in local land transactions, as Hays' original notes (unearthed from mason jars he buried on the peak) formed basis for later surveys—including those of A. L. Marhoff in 1906, establishing boundaries for the farm colony of "Cereal King" C. W. Post. (1969)

POST (Garza Co.)   US 84, 3 mi. NW
C. W. Post Rain Battles
Site of 1911–1914 dynamiting to produce rain, carried on by C. W. Post, Texas farm colonizer and cereal foods millionaire. After reading that rain often accompanies cannonading in war, Post planned "battles" to relieve drouths. He thought vertical air currents would condense vapor in atmosphere and cause rain. He first used dynamite airborne by kites, but soon replaced this dangerous method by setting off explosions on edge of caprock. Post's experiments were said to have been 40% effective, and cost $5,000. He battled drouth of farms until his death, 1914. (1967)

POST (Garza Co.)   US 84, 3 mi. NW at roadside park
Twin Chimneys (100 yds. N)
Used as a landmark in the 19th century by surveyors sighting from Duffy's Peak, located ten miles northeast. Jasper Hays, earliest recorded surveyor of this area, used the peaks during 1877–1878 for charting the Llano Ranch, later bought by C. W. Post, the cereal king. Hays established, in addition, lines from which section surveys were made. Civil Engineer A. L. Marhoff, using the original field notes and book of Hays, surveyed the land bought by Post, 1906. This included the section on which the town of Post was founded, 1907, as well as other property. (1970)

POST (Garza Co.)   US 84, entrance to city park
Post
Founded 1907 by industrialist C. W. Post. Early abundant water supply by windmills above caprock. Later from White River Lake. Extensive ranching and farming. Postex Cotton Mills, making sheets and pillowcases, furnish year-round employment. Service center for over 1,750 oil wells in county. (1967)

POST (Garza Co.)   US 380 at courthouse
Charles W. Post (1854–1914)
Internationally known creator of Post Cereals, advertising genius, inventor and innovator, founder of Post City in 1906. Through the purchase of the Curry Comb Ranch and adjacent land approximating 225,000 acres he began his dream of building self-contained model community of towns and farms. Mr. Post financed, supervised and built towns without profit to himself. Settlers were offered ownership of business or farm sites far below cost. Mr. Post planned community of debt-free private ownership in every field of endeavor, and sought to make his vision true to its purpose. (1967)

POST (Garza Co.)   US 380 at FM 669 in Post
Old Post High School
Built 1928, incorporating in lower walls native Garza County stones from the town's first (1909) school, erected soon after the founding of City of Post. This historic preservation occurred under leadership of Supt. John E. Watson, outstanding educator, veteran of World War I service in the heroic Rainbow Division. The Parent-Teachers' Association backed Watson's stand, and bond issue passed in spite of adverse circumstances. When later growth called for a larger educational complex to meet community needs, this became Post Junior High School. (1968)

POST (Garza Co.)   US 380, .5 mi. E
Terrace Cemetery Gateway
From Double "U," "Lazy S," Connell and Curry Comb Ranch canyons, round rocks were collected and made into gate piers in 1908 when cereal king C. W. Post founded Post City. George

379

Samson designed and with fellow Scotsman James Napier built the gateway. Samson was a community leader 50 years.
(1963)

POST (Garza Co.)
US 84, .1 mi. S
Garza County
Named in honor of The Garza family, natives of the Canary Islands. Pioneer settlers of San Antonio in 1731. A cattle raising county since its settlement, agricultural since 1910. Textile mills established in 1912. Post, the county seat.
(1965)

POST (Garza Co.)
US 84, 6 mi. SE in rest area
Llano Estacado
Stretching across the horizon as a range of flat-topped mountains is the caprock escarpment, eastern boundary of the vast Llano Estacado or "Staked Plains." The Llano, one of the world's most perfect plains regions, is an elongated oval extending from north to south. Some three quarters of it, 20 million acres, are in Texas. The remainder is in eastern New Mexico. Its naturally treeless surface, unbroken except for several canyons, slopes gradually from an altitude of 2,700 feet at its eastern edge to more than 4,000 feet along the New Mexico border. The caprock escarpment is the result of surface erosion that began in the early Pleistocene Period some 750,000 years ago. Composed of tough caliche, the caprock has protected the softer materials underlying it, thus resisting the erosive factors with varying success. The escarpment begins in Borden County 25 miles south of this point and extends northward, in a sweeping arc 170 miles into the Texas Panhandle. It rises from 300 feet to 1,000 feet above the lower plains at its base, giving the impression of having been thrust upward out of the surrounding land. First white man to visit the Great Plains was the Spanish Conquistador Francisco de Coronado who crossed them in 1541 on his search for the fabled Seven Cities of Cibola. He was especially impressed by the sea of grass which covered the soil so completely that the tracks of his expedition left no permanent mark. The Spaniards, it is said, staked their route so they would be guided on the return trip—hence the term "Staked" Plains. Because of the scarcity of surface water, the Llano was generally shunned by buffalo and Indians until the encroachment of settlers in the lower areas drove them onto it. The native grasses supported an immense ranching empire following the extinction of the buffalo. More recently the Llano has become one of the nation's leading cotton, wheat and grain sorghum producing areas.

POST (Garza Co.)
US 84, 8 mi. SE
O S Ranch
Founded on open range, 1878, brand was owned in 1881 by R. H. Overall. Acquired 1901 by W. E. Connell, who had about 200 sections of land. Ranch house a community center—for barbecues, roundups, parties. In 1907 it was site of election organizing Garza County.
(1966)

POTEET (Atascosa Co.)
4th St. at Ave. I
Poteet
The town of Poteet traces its history to the 1880s, when Francis Marion Poteet (1833–1907) established a mercantile store northeast of this area. A blacksmith and farmer as well as a merchant, Poteet began providing mail service to his customers. Poteet sold his business to Henry T. Mumme (1870–1947) before 1900. Mumme continued to offer postal service at the store, and in 1910 he and his wife Ida (1869–1942) donated 400 acres of land for a new townsite. Since the area had been referred to as Poteet as a result of the early mail service, the new town was named in honor of Francis Marion Poteet. Mumme moved his store to the new townsite in 1911. Mumme drilled the town's first artesian water well and is credited with introducing the cultivation of strawberries here. The artesian water, together with the sandy soil of the region, proved ideal for growing the berries. Known statewide for its superior quality strawberries, Poteet has been nicknamed the "Strawberry Capital of Texas." The town grew steadily after 1910, with the establishment of schools, churches, homes, and businesses. It was incorporated in 1926.
(1989)

POTH (Wilson Co.)
US 181, 4 mi. S
Beauregard Ranch
Founded 1852, by Augustin Toutant-Beauregard, of landed Creole gentry who traced lineage to 16th century Spanish nobility. Brother was Confederate General Pierre Gustave Toutant-Beauregard. Stone-mounted iron rings were part of scaffolding used to butcher hogs.
(1967)

380

POWELL (Navarro Co.)   *SH 31 in Powell*
The Powell Oil Field
One of the world's most noted petroleum fields. Discovered 1905; developed in three periods. A number of early shallow wells (800'–1,000' in Nacatoch sand) drilled by Claude Witherspoon, are still producing. Field's second and greatest era came as a result of three heartbreaking years of drilling. On Sunday, Jan. 7, 1923, the W. H. Warren–R. K. Blackshear "J. H. Burke No. 1" (2,933' in Woodbine sand) blew in a gusher, triggering a feverish drilling boom. As this was prior to spacing and proration regulations, derricks sprouted by the dozens. The site of "J. H. Burke No. 1" is one mile southwest of this marker. On May 8, 1923, another great gusher, the "J. K. Hughes–W. J. McKie No. 1" (2.25 mi. SW), blackened the area with oil which soon ignited, causing 15 deaths. This 8,000-barrel-a-day gusher defined the main pool. By fall, the six-square-mile field was outproducing Pennsylvania plus nine other oil states. On Nov. 23, 1923, came the peak day of 354,893 barrels. The population skyrocketed. Corn and cotton patches became townsites for Oil City, Tuckertown, Wildcat. In 1923, Powell ran over 30 million barrels; in 1924, over 40 million. It then declined, with its last million-barrel year in 1931. Waterflooding ushered in the third yield period in 1964.   (1973)

PRAIRIE VIEW (Waller Co.)   *FM 1098, off US 290, University campus*
Prairie View A&M University
Authorized by the Texas Legislature in 1876, the "Agricultural and Mechanical College for Colored Youth" was Texas' second state-supported institution of higher learning. As a land grant college, it occupied a 1,434-acre former slave plantation. Organized by the Texas A&M board of Directors, Prairie View has remained a part of the Texas A&M system. The first eight students enrolled on March 11, 1878, but low enrollment caused the school to close. The following year the "Prairie View Normal Institute" was organized with emphasis on preparing teachers in trade and agricultural subjects. A coeducational college, Prairie View's enrollment of 16 soon reached 60. In ten years, industrial training was added to the curriculum. Inter-collegiate athletics began in 1904. By 1931, the campus boasted 31 main buildings and 50 cottages. In 1934, the Southern Association of Colleges and Secondary Schools granted a Class "A" rating. In 1947, the institution became "Prairie View Agricultural and Mechanical College." Integrated during the 1960s, the name changed to "Prairie View A&M University" in 1973. The university's motto is "Prairie View produces productive people."   (1982)

PRESIDIO (Presidio Co.)   *FM 170, 4.5 mi. E, Fort Leaton State Historic Site*
El Fortín de San José (The Little Fort of Saint Joseph)
About 1773, the Spanish garrison at Presidio del Norte, present Ojinaga, Mexico, established El Fortín de San José in this vicinity to protect local farmers. The settlement retained the name after the post was abandoned about 1810. After Ben Leaton had acquired extensive property in the area in 1848, the community came to be called Fort Leaton. Ben Leaton's fortress is all that remains of the old settlement. Fort Leaton is neither the site of the original Presidio del Norte nor the Spanish Mission Apostal Santiago, as stated erroneously by earlier markers at this location.   (1978)

Presidio del Norte
Approximate site of Presidio del Norte de la Junta, established by Captain Alonzo Rubin de Celis in 1759–1760. Name of the post retained in part by the present town and county. In this vicinity the missions of San Antonio de los Publiques, San Francisco de los Julimes, Santa Maria la Redonda, San Pedro Alcantara, El Apostol Santiago, San Cristobal, were first established in 1683 by Don Juan Dominguez de Mendoza and Padre Fray Nicolas Lopez O. F. M. Maintained by Franciscan missionaries for the Christianizing and civilizing of the Apache Natages, Faraones, Publiques, Julimes, Jumanos, Zumas, and other Indian tribes. Administered and controlled in 1746 by the custodia of New Mexico.

PRESIDIO (Presidio Co.)   *O'Reily St. (US 67) in St. Francis Plaza*
Captain Henry Skillman, C.S.A.
Renowned southwestern mail and stagecoach man. Born in Kentucky. Came to Texas before 1846. Served as a U.S. Army scout in Mexican War. About 1851 established the first mail service from San Antonio to El Paso. When the first Butterfield Overland Stagecoach in 1858 made bid to establish fast service to the West Coast, was selected to drive perilous Comanche Indian area from Horsehead

Crossing on the Pecos to El Paso. Made it in 4 days without rest or relief, his 6-foot frame draped with revolvers and Bowie knives. A Confederate scout in the Civil War. From July 1862, when Federals seized El Paso and the Davis Mountains (to make the longest enemy occupation in Texas), served as liaison between regular Confederate troops and the C.S.A. patriots who plotted in their refugee colony in Juarez to recapture West Texas. Knowing country well, came and went at will. Spread false rumors of Confederates massing in deserts, to divert Federal troops from combat. Came to be most dreaded scout known to the occupation. Was hunted by special force commissioned to take him alive. In showdown at Spencer's Ranch near here on April 3, 1864, fought to his death.   (1964)

PRIDDY (Mills Co.)   *SH 16 in Priddy*
Zion Evangelical Lutheran Church
In the 1870s and 1880s many settlers of German ancestry began arriving in this area. In 1889, under the leadership of the Rev. R. Seils, Zion Evangelical Lutheran Church was organized. Early worship services were held in the Bismark schoolhouse (approx. 2 mi. S). Beginning with twenty-three charter members, the congregation grew steadily. By 1892, a small sanctuary was constructed and a cemetery was established on the church property (2 mi. SW). Another group of families began meeting together for worship services in the Priddy community, and in December 1903 organized St. John's Lutheran Church. Services were held in the Becker Mountain schoolhouse (approx. 2 mi. E). Soon both German Lutheran congregations were being served by the same minister. In 1929, the Zion congregation moved to Priddy and built a new sanctuary. In 1941, by mutual consent, the Zion and St. John's congregations joined together to become one church under the Zion Evangelical Lutheran Church name. A part of Mills County history for generations, this church continues to serve the community with many forms of outreach.   (1989)

PROCTER (Comanche Co.)   *US 67/377 in Proctor*
Confederate Texas Poet Mollie E. Moore (1844–1909)
During the Civil War, wrote poems Texans memorized, cut out of newspapers, sent their boys on the battlefront: About the deaths of heroes, Texans' units, Confederate victories and such topics. She also did social work and nursing at Camp Ford, Tyler. She was a lively, spirited girl who went horseback riding with a pistol strapped to her side. After war, became nationally known poet, novelist, columnist. Married a newspaper editor. Led New Orleans society 20 years. Near this marker site, at old Mooresville (now Proctor) often visited her brother's family.   (1965)

PROGRESO (Hidalgo Co.)   *US 281, 4 mi. E*
Battle of La Bolsa
In 1859 and early 1860, a series of raids on Texas settlements led by Juan N. Cortina (1824–1894) led to skirmishes with companies of Texas Rangers and U.S. soldiers. These conflicts became known as the Cortina Wars. On February 4, 1860, a battle occurred at La Bolsa Bend (ca. 1 mi. S) between Cortina's raiders and Capt. John S. "Rip" Ford's Texas Rangers. The Rangers successfully defended the riverboat Ranchero, traveling downstream from Rio Grande City, from an attack by Cortina's band. Cortina escaped into Mexico and later became a general in the Mexican Army.   (1991)

PROSPER (Collin Co.)   *Preston Road (SH 289) at Rock Hill Rd., 2 mi. S*
Site of Rock Hill
Probably named for the white rock escarpment on which it was built, Rock Hill was established by December 1854 when John Moore became its first postmaster. By the early 20th century the town boasted two schools, four churches, three doctors, a grist mill, general store, cotton gin, blacksmith, drugstore, dry goods and grocery and a population of 115. In 1902 the St. Louis and San Francisco Railroad bypassed the town, and within months most of the businesses, townspeople and churches had relocated to Prosper. The little community survived for several more years. In the mid-1930s an African American Baptist church was the only one remaining. The Anglo school closed in 1948; the black school closed in the 1960s. A general store, the last remnant of Rock Hill, was razed in 1973.   (2000)

PUTNAM (Callahan Co.)   *IH 20, 2 mi. E*
Burkett Pecan Tree
Pecan tree, bred from a native tree, 1900, by J. H. Burkett (1861–1945), Texas pecan industry leader.   (1966)

PYOTE (Ward Co.)
IH 20 westbound, exit 66
Rattlesnake Bomber Base (Pyote Army Air Base)
Nicknamed for the numerous rattlesnake dens that were uncovered during the construction, Pyote Army Air Base was established in 1942 to train replacement crews for bombers during World War II. Located on 2,700 acres of University of Texas land, the base consisted of two 8,400-ft. runways, five large hangars, and hundreds of buildings used to house 3,000 to 4,000 soldiers and 2,000 civilians. On Jan. 1, 1943, the 19th Bombardment Group (later known as the 19th Combat Crew Training School), a heavily-decorated fighting unit from the Pacific Theater, arrived to begin training B-17 bomber crews. Pyote came to be highly regarded as a top training field, and its crews set many new records for flying hours. This reputation continued after the transition to B-29s was made in July 1944. During the post-war years, the base served as a storage facility, at one time housing as many as 2,000 aircraft, including the Enola Gay, the plane that dropped the first atomic bomb. Pyote also was used for a short time as a radar station, but by 1966 it was no longer economical to maintain such a large base for so small an operation, and the facility was closed. (1984)

QUANAH (Hardeman Co.)
E. 11th St. (US 287), 1.1 mi E
Medicine Mound Depot, 1910
Built by Kansas City, Mexico & Orient Railway as passenger and freight station, in area where Chief Quanah Parker's Comanches prayed and rolled in gypsum, believing it was healing dust. Later, Santa Fe Station. Site of holdups and shooting. Has bullet holes, but escaped a 1935 fire that burned entire town. Retired from use, 1959; was moved via Highway 287 to its present site. (1964)

QUANAH (Hardeman Co.)
US 287 W, Quanah Garden Club Park
Hardeman County
Created February 1, 1858; recreated August 21, 1876; organized December 30, 1884. Named in honor of Bailey Hardeman, 1785–1836, signer of the Texas Declaration of Independence, and Thomas Jones Hardeman, 1788–1854, member of the Texas Congress and Legislature. County seat, Margarette, 1884–1890, Quanah, since, in honor of Quanah Parker, a Comanche chief. (1965)

QUANAH (Hardeman Co.)
222 S. Main St. (SH 6)
Simpson Building
After serving as manager of the Cameron lumberyard in Quanah and then as a general manager in Waco, L. Simpson began his own lumber company and returned to Quanah in 1906. In 1910, Simpson had this three-story commercial building constructed to house his offices; other local businesses, including the corner drug store from 1920 until 1998; and the Elks Lodge, which occupied the top floor. Featuring decorative brick detailing and a corner entry, the Simpson Building is a significant part of Quanah's architectural heritage. (2001)

QUANAH (Hardeman Co.)
300 blk. S Main St. (SH 6)
Hardeman County Courthouse
Hardeman County was created in 1858 and named for early Texas legislators Bailey and Thomas Jones Hardeman. It was not organized, however, until 1884 when the population had increased enough to have a formal county government. The community of Margaret (now in Foard County) was selected as first county seat, but after the Fort Worth and Denver City Railway laid out the townsite of Quanah along its line, voters elected to move the county seat to Quanah in 1890. A 1906 bond election secured funds for the construction of a new building to replace the 1890 county courthouse. The Commissioners Court selected architect R. H. Stuckey of Chillicothe and Tom Lovell & Sons of Denton to design and construct the building, respectively. Stuckey used a domed cupola, stone lintels over the windows, and ionic columns flanking the entryways to execute his Neoclassical design for the courthouse. Built of glazed tan brick with a raised basement of Indiana limestone, it was completed in 1908. Since its construction, the Hardeman County Courthouse has served as the center of politics and government for county residents. The square is a focal point for local festivals and community events. An anchor in Quanah's downtown historic district, the 1908 courthouse continues as a significant part of the community's architectural heritage. (2001)

QUANAH (Hardeman Co.)
409 S. Main St. (SH 6)
First Presbyterian Church of Quanah
This congregation was organized in 1892 at the home of Mrs. A. E. DeGraffenried by the Rev. Jacobs and eight charter members. This beaux arts classical style church building, erected by

Chillicothe contractor R. Henry Stuckey in 1909, features stucco over frame construction, an inset entry under large columns, arched stained glass windows, and an elaborate stained glass dome. This structure is a symbol of the church's continuing service to the community.

(Recorded Texas Historic Landmark 1995)

QUINLAN (Hunt Co.)
SH 34 at Spur 264, 1 mi. S
Roberts
In 1882, the Houston and Texas Central Railroad bought 100 acres of land from Texas Governor Oran Roberts. As the terminus of the company's Northeastern Line, Roberts quickly attracted business people. The town boasted a school for white students and another for black students, a post office with daily mail service, a doctor, a blacksmith, a carpenter, dry goods and grocers, general stores, and saloons. Roberts gained a reputation as a boomtown, full of opportunity and vice. In 1892 the bankrupt Houston and Texas Central sold its Northeastern Line to New Yorker Hetty Green who reorganized the railroad as the Texas Midland under the leadership of her son Edward "Ned" Green. A land dispute between the two railroad companies led Ned Green to purchase land just north of Roberts, establishing a depot there and platting the new town of Quinlan. Merchants and business people soon moved their facilities to Quinlan, followed by the First Missionary Baptist Church of Roberts and others wishing to escape Roberts' lawlessness. The Quinlan depot and post office were dedicated on October 17, 1894; the Roberts depot and telegraph office were promptly dismantled by railroad agents. A fire of unknown origin destroyed Roberts in 1895.
(1998)

QUINLAN (Hunt Co.)
Main St. (SH 34/276) at Church St.
Quinlan
The city of Quinlan began about 1892 as a stop on the Texas Midland Railroad. Owned by famed bond investor Hettie Green, called by the contemporary press "the witch of Wall Street," the railroad was operated by her son, Edward H. R. Green. Texas Midland became a subsidiary of the Houston & Texas Central Railroad, and the city which built up around a depot constructed here between the towns of Roberts and Greenville was named Quinlan in honor of George A. Quinlan, the general manager of the Houston & Texas Central Railroad. A post office opened in Quinlan in 1894, and by 1896 the city was incorporated. Harry Ford served as first mayor. Quinlan soon became the center of a large agricultural area, providing a railroad shipping point for growers of cotton and other crops. By the early 20th century the town boasted three cotton gins, numerous businesses and fraternal organizations, banks, schools, churches, and homes. Oil exploration and production overtook cotton farming as the area's economic base in the 1930s and 1940s, and the construction of Lake Tawakoni in the 1950s brought another economic boost to the community.
(1994)

QUITAQUE (Briscoe Co.)
SH 86, 7 mi. NW at roadside park
Trading Area of Jose Tafoya and Other Comancheros
In Quitaque area, Comancheros (peddlers in Comanche domain) from New Mexico traded flour and other goods to Indians. The barter (begun in 1700's) reached peak in 1864–1868, when Apaches, Comanches and Kiowas rustled horses and thousands of cattle "down in Texas," to use in trades. Jose Tafoya, who had wagons as well as pack mules, sold guns to Indians until U.S. Army caught and threatened to hang him in 1874 unless he enlisted as a frontier scout. There were many other Comancheros. Tafoya is an example of one who helped rid Texas of Indian marauders.
(1969)

QUITMAN (Wood Co.)
Main St. at Goode St. (SH 154) at courthouse
James Stephen Hogg (March 24, 1851–March 3, 1906)
Texas statesman whose nationally-acclaimed public career began at this site. The third son of Gen. Joseph L. and Lucanda (McMath) Hogg was born near Rusk. Orphaned during troubled Civil War era, he began at age 14 to earn his own way as a farmhand, clerk, printer's devil, typesetter, country editor. At 22, he was elected Justice of the Peace, Precinct 1, and headed Commissioners' Court of Wood County, 1874–75. He was admitted to the bar in 1875 and soon held higher offices: county attorney (1879–81), district attorney (1881–85), Texas attorney general (1887–90). Inaugurated on Jan. 20, 1891, he was the first native Texan to become governor of the state. He championed the common people. An intellectual and physical giant, personally fearless, he saw

Texas as victim of Wall Street greed, and corrected many injustices. To equalize business opportunities among great and small, he led in creating Texas Railroad Commission, hailed as a model throughout the world. Public office left him financially insecure. Later came wealth, which has been invested by his heirs in Texas mental health and culture. His wife was Sallie Stinson of Wood County. Their children—Will, Ima, Mike and Tom—were all philanthropists.
(1971)

QUITMAN (Wood Co.)
SH 37, Gov. Hogg Shrine Historic Site
James A. Stinson Home
Constructed in 1869 of virgin pine and oak by James A. Stinson, a widower who came to Texas in 1868 from Georgia after having served as a colonel in the Confederate Army. He brought with him his daughter Sallie. He bought extensive timber and farm lands in the eastern area of Wood County; operated a large sawmill which sent lumber throughout the state. Was also known as an early-day scientific farmer. Mrs. Nathan Jones, a widow with one daughter, Mary, became the second wife of Col. Stinson. They had two daughters, Lily and Cliffie, and one son, James F. In the parlor of the house, on April 22, 1874, Sallie Stinson married James Stephen Hogg, who later became the first native-Texan governor of the state. Col. Stinson was a Southern aristocrat, a progressive thinker and a great scholar of government. He probably had great influence on James S. Hogg's ideas on good government. Was a leader in the County and State Grange, an organization which strove to protect rural interests. He was also instrumental in getting enacted into law the bill creating experimental farm, Texas Agricultural and Mechanical College. Stinson's home was always open to young and old.
(1968)

QUITMAN (Wood Co.)
SH 37, Governor Hogg Shrine Historic Site
James Stephen Hogg's Early Home
Built in 1860s; bought Jan. 8, 1873, by James Stephen Hogg (1851–1906), who in 1874 married Sallie Stinson of Wood County. When the couple honeymooned in this cottage, young Hogg was editor-publisher of Quitman News and justice of the peace—start of a brilliant career which led to governorship of Texas, 1891–1895. Local clubs bought the cottage and moved it here in 1946. It was restored in 1952 by Gov. and Mrs. Hogg's only daughter, Miss Ima. Awarded Medallion Plate.
(1962)

QUITMAN (Wood Co.)
SH 37, 1.7 mi. S
Wood County
Created February 5, 1850. Organized August 5, 1850. Named in honor of George T. Wood, 1795–1858. Member of Congress of the Republic of Texas. An officer in the Mexican War. Governor of Texas, 1847–1849. Quitman, county seat.

RANDOLPH (Fannin Co.)
SH 121 Bus., .5 mi. NE
Lindsey-Randolph Cemetery
Tennessee native Thomas Lindsey (b. 1794) brought his family to this part of Fannin County in 1837. In the late 1840s, Lindsey donated four acres of his farmland for a school and cemetery. The first burial in the cemetery was for one of Lindsey's slaves. The one-room schoolhouse built next to the graveyard served as a community church where funeral services were held. Over the years, this cemetery has served residents of the surrounding area, including the community of Randolph, which was founded in 1887 on the Louisiana, Arkansas and Texas Railroad. The main street in Randolph was located about ¾ mile southwest of the Lindsey School and Cemetery, and a wooden sidewalk connected the two. In the middle 1890s, the Lindsey School was moved to Randolph, and the original school grounds were added to the cemetery. Among those buried here are Thomas Lindsey and his wife, Rebecca, and their son-in-law, the Rev. Burwell Cox, who organized several Presbyterian churches in the area. Other graves located here include those of businessmen, farmers, doctors, pioneer citizens and their descendants, and veterans of several wars.
(1984)

RANGER (Eastland Co.)
Loop 254 at Main St.
Site of First Oil Well Drilled in Eastland County
The J. H. McClesky No. 1 Discovery Well of the Ranger Pool was drilled by Warren Wagner under the supervision of W. K. Gordon of the Texas Pacific Coal and Oil Company, July 2–October 27, 1917. Initial production was 1600 barrels with three million feet of gas. Abandoned May 30, 1930 after producing 275,000 barrels of oil.
(1964)

RANGER (Eastland Co.)
Loop 254 at Main St.

Roaring Ranger

Boom of high excitement and strategic importance. When oil demand was high during World War I, Texas Pacific Coal Company General Manager W. K. Gordon, a believer in deep drilling, persuaded his company to make the venture that started Ranger's oil boom at McClesky No. 1 (1 mi. S). This blew in October 1917, as a 1700-barrels-a-day gusher. Later gushers yielded up to 7,000 and 11,000-barrels-a-day each. Ten daily trains brought in prospectors packed in the aisles or on tops of coaches. Ranger's dozen or so houses became a city of drillers, suppliers, oil company offices. Living quarters were so scarce that not only were beds of day-tour men occupied by the graveyard-tour men, but overstuffed chairs were also rented for sleeping. Food was hard to get and prices were high. For two rainy years, Ranger was a sea of mud. A sled taxied people across streets, or a man in hip boots carried them piggyback. However, money was plentiful, and forces of vice moved in. After five murders occurred in one day, law officers arrested many criminals and expelled gamblers and vagrants. Ranger's success overshadowed its troubles. It is said to have yielded in a year twice the wealth of best years in California and Klondike gold fields. (1967)

RANKIN (Upton Co.)
SH 349, 7 mi. NW

The Benedum Oil Field and Benedum Townsite (About 9 mi. E)

Field named in 1950 by Texas Railroad Commission in honor of Michael Late (Mike) Benedum, 1869–1959, who devoted 69 of his 90 years to the oil business, and won fortune and fame as "The Great Wildcatter." His work began in 1890. With a partner, Joe C. Trees, he discovered or developed oil fields in Illinois, West Virginia, Louisiana (the great Caddo Field); the Tuxpam in Mexico; deMares in Colombia, South America; and in Texas the Desdemona, Big Lake, Yates, East White Point, Susan Peak and Benavides. Discovery of Big Lake Field (1923) on University of Texas land tapped the great wealth of the Permian Basin, which opened in 1920 with a small discovery. Alford No. 1, original well in Benedum Field (later reclassified as a gas field), was completed Jan. 4, 1948, at depth of 12,011 feet by Slick-Urschel Oil Co., under a partnership agreement. The field later benefited by dedication of Benedum Townsite. The "Great Wildcatter" was an oil pioneer whose work enriched one of the world's large constitutional permanent university funds. Revenues from oil and gas operations give Texas the largest permanent public school fund in the world. (1965)

RANKIN (Upton Co.)
SH 329, 7 mi. NW

"Weir No. 1" Oil Well

Except for the original Yates Ranch gusher of 1926, most dramatic oil discovery in Upton County. Brought in December 6, 1961. West of this site 3.5 miles. First quadruple completion in West Texas, called by American Association of Petroleum Engineers the most important development of the year 1961—and the most prolific discovery in many years. Drilled to depth of 12,432 feet. Plugged back at 9,925 feet. Produced from upper, middle and lower Strawn zones, and from the bend, with perforations in lower detrital gas zone. Contractor was Brahaney Drilling Co. Discovery made by E. G. Rodman, W. D. Noel and Odessa Natural Gasoline Co., founded by Rodman and Noel, and affiliated with El Paso Natural Gas Products Co. Rodman and Noel, who began their Upton County operations in 1940, have been responsible for numerous significant discoveries in the Permian Basin of Texas and New Mexico, and have led in the establishment of a vast petrochemical complex in Odessa. This utilizes in the making of such things as plastics, many petroleum by-products once scrapped as waste. Such leadership and such wells as Weir No. 1 have enabled Upton County to remain for many years one of the outstanding production areas in Texas. (1964)

RANKIN (Upton Co.)
US 67, 5 mi. E

Rankin

Made Upton County seat in 1921. Named for F. E. Rankin, who gave site for railway station— the center of community life over and above its business dealings; was scene of cowboy dances of Saturday nights, church services on Sundays. Home of Rankin Museum and of World Champion Rodeo Stars Toots Mansfield and Allen Holder. (1964)

RANKIN (Upton Co.)
US 67, 0.5 mi. E

Upton County

Formed from Tom Green County. Created Feb. 26, 1887. Organized May 7, 1910. Named in honor of John Cunningham Upton, 1828–1862. A distinguished Confederate officer killed at

Manassas Aug. 30, 1862. County seat, Upland 1910–1921, Rankin since. A cattle and sheep raising country. Oil wells dot the county. (1936)

RANKIN (Upton Co.)   *205 E. 10th Ave, 2 blks. W of SH349*
Upland First Upton County Seat
Now abandoned, the town of Upland (10 miles N) was intended as a station on the rail line from St. Louis to Chihuahua, Mexico. It was also located near the stage route of the Butterfield mail line. Henry Halff and his son platted the townsite in 1908 and a school opened the same year. In 1910 Upland was named the first county seat and a stone courthouse was constructed later. Bypassed by new rail lines and suffering from a severe drought, the town declined. Homes and buildings were moved here by 1921 when Rankin became the new seat of government. (1980)

RANKIN (Upton Co.)   *US 67, 8.4 mi. W*
Rattlesnake Butte (¼ mi. S)
Named for wildlife seen here 1919 by University of Texas geology team of students and professors mapping county resources. A meandering formation, 2,600 ft. elevation, this is part of an uplift in southern Permian Basin; associated with uplift are county's oil fields. (1967)

RATCLIFF (Houston Co.)   *SH 7, 1 mi. W of Ratcliff*
Four C Mill
R. M. Keith, agent for Central Coal & Coke Co., Kansas City, Mo., in Oct. 1899, began purchasing the virgin pine timberlands of this region. Lumber for construction of a new mill was cut by a small sawmill bought by Keith, Jan. 10, 1901, from local landowner, J. H. Ratcliff. Although known as "Four C" Mill, it was operated by the Louisiana & Texas Lumber Co., organized by Keith in July 1901. The mill began sawing lumber in June 1902, producing 300,000 board feet per 11-hour day. The Texas Southeastern Railroad laid tracks from Lufkin; tram roads and tap lines were built into the forest to haul fresh-cut timber to the mill. The company built houses and a "company store" at the mill, and several logging camps in the forest to house and feed lumberjacks. Hostility erupted when town of Ratcliff was begun nearby, competing for the workers' trade. Between the mill and Ratcliff the company erected a 16-foot fence, which was dynamited several times, thwarting the attempts to establish a company-controlled town. By 1917, the company had exhausted the 120,000 acres it had purchased. The mill was shut down and dismantled in 1920, due to shortage of good timber. Nearby Ratcliff Lake was the Four C Millpond. (1973)

RATCLIFF (Houston Co.)   *SH 7 in Ratcliff*
Ratcliff
About 1875, a 32-wagon train of settlers came here from Georgia. Jesse H. Ratcliff (1844–1920) built a sawmill about 1885, drawing more people. Post office opened 1889, with Ratcliff as postmaster, and town soon had several stores. Professional men included Drs. H. L. McCall and Jack Jackson. Sold 1901 to Louisiana & Texas Lumber Co., then to Central Coal & Coke Co., sawmill became a vast complex, running until 1917, when it closed. Turning to logging or other enterprises, the community survived, although many residents moved away. The Ratcliff schools consolidated (1955) with Kennard. (1972)

RAYMONDVILLE (Willacy Co.)   *SH 186 right-of-way, 12 mi. E*
San Juan de Carricitos Land Grant
The largest land grant in South Texas, the San Juan de Carricitos lands were awarded to Don Jose Narciso Cavazos in 1792 by the the king of Spain. Comprising over one-half million acres, the grant included virtually all of present Willacy County, including the sites of the towns of Sebastian, Lyford, Raymondville, Lasara, San Perlita, and Port Mansfield. In 1793, Cavazos took formal possession of the land grant seven miles north of this site. Most of the grant was later sold by Cavazos' heirs, although some descendants still live within its boundaries. (1988)

RAYMONDVILLE (Willacy Co.)   *SH 186 at 3rd St.*
Willacy County
Formed from Cameron and Hidalgo counties; created March 11, 1911, recreated April 2, 1921; organized August 12, 1911, reorganized August 13, 1921. Named in honor of John G. Willacy; born November 10, 1859; member of the Texas Legislature 1900–1916; State Tax Commissioner, 1922–1926; County Seat, Sarita, 1911, Raymondville, since 1921. (1936)

RAYMONDVILLE (Willacy Co.)
427 S. 7th St. (US 77)
Edward Burleson Raymond

Founder of Raymondville. Born in a log house on Congress Avenue, Austin, son of Republic of Texas lawyer and newspaperman N. C. Raymond and wife Lucinda (Riggs), E. B. Raymond came on horseback to South Texas in 1870. After herding cattle uptrail to Kansas, he was hired about 1874 by Richard King to open El Sauz Ranch, and managed King-Kenedy interests for 37 years. He also developed a ranch of his own, married Juanita Rodriguez, and was the father of two sons, Fred N. and Edward Charles. When El Sauz Post Office was created in 1893, he was made postmaster. He was a school official and served 1898–1910 as a commissioner of Cameron County. Joining other ranchers in deeding right of way for St. Louis, Brownsville & Mexico Railway, he also donated a station site near his Las Majadas Ranch. Railway officials named the station in his honor. In 1904, the year rail service was formally inaugurated on the fourth of July, he organized Raymond Town & Improvement Co.; in 1907, became president of town's first bank; set up telephone exchange; built cotton gin. After his death, Raymondville became seat of government for new county of Willacy, created 1921. (1974)

RAYMONDVILLE (Willacy Co.)
SH 186, 8.4 mi. W
Great Salt Lake

Here has existed, since the first Spanish chronicler traversed the region, a Great Salt Lake which supplied all Northern Mexico with salt.

REAGOR SPRINGS (Ellis Co.)
US 287 at Old US 287 N
Richardson Cemetery (1 Mi. SW)

John I. Richardson (1839–1922), county surveyor, mason, and veteran of the 12th Texas Confederate Cavalry, married Ann Elizabeth Reagor (1849–1923) in 1865. Both were descendants of the family for which Reagor Springs was named. A cousin, Robert S. Reagor, was buried on the Richardsons' property in 1879. In 1890 the land was deeded for use as a cemetery. Also buried here are two of the Richardsons' six children. The Richardsons left Reagor Springs near the turn of the century. Other early area families also are buried in the cemetery, which contains thirty graves. Those interred in the Richardson Cemetery helped to forge Reagor Springs and early Ellis County. (1998)

RED OAK (Ellis Co.)
SH 342, 1 mi. S
Red Oak Cemetery

Originally known as the Kemble Cemetery, this graveyard began as a family burial ground. Abraham Kemble acquired the land on which the cemetery is located about 1860. He and his wife Mary were both buried here in 1867. In 1892, Kemble descendants gave the land to Liberty Baptist Church, later renamed First Baptist Church, Red Oak. The cemetery became a public burial ground after the turn of the century. Those interred here include generations of Kemble family members, area pioneers, and veterans of several wars, beginning with the Civil War. (1988)

REDWATER (Bowie Co.)
US 67 at FM 991
Redwater

The first community in this area was Mooresville (2 mi. E), settled in 1840 by the Charles Moores (1776–1852) family. It had disappeared before this town grew up near the Daniels and Spence sawmill in 1875. Because of mill workers' disregard for religion, the village was first named Ingersoll for the famous agnostic of that day, Robert Green Ingersoll (1833–1899). A branch of the St. Louis Southwestern (Cotton Belt) Railway arrived here in the late 1870s, attracting more upstanding citizens. William Thomas Fagan built two more sawmills in the early 1880s. English-born Earnest Thomas Page (1860–1937) opened a general store, which also housed the town's first post office (1881). Church-going townspeople objected to the name Ingersoll and suggested changing it to Redwater, for the color of spring and well water in the area. A town vote in 1894 made Redwater the official name. In 1914, a tornado destroyed many businesses here, but Redwater quickly rebuilt. The economy was based on farming and lumbering until 1941, when the Red River Army Ammunition Depot and Lone Star Ordnance Plant were built just north of town. The opening of the International Paper Mill in the 1970s has created new interest in lumbering and tree farming. (1975)

REFUGIO (Refugio Co.)   *US 183 at SH 202, 2 mi. N*
Sally Scull
Woman rancher, horse trader, champion "cusser." Ranched NW of here. In Civil War Texas, Sally Scull (or Skull) freight wagons took cotton to Mexico to swap for guns, ammunition, medicines, coffee, shoes, clothing and other goods vital to the Confederacy. Dressed in trousers, Mrs. Scull bossed armed employees; was sure shot with the rifle carried on her saddle or the two pistols strapped to her waist. Of good family, she had children cared for in New Orleans school. Often visited them. Loved dancing. Yet during the war, did extremely hazardous "man's work."
(1964)

REFUGIO (Refugio Co.)   *Commerce St. at E. Empresario St., 1 blk. E of US 77*
Refugio County
Organized in 1835 into the Mexican municipality of Refugio. Created a county of the same name March 17, 1836, organized 1837. Named for the Mission "Our Lady of Refuge" established in 1791 to civilize and Christianize the Indians. Refugio, the county seat.
(1936)

REFUGIO (Refugio Co.)   *US 77, .5 mi. S*
The Urrea Oaks
By tradition, camping place in March 1836, during Texas War for Independence, of Gen. José Urrea of Mexico. Strategically located, this was Urrea's staging area. Capt. Amon B. King came from Goliad with his Texas Volunteers to support the Refugio townsmen, who were taken into the safety of Mission Nuestra Señora del Refugio. Then Lt. Col. William Ward also arrived on March 13, and the "Battle of Refugio" began. Both King and Ward left protection of the mission, and Urrea won final victories over them, capturing King's command on March 15 and Ward's on March 22.
(1973)

RHOME (Wise Co.)   *US 287/81 bypass at SH 114*
First National Bank in Rhome
Prominent area businessman Dan Waggoner began this financial institution in 1904 as a branch of his privately-owned bank in Decatur (15 mi. NW). His son, W. T., served for a time as its president. Rhome's first bank was given a national charter in 1914 and grew steadily through the years. Its sound financial policies enabled it to survive the period of the Great Depression. Headquartered downtown for more than seventy years, the First National Bank in Rhome has been located at this site since 1975.
(1984)

RICHLAND SPRINGS (San Saba Co.)   *US 190 at FM 45*
John Duncan's Fort
A private, or settler's fort, built 1858. Cabins of 4 families (30 people) formed a stockade for defense against Indians. Daily a hunting party would go out for meat; other men stood guard. Residents went home to farm in spring, but through 1865 "forted up each fall."
(1968)

RICHMOND (Fort Bend Co.)   *US 90A, E in roadside park*
Mirabeau Buonaparte Lamar,
President of the Republic of Texas
Born 1798 in Georgia. Came to Texas 1835. Became involved immediately in movement for independence from Mexico. Upon fall of the Alamo and news of Goliad massacre, joined Texas Army as a private, as Houston moved eastward toward San Jacinto. In swiftly moving chain of events, Lamar was made a colonel on eve of Battle of San Jacinto. There he commanded cavalry with distinction and ten days later was named Secretary of War in the interim government. Elected vice-president in new nation's first government, was candidate of the Anti-Sam Houston faction for president in next election. He won, and took office in 1838 for 3-year term. During his administration, the Republic of Texas was recognized by Great Britain and France. He was known for his forceful Indian policy and for his opposition to annexation. He laid the foundation for first system of public education in Texas. By his decision, Austin was made capital of Texas. A poet and diplomat, he projected the writing of a history of Texas, but died in 1859, before book was well begun. His plantation was near Richmond. He is buried near here, in the Morton Cemetery.
(1965)

RICHMOND (Fort Bend Co.)   *US 90A, W bank of Brazos River, S Bridge*
Site of Fort Bend
Built in November, 1821 by William Little, William Smithers, Charles Beard, Joseph Polly and Henry Holster. Its name was given to the county when created in 1837.   (1965)

RICHMOND (Fort Bend Co.)   *200 block of 4th St.*
Jane Long Boarding House
Born in Maryland in 1798, Jane H. Wilkinson moved to Mississippi (1811) and became the ward of her famous relative, Gen. James Wilkinson, Field Commander of the United States Army. Jane married Dr. James Long in 1815 and later followed him on a filibustering expedition to free Texas from Spain. In 1821, Long led his forces into battle, leaving Jane alone with their daughter Ann and slave girl Kian at Point Bolivar, near Galveston. On Dec. 21, 1821, with snow falling, their food supply gone, and Kian ill, Jane gave birth to a daughter, then rose and got food and firewood for her family. Her heroism earned her the name "Mother of Texas." Later she learned of her husband's death in Mexico. During the period Texas was a colony and a republic, Jane Long operated two well-known boarding houses. She started the first in Brazoria in 1832; her guests included William B. Travis, Sam Houston, and Mirabeau B. Lamar. In 1837, Jane moved to Richmond and on this site opened another boarding house which became a center for social and political activities as well as lodging for prominent Texans and European visitors. Jane ran this hotel until her plantation near town became prosperous in the 1840s. She died in 1880 and is buried in Richmond's Morton Cemetery.   (1975)

RICHMOND (Fort Bend Co.)   *6th at Houston St.*
Erastus ("Deaf") Smith (April 17, 1787–November 30, 1837)
Most famous scout in Texas War for Independence. Obeyed Gen. Sam Houston's strategic order, then raised San Jacinto battle cry: "Fight for your lives! Vince's Bridge has been cut down." A native of New York, Smith settled here in 1821 in San Antonio. Trading in land and goods, he traveled Texas province, making him an invaluable guide for the army during the War for Independence. He married Guadalupe Ruiz Duran, and they had three daughters. Dying here in the home of Randall Jones (a friend), he was buried in Calvary Churchyard, Houston at 6th. His grave is now unidentified. (1973)

RICHMOND (Fort Bend Co.)   *US 90A, 1.5 mi. W in roadside park*
Dismounted Texas Cavalry
The 95,000 men of military age in Civil War Texas, unaccustomed to walking, preferred the daring and mobility of the cavalry used to scout the enemy, screen troop movements and make lightning attacks. 58,533 Texans joined it, riding their own horses or ones donated by citizens' groups. Many of Texas' 325,000 horses were sent to other states. Yet footsoldiers were needed, too. The state set up camps of instruction, to teach Texans to walk and fight. By mid-1862 the need for infantry was so great that the following units were unhorsed under strong protest: 6th Texas Cavalry Battalion, 13th, 16th, 18th, 22nd, 24th, 25th and 28th Texas Cavalry Regiments. On Aug. 15, 1863, a part of A. W. Terrell's Cavalry Regiment at Richmond was ordered to dismount and march to the defense of Galveston. On Sept. 11, an order to dismount still more men caused mutiny, and 91 rode their prized horses north to homes on the Indian frontier or to join other cavalry units. When 25 were tried later, only the officers were punished. Enlisted men returned to the regiment, and fought in such actions as the 1864 Red River Campaign to prevent a Federal invasion of Texas.

RIESEL (McLennan Co.)   *SH 6, in Riesel*
Riesel
Fertile soil, good water, and available rail transportation attracted cotton farmers to this area after the Civil War. They were soon joined by German settlers from Washington County led by the Rev. Friedrick Von Schleumbach. A nearby postal station known as Roddy first served the area, but a town developed here following construction of a cotton gin by William Henry Riesel in 1890. The townsite of Riesel was platted by the Rev. Von Schleumbach and the new settlement grew as an early agricultural center of southeastern McLennan County.   (1986)

RINGGOLD (Montague Co.)   *US 82, 1 mi. W*
Early Trails in Montague County
Lying on a direct line of travel from the United States to Mexico, California, and points west, the area now Montague County was once a network of trails. One of the first area roads forged by

white men was the Chihuahua Traders' Trail of 1840. Blazed by merchants hoping to open a trade route from Mexico to St. Louis, Mo., this road crossed present Montague County and left tracks for later travelers. In 1841 came the Texan-Santa Fe Expedition; though it failed to open regular commerce between the Republic of Texas and Northern Mexico, this delegation also left a road and enforced the claims of Texas to western territories. In 1849 U.S. Army Capt. Randolph B. Marcy charted a "California Trail," using parts of older routes. This soon grew into a thoroughfare for forty-niners and sturdy pioneers who came later. In 1858 the famous Butterfield Overland Mail Line came across the county; and in the 1870s, as Texas was building her image as a cattle empire, Montague County was crossed by two feeder branches of the Chisholm Trail. In 1882, the county's first railroad followed much of the Texan-Santa Fe Trail. Today Highway 82 partly traces Marcy's route and other roads parallel many of these early trails. (1969)

RINGGOLD (Montague Co.)
US 81, 5 mi. S in roadside park
Highways Paved with Gold
From time immemorial man has searched for a land where streets were paved with gold. As early as the 16th century he was in Texas, lured by Indian reports of "seven cities of gold." They never were found. But they provided the basis for legends of untold riches—stories still spun by some Texans. Surprisingly, perhaps, many of the "tall tales" are more fact than fiction. For instance, both this section of U.S. Highway 81 and a portion of adjacent U.S. Highway 287 are actually paved with gold! The story began in 1936 when the Texas Highway Department was paving the two highways here in Montague County. Sand for the concrete was taken from a nearby pit, opened three years earlier. The grains glistened with such intensity as they were mixed that a closer examination seemed prudent. So a small supply was sent to a Fort Worth laboratory for assay. Back came the report: the sand contained gold. The news sent the owner of the pit in feverish search of the mother lode. But in vain. Top assays on his extensive "soundings" came to no more than 54 cents per ton of ore. His ardor was cooled further when he learned the gold was not free but deeply imbedded in the sand. Disheartened, he settled back into routine sand production. From his pit, however, eventually came $250,000 in gold—all part of the sand. It has been reckoned that as much as $31,000 is distributed along 39 miles of roadway, some $25,000 in U.S. Highway 81 and $6,000 in U.S. Highway 287. The remainder has gone into other construction in the region, including numerous buildings in which concrete has been used. So it is that today's motorist has discovered the highways paved with gold and the "golden" cities which his predecessors sought in vain. (1963)

RIO GRANDE CITY (Starr Co.)
Ringgold Ave. at Fort Ringgold,
just N of US 83
Fort Ringgold
Established October 26, 1848, at Davis Landing by Capt. J. H. LaMotte, 1st U.S. Infantry, as Ringgold Barracks. Named in honor of Brevet Major David Ringgold, 4th U.S. Artillery, who died of wounds received at Palo Alto, May 8, 1846. Troops were withdrawn March 3, 1859. Reoccupied December 29, 1859. Abandoned in 1861. Reoccupied by U.S. troops in June 1865. General Robert E. Lee passed a few days here in 1856 and in 1860. (1936)

RIO GRANDE CITY (Starr Co.)
2nd St. (US 83) at West St.,
Old Cemetery Park
Site of Cortina Battle, Dec. 27, 1859
Crushing defeat for partisan leader Juan Cortina who in late 1859 laid waste the Lower Rio Grande Valley. Cortina's band of 450 were surprised here at daybreak by Maj. S. B. Heintzelman with U.S. Army troops, joined by Texas Rangers recruited by John S. ("Rip") Ford. Cortina fled to Mexico by horseback. Many of his men jumped into the Rio Grande. Regarrisoning of Ringgold barracks ended partisan raids for a time. But with the American Civil War (1861–1865) and Cortina's rise to power in Tamaulipas, raids were renewed—until Cortina was removed, 1875. (1970)

RIO GRANDE CITY (Starr Co.)
US 83, 2.5 mi. W
Site of the Mission San Agustin de Laredo a Vista
Established in 1749 as a part of Jose de Escandon's project to settle the region and civilize and Christianize the Indians.

RIO VISTA (Johnson Co.)
*SH 174, S of intersection with
N. Cleburne Whitney Rd.*

Henry Briden Cabin

Henry Briden (1825–1908) came to Texas from his native Germany in 1845 and served for two years as a Texas Ranger. In 1849, he and his wife, Lucinda Sevier (1831–75), became first permanent white settlers in what is now Johnson County, when they built this cabin on the east bank of Nolan's River (2.5 mi. northwest). The one-room log structure was later used as a barn when Briden erected a larger home nearby. In 1974, it was restored and moved to this site.   (1975)

RIO VISTA (Johnson Co.)
*SH 174, S of intersection with
N. Cleburne Whitney Rd.*

Early Cattle Trade

Famed for its beef since era of the Republic, Texas fed a great part of the Confederacy—both civilians and army—in the Civil War years, 1861–1865. Routes for beef supplying were many: Shreveport Trail to Vicksburg, Miss.; Alexandria Trail to Natchez, Miss.; Opelousas Trail to Woodville, Miss., and on to Mobile, Ala.; Old Government Road to Little Rock, Ark.; Oliver Loving's 1859 Trail North, to Indian Territory; trails to all army depots and even to Mexico. Cowboys had to swim cattle across rivers—even the Mississippi. After undergoing such hardships, one outfit was mistakenly arrested by Confederates. Lt. Col. J. F. Scurlock and son, from Johnson County, on a Texas beef drive into Southern Louisiana, were arrested by Federals and died in prison, of fever. Meredith Hart (1811–1864), a leading beef supplier, came to Johnson County in 1855, after fighting for the Texas Republic in 1836. In the 1850s, he sold beef to the U.S. Army. During the Civil War, he was one of the ranchers victimized by beef contractors using counterfeit money, but accepted losses in the faith that beef was feeding his sons and others on Confederate fighting fronts. Hart's home was 1½ miles west of Rio Vista.   (1965)

RISING STAR (Eastland Co.)
SH 36 at city park

Rising Star

First settlers—families of Andrew Agnew, Isaac Agnew, Fletcher Fields, David McKinley, Allis Smith, and W. W. Smith—arrived in a wagon train from Gregg County, Jan. 6, 1876. Area was known for hardships: Indian raids, vigilante activities, gunfights. But a stable community developed around log school-church building erected in 1876. First store was founded about 1879 by Thomas W. Anderson and son William. Post office established 1880. The most credible story as to how the town got its name is that the settlers suggested the name Star for the post office but it was rejected by the U.S. postal authorities as another Texas town had that name. The settlers argued all night over the name selection, looked up and saw the morning star as they started home from their meeting and agreed to call it Rising Star. The city was first incorporated in 1891. In a 1905 election, there was a vote to dissolve the corporation but the charter was restored later the same year. Rising Star is the home of Texas (1939–1941) poet laureate Lexie Dean Robertson. Unique local structure is city hall built of stone from buried petrified forest. Economy is based on ranching, farming (a chief crop is Spanish peanuts), commercial pecans, industry, oil.   (1968)

RIVERSIDE (Walker Co.)
FM 980, .5 mi. E near SH 19

Town of Riverside

Founded 1872 when Houston & Great Northern Railroad (later, International & Great Northern) was being built into the area. Walker County landowners gave earth, timber, and rock to the road in order to gain shipping facilities. Post office was moved here Feb. 23, 1872, from Newport (6 mi. SE), where wharves were idle when Trinity River was low. Riverside developed churches, a 4-teacher school, and two blocks of businesses, including stores, blacksmith shop, livery stable, saloon, barber shop, 2-story hotel, cotton gin. In the 1920s, Fuller's Earth Refining Plants were built.   (1972)

RIVIERA (Kleberg Co.)
US 77, 4 mi. N at roadside park

1766 Exploration of Diego Ortiz Parrilla

First expedition to give detailed descriptions of Texas' offshore islands and to refer to Corpus Christi bay by its present name. The exploration was ordered by the viceroy of New Spain in the midst of rumors that the English planned to encroach on Spanish territory. Parrilla, who had fought the Moors for Spain before holding positions of civil and military leadership in the New World, was ordered to expel any intruders. He began his trek at San Juan Bautista on the Rio Grande, September 13, 1766. At Corpus Christi Bay a detachment marched south to explore the coastal islands. Their report of uniformly bleak, treeless, waterless dunes (including this area) cast doubt on the feasibility of enemy occupation. At this point, torrential rains and floods impeded the party's progress. At La Bahia (present Matagorda Bay) Parrilla was luckily able to interview some of the soldiers serving along the coast and thus he obtained knowledge of the geography of the area and its Indians as far north as Trinity Bay. After several months Parrilla returned, having helped disprove rumors of the English intrusion and bearing vital information on the Texas Gulf Coast.   (1970)

RIVIERA (Kleberg Co.)
US 77, 4 mi. N at roadside park
Approximate Route of U.S. Army March to Rio Grande, 1846
Battle Road of General Zachary Taylor and largest U.S. Army fielded in first half of the 19th century. After annexation of former Republic of Texas was approved in 1845, the United States sent Taylor to occupy area below the Nueces—to support claim to all land east of the Rio Grande. In August, 1845, he reached Corpus Christi where he waited while U.S. and Mexico tried to reach boundary agreement. He also sent out engineers to map a road parallel to the gulf, where the U.S. Navy watched the crisis. His army—including on its rosters two later U.S. presidents and many later statesmen and generals—drilled throughout a rainy winter. On orders from Washington, it moved toward Rio Grande in March, 1846. Along its path were few people but much game—wild cattle, antelope, deer, mustang horses, wild turkeys. Although challenged about 70 miles south of here by a Mexican patrol, Taylor proceeded to occupy Rio Grande Valley. April attacks and May battles of Palo Alto and Resaca de la Palma caused the United States to declare war. Afterward many troops took this road and joined the fighting, which fixed the Rio Grande as boundary and gained for U.S. lands now in Arizona, California, Nevada and New Mexico.   (1968)

RIVIERA (Kleberg Co.)
US 77 at FM 771
Federal Raid from Camp Boveda, 1863
On Dec. 23, 1863, Capt. Jas. Speed of Gen. Napoleon J. T. Dana's Brownsville-based Federal Army force raided unguarded King Ranch. Objectives were to capture or kill Capt. Richard King and destroy the Confederate cotton trade. King, forewarned, evaded the enemy. At King Ranch, the raiders killed Francisco Alvarado; captured C. S. A. captains John Brown, Alvin Dix, W. S. Gregory and Jas. McClearly and Chaplain Hiram Chamberlain; rifled all buildings; dispersed ranch employees; declared the slaves free; confiscated all horses and mules; impounded Confederate government cotton, promising that if it were moved or burned, King's life would be the forfeit; and threatened further raids from Boveda by Col. E. J. Davis, former South Texas attorney turned Federal officer. Mrs. King and children moved to San Antonio for the war's duration; soon Col. J. S. "Rip" Ford's Confederate Cavalry came to protect the cotton road and ranch. At Camp (Rancho) Boveda, near a ford on Los Olmos Creek, were seven cypress-walled water wells, possibly used by Gen. Zachary Taylor in 1846. Campsite 2½ miles east of this point, on lot 2, block 15, Koch Subdivision Number One, present Poteet Ranch.   (1965)

RIVIERA (Kleberg Co.)
US 77 at FM 771
8 mi. E to Indian Burial Ground (Dietz Archeological Site)
Centuries old, this burial ground was once used by the primitive Karankawa Indians. A little-known group, this coastal tribe cared for Spanish Explorer Cabeza De Vaca when he was ship-wrecked in Texas in 1528. Although previously looted, the site produced over 20 skeletons when excavated by archeologists in 1927 and later. Also found were large quantities of burned human bones (suggesting ritual cannibalism), potsherds, arrowpoints, flint tools, fire implements, and shells. European explorers found the Karankawas unusually tall and muscular, but were repelled by their habits of tattooing and painting their bodies and smearing themselves with alligator grease to keep off insects. Much ritual attended Karankawa death, especially that of boys and young men, who were mourned for an entire year. Three times a day the family wept for the departed youth. After a year, the mourners purified themselves with smoke in a special rite. Ordinary persons were buried in shallow graves with some tools and ornaments, but Shamans (medicine men) were cremated during a ceremonial dance. Never very numerous, the Karankawas drifted into Mexico after the white man's diseases and enmity reduced them to a handful of survivors.   (1970)

ROARING SPRINGS (Motley Co.)

Broadway St. at depot

Roaring Springs Depot

Under the leadership of Samuel Lazarus (1855–1926), the Quanah, Acme & Pacific Railroad contributed much to Motley County's economic development. One of the townsites along the line, Roaring Springs was platted in 1912, one year before the tracks reached this point. This brick mission revival style depot was completed within a year, and handled passenger and freight traffic until 1971. Roaring Springs' oldest structure, it was purchased by the city in 1972. (1977)

ROBERT LEE (Coke Co.)

SH 208, 13 mi. NW

Panther Gap

Landmark on ancient Indian trail, and early route of travelers and military west of Fort Chadbourne (20 miles east) before the Civil War. After 1880, was used extensively to connect this area with the railroad at Colorado City. Named for panthers (cougars), which still roam the region. (1973)

ROBERT LEE (Coke Co.)

SH 158, 5.75 mi. NE

Southern Overland Mail, 1858–1861 (Butterfield Stage)

Passed near this site, providing for the first time combined passenger and mail service between Pacific and Atlantic coasts. Operating west from St. Louis and Memphis, John Butterfield's company used 1350 horses and mules and 90 Concord coaches and wagons. Stage traveled at a run, despite lack of good roads. A signal given approaching a station would have fresh horses ready and food on the table for crew and passengers. Route had stations 12 to 13 miles apart, and was sometimes changed to get water. Crew and passengers wore guns; to reduce danger of Indian attacks, mules (less coveted than horses) were used west of Ft. Belknap. The trip one way took 25 days—seven spent crossing Texas, from Preston (now under Lake Texoma) to Jacksboro, Ft. Belknap, Ft. Chadbourne and El Paso. One way fare for the 2700 miles was $200. Passengers rarely stopped off, because they might not find seats on a later stage. Merchants in Jacksboro and other towns used Butterfield's light freight service to make mail-order sales. Greatest contribution of the Overland stage was its carrying news; coaches also brought mail from the west one to 10 days faster than it came by ship. Service was ended in 1861 by the Civil War. (1966)

ROBERT LEE (Coke Co.)

SH 158, 1 mi. NE in roadside park

Coke County

Formed from Tom Green County. Created March 13, 1889. Organized April 23, 1889. Named in honor of Richard Coke, 1829–1896. Governor of Texas 1874–1876. Member of United States Senate 1878–1896. County seat, Hayrick, 1889; Robert Lee, since 1890. (1964)

ROBERT LEE (Coke Co.)

E. 7th Ave. (Spur 229) at Austin St.

Fence-Cutting War

This area was a center of hostilities during 1880's conflict between landless cattlemen trying to keep use of free grass and open range and those erecting barbed wire fences to create permanent ranches. On L. B. Harris Ranch (3 miles west of here) posts and wire worth $6,000 were burned by anti-fence group during crisis. War was brought on by severe drought in 1880's when men without land found best waterholes fenced in. Many ranchmen owned or leased land they fenced, but some overambitious ones enclosed public lands, farms, and small ranches belonging to homesteaders recently arrived in Texas. Widespread resentment prevailed against these fencers, who, by blocking a road, had little regard for convenience of travelers. When drought pushed landless cowmen to brink of financial ruin, violence was inevitable. They blamed barbed wire fences for their predicament. At first, cutting of fences that blocked roads or waterholes occurred, but soon all fences were threatened. Armed "Nippers" cut fences in almost every Texas county. Fence cutters were then viewed as outlaws rather than crusaders. When laws were passed in Gov. John Ireland's administration to stop the war, Texas had suffered much damage to its property and reputation. (1967)

ROBERT LEE (Coke Co.)

SH 208, .5 mi. SE

Robert Lee Cemetery

Established in 1891, two years after the founding of the city of Robert Lee. Developers L. B. Harris and Eugene Cartledge, as president and secretary of the Austin & Northern Land & Cattle Company, on Sept. 29, 1892, sold for $1.00 this 11.7-acre burial ground. Already site of several graves, it was deeded to Hayrick Lodge No. 696, A. F. & A. M., for "sole use as cemetery grounds for the members, relatives, and friends." Later it was named by the lodge. Buried here are 34 civil war veterans, as well as soldiers of later wars and members of many of the families in Robert Lee.

(1973)

ROBERT LEE (Coke Co.)
SH 158, 9 mi. SW
Edith, Original Site 1 mi. N
Settled by cattlemen who ran herds on open range, and stock-farming homesteaders. Development began in early 1880s after Winfield Scott, rancher, fenced his spread. Area had three schools, lodge hall, tabernacle, general store, cotton gin and blacksmith shop. The post office, established in 1890, was named for Edith Bonsall, an admired young lady of Ballinger. It closed in 1955. Dwindling schools combined, then consolidated with those of nearby Robert Lee. As trend toward urban living increased, Edith declined.

(1969)

ROBSTOWN (Nueces Co.)
SH 44 & South Violet Rd., 4 mi. E
Old Saint Anthony's Catholic Church
In Nov. 1909, the Rev. J. Goebels called a meeting to organize St. Anthony's parish for the recently settled German Catholic farm families in the community of Land Siding, later known as Violet. Louis Petrus donated five acres for a church site, and five additional acres were purchased. The parishioners began construction of the building in 1910, with John W. Hoelscher (1866–1941), one of the earliest settlers here, as foreman of the project. Originally measuring 26 ft. by 40 ft., the frame structure served as a schoolhouse and church. The congregation enlarged and extensively remodeled the building in 1919. Three towers were added at that time. A bell, purchased earlier from Spohn Sanitarium in Corpus Christi, was installed in one. The rectory, which served as a schoolhouse and living quarters for visiting priests, was attached to the church building in 1920. Members then fenced and landscaped the area. In 1952, the parish built a larger church, and this structure was moved to the parish mission of Our Lady of Mount Carmel in nearby Clarkwood community. In 1975, after that congregation erected a new church facility, the old St. Anthony's building was relocated 200 ft. east of its original site and restored as a museum by the Violet Historical Society.

(1978)

ROBSTOWN (Nueces Co.)
US 77, 3 mi. S
Martha (Reagan) Rabb (February 25, 1826–March 20, 1901)
Martha Reagan moved with her parents from Tennessee to Fayette County, Texas where she met and married John Rabb (1825–1872). In 1857, John and Martha moved their family to Nueces County and settled near Banquete, where John pursued cattle ranching under the Bow and Arrow brand. Rabb raised far more cattle than his ranch land could support by running his herds on the open range. He became one of the most successful cattlemen in the area, owning more than 10,000 head of cattle when he died in 1872. When Martha assumed control of the business, she took it in a dramatically different direction. Foreseeing the end of the free-range era, she capitalized on the panic and flight caused by violent raids along the Nueces strip and aggressively began to buy land here in 1875. Within a year, she owned more than 43,000 acres, some of which she bought for as little as 37 cents per acre. Enclosed within 40 miles of fence, the Rabb Ranch included this site and stretched from north of Robstown south to Driscoll, and was bordered on the west by the Petronilla and Banquete Creeks and on the east by present-day Callicoate Road (FM 1694). She became known as a "Texas Cattle Queen."

(1992)

ROBY (Fisher Co.)
SH 70 right-of-way, 1 mi. N
Roby Cemetery (½ mi. E)
Settlers began arriving in this area in the late 19th century. The oldest grave marker in the Roby cemetery, that of Mable W. Deming, bears the date 1884, one year prior to the organization of Fisher County and the establishment of the town of Roby. Brothers D. C. and M. L. Roby purchased over 4,000 acres of land in 1885. They had a townsite platted; donated sites for schools, churches, and a park; and designated the land containing Mable Deming's grave as a public cemetery. The original cemetery plot consisted of seven acres, and the brothers stipulated that no fee was to be levied for grave sites in that section. The Roby Cemetery served as the principal burial ground for citizens of Fisher County. In the late 1950s the county deeded the cemetery lands to the city of Roby. In 1975, the Roby Cemetery Association was chartered and accepted the deed to the cemetery property from the city. Later land acquisitions increased the graveyard's size to twenty-one

acres. Those interred in the Roby cemetery include pioneer settlers of Fisher County, veterans of the Civil War, and one former slave, "Aunt" Abbie Alborn, who came to this area from Tennessee in 1886. The graveyard serves as a reminder of the area's early history. (1988)

ROBY (Fisher Co.) *US 180 at SH 70, courthouse*
Fisher County
Site of old Indian trail from Mexico to settlements on Texas frontier. In this region in 1856, Colonel Robert E. Lee, then commanding the famed U.S. Second Cavalry (and later General-in-chief of the Confederate Army), campaigned against the Indians. County formed from Young and Bexar territories. Created 1876. Settled in 1877. Organized 1886. Named for Samuel Rhoads Fisher (1794–1839), a signer of the Texas Declaration of Independence, Secretary of the Navy in the Republic of Texas, 1836. Roby, county seat, named for landowners. (1965)

ROBY (Fisher Co.) *US 180 at SH 70, in park across from courthouse*
Roby
Located on land originally included in a land grant to Texas War for Independence veteran Thomas H. Cosby, the town of Roby was first platted in 1885. The land was purchased by D. C. and M. L. Roby of Mississippi, relatives of Cosby's second wife, Martha. The Robys hired Walton, Hill, and Walton, a Travis County law firm, to represent their interests, and instructed the attorneys to organize a town to be named county seat of Fisher County. On behalf of their clients, the attorneys donated land for churches, schools, a park, and a cemetery. Town lots were also given to settlers who would build homes within ninety days. In an election held in April 1886, Roby was declared the county seat. The first county court was held in a shed behind the V. H. Anderson house, which served as the town's first post office. A frame courthouse was built on the southwest corner of the town square and was replaced over the years by a succession of other structures. Schools, churches, and businesses were established as settlement in the town increased. Retaining its small town atmosphere, Roby remains a center of commerce for Fisher County. (1989)

ROCHELLE (McCulloch Co.) *US 190, N of intersection with FM 1121*
Rochelle Depot
J. F. Crew of Ohio purchased land here in 1902 and later moved to McCulloch County and founded the settlement of Rochelle. When the Fort Worth and Rio Grande Railroad built a line from Brownwood to Brady in 1902–1903, he was successful in having it routed through Rochelle. Later part of the Sante Fe system, the railroad played an important role in the area's early growth and agricultural development. The town's first depot burned and was replaced about 1912 by this frame structure. In 1956, it was moved to this site for use as a community center. (1982)

ROCKDALE (Milam Co.) *US 79, 2.5 mi. E*
La Recluta and La Escuelita
Jose Leal received six leagues of land in this area in 1833. In 1867, coal was discovered, and the railroad reached Rockdale in 1874. Not until 1890 did the first coal mine, owned by Herman Vogel, begin operation. Others opened, and more settlers came looking for work. Many workers came from Mexico, leaving behind a revolution. These immigrants settled on land owned by E.A. Camp. They sharecropped, growing enough for themselves, and worked in the mines. They named their settlement, just north of the International–Great Northern Railroad tracks, La Recluta, or "recruitment." Family names represented here include Ruiz, Flores, Casarez, Zapata, Aldama, Montoya and Lumbreras. The men, like many other industry workers at the time, received their pay in tokens, which were redeemable only for mine commissary purchases and doctor visits. Several men were trapped in an International Mine Company cave-in in 1913. Eight men and one mule awaited rescue for six days; one man did not survive. Yards away from the collapsed mine entrance is La Escuelita, the small schoolhouse built for the children of the community. Classes were taught in English, although most students spoke Spanish at home. As part of the Talbott Ridge School District, the students transferred to Rockdale schools in 1944, when the districts consolidated. In 1946, Rockdale merchants donated benches to La Escuelita building. In 1953, the school was deeded to the St. Joseph's Cemetery Association, the support group for the community's cemetery, where nearly 300 gravestones tell the stories of La Recluta's families, many of whom remain in the area. (2002)

ROCKDALE (Milam Co.)   *FM 908, 8 mi. NW*
Site of the Mission San Francisco Xavier de Los Dolores
Established by Franciscan missionaries in 1746 with the hope of civilizing and Christianizing the Coco, Mayeye, Orcoquiza, Karankawa and other tribes of Indians. The martyrdom of Padre Jose Ganzabal and the circumstances connected therewith caused the departure of the Indians and the Friars and the removal of this mission to the San Marcos River in 1755. Re-established in 1757 on the San Saba River for the conversion of the Lipan Apaches with the new name of Mission Santa Cruz de San Saba.

ROCKDALE (Milam Co.)   *140 W. Cameron Ave. (US 79)*
City of Rockdale
Rockdale began as a railroad town in 1874 along a new line of the International & Great Northern. It grew quickly as a shipping point and soon boasted churches, schools, cotton gins, grist mills, an opera house, a bank and newspaper. The City of Rockdale formally organized in 1875. Work on a city hall began at this site in 1895 on the design of Austin architect A. O. Watson. Completed years later, it provided space for city programs, social gatherings, school functions and political meetings, and housed the volunteer fire department for 80 years. Altered in the 1930s, resulting in the loss of a tall bell tower, the former city hall still serves as a reminder of Rockdale's early development.
(2005)

ROCKNE (Bastrop Co.)   *FM 535 right-of-way, in front of Sacred Heart Church*
Rockne
Rockne began as a small farming community. Phillip Goertz (1825–1900), considered to be the first German Catholic settler of the area, arrived from Germany in 1856 and purchased land along Walnut Creek. He was soon joined by more German Catholic immigrants who established family farms. The first church built by the settlers, Ascension of Christ Church, was erected on Walnut Creek in 1876 but was destroyed by an arsonist's fire in 1891. A new structure was completed in 1892 and named Sacred Heart Church. Rockne has been known by several names. First called Walnut Creek because of its proximity to the stream, it was known as Lehmanville when the Lehman post office was established in 1900, and as Hilbigville after William Hilbig opened a store here. In 1931, the children of Sacred Heart School were given the opportunity to permanently name their town. A vote was taken, with the children electing to name the community Rockne in honor of Knute Rockne, the famous Notre Dame University football player and head coach who had died in a plane crash in 1931. Rockne continues to be a rural community, with Sacred Heart Catholic Church at its center.
(1988)

ROCKPORT (Aransas Co.)   *SH 35, 10 mi. N*
Site of the Town of Lamar
Named for Mirabeau B. Lamar, 1798–1859. President of the Republic of Texas 1838–1841. Established in 1838. Made a port of entry in 1839. Sacked by Union troops Feb. 11, 1864. Survived until 1914 but never flourished.

ROCKPORT (Aransas Co.)   *5800 blk. SH 35N, 8.5 mi. N*
Mills Wharf
Mills Wharf, built by John Howard Mills in 1932, was a renowned center for waterfowl hunting and fishing from the 1930s until it was sold in 1960. It consisted of cottages, a cook house, a guide service office, a store, a tackle shop, and a unique wildlife museum with a famous duck, featured in "Ripley's Believe it or Not," which had an oyster permanently attached to its foot. The new "Hug the Coast" Highway 35 made the wharf accessible, thereby aiding the growth of the tourism industry in the area. In 1946, Herbert and Harry Mills bought the wharf from their parents and expanded the business with a unique seaplane service to drop off customers at remote fishing sites.   (2011)

ROCKPORT (Aransas Co.)   *SH 35, 4 mi. N*
Site of One of the Homes of James Power
Born in Ireland, 1789. Died in Live Oak Point, Texas, 1852. With James Hewetson, he was granted authority January 11, 1828 to settle 200 families in Texas. Served Texas under three flags as empresario, soldier, statesman. Signed the Texas Declaration of Independence. Ever a loyal son of his adopted country, honored and loved by his people.

ROCKPORT (Aransas Co.)
SH 35, .6 mi. N
Aransas County
Created September 18, 1871 from Refugio County. Organized in 1871 with Rockport as the county seat. Named for the river Nuestra Señora de Aranzazu. (1964)

ROCKPORT (Aransas Co.)
317 N. Fulton Beach Rd.
Home of George W. Fulton
Born at Philadelphia, June 8, 1810. Served in the Texan Army in 1836. A pioneer resident of Refugio County. After an engineering career of distinction elsewhere, he returned to Texas and became a cattle baron. Died October 31, 1893. The town of Fulton bears his name. (1964)

ROCKPORT (Aransas Co.)
317 N. Fulton Beach Rd.
Fulton Mansion
Built between 1874 and 1877 by George Ware Fulton (1810–1893) and his wife, Harriet Smith Fulton (1823–1910), this imposing residence was named "Oakhurst." The three-story French Second Empire style home is of plank wall construction, with a shell aggregate concrete basement and characteristic mansard roof. The house featured modern heating, ventilation, and plumbing systems and gas lighting. The Fulton family lived here until 1895.
(Recorded Texas Historic Landmark 1964)

ROCKPORT (Aransas Co.)
E. Orleans St., between N and S lanes of SH 35
Rockport
The town of Rockport was founded by cattlemen J. M. and T. H. Mathis in 1867. Originally a part of Refugio County, it became county seat of newly formed Aransas County in 1871. Shipping and fishing provided the primary economic base of the town in its early years. The railroad arrived in 1888 and with it came a decline in the shipping industry, although shipyards were in operation during World War I and World War II. Rockport has been a popular recreation center over the years, and tourism continues to be important to the local economy. (1988)

ROCKPORT (Aransas Co.)
1800 S. Church St. (SH 70)
Site of Heldenfels Shipyard
Shipping industries flourished on the Rockport waterfront by the 1880s. Heldenfels Shipyard was established here on 12.9 acres in October 1917. Four 281-foot wooden cargo vessels were to be built for military use in World War I; the "Baychester" was launched on July 31, 1919, and the "Zuniga" on September 9, 1919. At the height of construction, over 900 men were employed at the shipyard. The need for ships fell as the war ended. Despite hurricane damage to the shipyard on September 14, 1919, the "Jasper" and the "Manchester" were completed as barges in 1920, ending this vital war contract. (1996)

ROCKSPRINGS (Edwards Co.)
SH 55, 9.5 mi. NW
Mackenzie Trail (Merged at this point into SH 55)
When the U.S. Army built Forts Clark (70 mi. SW) and McKavett (90 mi. NE) this frontier trail connected the posts. After Fort Concho was established in 1867, the trail was extended farther north, to present San Angelo. It was later named for Col. Ranald S. Mackenzie, the commander of Fort Clark, who traveled it in his campaigns against hostile Indians. One of its landmarks was Mackenzie Lake (6.5 mi. N) which furnished water for the troops, for cattle drives up the trail, for settlers and for Texas Rangers on frontier patrols. (1977)

ROCKSPRINGS (Edwards Co.)
US 377 at Paint Rock Springs, 21 mi. NE of Rocksprings
Stopping Place on Ft. Clark–Ft. McKavett Military Road
One of many roads connecting U.S. Cavalry's frontier posts. This route led south to Ft. Clark and north to Ft. McKavett, 1852–1883. This spot, Paint Rock Springs, at head of South Llano River, was a natural midway rest stop, as it had abundant water. Here, too, Maj. John B. Jones' Frontier Battalion assembled in 1877 to begin the famous outlaw roundup, to make this area safe for settlement by ranchers. Besides its army uses, this road was open to immigrants, cattle drovers, pioneer ranchers, mail carriers, and freighters. (1967)

ROCKSPRINGS (Edwards Co.)

US 377, .25 mi. NE at park

The Rock Spring

Known to early Texans as one-inch flow of water out of rocks. Site of a camp for travelers and freighters. Occupants of land around the spring included W. J. Greer, with a sheep camp, 1882; Francis Winans, with a cattle and sheep ranch, 1884; A. O. Burr, farming, about 1885. Cattlemen, including Frank Gray, camped here during roundups. Outlaws in 1880s frequented a hut nearby. Rocksprings post office opened 1891 in townsite platted for a new county seat at center of Edwards County. The rock spring still seeps, in city and county historic park and playground. (1972)

ROCKSPRINGS (Edwards Co.)

SH 55 at US 377/SH 41, .6 mi. E

Rocksprings Cemetery

The town of Rocksprings traces its beginnings to 1889, when J. R. Sweeten dug the first water well in the area to serve new settlers. Three years later, in 1892, Sweeten donated two acres of land to be used as a community cemetery. There were some burials at this site prior to its formal designation as a cemetery. Two children, Willie J. Blackwell and Ben Smith, were interred here in 1891. Many of the people buried in the Rocksprings Cemetery in the early years were travelers passing through the area. Among the more than one thousand graves are those of victims of a devastating tornado which struck the town on April 12, 1927. Over the years, additional land acquisitions have increased the size of the cemetery. Iron fencing which once surrounded some grave sites was donated to scrap metal drives during World War II. The Rocksprings Cemetery Association, which originated in 1897, was formally chartered by the state in 1967. Through such projects as surveys and landscaping, the association continues to maintain the historic graveyard, which remains as a visible link to the community's past. (1989)

ROCKWALL (Rockwall Co.)

Goliad St. (SH 205) at West Rusk St., courthouse

Rockwall County

First settled in the 1840s, this region was a part of Kaufman County until 1873, when Rockwall County was created. With an area of 147 square miles, this is the smallest of Texas' 254 counties. The county and city of Rockwall were named for an underground formation of rock discovered in the early 1850s. Crossed by the Missouri, Kansas & Texas Railroad, Rockwall County is an area of fertile farmland. The location here of the aluminum industry and the creation of Lake Ray Hubbard from the east fork of the Trinity River diversified the local economy in recent years. (1976)

ROCKWALL (Rockwall Co.)

104 S. Goliad St. (SH 66)

East Trinity Lodge No. 157, A.F. & A.M.

A dispensation for the formation of the lodge was granted July 26, 1854, when Rockwall was part of Kaufman County. The Grand Lodge of Texas designated James Wilson as the first Master. John O. Heath served as Senior Warden and S. R. Barnes as Junior Warden. Barnes and Heath were among the earliest residents of the area to receive land grants in 1848. The lodge charter was issued January 18, 1855. The E. C. Heath Masonic Lodge, located six miles south, merged with East Trinity in 1968. (1980)

ROCKWALL (Rockwall Co.)

IH 30 at Ridge Rd. (FM 740)

Central National Road of the Republic of Texas

In an effort to improve overland transportation, the Republic of Texas Congress authorized the Central National Road in Feb. 1844. The roadway was to be 30 feet wide and cleared of stumps over 12 inches high. A survey team led by Major George W. Stell platted the route from near the mouth of Elm Fork on the Trinity River in present downtown Dallas, northeast to Kiomatia on the Red River. The highway linked a road leading south to Austin and San Antonio with a U.S. military highway extending north to St. Louis from Fort Towson in present Oklahoma. Running east from Dallas, the Central National Road turned northeast to cross the area that is now Rockwall County. Portions of FM 740, known locally as Ridge Road, follow the historic route. The earliest Rockwall County pioneers settled near the road about 1846. Sterling R. Barnes located his homestead about two miles south of the present site of Rockwall, and John O. Heath settled near the crossing of the east fork of the Trinity River. The towns of Heath, originally named "Black Hill" and later "Willow Springs," and Rockwall, the county seat, were founded along the highway. (1977)

ROCKWALL (Rockwall Co.)   *SH 205, 8 mi. SE in McLendon-Chisholm Community*
Chisholm Cemetery
Enoch P. Chisholm, a circuit-riding Methodist minister, brought his family to this area in the 1860s. The community which grew up here was named in his honor. Chisholm donated land for this graveyard in 1871, and in 1875 he became the first person interred in it. A chapel, also named for Chisholm, was built that same year on the cemetery grounds. At its peak, the town of Chisholm boasted a school, post office, Masonic lodge, cotton gin, and stores. Many early pioneers were interred in the Chisholm cemetery, and some of their descendants still reside in the area.   (1990)

ROMA (Starr Co.)   *US 83, 1 mi. W*
The Mier Expedition
A body of Texans intent on invading Mexico camped here on December 21, 1842. After being made prisoners at Salado, Mexico, they drew beans, white for life in prison, black for death. 17 members of the expedition were shot by order of General Santa Anna, March 25, 1843.

ROMA (Starr Co.)   *US 83, 3.5 mi. NW*
Mission Mier A Vista
In the vicinity of this site was Mission Mier A Vista. Established in 1750 as a part of Jose de Escandon's project to settle the region and civilize and Christianize the Indians.

ROMERO (Hartley Co.)   *US 54, 3.5 mi. NE at roadside park*
Chief of the Pastores, Casimiro Romero (1833–1912)
Moved to Texas, 1876, from New Mexico—wife and two children in a coach, goods in 14 wagons. Owned 6,000 sheep. A Castilian Spaniard by birth, Romero spoke for Pastores (sheep herders), who built eleven haciendas and plazas in Canadian River area. Cattle Rancher Chas. Goodnight in late 1876 made a pact with Romero to respect right of the Pastores to valley of Canadian River. But railroads and cattle ranchers in 1800s cut into sheep lands. Romero returned to New Mexico, selling Texas lands, 1897. He is memorialized in this area by town of Romero (3.5 mi SW of here).   (1970)

ROPESVILLE (Hockley Co.)   *US 82, .5 mi. S*
Site of Primrose School (About .5 mi. SW)
First public school in Hockley County; named for a wild prairie flower. In 1902 homesteaders had begun farming here. By 1909 their children needed education, so the parents hauled lumber by wagon from Big Spring (about 100 mi. S), donated labor, and built a one-room schoolhouse. Classes began Dec. 13, 1909, with pupils from the Ardis, Baker, Blankenship, Brown, Carter, Cowan, Dixon, Perritt, Rose, and Witherspoon families. The schoolhouse served as polling place, church, and public meeting hall until 1917, when Ropesville was established about a mile away, with better facilities.   (1974)

ROSENBERG (Fort Bend Co.)   *1117 First Street (SH 36)*
First Baptist Church of Rosenberg
In 1896, three Baptist men organized this church. T.E. Muse served as the first pastor from 1898 to 1900. The 1900 Galveston hurricane destroyed an unfinished church building. Services were held in a nearby church and in a rail car until a schoolhouse was purchased in 1901. In 1912, a brick sanctuary was built, with the first electric lights in town. Some baptism services were held in the Brazos River until the 1930s. New facilities were added over the years as the congregation grew. The church continues to serve the Rosenberg community.   (1996)

ROTAN (Fisher Co.)   *SH 92 at CR 251, 15.1 miles E*
Site of Hitson Community
Ranchers John and William Hittson were among the first to settle in this area in about 1870; the area around their homes became known as Hittson or Hitson. Fisher County was created in 1876, and settlement began to increase. A post office opened in 1885. A school began operation in 1888 and by 1896 Hitson had a general store operated by C. W. Morris as well as a Methodist church. The Hittson brothers were the major landowners in the area, but the community included a number of large farming families who cleared the fertile land and planted crops. Though the post office was moved to Swedonia in 1906, the community of Hitson continued to grow. Oil was discovered in the

area after World War I, providing an additional means of income for the townspeople as well as the Hitson School for a time. In 1925 there were 32 families with 120 school-age children living in the area. By 1940 the town had a school, a church, three businesses and scattered dwellings. As was the case in many small towns across Texas and the U.S. during World War II, most of the town's young people enlisted in the armed forces or moved to cities to take part in the war effort. With their labor force thus depleted, Hitson farmers were unable to survive. Small family farms were sold to larger enterprises. Most of the new owners lived in nearby Hamlin or Rotan. Hitson School was consolidated with Hamlin schools in 1947; the white frame church building used by the Hitson Baptist Church was moved to Roby in 1959 and by the end of the 20th century all that remained of the community were a few homes and a cemetery. (2000)

ROUND ROCK (Williamson Co.)   *N. Mays St. at US 79*
In Memory of the Pioneer Builders
Greenwood Masonic Institute, 1867–1881, one quarter mile west and Round Rock Institute, one half mile south, 1881–1891, under auspices Cumberland Presbyterian Church, 1881–1887 and the Southern Presbyterian Church 1887–1891, "Built for the people by the people" of Round Rock and vicinity. Erected by the State of Texas. (1936)

ROUND ROCK (Williamson Co.)   *Palm Valley Blvd. (US 79),*
.5 mi. W of Harrell Pkwy.
½ mi. S to the Site of Kenney Fort
First settlement in Williamson County. Erected as a home by Dr. Thomas Kenney and Joseph Barnhart in the spring of 1839 & served as a place of defense during Indian raids and rendezvous of the Santa Fe Expedition, 1841. Here the archives of the Republic of Texas enroute to Washington-on-the-Brazos were captured on Dec. 31, 1842 and returned to Austin. (1936)

ROUND ROCK (Williamson Co.)   *2500 Palm Valley Blvd. (US 79)*
Palm Valley Lutheran Church
In area first claimed in 1838 by white men. Valley bears name of the Anna Palm family, 1853 Swedish settlers. "Brushy," the first Lutheran Church (of logs), was built here by Andrew John Nelson and 3 hired men in 1861. This also housed early school. Congregation was formally organized Nov. 27, 1870. Second church, built 1872, was used for sessions of Palm Valley School. Present gothic revival style building was erected in 1894. (1970)

ROUND ROCK (Williamson Co.)   *Palm Valley Blvd. (US 79)*
The Double File Trail
As the Delaware Indians moved from their home in the "Redlands" of East Texas in 1828 to near present Nuevo Laredo, Mexico, they laid out this trace. It was named Double File Trail because two horsemen could ride side by side. The first settlement in Williamson County, Kenney Fort, was built here at the Brushy Creek crossing in 1838. It served as a way station and for Indian protection. In 1841, members of the Santa Fe Expedition assembled here. Texas Rangers, early Anglo-American settlers, surveying parties, and explorers also used this important route. (1979)

ROUND ROCK (Williamson Co.)   *W. Main St. at Round Rock Ave.*
Sam Bass' Death Site
An uneducated Indiana orphan who drifted to Texas as a youth, Sam Bass won fame racing his swift "Denton Mare," gambling, and robbing trains. A rich haul in Nebraska was followed by months of reckless spending. Bass liked to shower gold on people who fed or harbored him while he eluded law officers. In July 1878 he came to Round Rock to rob a bank, and was shot by Texas Rangers. Gallant to the last, refusing to name guilty partners, he became a hero to 19th century balladeers. His celebrated grave is situated in Old Round Rock Cemetery. (1981)

ROUND ROCK (Williamson Co.)   *RR 1431 near Brushy Creek, 6 mi. W*
Wilson-Leonard Brushy Creek Burial Site
In this vicinity is a prehistoric archeological site discovered in 1973 by a team of Texas Highway Department archeologists. Scientific excavations have produced evidence that the site was a major camping ground for prehistoric peoples, particularly during the Archaic Period (2,000–8,000 years ago). More than 150 fireplaces, numerous projectile Plainview points, and several types of spear

points have been uncovered. In 1982, archeologists discovered the skeleton of a human female, 10,000 to 13,000 years old, that became known as the "Leanderthal Lady." (1985)

ROUND TOP (Fayette Co.)

SH 237 at FM 1437

Early Texas Hotels and Inns

Two miles east, at Winedale, is the old "Sam Lewis Stopping Place" of the 1850s—a typical early Texas inn, now a University of Texas research center. Built 1834, as a settler's 2-room log cabin of hand-hewn cedar; then enlarged twice and (with work of local German craftsmen) improved in style, it was home after 1848 to Lewis, his wife, eight children; also entertained guests from passing stagecoaches. It was near roads connecting major Texas cities. Many roadside homes in early Texas were inns. The horseback traveler would shelter his pony in the barn, share family meals, get a room for the night. All stage lines depended on such accommodations—for changes of horses, for passengers' meals, and for overnight stops. With travel difficult at best, such inns rendered a service of great public necessity. A frontier inn might even be a dugout, where the guests rolled up in blankets and slept on the floor. (Travelers sometimes had to sleep under a tree, so any sort of sheltering house was usually welcomed.) Most stage stops dispatched and received U.S. mail for the community. Towns originated at many stops.

ROUND TOP (Fayette Co.)

SH 237 at city square

Round Top

On the Old San Felipe Trail, in memory of John C. Robison, participant of the Battle of Velasco; Joel W. Robison, McHenry Winburn, Isaac Lafayette Hill, Spencer Burton Townsend, Stephen Townsend, Veterans of San Jacinto; J. T. Townsend, John P. Townsend of the San Jacinto Campaign; Mayers Fisher Jones of the Santa Fe and Snively Expeditions; John Rufus Alexander of the Mier Expedition, and other Pioneers who resided in the vicinity. (1936)

ROXTON (Lamar Co.)

FM 137, 5 mi. W

Hickory Grove Cemetery

Widespread settlement of this area of Lamar County began in the late 1840s and early 1850s. By 1852 the Hickory Grove Methodist Episcopal Church, South, was established and this cemetery was in use. The earliest documented grave here is that of Mary Isabella Alexander (1832–1852). Also interred that year were Franklin Day (1827–1852) and Nancy Smith (1842–1852). By the 1870s the Hickory Grove Cemetery was fully established as a community burial ground. The Methodist Church was relocated in 1881, providing more space for grave sites where the sanctuary had once stood. Additional land acquisitions, including property deeded by Sam and Dicie Swan in 1889 and F. E. and M. E. Simpson in 1907, enlarged the cemetery grounds. A building referred to as "the shed" was built in the 1920s for funeral services, but it burned in 1949. The Hickory Grove Cemetery contains over 1,000 graves. The tombstones, diverse in style and size, serve as reminders of the area's pioneer heritage. Many mark the graves of infants and children and are a testament to the often harsh conditions of pioneer life. Others interred here include veterans of the Civil War, World War I, World War II, and Korea. A cemetery association maintains the historic graveyard. (1991)

RUN (Hidalgo Co.)

US 83, 7 mi. S at FM 493

Asadores Ranch

Salvador Cavazos Gallegos and his wife, María San Juana Anzaldua, founded Asadores Ranch in 1881 on the Mexican La Blanca land grant to Lino Cavazos. The Cavazos family raised cattle and horses and grew corn, beans and other crops along the Rio Grande. Cavazos family members and ranch workers formed a small but important community. The land remained in the Cavazos family until 1902 when it was sold to John Closner. The family retained a one acre burial site where Salvador Cavazos Gallegos and Maria San Juana Anzaldua were buried in 1886 and 1887. The cemetery continued to be used by the family into the 1940s. Asadores Ranch is an example of the many eighteenth and nineteenth century Hidalgo County ranch settlements. (2010)

RUNGE (Karnes Co.)

FM 81, off SH 72 in town square

Runge, Texas

Early Texas town. Near site where old ox-cart road from San Antonio to Indianola crossed the Ojo de Agua (Spanish name meaning "Eye of Water" or Spring) Creek. Here pioneer travelers

402

found essentials of water, wood, and grass. Numerous Indian artifacts found nearby indicate that Karankawas, Tonkawas, Apaches, and Comanches camped or hunted in vicinity. First Anglo-American settlement here, in early 1850s, was named Sulphur Spring; in the late 1850s and 1860s the place was called Mineral Spring. In 1886 a group of Cuero merchants known as H. Runge and Company bought a large tract of land on which they platted the townsite of Runge. The San Antonio & Aransas Pass Railroad, called the "Sap," extended its line from Kenedy toward Houston and built a depot, a switch, and stockpens at Runge. The first post office was established here September 20, 1887. By 1890 Runge had grown to be the largest town in Karnes County. The public schools were organized in 1891 and Runge citizens engaged in many typical pioneer social and civic activities, including weekly band concerts held in the town square. The economy of the region has been sustained by farming, ranching, dairying, and petroleum production.

(1965)

RUSK (Cherokee Co.)   *SH 110, 6 mi. NE*
Elm Grove Common School
Elm Grove, a Freedmen's community, was part of the county school system by 1884, when 69 school districts were set up by the Commissioners Court. Classes were held in a local church or in homes until the 1890s when a schoolhouse was erected on land given by R. B. and Caroline Wood. Built by Elm Grove citizens with donated materials, the building was originally one large room. A merger with other schools in 1917 increased the student population, and the interior was divided into three classrooms. The school closed in 1957 when it merged with Rusk schools.

(1997)

RUSK (Cherokee Co.)   *US 84, 3 mi. W at FM 347*
Little Bean's Cherokee Village
In the winter of 1819–1820 Chief John Bowles led about sixty Cherokee families from Arkansas to East Texas. Near this site a small settlement was established by a leader named Little Bean. They remained until 1839, when the Republic of Texas government forced the tribe to move to Oklahoma. The land later was opened to Anglo settlers. Early owners of the Indian village were Reza J. Banks and Lewis Rogers. Little Bean, who died in 1839, is thought to be buried in the vicinity of the village.

(1991)

RUSK (Cherokee Co.)   *US 69 at Avenue A*
Rusk Penitentiary Building
The abundance of iron ore for use in manufacturing prompted a commission appointed by Gov. Richard Coke in 1875 to select this region for a state penitentiary. In 1877, this 19,000-acre tract was purchased from T. Y. T. Jamison and his wife. Contractors Kanmacher and Denig of Columbus, Ohio, built this structure the following year. The walls are of two-and-a-half foot thick sandstone. The administrative offices, a hospital, chapel, dining area, and cells were housed here. The prisoners helped construct the Texas State Railroad from Rusk to Palestine. They built the "Old Alcalde" iron ore smelting furnace adjacent to this structure. The furnace produced iron products for construction throughout the United States and for use in the erection of many state buildings. Convict labor was used in the area at contract prices. In 1917, the Texas Legislature changed the facility to a state hospital for the mentally ill. The building was renovated and ready for occupancy by 1919 and operated under the name of Rusk State Hospital. The Department of Mental Health and Mental Retardation was designated as the governing body in 1963. This structure became the administrative center for the hospital.

(1979)

RUSK (Cherokee Co.)   *1100 SH 62*
James Stephen Hogg and Cherokee County
James Stephen Hogg was born in 1851 to Lucanda (McMath) and Joseph L. Hogg on the family's plantation near Rusk. After a political career in Wood County as justice of the peace, judge and prosecutor, he became Texas Attorney General in 1887. In 1890, he ran as the Democratic candidate for Governor. He returned to his native Rusk on April 19, 1890 to begin his campaign with a speech at Live Oak Park, where approximately 3,000 people gathered to hear him speak for almost three hours. His speech outlined his platform, which included the creation of the Texas Railroad Commission and the Alien Land Law, later considered among his greatest accomplishments as Governor.

(2004)

RUSK (Cherokee Co.)   *588 Main St. (SH 62) at courthouse*
Cherokee County
Cherokee County has a rich and varied history. Spanish and French explorers of the seventeenth century found Tejas and Hasinai Indians living in this area, and Spanish missions were established in the region. Driven out of the United States, the Cherokee Indians migrated to this area about 1822, and were here at the time of early Anglo-American colonization in the 1820s and 1830s. Under the administration of Republic of Texas President Mirabeau B. Lamar, the Cherokees were expelled from the area in 1839. Following formal creation of Cherokee County from Nacogdoches County in 1846, settlement of the area increased rapidly. Family farms and towns soon sprung up throughout the county. The building of roads and the advancement of railroads and river navigation contributed further to settlement. The chief economic base of the county from its beginning, agriculture remained a vital force as industrialization and business interests developed. The establishment of schools and churches formed the basis for the area's social history. Cherokee County has been the birthplace of two Texas governors, one governor of Wyoming, and one speaker of the Texas House of Representatives.   (Texas Sesquicentennial 1836–1986)

RUSK (Cherokee Co.)   *207 E. 6th St. (US 84)*
Bachelor Girl's Library Club
Formed by 15 young single women in 1902 with fewer than 50 books, this library club would later donate to the City of Rusk a volume of books that greatly contributed to an inventory in excess of 23,000 books. The book club, originally housed in downtown Rusk at the Acme Hotel, is believed to be the first public library established in Cherokee County. In 1904 the club changed its name to "The Maids and Matrons Library Club" and rescinded its rule prohibiting married members in order that several of its original founders who had since married could continue in the organization. The name of the club was changed once more in 1916 to the "Library Study Club." In 1936 the members formed a club for younger women called "The Thalian Study Club." The size of the library's holdings continued to grow so that by 1966 the club had for some years required the services of a paid librarian. That year the club donated all of its books and furnishings to the City of Rusk. In 1969 they became part of the permanent collection at the newly constructed Singletary Memorial Library building. The Library Study Club and its offspring the Thalian Club continued to support the Rusk Community Library.   (1993)

RUSK (Cherokee Co.)   *W. 6th St. (US 84), .25 mi. W of SH 62*
Site of Confederate Gun Factory
Built in 1862 by John L. Whitesarver, William H. Campbell and Benjamin F. Campbell. When unable to secure materials and tools for the manufacture of rifles, Colt-model pistols were made. A number of Negroes were employed.

RUSK (Cherokee Co.)   *W. 6th St. (US 84), .25 mi. W of SH 62*
Site of Rusk Public School No. 2 for African Americans
By 1884, the Rusk Public School District maintained two schools: No. 1 for its Anglo students and No. 2 for its African American students. A yearly average of 50 students met in a small house built here about 1895 to house Rusk Public School No. 2. In 1939, the Rusk Independent School District erected a new school building southeast of downtown Rusk for its African American students. Named after long-term principal G. W. Bradford, the facility was used until Rusk integrated its schools in the 1960s. Many graduates of this school became highly respected professionals.   (1993)

RUSK (Cherokee Co.)   *US 69, 1 mi. SE*
New Birmingham
Born during iron rush of 1880s. Population about 3000. Had 2 iron furnaces, "The Tassie Bell" and "The Star and Cresent," 15 brick business blocks included banks, ice plant, electric plant, pipe foundry, school and palacial southern hotel where Jay Gould and Grover Cleveland were guests. Street railway connected with Rusk. Became ghost town in 1890s due to financial troubles of iron companies.   (1966)

RUSK (Cherokee Co.)   *US 69, 3 mi. SE*
Site of Tassie Belle and Star and Crescent Iron Ore Furnaces
New Birmingham was a boomtown nearby in the late 1800s built around local iron ore operations. The furnaces, capable of producing 50 tons of iron daily, were named "Tassie Belle," after

the wife of town founder A. B. Blevins, and the "Star and Crescent." About 275 workmen were required to keep furnaces in continual operation. The town grew to over 3,000 people with a business district of 15 blocks including 32 mercantile houses, an ice plant, the spacious Southern Hotel, bottling works, and an early electric power plant. The 1893 panic bankrupted the industries and killed the town.

(1996)

SABINAL (Uvalde Co.)
US 90, 1 mi. W on west side of Sabinal River
Site of Camp Sabinal
Established July 12, 1856 by Captain Albert G. Brackett, Second U.S. Cavalry, as a protection to the San Antonio-El Paso road and frontier settlers. Occupied by Federal troops until November 1856. Later served as a Ranger camp.

SABINAL (Uvalde Co.)
Old US 90, .5 mi. E of SH 127
John M. Davenport (February 8, 1827–October 28, 1859)
Stock-raiser and captain of a company of volunteer Indian fighters. Killed near here by 30 Comanches. Inquest for him was first in area for Indian victim. Settlers and soldiers from Fort Inge trailed the band 200 miles. After battle, found Davenport's gun on one of the Indians. (1969)

SABINAL (Uvalde Co.)
US 90 at FM 187
Sabinal
Named by Spanish for Rio Sabina and cypress trees along river. Town founded in 1854 by Thomas B. Hammer, who operated a stage stop and was first postmaster. Despite Indian depredations, town thrived as settlers built homes, and a railroad reached here in 1881. In 1906, town was incorporated, telephone service started, city waterworks and volunteer fire department organized. In 1907, Sabinal Christian College was founded. Closed in 1917. Cotton industry was foremost in early 1900s. Today, farming and ranching flourish in community. (1967)

SABINE PASS (Jefferson Co.)
SH 87 W
Visit Historic Sabine Pass
Established in 1837 as Republic of Texas port of entry and customs office. In the Civil War had defenses of one cavalry, one artillery and three infantry companies. Guarded shipping against the Federal blockade, admitting to port vital factory goods, guns, gunpowder, medicines. Guarded access to upriver ports that loaded out cotton, received guns. Stood sentry over coastal troop movements by rail, wagon or horseback from Texas to eastern battles. Was swept in 1862 by yellow fever brought in by ships from Havana. Ailing men had to spike their guns. Lost Sabine City to the Federals, who burned Taylor's Bayou railroad bridge and planned to make coastal plantations their commissary. Recaptured in Jan. 1863 by Confederates, the pass made military history Sept. 8, 1863, when fewer than 50 men under Lt. Dick Dowling defeated large Federal fleet bringing in 5,000 troops to conquer Texas and cut her off from remainder of the Confederacy. Battlefield park and monument open to public. Now a commercial fishing and marine repair center. Entrance from the Gulf of Mexico of Sabine-Neches Waterway. Important because of the petrochemical and oil industry along the shores. (1969)

SABINE PASS (Jefferson Co.)
6100 Dowling (FM 332) at park
Fort Manhassett
To protect Texas against Federal invasion during the Civil War, Confederate General John B. Magruder ordered the construction of a fort at this site on September 4, 1863, four days before the famous Confederate victory won by Dick Dowling and his small company against Union ships and gunboats at Sabine Pass (7 mi. NE). After the Federal retreat, the Confederate Coastal Defense program continued, since Federal blockading vessels still patrolled Gulf waters and the threat of more invasions was feared. A storm on September 19 sent the Union patrol steamers out to sea, but drove ashore their coaling ship, the "Mannahassett". Confederate troops dismantled the ship and seized its cargo. Col. Valery Sulakowski, formerly of the Austrian Army, designed Fort Manhassett, whose name evidently was adapted from that of the captured ship. Major Getulius Kellersberger, a Swiss-born engineer who had settled in America some years earlier, oversaw the construction. By October 1863, five companies garrisoned the five redoubts of the new fort and manned its ten cannons. Fort Manhassett soldiers participated in the capture of two Union ironclad ships at Calcasieu Pass, Louisiana on May 6, 1864. (1991)

SABINE PASS (Jefferson Co.)

S. Gulfway Dr. (SH 87) at S. 9th St.

Beach Road

The Beach Road is the coastal section of the Texas Highway 87 system. Stretching along the Gulf of Mexico from Sabine Pass through Chambers County to Port Bolivar in Galveston County, it follows a historic route that proved vital to the early development of Jefferson County. Native Americans, early settlers, traders, cattlemen and Republic of Texas mail carriers all used the road. During the Civil War, Confederate forces used the route, which was generally known as the "Road from Galveston." By 1920, local residents found it difficult to travel on the unmaintained Beach Road. In 1923, commissioner W. A. Vaughan worked to improve the route using shell deposits from along the coast. Soon traffic to McFaddin Beach and westward to Port Bolivar increased dramatically, leading to a business boom in the area as firms built facilities for visitors. A larger effort by the state in the late 1920s called for a paved road with a ferry connection to Galveston. The project moved slowly, but in 1931, the Texas Highway Commission named the new roadway as part of State Highway 87. In the 1940s, during World War II, the highway contributed to coastal defense preparedness. The U.S. Immigration Service set up a barricaded checkpoint for through traffic and the Coast Guard patrolled it during that time. Over the years, hurricanes battered the highway and eroded the nearby coastline, resulting in tidal zone encroachment. Destruction caused by two storms in 1989 forced its closure, though sections of the route remain in use for local traffic. (2007)

SABINE PASS (Jefferson Co.)

Sabine Pass Battleground State Historical Park, 1 mi. SE

United States Forces at the Battle of Sabine Pass

Federal forces in the Civil War failed in most of their early efforts to capture Texas. In the fall of 1863, after taking New Orleans and Vicksburg, their leaders attacked western Louisiana in a renewed effort. They wished to divert valuable stocks of cotton from Confederate to Federal uses, and to cut off French troops who might come from Mexico to aid the Confederacy. General N. P. Banks, U.S.A., ordered 5,000 troops to go by sea, capture Sabine Pass, and establish a land base near the river. He wanted these men to rendezvous later with troops he was leading overland to the Red River for a sweep into Texas. Federal ships carrying men and materiel converged beyond the sandbars, and on Sept. 8, 1863, began to run north through Sabine Pass. They saw a Confederate installation, Fort Griffin, sitting above the pass, but got no response when they fired upon it while advancing. When they came within 1200 yards of the fort, however, fire was returned, crippling the gunboats Clifton and Sachem. After the battle, at least 56 men were dead or missing. Both gunboats surrendered and the rest of the fleet retreated. (1980)

Spanish-American War Fortifications

As tension mounted between the United States and Spain during the late 1890s, U.S. Representative Samuel Bronson Cooper of Texas recommended the War Department begin plans for the defense of the strategic Sabine Pass area. Maj. James B. Quinn of the Army Corps of Engineers in New Orleans was authorized to direct construction of two forts on land granted by Augustus F. Kountze. Work on the batteries was under way by May 1898, one month after the formal war declaration. Military efforts were coordinated with area residents by government engineer J. L. Brownlee. Although the emplacements were soon completed, the shore guns were never part of military action here. The Spanish-American War ended December 10, 1898, with the signing of the Treaty of Paris. Later efforts were made to locate permanently a military installation at the site following the war. The plans were dropped, however, by 1901. In 1913, fifteen years after the war, the fortifications were the site of a tragic accident, in which a Sabine boy was killed when an abandoned ammunition cache exploded. Evidence of the fortifications has been severely damaged by hurricanes, but the site remains a symbol of an important era in U.S. history. (1983)

Sabine Pass, Richard Dowling

In memory of Lt. Richard W. Dowling and his men. Texas remembers the faithfulness and valor of her sons and commends their heroic example to future generations. Thus it will be seen that we captured with forty-seven men two gunboats mounting thirteen guns of the heaviest caliber and about three hundred and fifty prisoners. All my men behaved like heroes, not a man flinched from his post. Our motto was victory or death. Official report of Lt. Richard W. Dowling. At this site on Sept. 8th, 1863 Dick Dowling and forty-seven men comprising Company F Texas Heavy Artillery, Jefferson Davis Guards C.S.A., from a mud fort repulsed an attack made by four warships and twelve hundred men of the Federal Army, thus saving Texas from invasion by the enemy. There is no parallel in ancient or modern warfare to the victory of Dowling and his men at Sabine Pass, considering the great odds against which they had to contend. Jefferson Davis.

Site of Fort Griffin (1863–1865)
Renowned for brilliant Civil War victory, Sept. 8, 1863. Confederates in this fort repulsed a fleet seeking to land thousands of Federal soldiers. Lt. Richard W. Dowling (1838–1867), in civilian life a Houston businessman, commanded the fort during the enemy assault. His men, mostly Irishmen from Galveston and Houston, had been comrades in arms since Feb. 1861. Sabine Pass, where Dowling's men (Co. F, Texas Heavy Artillery) were assigned in 1863, was a center for blockade-running, whereby Confederacy exported cotton and obtained in exchange vital goods such as medicines and arms. Here Co. F built Fort Griffin, named in honor of Lt. Col. W. H. Griffin, Confederate commander at Sabine City, and designated by Col. Valery Sulakowski, formerly of the Austrian Army. Fort Griffin was an earthwork strengthened with railroad iron and ship's timbers. It was unfinished when Confederates learned of the approach of 22 ships. Dowling kept watch, but ordered no response to the early shelling by the Federals. When first ships entered range of Fort Griffin's guns, however, the battle began. Dowling himself served as one of the gunners. The fort sent 137 shells toward the targets. Dowling monument (near here) tells of the victory.   (1969)

SAINT JO (Montague Co.)   US 82 at square
Stonewall Saloon
Built 1873 as saloon and trail drivers rest stop. After county prohibition, 1897, housed offices and bank. Named after Gen. "Stonewall" Jackson. Town's first permanent building, originally of native stone. Stuccoed in 1930's; wooden facade added in 1964.   (1967)

SAINT JO (Montague Co.)   US 82 at square
Head of Elm (Saint Jo)
1849—Capt. Randolph B. Marcy U.S. Government Survey Trip; 1854—Capt. John Pope surveying proposed Federal railroad; 1855—U.S. 2nd Cavalry Under Col. Albert Sidney Johnson en route to establish Texas frontier forts, reported settlement here; 1857—Col. James B. Llach heading "corn train" to Fort Belknap; 1860—First U.S. Post Office John W. Womble post master; 1873—Saint Jo founded on site by Capt. I. H. Boggess & I. A. Bowell.   (1964)

SALADO (Bell Co.)   IH 35, S of Salado Creek, on west side
Birthplace of White House Aide, Mary Elizabeth Carpenter
Great-granddaughter of builders. Daughter of Thomas S. and Mary Elizabeth (Robertson) Sutherland. First woman vice president of student body, University of Texas. Married Leslie Carpenter; has 2 children. In 1954 was president Women's National Press Club. First woman ever to serve as executive assistant to the vice president of the United States, 1961. First newswoman to be staff director and press secretary to a First Lady, Mrs. Lyndon B. Johnson. Outstanding Women of Texas series, 1967. Awarded Medallion Plate.

SALADO (Bell Co.)   IH 35W, south of Salado Creek
Robertson Home
Built by Col. E. S. C. Robertson and wife, Mary Elizabeth (Dickey). Rare ante-bellum plantation complex, comprising home, servant quarters, land, family cemetery, stables. Still a working ranch. The house, occupied by fifth generation of Robertsons, is an example of Classical Revival style. Shows Palladian influence in its recessed porches and gallery rooms forming terminal pavillions balancing a central gabled portico.   (1967)

SALADO (Bell Co.)   400 blk. Main St., off IH 35
Site of Thomas Arnold High School
Dr. Samuel J. Jones (1857–1918) and his wife, Charlotte Hallaran Jones (d. 1904), established Thomas Arnold High School on this site in 1890. The school, which was actually a private academy, occupied the stone buildings vacated by Salado College, where Dr. Jones taught. Named for Thomas Arnold (1795–1842), noted headmaster of Rugby School in England, the academy provided quality education during a time when there were few public high schools. After it closed in 1913, the facilities were again operated as Salado College until 1918, and as a public school until 1924, when the buildings burned.   (1975)

SALADO (Bell Co.)   *400 blk. Main St., off IH 35*
Stagecoach Inn
Constructed during the 1860s, the Stagecoach Inn was known as Salado Hotel and as Shady Villa before the current name was adopted in 1943. Military figures George Armstrong Custer and Robert E. Lee, and cattle baron Shanghai Pierce are among those thought to have stayed here. A good example of frontier vernacular architecture, the Stagecoach Inn features a two-story galleried porch with a second-story balustrade.   (1962)

SALADO (Bell Co.)   *400 blk. Main St., off IH 35*
Site of Salado College (across from Stagecoach Inn)
Founded 1856 with a gift by Col. C. S. Robertson of 100 acres of land. The Athens of Texas from 1858 to 1884. This marker rests on ground where the college building stood.

SALADO (Bell Co.)   *Main St., off IH 35, S end of bridge*
Dodd's Creek Bridge (Lenticular Truss Bridge)
One of many patented truss designs developed by American inventors and engineers in the mid- to late-19th century, this 87-foot lenticular truss bridge represents an unusual truss type in the United States. The lenticular design features a curved top and bottom chord which forms a lens shape. The patent, issued to William O. Douglas of Connecticut in 1878, was the only one given for a lenticular truss bridge in the United States. Most were constructed in the New England area and in New York State. Through the efforts of William Payson, a salesman for Douglas' Berlin Iron Bridge Company, Texas acquired at least a dozen truss bridges in the late 19th century. The Coryell County Commissioners Court contracted with the Berlin Iron Bridge Company to build four lenticular truss bridges for $16,500 in 1889. This bridge originally was located across Cowhouse Creek and later was moved to Dodd's Creek. In 1990 the Texas Historical Commission and the Texas Department of Transportation identified eight lenticular truss bridges surviving in Texas. Four of the spans were located in San Antonio; the other four were positioned on out-of-service roadways. The only examples of this rare bridge type west of the Mississippi; they are recognized as historically significant engineering structures. The Society for Industrial Archeology and Historic American Engineering Record, a branch of the National Park Service, also has recognized the importance of the Texas lenticular bridges as products of a short-lived but important period of bridge technology in 19th century engineering history. The Dodd's Creek Bridge was moved to this site in 1997 to improve the flow of traffic, protect pedestrians and enhance the Salado Historic District.   (2000)

SALADO (Bell Co.)   *Main St., off IH 35, S end of bridge*
Main Street Bridges
A number of bridges have been built over Salado Creek on Main Street since 1870. After the town of Salado was laid out in 1859, citizens crossed the creek using various combinations of rocks and logs. When local citizens and students at Salado College began to demand that a proper bridge be constructed across the creek, town officials voted to issue bonds to fund the project. The first bridge, built in 1868–69, was constructed by local volunteers. The cable wire suspension footbridge, with cedar crossbars and a wooden plank floor, was destroyed in a 1900 flood. The second bridge, a larger structure which would accommodate wagon as well as foot travel, was an iron bridge built by the King Bridge Company in 1892. Located a few yards west of the suspension footbridge, it rested on piers of rock and mortar, and was destroyed in a flood in 1913. Replaced a year later, the duplicate bridge was washed away in a 1921 flood. A concrete bridge was built across the creek in 1922. Anchored with reinforced steel set into the rock creek bed, it proved to be a more permanent solution than previous efforts to bridge the stream and continues to be a focal point in the town.   (1986)

SALADO (Bell Co.)   *Main St., off IH 35, S end of bridge*
Salado Creek
Gushing limestone springs, abundant fish, flowers, and trees have long made the banks of Salado Creek a good home site. Indians camped beside stream; Spanish explorers named it; the first Anglo-American settler was Archibald Willingham, 1851. College and town of Salado were built on creek, 1860. Stream once had 8 mills, thus was county industrial center. Chisholm Cattle Trail crossed it, as did Dallas–San Antonio Stage Line. The 35-mile creek is one of many which rise at the Balcones Fault—an outstanding North American region of springs.   (1967)

SALT FLAT (Hudspeth Co.)

US 62/180, 4.5 mi. E

Site of El Paso Salt War

Resentment over private control of the Salt Lakes in this region, often called Guadalupe Lakes, in 1877 led to the El Paso Salt War which entailed the loss of many lives and much property.

SALT FLAT (Hudspeth Co.)

US 62/180, 4.5 mi. E

Crow Springs (15 mi. N)

Named for birds habitually there in abundance, Crow Springs was an oasis for Indians for centuries. The Butterfield Overland Mail in 1858 built a stage relay station at the springs, but used it less than a year before shifting the route south, to go by Fort Davis. During the Apache Wars of the early 1880s, Texas Rangers and the U.S. 10th Cavalry camped at Crow Springs occasionally, to prevent Indians in New Mexico from joining the war leaders, Victorio and Nana, in Mexico. Today the springs are dry, the station has fallen to dust, and the crows have disappeared.   (1974)

SAN ANGELO (Tom Green Co.)

US 87, 3 mi. NW

Sheep and Goat Industry in Texas

Spanish explorers introduced sheep to the Southwest in the 1500s, and Spanish missions depended on the animals for food and clothing. The first Angora goats, known for the beauty and strength of their mohair, were brought to Texas in 1853 by Col. W. W. Haupt. Pioneer of modern sheep ranching in Texas from 1857 to 1867 was George Wilkins Kendall, who encouraged others with glowing reports of the industry's future while improving his own flocks. Kendall was one of the first to crossbreed the coarse-wooled Mexican Churro sheep with the fine-wooled Merino variety brought by European settlers. The land, climate, and vegetation of the Edwards Plateau area especially suited the raising of sheep and goats. After 1870, with new markets and abundant land, the industry boomed. Ranchers fought disease, predators, deadly plants, and drouths to build their flocks. Today Texas is the leading producer of sheep and goats in the nation, and San Angelo is the major market center for these animals and their wool. Research facilities such as the San Angelo Research and Extension Center, built in 1969 through the efforts of Gen. Earl Rudder, then president of the Texas A. & M. System, work for the industry's continued prosperity.   (1974)

SAN ANGELO (Tom Green Co.)

Irving at Beauregard Sts. (US 67), courthouse

Original Tom Green County

On Transcontinental Trail of California Gold Rush. Until 1846 a part of Bexar Land District, Republic of Texas. Private tracts were surveyed as early as 1847. German emigration company colony (90 mi. SE) had grants here, but in 1840s found Indians blocking settlement. Butterfield Overland Mail managers lived at stands in area, 1858–1861. R. F. Tankersley family established a permanent home in 1864 in future Tom Green County. By 1874 there were five settlements here, including Bismarck Farm, colony of 15 German immigrants. The county (12,756 sq. mi., 10½ times as large as state of Rhode Island) was created in 1874 and named for heroic Gen. Green (1814–1864), a state official and gallant Texas soldier. After a decade of progress, the original Tom Green County began losing outlying areas. Midland County—halfway between Fort Worth and El Paso on newly opened Texas & Pacific Railway—was created in 1885. Settlers remote from San Angelo petitioned for new counties in 1887, and the Texas Legislature created Crane, Loving, Upton, Ward and Winkler. Coke and Irion counties were cut out of Tom Green in 1889. Ector and Sterling were created in 1891. Last divisions—Glasscock (1893) and Reagan (1903)—gave Tom Green its present size. It remains influential in the region.   (1972)

SAN ANGELO (Tom Green Co.)

18 E. Avenue A

Municipal Swimming Pool

In September 1936, a devastating flood swept down the South Concho River, inundating much of the city of San Angelo. Among the many properties lost or severely damaged were the city's parks and its public swimming pool. Plans were made to rebuild the parks and construct a new municipal swimming pool, but a bond election held in 1937 to finance the project was defeated by the voters. Once it was determined that the federal government would assist with Works Progress Administration funds and labor for the project, a new bond election was held and passed by sixty-six votes. Work on the project began in March 1938 and was completed in October. Opening ceremonies were held on April 29, 1939. During its first two days of operation, the pool hosted 795 swimmers. Designed by John G. Becker, the Pueblo Revival complex features a two-story hexagonal stone structure flanked by one-story wings. Exposed vigas are symmetrically placed on the upper portion of the wings. The complex reflects the 1930s construction and planning activity of the Federal Works Progress Administration. (1989)

SAN ANGELO (Tom Green Co.)

630 S. Oakes St.,
Fort Concho Nat'l Historic Landmark

Fort Concho
The center of a line of forts extending from the northeastern border of Texas to El Paso. Was also northern point of southern chain of forts extending to Rio Grande, thence along that river to its mouth. Established 1867 (at then junction of Butterfield Trail, Goodnight Trail and road to San Antonio) by 4th Cavalry under Capt. George G. Huntt to protect frontier. By March 1, 1870, fort buildings were (in order of their construction) a commissary and quartermaster storehouse, hospital, five officers' quarters, a magazine and two barracks—all built of sandstone. Among those who commanded the post were: Gen. Wm. R. Shafter (later Major General of Volunteers, Spanish-American War and commanded troops at capture of Santiago de Cuba, July 1898); Maj. John P. Hatch (at one time fort was named in his honor); Gen. Wesley Merritt (first commander of Fort Davis after Civil War; was later superintendent of U.S. Military Academy at West Point); Gen. Ranald Slidell Mackenzie (who led attacks from this and other forts, credited with defeat of Indian resistance in Southwest); and Gen. Benjamin H. Grierson, commander of Negro troops of 10th Cavalry. On June 20, 1889, fort was abandoned as a military post and property passed into private ownership. (1970)

SAN ANGELO (Tom Green Co.)

630 S. Oakes St.,
Fort Concho Nat'l Historic Landmark

The Tenth Cavalry
Following the Civil War, the United States Congress authorized the creation of six regiments of black U.S. army troops. The Tenth Cavalry was organized in 1867 under the leadership of Col. Benjamin Grierson (1826–1911). The order creating black troops also specified that they would be commanded by white officers. Facing problems of racial discrimination at the regiment's headquarters in Fort Leavenworth, Kansas, Grierson wanted the Tenth Cavalry reassigned to the West, and they arrived at Fort Concho in the spring of 1875. The contributions of the men of the Tenth Cavalry to the settlement of the American West are of major importance. They took part in grueling scouting and mapping expeditions and campaigns against hostile Indians, often facing days without proper supplies or water on the High Plains. They were instrumental in the defeat of the Mescalero Apache Indians led by Chief Victorio in 1880. The men of the Tenth Cavalry were stationed at Fort Concho until 1882, when they were moved to Fort Davis. Transferred frequently after 1885, members of the unit eventually served throughout the world, including Cuba, North Africa, Germany, Korea, and Vietnam. (1987)

SAN ANGELO (Tom Green Co.)

US 87, 4 mi. SE

Tom Green County
A part of the Miller and Fisher grant, 1842. Created a county March 13, 1874. Organized January 5, 1875. Named in honor General Thomas Green, 1814–1864. A veteran of San Jacinto, member of the Somerall expedition. A Confederate officer. First mail routes to the Pacific converged here in 1858. County seat, Ben Ficklin, 1875. San Angelo since 1882.

SAN ANGELO (Tom Green Co.)

S. Bryant Blvd. (US 277)
access road at SH 306

Major Ben Ficklin, C.S.A. (1827–1871)
Called mystery man of the Confederacy. Educated at Virginia Military Institute. At age 18 served as a corporal in Mexican War. In 1850s worked with stagecoach and mail lines from Missouri to San Francisco. Helped to start the Pony Express line in 1860. Promoted idea of the railroad that later was the Union Pacific—the first to span the U.S. Was a soldier and state quartermaster in Virginia at start of Civil War. Appointed Confederate purchasing agent, his swagger and success in Europe excited Federal envy. Personally ran blockade and passed through New York and Washington on secret missions. In 1867 was awarded U.S. contract for weekly mail run from Fort Smith, Ark., to San Antonio and El Paso. Had his operational headquarters 3 miles below Fort Concho. Owned 640 acres of land here. Built corrals, blacksmith shop, storage rooms, adobe house, kitchen

and commissary. On a visit to Washington, died of swallowing fish bone. Was buried in Charlottesville, Va. Associates carried on the mail stage runs, later named town near Fort Concho for the late major. "Ben Ficklin" was first county seat of Tom Green, serving until was destroyed by flood in 1882.

(1964)

SAN ANGELO (Tom Green Co.) *US 87/277, 4 mi. S*
Site of Ben Ficklin
An early stage stand named in honor of Major Ben Ficklin, noted frontiersman, mail and stage contractor, who assisted in establishing the Pony Express. He carried the first message from the Governor of California to the Governor of Missouri. First county seat of Tom Green County, 1875–1882. Destroyed by flood, August 24, 1882.

SAN ANGELO (Tom Green Co.) *FM 584 at Hillside Dr., 2 mi. S of SH 306*
John R. ("Sarge") Nasworthy
(September 12, 1849–November 4, 1924)
Colorful pioneer and Texas Ranger who helped to create civilization and institutions of West Texas. Owned ranch land on which today is situated Lake Nasworthy—first conservation lake in this area. Born in Georgia. Served 1864–1865 in Confederate Army, during Civil War. Later came to Texas, living first at Bonham. After he moved west, he operated in Menard area as a buyer of beef cattle for United States Army mess halls at Fort Concho. In 1880s he was deputy county clerk and deputy sheriff of Tom Green County and the first treasurer of the City of San Angelo. He owned the first local brick kiln, a wagon yard, a livery stable, and the only hearse in town in the early days. He was second man to fence land, second man to grow cotton in the county. A county commissioner, 1910–1916, he promoted building of the old Chadbourne viaduct. A leader in church and philanthropic endeavors, he was a promoter of the Baptist Encampment at Christoval (then one of the largest religious gatherings in the South). He married Dena Von Fisher. The family had homes on Beauregard Street, Knickerbocker Road, Ben Ficklin Road and at Nasworthy Lake site. His six children carry on family tradition of community leadership.

(1970)

SAN ANTONIO (Bexar Co.) *IH-10 at Boerne Stage Road in Leon Springs*
(TxDOT park-and-ride parking lot)
First Officers Training Camp
The First World War came to America on April 6, 1917, when President Woodrow Wilson signed the declaration, passed by Congress, that a state of war existed between the United States of America and Germany. Immediately thereafter, eight camps were established in the U.S. to train officers for combat leadership. The first was at Leon Springs, Texas, and on May 8, 1917, three thousand volunteers assembled at Camp Funston on the Schasse Ranch (now a part of Camp Bullis near this site) for training in various branches of the army. They endured three months of intense training and 1,846 young men graduated on August 15, 1917, as second lieutenants. The length of their training resulted in the term "90-day wonders." Embodying their motto "Brave men shall not die because I faltered," the members of the first officers training camp served with distinction in the war, many of them highly decorated for valor in combat. Almost 300, many highly ranking colonels or generals, returned to active duty for service in World War II. Three of those trained here later became governors: Beauford Jester of Texas, James R. Beverley of Puerto Rico, and Charles H. Martin of Oregon. Many more "first campers" were prominent leaders in business, industry and government throughout Texas and the United States. Following their training and service, the former comrades in arms organized the "First Officers Training Camp Association" in 1931. Members residing in 30 states and several foreign countries gathered for annual meetings for more than fifty years. Now succeeded by generations of modern soldiers and officers, the First Officers Training Camp veterans leave a legacy of honor, courage and service to their country.

(1999)

SAN ANTONIO (Bexar Co.) *Loop 410 at Nacogdoches Rd.*
Route of El Camino Real
The main thoroughfare of early Texas, the Camino Real, or "King's Highway," followed ancient Indian and buffalo trails. It stretched 1,000 miles from Mexico to present Louisiana. Domingo Terán de los Ríos, first Governor of Texas, blazed the central section of the road in 1691. Called the "Trail of the Padres," it linked Monclova, Mexico with the Spanish missions of East Texas. Over the centuries, priests, soldiers, traders, and settlers used the Camino Real. The French adventurer

St. Denis probably traveled the road from Louisiana to the Rio Grande in 1714. San Antonio was a major stop on this frontier highway. Moses Austin followed the Camino Real to San Antonio in 1820 seeking colonization rights from Spain. Many Anglo-American settlers called it the "Old San Antonio Road." It joined this city with Nacogdoches, San Augustine, and other East Texas settlements. In 1915, the Texas Legislature appropriated $5,000 to mark the historic roadway across the state. The Daughters of the American Revolution, along with other patriotic groups, endorsed the project. V. N. Zivley surveyed the route and indicated the spacing for granite markers every five miles. Today many modern highways follow the path of the Camino Real. (1979)

SAN ANTONIO (Bexar Co.)
Alamo Plaza
The Alamo (Founding of the Mission and Origin of Name)
The San Antonio de Padua Mission was founded in San Antonio in 1716 by the Franciscan Father, Antonio Olivanes, and after merging with the San Francisco Solano Mission in 1718, it was officially founded as the San Antonio de Valero Mission. The present site was selected in 1724. It was named in honor of Saint Anthony de Padua and the Duke of Valero, a Spanish Viceroy. The cornerstone of this chapel was laid May 8, 1744. Founded for the purpose of Christianizing and educating the Indians, it later became a fortress and was the scene of many conflicts prior to the immortal siege of 1836. Its activity as a mission began to wane after 1765, and it was abandoned in 1793 and the mission archives were removed to San Fernando, the parish church. During Mexico's War for Independence from Spain, a company of Spanish soldiers from Alamo del Pamas Coahuila, Mexico, occupied the abandoned mission, using its buildings as barracks for a number of years. From this association probably originated the name, Alamo. According to some historians, the name "Alamo" was derived from a grove of cottonwood trees growing on the banks of the Acequia, "Alamo" being the Spanish word for cottonwood. (This is not an official Texas Historical Commission marker.)

SAN ANTONIO (Bexar Co.)
Alamo Plaza
The Defense of the Alamo
"Thermopylae had its messenger of defeat. The Alamo had none." The Alamo in 1836 consisted of this church, the convent and a large rectangular area or plaza, an enclosure of about six acres surrounded by walls with barracks on the west side of the Plaza. On February 23, 1836 Colonel William Barret Travis entered the Alamo with an approximate force of two hundred men. The siege, commanded by General Santa Anna and an army of several thousand Mexican soldiers, lasted nearly two weeks. At dawn on Sunday, March 6, the final assault was made, and in less than an hour the defenders slain. Later the bodies were burned by order of General Santa Anna. This victory in defeat was the means of uniting the colonists in a determined effort to resist further oppression and by armed force to secure permanent independence. "It was here that a gallant few, the bravest of the brave, threw themselves between the enemy and the settlements, determined never to surrender nor retreat. They redeemed their pledge to Texas with the forfeit of their lives—they fell the chosen sacrifice to Texas freedom."—Newell (This is not an official Texas Historical Commission marker.)

SAN ANTONIO (Bexar Co.)
Alamo Plaza
Adina de Zavala (November 28, 1861–March 1, 1955)
As the granddaughter of Lorenzo de Zavala (1789–1836), first vice-president of the Republic of Texas, young Adina de Zavala was exposed to vivid accounts of Texas' revolutionary and republican past. She became a guiding force in the preservation of many of Texas' most revered historic structures and sites, including the Alamo, Mission San Francisco de los Tejas in east Texas, and San Antonio's Spanish Governor's Palace. The "De Zavala Daughters," a women's group formed by Miss Adina in 1889, erected Texas' first historical markers and helped preserve San Antonio's Spanish missions. Her firm belief, later verified, was that remnants of Mission San Antonio de Valero, known in 1836 as the Alamo's long barracks, lay underneath the wooden exterior of buildings adjacent to the Alamo church. By 1893, as president of the De Zavala Chapter of the Daughters of Republic of Texas (DRT), Miss Adina had secured the adjacent property owner's commitment to give the chapter first purchase option. In 1907, upon hearing that the 2-story long barracks were about to be razed, Miss Adina barricaded herself inside the buildings for three days and nights in an effort that ultimately prevented their destruction. (1994)

SAN ANTONIO (Bexar Co.)   *Alamo Plaza*
Alamo Low Barracks and Main Gateway
Mission San Antonio de Valero, established nearby in 1718, was relocated here in 1724; by 1762, the mission plaza was enclosed by thick stone and adobe walls. The 11x 14-foot main gateway was located at this site along the south wall. In 1803, Spanish cavalry from San Carlos de Parras del Alamo, Mexico, occupied the secularized mission and built one-story (low) barracks inside the south wall on each side of the main gateway. The Alamo, as the complex came to be known, was occupied in 1835 by Mexican soldiers led by Gen. Cos. They fortified the main gateway with artillery pieces and a defensive lunette, a semi-circular enclosure with deep trenches. In December 1835, Texas patriots captured the Alamo, but by Feb. 23, 1836, were under siege by an armed force led by Gen. Santa Anna. Couriers departed the Alamo through the main gateway during the siege. On March 6, Mexican troops breached the main gateway and retook the Alamo. After the assault, some Mexican military observers and local residents stated that Col. James Bowie and others died in the low barracks. The low barracks and main gateway were leveled in 1871, melding Valero Plaza on the south with the Alamo's plaza to create an open space.   (1996)

SAN ANTONIO (Bexar Co.)   *204 Alamo Plaza, exterior wall of Menger Hotel*
Barbed Wire Demonstration
Once called "bobwire" by cowboys, barbed wire was a French invention first patented in the U.S. in 1867, but it did not gain favor with cattlemen until the late 1870s. Joseph Glidden of Dekalb, Illinois, received a patent for his barbed wire in 1874, and it was wire of his manufacture that was the first barbed wire fencing successfully demonstrated in Texas. In 1876, veteran salesman Pete McManus and his young partner, John Warne Gates, made their first demonstration of "the Glidden winner" barbed wire. Though speculation has placed this demonstration in San Antonio's bustling Military Plaza, it was here in the quiet "mudhole" of Alamo Plaza that McManus and Gates set up a barbed wire corral and then drove cattle into the pen. It is said that after the corral held the thundering animals under the astonished eyes of cowboys and cattlemen, the flamboyant Gates invited spectators into the Menger Hotel to place their orders. After the theatrical demonstration in Alamo Plaza, the market for barbed wire fencing suddenly exploded with large sales to Texas ranchers and others along the frontier. Pete McManus reportedly sold more barbed wire fencing than any salesman in the world. John W. "Bet-A-Million" Gates became the world's largest barbed wire manufacturer. He helped found the Texas Company (later Texaco) and developed the town of Port Arthur. Barbed wire fencing changed the landscape of the American West and with it the industries of ranching and agriculture. It made possible the introduction of cultivated cattle stock into the beef industry and opened up the fertile land to farmers and other homesteaders. Within 25 years nearly all the open range had become privately owned and was under fence.   (2000)

SAN ANTONIO (Bexar Co.)   *near 100 blk. E. Commerce St.*
Commerce Street Bridge
The main ford between San Fernando de Bexar (the city) and San Antonio de Valero (the Alamo), this river crossing has long been a focal point of history. At its footbridge on Feb 23, 1836, Alamo emissary Albert Martin met to parley with Santa Anna's aide, Juan Almonte, during the Texas War for Indepedence. Mayor John W. Smith employed R. T. Higginbotham to build a wooden bridge in 1842. The scene was painted by artist Herman Lungwitz in 1854. In the 1850s the bridge and river (then as now an asset to the city) were described by world travelers Frederick Olmsted and William Bollaert. It was a favorite spot of noted southern author Sidney Lanier while he lived here. A sign in English, Spanish, and German recognizing the local ethnic population division was placed on the bridge in the 1870s. Law-abiding Teutons were told brusquely, "Schnelles Reiten Uber Dise Brucke Is Verboten". Mexicans however, were warned, "Anda Despacio Con Su Caballo, O Teme La Ley", while Anglo-Americans, unlikely to truckle to authority or fear the law, had their pocketbooks threatened: "Walk your horse over the bridge or you will be fined." Present bridge replaces an 1880 iron structure. Linking old and new, it spans 250 years of recorded history.   (1971)

SAN ANTONIO (Bexar Co.)   *100 Dolorosa at courthouse*
Bexar County under Nine Governments
The administrative government of Bexar County, besides being the oldest in Texas, is distinguished by having served under nine governments. The community served under Spanish rule

from May, 1718, until January, 1811, when it was taken over by the revolutionary "Casas Regime." Only five weeks later, the "Counter-Revolutionary Junta of Bexar" overthrew the Casas government and eventually restored Spanish rule. In April, 1812, however, the "Republican Army of the North" deposed the provincial Spanish government and declared independence from Spain. Five months later the Spanish regained control, holding Texas until 1821. The fifth regime, "First Imperial Government of Mexico" was created when Mexico gained independence from Spain in 1821. The emperor relinquished control to army leaders within two years, however, and the "Republic of Mexico" was established. Texas gained independence from Mexico in 1836, thereby establishing Bexar's seventh government, the "Republic of Texas." In 1845, Texas became the twenty-eighth state of the United States and remained in the Union until 1861, when the Southern States seceded to form the Confederacy. Following the Civil War, U.S. rule returned to Bexar County in 1865.

(1967)

SAN ANTONIO (Bexar Co.)
100 Dolorosa at courthouse
The Canary Islanders
Earliest civilian colonists of San Antonio, this nucleus of pioneers from the Canary Islands formed the first organized civil government in Texas and founded the village of San Fernando de Bexar in 1731. Following a sea and land voyage of over a year, these weary travelers arrived at the Presidio (fort) of San Antonio early on March 9, 1731. Totaling 56 persons, they had emigrated to Texas from the Spanish Canary Islands near Africa, by order of King Phillip V. On July 2, they began to lay out a villa (village), choosing a site on the west side of the Plaza de las Yslas (present Main Plaza) for the church and a site on the east side for the Casa Real (government building). On July 9, the captain of the presidio, Juan Antonio de Almazan, read to the islanders the decree of the Viceroy naming them and their descendants "Hijos Dalgos," persons of nobility. The heads of the 16 families who settled in San Antonio were Juan Leal Goraz, Juan Curbelo, Juan Leal, Antonio Santos, Jose Padron, Manuel de Nis, Vicente Alvarez Travieso, Salvador Rodriguez, Jose Leal, Juan Delgado, Jose Cabrera, Juan Rodriguez Granadillo, Francisco de Arocha, Antonio Rodriguez, Lorenzo and Martin de Armas, and Felipe and Jose Antonio Perez.

(1971)

SAN ANTONIO (Bexar Co.)
Dwyer Ave. at E. Nueva St.
Erasmo Seguín
Born in San Antonio; descendant of Frenchman who settled in Mexico before 1714. Always a civic leader, helped found first public school in San Antonio, 1812. Went (1821) with Juan M. Veramendi to escort Austin Colony leaders to Bexar, and ever after befriended Stephen F. Austin and Anglo-American settlers. Seguin was postmaster of San Antonio, 1823–35, and deputy for Texas in National Congress of Mexico, 1823–24. After Santa Anna came to power as a liberal (1831), then made himself dictator, Seguin joined neighbors in sending him "San Antonio Remonstrances" (protests) in 1832, and called an opposition convention in 1834. Expelled from the postmastership by Santa Anna's brother-in-law, Gen. Cos, and made to flee from San Antonio on foot, he walked 33 miles to his ranch, Casa Blanca, where he recruited men to help patriots win siege of Bexar (Dec. 1835) and expel Gen. Cos. Early in 1836 he sent spies to the Nueces to watch for Santa Anna. He lodged David Crockett in his home, and provisioned the Alamo before the final siege. Persecuted by newcomers to Texas, he refused to go to Mexico with his son Juan, but with his wife Josefa Becerra retired to Casa Blanca (located in present Wilson County), where he died and was buried in 1857.

(1973)

SAN ANTONIO (Bexar Co.)
100 E. Houston St. at Soledad St.
Site of De la Garza House, Gardens and Mint
Erected on this site in 1734 for prominent Bexar citizens Geronimo and Javiera Cantu de la Garza, the De la Garza family home was designed by Geronimo's brother-in-law Pedro Flores Valdez. The complex occupied an entire city block and was crafted with limestone and plaster walls three feet thick. Extensive gardens included cottonwood, pecan, fig and peach trees. The Spanish government granted the property to Javiera de la Garza in 1736 after her husband's death. Two generations later, José Antonio de la Garza used the home's vault to safeguard the valuables of local merchants. In 1818 the Spanish Crown granted him permission to mint coins which became known as "jolas," a Spanish slang term for small currency of local issue used in the northeastern provinces of New Spain. The "jolas" replaced scarce Spanish silver in the value of a half "real," making the De la Garza home what was probably the first mint in Texas. During the Siege of Bexar in 1835,

414

Ben Milam's troops engaged in a two-day battle to commandeer the fortress-like compound as their headquarters. Milam died in the struggle to take the city. After the siege possession of the home returned to the family, in whose control it remained for the rest of the century. Six months of demolition were required to bring down the De la Garza home in 1912. At that time a large sum of money was found hidden in the house and a sixteen-pound cannonball was discovered embedded in the walls, inscribing another page in the De la Garza chapter of San Antonio history.   (1999)

SAN ANTONIO (Bexar Co.)

S. Alamo St. in Hemisfair Park, off IH 37

Acequia Madre de Valero
(Main irrigation ditch of Valero Mission)

One in a network of ditches begun by the Spanish and their Indian charges at the founding of San Antonio in 1718. Hand-dug and made of dressed limestone, the Acequia diverted water from San Antonio River through fields belonging to San Antonio de Valero Mission. Irrigation was the key to the growth of mission and town. The ditch paralleled present Broadway by Brackenridge Park and Alamo Street, then fed back into the river southwest of this section. It became part of modern waterworks after 1877. This section was restored, 1968.   (1968)

SAN ANTONIO (Bexar Co.)

Losoya St. at Commerce St.

San Antonio River Walk (Paseo Del Rio)

In September 1921 the flooding of the San Antonio River reached as high as eight feet in the center of the city. Loss of lives and property damage were high, and prompted city officials to take action to prevent a recurrence. The Olmos Dam was built and a city engineering report recommended filling and paving the river bend. Protests from the city Federation of Women's Clubs and the San Antonio Conservation Society convinced municipal leaders to view the river as an asset to be preserved. San Antonio architect Robert H. H. Hugman (1902–1980) developed beautification plans for the river area including walks, foot bridges, landscaping, and retail shops. In 1929 Hugman, W. P. Drought, and city leaders helped Congressman Maury Maverick, Mayor C. K. Quin, and Jack White develop support that led to a Federal Works Progress Administration (WPA) grant to fund the project. In 1938, Hugman was hired as the project architect and Edwin P. Arneson as the project engineer. By 1941 the River Walk was completed. During the 1960s voters approved a bond for improvements including extending the walk to the convention center. A source of pride for San Antonio, the River Walk is one of its most unique attractions.   (1997)

SAN ANTONIO (Bexar Co.)

IH 37 at Commerce St.,
Chamber of Commerce Bldg.

250th Anniversary of the Founding of San Antonio

Area was first explored and named by Spaniards in 1691. Colonial settlement began here May 1–5, 1718, with founding of Franciscan Mission San Antonio de Valero (later known as "The Alamo"). In vicinity of the mission was the Presidio San Antonio de Bexar, named for one of the great heroes of Spain, the Duc de Bexar, brother of the Viceroy of New Spain. The place was re-named San Fernando de Bexar, 1731, when it became a municipality—the first in all of Texas. But the name "San Antonio" persisted. Today it is San Antonio in the County of Bexar. In its lifetime it has given allegiance to nine governments, and from 1772 to 1824 it served as the provincial and territorial capital of Texas. HemisFair '68—a world's fair held here April 6 to October 6, 1968, on the 250th anniversary of the birth of the City of San Antonio—had as its theme "The Confluence of Civilizations in the Americas." It originated as a tribute to the diverse peoples who have occupied the Western Hemisphere from pre-Columbian times: Indians who were the first known inhabitants; proud Spanish conquerors and devout padres; the pioneering American settlers; and the immigrants from many different lands.   (1968)

SAN ANTONIO (Bexar Co.)

IH 35 frontage road near San Antonio stockyards

The Grass Fight

Near this site on Nov. 26, 1835, occurred the Grass Fight, one of the least decisive but certainly most unusual battles of the Texas War for Independence. For more than a month, the Texas forces, composed of both Anglo- and Mexican-Texans, had camped near San Antonio de Bexar waiting for an opportunity to engage the army of the Centralist Regime stationed in the city. Erastus "Deaf" Smith, a Texas scout, learned that a Mexican pack train carrying silver to pay the garrison would arrive in Bexar. On Nov. 26 Smith sighted an approaching caravan and alerted the Texas camp.

Col. James Bowie led about 100 volunteers, while others followed Col. Edward Burleson. Near the junction of Alazan, Apache and San Pedro Creeks, the Texans overtook the pack train. Soldiers from the garrison in Bexar rode to aid their comrades, but the Texans forced them to retreat and captured the pack animals. About 50 Mexican soldiers were killed in the clash; two Texans were wounded. In the packs the Texans found not silver but hay that Mexican troops had foraged for their livestock. Two weeks later, supported by a contingent under Juan N. Seguin, Ben Milam led Texan volunteers in the storming of Bexar, expelling the Centralist Army and setting the stage for the siege of the Alamo, Feb. 23–March 6, 1836. (1982)

SAN ANTONIO (Bexar Co.) *646 S Main, 4 blks. E of IH 10/IH 35*
Arsenal Magazine

At the urging of United States Secretary of War Jefferson Davis, land was secured at San Antonio in 1858 for an arsenal. In 1859, the state of Texas added 16 acres, and the arsenal became headquarters for the U.S. Army's Department of Texas. Under construction when the Civil War (1861–1865) began, this magazine was included in Federal property surrendered in 1861. The building was completed for Confederate Texas by local contractor J. H. Kampmann. Carefully spaced vents and cavities in the walls permitted air circulation and reduced the danger of sparks igniting stored gunpowder. The arsenal supplied arms for South Texas and frontier defense, as well as for the Sibley Expedition to New Mexico in 1862. Reoccupied by Federal forces in 1865, this became the principal supply depot for the line of forts defending frontier settlements. It served the U.S. Army until 1947, when the arsenal was closed. The long, narrow one-story structure features walls of extremely thick ashlar limestone construction. Details include end gables extended above the roofline, lintels which protrude as hood molds, and a date stone in relief over the side entry. (1977)

SAN ANTONIO (Bexar Co.) *8535 Mission Rd.*
Stinson Airport

Established by the Stinson family of aviation pioneers, Stinson Airport has witnessed the history of aviation from barnstormers to jets. Alabama native Katherine Stinson (1891–1977), hoping to win prize money to finance her musical education, convinced famed flight instructor Max Lillie of Chicago to take her on as a student in 1912. She became the fourth licensed woman pilot in the U. S. and began touring as a stunt pilot. Her family—mother Emma, sister Marjorie, and brothers Eddie and Jack—established the Stinson Aviation Company in Hot Springs, Arkansas. Marjorie and Eddie trained at the Wright Flying School in Ohio and also became pilots. In 1913, Max Lillie encouraged the Stinsons to move to San Antonio where the army had granted him permission to use the parade ground at Fort Sam Houston. Soon Katherine and Marjorie were offering instruction to U. S. and Canadian military pilots. The family leased 500 acres at this site from the city in 1916 and established Stinson Field. After the ban of civilian flights during World War I, Stinson Field became the city's civil airport in 1918. Charles Lindbergh kept an airplane and flew out of Stinson while he was stationed at Brooks Field. In the 1930s, commercial airlines began using the airport and construction of a new terminal building with Works Progress Administration funds enhanced the facility. During World War II it once again became an Army Air Corps training facility. Returned to civilian use after the war, Stinson Field became the primary general aviation airport for the city of San Antonio. (2001)

SAN ANTONIO (Bexar Co.) *Espada Rd., .5 mi. N of intersection with Loop 410*
Mission San Francisco de la Espada
Dam, Ditch and Aqueduct

Since water was vital to the permanency of San Francisco de la Espada Mission, the Franciscan missionaries and their Indian followers built a dam, irrigation ditch, and aqueduct. The 270-foot dam, an engineering feat which "curved the wrong way," was built across the San Antonio River. Lime salts in the water gradually cemented the dam's layers of brush, gravel, and rocks. Water transported by Espada ditch crossed Piedras Creek by way of the Espada Aqueduct. This, the only such structure in the United States, was built from 1740 to 1745. The alluvial valley produced crops of maize, beans, melons, calabashes, and cotton; however, deterioration had set in at Espada before its secularization in 1794. Even so, the dam, ditch, and aqueduct survived a century of Indian attacks, ravaging floods, and controversy before the Espada Ditch Company repaired the dam in 1895. In 1941, to help insure the preservation of this singular colonial aqueduct, the San Antonio Conservation Society purchased the adjacent lands. Further assurance came in 1965, when the

United States Department of Interior designated Espada Aqueduct as a registered national historic landmark.
(1970)

SAN ANTONIO (Bexar Co.)   *Graf Rd. at SH 122, at mission*
Mission San Juan Capistrano
Founded in March, 1731, by Franciscan missionaries on the banks of the San Antonio River; named for St. John of Capistrano, who in 1456 led a European religious crusade that saved the city of Belgrade from infidels. Mission San Juan was a successor to Mission San José de los Nazonis, established in 1716 in East Texas. It moved here due to the difficulty of defense. One of a complex of missions, San Juan was devoted to the cultural and religious conversion of the Coahuiltcan-speaking Indians of South Texas. During the uncertain early years, buildings were constructed, crops planted, and the Indians had to be continually persuaded to stay long enough to reap the benefits of civilization. Apache raids, cholera and smallpox epidemics, and harassment by the civil authorities also plagued the missions constantly. By 1762, however, San Juan had surplus harvests of corn, cotton, beans, chili peppers, watermelons, and cantaloupes. It also owned numerous cattle, sheep, goats, and horses. The 203 resident Indians lived in thatched huts; the chapel and convent were of stone. The mission was secularized in 1794. In 1967, when the buildings were restored, many artifacts relating to the three centuries of occupancy were unearthed.
(1968)

SAN ANTONIO (Bexar Co.)   *Rigsby Ave. (US 87) at Comanche Park*
Site of the Camp of Stephen F. Austin (October 20–26, 1835)
While assembling troops preparatory to the attack on the Mexican garrison at San Antonio. After his appointment on November 12 as Commissioner to the United States, the Texans, under Colonels Ben Milam and Frank W. Johnson stormed and captured San Antonio, December 10, 1835.

SAN ANTONIO (Bexar Co.)   *US 281 at FM 2537, 14 mi. S*
The Battle of the Medina
The Battle of the Medina was fought here on August 18, 1813 by an army of Spanish Royalists commanded by General José Joaquín Arredondo which defeated with terrific slaughter the Republican Army of the North composed of Anglo-Americans, Mexicans and Indians commanded by José Álvarez de Toledo. Thus ended an attempt to free Texas and Mexico from Spanish rule.   (1936)

SAN ANTONIO (Bexar Co.)   *W. Montgomery Rd. off US 90*
"Battle" of Adams Hill
Near this site, an early armed confrontation of the Civil War ended without bloodshed. On February 16, 1861 in San Antonio, General David E. Twiggs, commander of the U.S. Army Department of Texas, surrendered all federal military property in the state to forces under command of Ben McCulloch. Possession of the San Antonio Arsenal and 20 other installations statewide transferred to Texas forces, who permitted U.S. soldiers to march to the coast and leave Texas as soon as ships could be procured. After the outbreak of hostilities in the South in April, federal troops still in Texas were declared prisoners of war. There was, however, one unit still armed and not in Confederate custody. Marching southeast from Forts Bliss, Davis and Quitman in far west Texas were six companies of the 8th U.S. Infantry, a total of 347 men under the command of Lt. Col. I.V.D. Reeve. Here near San Lucas Spring, Col. Earl Van Dorn, Confederate commander of Texas, stationed 1300 men and six field pieces to meet Reeve. Federal troops took up a defensive position on Adams Hill, a half mile in front. After a six-week march from El Paso, Reeve's numbers were down to 270 men. On May 9, Van Dorn sent a demand for surrender, but Reeve refused. Reeve rejected a second flag of truce with the same mandate. Van Dorn succeeded with his third request—that Federal officers come over, see the Confederate strength and surrender peaceably. The move brought an end to the encounter without the firing of a shot. Reeve's men were made prisoners of war, interned and later exchanged. In February 1863, the last of the 8th U.S. Infantry left Texas in exchange for Confederate prisoners at Baton Rouge after more than 21 months of imprisonment.   (2007)

SAN ANTONIO (Bexar Co.)   *Acme Rd. at Castroville Rd. near US 90 at SH 151*
Chihuahua Trail
This is route of an old Indian road, often path for Apache and Comanche depredations in Texas. Passed Castroville, Uvalde, Horse-Head Crossing on the Pecos; went through Presidio into northern Mexico. In some stretches, water holes were 40 miles apart. Men chewed boots to slake thirst.

417

At smell of water, oxen ran. Texas' commercial use began in 1835. Leather, silver, other metals came here over the road in big-wheel Mexican carts. On south to seaports went some of the goods. In the Civil War, the route brought rope, hats, shoes, salt and other goods to Texas.   (1965)

SAN AUGUSTINE (San Augustine Co.)   *SH 147, 4 mi. N at cemetery entrance*
Antioch Church of Christ
William P. Defee, a medical doctor, arrived in Texas in 1833 and began preaching in homes. In 1836, he began this congregation. They met in a dirt-floored, log building on Rhoddy Anthony's property. The name "Antioch" was chosen because the disciples were first called Christians in Antioch. Anthony was selected elder and served for 50 years. About 1870, a new sanctuary was built on this land belonging to Stephen Passmore. The building served as a schoolhouse and community meeting place. This structure was completed in 1938.   (1979)

SAN AUGUSTINE (San Augustine Co.)   *SH 147, 1.5 mi. N*
Alexander Horton Cemetery
Pioneer, soldier, civic leader, and state legislator, Alexander Horton (1810–1894) came to Texas in 1824. He served as an aide-de-camp to Gen. Sam Houston at the Battle of San Jacinto, April 21, 1836. This cemetery is situated on property Horton bought in 1837. His home once stood adjacent to the plot. According to family tradition, the first grave here was that of Horton's brother William Wade, a Texas Ranger who died in 1849. Maintained by descendants, the cemetery contains about 20 graves, including those of Horton and other family members.   (1977)

SAN AUGUSTINE (San Augustine Co.)   *SH 21, .4 mi. E of Carrizo Creek*
Site of Battle of Fredonia
Climax of first Anglo-American rebellion in East Texas. In 1826 colonizer Hayden Edwards defied expulsion orders of Mexico and founded Republic of Fredonia—raising flag of "Independence, Liberty, and Justice." When Ayish Bayou settlers refused to join, he ordered their banishment. Fredonians, from log fort at this site, were ordered to take Ayish Bayou on Jan. 21, 1827. That day, however, without a shot, Stephen Prather's 9 white men and 60 Indians took the fort and 200 soldiers. At news of this, Edwards fled to the U.S., ending the Fredonian Rebellion.   (1966)

SAN AUGUSTINE (San Augustine Co.)   *128 E. Columbia (Spur 547)*
Sam Houston in San Augustine
Sam Houston (March 2, 1793–July 26, 1863) left home in 1809 and lived among the Cherokees. After two years he returned to the Anglo world; he opened a school, fought the British under Andrew Jackson, and was Governor of Tennessee. After a three-week marriage, Houston left the governorship and returned to the Cherokees; three years later, he came to Texas. Upon his arrival in San Augustine, Sam Houston opened a legal practice on this site. For the next thirty years he used "The Redlands" as a place of business, residence, or refuge. Houston is said to have recuperated from the Battle of San Jacinto in the home of Colonel Phillip Sublett, issuing his report of the battle from San Augustine. Following Houston's term as President of the Republic of Texas, the people of San Augustine elected him to serve them in the Texas House of Representatives during the Fourth and Fifth Congresses. Houston's divorce from Eliza Allen took place in San Augustine in 1837. He married Margaret Lea in 1840; though her health would not permit her to live in San Augustine, she made frequent visits. The early and strong support of the people of "The Redlands" for Sam Houston and Houston's love for them is documented in the history and lore of San Augustine and its people.   (1998)

SAN AUGUSTINE (San Augustine Co.)   *Corner of Livingston and Goldenway*
Jerusalem Memorial Christian Methodist Episcopal Church
Blacks in San Augustine worshiped together as early as 1845, when two slaves known as Sutton and Bartlett were granted licenses to preach in the Methodist Episcopal Church, South. They built a place of worship, referred to as the "Church on the Branch," on a lot thought to belong to local landholder George Teel. After the Civil War the fellowship declined invitations to join independent groups such as the African Methodist Episcopal Church, and remained part of the Methodist Episcopal Church, South. In 1866, the Methodist Episcopal Church, South, formed a separate conference for its black members, which was known as the Colored Methodist Episcopal (C.M.E.) Church. The San Augustine "Church on the Branch" joined the conference in 1870 under

the pastorate of the Rev. Sam Horton, but was not officially known as Jerusalem C.M.E. Church until 1946. The name Christian Methodist Episcopal Church was adopted in 1954. With its earliest history dating to the pre-Civil War era, Jerusalem Memorial C.M.E. Church is considered one of the oldest black congregations in the state. For over a century it has played an important role in the growth of Methodism in San Augustine.

(1983)

SAN AUGUSTINE (San Augustine Co.)   *SH 147, .5 mi. S*
Mission Nuestra Señora de los Dolores de los Ais
Established in 1716 by Padre Fray Antonio Margil de Jesus. Here faithful Franciscans labored for the purpose of civilizing and Christianizing the Ais Indians. Abandoned temporarily due to the French incursions from Louisiana in 1719. Restored by the Marquis of Aguayo in 1721. The mission also served to confirm the claim of the King of Spain to the Province of Texas.

SAN AUGUSTINE (San Augustine Co.)   *Columbia St., E of SH 21 at Spur 547*
¼ mi. N to Site of Early Texas Sawmill
Texas' first million-dollar industry—lumbering—was born to recorded history with the building of two sawmills in 1819. One, located on Ironosa Creek in present San Augustine County, was run by pioneer Wm. Ward; the other was in Nacogdoches. In 1825 yet another mill (¼ mi. N) was turning out about 500 board feet of lumber a day. Wm. Quirk was miller. In these times, trees were felled using an ax and a wedge. Then one end of each huge log was slung under a heavy cart and dragged to a stream or road. At the mill the logs were often stored in a mill pond, to keep them from rotting, and then they were sawed by various methods. Two primitive ones—soon abandoned—were pit sawing (a slow, exhausting two-man process) and the Muley-mill powered by animals. A later improvement was the sash saw, which was so nearly effortless that one old-timer claimed the attendant "could read the Bible or the *Galveston News* while the saw was cutting." In the mid-19th century, logging served as a pivot-point for dozens of subsidiary industries; railroad building and lumbering had a strong mutual influence and the gusto of loggers' lore is still alive in the rich heritage of the piney woods.

(1969)

SAN AUGUSTINE (San Augustine Co.)   *US 96 at SH 21*
San Augustine
An early eastern gate to Texas, in area claimed in 1600s by both France and Spain. To back her claim, Spain in 1691 charted from Mexico past this site El Camino Real (The King's Highway) and established nearby in 1717 Mission Dolores de los Aies. Inhabited by Ayish Indians and Spaniards until the later 1790s, when Richard Sims came and was soon followed by John Quinalty, Edmond Quirk and families of Broocks, Cullens, Cartwrights, Hortons, Hustons, Prathers and others. By 1824 the settlement had a water mill to grind corn meal; in 1826, a cotton gin. In the 1827 Battle of Ayish Bayou, Col. Prather and 69 men put down Fredonian uprising over land titles. The town was laid off in 1833 by Thomas McFarland. In 1836 it sent as delegates to sign Declaration of Independence S. W. Blount and E. O. LeGrand; fielded 3 companies to fight in the War for Independence. Its Republic of Texas statesmen included vice-president K. L. Anderson; J. A. Greer, secretary of the treasury; Wm. Holman, congressman; J. Pinckney Henderson, minister to England and France, and later the first governor of the state. Oran M. Roberts was 16th governor. Home of 1965 United States Ambassador to Australia Edward Clark. Many historic sites are marked.

(1966)

SAN AUGUSTINE (San Augustine Co.)   *SH 21, 7 mi. W*
Home of Thomas S. McFarland (1810–1880)
Surveyor, soldier and statesman. Aide-de-camp to Major Bullock in the Battle of Nacogdoches, 1832. Laid out the town of San Augustine in 1833. Soldier in the Texan Army, 1836. Member of the Congress of the Republic of Texas. Chief Justice, San Augustine County.

SAN BENITO (Cameron Co.)   *US 77 at SH 345*
Spiderweb Railroad
Col. Sam A. Robertson, who founded the town of San Benito in 1907, promoted and built the San Benito & Rio Grande Valley Railway. It was designed to provide a more accessible and efficient transportation system for the shipping of area farm products. Because of the railroad's intricate network of lines and spurs, it was commonly known as the Spiderweb Railroad. The first phases of the rail line were begun in 1911 under the supervision of Col. Robertson's brother Frank S. Robertson.

Construction of the feeder rail lines brought trackside loading facilities to the remote farming areas of the valley and assured the continuing development of brushland into irrigated farms. Trains carrying freight and passengers were soon making two round trips daily over routes that eventually stretched 128 miles. For many years the Spiderweb remained essential to the valley's development as one of the leading agricultural regions of the nation. Traffic on the line declined, however, because of improved roads, motor transportation and more centralized loading facilities. Today the history of the line serves as a reminder of the pioneer farmers and businessmen who were instrumental in the area's early growth. (1982)

SAN BENITO (Cameron Co.)
216 S. Sam Houston (SH 345)
Water District Building
Designed by Austin architects Endress and Walsh and built by contractor L. Fleming, the San Benito Land and Water Company building was completed in 1910 at a cost of $14,386. Thirty-foot pine beams and locally made brick were used to construct the home of the company. A fine example of the Mission Revival Style, the edifice features a red tile roof, wooden bracketed eaves, a stucco exterior, and curved gable parapets. The building has been home to many San Benito institutions, notably the irrigation and drainage districts. A beloved fixture of downtown San Benito, it stands as a memorial to the vital role of irrigation in valley life. (1997)

SAN DIEGO (Duval Co.)
404 E. Gravis Ave. (SH 359)
Duval County
Created by the Texas Legislature in 1858 and organized in 1879, Duval County played an important role in the economic and political development of South Texas. Early settlers came to this area in the mid-19th century from Mexico, and Anglo pioneers began arriving in the 1860s. The early economy was based on ranching and agriculture. In the late 1870s the railroad brought increased employment and population to the county. The discovery of oil, gas, and uranium in the early 1900s boosted the economy and caused increased settlement in the region. (1996)

SAN DIEGO (Duval Co.)
SH 44 at FM 3196, 11.7 mi. W
Felipe Valerio Store and Garage (1.5 mi. SE)
Built in 1905 by Felipe Valerio (1878–1953) and his wife Jesusa (1886–1973), the Valerio store was an integral part of the small community of La Rosita. Located approximately halfway between San Diego and Freer, the store provided groceries and other goods for residents of this rural area. An increase in business from the area oil boom in the 1930s led to the addition of a gas station and garage. The store also served as a bus station, and Felipe Valerio was local postmaster from 1917 to 1929. Construction of State Highway 44 led to the closing of the store in 1956. (1994)

SAN ELIZARIO (El Paso Co.)
1500 Main St. at Glorietta Rd.,
San Elizario Plaza
San Elizario
San Elizario was established in 1789 on the former site of Hacienda de los Tiburcios as a Spanish colonial fort known as the Presidio de San Elceario. The Presidio was moved from its original location (approx. 37 mi. S) in response to requests from settlers for military protection from Indian raids. It operated as a Spanish post until 1814, when troops withdrew during the Mexican War for Independence (1810–1821). During its years as a part of Mexico, the Presidio de San Elceario (now San Elizario) was occupied periodically by Mexican troops. A reduced military presence resulted in the fort's decline. American control of the area began in 1848, with the treaty of Guadalupe Hidalgo, which established the Rio Grande as the border between the United States and Mexico. When the county of El Paso was organized in 1850, the town of San Elizario was chosen first county seat and served as such until 1873. In 1877, it was the scene of a crisis known as the Salt War, in which local businessmen attempted to control the salt market that had operated since colonial times. Although San Elizario was bypassed by the railroad and has become a rural farming community, it remains an important element in the region's rich heritage. (1985)

Rodríguez-Chamuscado Expedition—1581
Inspired by Indian stories of settlements in present New Mexico and authorized by the Spanish Viceroy, Fray Agustín Rodríguez, a Franciscan priest, led a missionary expedition to the area. Ac-

420

companied by Fray Juan de Santa María, Fray Francisco López, nine soldiers, and nineteen Indian servants, he left Santa Barbara, Mexico, on June 5, 1581. The military escort was led by Francisco Sanchez, who, because of his red beard, was known as Chamuscado, "The Singed." Following the Rio Grande, the expedition reached El Paso del Norte. Proceeding through the pass, they spent the remainder of 1581 exploring the vast region from present western New Mexico to the Texas Panhandle. After Indians killed Fray Santa María in September 1581, plans were made to return for a report to the Spanish authorities. Despite the hostile environment, the two remaining missionaries chose to stay. Chamuscado led the others back through the Pass of the North, but died before reaching Santa Barbara. Believed to have been the first Spanish expedition to use the Pass of the North, the Rodríguez-Chamuscado Expedition marked the beginning of Spanish influence in the area. Their exploration opened the region, now the American Southwest, to later colonization.   (1981)

Espejo-Beltran Expedition—1582–1583
Following the Rodríguez-Chamuscado Expedition of 1581, there was increased interest in the area now known as New Mexico and Texas. There was also concern for the safety of Fray Rodríguez and Fray López, who had stayed in the area. In 1582, a Franciscan priest from Santa Barbara, Mexico, Fray Bernardino Beltran, formed an expedition to find the missionaries. His military escort was led by Antonio de Espejo, a former Santa Barbara merchant and rancher living in voluntary exile over a legal dispute with the Spanish authorities. The expedition departed the mining outpost of San Bartolome in November 1582. By the following January they had reached the El Paso area. In present New Mexico they learned that Fray Rodríguez and Fray López had been killed by Indians. Fray Beltran led a small party back to Mexico, but Espejo and several companions stayed to check the Indian stories of silver mines and wealthy pueblos. On their journey the Spaniards became the first explorers in the region from the Pecos River Valley to the Junta de los Rios, the junction of the Concho River and the Rio Grande. The reports of their explorations further heightened the interest in the area.   (1981)

Salt War
The Salt War rose from political conflicts in El Paso County and from controversies over control of the salt lakes east of El Paso, which for centuries had been a free source of salt for local residents. In 1877, Charles Howard, a former county judge who claimed ownership of the lakes, shot political adversary Luis Cardis over the issue of the salt beds. While under the protection of state troops in San Elizario, Howard and several of the troopers were killed by a riotous mob. Federal and state investigations of the Salt War led to the reestablishment of Ft. Bliss in 1878.   (1984)

SAN FELIPE (Austin Co.)   *FM 1458, 2 mi. N of IH 10 at roadside park*
San Felipe de Austin
First Anglo-American Capital of Texas. Came into being on July 26, 1823, as capital of the Austin Colony, by decree of the Mexican government. Father of Texas Stephen F. Austin had begun under the 1821 grant from Mexico the settlement of more than 1,000 families. The original colony ran from the coast on the south to the Old San Antonio Road on the north, and from the Lavaca River on the west to the San Jacinto River on the East. In this first American town in Texas lived Austin, William Barret Travis, Sam Houston, David G. Burnet and Jane Long. All settlers crossed its threshold for land grants. After the organization of other colonies, this continued to be the recognized center of Texas. It was capital of the Mexican Department of Brazos, site of the conventions of 1832 and 1833 and the consultation of 1835 where Texans aired grievances and tried to reach understanding with Mexico. The provisional government created with Henry Smith as governor in 1835 functioned here until it gave way to the convention declaring Texas independent of Mexico on March 2, 1836. Republic of Texas capitals were Columbia, Houston, Washington-on-the-Brazos and Austin.

Stephen Fuller Austin
Father of Texas. November 3, 1793–December 27, 1836. He planted the first Anglo-American colony in Texas, "The Old Three Hundred." In his several colonies he settled more than a thousand families. He was from 1823 until 1828 the actual ruler of Texas and thereafter its most influential leader. His own words are a fitting epitaph. "The prosperity of Texas has been the object of my labors—the idol of my existence. It has assumed the character of a religion—for the guidance of

my thoughts and actions," and he died in its service. No other state in the Union owes its existence more completely to one man than Texas does to Austin.

Early Roads to San Felipe

During the mid-1820s, when Stephen F. Austin was founding this town, the only roads in the area were wagon ruts or beaten trails marked by notched trees. Within a decade, however, the village of San Felipe, one of the first Anglo settlements in Texas, had become a hub from which eight or more roads projected. Many of these were small, intra-colony routes, but the main trails extended to major towns or joined "highways," such as the San Antonio Road (El Camino Real). A main route which passed through San Felipe was the Atascosita Road, connecting Goliad with the United States. It took its name from Atascosa (Spanish for "boggy") Spring near Liberty, which once was its main terminus. The Gotier Trace, another travel artery, was laid out about 1830 by pioneer James Gotier. It joined the northern and southern parts of Austin's colony and was used for decades. The San Felipe Road proper, which ran to Harrisburg, transported goods inland from the Gulf coast. Even the main thoroughfares, however, were dusty trails in the summer and impassable quagmires in the winter, often flooded by knee-deep water. Not until well into the 20th century did Texas begin to develop her present, outstanding highway system. (1969)

SAN FELIPE (Austin Co.)   *FM 1458 E at 6th St.*
San Felipe Town Hall

Successor to 1828 hall used by "Ayuntamiento" (town council). Conventions of 1832, 1833, and consultation of 1835—leading to Texas Revolution—met there. Burned during revolution in 1836. Two-story section of present structure was built about 1842 and may have served as county courthouse until 1847. It was joined to a one-story school after 1900; moved to this site, 1915. By old custom, council meets each Saturday before full moon. Awarded Medallion Plate.   (1970)

SAN GABRIEL (Milam Co.)   *FM 487, 6 mi. E*
Site of the Mission San Ildefonso

Established by Franciscan missionaries in 1749 with the hope of civilizing and Christianizing the Coco, Mayeye, Orcoquiza, Karankawa, and other tribes of Indians. The martyrdom of Padre Jose Ganzabal and the circumstances connected therewith caused the departure of the Indians and the Friars and the removal of this mission to the San Marcos River in 1755. Reestablished in 1762 on the Nueces River for the conversion of the Lipan Apaches with the new name of Mission San Lorenzo de la Santa Cruz.

SAN GABRIEL (Milam Co.)   *FM 487, 1.5 mi. E*
Site of the Mission Nuestra Señora de la Candelaria

Established by Franciscan missionaries in 1749 with the hope of civilizing and Christianizing the Coco, Mayeye, Orocoquiza, Karankawa, and other tribes of Indians. The martyrdom of Padre Jose Ganzabal and the circumstances connected therewith caused the departure of the Indians and the Friars and the removal of this mission to the San Marcos River in 1755. Reestablished in 1762 on the Sabinal River for the conversion of the Lipan Apaches with the same name of Nuesta Señora de la Candelaria.

SAN JUAN (Hidalgo Co.)   *US 83S, 5 mi. S at FM 1426*
San Antonio and Rio Grande Railway: "Old Flossie"

Beginning operations in 1909, the San Antonio and Rio Grande Railway Company became a branch of the St. Louis, Brownsville and Mexico Railway in 1912. Nicknamed "Old Flossie," it provided freight and passenger transportation to the new towns of Chapin (Edinburg) and San Juan during a crucial time in the area's development. Passenger service decreased after World War II, and the line was limited to freight service. It was absorbed by the Missouri Pacific system in 1956. By the late 1960s all service to San Juan and Edinburg ceased, the rails were removed, and the depots were razed.   (1991)

SAN MARCOS (Hays Co.)   *IH 35 frontage rd./US 81, 1.5 mi. N*
Hays County

Formed from Travis County. Created March 1, 1848. Organized August 7, 1848. Named in honor of John Coffee (Jack) Hays, 1817–1883. Captain of Texas Rangers. Colonel in the Mexican War. County seat, San Marcos.

SAN MARCOS (Hays Co.)   *Loop 82, Aquarena Springs Dr. at entrance to park*
San Marcos Springs
   Pouring forth millions of gallons of clear, icy water daily, these springs feed the San Marcos River and the 1,380-square-mile area in which it drains. The immense springs rise at the Balcones Escarpment, a geologic fault line which slices across the state, separating upland from lowland Texas. The abundance of fresh water made these springs a mecca for the Indians who inhabited Central Texas and later for the European explorers and settlers who followed. The name San Marcos was first given to a Texas river by the Alonso de Leon Expedition on April 26, 1689 (Saint Mark's Day). The name was not applied to the present river, however, until 1709. Other explorers inspected this area and in 1755 it became a temporary site for several Spanish missions. Almost a century later, in 1845, pioneers William W. Moon and Mike Sessom made a permanent settlement here. In 1851 Gen. Edward Burleson, William Lindsey, and Eli T. Merriman bought the adjacent land and on it laid out the town of San Marcos. Attracted by the scenic beauty of the area, A. B. Rogers started a park here in 1926. Over the years it has been developed into Aquarena Springs, one of Central Texas' most popular tourist attractions.   (1971)

SAN MARCOS (Hays Co.)   *SH 80 at Old Bastrop Rd. (CR 266), 2 mi. SE*
McGehee Crossing
   The Camino Real, also known as the Old San Antonio Road and the King's Highway, followed a route from Nacogdoches to the Rio Grande. Louis Juchereau de St. Denis (1676–1744) traveled the route to establish trade between the French in Louisiana and the Spanish of Coahuila province on the Rio Grande in 1714. The first settlement at the San Marcos River crossing of the road was Villa San Marcos de Neve, established by the Spanish in 1808. It was abandoned by 1812 due to the brewing Mexican Revolution. During their colonization efforts in 1820 and 1821, Moses Austin (1761–1821) and his son, Stephen F. Austin (1793–1836), very likely crossed the San Marcos River near this point. Thomas Gilmer McGehee (1810–1890) settled on the east side of the river on a Mexican land grant about 1846. In 1859, his nephew, Charles L. McGehee, Jr. (1837–1929), acquired 1200 acres of land bordered by the Camino Real and the river. Ten years later he sold the land to his cousin, George T. McGehee (1836–1926). Due to the McGehee family's association with this historic site, it became known as McGehee Crossing.   (1987)

SAN SABA (San Saba Co.)   *US 190, 5 mi. E*
Indian Signaling Grounds
   Heights used from pre-settlement days to 1870s by Comanches and others to send messages over long distances. Smoke once rose from here (Five Mile Hill); Chappel Hill, 2 mi. south; and old community of Sloan in West San Saba County. Tribes wintered at main village near Sloan; burial ground is on Chappel Hill. An early settler recalls Indians peering through cracks in cabin at night while she, children, and friend put ashes on fire and hid. She believed Indians would not enter a dark house. Another time she heard livestock being taken. Many pioneers saw signals on nearby hills. Indians communicated by means of smoke, at times mirrors. Codes were used to confuse enemies. Messages sent news and could gather or disperse tribes. The Comanches had an excellent smoke signal system, also imitated animal cries. These often warned settlers to prepare for attack. In some areas, whites later pre-empted signal grounds for use against the Indians. Mirabeau B. Lamar visited this area in 1837; later, as president of Republic of Texas, he had a forceful Indian policy. On banks of San Saba in 1847, German Emigration Company bought peace from the Comanches for $3,000 worth of beads, trinkets; and in 1850 at Wallace Creek, about 15 mi. southwest, the U.S. signed an Indian treaty.   (1967)

SAN SABA (San Saba Co.)   *US 190, 4 mi. E*
Site of Barnett-Hamrick Settlement, 1855–1895
   John W. Barnett and family with sons-in-law, Burrell L. and Tom P. C. Hamrick, settled large tract of land here. Founded community of Simpson Creek. Were first in area to farm as well as to irrigate crops. Were active in local commerce. Helped organize county. First camp meeting and one of first schools were held here.   (1969)

SAN SABA (San Saba Co.)   *US 190, .75 mi. E*
San Saba Lodge No. 225, A. F. & A. M.
   The history of San Saba is closely tied with the story of Freemasonry in the area, as many of those who helped organize San Saba County were Masons. Local Freemasons were already gathering as a

group when the first county courthouse was erected in 1857 and the Commissioners Court allowed the Masons to meet in the new building. Twelve Master Masons petitioned the Grand Lodge of Texas for dispensation to form a lodge; their petition was granted in May 1858. A full charter for San Saba Lodge No. 225 was granted in June 1859. Members of the lodge were county officials, community leaders, frontier trailblazers, Texas Rangers, sheriffs and Confederate soldiers. The lodge first focused on the need for a public school in San Saba as members built a combination school and lodge hall. The Texas Legislature granted an official charter to the San Saba Masonic College in 1863. Freemasonry grew in popularity and in 1863 the Royal Arch Masons were granted a dispensation for a San Saba chapter, remaining active until 1869. Despite a membership of 84 in 1879, San Saba lodge suffered the same financial hardships as most of the Texas lodges during Reconstruction. San Saba Lodge No. 225 surrendered its charter in 1882, due in part to perceived association with the San Saba mob, an outlaw vigilante group that terrorized the county during that era. A new lodge was organized in 1884, however, allowing Freemasonry to survive in San Saba.   (1999)

SAN SABA (San Saba Co.)   *US 190, .25 mi. E*
John H. "Shorty" Brown Cemetery
After living for a time in Arkansas, John H. "Shorty" Brown (1817–1896), his wife Jane Ann, and some of their children came here. Brown helped found San Saba in 1854 and became a civic leader. Although San Saba County provided a graveyard, Brown and his wife deeded this plot near their home for a family burial ground. Jane Ann, who bore 17 of Brown's 21 children, was probably the first burial here about 1874. Brown's son and a son-in-law who were murdered are buried here along with other family members and friends.   (1980)

SAN SABA (San Saba Co.)   *US 190, at E city limits*
San Saba County
On northeastern border of the Edwards Plateau. Created from Bexar County, Feb. 1, and organized May 3, of 1856. Named for San Saba River. County seat of same name. Area first explored in 1732 by Juan Antonio Bustillo y Zevallos. Anglo-American settlement began in 1840s. Economy based on ranching, farming and commercial quarrying of marble, sand and limestone. Principal crops are cotton, grains, peanuts, sorghums and clovers. Ranchers market wool and mohair. Known as "Pecan Capital of the World."   (1966)

SAN SABA (San Saba Co.)   *W. Wallace St. (US 190) at 2nd St.*
San Saba Church of Christ
San Saba County was organized in 1856, and in 1860 the commissioners court issued a block of land to each religious body; the Christian Church was one of these. The congregation traded their land for another block upon which they built a small frame structure. The first documented preacher of the Christian Church in San Saba was J. A. Henderson. For many years, services were conducted by lay elders and by traveling ministers. Popular religious debates held in San Saba often involved members of the Christian Church. The 20th century was ushered in by the 1904 division in the Christian Church, which led the San Saba congregation to choose the Church of Christ. Despite the split and such lean years as those of the depression era, the San Saba Church of Christ thrived, popular activities such as summer revivals increased membership in the church, with new facilities erected as needed. A controversy over the support of mission work resulted in the founding of a separate congregation in 1957, but the original San Saba congregation carried on and quickly regained its strength, flourishing in the 1970s. The San Saba Church of Christ upholds the unique traditions of its founders through worship, missionary, and community outreach programs in Texas and beyond.   (1998)

SAN SABA (San Saba Co.)   *US 190, 3 mi. W*
Harkeyville
A site once famous for its horses and racetrack. Riley Harkey (1832–1920) and Israel Harkey (1835–1914) were Indian scouts in Texas in 1850–1853. In 1855 they led their parents, Mathias and Catherine Harkey, to move here from Arkansas with other adult sons, daughters, in-laws, and grandchildren. The families ranched, and Mathias Harkey ran a country store for many years. Riley Harkey brought to Texas a fine, fleetfooted mare, who with her racing progeny drew crowds of enthusiasts to this site for half a century. Other sons and grandsons of Mathias Harkey also joined in the breeding, training, and racing of horses. Stores, blacksmith shop, and other businesses all

faced east on a single street overlooking the flat with its racetrack and baseball diamond. There was no post office, but the village was so well known that mail addressed to Harkeyville promptly arrived here. On Nov. 26, 1873, George W. Barnett (1823–1885) gave land for the first school; the schoolhouse was used also for church services and public meetings. The racetrack closed in 1970; the cotton gin burned in 1920, and was not rebuilt; school consolidated in 1929 with San Saba. The last store closed in 1954. A community hall, built 1973, marks site of the town.   (1974)

SAN SABA (San Saba Co.)   *US 190, 10.7 mi. W*
The John Robert Polk Ranch
Known as San Saba County property with history of longest continuous ownership by a single family. Texas settler Headley Polk, a kinsman of 1845–1849 United States President James K. Polk, bought from grantee Burke Trammel in 1849 a section of land a half-mile to the south of this marker. Headley's son, John Robert Polk (1853–1946), grew up in Lockhart and on the San Marcos River at the Mooney Mill, where he made fine furniture. In 1883, "Bob" and his wife Kate Word Polk moved to this property with their herd of cattle. Over the years they bought adjacent land until they had 2,000 acres with frontage of three and one-half miles on the San Saba River. The second tract of land in this county ever to be enclosed was fenced by Polk with the help of a man named Baker. Two schoolhouses were built at different times on this ranch, for the convenience of the Polk family and neighbors. In the early era, Polk trailed his Bar-P cattle to market; for years he belonged to the Texas Trail Drivers' Association. John Robert and Kate Polk were parents of a son, Headley (who died at 17, in 1904) and five daughters: Annie (later Mrs. W. W. Holman), Eupha (Mrs. Louis J. Bryan), Ivor Mac, Katie (Mrs. J. A. Sloan), and Lex.   (1971)

SAN YGNACIO (Zapata Co.)   *US 83 right-of-way, 5 mi. SE*
Old Ramireño
Old Ramireño was located on land granted to Don Jose Luis Ramirez by the King of Spain in 1784. Part of the colonization effort of Col. Jose de Escandon, Ramirez' grant was designated as Porción 5. A resident of Revilla (now Guerrero), Nuevo Santander (now Tamaulipas) in Mexico, Don Jose Luis Ramirez, his wife Maria Bacilia Martinez, and their children moved across the Rio Grande and established a home on their land in present Zapata County. Don Jose Luis and Maria Bacilia Martinez Ramirez had ten children. Their families and descendants formed the nucleus of the community of Ramireño. The men of the ill-fated Mier Expedition of 1842 camped at Ramireño during their march to Mexico, and the settlement was also the site of United States military activity during the Mexican Revolution and border raids of 1916–1917. The construction of Falcon Reservoir on the Rio Grande caused the relocation of several area communities, including Ramireño. The settlement founded by Don Jose Luis Ramirez was moved in 1953 to a site two miles from the original Ramirez Ranch. The hand-cut sandstone Ramirez ranch home was covered by the waters of Falcon Reservoir.   (1988)

SANDERSON (Terrell Co.)   *US 90, 10.2 mi. E*
Baxter's Curve Train Robbery
In the early hours of March 13, 1912, Ben Kilpatrick, a former sidekick of Butch Cassidy and Sundance Kid, and Ole Hobek attempted one of the last major train robberies in West Texas. The two robbers boarded the Galveston, Harrisburg, and San Antonio railroad train when it stopped at Dryden on the way to El Paso. They ordered the engineer on to Baxter's Curve, a sharp bend in the railway's rail bed. The baggage cars were uncoupled from the coaches, but while the two searched for valuables, Wells Fargo express manager David A. Trousdale bludgeoned one with an ice mallet and killed the other with the first robber's rifle. Kilpatrick and Hobek were buried in Sanderson, and Trousdale was recognized and rewarded for his bravery.   (2010)

SANDERSON (Terrell Co.)   *105 W. Hackberry St., 2 blks. N of*
                                                    W. Oak St. (US 90), courthouse
County Named for Texas Confederate
General Alexander W. Terrell (1827–1912)
Born in Virginia. Came to Texas in 1852. Dist. Judge 1857–1863. Entered Confederate service 1863 as Lt. Col. Commanded Terrell's Texas Cavalry. Assigned special duty to try to keep open vital supply sources of cotton—lifeblood of South. Led his unit in Red River Campaign 1864 to prevent Union invasion of Texas, being wounded at the Battle of Mansfield. Promoted to Briga-

dier General 1865. Went to Mexico rather than surrender at war's end, soon returned to Texas. As state legislator authored present primary election law. Minister to Turkey 1893–1897. Outstanding lawyer and public servant.

SANDERSON (Terrell Co.)

105 W. Hackberry St., 2 blks. N of W. Oak St. (US 90), courthouse

Terrell County

Formed from Pecos County. Created April 8, 1905. Organized September 19, 1905. Named in honor of Alexander Watkins Terrell, 1827–1912. A distinguished officer in the Confederate Army. Member of the Texas Legislature for sixteen years. Sanderson, the county seat.

SANDIA (Jim Wells Co.)

SH 359 at CR 364

Fort Casa Blanca, CSA

First building erected in area that is now Jim Wells County early as 1855. During the Civil War was on Confederate supply line that started in Corpus Christi, followed the Nueces here, went to Laredo, to Brownsville and back to Corpus Christi. When Federals were in Corpus Christi, Thomas Wright, the sutler, drove from here to other points. Casa Blanca was supplied by small boats that out-maneuvered Federals on Nueces Bay, slipped into the Nueces River, and came up Penitos Creek. They hauled guns, ammunition, medicine, and other wartime goods and took out cotton, "Currency of the Confederacy." The fort had walls 28" thick; an escape tunnel from its well led to the creek. Its one entryway, wide enough for a 2-wheel cart of 2 horses abreast, was closed with a heavy cypress door. Cypress shutters covered its few small windows. Corner parapets and portholes at 3 heights gave it emplacements for defense. It not only warehoused goods, but also provided shelter and water for drivers passing with wagons along the Cotton Road from San Antonio to Matamoros. For cotton wagons it meant safety from bandit chases and from killing thirsts. In the 20th century the fort has disappeared.

SANTA ANNA (Coleman Co.)

US 84, 1 mi. NW

Old Rock House

This site was claimed in 1857 under a Republic of Texas land certificate held by former State Representative Darwin Stapp of Victoria County. In 1869 he sold the tract to another absentee owner. By tradition, this house was built in the 1870s by John J. Brestow, a squatter who came to this area for his health. The one-room cabin was constructed of stone from the nearby Santa Anna mountains. Later owners, including Mrs. Sarah Himmins, rented the property to tenant farmers. Mr. and Mrs. C. D. Bruce, who purchased the land in 1947, restored the rock house and maintain it now as a museum. (1975)

SANTA ANNA (Coleman Co.)

US 84, .6 mi. NW

Coleman County

Formed from Travis and Brown Counties. Created February 1, 1858, organized October 6, 1864. Named in honor of Robert M. Coleman, 1799–1837, a signer of the Declaration of Independence, a hero of San Jacinto, organizer of first company of Texas Rangers. Coleman approved as county seat April 28, 1876. (1936)

SANTA ANNA (Coleman Co.)

Wallis Ave. (US 67/84)

Santa Anna, C.S.A.

Mountain and town named in honor of man in power here in 1840s, a Comanche chief friendly to Texans. Santa Anna in 1846 visited President Polk in Washington during U.S. negotiations to annex Texas. Also signed and kept until his death of cholera in 1849 peace treaties that allowed the German Emigration Company to settle lands north of the Llano River. Comanches used Santa Anna peaks as signal points. Early surveyors, travelers, explorers and settlers took them as guide points. In 1857, nearby United States Cavalry at Camp Colorado kept lookouts here. In the Civil War, 1861–1865, frontier rangers camped at foot of mountain, with sentries on height watching at the pass the military road from San Antonio northeastward to Fort Belknap, a strategic outpost guarding Texas from invasion by Indians and Federal troops. During the 1870s, thousands of longhorns went through the gap, over the western cattle trail. In 1879, "The Gap" had a store and post office to supply the cattle drives. When Gulf, Colorado and Santa Fe built here in 1886, settlers moved from the gap to the railroad, starting the present town. Quarries in the mountain yield fine sands for the manufacturing of glass. (1965)

SANTA ANNA (Coleman Co.) *1204 Wallis Ave. (US 67/84)*
The Turner House
Built 1886 by an attorney from Mississippi. Colonial architecture. House was enlarged from 8 to 12 rooms after 1903 purchase by Fred W. Turner, rancher and oilman. This was gathering place for area social and business leaders. Awarded Medallion Plate. (1968)

SANTA ANNA (Coleman Co.) *US 67/84, 3 mi. E*
Route of Old Military Road
Opened in 1850s for supply trains and cavalry travel along line of U.S. forts from Belknap on the Brazos to Fort Mason and to Fort Clark near the Rio Grande. Along this road passed great men, including Col. Robert E. Lee, later (1861–1865) General of Confederate forces in the Civil War. (1972)

SANTA FE (Galveston Co.) *SH 6 at Jackson Ave. in roadside park*
Dairy Industry in the Santa Fe Area
The railroad communities of Arcadia, Alta Loma, and Algoa, established in the 1890s, formed the nucleus of the Santa Fe area at the turn of the 20th century. Citrus and fig production, truck farming, and a burgeoning dairy industry dominated the local economy at that time. Creameries operating at Alta Loma and Arcadia produced and shipped large amounts of butter and milk to markets in Galveston and Houston by 1912. Dairy farming, unlike the citrus and fig industry, emerged as a major economic base in the area during the 1920s. According to local tradition they became so prevalent during this time that most everyone had a dairy. Trucks had supplanted trains for transporting dairy products to markets in Galveston and Houston by this time. Local citizens recalled catching rides on milk trucks before community bus service was available. Although able to recover from a crushing hoof and mouth epidemic in the mid-1920s, many small dairies were bought out by larger operations able to afford land leases for grazing purposes made necessary by stock laws of the 1930s restricting grazing on public lands. Though many dairies prospered with the introduction of automation in the 1950s, the gradual loss of workers to higher paying urban jobs resulted in the closing of all Santa Fe area dairies by the 1970s. (1993)

SANTA MARIA (Cameron Co.) *US 281, 8 mi. E at roadside park*
Near Routes of Alonso de Leon Expeditions
Some of the first systematic explorations of East Texas. Conducted by the Spanish between 1686 and 1690, de Leon's five expeditions were spurred by the fear that the French explorer La Salle, who had landed on the Texas coast in 1685, was claiming vast areas of the New World for France. Because Spain and France were bitter rivals, de Leon was directed to find and destroy any signs of French encroachment. His first trip, originating in Mexico in 1686, took him to the mouth of the Rio Grande, where he sounded the river's depth and took latitude observations. On the second expedition, begun in 1687, he crossed the river near present Roma and followed it to the mouth. Very likely his men traveled several miles away from the water to avoid mud, brush, and hidden Indians. He proceeded up the coast as far as a "Salt River," possibly Olmos Creek, which runs into Baffin Bay near the present town of Rivera. On his three later expeditions, de Leon found and burned the ruins of La Salle's "Fort St. Louis." He also established the first Spanish mission in East Texas, "San Francisco de los Tejas." Stimulated by both of these successes, Spain began her great enterprise of colonizing Texas. (1968)

SANTA MARIA (Cameron Co.) *US 281, 1.8 mi. E at FM 506*
Longoria Cemetery
The Longoria family were among the initial Spanish settlers to arrive in this region in the mid-1700s. Juan Rosas Longoria and Maria Salome Cano were among the men and women who founded permanent communities such as the Villa de Reynosa, establishing the Longoria family in the area. They and other pioneers introduced ranching into the area with techniques brought from southern Spain, many of which remained in use centuries later. In 1831 Irineo Longoria increased the family landholdings north of the Rio Grande by purchasing portions of the Llano Grande, La

427

Feria and Ojo de Agua land grants. He added these tracts to the land of his second wife, Maria Inez Cavazos. They established residence in the community of Santa Maria. The Longoria ranch stretched from what became Sebastian to the Rio Grande. The family also farmed the land and participated in the early development of irrigation systems in the Rio Grande valley. Juan Miguel Longoria (1815–1875) became the owner of the Longoria ranch in the mid-1800s. Married three times, he was the father of 17 children. His first wife was Soledad Cavazos. His second wife, Silveria Ruiz, became one of the first persons interred here upon her death before 1853. After his death, Juan Miguel's third wife, Teresa Guerra, became the family matriarch and managed the ranch from 1875 to 1909. Juan Miguel's grave is marked by an above-ground brick tomb. By the late 1990s, the cemetery was in a state of disrepair. Longoria descendants organized to restore the site and its estimated 371 graves to ensure the endurance of the Longoria Cemetery as a chronicle of the diverse history and heritage of Texas. (2000)

SANTA MARIA (Cameron Co.)
US 281, 1 mi. E at ranch gate
Rancho de Santa María
Part of Spain's 1777 La Feria Grant (12.5 leagues), partitioned into 6 units 1843. Here in 1850s was a sub-post of Fort Brown (28 mi. SE) and Fort Ringgold (65 mi. NW). This was proposed site in 1860s for "Homeville," this locality's first small-acreage promotion. Present compound, built 1870 by L. J. Hynes, has buildings for dairy, kitchen, ammunition. Hynes, first postmaster (1876), had stage depot, general store, telegraph office, shipping wharf on river. Chapel was built 1880. In 1892, Frank Rabb bought the ranch. In 1916 border troubles, U.S. Army established headquarters here. (1968)

SANTA MARIA (Cameron Co.)
US 281, .5 mi. E
Our Lady of Visitation Catholic Church
A rare South Texas snowstorm marked the cornerstone laying ceremonies for this church building, Dec. 29, 1880. The gothic revival edifice was constructed of bricks made at nearby El Rancho de Santa Maria, owned by L. J. Hynes, who gave land for the church. Built from plans drawn by Father Peter I. Keralum, O. M. I., the structure was dedicated June 29, 1882. The wooden steeple was blown off during a 1933 hurricane. Residents of Bluetown, Santa Maria, and neighboring communities worshiped here. (1977)

SARGENT (Matagorda Co.)
FM 457, 5.1 mi. SE
Confederate Defenses at the Mouth of Caney Creek
During the Civil War (1861–1865), Federal forces tried several times to seize Texas ports. Galveston was taken on Oct. 5, 1862, but recaptured by a Confederate Army on Jan. 1, 1863. Lt. Dick Dowling's troops stopped a Federal invasion at Sabine Pass on Sept. 8, 1863. Another thrust began on Nov. 7, 1863, when a Federal expedition under Maj. Gen. N. P. Banks seized Brownsville, then moved up the coast, capturing Corpus Christi, Aransas Pass, Pass Cavallo, and Port Lavaca (Dec. 26). Maj. Gen. John B. Magruder, Confederate commander of Texas, ordered fortification of the mouth of Caney Creek in an attempt to halt the invasion. In Jan. 1864, an earthen fortress, rifle pits, trench works, and four redoubts were erected near this site. Defended by 4000–6000 Confederates, the area was bombarded by Federal gunboats during January and February. No ground combat occurred at Caney Creek, but the preparations deterred a further Federal advance. In March 1864, Gen. Banks moved most of his troops to Louisiana and launched an unsuccessful invasion along Texas' eastern border. Removal of Federal forces from key Texas ports allowed blockade runners to continue transporting needed materials to Civil War Texas. (1976)

SARITA (Kenedy Co.)
US 77, 3 mi. N
Kenedy County
Created April 2, 1921, out of Cameron, Willacy and Hidalgo counties. Named for Captain Mifflin Kenedy, 1818–1895, sent to Texas in 1846 on United States Army supply boats. Commercial navigator of the Rio Grande 1848–1860. Sarita is the county seat.

SARITA (Kenedy Co.)
US 77, 7 mi. S
Site of General Zachary Taylor Camp
Under this tree General Zachary Taylor, commanding the Expeditionary Army of the United States, sent to Texas in 1845, encamped on March 15, 1846, while enroute with his troops from Corpus Christi to the Rio Grande. (1936)

SARITA (Kenedy Co.)

US 77, 20 mi. S, entrance to Armstrong Ranch

The Armstrong Ranch

In 1852, James H. Durst, son of a leading Nacogdoches, Texas family, purchased 83,219 acres of land here, part of the "La Barreta" Spanish land grant. In 1878, Mary Helena "Mollie" Durst, daughter of James and Mary Josephine Atwood Durst, married the noted Texas Ranger John Barkley Armstrong. Armstrong had served with Captain Leander McNelly and played a major role in bringing law and order to South Texas. He participated in the arrest of King Fisher and gained national fame for his capture of the notorious Texas outlaw John Wesley Hardin. Armstrong moved his family to the ranch home he built here. Their close friends and neighbors were the families of Captain Richard King and Captain Mifflin Kenedy. The ranch was an important site in the area; General Zachary Taylor had camped here prior to the Mexican War and for many years the ranch served as a stop on the stage route between Corpus Christi and Brownsville. Under Armstrong's guidance, the Armstrong Ranch became one of the legendary cattle ranches of Texas. His descendants have continued the tradition of family enterprise here through the 20th century.   (1983)

SARITA (Kenedy Co.)

US 77, 20 mi. S

The Armstrong Ranch House

This residence was begun in 1897, after John B. Armstrong moved the headquarters of his ranch from the Chicago pasture (7 mi. SE) to this site. Built in stages, the house was completed about 1900. The first portion was made of adobe and plastered over. Later a frame wing was added. Changes were made to the front porch after the destructive hurricane of 1919. This structure exemplifies the evolution of a South Texas ranch headquarters.   (1982)

SAVOY (Fannin Co.)

US 82, 3 mi. E

Little Jordan Cemetery

Sid H. (1833–1914) and Suzan Brown Pierce (1845–1923) donated this burial ground, near the Little Jordan Baptist Church (active 1850–1893). The Ector Baptist Church, organized by former Little Jordan members, deeded the cemetery to Savoy Baptist Church, 1953. Pioneers' heirs fenced the area in 1966.   (1973)

SAVOY (Fannin Co.)

US 82, .5 mi. E

Fort Warren (Site 6 mi. N)

First settlement and fort in Fannin County. Built in 1836 by Abel Warren, Indian trader from Arkansas, to protect his trading post. Constructed of Bois D'Arc wood, the structure had two-story guardhouses at all four corners. Kiowa, Tonkawa, Caddo, Wichita and other Indians came here to trade furs for paint, knives and trinkets. In Civil War, Fort Warren was a transport and food supply center, where goods were sent to Confederate Indian refugees and troops in Indian territory (to the north) and to soldiers in Louisiana and Arkansas.   (1968)

SAYERSVILLE (Bastrop Co.)

SH 95, .6 mi. NE at Gate 11

Rural Farms and Communities before Camp Swift

As the United States prepared for the possibility of war in 1940, the government selected this area for establishment of what would be Camp Swift, a training and shipment facility. The federal government quickly acquired property, giving landowners 30 days to leave and move structures. The displacement resulted not only in the loss of farms but also early rural communities, some dating to 19th-century settlement. Outlying areas of larger communities, including Sayersville, Elgin, McDade, Oak Hill and Waysie, were affected, as were dispersed rural settlements within the camp area, including Duck Pond, Piney, Spring Branch and Dogwood. Most of the displaced residents were farmers, although some worked in other occupations. Antoine Aussiloux, born in France, began operating a local winery in the late 19th century that prospered until refrigerated railroad cars began to deliver beer in the 1890s and later anti-saloon leagues and prohibition eliminated legalized alcohol production. Another area resident, Frank Dennison, constructed nearby facilities for lignite mining, part of the Sayers Mine. He built a village to house miners, and it was associated with a graveyard known as the Mexican Cemetery. Other area burial grounds located within present Camp Swift included Chandler Cemetery, New Hope Cemetery and a single gravesite. After World War II, the War Assets Administration began to sell some of the land, but many residents were unable to repurchase their former properties. The government eventually retained about 11,500 acres of the approximately 25,000-acre Camp Swift for use by the National Guard. Today, many residents continue to live in this area, and visible reminders throughout Camp Swift chronicle the history of the settlements displaced by wartime activities.   (2007)

SCHULENBURG (Fayette Co.)   *SH 77, .3 mi. N of US 90*
Schulenburg
German and Czech settlers used this gateway to the rolling hills of Fayette County. Settled by former residents of Lyons and High Hill in 1873, when the Galveston, Houston & San Antonio Railway reached here. Named for landowner Louis Schulenburg, town was incorporated in 1875.   (1970)

SCHULENBURG (Fayette Co.)   *SH 77, 1 mi. S*
Site of Former Town of Lyons
Early town of land grant of Keziah Cryer. Named for settler James Lyons, killed in 1837 by Indian raiders, who kidnapped his son Warren. In 1860s town had stores, Masonic Lodge, school, post office; and was on "Cotton Road" to Mexico, but it died in 1870s when the Southern Pacific Railroad was built.   (1972)

SCOTLAND (Archer Co.)   *US 281, W*
J. H. Meurer Home
German native John H. Meurer (b. 1850) settled his family in this area about 1900 when he became a land agent for H. J. Scott of the Clark and Plumb Company. In selling over 60,000 acres of land, Meurer helped to establish the towns of Windthorst (6 mi. S) and Scotland (named for H. J. Scott), both primarily German Catholic settlements. Meurer had this one-and-a-half story home built in 1911. The 11-room house with wraparound porch remained in the Meurer Family until 1941 when Saint Boniface Catholic Church purchased it to serve as a residence for parish priests.   (1982)

SEADRIFT (Calhoun Co.)   *SH 185*
Seadrift
Settlement here began in the 1840s when German immigrants disembarking at Indianola stayed in the vicinity. A post office was granted in 1888, its name inspired by debris that collected on the shore blown in by heavy storms from the Gulf of Mexico. In 1912, A. D. Powers founded the Seadrift Townsite Company, and the city was incorporated that December. By 1914, Seadrift had 3 churches, 2 banks, 4 hotels, factories, a telephone line, and a weekly newspaper called the Seadrift Success. Despite a severe 1919 hurricane, the city survived. Processing plants were established in the area beginning in the 1950s. The village of Seadrift continues to be a popular resort and recreation spot.   (1998)

SEAGOVILLE (Dallas Co.)   *US 175 at Seagoville Rd.*
Lee Cemetery
In 1870, James J. Lee (1820–1901), a Confederate Army veteran from Mississippi, donated land for this cemetery, stipulating that no charges were to be made for plots. The 1.125-acre tract was the first cemetery in southeast Dallas County. Among the 1,500 burials are Lee and members of his family; Gen. James S. Raines (1817–1880), an officer in the Mexican War, 1846; some 60 people of Mexican descent; and a slave brought here in 1855. Land deeded for hitching horses has become part of the parking lot. The burial ground is maintained by Lee Cemetery, Inc.   (1976)

SEBASTIAN (Willacy Co.)   *US 77 Bus. N at FM 1018*
Stagecoach to the Rio Grande C.S.A.
About ten miles east of this site during the Civil War was Paso Real ferry point on the Arroyo Colorado. As early as 1846 stage coaches had gone over Paso Real ferry (the name probably meant "The Kings Pass." It was a crossing for the Cotton Road, lifeline to the Confederacy. When Federal coastal blockades had cut off imports and exports for the entire South, this road moved cotton down to Matamoros so that it could be exchanged for guns, ammunition, medicines, cloth, shoes, blankets, and other vital goods. Besides the prized cotton loads that went past Paso Real, the stage coach connection there was of importance to Confederate and foreign businessmen, government agents, diplomats, and army personnel. This was area of conflict and intrigue. Bandits and army deserters watched the road for stages and cotton wagons to pilfer. Mysterious travelers went this way—sometimes a pursuing sheriff on the next stage. Of thirty-one stagelines in Confederate Texas

(hauling mail, soldiers, civilians) no other was more vital nor interesting to travel than this through Paso Real.

SEBASTIAN (Willacy Co.)
US 77 Bus. at FM 506, at post office
Sebastian
Originally part of the San Juan de Carricitos land grant, this townsite later was part of South Texas' famed King Ranch. Sebastian was known as Stillman Town Tract until 1906, when it was renamed to honor an officer of the Rock Island Railroad. In 1914, the Sebastian Realty Company was promoting the town in the hope that it would become a major agricultural center. During the early 20th-century period of lawlessness in South Texas, Sebastian experienced a bandit raid in which two members of the Austin family were killed. (1985)

SEGUIN (Guadalupe Co.)
SH 46, 8 mi. NW
Clear Spring Hall and Store
This area was settled by German immigrants in the 1840s and 1850s. Named for a water source later inundated by Lake Dunlap, the Clear Spring community never evolved into a town, but remained a rural settlement. A store built at this site in the 1870s by Johann Andreas Breustedt became the commercial and social center for the surrounding area. A saloon and community hall were added to the building in later years, and the Clear Spring Gin Company located behind the store was important to the local cotton industry. (1989)

SEGUIN (Guadalupe Co.)
SH 46, 7 mi. NW
Site of Dietz Community
In 1851, Jamaica native Jacob de Cordova (1808–1868) settled here. He selected this spot for its beauty, rich soil and nearby springs. He built his first home, "Wanderer's Retreat." It served as a stage stop on the San Antonio Road and as a mail delivery station. De Cordova, acting as a land agent, sold over 90,000 acres of Texas land including this site. Nine German bachelors purchased the property and it became known as "Bachelor's Hall" and "Nine Men's House." Two brothers, Ferdinand Michael and J. August Dietz, cowboys for de Cordova, bought out the other men and the community became "Dietz." Johann Phillip Stautzenberger (1838–1904) bought the land in 1861, built a substantial house and general store, and became the first postmaster. Formal education began in a small room adjacent to Stautzenberger's store with Frankfort School starting later. "The Frohsinn Maennerchor," a singing group, was organized in the schoolhouse. Later they adopted the present name of "Frohsinn Mixed Chorus of Clear Springs." In 1895, a group of farmers founded present-day Friedens Church in the school building. Consolidation of the schools, closing of the post office, and good roads and automobiles caused this early community to disappear. (1978)

SEGUIN (Guadalupe Co.)
US 90A, 5 mi. E
Battleground Prairie
Where 80 volunteers commanded by General Edward Burleson defeated Vicente Cordova and 75 Mexicans, Indians and Negroes, March 29, 1839, and drove them from Texas, ending the "Cordova Rebellion." 25 of the enemy were killed. Many volunteers were wounded, but none fatally. (1965)

SEGUIN (Guadalupe Co.)
US 90A, 3 mi. E
Tiemann School
Named for Theodore Tiemann, who sold one acre of land to the county school district for $5.00, Tiemann School provided educational, cultural, and recreational opportunities for citizens in this area. Beginning in 1903 as a one-room, one-teacher facility, the school eventually was enlarged to accommodate two teachers and many students. A gathering place for many community events, Tiemann school closed in 1943. Along with other area schools, it was annexed by the Seguin school system in 1949. (1990)

SEGUIN (Guadalupe Co.)
205 N. River St., 2 blks. N of US 90
Juan Nepomuceno Seguín (1806–1890)
Born in San Fernando de Béxar (San Antonio), son of Erasmo Seguín, whose ancestors came to America about 1700. Juan N. Seguín and his father in 1834 rallied fellow Texans against dictator Santa Anna. Young Juan Seguín raised Mexican-Texan troops, and fought in Siege of Bexar, 1835. He provided horses for soldiers of Col. W. B. Travis, further aiding as a courier during the Siege of the Alamo. Between fall of the Alamo and the Battle of San Jacinto, he led his Co. A, 2nd Regiment,

Texas Cavalry, as rear guard for Gen. Sam Houston, protecting the civilians fleeing in front of army of Santa Anna. His men and Moseley Baker's troops held San Felipe, preventing Mexican Army from crossing the Brazos there. Then Seguin's unit joined Gen. Sam Houston's army and fought in the Battle of San Jacinto. In May 1836, Seguin gave military burial to the ashes of the heroes of the Alamo. From 1837 to 1840 he served the Republic of Texas as a Senator. Town of Walnut Springs, on the Guadalupe, changed its name, Feb. 25, 1839, to "Seguin", to honor this hero. Juan N. Seguín married María Gertrudis Flores. At his death he was buried in Nuevo Laredo, where his grave is cared for by citizens of City of Seguin. (1970)

SEGUIN (Guadalupe Co.) *US 90, 1.9 mi. W*
Guadalupe County
Formed from Gonzales and Bexar counties. Created March 30, 1846. Organized July 13, 1846. Named for the Guadalupe River, to which this name was given by Alonso de Leon in 1689. Seguin, the county seat, named in honor of Juan Nepomuceno Seguin 1806–1890. (1965)

SEGUIN (Guadalupe Co.) *SH 123, 1.5 mi. S at Starcke Park*
The Guadalupe River
One of the earliest explored rivers in Texas. Named for our Lady of Guadalupe by Spaniard Alonso de Leon in 1689. During 1691–1693, Domingo Teran de los Rios, Spanish governor of Texas, maintained a colony on the Guadalupe. An early Anglo-American settlement, 30 or 40 families located along its bank, which formed a boundary of the Power-Hewetson Irish Colony. Near the mouth of the river, historic Victoria was founded, and 60 miles above was Gonzales, where the first shot for Texas freedom was fired, Oct. 2, 1835. The Guadalupe is 250 miles long. (1969)

SEGUIN (Guadalupe Co.) *SH 123, 1.5 mi. S in Starcke Park*
Saffold Dam
Named for William Saffold, who owned land here in the mid-1800s, Saffold Dam is typical of many mill dams built during the late 19th and early 20th centuries. Originally a natural rock outcropping, the dam was first improved by Henry Troell in the late 1800s when he added rock to the dam to raise the water level to power a cotton gin. The city of Seguin bought Troell's property in 1907 to further develop the river's hydroelectricity, and subsequent improvements have led to the establishment of a hydroelectric plant on the dam's south side. (1991)

SEMINOLE (Gaines Co.) *US 180, 20 mi. E*
Lake Mackenzie (¼ mi. N)
According to geologists, this dry salt lake may be the remains of an ancient river bed. Water from infrequent rains quickly evaporates, leaving a deposit of salt and alkali. The lake and nearby draw were named for Col. Ranald S. Mackenzie (1840–1889). During the 1870s, Col. Mackenzie led several U.S. Army expeditions across the Staked Plains and fought a series of Indian battles. He was instrumental in bringing hostile tribes under control and opening this area to settlement. West Texas pioneers named a number of natural landmarks in his honor. (1979)

SEMINOLE (Gaines Co.) *US 180 at SH 214*
Gaines County
Named for James L. Gaines, a signer of the Texas Declaration of Independence, this county was formed out of Bexar County in 1876. Anglo settlement of the area began about 1895, and the county was formally organized in 1905. Seminole was established as the county seat that year, and a courthouse was built in 1906. Ranching and farming were the most prominent and profitable occupations until the mid-1930s, when they were eclipsed by oil production. Gaines County encompasses 1,479 square miles, and Seminole and Seagraves are its two largest cities. (1989)

SEMINOLE (Gaines Co.) *US 180 at SH 214*
Seminole
Founded and designated county seat in 1905, same year county was organized. Took name from Seminole wells, Indian watering places to south and west. First store and post office were established in 1905 by W. B. Austin of nearby Caput. The courthouse was built in 1906. Seminole grew slowly, being chiefly important as a trading center. Arrival of the Midland & Northwestern Railroad (1918) and development of highways and oil resources all helped speed the town's later expansion. Today it is a business center for farming and petroleum industry. (1970)

SEMINOLE (Gaines Co.)   *US 385, 2 mi. S*
Historic Hackberry Grove
Earliest known human habitation in Gaines County. This small, unique grove of hackberry trees has survived in this arid land because of sub-irrigation provided by a very shallow draw. First officially reported by Col. W. R. ("Pecos Bill") Shafter, 24th Infantry, during his scouting of the north and western plains area in 1875. In this draw, Col. Shafter and his men found some 50 wells, 4 to 15 feet deep. Surrounding one well in the grove were evidences of use of roving bands of Indians as a seasonal campsite. A Fourth of July gathering of settlers in this grove in 1905 planned local organization of Gaines County, which had been created in 1876. In election of October 24, 1905, the first officers were selected and Seminole was named the county seat. Hackberry Grove and the shallow water well which is located here served Gaines Countians as an area for recreation and outdoor meetings until the early 1940s, when the discovery of oil and installation of a pump station caused the grove to be closed to the public.   (1968)

SEMINOLE (Gaines Co.)   *US 385, Gaines County Park*
Oil Industry in Gaines County
The first oil lease in Gaines County was in 1912 and the first drilling occurred in 1925. Ten years later the Landreth Co. brought in the first producing well. In 1936, Amerada Oil Co. opened up the Seminole pool, a major field that yielded 350 wells within a decade. Less than 50 years after that discovery, Gaines County had produced over one billion barrels of crude oil. With several active fields, Gaines ranks as one of the top oil producing counties in Texas. The petroleum industry accounts for much of this area's prosperity.   (1979)

SEYMOUR (Baylor Co.)   *US 82 at US 183, 9 mi. NE*
Baylor County
Created February 1, 1858. Organized April 23, 1879. Named in honor of Dr. Henry W. Baylor, 1818–1854, Indian fighter and Ranger captain. Served in the Mexican War. Seymour, the county seat.   (1964)

SEYMOUR (Baylor Co.)   *US 87/277 in roadside park, at NE city limits*
Near Route of the Western Trail
Principal cattle trail from Texas to Kansas and beyond from 1876 to 1887; superseded the Chisholm Trail after Dodge City replaced Abilene as the main intermediate northern beef market. As its name implies, the Western Trail ran west of the Chisholm Trail, by about 100 miles. Most of its feeder trails started in South Texas, although some made connections at San Antonio and Fort Griffin. Here in Baylor County the trail crossed the Brazos River passing half a mile east of Seymour, a major supply center. The herds bedded near Seymour Creek, at the site of the present fair grounds. The Millett Ranch (established 1874) served as a watering spot, and the Millett brothers—Eugene, Alonzo, and Hiram—were among the first users of the trail. From Seymour the route continued north, leaving Texas at Doan's Store on the Red River. It then ran through Oklahoma to Dodge City, lesser extensions proceeding to Nebraska, Wyoming, and Montana. During its life, the Western Trail moved hundreds of thousands of cattle north to stock ranges, Indian reservations, and markets. But after the fencing of the open range and building of the Texas & Pacific Railroad, it ceased to be used by the cattle industry.   (1972)

SEYMOUR (Baylor Co.)   *SH 114 and Hale Rd., 16 mi. SE*
Westover
Platted in 1910 on the Gulf, Texas and Western Railroad, Westover developed into a small market center providing goods and services for area farmers and ranchers. J. W. Stevens offered part of his ranchland for the townsite, which was given the maiden name of his mother-in-law. James H.B. Kyle served as first postmaster when the post office was established in 1910. Businesses, including a bank, barbershops, cotton gins and dry goods stores, as well as churches, a school and a cemetery were established to serve area residents. After the commercial area suffered a fire in 1921 and the rail line was abandoned in 1942, many settlers and businesses moved to Seymour.   (2002)

SEYMOUR (Baylor Co.)   *SH 114 at Hale Rd., 16 mi. SE*
Westover School
One-half mile east of this site is the location of the former Westover School, which served students in this part of Baylor County from 1910 until 1950. School classes first met in the Church of

Christ building in Westover until trustees constructed a frame schoolhouse in 1911. Six years later, that building was replaced by a two-story brick building, which held all eleven grades and included seven classrooms, a library and an auditorium. Enrollment reached 400 students by the 1930s, but with abandonment of the rail line in 1942 and the general movement of people from rural areas after World War II, the student population declined, and Westover School closed in 1950. (2002)

SHAFTER (Presidio Co.)   *SH 67, 5 mi. N*
Milton Faver (ca. 1829–December 1889)
The earliest large-scale cattleman to settle in the Big Bend, Milton (Don Meliton) Faver prospered against seemingly impossible odds to become the first cattle baron west of the Pecos. While operating a freighting business on the Chihuahua Trail, he moved his family to Presidio Del Norte and opened a general store about 1855. After accumulating a large herd of cattle in Mexico he moved his family and vaqueros to the mountain country north of Presidio and made his headquarters on Cibolo Creek in 1857. He established two other ranches at nearby La Cienega and La Morita. Springs flowed abundantly on all three ranches, providing water for livestock and agriculture. In the fertile fields surrounding the ranches, Faver devised and installed irrigation systems that supplied water for vegetables, grain, and large peach orchards. El Fortín del Cibolo, ranch headquarters, served as a supply station for the U.S. Army Quartermaster Division at Ft. Davis. Troops used the ranch as a point of departure for forays into Indian occupied regions to the west and north. Celebrated for his hospitality, Faver was known as a gentleman of means who lived in style. He died in December 1889 and was buried on his ranch at Cibolo. (1992)

SHAFTER (Presidio Co.)   *US 67, 4.5 mi. N*
Milton Faver Ranches
Milton Faver (ca.1822–1889), a native of the midwest United States, moved to this area in the 1850s from Presidio Del Norte, where he owned a general store and operated a freighting business on the Chihuahua Trail. By the 1880s, Faver controlled vast acreage in this part of the county, including most of the best permanent water sources, which he built into a formidable cattle, sheep, and goat ranching empire. Faver's three ranches—El Fortín Del Cibolo, El Fortín de la Cienega, and La Morita—comprised the largest single-owner landholdings in the county. Structures on the ranches, including dwellings, work rooms, fences, corrals, and irrigation systems, were built with traditional adobe and stone building methods. Census and tax records show that Faver owned the largest livestock herds in the county in the late 19th century. Following the deaths of Milton Faver in 1889, his wife Francisca in 1893, and his son Juan in 1913, and after a lawsuit, the ranchlands were sold by the Faver heirs. Other pioneer ranching families in the area, including George and Juliana Dawson (niece of Francisca Faver), and J. A. Pool, Sr., J.W. Pool, and their heirs, the Greenwood family, operated ranches on the former Faver lands until the late 20th century. (1995)

SHAMROCK (Wheeler Co.)   *IH 40, 10 mi. E at roadside park*
Greer County, Texas (To the East in Present Oklahoma)
Created 1860; until 1896, one of largest counties in Texas. Organized at old Mobeetie, northwest of here. In 1880s settlement was rapid; by 1892 nearly 2,500 pupils were in county's schools. A post office, jail and many houses were built, and over 60,000 cattle grazed the 3,480 square miles of the county's area. But for a half-century (1846–1896) the United States and Texas waged a heated dispute over Greer County. Controversy had origin in an 1819 treaty fixing the line between United States and Spanish territory. A map designating the Red River and 100th meridian as boundary lines was part of treaty; but map aroused dispute, for it incorrectly marked 100th meridian and showed only one fork of two-forked Red River. Texas claimed the north fork and meridian shown on map defined territory, and legislation and occupancy by Texans decided sovereignty. United States contended south fork (larger of the two) and true 100th meridian marked boundaries. Three joint survey commissions failed to settle the issue.The U.S. Supreme Court in 1896 ruled that the region was in 1819 part of the Union and thus was actually a part of Oklahoma. Named for John A. Greer, Senator, Secretary of State, Republic of Texas; Lieutenant Governor, 1847–1853. (1967)

SHAMROCK (Wheeler Co.)   *US 83 at Railroad Ave. (FM 2033)*
Shamrock Water Tower
Soon after residents voted to incorporate in March 1911, Shamrock officials identified the need for a reliable waterworks for the city. Prior to that time, citizens got their water from one of two

town wells or hauled it to town in barrels on wagons. A November 1912 election authorized the sale of bonds in the amount of $15,000 for a drinking water system that included a tower and reservoir on Railroad Avenue. In September 1915, city leaders accepted the bid of the Chicago Bridge and Iron Company of Chicago, Illinois to build the water tower. The all-steel structure was designed with a cylindrical tank with a hemispherical bottom, supported by four latticed channel columns held together with metal tie rods. The large tank has a capacity of 75,000 gallons, rising 176 feet above ground level. Workers utilized a steam threshing machine to raise the tower's standpipe. The tower was constructed of railway bridge grade steel riveted together using rivet grade steel. Engineers also had to account for the maximum pressure of panhandle winds upon the load of the structure plus the weight of the water. According to records of the CB&I Co., in business since 1889, this substantial tower is the tallest tank of its class ever built by the company, and it remains one of the tallest water tanks in Texas. Built to provide water to a growing community, the Shamrock water tower is also visible for about ten miles in any direction. Early 20th century travelers stopped here to water their horses or wagon teams in the concrete troughs under the tower, and travelers continue to mark their progress by the tower, an engineering and tourism icon. (2008)

SHEFFIELD (Pecos Co.)
US 290 at city park
Sheffield
Spanish explorers traveled Indian trails here in the Pecos River Valley as early as 1590. Later, U.S. Cavalry, a camel train, and stage and mail lines between San Antonio and San Diego, California, used the route. Nearby Pecos Spring attracted settlers to the area in the 1880s and '90s. Families lived in tents on the north side of the creek and hauled water from the spring. About 1890, a community water well was dug. Early residents were sheep and cattle ranchers. Mail and supplies had to be brought from San Angelo and Ozona. About 1901, Will Sheffield built a grocery and dry goods store approximately one mile from the spring. A post office opened with Will Sheffield as postmaster. Since he was the first to operate a store, the settlement was named for him. A saloon was opened, and in 1901 a school was begun with sixty-four pupils. After living for several years in tents, residents began building permanent homes. Garrett Bean purchased a section of land from the state where the present townsite is located and drew off town lots in 1905. Well-known Texas Ranger Frank Hamer got his start in law enforcement here. Sheffield offers churches and a trade center for area ranches. (1980)

SHELBYVILLE (Shelby Co.)
SH 87 at FM 417
First County Seat
Shelbyville, once known as Nashville, was the first county seat of government of the District of Tenaha or Shelby County. The first courthouse stood on this site. The settlement began before 1825. It became headquarters for the "Regulator-Moderator War." Troops were raised here to fight the Indians; for the Texas Army; and Confederate forces were organized here.

SHELBYVILLE (Shelby Co.)
SH 87, 1 mi. S
Site of Last Battle, August 14, 1844
Between Regulators and Moderators, warring factions in Shelby County, 1841–1844, who caused heavy sacrifice of life and property before General James Smith with Texas troops restored order.

SHELBYVILLE (Shelby Co.)
SH 147, 1.2 mi. W of SH 87
McWilliams Cemetery
This burial ground, originally known as Wayfare and later as McWilliams Graveyard, has served the Todd Springs community since early in the settlement's history. The community, named for landowner John D. Todd and area springs, was largely populated by African Americans. Before the Civil War, there were plantations in the area, including one owned by Irishman Robert McWilliams, who came here with wife Mary and his family from South Carolina in 1843. McWilliams died in 1864 and although this burial ground is named for him, he is buried in nearby Rather Cemetery. After the Civil War, many freedmen worked in the area as farmers; others labored in Center, Shelbyville and San Augustine. During the early 1900s, Todd Springs was a thriving community, with several businesses, an African American school and a lodge. However, the population declined during the 1930s and 1940s, as many residents moved to urban areas. This burial ground was officially established when N. K. and E. L. Boozer deeded property to trustees, although the land was used as a cemetery before that time. The oldest marked grave in McWilliams Cemetery, of Fennie

McClelland, dates to 1903; however, it is believed there are a number of earlier, unmarked burials here. Others interred include farmers, preachers, community leaders and veterans of conflicts dating to World War I. There are also a number of teachers buried here, including Johnny W. Lee, who also served as a school administrator. The cemetery features obelisks, grave slabs and Masonic lodge markers. Today, the McWilliams Cemetery Association maintains this burial ground, whose graves provide a record of African American pioneer families that settled Todd Springs. (2008)

SHEPHERD (San Jacinto Co.) *FM 223, 2 mi. E*
Near Site of Coushatta Indian Village
Inhabited from about 1835–1900 by members of the Coushatta tribe. Most of the Indians had small farms, but also worked for wages after crops were harvested. Burial pits excavated by archeologists (1968) revealed skeletal remains, ironstone dishes, glass beads (obtained in trade with Anglos), ornaments made from silver coins. (1969)

SHEPHERD (San Jacinto Co.) *Main St. (SH 150) W of FM 222*
Town of Shepherd
Originated in vicinity of old Drew's Landing, a Trinity River port for settlers bringing in goods and shipping cotton, tobacco, and other products to markets. An early nearby community was Big Creek. Into these pioneer settlements came Houston East & West Texas Railroad investors, including Benjamin A. Shepherd (1814–1891) of Houston, who in 1875 platted townsite here, naming it for himself. The town square was on west side of H. E. & W. T., which was completed beyond this point in 1879. The Shepherd post office opened Dec. 22, 1879, with Jack B. Noble as postmaster. A pioneer physician was Dr. William Herbert Beazley (1837–1919); Mrs. Jessie Fain operated an early hotel; Mrs. Jane Langham taught first public school session, in Methodist Church building. James Ephraim Tribe, a native of Canada, came here in 1895, was a carpenter, coffin maker, millwright, and wheelwright. A Baptist, he built a church edifice for that faith in 1896. Distinguished native son Robert Scott Lovett (1860–1932), became president of Southern Pacific and Union Pacific railroads and rendered outstanding civilian service to the nation during World War I. Once a center for the lumbering industry, Shepherd remains an important market town of Southeast Texas. (1972)

SHERMAN (Grayson Co.) *1815 Sam Rayburn Fwy. (US 75)*
Sherman Manufacturing Company
Sherman Seamless Bag Mill was founded here in 1891, to serve the cotton industry of North Central Texas. Elected to board of directors on March 18, 1891, were C. A. Andrews, Edward Eastburn, W. C. Eubank, Thomas Forbes, J. F. Jaques, J. C. Jones, Tom Randolph, Z. E. Raney, and J. C. Tassey to serve as chairman. Elegant cornerstone was shipped from Cromwell, Mass., to go into the original structure. Suffering from financial problems during those early years, the plant operated and closed intermittently. Acquired in 1906 by Wellington-Sears Company of New York, who added buildings and centered production upon single-filling flat duck. Purchased, 1946, by Ely Walker & Company of St. Louis, Missouri; wide sheeting became main product. Merged into Burlington Industries, Inc., 1955. Cornerstone of original building opened 1956. Disclosed old coins, 1891 newspapers, timetable for trains to Indian territory (now State of Oklahoma), saloon tokens and menu from Binkley Hotel coffee shop. A portion of the original structure remains as a useful part of this modern plant. Through Burlington's international organization, products made here are sold in market places throughout the world. (1967)

SHERMAN (Grayson Co.) *Texoma Pkwy. (SH 91) at Woodlake Rd.*
First Texas Interurban
Electric railways (trolleys) provided convenient travel between many Texas cities for more than forty years. The first interurban line was established in Grayson County, connecting the cities of Sherman and Denison. Founded in 1900 by Fred Fitch and John P. Crerar, the Denison and Sherman Railway began operations on May 1, 1901, with a single 10.5-mile track. The company built a power plant, offices, and a car barn near this site halfway between its passenger stations in the two cities. In order to provide water for the power plant, they built a dam below Tanyard Springs, creating a small lake. Named Wood Lake, it provided recreational facilities for passengers on the line's excursion trains. The Texas Traction Company, founded in 1906, began construction of a second interurban line from Dallas to McKinney in 1906. Merged with the Denison and Sherman

Railway in 1908, the company expanded its operations, eventually connecting a number of North Texas cities and changing its name to the Texas Electric Railway in 1917. The advent of automobile travel signalled the decline of the Texas Interurbans by the 1930s. The last train passed this site on December 31, 1948, on its route from Denison to Dallas. (1990)

SHERMAN (Grayson Co.)
100 W. Houston St. (SH 56) at courthouse
Grayson County
In the mainstream of Texas history for more than a century, this area was, in 1837, the site of Colonel Holland Coffee's Trading Post, a landmark structure at the Preston Bend crossing of the Red River. It was a focal point, beginning in 1842, for settlers of the important Peters colony. In 1846 the county was created from part of Fannin County by the 1st State Legislature. It was named for Peter W. Grayson, who immigrated to Texas in 1830, served in the Texas revolution, and was attorney general in the Republic. Also in 1846 the county was organized and Sherman was made county seat. The original townsite was 5-1/4 mi. W of here. It was moved to its present location, 1848. Honoree of the town name was Colonel Sidney Sherman, a hero of the Battle of San Jacinto. The place is distinguished for having had at least five courthouses and for its superior schools of the 19th century. It was once known as the "Athens of Texas." In 1858 the famous Butterfield Trail crossed the county and in the same period and later, a number of cattle trails and early railroads traversed the area. Today Lake Texoma, created 1939–1944, is a county approved tourist attraction. The Sherman-Denison region was named a Standard Metropolitan Statistical Area, 1967. Incise on back: Erected by Grayson County Historical Survey Committee. (1969)

SHERMAN (Grayson Co.)
100 W. Houston St. (SH 56) at courthouse
Peter W. Grayson
Peter Wagener Grayson was born in 1788 in Bardstown, Virginia (later part of Kentucky) to Benjamin and Caroline (Taylor) Grayson, members of a politically prominent family. He served in the War of 1812 and worked in Louisville as an attorney, businessman and legislator. Well-spoken in legal matters and also a poet, he nevertheless amassed substantial debts and privately combated mental illness. In 1830, Grayson wrote to Stephen F. Austin about acquiring land in Texas, and by 1832 he had established a plantation near Matagorda. He also became a friend and advisor to Austin. During Austin's imprisonment in Mexico City in 1834, Grayson and Spencer Jack went there with petitions in hopes of freeing the empresario. In December 1834, they secured Austin's bail, although he was not free to leave until the following summer. Settlers began preparations for revolution soon after Austin returned to Texas, and Grayson worked with him to outline an independent government. Grayson also served as president of the Council of War and aide-de-camp to both Austin and Gen. Edward Burleson. After Texas' victory at San Jacinto on April 21, 1836, Grayson acted as interpreter and Attorney General, signing the Treaties of Velasco on May 14, 1836. Grayson went with others to Washington, D.C. to gain recognition of the Texas Republic and discuss annexation to the United States, but the efforts were unsuccessful. He served as Texas Attorney General and as naval agent, and was Sam Houston's candidate for the Texas presidency in 1838. On July 9 of that year, though, while traveling through Tennessee, Grayson took his life, leaving a note that his previous mental illness had returned. In 1846, following the eventful annexation of Texas to the United States, the Texas Legislature created Grayson County, naming it for the Texas patriot. (2005)

SHERMAN (Grayson Co.)
100 W. Houston St. (SH 56) at courthouse
President T. Roosevelt's Visit to Grayson County
One of the most festive events in Sherman's early history, Theodore Roosevelt's 1905 appearance here marked the first visit of a president of the United States to Grayson County. Traveling to San Antonio to attend a reunion of the "Rough-Riders"—his special troops in the Spanish-American War—Roosevelt stopped first in Denison on that same day, April 5, and was there presented with a Texas-shaped floral piece from excited youngsters. His train proceeded then to Sherman, where a record crowd of 35,000 had come by buggy, horse, and special trains from as far away as 175 miles to see him. Led by a unit of Rough Riders, Roosevelt and his party rode up the banner-decked streets in nine handsome carriages. Passing between lines of Union and Confederate Civil War veterans, they arrived at the speaker's stand amid loud applause. Here (at this corner) he spoke for 15 minutes, praising Texas as "one of two or three greatest states in the Union". He emphasized his own heritage from the south and the north and his delight in national reunification. Within an

hour Roosevelt left for Dallas, having provided for the people of this area one of the most memorable occasions in their lives. (1971)

SHERMAN (Grayson Co.)

100 W. Houston St. (SH 56) at courthouse

Butterfield Overland Mail Route through Grayson County

In the mid-19th century, mail traffic between the eastern United States and the western states and territories was accomplished via Panama and Cape Horn. In 1857, Congress authorized the postmaster to contract a new overland mail service. The successful bidder for the southern route was John Butterfield, who agreed to convey mail twice weekly in 25 days per run. The "Oxbow Trail" originated at St. Louis, Missouri, and Memphis, Tennessee, then merged at Fort Smith, Arkansas. The stagecoaches traveled through Indian Territory (later Oklahoma) and across northern Texas to Tucson, Arizona, and on to Los Angeles and San Francisco, California, traveling 2,795 miles from St. Louis. The trail entered Grayson County by crossing the Red River at Colbert's Ferry and proceeding into Sherman. It crossed the county toward Gainesville in Cooke County en route to Franklin (later El Paso). The citizens of Sherman are credited with especially courting the mail route to use Colbert's Ferry instead of entering Texas near Preston (8 mi. upriver). Sherman became a distribution point in 1858, bringing mail service to Texas settlements. Waterman L. Ormsby of *The New York Herald* was the first through passenger on the Butterfield Trail in September 1858. He described Sherman as "a pleasant little village of about six hundred inhabitants," and chronicled the remainder of his trip across Grayson County, writing "our course lay across a fine rolling prairie, covered with fine grass, . . . the beautiful moonlight lit up the vast prairies making its sameness appear like the boundless sea and its hills like the rolling waves." The southern route was terminated in March 1861. The course of the trail is still visible in a number of locations in Grayson County. (1999)

SHERWOOD (Irion Co.)

Madison St. at Washington Ave., off US 67

Sherwood Courthouse (Built 1900–1901)

First permanent courthouse for Irion County, locally organized 1889. Replaced temporary housing in several buildings. Site was gift of Mr. and Mrs. Frank Ripley. Contractors: Martin and Moody. Stone was quarried nearby. Courthouse was used for dances, teachers' institutes, community events, yards for summer socials. Enclosed to keep out grazing stock, approach was by a stile over fence beside which were water troughs and hitching posts for teams and saddle horses. A 1936 election made Mertzon county seat. Once pride of area, this now is a community center. (1971)

SHILOH (DeWitt Co.)

SH 72, 4 mi. N

Shiloh

The small farming community of Shiloh began about 1847 with settlement by the McBride, Hamilton, McFarland, Odom, Anderson, and Woods families. In 1851 John Keith Rankin helped organize a Methodist Episcopal Church, whose members erected a building in 1852. Shiloh School, established in 1856, served the community until the early part of the 20th century. The first burial in the Shiloh Cemetery was that of Montraville Woods, son of Texas patriot Zadock Woods, in 1857. Woods Cemetery, as it is now called, is all that remains of the Shiloh community. (1983)

SHINER (Lavaca Co.)

SH 95 at Ponton Creek, 4 mi. N

Ponton Family

Virginians William (1772–1834) and Isabella (Moreland) Ponton came to Texas in 1829 from Missouri. With them were their children Andrew, Sarah Ann, and Mary Jane, and son-in-law James Patrick. Their son Joel Ponton arrived in 1834. The families received land in DeWitt's colony. William Ponton was the first recorded settler killed by Comanche Indians in the area that became Lavaca County. Joel Ponton and a companion were attacked in the same area in 1840; Joel survived with two arrows in his back. Ponton Creek was named for William. The Pontons and their neighbors stood up against the Mexican Army in the Battle of Gonzales and later fled the area in "The Runaway Scrape" in the wake of Santa Anna's victory at the Alamo. After the Texan victory at the Battle of San Jacinto, they returned to rebuild their homes from almost nothing. They endured Indian attacks and lived through the eras of the Republic of Texas, statehood, the Civil War, and Reconstruction. Exemplary pioneers, they were mothers and fathers, alcaldes, judges, tax collectors, commissioners, doctors, preachers, storekeepers, farmers, ranchers, and official peacemakers. The children and grandchildren of William and Isabella Ponton forged Lavaca County from a wilderness. The story of the Ponton family is a story of Texas. (1998)

SHINER (Lavaca Co.)

SH 95, .5 mi. N

Kasper Wire Works

Founded as outgrowth of an 1895 invention that used smooth wire discarded when barbed wire fencing was introduced in this area. August Kaspar, son of a Swiss Lutheran missionary to Texas, salvaged some of the plain wire and made a corn shuck basket for home use. A neighbor saw and bought the basket. Soon Kaspar disposed of his baskets as rapidly as he could make and put them to use in his own barn. In 1898 he began the full-time manufacture of wire baskets and horse muzzles. His backyard shop was equipped with little more than a pair of pliers and his inventive genius. A rented wagon was the original Kaspar show room. Arthur H. Kaspar, son of the founder, purchased the business in 1924. In 1949 a grandson, Don A. Kaspar, joined the organization. Kaspar Wire Works has progressed to assembly-line manufacturing of nationally and internationally distributed goods—including display racks, baskets, newspaper racks, wire shelving and many other products. The growth and success of Kaspar Wire Works was officially recognized in 1967 by the bestowal of The First Annual Governor's Expansion Award under the auspices of the Texas Industrial Commission.

(1970)

SHINER (Lavaca Co.)

US 90A at city hall

Shiner

Originated as German-Czech community of Half Moon, located west of present town. When the San Antonio & Aransas Pass Railroad came through in 1887, citizens moved to rail line, where H. B. Shiner, Victoria landowner, had given a townsite. Shiner was developed by cattlemen. Industries include brewery, wire works. City has museum.

(1969)

SIERRA BLANCA (Hudspeth Co.)

IH 10, 10 mi. W in roadside park

Claude Hudspeth (1877–1941)

State senator and member of U.S. House of Representatives from whom Hudspeth County was named. Became a ranch worker at age 9 and editor-publisher of an Ozona newspaper at 16. Was largely self-educated. Won seat in legislature in 1902—starting 29-year public career. He authored many bills to benefit working man. Served in Texas Senate 1907–1919. During this time, he studied law and was admitted to the bar, 1909. Served in U.S. Congress 1919–1931. Upheld sending U.S. force to defend El Pasoans endangered by Mexican Revolution fighting.

(1969)

SIERRA BLANCA (Hudspeth Co.)

IH 10 Bus. at FM 1111

Hudspeth County

Formed from El Paso County. Created February 16, 1917. Organized August 25, 1917. Named in honor of Claude Benton Hudspeth. Born in 1877. A native Texan, holder of large ranching interests, member of the Texas Legislature and the United States Congress. Sierra Blanca, the county seat.

SIERRA BLANCA (Hudspeth Co.)

IH 10 Bus. at FM 1111

America's Second Transcontinental Railroad (Joined Here in 1881)

Great achievement in American history. Victory for statesmen, including Henry Clay and John C. Calhoun, who early as 1845 had supported in the United States Congress the idea of a transcontinental railroad. This was effected in 1869, but a need remained—as advocated in the Congress—for a southern route. In 1869 the Southern Pacific began constructing such a line eastward from the West Coast. In 1871 the Texas & Pacific began building a line, under a special act of Congress, from East Texas to Southern California. They ran a dramatic race which reached its climax as construction crews for the two roads neared this site. Southern Pacific reached Sierra Blanca on Nov. 25, 1881—while crews of the T. & P. were 10 miles to the east of here. On Nov. 26, 1881, an agreement was reached by Jay Gould, for the Texas & Pacific, and Collis P. Huntington, for the Southern Pacific, whereby in Sierra Blanca the roads would "... approach, .. meet, .. and ... form one continuous line to the Pacific Ocean. ...." The lines were joined here on Dec. 15, 1881, and on Dec. 16 transcontinental service was inaugurated.

(1968)

SIERRA BLANCA (Hudspeth Co.)

IH 10 Bus. at FM 1111

The Killing of General J. J. Byrne
(Event Occurred 15 mi. S of Here in Quitman Canyon)

One of the final acts of violence in raiding led during 1880 by the feared Apache chieftain, Victorio. Just prior to this incident, Victorio's band—100 to 200 strong—had finished a sanguinary two years of raiding in Southwest Texas, New Mexico, and Mexico. His brilliant guerrilla tactics baffled his U.S. Army pursuers and earned their grudging admiration. J. J. Byrne, a surveyor and retired military man, had fought in U.S. Army in the Civil War (1861–1865), having been cited both for gallantry and meritorious conduct. At the time of his death, he was the lone passenger on the stage bound for Fort Davis. Drawn by small, swift Mexican mules, the coach left Fort Quitman, a former army post on the Rio Grande, August 13, 1880. As it entered a steep canyon Victorio's men attacked. Gen. Byrne was killed almost at once but the driver, Ed Walde, turned the stage and raced back to the fort for safety. Later in 1880 the United States and Mexico fielded 5,000 soldiers to hunt down Victorio, who was finally killed in Mexico. Thus ended the career of one of the most notable Indian chiefs in the Southwest. Byrne, born in Ireland about 1842, was buried near Fort Quitman but later reinterred in Fort Worth. (1973)

SILVER (Coke Co.)   RR 1672 at SH 208
First Producing Oil Well in Coke County
Sun Oil Company's well—No. 1 Allen Jameson—was staked in Sept. 1946 and struck oil Nov. 17. Intermittent drilling had gone on in Coke County for 30 years, but this discovery began a county-wide oil boom. Drilled by the Dallas firm of Roberts & Hawkins, the well hit pay dirt at 6,230 feet in fossil-bearing limestone 280 million years old. In a 24-hour test it flowed 168 barrels. Coke County recently ranked among the top quarter of oil-producing counties in Texas, with its 18 fields exceeding 6.4 million barrels annually. (1968)

SILVERTON (Briscoe Co.)   SH 207, 11 mi. NW
Archeological Sites at Mackenzie Reservoir and Tule Canyon
Before this area was covered by Mackenzie Reservoir, evidence of human occupancy was found at 77 recorded archeological sites. The earliest artifacts date back 10,000 years to a bison kill. Prehistoric occupancy is indicated by burial sites, shallow hearths, and stone tools. Gun flints, glass beads, and metal objects confirm 18th century European contact. By 1874, Col. Ranald S. Mackenzie's 4th Cavalry had driven the Indians from the Tule Canyon area, which had been a lush grazing ground for buffalo and antelope. (1979)

SILVERTON (Briscoe Co.)   SH 256, 10 mi. E at Sky High roadside rest area
William E. Schott
Briscoe County pioneer William E. Schott (1870–1941) was born in Ohio and moved to North Texas in 1885. Still legally a minor, he came to this area in 1890 and filed to a claim for the first of his later extensive landholdings. In 1891, he overcame the caprock barrier by building the first wagon road to Silverton, where in 1892 he helped organize Briscoe County. A major factor in the settlement of this region, Schott Cap Road (1.5 mi. N) was improved when auto travel began. Schott supported local education and encouraged improvement of cattle herds. He married (1907) Tina Kitchen; they had four children. (1975)

SILVERTON (Briscoe Co.)   SH 86/256 at courthouse
Briscoe County
Formed from Bexar Territory. Created August 21, 1876. Organized March 15, 1892. Named for Andrew Briscoe 1810–1849. Defender of Texan liberty at the Battle of Concepcion, the Capture of Bexar and the Battle of San Jacinto; Chief Justice of Harris County. Silverton is the County Seat. (1936)

SILVERTON (Briscoe Co.)   SH 207, 8 mi. S
Site of Reeves Post Office (.5 mi. E)
Since the railroad was 60 miles from this sparsely populated prairie, the establishment of Reeves post office opened a communication link for the early pioneers. Begun July 13, 1899, in the front room of postmaster Joseph H. Reeves' two-story frame home, the post office served 110 settlers. James U. Strickland bought the house and took over as postmaster August 24, 1905. He served until the facility closed on March 30, 1907, and mail was delivered to Silverton (8 mi. N). After Strickland sold the home to Forrest Leonard Weast in 1909, it was destroyed by fire.

SINTON (San Patricio Co.)   US 181, 6 mi. N
St. Paul
The town of St. Paul began in 1910, the result of a land promotion operation by developer George H. Paul and the Shary Land Company. George Paul purchased 70,000 acres of land from

local rancher J. J. Welder and divided the acreage into farm lots. The townsite of St. Paul was platted in December 1910, and Adolph, Robert, and John Shary formed the Shary Land Company to promote the new town. Agents representing the development team worked throughout the Midwest to publicize the new community and excursion trains departed Kansas City twice a month bringing prospective settlers to Texas. The town grew quickly, with the construction of homes, the three story Shary Hotel, retail stores, schools, and churches. The George H. Paul Company operated a huge company farm that employed as many as 300 workers, as well as the largest store in town, the George H. Paul farm store, which also housed a post office (established in 1910), telephone exchange, and a bank. By the 1920's prosperous cotton gins were in operation to process farmers' crops, and eight trains a day came through the busy St. Paul Depot. The town declined after World War II as many people moved to larger cities. (1994)

SKIDMORE (Bee Co.)
US 181, 10 mi. S at roadside park
Papalote Creek
A few yards south passes Papalote Creek, crossed by the fierce Karankawa Indians who found kite-shaped pebbles and named it Papalote, which means "kite-shaped" or "wing-shaped." Along its banks came the leaders of the Power and Hewetson Colonists, holding Mexican land grants in the 1830's. On its Rata tributary there is evidence the Mexican Army camped on its way to suppress the Texas Revolution. By 1857 the town of Papalote had emerged. It was the center of entertainment for the county, boasting of a circular dance hall built by cowboys trading steer yearlings at $3 a head for lumber. There were rooster fights, ring tournaments and horse races. In 1886, when the railroad came, the town was booming. After the turn of the century, however, Papalote began to die away. A land company sold lots to settlers from as far away as Hawaii. Expecting to grow citrus fruits, they were disillusioned when the first killing frost doomed the project. Threats of Pancho Villa's raids continued as late as 1916, when women and children hid in a brick schoolhouse. Then dancing was banned, and the dance hall became a school house on a full-time basis. Today there is no post office, only a rural route for the few remaining households. (1965)

SKIDMORE (Bee Co.)
US 181 at Sullivan St.
Aransas Creek Settlers
Earliest known residents were Karankawa Indians who named creek. On this stream was one of the most famous ranches in early Texas, occupied in 1805 by Don Martin De Leon, who in 1824 founded Victoria. In 1830s Irish colonists came by way of Copano Bay, settling down creek. Anglo-Americans from older settlements came by road and trail, stopping mainly up creek. Stockraising, trucking and freighting provided livelihoods in the rich, new prairie land. In 1850 Patrick Fadden sold to Ft. Merrill corn and vegetables from 1835 land grant of his uncle, Father John Thomas Malloy. Fadden and W. R. Hayes freighted supplies to settlers in 1860s. Hayes had early post office in his home, 1870; was county judge 1876–1892. John Wilson, an 1850s up creek settler, brought first Durham cattle to country; built one of first wooden fences, enclosing 600 acres of homesite with rough heart pine plank. On creek's north bank stood ranch of Frank O. Skidmore, founder of Skidmore, who gained fame for building first barbed wire fence and windmill in county. He promoted breeding of registered Herefords and in 1886 gave much of right-of-way to the San Antonio and Aransas Pass Railroad. (1967)

SMITH POINT (Chambers Co.)
FM 562, .75 mi. N near McNeir Cemetery
Sarah Ridge Paschal Pix
Born on the family plantation in the Cherokee Nation near present Rome, Georgia, Sarah Ridge (1814–1891) attended mission schools and girls' seminary. Her father Major Ridge was a Cherokee leader and friend of Sam Houston. Major Ridge, Sarah's brother John, and cousin were later assassinated for supporting the treaty that traded Indian lands for acreage in the West. This treaty led to the infamous "Trail of Tears." Sarah married a lawyer, George Washington Paschal, in 1837 and they settled in Arkansas. In 1847, the family and slaves moved to Galveston. During the 1850 yellow fever epidemic Sarah opened her home and treated many of the ill with an Indian remedy. After Sarah and Paschal were divorced, she married Charles C. Sisson Pix, an Englishman, in 1856 in the home of Republic of Texas President Mirabeau B. Lamar. Sarah traded her Galveston home for this land at Smith Point soon after her marriage. Pix cattle ranged from here to present Liberty. While Pix served in the Confederate Army, Sarah built the ranch into a large operation. With the end of slavery, the ranch declined. After Sarah divorced Pix in 1880, she remained on

the ranch with her widowed daughter Agnes Paschal McNeir and two grandsons. Heirs still own the land.   (1979)

SMITHLAND (Marion Co.)   *SH 49, 4 mi. E near intersection with FM 727*
Potter's Point (About 6 mi. S)
Site of one of most famous events in Texas. Robert Potter—a signer, Texas Declaration of Independence, a chief author of Republic's Constitution, first Secretary of Navy, Republic of Texas— settled 1837 on Caddo Lake. A former U.S. Congressman, he won election 1840 to Texas Senate. After Senate adjourned in 1842 he tried to arrest his political foe, William P. Rose. On night of March 1, 1842, Rose led armed men to Potter's home. At dawn Senator Potter jumped into the lake to swim for help, but was shot to death. He is buried in State Cemetery, Austin.   (1969)

SMITHVILLE (Bastrop Co.)   *SH 71, 3 mi. W*
Site of Early Bastrop County Fort
In the late 1820s, a group of families settled in this area as a part of Stephen F. Austin's second colony. Included in this group were the Winslow Turner, Stephan Cottle, and Ahijah M. Highsmith families, who came to Texas from Lincoln County, Missouri. They were later joined by other families, including the Whites, Crafts, Grimeses, Ridgeways, and Parkers. For defense purposes, they built a log fort at the juncture of the Colorado River and Alum Creek (south of this site) and placed their cabins near the fort. During the 1830s, settlers established churches, schools, and communities around the fort and in neighboring areas on land given to them in return for their colonization efforts. Alum Creek, Craft's Prairie, Yeupon, Cottletown, Antioch, and Mount Pleasant were some of the names given to these settlements. A post office was established, and a number of early sawmills in Bastrop County were located near the fort site. It is not certain when the fort was razed. Though no physical evidence remains, the site is important as a reminder of early Bastrop County settlement and of the harshness of life during the early years of colonization in Texas.   (1984)

SNYDER (Scurry Co.)   *US 84, 12 mi. NW*
McDermott
Named for S. P. McDermott, who had crossroads store and was an early postmaster. Began as a community called Dark, 1½ miles northeast. (School in area was named Bookout.) Town moved 1909 to the Roscoe, Snyder & Pacific Railroad. It had a hotel and a number of businesses. The Santa Fe was built in 1911, and the competing railroads made this a busy cattle shipping center, with full loading pens. Town moved 1915 to Santa Fe Railroad. The R. S. & P. tracks were taken up in 1942. The town had new population in the later 1940s, during county oil boom.   (1966)

SNYDER (Scurry Co.)   *US 84, 8.4 mi. NW*
Home County of Famous Frontiersman J. Wright Mooar
J. Wright Mooar was a champion hunter of buffalo, largest game animal in North America. A native of Vermont. He came west at age 19 and in 1870 began hunting to supply hides for market. In partnership with his brother, John W. Mooar, he established the first buffalo hunting camp in the Texas Panhandle in 1873. On October 7, 1876, at his first camp in Scurry County (2.8 miles south of this site on County Road 253, near the Old Mooar Ranch headquarters) J. Wright Mooar killed a rare albino buffalo, one of two known to have been killed in Texas. The albino hide was shown at the 1904 St. Louis World's Fair and on many other occasions. Mooar hunted regularly until 1879. In 1881 he helped furnish game and hay to construction crews building the Texas & Pacific Railroad in West Texas. During his career, he shot about 22,000 buffalo, a record probably unsurpassed. His ability to hit a vital spot from a distance of 1,000 feet or farther won the respect of Comanche Indian Chief Quanah Parker, who became a friend in later life. The Mooar brothers began ranching in 1877. Highly esteemed by their fellow citizens, they owned a livery stable in Colorado City from 1881 to 1905.   (1995)

SNYDER (Scurry Co.)   *US 84, 6 mi. NW*
Scurry County's Billionth Barrel of Oil
Petroleum discoveries in this county began in 1923, with recovery of oil in the San Andres Formation—eventually penetrated by over 2,000 shallow wells. In late 1948, rigs drilling deeper

than 6,000 feet tapped the Canyon Reef geological formation. Four exploratory wells—Sun Oil Company's Schattel; Magnolia's Winston; Standard Oil Company of Texas' Brown; Lion Oil Company's C. T. McLaughlin—and other extensive drilling defined a gigantic field covering 85,000 acres and containing oil reserves estimated to total at least four billion barrels. The local economy and growth rate improved greatly. Many farmers and ranchers who had fought years of drouth and adversity paid off debts, modernized their homes, and continued to live on their land. On Oct. 8, 1973, twenty-five years after the Canyon Reef discovery, Scurry County produced from that formation its billionth barrel of oil, and in a week of festivities paid tribute to the petroleum industry. The celebrated billionth barrel of oil came from the well near this marker. By 1973, Scurry County was producing 3.2 percent of all the oil recovered annually in the United States. (1975)

SNYDER (Scurry Co.)   *US 180, 12 mi. E in roadside park*
Greene Springs and Site of Archeological Discoveries (1.5 mi. SW)
Located at a place occupied by man for centuries, these springs compose the first live (running) water that flows into the south fork of the Clear Fork of the Brazos River. The waters, which collect in large potholes in a sandstone formation, have produced a constant flow since first discovered by settlers. For many centuries before, they were also visited by Indians. Food grinding holes and petroglyphs (rock carvings) on the sandstone creek walls give evidence of this early use. Since 1964, explorations by the Scurry Chapter, South Plains Archeological Society, have produced many artifacts such as stone knives and scrapers, beads, potsherds, and arrow points. In the 19th century, military units under Capt. R. B. Marcy (1849) and Gen. Robert E. Lee (1856) camped at Greene Springs. Somewhat later, buffalo hunters, freighters, and emigrants moving west and north stopped for water at this beautiful place. The springs were named about 1881 for J. L. "Jim" Greene, a horse rancher who moved here at that time. Greene and his family lived in two dugouts until their first house was built in 1890. Remains of the dugouts are still visible today in a nearby hill. (1968)

SNYDER (Scurry Co.)   *25th St. (US 180), at Ave. U, W of bridge*
Channel of Deep Creek
Once a spring-fed tributary of the Colorado River; heads and ends within Scurry County. In 1870's it supplied buffalo hunters living in hide-covered half dugouts. "Pete" Snyder's Trading Post, which eventually grew into the county-seat town of Snyder, was located on bank. Although state surveyors had officially named it Culvers Creek, famous buffalo hunters John and J. Wright Mooar called it Deep Creek in 1876, and soon the name became widely used. Played central role in early town life as a scene of picnics, horse races, and baptisms. (1969)

SNYDER (Scurry Co.)   *US 180, 6 mi. W*
The Block 97 Controversy
Notorious county land dispute arising from state practice of paying railroads in public land for trackage laid began in 1873 when Houston & Texas Central claimed, in error, some 300,000 acres of Block 97 which were in reserve for Texas & Pacific. Found in 1882, the error voided all deeds from H. & T. C. for lots in the reserve. Much land was unscrupulously resold, causing a decade of conflict over claims. Issue was decided only when 1899 Legislature, on authority of State Supreme Court, declared land to be state school land and gave settlers option to buy. (1972)

SNYDER (Scurry Co.)   *US 180, 12 mi. W in roadside park*
Scurry County
Formed from Young and Bexar Territories. Created August 21, 1876. Organized June 28, 1884. Named in honor of General William R. Scurry, 1821–1864. Member of the last Texas Congress. A distinguished officer in the Confederate Army. Snyder, the county seat.

SOCORRO (El Paso Co.)   *328 S. Nevarez, 1 blk. N of intersection with FM 258*
Socorro
Site of the mission and pueblo of Nuestra Señora de la Concepcion Del Pueblo de Socorro established by Don Antonio de Otermin and Father Fray Francisco Ayeta, O. F. M. in 1683. Maintained by Franciscan missionaries for the civilizing and Christianizing of the Piro, Thano and Gemex Indians, refugees after the Pueblo Revolt in New Mexico. (1964)

SOCORRO (El Paso Co.)   *328 S. Nevarez, 1 blk. N of intersection with FM 258*
Mission Nuestra Señora de las Purisima Concepcion Del Socorro
(Our Lady of the Immaculate Conception of Socorro)
Established in 1680 by Brother Antonio Guerra for Piros Indians, refugees from Old Socorro, N. M., this and 1682 mission at Ysleta (located 3.7 mi. W) are among oldest continuously occupied settlements in the Southwest. By 1750, town had 498 Indians and 54 Spaniards. Present church, built about 1840, exhibits Indian influence on basic Spanish mission style. Adobe brick walls are several feet thick.   (1963)

SOCORRO (El Paso Co.)   *10140 Socorro Rd. (FM 258)*
Casa Ortiz
Legend says this house was built before 1800. In 1840s, its owner was Jose Ortiz, whose cart train freighted salt from foot of Guadalupe Mountains to Durango; knives, sarapes, clothing to Santa Fe and Llano Estacado. There he traded with Comanches and other wild Indians for dried buffalo hides and meat. He was a "Comanchero, Salinero, Cibolero." Francisca Lujan, the widow of Epifanio Ortiz (1842?–1932), was last of family to live here, in 1940s. A fine example of New Spain's frontier architecture: thick adobe walls; cottonwood and willow vigas and latias with dirt roof.   (1973)

SOMERVILLE (Burleson Co.)   *SH 36, N city limits*
Harvey House
Fred Harvey, a native of England, began operation of his Santa Fe Railroad dining rooms in 1876. In 1900 a Harvey House opened in Somerville, Divisional Headquarters of the Santa Fe Line. The 2-story, galleried structure was 260 ft. long and contained a dining room, guest rooms, library and reading room. The Harvey House served travelers and railroad workers in an atmosphere of elegance. It became the social center of the town and boosted the local economy. The Harvey House closed in 1940 and was dismantled in 1943. The present depot is a part of the original building.   (1978)

SOMERVILLE (Burleson Co.)   *SH 36, north city limits*
1906 Reunion of Hood's Texas Brigade
In 1906, Somerville hosted the annual reunion of the Hood's Texas Brigade Association, a group established in 1872 for veterans of the celebrated Confederate unit. For two days, June 27–28, 74 veterans were honored with a celebration which included speeches, a baseball game, and a grand ball. The local events were planned under the direction of the association's president R. A. Brantley, Sr., and his daughter Mrs. Norton B. Wellborn, both of Somerville. Part of a tradition which ended in 1934, the reunion reflected the area's respect for the former Civil War soldiers.   (1981)

SOMERVILLE (Burleson Co.)   *SH 36, north city limits*
Somerville
Located where two branches of the Gulf, Colorado & Santa Fe Railway joined, town was named for Albert Somerville, first president of the railroad. First settlers arrived after town was surveyed about 1883; the post office was permanently established in 1897. Somerville boomed in the 1890s when local citizens persuaded a railroad tie plant to locate here. Santa Fe Railroad bought the operation in 1905. This is still an important industry. Incorporated in 1913, the town has become a recreation center since Lake Somerville was created in the 1960s.   (1974)

SOMERVILLE (Burleson Co.)   *SH 36 at CR 422*
Oaklawn Cemetery
Dating to 1900, this graveyard was first called the Somerville and Lyons Cemetery. Land was purchased by J.W. Lauderdale to establish a cemetery upon the death of his two-year-old son Charles on November 6, 1900. The name was changed to Oaklawn Cemetery in 1913. Among the more than 2000 burials are 22 Civil War veterans, 20 children between 1900–1905, and victims of a typhoid fever epidemic in 1903. The construction of the dam at Somerville in 1963 caused 16 people to be re-interred here from other graveyards. The cemetery is still in use.   (1996)

SOMERVILLE (Burleson Co.)   *SH 36, .25 mi. S of the bridge*
Yegua Creek
In 1690 the Spanish gave the name "San Francisco" to this 62-mile Brazos River tributary; but on an 1822 map, Stephen F. Austin, "Father of Texas," marked it "Yegua," Spanish for "mare."

Mustang mares and foals then grazed among the Indians on the timbered creek. In 1826, colonist John P. Coles built a mill on the stream. A measure signed in 1837 by Texas President Sam Houston made the Yegua a county boundary. Floods often devastated the area until Lake Somerville harnessed Yegua's waters in 1967. Now a recreation area, the lake and creek benefit crops, wild life, and vacationers. (1976)

SONORA (Sutton Co.)   *IH 10, 4 mi. E*
Sutton County
Has traces of culture at least 20,000 years old. Occupied by Apache Indians up to founding of Fort Terrett, 1852. Anglo-Texan settlement began 1879 at Sonora, a trading post on San Antonio–El Paso Road. Created April 1, 1887, from land then in Crockett County. Organized Nov. 4, 1890, with Sonora as the county seat. Named in honor of John S. Sutton (1821–1862), a member of Santa Fe Expedition, Texas Ranger and Indian fighter, soldier in Mexican War and colonel of Mounted Volunteers, who died of wounds received in Civil War Battle of Val Verde. (1965)

SONORA (Sutton Co.)   *E. Main St. at Walter St., 2 blks. NE of US 277*
Colonel John S. Sutton
At outbreak Civil War, this veteran soldier, Ranger, Indian fighter joined 7th Regiment Texas Mounted Volunteers. Elected Lt. Colonel, led five companies Arizona–New Mexico campaign designed to make Confederacy an ocean to ocean nation. Mortally wounded in Battle of Val Verde while leading rifle assault against enemy cannons, he refused immediate aid and motioned on his battalion which captured the battery. A memorial to Texans who served the Confederacy. (1962)

SONORA (Sutton Co.)   *E. Main St. at Walter St., 2 blks. NE of US 277*
Sutton County Courthouse
This building site of all land transactions incident to development of county. Water well, a few feet from building, was first water here, where sheepmen watered their flocks, hence locating here as a home. Father of founder of the townsite killed father of one of West Texas' most prominent families on site of Courthouse over argument concerning watering sheep. (1962)

SONORA (Sutton Co.)   *US 277, 3 mi. S*
About 200 yds. W is Site of Ghost Town Wentworth
Situated in 1880s at water well of A. J. Winkler, who platted townsite, gave title bond, and named place for Fort Terrett area rancher P. H. Wentworth. The residents occupied tents and picket homes. Principal building was two-story school, church, and hall of Dee Ora Lodge No. 715, A. F. & A. M. Town had a post office Aug. 1890–Aug. 1891. Postmaster was Thomas Stevenson, uncle of a future Texas Governor. Losing 1891 county seat election to Sonora, Wentworth citizens moved away. Lodge hall, relocated late 1891 in Sonora, served as school and community building until 1938. (1972)

SOUR LAKE (Hardin Co.).   *SH 105, .5 mi. NW*
Sour Lake, C.S.A.
Early-day health resort, with baths that attracted such Texans as Gen. Sam Houston. The healing waters had been used for years by the Indians. One spring's water, with high sulphuric acid content, primed telegraph batteries during the Civil War. This was of vital importance, for at best telegraph service was limited. Started in 1854, the 1861–1865 system went only from Shreveport to Marshall to Houston, and Houston to Galveston to Orange. A 20-word telegram sent from Shreveport to Houston in February, 1865 cost $36. (1964)

SOUR LAKE (Hardin Co.)   *SH 326 at Crosby St.*
Stephen Jackson (1803–1860)
Born in South Carolina, Stephen Jackson moved to Lorenzo de Zavala's colony in Texas in 1831. He received a labor of land (177 acres) to establish a farm. In 1835 Jackson was granted a league of land (4,428 acres), which included the later community of Sour Lake. In 1836 Jackson served in Captain Logan's company of the Texas Army and was awarded 320 acres of land in Milam County as bounty. He married Susan Choate (1807–1873) in 1838 and established their home near here. They are buried along with their children—Ambrose, Sarah, James A., Minerva, Stephen, and W. J. in the family cemetery (.5 mi. NW). (Texas Sesquicentennial 1836–1986)

445

SOUTH HOUSTON (Harris Co.)   *58 Spencer Hwy., 2 blks. E of SH 3*
First Airplane Flight over Texas
The first documented flight of a heavier-than-air flying machine in Texas occurred over this site on February 18, 1910, two weeks before the first military airplane flight by Lt. Benjamin Foulois at Fort Sam Houston in San Antonio. The South Houston flight was part of a land development promotion sponsored by the Western Land Corporation and the Houston "Post." French aviator Louis Paulhan, on a coast-to-coast flying exhibition tour of America, was commissioned to demonstrate his flying skills. The promoters arranged for special excursion trains to transport spectators to the site from downtown Houston. Headlines in the "Post" proclaimed, "This is the first opportunity for Texans to see a real demonstration of man's ability to fly. Don't fail to come and see demonstrated the greatest invention of the present era." A crowd of more than 2,500 people gathered on Friday, February 18th, to witness Paulhan's first Texas flight in his Farman biplane. Because of high winds and inclement weather, the aviator was not able to perform some of his most spectacular stunts, but the crowd was thrilled with the aerial display. A second flying exhibition on the following day drew almost 6,000 people.   (1991)

SPANISH FORT (Montague Co.)   *FM 103*
Town of Spanish Fort
Named San Teodora by Spanish. Important trading-post between French and Indians. During 18th century, Spain, resenting this encroachment on her territory, sent expedition to drive them out, suffered defeat by Indians who had been supplied with weapons and trained in war tactics by French. A monument marks the site: Red River Station. A frontier post for state militia, most northwestern outpost of Confederacy. Became thriving settlement and main crossing on Red River for vast herds of Texas cattle "going up" the Chisolm Trail to Northern markets. Town abandoned 1887. Thus trail driving through this area marked the advance of American settlement westward.

SPANISH FORT (Montague Co.)   *FM 103*
The Site of the 1759 Taovaya Victory over Spain
Col. Diego Ortiz Parilla, Commandant of Presidio San Saba (near the later site of Menard) had grave Indian problems in 1759. Priests and others were killed in Comanche attacks on Mission San Saba. Comanches and their friends were allied to Frenchmen, who were trading deep in Spanish domain. Parilla wished to whip the Comanches and expel the French. With 380 soldiers and Indian support to a total of 600 men, he left San Antonio in August. A victory over some Tonkawas on the Brazos as he marched north gave him false confidence. When he arrived at this site in October, he saw Red River forming a moat around a fort. His Apaches tried in vain to span the river and invade the fortified Taovaya Village. He saw 14 or more Frenchmen; a French flag was flying. Indians played drum and fife and had plenty of guns and ammunition. He bombarded the fort with cannons, but after losing 52 men in a 4-hour battle he was glad that nightfall gave him a chance to withdraw. He was pursued for many days as he retreated to Presidio San Saba, which he reached on Oct. 25, 1759. The Taovaya Indians were later known as Wichitas, and continued to resist white men until the 1870s.   (1976)

SPEARMAN (Hansford Co.)   *SH 15, 3 mi. NE*
Hansford County
Formed from Young and Bexar Territories. Created August 21, 1876. Organized March 11, 1889. Named in honor of John M. Hansford. Came to Texas in 1837. Member of the Texas Congress, judge of the Seventh Judicial District, 1840–1842. Died in 1844. Hansford, the county seat.   (1965)

SPEARMAN (Hansford Co.)   *SH 15/207, 6.5 mi. W*
Dodge City–Tascosa Trail
This road was surveyed during the Civil War to haul military supplies to Ft. Bascom, New Mexico Territory. Then came the buffalo hunters using the trail going to Dodge City hauling hides and buying supplies. Tascosa became a town in the early 1880s. Ox teams and mule teams hauled freight for the cowboy capital of the Panhandle and ranches that ran into hundreds of thousands of dollars annually. Herds from all the Panhandle trailed into Dodge over this route for a number of years. Kit Carson and his New Mexico volunteers came down this trail from Ft. Bascom in November, 1865 to fight a losing battle with the Indians at the first Adobe Walls site. Stage coaches ran weekly carrying mail and passengers over the 242 mile route. Post offices and stage stands out of

Tascosa were Little Blue, Cator's Zula Stockade, Hardesty Ranch in "No Man's Land," Jim Lanes Beaver Creek, Hines Crossing, Cimarron, Hoodoo Brown, Crooked Creek, on into Dodge. Brick for the courthouse at nearby ghost town of Hansford was hauled from Dodge City. Later freight came over this trail from Liberal, Kansas. Ranchers continued to use portions of the old trail until 1920 when the railroad built across the county and Spearman was built. Thus another old historic trail was fenced and plowed under. Hansford County Historical Survey Committee Twentieth Century Club.

(1963)

SPEARMAN (Hansford Co.)

SH 15/207, 6 mi. W

Hansford Cemetery

First burial ground set aside in this county. Earliest grave (1890) was that of Mrs. Alfie P. Magee, wife of the first sheriff. Also buried here: the Cator Brothers, founders of Zulu Stockade; and the Wright brothers, early ranchers. Only official cemetery in county until 1928; is still in use. (1967)

SPEARMAN (Hansford Co.)

SH 207, SW

Spearman

Founded 1917; incorporated 1921. Named for Thomas C. Spearman, a vice-president and head of the land department of the Santa Fe Railway. The Santa Fe Line was completed to Spearman in 1920, making this the first railroad shipping point in the county. Hansford County, created 1876 and organized 1889, relocated its county seat here in 1929. The courthouse was built 1931. Center for agriculture, wheat storage, ranching, and petroleum industry. Early 1960s growth included 25 new businesses in two years. Streets paved with brick make city distinctive. (1967)

SPEARMAN (Hansford Co.)

SH 207 right-of-way,
.4 mi. S of intersection with 13 St.

Lindberghs Land at Spearman

At ten minutes before 11:00 A.M. on Monday, September 24, 1934, a small monocoupe airplane landed in a pasture about ¼ mile west of this site. The pilot taxied his craft to a stop near a windmill, deplaned, and asked the curious resident, "Lady, can I park my plane in your back yard?" The day proved a momentous one for Spearman residents. The pilot was Charles Augustus Lindbergh (1902–1974), traveling from California to New York with his wife, Anne. With about one hundred miles' worth of fuel left in his plane, Lindbergh chose to stop in this small community to refuel in order to avoid the inevitable crowds his arrival would cause in a larger town. A passing motorist was sent into town to purchase fuel for the airplane while the Lindberghs rested, enjoyed refreshments, and gave their hostess a tour of the airplane. As news of the Lindberghs' landing spread, school children were excused from classes to see the famous aviator and watch the plane depart two hours later. Although brief in duration, the visit by Charles and Anne Morrow Lindbergh to this small rural community was a significant local event. (1989)

SPRINGLAKE (Lamb Co.)

US 385, 6.2 mi. S

Lamb County Sand Hills

A natural landmark, this chain of sand dunes extends for 130 miles and is three to five miles wide. Archeological findings show that the area was inhabited 6,000 years ago. Comanches camped in the sand hills because of wild game, vegetation, protection from the wind, and the availability of water. Spanish explorers and later Anglo-Americans used the old Indian trails that passed along the dunes. Early ranching did little damage to the area. However, in recent years, the sand hills have been destroyed by extensive farming and industrial operations. (1979)

SPUR (Dickens Co.)

SH 70, 6 mi. N

Site of Anderson's Fort or Soldier's Mound

Here behind extensive breastworks Major Thomas M. Anderson, Tenth U.S. Infantry, maintained a supply camp for the cavalry under General Ranald S. Mackenzie, Fourth U.S. Cavalry, who in 1874–1875 forced the Indians of the region onto reservations and opened the plains to white settlement.

STAFFORD (Fort Bend Co.)

US 90A at city hall

Buffalo Bayou, Brazos & Colorado, First Railroad in Texas

Planned 1840 to benefit the Republic of Texas by moving rich sugar and cotton crops from plantation areas. Chartered 1841 by 5th Congress of the Republic, in name of Harrisburg Railroad &

Trading Company. H.R.&T.C. did not succeed in building a railroad. Its holdings were transferred in 1847 to Gen. Sidney Sherman, a hero of the Battle of San Jacinto, who was backed by eastern capital and leading Texans—W. J. Hutchins, Gen. Hugh McLeod, Wm. Marsh Rice (benefactor of Rice University), B. A. Shepherd, James H. Stevens, and John Grant Tod (a former Texas naval officer). B. F. Terry (destined to lead Terry's Texas Rangers in the Civil War) and W. J. Kyle graded the roadbed. The first locomotive, "General Sherman," arrived 1852. In August 1853, the tracks extended 20 miles from Harrisburg to Stafford's Point, early Texas center of trade and social life. On Sept. 1, with fanfare, a special train brought a load of honored guests to join planters here for a barbecue-jubilee. Regular schedules were soon in operation. Stafford's Point, end of the line for two years, did much business. Buffalo Bayou, Brazos & Colorado in 1860 reached Alleyton—a distance of 80 miles from Harrisburg. (1967)

STAIRTOWN (Caldwell Co.)
SH 80 at FM 671, 2 mi. SE
Rafael Rios No. 1 (Located .8 mi. N on Farm Road 671)
Discovery well of Luling Field, a major Texas oil area. Wildcatter E.B. Davis drilled on land owned by R. Rios. Well came in Aug. 10, 1922, after 3 dry holes had been drilled in same area. Magnolia (now Mobil) Oil Co. bought field 1926. By 1969, production was 135,000,000 barrels. Incise on back: Donated by Mobil Oil Corporation. (1970)

STAMFORD (Jones Co.)
US 277 Bus., .25 mi. E of US 277
Stamford
Swedish native Swante Magnus Swenson and his two sons, Eric Pierson and Swen Albin Swenson, came to Texas in 1882 to establish the SMS ranches. In 1899, Eric P. and Swen A. Swenson donated a large section of land for a townsite on an extension of the Texas Central Railway. Railway president Henry McHarg named the new town Stamford for his hometown in Connecticut. A Cumberland Presbyterian Church was organized in members' homes and a post office was established in a railroad boxcar in 1899. The Bank of Stamford opened for business in January 1900 and the first train pulled out of the Stamford depot in February. Businesses, churches and utilities soon were established. The booming town was incorporated in January 1901 and P. P. Berthelot became the first mayor. Stamford relied primarily on agriculture for its economy. Cotton, Swenson's Herefords and other area livestock brought substantial income. The town also boasted a flour mill, cottonseed oil plant, iron foundry, gins, brick manufacturers and a railroad roundhouse. Both passenger and freight trains brought business to town. Stamford Collegiate Institution (later Stamford College), a Methodist school, opened in 1907. Oil was discovered near Stamford in 1935 and broadened the town's economic base still further. U. S. Army pilots trained at nearby Arledge Field during World War II. The town of Stamford thrived throughout the 20th century. Though the Burlington Northern Railroad (final proprietor of the railway through Stamford) abandoned the track in the late 1990s, the Swenson Land and Cattle Company remained in operation, and cotton, cattle and wheat continued to be among Stamford's leading industries at the dawn of the 21st century. (2000)

STAMFORD (Jones Co.)
US 277 at SH 92, .75 mi. W Stamford
Square at Reunion Headquarters
Texas Cowboy Reunion Oldtimers' Association
Founded 1930, jointly with Texas Cowboy Reunion—to "hand down to posterity, customs and traditions" of early cattle people who lived in dugouts and fought drouths, die-outs, heat and freeze-ups, raising the longhorns that finally brought settlement to the Southwest. Here (1930) were 335 men who had been cowboys prior to 1895. Besides regular cowmen, early members included musician Paul Whiteman, Editor Amon Carter, Ranger Captain Tom Hichman and Will Rogers, ex-cowhand, internationally famous entertainer and columnist. Colonel R. L. Penick was first president. In 1932, donation of a bull started building fund for bunkhouse and roundup hall standing nearby. Ranch donated site. The interior and exterior of the bunkhouse feature ranch brands of many members. Oldtimers' Reunion and Rodeo held 3 days annually (including July 4th) features chuckwagon meals, square dancing, and oldtimers' memories and songs. Town celebrates with cowboy parade and thousands come to see what is called "World's Largest Amateur Cowboy Show," with actual cowhands performing. These oldtimers represent the end of the open range and beginning of the era of barbed wire. They opened Texas' last frontier. (1969)

STANTON (Martin Co.)

IH 20, .5 mi. W

Martin County

On lower great plains of West Texas. Formed from Young and Bexar territories. Created Aug. 21, 1876, and organized Nov. 4, 1884. Named for Wyly Martin, member of Austin's Colony and Texas patriot. County seat established by the first commissioners court which authorized construction of courthouse in Stanton (then called Marienfeld). Early C. C. Slaughter Ranch headquarters, 12 miles northwest of Stanton at Mustang Spring, best campsite west of Big Spring. Economy based on grain sorghum; cotton farming; cattle ranching; petroleum.

(1966)

STANTON (Martin Co.)

IH 20, .5 mi. E

The J. E. Millhollon Ranch House

About 1900, J. E. and Nettie (Bell) Millhollon trailed their cattle from Glasscock to Martin County, acquiring this homesite and 34 sections of land. Business and church leaders in Stanton, the couple had this house erected in 1907 by N. H. Hunt of Big Spring, who built many structures along the Texas & Pacific Railroad. The restoration, begun 1970 by Mr. and Mrs. Mike Hull, is being continued by Mr. and Mrs. Norman Wright, who bought the property in 1974. Awarded Historical Building Marker.

(1974)

STANTON (Martin Co.)

300 St. Joseph St., courthouse

Old Martin County Jail

The cell block of this jail was originally included in the 1885 Martin County Courthouse, built the year after the organization of Martin County when Stanton was known as Marienfeld. When the courthouse was torn down following a 1908 bond election, the cells were retained as the nucleus of this rock jail building. Completed that same year, it included living quarters for the sheriff's family. It later served as a library and museum.

(1982)

STANTON (Martin Co.)

301 N St. Peter St.

Marienfeld

Former name of Stanton. Begun as German colony by 5 German Catholics from Kansas, who pitched tents here, near new Texas & Pacific Railroad in 1881. The site—with a water tank, section house, telegraph office bore name Grelton, but settlers had it changed to Marienfeld, German for "Field of Mary." County was created 1876 and named for Wylie Martin, senator in Republic of Texas. When the county organized, town became county seat. First commissioners court met here December 13, 1884. Through Protestant influence, town was renamed Stanton, 1870.   (1970)

STEPHENVILLE (Erath Co.)

SH 108, 5.1 mi. NW

Oak Dale Cemetery

Founders of Oak Dale community began arriving in 1867. They included: John R. Pickard; George Lidia, who became Pickard's son-in-law; the Rev. James M. Johnson, a Methodist minister; and William Jasper Mefferd. These men and their families, including Johnson's four sons, harvested timber along the Bosque River to build cabins and began farming the land. Samuel Johnson chose Oak Dale as the settlement's name for the abundance of the trees in the area. By 1868, the wives of both John Pickard and James Johnson were interred here on Pickard's land; the graves are now unmarked. The first marked burial is that of two-day-old Ruth Ann Johnson (d. 1877). Local residents established Oak Dale School, which consolidated with Stephenville in 1951. There were also a Baptist church and a Methodist church until the mid-20th century, when they likewise moved to the county seat. Today, Oak Dale Cemetery is a link to the early settlement, which began to decline in population during the Great Depression and World War II. It is the final resting place of generations of area residents, including military veterans of conflicts dating to the Civil War.   (2004)

STEPHENVILLE (Erath Co.)

US 281 at FM 1188, 10 mi. N

Morgan Mill Tabernacle

The community of Morgan Mill, named for early settler George Bryan Morgan, traces its history to the mid-19th century. A post office was established in 1877. Several community church congregations shared a brush arbor in the summers for revivals and other meetings. In 1910, the brush arbor was replaced with this permanent structure, named the Morgan Mill Tabernacle. In addition to serving the churches, the tabernacle also was used by the local school and other community organizations. It remains in use as a community gathering place.

(1994)

STEPHENVILLE (Erath Co.)
US 281, 5.5 mi. S
Wyatt-Boyd Ranch Complex
This is a rare example of a virtually complete 19th-century cross timbers farmstead. Thought to have been built in the early 1870s by James J. Wyatt, the Cumberland plan one-story rough limestone two-room ranch house was altered in the 1890s by J. H. Boyd and modified in the 1930s and 1940s. Other structures in the ranch complex include a single-room masonry dugout, two stone barns, and a rock base for an elevated cistern. (1987)

STERLING CITY (Sterling Co.)
US 87, 4 mi. E at Montvale Cemetery
Montvale
The community of Montvale was established in 1884 when the pioneer settlement of St. Elmo was relocated here. Then a part of Tom Green County, Montvale was located on the Shafter Military Trail, an early road from Fort Concho. A community school, the earliest in the area, was in operation by 1886. Three years later the town was platted by H. B. Tarver, the surveyor for Tom Green County. It is believed the settlement was named for a nearby hill referred to in Tarver's field notes at Mt. Vale. Early businesses in Montvale included the saddle and harness shop of R. B. Cummins and the general store and blacksmith shop of B. Z. Cooper. The town was also the site of a Methodist Church, a hotel, a post office and a variety of stores. About 1889, R. B. Cummins started the town of Cummins (5.4 mi. NW) upriver from Montvale. Both settlements began to decline in 1891 with the establishment of Sterling City (3.5 mi. NW) as the seat of government for the newly created Sterling County. A community cemetery is all that remains of the townsite of Montvale, a pioneer settlement that played an important role in the area's development. (1982)

STERLING CITY (Sterling Co.)
US 87, public square
Sterling County
This prairie region split by the North Concho River is old Comanche, Kickapoo, Kiowa, Lipan, and Wichita hunting ground. Possibly it was crossed by six or so Spanish explorations between 1540 and 1654. In the 1860s and 70s, Anglo-Americans hunted buffalo commercially in this area. An 1860s hunter, Capt. W. S. Sterling, had a dugout home on the creek that bears his name. In the 1870s, bandits Frank and Jesse James kept horse herds on a tributary of Sterling Creek. In 1874, the United States Army occupied Camp Elizabeth, a Fort Concho outpost hospital, about ten miles west of here. Ranchers from other counties began to bring in large cattle herds in the 1870s, to capitalize on free grass. After keeping out small herds for a time, they permitted actual settlers to share the range. Family men staked land claims, grew crops in the valleys, and opened stores, schools, and post offices. On March 4, 1891, on the petition of 150 citizens, the county was created out of part of Tom Green County, and named for its first regular resident. Sterling City became the county seat. Petroleum production has been important to the economy since the 1950s; yet the land essentially remains range country, grazed by cattle and sheep. (1976)

STERLING CITY (Sterling Co.)
US 87, 1.9 mi. W
Site of Town of Cummins (100 yds. SW)
The pioneer settlement of Cummins developed at this site about 1890 around the saddle and harness shop of the earliest permanent settler, Mississippi native Robert Benjamin Cummins (b. 1848). A post office opened here in 1890 with J. H. Kellis as postmaster. The following year the nearby town of Sterling City (1.9 mi. E) was founded. The two towns became rivals for the designation of county seat when the Texas Legislature created Sterling County from Tom Green County on March 4, 1891. An intense publicity campaign developed, aided by the writings of the respective town newspaper editors: W. L. Thurman of the Cummins paper, the "North Concho News," and S. R. Ezzell of the "Sterling Courier." An election, conducted May 20, 1891, appeared to be a victory for Cummins until several voting boxes were dismissed for technical reasons, resulting in a tie. A second election on July 7 gave Sterling City a 13-vote margin and it was named the county seat. Most Cummins businesses and residents had moved to Sterling City by the end of 1891. Nothing remains of the early townsite, which once included a school, saloon, meat market, mercantile, blacksmith shop, and grocery stores. (1981)

STERLING CITY (Sterling Co.)
US 87, 9 mi. NW
Site of Camp Elizabeth
Thought to have been established 1853. Used as an outpost hospital of Fort Concho, 1874–1886.

450

STINNETT (Hutchinson Co.)
SH 136/207, 10 mi. N
Drift Fence
Famed cattleman Charles Goodnight established one of the first ranches in the Texas Panhandle, the J A Ranch, in 1876. Later that year, Thomas S. Bugbee established the first cattle ranch in Hutchinson County. As a result of soaring beef prices cattle ranching proliferated in this region of the U.S. in the 1880s. The Texas Panhandle, with its open range and expansive grasslands, became the preferred winter grazing site for cattle migrating south from Colorado, New Mexico, Oklahoma, and Kansas. This seasonal influx of cattle disrupted the practice of area ranchers who went to great lengths to respect adjacent ranch boundaries. Members of the Panhandle Stock Association pooled their resources and in 1882–85 erected barbed wire barriers along a 200-mile stretch of the Panhandle including Hutchinson County to prevent cattle from drifting south into the fertile Canadian River Valley. The "drift fence" worked too well in the winters of 1886 and 1887 when thousands of cattle moving south ahead of strong storms stalled at the fence line and froze or were trampled to death. The staggering losses prompted federal and state legislation which limited fencing on public lands and the "drift fence" was removed or incorporated into private ranch fencing.
(Sesquicentennial of Texas Statehood 1845–1995)

STINNETT (Hutchinson Co.)
SH 136/207, 4 mi. N
First Battle of Adobe Walls (November 25, 1864)
Largest Indian battle in Civil War, 15 miles east, at ruins of Bent's Old Fort, on the Canadian. 3,000 Comanches and Kiowas, allies of the South, met 372 Federals under Col. Kit Carson, famous scout and mountain man. Though Carson made a brilliant defense—called greatest fight of his career—the Indians won. Some of the same Indians lost in 1874 Battle of Adobe Walls, though they outnumbered 700 to 29 the buffalo hunters whose victory helped open the Panhandle to settlement.
(1964)

STINNETT (Hutchinson Co.)
SH 207 at courthouse
Hutchinson County Courthouse
Hutchinson County, named for prominent judge and writer Anderson Hutchinson, was one of 54 counties created out of the District of Bexar in 1876 by the Texas Legislature. It was not until 1901, however, that the county was officially organized. That year a temporary county courthouse was erected in the county seat of Plemons. A permanent courthouse was built in Plemons by contractor E. E. Ackers. Stinnett replaced Plemons as Hutchinson County seat in 1926. The county courthouse was temporarily housed in an office building in downtown Stinnett in 1926 before this courthouse was erected in 1927 at a time of major oil discoveries in the area. Designed by Amarillo architect W. C. Townes and built by local contractor C. S. Lambie & Company, the Spanish renaissance revival style building also housed the county jail. It features brick construction with cut stone ornamentation, a 3-bay primary facade with grand entry bay, raised basement with end entries, metal sash windows and 2nd floor windows with round-arch stone lintels. Friezes at the east and west entrances of the courthouse depict the petroleum, farm and ranch, and cattle industries, historically the three principal commercial enterprises in the area.
(Recorded Texas Historic Landmark 1962)

STOCKDALE (Wilson Co.)
US 87, south side of bypass
Stockdale Cemetery
Before the Stockdale Cemetery was begun in the 1870s, most burials in the area took place in private, family graveyards. About 1873, however, a young man who was not related to any of the local settlers was thrown from his horse and killed. To provide a place for his burial, Dr. T. M. Batte gave one acre of land at this site, and the burial ground has been used by Stockdale citizens since that time. Additional acreage was purchased in 1881 and 1904, and in 1938, area resident Paul Ballard donated an acre of land for use by anyone who did not have a family plot and needed a place for burial. The earliest marked grave in the Stockdale Cemetery, that of Sallie A. Pope, is dated 1873. Many early settlers are buried here, including the town's founder, John R. King, and the first schoolteacher, Martin West. The cemetery also contains the graves of numerous war veterans and victims of a post–World War I flu epidemic. The women of Stockdale formed an organization in the early 1900s to care for the gravesites, and in 1965 the Stockdale Cemetery Association was formally organized. In use for more than 100 years, the Stockdale cemetery continues to serve the residents of the Stockdale area.
(1983)

STONEWALL (Gillespie Co.)   *US 290, 10 mi. E*
Lower South Grape Creek School
Area settlers built a log schoolhouse 1.5 miles south of here in 1871 along South Grape Creek. It was part of Luckenbach School Precinct No. 3 until 1889, when it was renamed Lower South Grape Creek and began to serve as District No. 21. The log schoolhouse was replaced with this structure in 1901. It is typical of early 1900s rural school buildings found in Texas' Hill Country. The stuccoed limestone building features an open plan and bell tower with a pyramidal roof. The school closed in 1960 and merged with the Fredericksburg School District.   (1994)

STONEWALL (Gillespie Co.)   *US 290, 3 mi. E to RR 1 in rest area*
Site of the Andreas Lindig Lime Kiln
First kiln, eastern Gillespie County. Built 1874 by Andreas Lindig, trained in his native Germany in quicklime making. On his homestead, he found rock to be hauled to this site by oxwagon, using 7 loads of rock for each "batch" of lime. Post oak wood, burned in a cooking bed, produced high heat which produced the lime. Besides that for his own use, he made lime commercially for neighbors. Lindig's home (built 1874, about .5 mi. S) shows endurance of cement made from his lime. So does the 1963–1969 "Texas White House," built nearby in 1897 by Willie Meier.   (1970)

STONEWALL (Gillespie Co.)   *US 290, 3 mi. E, at Lower Albert Rd.*
Andreas and Frederike Lindig Farmstead
German immigrants Andreas and Frederike Lindig arrived in Texas in 1869. They established a farmstead here in 1874 on 448 acres that included a main farmhouse, summer kitchen, barn, water well, and commercial lime kiln. Lindig used native post oak timbers to build a log farmhouse to which he added limestone shed rooms. They grew cash crops of peanuts, sweet potatoes, and cotton. Their sons Friedrich, Karl, and Christian built homes nearby. Andreas (d. 1898) and Frederike (d. 1913) are buried in the family cemetery (one-half mile SE). The property remained in the family until 1980.   (1995)

STONEWALL (Gillespie Co.)   *Stonewall Elementary School Campus*
The 36th President of the United States of America
Lyndon Baines Johnson
As a 12-year-old student attended classes of the 8th grade here at the old Stonewall school from October 1920 to June 1921.   (1971)

STONEWALL (Gillespie Co.)   *RR 1 N of US 290 at Lyndon B. Johnson State Park & Historic Site*
Lyndon Baines Johnson
The 36th President of the United States was born here on August 27, 1908; son of a state legislator (1905–1917), Sam Ealy Johnson, Jr., and Rebekah Baines Johnson, a teacher. The house was built in 1906 with the help of neighbors. The Johnsons and Baineses—early settlers—were ministers, Indian fighters, newspapermen, college professors, ranchers. Original house burned, and was rebuilt by the President.   (1967)

STONEWALL (Gillespie Co.)   *RR 1 N of US 290 at state historic site*
Trinity Lutheran Church
Was organized in June, 1902. This corner stone and surrounding stones formed the foundation for the second church which was dedicated in June, 1904.   (1904)

STRATFORD (Sherman Co.)   *US 54, 2.5 mi. NE in roadside park*
County Named for Sidney Sherman, C.S.A.
Born in Massachusetts, 1805. Led his crack Kentucky Militia Company to join Texas Army in War for Independence. Commanded cavalry wing, Battle of San Jacinto. Major-General and Congressman, Republic of Texas. Built second railroad west of Mississippi River. First engine to run in Texas was "General Sherman," named in his honor. Put in command of fortifying Galveston, most valued seaport in Texas, at outbreak of Civil War. Set up marine guard and batteries of cannon. Lost eldest son in Galveston recapture, 1863. Gen. Sherman died in 1873.

STRATFORD (Sherman Co.)
US 287, 2 mi. N in roadside park
Early Settlers on Coldwater Creek (Creek Located 6½ mi. S)
First area in Sherman County to be settled, and only live water for miles. First settler, buffalo hunter J. D. Rawlings, came 1870s. Later county judge. W. B. Slaughter acquired the Rawlings Place about 1894. Later ran bank and store in Stratford. John Lanners (arrived 1892) was a cowboy at Slaughter's ranch; acquired land and ran a mule-drawn supply line. One of largest spreads was owned by Thomas Snyder (also arrived in 1892). Among other prominent early settlers were J. H. Williams, freighter, and Geo. Loomis, merchant.
(1971)

STRATFORD (Sherman Co.)
US 287, 2 m. S
Sherman County
Formed from Young and Bexar Territories. Created August 21, 1876. Organized June 13, 1889. Named in Honor of General Sidney Sherman 1805–1873. Commander of the Left Wing of the Army at the Battle of San Jacinto; member of the Texas Congress 1842–1843. County seat, Coldwater, 1889; Stratford, since 1901.
(1936)

STRAWN (Palo Pinto Co.)
SH 16, 6 mi. N
Robinson School
In 1937, Guy U. Robinson led his neighbors to petition the county for a new common school district, in part to protest high school taxes in Strawn. Leo Ankenbauer sold two acres of land to school trustees, and craftsmen Bill Roberson and W. Proctor of Strawn completed this one-room, red brick schoolhouse in time for classes to begin in September 1937. Darker brick at the corners and around the windows and the door provide some ornament to the simple vernacular structure. In use only until 1943, when the number of pupils declined to two, Robinson School is a unique reminder of the county's rural educational history.
(2001)

STRAWN (Palo Pinto Co.)
SH 16, N city limits
Bethel Strawn, C.S.A.
An 1858 settler and leading citizen of Palo Pinto County. Enlisted 1864 in Co. B, 1st Frontier District, Texas State Troops, in Maj. Wm. Quayle's command. Saw service mainly in keeping down Indian depredations and protecting settlements that were furnishing food, salt, hides, leather, and other goods to aid the Confederate cause during the Civil War. In 1880, when Texas & Pacific Railroad built through western Palo Pinto County, a stop was named for Bethel Strawn, who owned land at that point. By 1885, Strawn settlement had grown into a town drawing off people from old Palo Pinto. During 20th century oil developments, the name Strawn is used for petroleum bearing formations of rock that underlie this county and other areas. Strawn minerals include coal, once mined locally. 36 Texas counties were named for men prominent in the Confederacy during the Civil War. One county, Val Verde, was named for a Civil War battlefield on which Texas troops were victorious during the New Mexico–Arizona Campaign of 1861–1862. 41 Texas towns were named for men who figured in the Civil War. Strawn, however, is the one geographical name commemorating a Texan in the Civil War.
(1965)

STRAWN (Palo Pinto Co.)
715 Central Avenue (SH 16)
Thomas House
Designed by Dallas architect Thomas J. Galbraith and completed in 1919, this house is an excellent regional example of the Prairie School style of architecture. Its strong historical associations with area ranches and with the Ranger Oil Boom lend additional significance to its place in the architectural history of Palo Pinto County. Rancher Randal Burton Thomas, Sr. (1886–1969), grew up in West Texas assisting his mother, Mary Ellen Satterfield Thomas, in running her family ranch. Having first arrived in Strawn from Bowling Green, Kentucky, by 1881, when railroads began to reach this area, their family was among the region's first settlers. The Ranger Oil Boom, begun in 1917 with McClesky No. 1 Well, brought new wealth to the family from the many producing wells on their properties. When Thomas began making plans to move into town, he designed this house with living quarters for his family on the north side and for Mary Ellen Satterfield Thomas on the south side. It remained their home until their deaths. The Thomas house features strong elements of the Prairie style, with its horizontality enhanced by the use of wide, projecting eaves. Designed to be heated with coal from the nearby mines in Thurber, the house features extensive use of concrete

and a red metal roof. Still in the Thomas family at the turn of the 21st century, the house is an important reminder of West Texas history and culture. (2002)

SUDAN (Lamb Co.)
US 84 between Commerce and Main Sts.
Old Watering Trough
One of Sudan's oldest structures. Built 1916, when Santa Fe Railway terminus here shipped out cattle of early ranches. Here ranchers watered herds and horses, traded, told yarns, hired hands. Trough also served mule teams, after the farming era began in the 1920's. (1966)

SUGAR LAND (Fort Bend Co.)
US 90A, city limits marker
Sugar Land
Founded 1853. Named by B. F. Terry and W. J. Kyle for sugar mill and plantation bought on their return with fortunes from California Gold Rush. The town's founders organized Terry's Texas Rangers at the start of the Civil War. Farming market. Site of Texas' only cane sugar refinery. Texas prison farms are located nearby.

SUGAR LAND (Fort Bend Co.)
US 90A at Imperial Sugar
The Sugar Land Refinery
Stephen F. Austin's colonists brought sugar cane to Fort Bend County in the 1820s. The Sugar Land area was once part of Oakland Plantation, where Nathaniel (1800–1884) and Matthew Williams (1805–1852) planted sugar cane about 1840. They began processing the cane in 1843 using a horse-powered mill and open-air cooking kettles. In 1853, the plantation and mill were purchased by William J. Kyle (1803–1864) and Benjamin F. Terry (1821–1861). They improved the mill and promoted a railroad for the area, which they named Sugar Land. Terry later helped organize the famed Confederate cavalry unit, Terry's Texas Rangers, and was killed in the Civil War (1861–1865). After the war, the operation was sold to Edward H. Cunningham (1835–1912), who expanded the sugar mill into a refinery. W. T. Eldridge (1862–1932) and Galveston business-man I. H. Kempner, Sr. (1873–1967) purchased the refinery in 1907. They began importing raw sugar to operate the refinery year-round because local cane was available only seasonally and in decreasing quantities in the early 1900s. Named by Kempner for the Imperial Hotel in New York City, the Imperial Sugar Company and the city of Sugar Land have grown steadily. During the 1970s, the Imperial Sugar Company produced more than three million pounds of refined cane sugar daily. (1978)

SULPHUR SPRINGS (Hopkins Co.)
SH 19/154, 5 mi. N in roadside park
Confederate Refugees in Texas, C.S.A
In the vicinity of Old Tarrant, south of here, the Civil War refugee family of Mrs. Amanda Stone, of Louisiana, was shown great kindness when rescued by Hopkins Countians after a road accident. The Stones saw the Texans share the little they had, even cooking the last tough old farm hen, to feed them. The Stones were but one of many families to flee from war lines to the comparative safety of Texas. Here, though Federal invasion repeatedly threatened, only a few coastal towns were under fire from the enemy. The family of Gen. Stand Watie, from Indian Territory, visited relatives in Wood County. Gen. Kirby Smith, with headquarters in Shreveport, rented homes in Marshall or Hempstead for his wife and babies. Like most refugees, the Stones when they visited in Hopkins County were heartbroken over loss of their old home to the enemy. In Texas they endured poverty, loneliness, and sorrow at deaths of two sons in the war. They had to lease farm land, to support the family and 90 slaves dependent upon them. Their young boys at one time carried pistols for safety when schoolmates resented their strange manners. Yet eventually they and most other refugees were grateful to Texas for its many generosities. (1965)

SULPHUR SPRINGS (Hopkins Co.)
SH 19/154 right of way, 4.5 mi. N
Townsite of Tarrant
Eldridge Hopkins, for whose family Hopkins County was named in 1846, donated this site for the county seat. Named for Gen. Edward H. Tarrant (1796–1858), Texas Ranger and Mexican War vet-eran, Tarrant Post Office was established in March, 1847. A two-story frame courthouse was begun in 1851, but lack of funds delayed completion for two years. Tarrant quickly grew into a thriving frontier town with a tannery, steam mill, blacksmith shop, brick kiln, and hotel. After 1851, it had a Masonic Lodge and school. During the 1850s, a newspaper, the "Texas Star," began publication,

and a Methodist college opened. Encircled by creeks, the town was difficult to reach in bad weather. The inconvenience of travel to Tarrant led Capt. Thomas M. Tolman in 1868 to transfer county records to Sulphur Springs, where Federal troops under his command were stationed after the Civil War to enforce Reconstruction laws. Despite local protests, county government remained there until civilian rule was restored in 1870. The return to Tarrant was brief, because the State Legislature in 1870 named Sulphur Springs as permanent county seat. Soon Tarrant began to decline. A rural community and old cemetery now mark the site of the first Hopkins County Seat. (1975)

SULPHUR SPRINGS (Hopkins Co.)   *IH 30/US 67, 9 mi. E at mile marker 134*
Hopkins County
Formed from Lamar and Nacogdoches Counties. Created March 25, 1846. Organized July 13, 1846. Named in honor of the pioneer Hopkins family which came to Texas from Kentucky and Indiana. County Seat, Tarrant (1846–1858); Sulphur Springs since.

SULPHUR SPRINGS (Hopkins Co.)   *US 67 at Gilmer St. (SH 154)*
Hopkins County Courthouse
The third Hopkins County Courthouse, built in 1882, was destroyed on Feb. 11, 1894 by a fire that also burned the jail and several nearby structures. Plans were soon made for a new court building to be erected on this corner rather than in the middle of the block where the first edifice stood. The site is unusual because most Texas courthouses are located in the center of the public square, not facing it. The new structure was designed by James Riely Gordon (1864–1937), popular courthouse architect from San Antonio, and constructed by the Dallas firm of Sonnefield and Emmins. Austin architect A. O. Watson was hired to inspect the work. He admired the plans but suggested bracing to strengthen the stonework. The building was completed on Aug. 22, 1895, at a final cost of $75,000. A clock for the tower was requested by some citizens, but county commissioners refused to provide funds for it. Made of red granite with contrasting sandstone trim, the Hopkins County Courthouse is a fine example of the massive Richardsonian Romanesque style which Gordon often used. The quarter-circular porches at the northwest and southwest corners mark entrances to the three-story edifice. (1975)

SULPHUR SPRINGS (Hopkins Co.)   *SH 154, 1 mi. S*
Shooks Chapel Methodist Church
This church traces its history to 1886, when area settlers organized a congregation of the Methodist Episcopal Church, South. The church was named for the Rev. W. A. Shook, who held the first revival here. The congregation met in a brush arbor or a nearby schoolhouse until a sanctuary was built on land donated by B. P. Joiner. Early worship services were led by student pastors who were often paid in produce. Associated with the church is a community cemetery, begun in 1889. A second sanctuary, built in 1916, was replaced by a new structure in 1974. (1988)

SUNDOWN (Hockley Co.)   *FM 303, 1.5 mi. S*
First Oil Well in Hockley County—
J. E. Guerry No. 1 (700 yds. SW)
On April 6, 1937, this well was completed by the Texas Company (Texaco, Inc.), flowing 502 barrels per day from a depth of 5,023 feet, on land owned by J. E. Guerry (1885–1956). The Guerry family purchased surface and ⅛ mineral rights on 177 acres, in 1929, from R. L. (Bob) Slaughter (1870–1938), who inherited over 16,000 acres of the Lazy S Ranch after death of his father, Col. C. C. Slaughter (1837–1919). Located in the vast Slaughter field, this well was the first of over 2,600 active wells in the county, which have produced over 400 million barrels of oil. (1973)

SURFSIDE BEACH (Brazoria Co.)   *SH 332, 1blk S of Intercoastal Waterway*
Sinking Site of the Blockade Runner "Acadia"
The sidewheel steamer "Acadia", owned by Canadians, set out on her maiden voyage in Dec. 1864 for Nassau, Havana, and Vera Cruz. Loaded with food, hardware, and clothing, she braved the Federal blockade to bring the goods to suffering Texans. Early on Feb. 6, 1865, in heavy fog she grounded in sticky clay 300 yards off this beach. Her crew and cargo came safely ashore. When the fog lifted, the foe sighted and shelled her, but could not board and burn the crippled ship, as Confederate Cavalry defended her from the shore. The "Acadia" then became a coastal landmark. (1977)

SWEENY (Brazoria Co.)
SH 35, .5 mi. W of Old Ocean

Sweeny Plantation

John Sweeny, Jr., after returning from the Texas Revolution, was given this plantation by his father, an extensive landholder. In 1837 slaves built the house, using only brick, nails and wood made on his land. Molasses, cotton, sugar were produced. Still owned by descendants.   (1965)

SWEETWATER (Nolan Co.)
IH 20, 4 mi. W to mile marker 240

W. A. S. P. Training Base: Avenger Field

Women's Airforce Service Pilots (WASP) trained here in military aircraft during World War II, from Feb. 21, 1943, through final graduation Day, Dec. 7, 1944. Avenger Field first served as a training base for British Royal Air Force Cadets in 1942, then for U.S. Army Air Forces Cadets Aug. 1942–April 1943. The WASP program was started under Gen. H. H. ("Hap") Arnold to train women to fly every kind of mission short of combat, releasing male pilots for overseas duty. Jacqueline Cochran was director of women pilots; Ethel A. Sheehy, WASP staff field executive; Nancy Harkness Love, WASP staff executive-ferrying division; and Leoti Clark Deaton, WASP staff executive-training bases. Of 25,000 girls who applied for WASP flight training, 1,830 were accepted; 1,074 won their silver wings. The WASPs flew 60 million miles on operational duty; 37 lost their lives serving their country. WASPs had civil service—not military—status, but were granted eligibility to apply for reserve commissions in the Air Corps after the WASP program ended when the Allies were winning the war in Europe and the U.S.A. pilot shortage was past. Avenger Field was closed after a short post-WASP span of service as a missile base.   (1972)

SWEETWATER (Nolan Co.)
SH 70, 3 mi. S of intersection with I-20

Site of U. S. Army Air Corps Plane Crash

At 6:05 A.M. on Friday, April 20, 1945, twenty-five Army Air Corps officers and enlisted men left Midland Army Air Field in a C-47 transport plane en route to Berry Army Air Field in Nashville, Tennessee. The flight crew consisted of the pilot, First Lieutenant James A. Bailey; the co-pilot, Captain John R. Rawls; and the flight engineer, Sergeant William H. Edwards. It was Sergeant Edwards' 36th birthday. Included among the passengers were eight officers and fourteen enlisted men. Two Sweetwater cab drivers spotted the plane on fire in mid-air. They notified their dispatcher, who alerted authorities at nearby Avenger Field. A crash landing message came from the plane itself at 6:30 A.M. Another C-47 flying just a few minutes behind the doomed aircraft never encountered a problem. After the crash, parts of the plane were found on a straight line almost two miles from the crash site. By 10:00 A.M. most of the bodies of the victims had been recovered from the smoldering wreckage and taken to funeral homes in Abilene and Sweetwater. The soldiers, whose ages ranged from 20 to 37, were buried in Arkansas, Florida, Illinois, Iowa, Massachusetts, Michigan, New Jersey, New York, North Carolina, Ohio, Oklahoma, Pennsylvania, Texas and Washington, D. C. Ten days after the crash, the Army Air Corps Aircraft Accident Classification Board met to determine its cause. It was the opinion of the regional safety officer that the craft had encountered a thunderstorm with only one of its two engines running, putting the plane into a roll. The plane's 4,000 hours of flight time, mainly spent towing gliders, probably caused a weakness in the tail and contributed to its disintegration in severe turbulence.   (2000)

SYLVESTER (Fisher Co.)
FM 1812, SE

Adair-Steadman Site

In this vicinity is a prehistoric archeological site discovered in 1969 near the clear fork of the Brazos River. Archeologists have conducted extensive scientific excavations and attribute most of the cultural materials to the Paleo-Indian period. The Adair-Steadman site was a large base campsite for makers of fluted points, who were part of the distinctive Folsom culture between nine and eleven thousand years ago. Prehistoric peoples chose to live here because of the availability of water at the time of occupation and the presence of a large stone resource area nearby. Stone tools and other material recovered include fluted point fragments, point preforms, channel flakes, scrapers, gravers, and large bifaces. Future archeological, geological, and paleontological studies of the site may yield sufficient data to reconstruct the physical appearance of the site during its period of occupation. One of the most significant locations of Folsom artifacts in North America, the Adair-Steadman site is important as a valuable source of information on the prehistory of the state, the nation, and the entire continent. It is protected from disturbance by federal and state antiquities laws.   (1984)

TAHOKA (Lynn Co.)   *US 380 at FM 212, 10 mi. E*
Grasslands (2 mi. S)
One of first land patents in South Plains, lying along a well-marked Indian trail used by explorers, U.S. Army, and (after 1880) the stages and freighters northbound from Colorado City. Grasslands Ranch (named for an estate of President Cleveland) was established 1888 by Enos L. Seeds, the 1889–1900 postmaster, who erected a fine frame house and first trading post on South Plains. Mrs. Seeds was the first permanent white woman resident in county. Nearby is grave of area's firstborn white child (a son of Mr. and Mrs. Todd Wilson). Community name is now Grassland.   (1970)

TAHOKA (Lynn Co.)   *US 87 at courthouse*
Lynn County
Created 1876 from Bexar Territory. Name honors G. W. Lynn, "one of those who baptized the altar of Texas with life blood at the Alamo." Tahoka Lake and Double Lakes Springs were watering places on Indian, Spanish, U.S. Army and cattle-driving trails. This was home land of nomadic Indians; visited by Spaniards, 1500s–1880s; used by New Mexicans grazing large herds of sheep in 1860s; site of last great buffalo hunts and the U.S. Cavalry's drive against Comanches, 1874–1877. Last cowboy-Indian skirmish occurred 1879 at Double Lakes. Earliest open-range cattlemen settled here in 1880s. First schools, Lynn and T-Bar, opened in 1902. In April 1903, county was organized, with Tahoka as county seat. The first officials: M. L. Elliott, county judge; S. N. McDaniel, county and district clerk; C. H. Doak, sheriff and tax collector; O. L. Miller, treasurer; A. S. Coughran, tax assessor; W. E. Porterfield, surveyor; J. E. Ketner, H. E. Baldridge, B. Humphries, and W. T. Petty, commissioners. The Santa Fe Railroad built to this point in 1910. This has since become a major agricultural area, ranking among top ten cotton counties in Texas—and one of the top twenty in the United States.   (1970)

TAYLOR (Williamson Co.)   *SH 95, .1 mi. N of FM 1331, Circleville*
C.S.A. Cotton Cards Factory
Near this site in 1862–65. Used power from the San Gabriel River. Chartered by Confederate Texas during re-tooling of agricultural economy to meet demands of the Civil War years. Because trade of bales of cotton for finished cloth was no longer practical, and textiles had to be made at home, Texas imported through neutral Mexico, at costs of $4 to $20 a pair, thousands of cotton cards—stiff brushes that made fluffy cotton into firm, smooth "batts" to be spun into yarn or thread, quilted or made into mattresses. The administration of Governor F. R. Lubbock (1861–1863) also acted to have cards made in Texas, in factories such as the one here, owned by Joseph Eubank, Jr. Heavy military demands (90,000 Texas men under arms; a 2,000 mile coastline-frontier to guard) plus reduced imports, caused fast expansion of industry. Arms and munitions plants were built. Land grants were used to encourage production. Private effort met the need, and produced vital supplies for both the military and civilian populations. Confederate quartermasters set up depots and shops for military goods. Production of salt and "King Cotton" was hiked to trade for scarce items. The state of Texas became a storehouse for the Confederacy.   (1964)

TAYLOR (Williamson Co.)   *SH 29, 8 mi. NW*
Sloan Home
Home built 1854 by David McCurdy Sloan (1827–1912) and wife, Mary Elizabeth Easley (1829–1890), who came to Texas from South Carolina. Finished lumber was hauled from Houston; rest hand-hewn in nearby river bottom, by slave labor. Awarded Medallion Plate.   (1965)

TAYLOR (Williamson Co.)   *400 Porter St. at E. 4th St. (US 79 Bus.)*
City of Taylor
When the International & Great Northern Railroad built across Williamson County in 1876, one of the towns created along its route was "Taylorsville", named for railroad executive Moses Taylor. Lots were sold in June, and the post office opened on August 9, 1876. The earliest settlers included railroad officials such as I.&G.N. president John R. Hoxie and agent Henry Dickson, and merchants such as C. P. Vance, who moved his general store from Circleville. John McMurray started a private school, and Moritmer R. Hoxie donated land for a cemetery. Methodist and Presbyterian churches were organized in 1876, and other congregations the following year. Located on a cattle trail, the new community soon became a major shipping point for cattle. A second rail line, the Missouri, Kansas & Texas, was extended to Taylorsville in 1882, spurring further growth. The town was

incorporated in 1882 with Daniel Moody, father of Texas governor Dan Moody (1893–1966), as its first mayor. In 1892 the city's name was shortened to "Taylor". By that time, cotton had joined cattle and the railroad as an important element in the local economy. Today light industry and diversified farming contribute to Taylor's prosperity.

TAYLOR (Williamson Co.)   *FM 619, 15 mi. SE*
Pioneer Publisher and Printer David Irvin Lawhon
(Buried ½ mi. NW of Here)

Born in Tennessee on June 15, 1811. While very young learned the printing trade and worked at it in some of the principal cities of the United States. Came to Nacogdoches, Texas, in November, 1835, in answer to pleas for volunteers for Texas Army. Was pressed into service publishing the "Texean and Emigrant's Guide," with essential war proclamations. Also printed handbills, patriotic songs and legal documents. His newspaper was one of several printed in Texas during War for Independence, 1836. In 1839, moved to what is now Jefferson County and engaged in cattle ranching. Served as captain of a Ranger company. Was county's chief justice during the days of the Republic of Texas. Moved to Bastrop County in 1861, where he tried farming; then moved to Williamson County where he died February 14, 1884. As a newspaper publisher and printer for the Army of the Revolution (1835–1836), an Indian fighter, frontiersman and judge, he contributed much to the early development of Texas. In 1840, David Lawhon married Nancy Carr, a daughter of one of Stephen F. Austin's "Old Three Hundred" settlers. Their eleven children carried on their pioneering spirit and tradition.   (1967)

TEAGUE (Freestone Co.)   *FM 1365, 6 mi. W*
1 mi. N to Birthplace of Harvey Means (1868–1943)

Noted Negro civic leader and barber to two generations of prominent Texans. An adventurous youth, Means began work at age 18 as shoe-shine boy in a West Texas barber shop. When rowdy cowboys demanded haircuts one day, Means (though inexperienced) complied with their wishes, and thus began a 54-year career. His last 31 years were spent in Fort Worth, where he helped establish a hospital and city park for black citizens. He led in civic, religious, and fraternal affairs and worked continually to improve race relations. His 10 children all attended college.   (1971)

TELEGRAPH (Kimble Co.)   *US 377*
Telegraph Store and Post Office

This Kimble County landmark was named for a nearby canyon from which trees were cut for telegraph poles in the mid-19th century. The store and post office were built about 1890–1900. The first commissioned postmistress was Ruth Holmes in 1900. For many years this has been the stopover place for vacationers along nearby south Llano River and travelers enroute to points south. The Telegraph post office was the Kimble County address of Texas Governor Coke R. Stevenson. The site retains the rustic charm of its early years, and has served the community for a century.   (1996)

TEMPLE (Bell Co.)   *SH 53, 9 mi. E*
Ocker Brethren Church

A group of deeply devoted followers of the Unity of the Brethren Faith were among the Czech immigrant families who settled in this area of eastern Bell County in the late 1870s and established the farming community of Ocker. The group initially worshiped informally in their homes. Annual visits from 1884 to 1891 by the Rev. Henry Juren and the Rev. Bohuslav Emil Lacjak encouraged them to organize. The Evangelical Congregation of the Bohemian and Moravian Brethren of Ocker was established in 1892. The dedication of their first church building, erected in 1893, was conducted by the Rev. Juren and the Rev. Adolph Chlumsky, noted early-day Czech community preachers. The church cemetery was established later that year. Membership in the church grew from 52 families in 1900 to 92 families in 1925. A new church/Sunday school building was erected at this site in 1931 to meet the spiritual needs of a growing congregation. By mid-1940, English had replaced Czech as the language used in Sunday School and worship services. The congregation was served by part-time pastors until 1981 when a full-time pastor was called. The church continues to serve the local community with spiritual guidance and outreach programs.   (1994)

TEMPLE (Bell Co.)   *SH 53, 7.5 mi. E at Seaton Rd.*
Seaton Cemetery
The community of Lost Prairie-Seaton was settled in the 1880s by Czechoslovakian immigrants, and at one time contained a post office, school, store and saloon. Charles Motl, Sr., donated two acres of land for a community cemetery following the death of Tomas Ondrasek in 1896. The Seaton National Cemetery Association was formed in 1897, and was eventually renamed the Seaton Cemetery Association. Among the 1,150 burials are those of veterans of World Wars I and II, and the Korean conflict. The cemetery continues to serve the community.   (1997)

TEMPLE (Bell Co.)   *IH 35 at Adams Ave.*
½ mi. N to Bird Creek Battlefield
Named in honor of Captain John Bird, who lost his life here May 26, 1839. With only 34 Texas Rangers, he met 240 Indians at this point, and routed them.   (1964)

TEMPLE (Bell Co.)   *1901 SW H. K. Dodgen Loop 363*
King's Daughters Hospital
The Temple Charter of the International Order of the King's Daughters and Sons, a Protestant ecumenical group, was formed in 1893 to provide medical care to indigent citizens. The group, made up largely of educated women, rented rooms in a small house and opened King's Daughters Hospital in 1896. In 1898 a board of trustees was elected which appointed the first staff physicians; Cornelia Parsons became hospital superintendent. By 1920 the King's Daughters organization had discontinued support of the hospital facility. Considered ahead of its time from its earliest days, King's Daughters Hospital remains a major provider of affordable modern medical care.   (1998)

TEMPLE (Bell Co.)   *1901 SW H. K. Dodgen Loop 363*
King's Daughters Hospital School of Nursing
Nursing training was implemented at King's Daughters Hospital from as early as 1897, and formal two-year classes began in 1903. In 1906, the hospital revised its charter to officially include a nurses' training school and the curriculum expanded to three years about 1910. Mary Julia Putts provided outstanding leadership as director in the 1920s. In difficult Depression years, an expanded curriculum and facilities helped the school survive, but a shortage of enrollees caused it to close its doors in 1948. The hospital began its own vocational nursing program in 1954. School alumnae formed an association in 1921 and served with distinction in both world wars.   (1998)

TENNESSEE COLONY (Anderson Co.)   *FM 321 at Spur 324, off US 287*
Tennessee Colony
Founded in 1838 by settlers who came from the Old South by wagons, seeking fertile, watered farm lands. Later their cotton shipped from Magnolia Ferry on the Trinity created great wealth. Early businesses were a general store, blacksmith shop, cabinet shop (which made furniture still found in area). Town was trade center for places as far away as Dallas. The plantation era reached a climax in grandeur on the properties of F. S. Jackson, a settler from Virginia. Circuit riders held religious services in homes until a log cabin church could be built, probably in late 1838; a second log church succeeded this one. Masons attended the lodge in Magnolia for years, but in 1857 obtained charter for Tyre Lodge No. 198, A. F. & A. M., in Tennessee Colony. They then worked to build a 2-story church-school-lodge hall, which was finished in 1860 (and was to be used until 1948). The schools were outstanding, especially those taught by a Mr. Hooker and by Professor Sidney Newsome. They drew patronage from Palestine and other area towns. Remembered students included Addison and Randolph Clark, later to become founders of a college that would be forerunner of Texas Christian University. Descendants of original colonists still live here.   (1971)

TENNYSON (Coke Co.)   *US 277 at FM 2333*
Tennyson
In area roamed by Indians for centuries. Tamed by open-range cattlemen in the late 1870's. Permanent settlement began in 1880's. A post office, named for British poet Alfred Tennyson, was established in 1894 with Mrs. Sarah E. Kiser as the first postmaster. Seven persons have held that office to date (1970). Over years, area has had several schools, but all are now closed. Near Mt. Margaret (height 335 feet), once locale of Indian activities, is now site of annual community homecoming (the Saturday before Labor Day) and Easter sunrise religious services each spring.   (1971)

TENNYSON (Coke Co.)   *US 277, near post office*
Mule Creek Cemetery (4.5 mi. SW)
Established by pioneers of Mule Creek community, a small frontier settlement founded in 19th century. Said to be named either for (1) an early horse and mule ranch, or (2) a stagecoach mule that died at a creek which runs nearby. The Abilene–Fort Concho Stage once served area. For years principal building here was a combination school-church. Since 20th century, shift to urban living has diminished population of Mule Creek. Inscriptions on tombstones chronicle history of community. In spring, grounds are covered with bluebonnets, state flower.   (1971)

TEXARKANA (Bowie Co.)   *US 71/59, 4.5 mi. N*
The French in Texas
Were explorers and traders for about a century. Claimed coastal Texas early as 1685, when La Salle established his Fort Saint Louis Colony. Another Fort Saint Louis, among Nassonite Indians, a few miles northwest of this marker, was founded in 1719 by a French captain, Benard De La Harpe, who came up the Red River. This fort was a center for trade with the Cadodacho (Caddoes) of Northeast Texas and the Wichita, Tawakoni, Tonkawa and other tribes of North Texas. Over 250,000 French and Caddo Indian artifacts have been found near here—including two millstones used in a flour mill near the fort. Although Spain claimed Texas earlier and during the time of La Harpe, this did not discourage the French; they traded as far south as the mouth of the Trinity until Louisiana was ceded to Spain in 1762. The chief French influence in East Texas was the Cavalier Saint Denis (1676–1744), who controlled Red River area of Louisiana, frequently coming into Texas. At first he prospected for silver and gold, as Spain had done. Later he found trading with the Indians was very profitable. The French had no policy against trading guns to Indians; partly for that reason they were more popular than the Spaniards.   (1966)

TEXARKANA (Bowie Co.)   *US 71/59, 4.5 mi. N*
Trammel's Trace
Entered Texas at this point. The 1813 road from St. Louis. Brought in great numbers of pioneers: Stephen F. Austin, his settlers, Sam Houston, James Bowie, David Crockett and others who died in the Texas Revolution. From here pointed Southwest. Crossed the Sulphur at Epperson Ferry, going south to Nacogdoches, linking "Southwest Trail" with the King's Highway to Mexico. Surveyed by Nicholas Trammel (born in Nashville, Tenn. 1780; died, LaGrange, Texas, 1852), one of a family of U.S. surveyors and scouts. Mapped many trails, but only this one bears his name.   (1965)

TEXARKANA (Bowie Co.)   *US 71/59, 4.5 mi. N*
First Disciples of Christ of Texas (9 mi. NW)
Worshiped in 1831 at McKinney's landing, where the McKinney family and a small group of neighbors met together for informal services. During the winter of 1841–1842, a traveling preacher from Illinois, G. Gates, organized the congregation into a church. He later wrote, "I remained with the brethren about a week . . . gathered scattered sheep and constituted a church of 16 members, with fair prospects for more." First leader of the group was Collin McKinney (1766–1861), who had come with his family from Kentucky to Texas in 1831, when Mexico governed the state. The worship services he started were in defiance of the laws of Mexico, which demanded the allegiance of each citizen to the Catholic religion. In 1836 he signed the Texas Declaration of Independence. Collin County and the city of McKinney bear his name. Between 1844 and 1846, the McKinney families and neighbors moved their congregation to Mantua, near Van Alstyne, where they met in a wooden church with a four-foot wall separating men from women. Five slaves of the family were members of the Mantua group. When the railroad built past Van Alstyne, they moved there and organized the First Christian Church, a direct descendant of the 1831 congregation.   (1967)

TEXARKANA (Bowie Co.)   *US 71, 2 mi. N*
Hatchel/Barkman Caddo Indian Village
Near here for 1,000 years, A.D. 800–1800, lived civilized Caddoes, who thought they were the sole survivors of a prehistoric flood and ancestors of all Indians. Their ceremonial mounds stood high above Red River. They had a significant role in exchanges between Puebloan Indians and the Mound-Builders in the East. They domesticated food plants such as corn, squash and beans and manufactured fine pottery. Because of pressure from Euro-American settlers, they left this area, and descendants are found in Oklahoma. Their village site is now under state protection.   (1981)

TEXARKANA (Bowie Co.) *901 State Line Avenue (US 71)*
Scott Joplin (November 24, 1868–April 1, 1917)
Black composer Scott Joplin, often called the "King of Ragtime Music," was born in Texarkana, Texas, five years before the townsite was platted in 1873. His family lived in this vicinity, and he attended nearby Orr School on Laurel Street. His early musical training came from his father, Giles Joplin, an ex-slave who played the fiddle, and mother, Florence Givens Joplin, who played the banjo. By tradition, a German music teacher realized Joplin's talent and gave him lessons. Joplin left home at age 14 and wandered through the Midwest entertaining in saloons and honky-tonks. In the 1890s, he was one of the originators of ragtime, a rhythmic new musical form that combined black and white musical traditions. Joplin's "Maple Leaf Rag," published in 1899, launched ragtime as a national fad. Joplin defended ragtime against those who called it frivolous and worked constantly to refine his music, which included over 30 piano rags. Demand for ragtime had declined by 1917, when Joplin died in New York City. Joplin's background is revealed in his most ambitious work, the black folk opera Treemonisha, set on a plantation "northeast of the town of Texarkana." It was not produced until the 1970s, when a revival of Joplin's music inspired public recognition of his genius.
(1976)

TEXARKANA (Bowie Co.) *US 67/SH 8 at FM 2149, 10 mi. SW*
Old Boston
Established while part of Mexico, to serve plantations on Red River. Mail came horseback from Arkansas. Named for W. J. Boston, first storekeeper. A battalion was formed here to fight in Texas Revolution. First Bowie County Seat, 1841. Large stores surrounded square and two-story brick courthouse. Became educational center with 3 fine private schools. Texas Governors Hardin R. Runnels and S. W. T. Lanham have lived here. New Boston (4 mi. N) founded on railroad, 1877. Boston (1 mi. S), exact county center, made county seat 1890, and this became "Old" Boston.
(1966)

TEXAS CITY (Galveston Co.) *29th St. at 25th Ave. (Loop 197)*
Texas City Memorial Cemetery
On April 16 and 17, 1947, disastrous explosions aboard two ships docked at the Texas City port killed hundreds of people. In the weeks that followed, relief workers led by the American Red Cross and other volunteers labored to identify the victims. Temporary morgues were set up in the Central High School gymnasium and at Camp Wallace, a former army post. Eventually, 444 people were confirmed dead, and an additional 143 were listed as missing. Sixty-three bodies were never identified. There was no public cemetery in Texas City in 1947. A burial committee appointed by local officials used donated funds to purchase this two-acre tract of land and made plans to bury the unidentified victims on Sunday, June 22. An interfaith and inter-racial funeral service was conducted before an estimated 5,000 mourners. Funeral homes from 28 towns provided individual caskets and hearses, and florists from throughout Texas donated flowers. The Texas City Memorial Cemetery is still reserved for the 63 people who, although unknown by name, are remembered each year at a memorial service on the 16th of April.
(1991)

TEXAS CITY (Galveston Co.) *1301 Loop 197 S at Dock Rd.*
The Texas City Disaster
On April 16, 1947, three ships—the Grandcamp, the High Flyer, and the Wilson B. Keene— were docked in the Texas City port. They were loaded with cargo, including ammonium nitrate fertilizer, bound for Europe to assist in the post–World War II recovery effort. At 8:33 A.M. the Texas City fire department responded to a call for assistance with a fire on the Grandcamp. As smoke billowed from the ship, spectators gathered to watch. The Grandcamp exploded at 9:12 A.M. with a tremendous force that was felt for miles around. A second explosion came at 1:10 A.M. on April 17, when the High Flyer's cargo caught fire, destroying the Wilson B. Keene as well. More than 550 people, including 27 firemen, were killed; flying pieces of concrete, steel, and glass injured thousands more; resulting fires took days to extinguish. Response to the disaster came immediately, with the American Red Cross coordinating relief efforts. Far-reaching effects of the Texas City disaster included the implementation of safety standards and revised emergency medical treatment procedures. Citizens determined to rebuild. By 1950, few physical reminders of the disaster remained, although the event retains a prominent place in state and national history.
(1990)

TEXAS CITY (Galveston Co.) *1301 Loop 197 S at Dock Rd.*
Texas City Terminal Railway Company
Minnesota investors and brothers Jacob R. and Henry H. Myers and Augustus B. Wolvin formed the Texas City improvement company in 1893 and developed a port facility and townsite here. By 1897 the company had built a rail spur line linking its port facilities with national railroad systems 4.5 miles inland. Wolvin acquired the company in 1898 and created the separate Texas City Company for the townsite and the Texas City Terminal Company (TCT) for the railway and docks. He persuaded the U. S. Congress to fund dredging of the channel for ocean-going vessels by 1904 and to designate Texas City as a U. S. port of customs in 1905. TCT official Hugh B. Moore persuaded the Pierce-Fordyce oil refinery company to move to the port industrial area in 1908. He continued to attract oil companies, and by the 1920s oil and petroleum refined products made up over 80 percent of the tonnage handled at the port. The Texas City Terminal railway company provided Texas City its early water, electric, and sewage utility systems and established the community's first telephone, newspaper, and banking operations. Despite a catastrophic 1947 dock explosion, national recession, and hurricane damage in 1983, TCT continued to expand and upgrade its port and rail facilities. (1994)

TEXAS CITY (Galveston Co.) *1301 Loop 197 S at Dock Rd.*
The First Texas City Refinery
The first oil refinery built in Texas City was established in 1908 by the Texas City Refining Company. Contractor J. C. Black and more than 100 craftsmen constructed the refinery. Processing equipment included eleven stills, storage tanks, and a boiler house. Railroad tank cars delivered crude oil for processing. The finished product was shipped by rail or carried by pipeline to the Texas City docks for loading on seagoing tankers. Through the years more land was purchased, extra storage tanks were built, and facilities were modernized as technology advanced. Petroleum products made during both world wars provided significant contributions to the nation's defense. World War II production demands caused Texas City's population to nearly triple. Despite economic shifts, natural disasters and accidents, oil industry fluctuations, and multiple owners, this refinery has been an integral part of the area for over eight decades, providing employment for hundreds of employees, and infusing millions of dollars into local, regional, and national economies. Now an upgraded, modern facility, the refinery's capacity for processing crude oil has grown from 1,500 barrels per day in 1908 to 130,000 barrels per day in the 1990s. (1996)

TEXON (Reagan Co.) *SH 67 at FM 1675*
The Town of Texon
Early travelers along many historic trails in this area found the region arid and inhospitable. Given (1876) to the University of Texas, the lands around this marker were leased to cattlemen. The Kansas City, Mexico & Orient Railroad built its line here in 1911, but did little local hauling. Development came after Frank Pickrell and Haymon Krupp of Texon Oil & Land Company drilled for oil. Their driller, Carl Cromwell, brought in Santa Rita No. 1, the first gusher in the Permian Basin, on May 28, 1923. Texon, first company town in the Permian Basin, was founded in 1924 by Big Lake Oil Company. Levi Smith, president of the firm, planned and supervised building of the town, and Ted Williams served as city manager for the company. Texon had stores, shops, a school, a physician, a dentist, a hospital, a theater, a park, a well-known baseball team, and many facilities for recreation. The post office opened in 1926. As many as 2,000 people lived here—boosters claimed up to 10,000—manning the drilling, a gasoline plant, an oil treating plant, and other operations. Plymouth Oil Company absorbed Big Lake Oil Company, then sold out to Marathon Oil Company. The company town was closed in 1962. (1977)

THE COLONY (Denton Co.) *S. Colony Blvd. at Blair Oaks Dr.*
The Hedgcoxe War
Distribution of land in the Peters Colony of North Texas triggered a dispute known as the Hedgcoxe War. The Texas Emigration and Land Co. organized the colony under an 1841 Republic of Texas law which allowed it to keep one-half of a settler's grant. After protests, this right was repealed, but in Feb. 1852 the company was compensated with 1,088,000 acres of vacant land within the colony. This action angered settlers and speculators with land certificates, who feared that the large grant would lower land values. At that time, the company's unpopular agent, English-born Henry O. Hedgcoxe, operated a land office on nearby Office Creek. On July 12 and 13, 1852, a

group of Dallas men broke in and examined the land records. They reported to a meeting in Dallas on July 15 that the company was defrauding the colonists. John J. Good (1827–82), later mayor of Dallas, then led a band of armed men to Hedgcoxe's office. Hedgcoxe escaped, but most of his files were seized and the office burned. After the raid, tensions quickly cooled. The law was amended so that settlers obtained their grants from the state rather than from the company agent. The company kept its land grant, however, and Hedgcoxe returned to help survey the tract. (1975)

THE GROVE (Coryell Co.)
SH 236, 6 mi. NE on PR 14
Mother Neff State Park
First official state park in Texas; suggested the idea for the state parks system. Originated with a 6-acre plot willed to Texas in 1916 by Mrs. Isabella E. Neff, mother of Pat M. Neff, governor of Texas 1921–1925. Because Texas then had no state parks, Mrs. Neff stated the land was to be used for religious, fraternal, political, and educational activities. Seeing the need for more such areas, 1923, the 39th Legislature created the State Parks Board. In 1934, Pat Neff deeded 250 acres, and other owners 3 acres, to enlarge the original tract. (1968)

THOMASTON (DeWitt Co.)
Fordtran Rd., 1 blk. off US 87
Thomaston (Founded 1872)
DeWitt County's first railroad town. Absorbed Price's Creek, 1848 settlement of Republic of Texas patriot, Judge David Murphree (1811–1866). Thomaston was named for State Legislator Nathan Thomas (1809–1891), who sold south part of townsite (in Refugio Amador survey) to Gulf, Western Texas & Pacific Railroad. North part of plat was donated (from Charles Lockhart survey) by John P. and Mary (Lockhart) Wright. Schoolteacher J. H. Moore and wife Lou (Thomas) built first house and owned cotton gin and grist mill. James Pridgen was first railroad agent, postmaster, and merchant. At peak, town had 500 people. (1973)

THORNTON (Limestone Co.)
SH 14, 2 mi. S
Eaton Cemetery
The Richard Eaton family came to Texas in 1833 as members of the Robertson Colony. They moved to this area about 1845 and established a home and farm. The oldest grave in this cemetery, which was established on the family farm, is that of Richard's first wife, Mary, who died about 1848. Also interred here are Richard Eaton and his second wife, Charity, as well as other members of their family and neighbors. There are both marked and unmarked graves in the Eaton Cemetery, the final resting place of many Texas pioneers. (1990)

THORNTON (Limestone Co.)
FM 1246 at CR 758
Site of Old Potter's Shop
The fine, white clay mined near here was used at this shop from the 1840s to 1912 to make pitchers, jars, crocks, churns, flower pots, and ornamental urns, which were used locally and shipped out of county. In the 1870s the shop, built by Alberry Johnson, was a major industry in Pottersville (later Oletha). Wm. C. Knox later bought the plant and hired J. L. Stone as the chief artisan. John Fowler then became owner and was joined by his son E. J. Fowler about 1900. Men dug kaolin clay from pits and hauled it to the plant, where mules provided labor to grind the clay to powder and it was fashioned into ceramics. Historically, kaolin—still mined today from the deposits nearby—has been used to make fine porcelain and china. It ranks with gas, oil, and stone as a major commercial resource in Limestone County. During the 19th century, vast natural resources throughout the state were creating new enterprises. Cattle and cotton headed the list of products, which also included lumber, iron ore, stone and salt, as well as finished articles such as cloth, iron kettles, soap, flour, brick, and matches. These businesses, although crude and not of the "luxury" type, initiated the industrial growth of Texas. (1967)

THREE RIVERS (Live Oak Co.)
FM 72, 4 blks. W of US 281
Site of Three Rivers Glass Factory
Opened 1922 by company headed by Charles R. Tips (b. 1892), the founder of town of Three Rivers. Powered by local natural gas, plant used quartzose sand mined in area to make glass bottles for milk and other beverages and jars for food and cosmetics, attaining annual gross sales of a million dollars. Sold in 1937 to Ball Glass Company, it was closed in 1938, but had shown Texas' potential in the industry. In later years, factory site became location of a warehouse. Glass with Three Rivers cipher is highly prized by collectors. (1973)

THREE RIVERS (Live Oak Co.)   *US 281, town square*
Three Rivers
Founded March 1913 by Charles R. Tips, an investor. Chartered June 12, 1913, as Hamilton-burg—named for local family. Town lot sale began July 4, 1913. Townsite renamed by U.S. Postal Department May 1, 1914, to mark fork of Three Rivers—Nueces, Atascosa and Frio. Present interests are ranching, farming, gas, oil and recreation.   (1967)

THROCKMORTON (Throckmorton Co.)   *US 283/183 at SH 79, N city limits*
Throckmorton Co.
Formed from Fannin and Bosque Counties. Created January 13, 1858. Organized March 18, 1879. Named in honor of Dr. William Edward Throckmorton, 1795–1843. A Revolutionary soldier. Father of James Webb Throckmorton, who became Governor of Texas in 1866. County seat Throckmorton.

THURBER (Erath Co.)   *IH 20S frontage rd., 1 mi. E of Thurber exit*
Site of Thurber Big Lake and Dairy
In 1891, a 20-acre "little lake" was built south of the Thurber town site to supply water to the community. It soon proved inadequate, however, and five years later a 150-acre "big lake" was constructed here about a mile southeast of town. Texas and Pacific Coal Company president R. D. Hunter organized a hunting and fishing club at the Big Lake for company executives and staff. Water from the lake irrigated company-owned farmland in the valley below, and provided water for the nearby Thurber dairy. The dairy's twin silos were still visible decades later.   (1995)

THURBER (Erath Co.)   *IH 20S frontage rd., 1 mi. E of Thurber exit*
Site of Thurber Brick Plant
Texas and Pacific Coal Company general manager W. K. Gordon, seeing potential in the shale mud found in Thurber, persuaded company president R. D. Hunter to build a brick plant here in 1897. Original machinery included 3 Ross-Keller brick presses powered by a Corliss steam engine nicknamed "Old Hunter." The operation covered 5 acres and employed 800 men. Brick manufactured here was used to pave roads throughout Texas, including Old Bankhead Highway (US 80), Austin's Congress Avenue, Fort Worth's Camp Bowie Boulevard, and the Galveston Sea Wall. The plant closed in 1931.   (1995)

THURBER (Erath Co.)   *IH 20S frontage rd., 1 mi. E of Thurber exit*
Site of Thurber's First Coal Mine
Hundred yards southeast of this site, at the base of the hill and at a depth of 65 feet, the first coal mine in this area was placed in operation by brothers William W. and Harvey E. Johnson. After Harvey's death in 1888, and because of labor and financial difficulties, William Johnson sold his mining interest to R. D. Hunter's Texas and Pacific Coal Company. Railroads provided a ready market for coal, and the company town of Thurber (named for investor H. K. Thurber) became completely unionized after a 1903 strike. The company employed 2,500 miners of 18 nationalities.   (1995)

THURBER (Erath Co.)   *IH 20S frontage rd., 1 mi. E of Thurber exit*
New York Hill
This area of Thurber developed after 1917, when the Texas and Pacific Coal Company expanded into the burgeoning oil industry following W. K. Gordon's discovery of the Ranger oil field. Renamed in 1918, the Texas Pacific Coal and Oil Company brought staff for its new oil division to Thurber from New York. Thirty-one houses were built here on New York Hill. Church Street climbed the hill from town, as did sidewalks and brick steps, some of which were still visible decades later. The buildings on the hill were removed in the 1930s when the company town was dismantled.   (1995)

THURBER (Erath Co.)   *IH 20 at SH 108*
Thurber
Most important mine site in Texas for 30 years. Coal here, probably known to Indians, was "discovered" in 1886 by W. W. Johnson, who with his brother Harvey sold out to Texas & Pacific Coal Company in 1888. (T. & P. Coal Company provided fuel for the Texas & Pacific Railroad, but was independently owned.) Town was named for H. K. Thurber, friend of T. & P. Coal Company

founders. Most dynamic firm member was Robert D. Hunter (1833–1902), developer of 7 of 15 mines. Next president was E. L. Marston, Hunter's son-in-law, who left mining largely to William K. Gordon (1862–1949), an engineer who brought daily output to 3,000 tons. Then in 1917, Gordon (backed by management of coal company) was primarily responsible for discovery of Ranger Oil Field, 20 miles west. Adoption of oil-burning railway locomotives cut demand for coal. Last mine here closed in 1921, and the 10,000 or more inhabitants of Thurber began to move away. The coal firm changed its name to Texas Pacific Coal and Oil Company and was sold in 1963 to Joseph E. Seagram & Sons, Inc., for $277,000,000.00. Renamed Texas Pacific Oil Company, it is now one of the largest independent domestic energy suppliers. Much coal (by estimate 127,000,000 tons) remains underground.

(1969)

TILDEN (McMullen Co.)   *SH 16, 5 mi. N*
Cross

This community (earlier known as Nopal, San Miguel, Franklin) is one of area's first permanent settlements. Named for Samuel C. Cross, who opened grocery store, became first postmaster, 1924. Post office closed, 1934. Gas well completed nearby, 1953, was largest in state at that time. Ranching also is important to economy.

(1967)

TILDEN (McMullen Co.)   *SH 16, 4.5 mi. N to Franklin Ranch Rd., W*
Franklin Ranch

Ranch founder, Ralph S. "Rafe" Franklin, was born in Louisiana, April 4, 1848. He came to McMullen County in the early 1860s with his family. He started this ranch about 1870, building it up until he owned 40,000 acres, one of the largest holdings in this area. On Nov. 4, 1870, he married Minerva Holland; their children were: Murray; Buddy; R. S. Jr.; Green; Felix; Chapman; Amy; Claude; Tom; John; Margaret; Sam; Julius. The ranch headquartered on San Miguel Creek. In 1913, the present ranch home was built at the same location. It was a travelers' refuge; relatives and friends from near and far visited often to attend parties, dances, picnics and other social gatherings. For a short time Franklin ran sheep and goats but changed to cattle. In 1902, he purchased a herd of Black Angus, the first in this part of the country. The old "San Antonio-Laredo Stage Road" traverses ranch, crossing San Miguel Creek below ranch home. During the Civil War much cotton passed over this road headed for the Mexican border. The Franklins were pioneers in truest sense—few were more dynamic than they in early McMullen County development. "Rafe" Franklin died March 14, 1913.

(1967)

TILDEN (McMullen Co.)   *SH 16, .5 mi. N of SH 72*
Camp Rio Frio, C.S.A.

A Civil War Home Guard post, acting as buffer to protect older settlements from Apaches and bandits. Scattered local men were members of the 29th Brigade, Texas Militia. Picket homes with dirt floors. Diet of prickly pear salad and fruit, Spanish dagger blooms, hominy, turkey, quail and deer meat. Homespun and linsey clothing dyed blue with Brazil root or gold with agarita. Such was local scene the home guard protected. Camp Rio Frio was later Dogtown, then became Tilden. It proved itself in a rugged era.

(1964)

TILDEN (McMullen Co.)   *SH 16, .5 mi. N of Wheeler Store*
San Caja Hill (Located 14 mi. S)

The name, originally "Sin Caja," means "without coffin" in Spanish and may refer to the grim aftermath of the Turkey Creek Indian Battle, which was fought a short distance west of the hill in December, 1872. The fight developed after raiding Indians had stolen livestock, chased young rancher Andrew Tullis, and dragged a herder to death at the J. Campbell Place. The day following the killing, 13 ranchers from Oakville overtook the band at Turkey (now "Hill") Creek. Five Indians were slain, while one white man, Sebastian Beall, had a tooth shot out. Others in the fight were Caleb Coker, Time Cude, John Edwards, Bob and Sam Nations, Tobe Odom, Cullen Sanders, Andrew and Woodie Tullis, Rans Tullos, Pleas Waller, John Wilson. The bones of the warriors, put in a cave in San Caja Hill, later mysteriously disappeared. They were supposedly removed by members of the same tribe. Legends of treasure also hinge upon the name of the hill, for "caja" can mean "box" or "chest." This is thought to refer to money hidden in boxes here by Mexican bandits who raided wagon trains and stages traveling on the nearby Laredo-Goliad Road. Other tales tell of silver from the rich San Saba mines once buried nearby, but now lost to history.

(1969)

TILDEN (McMullen Co.)
SH 72, 4.7 mi. W
Old San Antonio–Laredo Road

Shortly after the founding of Laredo, in 1755, the Spanish established a transportation-communication route across this site. The road provided necessary abundance of water and grass for travel across this arid region, and served as a vital link between San Antonio and Laredo for well over a century. Although under constant surveillance by hostile Indian tribes, this route was traversed by numerous notable people. Fray Gaspar Jose de Solis passed this site on Aug. 21, 1768, on return from an inspection of Spanish Texas missions. Stephen F. Austin, en route to Mexico City to seek a colonization grant, crossed here about March 18, 1822. On Feb. 26, 1828, Manuel de Mier y Teran passed on his way to survey Anglo-American strength in Mexican Texas. The Somervell Expedition, in punitive retaliation for a Mexican invasion of Texas, crossed here on Dec. 1, 1842, bound for Laredo. Before and after the Civil War the road was used as a military supply route from San Antonio to Forts Ewell (1852–1854), at Nueces River crossing, and McIntosh, at Laredo, and as a trade outlet for early settlers. Although abandoned after ranches were fenced and a railroad from San Antonio to Laredo was built in 1881, the road is still visible on the open range.
(1973)

TILDEN (McMullen Co.)
SH 72, 6 mi. NE
Site of County's First Settlement Yarbrough Bend
(5 mi. NE, on Frio River)

Founded 1858. Named for John Swanson Yarbrough, an original settler. Town contained about 30 log "picket houses." Settlers were often harassed by Indians, cattle thieves and wild animals. Other original settlers were: Dr. George Dilworth, John Moore, James Tope, N. H. Walker, Joe Walker and Benjamin Franklin Winters.
(1968)

TILDEN (McMullen Co.)
SH 72, 6 mi. E
5 mi. SE to Townsite of Wentz

Founded as market center for a 44,000-acre development. Thrived for 3 years, 1914–1916. Wentz Townsite was named for C. C. Wentz (1872–1957), agent of the Two Rivers Ranch Co. He promoted the townsite for the absentee Kansas landlords and was also a well-known businessman in West Virginia before coming to Texas. The town grew to have about 200 people by 1916. A limousine was hired to meet each train at Three Rivers and bring the mail to Wentz. A severe drouth in 1917, though, forced most citizens to move. The post office closed, 1921; the two schools in 1948.
(1968)

TILDEN (McMullen Co.)
SH 16 at SH 72, courthouse
Tilden

Settled 1858 as Rio Frio. Later called "Dog Town" because ranchers used many dogs to round up cattle. 1871 townsite was laid out as Colfax. Made county seat 1877. Renamed for S. J. Tilden, who won popular vote for U.S. President, 1876. Ranching and petroleum center. Noted for fine rural high school, annual rodeo, historic sites.
(1966)

TILDEN (McMullen Co.)
SH 16 at SH 72, courthouse
McMullen County

Created 1858. Organized 1862. Abandoned because of bandit activities in thicket area during the Civil War. Reorganized 1877, with Tilden as county seat. Named for John McMullen (1785–1853), founder with James McGloin of the Irish Colony at San Patricio: president pro tempore of the general council which governed Texas in 1836, on the eve of the Republic. Of the 254 Texas counties, 42 bear Indian, French or Spanish names. 10 commemorate such colonizers as McMullen and Stephen F. Austin, "Father of Texas." 12 honor Washington and other American patriots. 96 were named for men who fought in the Texas War for Independence (15 dying at the Alamo), signed the Declaration of Independence from Mexico, or served as statesmen in the Republic of Texas. 23 have the names of frontiersmen and pioneers. 11 honor American statesmen who worked for the annexation of Texas; 10, leaders in Texas since statehood, including jurists, ministers, educators, historians, statesmen; and 36, men prominent in the Confederacy during the Civil War. Rockwall and 8 others have geographical names. San Jacinto and Val Verde were named for battles; Live Oak and Orange, for trees; and Mason for a fort.
(1964)

TILDEN (McMullen Co.)
SH 16 at SH 72
Old Rock Store
Built about 1865 by Pat Cavanaugh, Irish stonemason, assisted by Dick Barker. Site of gun battles in Dog Town (now Tilden), "wide open" during lawless era of the 1860s and 1870s. Preserved since 1929 by Clifton Wheeler, owner. (1966)

TILDEN (McMullen Co.)
SH 16 on school campus
Old McMullen College
Established 1881 under leadership of Dr. John Van Epps Covey, founder of three Texas colleges—aided here by civic leaders S. F. Dixon, Dr. M. W. C. Frazier, C. F. H. Hiers, R. W. Johnson, M. F. Lowe and L. Wheeler. A 3-acre site was bought from James Lowe, and S. D. Frazier constructed the building. Funds were raised by subscription to defray initial costs. Dr. Covey, his wife, and the Rev. Woodlief Thomas were teachers during the first year. Accommodations were planned for 100 students. The curriculum included spelling, mathematics, geography, surveying, bookkeeping, logic, history, reading, Latin, other liberal arts courses. In September 1897, after 16 years of service, the college ended its career. Its building was turned over to the trustees of the newly-organized Tilden School District, and used as a public school until January 1926, when a new structure replaced it. Texas had numerous early schools with similar histories. Like McMullen College, these were founded by dedicated civic groups eager to see that young Texans were offered sound education. Most of these small local colleges had primitive facilities and endured repeated financial crises, but they held to ideals they were never able to attain. (1967)

TIMPSON (Shelby Co.)
US 59/84 right-of-way, 4.5 mi. E
George Washington Green
(December 22, 1858–December 14, 1937)
Georgia native George Washington Green grew up in Tennessee and in 1878 set out for Texas. He married Tempie Ann Fowler in Logansport, Louisiana, that year, and they settled in this part of Texas. Green worked first as a sharecropper, growing cotton and corn, before purchasing his first parcel of land in 1883. Two years later, as the Houston East & West Texas Railroad began to build its line through Shelby County, G. W. Green purchased more land on both sides of the rail line and soon became a prominent landowner in the area, operating a general store and cotton gin. The Bobo community, primarily a train stop, was established on Green's land and operated a post office from 1893 until 1898. The phrase "Tenaha, Timpson, Bobo and Blair," used by the railroad conductor to announce stops along the rail line, became very popular and was used as a cadence during World War I. In 1905, George Washington Green made a lasting contribution to the area when he developed Green's Lake as a recreational spot and water source for the railroad. From 1905 through the 1940s, families came to picnic, swim and fish, and churches held baptismal services in the lake. George and Tempie Green reared four children: Luther (1880–1956), R. H. "Cooter" (1889–1969), Inez (M. Drewery) (1895–1965) and Nubern (1900–1959). George died in 1937 and is buried in the Buena Vista Cemetery. His contributions to the development of the rail line and to the Bobo community remain a significant part of the history of Shelby County. (2001)

TOM BEAN (Grayson Co.)
SH 11, 2 mi. W
First United Methodist Church
This congregation was organized in the mid-1880s, growing out of brush arbor meetings at the Cedar campground near Whitemound. The original church building at Whitemound was moved, in 1906, to Tom Bean, where it burned in 1924. Methodists worshiped in the Presbyterian Church until it was destroyed by a tornado a short time later. A new edifice was built, serving both denominations until 1972. In 1974, the sanctuary was moved here, and the heritage of the old Perrin Air Force Base chapel was preserved when it was added to the facility. (1975)

TORNILLO (El Paso Co.)
SH 20 at O. T. Smith Road
Tornillo
The town of Tornillo derives its name from the Spanish word for screw-bean bush, a hardy firewood once prevalent in the area. Efforts to establish this site as a major agricultural center began when the United States Reclamation Service announced plans to build dam and reservoir projects on the Rio Grande. The Tornillo Townsite Company, founded by an El Paso investment

firm, mapped the townsite in 1909, and the Tornillo post office was established the same year. After the Elephant Butte project north of El Paso was completed, agricultural speculation in the valley increased. In about 1917, three leading agriculturists, J. B. Dale, Will T. Owen, and Louis J. Ivey, planted 600 acres of cotton in Tornillo. They harvested a successful crop and built the town's first cotton gin. Other farmers and businessmen, attracted by their success, settled here, and by the late 1920s Tornillo boasted several corporations, packing plants, and a cattle feeding operation, as well as several stores and a modern school system. The town's economy suffered during the Great Depression of the 1930s and never fully revived. Urban growth in nearby El Paso contributed to the decline of the settlement. Tornillo stands today as a symbol of early commercial development in El Paso County. (1983)

TOYAH (Reeves Co.)
IH 20 at FM 2903
Toyah
Began as division point, 1881 on T. & P. Railway, with shops, roundhouse, hotel, cafe. Water was hauled from Monahans and sold by the barrel. Stage took passengers and mail to Brogado. 1882 cattle shipping brought cowboy-detective Charles Siringo here to look for rustlers. (1964)

TRENTON (Fannin Co.)
US 69 Bus. at Hamilton St.
Trenton
The earliest Anglo settlers in this area, drawn to the fertile farmlands, probably came to the locality known as Wildcat Thicket in the mid-1800s. By the 1870s a community had begun to form, and settler A. J. Russell reportedly named Trenton for a hospital in which he had been treated during the Civil War. The railroad arrived in Trenton in 1881, the same year a post office was established, and the town began to boom. By 1885 there were several thriving businesses in operation. Trenton was incorporated in 1890. Dr. W. C. Holmes, a former Trenton mayor and active citizen, began to publish the weekly *Trenton Tribune* in 1909. The town maintained its size during the 20th century, outlasting many of its neighbors. Trenton remains a bustling community. (1999)

TRINIDAD (Henderson Co.)
SH 31 W of SH 274
The Malakoff Man
A sandstone image of a human head—carved by prehistoric men—was found near here in 1929 by workmen of Texas Clay Products Company. It was dug from gravel pit now under Cedar Creek Lake. The carving weighed 98 pounds, was 16 by 14 inches, with eyes 2½ inches wide. First stone was found at depth of 16½ feet. Two similar images were unearthed in same area in 1935 and 1939. Archaeologists date Malakoff "men" as many thousands of years old. Found near the images were fossil remains of extinct horse, elephant, camel species. Images now in Texas Memorial Museum. (1967)

TRINIDAD (Henderson Co.)
SH 31 W of SH 274
The Trinity River
Three main tributaries—the West, Elm, and East Forks—feed the Trinity from headwaters in North Texas. Discovery of prehistoric Malakoff man carved stone heads near this site in the 20th century revealed that humans inhabited the Trinity valley thousands of years ago. Indian villages dotted the river banks when European exploration began. French explorer Robert Cavalier Sieur de la Salle called this waterway the River of Canoes in 1687. Spaniard Alonso de Leon is credited with first using the name "Trinity" in 1690. The fertile Trinity flood plain drew Anglo-American settlers to this area during the Republic of Texas. Buffalo, first Henderson County seat, was founded a few miles upstream at a ferry crossing. Navigation of the Trinity has been proposed in a number of ambitious plans since the 1850s. Steamboats plied the river carrying cotton, cattle, and lumber to Galveston and other Gulf of Mexico ports until the 1870s. Arrival of the railroad ended the era of riverboat trade. Founded in 1881 on the St. Louis Southwestern Railroad, also known as the Cotton Belt, the town of Trinidad had a pump station to draw water for the boilers of steam locomotives. A ferry crossed the Trinity here until a bridge was erected in 1900. (1977)

TUCKER (Anderson Co.)
US 79/84 right-of-way at church
Green Bay A.M.E. Church
This congregation traces its history to 1866, when a group of black workers at the Long Lake Cotton Plantation gathered together informally to organize a church. The following year the owners

of the plantation designated a plot of land on which the workers built a sanctuary, known as Green Bay Church. In 1868, the congregation was formally recognized by the African Methodist Episcopal (A.M.E.) denomination and was renamed Green Bay A.M.E. Church. It was the first church in the Long Lake area. In 1870, members of the church organized a day school for their children which became known as Green Bay School. When the church was moved to this site in 1887, school classes were held in the church building until a new school facility was erected in 1899. The church continued to grow in its new location. Missionary activities included the establishment of two new congregations in the Tucker vicinity: New Salem Church and Bailey Chapel. Construction of a new sanctuary at this site began in 1956 and was completed in 1959. Still an active congregation, Green Bay A.M.E. Church continues to serve the community with worship and outreach.   (1989)

TUCKER (Anderson Co.)   *US 79, Green Bay Community Center*
Green Bay High School
Green Bay High School traces its origin to October 11, 1899, when eleven black men of the community formed a board of trustees and organized a school for the area's black children. The first school facility was provided by Green Bay Methodist Church. New school buildings erected in the early 1900s also housed the Mt. Sinai Masonic Lodge. Many dedicated teachers served in the Green Bay School, and students from a large rural area attended the school from its creation until desegregation of area school systems was achieved in 1966. (Texas Sesquicentennial 1836–1986)

TUCKER (Anderson Co.)   *SH 294, 2 mi. SW*
Site of Woodhouse School
Woodhouse School began with the consolidation of the Long Lake, Tucker and Magnolia schools into Consolidated Common School District No. 7. These were all small schools, each with two teachers: one for grades one through four and another for grades five through eight. In December 1937, William Phillip Bishop Woodhouse (1864–1951) deeded a portion of his landholdings to the school district for the construction of Woodhouse School. Most of the teachers from Long Lake, Tucker and Magnolia returned to teach at Woodhouse for its opening session in the fall of 1938. Originally serving grades one through eight, the school added a grade each year until 1942, when the first senior class graduated and the first yearbook was published. First superintendent of the school district was J.P. Brookshire, who remained in that position until 1939. The Work Projects Administration (WPA) built additional facilities for Woodhouse School in 1941, including an agriculture building, a cafeteria and a home economics cottage. Athletic programs centered around basketball, and Woodhouse fielded competitive boys' and girls' basketball teams throughout much of its history. Consolidation with the Four Pines School to create Westwood School signaled the closing of Woodhouse. The class of 1960 was the last to graduate from Woodhouse, although its facilities continued in use until 1979. Woodhouse remains an important part of the history of rural education in Anderson County.   (2001)

TULETA (Bee Co.)   *US 181*
Tuleta
The Rev. Peter Unzicker led a group of Illinois settlers here in 1906. Buying 53.4 acres of land of the original Uranga Grant and later Chittim-Miller Ranch, he founded Tuleta, named for the daughter of J. M. Chittim. A rail depot and post office were opened. In 1909 Pastor Unzicker organized one of Texas' first Mennonite churches. Townspeople established the innovative Tuleta Agricultural High School in 1910, with Miss Amanda Stoltzfus as principal. Once marketing center for this fertile farming area, Tuleta also had a Union Church and several business houses. (1978)

TULIA (Swisher Co.)   *SH 86, 17 mi. E*
Palo Duro Canyon
Two miles north of here General Ranald S. Mackenzie, 4th U. S. Cavalry, ordered shot the 1,450 horses captured from Indians in Battle of Palo Duro Canyon Sept. 28, 1874 to prevent their possible recovery by the Indians and to force the Indians to return to their reservations on foot.   (1936)

TULIA (Swisher Co.)   *Austin St. at 2nd St. (SH 86)*
Swisher County
Formed from Young and Bexar Territories. Created August 21, 1876. Organized July 17, 1890. Named in honor of James Gibson Swisher, 1794–1864, conspicuous for gallantry at the storming of Bexar, 1835, signer of the Texas Declaration of Independence, 1836. County seat, Tulia.   (1936)

TULIA (Swisher Co.)
US 87, 1 mi. S
Rose Hill Cemetery
The history of this community cemetery dates to October 1890, just three months after Swisher County was organized and Tulia was named county seat. The first recorded burial here is that of 18-year-old Louis H. Harral, who died on October 17, 1890. His parents, L. J. & N. J. Harral, obtained permission from landowner T. W. Adams to bury their son on this hillside south of the Middle Tule Creek. Twelve days later, 4-year old Robert Alonzo Hutchinson, son of W. B. & Virginia Hutchinson, died and was buried on the hill near Louis. In 1906 five acres of land surrounding the graves were officially set aside for a community cemetery. A cemetery association was formed in 1916 under the leadership of Lula B. Tomlinson, who named the cemetery Rose Hill. The association was officially chartered by the state in 1937, and continues to maintain the site. Among those interred here are numerous city and county elected officials, including two law enforcement officers killed in the line of duty: John Mosley (d. 1933) and Robert (Bob) Potter (d. Christmas Day, 1960). Also buried here are veterans of the Civil War, the Spanish American War, World War I, World War II, Korea and Vietnam. (1994)

TURKEY (Hall Co.)
SH 86, 9.3 mi. NE
The Ozark Trail at Tampico
In 1913, William Hope "Coin" Harvey, who operated a resort in the Ozark Mountains of Arkansas, founded the Ozark Trail Association as a private highway organization. Several Texas and New Mexico counties joined the effort, and the line went diagonally from St. Louis, Missouri to Santa Fe, New Mexico. As part of Harvey's plan, stops along the way featured white obelisks denoting, in the official Ozark Trail green lettering, town names, as well as directions and distances to other towns. The central Ozark route passed across Wellington, Texas, and a second southern route was built through the communities of Childress, Estelline, Tampico, Turkey, Quitaque, Silverton, Tulia, Nazareth and Dimmitt. J. E. Swepston of Tulia, elected Ozark Trail Association president in 1920, was instrumental in having the striking road markers placed in this area. At the time, Hall County had more than 1,000 farms and ranches, and ranchland continued to be divided into farms as more settlers arrived in the area. In 1924, however, with a government initiative to enact a national road-numbering system, the Ozark Trails and other private highways were abandoned or absorbed into the national road system. Adjacent to the Tampico marker was a service station and general store. In 1929, the Tampico oilfield started a short-lived boom in the community, which supported a school. After the oil supply proved minimal, the school consolidated into the Turkey school district. The obelisk, designated a State Archeological Landmark in 1999, remains as a tie to both the early efforts to increase automotive travel and to the community of Tampico. (2006)

TUSCOLA (Taylor Co.)
US 83 S, city limits at bridge
Jim Ned Creek
Probably named for Jim Ned, Delaware Indian chief. During Republic and early statehood of Texas (about 1840–1860), he was a scout for the Texas Militia on several campaigns against wild Indians in this area. Dams near junction of two main forks of creek create Lake Brownwood. Note: Marker has been vandalized. (1968)

TYLER (Smith Co.)
US 271, 5 mi. NE of Loop 323
Camp Fannin
Numerous military bases were expanded or established throughout Texas during World War II. Originally planned as an air corps installation, construction of Camp Fannin began in late 1942. Named in honor of Texas Revolutionary hero James Walker Fannin, Jr., the camp opened in the spring of 1943 and was formally dedicated in September. The main purpose of the camp was an Infantry Replacement Training Center (IRTC), and during its peak operation as many as 35,000 to 40,000 men were trained every four months to replace troops killed, wounded, or recalled from the war's battlefronts. In addition to the Infantry Training Center, the camp also included a German prisoner of war facility from 1943 to 1946, and a Women's Army Corps (WAC) installation in 1944. Camp Fannin had a tremendous impact on the local economy, employing about 3,000 civilian workers and giving rise to numerous new businesses catering to the military trade. Many of the camp's facilities were later acquired by business interests and are still in use. Soldiers stationed here, as well as at least one former German prisoner, returned to East Texas to settle after the war. (1989)

TYLER (Smith Co.)   *US 271, 2 mi. NE in roadside park*
Camp Ford
On this site during the Civil War was located Camp Ford, the largest prisoner of war compound for Union troops west of the Mississippi River. Named in honor of Col. John S. "Rip" Ford, who originally established a training camp here in 1862. It was converted in the summer of 1863 to a prison camp. It first consisted of four to five acres enclosed by a stockade sixteen feet high. In the spring of 1864 following the Confederate victories at Mansfield, Louisiana, and Mark's Mills, Arkansas, the enclosure was doubled to accommodate the large influx of prisoners. Approximately 4700 Federals were confined here during this period. This overcrowded condition was somewhat relieved through a series of prisoner of war exchanges between the North and the South. Union soldiers representing nearly one hundred different regiments plus sailors from gunboats and transports were confined here. In addition there were imprisoned Union sympathizers, spies, and even Confederate deserters. The prisoners constructed their own shelters ranging from log huts and burrows called "shebangs" to brush arbors and tents made of blankets. A spring located about 100 yards southwest of this marker furnished an ample supple of good water. Their meager rations, essentially the same as that of their guards, usually consisted of beef and corn meal and were sometimes supplemented by vegetables purchased from nearby farms. Although escape attempts were frequent, very few were successful, due to the long distance to Union lines and the difficulty in eluding the tracking hounds used by the Confederate guards. Even though conditions were primitive, it compared favorably with the other Civil War prison camps. Camp Ford continued to serve as a prison until the surrender of the Trans-Mississippi Department in May, 1865. It was later destroyed by Federal occupation troops.   (1962)

TYLER (Smith Co.)   *FM 14, 17 mi. N*
Head of Navigation on the Sabine River: Belzora Landing
A thriving port for Tyler and East Texas, from 1850s until arrival of railroads in 1870s. One of many ports established when settlers (as in eastern states) turned to rivers for transportation. In Texas, river-freighting proved rather disappointing. The long, winding rivers were difficult for even small, shallow-draft steamers to navigate. Boats on the Sabine fared very well, however, because of abundant rainfall and favorable terrain. For several months each year, light steamboats could ascend the river to Belzora. The "Galveston News" for that period included Belzora in listings of ports. In dry seasons it was local practice to load goods on barges, flatboats and other craft and wait for a freshet to send them downstream. In addition to the boat landing, Belzora had a ferry used by travel on the Dallas-to-Shreveport Post Road. The town had a dozen businesses, a post office and a combination church-schoolhouse. Ambitious plans for greater inland navigation, deepening of river channel, and building of locks and dams never materialized. Belzora, like many sister ports, became an historic relic—a ghost town.   (1970)

TYLER (Smith Co.)   *SH 64, 2.4 mi. W of Loop 323*
Smith County
Formed from Nacogdoches County. Created April 11, 1846. Organized July 13, 1846. Named in honor of General James Smith, pioneer soldier and statesman, friend of General Sam Houston, Thomas Rusk and J. Pinckney Henderson. Born September 10, 1792. Died December 25, 1855, buried with military honors at Henderson. Tyler, county seat.

TYLER (Smith Co.)   *W. Front St. (SH 31),*
Tyler Rose Park, Rose Garden Center
Smith County Rose Industry and the Tyler Rose Garden
A combination of sandy soil, year-round rainfall, and a long growing season make the Tyler area ideal for rose propagation. First known commercial production began here in the 1870s when industry pioneers such as G. A. McKee and Mathew Shamburger (1827–1888) sold rosebushes along with other nursery stock. Business expanded in the 1920s as more nurserymen began growing roses. Production was increased by new growing methods such as irrigation, introduced in 1924 by A. F. Watkins. The Texas Rose Festival was started in Oct. 1933 to publicize the industry. Scientific plant research, begun in the 1930s by J. C. Ratsek, Dr. E. W. Lyle, and others from the Tyler substation of the Texas Agricultural Experiment Station, was implemented by organization of the Texas Rose Foundation, Inc., in 1945. The Tyler Rose Garden, a 22-acre municipal park, was created in 1952. Nurseries donate the many varieties of plants, which are cared for by the city. Today the rose

industry is vital to the economy of Smith County. In 1973 the value of bushes and flowers shipped around the world by local nurseries totaled $9,000,000. One-half of the rosebushes produced each year in the United States come from the Tyler area.   (1975)

TYLER (Smith Co.)   *SH 155 at FM 344, 13 mi. SW*
Neches Saline, C.S.A.
Now covered by the waters of Lake Palestine, the Neches Saline was the source of salt for early settlers from over a wide area of East Texas. As early as 1765, the Spanish missionary Calahorra recorded the presence of salines in the area. An early manufacturing process for extracting salt from the saline involved drawing water from shallow wells and boiling it to the evaporation point, leaving the salt behind. The possibilities for commercial development of the Neches Saline became evident to the early settlers, and a small isolated settlement developed here before the Texas Revolution. Local salt making declined throughout the South between 1850 and 1861 as salt began to be imported from England. With the Federal embargo during the Civil War, salt began to be made locally again. It was reported that James S. O. Brooks, who had come to Texas from West Virginia, had twelve furnaces operating at the Neches Saline during the war and manufactured 100 bushels of salt per day to meet the needs of the Confederacy. Brooks leased the salt works to his son, William Bradford, in 1865. W. B. Brooks, who purchased the operation in 1871, apparently was the last owner and operator of the salt works at the Neches Saline.   (1965)

TYLER (Smith Co.)   *SH 64, 2.9 mi. SE*
Headache Springs, C.S.A. Medical Laboratory
A quarter mile north of this site is "Headache Springs," noted for its healing mineral waters. During the Civil War, as sea blockades cut off imports, a Confederate medical laboratory operated here. One of nine, and only one west of Mississippi River. For the government it made medicines and whiskey. The army at this time was buying medicinal herbs, including poke root, snakeroot, mullein, jimson weed, Jerusalem oak, nightshade, mistletoe and cherry bark. With mineral salts, these were the medicines of desperation.   (1965)

UMBARGER (Randall Co.)   *Buffalo Lake Rd., just S of US 60*
Umbarger
In 1895, Civil War veteran and farmer S. G. Umbarger established a wagon yard and sheds for travelers passing through this area. The area became known as Umbarger when the Pecos Valley Railroad, built in 1898, named a rail switch after him. By 1902, the community had a post office; in 1904, later citizens established a public school district. German-Catholic families, brought to the area by Pius Friemel, established St. Mary's Church, or Marienkirche, in 1908. During World War II, Italian prisoners of war were held in nearby Hereford. A group of them, trained in old world techniques, carved religious figures and painted the interior of the parish church, which remains a community center.   (2003)

UTOPIA (Uvalde Co.)   *Main St. (RR 187)*
Old Rock Store
Utopia's first building. Erected 1873 of native rock for R. H. Kincheloe, owner, by Joe Hastler, stone mason.   (1967)

UTOPIA (Uvalde Co.)   *Main St. (RR 187)*
Utopia
After an 1866 Indian raid on their nearby Little Creek home, R. H. Kincheloe and family moved here, built a home and in 1873 a 2-story rock store. They platted town as "Montana," giving land for churches, school, and community square. Post office moved from Waresville in 1883. Methodists had church here before town was founded. Baptists organized their church in 1883. Church of Christ congregation relocated here, 1902. New name praising climate was chosen by Postmaster George Barker. Stores and shops were built. Town is now a center for ranching, retirement, vacationing.   (1973)

UTOPIA (Uvalde Co.)   *Main St. (RR 187)*
Utopia Methodist Church
Established in 1866 as part of the Uvalde-Kerrville Mission, later in the Uvalde Circuit. Pecan grove behind present church was site of many pioneer camp meetings under brush arbors. The first

was held in 1868 by the Rev. A. J. Potter, noted Civil War chaplain and circuit rider. This Gothic sanctuary, built in early 1890s with members doing much of the work, is on a site given by the Rev. Irving Jones and R. H. Kincheloe. (1967)

UTOPIA (Uvalde Co.) Main St. (RR 187)
Old Waresville (¼ mi. W)
First non-military colony in Uvalde County. Founded 1852 by Capt. Ware, veteran of Battle of San Jacinto. Ware built first log cabin home (still standing). Other early settlers included Gideon Thompson, whose wife was first Anglo-American woman in Sabinal Canyon. Colony lost settlers in Indian raids, 1856–1866. Although the post office moved to Utopia in 1883, still here is the cemetery where Capt. Ware was buried in 1853; first store and post office built by Charles Durbon, 1856; homes of Joel Finley, John Ware, built of native stone, 1870s. (1966)

UVALDE (Uvalde Co.) Main St. (US 90) at 4th St.
USS Uvalde
Constructed and commissioned by the U.S. Navy in 1944, the "USS Uvalde" was a C-2 type cargo ship named to honor former United States Vice-President John Nance Garner and the county of his residence. The "Uvalde" was built by the Moore Drydock Company of Oakland, California, with an overall length of 459 feet. The "Uvalde" served the United States Navy during World War II and was most active in the campaigns of the Pacific Theater. After the war ended, the ship provided troop and cargo transport to vital outposts in the Western Pacific and earned the Occupation Service Medal for operations in Chinese waters. After service as part of the United Nations Force in the Korean Conflict, the "Uvalde" became part of the reserve fleet. In 1961, the ship was reactivated in response to the events of the Cold War, including the Berlin and Cuban missile crises. After earning numerous service awards and citations, the "USS Uvalde" was decommissioned in 1968. The city of Uvalde, which had remained interested in the ship's service record over the years, gladly accepted the navy's offer of several items of the vessel's equipment. The anchor and bell displayed at this site are reminders of the history of the ship and her crew. (Texas Sesquicentennial 1836–1986)

UVALDE (Uvalde Co.) Main St. (US 90) at Getty, town plaza
Uvalde County
Created 1850. Named for canyon which in turn had been named for the Spanish Army Captain Juan de Ugalde, who fought and routed Indians here in 1790. Over the years, "Ugalde" became "Uvalde." Many cattle, sheep, goats are raised; and Uvalde honey is famous for its flavor. Noted for fine hunting and scenic drives. Historic sites marked include 3 old forts, 2 Spanish missions, a Ranger camp. Home of Southwest Texas Junior College, Garner State Park and home (now museum and library) of John Nance Garner, first Texan elected vice-president of United States. (1965)

UVALDE (Uvalde Co.) Main St. (US 90) at Getty, town plaza
Early Texas Wagon Yards
Places of shelter for drivers, teams and wagons. Here travelers could cook bacon, eggs, beans, coffee; talk with friends and strangers. For people from the country, a wagon yard was both a hotel and a social center. Usually it was an open area flanked by a shed, stalls and feed rooms. It might cover a city block, and charges were 25¢ to $1.00 a day. Drivers pulled into yards, cared for teams, found cooking and sleeping space. Men or families might stay for weeks, await kin or goods coming by train or stage. Amusements were practical jokes, gossip, games, music by fiddle, guitar, harmonica. Young boys overcame bashfulness, learned to dance, roller skate, whip bullies. The yard was center for trading goods and horses; obtaining advice on travel, work, weather. Some yards were stops for stages and freighters. A block west of this site was wagon yard of F. A. Piper Company (predecessor of Horner's Store). Like many Texas merchants, Piper built and ran the wagon yard to aid customers, who used it free of charge. Modern transportation has made the wagon yard a relic of the past, but it has a secure place in the history of pioneer days in Texas. (1966)

UVALDE (Uvalde Co.) 301 N. Getty St. (US 83)
Original Site of Uvalde High School
Four years after Uvalde became a railroad shipping point, the people of the city built their first school building. Completed in 1885, the facility served all grade levels. The picketed structure

was constructed of cedar logs and erected on this site, which was donated by the town's founder, Reading W. Black. The demand for space quickly required a new four-room two-story structure. Four more rooms were added in 1891, the year of the first graduating class. Graduation ceremonies, which took place after completion of the tenth grade, were sometimes held in the Uvalde Opera House. The school building burned to the ground in 1898. Determined to continue to meet the educational needs of their children, Uvalde citizens erected a new building on this site in 1900. The two-story edifice cost $10,000 to build, and there was some controversy over its size. By 1907, Uvalde had become an independent school district, and even the modern 1900 structure was no longer adequate for the rapidly growing area. Plans for a larger Uvalde High School on West Main Street were carried out in 1908. The educational investments of the early citizens of Uvalde have been multiplied in the graduates of Uvalde High School. For more than a century, Uvalde students have become valuable community members. (1998)

UVALDE (Uvalde Co.) — 524 N Getty St. (US 83)
Schwartz House
Built in 1927 as the home of Lee Schwartz, local merchant and city alderman, and his wife Agnes (Racer), this house was designed by San Antonio architect Will A. Noonan. Constructed on land formerly owned by Mrs. Schwartz's mother, the house was built on the site of an earlier home. Features of the modest colonial revival style house include a pedimented entry, single entry door with sidelights, and groupings of multi-light windows. (Recorded Texas historic landmark 1997)

UVALDE (Uvalde Co.) — 332 N. Park St., 3 blks. N of US 90
John Nance Garner Home
Memorial to Ettie R. Garner, secretary to her husband in his long career as a statesman. John Nance Garner, born Nov. 22, 1868, was in Texas Legislature, 1898–1902; U.S. Congress, 1902–1932 (Speaker of the House in last term); Vice-President of the United States, 1933–1941. This home, built 1920, scene of visits of world figures, given to Uvalde by Vice-President Garner and son Tully in 1952. (1965)

UVALDE (Uvalde Co.) — 332 N. Park St., 3 blks. N of US 90
Judge John Nance Garner
Cherished by fellow citizens of Uvalde County for his acts of leadership, philanthropy and dedication to area progress. Able trial lawyer; rancher and banker. First elective office was County Judge. Benefactor, Southwest Texas Junior College. The good example and rare wit and wisdom of Judge Garner have inspired Southwest Texas and 20th Century America. Presented by the City of Uvalde. (1965)

VALERA (Coleman Co.) — US 67, .5 mi. W
Cleveland-Anson House
First fine house in area. Built in 1880 by George P. Cleveland, a sheep rancher. Structure of native stone and lumber hauled from Fort Worth by ox-wagon, has two-foot walls. Second owner was Englishman Billy Anson, son of the Earl of Litchfield. Awarded Medallion Plate. (1970)

VALLEY MILLS (Bosque Co.) — SH 6 at 5th St.
First Methodist Church of Valley Mills
Methodists in this area trace their history to the 1840s, when circuit-riding preachers began holding camp meetings on a nearby farm. In 1889, after the railroad caused Valley Mills to relocate south of the Bosque River, the Methodists built their first church, located in a residential area. In 1915, the congregation voted to move downtown. Brick structure, which features two inset temple-front entries with ionic columns, was completed by 1916. Art glass windows, corbelled brickwork, and a pressed metal roof that simulates tile are also prominent. (1991)

VALLEY VIEW (Cooke Co.) — IH 35, 3 mi. N at rest area
Kiowa Raid of 1868 (SW Part of County)
On Jan. 5–6, 1868, Chief Big Tree and 150 to 200 Kiowas raided Willa Walla Valley, Clear Creek and Blocker Creek. Burned homes; killed 13 people; scalped one woman alive. Captured 10 women and children; 3 escaped, 2 were ransomed. Raiders reached Elm Creek at Gainesville before blizzard forced withdrawal. More damage and deaths would have resulted if George Masoner had not

become the "Paul Revere" of valleys and warned settlers of impending danger. Indian raids such as this one were in retaliation for loss of hunting grounds to settlers. (1968)

VAN (Van Zandt Co.)   SH 110, 3 mi. N
Pruitt Baptist Church and Pruitt Community
Named for Adelia Pruitt, the first postmistress, the town of Pruitt began in the 1880s. It included a cotton gin, blacksmith shop, general store, barber shop, Woodmen of the World Lodge, drug store, school, Methodist Church, and Congregational Church. The Pruitt Baptist Church was organized in 1896 by Malinda Ashworth and E. R. Crocker. In 1912, a church building was erected for the Baptist congregation one mile west of this site. The sanctuary was moved in 1947 and replaced with a new structure in 1962. Many additions have been made to the building. The church continues to serve the area. (1996)

VAN (Van Zandt Co.)   IH 20, 1 mi. W at rest area
Park Dedicated to Memory of Texas State Highway Commission
Chairman Brady P. Gentry (March 25, 1895–Nov. 9, 1966)
A man whose public service was of highest order. Born on a farm near this site in Van Zandt County. Educated at Cumberland University (Tennessee) and Tyler Commercial College, was county attorney and county judge of Smith County. As chairman of Texas Highway Commission, 1939–1945, he traveled almost every Texas highway to learn road needs of state. Aided long-range financial strength of highway program by supporting the reservation of road-use revenue for road building. An authority on highway policy, Gentry served in 1943 as president of the American Association of State Highway Officials. In that capacity he aided post-war expansion in use of motor vehicles by implementing legislation to provide funds for farm-to-market roads and the first major expressways in the country. Interested in education, Gentry helped to establish Tyler Junior College. He served as U.S. Congressman, 1953–1957, for Third Congressional District of Texas. A member of committees for public works and roads, he helped design legislation for interstate highway system. Refused to vote along merely political lines. The preeminent position of the Texas Highway Department and the high quality of roads in Texas and the U.S. are a tribute to the ability of Brady P. Gentry. (1967)

The Free State of Van Zandt
Pioneer nickname appropriate to this area's many freedoms—particularly from want and fear. (Food was obtained with little effort; and although the Indians fought white men here as late as 1842, the settlers by 1847 slept in the open with no dread of Indians or wild animals.) According to tradition, Van Zandt county (created 1848) also by a legal accident had freedom from sharing debts of its parent county, Henderson—and was proud of that unusual advantage. Other parts of Texas share "free state" traditions. An 1826 "Republic of Fredonia" was proclaimed in Nacogdoches and endured for a few weeks. Along the Mexican border, citizens maintained in 1839–1840 the "Republic of The Rio Grande." Because it developed great self-reliance in recurring border troubles, Hidalgo County called itself a republic, 1852–1872. A Panhandle County formed the secessionist "Free State of Ochiltree" in the 1890s. All secessions have been brief. When Texas in 1845 voted to become a part of the United States, it was given (but declined) the right to become five states. Such movements as "The Free State of Van Zandt" soon lost force. Ten proud years as the Republic of Texas invoke unusual loyalty to the state. (1968)

VAN HORN (Culberson Co.)   IH 10, 2 mi. W at scenic overlook
Culberson County
Formed from El Paso County. Created March 10, 1911. Organized April 18, 1911. Named for David B. Culberson, 1830–1902, famous Constitutional lawyer, a Confederate officer, member of the Texas Legislature, member of the United States Congress. Van Horn, the county seat. (1964)

VAN HORN (Culberson Co.)   IH 10, 2 mi. W at scenic overlook
San Antonio–California Trail (3 mi. S)
One of Texas' first cross-country wagon trails. The San Antonio-El Paso section of this route was surveyed in 1848 by a party under the intrepid Indian fighter Jack Hays. Used first by emigrants and gold-seekers, it became part of the San Antonio–San Diego Mail Line (1857), one of America's pioneer mail services. Passengers on the line paid $200 (one-way) to share a swaying Concord coach

with 600 pounds of mail and braved bandits, dust, floods, and Indians to spend 27 days traveling 1,500 miles. Service ended in 1861 at the outbreak of the Civil War.   (1968)

VAN HORN (Culberson Co.)   *US 90, 12 mi. S*
Van Horn Wells (½ mi. W)
Only dependable water supply in miles of arid terrain. Used by Indians for centuries. Named for either Maj. Jefferson Van Horne (who passed here en route to establish fort at El Paso, in 1849), or for Lt. J. J. Van Horn (stationed here to fight Indians, 1859). Wagon trains from South Texas welcomed the "seep-water" from wells, as did soldiers on San Antonio–El Paso Military Road. Riders for "Jackass Mail" (San Antonio–San Diego) stopped here and the Butterfield Mail Line built a stage stand at Wells, 1859. Town of Van Horn grew up (12 mi. N) in 1880s.   (1970)

VAN HORN (Culberson Co.)   *US 90 at SH 54*
Clark Hotel
First permanent structure in Van Horn. Earliest portion (built 1901) housed original city post office. Main portion was built in 1905–06 by John Cox of concrete blocks handmade by crew on site. In 1911–12, when Culberson was newly organized, served as the county courthouse. Until 1918, when converted to hotel by Fred Clark, structure was site for theatrical programs and school graduations and housed a saloon, offices, and all kinds of shops.   (1971)

VAN HORN (Culberson Co.)   *SH 54, 32 mi. N*
Figure 2 Ranch
The lands which now lie within the boundaries of the Figure 2 Ranch were occupied in the 19th century by nomadic native American tribes. One of the last battles between Texas Rangers and Apache Indians occurred in the mountains west of this site in 1881. James Monroe Daugherty (1850–1942), who came to Texas from Missouri as a small child in 1851, served as a Confederate express rider at age 14. Following the Civil War he returned home to Denton County and became interested in the cattle business. He participated in numerous cattle drives and by 1872 purchased his first ranch. He was a charter member of the Texas and Southwestern Cattle Raisers Association. As his empire grew, Daugherty acquired additional ranches in several states. In 1900, he purchased land here and founded the Figure 2 Ranch. Taking up residence here by 1905, he was active in local politics and served as one of Culberson County's first commissioners upon its creation in 1911. Due to his failing health, Daugherty sold the Figure 2 Ranch in 1933 to legendary millionaire businessman James Marion West, Sr. (1871–1941) of Houston. Although West did not live at the ranch, he visited often and the property remained in his family until 1992.   (1994)

VAN HORN (Culberson Co.)   *US 180/62, Guadalupe Mountain*
                                                     National Park, 54 mi. N via SH 54
Ruins of "The Pinery" or "Pine Spring" Stage Stand
Built in 1858 as a station on the Butterfield Overland Mail Route, St. Louis to San Francisco. Abandoned in 1859, when the line was shifted to the Davis Mountain Route.   (1964)

VAN HORN (Culberson Co.)   *US 180/62, 3 mi. SW in roadside park,*
                                                     54 mi. N via SH 54

Guadalupe Peak
Guadalupe Peak, Texas' highest mountain at 8,751 feet, dominates one of the most scenic and least-known hinterlands of the old frontier. It lies behind and to the right of 8,078-foot El Capitan, the sheer cliff that rises more than 3,000 feet above this spot to mark the south end of the Guadalupe Range. Starkness of the mountainside belies the lushness which the Guadalupes conceal. Tucked away in their inner folds are watered canyons shaded by towering ponderosa pine, douglas fir, juniper and quaking aspen. McKittrick Canyon, scene of a four-mile trout stream, is also the habitat of the state's only known herd of wild elk. Deer and wild turkeys abound. Stories of hidden gold go back to Spanish days. The Conquistadores who rode north from Mexico wrote about fabulous deposits. Geronimo, the Apache chief, said the richest gold mines in the western world lay hidden in the Guadalupes. Legend holds that Ben Sublett, a colorful prospector of the 1880's, slipped off at night to a cave and returned with bags of nuggets. Probably less is known about the archeology of the Guadalupes than of any other area in the Southwest. Excavators have found spearheads, pictographs and human remains together with bones of long-extinct bison, dire wolf and musk ox in cliff

caves. At Hermit Cave in Last Chance Canyon, carbon-14 dating indicates occupancy 12,000 years ago. Geologically, the Guadalupes present a spectacular exposure of the famous Capitan prehistoric barrier reef, said to be the most extensive fossil organic reef known.

VEGA (Oldham Co.)   *US 385, 21 mi. N in rest area*
Old Tascosa
Old Tascosa, cowboy capital of the plains, lay one-half mile northeast. In its brief span it became the center of the open-range world, stamping ground for some of the West's most notorious bad men and focal point for cattle thieves and ranchmen. Because of the easy crossing of the Canadian River at the site, it early became a meeting place where Indians and Mexican traders (comancheros) exchanged contraband goods, including women and children. With the passing of the buffalo came the first permanent settlement, made by Mexican sheepherders in 1876. Charles Goodnight and Thomas S. Bugbee brought the first cattle to the free-grass empire the same year. Smaller ranchmen and nesters followed and the boom was on. Hundreds of miles from the general line of settlement, Tascosa lured the lawless and the lawmen: Billy the Kids and Pat Garretts. To accommodate those who "died with their boots on" in growing gunfights, a cemetery was set aside in 1879. It was named for the famed "Boot Hill" in Dodge City, Kansas, to which Tascosa was tied by cattle and freight trail. Heaviest toll in a single shoot out occurred March 21, 1886, when three cowboys and a restaurant owner died in a five-minute duel. All went to Boot Hill. The cattle trails, Tascosa's lifeblood, began to be pinched off with the coming of barbed wire, first commercial use of which was on the nearby Frying Pan Ranch in 1882. The noose was drawn still tighter when the vast XIT spread fenced its 3 million acres. By 1887 Tascosa was completely closed in. When the railroad bypassed it the same year, its fate was sealed. By the time the Oldham County seat was moved to Vega in 1915, only 15 residents remained. Sole remnants of the old town today are Boot Hill and courthouse. The site, however, is occupied by Cal Farley's Boys Ranch.

VEGA (Oldham Co.)   *US 385, 21 mi. N in rest area*
The Historic LS (Headquarters 3 mi. SE)
Great early ranch well known to badman Billy the Kid and other famed western characters. The LS was founded in 1870s by former Indian territory trader W. M. D. Lee and New York financier Lucien Scott. Through Lee's efforts, the LS had water and grass for over 100,000 cattle and sometimes drove 6 or 7 herds a year up the trail. When thefts followed Billy the Kid's visits, LS men rode west and brought back their cattle: and when Tascosa gunfights put men into Boot Hill graves, the LS escaped disaster. But drouth brought heavy losses in 1886; and grant of 3,000,000 acres of Panhandle lands to the XIT (State of Texas' payment for constructing capitol in Austin) cut old LS range in half. Lee left in 1890 to promote a ship canal in Houston. Scott died 1893. W. H. Gray and E. F. Swift of Chicago bought LS in 1905. Memorable LS men included foreman J. E. McAlister, later a Channing merchant. One of the $25-a-month cowboys was E. L Doheny, later a multi-millionaire oil man involved in 1920's Teapot Dome scandal. Ownership of brand and 96,000 acres of LS range passed to Col. C. T. Herring, rancher and civic leader of Amarillo; his estate still operates it.   (1968)

VEGA (Oldham Co.)   *US 385, 21 mi. N in rest area*
Oldham County
Formed from Young and Bexar Territories. Created August 21, 1876. Organized January 12, 1881. Named in honor of Williamson Simpson Oldham, 1813–1868, Arkansas lawyer and jurist member of the Confederate Senate from Texas. County seat, Tascosa, 1881. Vega, since 1915.   (1936)

VEGA (Oldham Co.)   *US 385 at courthouse*
Site of Old Tascosa (23 mi. NE)
Contains one of the famous Boot Hill Cemeteries of Wild West days and was the gathering place for pleasure-seeking cowboys, gamblers and "bad men" of the Panhandle in the 1870s and '80s. Outlaws such as Billy the Kid and lawmen like Pat Garrett and Bat Masterson walked its streets. At first an Indian camping place at a crossing on the Canadian River, then Mexican trading point and pastoral settlement, Atascosa (Boggy Place) rapidly became an open-range trading center and capital of a cattle empire from 1876 to 1877. Romero Plaza and Howard and Rinehart Store marked the boom in growth. Struggles between large ranch owners like Charles Goodnight and the "Little Men" of the plains were focused there. Became seat of Oldham County, 1880, and then legal capital

of ten unorganized counties. Progress spelled doom for the town. The railroad in 1887 created other important towns and barbed wire fences ended the vital trading routes and great roundups. The open ranges and cattle trails like the famous Dodge City Trail were gone. When county seat was moved to Vega in 1915, few residents remained. Today "Old Tascosa" retains only the courthouse and Boot Hill. Cal Farley's Boy's Ranch is located there.

VEGA (Oldham Co.)
US 385 at courthouse
County Named for Texas Confederate
Senator W. S. Oldham 1813–1868
Legislator, judge, newspaperman. Came to Texas from Arkansas. Member 1861 Texas Secession Convention. Chosen delegate to provisional Confederate Congress, Montgomery, Ala. Sent Arkansas to work for secession by Jefferson Davis 1861. Texas Confederate Senator 1862–1865. Influential defender of states rights, and granting president power to suspend writ of habeas corpus. A memorial to Texans who served the Confederacy.   (1963)

VERNON (Wilbarger Co.)
FM 2916, 3 mi. E of US 283, 13 mi. N
Doan's Crossing
A major route for cattle drives known primarily as the Western Trail developed from far South Texas to Dodge City, Kansas, in the 1870s. About 1876, trail drivers along the route began crossing the Red River near this site. In 1878, Ohio native Jonathan Doan established a trading post near the crossing and became the first person to permanently settle in Wilbarger County (organized in 1881). In the early 1880s he and his partner/nephew Corwin F. Doan recorded the passage of hundreds of thousands of cattle along this river crossing which became known as Doan's Crossing.   (1993)

VERNON (Wilbarger Co.)
FM 2916, 3 mi. E of US 283, 13 mi. N
The Doans' Adobe Building
Corwin F. Doan (1848–1929) settled here on Red River in 1878; erected this house in 1881. In his early picket store and later, permanent building, he had large stocks of goods to supply the cowboys who annually drove cattle in herds of thousands along the western trail. The village of "Doan's Crossing" had 14 or more buildings. Doan, his wife Lide (1850–1905), and their 3 children entertained people from all walks of life—English Lords to Indians—in this adobe house. Awarded Medallion Plate.   (1962)

VERNON (Wilbarger Co.)
US 287 at US183/283, courthouse
Early Wilbarger County
Organized 1858 and named in honor of Matthias and Josiah P. Wilbarger, early Texas settlers. Josiah, a surveyor, had become famous as the man who lived 12 years after being scalped by Comanches, 1833, near Austin. He had saved his life by putting a wool sock on his head; he was rescued next day by neighbors. An adobe house built 1878 by Jonathan and C. F. Doan, the first Wilbarger County settlers, marks the Red River crossing of the famous Western Cattle Trail. Vernon (formerly Eagle Flat) became county seat in 1881. The first railroad reached town, 1886.   (1968)

VERNON (Wilbarger Co.)
4600 College Dr. (US 70)
Red River Valley Museum
Features one of Texas' famed regional collections of Indian artifacts, tracing history of early man along the Red River. Before Chisholm Trail days, when thousands of cattle crossed Red River at nearby Doan's Crossing, Vernon area was home to tribes of Comanche, Kiowa, and Wichita. Mr. and Mrs. J. Henry Ray of Vernon spent 30 years gathering artifacts, which they donated to Wilbarger County, Oct. 14, 1963.

VERNON (Wilbarger Co.)
4600 College Dr. (US 70)
Wilbarger County
Formed from Bexar County. Created February 1, 1858. Organized October 10, 1881. Named for Josiah and Mathias Wilbarger, brothers who came to Texas in 1829. Josiah, scalped by Indians August, 1833, survived 11 years. Vernon, the county seat. Millions of cattle and horses were driven north through this county.   (1936)

VICTORIA (Victoria Co.)   US 87, 4 mi. NW
C.S.A. Camp Henry E. McCulloch
October 1861, on this site in Nuner Mott, a valley extending southwest in Victoria County, several infantry and two cavalry companies of the 6th Regiment Texas Infantry trained in this camp of instruction commanded by Col. R. R. Garland. Co. A, of Port Lavaca, under A. Ham Phillips, and Co. B, Victoria, under Jacob Rupley, were joined for eight months by troops from nearby towns. The 6th on May 22, 1862, was ordered to Gen. Van Dorn at Arkansas Post, where it was captured. Less than 100 of the 643 men survived the war.   (1963)

VICTORIA (Victoria Co.)   US 87, 1 mi. NW
Camp Henry E. McCulloch
At the suggestion of Confederate Col. Henry McCulloch, an area near this site north of Victoria, known as Nuner's Mott, was selected for the establishment of a military training camp in 1861. Troops from Bell, Bexar, Calhoun, Dewitt, Gonzales, Guadalupe, Matagorda, Travis, and Victoria counties began arriving that September. Col. Robert Garland of Virginia was appointed regimental commander. The entire regiment, now known as the Sixth Texas Infantry, trained at Camp McCulloch until May 1862. Captured at Arkansas Post in 1863, the regiment later fought in the battles of Missionary Ridge, Atlanta, Franklin, and Nashville before finally surrendering with the Army of Tennessee in North Carolina.   (1998)

VICTORIA (Victoria Co.)   US 59, 12 mi. NE in rest area
Victoria County
Inhabited briefly by adventurer Cabeza De Vaca in 1530s and French explorer La Salle in 1680's. Site of 1720 Mission Espiritu Santo de Zuniga. Mission friars, sent here to Christianize and civilize the Karankawa Indians, laid foundation for the cattle industry of Texas, their stray stock forming nucleus for later vast herds of wild cattle. Presidio La Bahia, founded 1721 with present Victoria County, has been restored on a later site, in Goliad. Civilian settlement began in 1824 with Martin De Leon's grant from the Mexican government to plant a colony on the Guadalupe River. Placido Benavides, son-in-law of De Leon, commanded Victoria militia, which as part of army of Gen. Sam Houston, opposed Mexican countrymen during the Texas Revolution. After the establishment of the Republic of Texas, Victoria County was officially organized in 1837. Many settlers from the Old South immigrated to the area. Navigation of Guadalupe River began 1854 with line of steamers between Victoria and Indianola. Kemper's Bluff was principal cotton loading point. Known as "Cradle of the Cattle Industry in Texas," county remained principally agricultural and ranching area until oil was discovered in later 1930s.   (1967)

VICTORIA (Victoria Co.)   US 59 SW at Guadalupe River Bridge
Guadalupe River
Discovered in this vicinity on April 14, 1689 by Alonso de Leon. Named in honor of "Our Lady of Guadalupe," patron saint of Mexico. Here at a ford, used since Indian days, Empresario Martin de Leon founded the town of Victoria in 1824.

VICTORIA (Victoria Co.)   US 59, 8 mi. SW in Coleto Creek roadside park
Victoria County, C.S.A.
Transportation, military and supply center in the Civil War. On one branch of the Cotton Road, which moved crop to Mexico for exchange on foreign markets for vital guns, ammunition, medicines and other goods. The 1861 vote favored secession 313 to 88. Troops furnished the Confederacy included 5 cavalry companies. County men were also in the 6th Texas Infantry, which trained at "Henry E. McCullock," a camp of instruction 4 miles from Victoria. Local men in Hood's, Ross' and Sibley's Brigades, Terry's Texas Rangers and Buchel's Cavalry were among the 90,000 Texans noted for mobility and daring who fought on every battlefront. Fort Esperanza, on Matagorda Island, was garrisoned by 100 Victoria militia, who were captured by 1,900 Federals. The people at home made cloth, tallow candles, shoe blacking from China berries, coffee substitutes from parched corn, dried potatoes or okra seeds. To block 1863 threat of Federal invasion, Gen. John B. Magruder, commander of the Dept. of Texas, destroyed the railroad from Port Lavaca to Victoria. Citizens sacrificed their fine river harbor, one of the two busiest in Texas, by felling trees and sinking boats in the shipping lanes.

WACO (McLennan Co.)   *US 84 at SH 31, 8 mi. E*
Waco
Founded 1849. Named for Waco Indians. Sent men to state frontier defense and Confederate Army in Civil War. Home of five C.S.A. generals. Center for medicine, recreation, financial institutions and manufacturing enterprises. Home of Baylor University, Paul Quinn College, Cameron Park and Annual Heart O'Texas Fair.

WACO (McLennan Co.)   *US 77 Bus. at Stanfield Dr.*
Sarah Ann Vouchere Walker
Widow of Jacob Walker, said to have been last man to die in the Alamo. Born in Louisiana in 1811. Married and came to Texas 1829, and to this area 1844. Received Republic of Texas Land Grant No. 1, Sabine County, a league and labor E. of the Brazos. Once rode horseback 300 mi. to warn Gen. Sam Houston of an impending Indian attack. Her burial site, about 100 ft. to the south, set aside in perpetuity by her grandson, George Anthony Stanfield. This marker erected by her descendants, through McLennan County Historical Survey Committee.   (1965)

WACO (McLennan Co.)   *IH 35, 10 mi. N in roadside park*
General Richard Harrison (1821–1876)
One of a trio of brothers—great grand-nephews of U.S. President Wm. Henry Harrison—who all gained rank of general in the Confederate Army during the Civil War. Richard Harrison was a physician and statesman prior to army service. Won his general's commission in Jan. 1865 in Mississippi. Moved to Texas, 1866, settling near older brother, Gen. Jas. E., and younger brother, Gen. Thos. Harrison. Practiced medicine, farmed, helped rebuild Texas economy, was a church leader. A trustee of Waco University, a forebear of Baylor University.   (1965)

WACO (McLennan Co.)   *IH 35, 2 mi. N*
McLennan County
Created January 22, 1850. Organized August 5, 1850. Named in honor of Neil McLennan, 1787–1867. Came to Texas in 1835. Located on the Bosque River in 1840. Built the first dwelling, a log cabin, in McLennan County. Waco, county seat.

WACO (McLennan Co.)   *IH 35 at University Parks Dr.*
Hebrew Rest
Jews settled in Waco in the 1850s. In 1869 the Hebrew Benevolent Association (HBA) was formed to assist the needy and provide interment in accordance with the laws and rites of Judaism. That year, the HBA acquired this property as a Jewish burial ground. It was named Hebrews' Rest. The first burial was of an 18-month old infant, Bessee Lyans, in July 1869. Hebrew Rest Cemetery was enlarged with purchases of additional land in 1893 and 1922. Many early leaders of Waco's Jewish community and prominent Wacoans are interred here.   (1986)

WACO (McLennan Co.)   *100 Texas Ranger Trail,*
N of IH 35 at University Parks Dr.
The Texas Rangers and the Fence Cutters
Before 1875 in Texas, cattle roamed over thousands of acres of public land, and free grazing became a tradition. After 1875, however, an increasing farm populace tended to protect crops and other property with barbed wire fences which were resented by stockraisers. Cattle losses in drouths of the 1880s provoked such widespread cutting of fences that the Texas government recognized this as a crime and in 1884 enacted laws and measures to curb the practice. Texas Rangers were dispatched by the governor at the call of county judges and sheriffs to apprehend the fence cutters. They operated from the Red River to the Rio Grande, and from the Panhandle to the pine woods of East Texas. Disguise and concealment were required, and one of the Rangers who won praise for his work pronounced it the most disagreeable duty in the world. The vigorous effort went on for some years. Finally, however, stockmen who had wanted to restore the open range were won over to fencing their own lands and using windmills to water their cattle herds. The Texas Rangers had in one more instance helped to stabilize life in the West.   (1976)

WACO (McLennan Co.)

Waco, County Seat of McLennan County

Within sight of this spot March 1, 1849, occurred the first sale of town lots at Waco Village, former home of Waco Indians. Shapley P. Ross, first settler, started Brazos Ferry in 1850. McLennan County was created same year, named for Neil McLennan, pioneer Scot whose cabin on the South Bosque River became first Anglo-American home in the area (1845). Waco, county seat, grew steadily as a center of trade, education, and industry for rich farm and ranch area. Completion of first Brazos River Bridge, 1870, and coming of first railroad, 1872, set city on the road to industrial expansion. At the turn of the century, Waco was one of Texas' major inland cotton exporters. Three Texas governors have resided in the city: Richard Coke (1874–1876), Sul Ross (1887–1891), and Pat M. Neff (1912–1925). Baylor University moved to Waco, 1886, and Texas Christian University was located here 1896–1910. Military training (1917–1918 and 1941–1966) made Waco famous in faraway places. Camp McArthur and aviation schools at Rich Field, Blackland, Waco Army Air Field, and Connally Air Force Base have been located here. Flood control dams on Brazos Basin (built 1954–1965) assure future water supply of the area and have opened much land for development in metropolitan Waco. (1967)

WACO (McLennan Co.)

#11 Lake Brazos Park North west of IH 35

Site of A. J. Moore High School

In 1875, Professor A. J. Moore of Paul Quinn College, concerned over the lack of quality education for Waco's Negro population, began teaching small groups of children in his home. He later founded the Second District Negro School. The first schoolhouse, a frame building that had been relocated east of this site, had formerly served as a hospital. In 1923, the frame schoolhouse was replaced with a brick building. The school was renamed for its founder, A. J. Moore, who served as principal from 1881 to 1905. As the first school in Waco designated to educate the city's Negro youth, A. J. Moore High School was an important institution in the community. Until 1952, Moore High housed students from grades one through twelve. From 1952 to 1971 it served grades seven through twelve only. Moore High was closed in 1971. More than 4,000 students were graduated from A. J. Moore High School during its nearly 100 years of service. Many of them have made significant contributions in the fields of education, medicine, religion, law, public health, business, engineering, law enforcement, social services, theater, sports, and military service. (1985)

WACO (McLennan Co.)

US 77, 11 mi. S

Fletcher Cemetery

This cemetery began with the 1868 burial of early settler Sample Carrigan, who is interred in an unmarked grave. The first marked burial site is that of Clinton A. Mahoney (1860–1868). The graveyard was used chiefly by the Carrigan, Needham, and Harris families until Catherine Carrigan Fletcher set aside three acres as a public cemetery in 1873. The burial ground served residents of several McLennan and Falls County communities, including Golinda, Mooreville, Robinson, Rosenthal, and Satin. A number of Civil War veterans are buried here. (1985)

WADSWORTH (Matagorda Co.)

SH 60 at Ave. F

Sacred Heart Catholic Church

Early residents of Wadsworth (est.1909) John H. and Anna Ottis received help from Galveston Bishop N.A. Gallagher, the Rev. George Montreuil, and other Catholics in the area to erect the 2-story Sacred Heart Catholic Church/School building in 1912 at the corner of 1st and Ave. H. Though the school closed after 2 years, Catholic services were continued. Road construction prompted the Rev. M.J. O'Regan and the congregation to reassemble the original sanctuary here in 1924. Sacred Heart continues to serve the community as a mission of Bay City's Holy Cross Catholic Church. (1993)

WAELDER (Gonzales Co.)

US 90 on building

Miller's Store

Erected 1900–1901 by R. L. Miller and sons. Now owned by 4th generation of family. First store established 1866. Unique bannister features wooden balls carved by the contractor "Cap" Smith. Bullet holes in awning testify to rowdy early era. Awarded Medallion Plate. (1968)

WAELDER (Gonzales Co.)   SH 97 at US 90
The Town of Waelder
In 1875 and 1876, when the Galveston, Harrisburg, and San Antonio Railroad built through Gonzales County, this town was laid out to serve as a shipping point for the surrounding agricultural and ranching area. Hopkinsville, a thriving community five miles north, moved here to become the nucleus of Waelder. Because of valuable services rendered to railroad interests in the early days, the G. H. and S. A. named the new town for the company attorney, Frederick Jacob Waelder (1820–1887). Born in Germany, Waelder spent most of his life in Texas where he was a lawyer, Representative in the State Legislature (1855–1859) and briefly an officer in the Confederate Army. He was also a leader of the German-Texas colonists in numerous undertakings. The town of Waelder, which grew to be the second largest in the county by 1900, can trace the history of its populace back to the three waves of German immigrants who settled in Texas from 1831 to 1900. Highly regarded by their neighbors, German citizens were considered frugal and industrious. Joining with Latin Americans and Old South Anglo-Americans, the two other largest ethnic groups in Texas, they have left a distinctive mark on the culture of the state.   (1968)

WALLIS (Austin Co.)   SH 36, 4 mi. N
Martin Allen (November 28, 1780–December 30, 1837)
As a young man Martin Allen assisted his father, Benjamin, in surveying roads in their native state of Kentucky. He married Elizabeth Vice in 1804 and by 1810 they and their three children were living in Louisiana. Martin joined the Gutierrez-Magee expedition's bid to rid Texas of Spanish rule in 1812–1813. His father and nephew were killed at the decisive battle of Medina. Martin, on a recruiting mission at the time, survived. After a brief stay in Arkansas Territory, the Allens moved back to northwest Louisiana about 1818 and settled in a community which shortly thereafter was named Allen's Settlement in Martin's honor. In 1821, Martin traveled to nearby Wharton County as one of Stephen F. Austin's "Old 300" colonists and was among the first settlers on the Colorado River. About 1834, the Allens purchased land here at Eight Mile Point (so named for its distance from San Felipe de Austin) from their son, Miles N. The Allens lived on this property for the rest of their lives. Allen family members operated a "public house" about ¼ mile east of here that was frequently visited by future hero of the Alamo, William B. Travis. Martin, a Texas War for Independence veteran, was buried near the "public house" in the Allen family cemetery.   (1993)

WALLISVILLE (Chambers Co.)   20136 IH 10 at Wallisville Heritage Park
Joseph Blancpain's French Trading Post
French trader Joseph Blancpain established a trading post in this vicinity in August 1754. He had been living in Natchitoches, Louisiana, where he was the owner of a mercantile store. With a small group of men, Blancpain arrived in August and soon opened trade with the Atakapan and related Indian tribes of this region. He had entered Spanish territory, and the Spanish soon received word of his presence. The Spanish governor ordered a detachment of soldiers to arrest the French. Aided by the Bidai Indians, the Spaniards located the settlement and attacked on October 10. The Frenchmen were imprisoned in Mexico City, where authorities concluded that Blancpain was an agent of the French government. He died in prison in Mexico on March 14, 1756, and the other members of his party were imprisoned in Spain for life. The Spanish established Presidio San Augustin de Ahumada and Mission Nuestra Señora de la Luz on the site of Blancpain's trading post. The complex was destroyed in a 1766 hurricane. One hundred years later the archeological remains of both the French and Spanish settlements were uncovered and were later entered in the National Register of Historic Places.   (Texas Sesquicentennial 1836–1986)

WALLISVILLE (Chambers Co.)   IH 10W, near Wallisville Liberty Rd.
Site of Old Wallisville
Settled in 1825 by Elisha H. R. Wallis, a pioneer from Georgia, on land in grant of Joseph Vehlein, a contractor working to place colonists in Texas. Chambers County was organized in 1858; Wallisville was made county seat. A post office was granted in 1859, and town became a thriving retail market. Many county records were burned in a courthouse fire in 1875. A brick and stone courthouse, with a jail and an unique hanging tower (for executions) was completed in 1886. By 1900 the town had 728 people, a shipyard, a lumber yard, a cotton gin, a skating rink, several stores and an export house. By land, there was daily hack service to Liberty; and sloops

made regular runs from here to Galveston. Chambers County's first newspaper, "Wallisville Age," was published here. The town remained county seat until 1908 when the courthouse was moved to Anahuac after the famous "County Seat Hog War" over issue of letting animals roam at large. In that year Wallisville lost few people, but in 1915 a storm almost destroyed the town. Part of the historic townsite is now included in Wallisville Reservoir, constructed by the United States Army Corps of Engineers.   (1968)

WALNUT SPRINGS (Bosque Co.)   *SH 144 at city park*
Captain J. J. Cureton, C.S.A. (1826–1881)
Indian fighter, lawman and rancher. Settled on the Palo Pinto County frontier, 1854. Led neighbors in defending homes during Indian raids. In 1860 helped rescue Cynthia Ann Parker, who had been taken 24 years before by Comanches. Captain in frontier troops during Civil War, defending Northwest Texas from Indians and northern invasion. Camp Cureton, Archer County C.S.A. outpost, was named for him. Sheriff of Bosque County, 1876–80. Grave is on Flat Top Ranch, near here.

WALNUT SPRINGS (Bosque Co.)   *SH 144 at city park*
James Buckner "Buck" Barry, C.S.A. (1821–1906)
Came to Texas from North Carolina in 1845. Fought in Mexican War and Indian campaigns. In the Civil War, commanded Confederate Cavalry Regiment in Texas outposts from Red River to Fort McKavett. Camps were a day's horseback ride apart. Patrols protected outer settlements and prevented Indian attacks and threatened Federal invasion from Indian Territory. Elected to Texas Legislature 1883. Died on ranch near here. Left personal records of his years in frontier defenses.

WASHINGTON (Washington Co.)   *FM 1155 to PR 12, Washington-on-the-Brazos*
State Historic Site
Washington County
To the memory of those courageous souls, the delegates to the Constitutional Convention held here March 1–17, 1836, who declared Texas free. Organized a Republic, and framed its constitution.

Washington-on-the-Brazos
This village—site of the signing of the Texas Declaration of Independence and first capital of the Republic of Texas—began in 1822 as a ferry crossing. Here the historic La Bahia Road (now Ferry Street) spanned the Brazos River. In 1834 a townsite was laid out and named, probably for Washington, Georgia, home of a leading settler. In 1835, as political differences with Mexico led toward war, the General Council (the Insurgent Texas Government) met in the town. Enterprising citizens then promoted the place as a site for the Convention of 1836 and, as a "bonus," provided a free meeting hall. Thus Texas Declaration of Independence came to be signed in an unfinished building owned by a gunsmith. The provisional government of the Republic was also organized in Washington, but was removed, March 17, as news of the advancing Mexican army caused a general panic throughout the region. The townspeople fled too on March 20, 1836, in the "runaway scrape." After the Texan victory at San Jacinto, the town thrived for a period. It was again Capital of Texas, 1842–1845; and became center of Washington State Park, 1916. It now contains historic buildings and "Barrington," home of Anson Jones, the last president of Texas.   (1969)

Andrew Robinson, Sr.
First settler of Stephen F. Austin's "Old 300" colonists to arrive in Texas. Came November 1821 with his wife Nancy and 2 children. In 1824 he received title to over 9,000 acres of land and was made a captain in the Colonial Militia. The town of Washington was surveyed on his grant and he became a co-founder of it. By 1830 he was operating a ferry at La Bahia crossing as well as a hotel and saloon. In 1835 he fought in the Battle of Gonzales, where his unit first carried into battle the original Lone Star Flag made by Sarah Dodson. He died 1852.   (1965)

WASHINGTON (Washington Co.)   *FM 912, 2 mi. SW*
Washington-on-the-Brazos
This frontier village was the setting for the convention that on March 2, 1836, wrote and signed the immortal Texas Declaration of Independence. In this first capital of the Republic of Texas, the constitution was drawn, the government organized. However, Washington was a target for Santa

Anna's army, and on March 17 the government had to flee. After the Texas victory at San Jacinto, April 21, 1836, Washington was again proposed as capital but Houston was selected instead. In 1842, the Republic's government returned to Washington and remained here during the term of Anson Jones, fourth and last President of Texas. Anson Jones, native of Massachusetts, in 1833 had come to Texas, where he at once began the practice of his profession, medicine. At the Battle of San Jacinto in the Texas Revolution, he took the field as surgeon of the 2nd Regiment. Later he served in the Texas Congress, was minister to the United States, secretary of state, a senator, and finally the president from 1844 to 1846. Upon annexation of Texas to the United States, Dr. Jones retired to Barrington, his plantation near Washington. He died in Houston on January 9, 1858. (1965)

WATER VALLEY (Tom Green Co.) — US 87, in Water Valley Cemetery
World War I Peace Monument
At the close of "The Great War," the citizens of Water Valley wanted to honor those of their community who had served overseas. They were inspired by a small family monument erected on the eastern ridge of Mount McLaughlin in 1902. On Armistice Day, November 11, 1918, at least ten men and a burro named "Come on" climbed the 2,410-foot rise of Mount McLaughlin two miles south of this site. They built five tiers of native fieldstone on the western end of the peak. Designed by local mason Harry Howard, the monument stands 22 feet high and measures 8 feet wide at its base. It bears the names of the Water Valley men who served in World War I: Herschel Ditmore, John Gillespie, Webb Gillespie, Earl Hanson, Chester Harden, Mark Harden, Ollie McCrary, John Runnels, Boone Rainey, Ulysis Rainey, J. H. Ruth, and Mark Trotter. Important facts about the war also are listed. The builders of this monument were Frank Demere, George Demere, Houston Ditmore, Harve Earnest, Will Garner, Pablo Garza, Harry Howard, S. L. Tate, Stanley Turner, and R. R. Wade. The monument continues to honor the heroes of Water Valley. Four of the veterans and five of the builders are interred in the Water Valley Cemetery. (1998)

WAXAHACHIE (Ellis Co.) — US 287, 6 mi. NW
Sardis School
Children of the Sardis community attended school in the Methodist church building from the early 1870s until a small two-room schoolhouse was constructed near this site in 1897. By 1915, the school population had grown such that a larger facility was needed. Over the years, the Sardis school system served as a source of leadership for the community. As the population dwindled and school bus service became available, consolidation with the Waxahachie School District began in 1937 and was completed in 1952. The c. 1915 schoolhouse remains in use as a community center. (Texas Sesquicentennial 1836–1986)

WAXAHACHIE (Ellis Co.) — US 77, 5 mi. N
Ellis County
Created December 20, 1849 from Navarro County. Organized August 5, 1850. Named in honor of Richard Ellis, 1781–1846. A Virginian by birth, and education jurist and statesman of Alabama, 1813–1825. Moved to Texas in 1825. President of the Constitutional Convention, March, 1836. Member, Congress of the Republic of Texas. Waxahachie, the county seat. (1964)

WAXAHACHIE (Ellis Co.) — US 77, 5 mi. N
Parsons' Cavalry, C.S.A.
Originally comprised of men from Ellis and surrounding counties. Organized for Civil War service at Rockett's Spring (4 mi. E of this site), Sept. 1861. Unit was trained and commanded by Col. William H. Parsons, Mexican War veteran, colorful duelist, editor, merchant, and lawyer. In a Confederate Brigade, this unit was joined with 12th, 19th, and 21st Texas Cavalry Regiments, Morgan's Battalion, and Pratt's Battery, to scout and fight in Missouri, Arkansas, Louisiana, and Indian Territory. It was famous for attacks on Federal ironclad ships, Red River Campaign, 1864. (1972)

WAXAHACHIE (Ellis Co.) — 604 W. Main (SH 287)
The Mahoney-Thompson House
Constructed in 1904 by Dennis Mahoney, contractor and builder. He came from Connecticut to Texas in late 1800s to build Trinity University in Waxahachie (now in San Antonio). Cornerstone

was laid March 21, 1902. He later moved to Waxahachie and erected this stately house, which later belonged to family of his son-in-law, W. B. Thompson. The building is now restored by the Ellis County Historical Museum and Art Gallery, Inc. (1969)

WAXAHACHIE (Ellis Co.)   *109 S. Jackson St. at E. Main St. (SH 287), courthouse*

Richard Ellis
By birth and education, a Virginian; through residence, 1813–1825, an Alabama jurist. In that year, Texas claimed him. As president of the Constitutional Convention in 1836 and as a member of the Congress of the young Republic, he steered the helm of state through troubled waters. Nurtured in the culture of the Old South, practiced in the application of the law, he exercised, in behalf of Texas, courage, vision, and leadership. Born February 14, 1781—Died December 20, 1846. "Leaving the old, both worlds at once they view, that stand upon the threshold of the new." (1936)

WAXAHACHIE (Ellis Co.)   *400 blk. E. Main St. (US 287) in Freedman's Memorial Plaza*

Bessie Coleman (1892–1926)
Born in Atlanta, Texas, pioneer aviatrix Bessie Coleman grew up and went to school in a Waxahachie neighborhood a few blocks north of this site. At age 23 she moved to Chicago and first expressed her desire to fly. Since there were no flight schools in this country that would teach African American women, Coleman learned to fly in France and obtained her international pilot's license in 1921. Upon her return to the United States, she was hailed as the first black woman pilot. Extremely popular, "Queen Bess," as she was known, performed as a barnstormer for integrated audiences at air shows and exhibitions around the country before her death in an air accident in Jacksonville, Florida. (2001)

WAXAHACHIE (Ellis Co.)   *US 77, Rogers St. Bridge over Waxahachie Creek*

Rogers Street Bridge
Located on an early Waxahachie Creek fording site that served pioneer settlers of the area, this truss bridge was built in 1889. It was manufactured by the Wrought Iron Bridge Company of Canton, Ohio, and was one of thirteen approved by Ellis County Commissioners from 1888 to 1890. The span provided an extension for Rogers Street, a road named for Emory Rogers, donor of the Waxahachie townsite. As part of an important early north-south commercial route, the Rogers Street Bridge was vital to the growth and development of the city. (1981)

WAYSIDE (Armstrong Co.)   *SH 207, 8 mi. NE in roadside park*

Roadside Park on Hamblen Drive
Named for Will H. Hamblen (1878–1952), who in 1890s pioneered a crude road (about 6 mi. N) into Palo Duro Canyon along old Indian trails. This cut 120 miles off settlers' trips to courthouse in Claude, but was steep and dangerous. Hamblen and his wife, Ada (1883–1955) ranched near Wayside after 1905. He worked unceasingly to get a passable road through Palo Duro. Elected county commissioner in 1928, he at last had a graded road built. By decision of the commissioners' court, this was dedicated in 1930 as Hamblen Drive. With its paving in 1954, a dream of a lifetime was realized. (1968)

WAYSIDE (Roberts Co.)   *SH 70, 6 mi. N of Pampa*

Wayside Community
Settlers came to this locality in 1876. The county was organized in 1889. Pioneer School District No. 5 originated by court order in 1890 to serve this area with schools known as Tallahone, Poole, and Wayside, taught usually in homes. In 1914, Frederic Foster of New York gave this 2-acre school site to the county. The district bought materials, and patrons erected this 28 by 36-foot schoolhouse, painting it red. It soon became the focus for the community—site for elections, church services, and other activities, as well as housing the Wayside School. The trustees in 1914 were James A. Poole, J. M. Story, and Early Talley. Despite enrollment fluctuations caused by drouths, oil booms, and other economic factors, Wayside prided itself on scholastic excellence. Beginning in 1929, high school students were transferred by bus into Pampa, Wayside District paying their tuition. In 1933–1934, all grades were transferred—an arrangement used until 1950, when Wayside consolidated with Pampa. White Deer Land Co., successor to original donor Frederic Foster, then deeded

the red schoolhouse for continuing community use to trustees Paul Caylor, R. E. Montgomery, and J. T. Roberts. Current trustees are C. W. Osborne, J. T. Rogers, and Jack Sloan. (1974)

WEATHERFORD (Parker Co.)
US 180, 10 mi. W
Porter Cemetery (.4 mi. N)
Robert Scott Porter (1795–1877), first Parker County judge, dedicated this land near his cabin as a family cemetery in 1867 after the death of his 3-year-old granddaughter Syrene E. Newberry. Judge Porter's grandson Elbert T. Doss (1847–1869) and the judge's daughter Mary, her husband W. G. Light, and the child were killed by Indians and buried here. This site may contain about 50 burials, but only 28 are identified. The graves of Judge Porter and his wife Nancy Ann (Pearce) (1806–1901) are here. Their daughter Elizabeth Jane Doss Upton (1826–1908) was the last burial. Porter family descendants restored this cemetery in 1976. (1978)

WEATHERFORD (Parker Co.)
US 180 at College Ave.
Weatherford
Founded 1856. Named for Jefferson Weatherford, state senator and a confederate soldier. Frontier people found protection here from constant Indian threat during Civil War. Long the only town between Fort Worth and El Paso. Home of Chandor Gardens and Texas Railroad Museum. Nearby is Double Log Cabin Museum. (1964)

WEATHERFORD (Parker Co.)
Front St., 2 blks. E of N. Main St.
in Greenwood Cemetery
The Dean of Texas Trail Drivers, Oliver Loving (1812–1867)
Founder of three major cattle trails, Oliver Loving came from Kentucky to Texas in 1845 and to Parker County about 1855. During the Civil War (1861–65), he supplied beef to Confederate forces. With Charles Goodnight as partner on a drive to New Mexico, Loving scouted ahead of the cattle, was badly wounded by Indians, lay five days without food before his rescue, and died of gangrene on Sept. 25, 1867. His dying wish was fulfilled when his son Joseph joined Goodnight to bring the body 600 miles by wagon for burial in this county. (1977)

WEATHERFORD (Parker Co.)
SH 171, 12 mi. S
Parsons Station
For more than 100 years, this was the site of the Parsons community, which developed around the homestead and ranch of Amsley Parsons, who came to the area with his family in 1854. Another early settler was Sam B. Kutch; the Kutch and Parsons families intermarried, and it was on Kutch's property that the Gulf, Colorado & Santa Fe rail line crossed on its way from Weatherford to Cresson and Cleburne. The rail line was built through the area in the 1880s. In addition to being a rail stop, Parsons community had a rail switching station and offices for telegraph, Western Union and Wells Fargo services. A post office opened in 1888 under the name Parsons after the originally requested name, Woodstock, was denied by Postal Service officials. The rail stop featured cattle pens for loading livestock of area ranchers onto rail cars that shipped them to Cleburne, from which they could be taken to other markets. Prominent ranch families in the vicinity were McFarland, Eddleman, Woodhouse and Buck, as well as Kutch, Parsons and others. Longtime area residents also remember a school named Paradise and a grocery store. The train that made the trip from Weatherford to Cleburne was known as Old Nancy Hanks, or Old Nancy, reportedly for a famous horse belonging to Abraham Lincoln's mother. Old Nancy was a cattle train, although passengers often hopped aboard for rides. In 1931, the county began construction on what became State Highway 171. The road's completion led to a decline in rail use and the ultimate end to Old Nancy's route, and few relics of the once vital area shipping point and community around Parsons Station remain. (2006)

WEBSTER (Harris Co.)
300 block of E NASA Pkwy. at
Old Galveston Rd., E of SH 3
Contributions to the Texas Rice Industry by Seito and Kiyoaki Saibara
Seito Saibara (1861–1939), former president of Doshisha University in Kyoto, Japan, and first Christian member of the Japanese Diet (parliament), arrived in the United States in 1901 to study theology, and with the desire to establish a Japanese colony in America. Saibara came to Texas in August 1903 at the invitation of the Houston Chamber of Commerce to advise farmers on the cultivation of rice, which was emerging as a major cash crop. He decided rice farming was the ideal

business for a colony, leased this tract of land (which he later purchased), and sent for his family. The oldest son, Kiyoaki Saibara (1884–1972), brought from Japan 300 pounds of Shinriki seed, a variety superior to native rice; and together, father and son planted a field near the canal (½ mile NE). Their first crops were utilized primarily for distribution as seed in Texas and Louisiana. The Saibaras built a house (250 yards S), and several families soon moved here from Japan, but the colonization effort failed because of disillusionment and homesickness of the new colonists. Seito Saibara aided the growth of the Texas rice industry with improved rice strains and agricultural techniques until his death, and Kiyoaki Saibara continued new development until his retirement in 1964.

(1974)

WECHES (Houston Co.)
SH 21, 4 mi. NE
Mission Santíssimo Nombre de María
Was founded in this vicinity summer 1690 on the banks of El San Miguel (Neches) River. Erected A. D. 1934 by De Zavala Chapter Texas Historical and Landmarks Association.

WECHES (Houston Co.)
SH 21 at entrance to Mission Tejas
State Historical Park
Mission San Francisco de los Tejas
First Spanish Mission in East Texas. Established in 1690 by Franciscan friars to convert the Tejas Indians. "Tejas", a Spanish rendition of the Indian word for "friend", was in time adopted as the state name. The founding party was led by Capt. Alonso de León, a veteran explorer making his fifth journey into Texas. He was to see if the Tejas desired a mission and to find any remaining threat of the Frenchman La Salle's expedition of 1685. Finding none, De León proceeded to this site. As the Tejas were willing to accept missionaries, he built a dwelling and church of rough-hewn logs near a brook. The church was dedicated on June 1, 1690. Leaving father Damian Massanet in charge, De León departed on July 4. Three years later, however, the mission was empty. Lack of sufficient defense, the isolated location, epidemics and the insincerity of the Indians (who took the Spaniard's gifts but not their religion) contributed to its failure. In 1693 it was abandoned, although later twice re-established and renamed. In spite of this, Spanish officials were inspired by the Tejas effort to make long-range plans for future expeditions, which marked the beginning of the Spanish mission and colonization movement in Texas.

(1968)

WECHES (Houston Co.)
SH 21 at entrance to Mission Tejas
State Historical Park
The Joseph R. Rice Log Cabin
Joseph Redmond Rice (1805–1866) cut timber, then his young wife, Willie Masters Rice (1809–1881), snaked the logs to a homesite 16 miles southwest of here. The cabin they built was a noted way-station on the San Antonio Road. They brought up nine children, enlarging their cabin several times. After a grandson built a frame home in 1919, the old cabin became a farm storage shed. The Texas Centennial Commission in 1936 marked its history, and in 1973 it was given to the state of Texas and moved here for restoration and exhibition.

(1976)

WECHES (Houston Co.)
CR 1580 off SH 21 at entrance to Weches Cemetery
Community of Weches
Located near the site of 17th-century Spanish missionary activity, this farming community had its beginnings with the settlement of the McLean, Conners, Patton, and Gregg families, who had all arrived in the area by 1840. Originally known as Neches for the nearby river, the similar name Weches was adopted in 1887 when post office officials informed residents that "Neches" had been assigned to another community. The following year Alfred Monroe Gregg set aside land for a church, school, and cemetery. The Weches post office closed in 1939.

(Texas Sesquicentennial 1836–1986)

WECHES (Houston Co.)
SH 21, 1 mi. SW
Weches CCC Camp
Weches Camp P-58-T was established by the Federal Civilian Conservation Corps (CCC) in June 19, 1933. Manned by Company 888, the Weches camp was the first CCC camp established in Houston County. It contained barracks, a mess hall, recreation area, post office and medical infirmary. Camp enrollees helped restore and develop the Davy Crockett National Forest and the

Historic 118-acre San Francisco Mission State Forest. They planted trees, built roads, developed park facilities and erected log structures and fire observation towers. The camp closed in November 1935.   (1994)

WEIMAR (Colorado Co.)   *US 90 at post office*
Town of Weimar
This land—once part of first Anglo-American Colony in Texas—grew into a townsite in 1873 with coming of the Galveston, Harrisburg, & San Antonio Rail Line. D. W. Jackson donated half of land for town, which was named for Weimar, Germany. Post office was established in 1873. Town incorporated 1875. By 1887 Weimar was enjoying a prosperous cotton economy, had many stores and 2 newspapers. Local opera house (150 yds. S), built about 1880, was one of the first between Houston and San Antonio. Present economy is based on agriculture. Population is 2,050.   (1970)

WELLINGTON (Collingsworth Co.)   *US 83, about 8 mi. N in roadside park*
Rocking Chair "Ranche" (1883–1893)
Owned by Scottish Earls of Aberdeen and Tweedmouth. The headquarters were at Aberdeen (about 7 mi. NE). Starting with 14,745 cattle, the Rocking Chair made profits for a few years, then failed. In north part of county are hills bearing its name. Also, town of Wellington was given that name at wish of Rocking Chair owners, who had a kinsman die at Waterloo where he was aide to the Duke of Wellington. W. E. Hughes in 1893 bought the land and added it to Mill Iron Ranch. Later the 235 sections were sold to others, to convert to farms and smaller ranches.   (1970)

WELLINGTON (Collingsworth Co.)   *US 83, 6 mi. N at Collingsworth County*
Pioneers Park
The Red River Plunge of Bonnie and Clyde
On June 10, 1933, Mr. and Mrs. Sam Pritchard and family saw from their home on the bluff (west) the plunge of an auto into Red River. Rescuing the victims, unrecognized as Bonnie Parker and Clyde and Buck Barrow, they sent for help. Upon their arrival, the local sheriff and police chief were disarmed by Bonnie Parker. Buck Barrow shot Pritchard's daughter while crippling the family car to halt pursuit. Kidnapping the officers, the gangsters fled. Bonnie and Clyde were fated to meet death in 1934. In this quiet region, the escapade is now legend.   (1975)

WELLINGTON (Collingsworth Co.)   *US 83, 2 mi. N*
Collingsworth County
Formed from Young and Bexar Territories. Created August 21, 1876. Organized November 4, 1890. Named in honor of James Collinsworth, 1806–1838, the first Chief Justice of the Republic of Texas. Signer of the Declaration of Independence at the Battle of San Jacinto. Secretary of State in Burnet's Cabinet. Wellington, the County Seat.   (1964)

WELLINGTON (Collingsworth Co.)   *US 83, 2 mi. S*
Capt. Randolph Marcy's Exploration Route
through Collingsworth County
In 1852, Capt. R. B. Marcy led a survey expedition along the Red River to document the river's channel and related streams. The team, which included Capt. G. B. McLellan of the Corps of Engineers, entered the Texas panhandle June 10, 1852 and arrived in what is now Collingsworth County on July 7. Traveling eastward through the southern part of the county, the team identified the sources and route of the Red River. The team left Texas north of Dodson and returned to Fort Arbuckle in present Oklahoma. Their survey later proved important in settling a boundary dispute between Texas and Oklahoma.   (2006)

WELLS (Cherokee Co.)   *US 69 in Wells*
Falvey Memorial United Methodist Church
In the late 1860s or early 1870s, Republic of Texas Army veteran James H. Bowman offered one hundred acres of land to the Rev. W. D. Lewis, Sr., of nearby Barsola, on the condition that he move to the Mt. Hope community for the purpose of establishing a Methodist church. The Rev. Mr. Lewis accepted the offer, and the Mt. Hope Methodist Episcopal Church, South, was organized by 1875. The Wells community was established in 1885 as the Kansas and Gulf Short Line Railroad was built through the area to the south of Mt. Hope. It was named for Major E. H. Wells, a railroad

engineer. Dr. J. C. Falvey and his wife, Matilda Falvey, settled in Wells that year. They joined the Mt. Hope Methodist congregation after it relocated to Wells in 1888. The congregation soon built a parsonage behind the new church. The church was a focal point for area Methodist pioneers. This congregation prospered for the remainder of the 19th century and well into the 20th. From 1948 to 1950 a new church building was constructed on this site in honor of Dr. J. C. and Mrs. Matilda Falvey by their son. The Falvey Memorial Methodist Church was dedicated in 1951. Active in the Mt. Hope and Wells communities from its earliest days, Falvey Memorial United Methodist Church continues to serve the area with programs of worship and service. These include ecumenical gatherings, such as a Bible reading marathon and Easter sunrise services at Mt. Hope Cemetery Tabernacle, as well as community outreach. Falvey Memorial United Methodist Church continues in the traditions of its founders. (2000)

WESLACO (Hidalgo Co.)
2415 E. US 83 Bus.
Camp Llano Grande
Occupied in 1916–1917 by Indiana, Nebraska, Minnesota, and North Dakota National Guard units, Camp Llano Grande was one of a line of encampments established along the Rio Grande in response to Mexican bandit raids into the U.S. Covering over 200 acres, it included a headquarters building, commissary, and recreational facilities. South of the railroad tracks were parade grounds, tent encampments, and stock pens. The camp was abandoned in March 1917, one month before the U.S. entered World War I, and former Llano Grande troops were called for war service in France.
(Texas Sesquicentennial 1836–1986)

WESLACO (Hidalgo Co.)
US 83, 1.5 mi. E, A&M Experiment Station
(inside building)
Citrus Fruit Developed in Rio Grande Valley—Red-Meat Grapefruit
Unique and colorful product of saline-alkaline soil of Rio Grande Valley of Texas. Bred of Thompson pink wood budded on sour orange rootstock. Two nurserymen, A. E. Henninger of Mission and Dr. J. R. Webb of Donna, discovered red fruit in their orchards in 1929. They cast lots and Henninger won right to get a patent. He named his variety "Ruby Red," and was issued U.S. Plant Patent No. 53. Dr. Webb's new strain, "Red Blush," is equally popular. Both varieties, with rose-colored meat and red-tinged rinds, are sweet, early, delectable fruits. (1966)

WEST (McLennan Co.)
IH 35 N access road between
Mangrum and Wiggins Sts.
The Crash at Crush (.5 mi. E)
A head-on collision between two locomotives was staged on Sept. 15, 1896, as a publicity stunt for the Missouri, Kansas & Texas Railroad. Over 30,000 spectators gathered at the crash site, named "Crush" for MKT passenger agent William G. Crush, who conceived the idea. About 4 P.M. the trains were sent speeding toward each other. Contrary to mechanics' predictions, the steam boilers exploded on impact, propelling pieces of metal into the crowd. Two persons were killed and many others injured, including Jarvis Deane of Waco, who was photographing the event. (1976)

WEST COLUMBIA (Brazoria Co.)
SH 36, 1 mi. NW
W. H. Abrams Well No. 1
In 1920, Texas & Pacific Railway official William H. Abrams (1843–1926) of Dallas owned this old plantation land, then considered fit only for pasture. He leased minerals rights to the Texas Company (now Texaco, Inc.), whose drilling reached a climax on July 20, 1920. At 7:45 that evening a massive jet of oil and gas erupted from a 2,754-foot depth, heralding a major discovery now known as West Columbia Field. W. H. Abrams No. 1 was a gusher. Three pipe lines were laid at once to draw the oil to earthen tanks, filled by powerful steam pumps with over 20,000 barrels daily. For Abrams, this wildcat well was a second bonus, as land he owned in Mitchell County produced the first oil in the Permian Basin in June 1920. Locally, land that sold for 10¢ an acre in 1840 and $5 an acre in 1888 now brought $96,000 an acre for mineral rights, irrespective of surface values. Yet the boom days were hazardous. Brazoria County oldtimers suffered along with oilfield workers, all living precariously and dangerously until the flow of oil money led to better schools, roads and general social conditions. Half a century later, the socio-economic significance of the West Columbia discovery could be acknowledged as a nationwide contribution. (1977)

WEST COLUMBIA (Brazoria Co.)   *FM 2852, Varner-Hogg Plantation State Historic Site*

The "Varner," 1835

Last home of James Stephen Hogg, first native Texan to be elected governor. Located on an 1824 Spanish land grant made to Martin Varner. House built by sugar planter C. R. Patton. Restored 1920. Given to the state, 1958, by Miss Ima Hogg. Awarded Medallion Plate.   (1964)

WEST COLUMBIA (Brazoria Co.)   *142 N. 14th St., just off E. Brazos Ave. (SH 35)*

Near Site of the First Capitol of the Republic of Texas

About 1833 Leman Kelsey built a story-and-a-half clapboard structure near this location. When Columbia became capital of the Republic of Texas in 1836, the building was one of two which housed the newly formed government. The first Republic of Texas Congress convened in Columbia. Here Sam Houston took office as President and Stephen F. Austin as Secretary of State. In 1837, the government moved to Houston. The 1900 storm destroyed the original capitol. The replica at this site was built in 1976–1977.   (1979)

WEST COLUMBIA (Brazoria Co.)   *SH 35 at E. Bernard St.*

Columbia

In September 1836 Columbia, now known as West Columbia, became capital of the Republic of Texas. This took place with the removal of the ad interim government here from Velasco. After the election called by ad interim President David G. Burnet, the first permanent government of the Republic went into operation here in Columbia in October. Inaugurated were President Sam Houston and Vice-President Mirabeau B. Lamar. Under their leadership the first duly elected Congress convened and the first Constitution of the Republic was ratified. Citizens of this vicinity served the Republic. Henry Smith of nearby Brazoria prior to this time had been the first Anglo-American governor of Texas, in the 1835–36 Revolutionary provisional government. In President Houston's cabinet he was secretary of the treasury. Stephen F. Austin, colonizer and Father of Texas, was secretary of state; under the heavy demands of that office, his health broke and he died here on December 27, 1836. In April 1837 at the wish of President Houston, the seat of government was moved to more adequate quarters in the city of Houston.   (1965)

WEST COLUMBIA (Brazoria Co.)   *SH 36, .5 mi. S*

Site of the Home of Josiah Hughes Bell, 1791–1838

One of the "Old Three Hundred" who came to Texas with Stephen F. Austin in 1821. First Alcalde of Austin's colony. On this tract of 6,642 acres, granted him in 1824, was later built the Town of Columbia, first Capital of the Republic.   (1964)

WEST POINT (Fayette Co.)   *SH 71, 1.5 mi. W*

Site of Woods' Fort

Used by colonists of this vicinity as a protection against Indian attacks, 1828–1842. Fortified residence of Zadock Woods, veteran of the War of 1812. One of the old "Three Hundred" of Austin's colonists. Oldest man killed in the "Dawson Massacre" September 18, 1842.

WESTBROOK (Mitchell Co.)   *IH 20, 2 mi. W in roadside park*

Discovery Well of the Permian Basin

The first commercial discovery oil well in the Permian Basin was named for W. H. Abrams, leasing agent for the Texas and Pacific land trust. The well first produced oil in February 1920 at a depth of 450 feet; but in June 1920, a better showing of oil was found at 2345–2410 feet. On July 16, 1920, the well was "shot" with nitroglycerin. As a crowd of 2,000 people looked on, a great eruption of oil, gas, water, and smoke shot from the mouth of the well almost to the top of the derrick. Shortly after, the well flowed at a rate of 129 barrels daily, but soon settled down to 20 barrels per day. From this well and a well nearby the Rio Grande Oil Company laid the first commercial oil pipeline in the Permian Basin. The first load of oil went through the pipeline on April 3, 1922. W. H. Abrams No. 1 was redesignated on May 1, 1968 as Westbrook southeast unit No. 701, formed to increase oil recovery from the Westbrook oil field by water flooding. This enhanced oil recovery technique has produced 67 million barrels of the more than 100 million barrels of oil recovered

from this field. Designated as major fields, only a small number produce 100 million barrels of oil or more. Fifty-six major fields are located in the Permian Basin, the fourth largest oil producing area in the U.S.
(1996)

WESTHOFF (DeWitt Co.)   *US 87 right-of-way*
Westhoff
Founded 1906 as Bello ("Beautiful View"), tent city of workers building Texas & New Orleans Railroad. Renamed 1909 for Wm. Westhoff (Aug. 8, 1831–March 19, 1911), local merchant and political leader. For a time town had 3 cotton gins, 13 stores. It remains a farming-ranching-uranium leasing center, inhabited by many ethnic groups.
(1970)

WESTHOFF (DeWitt Co.)   *US 87, SE at Church Road*
George Lord
George Lord was born in Essex County, England on April 21, 1816 to Felstead and Anna Siggs Lord. He immigrated to Canada in 1834 and worked there for two years. He then moved to New Orleans and joined other volunteers under a Capt. Lyons to serve in the military of the young Republic of Texas. They arrived in Galveston in 1837. As part of the Texan Army, Lord participated in a number of operations, including suppression of the Córdova Rebellion (1838) and the fight against Manuel Flores (1839). He also fought in Mexico with the Federalists before returning to Texas. He joined the Somervell Expedition to expel forces of Gen. Adrián Woll from the Republic, fighting at the Battle of Salado Creek (1842) with many notable Texas figures like John C. "Jack" Hays and William "Bigfoot" Wallace. Lord was among those who then followed Col. William Fisher into Mexico. Fisher's men were captured after fighting at Mier, and as part of the infamous "Black Bean Incident," ten percent were executed while the others remained imprisoned. Lord was not selected for execution; he survived the harsh conditions at Mexico's Perote Prison, returned to Texas and fought in the Mexican War as a Ranger. In 1849, Lord accompanied Jack Hays and others to California during the Gold Rush. Along the way, he wed Catherine "Kate" Myers (1832–1909) in Eagle Pass, Texas. The couple spent three years mining for gold; Kate sold pies to other miners while her husband collected gold dust. They returned to Texas with $7,000 worth of gold and settled near this site in DeWitt County, where they established a longhorn cattle ranch and reared 11 children. Lord died while working in his garden in 1895. Today, he is remembered as a Texas patriot.
(2004)

WESTPHALIA (Falls Co.)   *SH 320 at CR 379*
Frank and Julia Bockholt Home
The Johann and Theresia Bockholt family settled in this area in 1881. In 1933, their son Frank and his wife, Julia, inherited a portion of the estate. Both were active in community life, and he is remembered for his musical talent and his 52 years as organist at the Church of the Visitation. They built on to an existing two-room house at this site in 1912 and reared their large family here. The American Four Square design exhibits a transition between Craftsman and late Victorian styling, and the home retains its original detailing.
(2003)

WHARTON (Wharton Co.)   *101 W. Burleson, courthouse*
Wharton
The town of Wharton was founded as the seat of Wharton County in April 1846. Land for a courthouse, named Monterey Square, was given from the land grant of William Kincheloe, one of Stephen F. Austin's "Old Three Hundred" colonists who settled in this area in 1822. The townsite was surveyed by Virgel Stewart and William J. E. Heard, and the rich farmland attracted many settlers. The advent of railroads and irrigation brought increased settlement to the town, which remains a center of agricultural, educational, industrial, and medical services for a large area. (1986)

WHARTON (Wharton Co.)   *101 W. Burleson, courthouse*
Wharton County
Created April 3, 1846 from Matagorda, Jackson and Colorado Counties, organized same year. Named for William H. Wharton, 1806–1839, Texas Minister to the United States, 1836–1837, and his brother, John A. Wharton, 1809–1838, Adjutant at San Jacinto. Member of Congress of the Republic of Texas, 1837–1838. Wharton, the county seat.

WHEELER (Wheeler Co.)
US 83 at courthouse
Wheeler County
Formed from Young and Bexar Territories. Created August 21, 1876. Organized April 12, 1879. Named in honor of Royal T. Wheeler, 1810–1864. Associate Justice of the Supreme Court of Texas, 1844–1858; Chief Justice, 1858–1864. County seat, Mobeetie, 1879–1906. Wheeler since.

WHITE DEER (Carson Co.)
US 60, city limits
Last Great Panhandle Cattle Drive to Montana
Each spring and summer after 1880, many Texas herds went up the trail to northern states for fattening. For the cowboys, trail drives meant hard work. They had to turn stampedes, ford rivers and quicksand streams, and fight Indians and cattle thieves. They endured hunger, thirst, and other physical hardships. The last great Texas Panhandle drive was organized here at N Bar N (N - N) headquarters. Ranch manager was J.L. Harrison; trail boss, T.L. (Tom) Coffee. 100 cowboys drove 10 herds, each with 2500 cattle, or a total of 25,000 beeves, to Montana from April to September 1892. The cattle belonged to Niedringhaus brothers, German tinsmiths of St. Louis, who put into ranching a fortune made in enamel granite household wares. From 1882 to 1886, N Bar N leased range in Carson and neighboring counties from the Francklyn Land & Cattle Company, a British syndicate backed by Cunard Steamship Line. Afterward this range belonged to White Deer Land Company. The N Bar N outfit left here because White Deer Land Company wanted the range cleared of large herds. By 1907, the 650,000 acres of its land was offered for sale to small ranchers and farmers. It was fenced and the steam plow introduced to turn the rich, grassy sod.   (1965)

WHITE DEER (Carson Co.)
SH 60 at Main
Jackson General Store
This commercial structure was built at the original townsite of White Deer (0.5 mi. E). It was moved here in 1908, when the present townsite was established. It housed the general merchandise business of J. C. Jackson (d. 1966), a prominent leader in the development of White Deer. In his career as a public servant, Jackson was mayor, postmaster, county judge (1935–41), and precinct commissioner (1947–66). In addition, he and his wife Dolly (d. 1957) were founders of the First Presbyterian Church. The Jacksons maintained their home in the general store building for many years.   (Texas Sesquicentennial 1836–1986)

WHITEFLAT (Motley Co.)
SH 70 right-of-way
Whiteflat
This area of Motley County was first called "White Flat" due to the tall white needlegrass which covered the flat prairie land. A post office, named Whiteflat, was established for the rural settlement in 1890 at the request of W. R. Tilson. At its height, the community boasted four grocery stores, three service stations, three garages, two cafes, a hardware store, two gins, and three churches. A school, first housed in a one-room schoolhouse built by volunteers, opened in 1890. It was replaced by a four-room school in 1908, and in 1922 a new two-story brick structure was erected. It also served as a community gathering place. Dependent on an economy based on agriculture and small family farms, the community began to decline as a result of the depression and dust bowl years of the 1930s. The Whiteflat school closed in 1946, when it was consolidated with Matador Schools. The local churches disbanded in the 1960s; the post office closed in 1966 following the death of the last postmaster, Ida Morris; and the last remaining retail business, a grocery store and service station, closed in 1968.   (1991)

WHITESBORO (Grayson Co.)
SH 56, 5 mi. E
Sanborn Ranch
Established in late 1870's by H. B. Sanborn, one of the major promoters of barbed wire. Ranch (a showplace) was first large area in Texas to be fenced with barbed wire—a model demonstration project, contributing to decline of open-range West. In 1888, Sanborn founded City of Amarillo and thereafter sold ranch.   (1967)

WHITESBORO (Grayson Co.)
SH 56, near water well, Main St.
Whitesboro
Settlers moved to this site after Ambrose B. White (1811–1883) camped here on his way west from Illinois in 1848. His inn here was on the Butterfield Stage Route after 1858. The post office,

opened in 1860, was named for White, who surveyed (1869) the townsite with Dr. W. H. Trolinger (1827–1895), donor of land for a park. When Whitesboro incorporated in 1873, White was elected its first mayor. The Denison & Pacific Railroad, later part of the Missouri, Kansas, & Texas, arrived in 1879; The Texas & Pacific in 1881. Today the area's economy is based on recreational facilities and peanut production.   (1975)

WHITESBORO (Grayson Co.)   *SH 56, 1 mi. W*
Diamond Horse Ranch
Diamond Horse Ranch, founded 1850 by James R. and John Diamond. Joined later by their brother, George, who had founded paper that today is Houston "Post." Station 1858–1861, on Butterfield Stage Line. The Diamond brothers were political leaders and active in Texas frontier defense and Masonry. James is buried here.

WHITEWRIGHT (Grayson Co.)   *US 69 at FM 151*
Whitewright
Early settlers in this part of Grayson County established communities at Orangeville (4 mi. E), Pilot Grove (4 mi. S), and Kentucky Town (3 mi. W). In 1878, after the Missouri, Kansas, and Texas (MKT) railroad built a line southeast from Denison to this site, a new town was created and named for William Whitewright (1825–1898), a railroad official and vice president of the Union Trust Company of New York, the railroad's financial backer. Immediately upon the new town's founding, former citizens of Orangeville, Pilot Grove, and Kentucky Town moved to Whitewright. A post office was established in 1878, along with numerous homes and businesses. By 1894 the town boasted schools, churches, a newspaper, a college, and community organizations, as well as railroad depots, cotton gins, restaurants, drugstores, grocery stores, wagon yards and livery stables, lumberyards, hardware stores, blacksmith shops, and numerous other businesses. Serious fires in 1904 and 1911 almost destroyed the central business district, but the citizens soon rebuilt. The city of Whitewright no longer has passenger rail service, but it continues its role as an important marketing center for this area of Grayson County.   (1992)

WHITEWRIGHT (Grayson Co.)   *SH 11, 3 mi. W*
Kentucky Town
When first settled in 1830s was known as Annaliza. Renamed by Kentucky emigrants in 1858. Unique layout gave town protection against Indian attacks. On freight and stage routes. "Sacred Harp," a robust frontier gospel style of singing and composition, began here. During Civil War was Quantrill Gang rendezvous.   (1965)

WHITEWRIGHT (Grayson Co.)   *SH 160, 3.5 mi. S*
Bethel Baptist Church
This congregation grew from an early prayer group, established in the Bethel Community in 1875. A small group met in the schoolhouse, which also served as a community center, for weekly prayer and Bible study. On April 16, 1884, nine men and women met to organize the Bethel Baptist Church. These charter members were Mr. and Mrs. J. P. Autrey, Mr. and Mrs. B. F. Blanton, Mr. and Mrs. J. F. Holland, Mr. and Mrs. E. F. Jones, and Mrs. Sarah Miller. The Rev. Bob Thomas served as first pastor. The small congregation grew rapidly and soon had more than 150 members. In 1897, this property was deeded to Bethel Baptist Church by Mr. and Mrs. J. P. Autrey. In the same year, during the pastorate of J. M. Harder, a one-room sanctuary was constructed. A 1918 storm damaged the building, but it was repaired and the congregation continued to worship there until another was constructed in 1937. Throughout its history, Bethel Baptist Church has served as a focal point for the small community. The congregation continues to maintain the ideals and traditions of its pioneer founders.   (1984)

WHITNEY (Hill Co.)   *SH 22, N of S. San Jacinto St.*
Whitney Memorial Park
The construction of Whitney Dam caused the creation of this cemetery in 1950 for the reinterment of 1260 graves from six historic cemeteries in Hill and Bosque counties. Before Lake Whitney inundated several pioneer cemeteries, all of the gravesites and monuments were moved here and placed on nearly 24 acres purchased for the Brazos Valley graves. The Captain Wilson Cemetery was originally located about six miles southwest of Whitney and named for Civil War veteran

and politician J. M. C. Wilson. The earliest documented burial was from 1857. The Walling Bend Cemetery, dating from 1863, was named for Jesse Walling, who served in the Texas legislature. The two Schuler place cemeteries were located on the Bosque County side of Lake Whitney, and contained 14 graves, many of the Basye Family. The cemetery that served the Towash community was located about five miles west of Whitney. The earliest known burial was that of A. J. and J. J. Dyer in 1864. Their descendants included a member of the Texas Legislature, the first chief justice of Hill County and owners of a flour and grist mill. The DeGraffenreid graveyard, located about three miles west of Whitney, was the largest of the six cemeteries moved with 685 graves. (1996)

WHITSETT (Live Oak Co.)   US 281 at FM 99
Town of Whitsett
Situated on 1835 land grant of Mexico to John Houlihan. At this site in 1800s was water and a camp for cross-country drives of cattle hogs. Town arose in 1913 when San Antonio, Uvalde & Gulf Railroad was built and post office opened. Named for ranch family donating right-of-way and townsite. Soon shipped steers by thousands to Northern markets. International fame began 1924 when H. A. Coffey acquired 125 bee colonies, bred and sold queens. Besides beekeeping, area has oil and uranium production, farming, horse and cattle ranching, rock-gems and game hunting, fishing. (1973)

WICHITA FALLS (Wichita Co.)   US 281, 1.7 mi. S
Wichita County
Formed from Young Land District. Created February 1, 1858. Organized June 21, 1882. Named for the Wichita Indians who formerly resided here. County seat, Wichita Falls.

WICHITA FALLS (Wichita Co.)   US 287 at 8th St.
Wichita Falls Bank Robbery of 1896
On the afternoon of February 25, 1896, two cowboys, Foster Crawford and Elmer "Kid" Lewis, robbed the City National Bank, then located at Ohio and 7th Street (2 blocks east). They killed cashier Frank Dorsey, took about $410 cash, and fled on horseback. A posse of citizens and Texas Rangers captured the pair that night hiding in a thicket outside of town. The next day, after the Rangers departed, the anger of the townspeople turned to violence. On the night of February 26, a mob dragged the prisoners from the jail and lynched them in front of the bank building. (1978)

WILLIS (Montgomery Co.)   SH 75, south edge of Willis
Willis
Founded in 1870. Named for P. J. and R. S. Willis (large land and timber owners who formerly were merchants in area). They gave townsite, on the Houston & Great Northern Railroad. With the line came prosperity, and in 1874 Willis and Montgomery vied for county seat, but both eventually lost to Conroe. Willis boasted a college, opera house, numerous stores; and by 1895 had vast tobacco fields supporting 7 cigar factories. This industry faded when tariff on Cuban tobacco was lifted. Present industries are timber and livestock. (1970)

WILLS POINT (Van Zandt Co.)   SH 64 at CR 3415
Dallas–Shreveport Road
A trail established by Caddoan Native Americans and later used by French traders who traversed this area is known today as the Dallas–Shreveport Road. The trail emerged in the mid-1830s as a main route into North Texas for emigrants and cargo from the river port of Shreveport, Louisiana. Van Zandt County's first courthouse was built along the route at Jordan's Saline in 1848. Used extensively for troop movements during the Civil War, the route remained active with emigrants and ox teams into the 1900s. The route has greatly influenced settlement patterns in this area. (1995)

WILLS POINT (Van Zandt Co.)   SH 64 at CR 3415
County Seat War
Due to a surveyor's error, the county seat of Van Zandt County was located on private property in 1850. An election was called 27 years later because of discontent with the site. On May 28, 1877, County Judge Cadwell Walton Raines ordered court records moved to Wills Point from Canton. Many citizens objected, and about 200 armed men from around Canton marched on Wills Point. Governor R.B. Hubbard assigned militia troops to maintain order and fighting was

averted. The records were returned in October 1878 and the county seat ultimately remained in Canton.
(1997)

WILLS POINT (Van Zandt Co.) — *SH 64 at CR 3415*
William A. Wills

Tennessee native William A. Wills (1804–1864) moved to Texas with his wife, Mary Ann "Polly" (Phillips), and their children in 1847 and settled on the Dallas-Shreveport Road in what became Van Zandt County. They hosted many travelers in their home. In 1850, Wills served the county as tax assessor-collector and later held other public offices, including road overseer and Van Zandt County commissioner. As early as 1855, references in commissioners court minutes referred to the area surrounding his property as "Wills Point." When the town was laid out along the Texas and Pacific Railroad in 1873, it became known by the same name. Wills is buried in the White Rose Cemetery.
(2001)

WILSON (Lynn Co.) — *FM 211, west of town in roadside park*
Site of Mackenzie Cavalry Camp

At or near this spot, Colonel Ranald S. Mackenzie, with two companies of United States 4th Cavalry, was overtaken on Dec. 4, 1874, by a snowstorm. Forced to spend the night here without wood or water, or grass for the horses, troops called this the most miserable night of their duty in the Southwest. Several horses froze to death. Mackenzie was hunting here for straggling Indians, during last weeks of 1874 campaign to confine tribes to reservations. On Dec. 5 his troops reached Tahoka Lake, where they found shelter under a cliff.
(1967)

WILSON (Lynn Co.) — *FM 211, west of town in roadside park*
Spanish Explorers' Route

A prehistoric road discovered and used by Indians, Spaniards, United States Army units, and cattle drovers. It crossed the Llano Estacado from Gholson Spring (7 mi. E of present-day Slaton), to Tahoka Lake (3 mi. S of Wilson), then to Tobacco Creek, Big Spring, and the North Concho. Here passed many 17th century Spanish visitors: Father Salas, coming from New Mexico in 1629 on pleas of Jumano Indians to preach to them; Captains Hernan Martin and Diego del Castillo, exploring in 1650; Captain Diego de Guadalajara, seeking pearls and other treasure, in 1654.
(1967)

WIMBERLEY (Hays Co.) — *RM 12 at River Road*
Wimberley Mills

In 1848 William C. Winters (1809–1864), a veteran of San Jacinto, came to this valley and built a grist mill and sawmill on Cypress Creek. A settlement called Winters' Mill soon emerged from the wilderness. After a flood destroyed the millhouse about 1856, Winters moved to higher ground across the creek and built a new 2-story millhouse with a long millrace and tailrace. After Winters' death in 1864, his son-in-law John M. Cude operated the mill successfully and the village came to be called Cude's Mill. Pleasant Wimberley (1823–1919) in 1874 bought the mill complex which included a stone flour mill, French buhrstone grist mill, sawmill, shingle mill, and a one-stand cotton gin, powered by a 21-inch turbine type waterwheel. The "Wimberley Mills" Post Office, opened in 1880, soon was renamed "Wimberley." A short supply of cypress wood in the early 1880s caused the shingle mill to close. In 1893 the flour mill shut down. Because of the diminishing flow of Cypress Creek, the operation was converted to steam power in 1900 and the millhouse was rebuilt in order to continue in operation. The milling enterprise was abandoned in 1934, after over 85 years of service on Cypress Creek.
(1974)

WIMBERLEY (Hays Co.) — *RM 12 at River Rd.*
Winters-Wimberley House

William Carvin Winters (1809–1864) and his wife Lavinia Winters (1805–1891) came to Texas from Tennessee in 1834, along with other members of his family. William and his brothers, James Washington and John Frelan, fought in the Battle of San Jacinto, where William was severely wounded. William became a noted woodcarver and furniture craftsman in Walker County and in Seguin. The Winters family eventually settled in Hays County. William and Lavinia arrived between 1853 and 1855 and he built a mill on Cypress Creek in 1856. The mill became the economic hub of the village, which took on the name Winters' Mill. William built a homestead on this site in

1857–1858. From here he could survey his sawmill and gristmill with its power source, Cypress Creek. One of the first stone houses in the area, the Winters house boasted 18-inch thick limestone walls. After William's death, his daughter Nancy and her husband John Cude took over the mill and the village became known as Cude's Mill. They sold the mill and family home to Pleasant and Amanda Wimberley in 1874. With their son Zachary, the Wimberleys expanded their business to include the production of flour and sorghum molasses as well as a cotton gin. The village name soon changed to Wimberleyville, later Wimberley. Zachary Wimberley's son-in-law, John Will Pyland, lived in the homestead and kept the mill in business until 1925. The evolution of the house, with its various alterations and additions, reflects the changing needs of the families who occupied it. A village landmark for generations, the Winters-Wimberley house remained with Wimberley family descendants until the 1990s. (1999)

WINDOM (Fannin Co.)
FM 1743, 3 mi. S
The Sam Rayburn Homesite
Samual Taliaferro Rayburn (1882–1961), son of William Marion and Martha (Waller) Rayburn, was born in Tennessee; moved to Texas, 1887. Educated at East Texas State University and the University of Texas Law School, became lawmaker: Texas House of Representatives, 1906–1913 (House Speaker, 1911–1913), United States Congress, 1913–1961. World famous as Speaker, United States House of Representatives, 17 years, in terms of Presidents F. D. Roosevelt, Harry S Truman, Dwight Eisenhower, J. F. Kennedy. His homesite (1887–1912) was half a mile south of this marker. (1972)

WINDTHORST (Archer Co.)
SH 16 at Prideaux Rd., 10 mi. S via US 281
West Fork School
Begun in the early 1880s as the Baggett School, taught by landowner Silas Baggett, the West Fork School served students in this rural region for more than 60 years. In order to remain in the center of a dispersed agricultural community, the two-room school building was moved twice: once in 1886, when it was renamed New Hope, and again in the 1920s to this site, where it was called West Fork. By 1944, enrollment had declined to six children, and the school was closed. Students were reassigned to school in Antelope. The building was relocated to Archer City, where it served as a residence until it burned some years later. (2002)

WINDTHORST (Archer Co.)
SH 16 at Prideaux Rd., 10 mi. S via US 281
The Stone Houses
Named for shapes resembling teepees; an Indian ceremonial ground, yielding war paint. In famed "Battle of Stone Houses," Nov. 10, 1837, Lt. A. Van Benthousen and 18 Rangers (hunting stolen horses) were attacked 1.5 miles west of here by 150 Keechis. Ten Rangers and 50 Indians died in 3-hour battle. Indians fired the grass. Rangers lost their horses but escaped through a ravine and walked back to settlements. In 1874, area's first permanent home was built near the stone houses (and 5 mi. W of here) by English-born Dr. R. O. Prideaux (1884–1930), who helped organize this county. (1970)

WINDTHORST (Archer Co.)
US 281, 4.5 mi. S
Marcy Trail
Mapped 1849 by U.S. Army Capt. Randolph B. Marcy. Used for California gold rush; export of buffalo hides; West Texas settlers; cattle drives; 1859 Indian exodus from Texas. Route connected Texas Ranger frontier posts. Wagon ruts, water stops visible 3 miles to west. (1967)

WINDTHORST (Archer Co.)
US 281, 5 mi. S in roadside park
Bridwell Park
Donated to his countrymen by conservationist-philanthropist Joseph Sterling Bridwell (1885–1966) Missourian who moved to Texas in 1909. Drilling his first well in 1921 on W. T. Waggoner estate, in 1927 he formed Bridwell Oil Co., which ultimately produced 50 million barrels of petroleum. In 1932 he bought local ranch (with headquarters 5 mi. to NW), where he bred famous herd sire Larry Domino and other fine Herefords. A founder and president (1940) West Texas Chamber of Commerce, Bridwell gave nation the site for Sheppard Air Force Base. He and wife had 2 daughters. (1972)

WINK (Winkler Co.)
SH 115 at 3rd St.
Wink
On land ruled up to 1874 by Comanche Indians, later part of famed "W" Cattle Ranch. Town "born" in 1926 when Roy Westbrook's Permian Basin oil discovery 1.5 miles to the north brought in 10,000 to 20,000 people, initiated area's conversion to industrialization. Named for Col. C. M. Winkler, famed Texas Confederate soldier.

WINK (Winkler Co.)
SH 115 in Wink
Winkler County Discovery Well "Hendrick No. 1"; site 1.5 mi. NE
First of 612 wells in Hendrick Field, a very prolific, 10,000-acre West Texas oil pool. This area, called "Wildcatters' Graveyard," lay on the 30,000-acre T. G. Hendrick Ranch. Drillers Roy A. Westbrook & Associates leased land at 10 cents an acre. Well arrived dramatically, in great blasts of oil and rock, about midnight, Sept. 3, 1926. Its eventual depth was 3,049 feet. Total production when plugged in 1939 was 235,000 barrels. Data gathered here was vital in future drilling of El Capitan reef lime, a major oil-bearing geologic formation. (1972)

WINK (Winkler Co.)
105 Roy Orbison Dr. (FM 1232)
Roy Orbison
Roy Orbison (April 23, 1936–December 6, 1988) Roy Kelton Orbison was one of America's most famed rock and roll musicians. Born in Vernon (Wilbarger Co.), Orbison and family moved often and by 1946 they had settled in Wink. The Orbisons lived at 102 Langley Way (now 105 North Roy Orbison drive). As a high school student in Wink, Orbison formed his first band, the Wink Westerners (later the Teen Kings). He attended North Texas State University at which time the Teen Kings recorded "Ooby Dooby," a song which led to their signing by Sun Records in 1956. By the early 1960s, Orbison had signed with Monument Records, where he had his greatest commercial success, recording songs like "Only The Lonely (Know The Way I Feel)," "Crying," "In Dreams," "Running Scared" and "Oh! Pretty Woman." By this time, Orbison had perfected his unique, powerful singing voice, while focusing on complex melodies in his music. He also began to wear his familiar dark sunglasses during performances. By the mid-1960s, though, Orbison's career languished. In addition, he suffered a number of personal tragedies. In 1966, Orbison's wife, Claudette (Frady), died in a motorcycle accident; two years later, two of their three sons died in a fire. In 1969, Orbison remarried; he would have two more sons. In the late 1970s, other artists began covering Orbison's music and by the late 1980s, his career was revived. Orbison was inducted into the Rock and Roll Hall of Fame in 1987. In 1988, he recorded the album, *Mystery Girl*, which included the hit, "You Got It." Before it was finalized, Orbison died unexpectedly of a heart attack. The album was released posthumously and was a success. Today, Orbison continues to be remembered for his legacy of music, which has inspired generations of successful musicians. (2009)

WINNSBORO (Wood Co.)
SH 37, 1.5 mi. S
Lee Cemetery
North Carolina natives Benjamin Lee, his wife Alice, and their family came to this area about 1853, and soon acquired over 1,230 acres of land. The Lees operated a large cotton plantation with the help of their ten children and slave labor. Benjamin Lee became a community leader and was elected county commissioner one year after his arrival in the area. Currently covering over thirteen acres, this cemetery began as a small family burial ground in 1856, upon the death of Benjamin Lee. Alice Lee was the second person to be buried here, and their graves are included in the Lee family plot in the oldest section, surrounded by an iron fence. The graves of the four Lee sons, all of whom served in the Confederate Army, are also in the family plot. Although established as a family graveyard, the Lee Cemetery was expanded to include graves of neighbors and gradually became a public community cemetery. Many types of stones and grave markers can be seen here, including one above-ground brick vault burial. Members of the community interred here include banker Charles H. Morris; mayor and state legislator William D. Suiter; Doctor John B. Goldsmith; and newspaper publishers Homer R. and Mae O. Weir. (Texas Sesquicentennial 1836–1986)

WINONA (Smith Co.)
SH 155, 1 mi. N
The Kay House
South Carolina planter Francis Lemuel Kay (1814–1867) settled in Smith County in 1856. Between 1856 and 1860, Kay bought 640 acres of land and built this two-story home for his wife

Mary Ellen (Black) (1826–1896) and their eleven children. By 1860, Kay owned and operated 1,300 acres of farm and ranchland. The Kay family sold the property to the Combination Orchard Company in 1909, and the house became the headquarters for the company's pecan orchards. In 1937, the Hunt Oil Company bought the house and land and has continued to operate the pecan business. (1983)

WINONA (Smith Co.) SH 155, 2 mi. S
Elisha Everett Lott (February 24, 1820–January 17, 1864)
Elisha Everett Lott moved to Harrison County, Texas in 1840. Elected to the Republic of Texas Congress in 1842, he helped open this area of Texas for settlement. He moved here in 1845, and in 1846 was instrumental in the organization of Smith County and the selection of Tyler as the county seat. He helped promote steamboat navigation of the Sabine River and in 1853 was elected to the state senate. A Confederate veteran of the Civil War, Lott died at his Starrville home in 1864 and is buried near this site in the Lott family cemetery. (1991)

WINTERS (Runnels Co.) SH 153 at junction of FM 384 and FM 2111
Poe Chapel
Named in honor of William Wyatt Poe, who came to Texas from his native Alabama in late 1870. Married Jerusha Evaline Cline in 1885; had ten children. Moved family to Runnels County, 1904. Gave land for school and church buildings. Was school trustee. Three sons were later on school board. Family active in farming, civic and church affairs. Son, Howard, introduced 4-row tractor farming to area in 1930. Upon W. W. Poe's death, 1945, each child inherited a farm. Land is still farmed, mainly by his grandsons. (1967)

WOLFE CITY (Hunt Co.) SH 11, .7 mi. SE
Mt. Carmel Cemetery (.9 mi. S)
William J. ("Uncle Billy") Williams (1826–1918), whose family settled this area in 1844, set aside 3.5 acres of this cemetery in 1852 for burial of his two-year-old niece, Angelina Williams. Oldest gravestones are those of his parents, Elizabeth (1789–1861) and George Williams (1786–1863). First called Williams Cemetery, it became known as Mt. Carmel after a Methodist church by that name was built nearby in 1883. An open chapel was added to the property in 1891; another erected in 1920 still stands. Maintained by Mt. Carmel Cemetery Association, the site has grown to 37.6 acres and contains about 10,000 graves. (1975)

WOODLAWN (Harrison Co.) US 59, 1 mi. S
Woodlawn Baptist Church
Organized as Bethesda Baptist Church on July 21, 1850, with 13 charter members, most of whom had come from Mississippi or Alabama. Bethesda church building, erected in 1850, was moved in 1877 to a site donated by Capt. Henry L. Berry. For 95 years, until 1945, services were held only on the fourth Sunday of each month, sometimes furnishing an occasion for "dinner on the ground." In 1958, the congregation adopted its present name and completed this modern building on a site given by Mr. and Mrs. George C. Ives. (1974)

WOODVILLE (Tyler Co.) US 190, 1 mi. W
Tolar Kitchen
Built as home south of town in 1866 by Robert Tolar. Logs cut, squared and notched on site. Has "mud cat" chimney, roof of hand-rived shakes. Converted to "Cook House." Here 3 meals every day were cooked over open fireplace until 1960. Pots were cooked "full" for travelers who "dropped in." (1964)

WOODVILLE (Tyler Co.) US 69/287 at US 190
Tyler County (Crossroads to East Texas)
Home ground of civilized tribes of Indians. Visited 1756 by Spanish explorers, who were trying to keep French trading expeditions out of Texas. Site in 1831 of Fort Teran, commanded by Colonel Ellis Peter Bean, famous and colorful adventurer. The county was created an organized in 1846. It was named for President John Tyler, who signed the resolution to annex Texas to the United States. A 200-acre plot for a county seat was donated by a leading early settler, Josiah Wheat. It was named "Woodville" for George T. Wood, sponsor of the bill in the First Legislature of Texas which created the county. (Wood later served as Governor of Texas, from 1847 to 1849.) In the "Big Thicket."

Home of the annual Dogwood Festival. Economy is based on timber, oil, livestock. First county officials: William P. Sansour, chief justice; Ezekiel Green, George Kirkwood, Angelina Parker, Ivy Taylor, commissioners; James Sapp, sheriff; James Barclay, tax assessor and collector; J. Dobb and William Gray, justices of the peace; Harmon Frazier, surveyor; John C. Arnett, treasurer. 1966 county officials: Jeff R. Mooney, county judge; Joe I. Best, F. C. Hicks, Leon Fowler, H. H. Powell, commissioners; J. F. Boyd, treasurer; Tom Sawyer, county clerk; A. L. Thornton, tax assessor & collector; Clyde E. Smith, Jr., county attorney; Grady Ray, sheriff; B. M. Minter, county school superintendent; Hilda Coats, district clerk; Joe H. Loggins, E. E. Sheffield, Clarence Woodrome, L. L. Parrish, justices of the peace.

WOODVILLE (Tyler Co.)

*Dogwood at Charlton St., 1 blk. W of US 287
at Allan Shivers Library and Museum*

Texas Statesman Allan Shivers

One of Texas' strongest governors, a progressive, colorful, dynamic leader. Administration (1949–1957)—longest in state's history—was marked by winning fight for restoration of the Tidelands to Texas. In state Senate, 1935, where he was youngest man ever seated up to that time, he was author of Texas old-age pension and unemployment compensation laws. In 1947–1949 he served as lieutenant governor. As governor he made reforms in state hospitals, prisons, schools for deaf and exceptional children; created agencies for higher education, historical preservation, water resources, studies of alcoholism. In his administration highway mileage doubled. He had a moderate tax policy and a balanced budget. He was Chairman, National and Southern Governors Conferences, and Interstate Oil Compact Commission; President of the Council of State Governments. Born Oct. 5, 1907, in Lufkin, of pioneer East Texas family. Son of Robert A. and Easter Creasy Shivers. Attended Woodville schools; graduate of Port Arthur High School; University of Texas, B.A., 1931, LL.B., 1933. Married Marialice Shary, 1937. Has four children. Served in Europe in World War II. Is a Baptist and a Mason; lawyer, rancher, farmer, investor, civic leader.   (1966)

WORTHAM (Freestone Co.)

SH 14, N at Wortham Negro Cemetery

Blind Lemon Jefferson (1897–1929)

Born near Wortham. As a young street musician, played a guitar and sang spirituals and blues. Composed many of his songs, and had a distinctive vocal style. From Dallas' Deep Ellum District went to Chicago in 1920s with a talent scout: made 70 great jazz and blues recordings. One of America's outstanding, original musicians. Influenced Louis Armstrong, Bix Beiderbecke, Tommy Dorsey, Harry James, Bessie Smith, and other great artists.   (1967)

WORTHAM (Freestone Co.)

SH 14 at Main St.

City of Wortham

Situated on grant given 1834 by Mexico to Robert B. Longbotham (1797–1883), a Texas colonist from England who settled here in 1839. Years later, in 1871, when Houston & Texas Central Railway was planned through the area, R. B. Longbotham sold right of way through his land for token sum of $5, and townsite was bought from him by investors. Although town was platted as "Tehuacana," post office was established Nov. 10, 1871, as Longbotham, for original landowner. In 1874 name again changed, to honor Col. Luther Rice Wortham, a merchant instrumental in securing railway for area. Wortham was incorporated in 1910, but remained a modest market town until the 1920s, when rumors of oil attracted such prospectors as hotel man Conrad Hilton, who soon left when wells yielded salt water. A Thanksgiving Day gusher in 1924 opened the boom. Population leaped from 1,000 to over 30,000 at once. Law enforcement was impossible, housing inadequate, but in time the town met its obligations. Churches and schools prospered. The Municipal Band was the official band of 1926 United Confederate Veterans' Convention in Birmingham, Ala. Intensive drilling had ended the boom by later 1927. In 1972 a few wells are still pumping, and new horizons are being explored.   (1972)

WORTHAM (Freestone Co.)

SH 14 near intersection with Main St.

The Wortham Oil Boom

The City of Wortham rejected a well drilled by C. L. Witherspoon in 1912 when it produced gas, not water. However, oil and gas wells in 1919–1923 gave prosperity to neighbors north and south, and petroleum exploration began here. Discovery well for the Wortham Field, Roy Simmons No. 1 (1 mi. S), came in as a gusher on Nov. 27, 1924. Within three weeks over 300 drilling rigs were in the field. 3,509,768 barrels of oil were produced in Jan. 1925; total for the year was 16,838,150 barrels. Wasteful drilling slowed yield to 3,000 barrels a day by Sept. 1927, and the boom was concluded. (1972)

YOAKUM (Lavaca Co.) — US 77, N city limits
Yoakum
Located on DeWitt-Lavaca county line on land granted by Mexico in 1835 to settler John May. Cattle gathering area for Chisholm Trail. With coming of San Antonio & Aransas Pass Railroad in 1887, became transportation center. Named for rail official B. F. Yoakum, incorporated in 1889. Industries: beef, leather, canning plant. (1971)

YOAKUM (Lavaca Co.) — SH 111, E city limits
Ruins of Brushy Creek Church (Several Hundred Yards North)
On 50-acre site donated 1868 for church and school purposes by John H. and Stephen Dunn. In large Irish and Czech Catholic area near the Post Road Trading Station of Bovine it was 1876–1912 Church of St. Joseph's Parish, founded in 1860s by Father John Anthony Forest (1838–1911), third Bishop (1895–1911), Diocese of San Antonio. Parishioners built church 1869–1876 of stone from Muldoon, East Texas milled pine, and hand-hewn logs. Blacksmiths made nails and hinges on the site. Floor was of hard-packed, mortared clay. On Aug. 26, 1912, last mass was said here; church burned in 1932. (1973)

YOAKUM (DeWitt Co.) — US 77A at SH 111
Holy Cross Lutheran Church
Lutheran missionaries began serving settlers in the Yoakum area about 1888. The Rev. Cornelius Ziesmer and about ten families organized Holy Cross Lutheran Church on January 27, 1891. Early worship services were held in homes, the city hall, the old community opera house, and the Cumberland Presbyterian Church. The First Lutheran sanctuary, completed in October 1893 at the corner of Hochheim and Schwab Streets, was destroyed by a tornado the following month. The members worked together to build a new structure on the same site, and it was completed in January 1894. The Rev. W. C. Wolfsdorf became the congregation's first resident pastor that same year. Serving a predominantly German membership, the church grew quickly. Its activities have included worship, civic, and missionary endeavors. The congregation purchased property at this site in 1948, and a new sanctuary was built in 1951–1952 to serve the growing membership. An important part of local history for generations, Holy Cross Lutheran Church continues to be an integral part of the Yoakum community, still counting among its members descendants of its founding families. (1991)

YOAKUM (DeWitt Co.) — SH 111, 6.5 mi. W
Von Hugo–Von Clausewitz Family Cemetery (1,000 ft. S.)
The nearby oak grove served as a family cemetery from the 1870s, originally for two Prussian families immigrating to Texas in the 1850s. They sailed to the port of Indianola and settled here, close to Hochheim Prairie (3 mi. W). Carl Ottomar Gunther Theodor Von Hugo (1805–1875) originally owned the property; his is the oldest marked grave in the cemetery. He was born in Prussia and married Albertine Amalie Elise Elenore, Countess Zu Dohna (1813–1890), also a Prussian native. Gustav Adolph Frederick Von Clausewitz (1802–1874) owned the land adjacent to the cemetery. He was born at Berg, Prussia, and his passport for immigration was dated 1858. He married Elise Elenore Wilhelmine, Countess Zu Dohna (1817–1870), sister of Albertine Von Hugo. Both Von Clausewitz graves are now unmarked but are recorded in the family cemetery. The cemetery has some 14 known graves, and possibly others from before the turn of the century. Other family names represented in the cemetery by record are Barth, Bulwer, Nelson, Petering, and Stablefeld. Burials ceased evidently after the completion of nearby St. Ann's Church in 1906 and the location there of a church cemetery. (Texas Sesquicentennial 1836–1986)

YORKTOWN (Dewitt Co.) — SH 72, NE at city limits
DeWitt County
Created March 24, 1846, from Gonzales, Victoria and Goliad Counties. Organized July 13, 1846, with Cameron as the county seat. Named in honor of Green De Witt, a Texas empresario. Born in Kentucky February 12, 1787. Died in Mexico May 18, 1835. (1964)

YORKTOWN (DeWitt Co.)   *SH 72, NE at city limits*
Yorktown
Founded 1848 as way station on Old Indianola Trail. Chartered Aug. 2, 1854. Incorporated 1871. San Antonio & Aransas Pass Railroad reached here 1886. Town's first school organized 1853. Prospered as center of farming and ranching; later, of oil and gas. Pioneer strains are German, American, Pole, Czech, Spaniard, Mexican, Negro.   (1968)

YORKTOWN (DeWitt Co.)   *SH 119 at Lee Alvis Rd. (CR 2024)*
Lithuanians in Texas
Among the many European immigrants arriving in Texas in the mid-19th century was a small group of Lithuanians who settled in the Yorktown vicinity of De Witt County. Due to their eventual assimilation with the numerous German immigrants in the area, the Lithuanians and their contributions to the history of this region were overlooked for generations. Records reveal that the first Lithuanian family to settle in this area probably was that of David and Dora (Scholze) Stanchos. They arrived about 1852, making them among the earliest documented Lithuanian immigrants to America. By 1874 they were joined by about 70 more immigrants, most from the province of Gumbinnen in what was then part of east Prussia. Leaving their homeland for a variety of religious and political reasons, the Lithuanians arrived in Texas primarily through the ports of Galveston and Indianola. Establishing farms in the area, the Lithuanians became American citizens and contributed to the history and culture of this area. Men from the community fought on both sides of the American Civil War. A small graveyard south of Yorktown known as Jonischkies Cemetery contains the interments of many of these early settlers.   (1994)

YSLETA (El Paso Co.)   *IH 20 Bus., right-of-way, Alameda Avenue*
Oldest Mission in Texas
Originally founded in 1613 at Isleta Pueblo, in New Mexico, and dedicated in 1621 as San Antonio de Isleta. Removed to El Paso area, 1680 (during Pueblo revolt), by Tigua Indians who brought along the patron saint as they accompanied fleeing Spaniards. Re-established here in 1682, it has been named successively: Sacramento de Los Tiguas de Ysleta; Corpus Christi de Los Tiguas de Ysleta (1691); San Antonio de Los Tiguas de Ysleta (1744); and Nuestra Señora del Carmen (1874). Present chapel has walls and bells of 1744 building. Still ministers to the Tiguas.   (1970)

YSLETA (El Paso Co.)   *Alameda Ave. (Loop 20) at Finita Ln.*
Approximate Site of the Mission and Pueblo of San Antonio De Senecu
Established by Don Antonio De Otermin and Father Fray Francisco Ayeta, O. F. M. in 1682. Maintained by Franciscan missionaries for the civilizing and Christianizing of the Piro and Tompiro Indians.   (1964)

YSLETA (El Paso Co.)   *Alameda Ave. (Loop 20) at mission*
First Mission and Pueblo in Texas, Corpus Christi de la Ysleta
Established by Don Antonio De Otermin and Fray Francisco Ayeta O. F. M. in 1682. Maintained by Franciscan missionaries for the civilizing and Christianizing of the Tigua Indians, Pueblo Revolt refugees.   (1964)

ZAPATA (Zapata Co.)   *US 83, 5 mi. NW*
Zapata County
Formed from Webb and Starr Counties. Created January 22, 1858. Organized April 26, 1858. Named in honor of Antonio Zapata, a pioneer stockman of the region, supporter of the Republic of the Rio Grande. County seat, Carrizo, 1858. Name later changed to Zapata.

ZAPATA (Zapata Co.)   *US 83, 4 mi. NW*
Site of Uribeño
One of five Zapata County settlements inundated by the waters of Falcon Reservoir in the 1950s, Uribeño traces its origin to 1803, when Porción 41 was granted to José Nicolás Clemente Gutiérrez de Lara (1770–1805) for his service in the Spanish army. As required by the terms of the grant, José Nicolás Clemente worked to establish a ranch on his property against the odds of Indian raids, scorching heat, drought and periodic river flooding. He returned to his hometown of Revilla in Mexico just prior to his death, leaving behind his widow, María Josefa Martínez, and six children.

Development of the ranch on Porción 41 was delayed until after Mexico won its independence from Spain in 1821. After the war, some of José Nicolás Clemente's sons returned to the ranch; by 1826 all of his children had married and moved to the ranch, which was named Uribeño. By 1860, the population of the Uribeño community, which took its name from the Gutiérrez ranch, was 152. Located about two miles west of this site, it was a small, poor community, comprised primarily of farmers, herdsmen and laborers. Although no permanent church existed, visiting priests periodically held worship services. A cemetery, a schoolhouse and a small grocery store existed to serve the residents. When the United States government built Falcon Dam, Uribeño met the same fate as its neighboring towns, but its residents chose not to move the community to another site before the waters flooded the town. Only the cemetery was relocated to serve as a physical reminder of this early border community. (2001)

ZAPATA (Zapata Co.)   *SH 16, 12 mi. NE*
Bustamante (Rancho Las Comitas)
The unincorporated village of Bustamante, settled by Don Pedro Jose Bustamante and his family in 1822, is located on a 22,142-acre land grant awarded by the Mexican government to Bustamante in 1835. He brought other settlers, horses, cattle, sheep, and goats to help open up the frontier. An early sandstone blockhouse built by the Bustamante family provided protection from Indian raids. During the 1870s the village became the headquarters of Rancho Las Comitas, named for the Comita tree which grew on the property. Las Comitas gave rise to a community of homes, a school and a store, making the ranch almost self sufficient. Part of the land later was claimed by the State of Texas in a Supreme Court case. Numerous Bustamante family members are buried in three ranch cemeteries: the Bustamante Cemetery, the Cameron Cemetery, and the Garcia Cemetery. The community was officially named Bustamante in 1926 when a post office was established with Herlinda Bustamante as postmistress. Ranch life changed in the 1930s with the discovery of oil and gas in the area. Although much of the land was leased for exploration wells, the ranch is still in operation under the direction of Bustamante descendants. (1991)

ZAVALLA (Angelina Co.)   *SH 63, 8 mi. SE*
U.S. Forest Service in Texas
This area—heart of the Piney Woods and the East Texas forest industry—was, in 1933, cutover forests and worked-out farms. That year the Texas Legislature authorized the establishment of National Forests in this state. Today Angelina, Davy Crockett, Sabine and Sam Houston forests (the 4 National Forests in Texas) include over 658,000 acres. Under management, net growth exceeds 175,000,000 board feet with a value of over $7,000,000 yearly. In addition, forests offer extensive recreation areas. U.S. Forest Service offices have been in Lufkin since 1947. (1968)

ZEPHYR (Brown Co.)   *US 84/183 at CR 259, 1 mi. SE*
Zephyr Cemetery
The unincorporated town of Zephyr, located on land granted to early settlers Benjamin Head and Felix Wardziski, was established in the 1860s. As the settlement grew, a school was opened in the 1870s, and churches and businesses were established. Mail was delivered weekly from Brownwood. This cemetery has served the residents of Zephyr and the surrounding area since the 1870s. The earliest known burials in the graveyard are those of three children of the Staggs family, who died in 1878 and 1879. Another early grave is that of Ann Catherine Sewell Ward (1843–1879). The first official deed of cemetery property took place in 1899, although it was in use prior to that time. Subsequent land acquisitions have increased the size of the graveyard to more than seven acres. Among those buried here are thirty-three victims of the devastating tornado of May 29, 1909, which almost completely destroyed the town, and veterans of six wars: the Mexican War, the Civil War, World War I, World War II, Korea, and Vietnam. The Zephyr cemetery stands as a reminder of the pioneer spirit of the area's early settlers. It is maintained by the Zephyr Cemetery Association. (1988)

ZION HILL (Jasper Co.)   *US 96 about 7 mi. S of Jasper*
Zion Hill Missionary Baptist Church and Cemetery
Local tradition and Baptist church records indicate that the Zion Hill Missionary Baptist Church was organized in 1852 with the Rev. John Bean as first pastor. The first church building on this site is thought to have been a small log house. On August 15, 1853, Aurin Goodgame Horn donated 3

acres including the graveyard to the Zion Hill Baptist Church. The oldest marked grave is that of Joseph Wood, who was born in 1792 in North Carolina and died in Jasper County on September 16, 1854. The original church building was quickly replaced by a board-and-batten structure and in the 1880s, a large frame building. This stood until 1967, when it was demolished and replaced by a modern brick edifice outside the cemetery's north fence. Of over 1,186 graves in Zion Hill Cemetery, 36 are unmarked or unknown. Several were citizens of the Republic of Texas; 75 war veterans are interred on this site. The graves of 102 young children bear witness to the high infant mortality rate among pioneers. Another notable grave is that of the Rev. A. C. Sims (1845–1920), who was born in the Republic of Texas, served in the Confederate Army, and was a pastor of Zion Hill Baptist Church.

(1998)

Index

Wilson-Leonard Brushy Creek burial site, 401
Archer County, 20–21, 145, 219, 292, 307, 496
copper mines, 20
Archive War, 25
Argyle, 21
Arledge Ridge Cemetery, 50
Armistead, Robert Starke, 59
Armstrong, Mollie W., 66
Armstrong County, 93–94, 195–96, 485
jail, 94
Armstrong Ranch, 429
ranch house, 429
Army of the Republic of Texas
camp site of, 211, 275
Arroyo de Juan Lorenzo, 308
Arsenal magazine in San Antonio, 416
Asa Hill of Rutersville, 260
Asadores Ranch, 402
Atakapan Indians of Orange County, 349
Atascosa County, 242–43, 371–72, 380
Atascosito, 273
Athens, 24
machinery from first factory, 24
Austin, C.S.A., 26
Austin, Moses, 25
Austin, Preston Rose, 29
Austin, Stephen Fuller, 329, 421
campsite, 417
Austin County, 40, 232, 249, 332–33, 421–22, 482
Avenger Field, W.A.S.P. training base, 456
Aynesworth-Wright House, 28

Babb, Dot and Bianca, Indian captives, 89
Baby Head Cemetery, 280
Bachelor Girls' Library Club, 404
Badu House, 280
Bailey, "Brit," plantation, 30
Bailey, James Britton, 147
Bailey County, 155, 325–26
Baines, Joseph Wilson, 241
Baker, Jonathan Hamilton, 358
Baker Ranch School, 342
Balcones Fault, 28
Baldwin, Frank D., rescued captives, 270
Ballí, Padre J. Nicolas, 110, 376
Ballí Cemetery, 143
Ballinger, 31
Bandera Cemetery, 32
Bandera County, 31–32, 307
Bandera Pass, 31
Banquete, C.S.A., 32
barbed wire demonstration, 413
barbed wire fence in the Panhandle, 81
Barker Post Office, 33
Barnard's Trading Post No. 2, 187
Barnett-Hamrick settlement, 423

Barnhart, 33
Baron de Bastrop, Felipe Enrique Neri, 35
Barrett, Harrison, 118
Barroneña Ranch, 173
Barry, James Buckner, C.S.A., 483
Barry Scobee Mountain, 162
Barton Springs, 27
Bass, Sam, holdup, 242
site of death, 401
train robbery, 312
Bass, T. C., home, 137
Bastrop, early history, 35
Bastrop, Felipe Enrique Neri de, 35
Bastrop County, 34–36, 152–53, 304, 397, 429, 442
fort, 442
Battle Branch, 264
Battle Creek burial ground, 131
Battle of San Jacinto, 221
Mexican Cavalry, 221
battles
Adams Hill, 417
Adobe Walls, 51, 451
Agua Dulce, 5
Bird Creek, 459
Coleto, 158
Cortina, 391
Dove Creek, 311
El Perdido, 158
Fredonia, 418
Gonzales, 194
Gregg 1872 site, 80
Jones Creek, 171
La Bolsa, 382
Little Wichita, 20
Lyman's wagon train, 79
Medina, 417
Nacogdoches, 328
Neches, 98
North Fork of Red River, 270
Palmito Ranch, 65
Palo Duro Canyon, 81, 94
Pease River, 120
Plum Creek, 281
Sabine Pass, 406
San Jacinto, 221
Texas Rangers' of May 29, 1850, 7
Baxter's Curve train robbery, 425
Bayland Guards, 37
Bayland Orphanage, 37
Baylor, Gen. John R., 320
Baylor County, 48, 433
Baylor Park, 231
Beach Road, 406
Bean, Ellis P., 9
Bean, Judge Roy, 266
Bear Creek Methodist Church and Cemetery, 225

506

Sabine County, 181, 210, 316
Sabine Pass, 405
  Battle of, 406
  Richard Dowling, 406
Sabine River headwaters, 200
Sachse, William, cemetery, 180
Sacred Heart Catholic Church, 481
Saffold Dam, 432
Saibara, Seito and Kiyoaki, 486
Saint Anthony's Catholic Church, 395
Saint Dominic Catholic Church, 139
Saint John Catholic Church of Bomarton, 48
Saint John Lutheran Church, 34
Saint John's Catholic Church of Scurry Co.,
  215
Saint Joseph Catholic Church, 162
Saint Louis Church, 86
Saint Mark's School of Texas, 128
St. Paul, 440
Salado, Main Street bridges, 408
Salado, Stagecoach Inn, 408
Salado College, site of, 408
Salado Creek, 408
Salt War in El Paso Co., 409, 421
salt works
  C.S.A., in Lometa, 282
  C.S.A., in Llano, 279
  Graham, 197
Saltpetre mine, C.S.A., 105
Sam Houston Industrial and Training School,
  229
Sam Houston Oak, 193
Sams, Pleasant C., 42
San Angelo municipal swimming pool, 409
San Antonio–California Trail, 475
San Antonio–El Paso Road, 163
San Antonio–Laredo Road, 466
San Antonio & Rio Grande Railway, "Old
  Flossie", 422
San Antonio River Walk, 415
San Antonio Road
  See Camino Real
San Antonio, 250th Anniversary, 415
San Augustine, 419
  site of early sawmill, 419
San Augustine Church, 371
San Augustine County, 418–19
San Benito Water District building, 420
San Bernardo Avenue in Laredo, 267
San Caja Hill, 465
San Elizario, 420
San Felipe
  early roads, 422
  town hall, 422
San Felipe de Austin, 421
San Jacinto Campaign and capture of Mexican
  dispatches, 39
San Jacinto County, 97, 342, 372, 436

  courthouse, 97
San Jacinto River, west fork, 105
San Juan de Carricitos Land Grant, 387
San Marcos Springs, 423
San Patricio County, 19, 342, 378, 440
San Saba Church of Christ, 424
San Saba County, 42, 88, 389, 423–25
San Saba Lodge No. 225, A.F. & A.M., 423
San Saba Peak, 188
San Salomon Springs, 31
Sanborn Ranch, 492
Sand Hills
  Lamb Co., 447
  Monahans Sandhills State Park, 319
  Winkler Co., 249
Sand Springs, 137
Sanders, Harvey C., C.S.A., 333
Santa Anna, C.S.A., 426
Santa Anna Mound, 195
Santa Anna's camp, 100
Santa Anna's surrender ratified, 190
Santa Fe Railroad Terminus, 360
Santa Gertrudis campsite, Mexican activities
  1830's, 255
Santa Gertrudis, King Ranch headquarters, 254
Santa Margarita Crossing, 32
Santa Petronila Ranch, site of, 143
Santa Rita No. 1, 44
Sardis School, 484
Savage community, 271
sawmill, site of early Texas, 419
Scarborough, A. B., home of, 50
Schleicher County, 151–52
Scholten Railroad, 283
Schott, William E., 440
Schreiner College, 251
Schulenburg, 430
Schumacher Crossing on the Guadalupe River,
  227
Schwartz House, 474
Scull, Sally, 389
Scurry County, 145, 215, 233–34, 442–43
  billionth barrel of oil, 442
Scyene Meeting Place, site of, 130
Seadrift, 430
Seaton Cemetery, 459
Sebastian, 431
Seguín, Don Erasmo, 414
  Casa Blanca, 160
Seguín, Juan Nepomuceno, 431
Seminole, 432
Seminole Indian Scouts Cemetery, 54
Seminole Scout camp on Fort Clark, 54
Settler's Cemetery, 364
Seven Wells, 99
Sewell Park, 236
Shackelford County, 6–7, 322
  first natural gas well, 322

525

About the Editors

Betty Dooley Awbrey is a retired educator from San Antonio, Texas, and has been involved in educating gifted and bilingual children for thirty years. She continues her commitment to educating children through her volunteer work. She updates and expands each new edition since the death of her father, **Claude Dooley**, who compiled the original in 1978. He was a retired businessman and entrepreneur from Odessa, Texas.

Stuart Awbrey is retired from USAA and now enjoys gardening. He is an avid reader of Texas and American history. Betty and Stuart enjoy traveling and reside in Fair Oaks Ranch, Texas, north of San Antonio.